Get started with your **Connected Casebook**

Redeem your code below to access the **e-book** with search, highlighting, and note-taking capabilities; a **study center** complete with practice questions, explanations, and videos; **case briefing** and **outlining** tools to support efficient learning; and more.

1. Go to www.casebookconnect.com
2. Enter your access code in the box and click **Register**
3. Follow the steps to complete your registration and verify your email address

If you have already registered at CasebookConnect.com, simply log into your account and redeem additional access codes from your Dashboard.

ACCESS CODE:
Scratch off with care.

Is this a used casebook? Access code already redeemed? Purchase a digital version at **CasebookConnect.com/catalog**.

If you purchased a digital bundle with additional components, your additional access codes will appear below.

"I liked being able to search quickly while in class."

"Being able to highlight and easily create case briefs was a fantastic resource and time saver for me!"

"I loved the practice exercises and study questions; they really helped me learn the material!"

For technical support, please visit http://support.wklegaledu.com.

10051290-0002

CIVIL PROCEDURE

ASPEN CASEBOOK SERIES

CIVIL PROCEDURE

Doctrine, Practice, and Context

SIXTH EDITION

STEPHEN N. SUBRIN

Professor of Law
Northeastern University School of Law

MARTHA L. MINOW

Morgan and Helen Chu Dean and Professor of Law
Harvard University Law School

MARK S. BRODIN

Michael and Helen Lee Distinguished Scholar and Professor of Law
Boston College Law School

THOMAS O. MAIN

William S. Boyd Professor of Law
William S. Boyd School of Law
University of Nevada, Las Vegas

ALEXANDRA D. LAHAV

Ellen Ash Peters Professor of Law
University of Connecticut School of Law

Published by Wolters Kluwer in New York.

Wolters Kluwer Legal & Regulatory U.S. serves customers worldwide with CCH, Aspen Publishers, and Kluwer Law International products. (www.WKLegaledu.com)

To contact Customer Service, e-mail customer.service@wolterskluwer.com, call 1-800-234-1660, fax 1-800-901-9075, or mail correspondence to:

Wolters Kluwer
Attn: Order Department
PO Box 990
Frederick, MD 21705

Printed in the United States of America.

3 4 5 6 7 8 9

ISBN 978-1-5438-1560-3

Library of Congress Cataloging-in-Publication Data

Names: Subrin, Stephen, 1936– author. | Minow, Martha, 1954- author. | Brodin, Mark S., 1947– author. | Main, Thomas O., author. | Lahav, Alexandra D., author.
Title: Civil procedure : doctrine, practice, and context / Stephen N. Subrin, Professor of Law, Northeastern University School of Law; Martha L. Minow, Morgan and Helen Chu Dean and Professor of Law, Harvard University Law School; Mark S. Brodin, Michael and Helen Lee Distinguished Scholar Professor of Law, Boston College Law School; Thomas O. Main, William S. Boyd Professor of Law, William S. Boyd School of Law University of Nevada, Las Vegas; Alexandra D. Lahav, Ellen Ash Peters Professor of Law University of Connecticut School of Law.
Description: Sixth edition. | New York : Wolters Kluwer Legal & Regulatory U.S./Aspen Publishers, [2020] | Series: Aspen casebook series | Includes bibliographical references and index. | Summary: "Casebook intended for use in a first-year civil procedure course"—Provided by publisher.
Identifiers: LCCN 2019055392 | ISBN 9781543815603 (hardcover) | ISBN 9781543820911 (ebook)
Subjects: LCSH: Civil procedure—United States. | LCGFT: Casebooks (Law)
Classification: LCC KF8839 .C452 2020 | DDC 347.73/5—dc23
LC record available at https://lccn.loc.gov/2019055392

About Wolters Kluwer Legal & Regulatory U.S.

Wolters Kluwer Legal & Regulatory U.S. delivers expert content and solutions in the areas of law, corporate compliance, health compliance, reimbursement, and legal education. Its practical solutions help customers successfully navigate the demands of a changing environment to drive their daily activities, enhance decision quality and inspire confident outcomes.

Serving customers worldwide, its legal and regulatory portfolio includes products under the Aspen Publishers, CCH Incorporated, Kluwer Law International, ftwilliam.com and MediRegs names. They are regarded as exceptional and trusted resources for general legal and practice-specific knowledge, compliance and risk management, dynamic workflow solutions, and expert commentary.

I dedicate this book to over three decades of
Northeastern Law students who have insisted that intelligence,
compassion, and justice must go hand in hand, and to Joan,
who has done the same—and then some.
—Stephen N. Subrin

I dedicate this book to law students past and future in hopes
that you will work to make procedure more civil, and to Joe Singer,
who inspires accessible casebooks and other improvements of daily life.
—Martha L. Minow

I dedicate this edition to all those who devote their talents and energies
to the pursuit of justice in the courts across the land; and to Steve Subrin,
our constant inspiration.
—Mark S. Brodin

I dedicate this book to my parents, who always seem to know the way,
and to Paula, with whom I read maps.
—Thomas O. Main

I dedicate this edition to Martha, Steve, and my students,
from whom I have learned so much.
—Alexandra D. Lahav

SUMMARY OF CONTENTS

Contents   xi
Exercises   xxvii
Preface to the Sixth Edition   xxxi
Preface to the First Edition   xxxiii

CHAPTER 1
An Introduction to Civil Procedure   1

CHAPTER 2
Remedies and Stakes   105

CHAPTER 3
Thinking Like a Trial Lawyer, Pleadings, and Joinder   237

CHAPTER 4
Discovery   421

CHAPTER 5
The Right to Jury Trial and Judicial Control of Results 507

CHAPTER 6
Alternative Dispute Resolution   641

CHAPTER 7
**The Choice of an Appropriate Court: Personal Jurisdiction,
Notice, and Venue**   667

CHAPTER 8
**The Choice of an Appropriate Court: Subject Matter
Jurisdiction and Removal**   865

CHAPTER 9
Choice of Federal or State Law—The *Erie* Doctrine   929

CHAPTER 10
Finality and Preclusion   987

CHAPTER 11
Aggregate Litigation: It All Comes Together   1063

Case Files   1141
Carpenter v. Dee   1141
Warner v. City of New York   1233
Table of Cases   1283
Table of Statutes and Rules   1293
Index   1301

CONTENTS

Exercises   xxvii

Preface to the Sixth Edition   xxxi

Preface to the First Edition   xxxiii

CHAPTER 1

An Introduction to Civil Procedure   1

A. **What Students Should Know from the Start**   2

    1. Why Procedure Matters   2

    2. What Is "Civil Procedure"?   3

    3. Meeting the Players and the Institutions   4

      a. Parties   4

      b. Jurisdiction   5

      c. Remedies   6

    4. Sources for the Rules and Doctrines   6

    5. How to Approach Studying   7

    6. About This Book   9

    7. Law as Theater   10

      Milner S. Ball, *The Promise of American Law: A Theological,*
Humanistic View of Legal Process   10

B. **An Opening Case: The Power and Limits of Courts**   12

    1. Reading a Federal Rule of Civil Procedure   12

      Reading a Federal Rule   13

    2. Interpreting Rules and Statutes   13

    3. Background of *United States v. Hall*   14

      Reading the Case   17

    4. The Opinion   17

      United States v. Hall   17

      Review Questions   22

    5. The Significance of *Hall* Today   23

C. **The Right to Be Heard: Elements and History of Due Process**   25

    1. Introductory Case: *Goldberg v. Kelly*   26

      a. Background of *Goldberg v. Kelly*   26

      b. The Supreme Court's Opinion   27

      Goldberg v. Kelly   27

      Review Questions   33

      c. Context: History of Welfare Reform After *Goldberg v. Kelly*   35

    2. Due Process Values   35

      Frank L. Michelman, *The Supreme Court and Litigation Access*
Fees: The Right to Protect One's Rights   36

Tom R. Tyler and E. Allan Lind, *A Relational Model of Authority
   in Groups*   38
3. Costs of Notice and a Hearing   39
   a. The Cost of Process   39
      Mathews, Secretary of Health, Education, and Welfare v. Eldridge   40
      Review Questions   46
   b. Process Values, Costs, and Benefits   47
      Jerry L. Mashaw, *The Supreme Court's Due Process Calculus for
         Administrative Adjudication: Three Factors in Search of a Theory
         of Value*   47
      Louis Kaplow, *The Value of Accuracy in Adjudication: An
         Economic Analysis*   55
   c. The Cost of Notice: *Jones. v. Flowers*   60
      Jones v. Flowers   60
      Review Questions   69
4. Enemy Combatants and Due Process   70
      Hamdi v. Rumsfeld   70
      Review Questions   79
D. Access to Lawyers and to the Legal System   79
   1. Access to Court   80
      Boddie v. Connecticut   80
      Review Questions   85
   2. Access to a Lawyer   87
      *Lassiter v. Department of Social Services of Durham County,
         North Carolina*   87
      Review Questions   99
   3. Unbundling Legal Services   101
   4. Donated Legal Services   101
   5. The Comparative Perspective   101
      Practice Exercise No. 1: Applying the Due Process Clauses   102

CHAPTER 2
Remedies and Stakes   105

A. Introduction   105
B. Provisional Relief   106
   1. Securing the Judgment: Attachments, Garnishments, and
      Sequestration   107
      a. Development of the Law of Prejudgment Remedies   108
      Fuentes v. Shevin   109
      Review Questions   114
      b. Litigating Prejudgment Remedies After *Fuentes*   115
   2. Preserving the Status Quo   116
      Winter v. Natural Resources Defense Council, Inc.   116
      Review Questions   127
      Practice Exercise No. 2: Motion for a Preliminary Injunction   127

C. **Final Relief**   129
   1. Equitable Relief   129
     a.   The Standard for a Permanent Injunction   129
     Walgreen Co. v. Sara Creek Property Co.   130
     Review Questions   133
     b.   Types of Permanent Injunctions   134
     c.   Equitable Relief and the Judicial Role   135
     Brown v. Plata   136
     d.   Theories of Judicial Power Applied to Injunctive Relief   155
     Lon Fuller, *The Forms and Limits of Adjudication*   155
     Abram Chayes, *The Role of the Judge in Public Law Litigation*   159
     Practice Exercise No. 3: Equitable Relief in *Carpenter* and *Warner*   164
     e.   Enforcement of Equitable Relief   165
   2. Declaratory Relief   166
   3. Damages   166
     a.   Nominal Damages   167
     Carey v. Piphus   167
     Review Questions   173
     b.   Punitive Damages   174
     Practice Exercise No. 4: Damages in *Carpenter* and *Warner*   178
     c.   Enforcement of Damages   179
D. **Settlement**   180
   Steven Shavell, *Foundations of Economic Analysis of Law*   180
E. **Financing Litigation**   185
   1. The "American Rule"   185
   2. Fee-Shifting Statutes   186
   3. The Effect of Rule 68 Settlement Offers on Attorneys' Fees   187
     Marek v. Chesny   188
     Review Questions   196
     Practice Exercise No. 5: Revising Fed. R. Civ. P. 68   199
     a.   Conditional Offer of Settlement   200
     b.   Frivolous Claims   201
   4. Assessing the Value of Legal Services   202
     City of Riverside v. Rivera   202
     Review Questions   207
   5. The Contingency Fee   208
   6. Third-Party Litigation Financing   210
     Jonathan T. Molot, *Litigation Finance: A Market Solution to a*
        Procedural Problem   210
     Practice Exercise No. 6: Fee Arrangements in *Carpenter* and *Warner*   214
F. **Contempt**   214
   David Luban, *Legal Modernism*   215
   Walker v. City of Birmingham   217
   Review Questions   224
   Martin Luther King, Jr., *Letter From Birmingham City Jail*   226

CHAPTER 3

Thinking Like a Trial Lawyer, Pleadings, and Joinder   237

A. Introduction   237
B. The Stages and Essential Concepts of a Civil Litigation   237
C. Claims, Causes of Action, and Elements   247
    Practice Exercise No. 7: Initial Strategy Session in *Carpenter*   251
D. Pleadings and Amendments   251
    1. The Purpose and Doctrine of Complaints   252
      Conley v. Gibson   254
      a. The Lower Courts' Response to Notice Pleading   256
      b. A New Pleading Standard: Plausibility   257
      Bell Atlantic Corp. v. Twombly   258
      Review Questions   273
      c. The Aftermath of *Twombly*   273
      Ashcroft v. Iqbal   275
      Review Questions   284
      d. What Happened Next?   284
      e. Plausibility Pleading in Action   285
      f. Abrogating the Forms   287
      g. Frivolous Litigation   287
      h. Congressional Legislation and Pleading   288
      i. Winning a 12(b)(6) Motion   289
      Bower v. Weisman   289
      Review Questions   294
      The Four-Corners Rule   295
      Practice Exercise No. 8: Analyzing 12(b)(6) and 12(e) Motions
        in *Carpenter*   296
    2. Strategy Considerations   296
      Practice Exercise No. 9: Considering the *Warner* Complaint   297
    3. Technical Pleading Requirements   298
    4. Anonymous Plaintiffs   299
      *Freedom From Religion Foundation, Inc. v. Emanuel County
        School System*   299
      Review Question   304
    5. Answers, Motions, and Affirmative Defenses   305
      a. Preliminary Motions   305
      b. Motions to Dismiss   306
      c. Answers   309
      d. Admissions and Denials   309
      e. Affirmative Defenses   311
      Practice Exercise No. 10: Analyzing the Answer in *Carpenter*   313
      Review Exercise No. 1   314

6. Amendments   315
   Singletary v. Pennsylvania Department of Corrections   319
   Review Questions   327
   Krupski v. Costa Crociere S.p.A.   328
   Review Questions   334
   a. State Procedural Rules   334
   b. Calculating the Statute of Limitations Period   335
   Practice Exercise No. 11: Argument on Plaintiff's Motion
      to Amend in *Carpenter*   336
   c. Tips on Arguing Motions   338
E. The Historical Background of Civil Procedure   339
   1. The First Era: Common Law and Equity   339
      a. Common Law Procedure   339
      b. Equity Procedure   342
      c. Coming to America   343
   2. The Second Era: The Field Code   344
      David Dudley Field, *What Shall Be Done with the Practice
         of the Courts?*   345
      Review Question   347
      a. The Field Family   347
      b. The Politics of Procedure   347
      c. Transnational Civil Procedure   348
   3. The Third Era: Federal Rules of Civil Procedure   349
      a. The Rules of Decision Act, and the Process and
         Conformity Acts   349
      b. The Rules Enabling Act and the Drafting of the Federal
         Rules of Civil Procedure   350
      c. Trans-Substantive Procedure and Politics   354
      d. Procedural Rulemaking   354
   4. Are We Now in a Fourth Era?   355
      Chief Justice Warren E. Burger, *Agenda for 2000 A.D.—A Need
         for Systematic Anticipation*   358
      Simon H. Rifkind, *Are We Asking Too Much of Our Courts?*   359
      Frank E.A. Sander, *Varieties of Dispute Processing*   361
      Laura Nader, *Commentary*   362
      a. The Role of Procedural Rules   363
F. Sanctions   365
   Chaplin v. DuPont Advance Fiber Systems   367
   Review Questions   371
   a. Safe Harbor   372
   b. "Bad Faith" Is Not a Necessary Condition   373
   c. The Chilling Effect of Sanctions   374

d. Monetary and Nonmonetary Sanctions	374
e. State Procedure	375
f. Frivolous Litigation	376
g. Other Sources of Authority to Sanction	377
Practice Exercise No. 12: Reviewing the *Warner* Answer Under Rule 11	377
G. Simple Joinder	377
Cooper v. Fitzgerald	379
Review Questions	385
a. Joinder Is Only One Star in the Constellation of Procedure	387
b. The "Transaction or Occurrence" Test	387
c. Litigation Strategy	387
H. Counterclaims and Cross-Claims	388
Podhorn v. Paragon Group, Inc.	389
Review Questions	390
a. Revisiting Motions to Dismiss	391
b. The "Transaction or Occurrence" Test, Again	391
c. Cross-claims	392
Practice Exercise No. 13: Considering Counterclaims, Cross-Claims, and Rule 13(h) Additional Parties in *Carpenter*	392
I. Third-Party Practice	393
Gross v. Hanover Insurance Co.	393
Review Question	397
Practice Exercise No. 14: Considering an Impleader in *Warner*	398
J. An Introduction to Necessary and Indispensable Parties	398
Temple v. Synthes Corporation, Ltd.	399
Review Questions	400
Review Questions	402
Daynard v. Ness, Motley, Loadholdt, Richardson & Poole, P.A.	403
Review Questions	411
a. Considering Strategy	411
K. Interpleader	412
L. Intervention	413
United States v. Northern Indiana Public Service Co., et al.	413
Review Questions	416
a. Statutory Authority to Intervene	416
Review Exercise No. 2	416
Review Exercise No. 3	418
CHAPTER 4	
Discovery	421
A. Introduction	421
B. Discovery and Its Tensions	424
Wayne Brazil, *The Adversary Character of Civil Discovery*	424

       ABA Model Code of Professional Responsibility 428
       ABA Model Rules of Professional Conduct 429
C. **The Mechanics of Discovery** 434
  1. Mandatory Initial Disclosures 434
  2. Party-Controlled Discovery 436
    a. Depositions 436
    b. Written Interrogatories 437
    c. Production of Documents (Including ESI) and Things 438
    d. Physical and Mental Examinations 442
    e. Requests for Admissions 443
    f. Informal Discovery 443
    g. Experts 444
    h. A Brief Introduction to the Rules of Evidence 445
    Practice Exercise No. 15: Discovery Planning in *Carpenter* 449
  3. The Scope of Discovery 449
    Oxbow Carbon & Minerals LLC v. Union Pacific R.R. Co. 453
    Review Questions 460
    Alley v. MTD Products, Inc. 462
    Freedom's Path at Dayton v. Dayton Metro. Hous. Auth. 470
    Review Question 483
    Practice Exercise No. 16: Ethical Issues in Discovery 487
    Practice Exercise No. 17: Analyzing the Scope of Discovery 489
    Practice Exercise No. 18: Analyzing the Scope of Third-Party
      Discovery 490
    Practice Exercise No. 19: Analyzing Proportionality in Discovery 491
    Practice Exercise No. 20: Finding an Expert (and Expertise)
      in *Carpenter* 492
    Hickman v. Taylor 493
    Review Questions 499
D. **Procedural Rulemaking** 500
    Catherine T. Struve, *The Paradox of Delegation: Interpreting the*
      Federal Rules of Civil Procedure 500
    Stephen B. Burbank, *Ignorance and Procedural Law Reform* 501
    Laurens Walker, *Federal Civil Rulemaking* 502
    Letter of Transmittal from Justice Rehnquist 503
    Practice Exercise No. 21: Assessing the Rulemaking Process 506

CHAPTER 5

The Right to Jury Trial and Judicial Control of Results 507

A. Values and Historical Background 507
  1. Introduction 507
  2. The Debate over the American Civil Jury 509
    Jerome T. Frank, *Courts on Trial* 510
    Harry Kalven, *The Dignity of the Civil Jury* 512

Valerie P. Hans and Neil Vidmar, *Judging the Jury*   514
3. The Historical Background of the Modern American Civil Jury   523
B. **The Right to Jury Trial in Civil Cases in Federal Court**   524
Chauffeurs, Teamsters and Helpers, Local No. 391 v. Terry   525
Review Questions   534
Practice Exercise No. 22: Legislative Exercise Regarding Right
to Jury Trial   535
Practice Exercise No. 23: Law Firm Strategy Session Regarding
Jury Trial in *Warner*   536
C. **Jury Selection: Techniques and Purposes, Including Peremptory
Challenges**   536
1. Attorney Behavior   536
Valerie P. Hans and Neil Vidmar, *Judging the Jury*   539
Federal Jury Selection Statutes   540
2. Peremptory Challenges and Discrimination   541
D. **Summary Judgment**   548
1. An Extraordinary Remedy   551
Adickes v. S.H. Kress & Co.   551
Review Question   562
2. A Focal Point of Litigation   563
Celotex Corp. v. Catrett   563
Review Question   571
3. The Fact-Law Distinction   580
William Schwarzer, *Summary Judgment Under the Federal
Rules: Defining Genuine Issues of Material Fact*   581
4. Strategic Considerations   582
Practice Exercise No. 24: Summary Judgment Motion Session
in *Carpenter*   583
Practice Exercise No. 25: Summary Judgment Motion Session
in *Warner*   585
E. **Dismissal, Directed Verdicts, Judgments Notwithstanding the
Verdict, New Trial Motions, and Motions to Vacate Judgment**   585
1. Voluntary Dismissal   587
2. Involuntary Dismissal   588
3. Directed Verdict (Judgment as a Matter of Law)   588
4. Judgment Notwithstanding the Verdict (JNOV/Renewed
Judgment as a Matter of Law)   589
5. Motions for New Trial   591
6. Judgments as a Matter of Law and New Trial Motions
in More Detail   594
Galloway v. United States   594
Review Questions   608
Review Exercise No. 4   612
7. Motion to Vacate Judgment   615
Brandon v. Chicago Board of Education   616

F. Types of Verdicts, Bifurcation, Trifurcation, Instructions,
    Remittitur, and Additur   619
    1. Types of Verdicts   619
    2. Bifurcation and Trifurcation   620
    3. Jury Instructions   622
        Practice Exercise No. 26: Jury Instructions in *Carpenter*   625
    4. Remittitur and Additur   625
        Review Questions   627
        Practice Exercise No. 27: Motions to Challenge a Jury Verdict 628
G. Closing Arguments   629
    Lloyd Paul Stryker, *The Art of Advocacy*   629
    Practice Exercise No. 28: Closing Argument in *Carpenter*   632
H. Appeals   634
    Review Exercise No. 5   637

CHAPTER 6
Alternative Dispute Resolution   641
A. History of ADR in the Federal Courts   643
B. The Debate over ADR   644
C. Arbitration and Judicial Review   646
    1. Decisionmakers   646
    2. Source of Law   647
    3. Procedural Rules   647
    4. Appealing an Arbitration Award   648
    5. Policy Issues in Arbitration   648
        Practice Exercise No. 29: Applying the Federal Arbitration Act 649
D. The FAA and State Law   653
    Kindred Nursing Centers Limited Partnership v. Clark   653
    Review Questions   656
E. Recent Developments   658
    Review Exercise No. 6: Alternative Dispute Resolution Under
        Local Rule   660
    Practice Exercise No. 30: Alternative Dispute Resolution
        in *Carpenter*   663

CHAPTER 7
The Choice of an Appropriate Court: Personal Jurisdiction,
Notice, and Venue   667
A. Introduction and Overview   667
B. Jurisdiction over the Person or Property of the Defendant   668
C. The Traditional Conception of Personal Jurisdiction   669
    Pennoyer v. Neff   670
    Your Takeaway   675
    Review Questions   675
    Harris v. Balk   679

Review Questions   681
Hess v. Pawloski   682
Review Questions   683
D. The Modern Conception of Personal Jurisdiction   684
International Shoe Co. v. State of Washington   684
Your Takeaway   688
Review Questions   688
E. Note on Long-Arm Statutes   690
F. Note on Specific as Compared to General Jurisdiction   693
G. Note on Personal Jurisdiction in Federal Court   695
H. Minimum-Contacts Analysis in Operation   697
World-Wide Volkswagen Corp. v. Woodson   699
Your Takeaway   707
Review Questions   708
Calder v. Jones   710
Your Takeaway   712
Review Questions   712
Walden v. Fiore   715
Review Questions   720
Asahi Metal Industry Co., Ltd. v. Superior Court of California,
    Solano County   720
Your Takeaway   727
Review Questions   727
J. McIntyre Machinery, Ltd. v. Nicastro   730
Your Takeaway   743
Review Questions   744
Practice Exercise No. 31: Applying a Long-Arm Statute
    in *Carpenter v. Dee*   747
Bristol-Myers Squibb Co. v. Superior Court of California   749
Your Takeaway   759
Review Notes & Questions   759
Burger King Corp. v. Rudzewicz   762
Your Takeaway   771
Review Questions   771
Practice Exercise No. 32: Ruling on a Rule 12(b)(2) Motion
    to Dismiss in a Contract Action   773
I. Personal Jurisdiction in Cyberspace   774
Rao v. Era Alaska Airlines   774
Your Takeaway   780
Review Questions   781
Practice Exercise No. 33: Electronic Contacts and Virtual Presence   785
Practice Exercise No. 34: A Twenty-First-Century Fish Story   786
J. Jurisdiction Based on the Presence of Defendant's Property   787
Shaffer v. Heitner   788
Review Questions   796

K. Jurisdiction Based Solely on Personal Service Within
the Forum State 799
    Burnham v. Superior Court of California 799
    Review Questions 808
L. General Jurisdiction 810
    Goodyear Dunlop Tires Operations, S. A., et al. v. Brown et ux.,
        Co-Administrators of the Estate of Brown, et al. 811
    Your Takeaway 816
    Review Questions 816
    Daimler AG v. Bauman 818
    Your Takeaway 827
    Review Questions 828
    BNSF Railway Co. v. Tyrrell 830
    Your Takeaway 834
    Review Questions 834
M. Consent 836
    Carnival Cruise Lines, Inc. v. Shute 837
    Your Takeaway 841
    Review Questions 841
N. Notice 846
    Mullane v. Central Hanover Bank & Trust Co. 846
    Your Takeaway 850
    Review Questions 851
O. Venue and *Forum Non Conveniens* 853
    Piper Aircraft Co. v. Reyno 854
    Your Takeaway 859
    Review Questions 859
    Practice Exercise No. 35: Location, Location, Location 862
    Review Exercise No. 7 862
P. Note on Personal Jurisdiction Under International Law 863

CHAPTER 8
**The Choice of an Appropriate Court: Subject Matter
Jurisdiction and Removal** 865
A. Introduction to Subject Matter Jurisdiction 865
B. Federal Question Jurisdiction 868
    Louisville & Nashville Railroad Co. v. Mottley 869
    Review Questions 871
    Gunn v. Minton 877
    Review Questions 883
C. Diversity Jurisdiction 884
    1. Complete Diversity 886
        Ceglia v. Zuckerberg 888
        Review Questions 892

2. Amount in Controversy   893
   Hackman v. One Brands, LLC   895
   Review Questions   898
   Review Exercise No. 8   900
D. Supplemental Jurisdiction   901
   United Mine Workers of America v. Gibbs   902
   Review Questions   904
   Owen Equipment and Erection Co. v. Kroger   906
   Review Questions   910
   Finley v. United States   911
   The Supplemental Jurisdiction Statute: 28 U.S.C. §1367   915
   House Report No. 101-734   915
   Review Questions   917
   Practice Exercise No. 36: Challenging Subject Matter Jurisdiction
      in *Warner*   919
   Practice Exercise No. 37: Challenging Subject Matter Jurisdiction
      in *Carpenter*   919
E. Removal   920
   Review Questions   924
   Review Exercise No. 9   925

CHAPTER 9
Choice of Federal or State Law—The Erie Doctrine   929
   Erie Railroad Co. v. Tompkins   930
   Your Takeaway   934
   Review Questions   935
   Guaranty Trust Co. v. York   940
   Your Takeaway   943
   Review Questions   943
   Byrd v. Blue Ridge Rural Electric Cooperative, Inc.   944
   Your Takeaway   947
   Review Questions   948
   Hanna v. Plumer   949
   Your Takeaway   954
   Review Questions   955
   Walker v. Armco Steel Corp.   957
   Your Takeaway   961
   Review Questions   962
   Gasperini v. Center for Humanities, Inc.   964
   Your Takeaway   971
   Review Questions   972
   Shady Grove Orthopedic Associates v. Allstate Insurance Co.   973
   Your Takeaway   983
   Review Questions   984

Practice Exercise No. 38: Analyzing Vertical Choice of Law Issues
in *Carpenter*   984
Review Exercise No. 10   985

CHAPTER 10
Finality and Preclusion   987
A. Introduction   987
　　Restatement (Second) of Judgments   988
B. Claim Preclusion (*Res Judicata*)—"Speak Now or Forever Hold
　　Your Peace"   990
　　1. What Constitutes the "Same Claim"?   990
　　　　Restatement (Second) of Judgments   990
　　　　Car Carriers, Inc. v. Ford Motor Co.   992
　　　　Your Takeaway   997
　　　　Review Questions   997
　　2. What Constitutes a "Final Valid Judgment on the Merits"?   1001
　　　　Restatement of (Second) Judgments   1001
　　3. "The Parties Are the Same or Are in Privity"   1002
　　　　Taylor v. Sturgell   1003
　　　　Your Takeaway   1009
　　　　Review Questions   1009
　　　　Gonzalez v. Banco Central Corp.   1010
　　　　Review Questions   1014
　　　　Practice Exercise No. 39: Applying Claim Preclusion Doctrine
　　　　in *Carpenter*   1014
C. Issue Preclusion (Collateral Estoppel)   1015
　　1. Defined   1015
　　2. In Operation   1016
　　　　David P. Hoult v. Jennifer Hoult   1016
　　　　Review Questions   1018
　　3. "Essential to the Judgment"   1020
　　　　Jarosz v. Palmer   1020
　　　　Review Questions   1023
　　　　Practice Exercise No. 40: Applying Preclusion Doctrine in *Warner*   1025
　　4. Nonmutual Issue Preclusion   1025
　　　　Parklane Hosiery Co., Inc. v. Shore   1025
　　　　Review Questions   1030
　　5. Issue Preclusion in Mass Tort Litigation   1033
　　　　Hardy v. Johns-Manville Sales Corp.   1033
　　　　Review Questions   1037
　　6. Issue Preclusion in Trademark Law   1037
　　　　B & B Hardware, Inc. v. Hargis Industries, Inc.   1037
　　　　Review Questions   1044

D. The Counterweights to Finality   1045
    Federated Department Stores, Inc. v. Moitie   1045
    Review Questions   1051
    Practice Exercise No. 41: Preclusion and New Precedent
        in *Carpenter*   1053
    Allen v. McCurry   1054
    Review Questions   1058
    Review Exercise No. 11   1060

CHAPTER 11

Aggregate Litigation: It All Comes Together   1063

A. Introduction   1063
B. Class Action Practice, Policy, and Context   1066
   1. Introduction   1066
   2. Policy Concerns in Class Actions   1067
   3. History: Where Have We Been, Where Are We Going?   1069
C. Due Process Foundations   1070
   1. Adequacy of Representation   1070
     Allen R. Kamp, The History Behind Hansberry v. Lee   1070
     Hansberry v. Lee   1076
     Review Questions   1079
   2. Participation   1080
     Phillips Petroleum Co. v. Shutts   1081
     Review Questions   1088
D. The Class Action Rule   1090
   1. The Contours of the Federal Rule   1090
     a. Settlement Approval   1093
     b. Interlocutory Appeal   1093
     c. Appointing the Class Counsel   1093
     d. Attorneys' Fees   1094
   2. The Rule in Application   1094
     Wal-Mart Stores, Inc. v. Dukes   1095
     Review Questions   1110
     Practice Exercise No. 42: Class Certification in *Warner* 1112
E. Subject Matter Jurisdiction in Class Action and Other Complex
  Litigation   1112
   1. Subject Matter Jurisdiction over Class Actions   1113
   2. Subject Matter Jurisdiction over Mass Torts   1115
F. Revisiting the Judicial Role in Aggregate Settlements   1117
   1. Background on Agent Orange   1118
   2. Rethinking the Judicial Role and the Adversarial System   1118
     Martha Minow, *Judge for the Situation: Judge Jack Weinstein,*
       Creator of Temporary Administrative Agencies   1119
     Review Questions   1122

Practice Exercise No. 43: The Judicial Role in Aggregate Litigation 1123
G. Preclusion in Class Actions 1124
    Martin v. Wilks 1124
    Civil Rights Act of 1991 1136
    Review Questions 1137
    Practice Exercise No. 44: The Supreme Court Addresses the
        Constitutionality of Preclusion Under the Civil Rights Act 1137

Case Files 1141
Carpenter v. Dee 1141
Warner v. City of New York 1233
Table of Cases 1283
Table of Statutes and Rules 1293
Index 1301

EXERCISES

Practice Exercises

CHAPTER 1
No. 1: Applying the Due Process Clauses   102

CHAPTER 2
No. 2: Motion for a Preliminary Injunction   127
No. 3: Equitable Relief in *Carpenter* and *Warner*   164
No. 4: Damages in *Carpenter* and *Warner*   178
No. 5: Revising Fed. R. Civ. P. 68   199
No. 6: Fee Arrangements in *Carpenter* and *Warner*   214

CHAPTER 3
No. 7: Initial Strategy Session in *Carpenter*   251
No. 8: Analyzing 12(b)(6) and 12(e) Motions in *Carpenter*   296
No. 9: Considering the *Warner* Complaint   297
No. 10: Analyzing the Answer in *Carpenter*   313
No. 11: Argument on Plaintiff's Motion to Amend in *Carpenter*   336
No. 12: Reviewing the *Warner* Answer Under Rule 11   377
No. 13: Considering Counterclaims, Cross-Claims, and Rule 13(h)
         Additional Parties in *Carpenter*   392
No. 14: Considering an Impleader in *Warner*   398

CHAPTER 4
No. 15: Discovery Planning in *Carpenter*   449
No. 16: Ethical Issues in Discovery   487
No. 17: Analyzing the Scope of Discovery   489
No. 18: Analyzing the Scope of Third-Party Discovery   490
No. 19: Analyzing Proportionality in Discovery   491
No. 20: Finding an Expert (and Expertise) in *Carpenter*   492
No. 21: Assessing the Rulemaking Process   506

CHAPTER 5
No. 22: Legislative Exercise Regarding Right to Jury Trial   535
No. 23: Law Firm Strategy Session Regarding Jury Trial in *Warner*   536
No. 24: Summary Judgment Motion Session in *Carpenter*   583
No. 25: Summary Judgment Motion Session in *Warner*   585
No. 26: Jury Instructions in *Carpenter*   625
No. 27: Motions to Challenge a Jury Verdict   628
No. 28: Closing Argument in *Carpenter*   632

CHAPTER 6
No. 29: Applying the Federal Arbitration Act   649
No. 30: Alternative Dispute Resolution in *Carpenter*   663

CHAPTER 7
No. 31: Applying a Long-Arm Statute in *Carpenter v. Dee*   747
No. 32: Ruling on a Rule 12(b)(2) Motion to Dismiss in a Contract
         Action   773
No. 33: Electronic Contacts and Virtual Presence   785
No. 34: A Twenty-First-Century Fish Story   786
No. 35: Location, Location, Location   862

CHAPTER 8
No. 36: Challenging Subject Matter Jurisdiction in *Warner*   919
No. 37: Challenging Subject Matter Jurisdiction in *Carpenter*   919

CHAPTER 9
No. 38: Analyzing Vertical Choice of Law Issues in *Carpenter*   984

CHAPTER 10
No. 39: Applying Claim Preclusion Doctrine in *Carpenter*   1014
No. 40: Applying Preclusion Doctrine in *Warner*   1025
No. 41: Preclusion and New Precedent in *Carpenter*   1053

CHAPTER 11
No. 42: Class Certification in *Warner*   1112
No. 43: The Judicial Role in Aggregate Litigation   1123
No. 44: The Supreme Court Addresses the Constitutionality of
         Preclusion Under the Civil Rights Act   1137

Review Exercises

CHAPTER 3
No. 1   314
No. 2   416
No. 3   418

CHAPTER 5
No. 4   612
No. 5   637

CHAPTER 6
No. 6   660

CHAPTER 7
No. 7   862

CHAPTER 8
No. 8   900
No. 9   925

CHAPTER 9
No. 10   985

CHAPTER 10
No. 11   1060

PREFACE TO THE SIXTH EDITION

Twenty years have passed since our first edition. We remain grateful to the dozens of professors who have adopted our book, many of whom have given us suggestions through the years that we have incorporated. Please continue to advise and question us. In particular, we seek your input as we begin to develop a set of online materials to enhance the teaching and learning of this subject.

With each edition of this book we return to the principles, insights, and goals that animated the first edition. First, we continue to think that setting cases in context is important to help students better understand doctrine. Doctrine becomes meaningful when set in its historical and sociopolitical context. In this edition we have endeavored to add more context to some of the more recent cases. That context often conveys the importance of procedure as the backbone to the vindication of substantive rights. The evolution of doctrine is often complex, and the facts on the ground often defy familiar and tidy ideological narratives. For those interested, an important part of the book's origin story is set forth in Stephen N. Subrin, *Teaching Civil Procedure While You Watch It Disintegrate*, 59 Brooklyn L. Rev. 1155 (1993). Then, as now, we think it important to be honest (even if critical) about the state of the field of civil procedure.

We hope the book gives students the ability to understand this complexity while still keeping a clear grasp of doctrine. Part and parcel of this commitment involves giving somewhat longer excerpts of cases than other books do. We think that this encourages critical thinking and perspective as well as acclimating students to how cases appear in the real world. The cases are edited, however, and we note that those edits are not always tracked in the text with ellipses or other notes. Footnotes have been kept to their original numbering, but most have been deleted.

Beginning with the first edition and continuing with each edition thereafter, we have looked for ways to help students learn by doing. We strongly believe that practice—engaging in how lawyers actually use procedure—is essential to understanding the doctrine and essential to becoming a successful ethical professional. We have added more practice exercises and improved others. In the Fifth Edition we replaced one of the two main cases that is used in practices exercises and in comments and questions throughout the text. This edition continues to use the materials from the litigation challenging New York City's stop-and-frisk policy. This case offers a good teaching tool for procedure; its high profile and its public nature offer a nice contrast to the jeep rollover case (the other case woven throughout the book), yet it is still an accessible set of trial documents. We thank Darius Charney at the Center for Constitutional

Rights and our research assistants, Scott Garosshen and Kimberly Sharpe, for helping us create this set of materials. We once again thank Jane Picker for her assistance creating that earlier set of materials for the City of Cleveland firefighters case used in previous editions. And of course we thank Jeffrey Stern for sharing the *Carpenter v. Dee* case materials, which still constitute the backbone of the practice component of this book.

In this edition we have updated and, where possible, streamlined the materials. We have completely revised the materials on discovery and alternative dispute resolution. We have also replaced the "Comments and Questions" sections with new categories: "Review Questions," which are aimed at helping students' understanding of the doctrine at issue; "Questions to Ponder," which encourage students to consider larger policy questions and to reflect on larger, systemic issues raised by the doctrine; and "Want to Know More?" boxes which provide more information about the academic and political debates surrounding procedural law. We thank our research assistants, Daniel Hanley, Demery Ormerod, Jesslin Wooliver, and Connor S. Romm for sharing their insights and helping us prepare this Sixth Edition.

The principal founder of this casebook, Steve Subrin, retired in 2016 after 45 years of teaching. A voluminous festschrift celebrating his profound contributions to the field of civil procedure is printed at *Through a Glass Starkly: Civil Procedure Re-Assessed*, 15 Nev. L.J. 1091-1692 (2015). Yet words fail to capture the mentorship, camaraderie, humor, grace, energy, knowledge, and genius that Steve brings to each personal relationship and to every scholarly project. Every page of this book reflects Steve's vision, passion, and humanity, as well as his love of procedure. His co-authors are immensely grateful for the opportunity to work with him, and we are truly honored to share the book with him. His vision continues to guide and inspire the production of this book.

Stephen N. Subrin
Martha L. Minow
Mark S. Brodin
Thomas O. Main
Alexandra D. Lahav
December 2019

PREFACE TO THE FIRST EDITION

The impetus for this book grew out of our own experience as law students and professors. We find that students learn most effectively when legal doctrine, its context, and how doctrine actually works in practice are integrated. Empirical and theoretical research support the notion that we learn and remember at our best as a result of intense, sustained experiences in which we must perform concrete tasks that call upon a number of our faculties. Many of our deepest learning experiences have come from teaching a new course, helping a client solve a problem, or writing an article or a book—experiences that call upon a combination of knowledge, insight, values, clarity, advocacy, judgment, and endurance. These are the lessons that stick.

We wanted a civil procedure course that created a more unified learning experience. Civil procedure doctrine can seem remote from the reality of torts, crimes, contracts, and land. And yet perhaps no other legal subject so calls into question the major issues of law and practicing law in the United States: separation of powers, federalism, the adversarial relationship, efficiency, fairness, power and powerlessness, justice, and fees. In a civil procedure course one finds, for example, the conceptual challenges of *Erie,* the ethical dimensions of discovery, and the practical necessities of hard and fast rules. Moreover, this is a field in flux, and studying the underlying values and historical context of procedure helps one make some sense of the inherent uncertainty and change.

Often students say that they know the doctrine, yet (frustratingly) they cannot meaningfully apply it. We wanted to develop a course in which students applied the doctrine they were learning. Seven years ago, Steve Subrin and several of his students at Northeastern University School of Law confronted the challenge of creating a more unified civil procedure course. They put two real cases, with practice-oriented exercises, at the center of a contextual, philosophic, and multidisciplinary study of civil procedure. They reprinted fewer opinions, but retained more of the procedure and factual context by not severely editing them. They also reprinted longer excerpts of pertinent articles to demonstrate the flow of an extended argument. The students were given challenging questions to contemplate or answer, but they were not given questions that required additional reading or expert knowledge. Finally, they employed *orientation essays* to illuminate certain doctrines and to elucidate the contextual and practical environments that influenced, and were influenced by, those doctrines.

We have remained true to the vision of Steve Subrin and his students—the vision of creating a civil procedure course that not only taught the doctrine but also applied it and illuminated the integral role of civil procedure in every substantive area of the law. Many features of this book promote that vision:

- Orientation essays that focus on doctrine, practice, or context, or a combination of these.
- Pleadings and files of two real cases are threaded throughout the book.
- To maintain a manageable size yet cover all of the essentials, the authors have carefully edited the book's cases.
- There is complete integration of contextual materials and practice exercises.
- Thomas Main helped design the founding materials as a law student, and became a co-author of this text as he entered practice and added a law-practice perspective to this course.
- Martha Minow and Mark Brodin brought original materials and different perspectives that contributed to this effort to reinvent a course in civil procedure.

We are grateful to those who aided and abetted this project. In particular, Jeff Stern, a distinguished trial lawyer at Sugarman, Rogers, Barshak & Cohen in Boston, Massachusetts, helped us develop the materials for the wrongful death action involving the roll-over of a Jeep. Jane Picker, Ken Kowalski, and the Fair Employment Law Clinic at Cleveland-Marshall College of Law, Cleveland State University, helped us develop the materials for the Title VII class action against the Cleveland Ohio Fire Department. In both cases, we have changed the names and, in a few instances for pedagogical purposes, certain facts.

Many Northeastern University School of Law students and graduates inspired Steve's vision for this book, and participated in its initial preparation and later iterations. He gives special thanks to Mary Azzarito, John Becker, David Brenner, Kent Brintnall, Kevin Brown, Shawn Bush, Genna Carver, Stephanie Cucurullo, Rachel Dimitruk, Liz Goldstein, Amy Hubert, Vik Kanwar, Dovie King, Amber Klinge, Aileen Lachs, Laura Matlow, Mark McGrath, David Plotkin, Judy Prosper, Sasha Rosebush, Joel Rosen, Nicole Voigt, Jason Walta, Angela Wessels, and Debra Williams.

Martha thanks Laurie Corzett, Katie Cook, Naomi Ronen, and many generations of civil procedure students.

Mark thanks the hundreds of civil procedure students over the years who, he insists, have taught him far more than he has taught them.

Thomas thanks Grace Petrola, Sandy Heffley, and countless others who contributed time and expertise to this project. He also thanks Hill & Barlow, Boston, Massachusetts, and Platinum Equity Holdings, Los Angeles, California, who wittingly shared (and in important respects shouldered) his commitment to this text.

All of the authors sincerely thank Greg Pingree for helping to clarify the collective voice of this book. The authors also thank Bernard Johnston, Melody

Davies, and Jay Boggis of Aspen Publishers for their assistance and patience. And finally, the authors thank Carol McGeehan, our Acquisitions Editor, for her support, guidance, and belief in this project. The final product is truly a collaborative effort.

Stephen N. Subrin
Martha L. Minow
Mark S. Brodin
Thomas O. Main
February 2000

CIVIL PROCEDURE

CHAPTER 1

An Introduction to Civil Procedure

The rules and laws governing civil litigation are the domain of lawyers and not the typical subject for popular culture or public debate. Nonetheless, as this introduction explores, civil procedure rules and practices centrally structure private dispute resolution and many public controversies. This introduction also provides a brief explanation of sources for key rules and doctrines, suggestions for studying, and comments on the unique features of this casebook. Especially for students interested in theoretical understandings of law, the introduction offers analysis of law itself as a kind of theater with rules and practices for translating social harms into a drama recognized by the legal world.

The opening section introduces a central theme of the course through discussion of one notable case, *United States v. Hall*, 472 F.2d 261 (5th Cir. 1972). The theme is that the law imposes limitations on the power of courts. The doctrinal issue is the reach of the courts' contempt power—whether a court has power to hold a nonparty in contempt. Arising in the larger context of a school desegregation suit, *Hall* presents judicial analysis of both common law precedents and a rule about judicial power to punish nonparties for violating a court order.

The second section of this chapter addresses the constitutional foundations for due process, or the right to be heard, a right that guides the structure of procedure in the United States. Because landmark Supreme Court opinions have addressed the scope of due process in reviewing decisions by administrative agencies, these opinions provide the centerpiece, but the frameworks and values that emerge pervade procedural rules and practices in the courts as well. Indeed, the values behind due process are critical to the doctrines governing access to court, jurisdiction, and preclusion, which are developed in later parts of the book.

The final section of this chapter considers access to the courts and to lawyers. Access to the courts is prior to every other topic in the field of procedure.

This chapter considers initial access to the court system and to representation, while other parts of the book continue the thread in considering how various procedural rules affect litigants' access to justice.

A. WHAT STUDENTS SHOULD KNOW FROM THE START

1. Why Procedure Matters

Most starting law students have some sense of the subjects to be addressed in criminal law, property, contracts, and torts. The media and personal encounters make these fields familiar to nonlawyers. Many students have signed leases for apartments and entered into oral or written employment contracts. Some have been involved in automobile accidents or injured by defective products. Others have had close encounters with the criminal law through following highly visible murder trials, serving on juries, or watching the experiences of friends and family members. However, few students, if any, have thought about why some cases are in federal court and some in state court, or whether an accident victim may file successive suits for each separate injury suffered in an incident, or what steps initiate and terminate a lawsuit.

Yet from the moment a lawyer meets a prospective client and begins to learn the details of the problem for which assistance is sought, the lawyer must think about such procedural dimensions. How could the client's story be translated into a "complaint," which is the document that commences litigation? What elements would comprise a viable "claim for relief" and thus survive the defendant's available procedural challenges, which may charge lack of jurisdiction, improper venue, failure to join a necessary party, or failure to plead with sufficient specificity? How can the "discovery" (pretrial fact investigation) process be used to develop evidence sufficient to support the "allegations" in the complaint? Is the amount of money likely to be recovered on a prevailing claim adequate to make the litigation worth the costs, including attorneys' fees? Or should the lawyer encourage the client to drop the claim, settle the claim, or pursue mediation or another alternative to litigation?

Even lawyers who never plan to go to court (the majority of the profession) must concern themselves with procedural matters. The business lawyer who drafts a contract must consider what could happen if either party fails to perform and litigation arises. Will my client have to chase the breaching party to its distant home state to file a suit to enforce the contract, or will we have to defend a suit charging breach in that distant forum? Should we negotiate for a "forum selection clause" and a "choice of law clause" to specify where any litigation over the contract would take place and under what rules? Should we include an arbitration provision?

The skills used in mastering the world of procedure are highly useful in other legal endeavors. Drafting complaints and answers helps lawyers refine the skill of sorting out points of agreement and disagreement. Studying the Federal

Rules of Civil Procedure and procedural statutes highlights the delicate art of statutory construction and interpretation. Mastering the line of Supreme Court opinions governing personal jurisdiction involves close reading of evolving case law and learning to see how legal concepts and factual distinctions matter over time in judge-made law. Fact gathering and managing information to prepare for litigation are skills crucial even to lawyers who never pursue court actions.

Although at times procedure may seem to involve petty details (do weekends count in assessing when a ten-day deadline kicks in?), it also engages the largest questions law can engage: What should a society value? How should it resolve disputes? What role should citizens have in governance? What are the roles and limits of democratic institutions such as legislatures? What power should be held and used by the nonmajoritarian institution of the court? Can words restrict the actions of people entrusted with power? What can remedy a wrong? What is a lie? How should economic disparities affect access to justice? These large questions underlie and shape the subject. Now let us consider what that subject is.

2. What Is "Civil Procedure"?

The "civil" in "civil procedure" means noncriminal. A criminal case may result in imprisonment or a fine, and the moving party is always the government; in a civil case the remedies include monetary compensation or an order directing the defendant to do or stop doing something. Often, both plaintiff and defendant are private parties, although in some instances the government may be either plaintiff or defendant.

"Procedure" is meant to contrast with "substance." The rights and duties governing daily activities of people and institutions constitute substantive law. For instance, a torts course covers the various forms of conduct about which a plaintiff can complain and obtain redress under such doctrines as negligence, assault, and defamation; the doctrines themselves are composed of elements that a litigant must prove before a court can order a remedy.

In contrast, a procedure course concentrates on the *methods* by which the substantive law can be enforced, typically, although not exclusively, by courts. Thus, procedure determines how disputes are channeled into a legal form; civil procedure addresses the channeling of disputes into courts and the methods for resolving them there. The topics range from the mundane, such as what documents must be filed and when, to those basic to defining governmental power in the United States. The procedural laws define the balance of power between the federal government and the states, including what power to resolve disputes is retained by the states and what by the federal government (subject matter jurisdiction) and which source of law—state or federal—applies to a dispute when it is litigated (the federalism issue epitomized by the case of *Erie Railroad v. Tomkins*, 304 U.S. 64 (1938)). Procedural law also defines the scope of the government's power, including when a person's liberty may be affected by the courts (due process, personal jurisdiction). Every issue, even the most mundane or technical, also involves important social policies and values. The doctrine of pleadings, for example, controls the ability of plaintiffs to access the court system. Summary judgment raises the fundamental question of whether disputes should be resolved by the professional judge or by lay citizens summoned to serve on juries. In sum, the civil procedure course concerns the premises and operations of the adversarial system of justice, the scope of due process, the ethical issues posed for a lawyer entrusted with representing the interests of another, and the proper balance between efficiency and fairness.

The basic line between procedure and substance, so central to the definition of civil procedure, will not always be clear or obvious. Indeed, in this respect, the debates over the line between procedure and substance mirror debates over most other lines drawn by the law. Procedure and substance are often closely connected as well as mutually defining; because some rules depend on the distinction between procedure and substance, that distinction itself at times becomes the site of disputes.

3. Meeting the Players and the Institutions

If substantive law announces norms and the consequences for their breach, procedural law converts a conflict over norms and breach into a case amenable to trial. Procedures translate conflicts into cases capable of being brought to trial, even when the dispute never gets that far and instead ends in settlement or moves through alternative processes such as mediation or arbitration. Procedural law translates disputants into parties. As parties, people appear in court; party or potential party status affects even out-of-court conversations. This section will briefly introduce procedural terms used in the federal courts, terms that you need to know in order to work with the materials in this chapter. A more comprehensive survey of terms appears in Chapter 3, which describes both the elements and stages of a lawsuit. You will soon see why civil procedure is often described as "lawyers' law," because the basic vocabulary is foreign to nonlawyers, and that vocabulary actually reflects institutions and professional practices that compose the world of lawyers.

a. Parties

The complaining party, who may be an individual, a corporation, or a collection of individuals, becomes the *plaintiff* or plaintiffs; those named in terms of fault or responsibility for the plaintiffs' claims become the *defendant* or defendants. Thus identified, the plaintiffs and defendants are adversaries on opposite sides of the lawsuit. Historically in the American system, progress in pursuing a civil case depends on the parties' initiatives rather than on the decision of a judge or prosecutor. Even with court changes, enlarging the roles of judges and administrators as managers of the docket, the tradition of party control in practice puts the burden on the parties' lawyers. Lawyers, in turn, will be influenced by their own assessment of the merits of their client's position, by their predictions of the outcome, and by the method they will use for assessing attorneys' fees. The general rule is that each party pays its own attorneys' fees, so estimates of the party's ability to pay influence the attorney. Many lawyers in the tort field offer clients contingency fee arrangements, meaning a promise by the client to give the lawyer a percentage (typically one-third) of any recovered damages, with no obligation to pay if there is no recovery. Some statutes require that a losing defendant pay the attorneys' fees incurred by a prevailing plaintiff. Variations in these payment methods affect the attorney's calculus of the costs and risks of filing the suit, undertaking extensive investigation, hiring expert witnesses, and settling before trial or before judgment.

Sometimes, disputes involve more than two sides, such that simple opposition cannot capture the varied interests and obligations at issue. The Federal Rules of Civil Procedure permit plaintiffs and defendants to construct lawsuits that vary the bipolar two-party lawsuit structure through devices such as joinder, intervention, class action, and interpleader, each of which will be explored later in the course.

b. Jurisdiction

This general term refers to the power of a tribunal over a case. It is a significant issue addressed in this course because the United States has so many jurisdictions: state courts, federal courts, courts of the United States territories, and tribal courts. Jurisdiction actually has two dimensions: *jurisdiction over the subject matter* and *jurisdiction over the person*. To have subject matter jurisdiction, a court must be authorized by the Constitution and statutes to decide cases dealing with this kind of subject. The federal district (trial) courts have power to hear the kinds of lawsuits specified by Congress under two main categories: (i) the suit raises a federal question, under federal statutes or the U.S. Constitution, or (ii) the suit involves parties satisfying diversity of citizenship (the plaintiff and defendant are citizens of different states or one of them is a citizen of a foreign country) *and* more than a statutory minimum amount is in controversy (currently set by Congress at $75,000). Specialized courts (dealing, for example, with patents or tax matters) have even more restricted spheres of subject matter jurisdiction. State trial courts include some with *general jurisdiction*—able to decide most cases—and those with *specialized jurisdiction*, such as the housing court (for landlord/tenant matters) or juvenile court (for offenses by minors).

Trial courts hear the initial dispute and presentation of evidence; appellate courts review the record developed in the course of the trial in light of claims of error in legal interpretation or application. The federal system has thirteen U.S. Courts of Appeals, each of which hears cases from a geographic area called a circuit. An appeal from a federal district court in Texas, for example, will be heard in the U.S. Court of Appeals for the Fifth Circuit. The Supreme Court of the United States is the court of last resort in the federal system. It has discretionary appellate jurisdiction over cases coming from the federal courts of appeals, as well as from state supreme courts if, and only if, those cases depend on an issue of federal law. State systems have varying names for their trial, appellate, and highest courts.

Jurisdiction over the person, or personal jurisdiction, must also be satisfied before a court can proceed with a case. This means that the court selected by the plaintiff must have authority to direct the defendant to appear and to bind the defendant with a judgment. Thus, the defendant must be subject to suit in the state in which the court is located, which in turn means that the defendant resides there or has engaged in conduct with sufficient connection to the state to make it fair to impose personal jurisdiction there.

c. Remedies

There are various kinds of relief a court may order after being persuaded that the plaintiff's claims are meritorious. Remedies may include money damages to compensate the plaintiff; money damages to punish the defendant; a declaration of the rights and duties of the parties; and orders, called injunctions, that direct the defendant to stop the harmful conduct or to start new conduct as required by law.

4. Sources for the Rules and Doctrines

The rules governing civil procedure come from several sources. Most law school civil procedure courses focus heavily on the federal courts and thus rely substantially on the Federal Rules of Civil Procedure. Congress has authorized the Supreme Court to prescribe rules to govern the conduct of federal district courts and courts of appeals (as well as rules of evidence), so long as those rules do not "abridge, enlarge or modify any substantive right." 28 U.S.C. § 2072(b).[1] Congress specified the mechanism for developing these rules: the Judicial Conference, composed of the Chief Justice of the Supreme Court, the chief judge of each court of appeals, one district judge from each regional circuit, and the chief judge of the Court of International Trade, authorizes the appointment of a standing committee that screens proposed rules. *See* 28 U.S.C. § 2073. The Judicial Conference also authorizes the appointment of advisory committees to focus on particular topics, such as civil rules or evidence rules. The advisory committees, comprising judges, practitioners, and scholars, consider proposed amendments and new rules, gather comments from judges and lawyers, and send revised proposals to the standing Committee on Practice and Procedure. That committee reports to the Judicial Conference, which recommends rule changes to the Supreme Court. The Supreme Court then decides whether to transmit such proposed rules to Congress, which in turn has the chance to reject the proposal or else, through inaction, let the proposal become part of the rules. 28 U.S.C. § 2074. In addition, Congress has on its own initiative

---

1. Congressional enactments are codified and organized by numbered titles. Title 28 collects the laws governing the federal judiciary and judicial procedure.

adopted legislation to alter one or more rules or promote alternative processes for reforming rules. *See, e.g.*, Civil Justice Reform Act of 1990, Pub. L. No. 101-650, 104 Stat. 5089 (codified as amended at 28 U.S.C. §§ 471-482). Federal district courts also have large numbers of local rules. Approximately half of the states have adopted the Federal Rules of Civil Procedure for their own state procedural rules.

No less important, however, are court-made doctrines. Some predate the codified rules of procedure; some interpret those rules; and some interpret constitutional or legislative norms to provide for procedural rules. Thus, for example, the doctrines governing a right to a hearing and what a hearing must include interpret the Due Process Clauses of the Fifth and Fourteenth Amendments to the U.S. Constitution. The doctrines governing the remedial powers of the courts grow from common law practices and statutory interpretation. The doctrine of personal jurisdiction stems from the Due Process Clauses of the Fifth and Fourteenth Amendments as well as interpretations of state statutes. Subject matter jurisdiction involves judicial interpretations of Article III of the U.S. Constitution and of statutes governing the courts. Allocation of power between the trial judge and jury depends on interpretations of the Seventh Amendment, common law and constitutional doctrines about burden of proof, as well as judicial interpretation of rules governing juries and the conduct of trials. Doctrines addressing the effects of a prior judgment on a subsequent lawsuit—the preclusion, or *res judicata* rules—grow from common law decisions as well as from interpretations of the Full Faith and Credit Clause of the Constitution (Art. IV, § 1), the Due Process Clauses, and judicial interpretations of statutes. Finally, special rules governing complex litigation have grown not only from the Federal Rules of Civil Procedure but also from congressional action, precedents, and the work of a multidistrict panel of judges addressing the subject.

Procedural design and rules, as well as judicial interpretations of these rules, can generate political debate and controversy. In this sense, procedure is no different than the substantive law you will learn in courses such as torts or criminal law. In later chapters, we will see how the courts have reinterpreted the Federal Rules over time and the criticisms of those reinterpretations.

5. How to Approach Studying

Learning procedure, like learning most of the law, requires that you actively engage the materials. Develop a habit of pursuing questions and imagining the events surrounding the materials you read. Ultimately, you will be required to apply the law to new fact situations, so memorizing and repeating rules is not enough. Rather than memorizing the materials, you will get more out of the course if you focus your time in some or all of these ways:

   a. *Carefully read all assignments before class, and read them critically*. For example, you might ask: Why was the case decided this way? Does the doctrine announced by the court make sense? Does its application to this circumstance make sense? Try to articulate the reasons for your reactions. What alternatives are there, and would they be better? Generate hypothetical situations or "what ifs." What if the facts were slightly different? Do you think that would produce a different result in the eyes of the court that produced the opinion? Should it produce a different result? What if the motion were a different motion? What if the case were in state rather than federal court? What if the judge sat without a jury?

b. *Ask where a given case is in the life cycle of procedure.* Has there already been a trial, and is the case now on appeal—and if so, in what court? Or is the case at an earlier stage, such as a challenge to the complaint through a motion to dismiss? Is a trial court's grant or rejection of such a motion now on appeal? These questions will arise in all your courses; become aware of the procedural posture of every case you study. Also ask what will happen next, procedurally. For example, is the next step a trial? An appeal?

c. *Look up what you do not know.* If a rule or statute is mentioned and seems relevant, look it up. It will often be in your rule and statute supplement. *Black's Law Dictionary* is also a good resource.

d. *Always start with a close reading of the language of the relevant rule or statute, just as courts do.* Consider if there are any ambiguous words; in what ways can the ambiguity be resolved?

e. *Think hard about facts.* You might ask: What "facts" are described in the judicial opinion? What is the source for those facts—an adversarial trial, the statements in the plaintiff's complaint, an empirical study, one witness's sworn statement? What is contested or contestable about the facts? What could resolve the contest? Which facts seem crucial to the judgment by a court or by you? Legal doctrine, abstracted from facts, is slippery if not worthless. It is the facts of any case that shape its ultimate result, putting the matter on one side or another of a legal rule or convincing a decision maker to change the rule. A wise lawyer once said, "I could find the law easier than the facts. When I was stumped or made a mistake, it was usually because of elusive facts."

f. *Try to make sense of what you read by learning about its historical and political context.* This book offers sources toward that end. Statutes and cases are made by people who reflect the times in which they live and respond to the world they have known. Many procedural issues are explicable only in relationship to prior debates and reforms. Being mindful of such context will help you remember and understand the law and will also help you explain it and persuade others about your views.

g. *Remember that law is about real people and groups.* Ask what effect the law has on them and what happened after the cases were over. What do these outcomes make you think about the policies and rules you have studied?

h. *Develop your own study materials as the course proceeds.* There is no single way to do this. Some people use outlines that they construct from their notes on the readings and class discussions. An outline can help you to get your hands around the material and to manage the large amount of information and analysis you will need to know by the end of the course. It is best to do this as you go along. Include not only cases and their results but also statements of rules and exceptions, as well as the values and policies underlying the rules and judicial interpretations of them.

i. *Form a study group to discuss and debate the materials with your classmates to help you* practice *law rather than memorizing it.* For example, you might propose hypotheticals and try to work them out together. By the middle of the course, take a look at old exams and tackle them together, or use the practice questions provided in this book. You want to get in the habit of applying doctrine, forming arguments, predicting court action, and evaluating unsatisfactory decisions. All of this is easier and more fun to do when learning with and from other students.

j. *Do not worry if many aspects of this and other courses do not make immediate sense or hang entirely together.* Much understanding of law depends on understanding each part's relationship to the others; many aspects of each course will make more sense as you learn other aspects. Be patient and determined.

6. About This Book

This book includes leading and illustrative judicial opinions, relevant statutes and rules, and exercises that place you in the role of lawyer and judge to help develop the critical skills of analysis, research, fact investigation, strategy formulation, document drafting, written and oral advocacy, and ability to make informed judgments in the face of necessarily limited information. The book further includes historical, empirical, and jurisprudential materials to help you see the litigation system in its broader contexts and to expose the value choices behind both the existing system and proposals for reform. Understanding the context in which rules are made and interpreted and the policies that they embody is critical to becoming a great advocate because advocates draw on context, values, and policies in framing their arguments and convincing the courts to rule in favor of their clients. In this way, doctrine, context, and practice are linked to one another—to become an accomplished practitioner you will need to master both doctrine and context.

The aspiring lawyer who uses this book should become a problem solver, considering each case and issue from the perspective of a legal practitioner who faces key decisions along the path of litigation. Based on an initial meeting with a potential client, the lawyer asks: Is there a claim for relief? What remedies are available, and do they make litigation worthwhile? Who will pay attorneys' fees? What is an appropriate court? Who should be designated as a party? What should the complaint include? What facts should be investigated through discovery? When should settlement be pursued? What motions should be filed and when?

For focus and coherence, this book continually uses the files of two actual cases. The first, brought by a surviving spouse, is a wrongful death action arising out of a motor vehicle accident. The second is a civil rights suit alleging that New York City's stop-question-and frisk program was racially discriminatory. By offering materials that reveal how these two cases move through the litigation process, the book provides chronological set pieces around which you can organize and remember what you have learned. The two cases also permit a realistic and sophisticated exploration of procedural doctrine and procedural decision making. They allow you to see the relationship between decisions made early on and those made in the later stages of the litigation. They also vividly demonstrate the importance of facts and how one arranges them into different stories for different audiences or purposes. Because practicing lawyers follow through with individual cases, rather than jump each day to new problems, these materials simulate real features of practice, in which procedural topics remain interconnected in the life history of particular cases. Finally, the two cases provide a good deal of substantive law, to create a realistic sense of the interplay between substance and process.

7. Law as Theater

Fundamentally, legal procedures enable the process of translating harms in the world into terms that are recognized by lawyers and judges. Crucial to that process of translation are the facts and the substantive law (rules of contract, tort, and so forth). Yet also vital are elements of presentation: style, tone, rhetoric, and drama. For the process to succeed, such elements must combine to form the appearance of fairness and impartiality, both to the specific players in a given legal dispute and to the society at large. Professor Milner Ball has proposed a way of understanding these elements by exploring the significance of metaphor and the function of courts as theater.

Milner S. Ball, The Promise of American Law: A Theological, Humanistic View of Legal Process
48-62, 136-138 (1981) Reprinted with permission of University of Georgia Press.

THE ELEMENT OF METAPHOR

The elements of presentation—rules of evidence, the case of the opposing side, the dynamics of the proceeding (including surprise and improvisation), the quality of evidence and witnesses, and the compellingness of the law—are considered just as carefully by an attorney as are the facts and the law. The dominant element in the presentation with which he will be concerned is the need to persuade the appropriate decisionmakers, first to a judgment that the claim is judicially cognizable, and then to a judgment favorable to the party represented. The consequential logic, which to a degree governs the selection of facts and law, coupled with the attorney's need for a persuasive presentation, distinguishes the legal case from a scientific investigation. . . . The methods are better understood as those of playwrights, actors, and directors, and may be described as the making of metaphor.

The passage from fact to metaphor is what the advocate seeks. It is the passage from the materials of fact and law (the text) by means of courtroom presentation (the performance) to a persuasive statement of what is to be done in a given situation (the metaphor).

THE FUNCTIONS OF JUDICIAL THEATER

REDIRECTING AGGRESSION

. . . [T]he theatrical character of lawsuits . . . allows them to redirect aggression. Aggression, the need to fight and have revenge, is acted out and is thereby ritually expressed and controlled. It is in this sense that "[t]he right to sue and defend in the courts is the alternative of force."

Acceptance of judicial proceedings must be voluntary and is consequently dependent upon the perceived fairness of the courts. . . .

Participants . . . bring with them a willing suspension of disbelief. It is manifested in their willingness to observe the rules and forms of the proceedings, their willingness to abide by the outcome of the proceedings, and their willingness not to dismiss the legitimacy of the legal system, characterized though it may be by curious formulae, arcane rites, and untoward results. Like the license granted theater, this willingness will answer for any sustained length of time only to the system's reasonable degree of success in doing what it promises, in this case, justice.

ENCOURAGING IMPARTIALITY

Courts may not always or even frequently do justice, but their theatrical quality does contribute to their potential for doing justice by encouraging disinterestedness in the decision-makers. As actors, the judge and jury are asked to play parts in a government of laws and not of people. Fulfillment of the roles enables judgments that rise above prejudice and that, therefore, will more likely be just. . . .

THE PERFORMANCE AS A WHOLE

If the advocate's presentation of his client's case is a form of theater which is played to the judge or jury and which contributes to judgment, there is also the theater of the courtroom itself—embracing all that goes on within—played to the public at large. It is the function of this drama to provide an image of legitimate society. In this sense, it is importantly an end in itself. As is true of theater generally, so of judicial theater: the performance is the "good" consumed. The courts are not so much in the business of producing decisions—finding facts, fixing liability, convicting the guilty, protecting the innocent, etc.—as they are of giving a performance. . . .

B. AN OPENING CASE: THE POWER AND LIMITS OF COURTS

In *United States v. Hall*, 472 F.2d 261 (5th Cir. 1972), the Court of Appeals for the Fifth Circuit asks whether the district court judge may punish—or indeed do anything to—someone who was not a party to the relevant lawsuit. What are the limits of judicial power as announced in this opinion? Have those limits changed because of this decision, or does this decision simply confirm pre-existing limits? When the court looks to a rule to answer the question before it, where does that rule come from? When there is more than one relevant rule, what should a court do? When applying established rules to new facts, does the court change the rules, and if so, how?

1. Reading a Federal Rule of Civil Procedure

Civil procedure may differ from your other classes in that statutes and rules (in addition to judicial decisions) are central to this subject. Many of the cases you read will be interpretations of procedural rules. *United States v. Hall*, the introductory case in this book, required the judge to interpret Rule 65 of the Federal Rules of Civil Procedure. Lawyers and judges interpret the Federal Rules using the same tools that they use to interpret statutes. But the Federal Rules differ from other laws in two ways that are useful to know. First, the process for passing Federal Rules differs from that for statutes because the Federal Rules are written by the advisory committee to the Committee on the Rules of Practice and Procedure, approved by the Supreme Court and ratified by Congress. By contrast, federal statutes are passed by both houses and presented to the President. When judges interpret the Federal Rules, they are interpreting rules written by the judicial branch rather than the legislative. Nevertheless, the Federal Rules have the force of statutes; after a Federal Rule comes into effect, any law that conflicts with that rule is supplanted. *See* 28 U.S.C. § 2072 (2012).

The Federal Rules are accompanied by a set of comments written by the advisory committee, known as "Advisory Committee Notes," which appear at the end of each rule. There is a dispute as to how these comments are to be used to help courts and litigants understand the meaning of the Federal Rules. Most judges see these comments as analogous to legislative history, to be referred to or ignored depending on one's philosophy of statutory interpretation. Some scholars argue that the Notes ought to be seen as definitive because of the process by which rules are adopted. *See* Catherine Struve, *The Paradox of Delegation: Interpreting the Federal*

Rules of Civil Procedure, 150 U. Pa. L. Rev. 1099 (2002). Disputes over the weight of the comments suggest the potentially significant disagreements over the scope and meaning of the rules as well as the elements of their interpretation.

READING A FEDERAL RULE

Here is a recommended approach to reading a Federal Rule:

Look at the structure of the rule. Before you read the entire rule, first look at its structure. Most rules have different parts addressing particular questions that might arise in the course of their application. Often these are in bold. At this point it is useful to step back and ask yourself: What is this rule about? At what point in the litigation does this rule become relevant? Think about the rule in the larger context of the lawsuit (the forest) before delving into its more specific language (the trees).

Read the text of the rule carefully. Then read it again. Careful reading is the key to interpreting rules and statutes. This is difficult because rules have no narrative. Instead, the case or hypothetical assigned with the rule provides the story. You might see yourself as trying to figure out how the rule will affect the way the story turns out. As you read the rule the second time, ask yourself which of the provisions of the rule are relevant to the problem that arises in the case or hypothetical you have been assigned. Of those provisions, what are alterative interpretations that will benefit one side or the other? How would you choose between them if you were the judge? Which interpretation is best for this litigant, which is best for society, and which fits most neatly with your ideas about how judges should interpret legal texts?

Interpreting the rule. Sometimes the plain text of the rule will be clear. Other times, the words used will be subject to different interpretations; in other words, parts of the rule will be ambiguous. Often a term that seems clear on an initial reading can seem more ambiguous in context and application. As you read the *Hall* case and Rule 65, consider what parts of the rule are ambiguous and what parts are clear. Then consider what tools the defendant uses to interpret the rule and what interpretive tools the judge uses to reach a different conclusion. Which approach do you find more convincing?

---

2. Interpreting Rules and Statutes

The same interpretative strategies are generally used for interpreting rules and statutes. You will encounter various methods of statutory interpretation as you move through the course and may choose to take a course devoted to statutory interpretation. As an introduction, three tools are useful to know:

Plain meaning. The first place that a court is to look for meaning is the text of the statute. Courts begin with the statute itself. But, of course, words do not exist in a vacuum. Sometimes the statute will specifically define a word. Other times the context in which the word is being used provides a basis for how it should be interpreted. If a term is not specifically defined in the statute, courts may interpret its "ordinary" meaning, sometimes relying on a dictionary.

Justice Scalia, an ardent proponent of the plain text tool of statutory interpretation, explained that statutory construction "is a holistic endeavor. A provision that may seem ambiguous in isolation is often clarified by the remainder of the statutory scheme—because the same terminology is used elsewhere in a context that makes its meaning clear, or because only one of the permissible meanings produces a substantive effect that is compatible with the rest of the law." *United Savings Ass'n. of Tex. v. Timbers of Inwood Forest Associates,* 484 U.S. 365, 371 (1988).

Purpose. Judges will also look to the purpose of the statute to interpret it, sometimes expressed in a statement of findings and purposes. Justice Jackson summarized this approach: "[C]ourts will construe the details of an act in conformity with its dominating general purpose, will read text in the light of context and will interpret the text so far as the meaning of the words fairly permits so as to carry out in particular cases the generally expressed legislative policy." *SEC v. C.M. Joiner Leasing Corp.,* 320 U.S. 344, 350-351 (1943). The general purpose of the Federal Rules of Civil Procedure is set forth in Rule 1. After reading the *Hall* case, consider to what extent Rule 1 provides justification for the parties' desired results and the court's ultimate decision.

Legislative history. Courts will sometimes use legislative history—contemporaneous statements by lawmakers and other materials—to illuminate the meaning of the text and the purpose of the statute as a whole. The use of legislative history is controversial. One of the difficulties of using legislative history is that legislators who voted for a law may not all agree as to its purpose or likely effects. With respect to the Federal Rules, we have a more definitive expression of the intent of the rules drafters in the form of the "Advisory Committee Notes." Courts and litigators rely on these Notes to shed light on how language in the rule ought to be interpreted. Not all judges agree, however, on the force that ought to be given to the Notes when interpreting rules. Justice Scalia summarized this position: "The Advisory Committee's insights into the proper interpretation of a Rule's text are useful to the same extent as any scholarly commentary. But the Committee's *intentions* have no effect on the Rule's meaning. Even assuming that we and the Congress that allowed the Rule to take effect read and agreed with those intentions, it is the text of the Rule that controls." *Krupski v. Costa Crociere S.p.A.,* 130 S. Ct. 2485, 2499 (2010) (Scalia, J., concurring).

3. Background of *United States v. Hall*

Eric Hall was arrested on March 9, 1972 for violating an emergency ex parte injunction issued pursuant to one of a series of decisions involving the Duval County, Florida public schools, then the thirteenth largest school district in the country.[2] Duval County maintained a dual school system divided along racial

---

2. Thanks to Vik Kanwar and Dovie Yoana King, then-students of Northeastern University School of Law, for their research. Mr. Kanwar is now the Associate Director of International Programs and an Adjunct Professor at Southwestern Law School in Los Angeles. Ms. King is a public interest attorney.

lines despite the U.S. Supreme Court's decision in *Brown v. Board of Education*, 347 U.S. 482 (1954), forbidding such deliberate segregation. In 1960, a group of black parents sued the school board on behalf of their school-aged children. The court found that the school board had maintained a racially divided school system "as a matter of policy, custom and usage" and had "not adopted any plan whatever for eliminating racial discrimination in the public school system. . . ." *Braxton v. Board of Public Instruction for Duval County*, 326 F.2d 616, 621 (5th Cir. 1964).

By 1971, the Duval County School Board remained either incapable of or unwilling to comply with the court's order. Only 60 of the 30,000 black students in the school system participated in desegregated schooling; most black students attended all-black schools, even if that required commuting to distant schools. *Mims v. Duval County School Board*, 329 F. Supp. 123, 125 (D. Fla. 1971). The district court therefore ordered remedial action, including a plan to pair Ribault and Raines High Schools, which would yield two integrated schools. This decision was in line with the Supreme Court's 1971 opinion in *Swann v. Charlotte-Mecklenburg Board of Education*, 402 U.S. 1 (1971), which detailed the duties of school districts and the powers of district courts to ensure plans to work realistically and effectively to end racial segregation in public schools.

Soon after the court's desegregation order was put into effect, racial violence erupted at Ribault High School—the formerly predominantly white school. In response to the violence, administrators shut down the school on at least two occasions. These and subsequent events were reported in Otis Perkins, *End to Disruptions at Schools Ordered Here*, Florida Times-Union, March 6, 1972. On February 18, 1972, black students at Ribault organized a walkout; white students and black students then engaged in fights that damaged school property. Despite the participation of both groups of students, school officials blamed the black students and charged and suspended 12 of them. The administrators then recruited 30 extra teachers to be present on campus. The administration also alerted sheriffs in the vicinity, rearranged lunch schedules, and eliminated one class period to avoid confrontations between the racial groups. Then, a white faculty member removed from the cafeteria bulletin board several posters relating to Black History week, including one with a picture of philosopher and prisoner advocate Angela Davis and the caption, "THIS IS WAR."[3] Black students replaced the posters, and then white students took them down. This incident produced a 20-minute delay in classes, and 50 white students and 125 black students then gathered on the school patio in a "free for all" fight. Black students then tried to organize another boycott.

School authorities held black students largely responsible for the unrest that day. The authorities also believed that black adults from outside the school were encouraging students to defy police and school authorities. The school administrators petitioned the district court for injunctive relief to bar such outsiders from school premises. In response, the court issued an ex parte injunction on Sunday, March 5, 1972. Among those intended to be covered by

---

3. Angela Davis became a fugitive after August 7, 1970 when she was accused of involvement in Jonathan Jackson's attempted hostage trade for the Soledad Brothers—an effort that ended in a deadly shootout. She later became a philosopher and university professor.

the injunction were members of the Florida Black Front, an organization that modeled itself on the Black Panthers. The injunction was served directly on some members of that group, but not to Eric Hall, who was associated with the group. Eric Hall's lawyer, William Sheppard, recalled that Eric intended to go to the school to support the black students following the incident over the posters. Whether Hall supported or opposed integration was not entirely clear; he did seek to inspire active strategies for asserting rights.[4]

Hall learned of the injunction from another member of the Black Front. He asked his lawyer what would happen if he went to the high school. Sheppard recalled his response: "I told him honestly that I thought he'd get picked up in three minutes." Sheppard also recalls that Hall next telephoned the famous leftist lawyer, William Kunstler, for a second opinion.[5] Kunstler reportedly told Hall that as a nonparty to the suit, he could do what he wanted to do. Hall entered the campus, was immediately arrested, and was then charged with contempt. The case that bears his name has been cited with approval by the U.S. Supreme Court. *See Washington v. Washington State Commercial Passenger Fishing Vessel Ass'n.*, 443 U.S. 658, 692 n.32 (1979); *Golden State Bottling Co. v. NLRB*, 414 U.S. 168, 180 (1973).

Duval County never fully integrated its school system, and controversy still surrounds its schools. Despite a court-approved agreement with the National Association for the Advancement of Colored People (NAACP) in 1996, Duval County administrators prefer voluntary integration through specialized magnet programs. The NAACP, by contrast, favors a school choice plan limiting students' options in order to ensure racial balance in the schools and is concerned that the school system plans to build new schools solely in predominantly white suburbs. The school board filed a motion to end the federal court involvement in the system. The litigation ultimately ended in 2001 when the Eleventh Circuit, over the NAACP's objection, lifted the injunction and ended the suit because, in the court's estimation, its purpose had been achieved. *N.A.A.C.P., Jacksonville Branch v. Duval County School*, 273 F.3d 960 (2001).

A final word or two on the principals involved in the case: The senior judge on the appellate panel assigned to the case, Judge John Minor Wisdom, was one of the champions of the civil rights movement who enforced Supreme Court school desegregation rulings despite personal attacks and threats of physical violence.

Less than a week after completing his jail term for contempt, Eric Hall was shot by a security guard in a Jacksonville, Florida nightclub. After his photograph appeared in a newspaper story about the incident, a former parole officer from southern Florida recognized him as someone known as Kenneth Hall, wanted for robbery in southern Florida. Hall was removed from his hospital bed and tried and convicted in southern Florida. Reportedly, by the early 1980s, he had become a prisoners' rights activist.

---

4. Interviews by Vik Kanwar with William Sheppard, Jan. 10, 1998, and Mar. 17, 1998.
5. Kunstler, a cofounder of the Center for Constitutional Rights, represented the Chicago 7 defendants and many Black Panthers.

> ## READING THE CASE
>
> As you read the opinions in this and other cases that follow, please consider the following different ways you can analyze opinions in procedural cases and be prepared to discuss them in class. These methods will serve you well for the entire course and beyond.
>
> *The underlying story.* It is often helpful to begin by trying to figure out what led to the dispute prior to the lawsuit. Who were the parties, what did they do prior to the litigation that led to the dispute, and what do they want to achieve in the lawsuit?
>
> *The procedural posture.* Follow and understand the procedure. This approach has three aspects: (1) You must consider the precise procedural question before each court. (2) You should analyze what procedural steps took place previously. This will help you preview procedural concepts before you get to them in greater detail, and it will help you review what you already know. (3) Finally, you should also consider the outcome at each level of court, from trial through the appellate process. In the case below, you might ask what the circuit court did with the district court decision. Also ask what will happen next in the case now that the circuit court has spoken.
>
> *Lawyer and judge strategies.* Consider the strategies of each of the participants. Why did the lawyers act as they did? This includes analyzing why they made their procedural choices and why plaintiffs seek particular types of relief. What is the judge's strategy in writing the opinion? When looking at cases with multiple opinions, such as concurrences or dissents, especially at the Supreme Court level, you might ask what are the Justices' strategies in writing their opinions? The judges may be trying to gain votes from other judges, and to influence future behavior and subsequent decisions.
>
> *Holdings and procedural doctrine.* Some students and teachers like to start with this step. Try to articulate what the case holds. What doctrine will lawyers and legislators take from the case? Is there reasoning that will be valuable to later cases? How closely does the judge try to link the decision to the facts of the particular case?
>
> *Other viewpoints of your choice.* You might consider judicial opinions from the points of view of other disciplines that interest you. For example, take history: What does this case tell you about the procedural, intellectual, and factual history of the times? If you like novels, consider the plot and characters involved. If you like film, imagine the courtroom scenes and others that precede and follow them.

4. The Opinion

United States v. Hall
472 F.2d 261 (5th Cir. 1972)

WISDOM, Circuit Judge:*

This case presents the question whether a district court has power to punish for criminal contempt a person who, though neither a party nor bearing any legal relationship to a party, violates a court order designed to protect the court's judgment in a school desegregation case. We uphold the district court's

---

* *Eds.' Note:* In this case and throughout this book we have omitted textual citations; textual omissions are indicated with ellipses. We have retained the original footnote numbering.

conclusion that in the circumstances of this case it had this power, and affirm the defendant's conviction for contempt.

On June 23, 1971, the district court entered a "Memorandum Opinion and Final Judgment" in the case of *Mims v. Duval County School Board*. The court required the Duval County Florida school board to complete its desegregation of Duval County schools, in accordance with the Supreme Court's decision in *Swann v. Charlotte-Mecklenburg Board of Education*, 402 U.S. 1 (1971), by pairing and clustering a number of schools which had theretofore been predominantly one-race schools. This order culminated litigation begun eleven years before, *Braxton v. Board of Public Instruction*. This Court affirmed the district court's order in *Mims v. Duval County School Board*, 447 F.2d 1330 (5th Cir. 1971). The district court retained jurisdiction to enter such orders as might be necessary in the future to effectuate its judgment.

Among the schools marked for desegregation under the plan approved by the district court was Ribault Senior High School, a predominantly white school. The plan directed pairing of Ribault with William E. Raines Senior High School, a predominantly black school, so that the black enrollment would be 59 percent at Raines and 57 percent at Ribault. After the desegregation order was put into effect racial unrest and violence developed at Ribault, necessitating on one occasion the temporary closing of the school. On March 5, 1972, the superintendent of schools and the sheriff of Jacksonville filed a petition for injunctive relief in the case with the district court. This petition alleged that certain black adult "outsiders" had caused or abetted the unrest and violence by their activities both on and off the Ribault campus. The petition identified the appellant Eric Hall, allegedly a member of a militant organization known as the "Black Front," as one of several such outsiders who, in combination with black students and parents, were attempting to prevent the normal operation of Ribault through student boycotts and other activities. As relief the petitioners requested an order "restraining all Ribault Senior High School students and any person acting independently or in concert with them from interfering with the orderly operation of the school and the Duval County School system, and for such other relief as the court may deem just and proper."

At an *ex parte* session on March 5, 1972, the district court entered an order providing in part:

1. All students of Ribault Senior High School, whether in good standing or under suspension, and other persons acting independently or in concert with them and having notice of this order are hereby enjoined and restrained from
   (a) Obstructing or preventing the attendance in classes of students and faculty members;
   (b) Harassing, threatening or intimidating any faculty, staff member or employee of Ribault Senior High School or the Duval County School Board;
   (c) Harassing, threatening or intimidating any student en route to and from school;
   (d) Destroying or attempting to destroy, defacing or attempting to deface any structure, buildings, materials or equipment of Ribault Senior High School or the Duval County School Board;

(e) Committing any other act to disrupt the orderly operation of Ribault Senior High School or any other school of the Duval County School System;

2. Until further order of this Court, no person shall enter any building of the Ribault Senior High School or go upon the school's grounds except the following:

(a) Students of Ribault Senior High School while attending classes or official school functions;

(b) The faculty, staff, and administration of Ribault Senior High School and other employees of the Duval County School Board having assigned duties at the school;

(c) Persons having business obligations which require their presence on the school's premises;

(d) Parents of Ribault Senior High School students or any other person who has the prior permission of the principal or his designee to be present on the school's premises;

(e) Law enforcement officials of the City of Jacksonville, the State of Florida or the United States Government.

The order went on to provide that "anyone having notice of this order who violates any of the terms thereof shall be subject to arrest, prosecution and punishment by imprisonment or fine, or both, for criminal contempt under the laws of the United States of America. . . ." The court ordered the sheriff to serve copies of the order on seven named persons, *including Eric Hall*. Hall was neither a party plaintiff nor a party defendant in the *Mims* litigation, and in issuing this order the court did not join Hall or any of the other persons named in the order as parties.

On March 9, 1972, four days after the court issued its order, Hall violated that portion of the order restricting access to Ribault High School by appearing on the Ribault campus. When questioned by a deputy United States marshal as to the reasons for his presence, Hall replied that he was on the grounds of Ribault for the purpose of violating the March 5 order. The marshal then arrested Hall and took him into custody. After a nonjury trial, the district court found Hall guilty of the charge of criminal contempt and sentenced him to sixty days' imprisonment.

On this appeal Hall raises two related contentions. Both contentions depend on the fact that Hall was not a party to the *Mims* litigation and the fact that, in violating the court's order, he was apparently acting independently of the *Mims* parties. He first points to the common law rule that a nonparty who violates an injunction solely in pursuit of his own interests cannot be held in contempt. Not having been before the court as a party or as the surrogate of a party, he argues that in accordance with this common law rule he was not bound by the court's order. Second, he contends that Rule 65(d) of the Federal Rules of Civil Procedure prevents the court's order from binding him, since Rule 65(d) limits the binding effect of injunctive orders to "parties to the action, their officers, agents, servants, employees, and attorneys, and . . . those persons in active concert or participation with them who receive actual notice of the order by personal service or otherwise." We reject both contentions.

For his first contention, that a court of equity has no power to punish for contempt a nonparty acting solely in pursuit of his own interests, the appellant relies heavily on the two leading cases of *Alemite Manufacturing Corp. v. Staff*, 42 F.2d 832 (2d Cir. 1930), and *Chase National Bank v. City of Norwalk*, 291 U.S. 431 (1934). In *Alemite* the district court had issued an injunction restraining the defendant and his agents, employees, associates, and confederates from infringing the plaintiff's patent. Subsequently a third person, not a party to the original suit and acting entirely on his own initiative, began infringing the plaintiff's patent and was held in contempt by the district court. The Second Circuit reversed in an opinion by Judge Learned Hand, stating that "it is not the act described which the decree may forbid, but only that act when the defendant does it." 42 F.2d at 833. In *Chase National Bank* the plaintiff brought suit against the City of Norwalk to obtain an injunction forbidding the removal of poles, wires, and other electrical equipment belonging to the plaintiff. The district court issued a decree enjoining the City, its officers, agents, and employees, "and all persons whomsoever to whom notice of this order shall come" from removing the equipment or otherwise interfering with the operation of the plaintiff's power plant. The Supreme Court held that the district court had violated "established principles of equity jurisdiction and procedure" insofar as its order applied to persons who were not parties, associates, or confederates of parties, but who merely had notice of the order. *See also Regal Knitwear Co. v. NLRB*, 324 U.S. 9, 13 (1945); *Scott v. Donald*, 165 U.S. 107 (1896).

This case is different. In *Alemite* and *Chase National Bank* the activities of third parties, however harmful they might have been to the plaintiffs' interests, would not have disturbed in any way the adjudication of rights and obligations as between the original plaintiffs and defendants. Infringement of the *Alemite* plaintiff's patent by a third party would not have upset the defendant's duty to refrain from infringing or rendered it more difficult for the defendant to perform that duty. Similarly, the defendant's duty in *Chase National Bank* to refrain from removing the plaintiff's equipment would remain undisturbed regardless of the activities of third parties, as would the plaintiff's right not to have its equipment removed by the defendant. The activities of Hall, however, threatened both the plaintiffs' right and the defendant's duty as adjudicated in the *Mims* litigation. In *Mims* the plaintiffs were found to have a constitutional right to attend an integrated school. . . . In short, the activities of persons contributing to racial disorder at Ribault imperiled the court's fundamental power to make a binding adjudication between the parties properly before it.

Courts of equity have inherent jurisdiction to preserve their ability to render judgment in a case such as this. This was the import of the holding in *United States v. United Mine Workers of America*, 330 U.S. 258 (1947). There the district court had issued a temporary restraining order forbidding a union from striking, though there was a substantial question of whether the Norris-LaGuardia Act had deprived the district court of jurisdiction to issue such an order. The Supreme Court upheld the defendants' contempt conviction for violation of this order. As an alternative holding the Court stated that the contempt conviction would have been upheld even if the district court had ultimately been found to be without jurisdiction. This holding affirmed the power of a court of equity to issue an order to preserve the status quo in order to protect its ability to render judgment in a case over which it might have jurisdiction. . . .

The integrity of a court's power to render a binding judgment in a case over which it has jurisdiction is at stake in the present case. . . .

The principle that courts have jurisdiction to punish for contempt in order to protect their ability to render judgment is also found in the use of *in rem* injunctions. Federal courts have issued injunctions binding on all persons, regardless of notice, who come into contact with property which is the subject of a judicial decree. . . . A court entering a decree binding on a particular piece of property is necessarily faced with the danger that its judgment may be disrupted in the future by members of an undefinable class—those who may come into contact with the property. The *in rem* injunction protects the court's judgment. The district court here faced an analogous problem. The judgment in a school case, as in other civil rights actions, inures to the benefit of a large class of persons, regardless of whether the original action is cast in the form of a class action. . . . At the same time court orders in school cases, affecting as they do large numbers of people, necessarily depend on the cooperation of the entire community for their implementation.

As this Court is well aware, school desegregation orders often strongly excite community passions. School orders are, like *in rem* orders, particularly vulnerable to disruption by an undefinable class of persons who are neither parties nor acting at the instigation of parties. In such cases, as in voting rights cases, courts must have the power to issue orders similar to that issued in this case, tailored to the exigencies of the situation and directed to protecting the court's judgment. . . .

The appellant also asserts that Rule 65(d) of the Federal Rules of Civil Procedure prevents the court's order from binding him.[73]

He points out that he was not a party to the original action, nor an officer, agent, servant, employee, or attorney of a party, and denies that he was acting in "active concert or participation" with any party to the original action.

In examining this contention we start with the proposition that Rule 65 was intended to embody "the common-law doctrine that a decree of injunction not only binds the parties defendant but also those identified with them in interest, in 'privity' with them, represented by them or subject to their control." . . . Literally

---

73. Rule 65(d) provides:

Form and Scope of Injunction or Restraining Order. Every order granting an injunction and every restraining order shall set forth the reasons for its issuance; shall be specific in terms; shall describe in reasonable detail, and not by reference to the complaint or other document, the act or acts sought to be restrained; and is binding only upon the parties to the action, their officers, agents, servants, employees, and attorneys, and upon those persons in active concert or participation with them who receive actual notice of the order by personal service or otherwise.

Eds.' Note: When you compare the version of Rule 65 reproduced in the opinion to that in your Federal Rules supplement, you will note that the version of Rule 65(d) in effect in 1972 is similar in substance to the modern rule, but the format is quite different. This is because all of the Federal Rules were restyled in 2007.

read, Rule 65(d) would forbid the issuance of *in rem* injunctions. But courts have continued to issue *in rem* injunctions notwithstanding Rule 65(d), since they possessed the power to do so at common law and since Rule 65(d) was intended to embody rather than to limit their common law powers.

Similarly, we conclude that Rule 65(d), as a codification rather than a limitation of courts' common-law powers, cannot be read to restrict the inherent power of a court to protect its ability to render a binding judgment. We hold that Hall's relationship to the *Mims* case fell within that contemplated by Rule 65(d). By deciding *Mims* and retaining jurisdiction the district court had, in effect, adjudicated the rights of the entire community with respect to the racial controversy surrounding the school system. Moreover, as we have noted, in the circumstances of this case third parties such as Hall were in a position to upset the court's adjudication. This was not a situation which could have been anticipated by the draftsmen of procedural rules. In meeting the situation as it did, the district court did not overstep its powers.

We do not hold that courts are free to issue permanent injunctions against all the world in school cases. Hall had notice of the court's order. Rather than challenge it by the orderly processes of law, he resorted to conscious, willful defiance. *See Walker v. Birmingham*, 388 U.S. 307 (1967).

It is true that this order was issued without a hearing, and that ordinarily injunctive relief cannot be granted without a hearing. *See* 7 J. Moore, *Moore's Federal Practice* ¶ 65.04[3] & n.8a (1972). But we need not hold that this order has the effect of a preliminary or permanent injunction. Rather, the portion of the court's order here complained of may be characterized as a temporary restraining order, which under Rule 65(b) may be issued *ex parte*. . . .

We hold, then, that the district court had the inherent power to protect its ability to render a binding judgment between the original parties to the *Mims* litigation by issuing an interim *ex parte* order against an undefinable class of persons. We further hold that willful violation of that order by one having notice of it constitutes criminal contempt. The judgment of the district court is affirmed.

REVIEW QUESTIONS

Try to answer the following questions about the case to test your understanding.

1. Who is suing whom in this case and in what court? Can you describe the dispute between Mr. Hall and the government in your own words?
2. What is an *in rem* injunction? How would you go about finding out? One way would be to look it up in a legal dictionary, such as *Black's Law Dictionary*. It defines the term *in rem* as follows: "Involving or determining the status of a thing, and therefore the rights of persons generally with respect to that thing." "In Rem," *Black's Law Dictionary* (11th ed. 2019). The term *injunction* means "a court order commanding or preventing an action." "Injunction," *Black's Law Dictionary* (11th ed. 2019). Can you articulate in your own words what the court order in this case commanded? An *in rem* injunction

sometimes refers to an injunction with respect to land as against the whole world. A litigant can ask a court to determine his or her ownership of a property with respect to anyone, even people who are not before the court such as future heirs.

3. Why is it a problem for the government that Mr. Hall was not a party to the first suit in which the injunction was issued?

4. How would you describe the scope of the injunction that was issued?

5. What are Hall's arguments against his being held in contempt, even though he had actual notice of the injunction? What do you think the government argued on the other side?

6. Does Rule 65(d)(2) allow the judge to enforce an injunction against a non-party? Under what theory? Look carefully at the language of the rule and revisit Judge Wisdom's reasoning. Can you articulate how you would use the language of the rule to argue both sides?

> (2) *Persons Bound.* The order binds only the following who receive actual notice of it by personal service or otherwise:
>   (A) the parties;
>   (B) the parties' officers, agents, servants, employees, and attorneys; and
>   (C) other persons who are in active concert or participation with anyone described in Rule 65(d)(2)(A) or (B).

5. The Significance of *Hall* Today

A controversial current iteration of the same problem raised in *Hall* is the national injunction, sometimes called a nationwide or universal injunction. In terms of politics, these injunctions have limited both Democratic and Republican administrations. In 2015, a district judge in Texas issued an injunction barring the federal government from enforcing an executive order issued by President Obama granting temporary reprieve and work authority to immigrant parents of persons lawfully in the United States (either citizens or permanent residents). The plaintiff was the State of Texas, but the injunction encompassed the entirety of the United States. In 2016, a district judge in Texas issued an injunction barring the federal government from enforcing a Department of Education policy requiring that public schools provide facilities (such as restrooms) that match their students' gender identity. The plaintiffs were sixteen states that did not wish to comply with the policy, but the injunction encompassed the entirety of the United States. In 2017, a federal district judge in Illinois issued an injunction barring the federal government from withholding federal funding to "sanctuary jurisdictions," states or local governments that refused to cooperate with immigration enforcement. And in 2017, several district court judges enjoined the federal government from enforcing various versions of an executive order barring nationals from several predominantly Muslim countries from entering the United States, a policy that was ultimately upheld by the Supreme Court in *Trump v. Hawaii*, 138 S. Ct. 2392 (2018).

In his concurrence in *Trump v. Hawaii*, Justice Clarence Thomas analyzed the district courts' power to grant universal injunctions and concluded that the courts have no power to order such injunctions: "These injunctions are a recent development, emerging for the first time in the 1960s and dramatically increasing in popularity only very recently. And they appear to conflict with several traditional rules of equity, as well as the original understanding of the judicial role." *Id.* at 2426. Justice Thomas explained "as a general rule, American courts of equity did not provide relief beyond the parties to the case. If their injunctions advantaged nonparties, that benefit was merely incidental. Injunctions barring public nuisances were an example. While these injunctions benefited third parties, that benefit was merely a consequence of providing relief to the plaintiff." *Id.* at 2427.

One's view of the propriety of national or universal injunctions depends on one's view of the role of the courts. Some people understand the role of the courts as primarily *dispute resolution*, that is, to resolve the dispute between the parties before the judge. Under that view, a judge who rules against a party not before the court is overstepping her bounds. Others understand the role of the court as primarily about *law declaration*. Many people understand the role of the courts as a little bit of both: In the process of deciding a case, the judge will also declare the law for future litigants. It is really a question of emphasis. How much should the judicial role focus on law declaration versus dispute resolution? Justice Thomas, for example, thinks that the courts should focus on dispute resolution, writing disapprovingly of judges like Judge Wisdom: "By the latter half of the 20th century, however, some jurists began to conceive of the judicial role in terms of resolving general questions of legality, instead of addressing those questions only insofar as they are necessary to resolve individual cases and controversies." *Id.* at 2428.

National injunctions have surfaced in the years when the executive has exercised more unilateral power than any time in recent memory. Indeed, it is impossible to understand the phenomenon of national injunctions without understanding the recent relationship among the courts, Congress, and the executive branch. Most of these cases have involved states bringing suit to resist executive orders they claim are unlawful. It is often hard to separate the substantive question (was this policy lawful and meritorious?) from the procedural question (should the injunctive remedy be national, or should it only apply to the parties before the court?). Notably, and as we shall see in his dissent in *Hamdi v. Rumsfeld* later in this chapter, Justice Thomas believes in deference to the power of the executive branch, a subject you will learn more about in your constitutional law class. Thus, the questions of procedure are bound up in questions of the proper scope of executive power and the important policy and constitutional question of who in our governmental system ought to be empowered to check executive overreaching. Since these cases are brought in a district court, which must decide whether to issue an injunction, it raises a second, equally important, policy question: Should one judge, potentially an outlier, make policy for the nation? If so, under what circumstances?

You should know that members of the legal profession differ in their answers to these questions, which go to the heart of our constitutional order.

WANT TO KNOW MORE?

For scholarship arguing that national injunctions exceed the court's powers (some of it cited by the Supreme Court), *see* Samuel L. Bray, *Multiple Chancellors: Reforming the National Injunction*, 131 Harv. L. Rev. 417 (2017); Michael T. Morley, *Nationwide Injunctions, Rule 23(b)(2), and the Remedial Powers of the Lower Courts*, 97 B.U. L. Rev. 615 (2017).

For scholarship arguing that national injunctions may be warranted in some cases, *see* Suzette M. Malveaux, *Class Actions, Civil Rights, and the National Injunction*, 131 Harv. L. Rev. F. 56 (2017); Amanda Frost, *In Defense of Nationwide Injunctions*, 93 N.Y.U. L. Rev. 1065 (2018).

C. THE RIGHT TO BE HEARD: ELEMENTS AND HISTORY OF DUE PROCESS

> "... *nor shall any State deprive any person of life, liberty, or property, without due process of law* ..."
>
> *U.S. Constitution, amend. XIV, § 1.*

The phrase "due process of law" is the Constitution's most basic notion of procedure. But what does it mean? The phrase most simply refers to a right to be heard, but as interpreted by theorists and courts, the meaning of that right has evolved and changed shape over time. A heated debate over these issues in the context of a highly charged political period produced six separate opinions in the Supreme Court case of *Joint Anti-Fascist Refugee Committee v. McGrath*, 341 U.S. 123 (1951). In that case, three organizations challenged the decision of the Attorney General of the United States both to list them as "totalitarian, fascist, communist, or subversive" and to furnish that information to the Loyalty Review Board of the United States Civil Service Commission. The three organizations claimed that this governmental action was taken without notice to them or an opportunity for them to present a defense, and injured them in a national climate that was decidedly anti-Communist. The majority view of the Supreme Court Justices interpreted "due process" to require that the organizations be given the opportunity to be heard and to present their own evidence before being labeled pejoratively by the Attorney General.

In his concurring opinion in the case, Justice Felix Frankfurter suggested two reasons for notice and hearing: "No better instrument has been devised for *arriving at truth* than to give a person in jeopardy of a serious loss notice of the case against him and opportunity to meet it. Nor has a better way been found for *generating the feeling*, so important to a popular government, *that justice has been done.*" *Id.* at 171-172 (emphasis added). He explained: "The heart of the matter is that democracy implies respect for the elementary rights of men, however suspect or unworthy; a democratic government must therefore practice

---

* *Eds.' Note:* The Fourteenth Amendment specifically sets limits on what state governments may do. For limitations on the federal government, see Amendment Five: "nor [shall any person] be deprived of life, liberty, or property, without due process of law."

fairness; and fairness can rarely be obtained by secret, one-sided determination of facts decisive of rights." *Id.* at 170.

At the same time, Justice Frankfurter acknowledged that "'due process,' unlike some legal rules, is not a technical conception with a fixed content unrelated to time, place and circumstances. Expressing as it does in its ultimate analysis respect enforced by law for that feeling of just treatment which has been evolving through centuries of Anglo-American constitutional history and civilization, 'due process' cannot be imprisoned within the treacherous limits of any formula. . . . It is a delicate process of adjustment inescapably involving the exercise of judgment by those whom the Constitution entrusted with the unfolding of the process." *Id.* at 162-163.

1. Introductory Case: *Goldberg v. Kelly*

Nearly twenty years after *Joint Anti-Fascist Refugee Committee v. McGrath*, a group of attorneys for poor people gave the Justices a further opportunity to interpret due process. *Goldberg v. Kelly* posed the question: Does due process require notice and a hearing before the government terminates public assistance (or welfare) benefits? As you read the background to the case and the Supreme Court opinions, consider the values behind the idea of due process and the specific contours that idea took in this setting.

a. Background of *Goldberg v. Kelly*

Presidents John F. Kennedy and Lyndon B. Johnson promoted programs to address poverty; these became the "War on Poverty" declared by President Johnson in 1964. These federal programs included public assistance, health care, housing assistance, job training, public education, and legal services for poor people. Activists and lawyers working on behalf of poor people found a model in the civil rights movement. "Activists, perhaps naively and certainly optimistically, viewed the federal courts as the ultimate protectors of individual rights and, under the appropriate circumstances, arbiters of social change." Martha F. Davis, *Brutal Need: Lawyers and the Welfare Rights Movement*, 1960-1973, at 1 (1993).

Activists and lawyers hoped to use law to make public assistance more certain and reliable, even though the state had long treated welfare as a gift rather than a right. Even progressive lawyers in the 1960s stopped short of arguing that the Constitution mandated welfare as a right. Instead, the lawyers argued that once an individual established eligibility, under a statute, for public assistance, the state had to comply with constitutional principles, such as equal protection and the right to travel in the implementation of the benefit. Before *Goldberg v. Kelly*, federal and state welfare laws had allowed benefits to be terminated as soon as a caseworker determined that the recipient was ineligible. Sometimes, caseworkers used the threat of termination to shake up recipients and make them pliant.

For due process to apply, however, public assistance had to fit somehow the predicates of "life, liberty, or property." Here, a landmark article written by Charles Reich helped. The Yale Law School professor argued that government benefits including licenses and jobs, as well as welfare payments, effectively operate like property and deserve legal protections like property, if the state is not to require extraordinary abilities to coerce those who depend on these resources. Legislative changes have altered the underlying benefits program established in the 1970s, as described in a section that follows the Court's opinion in *Goldberg v. Kelly*.

b. The Supreme Court's Opinion

Goldberg v. Kelly
397 U.S. 254 (1970)

Justice BRENNAN delivered the opinion of the Court:

The question for decision is whether a State that terminates public assistance payments to a particular recipient without affording him the opportunity for an evidentiary hearing prior to termination denies the recipient procedural due process in violation of the Due Process Clause of the Fourteenth Amendment.

This action was brought in the District Court for the Southern District of New York by residents of New York City receiving financial aid under the federally assisted program of Aid to Families with Dependent Children (AFDC) or under New York State's general Home Relief program.[9] Their complaint alleged that the New York State and New York City officials administering these programs terminated, or were about to terminate, such aid without prior notice and hearing, thereby denying them due process of law. At the time the suits were filed there was no requirement of prior notice or hearing of any kind before termination of financial aid. However, the State and city adopted procedures for notice and hearing after the suits were brought, and the plaintiffs, appellees here, then challenged the constitutional adequacy of those procedures.

The State Commissioner of Social Services amended the State Department of Social Services' Official Regulations to require that local social services officials proposing to discontinue or suspend a recipient's financial aid do so . . . [by] giving notice to the recipient of the reasons for a proposed discontinuance or suspension at least seven days prior to its effective date, with notice also that upon request the recipient may have the proposal reviewed by a local welfare official holding a position superior to that of the supervisor who approved the proposed discontinuance or suspension, and, further, the recipient may submit, for purposes of the review, a written statement to demonstrate why his grant should not be discontinued or suspended. The decision by the reviewing official whether to discontinue or suspend aid must be made expeditiously, with written notice of the decision to the recipient. . . .

---

9. AFDC was established by the Social Security Act of 1935, 49 Stat. 627, as amended, 42 U.S.C. §§ 601-610 (1964 ed. and Supp. IV). It is a categorical assistance program supported by federal grants-in-aid but administered by the state according to regulations of the Secretary of Health, Education and Welfare. . . . Home Relief is a general assistance program financed and administered solely by New York state and local governments. . . .

[Under an additional city procedure, a] caseworker who has doubts about the recipient's continued eligibility must first discuss them with the recipient. If the caseworker concludes that the recipient is no longer eligible, he recommends termination of aid to a unit supervisor. If the latter concurs, he sends the recipient a letter stating the reasons for proposing to terminate aid and notifying him that within seven days he may request that a higher official review the record, and may support the request with a written statement prepared personally or with the aid of an attorney or other person. If the reviewing official affirms the determination of ineligibility, aid is stopped immediately and the recipient is informed by letter of the reasons for the action. Appellees' challenge to this procedure emphasizes the absence of any provisions for the personal appearance of the recipient before the reviewing official, for oral presentation of evidence, and for confrontation and cross-examination of adverse witnesses. However, the letter does inform the recipient that he may request a post-termination "fair hearing." This is a proceeding before an independent state hearing officer at which the recipient may appear personally, offer oral evidence, confront and cross-examine the witnesses against him, and have a record made of the hearing. If the recipient prevails at the "fair hearing" he is paid all funds erroneously withheld. . . . A recipient whose aid is not restored by a "fair hearing" decision may have judicial review. . . .

The constitutional issue to be decided, therefore, is the narrow one whether the Due Process Clause requires that the recipient be afforded an evidentiary hearing before the termination of benefits. The District Court held that only a pre-termination evidentiary hearing would satisfy the constitutional command, and rejected the argument of the state and city officials that the combination of the post-termination "fair hearing" with the informal pre-termination review disposed of all due process claims. . . . Although state officials were party defendants in the action, only the Commissioner of Social Services of the City of New York appealed. We noted probable jurisdiction. . . . We affirm. . . .

Appellant does not contend that procedural due process is not applicable to the termination of welfare benefits. Such benefits are a matter of statutory entitlement for persons qualified to receive them. Their termination involves state action that adjudicates important rights. The constitutional challenge cannot be answered by an argument that public assistance benefits are "a 'privilege' and not a 'right.'" *Shapiro v. Thompson*, 394 U.S. 618, 627 n.6 (1969). Relevant constitutional restraints apply as much to the withdrawal of public assistance benefits as to disqualification for unemployment compensation, *Sherbert v. Verner*, 374 U.S. 398 (1963); or to denial of a tax exemption, *Speiser v. Randall*, 357 U.S. 513 (1958); or to discharge from public employment, *Slochower v. Board of Higher Education*, 350 U.S. 551 (1956). The extent to which procedural due process must be afforded the recipient is influenced by the extent to which he may be "condemned to suffer grievous loss," *Joint Anti-Fascist Refugee Committee v. McGrath*, 341 U.S. 123, 168 (1951) (Frankfurter, J., concurring), and depends upon whether the recipient's interest in avoiding that loss outweighs the governmental interest in summary adjudication. Accordingly, as we said in *Cafeteria & Restaurant Workers Union v. McElroy*, 367 U.S. 886, 895 (1961), "consideration of what procedures due process may require under any given set of circumstances must begin with a determination of the precise nature of the government function involved as well as of the private interest that has been affected by governmental action." *See also Hannah v. Larche*, 363 U.S. 420, 440, 442 (1960).

It is true, of course, that some governmental benefits may be administratively terminated without affording the recipient a pre-termination evidentiary hearing. But we agree with the District Court that when welfare is discontinued, only a pre-termination evidentiary hearing provides the recipient with procedural due process. For qualified recipients, welfare provides the means to obtain essential food, clothing, housing, and medical care. Thus the crucial factor in this context—a factor not present in the case of the blacklisted government contractor, the discharged government employee, the taxpayer denied a tax exemption, or virtually anyone else whose governmental entitlements are ended—is that termination of aid pending resolution of a controversy over eligibility may deprive an eligible recipient of the very means by which to live while he waits. Since he lacks independent resources, his situation becomes immediately desperate. His need to concentrate upon finding the means for daily subsistence, in turn, adversely affects his ability to seek redress from the welfare bureaucracy.

Moreover, important governmental interests are promoted by affording recipients a pre-termination evidentiary hearing. From its founding the Nation's basic commitment has been to foster the dignity and well-being of all persons within its borders. We have come to recognize that forces not within the control of the poor contribute to their poverty. This perception, against the background of our traditions, has significantly influenced the development of the contemporary public assistance system. Welfare, by meeting the basic demands of subsistence, can help bring within the reach of the poor the same opportunities that are available to others to participate meaningfully in the life of the community. At the same time, welfare guards against the societal malaise that may flow from a widespread sense of unjustified frustration and insecurity. Public assistance, then, is not mere charity, but a means to "promote the general Welfare, and secure the Blessings of Liberty to ourselves and our Posterity." The same governmental interests that counsel the provision of welfare, counsel as well its uninterrupted provision to those eligible to receive it; pre-termination evidentiary hearings are indispensable to that end.

Appellant does not challenge the force of these considerations but argues that they are outweighed by countervailing governmental interests in conserving fiscal and administrative resources. These interests, the argument goes, justify the delay of any evidentiary hearing until after discontinuance of the grants. Summary adjudication protects the public fisc by stopping payments promptly upon discovery of reason to believe that a recipient is no longer eligible. Since most terminations are accepted without challenge, summary adjudication also conserves both the fisc and administrative time and energy by reducing the number of evidentiary hearings actually held.

We agree with the District Court, however, that these governmental interests are not overriding in the welfare context. The requirement of a prior hearing doubtless involves some greater expense, and the benefits paid to ineligible recipients pending decision at the hearing probably cannot be recouped, since these recipients are likely to be judgment-proof. But the State is not without weapons to minimize these increased costs. Much of the drain on fiscal and administrative resources can be reduced by developing procedures for prompt pre-termination hearings and by skillful use of personnel and facilities. Indeed, the very provision for a post-termination evidentiary hearing in New York's Home Relief program is itself cogent evidence that the State recognizes the primacy of the public interest in correct eligibility determinations and therefore in the provision of procedural safeguards. Thus, the interest of the eligible recipient in uninterrupted receipt of public assistance, coupled with the State's interest that his payments not be erroneously terminated, clearly outweighs the State's competing concern to prevent any increase in its fiscal and administrative burdens. . . .

We also agree with the District Court, however, that the pre-termination hearing need not take the form of a judicial or quasi-judicial trial. We bear in mind that the statutory "fair hearing" will provide the recipient with a full administrative review.[10] Accordingly, the pre-termination hearing has one function only: to produce an initial determination of the validity of the welfare department's grounds for discontinuance of payments in order to protect a recipient against an erroneous termination of his benefits. . . . Thus, a complete record and a comprehensive opinion, which would serve primarily to facilitate judicial review and to guide future decisions, need not be provided at the pre-termination stage. We recognize, too, that both welfare authorities and recipients have an interest in relatively speedy resolution of questions of eligibility, that they are used to dealing with one another informally, and that some welfare departments have very burdensome caseloads. These considerations justify the limitation of the pre-termination hearing to minimum procedural safeguards, adapted to the particular characteristics of welfare recipients, and to the limited nature of the controversies to be resolved. We wish to add that we, no less than the dissenters, recognize the importance of not imposing upon the States or the Federal Government in this developing field of law any procedural requirements beyond those demanded by rudimentary due process. . . .

In the present context these principles require that a recipient have timely and adequate notice detailing the reasons for a proposed termination, and an effective opportunity to defend by confronting any adverse witnesses and by presenting his own arguments and evidence orally. These rights are important in cases such as those before us, where recipients have challenged proposed terminations as resting on incorrect or misleading factual premises or on misapplication of rules or policies to the facts of particular cases.

---

10. Due process does not, of course, require two hearings. If, for example, a state simply wishes to continue benefits until after a "fair" hearing, there will be no need for a preliminary hearing.

We are not prepared to say that the seven-day notice currently provided by New York City is constitutionally insufficient per se, although there may be cases where fairness would require that a longer time be given. Nor do we see any constitutional deficiency in the content or form of the notice. New York employs both a letter and a personal conference with a caseworker to inform a recipient of the precise questions raised about his continued eligibility. Evidently the recipient is told the legal and factual bases for the Department's doubts. This combination is probably the most effective method of communicating with recipients.

The city's procedures presently do not permit recipients to appear personally with or without counsel before the official who finally determines continued eligibility. Thus a recipient is not permitted to present evidence to that official orally, or to confront or cross-examine adverse witnesses. These omissions are fatal to the constitutional adequacy of the procedures.

The opportunity to be heard must be tailored to the capacities and circumstances of those who are to be heard. It is not enough that a welfare recipient may present his position to the decision maker in writing or secondhand through his caseworker. Written submissions are an unrealistic option for most recipients, who lack the educational attainment necessary to write effectively and who cannot obtain professional assistance. Moreover, written submissions do not afford the flexibility of oral presentations; they do not permit the recipient to mold his argument to the issues the decision maker appears to regard as important. Particularly where credibility and veracity are at issue, as they must be in many termination proceedings, written submissions are a wholly unsatisfactory basis for decision. The secondhand presentation to the decision maker by the caseworker has its own deficiencies; since the caseworker usually gathers the facts upon which the charge of ineligibility rests, the presentation of the recipient's side of the controversy cannot safely be left to him. Therefore a recipient must be allowed to state his position orally. Informal procedures will suffice; in this context due process does not require a particular order of proof or mode of offering evidence. . . .

In almost every setting where important decisions turn on questions of fact, due process requires an opportunity to confront and cross-examine adverse witnesses. . . . Welfare recipients must therefore be given an opportunity to confront and cross-examine the witnesses relied on by the department.

"The right to be heard would be, in many cases, of little avail if it did not comprehend the right to be heard by counsel." *Powell v. Alabama*, 287 U.S. 45, 68-69 (1932). We do not say that counsel must be provided at the pre-termination hearing, but only that the recipient must be allowed to retain an attorney if he so desires. . . .

Finally, the decision maker's conclusion as to a recipient's eligibility must rest solely on the legal rules and evidence adduced at the hearing. To demonstrate compliance with this elementary requirement, the decision maker should state the reasons for his determination and indicate the evidence he relied on, though his statement need not amount to a full opinion or even formal findings of fact and conclusions of law. And, of course, an impartial decision maker is essential. We agree with the District Court that prior involvement in some aspects of a case will not necessarily bar a welfare official from acting as a decision maker. He should not, however, have participated in making the determination under review. Affirmed.

Justice BLACK, dissenting:

In the last half-century the United States, along with many, perhaps most, other nations of the world, has moved far toward becoming a welfare state, that is, a nation that for one reason or another taxes its most affluent people to help support, feed, clothe, and shelter its less fortunate citizens. The result is that today more than nine million men, women, and children in the United States receive some kind of state or federally financed public assistance in the form of allowances or gratuities, generally paid them periodically, usually by the week, month, or quarter. Since these gratuities are paid on the basis of need, the list of recipients is not static, and some people go off the lists and others are added from time to time. These ever-changing lists put a constant administrative burden on government and it certainly could not have reasonably anticipated that this burden would include the additional procedural expense imposed by the Court today.

. . . [W]hen federal judges use this judicial power for legislative purposes, I think they wander out of their field of vested powers and transgress into the area constitutionally assigned to the Congress and the people. That is precisely what I believe the Court is doing in this case. Hence my dissent.

The more than a million names on the relief rolls in New York, and the more than nine million names on the rolls of all the 50 States were not put there at random. The names are there because state welfare officials believed that those people were eligible for assistance. Probably in the officials' haste to make out the lists many names were put there erroneously in order to alleviate immediate suffering, and undoubtedly some people are drawing relief who are not entitled under the law to do so. Doubtless some draw relief checks from time to time who know they are not eligible, either because they are not actually in need or for some other reason. Many of those who thus draw undeserved gratuities are without sufficient property to enable the government to collect back from them any money they wrongfully receive. But the Court today holds that it would violate the Due Process Clause of the Fourteenth Amendment to stop paying those people weekly or monthly allowances unless the government first affords them a full "evidentiary hearing" even though welfare officials are persuaded that the recipients are not rightfully entitled to receive a penny under the law. In other words, although some recipients might be on the lists for payment wholly because of deliberate fraud on their part, the Court holds that the government is helpless and must continue, until after an evidentiary hearing, to pay money that it does not owe, never has owed, and never could owe. I do not believe there is any provision in our Constitution that should thus paralyze the government's efforts to protect itself against making payments to people who are not entitled to them.

Particularly do I not think that the Fourteenth Amendment should be given such an unnecessarily broad construction. That Amendment came into being primarily to protect Negroes from discrimination, and while some of its language can and does protect others, all know that the chief purpose behind it was to protect ex-slaves. . . .

I would have little, if any, objection to the majority's decision in this case if it were written as the report of the House Committee on Education and Labor, but as an opinion ostensibly resting on the language of the Constitution I find it woefully deficient. . . .

The procedure required today as a matter of constitutional law finds no precedent in our legal system. Reduced to its simplest terms, the problem in this case is similar to that frequently encountered when two parties have an ongoing legal relationship that requires one party to make periodic payments to the other. Often the situation arises where the party "owing" the money stops paying it and justifies his conduct by arguing that the recipient is not legally entitled to payment. The recipient can, of course, disagree and go to court to compel payment. But I know of no situation in our legal system in which the person alleged to owe money to another is required by law to continue making payments to a judgment-proof claimant without the benefit of any security or bond to insure that these payments can be recovered if he wins his legal argument. . . .

The Court apparently feels that this decision will benefit the poor and needy. In my judgment the eventual result will be just the opposite. . . . Thus the end result of today's decision may well be that the government, once it decides to give welfare benefits, cannot reverse that decision until the recipient has had the benefits of full administrative and judicial review, including, of course, the opportunity to present his case to this Court. Since this process will usually entail a delay of several years, the inevitable result of such a constitutionally imposed burden will be that the government will not put a claimant on the rolls initially until it has made an exhaustive investigation to determine his eligibility. . . .

For the foregoing reasons I dissent from the Court's holding. The operation of a welfare state is a new experiment for our Nation. For this reason, among others, I feel that new experiments in carrying out a welfare program should not be frozen into our constitutional structure. They should be left, as are other legislative determinations, to the Congress and the legislatures that the people elect to make our laws.

[Chief Justice BURGER and Justice STEWART also dissented.]

REVIEW QUESTIONS

1. In what court did this case start—and where did it end? SDNY → SCOTUS
2. Notice that the plaintiffs filed their case in federal court rather than state court, although both forums were open to them. Why might they have made this strategic decision?
3. Which Due Process Clause is invoked in this case—the Fifth or Fourteenth Amendment—and why? 14
4. Describe the underlying story: Who are the plaintiffs and defendants, and how do they disagree? What happened that led to the disagreement, and what do the parties want to achieve through the lawsuit?
5. Does the Supreme Court rule that welfare is property for purposes of triggering the due process protections? How does the majority on the Court

deal with this question? Does the Court respond to Justice Black's argument in dissent? What are the strongest elements of Justice Black's view?

6. What would be the "full service," maximum elements of procedure that could ever be "due"? Use the formal court trial as a model for comparing expansive elements of process with the narrower elements at issue in *Goldberg v. Kelly*. Consider the following elements that could be part of an adjudicative process:

- advance notice,
- access to counsel,
- the opportunity to testify in person,
- language translation services,
- the opportunity to cross-examine witnesses,
- the requirement of a written record of testimony,
- the requirement of a statement of reasons accompanying the decision.

Which elements of process does the *Goldberg* Court find necessary in the termination of welfare benefits, and which ones not necessary? What principles or factors affect this set of distinctions? What facts does the Court assume in reaching its conclusion?

QUESTIONS TO PONDER

1. Justice Black argues that the decision giving beneficiaries additional process will actually work to their disadvantage. What do you make of this argument? Who will pay for the additional process required by the Court? Will the money available for benefits need to be reduced by the administrative costs in conducting pre-termination hearings? How will the Court's opinion influence termination decisions by the state agency? How will the Court's opinion influence the agency's initial decisions about who is eligible for benefits? Do you think that cost should be taken into account when determining the scope of rights under the Constitution?

2. What values are served by the particular elements of process discussed by the majority? Remember Justice Frankfurter's emphasis on arriving at the truth and on generating the feeling that justice has been done in *Joint Anti-Fascist Refugee Committee v. McGrath, supra*. Some researchers have found that people report greater perceptions of satisfaction with dispute resolution based on their perceptions of the process than on the actual results. *See, e.g.*, E. Allan Lind & Tom R. Tyler, *The Social Psychology of Procedural Justice* (1988); John Thibaut & Laurens Walker, *Procedural Justice: A Psychological Analysis* (1975).

c. Context: History of Welfare Reform After *Goldberg v. Kelly*

The scope and content of welfare benefits has changed drastically since the *Goldberg* decision was rendered. In 1996, Congress enacted the Personal Responsibility and Work Opportunity Reconciliation Act of 1996 (PRWORA), Pub. L. No. 104-193, 110 Stat. 2105, which explicitly declared that welfare benefits under the law are not entitlements and also granted flexibility to the states to limit the benefits, based on fiscal constraints. Given that the decision in *Goldberg* was based on the finding that welfare benefits were an entitlement, some observers predicted that this change would lead courts to find that no due process protections attach when an individual is denied or terminated from the temporary assistance program. In *Cleveland Board of Education v. Loudermill*, 470 U.S. 532 (1985), the Supreme Court made clear that the legislature may determine the scope of a government entitlement but *cannot* determine what minimum level of process must attach to satisfy constitutional requirements once that entitlement is granted. Courts have found that at least some due process protections still apply under PRWORA. The Colorado Court of Appeals, for example, ruled that welfare benefit recipients had a limited property right in the continued receipt of benefits under PRWORA and were entitled to due process, which was violated by the state's use of sanction notices that lacked full or accurate information about the sanctions and the appeal process. *Weston v. Cassata*, 37 P.3d 469 (Colo. App. 2001), *cert. denied*, 536 U.S. 923 (2002). The Supreme Court of Appeals of West Virginia held that, under PRWORA, former recipients of welfare benefits had no due process right to a pre-termination hearing when benefits were terminated due to a five-year time limit placed on assistance. *State ex rel. K.M. v. West Virginia Dept. of Health and Human Resources*, 575 S.E.2d 393 (W. Va. 2002). Even so, the court held that the state appeals system violated due process because it prevented review of the decision to refuse a six-month extension.

Since PRWORA, most states have retained their previous welfare systems, including hearing requirements. Wisconsin, however, has privatized its administration of welfare benefits; local nongovernmental agencies administer the program, including initial hearings and terminations. *See* Vicki Lens, *Bureaucratic Disentitlement After Welfare Reform: Are Fair Hearings the Cure?*, 12 Geo. J. Poverty on L. & Pol'y 13 (2005). Do you think due process should apply to a private corporation under contract with the state that terminates an individual's benefits? For a discussion of this issue, see David J. Kennedy, *Due Process in a Privatized Welfare System*, 64 Brook. L. Rev. 231 (1998).

2. Due Process Values

In the following excerpt, Frank Michelman identifies values behind process in his discussion of access fees, such as filing fees, that make it difficult if not impossible for impoverished individuals to file lawsuits. Which of the values he identifies persist, even for potential parties who have little or no chance of prevailing on the merits?

In the second excerpt, Tom Tyler and Allan Lind consider procedural values in light of social psychology and political stability. Again, consider what aspects of their argument stand independent from any claims by parties that should prevail on the merits. Can and should the legitimacy of the legal system be secured by procedural rights, even if outcomes are systematically biased against certain groups?

Frank L. Michelman, The Supreme Court and Litigation Access Fees: The Right to Protect One's Rights

1973 Duke L.J. 1153, 1172-1177

[T]here are generally accepted reasons for making litigation possible. I think we take little risk of serious distortion if we try to frame those reasons in terms of the values (ends, interests, purposes) that are supposed to be furthered by allowing persons to litigate.

I have been able to identify four discrete, though interrelated, types of such values, which may be called *dignity values, participation values, deterrence values,* and (to choose a clumsily neutral term) *effectuation values. Dignity values* reflect concern for the humiliation or loss of self-respect which a person might suffer if denied an opportunity to litigate. *Participation values* reflect an appreciation of litigation as one of the modes in which persons exert influence, or have their wills "counted" in societal decisions they care about. *Deterrence values* recognize the instrumentality of litigation as a mechanism for influencing or constraining individual behavior in ways thought socially desirable.[73] *Effectuation values* see litigation as an important means through which persons are enabled to get, or are given assurance of having, whatever we are pleased to regard as rightfully theirs. . . .

Dignity values. These seem most clearly offended when a person confronts a formal, state-sponsored, public proceeding charging wrongdoing, failure, or defect, and the person is either prevented from responding or forced to respond without the assistance and resources that a self-respecting response necessitates.

The damage to self-respect from the inability to defend oneself properly seems likely to be most severe in the case of criminal prosecution, where representatives of civil society attempt in a public forum to brand one a violator of important societal norms. . . .

---

73. A possibly more accurate (but less distinct) label would have been "social welfare values." The category is intended to stand for all interpretations of litigation as a means for maximizing value across society, as distinguished from securing to the victorious party his due. In a given case, value maximization might be effectuated through an act of redistribution of wealth (the immediate impact of the judgment or decree itself), rather than through an act of (negative or affirmative) deterrence strictly speaking (the impact on future behavior of knowledge of the decision and its grounds).

Of course, one immediately sees that there are some nominally "civil" contexts where the would-be litigant is trying to fend off accusatory action by the government threatening rather dire and stigmatizing results (for example, a proceeding to divest a parent of custody of a child on grounds of unfitness), which are exceedingly difficult to distinguish from standard criminal contexts in dignity value terms. Still these cases do not by themselves show that the dignity notion is uncontainable. Challenging though it may be in a few cases to draw the line between the quasi-criminal and the noncriminal context, the determination usually will not be insuperably difficult.

But this is hardly to say that dignity considerations are entirely absent from civil contexts. Perhaps there is something generally demeaning, humiliating, and infuriating about finding oneself in a dispute over legal rights and wrongs and being unable to uphold one's own side of the case. How serious these effects are seems to depend on various factors including, possibly, the identity of the adversary (is it the government?), the origin of the argument (did the person willingly start it himself?), the possible outcomes (will the person, or others, feel that he has been determined to be a wrongdoer?), and how public the struggle has become (has it reached the courts yet?). . . .

Participation values. The illumination that may sometimes flow from viewing litigation as a mode of politics has escaped neither courts nor legal theorists. But I can see no way of trenchantly deploying that insight so as to rank litigation contexts for purposes of a selective access-fee relief rule. (Certainly the Supreme Court's emergent rule cannot be construed to reflect any such ranking.)

But if participation values cannot help us differentiate among litigation contexts, they can contribute significantly to the argument for a broad constitutional right of court access. Participation values are at the root of the claim that such a right can be derived from the first amendment, a claim that I shall not pursue. And they also help inspire the analogy between general litigation rights and general voting rights. . . .

Deterrence values. Litigation is often, and enlighteningly, viewed as a process, or part of a process, for constraining all agents in society to the performance of duties and obligations imposed with a view to social welfare. A possible link between deterrence values and access fees is, of course, supplied by the obvious frustration of those values which results if the person in the best position, or most naturally motivated, to pursue judicial enforcement of such constraints is prevented by access fees from doing so. . . .

Effectuation values. In the effectuation perspective we view the world from the standpoint of the prospective litigant as distinguished from that of society as a whole or as a collectivity. Value is ascribed to the actual protection and realization of those interests of the litigant which the law purports to protect and effectuate (in this perspective one would shamelessly refer to those interests as the litigant's "rights") and more generally to a prevailing assurance that those interests will be protected; and litigation is regarded as a process, or as a part of a process, for providing such protection and assurance. . . .

Tom R. Tyler and E. Allan Lind, A Relational Model of Authority in Groups

25 Advances in Experimental Social Psychology 115, 133-140 (1992)

The research . . . shows that a key factor affecting legitimacy across a variety of settings is the person's evaluation of the fairness of the procedures used by the authority in question. The studies that have included behavioral measures show much the same pattern of results with respect to measures of obedience and other behaviors linked to authority. Evaluations of both the favorability of the authority's decision and its fairness, in distributive justice terms, have occasionally been found to exert an effect on legitimacy independent of that exerted by procedural fairness. Nevertheless, it is clear that in terms of both the strength of effects and the ubiquity of effects, neither outcome factor is nearly as important as procedural justice in determining whether an authority is viewed as legitimate.[12]

Why is procedural justice so central to legitimacy? One explanation can be found in some of the original theorizing on procedural justice issues. In their discussion of the problems of dispute resolution in groups, Thibaut and Walker (1975) noted the potential harm that the process of resolving disputes could do to social relationships within a group or society: poorly resolved disputes can threaten enduring relationships. They suggested that the use of procedures regarded by all parties as fair facilitates the maintenance of positive relations among group members—preserving the "fabric of society"—even in the face of the conflict of interest that exists in any group whose members have different preference structures and different beliefs with respect to what the group should strive for and how it should manage its affairs (Thibaut & Walker, 1975, p. 67).

A second reason for the pre-eminence of procedural justice concerns in judgments of the legitimacy of authority is found in another analysis by Thibaut and Walker (1978). In many social situations it is not at all clear what decision or action is correct in an objective sense. Indeed, it could be argued that most group decisions concern questions for which, at least at the time the decision is made, there is no way of knowing what course of action will work out best. In these circumstances, Thibaut and Walker argue, what is critical to good decision making is the appearance of fairness, and fairness is most obviously achieved when procedures that are accepted as just are used to generate the decision. In other words, absent objective indicators of the correctness of a decision, the best guarantee of decision quality is the use of good—which is to say fair—procedures. . . .

A third and final reason for the importance accorded procedural justice concerns in judgments of legitimacy has to do with links between perceptions of procedures and other cognitions about groups. In an earlier analysis (Lind & Taylor, 1988) we have argued that procedures are widely viewed as essential

---

12. As noted above, it is important to distinguish personal satisfaction from attitudes such as legitimacy. We are not saying that people are happier if they receive unfavorable outcomes through a fair procedure. We are saying, however, that they are: (1) more likely to accept the decision, and (2) less likely to blame the authorities and/or institutions they have dealt with. As a consequence, they are more likely to follow the authority's directives in the future.

elements of groups, that perceptions of procedures are key features of cognitions about groups. It is no accident, for example, that the drafting of a constitution is generally one of the first enterprises of any group that intends to function on a continuing basis. Through the design of procedures a group gives itself form and makes specific its values and goals. Because procedures are widely viewed as manifestations of group values, we argue, they take on enormous symbolic significance in cognitions about groups. According to this line of thought, perceptions of procedures have greater impact on evaluations of groups than do perceptions of outcomes, because outcomes are generally viewed as one-time responses to particular situations while procedures have an enduring quality that makes an unfair procedure much more threatening than a single unfair outcome. In much the same way, the procedures used by an authority to reach a decision might be seen as an expression of the authority's values, and the judgment that an authority uses unfair procedures might be viewed with greater concern than the judgment that a particular decision is unfair.

Whatever the explanation, the results reviewed above suggest that the use of fair procedures is an important element, perhaps the key element, for the effective exercise of legitimate authority. . . .

Effectively exercising authority is a core issue within any organized group. Hence, the questions which we have been examining are always important. But they become especially important in situations of resource scarcity, where social conflict is more likely and where allocation is especially problematic. As we noted above, the empowerment of authorities seems to be a response of groups to problems such as social conflict and the allocation of scarce or diminishing resources, and yet it is precisely in such situations that the actions of authorities are most likely to be controversial. . . .

The possibility of heightened social conflict was viewed as especially problematic for American government authorities during the 1970s because the United States was in an historic period during which it seemed particularly vulnerable to social unrest. Alienation from and distrust of legal, political, and industrial authorities was quite high. Since the legitimacy of authorities is often viewed as a "cushion of support" that helps societies to survive difficult periods in history, the weakness of the support underlying the American legal, political, and economic systems seemed to point to a potentially dangerous vulnerability to destructive social unrest. . . .

3. Costs of Notice and a Hearing

Process has costs. What role should costs play in determining how much process is due in a given circumstance?

a. The Cost of Process

The Supreme Court addressed this issue in *Mathews v. Eldridge*, which followed shortly after *Goldberg v. Kelly*. As you read *Eldridge*, consider whether the Court simply applies *Goldberg*'s standard for interpreting how much process is due or, instead, changes the standard.

Mathews, Secretary of Health, Education, and Welfare v. Eldridge
424 U.S. 319 (1976)

Justice POWELL delivered the opinion of the Court:

The issue in this case is whether the Due Process Clause of the Fifth Amendment requires that prior to the termination of Social Security disability benefit payments the recipient be afforded an opportunity for an evidentiary hearing.

Cash benefits are provided to workers during periods in which they are completely disabled under the disability insurance benefits program created by the 1956 amendments to Title II of the Social Security Act. 70 Stat. 815, 42 U.S.C. §423. Respondent Eldridge was first awarded benefits in June 1968. In March 1972, he received a questionnaire from the state agency charged with monitoring his medical condition. Eldridge completed the questionnaire, indicating that his condition had not improved and identifying the medical sources, including physicians, from whom he had received treatment recently. The state agency then obtained reports from his physician and a psychiatric consultant. After considering these reports and other information in his file the agency informed Eldridge by letter that it had made a tentative determination that his disability had ceased in May 1972. The letter included a statement of reasons for the proposed termination of benefits, and advised Eldridge that he might request reasonable time in which to obtain and submit additional information pertaining to his condition.

In his written response, Eldridge disputed one characterization of his medical condition and indicated that the agency already had enough evidence to establish his disability. The state agency then made its final determination that he had ceased to be disabled in May 1972. This determination was accepted by the Social Security Administration (SSA), which notified Eldridge in July that his benefits would terminate after that month. The notification also advised him of his right to seek reconsideration by the state agency of this initial determination within six months.

Instead of requesting reconsideration Eldridge commenced this action challenging the constitutional validity of the administrative procedures established by the Secretary of Health, Education and Welfare for assessing whether there exists a continuing disability. He sought an immediate reinstatement of benefits pending a hearing on the issue of his disability. 361 F. Supp. 520 (W.D. Va. 1973). The Secretary moved to dismiss on the grounds that Eldridge's benefits had been terminated in accordance with valid administrative regulations and procedures and that he had failed to exhaust available remedies. In support of his contention that due process requires a pre-termination hearing, Eldridge relied exclusively upon this Court's decision in *Goldberg v. Kelly,* 397 U.S. 254 (1970), which established a right to an "evidentiary hearing" prior to termination of welfare benefits. The Secretary contended that *Goldberg* was not controlling since eligibility for disability benefits, unlike eligibility for welfare benefits, is not based on financial need and since issues of credibility and veracity do not play a significant role in the disability entitlement decision, which turns primarily on medical evidence. . . .

Procedural due process imposes constraints on governmental decisions which deprive individuals of "liberty" or "property" interests within the meaning of the Due Process Clause of the Fifth or Fourteenth Amendment. The Secretary does not contend that procedural due process is inapplicable to terminations of Social Security disability benefits. . . . Rather, the Secretary contends that the existing administrative procedures, detailed below, provide all the process that is constitutionally due before a recipient can be deprived of that interest.

This Court consistently has held that some form of hearing is required before an individual is finally deprived of a property interest. *Wolff v. McDonnell*, 418 U.S. 539, 557-558 (1974). The "right to be heard before being condemned to suffer grievous loss of any kind, even though it may not involve the stigma and hardships of a criminal conviction, is a principle basic to our society." *Joint Anti-Fascist Comm. v. McGrath*, 341 U.S. 123, 168 (1951) (Frankfurter, J., concurring). The fundamental requirement of due process is the opportunity to be heard "at a meaningful time and in a meaningful manner." Eldridge agrees that the review procedures available to a claimant before the initial determination of ineligibility becomes final would be adequate if disability benefits were not terminated until after the evidentiary hearing stage of the administrative process. The dispute centers upon what process is due prior to the initial termination of benefits, pending review.

In recent years this Court increasingly has had occasion to consider the extent to which due process requires an evidentiary hearing prior to the deprivation of some type of property interest even if such a hearing is provided thereafter. In only one case, *Goldberg v. Kelly*, 397 U.S. at 266-271, has the Court held that a hearing closely approximating a judicial trial is necessary. In other cases requiring some type of pre-termination hearing as a matter of constitutional right the Court has spoken sparingly about the requisite procedures. *Sniadach v. Family Finance Corp.*, 395 U.S. 337 (1969), involving garnishment of wages, was entirely silent on the matter. In *Fuentes v. Shevin*, 407 U.S. 67, 96-97 (1972), the Court said only that in a replevin suit between two private parties the initial determination required something more than an *ex parte* proceeding before a court clerk. Similarly, *Bell v. Burson*, 402 U.S. 535, 540 (1971), held, in the context of the revocation of a state-granted driver's license, that due process required only that the pre-revocation hearing involve a probable-cause determination as to the fault of the licensee, noting that the hearing "need not take the form of a full adjudication of the question of liability." In *Arnett v. Kennedy*, 416 U.S. 134 (1974), we sustained the validity of procedures by which a federal employee could be dismissed for cause. They included notice of the action sought, a copy of the charge, reasonable time for filing a written response, and an opportunity for an oral appearance. Following dismissal, an evidentiary hearing was provided.

These decisions underscore the truism that "'[d]ue process,' unlike some legal rules, is not a technical conception with a fixed content unrelated to time, place and circumstances." *Cafeteria Workers v. McElroy*, 367 U.S. 886, 895 (1961). "[D]ue process is flexible and calls for such procedural protections as the particular situation demands." *Morrissey v. Brewer*, 408 U.S. 471, 481 (1972). Accordingly, resolution of the issue whether the administrative procedures provided here are constitutionally sufficient requires analysis of the governmental and private interests that are affected. More precisely, our prior decisions indicate that identification of the specific dictates of due process generally requires consideration of three distinct factors: First, the private interest that will be affected by the official action; second, the risk of an erroneous deprivation of such interest through the procedures used, and the probable value, if any, of additional or substitute procedural safeguards; and finally, the Government's interest, including the function involved and the fiscal and administrative burdens that the additional or substitute procedural requirement would entail. *See, e.g., Goldberg v. Kelly.*

The principal reasons for benefits terminations are that the worker is no longer disabled or has returned to work. As Eldridge's benefits were terminated because he was determined to be no longer disabled, we consider only the sufficiency of the procedures involved in such cases.

The continuing-eligibility investigation is made by a state agency acting through a "team" consisting of a physician and a nonmedical person trained in disability evaluation. The agency periodically communicates with the disabled worker, usually by mail—in which case he is sent a detailed questionnaire—or by telephone, and requests information concerning his present condition, including current medical restrictions and sources of treatment, and any additional information that he considers relevant to his continued entitlement to benefits.

Information regarding the recipient's current condition is also obtained from his sources of medical treatment. If there is a conflict between the information provided by the beneficiary and that obtained from medical sources such as his physician, or between two sources of treatment, the agency may arrange for an examination by an independent consulting physician. Whenever the agency's tentative assessment of the beneficiary's condition differs from his own assessment, the beneficiary is informed that benefits may be terminated, provided a summary of the evidence upon which the proposed determination to terminate is based, and afforded an opportunity to review the medical reports and other evidence in his case file. He also may respond in writing and submit additional evidence.

The state agency then makes its final determination, which is reviewed by an examiner in the SSA Bureau of Disability Insurance. If, as is usually the case, the SSA accepts the agency determination it notifies the recipient in writing, informing him of the reasons for the decision, and of his right to seek de novo reconsideration by the state agency. Upon acceptance by the SSA, benefits are terminated effective two months after the month in which medical recovery is found to have occurred.

If the recipient seeks reconsideration by the state agency and the determination is adverse, the SSA reviews the reconsideration determination and notifies the recipient of the decision. He then has a right to an evidentiary hearing before an SSA administrative law judge. The hearing is nonadversary, and the SSA is not represented by counsel. As at all prior and subsequent stages of the administrative process, however, the claimant may be represented by counsel or other spokesmen. . . .

Despite the elaborate character of the administrative procedures provided by the Secretary, the courts below held them to be constitutionally inadequate, concluding that due process requires an evidentiary hearing prior to termination. In light of the private and governmental interests at stake here and the nature of the existing procedures, we think this was error.

Since a recipient whose benefits are terminated is awarded full retroactive relief if he ultimately prevails, his sole interest is in the uninterrupted receipt of this source of income pending final administrative decision on his claim. His potential injury is thus similar in nature to that of the welfare recipient in *Goldberg,* the nonprobationary federal employee in *Arnett,* and the wage earner in *Sniadach.*

Only in *Goldberg* has the Court held that due process requires an evidentiary hearing prior to a temporary deprivation. It was emphasized there that welfare assistance is given to persons on the very margin of subsistence. . . . Eligibility for disability benefits, in contrast, is not based upon financial need. Indeed, it is wholly unrelated to the worker's income or support from many other sources, such as earnings of other family members, workmen's compensation awards, tort claims awards, savings, private insurance, public or private pensions, veterans' benefits, food stamps, public assistance, or the "many other important programs, both public and private, which contain provisions for disability payments affecting a substantial portion of the work force. . . ." *Richardson v. Belcher,* 404 U.S. 84, 85-87 (Douglas, J., dissenting).

As *Goldberg* illustrates, the degree of potential deprivation that may be created by a particular decision is a factor to be considered in assessing the validity of any administrative decisionmaking process. The potential deprivation here is generally likely to be less than in *Goldberg,* although the degree of difference can be overstated. . . . Thus, in contrast to the discharged federal employee in *Arnett,* there is little possibility that the terminated recipient will be able to find even temporary employment to ameliorate the interim loss.

As we recognized last Term in *Fusari v. Steinberg,* 419 U.S. 379, 389 (1975), "the possible length of wrongful deprivation of . . . benefits [also] is an important factor in assessing the impact of official action on the private interests." The Secretary concedes that the delay between a request for a hearing before an administrative law judge and a decision on the claim is currently between 10 and 11 months. Since a terminated recipient must first obtain a reconsideration decision as a prerequisite to invoking his right to an evidentiary hearing, the delay between the actual cutoff of benefits and final decision after a hearing exceeds one year.

In view of the torpidity of this administrative review process, and the typically modest resources of the family unit of the physically disabled worker, the hardship imposed upon the erroneously terminated disability recipient may be significant. Still, the disabled worker's need is likely to be less than that of a welfare recipient. In addition to the possibility of access to private resources, other forms of government assistance will become available where the termination of disability benefits places a worker or his family below the subsistence level. In view of these potential sources of temporary income, there is less reason here than in *Goldberg* to depart from the ordinary principle, established by our decisions, that something less than an evidentiary hearing is sufficient prior to adverse administrative action.

An additional factor to be considered here is the fairness and reliability of the existing pre-termination procedures, and the probable value, if any, of additional procedural safeguards. Central to the evaluation of any administrative process is the nature of the relevant inquiry. *See Mitchell v. W.T. Grant Co.*, 416 U.S. 600, 617 (1974); Friendly, *Some Kind of Hearing*, 123 U. Pa. L. Rev. 1267, 1281 (1975). In order to remain eligible for benefits the disabled worker must demonstrate by means of "medically acceptable clinical and laboratory diagnostic techniques," 42 U.S.C. §423(d)(3), that he is unable "to engage in any substantial gainful activity by reason of any medically determinable physical or mental impairment. . . ." In short, a medical assessment of the worker's physical or mental condition is required. This is a more sharply focused and easily documented decision than the typical determination of welfare entitlement. In the latter case, a wide variety of information may be deemed relevant, and issues of witness credibility and veracity often are critical to the decisionmaking process. *Goldberg* noted that in such circumstances "written submissions are a wholly unsatisfactory basis for decision."

By contrast, the decision whether to discontinue disability benefits will turn, in most cases, upon "routine, standard, and unbiased medical reports by physician specialists," *Richardson v. Perales*, 402 U.S. 389, 404 (1971), concerning a subject whom they have personally examined. . . . To be sure, credibility and veracity may be a factor in the ultimate disability assessment in some cases. But procedural due process rules are shaped by the risk of error inherent in the truth-finding process as applied to the generality of cases, not the rare exceptions. The potential value of an evidentiary hearing, or even oral presentation to the decisionmaker, is substantially less in this context than in *Goldberg*.

The decision in *Goldberg* also was based on the Court's conclusion that written submissions were an inadequate substitute for oral presentation because they did not provide an effective means for the recipient to communicate his case to the decisionmaker. Written submissions were viewed as an unrealistic option, for most recipients lacked the "educational attainment necessary to write effectively" and could not afford professional assistance. In addition, such submissions would not provide the "flexibility of oral presentations" or "permit the recipient to mold his argument to the issues the decision maker appears to regard as important." 397 U.S., at 269. In the context of the disability-benefits-entitlement assessment the administrative procedures under review here fully answer these objections. . . .

A further safeguard against mistake is the policy of allowing the disability recipient's representative full access to all information relied upon by the state agency. In addition, prior to the cutoff of benefits the agency informs the recipient of its tentative assessment, the reasons therefor, and provides a summary of the evidence that it considers most relevant. Opportunity is then afforded the recipient to submit additional evidence or arguments, enabling him to challenge directly the accuracy of information in his file as well as the correctness of the agency's tentative conclusions. These procedures, again as contrasted with those before the Court in *Goldberg*, enable the recipient to "mold" his argument to respond to the precise issues which the decisionmaker regards as crucial. . . .

In striking the appropriate due process balance the final factor to be assessed is the public interest. This includes the administrative burden and other societal costs that would be associated with requiring, as a matter of constitutional right, an evidentiary hearing upon demand in all cases prior to the termination of disability benefits. The most visible burden would be the incremental cost resulting from the increased number of hearings and the expense of providing benefits to ineligible recipients pending decision. No one can predict the extent of the increase, but the fact that full benefits would continue until after such hearings would assure the exhaustion in most cases of this attractive option. Nor would the theoretical right of the Secretary to recover undeserved benefits result, as a practical matter, in any substantial offset to the added outlay of public funds. The parties submit widely varying estimates of the probable additional financial cost. We only need say that experience with the constitutionalizing of government procedures suggests that the ultimate additional cost in terms of money and administrative burden would not be insubstantial.

Financial cost alone is not a controlling weight in determining whether due process requires a particular procedural safeguard prior to some administrative decision. But the Government's interest, and hence that of the public, in conserving scarce fiscal and administrative resources is a factor that must be weighed. At some point the benefit of an additional safeguard to the individual affected by the administrative action and to society in terms of increased assurance that the action is just, may be outweighed by the cost. Significantly, the cost of protecting those whom the preliminary administrative process has identified as likely to be found undeserving may in the end come out of the pockets of the deserving since resources available for any particular program of social welfare are not unlimited.

But more is implicated in cases of this type than ad hoc weighing of fiscal and administrative burdens against the interests of a particular category of claimants. The ultimate balance involves a determination as to when, under our constitutional system, judicial-type procedures must be imposed upon administrative action to assure fairness. We reiterate the wise admonishment of Mr. Justice Frankfurter that differences in the origin and function of administrative agencies "preclude wholesale transplantation of the rules of procedure, trial, and review which have evolved from the history and experience of courts." *FCC v. Pottsville*

Broadcasting Co., 309 U.S. 134, 143 (1940). The judicial model of an evidentiary hearing is neither a required, nor even the most effective, method of decision-making in all circumstances. The essence of due process is the requirement that "a person in jeopardy of serious loss [be given] notice of the case against him and opportunity to meet it." *Joint Anti-Fascist Comm. v. McGrath*, 341 U.S., at 171-172 (Frankfurter, J., concurring). All that is necessary is that the procedures be tailored, in light of the decision to be made, to "the capacities and circumstances of those who are to be heard," *Goldberg v. Kelly*, 397 U.S., at 268-269 (footnote omitted), to insure that they are given a meaningful opportunity to present their case. In assessing what process is due in this case, substantial weight must be given to the good-faith judgments of the individuals charged by Congress with the administration of social welfare programs that the procedures they have provided assure fair consideration of the entitlement claims of individuals. *See Arnett v. Kennedy*, 416 U.S. 17, 202 (White, J., concurring in part and dissenting in part). This is especially so where, as here, the prescribed procedures not only provide the claimant with an effective process for asserting his claim prior to any administrative action, but also assure a right to an evidentiary hearing, as well as to subsequent judicial review, before the denial of his claim becomes final.

We conclude that an evidentiary hearing is not required prior to the termination of disability benefits and that the present administrative procedures fully comport with due process. The judgment of the Court of Appeals is

Reversed.

Justice STEVENS took no part in the consideration or decision of this case.

Justice BRENNAN, with whom Justice MARSHALL concurs, dissented:

. . . [T]he Court's consideration that a discontinuance of disability benefits may cause the recipient to suffer only a limited deprivation is no argument. It is speculative. Moreover, the very legislative determination to provide disability benefits, without any prerequisite determination of need in fact, presumes a need by the recipient which is not this Court's function to denigrate. Indeed, in the present case, it is indicated that because disability benefits were terminated there was a foreclosure upon the Eldridge home and the family's furniture was repossessed, forcing Eldridge, his wife, and their children to sleep in one bed. Finally, it is also no argument that a worker, who has been placed in the untenable position of having been denied disability benefits, may still seek other forms of public assistance.

REVIEW QUESTIONS

1. Can you articulate the three-factor test that the Court puts forth in this case? This is the test that courts have used to decide due process questions since this decision was issued.
2. Formally speaking, *Eldridge* does not overrule *Goldberg*, yet comes out differently. Can you explain how? Try to write down the test in *Goldberg* and that in *Eldridge* side by side. Note that *Goldberg* articulates a balancing

test, whereas the test in *Mathews v. Eldridge* is a factor test. Looking at the two tests, what is your opinion on the question of whether *Mathews v. Eldridge* overrules *Goldberg*?

3. How are *Goldberg* and *Mathews v. Eldridge* different? For example, one involves state action and is decided under the Fourteenth Amendment, while the other federal action under the Fifth. What other differences between the two cases can you list? Which ones should matter?

QUESTIONS TO PONDER

The membership of the Court changed between the times of the decisions in *Goldberg* and *Mathews*. Sitting in 1970 were Justices Hugo Black, Harry A. Blackmun, William J. Brennan, Warren E. Burger, William O. Douglas, John M. Harlan, Thurgood Marshall, Potter Stewart, and Byron R. White. By 1976, President Nixon's nominees, Lewis F. Powell and William H. Rehnquist, had replaced Hugo Black and John Harlan, and President Ford's nominee, John Paul Stevens, replaced William O. Douglas (although Justice Stevens did not participate in the *Mathews* decision). How relevant is this to explaining the results? What would you want to know about the history of the period to understand why the Court changed its approach between 1970 and 1976?

Congress responded to *Mathews* in 1983 by requiring pre-termination hearings for disability benefits upon request. 42 U.S.C. § 423(g), *amended by* Pub. L. No. 97-455 (1983). Continuation of aid is provided while termination is under appeal. That aid is not required to be paid back unless there is a showing that the recipient did not appeal in good faith.

b. Process Values, Costs, and Benefits

How does the factor test build upon or move away from the basic values of due process? Analysis from two leading commentators helps address this question.

Jerry L. Mashaw, *The Supreme Court's Due Process Calculus for Administrative Adjudication: Three Factors in Search of a Theory of Value*
44 U. Chi. L. Rev. 28, 28-30, 46-59 (1976)

During the 1970s the Supreme Court has undertaken an intensive review of administrative hearing procedures for conformity with constitutional requirements of due process of law. The landmark case of *Goldberg v. Kelly* in 1970 confirmed the Court's unwillingness to limit its review by traditional notions of property interests and also suggested, in its specification of the constitutionally requisite elements of adjudicatory procedure, that the Court was prepared to assume a highly interventionist posture. What followed was a "due process revolution"—a flood of cases seeking to extend, or simply to apply, *Goldberg*'s precepts.

The basic task that this burgeoning due process case load has presented to the courts has been to give content to the requirements of due process while maintaining an appropriate judicial role in the design of administrative procedures. Although *Goldberg* may have indicated the Court's willingness to impose a detailed model of requisite adjudicatory procedure upon a particular administrative function, no recent Supreme Court has believed that a single model is readily and consistently applicable to all administrative functions. What is required, therefore, are general criteria for review that will lend consistency and principle to the Court's decisions while permitting different administrative functions to be reviewed on their own terms. At the same time, those general criteria should be sufficiently concrete to structure administrative behavior without resort to a judicial test of every procedure that lacks some element of the paradigm process advanced by *Goldberg*.

In the Court's latest attempt to formulate this due process calculus, *Mathews v. Eldridge*, Justice Powell's majority opinion articulates a set of criteria with a comprehensiveness that suggests a preliminary integration of the Court's recent efforts. In the majority's words, from which there is no dissent, the Court must consider:

> first, the private interest that will be affected by the official action; second, the risk of an erroneous deprivation of such interest through the procedures used, and the probable value, if any, of additional or substitute procedural safeguards; and finally, the Government's interest, including the function involved and the fiscal and administrative burdens that the additional or substitute procedural requisites would entail.

Although this functional formulation impliedly invites an intrusive, particularistic review and specification of procedures, it is tempered by judicial restraint. "In assessing what process is due in this case, substantial weight must be given to the good-faith judgment of the individuals charged by Congress with the administration of the social welfare system that the procedures they have provided assure fair consideration of the entitlement claims of individuals."

The thesis of this article is that the *Eldridge* approach is unsatisfactory both as employed in that case and as a general formulation of due process review of administrative procedures. The failing of *Eldridge* is its focus on questions of technique rather than on questions of value. That focus, it is argued, generates an inquiry that is incomplete because unresponsive to the full range of concerns embodied in the due process clause. . . .

The Supreme Court's analysis in *Eldridge* is not informed by systematic attention to any theory of the values underlying due process review. The approach is implicitly utilitarian but incomplete, and the Court overlooks alternative theories that might have yielded fruitful inquiry. My purpose is, first, to articulate the limits of the Court's utilitarian approach, both in *Eldridge* and as a general schema for evaluating administrative procedures, and second, to indicate the strengths and weaknesses of three alternative theories—individual dignity, equality, and tradition. These theories, at the level of abstraction here presented, require little critical justification: they are widely held, respond to strong currents in the philosophic literature concerning law, politics, and ethics, and are supported either implicitly or explicitly by the Supreme Court's due process jurisprudence.[61]

A. UTILITARIANISM

Utility theory suggests that the purpose of decisional procedures—like that of social action generally—is to maximize social welfare. Indeed, the three-factor analysis enunciated in *Eldridge* appears to be a type of utilitarian, social welfare function. That function first takes into account the social value at stake in a legitimate private claim; it discounts that value by the probability that it will be preserved through the available administrative procedures, and it then subtracts from that discounted value the social cost of introducing additional procedures. When combined with the institutional posture of judicial self-restraint, utility theory can be said to yield the following plausible decision-rule: "Void procedures for lack of due process only when alternative procedures would so substantially increase social welfare that their rejection seems irrational."

The utilitarian calculus is not, however, without difficulties. The *Eldridge* Court conceives of the values of procedure too narrowly: it views the sole purpose of procedural protections as enhancing accuracy, and thus limits its calculus to the

---

61. In early due process cases, the Supreme Court concentrated on tradition. The oft-cited statement in *Davidson v. New Orleans*, 96 U.S. 97, 104 (1878), that the Court's approach to due process problems should be "by the gradual process of judicial inclusion and exclusion," epitomizes the conservative, precedent-oriented, historical approach. As governmental functions increased, however, the Court was faced with due process problems that had no compelling historical analogies. If the Court was not to be a continual stumbling block to "progress," a more flexible approach was needed. Indeed, the history of due process in the Supreme Court might be characterized as a continuous search for a theory of due process review that combines the legitimacy of the evolutionary theory with a flexibility that permits adaptation to contemporary circumstances. Dignitary or natural right, utilitarian, and egalitarian theories have all been incorporated to this end.

Dignitary ideas, although used occasionally in a supportive role both before 1900 and in some contemporary cases, were employed most frequently as the primary mode of analysis from about 1933 through the early 1950s. The proliferation of new government functions associated with the New Deal legislation and, later, with emergency war measures, stimulated a judicial reaction that was captured in the Court's emphasis on individual rights and dignitary values. The reactive natural rights style, predicated upon the Justices' perception of the "fair" solution in each case, had an ad hoc quality that soon became disturbing. The apparent inconsistency of the Supreme Court's due process jurisprudence led Sanford Kadish in a seminal article to describe the Supreme Court's decisions as in "chaotic array." Kadish, *Methodology and Criteria in Due Process Adjudication—A Survey and Criticism*, 66 Yale L.J. 319 (1957).

In the late 1950s and early 1960s, various utilitarian formulations began to supply a structure for analysis. In *Cafeteria & Restaurant Workers Local 473 v. McElroy*, 367 U.S. 886, 895 (1961), for example, the Court, per Mr. Justice Stewart, stated that two factors must be considered in due process cases: "the precise nature of the government function involved . . . [and] of the private interest that has been affected by government action." The statement of the utilitarian approach culminates in the *Eldridge* opinion's three-factor calculus.

Equality as a due process value has received considerable attention in criminal (or quasi-criminal) cases, but little outside that area. Perhaps the best example of the explicit use of equality concerns with respect to an administrative function is found in *Ashbacker Radio Corp. v. FCC*, 326 U.S. 327, 330 (1945). There, the Court, per Mr. Justice Douglas, stated that the right to a hearing "becomes an empty thing" unless all parties affected by the process have an equal opportunity to be heard.

benefits or costs that flow from correct or incorrect decisions. No attention is paid to "process values" that might inhere in oral proceedings or to the demoralization costs that may result from the grant-withdrawal-grant-withdrawal sequence to which claimants like *Eldridge* are subjected. Perhaps more important, as the Court seeks to make sense of a calculus in which accuracy is the sole goal of procedure, it tends erroneously to characterize disability hearings as concerned almost exclusively with medical impairment and thus concludes that such hearings involve only medical evidence, whose reliability would be little enhanced by oral procedure. As applied by the *Eldridge* Court the utilitarian calculus tends, as cost-benefit analyses typically do, to "dwarf soft variables" and to ignore complexities and ambiguities.

The problem with a utilitarian calculus is not merely that the Court may define the relevant costs and benefits too narrowly. However broadly conceived, the calculus asks unanswerable questions. For example, what is the social value, and the social cost, of continuing disability payments until after an oral hearing for persons initially determined to be ineligible? Answers to those questions require a technique for measuring the social value and social cost of government income transfers, but no such technique exists. Even if such formidable tasks of social accounting could be accomplished, the effectiveness of oral hearings in forestalling the losses that result from erroneous terminations would remain uncertain. In the face of these pervasive indeterminacies the *Eldridge* Court was forced to retreat to a presumption of constitutionality.

Finally, it is not clear that the utilitarian balancing analysis asks the constitutionally relevant questions. The due process clause is one of those Bill of Rights protections meant to insure individual liberty in the face of contrary collective action. Therefore, a collective legislative or administrative decision about procedure, one arguably reflecting the intensity of the contending social values and representing an optimum position from the contemporary social perspective, cannot answer the constitutional question of whether due process has been accorded. A balancing analysis that would have the Court merely redetermine the question of social utility is similarly inadequate. There is no reason to believe that the Court has superior competence or legitimacy as a utilitarian balancer except as it performs its peculiar institutional role of insuring that libertarian values are considered in the calculus of decision. . . .

B. INDIVIDUAL DIGNITY

The increasingly secular, scientific, and collectivist character of the modern American state reinforces our propensity to define fairness in the formal, and apparently neutral language of social utility. Assertions of natural or "inalienable" rights seem, by contrast, somewhat embarrassing. Their ancestry, and therefore their moral force, are increasingly uncertain. Moreover, their role in the history of the due process clause makes us apprehensive about their eventual reach. It takes no peculiar acuity to see that the tension in procedural due process cases is the same as that in the now discredited substantive due process jurisprudence—a tension between the efficacy of the state and the individual's right to freedom from coercion or socially imposed disadvantage.

Yet the popular moral presupposition of individual dignity, and its political counterpart, self-determination, persist. State coercion must be legitimized, not only by acceptable substantive policies, but also by political processes that respond to a democratic morality's demand for participation in decisions affecting individual and group interests. At the level of individual administrative decisions this demand appears in both the layman's and the lawyer's language as the right to a "hearing" or "to be heard," normally meaning orally and in person. To accord an individual less when his property or status is at stake requires justification, not only because he might contribute to accurate determinations, but also because a lack of personal participation causes alienation and a loss of that dignity and self-respect that society properly deems independently valuable. . . .

Notwithstanding its difficulties, the dignitary theory of due process might have contributed significantly to the *Eldridge* analysis. The questions of procedural "acceptability" which the theory poses may initially seem vacuous or at best intuitive, but they suggest a broader sensitivity than the utilitarian factor analysis to the nature of governmental decisions. Whereas the utilitarian approach seems to require an estimate of the quantitative value of the claim, the dignitary approach suggests that the Court develop a qualitative appraisal of the type of administrative decision involved. While the disability decision in *Eldridge* may be narrowly characterized as a decision about the receipt of money payments, it may also be considered from various qualitative perspectives which seem pertinent in view of the general structure of the American income-support system.

That system suggests that a disability decision is a judgment of considerable social significance, and one that the claimant should rightly perceive as having a substantial moral content. The major cash income-support programs determine eligibility, not only on the basis of simple insufficiency of income, but also, or exclusively, on the basis of a series of excuses for partial or total nonparticipation in the work force: agedness, childhood, family responsibility, injury, disability. A grant under any of these programs is an official, if sometimes grudging, stamp of approval of the claimant's status as a partially disabled worker or nonworker. It proclaims, in effect, that those who obtain it have encountered one of the politically legitimate hazards to self-sufficiency in a market economy. The recipients, therefore, are entitled to society's support. Conversely, the denial of an income maintenance claim implies that the claim is socially illegitimate, and the claimant, however impecunious, is not excused from normal work force status.

These moral and status dimensions of the disability decision indicate that there is more at stake in disability claims than temporary loss of income. They also tend to put the disability decision in a framework that leads away from the superficial conclusion that disability decisions are a routine matter of evaluating medical evidence. Decisions with substantial "moral worth" connotations are generally expected to be highly individualized and attentive to subjective evidence. The adjudication of such issues on the basis of documents submitted largely by third parties and by adjudicators who have never confronted the claimant seems inappropriate. Instead, a court approaching an analysis of the disability claims process from the dignitary perspective might emphasize those aspects of disability decisions that focus on a particular claimant's vocational characteristics, his unique response to his medical condition, and the ultimate predictive judgment of whether the claimant should be able to work.

C. EQUALITY

Notions of equality can . . . significantly inform the evaluation of any administrative process. One question we might ask is whether an investigative procedure is designed in a fashion that systematically excludes or undervalues evidence that would tend to support the position of a particular class of parties. If so, those parties might have a plausible claim that the procedure treated them unequally. Similarly, in a large-scale inquisitorial process involving many adjudicators, the question that should be posed is whether like cases receive like attention and like evidentiary development so that the influence of such arbitrary factors as location are minimized. In order to take such equality issues into account, we need only to broaden our due process horizons to include elements of procedural fairness beyond those traditionally associated with adversary proceedings. These two inquiries might have been pursued fruitfully in *Eldridge*. First, is the state agency system of decision making, which is based on documents, particularly disadvantageous for certain classes of claimants? There is some tentative evidence that it is. Cases such as *Eldridge* involving muscular or skeletal disorders, neurological problems, and multiple impairments, including psychological overlays, are widely believed to be both particularly difficult, due to the subjectivity of the evidence, and particularly prone to be reversed after oral hearing.

Second, does the inquisitorial process at the state agency level tend to treat like cases alike? If the GAO's[14] study is indicative, the answer is decidedly no. According to that study, many, perhaps half, of the decisions are made on the basis of records that other adjudicators consider so inadequate that a decision could not be rendered. The relevance of such state agency variance to *Eldridge*'s claim is twofold: first, it suggests that state agency determinations are unreliable and that further development at the hearing stage might substantially enhance their reliability; alternatively, it may suggest that the hierarchical or bureaucratic mode of decision making, with overhead control for consistency, does not accurately describe the Social Security disability system. And if consistency is not feasible under this system, perhaps the more compelling standard for evaluating the system is the dignitary value of individualized judgment, which . . . implies claimant participation.

---

14. The Federal General Accounting Office surveyed state disability determinations to assess consistency. The study found definite inconsistencies both among state agencies and between state agencies and the federal adjudicators.

D. TRADITION OR EVOLUTION

Judicial reasoning, including reasoning about procedural due process, is frequently and self-consciously based on custom or precedent. In part, reliance on tradition or "authority" is a court's institutional defense against illegitimacy in a political democracy. But tradition serves other values, not the least of which are predictability and economy of effort. More importantly, the inherently conservative technique of analogy to custom and precedent seems essential to the evolutionary development and the preservation of the legal system. Traditional procedures are legitimate not only because they represent a set of continuous expectations, but because the body politic has survived their use.

The use of tradition as a guide to fundamental fairness is vulnerable, of course, to objection. Since social and economic forces are dynamic, the processes and structures that proved functional in one period will not necessarily serve effectively in the next. Indeed, evolutionary development may as often end in the extinction of a species as in adaptation and survival. For this reason alone tradition can serve only as a partial guide to judgment.

Furthermore, it may be argued that reasoning by analogy from traditional procedures does not actually provide a perspective on the values served by due process. Rather, it is a decisional technique that requires a specification of the purposes of procedural rules merely in order that the decision maker may choose from among a range of authorities or customs the particular authority or custom most analogous to the procedures being evaluated.

This objection to tradition as a theory of justification is weighty, but not devastating. What is asserted by an organic or evolutionary theory is that *the purposes of legal rules cannot be fully known*. Put more cogently, while procedural rules, like other legal rules, should presumably contribute to the maintenance of an effective social order, we cannot expect to know precisely how they do so and what the long-term effects of changes or revisions might be. Our constitutional stance should therefore be preservative and incremental, building carefully, by analogy, upon traditional modes of operation. So viewed, the justification "we have always done it that way" is not so much a retreat from reasoned and purposive decision making as a profound acknowledgment of the limits of instrumental rationality.

Viewed from a traditionalist's perspective, the Supreme Court's opinion in *Eldridge* may be said to rely on the traditional proposition that property interests may be divested temporarily without hearing, provided a subsequent opportunity for contest is afforded. *Goldberg v. Kelly* is deemed an exceptional case, from which *Eldridge* is distinguished.

CONCLUSION

The preceding discussion has emphasized the way that explicit attention to a range of values underlying due process of law might have led the *Eldridge* Court down analytic paths different from those that appear in Justice Powell's opinion. The discussion has largely ignored, however, arguments that would justify the result that the Court reached in terms of the alternative value theories here advanced. Those arguments are now set forth.

First, focus on the dignitary aspects of the disability decision can hardly compel the conclusion that an oral hearing is a constitutional necessity prior to the termination of benefits when a full hearing is available later. Knowledge that an oral hearing will be available at some point should certainly lessen disaffection and alienation. Indeed, Eldridge seemed secure in the knowledge that a just procedure was available. His desire to avoid taking a corrective appeal should not blind us to the support of dignitary values that the de novo appeal provides.

Second, arguments premised on equality do not necessarily carry the day for the proponent of prior hearings. The Social Security Administration's attempt to routinize and make consistent hundreds of thousands of decisions in a nation-wide income-maintenance program can be criticized both for its failures in its own terms and for its tendency to ignore the way that disability decisions impinge upon perceptions of individual moral worth. On balance, however, the program that Congress enacted contains criteria that suggest a desire for both consistency and individualization. No adjudicatory process can avoid tradeoffs between the pursuit of one or the other of these goals. Thus a procedural structure incorporating (1) decisions by a single state agency based on a documentary record and subject to hierarchical quality review, followed by (2) appeal to de novo oral proceedings before independent administrative law judges, is hardly an irrational approach to the necessary compromise between consistency and individualization.

Explicit and systematic attention to the values served by a demand for due process nevertheless remains highly informative in *Eldridge* and in general. The use of analogy to traditional procedures might have helped rationalize and systematize a concern for the "desperation" of claimants that seems as impoverished in *Eldridge* as it seems profligate in *Goldberg*; and the absence in *Eldridge* of traditionalist, dignitary, or egalitarian considerations regarding the disability adjudication process permitted the Court to overlook questions of both fact and value—questions that, on reflection, seem important. The structure provided by the Court's three factors is an inadequate guide for analysis because its neutrality leaves it empty of suggestive value perspectives.

Furthermore, an attempt by the Court to articulate a set of values that informs due process decision making might provide it with an acceptable judicial posture from which to review administrative procedures. The *Goldberg* decision's approach to prescribing due process—specification of the attributes of adjudicatory hearings by analogy to judicial trial—makes the Court resemble an administrative engineer with an outdated professional education. It is at once intrusive and ineffectual. Retreating from this stance, the *Eldridge* Court relies on the administrator's good faith—an equally troublesome posture in a political system that depends heavily on judicial review for the protection of countermajoritarian values. . . .

Louis Kaplow, The Value of Accuracy in Adjudication: An Economic Analysis

23 J. Legal Stud. 307, 307-311, 356-357, 370-376, 389-399 (1994)

I. INTRODUCTION

. . . Accuracy is a central concern with regard to a wide range of legal rules. One might go so far as to say that a large portion of the rules of civil, criminal, and administrative procedure and rules of evidence involve an effort to strike a balance between accuracy and legal costs. . . .

Accurate damage determination may improve individuals' incentives to behave properly. If I contemplate committing an act that is unusually harmful, I will be more careful or more likely to refrain from the act if I will be held responsible for the true, higher level of harm, rather than for the lower, average level of harm for the class of acts. (Similarly, if my act is less harmful than is usual, holding me liable for an accordingly low amount will prevent excessive deterrence of my activity or avoid creating excessive incentives to be cautious.) In contrast, if at the time I act I am unaware whether my act will cause an atypically high or low level of harm, knowledge that an adjudicator will determine harm precisely ex post will not cause me to adjust my behavior accordingly. . . .

Determining the value of accuracy with regard to future events consists largely of identifying the social benefits associated with different outcomes. For example, with entitlements to social security disability payments, one would be concerned with the benefit of supporting the truly disabled, the implicit cost of public expenditures, and the extent to which giving payments to those not truly disabled produces benefits that fall short of the cost of public funds. While this formulation does not appear to deviate substantially from conventional understandings . . . arguments about accuracy in this context often confuse changes in accuracy with implicit changes in the burden of proof. . . .

Initially, it is useful to define a shift in the burden of proof in isolation—that is, taking as given all other aspects of the system, including its accuracy. When a decision-maker hears all the evidence, there inevitably remains some uncertainty about what actually happened. A higher proof burden is taken here to mean that the decision-maker must have a higher level of confidence that the party is responsible for committing the illegal act in order to impose a sanction. Thus, raising the burden of proof increases the rate of mistaken acquittals and decreases the rate of mistaken convictions.

In contrast, increasing accuracy [reduces] the rate of mistaken acquittals and convictions. This arises when better information is available to the decision-maker or a more capable decision-maker is used. For a given burden of proof, better information or better analysis of given information reduces mistakes of both types. . . .

Consider some alternative policies. Suppose there is a subsidy of defendants' legal counsel and a simultaneous downward shift in the express burden of proof to an extent that the portion of detected individuals who are ultimately convicted remains the same. Then, the only effect would be on accuracy.

The question thus becomes whether the additional accuracy is worth the cost, the burden-of-proof question being disposed of separately. For example, what if increasing resources available to the prosecution by the same amount increased accuracy more? Then, one could accompany this change by an increase in the express burden of proof, producing more accuracy at the same cost. Similarly, if what one really desired in advocating a subsidy to defendants' legal counsel was making the de facto burden of proof higher, one might accomplish this directly or through other indirect means (such as by reducing resources available to the prosecution). Thus, it is possible in principle to view accuracy and the burden of proof separately. Any policies affecting both can be analyzed with regard to each component because if one aspect is desirable and the other not, it would be possible to benefit from the former and do without the latter. . . .

1. THE VALUE OF ACCURACY

Consider a scenario in which individuals apply for disability benefits. Eligibility for benefits depends on whether one is disabled. The system of adjudication involves two types of mistakes. . . . Some disabled individuals will be mistakenly denied benefits, and some individuals who are not disabled will be mistakenly granted benefits. Expenditures to increase accuracy are assumed to reduce both types of errors, so that with more accurate procedures a higher portion of the truly disabled receive benefits, and fewer individuals who are not disabled receive benefits. . . .

In order to assess the value of accuracy, consider first the effect on the disabled. Providing more of them benefits has an element of social gain and a cost. The gain corresponds to the social value of a disabled person receiving benefits, rather than being left to other means of support. The cost is that of the funds, which may be supplied by increasing taxes, diverting revenue from other programs, or reducing benefit levels. The net effect should be positive, for otherwise it would be best to eliminate the program.

Second, consider those not disabled. Denying them benefits involves a cost (for, after all, providing payments to those not disabled is not a complete waste of resources) and a gain. The gain here corresponds to the cost with the truly disabled: reducing expenditures allows one to reduce taxes, increase funding of other programs, or raise benefit levels. The net effect here should be positive as well, for otherwise it would be best to expand the program to include those not disabled.

Finally, there is the cost of providing more accurate procedures themselves. Because this cost must be financed, it also has the character described previously. To determine whether a posited increase in accuracy is desirable, one would determine how much it reduced each type of error and sum the gains and losses just described.

An alternative way to view this cost-benefit calculus is to group all the financial costs and benefits together. More disabled receiving benefits increases the revenue requirement; fewer individuals who are not disabled receiving benefits reduces required revenues; and enhanced accuracy affects administrative costs.

Taken together, the net effect on direct costs could be positive or negative. To determine whether increasing accuracy is desirable, one would add to this the benefit of more disabled individuals receiving payments and the cost that fewer individuals not disabled receive payments.

2. CLAIMANTS' INCENTIVES TO PRESENT INFORMATION

Subsection 1 indicates that the appropriate level of accuracy is determined by a number of factors. But the claimant will only be concerned with the value of benefits to himself and the costs he incurs in attempting to demonstrate eligibility. Thus, claimants' incentives to provide information to enhance their chance of receiving benefits will be excessive because claimants do not take into account the cost of providing benefits.

To illustrate, suppose that a claimant seeks to receive $10,000 in public benefits. To receive these benefits, the claimant would be willing to spend up to $9,999. But the social benefit of the claimant being found eligible is always less—and often much less—than this amount. The reason is that paying the $10,000 in benefits involves an expenditure of public funds, which may require increasing taxes, reducing others' benefits, or cutting other programs. Hence, the social value of the transfer is less than the private value, regardless of whether the claimant is truly eligible or ineligible.

In practice, of course, claimants usually would choose to spend far less than $9,999. For example, if a claimant can spend $500 to achieve a 95 percent chance of receiving benefits, he surely would not spend an additional $9,499 to increase the probability to 100 percent, even if this were possible. The argument in the previous paragraph, however, applies equally to incentives at the margin. When a claimant contemplates an additional expenditure to increase the likelihood of receiving benefits, he considers only the cost of the expenditure and the gain from receiving the benefits, and not the social cost of funding the program. Therefore, whatever the amount individuals choose to spend, the amount will be socially excessive unless they are restrained or discouraged from undertaking as much effort in establishing eligibility as they would like. A system designed to determine benefit eligibility should generally constrain to some extent the ability of individuals to expend resources establishing their claims.

3. COURTS AND COMMENTATORS' VIEWS

Much of the attention to accuracy in the context of benefit eligibility has been with regard to the Supreme Court's approach to procedural due process that was first articulated precisely in *Mathews v. Eldridge*: "Identification of the specific dictates of due process generally requires consideration of three distinct factors: First, the private interest that will be affected by the official action; second, the risk of an erroneous deprivation of such interest through the procedures used, and the probable value, if any, of additional or substitute procedural safeguards; and finally, the Government's interest, including the function involved and the fiscal and administrative burdens that the additional or substitute procedural requirement would entail." Much subsequent criticism has focused either on whether the Court in this case or others applied this analysis correctly or on the appropriateness of a cost-benefit framework. The present discussion will instead concern whether the cost-benefit framework is properly conceived. . . .

A generous interpretation of the Court's discussion suggests that the first factor refers to the interest of the disabled in receiving benefits, the second to the reduction of false negatives, and the third to costs of the added procedure plus something else, presumably involving the cost of paying benefits to the ineligible. . . . Even so, this interpretation is not really a formulation. Rather, it is a heterogeneous listing of relevant factors. There is little care either in specifying each relevant component or in ruling out irrelevant ones. And it does not attempt to indicate how the components fit together. These limitations of the Court's test need not create significant problems as long as those who apply the test take it to represent a more coherent formulation. It does not appear, however, that clear thinking always results. In particular, there seems to be systematic confusion about the relationship between accuracy and the burden of proof. . . .

This confusion is reflected in the Court's third factor, which is generally seen as suggesting that government functions will be adversely affected, even aside from the added costs incurred in funding additional procedural safeguards. This seems to assume that the added procedure will involve an increase in the rate at which benefits are paid to individuals who are not disabled. Procedures that increase accuracy in isolation do not produce this sort of effect: more accuracy would reduce the rate of mistaken grants of benefits. Instead, this pattern of results—a higher rate of granting benefits to both the disabled and those who are not disabled—is what follows from a reduction in the implicit burden of proof. In other words, the Court and subsequent interpreters and commentators implicitly have in mind procedures that involve a de facto shift in the burden of proof, without regard to their effect on accuracy.

This makes the Court's test and discussion of it easier to understand. The origin is apparent: those who challenge existing procedures are individuals who lose under them, and they will seek an additional procedure that will improve their circumstances. But there remains the problem of justification. Is there a constitutional requirement that burdens of proof not be too high in determining benefit eligibility? If not, what is the basis for demanding a reduction in the burden of proof? . . .

C. ACCURACY IN ESTABLISHING FUTURE RIGHTS AND OBLIGATIONS

1. THE RIGHT TO APPEAR

In the context of determining future entitlements, a commonly expressed objection to employing an economic analysis to determine appropriate procedures is that the process value of allowing individuals to be heard is ignored.

There remains some question, however, about the justification for such a process value—in particular, one not already subsumed in the value of accuracy or in setting the burden of proof.

One suspects that claimants who object to not being heard are those who are, for example, denied benefits. If only losers complain, however, one should be suspicious that the complaint is motivated by a concern for the result, and thus an objection to a lack of process may implicitly be an instrumental argument. An entirely plausible reason to object to not being heard is that one may believe (perhaps feel certain) that the decision was adverse precisely because the decision-maker was deprived of information one had to offer. Thus, the decision may have been inaccurate. . . .

To test this, one must consider a hypothetical situation—one probably too far removed from the typical disappointed applicant's mind for him to take seriously—in which the applicant is heard but it is certain that the decision would be unaffected by the hearing. Would individuals value appearing if they knew in advance that they would be ignored or that they would be "heard" but that hearing them could have no effect whatever on the decision?

From one perspective, this is simply an empirical question that could be tested directly. There is indirect evidence relevant to how much people value such appearances for their own sake. One type of evidence noted previously is the high rate of settlement in most civil litigation. Another is the form of dispute resolution typically specified by contract, and these often are of a simple sort. Of particular relevance for *Mathews v. Eldridge*, individuals' private disability contracts presumably do not provide for personal appearances in formal hearings. Moreover, in such instances, individuals who agree to summary procedures forgo not only the benefits of greater personal involvement per se but also any positive effect such involvement may have on the accuracy of outcomes. Finally, it is important to recall . . . that individuals' incentives to promote their interests in claims proceedings, by personal appearance or otherwise, tend to be socially excessive. Thus, even if individuals, at the time disputes arose, did value further participation and were willing to pay for it, satisfying such preferences may be socially undesirable. . . .

2. Appearances and Legitimacy

Perhaps a system that allows additional procedures appears to be more "legitimate." Consider first the possibility that the system would be seen as more legitimate because it would appear to be more accurate. If the procedures indeed make the system more accurate, this suggests that accuracy is more valuable than economic analysis typically assumes. The idea may be that compliance with legal commands is enhanced not only by more precisely tailored incentives but also by a belief that the system functions well.

A second possibility is that additional procedures would make the system appear more legitimate even though it is not assumed that the procedures make it more accurate. Again, there is the problem from Subsection 1 that few if any individuals actually focus carefully on a hypothetical situation in which a new procedure is added and it has no effect on the outcome. If such a procedure were, nonetheless, seen as contributing to legitimacy, one would wish to know why. One possibility is that a procedure enhances legitimacy because it furthers the sorts of values addressed in Subsection 1. . . . In recent decades, one has heard more complaints about the litigation explosion, the excessive monetary cost and other burdens associated with particular types of lawsuits, and excessive procedures delaying or denying justice than about a serious shortage of procedures or an inadequacy of opportunities to be involved with lawyers or the legal system. Although such views in substantial part involve an unsophisticated understanding of the legal system, an approach that privileged them may warrant less accuracy and concern for procedure than indicated by the economic analysis presented here. . . .

Some commentators have remarked that a cost-benefit calculus such as that employed in *Mathews v. Eldridge* is not obviously suited to implementation by appellate courts rather than by legislative bodies or specialized agencies. Moreover, the Due Process Clause is a component of the Bill of Rights, much of which is designed to protect individuals against potential government abuse. Thus, it is not necessarily appropriate for the courts' tests of the constitutionality of procedures to mirror an economic analysis designed to determine which procedures are socially best.

c. The Cost of Notice

Both notice and a meaningful hearing are required under our due process jurisprudence. Now consider the question of cost versus accuracy as applied to the issue of notice.

Jones v. Flowers
547 U.S. 220 (2006)

Chief Justice ROBERTS delivered the opinion of the Court.

Before a State may take property and sell it for unpaid taxes, the Due Process Clause of the Fourteenth Amendment requires the government to provide the owner "notice and opportunity for hearing appropriate to the nature of the case." *Mullane v. Central Hanover Bank & Trust Co.,* 339 U.S. 306, 313 (1950). We granted certiorari to determine whether, when notice of a tax sale is mailed to the owner and returned undelivered, the government must take additional reasonable steps to provide notice before taking the owner's property.

I

In 1967, petitioner Gary Jones purchased a house at 717 North Bryan Street in Little Rock, Arkansas. He lived in the house with his wife until they separated in 1993. Jones then moved into an apartment in Little Rock, and his wife continued to live in the North Bryan Street house. Jones paid his mortgage each month for 30 years, and the mortgage company paid Jones' property taxes. After Jones paid off his mortgage in 1997, the property taxes went unpaid, and the property was certified as delinquent.

In April 2000, respondent Mark Wilcox, the Commissioner of State Lands (Commissioner), attempted to notify Jones of his tax delinquency, and his right to redeem the property, by mailing a certified letter to Jones at the North Bryan Street address. The packet of information stated that unless Jones redeemed the property, it would be subject to public sale two years later on April 17, 2002. Nobody was home to sign for the letter, and nobody appeared at the post office to retrieve the letter within the next 15 days. The post office returned the unopened packet to the Commissioner marked " 'unclaimed.' "

Two years later, and just a few weeks before the public sale, the Commissioner published a notice of public sale in the Arkansas Democrat Gazette. No bids were submitted, which permitted the State to negotiate a private sale of the property. Several months later, respondent Linda Flowers submitted a purchase offer. The Commissioner mailed another certified letter to Jones at the North Bryan Street address, attempting to notify him that his house would be sold to Flowers if he did not pay his taxes. Like the first letter, the second was also returned to the Commissioner marked "unclaimed." Flowers purchased the house, which the parties stipulated in the trial court had a fair market value of $80,000, for $21,042.15. Immediately after the 30-day period for postsale redemption passed, Flowers had an unlawful detainer notice delivered to the property. The notice was served on Jones' daughter, who contacted Jones and notified him of the tax sale.

Jones filed a lawsuit in Arkansas state court against the Commissioner and Flowers, alleging that the Commissioner's failure to provide notice of the tax sale and of Jones' right to redeem resulted in the taking of his property without due process. The Commissioner and Flowers moved for summary judgment on the ground that the two unclaimed letters sent by the Commissioner were a constitutionally adequate attempt at notice, and Jones filed a cross-motion for summary judgment. The trial court granted summary judgment in favor of the Commissioner and Flowers. It concluded that the Arkansas tax sale statute, which set forth the notice procedure followed by the Commissioner, complied with constitutional due process requirements.

Jones appealed, and the Arkansas Supreme Court affirmed the trial court's judgment. The court noted our precedent stating that due process does not require actual notice, and it held that attempting to provide notice by certified mail satisfied due process in the circumstances presented.

. . . . We hold that when mailed notice of a tax sale is returned unclaimed, the State must take additional reasonable steps to attempt to provide notice to the property owner before selling his property, if it is practicable to do so. Under the circumstances presented here, additional reasonable steps were available to the State. We therefore reverse the judgment of the Arkansas Supreme Court.

II

A

Due process does not require that a property owner receive actual notice before the government may take his property. Rather, we have stated that due process requires the government to provide "notice reasonably calculated, under all the circumstances, to apprise interested parties of the pendency of the action and afford them an opportunity to present their objections." *Mullane,* 339 U.S., at 314. The Commissioner argues that once the State provided notice reasonably calculated to apprise Jones of the impending tax sale by mailing him a certified letter, due process was satisfied. The Arkansas statutory scheme is reasonably calculated to provide notice, the Commissioner continues, because it provides for notice by certified mail to an address that the property owner is responsible for keeping up to date. The Commissioner notes this Court's ample precedent condoning notice by mail, and adds that the Arkansas scheme exceeds constitutional requirements by requiring the Commissioner to use certified mail.

. . . [W]e have never addressed whether due process entails further responsibility when the government becomes aware prior to the taking that its attempt at notice has failed. That is a new wrinkle, and we have explained that the "notice required will vary with circumstances and conditions." *Walker v. City of Hutchinson,*352 U.S. 112, 115 (1956). The question presented is whether such knowledge on the government's part is a "circumstance and condition" that varies the "notice required."

The Courts of Appeals and State Supreme Courts have addressed this question on frequent occasions, and most have decided that when the government learns its attempt at notice has failed, due process requires the government to do something more before real property may be sold in a tax sale. Many States already require in their statutes that the government do more than simply mail notice to delinquent owners, either at the outset or as a followup measure if initial mailed notice is ineffective.

In *Mullane,* we stated that "when notice is a person's due . . . [t]he means employed must be such as one desirous of actually informing the absentee might reasonably adopt to accomplish it," 339 U.S., at 315, and that assessing the adequacy of a particular form of notice requires balancing the "interest of the State" against "the individual interest sought to be protected by the Fourteenth Amendment," *id.,* at 314. . . .

We do not think that a person who actually desired to inform a real property owner of an impending tax sale of a house he owns would do nothing when a certified letter sent to the owner is returned unclaimed. If the Commissioner prepared a stack of letters to mail to delinquent taxpayers, handed them to the postman, and then watched as the departing postman accidentally dropped the letters down a storm drain, one would certainly expect the Commissioner's office to prepare a new stack of letters and send them again. No one "desirous of actually informing" the owners would simply shrug his shoulders as the letters disappeared and say "I tried." Failure to follow up would be unreasonable, despite the fact that the letters were reasonably calculated to reach their intended recipients when delivered to the postman.

By the same token, when a letter is returned by the post office, the sender will ordinarily attempt to resend it, if it is practicable to do so. This is especially true when, as here, the subject matter of the letter concerns such an important and irreversible prospect as the loss of a house. Although the State may have made a reasonable calculation of how to reach Jones, it had good reason to suspect when the notice was returned that Jones was "no better off than if the notice had never been sent." Deciding to take no further action is not what someone "desirous of actually informing" Jones would do; such a person would take further reasonable steps if any were available.

In prior cases, we have required the government to consider unique information about an intended recipient regardless of whether a statutory scheme is reasonably calculated to provide notice in the ordinary case. In *Robinson v. Hanrahan,* [409 U.S. 38 (1972),] we held that notice of forfeiture proceedings sent to a vehicle owner's home address was inadequate when the State knew that the property owner was in prison. In *Covey v. Town of Somers,* 351 U.S. 141 (1956), we held that notice of foreclosure by mailing, posting, and publication was inadequate when town officials knew that the property owner was incompetent and without a guardian's protection.

The Commissioner points out that in these cases, the State was aware of such information *before* it calculated how best to provide notice. But it is difficult to explain why due process would have settled for something less if the government had learned after notice was sent, but before the taking occurred, that the property owner was in prison or was incompetent. Under *Robinson* and *Covey,* the government's knowledge that notice pursuant to the normal procedure was ineffective triggered an obligation on the government's part to take additional steps to effect notice. That knowledge was one of the "practicalities and peculiarities of the case" that the Court took into account in determining whether constitutional requirements were met. It should similarly be taken into account in assessing the adequacy of notice in this case. The dissent dismisses the State's knowledge that its notice was ineffective as "learned long after the fact," . . . but the notice letter was promptly returned to the State two to three weeks after it was sent, and the Arkansas statutory regime precludes the State from taking the property for two *years* while the property owner may exercise his right to redeem.

It is certainly true . . . that the failure of notice in a specific case does not establish the inadequacy of the attempted notice; in that sense, the constitutionality of a particular procedure for notice is assessed *ex ante,* rather than *post hoc*. But if a feature of the State's chosen procedure is that it promptly provides additional information to the government about the effectiveness of notice, it does not contravene the *ex ante* principle to consider what the government does with that information in assessing the adequacy of the chosen procedure. After all, the State knew *ex ante* that it would promptly learn whether its effort to effect notice through certified mail had succeeded. It would not be inconsistent with the approach the Court has taken in notice cases to ask, with respect to a procedure under which telephone calls were placed to owners, what the State did when no one answered. Asking what the State does when a notice letter is returned unclaimed is not substantively different.

The Commissioner has three further arguments for why reasonable followup measures were not required in this case. First, notice was sent to an address that Jones provided and had a legal obligation to keep updated. Second, "after failing to receive a property tax bill and pay property taxes, a property holder is on inquiry-notice that his property is subject to governmental taking." Third, Jones was obliged to ensure that those in whose hands he left his property would alert him if it was in jeopardy. None of these contentions relieves the State of its constitutional obligation to provide adequate notice.

The Commissioner does not argue that Jones' failure to comply with a statutory obligation to keep his address updated forfeits his right to constitutionally sufficient notice, and we agree. In *Robinson,* we noted that Illinois law required each vehicle owner to register his address with the secretary of state, and that the State's vehicle forfeiture scheme provided for notice by mail to the address listed in the secretary's records. See 409 U.S., at 38, n.1. But we found that the State had not provided constitutionally sufficient notice, despite having followed its reasonably calculated scheme, because it knew that Robinson could not be reached at his address of record. . . .

As for the Commissioner's inquiry notice argument, the common knowledge that property may become subject to government taking when taxes are not paid does not excuse the government from complying with its constitutional obligation of notice before taking private property. We have previously stated the opposite: An interested party's "knowledge of delinquency in the payment of taxes is not equivalent to notice that a tax sale is pending." . . . Arkansas affords even a delinquent taxpayer the right to settle accounts with the State and redeem his property, so Jones' failure to pay his taxes in a timely manner cannot by itself excuse inadequate notice.

Finally, the Commissioner reminds us of a statement from *Mullane* that the State can assume an owner leaves his property in the hands of one who will inform him if his interest is in jeopardy. But in this passage, Justice Jackson writes of "libel of a ship, attachment of a chattel[,] or entry upon real estate in the name of law"—such "seiz[ures]" of property, he concluded, "may reasonably be expected to come promptly to the owner's attention." An occupant, however, is not charged with acting as the owner's agent in all respects, and it is quite a leap from Justice Jackson's examples to conclude that it is an obligation of tenancy to follow up with certified mail of unknown content addressed to the owner. In fact, the State makes it impossible for the occupant to learn why the Commissioner is writing the owner, because an occupant cannot call for a certified letter without first obtaining the owner's signature. For all the occupant knows, the Commissioner of State Lands might write to certain residents about a variety of matters he finds important, such as state parks or highway construction; it would by no means be obvious to an occupant observing a certified mail slip from the Commissioner that the owner is in danger of losing his property.

In any event, there is no record evidence that notices of attempted delivery were left at 717 North Bryan Street.

Jones should have been more diligent with respect to his property, no question. People must pay their taxes, and the government may hold citizens accountable for tax delinquency by taking their property. But before forcing a citizen to satisfy his debt by forfeiting his property, due process requires the government to provide adequate notice of the impending taking.

B

. . . For the reasons stated, we conclude the State should have taken additional reasonable steps to notify Jones, if practicable to do so. The question remains whether there were any such available steps. . . . [I]f there were no reasonable additional steps the government could have taken upon return of the unclaimed notice letter, it cannot be faulted for doing nothing.

We think there were several reasonable steps the State could have taken. What steps are reasonable in response to new information depends upon what the new information reveals. The return of the certified letter marked "unclaimed" meant either that Jones still lived at 717 North Bryan Street, but was not home when the postman called and did not retrieve the letter at the post office, or that Jones no longer resided at that address. One reasonable step primarily addressed to the former possibility would be for the State to resend the notice by regular mail, so that a signature was not required. The Commissioner says that use of certified mail makes actual notice more likely, because requiring the recipient's signature protects against misdelivery. But that is only true, of course, when someone is home to sign for the letter, or to inform the mail carrier that he has arrived at the wrong address. Otherwise, . . . the use of certified mail might make actual notice less likely in some cases—the letter cannot be left like regular mail to be examined at the end of the day, and it can only be retrieved from the post office for a specified period of time. Following up with regular mail might also increase the chances of actual notice to Jones if—as it turned out—he had moved. Even occupants who ignored certified mail notice slips addressed to the owner (if any had been left) might scrawl the owner's new address on the notice packet and leave it for the postman to retrieve, or notify Jones directly.

Other reasonable followup measures, directed at the possibility that Jones had moved as well as that he had simply not retrieved the certified letter, would have been to post notice on the front door, or to address otherwise undeliverable mail to "occupant." Most States that explicitly outline additional procedures in their tax sale statutes require just such steps. Either approach would increase the likelihood that the owner would be notified that he was about to lose his property, given the failure of a letter deliverable only to the owner in person. That is clear in the case of an owner who still resided at the premises. It is also true in the case of an owner who has moved: Occupants who might disregard a certified mail slip not addressed to them are less likely to ignore posted notice, and a letter addressed to them (even as "occupant") might be opened and read. In either case, there is a significant chance the occupants will alert the owner, if only because a change in ownership could well affect their own occupancy. In fact, Jones first learned of the State's effort to sell his house when he was alerted by one of the occupants—his daughter—after she was served with an unlawful detainer notice.

Jones believes that the Commissioner should have searched for his new address in the Little Rock phonebook and other government records such as income tax rolls. We do not believe the government was required to go this far. . . . An open-ended search for a new address—especially when the State obligates the taxpayer to keep his address updated with the tax collector—imposes burdens on the State significantly greater than the several relatively easy options outlined above.

The Commissioner complains about the burden of even those additional steps. . . The Commissioner has offered no estimate of how many notice letters are returned, and no facts to support the dissent's assertion that the Commissioner must now physically locate "tens of thousands of properties every year." . . . Successfully providing notice is often the most efficient way to collect unpaid taxes, . . . but rather than taking relatively easy additional steps to effect notice, the State undertook the burden and expense of purchasing a newspaper advertisement, conducting an auction, and then negotiating a private sale of the property to Flowers.

The Solicitor General argues that requiring further effort when the government learns that notice was not delivered will cause the government to favor modes of providing notice that do not generate additional information—for example, starting (and stopping) with regular mail instead of certified mail. We find this unlikely, as we have no doubt that the government repeatedly finds itself being asked to prove that notice was sent and received. Using certified mail provides the State with documentation of personal delivery and protection against false claims that notice was never received. That added security, however, comes at a price—the State also learns when notice has *not* been received. We conclude that, under the circumstances presented, the State cannot simply ignore that information in proceeding to take and sell the owner's property. . . .

Though the Commissioner argues that followup measures are not constitutionally required, he reminds us that the State did make some attempt to follow up with Jones by publishing notice in the newspaper a few weeks before the public sale. Several decades ago, this Court observed that "[c]hance alone" brings a person's attention to "an advertisement in small type inserted in the back pages of a newspaper," *Mullane,* 339 U.S., at 315, and that notice by publication is adequate only where "it is not reasonably possible or practicable to give more adequate warning," *id.,* at 317. Following up by publication was not constitutionally adequate under the circumstances presented here because, as we have explained, it was possible and practicable to give Jones more adequate warning of the impending tax sale. . . .

* * *

There is no reason to suppose that the State will ever be less than fully zealous in its efforts to secure the tax revenue it needs. The same cannot be said for the State's efforts to ensure that its citizens receive proper notice before the State takes action against them. In this case, the State is exerting extraordinary power against a property owner—taking and selling a house he owns. It is not too much to insist that the State do a bit more to attempt to let him know about it when the notice letter addressed to him is returned unclaimed.

The Commissioner's effort to provide notice to Jones of an impending tax sale of his house was insufficient to satisfy due process given the circumstances of this case. The judgment of the Arkansas Supreme Court is reversed, and the case is remanded for proceedings not inconsistent with this opinion.

It is so ordered.

Justice Alito took no part in the consideration or decision of this case.

Justice Thomas, with whom Justice Scalia and Justice Kennedy join, dissenting.

. . . Because, under this Court's precedents, the State's notice methods clearly satisfy the requirements of the Due Process Clause, I respectfully dissent.

I

. . . Balancing a State's interest in efficiently managing its administrative system and an individual's interest in adequate notice, this Court has held that a State must provide "notice reasonably calculated, under all the circumstances, to apprise interested parties of the pendency of the action." . . . "[H]eroic efforts," however, are not required. *Dusenbery v. United States,* 534 U.S. 161, 170 (2002). . . .

The methods of notice employed by Arkansas were reasonably calculated to inform petitioner of proceedings affecting his property interest and thus satisfy the requirements of the Due Process Clause. The State mailed a notice by certified letter to the address provided by petitioner. The certified letter was returned to the State marked "unclaimed" after three attempts to deliver it. The State then published a notice of public sale containing redemption information in the Arkansas Democrat Gazette newspaper. After Flowers submitted a purchase offer, the State sent yet another certified letter to petitioner at his record address. That letter, too, was returned to the State marked "unclaimed" after three delivery attempts.

Arkansas' attempts to contact petitioner by certified mail at his "record address," without more, satisfy due process. Because the notices were sent to the address provided by petitioner himself, the State had an especially sound basis for determining that notice would reach him. Moreover, Arkansas exceeded the constitutional minimum by additionally publishing notice in a local newspaper. Due process requires nothing more—and certainly not here, where petitioner had a statutory duty to pay his taxes and to report any change of address to the state taxing authority.

My conclusion that Arkansas' notice methods satisfy due process is reinforced by the well-established presumption that individuals, especially those owning property, act in their own interest. . . . Consistent with this observation, Arkansas was free to "indulge the assumption" that petitioner had either provided the state taxing authority with a correct and up-to-date mailing address—as required by state law—"or that he . . . left some caretaker under a duty to let him know that [his property was] being jeopardized."

The Court does not conclude that certified mail is inherently insufficient as a means of notice, but rather that "the government's knowledge that notice pursuant to the normal procedure was ineffective triggered an obligation on the government's part to take additional steps to effect notice." I disagree.

First, whether a method of notice is reasonably calculated to notify the interested party is determined *ex ante, i.e.,* from the viewpoint of the government agency at the time its notice is sent. . . . Relatedly, we have refused to evaluate the reasonableness of a particular method of notice by comparing it to alternative methods that are identified after the fact. Today the Court appears to abandon both of these practices. Its rejection of Arkansas' selected method of notice—a method this Court has repeatedly concluded is constitutionally sufficient—is based upon information that was unavailable when notice was sent. Indeed, the Court's proposed notice methods—regular mail, posting, and addressing mail to "'occupant,'"—are entirely the product of *post hoc* considerations, including the discovery that members of petitioner's family continued to live in the house.

. . . Under the majority's logic, each time a doubt is raised with respect to whether notice has reached an interested party, the State will have to consider additional means better calculated to achieve notice. Because this rule turns on speculative, newly acquired information, it has no natural end point, and, in effect, requires the States to achieve something close to actual notice. . . .

The only circumstances in which this Court has found notice by mail and publication inadequate under the Due Process Clause involve situations where the state or local government knew at the outset that its notice efforts were destined to fail and knew how to rectify the problem prior to sending notice. See *Robinson v. Hanrahan,* 409 U.S. 38, 39 (1972) *(per curiam)* (intended recipient known to be in jail); *Covey v. Town of Somers,* 351 U.S. 141, 145 (1956) (intended recipient known to be incompetent and without a guardian).

In *Robinson,* the State, having arrested petitioner and having detained him in county jail, immediately instituted forfeiture proceedings against his automobile and mailed notice of those proceedings to his residential address. 409 U.S., at 38. . . . Because the State knew beforehand that Robinson was not at, and had no access to, the address to which it sent the notice, this Court held that the State's efforts were not "'reasonably calculated'" to notify him of the pending proceedings. *Id.,* at 40. . . .

By contrast, Arkansas did not know at the time it sent notice to petitioner that its method would fail, and Arkansas did not know that petitioner no longer lived at the record address simply because letters were returned "unclaimed." . . . The State cannot be charged to correct a problem of petitioner's own creation and of which it was not aware.[5] Even if the State had divined that petitioner was no longer at the record address, its publication of notice in a local newspaper would have sufficed because *Mullane* authorizes the use of publication when the record address is unknown. . . .

II

The Court's proposed methods, aside from being constitutionally unnecessary, are also burdensome, impractical, and no more likely to effect notice than the methods actually employed by the State. . . . These administrative burdens are not compelled by the Due Process Clause. Here, Arkansas has determined that its law requiring property owners to maintain a current address with the state taxing authority, in conjunction with its authorization to send property notices to the record address, is an efficient and fair way to administer its tax collection system. The Court's decision today forecloses such a reasonable system and burdens the State with inefficiencies caused by delinquent taxpayers. . . . Accordingly, I would affirm the judgment of the Arkansas Supreme Court.

REVIEW QUESTIONS

1. Can you articulate the test that the Court applies to determine what type of notice is required?
2. Does that test resolve the controversy over whether Arkansas' notice was sufficient? If not, what other considerations does the Court turn to?
3. Does looking at the issue of whether the notice in this case was adequate depend on whether one evaluates the notice *ex post* or *ex ante*? Is it ever possible for a court to evaluate a case *ex ante* when it will always receive the case after the worst has already happened? (Which is to say, all the people who did receive the letter by certified mail will never claim that the notice is inadequate, because they received it.)

WANT TO KNOW MORE?

The substantial literature bringing economic analysis into procedure and administration of justice includes Judge Richard A. Posner's general work, Economic Analysis of Law (5th ed. 1998); an argument for replacing fairness concerns with analysis from welfare economics advanced by Louis Kaplow and Steven Shavell, *Fairness Versus Welfare*, 114 Harv. L. Rev. 971 (2001); empirical work such as Geoffrey P. Miller, *The Legal-Economic Analysis of Comparative Civil Procedure*, 45 Am. J. Comp. L. 905 (1997); and the articles reviewed in William M. Landes, *The Empirical Side of Law & Economics*, 70 U. Chi. L. Rev. 167 (2003). A good general overview is Robert Bone, *The Economics of Civil Procedure* (2003). For criticism of these approaches, *see* Michael B. Dorff, *Why Welfare Depends on Fairness: A Reply to Kaplow and Shavell*, 75 S. Cal. L. Rev. 847 (2002); Herbert Hovenkamp, *Positivism in Law & Economics*, 78 Cal. L. Rev. 815 (1990); and Arthur A. Leff, *Economic Analysis of Law: Some Realism About Nominalism*, 60 Va. L. Rev. 45 (1974).

As the Kaplow excerpt indicates, litigation has a private and a public function. The private function is to provide a resolution to a controversy between two people. But that process has implications for the society as a whole, in terms of the cost to the broader society of providing a forum for adjudication, as well as the cost to society of inaccurate results and, perhaps, suboptimal incentives such as over- or under-deterrence of misconduct. For a discussion, see Steven Shavell, *The Fundamental Divergence Between the Private and the Social Motive to Use the Legal System*, 26 J. Legal Stud. 575 (1997). These issues will arise again in the discussion of settlement and of the jury right later in the course.

4. Enemy Combatants and Due Process

The following case applies due process to a new context, considering the application of due process doctrine to the United States' response to terrorist attacks.

Only four justices signed on to the main opinion. To become a majority opinion, five justices must sign on. The main opinion reprinted below is called a plurality. Two justices agreed with some parts of Justice O'Connor's plurality decision but not all of her reasoning. And three justices dissented. For purposes of understanding the significance of this decision in terms of due process, the most important decisions are reprinted below.

As you read the case, consider what framework is best suited to the question presented to the Supreme Court: the criminal law framework described in Justice Scalia's dissent, or the more administrative approach described by the plurality.

Hamdi v. Rumsfeld
542 U.S. 507 (2004)

Justice O'CONNOR announced the judgment of the Court, and delivered an opinion, in which THE CHIEF JUSTICE, Justice KENNEDY, and Justice BREYER join:

At this difficult time in our Nation's history, we are called upon to consider the legality of the Government's detention of a United States citizen on United States soil as an "enemy combatant" and to address the process that is constitutionally owed to one who seeks to challenge his classification as such. The United States Court of Appeals for the Fourth Circuit held that petitioner Yaser Hamdi's detention was legally authorized and that he was entitled to no further opportunity to challenge his enemy-combatant label. We now vacate and remand. We hold that although Congress authorized the detention of combatants in the narrow circumstances alleged here, due process demands that a citizen held in the United States as an enemy combatant be given a meaningful opportunity to contest the factual basis for that detention before a neutral decisionmaker.

I

On September 11, 2001, the al Qaeda terrorist network used hijacked commercial airliners to attack prominent targets in the United States. Approximately 3,000 people were killed in those attacks. One week later, in response to these "acts of treacherous violence," Congress passed a resolution authorizing the President to "use all necessary and appropriate force against those nations, organizations, or persons he determines planned, authorized, committed, or aided the terrorist attacks" or "harbored such organizations or persons, in order to prevent any future acts of international terrorism against the United States by such nations, organizations or persons." Authorization for Use of Military Force (AUMF), 115 Stat. 224. Soon thereafter, the President ordered United States Armed Forces to Afghanistan, with a mission to subdue al Qaeda and quell the Taliban regime that was known to support it.

This case arises out of the detention of a man whom the Government alleges took up arms with the Taliban during this conflict. His name is Yaser Esam Hamdi. Born in Louisiana in 1980, Hamdi moved with his family to Saudi Arabia as a child. By 2001, the parties agree, he resided in Afghanistan. At some point that year, he was seized by members of the Northern Alliance, a coalition of military groups opposed to the Taliban government, and eventually was turned over to the United States military. The Government asserts that it initially detained and interrogated Hamdi in Afghanistan before transferring him to the United States Naval Base in Guantanamo Bay in January 2002. In April 2002, upon learning that Hamdi is an American citizen, authorities transferred him to a naval brig in Norfolk, Virginia, where he remained until a recent transfer to a brig in Charleston, South Carolina. The Government contends that Hamdi is an "enemy combatant," and that this status justifies holding him in the United States indefinitely—without formal charges or proceedings—unless and until it makes the determination that access to counsel or further process is warranted.

In June 2002, Hamdi's father, Esam Fouad Hamdi, filed the present petition for a writ of habeas corpus under 28 U.S.C. § 2241 in the Eastern District of Virginia, naming as petitioners his son and himself as next friend. The elder Hamdi alleges in the petition that he has had no contact with his son since the Government took custody of him in 2001, and that the Government has held his son "without access to legal counsel or notice of any charges pending against him." The petition contends that Hamdi's detention was not legally authorized. It argues that, "[a]s an American citizen, . . . Hamdi enjoys the full protections of the Constitution," and that Hamdi's detention in the United States without charges, access to an impartial tribunal, or assistance of counsel "violated and continue[s] to violate the Fifth and Fourteenth Amendments to the United States Constitution." . . . Hamdi's father has asserted in documents found elsewhere in the record that his son went to Afghanistan to do "relief work," and that he had been in that country less than two months before September 11, 2001, and could not have received military training. The 20-year-old was traveling on his own for the first time, his father says, and "[b]ecause of his lack of experience, he was trapped in Afghanistan once the military campaign began."

. . . [T]he Government filed a response and a motion to dismiss the petition. It attached to its response a declaration from one Michael Mobbs (hereinafter Mobbs Declaration), who identified himself as Special Advisor to the Under Secretary of Defense for Policy. . . .

Mobbs then set forth what remains the sole evidentiary support that the Government has provided to the courts for Hamdi's detention. The declaration states that Hamdi "traveled to Afghanistan" in July or August 2001, and that he thereafter "affiliated with a Taliban military unit and received weapons training." It asserts that Hamdi "remained with his Taliban unit following the attacks of September 11" and that, during the time when Northern Alliance forces were "engaged in battle with the Taliban," "Hamdi's Taliban unit surrendered" to those forces, after which he "surrender[ed] his Kalishnikov assault rifle" to them. The Mobbs Declaration also states that, because al Qaeda and the Taliban "were and are hostile forces engaged in armed conflict with the armed forces of the United States," "individuals associated with" those groups "were and continue to be enemy combatants." Mobbs states that Hamdi was labeled an enemy combatant "[b]ased upon his interviews and in light of his association with the Taliban." According to the declaration, a series of "U.S. military screening team[s]" determined that Hamdi met "the criteria for enemy combatants," and "[a] subsequent interview of Hamdi has confirmed the fact that he surrendered and gave his firearm to Northern Alliance forces, which supports his classification as an enemy combatant. . . ."

The District Court found that the Mobbs Declaration fell "far short" of supporting Hamdi's detention. It criticized the generic and hearsay nature of the affidavit, calling it "little more than the government's 'say-so.'" It ordered the Government to turn over numerous materials for in camera review . . . indicat[ing] that all of these materials were necessary for "meaningful judicial review" of whether Hamdi's detention was legally authorized and whether Hamdi had received sufficient process to satisfy the Due Process Clause of the Constitution and relevant treaties or military regulations. . . .

The Fourth Circuit reversed, . . . stress[ing] that, because it was "undisputed that Hamdi was captured in a zone of active combat in a foreign theater of conflict," no factual inquiry or evidentiary hearing allowing Hamdi to be heard or to rebut the Government's assertions was necessary or proper. Concluding that the factual averments in the Mobbs Declaration, "if accurate," provided a sufficient basis upon which to conclude that the President had constitutionally detained Hamdi pursuant to the President's war powers, it ordered the habeas petition dismissed.

II

[Justice O'CONNOR then explained that the AUMF authorized capture and detention of individuals who were part of hostile forces taking up arms against the United States in Afghanistan. This satisfied 18 U.S.C. §4001(a), which states that "[n]o citizen shall be imprisoned or otherwise detained by the United States except pursuant to an Act of Congress."]

III

Even in cases in which the detention of enemy combatants is legally authorized, there remains the question of what process is constitutionally due to a citizen who disputes his enemy-combatant status. Hamdi argues that he is owed a meaningful and timely hearing and that "extra-judicial detention [that] begins and ends with the submission of an affidavit based on third-hand hearsay" does not comport with the Fifth and Fourteenth Amendments. The Government counters that any more process than was provided below would be both unworkable and "constitutionally intolerable." . . .

C

. . . The ordinary mechanism that we use for balancing such serious competing interests, and for determining the procedures that are necessary to ensure that a citizen is not "deprived of life, liberty, or property, without due process of law," U.S. Const., Amdt. 5, is the test that we articulated in *Mathews v. Eldridge*, 424 U.S. 319 (1976). *Mathews* dictates that the process due in any given instance is determined by weighing "the private interest that will be affected by the official action" against the Government's asserted interest, "including the function involved" and the burdens the Government would face in providing greater process. 424 U.S., at 335. The *Mathews* calculus then contemplates a judicious balancing of these concerns, through an analysis of "the risk of an erroneous deprivation" of the private interest if the process were reduced and the "probable value, if any, of additional or substitute procedural safeguards." *Ibid*. We take each of these steps in turn.

1

It is beyond question that substantial interests lie on both sides of the scale in this case. Hamdi's "private interest . . . affected by the official action," is the most elemental of liberty interests—the interest in being free from physical detention by one's own government. . . . Moreover, as critical as the Government's interest may be in detaining those who actually pose an immediate threat to the national security of the United States during ongoing international conflict, history and common sense teach us that an unchecked system of detention carries the potential to become a means for oppression and abuse of others who do not present that sort of threat. . . . We reaffirm today the fundamental nature of a citizen's right to be free from involuntary confinement by his own government without due process of law, and we weigh the opposing governmental interests against the curtailment of liberty that such confinement entails.

2

On the other side of the scale are the weighty and sensitive governmental interests in ensuring that those who have in fact fought with the enemy during a war do not return to battle against the United States. As discussed above, the law of war and the realities of combat may render such detentions both necessary and appropriate, and our due process analysis need not blink at those realities. Without doubt, our Constitution recognizes that core strategic matters of warmaking belong in the hands of those who are best positioned and most politically accountable for making them.

The Government also argues at some length that its interests in reducing the process available to alleged enemy combatants are heightened by the practical difficulties that would accompany a system of trial-like process. In its view, military officers who are engaged in the serious work of waging battle would be unnecessarily and dangerously distracted by litigation half a world away, and discovery into military operations would both intrude on the sensitive secrets of national defense and result in a futile search for evidence buried under the rubble of war. To the extent that these burdens are triggered by heightened procedures, they are properly taken into account in our due process analysis.

3

Striking the proper constitutional balance here is of great importance to the Nation during this period of ongoing combat. But it is equally vital that our calculus not give short shrift to the values that this country holds dear or to the privilege that is American citizenship. It is during our most challenging and uncertain moments that our Nation's commitment to due process is most severely tested; and it is in those times that we must preserve our commitment at home to the principles for which we fight abroad. . . .

We therefore hold that a citizen-detainee seeking to challenge his classification as an enemy combatant must receive notice of the factual basis for his classification, and a fair opportunity to rebut the Government's factual assertions before a neutral decisionmaker. "For more than a century the central meaning of procedural due process has been clear: 'Parties whose rights are to be affected are entitled to be heard; and in order that they may enjoy that right they must first be notified.' It is equally fundamental that the right to notice and an opportunity to be heard 'must be granted at a meaningful time and in a meaningful manner.'" *Fuentes v. Shevin*, 407 U.S. 67, 80 (1972) (quoting *Baldwin v. Hale*, 1 Wall. 223, 233, 17 L. Ed. 531 (1864)). These essential constitutional promises may not be eroded.

At the same time, the exigencies of the circumstances may demand that, aside from these core elements, enemy-combatant proceedings may be tailored to alleviate their uncommon potential to burden the Executive at a time of ongoing military conflict. Hearsay, for example, may need to be accepted as the most reliable available evidence from the Government in such a proceeding. Likewise, the Constitution would not be offended by a presumption in favor of the Government's evidence, so long as that presumption remained a rebuttable one and fair opportunity for rebuttal were provided. Thus, once the Government puts forth credible evidence that the habeas petitioner meets the enemy-combatant criteria, the onus could shift to the petitioner to rebut that evidence with more persuasive evidence that he falls outside the criteria. A burden-shifting scheme of this sort would meet the goal of ensuring that the errant tourist, embedded journalist, or local aid worker has a chance to prove military error while giving due regard to the Executive once it has put forth meaningful support for its conclusion that the detainee is in fact an enemy combatant. In the words of *Mathews*, process of this sort would sufficiently address the "risk of an erroneous deprivation" of a detainee's liberty interest while eliminating certain procedures that have questionable additional value in light of the burden on the Government. 424 U.S., at 335.

We think it unlikely that this basic process will have the dire impact on the central functions of warmaking that the Government forecasts. The parties agree that initial captures on the battlefield need not receive the process we have discussed here; that process is due only when the determination is made to continue to hold those who have been seized. The Government has made clear in its briefing that documentation regarding battlefield detainees already is kept in the ordinary course of military affairs. Any factfinding imposition created by requiring a knowledgeable affiant to summarize these records to an independent tribunal is a minimal one. Likewise, arguments that military officers ought not have to wage war under the threat of litigation lose much of their steam when factual disputes at enemy-combatant hearings are limited to the alleged combatant's acts. This focus meddles little, if at all, in the strategy or conduct of war, inquiring only into the appropriateness of continuing to detain an individual claimed to have taken up arms against the United States. While we accord the greatest respect and consideration to the judgments of military authorities in matters relating to the actual prosecution of a war, and recognize that the scope of that discretion necessarily is wide, it does not infringe on the core role of the military for the courts to exercise their own time-honored and constitutionally mandated roles of reviewing and resolving claims like those presented here. . . .

IV

Hamdi asks us to hold that the Fourth Circuit also erred by denying him immediate access to counsel upon his detention and by disposing of the case without permitting him to meet with an attorney. Since our grant of certiorari in this case, Hamdi has been appointed counsel, with whom he has met for consultation purposes on several occasions, and with whom he is now being granted unmonitored meetings. He unquestionably has the right to access to counsel in connection with the proceedings on remand. No further consideration of this issue is necessary at this stage of the case.

The judgment of the United States Court of Appeals for the Fourth Circuit is vacated, and the case is remanded for further proceedings.

It is so ordered.

[The opinion of Justice SOUTER, with whom Justice GINSBURG joins, concurring in part, dissenting in part, and concurring in the judgment, is omitted.]

Justice SCALIA, with whom Justice STEVENS joins, dissenting:

I

. . . The gist of the Due Process Clause, as understood at the founding and since, was to force the Government to follow those common-law procedures traditionally deemed necessary before depriving a person of life, liberty, or property. When a citizen was deprived of liberty because of alleged criminal conduct, those procedures typically required committal by a magistrate followed by indictment and trial. The Due Process Clause "in effect affirms the right of trial according to the process and proceedings of the common law." . . .

These due process rights have historically been vindicated by the writ of habeas corpus. In England before the founding, the writ developed into a tool for challenging executive confinement.

The writ of habeas corpus was preserved in the Constitution—the only common-law writ to be explicitly mentioned. *See* Art. I, §9, cl. 2. Hamilton lauded "the establishment of the writ of habeas corpus" in his Federalist defense as a means to protect against "the practice of arbitrary imprisonments . . . in all ages, [one of] the favourite and most formidable instruments of tyranny." The Federalist No. 84, at 444. . . .

II

The allegations here, of course, are no ordinary accusations of criminal activity. Yaser Esam Hamdi has been imprisoned because the Government believes he participated in the waging of war against the United States. The relevant question, then, is whether there is a different, special procedure for imprisonment of a citizen accused of wrongdoing *by aiding the enemy in wartime*.

A

Justice O'Connor, writing for a plurality of this Court, asserts that captured enemy combatants (other than those suspected of war crimes) have traditionally been detained until the cessation of hostilities and then released. That is probably an accurate description of wartime practice with respect to enemy *aliens*. The tradition with respect to American citizens, however, has been quite different. Citizens aiding the enemy have been treated as traitors subject to the criminal process.

. . . The Constitution provides: "Treason against the United States, shall consist only in levying War against them, or in adhering to their Enemies, giving them Aid and Comfort"; and establishes a heightened proof requirement (two witnesses) in order to "convic[t]" of that offense. Art. III, §3, cl. 1.

B

There are times when military exigency renders resort to the traditional criminal process impracticable. . . .

Our Federal Constitution contains a provision explicitly permitting suspension, but limiting the situations in which it may be invoked: "The Privilege of the Writ of Habeas Corpus shall not be suspended, unless when in Cases of Rebellion or Invasion the public Safety may require it." Art. I, §9, cl. 2. Although this provision does not state that suspension must be effected by, or authorized by, a legislative act, it has been so understood, consistent with English practice and the Clause's placement in Article I.

The Suspension Clause was by design a safety valve, the Constitution's only "express provision for exercise of extraordinary authority because of a crisis," *Youngstown Sheet & Tube Co. v. Sawyer*, 343 U.S. 579, 650 (1952) (Jackson, J., concurring).

* * *

V

. . . Hamdi is entitled to a habeas decree requiring his release unless (1) criminal proceedings are promptly brought, or (2) Congress has suspended the writ of habeas corpus. A suspension of the writ could, of course, lay down conditions for continued detention, similar to those that today's opinion prescribes under the Due Process Clause. But there is a world of difference between the people's representatives' determining the need for that suspension (and prescribing the conditions for it), and this Court's doing so. . . .

Having . . . discarded the categorical procedural protection of the Suspension Clause; the plurality then proceeds, under the guise of the Due Process Clause, to prescribe what procedural protections it thinks appropriate. It "weigh[s] the private interest . . . against the Government's asserted interest," (internal quotation marks omitted), and—just as though writing a new Constitution—comes up with an unheard-of system in which the citizen rather than the Government bears the burden of proof, testimony is by hearsay rather than live witnesses, and the presiding officer may well be a "neutral" military officer rather than judge and jury. It claims authority to engage in this sort of "judicious balancing" from *Mathews v. Eldridge*, 424 U.S. 319 (1976), a case involving . . . *the withdrawal of disability benefits*! Whatever the merits of this technique when newly recognized property rights are at issue (and even there they are questionable), it has no place where the Constitution and the common law already supply an answer.

There is a certain harmony of approach in the plurality's making up for Congress's failure to invoke the Suspension Clause and its making up for the Executive's failure to apply what it says are needed procedures—an approach that reflects what might be called a Mr. Fix-it Mentality. The plurality seems to view it as its mission to Make Everything Come Out Right, rather than merely to decree the consequences, as far as individual rights are concerned, of the other two branches' actions and omissions. . . . The problem with this approach is not only that it steps out of the courts' modest and limited role in a democratic society; but that by repeatedly doing what it thinks the political branches ought to do it encourages their lassitude and saps the vitality of government by the people. . . .

Because the Court has proceeded to meet the current emergency in a manner the Constitution does not envision, I respectfully dissent.

Justice THOMAS, dissenting:

The Executive Branch, acting pursuant to the powers vested in the President by the Constitution and with explicit congressional approval, has determined that Yaser Hamdi is an enemy combatant and should be detained. That detention falls squarely within the Federal Government's war powers, and we lack the expertise and capacity to second-guess that decision. As such, petitioners' habeas challenge should fail, and there is no reason to remand the case. . . .

Although I do not agree with the plurality that the balancing approach of *Mathews v. Eldridge*, 424 U.S. 319 (1976) is the appropriate analytic tool with which to analyze this case, I cannot help but explain that the plurality misapplies its chosen framework, one that if applied correctly would probably lead to the result I have reached. The plurality devotes two paragraphs to its discussion of the Government's interest, though much of those two paragraphs explain why the Government's concerns are misplaced. . . . At issue here is the . . . significant interest of the security of the Nation. The Government seeks to further that interest by detaining an enemy soldier not only to prevent him from rejoining the ongoing plains, detention can serve to gather critical intelligence regarding the intentions and capabilities of our adversaries, a function that the Government avers has become all the more important in the war on terrorism.

Additional process, the Government explains, will destroy the intelligence gathering function. It also does seem quite likely that, under the process envisioned by the plurality, various military officials will have to take time to litigate this matter. And though the plurality does not say so, a meaningful ability to challenge the Government's factual allegations will probably require the Government to divulge highly classified information to the purported enemy combatant, who might then upon release return to the fight armed with our most closely held secrets.

The plurality manages to avoid these problems by discounting or entirely ignoring them. . . .

The plurality next opines that "[w]e think it unlikely that this basic process will have the dire impact on the central functions of warmaking that the Government forecasts." . . . [T]his highlights serious difficulties in applying the plurality's balancing approach here. First, in the war context, we know neither the strength of the Government's interests nor the costs of imposing additional process.

Second, it is at least difficult to explain why the result should be different for other military operations that the plurality would ostensibly recognize as "central functions of warmaking." . . . Because a decision to bomb a particular target might extinguish *life* interests, the plurality's analysis seems to require notice to potential targets. . . . I offer these examples not because I think the plurality would demand additional process in these situations but because it clearly would not. The result here should be the same. . . .

Undeniably, Hamdi has been deprived of a serious interest, one actually protected by the Due Process Clause. Against this, however, is the Government's overriding interest in protecting the Nation. . . .

REVIEW QUESTIONS

1. The *Hamdi* decision is a plurality decision, meaning that a majority of the Justices agreed on the outcome but not on the reasoning. Here, six Justices concurred on the judgment, that is, on the ultimate decision to vacate the Fourth Circuit decision and remand to the district court. Four Justices (O'Connor, Roberts, Kennedy, Breyer) signed on to the plurality opinion reprinted here. What type of hearing do they propose for the accused? How do they determine this? Contrast the position of Justice O'Connor's plurality opinion with the dissent of Justices Scalia and Stevens. What rules would they apply? Finally, how would Justice Thomas balance the interests at stake differently than the majority?

2. You may wonder about the precedential value of a plurality decision. The Supreme Court has held that "[w]hen a fragmented Court decides a case and no single rationale explaining the result enjoys the assent of five Justices, 'the holding of the Court may be viewed as that position taken by those Members who concurred in the judgments on the narrowest grounds. . . .'" *Marks v. United States*, 430 U.S. 188, 193 (1977).

WANT TO KNOW MORE?

The law surrounding the use of military commissions to try detainees is still evolving. For a description of its evolution, *see* Stephen I. Vladeck, *Military Courts and Article III*, 103 Geo. L.J. 933, 937 (2015). If you are curious about the history of habeas corpus, which can be suspended only by congressional action, *see* Amanda L. Tyler, *Habeas Corpus in War Time: From the Tower of London to Guantanamo Bay* (2017).

D. ACCESS TO LAWYERS AND TO THE LEGAL SYSTEM

When should the due process right to be heard ensure a right to a lawyer? When should that right encompass rights of access to the formal setting of the courtroom? The following due process cases address these questions. Complicating the question of access to a lawyer is the issue of communication between clients and lawyers who may come from different social, economic, and cultural worlds. Questions of access could be resolved outside the constitutional framework through legislation, voluntary contributions by the bar, or the creation of cheaper, quicker processes inside and outside the formal judicial setting. When would such alternatives be desirable?

We start by considering the very basic question of whether and when the court system can charge for access to the court itself.

1. Access to Court

Boddie v. Connecticut
401 U.S. 371 (1971)

Justice HARLAN delivered the opinion of the Court:

Appellants, welfare recipients residing in the State of Connecticut, brought this action in the Federal District Court for the District of Connecticut on behalf of themselves and others similarly situated, challenging, as applied to them, certain state procedures for the commencement of litigation, including requirements for payment of court fees and costs for service of process, that restrict their access to the courts in their effort to bring an action for divorce.

It appears from the briefs and oral argument that the average cost to a litigant for bringing an action for divorce is $60. Section 52-259 of the Connecticut General Statutes provides: "There shall be paid to the clerks of the supreme court or the superior court, for entering each civil cause, forty-five dollars. . . ." An additional $15 is usually required for the service of process by the sheriff, although as much as $40 or $50 may be necessary where notice must be accomplished by publication.

There is no dispute as to the inability of the named appellants in the present case to pay either the court fees required by statute or the cost incurred for the service of process. The affidavits in the record establish that appellants' welfare income in each instance barely suffices to meet the costs of the daily essentials of life and includes no allotment that could be budgeted for the expense to gain access to the courts in order to obtain a divorce. Also undisputed is appellants' "good faith" in seeking a divorce.

Assuming, as we must on this motion to dismiss the complaint, the truth of the undisputed allegations made by the appellants, it appears that they were unsuccessful in their attempt to bring their divorce actions in the Connecticut courts, simply by reason of their indigency. The clerk of the Superior Court returned their papers "on the ground that he could not accept them until an entry fee had been paid." Subsequent efforts to obtain a judicial waiver of the fee requirement and to have the court effect service of process were to no avail.

Appellants thereafter commenced this action in the Federal District Court seeking a judgment declaring that Connecticut's statute and service of process provisions, "requiring payment of court fees and expenses as a condition precedent to obtaining court relief [are] unconstitutional [as] applied to these indigent [appellants] and all other members of the class which they represent." As further relief, appellants requested the entry of an injunction ordering the appropriate officials to permit them "to proceed with their divorce actions without payment of fees and costs." Our conclusion is that, given the basic position of the marriage relationship in this society's hierarchy of values and the concomitant state monopolization of the means for legally dissolving this relationship, due process does prohibit a State from denying, solely because of inability to pay, access to its courts to individuals who seek judicial dissolution of their marriages.

At its core, the right to due process reflects a fundamental value in our American constitutional system. Our understanding of that value is the basis upon which we have resolved this case.

Perhaps no characteristic of an organized and cohesive society is more fundamental than its erection and enforcement of a system of rules defining the various rights and duties of its members, enabling them to govern their affairs and definitively settle their differences in an orderly, predictable manner. Without such a "legal system," social organization and cohesion are virtually impossible; with the ability to seek regularized resolution of conflicts individuals are capable of interdependent action that enables them to strive for achievements without the anxieties that would beset them in a disorganized society. Put more succinctly, it is this injection of the rule of law that allows society to reap the benefits of rejecting what political theorists call the "state of nature."

American society, of course, bottoms its systematic definition of individual rights and duties, as well as its machinery for dispute settlement, not on custom or the will of strategically placed individuals, but on the common-law model. It is to courts, or other quasi-judicial official bodies, that we ultimately look for the implementation of a regularized, orderly process of dispute settlement. Within this framework, those who wrote our original Constitution, in the Fifth Amendment, and later those who drafted the Fourteenth Amendment, recognized the centrality of the concept of due process in the operation of this system. Without this guarantee that one may not be deprived of his rights, neither liberty nor property, without due process of law, the State's monopoly over techniques for binding conflict resolution could hardly be said to be acceptable under our scheme of things. Only by providing that the social enforcement mechanism must function strictly within these bounds can we hope to maintain an ordered society that is also just. It is upon this premise that this Court has through years of adjudication put flesh upon the due process principle. . . .

Such litigation has, however, typically involved rights of defendants—not, as here, persons seeking access to the judicial process in the first instance. This is because our society has been so structured that resort to the courts is not usually the only available, legitimate means of resolving private disputes. Indeed, private structuring of individual relationships and repair of their breach is largely encouraged in American life, subject only to the caveat that the formal judicial process, if resorted to, is paramount. Thus, this Court has seldom been asked to view access to the courts as an element of due process. The legitimacy of the State's monopoly over techniques of final dispute settlement, even where some are denied access to its use, stands unimpaired where recognized, effective alternatives for the adjustment of differences remain. But the successful invocation of this governmental power by plaintiffs has often created serious problems for defendants' rights. For at that point, the judicial proceeding becomes the only effective means of resolving the dispute at hand and denial of a defendant's full access to that process raises grave problems for its legitimacy.

Recognition of this theoretical framework illuminates the precise issue presented in this case. As this Court on more than one occasion has recognized, marriage involves interests of basic importance in our society. *See, e.g., Loving v. Virginia*, 388 U.S. 1 (1967); *Skinner v. Oklahoma*, 316 U.S. 535 (1942); *Meyer v. Nebraska*, 262 U.S. 390 (1923). It is not surprising, then, that the States have seen fit to oversee many aspects of that institution. . . .

[A]lthough they assert here due process rights as would-be plaintiffs, we think appellants' plight, because resort to the state courts is the only avenue to dissolution of their marriages, is akin to that of defendants faced with exclusion from the only forum effectively empowered to settle their disputes. Resort to the judicial process by these plaintiffs is no more voluntary in a realistic sense than that of the defendant called upon to defend his interests in court. For both groups this process is not only the paramount dispute-settlement technique, but, in fact, the only available one. In this posture we think that this appeal is properly to be resolved in light of the principles enunciated in our due process decisions that delimit rights of defendants compelled to litigate their differences in the judicial forum.

These due process decisions, representing over a hundred years of effort by this Court to give concrete embodiment to this concept, provide, we think, complete vindication for appellants' contentions. In particular, precedent has firmly embedded in our due process jurisprudence two important principles upon whose application we rest our decision in the case before us.

Prior cases establish, first, that due process requires, at a minimum, that absent a countervailing state interest of overriding significance, persons forced to settle their claims of right and duty through the judicial process must be given a meaningful opportunity to be heard. . . .

Due process does not, of course, require that the defendant in every civil case actually have a hearing on the merits. . . . What the Constitution does require is "an opportunity . . . granted at a meaningful time and in a meaningful manner," *Armstrong v. Manzo*, 380 U.S. 545, 552 (1965) (emphasis added), "for [a] hearing appropriate to the nature of the case," *Mullane v. Central Hanover Bank & Trust Co.*, 339 U.S. 306, 313 (1950).

Our cases further establish that a statute or a rule may be held constitutionally invalid as applied when it operates to deprive an individual of a protected right although its general validity as a measure enacted in the legitimate exercise of state power is beyond question. Thus, in cases involving religious freedom, free speech or assembly, this Court has often held that a valid statute was unconstitutionally applied in particular circumstances because it interfered with an individual's exercise of those rights.

No less than these rights, the right to a meaningful opportunity to be heard within the limits of practicality, must be protected against denial by particular laws that operate to jeopardize it for particular individuals. . . .

The State's obligations under the Fourteenth Amendment are not simply generalized ones; rather, the State owes to each individual that process which, in light of the values of a free society, can be characterized as due.

Drawing upon the principles established by the cases just canvassed, we conclude that the State's refusal to admit these appellants to its courts, the sole means in Connecticut for obtaining a divorce, must be regarded as the equivalent of denying them an opportunity to be heard upon their claimed right to a dissolution of their marriages, and, in the absence of a sufficient countervailing justification for the State's action, a denial of due process.

The arguments for this kind of fee and cost requirement are that the State's interest in the prevention of frivolous litigation is substantial, its use of court fees and process costs to allocate scarce resources is rational, and its balance between the defendant's right to notice and the plaintiff's right to access is reasonable.

In our opinion, none of these considerations is sufficient to override the interest of these plaintiff-appellants in having access to the only avenue open for dissolving their allegedly untenable marriages. . . .

We are thus left to evaluate the State's asserted interest in its fee and cost requirements as a mechanism of resource allocation or cost recoupment. Such a justification was offered and rejected in *Griffin v. Illinois*, 351 U.S. 12 (1956). In *Griffin* it was the requirement of a transcript beyond the means of the indigent that blocked access to the judicial process. While in *Griffin* the transcript could be waived as a convenient but not necessary predicate to court access, here the State invariably imposes the costs as a measure of allocating its judicial resources. Surely, then, the rationale of *Griffin* covers this case.

In concluding that the Due Process Clause of the Fourteenth Amendment requires that these appellants be afforded an opportunity to go into court to obtain a divorce, we wish to re-emphasize that we go no further than necessary to dispose of the case before us, a case where the bona fides of both appellants' indigency and desire for divorce are here beyond dispute. We do not decide that access for all individuals to the courts is a right that is, in all circumstances, guaranteed by the Due Process Clause of the Fourteenth Amendment so that its exercise may not be placed beyond the reach of any individual, for, as we have already noted, in the case before us this right is the exclusive precondition to the adjustment of a fundamental human relationship. . . .

Reversed.

[Justice Douglas's concurring opinion is omitted.]

Justice Brennan, concurring in part:

I join the Court's opinion to the extent that it holds that Connecticut denies procedural due process in denying the indigent appellants access to its courts for the sole reason that they cannot pay a required fee. . . .

But I cannot join the Court's opinion insofar as today's holding is made to depend upon the factor that only the State can grant a divorce and that an indigent would be locked into a marriage if unable to pay the fees required to obtain a divorce. A State has an ultimate monopoly of all judicial process and attendant enforcement machinery. As a practical matter, if disputes cannot be successfully settled between the parties, the court system is usually "the only forum effectively empowered to settle their disputes. Resort to the judicial process by these plaintiffs is no more voluntary in a realistic sense than that of the defendant called upon to defend his interests in court." . . . The right to be heard in some way at some time extends to all proceedings entertained by courts. The possible distinctions suggested by the Court today will not withstand analysis.

In addition, this case presents a classic problem of equal protection of the laws. The question that the Court treats exclusively as one of due process inevitably implicates considerations of both due process and equal protection. Certainly, there is at issue the denial of a hearing, a matter for analysis under the Due Process Clause. But Connecticut does not deny a hearing to everyone in these circumstances; it denies it only to people who fail to pay certain fees. The validity of this partial denial, or differentiation in treatment, can be tested as well under the Equal Protection Clause.

In *Griffin v. Illinois*, 351 U.S. 12, 76 S.Ct. 585, 100 L. Ed. 891 (1956), we held under the Equal Protection Clause as well as the Due Process Clause that a State may not deny a free transcript to an indigent, where the transcript is necessary for a direct appeal from his conviction. Subsequently, we have applied and extended that principle in numerous criminal cases. . . . The rationale of *Griffin* covers the present case. Courts are the central dispute-settling institutions in our society. They are bound to do equal justice under law, to rich and poor alike. They fail to perform their function in accordance with the Equal Protection Clause if they shut their doors to indigent plaintiffs altogether. Where money determines not merely 'the kind of trial a man gets,' but whether he gets into court at all, the great principle of equal protection becomes a mockery. A State may not make its judicial processes available to some but deny them to others simply because they cannot pay a fee. In my view, Connecticut's fee requirement, as applied to an indigent, is a denial of equal protection.

Justice BLACK, dissenting:

This is a strange case and a strange holding. Absent some specific federal constitutional or statutory provision, marriage in this country is completely under state control, and so is divorce. When the first settlers arrived here the power to grant divorces in Great Britain was not vested in that country's courts but in its Parliament. . . . It is not by accident that marriage and divorce have always been considered to be under state control. The institution of marriage is of peculiar importance to the people of the States. . . .

The Court here holds, however, that the State of Connecticut has so little control over marriages and divorces of its own citizens that it is without power to charge them practically nominal initial court costs when they are without ready money to put up those costs. The Court holds that the state law requiring payment of costs is barred by the Due Process Clause of the Fourteenth Amendment of the Federal Constitution. Two members of the majority believe that the Equal Protection Clause also applies. I think the Connecticut court costs law is barred by neither of those clauses.

It is true, as the majority points out, that the Court did hold in *Griffin v. Illinois*, 351 U.S. 12 (1956), that indigent defendants in criminal cases must be afforded the same right to appeal their convictions as is afforded to a defendant who has ample funds to pay his own costs. . . . [T]here are strong reasons for distinguishing between the two types of cases.

Criminal defendants are brought into court by the State or Federal Government to defend themselves against charges of crime. They go into court knowing that they may be convicted, and condemned to lose their lives, their liberty, or their property, as a penalty for their crimes. Because of this great governmental power the United States Constitution has provided special protections for people charged with crime. . . .

Civil lawsuits, however, are not like government prosecutions for crime. Civil courts are set up by government to give people who have quarrels with their neighbors the chance to use a neutral governmental agency to adjust their differences. In such cases the government is not usually involved as a party, and there is no deprivation of life, liberty, or property as punishment for crime. Our Federal Constitution, therefore, does not place such private disputes on the same high level as it places criminal trials and punishment. There is consequently no necessity, no reason, why government should in civil trials be hampered or handicapped by the strict and rigid due process rules the Constitution has provided to protect people charged with crime.

. . . The rules set out in the Constitution itself provide what is governmentally fair and what is not. Neither due process nor equal protection permits state laws to be invalidated on any such nonconstitutional standard as a judge's personal view of fairness. The people and their elected representatives, not judges, are constitutionally vested with the power to amend the Constitution. . . .

REVIEW QUESTIONS

1. Which of these values are crucial to the majority opinion, and why? What is their role in the Court's analysis?
   a. The interests of individuals involved in marriage and divorce are so fundamental that the state must act very carefully in governing them.
   b. The state monopoly over the techniques of binding conflict resolution in the area of divorce cannot be conducted in a mode that deprives an individual of liberty or property.
   c. The state monopoly over the techniques of binding conflict resolution cannot be conducted in a mode that deprives an individual of liberty or property.
   d. The individual plaintiffs have untenable marriages.
   e. The state here offers no mechanisms for waiving access fees for divorce upon demonstration of the parties' indigency.
2. Which of the rationales offered by Justice Black in dissent do you find most persuasive?

    a. Accommodation of indigents in criminal litigation is not a compelling analogy for the treatment of indigents in civil litigation, where the state itself does not threaten to deprive a person of life, liberty, or property.

    b. Nothing in the language of the Constitution empowers a judge to invalidate state laws on the basis of personal views of fairness.

    c. Dissatisfaction with the system should lead to action by the people and their elected representatives, not by judges.

3. What rejoinders does the majority offer to the arguments in the dissent? Which do you find most persuasive?

QUESTIONS TO PONDER

1. In what kinds of cases do you think limiting fee waiver for indigency would be appropriate? For example, in *United States v. Kras*, 409 U.S. 434 (1973), the Court rejected an indigent person's request to waive the filing fee for bankruptcy protection on due process grounds. In part the Court reasoned that filing bankruptcy was not a fundamental right, and therefore access to bankruptcy court not protected. By contrast, the Court supported an indigent mother's claim to waive the costs of a transcript necessary to appeal a civil court judgment terminating her parental rights for abuse or neglect. *M.L.B. v. S.L.J.*, 519 U.S. 102 (1996). The parent-child relationship is considered a fundamental right. In *M.L.B.*, the Court relied both on the due process analysis of the majority in *Boddie* and the equal protection rationale suggested by Justice Brennan's concurrence.

2. Fee waiver for indigent litigants has come up in prisoner litigation as well. The Prison Litigation Reform Act (PLRA) mandates that prisoners who are granted leave to proceed *in forma pauperis,* that is, who are indigent, must still pay their fees but on an installment basis, although it does have a safety valve for prisoners who cannot even pay installments. 28 U.S.C. § 1915(b)(1)-(4) (2012). However, the law also limits prisoners ability to file. It states that prisoners must pay the full fee when they "on 3 or more prior occasions, while incarcerated or detained in any facility, [have] brought an action or appeal in a court of the United States that was dismissed on the grounds that it is frivolous, malicious, or fails to state a claim upon which relief may be granted[,]" unless they are filing a habeas petition or they are in "imminent danger of serious physical injury." *Id.* at § 1915(g). In a concurring opinion denying a prisoner in forma pauperis status, D.C. Circuit Judge Tatel wrote:

> I have grave doubts that the PLRA's three-strikes provision may be constitutionally applied to indigent prisoners who seek access to the courts in order to bring claims involving fundamental constitutional rights. In

the appropriate case, this court should address this unsettled issue. In so suggesting, I fully understand that Congress was responding to a very real problem when it enacted the PLRA. It is undoubtedly true that much prisoner litigation is not only frivolous and abusive, but also imposes substantial costs on the federal courts. That said, it is also undoubtedly true that some prisoners have legitimate constitutional claims. So while faithfully honoring Congress's goal of reducing abusive litigation, the federal courts remain constitutionally obligated to hear such claims, for "[o]nly by zealously guarding the rights of the most humble, the most unorthodox and the most despised among us can freedom flourish and endure in our land." *Bridges v. Wixon*, 326 U.S. 135, 166 (1945).

Thomas v. Holder, 750 F.3d 899, 909 (D.C. Cir. 2014).

Do you think that the PLRA provision limiting indigent prisoner's access to courts is constitutional? Why or why not? So far most courts have upheld the provision on grounds that prisoners could sue by borrowing money or by filing in state court. *See, e.g., Lewis v. Sullivan*, 279 F.3d 526, 530 (7th Cir. 2002).

2. Access to a Lawyer

Even when a person is able to appear before the court, they may find it difficult to make their case without a lawyer to guide them. The case below addresses the question of when due process requires access to legal assistance.

Lassiter v. Department of Social Services of Durham County, North Carolina
452 U.S. 18 (1981)

Justice STEWART delivered the opinion of the Court:

In the late spring of 1975, after hearing evidence that the petitioner, Abby Gail Lassiter, had not provided her infant son William with proper medical care, the District Court of Durham County, N.C., adjudicated him a neglected child and transferred him to the custody of the Durham County Department of Social Services, the respondent here. A year later, Ms. Lassiter was charged with first-degree murder, was convicted of second-degree murder, and began a sentence of 25 to 40 years of imprisonment.[1] In 1978 the Department petitioned the court

---

1. The North Carolina Court of Appeals, in reviewing the petitioner's conviction, indicated that the murder occurred during an altercation between Ms. Lassiter, her mother, and the deceased:

> "Defendant's mother told [the deceased] to 'come on.' They began to struggle and deceased fell or was knocked to the floor. Defendant's mother was beating deceased with a broom. While deceased was still on the floor and being beaten with the broom, defendant entered the apartment. She went into the kitchen and got a butcher knife. She took the knife and began stabbing

to terminate Ms. Lassiter's parental rights because, the Department alleged, she "has not had any contact with the child since December of 1975" and "has willfully left the child in foster care for more than two consecutive years without showing that substantial progress has been made in correcting the conditions which led to the removal of the child, or without showing a positive response to the diligent efforts of the Department of Social Services to strengthen her relationship to the child, or to make and follow through with constructive planning for the future of the child."

Ms. Lassiter was served with the petition and with notice that a hearing on it would be held. Although her mother had retained counsel for her in connection with an effort to invalidate the murder conviction, Ms. Lassiter never mentioned the forthcoming hearing to him (or, for that matter, to any other person except, she said, to "someone" in the prison). At the behest of the Department of Social Services' attorney, she was brought from prison to the hearing, which was held August 31, 1978. The hearing opened, apparently at the judge's insistence, with a discussion of whether Ms. Lassiter should have more time in which to find legal assistance. Since the court concluded that she "has had ample opportunity to seek and obtain counsel prior to the hearing of this matter, and [that] her failure to do so is without just cause," the court did not postpone the proceedings. Ms. Lassiter did not aver that she was indigent, and the court did not appoint counsel for her.

A social worker from the respondent Department was the first witness. She testified that in 1975 the Department "received a complaint from Duke Pediatrics that William had not been followed in the pediatric clinic for medical problems and that they were having difficulty in locating Ms. Lassiter. . . ." She said that in May 1975 a social worker had taken William to the hospital, where doctors asked that he stay "because of breathing difficulties [and] malnutrition and [because] there was a great deal of scarring that indicated that he had a severe infection that had gone untreated." The witness further testified that, except for one "prearranged" visit and a chance meeting on the street, Ms. Lassiter had not seen William after he had come into the State's custody, and that neither Ms. Lassiter nor her mother had "made any contact with the Department of Social Services regarding that child." When asked whether William should be placed in his grandmother's custody, the social worker said he should not, since the grandmother "has indicated to me on a number of occasions that she was not able to take responsibility for the child" and since "I have checked with people in the community and from Ms. Lassiter's church

---

the deceased who was still prostrate. The body of deceased had seven stab wounds. . . ." *State v. Lassiter*, No. 7614SC1054 (N.C. Ct. App. June 1, 1977).

After her conviction was affirmed on appeal, Ms. Lassiter sought to attack it collaterally. Among her arguments was that the assistance of her trial counsel had been ineffective because he had failed to "seek to elicit or introduce before the jury the statement made by [Ms. Lassiter's mother,] 'And I did it, I hope she dies.' " Ms. Lassiter's mother had, like Ms. Lassiter, been indicted on a first-degree murder charge; however, the trial court granted the elder Ms. Lassiter's motion for a nonsuit. The North Carolina General Court of Justice, Superior Court Division, denied Ms. Lassiter's motion for collateral relief. File No. 76-CR-3102 (Mar. 20, 1979).

who also feel that this additional responsibility would be more than she can handle." The social worker added that William "has not seen his grandmother since the chance meeting in July of '76 and that was the only time."

After the direct examination of the social worker, the judge said:

> I notice we made extensive findings in June of '75 that you were served with papers and called the social services and told them you weren't coming; and the serious lack of medical treatment. And, as I have said in my findings of the 16th day of June '75, the Court finds that the grandmother, Ms. Lucille Lassiter, mother of Abby Gail Lassiter, filed a complaint on the 8th day of May, 1975, alleging that the daughter often left the children, Candina, Felicia and William L. with her for days without providing money or food while she was gone.

Ms. Lassiter conducted a cross-examination of the social worker, who firmly reiterated her earlier testimony. The judge explained several times, with varying degrees of clarity, that Ms. Lassiter should only ask questions at this stage; many of her questions were disallowed because they were not really questions, but arguments.

Ms. Lassiter herself then testified, under the judge's questioning, that she had properly cared for William. Under cross-examination, she said that she had seen William more than five or six times after he had been taken from her custody and that, if William could not be with her, she wanted him to be with her mother since, "He knows us. Children know they family. . . . They know they people, they know they family and that child knows us anywhere. . . . I got four more other children. Three girls and a boy and they know they little brother when they see him." Ms. Lassiter's mother was then called as a witness. She denied, under the questioning of the judge, that she had filed the complaint against Ms. Lassiter, and on cross-examination she denied both having failed to visit William when he was in the State's custody and having said that she could not care for him.

The court found that Ms. Lassiter "has not contacted the Department of Social Services about her child since December, 1975, has not expressed any concern for his care and welfare, and has made no efforts to plan for his future." Because Ms. Lassiter thus had "wilfully failed to maintain concern or responsibility for the welfare of the minor," and because it was "in the best interests of the minor," the court terminated Ms. Lassiter's status as William's parent.

On appeal, Ms. Lassiter argued only that, because she was indigent, the Due Process Clause of the Fourteenth Amendment entitled her to the assistance of counsel, and that the trial court had therefore erred in not requiring the State to provide counsel for her. The North Carolina Court of Appeals decided that "[while] this State action does invade a protected area of individual privacy, the invasion is not so serious or unreasonable as to compel us to hold that appointment of counsel for indigent parents is constitutionally mandated." *In re Lassiter*, 43 N.C. App. 525. The Supreme Court of North Carolina summarily denied Ms. Lassiter's application for discretionary review, and we granted certiorari to consider the petitioner's claim under the Due Process Clause of the Fourteenth Amendment.

For all its consequence, "due process" has never been, and perhaps can never be, precisely defined. "[Unlike] some legal rules," this Court has said, due process "is not a technical conception with a fixed content unrelated to time, place and circumstances." *Cafeteria Workers v. McElroy*, 367 U.S. 886, 895. Rather, the phrase expresses the requirement of "fundamental fairness," a requirement whose meaning can be as opaque as its importance is lofty. Applying the Due Process Clause is therefore an uncertain enterprise which must discover what "fundamental fairness" consists of in a particular situation by first considering any relevant precedents and then by assessing the several interests that are at stake.

Precedent

The pre-eminent generalization that emerges from this Court's precedents on an indigent's right to appointed counsel is that such a right has been recognized to exist only where the litigant may lose his physical liberty if he loses the litigation. Thus, when the Court overruled the principle of *Betts v. Brady*, 316 U.S. 455, that counsel in criminal trials need be appointed only where the circumstances in a given case demand it, the Court did so in the case of a man sentenced to prison for five years. *Gideon v. Wainwright*, 372 U.S. 335. And thus *Argersinger v. Hamlin*, 407 U.S. 25, established that counsel must be provided before any indigent may be sentenced to prison, even where the crime is petty and the prison term brief.

That it is the defendant's interest in personal freedom, and not simply the special Sixth and Fourteenth Amendments right to counsel in criminal cases, which triggers the right to appointed counsel is demonstrated by the Court's announcement in *In re Gault*, 387 U.S. 1, that "the Due Process Clause of the Fourteenth Amendment requires that in respect of proceedings to determine delinquency *which may result in commitment to an institution in which the juvenile's freedom is curtailed*," the juvenile has a right to appointed counsel even though those proceedings may be styled "civil" and not "criminal." *Id*. at 41 (emphasis added). Similarly, four of the five Justices who reached the merits in *Vitek v. Jones*, 445 U.S. 480, concluded that an indigent prisoner is entitled to appointed counsel before being involuntarily transferred for treatment to a state mental hospital. The fifth Justice differed from the other four only in declining to exclude the "possibility that the required assistance may be rendered by competent laymen in some cases." *Id*. at 500 (separate opinion of Powell, J.).

Significantly, as a litigant's interest in personal liberty diminishes, so does his right to appointed counsel. In *Gagnon v. Scarpelli*, 411 U.S. 778, the Court gauged the due process rights of a previously sentenced probationer at a probation-revocation hearing. In *Morrissey v. Brewer*, 408 U.S. 471, 480, which involved an analogous hearing to revoke parole, the Court had said: "Revocation deprives an individual, not of the absolute liberty to which every citizen is entitled, but only of the conditional liberty properly dependent on observance of special parole restrictions." Relying on that discussion, the Court in *Scarpelli* declined to hold that indigent probationers have, per se, a right to counsel at revocation hearings, and instead left the decision whether counsel should be appointed to be made on a case-by-case basis.

Finally, the Court has refused to extend the right to appointed counsel to include prosecutions which, though criminal, do not result in the defendant's loss of personal liberty. The Court in *Scott v. Illinois*, 440 U.S. 367, for instance, interpreted the "central premise of *Argersinger*" to be "that actual imprisonment is a penalty different in kind from fines or the mere threat of imprisonment," and the Court endorsed that premise as "eminently sound and [warranting] adoption of actual imprisonment as the line defining the constitutional right to appointment of counsel." *Id.*, at 373. The Court thus held "that the Sixth and Fourteenth Amendments to the United States Constitution require only that no indigent criminal defendant be sentenced to a term of imprisonment unless the State has afforded him the right to assistance of appointed counsel in his defense." *Id.*, at 373-374.

In sum, the Court's precedents speak with one voice about what "fundamental fairness" has meant when the Court has considered the right to appointed counsel, and we thus draw from them the presumption that an indigent litigant has a right to appointed counsel only when, if he loses, he may be deprived of his physical liberty. It is against this presumption that all the other elements in the due process decision must be measured.

The case of *Mathews v. Eldridge*, 424 U.S. 319, 335, propounds three elements to be evaluated in deciding what due process requires, viz., the private interests at stake, the government's interest, and the risk that the procedures used will lead to erroneous decisions. We must balance these elements against each other, and then set their net weight in the scales against the presumption that there is a right to appointed counsel only where the indigent, if he is unsuccessful, may lose his personal freedom.

This Court's decisions have by now made plain beyond the need for multiple citation that a parent's desire for and right to "the companionship, care, custody, and management of his or her children" is an important interest that "undeniably warrants deference and, absent a powerful countervailing interest, protection." *Stanley v. Illinois*, 405 U.S. 645, 651. Here the State has sought not simply to infringe upon that interest, but to end it. If the State prevails, it will have worked a unique kind of deprivation. A parent's interest in the accuracy and justice of the decision to terminate his or her parental status is, therefore, a commanding one.

Since the State has an urgent interest in the welfare of the child, it shares the parent's interest in an accurate and just decision. For this reason, the State may share the indigent parent's interest in the availability of appointed counsel. If, as our adversary system presupposes, accurate and just results are most likely to be obtained through the equal contest of opposed interests, the State's interest in the child's welfare may perhaps best be served by a hearing in which both the parent and the State acting for the child are represented by counsel, without whom the contest of interests may become unwholesomely unequal. North Carolina itself acknowledges as much by providing that where a parent files a written answer to a termination petition, the State must supply a lawyer to represent the child. N.C. Gen. Stat. §7A-289.29 (Supp. 1979).

The State's interests, however, clearly diverge from the parent's insofar as the State wishes the termination decision to be made as economically as possible and, thus wants to avoid both the expense of appointed counsel and the cost of the lengthened proceedings his presence may cause. But though the State's pecuniary interest is legitimate, it is hardly significant enough to overcome private interests as important as those here, particularly in light of the concession in the respondent's brief that the "potential costs of appointed counsel in termination proceedings . . . is [sic] admittedly *de minimis* compared to the costs in all criminal actions."

risk of errors

Finally, consideration must be given to the risk that a parent will be erroneously deprived of his or her child because the parent is not represented by counsel. North Carolina law now seeks to assure accurate decisions by establishing the following procedures: A petition to terminate parental rights may be filed only by a parent seeking the termination of the other parent's rights, by a county department of social services or licensed child-placing agency with custody of the child, or by a person with whom the child has lived continuously for the two years preceding the petition. §7A289.24. A petition must describe facts sufficient to warrant a finding that one of the grounds for termination exists, §7A289.25(6), and the parent must be notified of the petition and given 30 days in which to file a written answer to it, §7A289.27. If that answer denies a material allegation, the court must, as has been noted, appoint a lawyer as the child's guardian ad litem and must conduct a special hearing to resolve the issues raised by the petition and the answer. §7A-289.29. If the parent files no answer, "the court shall issue an order terminating all parental and custodial rights . . . ; provided the court shall order a hearing on the petition and may examine the petitioner or others on the facts alleged in the petition." §7A289.28. Findings of fact are made by a court sitting without a jury and must "be based on clear, cogent, and convincing evidence." §7A289.30. Any party may appeal who gives notice of appeal within 10 days after the hearing. §7A289.34.

The respondent argues that the subject of a termination hearing—the parent's relationship with her child—far from being abstruse, technical, or unfamiliar, is one as to which the parent must be uniquely well informed and to which the parent must have given prolonged thought. The respondent also contends that a termination hearing is not likely to produce difficult points of evidentiary law, or even of substantive law, since the evidentiary problems peculiar to criminal trials are not present and since the standards for termination are not complicated. In fact, the respondent reports, the North Carolina Departments of Social Services are themselves sometimes represented at termination hearings by social workers instead of by lawyers.

Yet the ultimate issues with which a termination hearing deals are not always simple, however commonplace they may be. Expert medical and psychiatric testimony, which few parents are equipped to understand and fewer still to confute, is sometimes presented. The parents are likely to be people with little education, who have had uncommon difficulty in dealing with life, and who are, at the hearing, thrust into a distressing and disorienting situation. That these factors may combine to overwhelm an uncounseled parent is evident from the findings some courts have made. . . . The respondent is able to point to no presently authoritative case, except for the North Carolina judgment now before us, holding that an indigent parent has no due process right to appointed counsel in termination proceedings.

The dispositive question, which must now be addressed, is whether the three *Eldridge* factors, when weighed against the presumption that there is no right to appointed counsel in the absence of at least a potential deprivation of physical liberty, suffice to rebut that presumption and thus to lead to the conclusion that the Due Process Clause requires the appointment of counsel when a State seeks to terminate an indigent's parental status. . . .

If, in a given case, the parent's interests were at their strongest, the State's interests were at their weakest, and the risks of error were at their peak, it could not be said that the *Eldridge* factors did not overcome the presumption against the right to appointed counsel, and that due process did not therefore require the appointment of counsel. But since the *Eldridge* factors will not always be so distributed, and since "due process is not so rigid as to require that the significant interests in informality, flexibility and economy must always be sacrificed," *Gagnon v. Scarpelli*, 411 U.S. at 788, neither can we say that the Constitution requires that appointment of counsel in every parental termination proceeding. We therefore adopt the standard found appropriate in *Gagnon v. Scarpelli*, and leave the decision whether due process calls for the appointment of counsel for indigent parents in termination proceedings to be answered in the first instance by the trial court, subject, of course, to appellate review. . . .

The Department of Social Services was represented at the hearing by counsel, but no expert witnesses testified, and the case presented no specially troublesome points of law, either procedural or substantive. While hearsay evidence was no doubt admitted, and while Ms. Lassiter no doubt left incomplete her defense that the Department had not adequately assisted her in rekindling her interest in her son, the weight of the evidence that she had few sparks of such an interest was sufficiently great that the presence of counsel for Ms. Lassiter could not have made a determinative difference. True, a lawyer might have done more with the argument that William should live with Ms. Lassiter's mother—but that argument was quite explicitly made by both Lassiters, and the evidence that the elder Ms. Lassiter had said she could not handle another child, that the social worker's investigation had led to a similar conclusion, and that the grandmother had displayed scant interest in the child once he had been removed from her daughter's custody was, though controverted, sufficiently substantial that the absence of counsel's guidance on this point did not render the proceedings fundamentally unfair.

Finally, a court deciding whether due process requires the appointment of counsel need not ignore a parent's plain demonstration that she is not interested in attending a hearing. Here, the trial court had previously found that Ms. Lassiter had expressly declined to appear at the 1975 child custody hearing, Ms. Lassiter had not even bothered to speak to her retained lawyer after being notified of the termination hearing, and the court specifically found that Ms. Lassiter's failure to make an effort to contest the termination proceeding was without cause. In view of all these circumstances, we hold that the trial court did not err in failing to appoint counsel for Ms. Lassiter. . . .

For the reasons stated in this opinion, the judgment is affirmed.

[Chief Justice BURGER'S concurring opinion is omitted.]

Justice BLACKMUN, with whom Justice BRENNAN and Justice MARSHALL join, dissenting:

The Court today denies an indigent mother the representation of counsel in a judicial proceeding initiated by the State of North Carolina to terminate her parental rights with respect to her youngest child. The Court most appropriately recognizes that the mother's interest is a "commanding one," and it finds no countervailing state interest of even remotely comparable significance. Nonetheless, the Court avoids what seems to me the obvious conclusion that due process requires the presence of counsel for a parent threatened with judicial termination of parental rights, and, instead, revives an ad hoc approach thoroughly discredited nearly 20 years ago in *Gideon v. Wainwright*, 372 U.S. 335 (1963). Because I believe that the unique importance of a parent's interest in the care and custody of his or her child cannot constitutionally be extinguished through formal judicial proceedings without the benefit of counsel, I dissent.

This Court is not unfamiliar with the problem of determining under what circumstances legal representation is mandated by the Constitution. In *Betts v. Brady*, 316 U.S. 455 (1942), it reviewed at length both the tradition behind the Sixth Amendment right to counsel in criminal trials and the historical practices of the States in that area. The decision in *Betts*—that the Sixth Amendment right to counsel did not apply to the States and that the due process guarantee of the Fourteenth Amendment permitted a flexible, case-by-case determination of the defendant's need for counsel in state criminal trials—was overruled in *Gideon v. Wainwright*, 372 U.S., at 345. . . .

Outside the criminal context, however, the Court has relied on the flexible nature of the due process guarantee whenever it has decided that counsel is not constitutionally required. The special purposes of probation revocation determinations, and the informal nature of those administrative proceedings, including the absence of counsel for the State, led the Court to conclude that due process does not require counsel for probationers. *Gagnon v. Scarpelli*, 411 U.S. 778, 785-789 (1973). In the case of school disciplinary proceedings, which are brief, informal, and intended in part to be educative, the Court also found no requirement for legal counsel. *Goss v. Lopez*, 419 U.S. 565, 583 (1975). Most recently, the Court declined to intrude the presence of counsel for a minor facing voluntary civil commitment by his parent, because of the parent's substantial role in that decision and because of the decision's essentially medical and informal nature. *Parham v. J.R.*, 442 U.S. 584, 604-609 (1979).

In each of these instances, the Court has recognized that what process is due varies in relation to the interests at stake and the nature of the governmental proceedings. Where the individual's liberty interest is of diminished or less than fundamental stature, or where the prescribed procedure involves informal decisionmaking without the trappings of an adversarial trial-type proceeding, counsel has not been a requisite of due process. Implicit in this analysis is the fact that the contrary conclusion sometimes may be warranted. Where an individual's liberty interest assumes sufficiently weighty constitutional significance, and the State by a formal and adversarial proceeding seeks to curtail that interest, the right to counsel may be necessary to ensure fundamental fairness. To say this is simply to acknowledge that due process allows for the adoption of different rules to address different situations or contexts.

It is not disputed that state intervention to terminate the relationship between petitioner and her child must be accomplished by procedures meeting the requisites of the Due Process Clause. Nor is there any doubt here about the kind of procedure North Carolina has prescribed. North Carolina law requires notice and a trial-type hearing before the State on its own initiative may sever the bonds of parenthood. The decisionmaker is a judge, the rules of evidence are in force, and the State is represented by counsel. The question, then, is whether proceedings in this mold, that relate to a subject so vital, can comport with fundamental fairness when the defendant parent remains unrepresented by counsel. As the Court today properly acknowledges, our consideration of the process due in this context, as in others, must rely on a balancing of the competing private and public interests, an approach succinctly described in *Mathews v. Eldridge*. As does the majority, I evaluate the "three distinct factors" specified in *Eldridge*. . . .

At stake here is "the interest of a parent in the companionship, care, custody, and management of his or her children." *Stanley v. Illinois*, 405 U.S. 645, 651 (1972). This interest occupies a unique place in our legal culture, given the centrality of family life as the focus for personal meaning and responsibility. "[Far] more precious . . . than property rights," *May v. Anderson*, 345 U.S. 528, 533 (1953), parental rights have been deemed to be among those "essential to the orderly pursuit of happiness by free men," *Meyer v. Nebraska*, 262 U.S. 390, 399 (1923), and to be more significant and priceless than " 'liberties which derive merely from shifting economic arrangements.' " *Stanley v. Illinois*, 405 U.S., at 651, quoting *Kovacs v. Cooper*, 336 U.S. 77, 95 (1949) (Frankfurter, J., concurring). Accordingly, although the Constitution is verbally silent on the specific subject of families, freedom of personal choice in matters of family life long has been viewed as a fundamental liberty interest worthy of protection under the Fourteenth Amendment. Within the general ambit of family integrity, the Court has accorded a high degree of constitutional respect to a natural parent's interest both in controlling the details of the child's upbringing, and in retaining the custody and companionship of the child.

In this case, the State's aim is not simply to influence the parent-child relationship but to extinguish it. A termination of parental rights is both total and irrevocable. Unlike other custody proceedings, it leaves the parent with no right to visit or communicate with the child, to participate in, or even to know about, any important decision affecting the child's religious, educational, emotional, or physical development. . . .

The magnitude of this deprivation is of critical significance in the due process calculus, for the process to which an individual is entitled is in part determined "by the extent to which he may be 'condemned to suffer grievous loss.' " *Goldberg v. Kelly*, 397 U.S. 254, 263 (1970), quoting *Joint Anti-Fascist Refugee Committee v. McGrath*, 341 U.S. 123, 168 (1951) (Frankfurter, J., concurring). Surely there can be few losses more grievous than the abrogation of parental rights. Yet the Court today asserts that this deprivation somehow is less serious than threatened losses deemed to require appointed counsel, because in this instance the parent's own "personal liberty" is not at stake.

I do not believe that our cases support the "presumption" asserted, that physical confinement is the only loss of liberty grievous enough to trigger a right to appointed counsel under the Due Process Clause. Indeed, incarceration has been found to be neither a necessary nor a sufficient condition for requiring counsel on behalf of an indigent defendant. The prospect of canceled parole or probation, with its consequent deprivation of personal liberty, has not led the Court to require counsel for a prisoner facing a revocation proceeding. On the other hand, the fact that no new incarceration was threatened by a transfer from prison to a mental hospital did not preclude the Court's recognition of adverse changes in the conditions of confinement and of the stigma that presumably is associated with being labeled mentally ill. *Vitek v. Jones*, 445 U.S. 480, 492, 494 (1980). For four Members of the Court, these "other deprivations of liberty," coupled with the possibly diminished mental capacity of the prisoner, compelled the provision of counsel for any indigent prisoner facing a transfer hearing.

Moreover, the Court's recourse to a "pre-eminent generalization," misrepresents the importance of our flexible approach to due process. . . .

Rather than opting for the insensitive presumption that incarceration is the only loss of liberty sufficiently onerous to justify a right to appointed counsel, I would abide by the Court's enduring commitment to examine the relationships among the interests on both sides, and the appropriateness of counsel in the specific type of proceeding. The fundamental significance of the liberty interests at stake in a parental termination proceeding is undeniable, and I would find this first portion of the due process balance weighing heavily in favor of refined procedural protections. The second *Eldridge* factor, namely, the risk of error in the procedure provided by the State, must then be reviewed with some care.

The method chosen by North Carolina to extinguish parental rights resembles in many respects a criminal prosecution. Unlike the probation revocation procedure reviewed in *Gagnon v. Scarpelli*, on which the Court so heavily relies, the termination procedure is distinctly formal and adversarial. The State initiates the proceeding by filing a petition in district court.

In addition, the proceeding has an obvious accusatory and punitive focus. In moving to terminate a parent's rights, the State has concluded that it no longer will try to preserve the family unit, but instead will marshal an array of public resources to establish that the parent-child separation must be made permanent. . . .

[T]he State here has prescribed virtually all the attributes of a formal trial as befits the severity of the loss at stake in the termination decision—every attribute, that is, except counsel for the defendant parent. The provision of counsel for the parent would not alter the character of the proceeding, which is already adversarial, formal, and quintessentially legal. It, however, would diminish the prospect of an erroneous termination, a prospect that is inherently substantial, given the gross disparity in power and resources between the State and the uncounseled indigent parent.

The prospect of error is enhanced in light of the legal standard against which the defendant parent is judged. As demonstrated here, that standard commonly adds another dimension to the complexity of the termination proceeding. Rather than focusing on the facts of isolated acts or omissions, the State's charges typically address the nature and quality of complicated ongoing relationships among parent, child, other relatives, and even unrelated parties. . . .

The legal issues posed by the State's petition are neither simple nor easily defined. The standard is imprecise and open to the subjective values of the judge. A parent seeking to prevail against the State must be prepared to adduce evidence about his or her personal abilities and lack of fault, as well as proof of progress and foresight as a parent that the State would deem adequate and improved over the situation underlying a previous adverse judgment of child neglect. The parent cannot possibly succeed without being able to identify material issues, develop defenses, gather and present sufficient supporting nonhearsay evidence, and conduct cross-examination of adverse witnesses.

The Court, of course, acknowledges, that these tasks "may combine to overwhelm an uncounseled parent." I submit that that is a profound understatement. . . .

The risk of error . . . is several-fold. The parent who actually has achieved the improvement or quality of parenting the State would require may be unable to establish this fact. The parent who has failed in these regards may be unable to demonstrate cause, absence of willfulness, or lack of agency diligence as justification. And errors of fact or law in the State's case may go unchallenged and uncorrected. Given the weight of the interests at stake, this risk of error assumes extraordinary proportions. By intimidation, inarticulateness, or confusion, a parent can lose forever all contact and involvement with his or her offspring.

The final factor to be considered, the interests claimed for the State, do not tip the scale against providing appointed counsel in this context. The State hardly is in a position to assert here that it seeks the informality of a rehabilitative or educative proceeding into which counsel for the parent would inject an unwelcome adversarial edge. As the Assistant Attorney General of North Carolina declared before this Court, once the State moves for termination, it "has made a decision that the child cannot go home and should not go home. It no longer has an obligation to try and restore that family."

The State may, and does, properly assert a legitimate interest in promoting the physical and emotional well-being of its minor children. But this interest is not served by terminating the rights of any concerned, responsible parent. . . .

The State also has an interest in avoiding the cost and administrative inconvenience that might accompany a right to appointed counsel. But, as the Court acknowledges, the State's fiscal interest "is hardly significant enough to overcome private interests as important as those here." . . .

The Court's analysis is markedly similar to mine; it, too, analyzes the three factors listed in *Mathews v. Eldridge*, and it, too, finds the private interest weighty, the procedure devised by the State fraught with risks of error, and the countervailing governmental interest insubstantial. Yet, rather than follow this balancing process to its logical conclusion, the Court abruptly pulls back and announces that a defendant parent must await a case-by-case determination of his or her need for counsel. . . .

The Court's own precedents make this clear. In *Goldberg v. Kelly*, the Court found that the desperate economic conditions experienced by welfare recipients as a class distinguished them from other recipients of governmental benefits. In *Mathews v. Eldridge*, the Court concluded that the needs of Social Security disability recipients were not of comparable urgency, and, moreover, that existing pre-termination procedures, based largely on written medical assessments, were likely to be more objective and evenhanded than typical welfare entitlement decisions. . . .

Moreover, the case-by-case approach advanced by the Court itself entails serious dangers for the interests at stake and the general administration of justice. . . .

The problem of inadequate representation is painfully apparent in the present case. . . .

It is perhaps understandable that the District Court judge experienced difficulty and exasperation in conducting this hearing. But both the difficulty and the exasperation are attributable in large measure, if not entirely, to the lack of counsel. An experienced attorney might have translated petitioner's reaction and emotion into several substantive legal arguments. The State charged petitioner with failing to arrange a "constructive plan" for her child's future or to demonstrate a "positive response" to the Department's intervention. A defense would have been that petitioner had arranged for the child to be cared for properly by his grandmother, and evidence might have been adduced to demonstrate the adequacy of the grandmother's care of the other children. The Department's own "diligence" in promoting the family's integrity was never put in issue during the hearing, yet it is surely significant in light of petitioner's incarceration and lack of access to her child. Finally, the asserted willfulness of petitioner's lack of concern could obviously have been attacked since she was physically unable to regain custody or perhaps even to receive meaningful visits during 21 of the 24 months preceding the action.

Petitioner plainly has not led the life of the exemplary citizen or model parent. It may well be that if she were accorded competent legal representation, the ultimate result in this particular case would be the same. But the issue before the Court is not petitioner's character; it is whether she was given a meaningful opportunity to be heard when the State moved to terminate absolutely her parental rights. In light of the unpursued avenues of defense, and of the experience petitioner underwent at the hearing, I find virtually incredible the Court's conclusion today that her termination proceeding was fundamentally fair. . . .

Finally, I deem it not a little ironic that the Court on this very day grants, on due process grounds, an indigent putative father's claim for state-paid blood grouping tests in the interest of according him a meaningful opportunity to disprove his paternity, *Little v. Streater*, but in the present case rejects, on due process grounds, an indigent mother's claim for state-paid legal assistance when the State seeks to take her own child away from her in a termination proceeding. In *Little v. Streater*, the Court stresses and relies upon the need for "procedural fairness," the "compelling interest in the accuracy of [the] determination," the "not inconsiderable" risk of error, the indigent's "fac[ing] the State as an adversary," and "fundamental fairness. . . ."

If the Court in *Boddie v. Connecticut*, 401 U.S. 371 (1971), was able to perceive as constitutionally necessary the access to judicial resources required to dissolve a marriage at the behest of private parties, surely it should perceive as similarly necessary the requested access to legal resources when the State itself seeks to dissolve the intimate and personal family bonds between parent and child. It will not open the "floodgates" that, I suspect, the Court fears. On the contrary, we cannot constitutionally afford the closure that the result in this sad case imposes upon us all. I respectfully dissent.

[Justice STEVENS's dissenting opinion is omitted.]

REVIEW QUESTIONS

1. What is the standard for determining whether appointing a lawyer is required?
2. What are the costs and benefits of the *Lassiter* Court's decision that the right to publicly funded counsel is a case by case decision?
3. Who are the parties to this case and who is missing? In the termination of parental rights at issue in *Lassiter*, the state assumes the role of moving party, or plaintiff, and the parent is the defendant. The child is not a party to the lawsuit. Even if the parent has no attorney, the state agency will have counsel, and in many circumstances, the child will also have an attorney, a guardian *ad litem* (pending the litigation), appointed by the court to protect his or her interests.

QUESTIONS TO PONDER

1. Does the issue of access to counsel have to be addressed at the federal level? After *Lassiter* was decided, North Carolina amended its statutes to make legal representation available for indigent parents facing termination of parental rights. *See* N.C. Gen. Stat. § 7(b)-1109(b) (1999). Some state courts interpreted their own due process clauses as requiring provision of counsel in parental termination hearings. *See, e.g., In re Ella R.B.*, 30 N.Y.2d 352 (1972); *In re K.L.J.*, 813 P.2d 276 (Alaska 1991). Now many other states have created a statutory right. A 2010 study found that in all but six states, parents have an absolute right to counsel in termination proceedings. However, as with the right to defense counsel in criminal proceedings, there are many problems of funding and training that stand in the way of quality representation. Vivek Sankaran,

A National Survey on a Parent's Right to Counsel in Termination of Parental Rights and Dependency Cases, http://youthrightsjustice.org/Documents/SurveyParentRighttoCounsel.pdf.

2. Would it be better if access to a lawyer were a bright line rule rather than a multi-factor standard? How important is context to the determination of whether access to counsel is required? The Court had an opportunity to revisit its decision in *Lassiter* in 2011, and it decided not to change the standard in a case that concerned jailing for contempt for failure to pay child support. *Turner v. Rogers*, 131 S. Ct. 2507 (2011). In South Carolina, orders for payment of child support could be enforced by a civil contempt order. Michael Turner admitted that he had not paid child support but claimed that he was unable to work and therefore unable to pay. Before issuing a civil contempt order and sentencing a defendant to jail time, the judge was supposed to fill out a form that included a question about ability to pay. In Mr. Turner's case, the judge did not answer this question and sentenced him to a year in jail. The Supreme Court had previously held that under the Sixth Amendment of the federal Constitution, defendants have a right to counsel in criminal proceedings, *Gideon v. Wainwright*, 372 U.S. 335 (1963), and in criminal contempt proceedings, *United States v. Dixon*, 509 U.S. 688, 696 (1993). But in the case of civil contempt, the Court found that there is no right to counsel because "once a civil contemnor complies with the underlying order, he is purged of the contempt and is free." The Court also relied on the informality of this civil contempt proceeding as a rationale for limiting the right to counsel, explaining:

> A requirement that the State provide counsel to the noncustodial parent in these cases could create an asymmetry of representation that would "alter significantly the nature of the proceeding." Doing so could mean a degree of formality or delay that would unduly slow payment to those immediately in need. And, perhaps more important for present purposes, doing so could make the proceedings *less* fair overall, increasing the risk of a decision that would erroneously deprive a family of the support it is entitled to receive. The needs of such families play an important role in our analysis.

Ultimately, the Court suggested using other procedures, including "(1) notice to the defendant that his "ability to pay" is a critical issue in the contempt proceeding; (2) the use of a form (or the equivalent) to elicit relevant financial information; (3) an opportunity at the hearing for the defendant to respond to statements and questions about his financial status (e.g., those triggered by his responses on the form); and (4) an express finding by the court that the defendant has the ability to pay." Do you think these procedures would be enough to protect litigants like Michael Turner?

3. Unbundling Legal Services

The use of alternatives to the provision of counsel, which is very expensive, has become a possible avenue for providing assistance to people who cannot afford legal services. These are sometimes called "unbundled legal services" because they provide some of the services a lawyer might offer piecemeal through instruction pamphlets or other limited forms of legal advice. An important question is whether having a lawyer actually helps litigants more than the provision of legal information or nothing at all. Studies of the question have reached different conclusions depending on a variety of factors, including the informality of the court procedures. *Compare* D. James Greiner & Cassandra Wolos Pattanayak, *Randomized Evaluation in Legal Assistance: What Difference Does Representation (Offer and Actual Use) Make?*, 121 Yale L.J. 2118 (2012) (finding that offers of representation delayed proceedings and did not cause a robust increase in the probability of success in unemployment proceedings), *with* D. James Greiner et al., *The Limits of Unbundled Legal Assistance: A Randomized Study in a Massachusetts District Court and Prospects for the Future*, 126 Harv. L. Rev. 901, 922 (2013) (finding that offers of representation improved outcomes in eviction proceedings in housing court). For more on the possibilities, see Rebecca L. Sandefur & Thomas M. Clarke, *Designing the Competition: A Future of Roles Beyond Lawyers? The Case of the USA*, 67 Hastings L.J. 1467 (2016).

4. Donated Legal Services

People who cannot afford to pay lawyers may find access to legal representation through the donated legal services of individual lawyers or law firms. A long tradition of such *pro bono publico*[16] service among lawyers today takes many forms, and some estimate that pro bono services provide one-quarter to almost one-third of the civil legal needs of the poor. *See, e.g.,* Rebecca L. Sandefur, *Lawyers' Pro Bono Service and American-Style Civil Legal Assistance*, 41 Law & Soc'y Rev. 79 (2007). The American Bar Association has consistently rejected proposals for a mandatory pro bono service duty. Should all law schools institute mandatory pro bono programs? Should all states? In 2012, the New York courts adopted a rule requiring applicants for admission to the bar to have completed 50 hours of pro bono services. Do you support this decision?

5. The Comparative Perspective

Most other Western democracies uphold a general right to counsel in civil litigation and do not leave the matter to legislation, which can be repealed. Two years before the Supreme Court's decision, the European Court of Human

---

16. *Pro bono publico* means for the public good or general welfare; pro bono legal work is usually understood as offering services to indigents without charge. *Pro bono publico, Black's Law Dictionary* 1203 (6th ed. 1990).

Rights held that the right to a fair hearing in civil cases included the right to counsel. *Airey v. Ireland*, judgment of 9 October 1979, Series A no. 32. *See also Steel and Morris v. The United Kingdom*, no. 68416/01, ECHR 2005-II. While these cases did not declare a right to counsel in *all* civil litigation, both provided for a right to counsel in any circumstances in which individuals cannot adequately represent themselves, including divorce proceedings and defamation suits. The rulings apply to the 45 European nations that are signatories to the European Convention on Human Rights. A right to counsel in civil litigation has also been included in almost all European constitutions, as well as those of Canada and South Africa. *See* Andrew Scherer, *Securing a Civil Right to Counsel: The Importance of Collaborating*, 30 N.Y.U. Rev. L. & Soc. Change 675, 680 (2006).

PRACTICE EXERCISE NO. 1: APPLYING THE DUE PROCESS CLAUSES

A new client, Graciela Rodriguez, who is a 76-year-old woman and a resident of San Antonio, Texas, has come to your office with the following story.[*] In 2010, Ms. Rodriguez received a citation for driving without insurance when a truck ran into her car while she was driving back from leaving flowers at a cemetery. She received a citation. Ms. Rodriguez worked for many years as a nurse's assistant and school nurse. Now she works as a home health aide. Because her license has been suspended, she has to travel by bus. It takes her approximately five hours to commute to her job every day, taking three different buses. Bus travel is especially difficult for Ms. Rodriguez because she takes medications that make it dangerous for her to be exposed to heat. In one incident, she was taken to the hospital because she was dangerously overheated after being on a bus for a long time.

Over several years, Ms. Rodriguez worked to pay off the fee for her citation ($400) and the license reinstatement fee ($100). In early 2017, when she thought she had paid these charges, Ms. Rodriguez went to the Texas Department of Public Safety to renew her license. It was only then that she learned for the first time that her license was suspended for failure to pay something called "Driver Responsibility Program" charges and that, as a result, she could not renew her license. Ms. Rodriguez had never received any pre-suspension notice of this program, of any surcharges, or of available alternatives for indigent persons. She now owes approximately $600 in Driver's Responsibility Program charges and has been put on an installment plan requiring her to pay $13.33 per month. She cannot afford to make these payments, but even if she could it would take her nearly four years to pay off her surcharges. In the meantime, she is unable to visit her family very often and arrives at work only with great difficulty.

---

[*]This problem is based on a real case, *Rodriguez et al. v. Mach et al.*, Case 5:18-cv-01265 (filed 12/5/18). The Texas Legislature repealed the Driver Responsibility Program at least in part in response to this lawsuit. Tex. Transp. Code Ann. § 708 et seq., *repealed by* 2019 Tex. Sess. Law Serv. Ch. 1094 (H.B. 2048) (Vernon's).

Your research into the applicable laws yields the following information. The Driver Responsibility Program is administered under a state statute that provides that any driver convicted of certain offenses (all of which carry their own court-imposed penalties) will automatically have an additional surcharge imposed on them every year following even a single offense. Driving without proof of insurance, for example, results in a surcharge of $250 per year for three years. The state receives a significant revenue stream from the program. Roughly half of that revenue is deposited into the state's general fund, and the other half into a dedicated fund for trauma facilities and higher education in the medical field.

Texas law requires that the Department of Public Safety waive "all surcharges" for a person who is indigent. But letters sent out to indebted drivers do not provide this information, and many (like Ms. Rodriguez) do not receive such notifications. To prove indigence, the statute requires that the individual provide the following documentation: a copy of their tax return, a copy of their statement of wages, or documentation from a federal or state agency that they receive assistance from a specific list of federal government programs. Nonpayment of surcharges under the DRP results in automatic license suspension. The state conducts no inquiry into an individual's ability to pay or whether the nonpayment was willful before it suspends their license and offers no opportunity for a hearing prior to suspension. It is not clear how a person is supposed to avoid suspension of their license for failure to pay a surcharge due to indigence. The Supreme Court has recognized a persons' driver's license as a property interest. *See Bell v. Burson*, 402 U.S. 535, 539 (1971).

Be prepared to discuss the following questions in class:

- Based on the cases you have read, does Ms. Rodriguez have a due process claim?
- What arguments would you make on her behalf? What arguments would the state make against you, and how would you respond?
- If the state wanted to retain the Driver Responsibility Program, how should it change its processes, if at all?

CHAPTER 2

Remedies and Stakes

A. INTRODUCTION

Voltaire wrote: "I was never ruined but twice: once when I lost a lawsuit, and once when I won one." *An Editor's Treasury: A Continuing Anthology of Prose, Verse, and Literary Curiosities* 1032 (Herbert Meyer ed. 1968). The costs — economic and emotional — of litigation should never be underestimated; what, then, are the benefits? The ability of courts to order remedies stands as the most concrete benefit, and these remedies can include money damages, orders to direct a defendant to cease the offending behavior or to undertake new behavior, and declarations of rights and duties. Although most remedies must await the plaintiffs' success in demonstrating entitlement to relief, courts are also authorized under special circumstances to order provisional, temporary relief even before the litigation is completed.

This chapter explores the range of remedial options as well as the practices limiting their availability. In other words, this chapter covers the results that litigation can be used to achieve for clients. The end of litigation should always be on the lawyer's mind in considering whether to bring a case and what to ask for in the complaint (addressed in the next chapter). What a party seeks to achieve in litigation also determines when parties will settle and for how much. The chapter also introduces attorneys' fees and the ways individuals and corporations can finance litigation. For example, under limited circumstances, one party may be ordered to pay another party's attorneys' fees. These issues are included because the ways litigation is financed — through fee shifting or other methods — affects the plaintiffs' decision to bring a case at all and to see their case through. As a result, attorneys' fees have an impact on deterrence and settlement just as money damages and other remedies do. Broadly speaking, judicial power over remedies can be understood as part of the larger topic of what is at stake in litigation.

The chapter closes with a section on judicial power to enforce court-ordered remedies through use of the contempt power, revisiting some themes introduced in Chapter 1. The final section also raises the question of the availability of methods other than litigation to achieve goals. For example, peaceful protest is an alternative to the courts often pursued by social movements.

As you learn about the remedies early in the litigation, such as attachments, temporary restraining orders and preliminary injunctions, and remedies that come at the end of litigation, such as damages, injunctions, and declaratory judgments, consider the context in which plaintiffs seek these remedies. When are they appropriate and how does the doctrine police their use? Consider also the historical context that gave rise to various attorneys' fee regimes and litigation financing — how do changing economic and policy climates influence the doctrine?

B. PROVISIONAL RELIEF

Should a plaintiff ever be able to use the law to obtain relief before proving the elements of the claim? Exceptional, but still frequently used, are devices for *securing the judgment* and for *maintaining the status quo*. Both stem from the equity powers of courts. The remedies in equity primarily were injunctive relief, while at law the remedies ordinarily were limited to money damages.

The Federal Rules of Civil Procedure joined law and equity in the federal court system in 1938. Originally, on this continent these two judicial systems were largely separate and reflected the English judicial system, which had separate courts of law and equity until the passage of the Judicature Acts of the 1870s. The law and equity courts in England evolved as complementary systems, with the King's equity courts affording relief where the common law courts, the only courts with juries, did not. Equitable relief was a last resort, available when the formalities and limitations of the common law system precluded a just result. Nevertheless, equitable relief is now common in the merged system and is explicitly provided for by some statutes.

Before the merger, law and equity involved different sets of procedures. For example, no jury existed at equity; the jury served only the law courts. This fact still limits when a jury is available in federal court, as we will see in the materials on the jury right in Chapter 5. As interpreted by the Supreme Court, the Seventh Amendment directs courts to use tests informed by the historical line between equity and common law jurisdictions in determining which cases will have a jury, if the parties so request. Pleadings at law faced strict categories; joinder was a rarity. Fact-finding mechanisms now known as discovery originated with equity. Yet common law courts in the United States permitted some discovery by the mid-nineteenth century. Similarly, equity courts would find procedural ways to refer particular factual issues to common law courts to be decided by a jury. Over time, a kind of interdependency grew between the two systems, which made merger all the more welcome. Currently, the Federal Rules cover the entire system of merged law and equity and tend to reflect the flexibility of equity rather than the rigidity of law. Vestiges of the old division remain, however, in the tensions between justice and efficiency, and in many standards and rules.

1. Securing the Judgment: Attachments, Garnishments, and Sequestration

Plaintiffs often bring a civil lawsuit in order to obtain or recover real or personal property or to receive money. Their lawyers would very much like to "tie up" defendants' property, pending the outcome of litigation. Sometimes, this is called "securing the judgment." For instance, a plaintiff's lawyer would like to put an attachment or a lien on real estate belonging to the defendant so that they cannot sell it. The real estate could be the subject of the lawsuit or could be unrelated, but would represent the defendant's assets and thus their ability to pay the judgment. Alternatively, a plaintiff's attorney could seek a preliminary injunction to enjoin the defendant from transferring the real estate. In many jurisdictions, lawyers, after obtaining a lien, a restraining order, or a preliminary injunction, will then file a notice of *lis pendens* in the registry of deeds, warning anyone who may want to acquire an interest in the realty of the pending litigation that the attachment could prevent them from obtaining unburdened title to the property.

More frequently, plaintiffs' lawyers prefer to trigger a process that would direct a public official, such as a sheriff, to take defendants' personal property to a neutral location or order the defendants' banks or employers to cut off the defendants' access to funds or wages. This process, often called sequestration, attaches property or funds pending the outcome of litigation; often this procedure removes property from the person in possession, pending some further action or proceedings affecting the property. This helps plaintiffs in two major ways. First, plaintiffs are assured that the defendants' resources will be available to collect if the plaintiffs win their lawsuits. If the property that has been secured is the very item at issue in the lawsuit (for instance, an installment vendor as plaintiff has sought to *replevy* the merchandise sold to the defendant), then the winning plaintiff will have less trouble turning a paper victory in court into actual recovery of the asset in question. Second, tying up a defendant's asset—such as a bank account or wages—puts intense pressure on the defendant to settle, regardless of the merits of the case. Plaintiffs generally like to secure such attachments prior to notifying defendants. Otherwise, defendants could harm or transfer the asset or dissipate the money before the end of the lawsuit.

The plaintiff (or other party seeking the injunction) may post a bond to cover any losses the enjoined party would face from damages, court costs, and attorneys' fees should the injunction turn out to have been erroneously granted.

With the moving party's bond in place, the court will issue an attachment order, which can involve literally seizing the property (through sequestration) or placing it under a *receiver*. A receiver is an official designated by the court to "hold and manage property . . . [m]ost frequently [] corporate property" usually because the property may be "endangered by fraud, by mismanagement or by dissension." Alternatively, the court may require the enjoined party to post a monetary bond to ensure compliance and pay for any judgment that will be rendered against him or her. *See Developments in the Law — Injunctions*, 78 Harv. L. Rev. 1086, 1091-1093 (1964).

a. Development of the Law of Prejudgment Remedies

Prior to the late 1960s, methods of securing the judgment before trial faced minimal or no restrictions. Indeed, in many jurisdictions a lawyer could commence a lawsuit by attaching the defendant's property prior to notifying the defendant of either the attachment or the suit. A plaintiff's lawyer would at that time *trustee* (or attach) any of the defendants' bank accounts that could be located; under this procedure, the banks would be directed to pay no funds to the defendants, even before the defendants received notice. Lawyers had commenced suits in this fashion for centuries (or at least this was the common belief), and they took the legality of these practices for granted.

In the 1960s, however, reflecting the due process revolution in the courts, some lawyers challenged these deprivations of property as violations of the Fourteenth Amendment's guarantee of due process and similar state constitutional provisions. Landmark cases, many brought by legal services lawyers defending poor clients when creditors sought to seize their limited assets or installment sales purchases, successfully established that (1) due process guarantees applied to prejudgment contexts and (2) insufficient procedural protections had been in place.

In June 1969, the Supreme Court struck down Wisconsin's prejudgment wage garnishment statute in *Sniadach v. Family Finance Corp.*, 395 U.S. 337 (1969). The Court ruled that an employee was entitled under the Constitution to notice and a hearing before the attachment of wages. In *Goldberg v. Kelly*, 397 U.S. 254 (1970), the Court held that due process required notice and a hearing prior to the termination of public welfare benefits. Other cases extended the requirement of notice and a right to be heard prior to even a temporary deprivation of property or liberty. *See Bell v. Burson*, 402 U.S. 535 (1971) (suspension of a driver's license); *Stanley v. Illinois*, 405 U.S. 645 (1971) (removal of custody of children from unwed father after death of mother). The next reading, *Fuentes v. Shevin*, 407 U.S. 67 (1972), followed these cases; it was argued on November 8, 1971, when the Court lacked two members. By the time the opinion was issued, Justices Powell and Rehnquist were seated on the Court, although they played no role in the decision.

Fuentes v. Shevin
407 U.S. 67 (1972)

Justice STEWART delivered the opinion of the Court:

We here review the decisions of two three-judge federal District Courts that upheld the constitutionality of Florida and Pennsylvania laws authorizing the summary seizure of goods or chattels in a person's possession under a writ of replevin. Both statutes provide for the issuance of writs ordering state agents to seize a person's possessions, simply upon the ex parte application of any other person who claims a right to them and posts a security bond. Neither statute provides for notice to be given to the possessor of the property, and neither statute gives the possessor an opportunity to challenge the seizure at any kind of prior hearing. The question is whether these statutory procedures violate the Fourteenth Amendment's guarantee that no State shall deprive any person of property without due process of law.

I

The appellant in No. 5039, Margarita Fuentes, is a resident of Florida. She purchased a gas stove and service policy from the Firestone Tire and Rubber Co. (Firestone) under a conditional sales contract calling for monthly payments over a period of time. A few months later, she purchased a stereophonic phonograph from the same company under the same sort of contract. The total cost of the stove and stereo was about $500, plus an additional financing charge of over $100. Under the contracts, Firestone retained title to the merchandise, but Mrs. Fuentes was entitled to possession unless and until she should default on her installment payments. For more than a year, Mrs. Fuentes made her installment payments. But then, with only about $200 remaining to be paid, a dispute developed between her and Firestone over the servicing of the stove. Firestone instituted an action in a small-claims court for repossession of both the stove and the stereo, claiming that Mrs. Fuentes had refused to make her remaining payments. Simultaneously with the filing of that action and before Mrs. Fuentes had even received a summons to answer its complaint, Firestone obtained a writ of replevin ordering a sheriff to seize the disputed goods at once.

In conformance with Florida procedure, Firestone had only to fill in the blanks on the appropriate form documents and submit them to the clerk of the small-claims court. The clerk signed and stamped the documents and issued a writ of replevin. Later the same day, a local deputy sheriff and an agent of Firestone went to Mrs. Fuentes' home and seized the stove and stereo.

Shortly thereafter, Mrs. Fuentes instituted the present action in a federal district court, challenging the constitutionality of the Florida prejudgment replevin procedures under the Due Process Clause of the Fourteenth Amendment. She sought declaratory and injunctive relief against continued enforcement of the procedural provisions of the state statutes that authorize prejudgment replevin.

II

Under the Florida statute challenged here, "[a]ny person whose goods or chattels are wrongfully detained by any other person . . . may have a writ of replevin to recover them. . . ." Fla. Stat. Ann. §78.01 (Supp. 1972-1973). There is no requirement that the applicant make a convincing showing before the seizure that the goods are, in fact, "wrongfully detained." Rather, Florida law automatically relies on the bare assertion of the party seeking the writ that he is entitled to one and allows a court clerk to issue the writ summarily. It requires only that the applicant file a complaint, initiating a court action for repossession and reciting in conclusory fashion that he is "lawfully entitled to the possession" of the property, and that he file a security bond in at least double the value of the property to be replevied conditioned that plaintiff will prosecute his action to effect and without delay and that if defendant recovers judgment against him in the action, he will return the property, if return thereof is adjudged, and will pay defendant all sums of money recovered against plaintiff by defendant in the action. Fla. Stat. Ann. §78.07 (Supp. 1972-1973). On the sole basis of the complaint and bond, a writ is issued "command[ing] the officer to whom it may be directed to replevy the goods and chattels in possession of defendant . . . and to summon the defendant to answer the complaint." Fla. Stat. Ann. §78.08 (Supp. 1972-1973). If the goods are "in any dwelling house or other building or enclosure," the officer is required to demand their delivery; but if they are not delivered, "he shall cause such house, building or enclosure to be broken open and shall make replevin according to the writ. . . ." Fla. Stat. Ann. §78.10 (Supp. 1972-1973).

Thus, at the same moment that the defendant receives the complaint seeking repossession of property through court action, the property is seized from him. He is provided no prior notice and allowed no opportunity whatever to challenge the issuance of the writ. After the property has been seized, he will eventually have an opportunity for a hearing, as the defendant in the trial of the court action for repossession, which the plaintiff is required to pursue. And he is also not wholly without recourse in the meantime. For under the Florida statute, the officer who seizes the property must keep it for three days, and during that period the defendant may reclaim possession of the property by posting his own security bond in double its value. But if he does not post such a bond, the property is transferred to the party who sought the writ, pending a final judgment in the underlying action for repossession.

The Pennsylvania law differs, though not in its essential nature, from that of Florida. As in Florida, a private party may obtain a prejudgment writ of replevin through a summary process of ex parte application to a prothonotary. As in Florida, the party seeking the writ may simply post with his application a bond in double the value of the property to be seized. Pa. Rule Civ. Proc. 1073(a). There is no opportunity for a prior hearing and no prior notice to the other party. On this basis, a sheriff is required to execute the writ by seizing the specified property. Unlike the Florida statute, however, the Pennsylvania law does not require that there ever be opportunity for a hearing on the merits of the conflicting claims to possession of the replevied property. The party seeking the writ is not obliged to initiate a court action for repossession. Indeed, he need not even formally allege that he is lawfully entitled to the property. The most that is required is that he file an "affidavit of the value of the property to be replevied." Pa. Rule Civ. Proc. 1073(a). If the party who loses property through replevin seizure is to get even a post-seizure hearing, he must initiate a lawsuit himself. He may also, as under Florida law, post his own counterbond within three days after the seizure to regain possession. Pa. Rule Civ. Proc. 1076. . . .

IV

For more than a century the central meaning of procedural due process has been clear: "Parties whose rights are to be affected are entitled to be heard; and in order that they may enjoy that right they must first be notified." . . . It is equally fundamental that the right to notice and an opportunity to be heard "must be granted at a meaningful time and in a meaningful manner." *Armstrong v. Manzo*, 380 U.S. 545, 552.

The primary question in the present cases is whether these state statutes are constitutionally defective in failing to provide for hearings "at a meaningful time." The Florida replevin process guarantees an opportunity for a hearing after the seizure of goods, and the Pennsylvania process allows a post-seizure hearing if the aggrieved party shoulders the burden of initiating one. But neither the Florida nor the Pennsylvania statute provides for notice or an opportunity to be heard before the seizure. The issue is whether procedural due process in the context of these cases requires an opportunity for a hearing before the State authorizes its agents to seize property in the possession of a person upon the application of another.

The constitutional right to be heard is a basic aspect of the duty of government to follow a fair process of decision making when it acts to deprive a person of his possessions. The purpose of this requirement is not only to ensure abstract fair play to the individual. Its purpose, more particularly, is to protect his use and possession of property from arbitrary encroachment — to minimize substantively unfair or mistaken deprivations of property, a danger that is especially great when the State seizes goods simply upon the application of and for the benefit of a private party. So viewed, the prohibition against the deprivation of property without due process of law reflects the high value, embedded in our constitutional and political history, that we place on a person's right to enjoy what is his, free of governmental interference.

. . . It has long been recognized that "fairness can rarely be obtained by secret, one-sided determination of facts decisive of rights. . . . [And] no better instrument has been devised for arriving at truth than to give a person in jeopardy of serious loss notice of the case against him and opportunity to meet it." *Joint Anti-Fascist Refugee Committee v. McGrath*, 341 U.S. 123, 170-172.

If the right to notice and a hearing is to serve its full purpose, then, it is clear that it must be granted at a time when the deprivation can still be prevented. . . .

The Florida and Pennsylvania prejudgment replevin statutes fly in the face of this principle. To be sure, the requirements that a party seeking a writ must first post a bond, allege conclusorily that he is entitled to specific goods, and open himself to possible liability in damages if he is wrong, serve to deter wholly unfounded applications for a writ. But those requirements are hardly a substitute for a prior hearing, for they test no more than the strength of the applicant's own belief in his rights. . . .

The minimal deterrent effect of a bond requirement is, in a practical sense, no substitute for an informed evaluation by a neutral official. More specifically, as a matter of constitutional principle, it is no replacement for the right to a prior hearing that is the only truly effective safeguard against arbitrary deprivation of property. . . .

V

The right to a prior hearing, of course, attaches only to the deprivation of an interest encompassed within the Fourteenth Amendment's protection. In the present cases, the Florida and Pennsylvania statutes were applied to replevy chattels in the appellants' possession. The replevin was not cast as a final judgment; most, if not all, of the appellants lacked full title to the chattels; and their claim even to continued possession was a matter in dispute. Moreover, the chattels at stake were nothing more than an assortment of household goods. Nonetheless, it is clear that the appellants were deprived of possessory interests in those chattels that were within the protection of the Fourteenth Amendment.

A

A deprivation of a person's possessions under a prejudgment writ of replevin, at least in theory, may be only temporary. The Florida and Pennsylvania statutes do not require a person to wait until a post-seizure hearing and final judgment to recover what has been replevied. Within three days after the seizure, the statutes allowing him to recover the goods if he, in return, surrenders other property—a payment necessary to secure a bond in double the value of the goods seized from him. But it is now well settled that a temporary, nonfinal deprivation of property is nonetheless a "deprivation" in the terms of the Fourteenth Amendment. *Sniadach v. Family Finance Corp.*, 395 U.S. 337; *Bell v. Burson*, 402 U.S. 535. Both *Sniadach* and *Bell* involved takings of property pending a final judgment in an underlying dispute. In both cases, the challenged statutes included recovery provisions, allowing the defendants to post security to quickly regain the property taken from them. Yet the Court firmly held that these were deprivations of property that had to be preceded by a fair hearing.

B

The appellants who signed conditional sales contracts lacked full legal title to the replevied goods. The Fourteenth Amendment's protection of "property," however, has never been interpreted to safeguard only the rights of undisputed ownership. Rather, it has been read broadly to extend protection to "any significant property interest," including statutory entitlements.

. . . Clearly, the [appellant's] possessory interest in the goods, dearly bought and protected by contract, was sufficient to invoke the protection of the Due Process Clause. . . .

It is enough to invoke the procedural safeguards of the Fourteenth Amendment that a significant property interest is at stake, whatever the ultimate outcome of a hearing on the contractual right to continued possession and use of the goods.

C

Nevertheless, the District Courts rejected the appellants' constitutional claim on the ground that the goods seized from them — a stove, a stereo, a table, a bed, and so forth — were not deserving of due process protection, since they were not absolute necessities of life. The courts based this holding on a very narrow reading of *Sniadach v. Family Finance Corp., supra,* and *Goldberg v. Kelly, supra,* in which this Court held that the Constitution requires a hearing before prejudgment wage garnishment and before the termination of certain welfare benefits. They reasoned that *Sniadach* and *Goldberg,* as a matter of constitutional principle, established no more than that a prior hearing is required with respect to the deprivation of such basically "necessary" items as wages and welfare benefits.

This reading of *Sniadach* and *Goldberg* reflects the premise that those cases marked a radical departure from established principles of procedural due process. They did not. Both decisions were in the mainstream of past cases, having little or nothing to do with the absolute "necessities" of life but establishing that due process requires an opportunity for a hearing before a deprivation of property takes effect. . . .

The household goods, for which the appellants contracted and paid substantial sums, are deserving of similar protection. While a driver's license, for example, "may become (indirectly) essential in the pursuit of a livelihood," *ibid.,* a stove or a bed may be equally essential to provide a minimally decent environment for human beings in their day-to-day lives. It is, after all, such consumer goods that people work and earn a livelihood in order to acquire.

No doubt, there may be many gradations in the "importance" or "necessity" of various consumer goods. Stoves could be compared to television sets, or beds could be compared to tables. But if the root principle of procedural due process is to be applied with objectivity, it cannot rest on such distinctions. The Fourteenth Amendment speaks of "property" generally. . . .

VI

There are "extraordinary situations" that justify postponing notice and opportunity for a hearing. *Boddie v. Connecticut,* 401 U.S. at 379. These situations, however, must be truly unusual. Only in a few limited situations has this Court allowed outright seizure without opportunity for a prior hearing. First, in each case, the seizure has been directly necessary to secure an important governmental or general public interest. Second, there has been a special need for very prompt action. Third, the State has kept strict control over its monopoly of legitimate force; the person initiating the seizure has been a government official responsible for determining, under the standards of a narrowly drawn statute, that it was necessary and justified in the particular instance. Thus, the Court has allowed summary seizure of property to collect the internal revenue of the United States, to meet the needs of a national war effort, to protect against the economic disaster of a bank failure, and to protect the public from misbranded drugs and contaminated food.

The Florida and Pennsylvania prejudgment replevin statutes serve no such important governmental or general public interest. . . .

Nor do the broadly drawn Florida and Pennsylvania statutes limit the summary seizure of goods to special situations demanding prompt action. . . .

The statutes, moreover, abdicate effective state control over state power. Private parties, serving their own private advantage, may unilaterally invoke state power to replevy goods from another. No state official participates in the decision to seek a writ; no state official reviews the basis for the claim to repossession; and no state official evaluates the need for immediate seizure. There is not even a requirement that the plaintiff provide any information to the court on these matters. The State acts largely in the dark. . . .

VIII

We hold that the Florida and Pennsylvania prejudgment replevin provisions work a deprivation of property without due process of law insofar as they deny the right to a prior opportunity to be heard before chattels are taken from their possessor. . . .

For the foregoing reasons, the judgments of the District Courts are vacated and these cases are remanded for further proceedings consistent with this opinion. It is so ordered.

[Justice WHITE's dissenting opinion is omitted.]

REVIEW QUESTIONS

1. What is the primary question in *Fuentes v. Shevin*?
2. The Fourteenth Amendment is implicated only when a state has acted to deprive someone of life, liberty, or property. What did Ms. Fuentes allege as her deprivation in this case? Can you describe what was the state action here sufficient to trigger Fourteenth Amendment protections?
3. If Firestone had sued in federal court, what rule would govern the ability of a plaintiff to seize property for purposes of securing the action? Look at Fed. R. Civ. P. 64. You will notice that the rule does not provide procedures for seizing property—these are governed by state laws such as those in Pennsylvania and Florida that were the subject of this suit.

b. Litigating Prejudgment Remedies After *Fuentes*

It is important to remember that due process protections are only triggered by state action. In *Flagg Brothers, Inc. v. Brooks*, 436 U.S. 149 (1978), for example, the Supreme Court made clear that due process is not part of self-help remedies; the Supreme Court clarified this because no overt official involvement occurs where a creditor threatens to sell repossessed goods to satisfy a debt.

When courts take action, however, this will usually trigger due process. Consider *Connecticut v. Doehr*, 501 U.S. 1 (1991), where a unanimous Supreme Court held that a state statute authorizing prejudgment attachment of real estate without prior notice or hearing afforded to the property owner, without a showing of extraordinary circumstances, and without a requirement that the party seeking the attachment post a monetary bond, violated the Due Process Clause of the Fourteenth Amendment. In that case, petitioner John F. DiGiovanni sought to attach $75,000 in value of the home of Brian K. Doehr as a precaution to protect a potential damage award if DiGiovanni prevailed in his then-pending civil suit claiming Doehr committed assault and battery. DiGiovanni obtained such an attachment solely on the basis of an affidavit with five one-sentence paragraphs asserting that he had been assaulted by Doehr, incurred medical expenses, and therefore offered facts sufficient to show probable cause that he would prevail in the civil suit. Because the attachment would burden Doehr's property interest by impairing his ability to sell it or obtain a loan or mortgage, because DiGiovanni had no prior claim to the property, and because the risk of an erroneous deprivation was substantial given the predicate of a secret and one-sided affidavit, the Due Process Clause compelled an opportunity for an adversarial pre-attachment hearing. Four of the Justices noted further that in their view, due process would require the moving party to post a bond or other security in addition to showing exigent circumstances. In the criminal context, the Supreme Court ruled that, absent exigent circumstances, the Fifth Amendment's Due Process Clause requires the government to afford notice and a meaningful opportunity to be heard before seizing, under a federal forfeiture statute, property used or intended to be used in a drug-related offense. *United States v. James Daniel Good Real Property*, 510 U.S. 493 (1993). As a post-conviction measure and an extra deterrent to crime, the federal government and many states have authorized prosecutors to seize goods used in the commission of the crime or purchased with the proceeds of the crime. The Court made clear, however, that neither the law enforcement purpose nor compliance with Fourth Amendment rules about criminal searches and seizures exempts the government from the requirements of due process. The Court distinguished its prior decision permitting seizure of movable property, such as a yacht, without prior notice or hearing, *Calero-Toldeo v. Pearson Yacht Leasing Co.*, 416 U.S. 663 (1974), because real property cannot be moved or concealed and owners are less able to frustrate governmental interests in forfeitable real property. In 2019, the Court held that states using civil forfeiture to seize property allegedly used in the commission of a crime was subject to both due process protections and the Eighth Amendment prohibition on excessive fines. *Timbs v. Indiana*, 139 S. Ct. 682 (2019).

2. Preserving the Status Quo

Sometimes a plaintiff wants to ensure that the defendant will stop engaging in a harmful activity or refrain from undertaking one. Yet during the pendency of the litigation, the defendant may act in harmful ways that would make a final remedy inadequate or unable to protect the plaintiff. In that situation, the Federal Rules make available forms of provisional relief known as temporary restraining orders (TROs) and preliminary injunctions. Typically such orders are issued after a short hearing. In the case of TROs, the Federal Rules limit the order to ten days (with a possible ten-day extension). *See* Fed. R. Civ. P. 65(b). In an emergency, a TRO may even be issued without prior notice or participation of the party to be bound.

The standard for a preliminary injunction requires courts to choose between incommensurable values and make judgments in the face of gross uncertainty. Courts in this context are charged with defining the "public interest," although in political life there is no widespread agreement about what that is. In the face of uncertainty about the magnitude and probability of harm, courts are nevertheless called upon to issue decisions. Consider these challenges, as well as what it means to "preserve the status quo" pending the outcome of the litigation, as you read the following case.

Winter v. Natural Resources Defense Council, Inc.
555 U.S. 7 (2008)

Chief Justice ROBERTS delivered the opinion of the Court.

"To be prepared for war is one of the most effectual means of preserving peace." 1 Messages and Papers of the Presidents 57 (J. Richardson comp. 1897). So said George Washington in his first Annual Address to Congress, 218 years ago. One of the most important ways the Navy prepares for war is through integrated training exercises at sea. These exercises include training in the use of modern sonar to detect and track enemy submarines, something the Navy has done for the past 40 years. The plaintiffs complained that the Navy's sonar training program harmed marine mammals, and that the Navy should have prepared an environmental impact statement before commencing its latest round of training exercises. The Court of Appeals upheld a preliminary injunction imposing restrictions on the Navy's sonar training, even though that court acknowledged that "the record contains no evidence that marine mammals have been harmed" by the Navy's exercises. 518 F.3d 658, 696 (C.A.9 2008).

The Court of Appeals was wrong, and its decision is reversed.

I

The Navy deploys its forces in "strike groups," which are groups of surface ships, submarines, and aircraft centered around either an aircraft carrier or an amphibious assault ship. Seamless coordination among strike-group assets is critical. Before deploying a strike group, the Navy requires extensive integrated training in analysis and prioritization of threats, execution of military missions, and maintenance of force protection.

Antisubmarine warfare is currently the Pacific Fleet's top war-fighting priority. Modern diesel-electric submarines pose a significant threat to Navy vessels because they can operate almost silently, making them extremely difficult to detect and track. Potential adversaries of the United States possess at least 300 of these submarines.

The most effective technology for identifying submerged diesel-electric submarines within their torpedo range is active sonar, which involves emitting pulses of sound underwater and then receiving the acoustic waves that echo off the target. Active sonar is a particularly useful tool because it provides both the bearing and the distance of target submarines; it is also sensitive enough to allow the Navy to track enemy submarines that are quieter than the surrounding marine environment. This case concerns the Navy's use of "mid-frequency active" (MFA) sonar, which transmits sound waves at frequencies between 1 kHz and 10 kHz.

Not surprisingly, MFA sonar is a complex technology, and sonar operators must undergo extensive training to become proficient in its use. . . . The Navy conducts regular training exercises under realistic conditions to ensure that sonar operators are thoroughly skilled in its use in a variety of situations.

The waters off the coast of southern California (SOCAL) are an ideal location for conducting integrated training exercises, as this is the only area on the west coast that is relatively close to land, air, and sea bases, as well as amphibious landing areas. At issue in this case are the Composite Training Unit Exercises and the Joint Tactical Force Exercises, in which individual naval units (ships, submarines, and aircraft) train together as members of a strike group. . . . The use of MFA sonar during these exercises is "mission-critical," given that MFA sonar is the only proven method of identifying submerged diesel-electric submarines operating on battery power. *Id.,* at 568-571.

Sharing the waters in the SOCAL operating area are at least 37 species of marine mammals, including dolphins, whales, and sea lions. The parties strongly dispute the extent to which the Navy's training activities will harm those animals or disrupt their behavioral patterns. The Navy emphasizes that it has used MFA sonar during training exercises in SOCAL for 40 years, without a single documented sonar-related injury to any marine mammal. The Navy asserts that, at most, MFA sonar may cause temporary hearing loss or brief disruptions of marine mammals' behavioral patterns.

The plaintiffs are the Natural Resources Defense Council, Jean-Michael Cousteau (an environmental enthusiast and filmmaker), and several other groups devoted to the protection of marine mammals and ocean habitats. They contend that MFA sonar can cause much more serious injuries to marine mammals than the Navy acknowledges, including permanent hearing loss, decompression sickness, and major behavioral disruptions. According to the plaintiffs, several mass strandings of marine mammals (outside of SOCAL) have been "associated" with the use of active sonar. They argue that certain species of marine mammals—such as beaked whales—are uniquely susceptible to injury from active sonar; these injuries would not necessarily be detected by the Navy, given that beaked whales are "very deep divers" that spend little time at the surface.

II

The procedural history of this case is rather complicated. The Marine Mammal Protection Act of 1972 (MMPA), 86 Stat. 1027, generally prohibits any individual from "taking" a marine mammal, defined as harassing, hunting, capturing, or killing it. 16 U.S.C. §§1362(13), 1372(a). The Secretary of Defense may "exempt any action or category of actions" from the MMPA if such actions are "necessary for national defense." §1371(f)(1). In January 2007, the Deputy Secretary of Defense—acting for the Secretary—granted the Navy a 2-year exemption from the MMPA for the training exercises at issue in this case. Pet. App. 219a-220a. The exemption was conditioned on the Navy adopting several mitigation procedures, including: (1) training lookouts and officers to watch for marine mammals; (2) requiring at least five lookouts with binoculars on each vessel to watch for anomalies on the water surface (including marine mammals); (3) requiring aircraft and sonar operators to report detected marine mammals in the vicinity of the training exercises; (4) requiring reduction of active sonar transmission levels by 6 dB if a marine mammal is detected within 1,000 yards of the bow of the vessel, or by 10 dB if detected within 500 yards; (5) requiring complete shutdown of active sonar transmission if a marine mammal is detected within 200 yards of the vessel; (6) requiring active sonar to be operated at the "lowest practicable level"; and (7) adopting coordination and reporting procedures.

The National Environmental Policy Act of 1969 (NEPA), 83 Stat. 852, requires federal agencies "to the fullest extent possible" to prepare an environmental impact statement (EIS) for "every . . . major Federal actio[n] significantly affecting the quality of the human environment." 42 U.S.C. §4332(2)(C) (2000 ed.). An agency is not required to prepare a full EIS if it determines—based on a shorter environmental assessment (EA)—that the proposed action will not have a significant impact on the environment. 40 CFR §§1508.9(a), 1508.13 (2007).

In February 2007, the Navy issued an EA concluding that the 14 SOCAL training exercises scheduled through January 2009 would not have a significant impact on the environment. The EA divided potential injury to marine mammals into two categories: Level A harassment, defined as the potential destruction or loss of biological tissue (*i.e.*, physical injury), and Level B harassment, defined as temporary injury or disruption of behavioral patterns such as migration, feeding, surfacing, and breeding.

The Navy's computer models predicted that the SOCAL training exercises would cause only eight Level A harassments of common dolphins each year, and that even these injuries could be avoided through the Navy's voluntary mitigation measures, given that dolphins travel in large pods easily located by Navy lookouts. The EA also predicted 274 Level B harassments of beaked whales per year, none of which would result in permanent injury. Beaked whales spend little time at the surface, so the precise effect of active sonar on these mammals is unclear. Erring on the side of caution, the Navy classified all projected harassments of beaked whales as Level A. In light of its conclusion that the SOCAL training exercises would not have a significant impact on the environment, the Navy determined that it was unnecessary to prepare a full EIS. See 40 CFR §1508.13.

Shortly after the Navy released its EA, the plaintiffs sued the Navy, seeking declaratory and injunctive relief on the grounds that the Navy's SOCAL training exercises violated NEPA, the Endangered Species Act of 1973 (ESA), and the Coastal Zone Management Act of 1972 (CZMA). The District Court granted plaintiffs' motion for a preliminary injunction and prohibited the Navy from using MFA sonar during its remaining training exercises. . . .

The Navy filed an emergency appeal, and the Ninth Circuit stayed the injunction pending appeal. After hearing oral argument, the Court of Appeals agreed with the District Court that preliminary injunctive relief was appropriate. The appellate court concluded, however, that a blanket injunction prohibiting the Navy from using MFA sonar in SOCAL was overbroad, and remanded the case to the District Court "to narrow its injunction so as to provide mitigation conditions under which the Navy may conduct its training exercises." 508 F.3d 885, 887 (2007).

On remand, the District Court entered a new preliminary injunction allowing the Navy to use MFA sonar only as long as it implemented the following mitigation measures (in addition to the measures the Navy had adopted pursuant to its MMPA exemption): (1) imposing a 12-mile "exclusion zone" from the coastline; (2) using lookouts to conduct additional monitoring for marine mammals; (3) restricting the use of "helicopter-dipping" sonar; (4) limiting the use of MFA sonar in geographic "choke points"; (5) shutting down MFA sonar when a marine mammal is spotted within 2,200 yards of a vessel; and (6) powering down MFA sonar by 6 dB during significant surface ducting conditions, in which sound travels further than it otherwise would due to temperature differences in adjacent layers of water. 530 F. Supp. 2d 1110, 1118-1121 (C.D. Cal. 2008). The Navy filed a notice of appeal, challenging only the last two restrictions.

The Navy then sought relief from the Executive Branch. The President, pursuant to 16 U.S.C. §1456(c)(1)(B), granted the Navy an exemption from the CZMA. Section 1456(c)(1)(B) permits such exemptions if the activity in question is "in the paramount interest of the United States." The President determined that continuation of the exercises as limited by the Navy was "essential to national security." He concluded that compliance with the District Court's injunction would "undermine the Navy's ability to conduct realistic training exercises that are necessary to ensure the combat effectiveness of . . . strike groups."

Simultaneously, the Council on Environmental Quality (CEQ) authorized the Navy to implement "alternative arrangements" to NEPA compliance in light of "emergency circumstances." See 40 CFR §1506.11. The CEQ determined that alternative arrangements were appropriate because the District Court's injunction "create[s] a significant and unreasonable risk that Strike Groups will not be able to train and be certified as fully mission capable." Under the alternative arrangements, the Navy would be permitted to conduct its training exercises under the mitigation procedures adopted in conjunction with the exemption from the MMPA. The CEQ also imposed additional notice, research, and reporting requirements.

In light of these actions, the Navy then moved to vacate the District Court's injunction with respect to the 2,200-yard shutdown zone and the restrictions on training in surface ducting conditions. The District Court refused to do so, 527 F. Supp. 2d 1216 (2008), and the Court of Appeals affirmed. . . .

We granted certiorari, . . . and now reverse and vacate the injunction.

III

A

A plaintiff seeking a preliminary injunction must establish that he is likely to succeed on the merits, that he is likely to suffer irreparable harm in the absence of preliminary relief, that the balance of equities tips in his favor, and that an injunction is in the public interest.

The District Court and the Ninth Circuit concluded that plaintiffs have shown a likelihood of success on the merits of their NEPA claim. The Navy strongly disputes this determination, arguing that plaintiffs' likelihood of success is low because the CEQ reasonably concluded that "emergency circumstances" justified alternative arrangements to NEPA compliance. 40 CFR §1506.11. . . . [P]laintiffs contend that the CEQ's actions violated the separation of powers by readjudicating a factual issue already decided by an Article III court. Moreover, they assert that the CEQ's interpretations of NEPA are not entitled to deference because the CEQ has not been given statutory authority to conduct adjudications.

The District Court and the Ninth Circuit also held that when a plaintiff demonstrates a strong likelihood of prevailing on the merits, a preliminary injunction may be entered based only on a "possibility" of irreparable harm. The lower courts held that plaintiffs had met this standard because the scientific studies, declarations, and other evidence in the record established to "a near certainty" that the Navy's training exercises would cause irreparable harm to the environment. 530 F. Supp. 2d, at 1118.

The Navy challenges these holdings, arguing that plaintiffs must demonstrate a likelihood of irreparable injury—not just a possibility—in order to obtain preliminary relief. On the facts of this case, the Navy contends that plaintiffs' alleged injuries are too speculative to give rise to irreparable injury, given that ever since the Navy's training program began 40 years ago, there has been no documented case of sonar-related injury to marine mammals in SOCAL. And even if MFA sonar does cause a limited number of injuries to individual *marine mammals*, the Navy asserts that plaintiffs have failed to offer evidence of species-level harm that would adversely affect *their* scientific, recreational, and ecological interests. For their part, plaintiffs assert that they would prevail under any formulation of the irreparable injury standard, because the District Court found that they had established a "near certainty" of irreparable harm.

We agree with the Navy that the Ninth Circuit's "possibility" standard is too lenient. Our frequently reiterated standard requires plaintiffs seeking preliminary relief to demonstrate that irreparable injury is *likely* in the absence of an injunction. Issuing a preliminary injunction based only on a possibility of irreparable harm is inconsistent with our characterization of injunctive relief as an extraordinary remedy that may only be awarded upon a clear showing that the plaintiff is entitled to such relief.

It is not clear that articulating the incorrect standard affected the Ninth Circuit's analysis of irreparable harm. Although the court referred to the "possibility" standard, and cited Circuit precedent along the same lines, it affirmed the District Court's conclusion that plaintiffs had established a "'near certainty'" of irreparable harm. At the same time, however, the nature of the District Court's conclusion is itself unclear. The District Court originally found irreparable harm from sonar-training exercises generally. But by the time of the District Court's final decision, the Navy challenged only two of six restrictions imposed by the court. The District Court did not reconsider the likelihood of irreparable harm in light of the four restrictions not challenged by the Navy. This failure is significant in light of the District Court's own statement that the 12-mile exclusion zone from the coastline—one of the unchallenged mitigation restrictions—"would bar the use of MFA sonar in a significant portion of important marine mammal habitat."

We also find it pertinent that this is not a case in which the defendant is conducting a new type of activity with completely unknown effects on the environment. . . . [T]he plaintiffs are seeking to enjoin—or substantially restrict—training exercises that have been taking place in SOCAL for the last 40 years. . . . . .

As explained in the next section, even if plaintiffs have shown irreparable injury from the Navy's training exercises, any such injury is outweighed by the public interest and the Navy's interest in effective, realistic training of its sailors. A proper consideration of these factors alone requires denial of the requested injunctive relief. For the same reason, we do not address the lower courts' holding that plaintiffs have also established a likelihood of success on the merits.

B

A preliminary injunction is an extraordinary remedy never awarded as of right. In each case, courts "must balance the competing claims of injury and must consider the effect on each party of the granting or withholding of the requested relief." "In exercising their sound discretion, courts of equity should pay particular regard for the public consequences in employing the extraordinary remedy of injunction." In this case, the District Court and the Ninth Circuit significantly understated the burden the preliminary injunction would impose on the Navy's ability to conduct realistic training exercises, and the injunction's consequent adverse impact on the public interest in national defense.

This case involves "complex, subtle, and professional decisions as to the composition, training, equipping, and control of a military force," which are "essentially professional military judgments." We "give great deference to the professional judgment of military authorities concerning the relative importance of a particular military interest." As the Court emphasized just last Term, "neither the Members of this Court nor most federal judges begin the day with briefings that may describe new and serious threats to our Nation and its people." Here, the record contains declarations from some of the Navy's most senior officers, all of whom underscored the threat posed by enemy submarines and the need for extensive sonar training to counter this threat. . . .

We accept these officers' assertions that the use of MFA sonar under realistic conditions during training exercises is of the utmost importance to the Navy and the Nation.

These interests must be weighed against the possible harm to the ecological, scientific, and recreational interests that are legitimately before this Court. Plaintiffs have submitted declarations asserting that they take whale watching trips, observe marine mammals underwater, conduct scientific research on marine mammals, and photograph these animals in their natural habitats. Plaintiffs contend that the Navy's use of MFA sonar will injure marine mammals or alter their behavioral patterns, impairing plaintiffs' ability to study and observe the animals.

While we do not question the seriousness of these interests, we conclude that the balance of equities and consideration of the overall public interest in this case tip strongly in favor of the Navy. For the plaintiffs, the most serious possible injury be harm to an unknown number of the marine mammals that they study and observe. In contrast, forcing the Navy to deploy an inadequately trained antisubmarine force jeopardizes the safety of the fleet. Active sonar is the only reliable technology for detecting and tracking enemy diesel-electric submarines, and the President—the Commander in Chief—has determined that training with active sonar is "essential to national security."

The public interest in conducting training exercises with active sonar under realistic conditions plainly outweighs the interests advanced by the plaintiffs. Of course, military interests do not always trump other considerations, and we have not held that they do. In this case, however, the proper determination of where the public interest lies does not strike us as a close question.

C

Despite the importance of assessing the balance of equities and the public interest in determining whether to grant a preliminary injunction, the District Court addressed these considerations in only a cursory fashion. . . . The subsequent Ninth Circuit panel framed its opinion as reviewing the District Court's exercise of discretion, but that discretion was barely exercised here.

The Court of Appeals held that the balance of equities and the public interest favored the plaintiffs, largely based on its view that the preliminary injunction would not in fact impose a significant burden on the Navy's ability to conduct its training exercises and certify its strike groups. The court deemed the Navy's concerns about the preliminary injunction "speculative" because the Navy had not operated under similar procedures before. But this is almost always the case when a plaintiff seeks injunctive relief to alter a defendant's conduct. The lower courts failed properly to defer to senior Navy officers' specific, predictive judgments about how the preliminary injunction would reduce the effectiveness of the Navy's SOCAL training exercises. . . . The Court of Appeals concluded its opinion by stating that "the Navy may return to the district court to request relief on an emergency basis" if the preliminary injunction "actually result[s] in an inability to train and certify sufficient naval forces to provide for the national defense." This is cold comfort to the Navy. The Navy contends that the injunction will hinder efforts to train sonar operators under realistic conditions, ultimately leaving strike groups more vulnerable to enemy submarines. Unlike the Ninth Circuit, we do not think the Navy is required to wait until the injunction "actually result[s] in an inability to train . . . sufficient naval forces for the national defense" before seeking its dissolution. By then it may be too late.

IV

As noted above, we do not address the underlying merits of plaintiffs' claims. While we have authority to proceed to such a decision at this point, doing so is not necessary here. . . .

At the same time, what we have said makes clear that it would be an abuse of discretion to enter a permanent injunction, after final decision on the merits, along the same lines as the preliminary injunction. An injunction is a matter of equitable discretion; it does not follow from success on the merits as a matter of course.

The factors examined above—the balance of equities and consideration of the public interest—are pertinent in assessing the propriety of any injunctive relief, preliminary or permanent. . . . Given that the ultimate legal claim is that the Navy must prepare an EIS, not that it must cease sonar training, there is no basis for enjoining such training in a manner credibly alleged to pose a serious threat to national security. This is particularly true in light of the fact that the training has been going on for 40 years with no documented episode of harm to a marine mammal. A court concluding that the Navy is required to prepare an EIS has many remedial tools at its disposal, including declaratory relief or an injunction tailored to the preparation of an EIS rather than the Navy's training in the interim. In the meantime, we see no basis for jeopardizing national security, as the present injunction does. Plaintiffs confirmed at oral argument that the preliminary injunction was "the whole ball game," and our analysis of the propriety of preliminary relief is applicable to any permanent injunction as well.

. . .

President Theodore Roosevelt explained that "the only way in which a navy can ever be made efficient is by practice at sea, under all the conditions which would have to be met if war existed." President's Annual Message, 42 Cong. Rec. 67, 81 (1907). We do not discount the importance of plaintiffs' ecological, scientific, and recreational interests in marine mammals. Those interests, however, are plainly outweighed by the Navy's need to conduct realistic training exercises to ensure that it is able to neutralize the threat posed by enemy submarines. The District Court abused its discretion by imposing a 2,200-yard shutdown zone and by requiring the Navy to power down its MFA sonar during significant surface ducting conditions. The judgment of the Court of Appeals is reversed, and the preliminary injunction is vacated to the extent it has been challenged by the Navy.

It is so ordered.

Justice GINSBURG, with whom Justice SOUTER joins, dissenting.

. . . I would hold that, in imposing manageable measures to mitigate harm until completion of the EIS, the District Court conscientiously balanced the equities and did not abuse its discretion. . . .

As the procedural history indicates, the courts below determined that an EIS was required for the 14 exercises. The Navy does not challenge that decision in this Court. Instead, the Navy defends its failure to complete an EIS before launching the exercises based upon CEQ's "alternative arrangements" — arrangements the Navy sought and obtained in order to overcome the lower courts' rulings. As explained below, the Navy's actions undermined NEPA and took an extraordinary course.

II

. . . . The EIS is NEPA's core requirement. This Court has characterized the requirement as "action-forcing." In addition to discussing potential consequences, an EIS must describe potential mitigation measures and alternatives to the proposed course of action. The EIS requirement "ensures that important effects will not be overlooked or underestimated only to be discovered after resources have been committed or the die otherwise cast."

"Publication of an EIS . . . also serves a larger informational role." It demonstrates that an agency has indeed considered environmental concerns, and "perhaps more significantly, provides a springboard for public comment." At the same time, it affords other affected governmental bodies "notice of the expected consequences and the opportunity to plan and implement corrective measures in a timely manner."

In light of these objectives, the timing of an EIS is critical. . . . An EIS must be prepared "early enough so that it can serve practically as an important contribution to the decisionmaking process and will not be used to rationalize or justify decisions already made."

The Navy's publication of its EIS in this case, scheduled to occur *after* the 14 exercises are completed, defeats NEPA's informational and participatory purposes. The Navy's inverted timing, it bears emphasis, is the very reason why the District Court had to confront the question of mitigation measures at all. . . .

The Navy had other options. Most importantly, it could have requested assistance from Congress. The Government has sometimes obtained congressional authorization to proceed with planned activities without fulfilling NEPA's requirements.

Rather than resorting to Congress, the Navy "sought relief from the Executive Branch." *Ante,* at 373. . . .

CEQ's hasty decision on a one-sided record is no substitute for the District Court's considered judgment based on a two-sided record. More fundamentally, even an exemplary CEQ review could not have effected the short circuit the Navy sought. CEQ lacks authority to absolve an agency of its statutory duty to prepare an EIS. . . . The Navy's alternative course—rapid, self-serving resort to an office in the White House—is surely not what Congress had in mind when it instructed agencies to comply with NEPA "to the fullest extent possible." 42 U.S.C. §4332.

III

A

Flexibility is a hallmark of equity jurisdiction. . . . Consistent with equity's character, courts do not insist that litigants uniformly show a particular, predetermined quantum of probable success or injury before awarding equitable relief. Instead, courts have evaluated claims for equitable relief on a "sliding scale," sometimes awarding relief based on a lower likelihood of harm when the likelihood of success is very high. 11A C. Wright, A. Miller, & M. Kane, Federal Practice and Procedure §2948.3, p. 195 (2d ed. 1995). This Court has never rejected that formulation, and I do not believe it does so today.

Equity's flexibility is important in the NEPA context. Because an EIS is the tool for *uncovering* environmental harm, environmental plaintiffs may often rely more heavily on their probability of success than the likelihood of harm. The Court is correct that relief is not warranted "simply to prevent the possibility of some remote future injury." "However, the injury need not have been inflicted when application is made or be certain to occur; a strong threat of irreparable injury before trial is an adequate basis." I agree with the District Court that NRDC made the required showing here.

B

The Navy's own EA predicted substantial and irreparable harm to marine mammals. Sonar is linked to mass strandings of marine mammals, hemorrhaging around the brain and ears, acute spongiotic changes in the central nervous system, and lesions in vital organs. . . .

The majority acknowledges the lower courts' findings, but also states that the EA predicted "only eight Level A harassments of common dolphins each year" and "274 Level B harassments of beaked whales per year, none of which would result in permanent injury." Those numbers do not fully capture the EA's predictions.

The EA classified the harassments of beaked whales as Level A, not Level B. . . . The record reflects "the known sensitivity of these species to tactical sonar," (National Oceanic and Atmospheric Administration letter), and as the majority acknowledges, beaked whales are difficult to study. Further, as the Ninth Circuit noted, "the EA . . . maintained that the methodology used was based on the 'best available science.' "[4]

In my view, this likely harm — 170,000 behavioral disturbances, including 8,000 instances of temporary hearing loss; and 564 Level A harms, including 436 injuries to a beaked whale population numbering only 1,121 — cannot be lightly dismissed, even in the face of an alleged risk to the effectiveness of the Navy's 14 training exercises. There is no doubt that the training exercises serve critical interests. But those interests do not authorize the Navy to violate a statutory command, especially when recourse to the Legislature remains open. . . .

In light of the likely, substantial harm to the environment, NRDC's almost inevitable success on the merits of its claim that NEPA required the Navy to prepare an EIS, the history of this litigation, and the public interest, I cannot agree that the mitigation measures the District Court imposed signal an abuse of discretion. Cf. *Amoco Production Co. v. Gambell,* 480 U.S. 531, 545, 107 S. Ct. 1396, 94 L. Ed. 2d 542 (1987) ("Environmental injury, by its nature, can seldom be adequately remedied by money damages and is often permanent or at least of long duration, *i.e.,* irreparable. If such injury is sufficiently likely, therefore, the balance of harms will usually favor the issuance of an injunction to protect the environment.").

For the reasons stated, I would affirm the judgment of the Ninth Circuit.

---

4. The majority reasons that the environmental harm deserves less weight because the training exercises "have been taking place in SOCAL for the last 40 years," such that "this is not a case in which the defendant is conducting a new type of activity with completely unknown effects on the environment." But the EA explains that the proposed action is not a continuation of the "status quo training." Instead, the EA is based on the Navy's proposal to employ a "surge" training strategy, in which the commander "would have the option to conduct two concurrent major range events."

REVIEW QUESTIONS

1. What is the test for determining whether a court may issue a preliminary injunction?

2. You should have noted that the test has four factors. Unlike the due process test in *Mathews v. Eldridge*, these factors are not weighed against each other. Rather, each of the factors must be met at some threshold level. One dispute among the lower courts is what to do when the likelihood of irreparable injury is high and the likelihood of success on the merits is relatively low, or if the likelihood of success on the merits is high, but the likelihood of irreparable injury is relative low. Can you find the dispute in the text of the case between the majority and the dissent over this issue? The dissent argues that the plaintiffs' likelihood of success on the merits is "almost inevitable." If that is the case, does that mean that the other factors should not matter as much?

3. How does the court's evaluation of the likelihood of success on the merits affect a final merits determination? The plaintiffs told the Supreme Court in *Winter v. NRDC* that the preliminary injunction was the "whole ball game." Can you articulate why that was the case? Consider the extent to which issuing the injunction changes the status quo. To the extent that a court views "preserving the status quo" as important, litigators will sometimes debate what the status quo means. In *Winter*, is the status quo continuing with the sonar program or, instead, suspending it? Sometimes courts refer to the status quo as the "last, peaceable, uncontested status of the parties." Is that clarification helpful?

4. Look at Federal Rule of Civil Procedure 65 and compare the process for obtaining a preliminary injunction that you just learned about with the process for obtaining a temporary restraining order (TRO). How would you describe the differences? As you learned in Chapter 1, due process requires notice and a hearing prior to a deprivation. Why do you think TROs can be granted without the other side present (*ex parte*)?

PRACTICE EXERCISE NO. 2:
MOTION FOR A PRELIMINARY INJUNCTION

Generic Comics is a comic book publisher in the United States. Its properties include thousands of comic book characters. It uses or licenses the use of its characters on products, for special events, and in connection with animated and live-action television series, television motion pictures, and feature films. Among these properties are a series of comic books called Justice, Inc. and the characters appearing in those books. Justice, Inc. is a group of superheroes who save the world from a group of recognizable villains.

In 2004, Generic Comics entered into an agreement with a movie studio, Motion Pictures, pursuant to which Generic Comics licensed the exclusive right to create, produce, distribute, and market theatrical motion pictures based on the "Justice Inc. Property" (or "Property"), defined in the agreement as "the Justice Inc. comic book series" and including "all related characters." The scope of the grant of rights was broad, although the media within which they could be exploited (i.e., theatrical motion pictures) was narrow. Generic Comics received $3 million for the license as well as a percentage of the gross proceeds. It also retained some rights, which are at the center of this dispute. These are summed up in ¶ 8 of the Agreement:

> 8. Generic Comics reserves all television rights [based on the Property] (other than television rights with respect to the Pictures produced hereunder). Generic Comics shall not, without Motion Picture's prior written consent, which consent may be withheld in Motion Picture's sole discretion, produce, distribute, or exploit or authorize the production, distribution, or exploitation of any live-action motion picture for free television exhibition, pay television exhibition, non-theatrical exhibition, or home video exhibition or any feature-length animated motion picture for non-theatrical exhibition or home video exhibition.

In early 2018, after ten years in development, Motion Pictures released a feature film called "Justice, Inc." and launched an extensive media and promotional campaign costing approximately $70 million. The movie generated $250 million in gross receipts from foreign and domestic sales, as well as millions more from sales of videotapes, DVDs, and associated merchandising. Motion Pictures estimates that it will net a profit of approximately $130 million and that Generic Comics will receive approximately $5 million over the life of the film. Motion Pictures is preparing a sequel to the film.

At the same time that the "Justice, Inc." movie was released, Generic Comics developed a weekly thirty-minute television series called "Justice Task Force." In this series, siblings of the original Justice, Inc. characters travel to an alternate universe where the villains in the "Justice, Inc." comic books are reimagined as heroes. Notwithstanding Generic Comics' claim that they took care to eliminate any elements reminiscent of Justice, Inc. in the "Justice Task Force" television show, the promotional material for the show, including television previews, referenced Justice, Inc. and associated characters. Generic Comics entered into broadcast licenses with television stations across the country and is currently in the process of selling advertising for the first season of the show. Generic Comics expects the show to run for five seasons, netting a total of approximately $60 million.

Motion Pictures filed a lawsuit in United States Federal Court for the Southern District of California in July 2018 seeking to enjoin Generic Comics from advertising or airing the "Justice Task Force" television show and requiring Generic Comics to remove all characters related to "Justice, Inc." from that show before airing. Motion Pictures argues that the term "live-action motion picture for free television" in ¶ 8 of the Agreement includes the television program "Justice Task Force." Generic Comics disputes this assertion, stating that although the term is ambiguous it can only refer to a long-form film, not short television episodes lasting under one hour. Motion Pictures asserts that it will suffer irreparable harm because the series will dilute the value of the Justice, Inc. franchise, especially if the television series is of low quality.

Prepare to argue in favor of each side in the preliminary injunction motion in this case. Make sure you have developed arguments for each of the four factors of the preliminary injunction standard.

C. FINAL RELIEF

1. Equitable Relief

At the conclusion of trial, if the plaintiff prevails, the court may issue an award for money damages, historically considered a remedy at law, or instead the court may order equitable relief such as a permanent injunction—like a preliminary injunction but with enduring effect—to direct the defendant to halt the offending conduct or perform acts under a legal duty. The distinction between law and equity has its roots in English law, when there were specialized courts of equity who would grant remedies that courts of law could not. The usual remedy available in the law courts was money damages; the equity courts, in contrast, offered injunctions; an accounting (reviewing of financial books, with reallocation of any monies wrongly placed in one account rather than another); rescission and reformation of contracts; and other tailor-made remedies. In the contemporary American federal system, which has merged law and equity, courts can consider requests for both kinds of relief. However, equitable relief is supposed to be available only when money damages would not be adequate.

a. The Standard for a Permanent Injunction

Historically, courts announced that a permanent injunction, like a preliminary injunction, would issue only to avoid irreparable injury. Unlike the test for a preliminary injunction, the inquiry leading to a permanent injunction does not involve predicting the likelihood of plaintiff success on the merits because the merits have already been decided. The other requirements are the same. Plaintiff must prove "(1) that it has suffered an irreparable injury; (2) that remedies available at law, such as monetary damages, are inadequate to compensate for that injury; (3) that, considering the balance of hardships between the plaintiff and defendant, a remedy in equity is warranted; and (4) that the public interest would not be disserved by a permanent injunction." *eBay Inc. v. MercExchange, L.L.C.*, 547 U.S. 388 (2006). Yet some courts have minimized the importance of this traditional requirement and instead called for evaluating the choice between money damages and an injunction in light of the relative ease of specifying each. Consider and assess the argument for this kind of analysis offered in the following case.

Walgreen Co. v. Sara Creek Property Co.
966 F.2d 273 (7th Cir. 1992)

POSNER, Circuit Judge:

This appeal from the grant of a permanent injunction raises fundamental issues concerning the propriety of injunctive relief. The essential facts are simple. Walgreen has operated a pharmacy in the Southgate Mall in Milwaukee since its opening in 1951. Its current lease, signed in 1971 and carrying a 30-year, 6-month term, contains, as had the only previous lease, a clause in which the landlord, Sara Creek, promises not to lease space in the mall to anyone else who wants to operate a pharmacy or a store containing a pharmacy. Such an exclusivity clause, common in shopping-center leases, is occasionally challenged on antitrust grounds—implausibly enough, given the competition among malls; but that is an issue for another day, since in this appeal Sara Creek does not press the objection it made below to the clause on antitrust grounds.

In 1990, fearful that its largest tenant—what in real estate parlance is called the "anchor tenant"—having gone broke was about to close its store, Sara Creek informed Walgreen that it intended to buy out the anchor tenant and install in its place a discount store operated by Phar-Mor Corporation, a "deep discount" chain, rather than, like Walgreen, just a "discount" chain. Phar-Mor's store would occupy 100,000 square feet, of which 12,000 would be occupied by a pharmacy the same size as Walgreen's. The entrances to the two stores would be within a couple of hundred feet of each other.

Walgreen filed this diversity suit for breach of contract against Sara Creek and Phar-Mor and asked for an injunction against Sara Creek's letting the anchor premises to Phar-Mor. After an evidentiary hearing, the judge found a breach of Walgreen's lease and entered a permanent injunction against Sara Creek's letting the anchor tenant premises to Phar-Mor until the expiration of Walgreen's lease. He did this over the defendants' objection that Walgreen had failed to show that its remedy at law—damages—for the breach of the exclusivity clause was inadequate. Sara Creek had put on an expert witness who testified that Walgreen's damages could be readily estimated, and Walgreen had countered with evidence from its employees that its damages would be very difficult to compute, among other reasons because they included intangibles such as loss of goodwill.

Sara Creek reminds us that damages are the norm in breach of contract as in other cases. Many breaches, it points out, are "efficient" in the sense that they allow resources to be moved into a more valuable use. Perhaps this is one—the value of Phar-Mor's occupancy of the anchor premises may exceed the cost to Walgreen of facing increased competition. If so, society will be better off if Walgreen is paid its damages, equal to that cost, and Phar-Mor is allowed to move in rather than being kept out by an injunction. That is why injunctions are not granted as a matter of course, but only when the plaintiff's damages remedy is inadequate. Walgreen's is not, Sara Creek argues; the projection of business losses due to increased competition is a routine exercise in calculation. Damages representing either the present value of lost future profits or (what should be the equivalent, *Carusos v. Briarcliff, Inc.*, 76 Ga. App. 346, 351-52 (1947)) the diminution in the value of the leasehold have either been awarded or deemed the proper remedy in a number of reported cases for breach of an exclusivity clause in a shopping-center lease. . . . Why, Sara Creek asks, should they not be adequate here?

Sara Creek makes a beguiling argument that contains much truth, but we do not think it should carry the day. For if, as just noted, damages have been awarded in some cases of breach of an exclusivity clause in a shopping-center lease, injunctions have been issued in others. . . . The choice between remedies requires a balancing of the costs and benefits of the alternatives. *Hecht Co. v. Bowles*, 321 U.S. 321, 329 (1944); *Yakus v. United States*, 321 U.S. 414, 440 (1944). The task of striking the balance is for the trial judge, subject to deferential appellate review in recognition of its particularistic, judgmental, fact-bound character. . . . As we said in an appeal from a grant of a preliminary injunction — but the point is applicable to review of a permanent injunction as well — "The question for us [appellate judges] is whether the [district] judge exceeded the bounds of permissible choice in the circumstances, not what we would have done if we had been in his shoes. . . ."

The plaintiff who seeks an injunction has the burden of persuasion — damages are the norm, so the plaintiff must show why his case is abnormal. But when, as in this case, the issue is whether to grant a permanent injunction, not whether to grant a temporary one, the burden is to show that damages are inadequate, not that the denial of the injunction will work irreparable harm. "Irreparable" in the injunction context means not rectifiable by the entry of a final judgment. . . . It has nothing to do with whether to grant a permanent injunction, which, in the usual case anyway, is the final judgment. The use of "irreparable harm" or "irreparable injury" as synonyms for inadequate remedy at law is a confusing usage. It should be avoided.

The benefits of substituting an injunction for damages are twofold. First, it shifts the burden of determining the cost of the defendant's conduct from the court to the parties. If it is true that Walgreen's damages are smaller than the gain to Sara Creek from allowing a second pharmacy into the shopping mall, then there must be a price for dissolving the injunction that will make both parties better off. Thus, the effect of upholding the injunction would be to substitute for the costly processes of forensic fact determination the less costly processes of private negotiation. Second, a premise of our free-market system, and the lesson of experience here and abroad as well, is that prices and costs are more accurately determined by the market than by government. . . .

The costs and benefits of the damages remedy are the mirror of those of the injunctive remedy. The damages remedy avoids the cost of continuing supervision and third-party effects, and the cost of bilateral monopoly as well. It imposes costs of its own, however, in the form of diminished accuracy in the determination of value, on the one hand, and of the parties' expenditures on preparing and presenting evidence of damages, and the time of the court in evaluating the evidence, on the other.

The weighing up of all these costs and benefits is the analytical procedure that is or at least should be employed by a judge asked to enter a permanent injunction, with the understanding that if the balance is even the injunction should be withheld. The judge is not required to explicate every detail of the analysis and he did not do so here, but as long we are satisfied that his approach is broadly consistent with a proper analysis we shall affirm; and we are satisfied here. The determination of Walgreen's damages would have been costly in forensic resources and inescapably inaccurate. . . . The lease had ten years to run. So Walgreen would have had to project its sales revenues and costs over the next ten years, and then project the impact on those figures of Phar-Mor's competition, and then discount that impact to present value. All but the last step would have been fraught with uncertainty. . . .

Damages are not always costly to compute, or difficult to compute accurately. . . . But this is not such a case and here damages would be a costly and inaccurate remedy; and on the other side of the balance some of the costs of an injunction are absent and the cost that is present seems low. The injunction here, like one enforcing a covenant not to compete (standardly enforced by injunction), is a simple negative injunction—Sara Creek is not to lease space in the Southgate Mall to Phar-Mor during the term of Walgreen's lease—and the costs of judicial supervision and enforcement should be negligible. There is no contention that the injunction will harm an unrepresented third party. It may harm Phar-Mor but that harm will be reflected in Sara Creek's offer to Walgreen to dissolve the injunction. (Anyway, Phar-Mor is a party.) . . .

The only substantial cost of the injunction in this case is that it may set off a round of negotiations between the parties. In some cases, illustrated by *Boomer v. Atlantic Cement Co.*, 26 N.Y.2d 219 (1970), this consideration alone would be enough to warrant the denial of injunctive relief. The defendant's factory was emitting cement dust that caused the plaintiffs harm monetized at less than $200,000, and the only way to abate the harm would have been to close down the factory, which had cost $45 million to build. An injunction against the nuisance could therefore have created a huge bargaining range (could, not would, because it is unclear what the current value of the factory was), and the costs of negotiating to a point within it might have been immense. If the market value of the factory was actually $45 million, the plaintiffs would be tempted to hold out for a price to dissolve the injunction in the tens of millions and the factory would be tempted to refuse to pay anything more than a few hundred thousand dollars. Negotiations would be unlikely to break down completely, given such a bargaining range, but they might well be protracted and costly. There is nothing so dramatic here. Sara Creek does not argue that it will have to close the mall if enjoined from leasing to Phar-Mor. Phar-Mor is not the only potential anchor tenant. *Liza Danielle, Inc. v. Jamko, Inc.*, 408 So. 2d 735, 740 (Fla. App. 1982), on which Sara Creek relies, presented the converse case where the grant of the injunction would have forced an existing tenant to close its store. The size of the bargaining range was also a factor in the denial of injunctive relief in *Gitlitz v. Plankinton Building Properties, Inc.*, 228 Wis. 334, 339-40 (1938).

To summarize, the judge did not exceed the bounds of reasonable judgment in concluding that the costs (including forgone benefits) of the damages remedy would exceed the costs (including forgone benefits) of an injunction. . . .

REVIEW QUESTIONS

1. What is the standard for applying a permanent injunction? How does it differ from the standard for applying a preliminary injunction?
2. Did the appellate court simply apply or instead modify the standard for issuing permanent injunctions?
3. The precise question before the Court of Appeals for the Seventh Circuit was whether the district court had exceeded the bounds of reasonable discretion in issuing the injunction. Why? Because the standard of appellate review is "abuse of discretion," which is supposed to be deferential to the district court's findings of fact. On questions of law, however, the appellate court does not defer to the district court's rulings.

QUESTIONS TO PONDER

1. One way to understand the facts in *Walgreen Co. v. Sara Creek Property* draws on the concept of bilateral monopoly in economics. A bilateral monopoly involves a single buyer and a single seller who must negotiate a price even though, in the general market, the seller is a dominant seller and thus can charge a higher-than-market price, and in the general market the buyer dominates and thus can pay a lower-than-market price. The result of their negotiation could end up anywhere between the higher price that the seller can command and the lower price that the buyer can demand, and will reflect their relative bargaining power. In this case, the landlord, as seller of space, has bargaining power in part because Walgreen Co. is established in the mall and would not want to leave. Yet Walgreen Co., as the buyer of space, has bargaining power because its general position in the market enabled it to negotiate the exclusivity clause in the first place. The economic analysis suggests that actual bargaining power will be necessary to work out a deal rather than a general market assessment of the value of the breached clause at issue.
2. How should courts compare monetary and non-monetary relief? For example, do you think it would be possible or desirable to imagine money damages as an alternative to an injunctive order directing officials to improve prison conditions? Is the type of analysis Judge Posner applies in *Walgreen* only applicable to cases involving business dealings?

b. Types of Permanent Injunctions

Professor Owen Fiss grouped injunctions into three categories: preventative injunctions, reparative injunctions, and structural injunctions. A preventative injunction prevents future wrongs, such as for example an order forbidding Sara Creek from leasing to Phar-Mor. A reparative injunction attempts to alleviate the effects of a past wrong. For example, if the result of an election was tainted by fraud, a court might order a new election. *See, e.g., Foulkes v. Hays*, 85 Wash. 2d 629 (1975). Finally, a structural injunction involves an injunction that commits judicial resources to bring about institutional reform. Examples of such injunctions include the desegregation of racially segregated schools, the improvement of prison conditions found to violate the Eighth Amendment ban on cruel and unusual punishment, the alteration of institutions for persons with mental disabilities in light of demonstrated statutory violations, and the redirection of public housing management found to violate statutory and constitutional guarantees. *See, e.g., Finney v. Hutto*, 410 F. Supp. 251 (E.D. Ark. 1976) (prison conditions); *Halderman v. Pennhurst State School and Hosp.*, 673 F.2d 647 (3d Cir. 1982) (en banc) (mental hospital); *Perez v. Bos. Hous. Auth.*, 379 U.S. 703 (1980) (public housing); *Swann v. Charlotte-Mecklenburg Bd. of Educ.*, 402 U.S. 1 (1971) (school desegregation). These injunctive orders often are very specific, indicating, for example, how the defendants should assign and transport students and teachers to schools; how patients should be evaluated and treated; how health and safety standards in housing should be devised and administered; and what resources should be available to individual prisoners. To assist a court in monitoring the implementation of such orders, judges have exercised their authority to appoint judicial officers, such as masters or monitors. *See* Fed. R. Civ. P. 53. As you read *Brown v. Plata*, 563 U.S. 493 (2011), reproduced below, consider how specific the injunction granted by the district court three-judge panel was, and how general. The three-judge panel ordered the California prison system to reduce overcrowding to a very specific level, but gave the state a great deal of leeway in how to produce this result.

Settlement of lawsuits that seek injunctive relief can produce *consent decrees*, which are settlements negotiated by parties but approved and enforced by the court which retains jurisdiction over the dispute. This form of dispute resolution resembles both a private contract and a court judgment. It is often used to terminate public law and institutional reform litigation where the goal is to ensure enforcement of a statute or government regulation, such as antitrust and employment discrimination regulations. Although the terms of the consent decree must be approved by the court, the parties contribute language, ideas, and voluntary compliance to the process. Violations of either kind of consent decree can trigger judicial enforcement through contempt hearings and sanctions. A court may approve a consent decree after finding liability or violation by the defendant; alternatively, the parties may propose and the judge may approve a consent decree prior to such a finding. This flexibility promotes settlement, but also may prompt questions about the use of judicial resources to enforce a privately constructed settlement. If you want to know more, a good introduction to consent decrees generally is Larry Kramer, *Consent Decrees and the Rights of Third Parties*, 87 Mich. L. Rev. 321 (1988). For a discussion on whether the courts should use their power to enforce quasi-private agreements such as consent decrees, *see* Jeremy A. Ralkin and Neal E. Devins, *Averting Government by Consent Decree: Constitutional Limits on the Enforcement of Settlements with the Federal Government*, 40 Stan. L. Rev. 203 (1987).

What difference would it make — to the parties and to the public — for a court to enforce a consent decree right after the suit is filed, compared with one produced after the introduction of massive evidence at trial? *See United States v. Am. Telephone and Telegraph Co.*, 522 F. Supp. 131 (D.D.C. 1982). The Supreme Court has addressed further questions about consent decrees, such as the binding of third parties and the circumstances permitting modification. *See Martin v. Wilks*, 490 U.S. 755 (1989) (effect on third parties); *Rufo v. Inmates of the Suffolk Cnty. Jail*, 502 U.S. 367 (1992) (modification permitted in light of significant change in facts or law warranting suitably tailored revision).

Courts often issue injunctions or use consent decrees without a termination date. Injunctions and consent decrees addressing school desegregation, prison conditions, and improvement of foster care systems can last for years or even decades. How do they end? Termination of the relief and associated judicial monitoring typically ends with a motion by one or both parties, triggered either by compliance or a demonstration of changed circumstances. At times, the court will shift the burden of proof on the motion to terminate the relief from plaintiff to defendant, depending on the kind of case and the particular factual circumstances.

c. Equitable Relief and the Judicial Role

When a court issues an injunction, especially an injunction against a public agency or institution, this raises questions about the appropriate relationship between the courts deciding constitutional questions and the power of the legislature to decide budgetary issues. For example, in litigation over the prison conditions, a court deciding the constitutional question of whether prison conditions violate the Eighth Amendment's prohibition on cruel and unusual punishment implicates legislative budgetary decisions such as how much money will be allocated to the prison system. As you read the Supreme Court opinion below and the two scholarly articles that follow, consider how well the positions taken by the Justices track the critiques presented by the scholars and your own view on the court's power and its appropriate limitations.

Before reading on, a bit of background on the special procedures required by statute in prison reform litigation would be helpful. Congress passed the Prison Litigation Reform Act of 1996 (PLRA), Pub. L. No. 104-34, 110 Stat. 1321 (codified as amended at 11 U.S.C. § 523(a) (2000), at 18 U.S.C. §§ 3624(a) and 3626 (2000), and in scattered sections of 28 and 42 U.S.C.). The purpose of the statute was to limit prison reform litigation. The PLRA requires that an injunction, such as that issued in the case below, be issued only after a hearing by a three-judge panel. The statute (i) limits the remedies courts can provide, 18 U.S.C. § 3626 (2000), (ii) imposes a two-year expiration date on injunctions; and (iii) requires that an injunction will terminate unless the court makes a new finding that affirmative relief is still required to end an ongoing constitutional violation. 18 U.S.C. § 3626(b)(1)(A)(i), (b)(3) (2000). After the expiration date, the PLRA shifts the burden from the defendant to the plaintiff. While this shift imposes new burdens on plaintiffs, it has not prevented some long-term prison litigation aimed at structural reform, as the case below demonstrates. As you read the case, consider what limits should be placed on the judicial power to issue structural injunctions.

Brown v. Plata
563 U.S. 493 (2011)

Justice KENNEDY delivered the opinion of the Court.

This case arises from serious constitutional violations in California's prison system. The violations have persisted for years. They remain uncorrected. The appeal comes to this Court from a three-judge District Court order directing California to remedy two ongoing violations of the Cruel and Unusual Punishments Clause, a guarantee binding on the States by the Due Process Clause of the Fourteenth Amendment. . . .

The appeal presents the question whether the remedial order issued by the three-judge court is consistent with requirements and procedures set forth in a congressional statute, the Prison Litigation Reform Act of 1995 (PLRA). 18 U.S.C. §3626. The order leaves the choice of means to reduce overcrowding to the discretion of state officials. But absent compliance through new construction, out-of-state transfers, or other means—or modification of the order upon a further showing by the State—the State will be required to release some number of prisoners before their full sentences have been served. High recidivism rates must serve as a warning that mistaken or premature release of even one prisoner can cause injury and harm. The release of prisoners in large numbers—assuming the State finds no other way to comply with the order—is a matter of undoubted, grave concern.

At the time of trial, California's correctional facilities held some 156,000 persons. This is nearly double the number that California's prisons were designed to hold, and California has been ordered to reduce its prison population to 137.5% of design capacity. By the three-judge court's own estimate, the required population reduction could be as high as 46,000 persons. Although the State has reduced the population by at least 9,000 persons during the pendency of this appeal, this means a further reduction of 37,000 persons could be required. As will be noted, the reduction need not be accomplished in an indiscriminate manner or in these substantial numbers if satisfactory, alternate remedies or means for compliance are devised. The State may employ measures, including good-time credits and diversion of low-risk offenders and technical parole violators to community-based programs, that will mitigate the order's impact. The population reduction potentially required is nevertheless of unprecedented sweep and extent.

Yet so too is the continuing injury and harm resulting from these serious constitutional violations. For years the medical and mental health care provided by California's prisons has fallen short of minimum constitutional requirements and has failed to meet prisoners' basic health needs. Needless suffering and death have been the well-documented result. Over the whole course of years during which this litigation has been pending, no other remedies have been found to be sufficient. Efforts to remedy the violation have been frustrated by severe overcrowding in California's prison system. Short-term gains in the provision of care have been eroded by the long-term effects of severe and pervasive overcrowding. . . .

This Court now holds that the PLRA does authorize the relief afforded in this case and that the court-mandated population limit is necessary to remedy the violation of prisoners' constitutional rights. The order of the three-judge court, subject to the right of the State to seek its modification in appropriate circumstances, must be affirmed.

I

The degree of overcrowding in California's prisons is exceptional. California's prisons are designed to house a population just under 80,000, but at the time of the three-judge court's decision the population was almost double that. The State's prisons had operated at around 200% of design capacity for at least 11 years. Prisoners are crammed into spaces neither designed nor intended to house inmates. As many as 200 prisoners may live in a gymnasium, monitored by as few as two or three correctional officers. As many as 54 prisoners may share a single toilet.

. . . In 2006, then-Governor Schwarzenegger declared a state of emergency in the prisons, as "'immediate action is necessary to prevent death and harm caused by California's severe prison overcrowding.'" The consequences of overcrowding identified by the Governor include "'increased, substantial risk for transmission of infectious illness'" and a suicide rate "'approaching an average of one per week.'"

Prisoners in California with serious mental illness do not receive minimal, adequate care. Because of a shortage of treatment beds, suicidal inmates may be held for prolonged periods in telephone-booth sized cages without toilets. . . . Wait times for mental health care range as high as 12 months. In 2006, the suicide rate in California's prisons was nearly 80% higher than the national average for prison populations; and a court-appointed Special Master found that 72.1% of suicides involved "some measure of inadequate assessment, treatment, or intervention, and were therefore most probably foreseeable and/or preventable."

Prisoners suffering from physical illness also receive severely deficient care. California's prisons . . . have only half the clinical space needed to treat the current population. . . . The number of staff is inadequate, and prisoners face significant delays in access to care. A prisoner with severe abdominal pain died after a 5-week delay in referral to a specialist; a prisoner with "constant and extreme" chest pain died after an 8-hour delay in evaluation by a doctor; and a prisoner died of testicular cancer after a "failure of MDs to work up for cancer in a young man with 17 months of testicular pain." California Prison Health Care Receivership Corp., K. Imai, Analysis of CDCR Death Reviews 2006, pp. 6-7 (Aug. 2007). . . . Many more prisoners, suffering from severe but not life-threatening conditions, experience prolonged illness and unnecessary pain.

These conditions are the subject of two federal cases. The first to commence, *Coleman v. Brown,* was filed in 1990. *Coleman* involves the class of seriously mentally ill persons in California prisons. Over 15 years ago, in 1995, after a 39-day trial, the *Coleman* District Court found "overwhelming evidence of the systematic failure to deliver necessary care to mentally ill inmates" in California prisons. *Coleman v. Wilson,* 912 F. Supp. 1282, 1316 (E.D. Cal.). . . .

In 2007, 12 years after his appointment, the Special Master in *Coleman* filed a report stating that, after years of slow improvement, the state of mental health care in California's prisons was deteriorating. The Special Master ascribed this change to increased overcrowding. . . . Prisons had retained more mental health staff, but the "growth of the resource [had] not matched the rise in demand." . . . The Special Master concluded that many early "achievements have succumbed to the inexorably rising tide of population, leaving behind growing frustration and despair."

. . . The second action, *Plata v. Brown,* involves the class of state prisoners with serious medical conditions. After this action commenced in 2001, the State conceded that deficiencies in prison medical care violated prisoners' Eighth Amendment rights. The State stipulated to a remedial injunction. The State failed to comply with that injunction, and in 2005 the court appointed a Receiver to oversee remedial efforts. The court found that "the California prison medical care system is broken beyond repair," resulting in an "unconscionable degree of suffering and death." . . .

Prisons were unable to retain sufficient numbers of competent medical staff, and would "hire any doctor who had 'a license, a pulse and a pair of shoes.'" Medical facilities lacked "necessary medical equipment" and did "not meet basic sanitation standards." "Exam tables and counter tops, where prisoners with . . . communicable diseases are treated, [were] not routinely disinfected."

In 2008, three years after the District Court's decision, the Receiver described continuing deficiencies in the health care provided by California prisons. . . .

A report by the Receiver detailed the impact of overcrowding on efforts to remedy the violation. The Receiver explained that "overcrowding, combined with staffing shortages, has created a culture of cynicism, fear, and despair which makes hiring and retaining competent clinicians extremely difficult." "[O]vercrowding, and the resulting day to day operational chaos of the [prison system], creates regular 'crisis' situations which . . . take time [and] energy . . . away from important remedial programs." Overcrowding had increased the incidence of infectious disease, and had led to rising prison violence and greater reliance by custodial staff on lockdowns, which "inhibit the delivery of medical care and increase the staffing necessary for such care." . . .

The *Coleman* and *Plata* plaintiffs, believing that a remedy for unconstitutional medical and mental health care could not be achieved without reducing over-crowding, moved their respective District Courts to convene a three-judge court empowered under the PLRA to order reductions in the prison population. . . .

The three-judge court heard 14 days of testimony and issued a 184-page opinion, making extensive findings of fact. The court ordered California to reduce its prison population to 137.5% of the prisons' design capacity within two years. Assuming the State does not increase capacity through new construc-tion, the order requires a population reduction of 38,000 to 46,000 persons. Because it appears all but certain that the State cannot complete sufficient con-struction to comply fully with the order, the prison population will have to be reduced to at least some extent. The court did not order the State to achieve this reduction in any particular manner. Instead, the court ordered the State to for-mulate a plan for compliance and submit its plan for approval by the court. . . .

The State appealed. . . .

II

As a consequence of their own actions, prisoners may be deprived of rights that are fundamental to liberty. Yet the law and the Constitution demand rec-ognition of certain other rights. Prisoners retain the essence of human dignity inherent in all persons. Respect for that dignity animates the Eighth Amendment prohibition against cruel and unusual punishment. . . .

To incarcerate, society takes from prisoners the means to provide for their own needs. Prisoners are dependent on the State for food, clothing, and nec-essary medical care. . . . A prison that deprives prisoners of basic sustenance, including adequate medical care, is incompatible with the concept of human dignity and has no place in civilized society.

If government fails to fulfill this obligation, the courts have a responsibility to remedy the resulting Eighth Amendment violation. Courts must be sensitive to the State's interest in punishment, deterrence, and rehabilitation, as well as the need for deference to experienced and expert prison administrators faced with the difficult and dangerous task of housing large numbers of convicted crimi-nals. Courts nevertheless must not shrink from their obligation to "enforce the constitutional rights of all 'persons,' including prisoners." *Cruz v. Beto*, 405 U.S. 319, 321 (1972) (per curiam). Courts may not allow constitutional violations to continue simply because a remedy would involve intrusion into the realm of prison administration.

Courts faced with the sensitive task of remedying unconstitutional prison conditions must consider a range of available options, including appointment of special masters or receivers and the possibility of consent decrees. When necessary to ensure compliance with a constitutional mandate, courts may enter orders placing limits on a prison's population. By its terms, the PLRA restricts the circumstances in which a court may enter an order "that has the purpose or effect of reducing or limiting the prison population." 18 U.S.C. §3626(g)(4). The order in this case does not necessarily require the State to release any prisoners. The State may comply by raising the design capacity of its prisons or by transferring prisoners to county facilities or facilities in other States. Because the order limits the prison population as a percentage of design capacity, it nonetheless has the "effect of reducing or limiting the prison population." *Ibid.*

Under the PLRA, only a three-judge court may enter an order limiting a prison population. §3626(a)(3)(B). . . .

The three-judge court must then find by clear and convincing evidence that "crowding is the primary cause of the violation of a Federal right" and that "no other relief will remedy the violation of the Federal right." 18 U.S.C. §3626(a)(3)(E). As with any award of prospective relief under the PLRA, the relief "shall extend no further than necessary to correct the violation of the Federal right of a particular plaintiff or plaintiffs." §3626(a)(1)(A). The three-judge court must therefore find that the relief is "narrowly drawn, extends no further than necessary . . . and is the least intrusive means necessary to correct the violation of the Federal right." *Ibid.* In making this determination, the three-judge court must give "substantial weight to any adverse impact on public safety or the operation of a criminal justice system caused by the relief." *Ibid.* Applying these standards, the three-judge court found a population limit appropriate, necessary, and authorized in this case.

This Court's review of the three-judge court's legal determinations is *de novo*, but factual findings are reviewed for clear error. Deference to trial court fact-finding reflects an understanding that "[t]he trial judge's major role is the determination of fact, and with experience in fulfilling that role comes expertise." The three-judge court oversaw two weeks of trial and heard at considerable length from California prison officials, as well as experts in the field of correctional administration. . . . The three-judge court's findings of fact may be reversed only if this Court is left with a " 'definite and firm conviction that a mistake has been committed.' "

The State contends that it was error to convene the three-judge court without affording it more time to comply with the prior orders in *Coleman* and *Plata*. . . .

Before a three-judge court may be convened to consider whether to enter a population limit, the PLRA requires that the court have "previously entered an order for less intrusive relief that has failed to remedy the deprivation of the Federal right sought to be remedied." 18 U.S.C. §3626(a)(3)(A)(i). . . .

Having engaged in remedial efforts for 5 years in *Plata* and 12 in *Coleman*, the District Courts were not required to wait to see whether their more recent efforts would yield equal disappointment. . . . The *Coleman* and *Plata* courts acted reasonably when they convened a three-judge court without further delay.

Once a three-judge court has been convened, the court must find additional requirements satisfied before it may impose a population limit. The first of these requirements is that "crowding is the primary cause of the violation of a Federal right." 18 U.S.C. §3626(a)(3)(E)(i).

The three-judge court found the primary cause requirement satisfied by the evidence at trial. . . . Because the "district court is 'better positioned' . . . to decide the issue," our review of the three-judge court's primary cause determination is deferential. *Salve Regina College v. Russell,* 499 U.S. 225, 233 (1991). . . .

. . . The three-judge court acknowledged that the violations were caused by factors in addition to overcrowding and that reducing crowding in the prisons would not entirely cure the violations. . . .

As this case illustrates, constitutional violations in conditions of confinement are rarely susceptible of simple or straightforward solutions. In addition to overcrowding the failure of California's prisons to provide adequate medical and mental health care may be ascribed to chronic and worsening budget shortfalls, a lack of political will in favor of reform, inadequate facilities, and systemic administrative failures. The *Plata* District Judge, in his order appointing the Receiver, compared the problem to "'a spider web, in which the tension of the various strands is determined by the relationship among all the parts of the web, so that if one pulls on a single strand, the tension of the entire web is redistributed in a new and complex pattern.'" (quoting Fletcher, *The Discretionary Constitution: Institutional Remedies and Judicial Legitimacy*, 91 Yale L.J. 635, 645 (1982)). Only a multifaceted approach aimed at many causes, including overcrowding, will yield a solution.

The PLRA should not be interpreted to place undue restrictions on the authority of federal courts to fashion practical remedies when confronted with complex and intractable constitutional violations. Congress limited the availability of limits on prison populations, but it did not forbid these measures altogether. See 18 U.S.C. §3626. . . .

Courts should presume that Congress was sensitive to the real-world problems faced by those who would remedy constitutional violations in the prisons and that Congress did not leave prisoners without a remedy for violations of their constitutional rights. . . . A finding that overcrowding is the "primary cause" of a violation is therefore permissible, despite the fact that additional steps will be required to remedy the violation.

. . . The three-judge court was also required to find by clear and convincing evidence that "no other relief will remedy the violation of the Federal right." §3626(a)(3)(E)(ii).

The State argues that the violation could have been remedied through a combination of new construction, transfers of prisoners out of State, hiring of medical personnel, and continued efforts by the *Plata* Receiver and *Coleman* Special Master. The order in fact permits the State to comply with the population limit by transferring prisoners to county facilities or facilities in other States, or by constructing new facilities to raise the prisons' design capacity. And the three-judge court's order does not bar the State from undertaking any other remedial efforts. If the State does find an adequate remedy other than a population limit, it may seek modification or termination of the three-judge court's order on that basis. The evidence at trial, however, supports the three-judge court's conclusion that an order limited to other remedies would not provide effective relief. . . .

The common thread connecting the State's proposed remedial efforts is that they would require the State to expend large amounts of money absent a reduction in overcrowding. The Court cannot ignore the political and fiscal reality behind this case. California's Legislature has not been willing or able to allocate the resources necessary to meet this crisis absent a reduction in overcrowding. There is no reason to believe it will begin to do so now, when the State of California is facing an unprecedented budgetary shortfall. As noted above, the legislature recently failed to allocate funds for planned new construction. Without a reduction in overcrowding, there will be no efficacious remedy for the unconstitutional care of the sick and mentally ill in California's prisons.

The PLRA states that no prospective relief shall issue with respect to prison conditions unless it is narrowly drawn, extends no further than necessary to correct the violation of a federal right, and is the least intrusive means necessary to correct the violation. 18 U.S.C. §3626(a). When determining whether these requirements are met, courts must "give substantial weight to any adverse impact on public safety or the operation of a criminal justice system." *Ibid.*

The three-judge court acknowledged that its order "is likely to affect inmates without medical conditions or serious mental illness." . . .

The population limit imposed by the three-judge court does not fail narrow tailoring simply because it will have positive effects beyond the plaintiff class. Narrow tailoring requires a " ' "fit" between the [remedy's] ends and the means chosen to accomplish those ends.' " The scope of the remedy must be proportional to the scope of the violation, and the order must extend no further than necessary to remedy the violation. . . .

This case is unlike cases where courts have impermissibly reached out to control the treatment of persons or institutions beyond the scope of the violation. Even prisoners with no present physical or mental illness may become afflicted, and all prisoners in California are at risk so long as the State continues to provide inadequate care. Prisoners in the general population will become sick, and will become members of the plaintiff classes, with routine frequency; and overcrowding may prevent the timely diagnosis and care necessary to provide effective treatment and to prevent further spread of disease. Relief targeted only at present members of the plaintiff classes may therefore fail to adequately protect future class members who will develop serious physical or mental illness. Prisoners who are not sick or mentally ill do not yet have a claim that they have been subjected to care that violates the Eighth Amendment, but in no sense are they remote bystanders in California's medical care system. They are that system's next potential victims.

A release order limited to prisoners within the plaintiff classes would, if anything, unduly limit the ability of State officials to determine which prisoners should be released. As the State acknowledges in its brief, "release of seriously mentally ill inmates [would be] likely to create special dangers because of their recidivism rates." The order of the three-judge court gives the State substantial flexibility to determine who should be released. If the State truly believes that a release order limited to sick and mentally ill inmates would be preferable to the order entered by the three-judge court, the State can move the three-judge court for modification of the order on that basis. The State has not requested this relief from this Court. . . .

Although the three-judge court's order addresses the entire California prison system, it affords the State flexibility to accommodate differences between institutions. There is no requirement that every facility comply with the 137.5% limit. Assuming no constitutional violation results, some facilities may retain populations in excess of the limit provided other facilities fall sufficiently below it so the system as a whole remains in compliance with the order. . . . The alternative—a series of institution-specific population limits—would require federal judges to make these choices. . . .

Nor is the order overbroad because it limits the State's authority to run its prisons, as the State urges in its brief. . . . The State may choose how to allocate prisoners between institutions; it may choose whether to increase the prisons' capacity through construction or reduce the population; and, if it does reduce the population, it may decide what steps to take to achieve the necessary reduction. . . .

. . . The State's desire to avoid a population limit, justified as according respect to state authority, creates a certain and unacceptable risk of continuing violations of the rights of sick and mentally ill prisoners, with the result that many more will die or needlessly suffer. The Constitution does not permit this wrong.

In reaching its decision, the three-judge court gave "substantial weight" to any potential adverse impact on public safety from its order. The court devoted nearly 10 days of trial to the issue of public safety, and it gave the question extensive attention in its opinion. Ultimately, the court concluded that it would be possible to reduce the prison population "in a manner that preserves public safety and the operation of the criminal justice system."

The PLRA's requirement that a court give "substantial weight" to public safety does not require the court to certify that its order has no possible adverse impact on the public. A contrary reading would depart from the statute's text by replacing the word "substantial" with "conclusive." Whenever a court issues an order requiring the State to adjust its incarceration and criminal justice policy, there is a risk that the order will have some adverse impact on public safety in some sectors. . . . A court is required to consider the public safety consequences of its order and to structure, and monitor, its ruling in a way that mitigates those consequences while still achieving an effective remedy of the constitutional violation.

This inquiry necessarily involves difficult predictive judgments regarding the likely effects of court orders. Although these judgments are normally made by state officials, they necessarily must be made by courts when those courts fashion injunctive relief to remedy serious constitutional violations in the prisons. These questions are difficult and sensitive, but they are factual questions and should be treated as such. Courts can, and should, rely on relevant and informed expert testimony when making factual findings. . . .

The three-judge court credited substantial evidence that prison populations can be reduced in a manner that does not increase crime to a significant degree. Some evidence indicated that reducing overcrowding in California's prisons could even improve public safety. Then-Governor Schwarzenegger, in his emergency proclamation on overcrowding, acknowledged that "'overcrowding causes harm to people and property, leads to inmate unrest and misconduct, . . . and increases recidivism as shown within this state and in others.'". . .

Expert witnesses produced statistical evidence that prison populations had been lowered without adversely affecting public safety in a number of jurisdictions, including certain counties in California, as well as Wisconsin, Illinois, Texas, Colorado, Montana, Michigan, Florida, and Canada. . . .

The court found that various available methods of reducing overcrowding would have little or no impact on public safety. Expansion of good-time credits would allow the State to give early release to only those prisoners who pose the least risk of reoffending. Diverting low-risk offenders to community programs such as drug treatment, day reporting centers, and electronic monitoring would likewise lower the prison population without releasing violent convicts. The State now sends large numbers of persons to prison for violating a technical term or condition of their parole, and it could reduce the prison population by punishing technical parole violations through community-based programs. This last measure would be particularly beneficial as it would reduce crowding in the reception centers, which are especially hard hit by overcrowding. The court's order took account of public safety concerns by giving the State substantial flexibility to select among these and other means of reducing overcrowding.

The State submitted a plan to reduce its prison population in accordance with the three-judge court's order, and it complains that the three-judge court approved that plan without considering whether the specific measures contained within it would substantially threaten public safety. . . . Courts should presume that state officials are in a better position to gauge how best to preserve public safety and balance competing correctional and law enforcement concerns. The decision to leave details of implementation to the State's discretion protected public safety by leaving sensitive policy decisions to responsible and competent state officials. . . .

III

Establishing the population at which the State could begin to provide constitutionally adequate medical and mental health care, and the appropriate time frame within which to achieve the necessary reduction, requires a degree of judgment. . . . Courts have substantial flexibility when making these judgments. . . .

Nevertheless, the PLRA requires a court to adopt a remedy that is "narrowly tailored" to the constitutional violation and that gives "substantial weight" to public safety. 18 U.S.C. §3626(a). When a court is imposing a population limit, this means the court must set the limit at the highest population consistent with an efficacious remedy. The court must also order the population reduction achieved in the shortest period of time reasonably consistent with public safety.

The three-judge court concluded that the population of California's prisons should be capped at 137.5% of design capacity. This conclusion is supported by the record. Indeed, some evidence supported a limit as low as 100% of design capacity. . . .

Although the three-judge court concluded that the "evidence in support of a 130% limit is strong," it found that some upward adjustment was warranted in light of "the caution and restraint required by the PLRA." The three-judge court noted evidence supporting a higher limit. In particular, the State's Corrections Independent Review Panel had found that 145% was the maximum "operable capacity" of California's prisons, although the relevance of that determination was undermined by the fact that the panel had not considered the need to provide constitutionally adequate medical and mental health care, as the State itself concedes. . . . After considering, but discounting, this evidence, the three-judge court concluded that the evidence supported a limit lower than 145%, but higher than 130%. It therefore imposed a limit of 137.5%.

This weighing of the evidence was not clearly erroneous. . . . In light of substantial evidence supporting an even more drastic remedy, the three-judge court complied with the requirement of the PLRA in this case.

The three-judge court ordered the State to achieve this reduction within two years. At trial and closing argument before the three-judge court, the State did not argue that reductions should occur over a longer period of time. The State later submitted a plan for court approval that would achieve the required reduction within five years, and that would reduce the prison population to 151% of design capacity in two years. The State represented that this plan would "safely reach a population level of 137.5% over time." The three-judge court rejected this plan because it did not comply with the deadline set by its order. . . .

Particularly in light of the State's failure to contest the issue at trial, the three-judge court did not err when it established a 2-year deadline for relief. Plaintiffs proposed a 2-year deadline, and the evidence at trial was intended to demonstrate the feasibility of a 2-year deadline. Notably, the State has not asked this Court to extend the 2-year deadline at this time.

The three-judge court, however, retains the authority, and the responsibility, to make further amendments to the existing order or any modified decree it may enter as warranted by the exercise of its sound discretion. . . . A court that invokes equity's power to remedy a constitutional violation by an injunction mandating systemic changes to an institution has the continuing duty and responsibility to assess the efficacy and consequences of its order. . . .

These observations reflect the fact that the three-judge court's order, like all continuing equitable decrees, must remain open to appropriate modification. They are not intended to cast doubt on the validity of the basic premise of the existing order. The medical and mental health care provided by California's prisons falls below the standard of decency that inheres in the Eighth Amendment. This extensive and ongoing constitutional violation requires a remedy, and a remedy will not be achieved without a reduction in overcrowding. The relief ordered by the three-judge court is required by the Constitution and was authorized by Congress in the PLRA. The State shall implement the order without further delay.

The judgment of the three-judge court is affirmed.

It is so ordered.

APPENDIX B

Mule Creek State Prison
Aug. 1, 2008

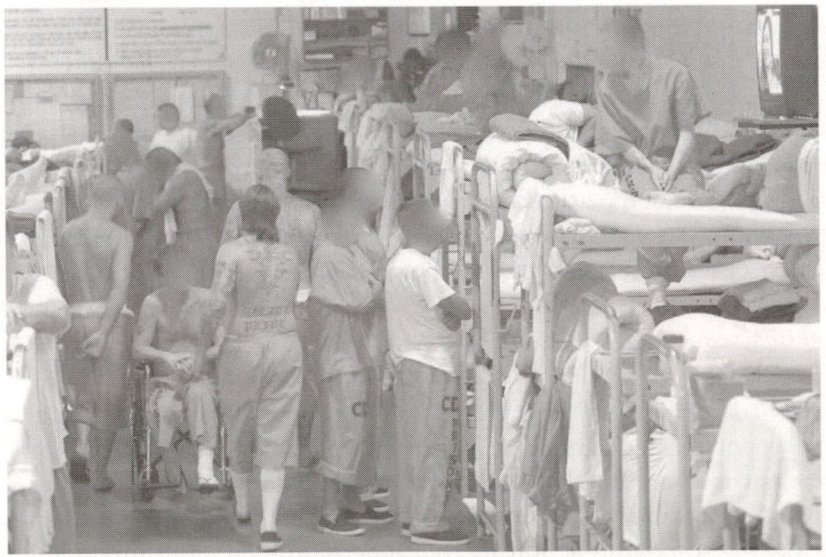

California Institution for Men
Aug. 7, 2006

Salinas Valley State Prison
July 29, 2008
Correctional Treatment Center
(dry cages/holding cells for people waiting for mental health crisis bed)

Justice SCALIA, with whom Justice THOMAS joins, dissenting.

Today the Court affirms what is perhaps the most radical injunction issued by a court in our Nation's history: an order requiring California to release the staggering number of 46,000 convicted criminals.

There comes before us, now and then, a case whose proper outcome is so clearly indicated by tradition and common sense, that its decision ought to shape the law, rather than vice versa. One would think that, before allowing the decree of a federal district court to release 46,000 convicted felons, this Court would bend every effort to read the law in such a way as to avoid that outrageous result. Today, quite to the contrary, the Court disregards stringently drawn provisions of the governing statute, and traditional constitutional limitations upon the power of a federal judge, in order to uphold the absurd.

The proceedings that led to this result were a judicial travesty. I dissent because the institutional reform the District Court has undertaken violates the terms of the governing statute, ignores bedrock limitations on the power of Article III judges, and takes federal courts wildly beyond their institutional capacity.

I

The Prison Litigation Reform Act (PLRA) states that "[p]rospective relief in any civil action with respect to prison conditions shall extend no further than necessary to correct the violation of the Federal right of a particular plaintiff or plaintiffs"; that such relief must be "narrowly drawn, [and] exten[d] no further than necessary to correct the violation of the Federal right"; and that it must be "the least intrusive means necessary to correct the violation of the Federal right." 18 U.S.C. §3626(a)(1)(A). In deciding whether these multiple limitations have been complied with, it is necessary to identify with precision what is the "violation of the Federal right of a particular plaintiff or plaintiffs" that has been alleged. What has been alleged here, and what the injunction issued by the Court is tailored (narrowly or not) to remedy is the running of a prison system with inadequate medical facilities. That may result in the denial of needed medical treatment to "a particular [prisoner] or [prisoners]," thereby violating (according to our cases) his or their Eighth Amendment rights. But the mere existence of the inadequate system does not subject to cruel and unusual punishment the entire prison population in need of medical care, including those who receive it. . . .

. . . [I]t is inconceivable that anything more than a small proportion of prisoners in the plaintiff classes have personally received sufficiently atrocious treatment that their Eighth Amendment right was violated—which, as the Court recognizes, is why the plaintiffs do not premise their claim on "deficiencies in care provided on any one occasion." Rather, the plaintiffs' claim is that they are all part of a medical system so defective that some number of prisoners will inevitably be injured by incompetent medical care, and that this number is sufficiently high so as to render the system, as a whole, unconstitutional.

. . . [T]he PLRA requires plaintiffs to establish that the systemwide injunction entered by the District Court was "narrowly drawn" and "extends no further than necessary" to correct "the violation of the Federal right of a particular plaintiff or plaintiffs." If (as is the case) the only viable constitutional claims consist of individual instances of mistreatment, then a remedy reforming the system as a whole goes far beyond what the statute allows.

It is also worth noting the peculiarity that the vast majority of inmates most generously rewarded by the release order—the 46,000 whose incarceration will be ended—do not form part of any aggrieved class even under the Court's expansive notion of constitutional violation. Most of them will not be prisoners with medical conditions or severe mental illness; and many will undoubtedly be fine physical specimens who have developed intimidating muscles pumping iron in the prison gym.

Even if I accepted the implausible premise that the plaintiffs have established a systemwide violation of the Eighth Amendment, I would dissent from the Court's endorsement of a decrowding order. That order is an example of what has become known as a "structural injunction." As I have previously explained, structural injunctions are radically different from the injunctions traditionally issued by courts of equity, and presumably part of "the judicial Power" conferred on federal courts by Article III:

> "The mandatory injunctions issued upon termination of litigation usually required 'a single simple act.' H. McClintock, Principles of Equity §15, pp. 32-33 (2d ed. 1948). Indeed, there was a 'historical prejudice of the court of chancery against rendering decrees which called for more than a single affirmative act.' *Id.*, §61, at 160. And where specific performance of contracts was sought, it was the categorical rule that no decree would issue that required ongoing supervision. . . . Compliance with these 'single act' mandates could, in addition to being simple, be quick; and once it was achieved the contemnor's relationship with the court came to an end, at least insofar as the subject of the order was concerned. Once the document was turned over or the land conveyed, the litigant's obligation to the court, and the court's coercive power over the litigant, ceased. . . . The court did not engage in any ongoing supervision of the litigant's conduct, nor did its order continue to regulate its behavior." *Mine Workers v. Bagwell*, 512 U.S. 821, 841-842 (1994) (Scalia, J., concurring).

Structural injunctions depart from that historical practice, turning judges into long-term administrators of complex social institutions such as schools, prisons, and police departments. Indeed, they require judges to play a role essentially indistinguishable from the role ordinarily played by executive officials. Today's decision not only affirms the structural injunction but vastly expands its use, by holding that an entire system is unconstitutional because it *may produce* constitutional violations.

The drawbacks of structural injunctions have been described at great length elsewhere. This case illustrates one of their most pernicious aspects: that they force judges to engage in a form of factfinding-as-policymaking that is outside the traditional judicial role. The factfinding judges traditionally engage in involves the determination of past or present facts based (except for a limited set of materials of which courts may take "judicial notice") exclusively upon a closed trial record. That is one reason why a district judge's factual findings are entitled to plain-error review: because having viewed the trial first hand he is in a better position to evaluate the evidence than a judge reviewing a cold record. In a very limited category of cases, judges have also traditionally been called upon to make some predictive judgments: which custody will best serve the interests of the child, for example, or whether a particular one-shot injunction will remedy the plaintiff's grievance. When a judge manages a structural injunction, however, he will inevitably be required to make very broad empirical predictions necessarily based in large part upon policy views—the sort of predictions regularly made by legislators and executive officials, but inappropriate for the Third Branch.

This feature of structural injunctions is superbly illustrated by the District Court's proceeding concerning the decrowding order's effect on public safety. The PLRA requires that, before granting "[p]rospective relief in [a] civil action with respect to prison conditions," a court must "give substantial weight to any adverse impact on public safety or the operation of a criminal justice system caused by the relief." 18 U.S.C. §3626(a)(1)(A). Here, the District Court discharged that requirement by making the "factual finding" that "the state has available methods by which it could readily reduce the prison population to 137.5% design capacity or less without an adverse impact on public safety or the operation of the criminal justice system." It found the evidence "clear" that prison overcrowding would "perpetuate a criminogenic prison system that itself threatens public safety," and volunteered its opinion that "[t]he population could be reduced even further with the reform of California's antiquated sentencing policies and other related changes to the laws." It "reject[ed] the testimony that inmates released early from prison would commit additional new crimes," finding that "shortening the length of stay through earned credits would give inmates incentives to participate in programming designed to lower recidivism," and that "slowing the flow of technical parole violators to prison, thereby substantially reducing the churning of parolees, would by itself improve both the prison and parole systems, and public safety." It found that "the diversion of offenders to community correctional programs has significant beneficial effects on public safety," and that "additional rehabilitative programming would result in a significant population reduction while improving public safety."

The District Court cast these predictions (and the Court today accepts them) as "factual findings," made in reliance on the procession of expert witnesses that testified at trial. Because these "findings" have support in the record, it is difficult to reverse them under a plain-error standard of review. And given that the District Court devoted nearly 10 days of trial and 70 pages of its opinion to this issue, it is difficult to dispute that the District Court has discharged its statutory obligation to give "substantial weight to any adverse impact on public safety."

But the idea that the three District Judges in this case relied solely on the credibility of the testifying expert witnesses is fanciful. *Of course* they were relying largely on their own beliefs about penology and recidivism. And *of course* different district judges, of different policy views, would have "found" that rehabilitation would not work and that releasing prisoners would increase the crime rate. I am not saying that the District Judges rendered their factual findings in bad faith. I am saying that it is impossible for judges to make "factual findings" without inserting their own policy judgments, when the factual findings *are* policy judgments. What occurred here is no more judicial factfinding in the ordinary sense than would be the factual findings that deficit spending will not lower the unemployment rate, or that the continued occupation of Iraq will decrease the risk of terrorism. Yet, because they have been branded "factual findings" entitled to deferential review, the policy preferences of three District Judges now govern the operation of California's penal system.

It is important to recognize that the dressing-up of policy judgments as factual findings is not an error peculiar to this case. It is an unavoidable concomitant of institutional-reform litigation. When a district court issues an injunction, it must make a factual assessment of the anticipated consequences of the injunction. And when the injunction undertakes to restructure a social institution, assessing the factual consequences of the injunction is necessarily the sort of predictive judgment that our system of government allocates to other government officials.

But structural injunctions do not simply invite judges to indulge policy preferences. They invite judges to indulge *incompetent* policy preferences. Three years of law school and familiarity with pertinent Supreme Court precedents give no insight whatsoever into the management of social institutions. Thus, in the proceeding below the District Court determined that constitutionally adequate medical services could be provided if the prison population was 137.5% of design capacity. This was an empirical finding it was utterly unqualified to make. Admittedly, the court did not generate that number entirely on its own; it heard the numbers 130% and 145% bandied about by various witnesses and decided to split the difference. But the ability of judges to spit back or even average-out numbers spoon-fed to them by expert witnesses does not render them competent decisionmakers in areas in which they are otherwise unqualified. . . .

My general concerns associated with judges' running social institutions are magnified when they run prison systems, and doubly magnified when they force prison officials to release convicted criminals. As we have previously recognized:

> "[C]ourts are ill equipped to deal with the increasingly urgent problems of prison administration and reform. . . . Running a prison is an inordinately difficult undertaking that requires expertise, planning, and the commitment of resources, all of which are peculiarly within the province of the legislative and executive branches of government. Prison is, moreover, a task that has been committed to the responsibility of those branches, and separation of powers concerns counsel a policy of judicial restraint. Where a state penal system is involved, federal courts have . . . additional reason to accord deference to the appropriate prison authorities." *Turner v. Safley*, 482 U.S. 78, 84-85 (1987) (internal quotation marks omitted).

These principles apply doubly to a prisoner-release order. . . .

II

The Court's opinion includes a bizarre coda noting that "[t]he State may wish to move for modification of the three-judge court's order to extend the deadline for the required reduction to five years." *Ante,* at 1947. . . . It also invites the District Court to "consider whether it is appropriate to order the State to begin without delay to develop a system to identify prisoners who are unlikely to reoffend," and informs the State that it "should devise systems to select those prisoners least likely to jeopardize public safety." *Ibid.* (What a good idea!)

The legal effect of this passage is unclear—I suspect intentionally so. If it is nothing but a polite remainder to the State and to the District Court that the injunction is subject to modification, then it is entirely unnecessary. . . .

I suspect, however, that this passage is a warning shot across the bow, telling the District Court that it had *better* modify the injunction if the State requests what we invite it to request. Such a warning, if successful, would achieve the benefit of a marginal reduction in the inevitable murders, robberies, and rapes to be committed by the released inmates. But it would achieve that at the expense of intellectual bankruptcy, as the Court's "warning" is entirely alien to ordinary principles of appellate review of injunctions. . . .

Of course what is really happening here is that the Court, overcome by common sense, disapproves of the results reached by the District Court, but cannot remedy them (it thinks) by applying ordinary standards of appellate review. It has therefore selected a solution unknown in our legal system: A deliberately ambiguous set of suggestions on how to modify the injunction, just deferential enough so that it can say with a straight face that it is "affirming," just stern enough to put the District Court on notice that it will likely get reversed if it does not follow them. . . . That we are driven to engage in these extralegal activities should be a sign that the entire project of permitting district courts to run prison systems is misbegotten.

But perhaps I am being too unkind. The Court, or at least a majority of the Court's majority, must be aware that the judges of the District Court are likely to call its bluff, since they know full well it cannot possibly be an abuse of discretion to refuse to accept the State's proposed modifications in an injunction that has just been approved (*affirmed*) in its present form. An injunction, after all, does not have to be perfect; only good enough for government work, which the Court today says this *is*. So perhaps the coda is nothing more than a ceremonial washing of the hands—making it clear for all to see, that if the terrible things sure to happen as a consequence of this outrageous order do happen, they will be none of this Court's responsibility. After all, did we not want, and indeed even suggest, something better?

III

In view of the incoherence of the Eighth Amendment claim at the core of this case, the nonjudicial features of institutional reform litigation that this case exemplifies, and the unique concerns associated with mass prisoner releases, I do not believe this Court can affirm this injunction. . . .

The District Court's order that California release 46,000 prisoners extends "further than necessary to correct the violation of the Federal right of a particular plaintiff or plaintiffs" who have been denied needed medical care. 18 U.S.C. §3626(a)(1)(A). It is accordingly forbidden by the PLRA—besides defying all sound conception of the proper role of judges.

Justice ALITO, with whom THE CHIEF JUSTICE joins, dissenting.
. . . The Constitution does not give federal judges the authority to run state penal systems. Decisions regarding state prisons have profound public safety

and financial implications, and the States are generally free to make these decisions as they choose.

The Eighth Amendment imposes an important—but limited—restraint on state authority in this field. The Eighth Amendment prohibits prison officials from depriving inmates of "the minimal civilized measure of life's necessities." *Rhodes v. Chapman*, 452 U.S. 337, 347 (1981). . . .

In this case, a three-judge court exceeded its authority under the Constitution and the PLRA. The court ordered a radical reduction in the California prison population without finding that the current population level violates the Constitution.

. . . Instead of crafting a remedy to attack the specific constitutional violations that were found—which related solely to prisoners in the two plaintiff classes—the lower court issued a decree that will at best provide only modest help to those prisoners but that is very likely to have a major and deleterious effect on public safety.

The three-judge court ordered the premature release of approximately *46,000 criminals — the equivalent of three Army divisions.*

. . . I would reverse the decision below for three interrelated reasons. First, the three-judge court improperly refused to consider evidence concerning present conditions in the California prison system. Second, the court erred in holding that no remedy short of a massive prisoner release can bring the California system into compliance with the Eighth Amendment. Third, the court gave inadequate weight to the impact of its decree on public safety. . . .

. . . Here, the majority and the court below maintain that no remedy short of a massive release of prisoners from the general prison population can remedy the State's failure to provide constitutionally adequate health care. This argument is implausible on its face and is not supported by the requisite clear and convincing evidence. . . .

I do not dispute that general overcrowding *contributes* to many of the California system's healthcare problems. But it by no means follows that reducing overcrowding is the only or the best or even a particularly good way to alleviate those problems. . . . Although some class members will presumably be among those who are discharged, the decrease in the number of prisoners needing mental health treatment or other forms of extensive medical care will be much smaller than the total number of prisoners released, and thus the release will produce at best only a modest improvement in the burden on the medical care system.

The record bears this out. The Special Master stated dramatically that even releasing 100,000 inmates (two-thirds of the California system's entire inmate population!) would leave the problem of providing mental health treatment "largely unmitigated." Similarly, the Receiver proclaimed that "'those . . . who think that population controls will solve California's prison health care problems . . . are simply wrong.'"

The State proposed several remedies other than a massive release of prisoners, but the three-judge court, seemingly intent on attacking the broader problem of general overcrowding, rejected all of the State's proposals. In doing so, the court made three critical errors.

First, the court did not assess those proposals and other remedies in light of conditions proved to exist at the time the release order was framed. Had more recent evidence been taken into account, a less extreme remedy might have been shown to be sufficient.

Second, the court failed to distinguish between conditions that fall below the level that may be desirable as a matter of public policy and conditions that do not meet the minimum level mandated by the Constitution. To take one example, the court criticized the California system because prison doctors must conduct intake exams in areas separated by folding screens rather than in separate rooms, creating conditions that "do not allow for appropriate confidentiality." *Id.,* at 88a. But the legitimate privacy expectations of inmates are greatly diminished, see *Hudson v. Palmer,* 468 U.S. 517, 525-526 (1984), and this Court has never suggested that the failure to provide private consultation rooms in prisons amounts to cruel and unusual punishment.

Third, the court rejected alternatives that would not have provided "'immediate'" relief. But nothing in the PLRA suggests that public safety may be sacrificed in order to implement an immediate remedy rather than a less dangerous one that requires a more extended but reasonable period of time.

If the three-judge court had not made these errors, it is entirely possible that an adequate but less drastic remedial plan could have been crafted. . . .

. . . Plaintiffs proposed not only a systemwide population cap, but also a lower population cap for inmates in specialized programs. The three-judge court rejected this proposal, and its response exemplified what went wrong in this case. One judge complained that this remedy would be deficient because it would protect only the members of the plaintiff classes. The judge stated:

> "The only thing is we would be protecting the class members. And maybe that's the appropriate thing to do. I mean, that's what this case is about, but it would be . . . difficult for me to say yes, and the hell with everybody else." *Id.,* at 2915:23-2916:2.

Overstepping his authority, the judge was not content to provide relief for the classes of plaintiffs on whose behalf the suit before him was brought. Nor was he content to remedy the only constitutional violations that were proved — which concerned the treatment of the members of those classes. Instead, the judge saw it as his responsibility to attack the general problem of overcrowding.

III

. . . When a trial court selects between the competing views of experts on broad empirical questions such as the efficacy of preventing crime through the incapacitation of convicted criminals, the trial court's choice is very different from a classic finding of fact and is not entitled to the same degree of deference on appeal. . . .

Commenting on the testimony of an expert who stated that he could not be certain about the effect of the massive prisoner discharge on public safety, the three-judge court complained that "[s]uch equivocal testimony is not helpful." *Id.*, at 247a. But testimony pointing out the difficulty of assessing the consequences of this drastic remedy would have been valued by a careful court duly mindful of the overriding need to guard public safety. . . .

The members of the three-judge court and the experts on whom they relied may disagree with key elements of the crime-reduction program that the State of California has pursued for the past few decades, including "the shift to inflexible determinate sentencing and the passage of harsh mandatory minimum and three-strikes laws." And experts such as the Receiver are entitled to take the view that the State should "re-thin[k] the place of incarceration in its criminal justice system." But those controversial opinions on matters of criminal justice policy should not be permitted to override the reasonable policy view that is implicit in the PLRA—that prisoner release orders present an inherent risk to the safety of the public.

. . . I fear that today's decision, like prior prisoner release orders, will lead to a grim roster of victims. I hope that I am wrong.

In a few years, we will see.

d. Theories of Judicial Power Applied to Injunctive Relief

As you read the excerpts from Lon Fuller and Abram Chayes below, consider the following questions: What are the sources for the criteria and judgments used by Fuller and Chayes in the debate over the function and capacities of courts? Fuller relies on a notion of rationality at the core of the judicial process. Is this notion intrinsic to due process? Is it intrinsic to the ideal of a court or to the reality of courts as operated in the contemporary United States? Chayes relies on examples of courts engaged in innovative practices. Do such examples give hope for the capacity of all courts, or do they merely illuminate the abilities of extraordinary judges? Where, if at all, do commitments to democratic participation and accountability to the broad public fit in his scheme?

Lon Fuller, The Forms and Limits of Adjudication
92 Harv. L. Rev. 353 (1978)

Attention is now directed to the question, What kinds of tasks are inherently unsuited to adjudication? The test here will be that used throughout. If a given task is assigned to adjudicative treatment, will it be possible to preserve the meaning of the affected party's participation through proofs and arguments?

[For purposes of addressing the question of limits, t]his section introduces a concept—that of the "polycentric task"—which has been derived from Michael Polanyi's book *The Logic of Liberty* (1951). In approaching that concept it will be well to begin with a few examples.

Some months ago a wealthy lady by the name of Timken died in New York leaving a valuable, but somewhat miscellaneous, collection of paintings to the Metropolitan Museum and the National Gallery "in equal shares," her will indicating no particular apportionment. When the will was probated the judge remarked something to the effect that the parties seemed to be confronted with a real problem. The attorney for one of the museums spoke up and said, "We are good friends. We will work it out somehow or other." What makes this problem of effecting an equal division of the paintings a polycentric task? It lies in the fact that the disposition of any single painting has implications for the proper disposition of every other painting. If it gets the Renoir, the Gallery may be less eager for the Cézanne but all the more eager for the Bellows, etc. If the proper apportionment were set for argument, there would be no clear issue to which either side could direct its proofs and contentions. Any judge assigned to hear such an argument would be tempted to assume the role of mediator or to adopt the classical solution: Let the older brother (here the Metropolitan) divide the estate into what he regards as equal shares, let the younger brother (the National Gallery) take his pick.

As a second illustration suppose in a socialist regime it were decided to have all wages and prices set by courts which would proceed after the usual forms of adjudication. It is, I assume, obvious that here is a task that could not successfully be undertaken by the adjudicative method. . . .

We may visualize this kind of situation by thinking of a spider web. A pull on one strand will distribute tensions after a complicated pattern throughout the web as a whole. Doubling the original pull will, in all likelihood, not simply double each of the resulting tensions but will create a different complicated pattern of tensions. This would certainly occur, for example, if the doubled pull caused one or more of the weaker strands to snap. This is a "polycentric" situation because it is "many centered"—each crossing of strands is a distinct center for distributing tensions. . . .

It should be carefully noted that a multiplicity of affected persons is not an invariable characteristic of polycentric problems. This is sufficiently illustrated in the case of Mrs. Timken's will. That case also illustrated the fact that rapid changes with time are not an invariable characteristic of such problems. On the other hand, in practice polycentric problems of possible concern to adjudication will normally involve many affected parties and a somewhat fluid state of affairs. Indeed, the last characteristic follows from the simple fact that the more interacting centers there are, the more the likelihood that one of them will be affected by a change in circumstances, and, if the situation is polycentric, this change will communicate itself after a complex pattern to other centers. . . .

Now, if it is important to see clearly what a polycentric problem is, it is equally important to realize that the distinction involved is often a matter of degree. There are polycentric elements in almost all problems submitted to adjudication. A decision may act as a precedent, often an awkward one, in some situation not foreseen by the arbiter. Again, suppose a court in a suit between one litigant and a railway holds that it is an act of negligence for the railway not to construct an underpass at a particular crossing. There may be nothing to distinguish this crossing from other crossings on the line. As a matter of statistical probability it may be clear that constructing underpasses along the whole line would cost more lives (through accidents in blasting, for example) than would be lost if the only safety measure were the familiar "Stop, Look & Listen" sign. If so, then what seems to be a decision simply declaring the rights and duties of two parties is in fact an inept solution for a polycentric problem, some elements of which cannot be brought before the court in a simple suit by one injured party against a defendant railway. In lesser measure, concealed polycentric elements are probably present in almost all problems resolved by adjudication. It is not, then, a question of distinguishing black from white. It is a question of knowing when the polycentric elements have become so significant and predominant that the proper limits of adjudication have been reached. . . .

The final question to be addressed is this: When an attempt is made to deal by adjudicative forms with a problem that is essentially polycentric, what happens? As I see it, three things can happen, sometimes all at once. *First*, the adjudicative solution may fail. Unexpected repercussions make the decision unworkable; it is ignored or modified, sometimes repeatedly. *Second*, the purported arbiter ignores judicial proprieties—he "tries out" various solutions in posthearing conferences, consults parties not represented at the hearings, guesses at facts not proved and not properly matters for anything like judicial notice. *Third*, instead of accommodating his procedures to the nature of the problem he confronts, he may reformulate the problem so as to make it amenable to solution through adjudicative procedures.

Only the last of these needs illustration. Suppose it is agreed that an employer's control over promotions shall be subject to review through arbitration. Now obviously an arbiter cannot decide whether when Jones was made a Machinist Class A there was someone else more deserving in the plant, or whether, in view of Jones' age, it would have been better to put him in another job with comparable pay. This is the kind of allocative problem for which adjudication is utterly unsuited. There are, however, two ways of obtaining a workable control over promotions through arbitration. One of these is through the posting of jobs; when a job is vacant, interested parties may apply for promotion into it. At the hearing, only those who have made application are entitled to be considered, and of course only the posted job is in issue. Here the problem is simplified in advance to the point where it can be arbitrated, though not without difficulty, particularly in the form of endless arguments as to whether there was in fact a vacancy that ought to have been posted, and whether a claimant filed his application on time and in the proper form, etc. The other way of accommodating the problem to arbitration is for the arbiter to determine not who should be promoted but who *has* been promoted. That is, the contract contains certain "job descriptions" with the appropriate rate for each; the claimant asserts that he is in fact doing the work of a Machinist A, though he is still assigned the pay and title of a Machinist B. The controversy has two parties—the company and the claimant as represented by the union—and a single factual issue, is the claimant in fact doing the work of a Machinist A?

In practice the procedure of applying for appointment to posted jobs will normally be prescribed in the contract itself, so that the terms of the agreement keep the arbitrator's function with respect to promotions within manageable limits. The other method of making feasible a control of promotions through arbitration will normally result from the arbitrator's own perception of the limitations of his role. The contract may simply contain a schedule of job rates and job classifications and a general clause stating that "discharges, promotions, and layoffs shall be subject to the grievance procedure." If the arbitrator were to construe such a contract to give him general supervision over promotions, he would embark himself upon managerial tasks wholly unsuited to solution by any arbitrative procedure. An instinct toward preserving the integrity of his role will move him, therefore, to construe the contract in the manner already indicated, so that he avoids any responsibility with respect to the assignment of duties and merely decides whether the duties actually assigned make appropriate the classification assigned by the company to the complaining employee. . . .

In closing this discussion of polycentricity, it will be well to caution against two possible misunderstandings. The suggestion that polycentric problems are often solved by a kind of "managerial intuition" should not be taken to imply that it is an invariable characteristic of polycentric problems that they resist rational solution. There are rational principles for building bridges of structural steel. But there is no rational principle which states, for example, that the angle between girder A and girder B must always be 45 degrees. This depends on the bridge as a whole. One cannot construct a bridge by conducting successive separate arguments concerning the proper angle for every pair of intersecting girders. One must deal with the whole structure.

Finally, the fact that an adjudicative decision affects and enters into a polycentric relationship does not of itself mean that the adjudicative tribunal is moving out of its proper sphere. On the contrary, there is no better illustration of a polycentric relationship than an economic market, and yet the laying down of rules that will make a market function properly is one for which adjudication is generally well suited. The working out of our common law of contracts case by case has proceeded through adjudication, yet the basic principle underlying the rules thus developed is that they should promote the free exchange of goods in a polycentric market. The court gets into difficulty, not when it lays down rules about contracting, but when it attempts to write contracts. . . .

Abram Chayes, The Role of the Judge in Public Law Litigation
89 Harv. L. Rev. 1281 (1976)

. . . We are witnessing the emergence of a new model of civil litigation and, I believe, our traditional conception of adjudication and the assumptions upon which it is based provide an increasingly unhelpful, indeed misleading framework for assessing either the workability or the legitimacy of the roles of judge and court within this model.

In our received tradition, the lawsuit is a vehicle for settling disputes between private parties about private rights. The defining features of this conception of civil adjudication are:

1. The lawsuit is *bipolar*. Litigation is organized as a contest between two individuals or at least two unitary interests, diametrically opposed, to be decided on a winner-take-all basis.
2. Litigation is *retrospective*. The controversy is about an identified set of completed events: whether they occurred, and if so with what consequences for the legal relations of the parties.
3. *Right and remedy are interdependent.* The scope of the relief is derived more or less logically from the substantive violation under the general theory that the plaintiff will get compensation measured by the harm caused by the defendant's breach of duty — in contract by giving plaintiff the money he would have had absent the breach; in tort by paying the value of the damage caused.
4. The lawsuit is a *self-contained* episode. The impact of the judgment is confined to the parties. If plaintiff prevails there is a simple compensatory transfer, usually of money, but occasionally the return of a thing or the performance of a definite act. If defendant prevails, a loss lies where it has fallen. In either case, entry of judgment ends the court's involvement.
5. The process is *party-initiated* and *party-controlled*. The case is organized and the issues defined by exchanges between the parties. Responsibility for fact development is theirs. The trial judge is a neutral arbiter of their interactions who decides questions of law only if they are put in issue by an appropriate move of a party. . . .

Whatever its historical validity, the traditional model is clearly invalid as a description of much current civil litigation in the federal district courts. Perhaps the dominating characteristic of modern federal litigation is that lawsuits do not arise out of disputes between private parties about private rights. Instead, the object of litigation is the vindication of constitutional or statutory policies. The shift in the legal basis of the lawsuit explains many, but not all, facets of what is going on "in fact" in federal trial courts. For this reason, although the label is not wholly satisfactory, I shall call the emerging model "public law litigation."

The characteristic features of the public law model are very different from those of the traditional model. The party structure is sprawling and amorphous, subject to change over the course of the litigation. The traditional adversary relationship is suffused and intermixed with negotiating and mediating processes at every point. The judge is the dominant figure in organizing and guiding the case, and he draws for support not only on the parties and their counsel, but on a wide range of outsiders—masters, experts, and oversight personnel. Most important, the trial judge has increasingly become the creator and manager of complex forms of ongoing relief, which have widespread effects on persons not before the court and require the judge's continuing involvement in administration and implementation. School desegregation, employment discrimination, and prisoners' or inmates' rights cases come readily to mind as avatars of this new form of litigation. But it would be mistaken to suppose that it is confined to these areas. Antitrust, securities fraud and other aspects of the conduct of corporate business, bankruptcy and reorganizations, union governance, consumer fraud, housing discrimination, electoral reapportionment, environmental management—cases in all these fields display in varying degrees the features of public law litigation. . . .

II. The Public Law Litigation Model

Sometime after 1875, the private law theory of civil adjudication became increasingly precarious in the face of a growing body of legislation designed explicitly to modify and regulate basic social and economic arrangements. At the same time, the scientific and deductive character of judicial lawmaking came under attack, as the political consequences of judicial review of that legislation became urgent.

These developments are well known and have become an accepted part of our political and intellectual history. I want to address in somewhat greater detail the correlative changes that have occurred in the procedural structure of the lawsuit. Most discussion of these procedural developments, while recognizing that change has been far-reaching, proceeds on the assumption that the new devices are no more than piecemeal "reforms" aimed at improving the functional characteristics or the efficacy of litigation conducted essentially in the traditional mode. I suggest, however, that these developments are interrelated as members of a recognizable, if changing, system and that taken together they display a new model of judicial action and the judicial role, both of which depart sharply from received conceptions.

A. The Demise of Bipolar Structure

Joinder of parties, which was strictly limited at common law, was very liberalized under the codes to conform with the approach of equity calling for joinder of all parties having an "interest" in the controversy. The codes, however, did not at first produce much freedom of joinder. Instead, the courts defined the concept of "interest" narrowly to exclude those without an independent legal right to the remedy to be given in the main dispute. . . .

. . . Today, the Supreme Court is struggling manfully, but with question-able success, to establish a formula for delimiting who may sue that stops short of "anybody who might be significantly affected by the situation he seeks to litigate."

"Anybody" — even "almost anybody" — can be a lot of people, particularly where the matters in issue are not relatively individualized private transactions or encounters. Thus, the stage is set for the class action. . . . Whatever the resolution of the current controversies surrounding class actions, I think it unlikely that the class action will ever be taught to behave in accordance with the precepts of the traditional model of adjudication. The class suit is a reflection of our growing awareness that a host of important public and private interactions — perhaps the most important in defining the conditions and opportunities of life for most people — are conducted on a routine or bureaucratized basis and can no longer be visualized as bilateral transactions between private individuals. From another angle, the class action responds to the proliferation of more or less well-organized groups in our society and the tendency to perceive interests as group interests, at least in very important aspects. . . .

B. The Triumph of Equity

One of the most striking procedural developments of this century is the increasing importance of equitable relief. It is perhaps too soon to reverse the traditional maxim to read that money damages will be awarded only when no suitable form of specific relief can be devised. But surely, the old sense of equitable remedies as "extraordinary" has faded.

I am not concerned here with specific performance — the compelled transfer of a piece of land or a unique thing. This remedy is structurally little different from traditional money-damages. It is a one-time, one-way transfer requiring for its enforcement no continuing involvement of the court. Injunctive relief, however, is different in kind, even when it takes the form of a simple negative order. Such an order is a presently operative prohibition, enforceable by contempt, and it is a much greater constraint on activity than the risk of future liability implicit in the damage remedy. Moreover, the injunction is continuing. Over time, the parties may resort to the court for enforcement or modification of the original order in light of changing circumstances. Finally, by issuing the injunction, the court takes public responsibility for any consequences of its decree that may adversely affect strangers to the action.

Beyond these differences, the prospective character of the relief introduces large elements of contingency and prediction into the proceedings. Instead of a dispute retrospectively oriented toward the consequences of a closed set of events, the court has a controversy about future probabilities. Equitable doctrine, naturally enough, given the intrusiveness of the injunction and the contingent nature of the harm, calls for a balancing of the interests of the parties. And if the immediate parties' interests were to be weighed and evaluated, it was not too difficult to proceed to a consideration of other interests that might be affected by the order. . . .

c. The Changing Character of Factfinding

The traditional model of adjudication was primarily concerned with assessing the consequences for the parties of specific past instances of conduct. This retrospective orientation is often inapposite in public law litigation, where the lawsuit generally seeks to enjoin future or threatened action, or to modify a course of conduct presently in train or a condition presently existing. In the former situation the question whether threatened action will materialize, in what circumstances, and with what consequences can, in the nature of things, be answered only by an educated guess. In the latter case, the inquiry is only secondarily concerned with how the condition came about, and even less with the subjective attitudes of the actors, since positive regulatory goals are ordinarily defined without reference to such matters. Indeed, in dealing with the actions of large political or corporate aggregates, notions of will, intention, or fault increasingly become only metaphors.

In the remedial phases of public law litigation, factfinding is even more clearly prospective. . . . [T]he contours of relief are not derived logically from the substantive wrong adjudged, as in the traditional model. The elaboration of a decree is largely a discretionary process within which the trial judge is called upon to assess and appraise the consequences of alternative programs that might correct the substantive fault. In both the liability and remedial phases, the relevant inquiry is largely the same: How can the policies of a public law best be served in a concrete case?

In public law litigation, then, factfinding is principally concerned with "legislative" rather than "adjudicative" fact. And "fact evaluation" is perhaps a more accurate term than "factfinding." The whole process begins to look like the traditional description of legislation: Attention is drawn to a "mischief," existing or threatened, and the activity of the parties and court is directed to the development of on-going measures designed to cure that mischief. Indeed, if, as is often the case, the decree sets up an affirmative regime governing the activities in controversy for the indefinite future and having binding force for persons within its ambit, then it is not very much of a stretch to see it as, pro tanto, a legislative act. . . .

The courts, it seems, continue to rely primarily on the litigants to produce and develop factual materials, but a number of factors make it impossible to leave the organization of the trial exclusively in their hands. With the diffusion of the party structure, fact issues are no longer sharply drawn in a confrontation between two adversaries, one asserting the affirmative and the other the negative. The litigation is often extraordinarily complex and extended in time, with a continuous and intricate interplay between factual and legal elements. It is hardly feasible and, absent a jury, unnecessary to set aside a contiguous block of time for a "trial stage" at which all significant factual issues will be presented.

The scope of the fact investigation and the sheer volume of factual material that can be exhumed by the discovery process pose enormous problems of organization and assimilation. All these factors thrust the trial judge into an active role in shaping, organizing and facilitating the litigation. We may not yet have reached the investigative judge of the continental systems, but we have left the passive arbiter of the traditional model a long way behind.

d. The Decree

The centerpiece of the emerging public law model is the decree. It differs in almost every relevant characteristic from relief in the traditional model of adjudication, not the least in that it is the centerpiece. The decree seeks to adjust future behavior, not to compensate for past wrong. It is deliberately fashioned rather than logically deduced from the nature of the legal harm suffered. It provides for a complex, on-going regime of performance rather than a simple, one-shot, one-way transfer. Finally, it prolongs and deepens, rather than terminates, the court's involvement with the dispute. . . .

I suggested above that a judicial decree establishing an ongoing regime of conduct is pro tanto a legislative act. But in actively shaping and monitoring the decree, mediating between the parties, developing his own sources of expertise and information, the trial judge has passed beyond even the role of legislator and has become a policy planner and manager.

e. A Morphology of Public Law Litigation

The public law litigation model portrayed in this paper reverses many of the crucial characteristics and assumptions of the traditional concept of adjudication:

1. The scope of the lawsuit is not exogenously given but is shaped primarily by the court and parties.
2. The party structure is not rigidly bilateral but sprawling and amorphous.
3. The fact inquiry is not historical and adjudicative but predictive and legislative.
4. Relief is not conceived as compensation for past wrong in a form logically derived from the substantive liability and confined in its impact to the immediate parties; instead, it is forward looking, fashioned ad hoc on flexible and broadly remedial lines, often having important consequences for many persons including absentees.
5. The remedy is not imposed but negotiated.
6. The decree does not terminate judicial involvement in the affair: its administration requires the continuing participation of the court.
7. The judge is not passive, his function limited to analysis and statement of governing rules; he is active, with responsibility not only for credible fact evaluation but for organizing and shaping the litigation to ensure a just and viable outcome.

8. The subject matter of the lawsuit is not a dispute between private individuals about private rights, but a grievance about the operation of public policy.

In fact, one might say that, from the perspective of the traditional model, the proceeding is recognizable as a lawsuit only because it takes place in a courtroom before an official called a judge. But that is surely too sensational in tone. All of the procedural mechanisms outlined above were historically familiar in equity practice. It is not surprising that they should be adopted and strengthened as the importance of equity has grown in modern times. . . .

IV. SOME THOUGHTS ON LEGITIMACY

. . . As the traditional model has been displaced in recent years, . . . questions of judicial legitimacy and accountability have reasserted themselves. . . .

In my view, judicial action only achieves such legitimacy by responding to, indeed by stirring, the deep and durable demand for justice in our society. I confess some difficulty in seeing how this is to be accomplished by erecting the barriers of the traditional conception to turn aside, for example, attacks on exclusionary zoning and police violence, two of the ugliest remaining manifestations of official racism in American life. In practice, if not in words, the American legal tradition has always acknowledged the importance of substantive results for the legitimacy and accountability of judicial action. . . .

PRACTICE EXERCISE NO. 3: EQUITABLE RELIEF IN *CARPENTER* AND *WARNER*

Equitable remedies, including injunctions and declaratory relief, combine with money damages to create the range of possible remedies available in a lawsuit. How does a plaintiff come to know what relief to seek? It helps to consult a lawyer to learn about what relief might be available and in what scope. The lawyer, in turn, will investigate relevant case law, assess probabilities of success in the litigation, and estimate the costs of litigation. But even before this kind of investigation, the lawyer's counsel about the contrasts between equitable and damage remedies can help a client clarify goals and choices. It is this kind of advice that you should try to develop in this exercise in the context of two situations, both of which became real cases. These two cases will recur throughout this book to show unfolding stages of litigation and decision points for lawyers and clients. As you read the following descriptions, keep in mind the differences between the types of final relief that may be sought in each case. Imagine that the plaintiff(s) in each case have asked you what kind of relief they could obtain if they prevail in their lawsuits. What would you tell them?

1. The *Carpenter* Case: Nancy Carpenter wants to file a suit in Massachusetts following the death of her husband, Charles Carpenter, who was a passenger in a Jeep CJ-7. Randall Dee was driving the jeep at the time of the fatal accident. Dee allegedly lost control of the jeep, and it rolled over, pinning Charles Carpenter under the vehicle and killing him. Dee could have been acting recklessly in at least the following acts and omissions: speeding, failing to stop at an intersection, and modifying the jeep with the use of a suspension lift kit and hugely oversized tires. At the time of the incident, the jeep was owned by Twyla Burrell, the ex-girlfriend of Randall Dee. Burrell maintained a minimum liability insurance policy on the jeep, worth a total of $10,000. You have not yet had the jeep inspected.

Apparently, Randall Dee is not a wealthy man. He is unmarried and lives with his brother in a house they bought from the estate of their deceased father. Randall Dee's interest in the home may be his only substantial asset.

2. The *Warner* Case: Jacob Warner and William Moore want to file a suit against the City of New York and others. Warner and Moore were detained for a period of time by New York City Police, and were patted down in what is known as a stop and frisk. Warner, Moore, and many other persons of color, were stopped and searched by City Police not because of any criminal wrongdoing, but rather because of their race. The lawsuit will pursue the theory that the City adopted and implemented this stop-and-frisk policy, and that that policy violates several laws, including the Fourth Amendment's prohibition on unreasonable search and seizure.

Given their claims, what would you tell each client about potential equitable relief? Assume that the Federal Rules of Civil Procedure or identical state rules apply; you will want to re-read Fed. R. Civ. P. 65. What kinds of injunctions could be available — and how would they redress the plaintiffs' injuries? Is there any way to indicate that monetary damages would be inadequate, and that therefore equitable relief would be in order?

e. Enforcement of Equitable Relief

Sometimes described as "the least dangerous branch," courts lack police or other direct resources to ensure enforcement of their rulings. Thus, even when a plaintiff wins and a court renders a final judgment, the dispute may not be over. First, the claimant needs a document, which is entitled a judgment, Fed. R. Civ. P. 58. *See also* Fed. R. Civ. P. 54(a) ("judgment" in federal court applies to decrees including equitable decrees). Executing or enforcing that judgment, when the defendant does not comply voluntarily, can lead to further proceedings. Under Fed. R. Civ. P. 70, the court can enforce some equitable decrees by appointing a person to engage in the required behavior (such as conveying title to property) at the cost of the disobedient party.

If the recalcitrant defendant in a civil proceeding fails to comply with an equitable order, the conduct could lead to civil or even criminal contempt proceedings. A civil contempt proceeding takes one of two forms. First, an action by the party who has suffered provable damages as a result of the other party's contumacious conduct may recover those damages in an action that is referred to as a civil compensatory contempt action. In the second form, referred to as civil coercive contempt action, the party who is engaged in the contumacious conduct is placed in jail (or faces some similar imposition) until they comply. Both of these forms of civil contempt actions would be conducted pursuant to the Federal Rules of Civil Procedure.

If the court wishes to punish a contemnor for their conduct, the judge must instead follow the basic rules of criminal procedure, including a requirement of proof beyond a reasonable doubt. The punishment could be as modest as a $100 fine or as severe as a lengthy jail term, but the proceeding will still fall within the category of criminal contempt, thereby triggering the constitutional protections due criminal defendants. Criminal contempt differs from civil compensatory contempt because the former is prosecuted by the state (not a party). And criminal contempt differs from civil coercive contempt because, with criminal contempt, the punishment is not optional; by contrast, someone facing civil coercive contempt is said to have the "keys to the jail" in their pocket—which is to say that they can avoid any punishment by complying with the court order.

2. Declaratory Relief

Sometimes, the relief a party wants most is a clarification of the law as applied to particular facts. For example, an investor may be reluctant to finance an entrepreneur without a clear announcement that the proposed enterprise will breach no patents owned by someone else; or the administrator of a new governmental task force may want a declaratory judgment that the meetings will be held in private before proceeding with the risk of litigation over this issue. Congress has empowered courts to issue clarifications, or declaratory judgments, under the Declaratory Judgment Act, 28 U.S.C. §§ 2201 and 2202, and most states have similar legislation authorizing suits that permit parties to obtain a declaration of rights. Also, a request for a declaratory judgment may be coupled with a request for other relief, including damages or an injunction. The difficulty posed by declaratory relief on its own arises from the constitutional requirement that courts refrain from acting in the absence of a concrete, live controversy; Article III of the Constitution limits federal courts to considering only actual cases or controversies, rather than hypothetical issues.

3. Damages

Stemming from law rather than equity, the remedy of money damages poses often difficult questions of valuation. How much money does a specific legal violation warrant? The substantive law governing contracts, torts, antitrust, and other matters will give considerable direction to a court about the measurement of damages in terms of compensation, replacement value, expectation interests, and the like. More ambiguity arises in the context of efforts to enforce constitutional rights since the U.S. Constitution itself gives no indication about how to measure monetary damages. Indeed, the very procedural predicate for a suit for monetary damages under the U.S. Constitution stems from a federal statute, 42 U.S.C. § 1983, authorizing suits by individuals against every person acting under the color of law who deprives an individual of "rights, privileges or immunities secured by the Constitution and laws," leaving courts to determine the measurement of damages to be awarded for such deprivations unless injunctive relief is granted instead.

a. Nominal Damages

The following case considers the measurement of monetary damages in light of a prior precedent holding that public school officials cannot suspend enrolled students without first holding a due process hearing. *Goss v. Lopez*, 419 U.S. 565 (1975). What, if any, monetary damages should a public school student receive if suspended without a prior hearing?

Carey v. Piphus
435 U.S. 247 (1978)

Justice POWELL delivered the opinion of the Court:

In this case, brought under 42 U.S.C. §1983, we consider the elements and prerequisites for recovery of damages by students who were suspended from public elementary and secondary schools without procedural due process. The Court of Appeals for the Seventh Circuit held that the students are entitled to recover substantial nonpunitive damages even if their suspensions were justified, and even if they do not prove that any other actual injury was caused by the denial of procedural due process. We disagree, and hold that in the absence of proof of actual injury, the students are entitled to recover only nominal damages.

I

Respondent Jarius Piphus was a freshman at Chicago Vocational High School during the 1973-1974 school year. On January 23, 1974, during school hours, the school principal saw Piphus and another student standing outdoors on school property passing back and forth what the principal described as an irregularly shaped cigarette. The principal approached the students unnoticed and smelled what he believed was the strong odor of burning marihuana. He also saw Piphus try to pass a packet of cigarette papers to the other student. When the students became aware of the principal's presence, they threw the cigarette into a nearby hedge.

The principal took the students to the school's disciplinary office and directed the assistant principal to impose the "usual" 20-day suspension for violation of the school rule against the use of drugs. The students protested that they had not been smoking marihuana, but to no avail. Piphus was allowed to remain at school, although not in class, for the remainder of the school day while the assistant principal tried, without success, to reach his mother. . . .

A suspension notice was sent to Piphus' mother, and a few days later two meetings were arranged among Piphus, his mother, his sister, school officials, and representatives from a legal aid clinic. The purpose of the meetings was not to determine whether Piphus had been smoking marihuana, but rather to explain the reasons for the suspension. Following an unfruitful exchange of views, Piphus and his mother, as guardian ad litem, filed suit against petitioners in Federal District Court under 42 U.S.C. §1983 and its jurisdictional counterpart, 28 U.S.C. §1343, charging that Piphus had been suspended without due process of law in violation of the Fourteenth Amendment. The complaint sought declaratory and injunctive relief, together with actual and punitive damages in the amount of $3,000. Piphus was readmitted to school under a temporary restraining order after eight days of his suspension.

Respondent Silas Brisco was in the sixth grade at Clara Barton Elementary School in Chicago during the 1973-1974 school year. On September 11, 1973, Brisco came to school wearing one small earring. The previous school year the school principal had issued a rule against the wearing of earrings by male students because he believed that this practice denoted membership in certain street gangs and increased the likelihood that gang members would terrorize other students. Brisco was reminded of this rule, but he refused to remove the earring, asserting that it was a symbol of black pride, not of gang membership.

The assistant principal talked to Brisco's mother, advising her that her son would be suspended for 20 days if he did not remove the earring. Brisco's mother supported her son's position, and a 20-day suspension was imposed. Brisco and his mother, as guardian ad litem, filed suit in Federal District Court under 42 U.S.C. §1983 and 28 U.S.C. §1343, charging that Brisco had been suspended without due process of law in violation of the Fourteenth Amendment. The complaint sought declaratory and injunctive relief, together with actual and punitive damages in the amount of $5,000. Brisco was readmitted to school during the pendency of proceedings for a preliminary injunction after 17 days of his suspension.

Piphus' and Brisco's cases were consolidated for trial and submitted on stipulated records. The District Court held that both students had been suspended without procedural due process. It also held that petitioners were not entitled to qualified immunity from damages under the second branch of *Wood v. Strickland*, 420 U.S. 308 (1975), because they "should have known that a lengthy suspension without any adjudicative hearing of any type" would violate procedural due process. . . . Despite these holdings, the District Court declined to award damages because: "Plaintiffs put no evidence in the record to qualify their damages, and the record is completely devoid of any evidence which could even form the basis of a speculative inference measuring the extent of their injuries. Plaintiffs' claims for damages therefore fail for complete lack of proof."

The court also stated that the students were entitled to declaratory relief and to deletion of the suspensions from their school records, but for reasons that are not apparent the court failed to enter an order to that effect. Instead, it simply dismissed the complaints. No finding was made as to whether respondents would have been suspended if they had received procedural due process.

On respondents' appeal, the Court of Appeals reversed and remanded. It first held that the District Court erred in not granting declaratory and injunctive relief. It also held that the District Court should have considered evidence submitted by respondents after judgment that tended to prove the pecuniary value of each day of school that they missed while suspended. The court said, however, that respondents would not be entitled to recover damages representing the value of missed school time if petitioners showed on remand "that there was just cause for the suspension[s] and that therefore [respondents] would have been suspended even if a proper hearing had been held."

Finally, the Court of Appeals held that even if the District Court found on remand that respondents' suspensions were justified, they would be entitled to recover substantial "nonpunitive" damages simply because they had been denied procedural due process. *Id.*, at 31. Relying on its earlier decision in *Hostrop v. Board of Junior College Dist. No. 515*, 523 F.2d 569 (7th Cir. 1975), *cert. denied*, 425 U.S. 963 (1976), the court stated that such damages should be awarded "even if, as in the case at bar, there is no proof of individualized injury to the plaintiff, such as mental distress. . . ." 545 F.2d, at 31. We granted certiorari to consider whether, in an action under §1983 for the deprivation of procedural due process, a plaintiff must prove that he actually was injured by the deprivation before he may recover substantial "nonpunitive" damages. 430 U.S. 964 (1977).

II

Title 42 U.S.C. §1983, Rev. Stat. §1979, derived from §1 of the Civil Rights Act of 1871, 17 Stat. 13, provides:

> Every person who, under color of any statute, ordinance, regulation, custom, or usage, of any State or Territory, subjects, or causes to be subjected, any citizen of the United States or other person within the jurisdiction thereof to the deprivation of any rights, privileges, or immunities secured by the Constitution and laws, shall be liable to the party injured in an action at law, suit in equity, or other proper proceeding for redress.

The legislative history of §1983, elsewhere detailed, *e.g.*, *Monroe v. Pape*, 365 U.S. 167, 172-183 (1961); *id.*, at 225-234 (Frankfurter, J., dissenting in part), demonstrates that it was intended to "[create] a species of tort liability" in favor of persons who are deprived of "rights, privileges, or immunities secured" to them by the Constitution.

Petitioners contend that the elements and prerequisites for recovery of damages under this "species of tort liability" should parallel those for recovery of damages under the common law of torts. In particular, they urge that the purpose of an award of damages under §1983 should be to compensate persons for injuries that are caused by the deprivation of constitutional rights; and, further, that plaintiffs should be required to prove not only that their rights were violated, but also that injury was caused by the violation, in order to recover substantial damages. Unless respondents prove that they actually were injured by the deprivation of procedural due process, petitioners argue, they are entitled at most to nominal damages.

Respondents seem to make two different arguments in support of the holding below. First, they contend that substantial damages should be awarded under §1983 for the deprivation of a constitutional right whether or not any injury was caused by the deprivation. This, they say, is appropriate both because constitutional rights are valuable in and of themselves, and because of the need to deter violations of constitutional rights. Respondents believe that this view reflects accurately that of the Congress that enacted §1983. Second, respondents argue that even if the purpose of a §1983 damages award is, as petitioners contend, primarily to compensate persons for injuries that are caused by the deprivation of constitutional rights, every deprivation of procedural due process may be presumed to cause some injury. This presumption, they say, should relieve them from the necessity of proving that injury actually was caused.

A

Insofar as petitioners contend that the basic purpose of a §1983 damages award should be to compensate persons for injuries caused by the deprivation of constitutional rights, they have the better of the argument. Rights, constitutional and otherwise, do not exist in a vacuum. Their purpose is to protect persons from injuries to particular interests, and their contours are shaped by the interests they protect. . . .

The Members of the Congress that enacted §1983 did not address directly the question of damages, but the principle that damages are designed to compensate persons for injuries caused by the deprivation of rights hardly could have been foreign to the many lawyers in Congress in 1871. Two other sections of the Civil Rights Act of 1871 appear to incorporate this principle, and no reason suggests itself for reading §1983 differently. To the extent that Congress intended that awards under §1983 should deter the deprivation of constitutional rights, there is no evidence that it meant to establish a deterrent more formidable than that inherent in the award of compensatory damages.[10]

_____

10. This is not to say that exemplary or punitive damages might not be awarded in a proper case under §1983 with the specific purpose of deterring or punishing violations of constitutional rights. [The Court cited several lower court decisions upholding punitive awards in §1983 cases.] Although we imply no approval or disapproval of any of these cases, we note that there is no basis for such an award in this case. The District Court specifically found that petitioners did not act with malicious intention to deprive respondents of their rights or to do them other injury, and the Court of Appeals approved only the award of "non-punitive" damages. We also note that the potential for liability of §1983 defendants for attorney's fees, see Civil Rights Attorney's Fees Awards Act of 1976, 42 U.S.C. §1988, provides additional—and by no means inconsequential—assurance that agents of the State will not deliberately ignore due process rights.

B

It is less difficult to conclude that damages awards under §1983 should be governed by the principle of compensation than it is to apply this principle to concrete cases. But over the centuries the common law of torts has developed a set of rules to implement the principle that a person should be compensated fairly for injuries caused by the violation of his legal rights. These rules, defining the elements of damages and the prerequisites for their recovery, provide the appropriate starting point for the inquiry under §1983 as well.

It is not clear, however, that common-law tort rules of damages will provide a complete solution to the damages issue in every §1983 case. In some cases, the interests protected by a particular branch of the common law of torts may parallel closely the interests protected by a particular constitutional right. In such cases, it may be appropriate to apply the tort rules of damages directly to the §1983 action. In other cases, the interests protected by a particular constitutional right may not also be protected by an analogous branch of the common law torts. In those cases, the task will be the more difficult one of adapting common-law rules of damages to provide fair compensation for injuries caused by the deprivation of a constitutional right.

Although this task of adaptation will be one of some delicacy—as this case demonstrates—it must be undertaken. The purpose of §1983 would be defeated if injuries caused by the deprivation of constitutional rights went uncompensated simply because the common law does not recognize an analogous cause of action. . . .

C

The Due Process Clause of the Fourteenth Amendment provides: "[N]or shall any State deprive any person of life, liberty, or property, without due process of law." This Clause "raises no impenetrable barrier to the taking of a person's possessions," or liberty, or life. *Fuentes v. Shevin*, 407 U.S. 67, 81 (1972). Procedural due process rules are meant to protect persons not from the deprivation, but from the mistaken or unjustified deprivation of life, liberty, or property. Thus, in deciding what process constitutionally is due in various contexts, the Court repeatedly has emphasized that "procedural due process rules are shaped by the risk of error inherent in the truth-finding process."

In this case, the Court of Appeals held that if petitioners can prove on remand that "[respondents] would have been suspended even if a proper hearing had been held," 545 F.2d, at 32, then respondents will not be entitled to recover damages to compensate them for injuries caused by the suspensions. The court thought that in such a case, the failure to accord procedural due process could not properly be viewed as the cause of the suspensions. The court suggested that in such circumstances, an award of damages for injuries caused by the suspensions would constitute a windfall, rather than compensation, to respondents.

545 F.2d at 32. We do not understand the parties to disagree with this conclusion. Nor do we.

The parties do disagree as to the further holding of the Court of Appeals that respondents are entitled to recover substantial — although unspecified — damages to compensate them for "the injury which is 'inherent in the nature of the wrong,'" 545 F.2d, at 31, even if their suspensions were justified and even if they fail to prove that the denial of procedural due process actually caused them some real, if intangible, injury. Respondents, elaborating on this theme, submit that the holding is correct because injury fairly may be "presumed" to flow from every denial of procedural due process. Their argument is that in addition to protecting against unjustified deprivations, the Due Process Clause also guarantees the "feeling of just treatment" by the government. *Anti-Fascist Committee v. McGrath*, 341 U.S.123, 162 (1951) (Frankfurter, J., concurring). They contend that the deprivation of protected interests without procedural due process, even where the premise for the deprivation is not erroneous, inevitably arouses strong feelings of mental and emotional distress in the individual who is denied this "feeling of just treatment." They analogize their case to that of defamation per se, in which "the plaintiff is relieved from the necessity of producing any proof whatsoever that he has been injured" in order to recover substantial compensatory damages. C. McCormick, *Law of Damages* §116 at 423 (1935).

. . . Petitioners' argument is . . . that such injury cannot be presumed to occur, and that plaintiffs at least should be put to their proof on the issue, as plaintiffs are in most tort actions.

We agree with petitioners in this respect. As we have observed in another context, the doctrine of presumed damages in the common law of defamation per se "is an oddity of tort law, for it allows recovery of purportedly compensatory damages without evidence of actual loss." The doctrine has been defended on the grounds that those forms of defamation that are actionable per se are virtually certain to cause serious injury to reputation, and that this kind of injury is extremely difficult to prove. Moreover, statements that are defamatory per se by their very nature are likely to cause mental and emotional distress, as well as injury to reputation, so there arguably is little reason to require proof of this kind of injury either. But these considerations do not support respondents' contention that damages should be presumed to flow from every deprivation of procedural due process. . . .

First, it is not reasonable to assume that every departure from procedural due process, no matter what the circumstances or how minor, inherently is as likely to cause distress as the publication of defamation per se is to cause injury to reputation and distress. . . .

Moreover, where a deprivation is justified but procedures are deficient, whatever distress a person feels may be attributable to the justified deprivation rather than to deficiencies in procedure. But as the Court of Appeals held, the injury caused by a justified deprivation, including distress, is not properly compensable under §1983. This ambiguity in causation, which is absent in the case of defamation per se, provides additional need for requiring the plaintiff to convince the trier of fact that he actually suffered distress because of the denial of procedural due process itself.

Finally, we foresee no particular difficulty in producing evidence that mental and emotional distress actually was caused by the denial of procedural due process itself. . . . In sum, then, although mental and emotional distress caused by the denial of procedural due process itself is compensable under §1983, we hold that neither the likelihood of such injury nor the difficulty of proving it is so great as to justify awarding compensatory damages without proof that such injury actually was caused. . . .

Because the right to procedural due process is "absolute" in the sense that it does not depend upon the merits of a claimant's substantive assertions, and because of the importance to organized society that procedural due process be observed, *see Boddie v. Connecticut*, 401 U.S. 371, 375 (1971); *Anti-Fascist Committee v. McGrath*, 341 U.S. at 171-172 (Frankfurter, J., concurring), we believe that the denial of procedural due process should be actionable for nominal damages without proof of actual injury. We therefore hold that if, upon remand, the District Court determines that respondents' suspensions were justified, respondents nevertheless will be entitled to recover nominal damages not to exceed one dollar from petitioners.

The judgment of the Court of Appeals is reversed, and the case is remanded for further proceedings consistent with this opinion.

REVIEW QUESTIONS

1. What is the holding of the case? If you were advising a school about the risks of losing a lawsuit if they fail to provide students with a hearing prior to suspension, what would you tell them?

2. Under what circumstances could the plaintiffs have obtained more than nominal damages for a due process violation?

3. What is the purpose of damages according to the Court? In your torts class you may learn that damages may serve a compensatory purpose and have a deterrent effect. Some of the time, these two goals work in tandem — by compensating the plaintiff for her injury, the defendant is also deterred. But that is not the case here, because the defendant need only pay a nominal amount. How is the defendant to be deterred?

4. In footnote ten, the Court suggests that having to pay the plaintiff's attorneys fees could be enough of a deterrent in some cases. We will discuss attorneys' fees later in this chapter, but you should know that courts are sometimes reluctant to award substantial attorneys' fees when the amount of damages is very low, because it seems disproportionate and courts have discretion as to the fee award.

5. Imagine that you are counsel to a school board. What would you tell your client about what procedures they should create for school suspensions?

QUESTIONS TO PONDER

Valuations problems arise even where damages are sought for harm to a building or piece of land. For example, what is the value of a historic landmark like an old railroad station that has been preserved for nearly one hundred years but is then destroyed by someone's negligence? Or what is the fair market value of a church that means much to its congregants, yet would have a very modest value if sold at an auction? These and more issues surfaced in *Trinity Church in the City of Boston v. John Hancock Mut. Life Ins. Co.*, 399 Mass. 43 (1987), when Trinity Church claimed that the life insurance company and other defendants caused structural damage to the church building while constructing the John Hancock Tower Building. The construction undermined the structural integrity of the church building — some of the damage could be repaired, but some of the damage merely shortened the projected useful life of the building. The defendants were undoubtedly responsible for the immediate repair costs. But the interesting question was whether those defendants should also be held monetarily responsible (now) for the fact that the church will, in the relatively distant future, collapse some number of years sooner than it otherwise would have. What do you think?

b. Punitive Damages

So far we have seen that nominal damages direct a token amount to signify the recognition of harm. Compensatory damages seek to return the plaintiff to the position he or she enjoyed prior to the harm. Sometimes, further monetary relief seems appropriate to deter future wrongful conduct and to express public disapproval of the injuring behavior. The common law thus developed *punitive damages*, typically left to the jury to assess, based on "'the gravity of the wrong and the need to deter similar wrongful conduct.'" *Pacific Mutual Life Ins. Co. v. Haslip*, 499 U.S. 1 (1991).

What kind of proof and what legal standard are needed for punitive damages? In typical common law cases, the moving party must show that the defendant acted egregiously, and usually this involves acting with malice or with reckless or callous indifference. The interaction between this standard and an underlying claim that itself requires demonstration of defendant's intention or state of mind can be very complex. In *Kolstad v. Am. Dental Assn.*, 527 U.S. 526 (1999), the Supreme Court held that although a plaintiff may seek punitive damages in a Title VII employment discrimination case, success in proving intentional discrimination does not itself guarantee evidence to support punitive damages. The Court rejected a standard of egregiousness and approved the standard of malice or reckless or callous indifference for demonstrating a basis for punitive damages. The Court also ruled that common law agency principles would limit liability on supervisors or the entire entity for conduct by individuals that might itself justify punitive damages.

The jury determination of punitive damages is reviewed by the trial and appellate courts under a standard of reasonableness. Reformers have argued that punitive damage awards are increasing in frequency, amounts, and unpredictability. *See*, *e.g.*, Cass R. Sunstein, Daniel Kahneman, and David Schkade, *Assessing Punitive Damages*, 107 Yale L.J. 2071 (1998). Others respond that the problems have been much overstated and reflect faulty generalizations from a few outlying cases. *See, e.g.*, Geoffrey T. Miller, *Behind the Battle Lines: A Comparative Analysis of the Necessity to Enact Comprehensive Federal Products Liability Reforms*, 45 Buff. L. Rev. 241 (1997); Product Liability Fairness Act, 1995: Hearings on S. 565 Before the S. Subcomm. on Consumer Affairs, Foreign Commerce, and Tourism, 104th Cong. 505 (1995) (testimony of Dr. Stephen Daniels, Senior Research Fellow, American Bar Foundation).

Besides generating legislative proposals, the debate over punitive damages has inspired a search by litigants for federal constitutional authority to limit the scope of punitive damages. The Supreme Court has rejected arguments that the Excessive Fines Clause of the Eighth Amendment sets a limit on punitive damages, *Browning-Ferris Indus. of Vermont v. Kelco Disposal, Inc.*, 492 U.S. 257 (1989), and instead has concluded that the Due Process Clause of the Fourteenth Amendment limits jury and judicial discretion in this area. *Pacific Mutual Life Ins. Co. v. Haslip, supra.*

Oregon's constitution prohibited judicial review of a punitive damages verdict unless the court could say that there was *no* evidence for the verdict. This rule was overturned by the Supreme Court in *Honda Motor Co. v. Oberg*, 512 U.S. 415 (1994). After reviewing eighteenth- and nineteenth-century English and American cases addressing excessive damages, the Supreme Court reasoned that judicial review had long been an important part of the process of awarding punitive damages. Oregon's constitutional provision to the contrary departed from tradition and thus presumptively violated due process without adequate substitutes to guard against arbitrary awards. Justice Ginsburg, joined by Chief Justice Rehnquist, dissented, not from the idea that due process should restrict punitive damage procedures, but from the application of due process to the Oregon context.

The Supreme Court has reviewed punitive damages awards in a number of cases and found them excessive and therefore a violation of due process. The main issue in many of these cases is the proportionality of punitive damages to compensatory damages. In *BMW v. Gore*, 517 U.S. 559 (1996), the Court rejected a punitive damages award in Alabama on such grounds. In that case, Dr. Ira Gore sued the auto distributor, BMW of North America, for fraud after discovering that the $40,000 new auto he had purchased from an authorized dealer had been repainted. BMW admitted a nationwide nondisclosure policy on its routine practice of repairing and repainting damaged new cars where the damage amounted to less than 3 percent of the car's total value. An Alabama jury found BMW liable for $4,000 diminution in value to Gore's car, then imposed $4 million in punitive damages, calculated by multiplying Gore's $4,000 in damages by the approximate number of undisclosed repaintings nationwide. The Alabama Supreme Court reduced the award to $2 million after concluding that the jury had erred in including in its calculations BMW's acts outside the jurisdiction.

Writing for the majority, Justice Stevens, who also had written the majority opinion in *Honda*, found the $2 million punitive damages grossly excessive in light of the state's legitimate interests in punishing and deterring illegal conduct within the state. The Court identified three "guideposts" to clarify what constitutes unconstitutional excessiveness in punitive damage awards. Most important is (1) how reprehensible is the defendant's conduct? Less important, but also relevant are (2) the ratio of the award to the actual or potential harm inflicted and (3) a comparison of the award to civil or criminal penalties that could be imposed for comparable misconduct. The Court found BMW's conduct not reprehensible because it only involved monetary loss, it reflected a reasonable effort to comport with uninterpreted state statutes, and it ceased upon a finding of unlawfulness. Noting that no "mathematical bright line" could demarcate constitutionality, the Court found the 500:1 ratio of award to damages excessive in light of precedents and reason and when compared with comparable legislatively created sanctions. A concurring opinion by Justice Breyer cited procedural defects in the Alabama judicial review of punitive awards.

Dissenting opinions by Justices Scalia and Ginsburg expressed concern about this federal intrusion into state law. Justice Scalia expressed the view that the Fourteenth Amendment affords "an opportunity to contest the reasonableness of a damages judgment in state court; but [not a] federal guarantee [that] a damages award actually be reasonable." *BMW*, 517 U.S. at 599.

In 2003, the Supreme Court held that an award of $145 million in punitive damages violated due process in a case where the compensatory judgment amounted to $1 million. In *State Farm Mut. Aut. Ins. Co. v. Campbell*, 538 U.S. 408 (2003), Mr. and Mrs. Curtis Campbell claimed that their insurance company's refusal to settle a claim falling within the limits of their insurance policy constituted bad faith, fraud, and intentional infliction of emotional distress. As later established at trial on the underlying claim, the Campbells were 100 percent responsible for an automobile accident that killed one individual and rendered another permanently disabled, yet their insurance company resisted settlement and pursued trial and appeals in the state courts. In their suit against State Farm Mutual Automobile Insurance Co., the Campbells introduced evidence that the insurance company declined to settle the underlying claim as part of a national scheme to meet corporate fiscal goals by capping the payouts on claims and engaging in fraudulent practices nationwide. Applying the guideposts for interpreting due process from *BMW v. Gore*, the Court reasoned first that "the reprehensibility guidepost does not permit courts to expand the scope of the case so that a defendant may be punished for any malfeasance," and therefore, damages should arise only in relation to the specific type of conduct that harmed the plaintiffs, not to the company's nationwide policies. Applying the second guidepost, the Court reasoned that there should be a presumption against an award with a 145:1 ratio between harm or potential harm suffered by the plaintiff and the punitive damages award, and consideration of the defendant's wealth could not justify an otherwise unconstitutional award. Using the third guidepost—the disparity between the punitive damages award and the civil penalties authorized in comparable cases—the Court found that $145 million in punitive damage "dwarfed" the $10,000 authorized under state law for an act of fraud. Further, the Court reasoned that the substantial compensatory damage award itself included a punitive element, and its $1 million level indicated the approximate level for a proper measure of punitive damages in the case. Justices Scalia, Thomas, and Ginsburg dissented. In her dissent, Justice Ginsburg questioned the Court's substitution of its judgment for that of the state courts and emphasized that the trial court specifically found that State Farm's national scheme was directly relevant to the Campbells' case. Justice Ginsburg also observed that the Court had swiftly converted guideposts into "instructions that begin to resemble marching orders." 538 U.S. at 439.

In *Philip Morris USA v. Williams*, 549 U.S. 346 (2007), the Court addressed whether a jury can increase punitive damages in order to punish a defendant for harming non-parties. A suit was brought on behalf of deceased smoker Jesse D. Williams, alleging negligence and deceit by tobacco company Philip Morris. At trial, after plaintiff's attorney made reference to all the past Oregon smokers that were likely harmed by Philip Morris, defense counsel requested an instruction to the jury clarifying that they could not increase punitive damages to punish Philip Morris for harm to such non-parties. The request was denied. The jury went on to award $821,000 in compensatory damages and $79.5 million in punitive damages. Writing for the Court, Justice Breyer explained that allowing punitive damages for harm to non-parties would indeed constitute a taking of defendants' property without due process of law. Because non-parties would not be present, defendants would be deprived of the right to present every available defense. At the same time, the Court held that harm to non-parties would still be relevant to the level of reprehensibility of defendant's conduct, and remanded the case to the Oregon Supreme Court for reconsideration under the clarified standard. "This nuance eludes me," Justice Stevens wrote in his dissent, arguing that punishing for reprehensibility due to third-party harm is the same as punishing for the third-party harm itself. Justice Ginsburg also dissented, joined by Justices Thomas and Scalia, arguing that the punitive damages awarded in the case were in fact the result of a judgment of reprehensibility, and thus legitimate.

The subsequent history of the case illustrates the limits of the reach of the federal courts. On remand, the Oregon Supreme Court held on independent state law grounds that the trial court had not erred in refusing to adopt the defendant's proffered jury instructions, reinstating the original verdict. *Williams*

v. Philip Morris, Inc., 176 P.3d 1255 (2008). The defendant again appealed, and although the Supreme Court initially granted certiorari, 553 U.S. 1093 (2008), it subsequently denied the writ of certiorari as improvidently granted, 556 U.S. 178 (2009).

The Supreme Court's most recent word on the subject came in a case involving the *Exxon Valdez* oil spill. *Exxon Shipping Co. v. Baker*, 554 U.S. 471 (2008). A jury had issued a punitive damages award of $2.5 billion arising out of the grounding of the supertanker the *Exxon Valdez* and the resulting oil spill on the coast of Alaska in 1989. The question before the Court was whether this punitive damages award was reasonable under maritime law, a species of federal common law (which you will learn more about when you learn *Erie* doctrine in Chapter 9). Unlike the previous cases, *Baker* was not a due process case. Expressing concern over variability in punitive damages awards and relying on studies demonstrating relatively low ratios between compensatory and punitive damages, the Court held that the appropriate award would represent a 1:1 ratio between punitive and compensatory damages. This limited the award amount to $507.5 million. For a critique of the Court's reliance on statistical studies of punitive damages awards, *see* Theodore Eisenberg, M. Heise, and M. Wells, *Variability in Punitive Damages: Empirically Assessing* Exxon Shipping Co. v. Baker, 166 J. Inst. & Theoretical Econ. 5 (2010).

QUESTIONS TO PONDER

1. One difficult question courts now face is what should be the appropriate relationship between compensatory and punitive damages. Do you think punitive damages should be proportional to compensatory damages? Can you construct arguments on both sides?

2. Given that the rationale that punitive damages are to punish the defendant or deter them from engaging in reprehensible conduct, is a 1:1 ratio of punitive to compensatory damages enough?

3. Can an appropriate ratio be determined as a rule for all cases, or do courts need greater discretion?

4. If not based on compensatory damages, on what should limits on punitive damages be based?

PRACTICE EXERCISE NO. 4:
DAMAGES IN *CARPENTER* AND *WARNER*

Imagine that the *Carpenter* and *Warner* plaintiffs have asked you to predict the scope of damages they could receive if they prevailed in their claims.

1. What types and categories of damages would be available for Nancy Carpenter, the plaintiff in the *Carpenter* case? Of what significance is the fact that she was pregnant at the time her husband Charles was

killed? (How *specifically* would this affect her recoverable damages?) If it is ultimately determined that Charles did not die instantly, but rather remained conscious for minutes or hours after the accident, does this affect the amount of recoverable damages? Substantive law usually guides answers to these questions, and we expect you to use the statutes in the Case Files to answer these questions about what types and categories of damages may be recoverable. We only want you to begin thinking about specific dollar amounts; what specific information will you need to value these claims? What witnesses, including experts, would you need to establish such value(s) at trial? (You may wish to take an early look at the letter from the valuation expert that is intended primarily for use in a later Practice Exercise. That letter, prepared by Economics Specialists of Boston, Inc., appears in the Case Files.)

2. What types and categories of damages would be available to the named plaintiffs in the *Warner* case? In light of *Carey v. Piphus*, what information would you seek from your client in order to prove damages? What limitations are there on the damages you can seek and how would you explain these limitations to your clients?

c. Enforcement of Damages

If the defendant refuses to pay money damages, the plaintiff must first be sure to obtain a judgment, which in federal court is described in Fed. R. Civ. P. 58. That judgment must be entered in the docket. Fed. R. Civ. P. 79(a); *see also* Forms 70 and 71 (at the end of the Federal Rules). The original judgment merely identifies the defendant's obligation to the plaintiff; it does not order payment (compared with an injunction, which directly orders conduct). Fed. R. Civ. P. 69 provides the process for enforcing a judgment for the payment of money. This involves a writ of execution, absent an alternative specified by the court or a relevant federal statute. Federal law does not provide many details of the enforcement process; therefore, the law of the state in which enforcement is sought will govern. State laws permit the use of proceedings to supplement or aid the enforcement of a judgment; these may include actions for garnishment of wages, contempt, and appointment of a receiver.

To collect from a defendant who does not pay on his own initiative, the plaintiff (now called the judgment creditor because she is owed a sum by the defendant/judgment debtor) must initiate another legal proceeding. Some state statutes permit judgment creditors to obtain a lien on property by recording the judgment in a registry of deeds or in the location for filings under the Uniform Commercial Code. The judgment creditor also can obtain a writ of execution for a piece of defendant's property, which authorizes the sheriff to seize the property, sell it — generally at public auction — and turn over the proceeds to the plaintiff. Through a discovery process, the plaintiff may even compel the defendant to disclose the location of assets to satisfy the judgment. Another option for the plaintiff is to execute the judgment against the income of the defendant, resulting in garnishment of wages if the defendant does not pay the installment as ordered. Even if assets exist or income exists, however, the plaintiff may have difficulty taking control of them. Many state statutes exempt certain property from liens so that the defendant can remain able to house, clothe, and feed his or her family; many statutes also limit wage garnishment. (It is worth asking, to what extent should due process "notice and right to be heard" principles apply to procedures to execute a final judgment?)

Other hurdles for the plaintiff include the sheltering effects of bankruptcy, under which the defendant's total assets may be outweighed by total debts, and the prioritization of creditors, which assures secured creditors first dibs on the defendant's assets.

It may also be difficult or impossible to collect on a judgment because of a lack of assets owned by the judgment debtor, because assets are exempt, or because prior liens exist. Consequently, plaintiffs and their lawyers often try to locate defendants who have insurance or sufficient assets to pay a judgment without causing the plaintiff to spend additional money and time to collect.

D. SETTLEMENT

The vast majority of cases settle before trial. Settlement occurs when a plaintiff agrees to abandon his legal claim(s) in exchange for payment or other relief by the defendant. A settlement is a contract and is subject to the laws governing contracts. Behind the scenes of litigation, parties are often negotiating a settlement price. Why do parties choose to settle? Steven Shavell provides an economic analysis of settlement in the following excerpt.

Steven Shavell, Foundations of Economic Analysis of Law
401-407, 410 (2004)

I now take up the question of whether parties will reach a settlement or instead go to trial. A settlement is a legally enforceable agreement, usually involving a payment from the defendant to the plaintiff, in which the plaintiff agrees not to pursue his claim further. If the parties do not reach a settlement, we will assume that they go to trial, that is, that the court will determine the outcome of their case. . . .

Simple model. Let us suppose for simplicity that the plaintiff and the defendant each has somehow formed beliefs—which may differ—about the trial outcome. Then we can discuss settlement possibilities in terms of two quantities. Consider first the minimum amount that the plaintiff would accept in settlement. Assuming that the plaintiff is risk neutral, this minimum acceptable amount equals his expected gain from trial less the cost of going to trial. For instance, if the plaintiff believes he will prevail with probability 70 percent, would obtain $100,000 upon prevailing, and the trial would involve expenses to him of $20,000, the minimum amount he would accept in settlement is 70% × $100,000 – $20,000 = $70,000 – $20,000 = $50,000; if he were offered anything less than this amount, he would be better off going to trial. If the defendant believes the odds of the plaintiff's winning are, say, only 50 percent, and the defendant's trial costs would be $25,000, then he would pay at most 50% × $100,000 + $25,000 = $50,000 + $25,000 = $75,000 in settlement.

It is evident that *if the plaintiff's minimum acceptable amount is less than the defendant's maximum acceptable amount, a mutually beneficial settlement is possible* — a settlement equal to any amount in between these two figures would be preferable to a trial for each party. Thus, if the plaintiff's minimum is $50,000 and defendant's maximum is $75,000, any amount in between, such as $60,000, would be preferred by each to going to trial. But if the plaintiff's chances of winning were only 20 percent, the defendant's maximum amount would be $20,000 + $25,000 = $45,000, so the most he would pay is less than the minimum $50,000 that the plaintiff would be willing to accept, and settlement could not occur.

Can more be said about when a mutually beneficial settlement will exist? That is, under what conditions will the plaintiff's minimum acceptable demand be less than the defendant's maximum acceptable payment? It is clear that if the plaintiff and the defendant have the same beliefs about the trial outcome, then there should always exist mutually beneficial settlements, because they can each escape trial costs by settling. Suppose that they both believe that $50,000 is the expected judgment the defendant will have to pay if there is a trial. Then the trial costs that the plaintiff would bear would lead to his willingness to accept a lower figure than $50,000; if his trial costs would be $10,000, he would accept $40,000, and so forth. Conversely, any trial costs that the defendant would have to bear would increase above $50,000 what he would be willing to pay; if his trial costs would be $10,000, he would be willing to pay $60,000. Thus, the settlement range would be from $40,000 to $60,000. For settlement possibilities to be eliminated, the plaintiff's minimum amount must rise far enough from $40,000 and/or the defendant's fall far enough from $60,000 such that the plaintiff's minimum turns out to exceed the defendant's maximum. That can occur only if they have different beliefs about the trial outcome. This line of thought suggests the following conclusion: A mutually beneficial settlement amount exists as long as the plaintiff's and defendant's estimates of the expected judgment do not diverge too much. Indeed, it can be shown that *a mutually beneficial settlement exists as long as the plaintiff's estimate of the expected judgment does not exceed the defendant's estimate by more than the sum of their costs of trial*. . . .

Interpretation of the model. A number of comments may help us to interpret and understand the foregoing model.

(a) *Does the existence of a mutually beneficial settlement amount imply that settlement will occur?* Although we know that there cannot be a settlement when a mutually beneficial settlement amount does *not* exist, what can be said about the outcome when a mutually beneficial settlement amount does exist? The answer is that there may or may not be a settlement, depending on the nature of bargaining between the parties and the information they have about each other. . . .

(b) *Parties' beliefs*. The effect of parties' beliefs on the existence of mutually beneficial settlement amounts, and thus on the tendency toward settlement, can be easily understood from the italicized conditions stated in the preceding section. Specifically, the greater the amount by which the plaintiff's estimate the likelihood of winning exceeds the defendant's, the smaller the tendency toward settlement, because it is the excess of the plaintiff's expected judgment over the defendant's expected payment that leads to trial. It is important to emphasize that what leads to trial is not that a plaintiff is confident of winning, but rather that he is *more* confident than the defendant thinks he has a right to be. . . .

Of course, if the plaintiff assesses his chances of winning as lower than the defendant assesses the plaintiff's chances, there will be a range of mutually beneficial settlements. If, for example, the plaintiff thinks his chances of winning are 30 percent and the defendant thinks the plaintiff's chances are 50 percent, then, given the figures mentioned above, the plaintiff would accept any amount over $50,000, and the defendant would pay any amount up to $80,000. (Note also that in such cases, this italicized condition automatically holds, because the difference in the plaintiff's expected gain and defendant's expected loss is negative and therefore definitely is less than the sum of trial costs.)

What would we expect the parties' beliefs about the likelihood of trial outcomes to be? The parties may, and often will, be in possession of different information about a case when it begins. For instance, the defendant may know more about whether he would be found liable than the plaintiff knows. Also, the two sides may initially have in mind different legal arguments that they can make. But the parties may elect to share information or may be forced to do so . . . and parties often can independently acquire information that the other side possesses (for instance, plaintiff could interview witnesses to an accident and learn more about the defendant's behavior). To the degree that the parties do come to similar beliefs, settlement becomes more likely.

We would not predict, though, that beliefs will always converge. For example, the parties might not want to share certain legal arguments with each other, believing that if a trial comes about, they would lose the advantage of surprise; yet in light of these arguments, each party might believe it is more likely to win than the other. Another factor standing in the way of convergence of beliefs is the element of natural optimism about one's chances. . . .

But, by and large, especially because parties have legal counsel who are likely to be familiar with the same body of law and because of opportunities for acquisition of information about facts material to disputes, we would expect beliefs about trial outcomes to be relatively close by the time of a trial, leading toward settlement.

(c) *Judgment amount.* If the size of the judgment rises, then the likelihood of trial rises, other things being constant. This is because the effect of a divergence in the assessments of the likelihood of winning is magnified if the judgment that would be awarded becomes larger. If there is, for instance, a 20 percent difference in beliefs and the judgments award would be $10,000, the difference in expected judgments would be only $2,000, perhaps not enough to exceed the sum of legal costs of trial and thus not enough to cause trial. But if the judgment would be $1,000,000, the 20 percent difference in trial outcomes would signify a $200,000 difference in expected awards, and thus be more likely to exceed the sum of trial costs, leading to trial.

Another point about the judgment amount is that, although we have assumed for simplicity that the parties agree on what the judgment amount would be, that might not be so. Differences in the parties' beliefs about the amount that would be won affect their expected judgments and thus the existence of mutually beneficial settlements, according to the italicized condition. If the plaintiff thinks he would win a larger amount than the defendant thinks, then again this would lead toward trial. . . .

(d) *Legal expenses.* The larger are the legal expenses of either party, the greater are the chances of settlement, clearly, since the sum of legal costs will rise, and thus the greater will be the likelihood that the sum of legal costs will exceed any excess of the plaintiff's expectation over the defendant's expectation. One would expect legal expenses to rise with the size of the potential judgment. This factor tends to increase the chances of settlement for large stakes cases, and thus works opposite to the tendency just discussed in (c) toward litigation.

(e) *Risk aversion.* When we introduce risk aversion into the basic model, we see that it leads to a greater likelihood of settlement. The reason is simply that a trial is a risky venture because its outcome is unknown. To a risk-averse party, settlement is more attractive than it is to a risk-neutral party. Further, as the degree of risk aversion of either party increases, or as the amount at stake increases—the size of the judgment or the size of legal fees—settlement becomes more likely, other things being equal. . . .

Actual amount of trial versus settlement. In fact, the vast majority of cases settle. Data on state courts show that over 96 percent of civil cases do not go to trial. Similarly, recent data on federal courts demonstrate that, for fiscal year 2001, almost 98 percent of federal civil cases were resolved without trial. These figures, however, may either overstate or understate the true rate: Because cases that are not tried may have been dismissed by a court, 96 percent or 98 percent is the settlement rate plus the dismissal rate, not the settlement rate; but because many disputes are settled before any complaint is filed, 96 percent or 98 percent may understate the settlement rate. In any event, it is evident that the vast majority of cases settle.

MORE TO PONDER

Why do lawsuits settle? Shavell offers an economic model in which settlement is an efficient way to avoid the costs of litigation. Consider why Professor Shavell calls his model the "simple model." What assumptions must be made, and what other factors might change the analysis or provide for an unexpected result?

Others have argued that there are values not captured by the concept of efficiency. For example, in his classic article condemning settlement, Professor Owen Fiss argues that settlement often involves a stark imbalance of bargaining power, that consent is often coerced, and that the bargain may be struck by someone without authority. Owen Fiss, *Against Settlement*, 93 Yale L.J. 1073 (1984). In such situations, the interests of the party are not properly represented, and the party is often misinformed. What, if anything, should courts do when they suspect a settlement is coerced? What, if anything, should a court do when a judge thinks that parties are making a mistake *not* to settle? The general answer is nothing—the value of litigant autonomy means that people can pursue a case even if the court thinks their choices are irrational. The same is generally considered true when parties settle.

Settlement can often be motivated by more than the brute economics of legal costs and payment of damages. For example, a defendant may be extremely concerned with the public nature of a trial and might seek a confidential settlement to protect itself from negative publicity, copycat litigation, or other related costs. Should a defendant be allowed to obtain secrecy as a condition of settlement? People differ on this question. Some argue that confidential settlements are too costly because they often conceal public harm, and there has been a recent rise of legislation prohibiting or reducing confidential settlements in certain areas. Others argue that even if secrecy as a condition of settlement is barred, people will still settle secretly; they will just do it before filing. If you want to read more about these issues, the following articles might interest you: Alison Lothes, *Quality, Not Quantity: An Analysis of Confidential Settlements and Litigants' Economic Incentives*, 154 U. Pa. L. Rev. 433 (2005); Scott A. Moss, *Illuminating Secrecy: A New Economic Analysis of Confidential Settlements*, 105 Mich. L. Rev. 867 (2007) (an economic analysis of confidential settlements reaching counterintuitive results); Jon Bauer, *Buying Witness Silence: Evidence Suppressing Settlements and Lawyer's Ethics*, 87 Or. L. Rev. 481 (2008) (discussing the ethical dimensions of secret settlements).

Finally, some cases might settle because parties do not want to publicize the true value of a case. In a well-known law review article, Marc Galanter argued that repeat players may settle high value suits and bring low value suits to trial in order to push down the value of settlement in the run of cases. *See* Marc Galanter, *Why the "Haves" Come Out Ahead: Speculations on the Limits of Legal Change*, 9 L. & Soc'y Rev. 95 (1974). A repeat player might find it worthwhile to invest much more than seems efficient to try a case in order to obtain a low verdict that it can then use to depress settlement values in a number of other cases.

While everyone knows that most cases settle, there is little empirical evidence of exactly what proportion of cases settle as opposed to being resolved in other ways by courts during pretrial process (such as on a motion to dismiss or by summary judgment) or through arbitration. It is wrong to assume that a case will either settle or go to trial, because there are many intermediate means of resolving a case, which you will begin learning about in the next chapter. And sometimes cases *both* settle *and* go to trial, such as when parties enter into a high-low agreement. The parties may agree on a floor and a ceiling of damages prior to going to trial. If the plaintiff loses, she still receives the lower bound that the defendant agreed to; if she wins, she can only receive the upper bound. This is a way for parties to reduce the risk of going to trial when they cannot agree on a settlement number.

E. FINANCING LITIGATION

The way litigation is financed has an inextricable effect on plaintiffs' remedies and on settlement, creating incentives or disincentives to bring lawsuits, to settle them early, or to pursue them to trial. In most cases in the United States, each party is responsible for paying her own attorneys' fees. This is known as the "American Rule." That rule and alterations to it (by statute, regulation, or judicial decision) have significant effect on lawyers' decisions to take a case and on the timing of settlement. In some areas of the law, such as civil rights litigation and some consumer protection laws, fee-shifting statutes require the defendant to pay the plaintiff's reasonable attorneys' fees if plaintiff prevails. *See, e.g.*, 42 U.S.C. § 1988. In other areas of the law, especially but not exclusively personal injury cases, the practice of contingency fees allows the plaintiff to finance the litigation by agreeing to pay the lawyer a percentage of her recovery, often 30 percent, in lieu of an hourly fee. Finally, an emerging and controversial business model involves third-party financing of litigation. Judicial rules, ethical rules, and statutes governing fee arrangements and awards are crucial to an understanding of what litigation can bring to parties, and more broadly, of how the American legal system operates.

1. The "American Rule"

Under the "American Rule," the losing party does not pay the prevailing party's attorneys' fees. As the name might imply, this is not the rule everywhere else. In England and much of Europe, for example, losing parties typically are required to pay the opposing lawyer's fees as well as their own lawyer's fees; costs follow victory. What differences emerge in practice under these rules?

Defenders of the American Rule maintain that it permits the poor, as well as the rich, to litigate. Poor folks would not otherwise be able to sue, the argument goes, because of the fear that if they lose they will have to pay the opponent's legal fees. Moreover, the American Rule encourages innovative claims, while the English Rule directs plaintiffs, and their lawyers, to be more risk averse.

Advocates of the English Rule emphasize that it deters frivolous or marginal litigation and that it more fully compensates the prevailing party for the troubles of litigation. It is worth noting that in practice, the English Rule exempts cases where the losing party's lawyer is financed through legal aid, which, in turn, is available to low-income people. Also, in the English practice a taxing officer determines fees (for both solicitors and barristers) with reference to a fee schedule, which tends to run 60-70 percent of actual fees. Insurance may also cover some of the costs. Further, applications for taxation of costs may be made at points before the end of the litigation, such as the award of preliminary relief, and therefore fees may be awarded to a party that does not prevail in the end. In Germany, the losing party pays fees to the degree that the winning party was successful, or what may be known as "less-than-full" fee compensation. Thus, "if the remedy sought was payment of 300,000 euros, and if the plaintiff is successful only in relation to the amount of 100,000 euros, the plaintiff has to bear two-thirds of the costs." *See* Peter F. Schlosser, *Lectures on Civil-Law Litigation Systems and American Cooperation with Those Systems*, 45 U. Kan. L. Rev. 9, 18 (1996). This rule deters plaintiffs from seeking enormous damages.

American economists have debated the effect of these two attorneys' fees models on attorney conduct For different points of view, *see* Steven Shavell, *Suit, Settlement and Trial: A Theoretical Analysis Under Alternative Methods for the Allocation of Legal Costs*, 11 J. Legal Stud. 55 (1982), and John J. Donohue III, *Opting for the British Rule, or If Posner and Shavell Can't Remember the Coase Theorem, Who Will?*, 104 Harv. L. Rev. 1093 (1991).

2. Fee-Shifting Statutes

Even at common law, the American Rule governing attorneys' fees had exceptions. The Supreme Court has concluded that when a party acts in "bad faith," courts have inherent authority to assess fees to reimburse the opposing party. Some courts have ruled that when a lawyer or litigant acts in a way that creates a "common fund" for the benefit of others, the resulting fund can be "taxed" for the fair value of the lawyer's work, to prevent a windfall to the beneficiaries. In the 1960s and 1970s, some lower federal courts adopted the theory that losing defendants could be ordered to pay plaintiffs' attorneys' fees where those plaintiffs acted as "private attorneys general." The Supreme

Court rejected this theory in *Alyeska Pipeline Serv. Co. v. Wilderness Soc'y*, 421 U.S. 240 (1975), and concluded that Congress, rather than the courts, should determine the kinds of cases warranting a fee shift. The Court recognized that a fee shift fundamentally provides an incentive to plaintiffs to file suit, an incentive to lawyers to represent those plaintiffs, and a deterrent to defendants at risk of such suits.

Congress responded to *Alyeska* by adopting the Civil Rights Attorney's Fees Act of 1976, 42 U.S.C. § 1988. By 1995, Congress had included fee-shifting provisions in over 180 pieces of legislation that addressed topics ranging from environmental protection and civil rights to intellectual property and banking. *See, e.g.*, Clean Air Act Amendments of 1977, 42 U.S.C. § 7622(e)(2); Equal Access to Justice Act, 28 U.S.C. § 2412(b); Handicapped Children's Protection Act of 1988, 20 U.S.C. § 1415(e)(4)(B); Patent Infringement Act, 35 U.S.C. § 285; Electronic Fund Transfer Act, 15 U.S.C. § 1693m(a) and (f). By creating monetary incentives for attorneys to pursue these and other claims, Congress intended to promote enforcement of selected federal statutory rights.

Yet unlike the English Rule, which directs that the loser pay the attorneys' fees of the opponent, many of these American statutes, as interpreted by the courts, provide only for shifting *prevailing* plaintiffs' fees to the defendants; a losing plaintiff is not obliged to pay the defendants' attorneys' fees. This pro-plaintiff, one-way shift structure encourages enforcement efforts without penalizing the unsuccessful plaintiff. Yet even under a statute with this structure, a court may order the plaintiff who brings a totally frivolous or groundless suit to pay the defendant's attorneys' fees. *See, e.g., Fox v. Vice*, 131 S. Ct. 2205 (2011). Such sanctions are also available under Fed. R. Civ. P. 11, which provides that a court may order "payment of some or all of the reasonable attorneys' fees and other expenses" as a sanction for filing a pleading or motion without adequate inquiry, unwarranted by existing law or fact, or based on a frivolous argument for new law.

Finally, some states have adopted "loser pays" legislation, requiring losing parties in some civil cases to pay their opponents' legal fees. *See* Tex. Civ. Proc. & Rem. Code § 42.004 (West 2015).

3. The Effect of Rule 68 Settlement Offers on Attorneys' Fees

As a monetary incentive and deterrent, attorneys' fees become part of the package of possibilities that influence settlement of lawsuits. If Congress authorizes attorneys' fees for a prevailing plaintiff, then the defendant must include the possible liability for plaintiff's attorneys' fees in the calculus of the costs and benefits of proceeding to trial, compared with the costs and benefits of settlement. Similarly, the plaintiff must consider the risk of losing not only on the merits, but also of forgoing attorneys' fees, in deciding whether to file initially, as well as whether to proceed or to settle. How should a statutory policy promoting certain kinds of lawsuits be reconciled with a judicial policy promoting settlement? When should the value of attorneys' fees themselves be on the bargaining table for settlement of a lawsuit? The following cases address these complex issues.

Marek v. Chesny
473 U.S. 1 (1985)

Chief Justice BURGER delivered the opinion of the Court:

We granted certiorari to decide whether attorney's fees incurred by a plaintiff subsequent to an offer of settlement under Federal Rule of Civil Procedure 68 must be paid by the defendant under 42 U.S.C. §1988, when the plaintiff recovers a judgment less than the offer.

I

Petitioners, three police officers, in answering a call on a domestic disturbance, shot and killed respondent's adult son. Respondent, in his own behalf and as administrator of his son's estate, filed suit against the officers in the United States District Court under 42 U.S.C. §1983 and state tort law.

Prior to trial, petitioners made a timely offer of settlement "for a sum, including costs now accrued and attorney's fees, of ONE HUNDRED THOUSAND ($100,000) DOLLARS." Respondent did not accept the offer. The case went to trial and respondent was awarded $5,000 on the state-law "wrongful death" claim, $52,000 for the §1983 violation, and $3,000 in punitive damages.

Respondent filed a request for $171,692.47 in costs, including attorney's fees. This amount included costs incurred after the settlement offer. Petitioners opposed the claim for postoffer costs, relying on Federal Rule of Civil Procedure 68, which shifts to the plaintiff all "costs" incurred subsequent to an offer of judgment not exceeded by the ultimate recovery at trial. Petitioners argued that attorney's fees are part of the "costs" covered by Rule 68, The District Court agreed with petitioners and declined to award respondent "costs, including attorney's fees, incurred after the offer of judgment." 547 F. Supp. 542, 547 (N.D. Ill. 1982). The parties subsequently agreed that $32,000 fairly represented the allowable costs, including attorney's fees, accrued prior to petitioners' offer of settlement. Respondent appealed the denial of postoffer costs.

The Court of Appeals reversed. The court rejected what it termed the "rather mechanical linking up of Rule 68 and section 1988." It stated that the District Court's reading of Rule 68 and §1988, while "in a sense logical," would put civil rights plaintiffs and counsel in a "predicament" that "cuts against the grain of section 1988." Plaintiffs' attorneys, the court reasoned, would be forced to "think very hard" before rejecting even an inadequate offer, and would be deterred from bringing good-faith actions because of the prospect of losing the right to attorney's fees if a settlement offer more favorable than the ultimate recovery were rejected. The court concluded that "[t]he legislators who enacted section 1988 would not have wanted its effectiveness blunted because of a little known rule of court." We granted certiorari. We reverse.

II

Rule 68 provides that if a timely pretrial offer of settlement is not accepted and "the judgment finally obtained by the offeree is not more favorable than the offer, the offeree must pay the costs incurred after the making of the offer." The plain purpose of Rule 68 is to encourage settlement and avoid litigation. The Rule prompts both parties to a suit to evaluate the risks and costs of litigation, and to balance them against the likelihood of success upon trial on the merits. This case requires us to decide whether the offer in this case was a proper one under Rule 68, and whether the term "costs" as used in Rule 68 includes attorney's fees awardable under 42 U.S.C. §1988.

. . . [Does] the term "costs" in Rule 68 include[] attorney's fees awardable under 42 U.S.C. §1988[?] By the time the Federal Rules of Civil Procedure were adopted in 1938, federal statutes had authorized and defined awards of costs to prevailing parties for more than 85 years. *See* Act of Feb. 26, 1853, 10 Stat. 161; *see generally Alyeska Pipeline Service Co. v. Wilderness Society*, 421 U.S. 240 (1975). Unlike in England, such "costs" generally had not included attorney's fees; under the "American Rule," each party had been required to bear its own attorney's fees. The "American Rule" as applied in federal courts, however, had become subject to certain exceptions by the late 1930's. Some of these exceptions had evolved as a product of the "inherent power in the courts to allow attorney's fees in particular situations." *Alyeska, supra*, at 259. . . .

The authors of Federal Rule of Civil Procedure 68 were fully aware of these exceptions to the American Rule. The Advisory Committee's Note to Rule 54(d), 28 U.S.C. App., p. 621, contains an extensive list of the federal statutes which allowed for costs in particular cases; of the 35 "statutes as to costs" set forth in the final paragraph of the Note, no fewer than 11 allowed for attorney's fees as part of costs. Against this background of varying definitions of "costs," the drafters of Rule 68 did not define the term; nor is there any explanation whatever as to its intended meaning in the history of the Rule.

In this setting, given the importance of "costs" to the Rule, it is very unlikely that this omission was mere oversight; on the contrary, the most reasonable inference is that the term "costs" in Rule 68 was intended to refer to all costs properly awardable under the relevant substantive statute or other authority. In other words, all costs properly awardable in an action are to be considered within the scope of Rule 68 "costs." Thus, absent congressional expressions to the contrary, where the underlying statute defines "costs" to include attorney's fees, we are satisfied such fees are to be included as costs for purposes of Rule 68. . . .

Here, respondent sued under 42 U.S.C. §1983. Pursuant to the Civil Rights Attorney's Fees Awards Act of 1976, 90 Stat. 2641, as amended, 42 U.S.C. §1988, a prevailing party in a §1983 action may be awarded attorney's fees "as part of the costs." Since Congress expressly included attorney's fees as "costs" available to a plaintiff in a §1983 suit, such fees are subject to the cost-shifting provision of Rule 68. This "plain meaning" interpretation of the interplay between Rule 68 and §1988 is the only construction that gives meaning to each word in both Rule 68 and §1988.

Unlike the Court of Appeals, we do not believe that this "plain meaning" construction of the statute and the Rule will frustrate Congress' objective in §1988 of ensuring that civil rights plaintiffs obtain " 'effective access to the judicial process.' " *Hensley v. Eckerhart*, 461 U.S. 424, 429 (1983), *quoting* H.R. Rep. No. 94-1558, p. 1 (1976). Merely subjecting civil rights plaintiffs to the settlement provision of Rule 68 does not curtail their access to the courts, or significantly deter them from bringing suit. Application of Rule 68 will serve as a disincentive for the plaintiffs' attorney to continue litigation after the defendant makes a settlement offer. There is no evidence, however, that Congress, in considering §1988, had any thought that civil rights claims were to be on any different footing from other civil claims insofar as settlement is concerned. Indeed, Congress made clear its concern that civil rights plaintiffs not be penalized for "helping to lessen docket congestion" by settling their cases out of court. . . .

Moreover, Rule 68's policy of encouraging settlements is neutral, favoring neither plaintiffs nor defendants; it expresses a clear policy of favoring settlement of all lawsuits. Civil rights plaintiffs — along with other plaintiffs — who reject an offer more favorable than what is thereafter recovered at trial will not recover attorney's fees for services performed after the offer is rejected. But, since the Rule is neutral, many civil rights plaintiffs will benefit from the offers of settlement encouraged by Rule 68. . . .

To be sure, application of Rule 68 will require plaintiffs to "think very hard" about whether continued litigation is worthwhile; that is precisely what Rule 68 contemplates. This effect of Rule 68, however, is in no sense inconsistent with the congressional policies underlying §1983 and §1988. Section 1988 authorizes courts to award only "reasonable" attorney's fees to prevailing parties. In *Hensley v. Eckerhart, supra*, we held that "the most critical factor" in determining a reasonable fee "is the degree of success obtained." *Id.*, at 436. We specifically noted that prevailing at trial "may say little about whether the expenditure of counsel's time was reasonable in relation to the success achieved." *Ibid.* In a case where a rejected settlement offer exceeds the ultimate recovery, the plaintiff — although technically the prevailing party — has not received any monetary benefits from the postoffer services of his attorney. This case presents a good example: the $139,692 in postoffer legal services resulted in a recovery $8,000 less than petitioners' settlement offer. Given Congress' focus on the success achieved, we are not persuaded that shifting the postoffer costs to respondent in these circumstances would in any sense thwart its intent under §1988.

Rather than "cutting against the grain" of §1988, as the Court of Appeals held, we are convinced that applying Rule 68 in the context of a §1983 action is consistent with the policies and objectives of §1988. Section 1988 encourages plaintiffs to bring meritorious civil rights suits; Rule 68 simply encourages settlements. There is nothing incompatible in these two objectives.

III

Congress, of course, was well aware of Rule 68 when it enacted §1988, and included attorney's fees as part of recoverable costs. The plain language of Rule 68 and §1988 subjects such fees to the cost-shifting provision of Rule 68. Nothing revealed in our review of the policies underlying §1988 constitutes "the necessary clear expression of congressional intent" required "to exempt . . . [the] statute from the operation of" Rule 68. *Califano v. Yamasaki*, 442 U.S. 682, 700 (1979). We hold that petitioners are not liable for costs of $139,692 incurred by respondent after petitioners' offer of settlement. The judgment of the Court of Appeals is Reversed.

[Concurring opinions of Justices POWELL and REHNQUIST are omitted.]

Justice BRENNAN, with whom Justice MARSHALL and Justice BLACKMUN join, dissenting:

The question presented by this case is whether the term "costs" as it is used in Rule 68 of the Federal Rules of Civil Procedure and elsewhere throughout the Rules refers simply to those taxable costs defined in 28 U.S.C. §1920 and traditionally understood as "costs" — court fees, printing expenses, and the like — or instead includes attorney's fees when an underlying fees-award statute happens to refer to fees "as part of" the awardable costs. Relying on what it recurrently emphasizes is the "plain language" of one such statute, 42 U.S.C. §1988, the Court today holds that a prevailing civil rights litigant entitled to fees under that statute is per se barred by Rule 68 from recovering any fees for work performed after rejecting a settlement offer where he ultimately recovers less than the proffered amount in settlement.

I dissent. The Court's reasoning is wholly inconsistent with the history and structure of the Federal Rules, and its application to the over 100 attorney's fees statutes enacted by Congress will produce absurd variations in Rule 68's operation based on nothing more than picayune differences in statutory phraseology. Neither Congress nor the drafters of the Rules could possibly have intended such inexplicable variations in settlement incentives. Moreover, the Court's interpretation will "seriously undermine the purposes behind the attorney's fees provisions" of the civil rights laws, *Delta Air Lines, Inc. v. August*, 450 U.S. 346, 378 (1981) (Rehnquist, J., dissenting) — provisions imposed by Congress pursuant to §5 of the Fourteenth Amendment. Today's decision therefore violates the most basic limitations on our rulemaking authority as set forth in the Rules Enabling Act, 28 U.S.C. §2072, and as summarized in *Alyeska Pipeline Co. v. Wilderness Society*, 421 U.S. 240 (1975). Finally, both Congress and the Judicial Conference of the United States have been engaged for years in considering possible amendments to Rule 68 that would bring attorney's fees within the operation of the

Rule. That process strongly suggests that Rule 68 has not previously been viewed as governing fee awards, and it illustrates the wisdom of deferring to other avenues of amending Rule 68 rather than ourselves engaging in "standardless judicial lawmaking." *Delta Air Lines, Inc. v. August, supra*, 450 U.S. at 378 (Rehnquist, J., dissenting).

I

The Court's "plain language" analysis, goes as follows: Section 1988 provides that a "prevailing party" may recover "a reasonable attorney's fee as part of the costs." Rule 68 in turn provides that, where an offeree obtains a judgment for less than the amount of a previous settlement offer, "the offeree must pay the costs incurred after the making of the offer." Because "attorney's fees" are "costs," the Court concludes, the "plain meaning" of Rule 68 per se prohibits a prevailing civil rights plaintiff from recovering fees incurred after he rejected the proposed out-of-court settlement.

The Court's "plain language" approach is, as Judge Posner's opinion for the court below noted, "in a sense logical." 720 F.2d 474, 478 (7th Cir. 1983). However, while the starting point in interpreting statutes and rules is always the plain words themselves, "[t]he particular inquiry is not what is the abstract force of the words or what they may comprehend, but in what sense were they intended to be understood or what understanding they convey when used in the particular act," We previously have been confronted with "superficially appealing argument[s]" strikingly similar to those adopted by the Court today, and we have found that they "cannot survive careful consideration." *Roadway Express, Inc. v. Piper*, 447 U.S. 752, 758 (1980). So it is here. . . .

For a number of reasons, "costs" as that term is used in the Federal Rules should be interpreted uniformly in accordance with the definition of costs set forth in §1920:

First. The limited history of the costs provisions in the Federal Rules suggests that the drafters intended "costs" to mean only taxable costs traditionally allowed under the common law or pursuant to the statutory predecessor of §1920. Nowhere was it suggested that the meaning of taxable "costs" might vary from case to case depending on the language of the substantive statute involved — a practice that would have cut against the drafters' intent to create uniform procedures applicable to "every action" in federal court. Fed. Rule Civ. Proc. 1.

Second. The Rules provide that "costs" may automatically be taxed by the clerk of the court on one day's notice, Fed. Rule Civ. Proc. 54(d) — strongly suggesting that "costs" were intended to refer only to those routine, readily determinable charges that could appropriately be left to a clerk, and as to which a single day's notice of settlement would be appropriate. Attorney's fees, which are awardable only by the court and which frequently entail lengthy disputes and hearings, obviously do not fall within that category.

Third. When particular provisions of the Federal Rules are intended to encompass attorney's fees, they do so explicitly. Eleven different provisions of the Rules authorize a court to award attorney's fees as "expenses" in particular circumstances, demonstrating that the drafters knew the difference, and intended a difference, between "costs," "expenses," and "attorney's fees."

Fourth. With the exception of one recent Court of Appeals opinion and two recent District Court opinions, the Court can point to no authority suggesting that courts or attorneys have ever viewed the cost-shifting provisions of Rule 68 as including attorney's fees. . . .

Fifth. We previously have held that words and phrases in the Federal Rules must be given a consistent usage and be read *in pari materia*, reasoning that to do otherwise would "attribute a schizophrenic intent to the drafters." *Id.*, at 353. Applying the Court's "plain language" approach consistently throughout the Rules, however, would produce absurd results that would turn statutes like §1988 on their heads and plainly violate the restraints imposed on judicial rulemaking by the Rules Enabling Act. For example, Rule 54(d) provides that "costs shall be allowed as of course to the prevailing party unless the court otherwise directs." Similarly, the plain language of Rule 68 provides that a plaintiff covered by the Rule "must pay the costs incurred after the making of the offer"—language requiring the plaintiff to bear both his post-offer costs and the defendant's postoffer costs. If "costs" as used in these provisions were interpreted to include attorney's fees by virtue of the wording of §1988, losing civil rights plaintiffs would be required by the "plain language" of Rule 54(d) to pay the defendant's attorney's fees, and prevailing plaintiffs falling within Rule 68 would be required to bear the defendant's postoffer attorney's fees.

Had it addressed this troubling consequence of its "plain language" approach, perhaps the Court would have acknowledged that such a reading would conflict directly with §1988, which allows an award of attorney's fees to a prevailing defendant only where "the suit was vexatious, frivolous, or brought to harass or embarrass the defendant," and that the substantive standard set forth in §1988 therefore overrides the otherwise "plain meaning" of Rules 54(d) and 68. But that is precisely the point, and the Court cannot have it both ways. . . .

Sixth. As with all of the Federal Rules, the drafters intended Rule 68 to have a uniform, consistent application in all proceedings in federal court. In accordance with this intent, Rule 68 should be interpreted to provide uniform, consistent incentives "to encourage the settlement of litigation." *Delta Air Lines, Inc. v. August, supra*, 450 U.S. at 352. Yet today's decision will lead to dramatically different settlement incentives depending on minor variations in the phraseology of the underlying fees-award statutes—distinctions that would appear to be nothing short of irrational and for which the Court has no plausible explanation.

Congress has enacted well over 100 attorney's fees statutes, many of which would appear to be affected by today's decision. . . . Under the "plain language" approach of today's decision, Rule 68 will operate to include the potential loss of otherwise recoverable attorney's fees as an incentive to settlement in litigation under these statutes. . . .

The result is to sanction a senseless patchwork of fee shifting that flies in the face of the fundamental purpose of the Federal Rules—the provision of uniform and consistent procedure in federal courts. Such a construction will "introduce into [Rule 68] distinctions unrelated to its goal . . . and [will] result in virtually random application of the Rule." . . .

In sum, there is nothing in the history and structure of the Rules or in the history of any of the underlying attorney's fee statutes to justify such incomprehensible distinctions based simply on fine linguistic variations among the underlying fees-award statutes—particularly where, as in *Roadway Express*, the cost provision can be read as embodying a uniform definition derived from §1920. As partners with Congress, we have a responsibility not to carry "plain language" constructions to the point of producing "untenable distinctions and unreasonable results." *American Tobacco Co. v. Patterson*, 456 U.S. 63, 71 (1982). . . .

II

A

Although the Court's opinion fails to discuss any of the problems reviewed above, it does devote some space to arguing that its interpretation of Rule 68 "is in no sense inconsistent with the congressional policies underlying §1983 and §1988." The Court goes so far as to assert that its interpretation fits in smoothly with §1988 as interpreted by *Hensley v. Eckerhart*, 461 U.S. 424 (1983).

The Court is wrong. Congress has instructed that attorney's fee entitlement under §1988 be governed by a reasonableness standard. Until today the Court always has recognized that this standard precludes reliance on any mechanical "bright-line" rules automatically denying a portion of fees, acknowledging that such "mathematical approach[es]" provide "little aid in determining what is a reasonable fee in light of all the relevant factors." 461 U.S. at 435-436, n.11. Although the starting point is always "the number of hours reasonably expended on the litigation," this "does not end the inquiry": a number of considerations set forth in the legislative history of §1988 "may lead the district court to adjust the fee upward or downward." *Id.*, at 433-434. We also have emphasized that the district court "necessarily has discretion in making this equitable judgment" because of its "superior understanding of the litigation." *Id.*, at 437. Section 1988's reasonableness standard is, in sum, "acutely sensitive to the merits of an action and to antidiscrimination policy." *Roadway Express, Inc. v. Piper*, 447 U.S. at 762.

Rule 68, on the other hand, is not "sensitive" at all to the merits of an action and to antidiscrimination policy. It is a mechanical per se provision automatically shifting "costs" incurred after an offer is rejected, and it deprives a district court of all discretion with respect to the matter by using "the strongest verb of its type known to the English language — 'must.'" *Delta Air Lines, Inc. v. August, supra*, 450 U.S. at 369. The potential for conflict between §1988 and Rule 68 could not be more apparent.

Of course, a civil rights plaintiff who unreasonably fails to accept a settlement offer, and who thereafter recovers less than the proffered amount in settlement, is barred under §1988 itself from recovering fees for unproductive work performed in the wake of the rejection. This is because "the extent of a plaintiff's success is a crucial factor in determining the proper amount of an award of attorney's fees," 461 U.S. at 440 (emphasis added); hours that are "excessive, redundant, or otherwise unnecessary" must be excluded from that calculus, *id.*, at 434. To this extent, the results might sometimes be the same under either §1988's reasonableness inquiry or the Court's wooden application of Rule 68. Had the Court allowed the Seventh Circuit's remand in the instant case to stand, for example, the District Court after conducting the appropriate inquiry might well have determined that much or even all of the respondent's postoffer fees were unreasonably incurred and therefore not properly awardable.

But the results under §1988 and Rule 68 will not always be congruent, because §1988 mandates the careful consideration of a broad range of other factors and accords appropriate leeway to the district court's informed discretion. Contrary to the Court's protestations, it is not at all clear that "[t]his case presents a good example" of the smooth interplay of §1988 and Rule 68, *ante*, at 9, because there has never been an evidentiary consideration of the reasonableness or unreasonableness of the respondent's fee request. It is clear, however, that under the Court's interpretation of Rule 68 a plaintiff who ultimately recovers only slightly less than the proffered amount in settlement will per se be barred from recovering trial fees even if he otherwise "has obtained excellent results" in litigation that will have far-reaching benefit to the public interest. . . .

To discuss but one example, Rule 68 allows an offer to be made any time after the complaint is filed and gives the plaintiff only 10 days to accept or reject. The Court's decision inevitably will encourage defendants who know they have violated the law to make "low-ball" offers immediately after suit is filed and before plaintiffs have been able to obtain the information they are entitled to by way of discovery to assess the strength of their claims and the reasonableness of the offers. The result will put severe pressure on plaintiffs to settle on the basis of inadequate information in order to avoid the risk of bearing all of their fees even if reasonable discovery might reveal that the defendants were subject to far greater liability. Indeed, because Rule 68 offers may be made recurrently without limitation, defendants will be well advised to make ever-slightly-larger offers throughout the discovery process and before plaintiffs have conducted all reasonably necessary discovery.

This sort of so-called "incentive" is fundamentally incompatible with Congress' goals. Congress intended for "private citizens . . . to be able to assert their civil rights" and for "those who violate the Nation's fundamental laws" not to be able "to proceed with impunity." . . .

Other difficulties will follow from the Court's decision. For example, if a plaintiff recovers less money than was offered before trial but obtains potentially far-reaching injunctive or declaratory relief, it is altogether unclear how the Court intends judges to go about quantifying the "value" of the plaintiff's success. . . .

B

Indeed, the judgment of the Court of Appeals below turned on its determination that an interpretation of Rule 68 to include attorney's fees is beyond the pale of the judiciary's rulemaking authority. *Ibid.* Congress has delegated its authority to this Court "to prescribe by general rules . . . the practice and procedure of the district courts and courts of appeals of the United States in civil actions." 28 U.S.C. §2072. This grant is limited, however, by the condition that "[s]uch rules shall not abridge, enlarge or modify any substantive right." *Ibid.* The right to attorney's fees is "substantive" under any reasonable definition of that term.

REVIEW QUESTIONS

1. Can you list the maxims of statutory interpretation that Justice Brennan uses in his analysis of the interaction between § 1988 and Rule 68? These approaches are useful in analyzing all statutes.

2. The majority and dissent apply the "plain meaning" of the statute yet reach different results. Can you articulate the argument on each side? Which do you find most convincing and why?

MORE TO PONDER

1. The ruling in *Marek v. Chesny* encourages parties to make realistic offers to their opponent by penalizing the party who refuses an offer of judgment and later receives a less favorable judgment at trial. But before *Marek*, the penalty was minor. It provided for a shift only of "costs" as a penalty, and costs (such as filing fees) are generally quite small. *Marek* adds teeth to the penalty in civil rights cases by construing "costs" to include attorneys' fees. This means that where a fee-shifting statute allows a prevailing party to recover attorneys' fees as part of costs, Rule 68 can curtail any fees otherwise due if the prevailing party rejected a settlement offer more favorable than the ultimate judgment. Fee-shifting statutes that do not include attorneys' fees as part of costs apparently avoid this operation of Rule 68.

2. *Marek* was decided at a time when § 1988 (the Civil Rights Attorney's Fees Act) was the most commonly used of the federal fee-shifting

statutes and the most common exception to the American Rule. Before this case was decided, the Supreme Court had interpreted § 1988 as authorizing courts to order defendants to pay the attorneys' fees of prevailing plaintiffs, but generally *not* to authorize courts to order plaintiffs to pay the attorneys' fees of prevailing defendants. *Christiansburg Garment Co. v. EEOC*, 434 U.S. 412 (1978)). The exception is where the plaintiffs suit is "frivolous, unreasonable, or without foundation.". *Marek* is therefore a "one-way" fee-shift rule, permitting shifts of attorneys' fees only from plaintiff to defendant; it is a "pro-plaintiff" rule, given the Court's view of the importance of encouraging enforcement of the civil rights laws.

3. Consider the plaintiff who wins a lawsuit brought under § 1983. Normally that plaintiff would then be entitled also to obtain attorneys' fees under § 1988. *Marek* ruled that Fed. R. Civ. P. 68 includes attorneys' fees within the scope of "costs" that can be shifted to the plaintiff who rejects a settlement offer that turns out to be greater than ultimate recovery. In the following simple hypothetical, how much must defendant pay in attorneys' fees?

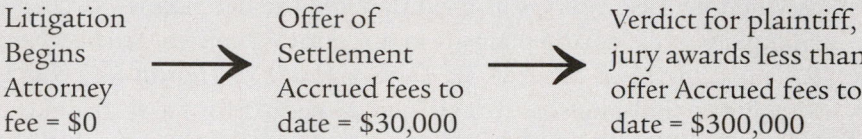

| Litigation Begins Attorney fee = $0 | → | Offer of Settlement Accrued fees to date = $30,000 | → | Verdict for plaintiff, jury awards less than offer Accrued fees to date = $300,000 |

By rejecting a settlement offer that exceeded ultimate judgment, under Fed. R. Civ. P. 68, the plaintiff now cannot shift to the defendant his attorneys' fees incurred after rejecting the settlement offer and will have to pay those fees unless the plaintiff's prior arrangement with the attorney imposed no such obligation on the plaintiff. Under what circumstances might an attorney sign such a contract?

4. The basic idea in *Marek*'s majority view is that the value of the attorneys' work up until the settlement offer deserves acknowledgment, but that the attorneys' work subsequent to a rejected settlement offer is not worthwhile when the ultimate recovery is less than the offer. But can the plaintiff who rejected the settlement offer now be liable for the defendant's attorneys' fees? The language of Fed. R. Civ. P. 68 suggests as much, once "costs" is construed to include "fees": "If the judgment finally obtained by the offeree is not more favorable than the offer, the offeree must pay the costs incurred after the making of the offer." Yet the Court in *Marek* does not direct the plaintiff to pay the attorneys' fees of the defendant that were incurred subsequent to the rejection of the settlement offer. The opinion's only comment on this issue appears

in its footnote 1, where the Court notes that the District Court refused to shift the petitioner-defendant's attorneys' fees to the respondent-plaintiff, and the petitioner-defendant did not contest this issue before the Supreme Court.

5. The *Marek* decision makes sense in light of the interpretation of § 1988. Because § 1988 has been construed as a one-way shift (absent extreme circumstances), the courts will not direct plaintiffs in § 1983 cases to pay the attorneys' fees of defendants even if Fed. R. Civ. P. 68 is triggered. Moreover, a defendant who makes a successful Rule 68 offer still is not a "prevailing party" if the plaintiff did have some recovery. Several courts thus have concluded that a defendant cannot recover its fees after making a successful Rule 68 offer. *See, e.g., EEOC v. Bailey Ford, Inc.*, 26 F.3d 570, 571 (5th Cir. 1994); *Payne v. Milwaukee Cnty.*, 288 F.3d 1021, 1027 (7th Cir. 2002). Is an accepted settlement offer adequate to be substantially "prevailing" for purposes of triggering attorneys' fees under § 1988 (or other fee-shifting statutes that permit a shift of fees to benefit the prevailing party)? It is if the accepted Rule 68 offer is filed with the court and signed as a judgment by the clerk. You may review the language of Rule 68(a) on this point. If there is no judgment, such as when litigation serves as a catalyst for the defendant's decision to change its policies, the plaintiff is not entitled to fees. *See Buckhannon Bd. and Care Home, Inc. v. W. Va. Dept. of Health & Human Res.*, 532 U.S. 598 (2001) (holding that federal laws providing for fee shifting to prevailing parties are inapplicable in the absence of an actual judgment or court-approved settlement). When cases to which no fee-shifting statute applies settle, there is no need to file the settlement with the court. Instead, the plaintiff simply dismisses the suit with prejudice.

6. A series of additional Supreme Court decisions have addressed fee shifting, largely acting to limit access to fees. Plaintiffs cannot obtain attorneys' fees when their lawsuit was merely a "catalyst" that led the defendant to change an illegal practice. *Buckhannon,* 532 U.S. at 600-601. Nor can plaintiffs be awarded attorneys' fees when they obtain a preliminary injunction if that injunction is subsequently dissolved or reversed. *Sole v. Wyner*, 551 U.S. 74, 86 (2007).

7. You should also know that Fed. R. Civ. P. 54(d) provides that costs other than attorneys' fees are to be awarded to prevailing parties unless the court otherwise directs or particular statutory provisions apply. Although "costs" covered by federal awards of costs to prevailing parties are usually quite limited, they can include the costs of a plaintiff's experts following a judgment for the plaintiff. Expert fees may be paid for by the other side under Fed. R. Civ. P. 26(a)(4)(C), which authorizes the judge to require a party seeking discovery to pay the reasonable fee of an expert responding to the discovery, or a fair portion of the fees

and expenses incurred by the opposing party in obtaining facts and opinions from the expert.

8. By its own terms, Rule 68 requires that offers allow judgment to be taken for both damages and costs. After *Marek*, if an underlying statute defines attorneys' fees as costs, then attorneys' fees must also be included in Rule 68 offers. The Court in *Marek* noted that this requirement can be met either by an offer that includes or specifies an amount for costs, or by an offer that does not include costs but that nevertheless allows judgment to be taken, costs to be determined and awarded by the court. If a rejected offer does not include costs, final judgment will be compared to the amount of the offer. In contrast, if a rejected offer includes costs, the final judgment will presumably be compared to the amount of the offer minus the costs accrued at the time of the offer. Thus, courts must often determine whether an offer included costs in order to determine whether Rule 68 applies. Unfortunately, Rule 68 does not provide guidance on how to draft a Rule 68 offer, nor how courts are to interpret such offers. If a defendant has offered "$100,000 with costs," has the defendant offered $100,000 including costs, or $100,000 in addition to costs? Courts have struggled with such ambiguities and have often reached contrary results. *See, e.g., Kyreakakis v. Paternoster*, 732 F. Supp. 1287 (D.N.J. 1990); *Christian v. R. Wood Motors, Inc.*, 1995 WL 238981 (N.D.N.Y. 1995). Other complications, such as claims involving requests for injunctive relief, have proved equally difficult.

PRACTICE EXERCISE NO. 5: REVISING FED. R. CIV. P. 68

States have been experimenting with methods for encouraging settlement that are more robust than Rule 68. For example, as part of tort reform measures the State of Georgia adopted the following provision:

> If a defendant makes an offer of settlement which is rejected by the plaintiff, the defendant shall be entitled to recover reasonable attorney's fees and expenses of litigation incurred by the defendant . . . from the date of the rejection of the offer of settlement through the entry of judgment if the final judgment is one of no liability or the final judgment obtained by the plaintiff is less than 75 percent of such offer of settlement.

O.C.G.A. § 9-11-68(b)(1) (West 2015), *limited on constitutional grounds by Fowler Prop., Inc. v. Dowland*, 646 S.E.2d 197, 197 (Ga. 2007) (holding that statute could not be applied retroactively). Texas has enacted an offer of settlement statute that is trigged when "a settlement offer is made and rejected and the judgment to be rendered will be significantly less favorable to the rejecting party than was the settlement offer." Tex. Civ. Prac. & Rem. Code § 42.004 (West 2011). In that event, the party rejecting settlement must pay all the offering party's costs, including reasonable attorneys' fees, with the caveat that "[t]he litigation costs that may be awarded under this chapter to any party may not be greater than the total amount that the claimant recovers or would recover before adding an award of litigation costs under this chapter in favor of the claimant or subtracting as an offset an award of litigation costs under this chapter in favor of the defendant." Some states have offer of settlement rules geared to specific type of cases. For example, Maryland enacted an offer of judgment statute applicable to medical malpractice claims. Md. Code, Cts. & Jud. Proc., § 3-2A-08A(f) (West 2015).

Imagine that you have been appointed to an Advisory Committee considering proposed changes to Fed. R. Civ. P. 68; what would you recommend? As you draft your revisions, keep in mind the *Marek* dissent's concern that the Rules Enabling Act boundaries may be breached by a procedural rule with substantive effects. Try to work out the specific language for a new rule, and explain what you are pursuing and how the rule would handle different cases.

For detailed analysis of the problems under the current regime and for alternative approaches, *see* Danielle M. Shelton, *Rewriting Rule 68: Realizing the Benefits of the Federal Settlement Rule by Injecting Certainty into Offers of Judgment*, 91 Minn. L. Rev. 865 (2007); Robert G. Bone, *"To Encourage Settlement": Rule 68, Offers of Judgment, and the History of the Federal Rules of Civil Procedure*, 102 Nw. U. L. Rev. 1561 (2008).

a. Conditional Offer of Settlement

What if the defendant offers a settlement whose terms include waiver of the attorneys' fees, notwithstanding a statutory provision calling for the defendant to pay the fee of a prevailing plaintiff? In *Evans v. Jeff D.*, 475 U.S. 717 (1986), the lawyers for a class-action plaintiff group of children with disabilities faced precisely this question when the defendant offered to settle and provide "virtually all of the injunctive relief" to improve the children's health care treatment as sought in the complaint—provided that the plaintiffs would waive statutory attorneys' fees. The plaintiff's attorney claimed that this offer violated the statute and would undermine its purpose of promoting precisely this kind of successful lawsuit. The lawyer claimed that he faced an ethical conflict between the interests of his current client and the interests of potential future clients with similar claims whose cases he would not be able to take because of the risk of forgoing attorneys' fees even in a successful case. The Supreme Court rejected this argument:

> Although respondents contend that Johnson, as counsel for the class, was faced with an "ethical dilemma" when petitioners offered him relief greater than that which he could reasonably have expected to obtain for his clients at trial (if only he would stipulate to a waiver of the statutory fee award), . . . we do not believe that the "dilemma" was an "ethical" one in the sense that Johnson had to choose between conflicting duties under the prevailing norms of professional

conduct. Plainly Johnson had no *ethical* obligation to seek a statutory fee award. His ethical duty was to serve his clients loyally and competently. Since the proposal to settle the merits was more favorable than the probable outcome of the trial, Johnson's decision to recommend acceptance was consistent with the highest standards of our profession.

475 U.S. at 727-728.

QUESTIONS TO PONDER

1. Special problems in *Evans v. Jeff D.* arose because the case was a class action composed of children with disabilities. Therefore, the option of a full discussion between attorney and client about whether to accept a settlement that waives attorneys' fees was unavailable. Could an individual, competent adult client make a sensible choice about whether or not to waive attorneys' fees as part of a settlement offer?

2. Perhaps the most widespread response to the issue presented in *Evans v. Jeff D.* is the use of contractual provisions between lawyers and their clients that forbid the client from waiving court-awarded fees. Are there any problems with this kind of agreement? Should the rules of professional ethics forbid it?

3. Taking *Evans v. Jeff D.* and *Marek v. Chesny* together, what policies provide the basis for the federal tendency toward settlement and toward litigation encouraged by pro-plaintiff fee shifts? Would you strike the balance differently? What factors are most relevant to this judgment? Note how the balance affects (a) when lawsuits should be filed; (b) when already filed lawsuits should be settled; and (c) when lawsuits should be followed through to judgments and precedential effects.

---

b. Frivolous Claims

As noted in the introduction to this section, a defendant may receive an award of fees under § 1988 in lawsuits bringing frivolous claims, but only for fees and costs that the defendant would not have incurred but for the frivolous claims. *Fox v. Vice*, 131 S. Ct. 2205 (2011). Defining a frivolous claim is notoriously difficult. In *Fox*, Justice Kagan explained:

> ... In enacting §1988, we stated, Congress sought "to protect defendants from burdensome litigation having no legal or factual basis." Accordingly, §1988 authorizes a district court to award attorney's fees to a defendant "upon a finding that the plaintiff's action was frivolous, unreasonable, or without foundation." ... These standards would be easy to apply if life were like the movies, but that is usually not the case. In Hollywood, litigation most often concludes with a dramatic verdict that leaves one party fully triumphant and the other utterly prostrate. The court in such a case would know exactly how to award fees (even

if that anti-climactic scene is generally left on the cutting-room floor). But in the real world, litigation is more complex, involving multiple claims for relief that implicate a mix of legal theories and have different merits. Some claims succeed; others fail. Some charges are frivolous; others (even if not ultimately successful) have a reasonable basis. In short, litigation is messy, and courts must deal with this untidiness in awarding fees.

131 S. Ct. at 2214.

The issue of frivolous claims is raised here because fee shifting enables litigation, raising concerns in some circles that it enables too much litigation. These issues will be revisited in Chapter 3's discussion of pleadings doctrine and sanctions under Fed. R. Civ. P. 11.

4. Assessing the Value of Legal Services

When a court awards attorneys' fees, how should those fees be calculated? Billing practices by attorneys vary widely. Traditionally, lawyers in this country have billed for each hour of service, but lawyers charge different hourly rates based on their years of experience, demonstrated expertise, access to colleagues with other expertise, or other reputational features. Percentage contingent fees are a long-standing alternative, especially in the field of personal injuries; the attorney and client agree by contract that the attorney will share a specified percentage of any award or settlement. Increasingly, lawyers explore other billing practices, including set fees for certain services, yearly salary (for in-house counsel, prepaid legal services plans, or legal aid lawyers), or a mixture of methods. Should the attorneys' fees awarded under a fee-shifting statute be subjected to a judicial inquiry as to their reasonableness — and if so, how should they be measured? Should the court inquire about the relationship between the fees and the amount recovered? The following case illuminates these questions.

City of Riverside v. Rivera
477 U.S. 561 (1986)

Justice BRENNAN announced the judgment of the Court and delivered an opinion in which Justice MARSHALL, Justice BLACKMUN and Justice STEVENS join:

The issue presented in this case is whether an award of attorney's fees under 42 U.S.C. §1988 is per se "unreasonable" within the meaning of the statute if it exceeds the amount of damages recovered by the plaintiff in the underlying civil rights action.

I

Respondents, eight Chicano individuals, attended a party on the evening of August 1, 1975, at the Riverside, California, home of respondents Santos and Jennie Rivera. A large number of unidentified police officers, acting without a warrant, broke up the party using tear gas and, as found by the District Court, "unnecessary physical force." Many of the guests, including four of the respondents, were arrested. The District Court later found that "[t]he party was not creating a disturbance in the community at the time of the break-in." . . . Criminal charges against the arrestees were ultimately dismissed for lack of probable cause.

On June 4, 1976, respondents sued the city of Riverside, its Chief of Police, and 30 individual police officers under 42 U.S.C. §§1981, 1983, 1985(3), and 1986 for allegedly violating their First, Fourth, and Fourteenth Amendment rights. The complaint, which also alleged numerous state-law claims, sought damages and declaratory and injunctive relief. On August 5, 1977, 23 of the individual police officers moved for summary judgment; the District Court granted summary judgment in favor of 17 of these officers. The case against the remaining defendants proceeded to trial in September 1980. The jury returned a total of 37 individual verdicts in favor of the respondents and against the city and five individual officers, finding 11 violations of §1983, 4 instances of false arrest and imprisonment, and 22 instances of negligence. Respondents were awarded $33,350 in compensatory and punitive damages: $13,300 for their federal claims, and $20,050 for their state-law claims.

Respondents also sought attorney's fees and costs under §1988. They requested compensation for 1,946.75 hours expended by their two attorneys at a rate of $125 per hour, and for 84.5 hours expended by law clerks at a rate of $25 per hour, a total of $245,456.25. The District Court found both the hours and rates reasonable, and awarded respondents $245,456.25 in attorney's fees. The court rejected respondents' request for certain additional expenses, and for a multiplier sought by respondents to reflect the contingent nature of their success and the high quality of their attorneys' efforts.

Petitioners appealed only the attorney's fees award, which the Court of Appeals for the Ninth Circuit affirmed. *Rivera v. City of Riverside*, 679 F.2d 795 (1982). Petitioners sought a writ of certiorari from this Court. We granted the writ, vacated the Court of Appeals' judgment, and remanded the case for reconsideration in light of *Hensley v. Eckerhart*, 461 U.S. 424 (1983). On remand, the District Court held two additional hearings, reviewed additional briefing, and reexamined the record as a whole. The court made extensive findings of fact and conclusions of law, and again concluded that respondents were entitled to an award of $245,456.25 in attorney's fees, based on the same total number of hours expended on the case and the same hourly rates. The court again denied respondents' request for certain expenses and for a multiplier.

Petitioners again appealed the fee award. And again, the Court of Appeals affirmed, finding that "the district court correctly reconsidered the case in light of *Hensley*. . . ." 763 F.2d 1580, 1582 (1985). The Court of Appeals rejected three arguments raised by petitioners. First, the court rejected petitioners' contention that respondents' counsel should not have been compensated for time spent litigating claims other than those upon which respondents ultimately prevailed.

Emphasizing that the District Court had determined that respondents' attorneys had "spent no time on claims unrelated to the successful claims," *ibid.*, the Court of Appeals concluded that "[t]he record supports the district court's findings that all of the plaintiffs' claims involve a 'common core of facts' and that the claims involve related legal theories." *Ibid.* The court also observed that, consistent with *Hensley*, the District Court had "considered the degree of success [achieved by respondents' attorneys] and found a reasonable relationship between the extent of that success and the amount of the fee award." 763 F.2d, at 1582. Second, the Court of Appeals rejected the argument that the fee award was excessive because it exceeded the amount of damages awarded by the jury. Examining the legislative history of §1988, the court found no support for the proposition that an award of attorney's fees may not exceed the amount of damages recovered by a prevailing plaintiff. Finally, the court found that the District Court's "extensive findings of fact and conclusions of law" belied petitioners' claim that the District Court had not reviewed the record to determine whether the fee award was justified. . . .

II

A

. . . Congress enacted the Civil Rights Attorney's Fees Awards Act of 1976, 42 U.S.C. §1988, which authorized the district courts to award reasonable attorney's fees to prevailing parties in specified civil rights litigation. [T]he statute itself does not explain what constitutes a reasonable fee. . . .

Hensley v. Eckerhart, 461 U.S. 424 (1983), announced certain guidelines for calculating a reasonable attorney's fee under §1988. *Hensley* stated that "[t]he most useful starting point for determining the amount of a reasonable fee is the number of hours reasonably expended on the litigation multiplied by a reasonable hourly rate." *Id.*, at 433. This figure, commonly referred to as the "lodestar," is presumed to be the reasonable fee contemplated by §1988. The opinion cautioned that "[t]he district court . . . should exclude from this initial fee calculation hours that were not 'reasonably expended'" on the litigation. *Id.*, at 434 (quoting Senate Report, at 6). . . .

B

Petitioners argue that the District Court failed properly to follow *Hensley* in calculating respondents' fee award. We disagree. The District Court carefully considered the results obtained by respondents pursuant to the instructions set forth in *Hensley*, and concluded that respondents were entitled to recover attorney's fees for all hours expended on the litigation. First, the court found that "[t]he amount of time expended by counsel in conducting this litigation was reasonable and reflected sound legal judgment under the circumstances." The court also determined that counsel's excellent performances in this case entitled them to be compensated at prevailing market rates, even though they were relatively young when this litigation began. *See Johnson*, 488 F.2d, at 718-719 ("If a young attorney demonstrates the skill and ability, he should not be penalized for only recently being admitted to the bar").

The District Court then concluded that it was inappropriate to adjust respondents' fee award downward to account for the fact that respondents had prevailed only on some of their claims, and against only some of the defendants. The court first determined that "it was never actually clear what officer did what until we had gotten through with the whole trial," so that "[u]nder the circumstances of this case, it was reasonable for plaintiffs initially to name thirty-one individual defendants . . . as well as the City of Riverside as defendants in this action." . . .

The District Court also considered the amount of damages recovered, and determined that the size of the damages award did not imply that respondents' success was limited:

> [T]he size of the jury award resulted from (a) the general reluctance of jurors to make large awards against police officers, and (b) the dignified restraint which the plaintiffs exercised in describing their injuries to the jury. For example, although some of the actions of the police would clearly have been insulting and humiliating to even the most insensitive person and were, in the opinion of the Court, intentionally so, plaintiffs did not attempt to play up this aspect of the case.

Id., at 188-189. The court paid particular attention to the fact that the case "presented complex and interrelated issues of fact and law," *id.*, at 187, and that "[a] fee award in this civil rights action will . . . advance the public interest." . . .

Based on our review of the record, we agree with the Court of Appeals that the District Court's findings were not clearly erroneous. We conclude that the District Court correctly applied the factors announced in *Hensley* in calculating respondents' fee award, and that the court did not abuse its discretion in awarding attorney's fees for all time reasonably spent litigating the case.

III

Petitioners, joined by the United States as amicus curiae, maintain that *Hensley*'s lodestar approach is inappropriate in civil rights cases where a plaintiff recovers only monetary damages. In these cases, so the argument goes, use of the lodestar may result in fees that exceed the amount of damages recovered and that are therefore unreasonable. Likening such cases to private tort actions, petitioners and the United States submit that attorney's fees in such cases should be proportionate to the amount of damages a plaintiff recovers. Specifically, they suggest that fee awards in damages cases should be modeled upon the contingent-fee arrangements commonly used in personal injury litigation. In this case, assuming a 33% contingency rate, this would entitle respondents to recover approximately $11,000 in attorney's fees.

The amount of damages a plaintiff recovers is certainly relevant to the amount of attorney's fees to be awarded under §1988. *See Johnson*, 488 F.2d, at 718. It is, however, only one of many factors that a court should consider in calculating an award of attorney's fees. We reject the proposition that fee awards under §1988 should necessarily be proportionate to the amount of damages a civil rights plaintiff actually recovers.

A

As an initial matter, we reject the notion that a civil rights action for damages constitutes nothing more than a private tort suit benefiting only the individual plaintiffs whose rights were violated. Unlike most private tort litigants, a civil rights plaintiff seeks to vindicate important civil and constitutional rights that cannot be valued solely in monetary terms. . . .

B

A rule that limits attorney's fees in civil rights cases to a proportion of the damages awarded would seriously undermine Congress' purpose in enacting §1988. Congress enacted §1988 specifically because it found that the private market for legal services failed to provide many victims of civil rights violations with effective access to the judicial process. These victims ordinarily cannot afford to purchase legal services at the rates set by the private market. . . . Moreover, the contingent fee arrangements that make legal services available to many victims of personal injuries would often not encourage lawyers to accept civil rights cases, which frequently involve substantial expenditures of time and effort but produce only small monetary recoveries. . . .

Justice POWELL's concurrence is omitted. Chief Justice BURGER, dissenting:

I join Justice Rehnquist's dissenting opinion. I write only to add that it would be difficult to find a better example of legal nonsense than the fixing of attorney's fees by a judge at $245,456.25 for the recovery of $33,350 damages.

The two attorneys receiving this nearly quarter-million-dollar fee graduated from law school in 1973 and 1974; they brought this action in 1975, which resulted in the $33,350 jury award in 1980. Their total professional experience when this litigation began consisted of Gerald Lopez' 1-year service as a law clerk to a judge and Roy Cazares' two years' experience as a trial attorney in the Defenders' Program of San Diego County. For their services the District Court found that an hourly rate of $125 per hour was reasonable.

Can anyone doubt that no private party would ever have dreamed of paying these two novice attorneys $125 per hour in 1975, which, considering inflation, would represent perhaps something more nearly a $250 per hour rate today? . . .

This fee award plainly constitutes a grave abuse of discretion which should be rejected by this Court—particularly when we have already vacated and remanded this identical fee award previously—rather than simply affirming the District Court's findings as not being either "clearly erroneous" or an "abuse of discretion." The Court's result will unfortunately only add fuel to the fires of public indignation over the costs of litigation.

Justice REHNQUIST, with whom THE CHIEF JUSTICE, Justice WHITE, and Justice O'CONNOR join, dissenting:

I see no escape from the conclusion that the District Court's finding that respondents' attorneys "reasonably" spent 1,946.75 hours to recover a money judgment of $33,350 is clearly erroneous, and that therefore the District Court's award of $245,456.25 in attorney's fees to respondents should be reversed. The Court's affirmance of the fee award emasculates the principles laid down in *Hensley*, and turns §1988 into a relief Act for lawyers.

A brief look at the history of this case reveals just how "unreasonable" it was for respondents' lawyers to spend so much time on it. Respondents filed their initial complaint in 1976, seeking injunctive and declaratory relief and compensatory and punitive damages from the city of Riverside, its Chief of Police, and 30 police officers, based on 256 separate claims allegedly arising out of the police breakup of a single party. Prior to trial, 17 of the police officers were dismissed from the case on motions for summary judgment, and respondents dropped their requests for injunctive and declaratory relief. More significantly, respondents also dropped their original allegation that the police had acted with discriminatory intent. The action proceeded to trial, and the jury completely exonerated nine additional police officers. Respondents ultimately prevailed against only the city and five police officers on various §1983, false arrest and imprisonment, and common negligence claims. No restraining orders or injunctions were ever issued against petitioners, nor was the city ever compelled to change a single practice or policy as a result of respondents' suit. The jury awarded respondents a total of $33,350 in compensatory and punitive damages. Only about one-third of this total, or $13,300, was awarded to respondents based on violations of their federal constitutional rights. . . .

The analysis of whether the extraordinary number of hours put in by respondents' attorneys in this case was "reasonable" must be made in light of both the traditional billing practices in the profession, and the fundamental principle that the award of a "reasonable" attorney's fee under §1988 means a fee that would have been deemed reasonable if billed to affluent plaintiffs by their own attorneys. . . .

REVIEW QUESTIONS

1. What is the rule for determining reasonable attorneys' fees articulated by the majority?
2. The dissent claims that it was wasteful to spend $245,456.25 in attorneys' fees to win $33,350 in compensation. What is the plurality's response?
3. Consider the benefits and costs of adopting a proportional compensation scheme for attorney's fees. For example, how would a court calculate fees for injunctive relief? What should the courts do in cases where only nominal damages are awarded?

QUESTIONS TO PONDER

1. Should the public's perception of fee awards greater than the amount of compensation matter to the Supreme Court?

2. Should attorneys' fees be calculated any differently when the relief is injunctive, versus when the relief is money damages? Why or why not?

3. Does the central difficulty in *City of Riverside* stem from hourly billing? What other ways of assessing the value of lawyers' work could provide compensation and incentive to lawyers to undertake appropriate cases? Most attorneys in private practice base their fees on the number of hours they work on a matter, often billing in six-minute increments. Annual billings in excess of 2,000 hours per year is common in larger firms and firms link billed hours to substantial bonuses awarded to their associates. The hourly billing model raises three concerns. First, hourly billing may encourage inefficiency. Second, it may encourage excessive litigation. Third, it may encourage fraud. It is difficult to determine how much unethical billing goes on. In the increasingly tight legal market, clients are extremely cost sensitive and firms are increasingly required to justify their bills with detailed explanations of the work performed. A 1991 study found that most lawyers denied engaging in unethical billing practices such as "padding" hours. *See* William G. Ross, *The Ethics of Hourly Billing by Attorneys*, 44 Rutgers L. Rev. 1 (1991). A number of studies have confirmed this finding since then.

4. As you learn more about the process of civil litigation, consider how the Rules of Civil Procedure might provide opportunities for increasing billed hours in ways that do not necessarily benefit the client. The discovery process, which you will read about in Chapter 4, has been a particular subject of criticism for encouraging unnecessary attorney labor and a concomitant increase in fees. Some law firms have sought to encourage business by switching to a flat rate approach, such as billing a flat rate per task. Another alternative is the contingency fee, discussed next.

5. The Contingency Fee

An American innovation, the contingency fee is the leading alternative to hourly billing by attorneys. Typically, the client signs an agreement drafted by the attorney that promises to pay the attorney a specified percentage, usually one-third, of any recovery achieved through the litigation, and simultaneously makes it clear that the client will owe no fee if there is no recovery. Under state judicial and ethics rules, such arrangements do not violate traditional norms against champerty, in which a person not a party to a suit agrees to invest in it in return for a share in the profits, while also providing for judicial review to ensure reasonable terms in contingency agreements.

What effect does this billing practice have on attorneys? The contingency fee in a real sense makes the lawyer an investor or joint venturer with the client. To proceed with the lawsuit, the lawyer has to invest time and potentially further resources for experts, court costs, and investigative work. The lawyer therefore must make judgments about which cases are worth taking "on speculation"; some must pay off if the lawyer is to stay in business over time.

The contingency fee also affects how much time a lawyer puts into a case, what the lawyer does with that time, and how the lawyer views settlements (and clients). One economic analysis suggests that the lawyer "should continue to devote hours to [a given contingency fee case] only as long as each additional hour increased his fee by at least as much as his opportunity cost," meaning the cost of forgoing work on another matter. Kevin M. Clermont and John D. Currivan, *Improving on the Contingent Fee*, 63 Cornell L. Rev. 529 (1978). Perhaps lawyers paid on a contingent fee basis will spend fewer hours on a case than would be optimal for the client (if the case appears to be a losing one), and lawyers paid on an hourly basis will put in more than the optimal number of hours. One study, based on court records and interviews with 371 hourly fee lawyers and 267 contingent fee lawyers from 12 state and federal courts concluded that:

> . . . the contingent fee lawyer appears sensitive to the potential return to be achieved from a case, which is closely related to the stakes. The hourly fee lawyer's return from a case is not as tied to stakes, and other types of considerations (*e.g.*, the client's goals, the nature of the forum, etc.) have a greater influence.

Herbert M. Kritzer, William L.F. Felstiner, Austin Sarat, and David M. Trubek, *The Impact of Fee Arrangement on Lawyer Effort*, 19 Law & Soc'y Rev. 251, 271 (1985).

In *Venegas v. Mitchell*, 495 U.S. 82 (1990), the Supreme Court considered whether a federal fee-shifting statute invalidates contingent-fee contracts that would require a prevailing plaintiff to pay his attorney more than the statutory award against the defendant. Mitchell was hired three months before the trial of Venegas' civil rights suit against city police officers (alleging false arrest and perjured trial), after the bulk of preparation had been completed. Mitchell obtained a $10,000 non-refundable retainer and a right to share in 40 percent of the gross amount of any recovery. After trial, the defendants unsuccessfully moved to set aside the judgment and then appealed. Mitchell pursued and obtained statutory attorneys' fees under 42 U.S.C. § 1988, which the court calculated by multiplying the hours of attorney time by a market-based hourly rate. Mitchell then sought 40 percent of the judgment proceeds. The court agreed to enforce the contingency fee arrangement. On review, the Supreme Court concluded that private fee arrangements may exist alongside statutory fee shifts, and therefore permitted enforcement of the contingency fee arrangement at issue. Perhaps the problem in the case arose from the method for assessing the value of the lawyer's time.

An advocacy group called Common Good has launched a proposal to coordinate incentives to settle and attorneys' fees by limiting the scope of contingency fees (essentially limited to tort cases). *See* Adam Liptak, *In 13 States, a Push to Limit Lawyers' Fees*, N.Y. Times, May 26, 2003. The proposal would limit the fees in many cases to 10 percent of the first $100,000 of a settlement, with 5 percent of any further settlement amount. Under the proposal, at the start of the case a plaintiff's attorney must write the defendant's attorney with a description of the injury and explanation of the defendant's liability. If the defense responds with a settlement offer and the plaintiff accepts it, the cap on the contingency fee for the plaintiff's attorney would apply. If that attorney neglected to send such a letter at all, the fee would be similarly capped regardless of how many hours or what degree of success for the plaintiff emerge. Consider how the proposal would affect the adversary system, the settlement rate, and the balance of power between plaintiff and defendant; would you support the proposal?

6. Third-Party Litigation Financing

Traditionally, contingency fee lawyers self-funded litigation. The newest development in litigation financing is financing by third-party investors. Consider the limits and possibilities of third-party litigation financing laid out in the following excerpt.

Jonathan T. Molot, Litigation Finance: A Market Solution to a Procedural Problem
99 Geo. L.J. 65, 92-100 (2010)

There are several different ways that U.S. investors have sought to profit from investments in litigation claims, each of which is briefly discussed below.

a. The Cash Advance Industry for Personal Injury Victims. Over the last decade or so, a relatively new "cash advance" industry has developed. Cash advance firms offer personal injury victims cash advances while their personal injury lawsuits are pending. Most of these firms structure their advances as nonrecourse loans. The transactions are loans insofar as the cash advance firm charges a fixed interest rate on the funds advanced, rather than receiving a specified percentage of the plaintiffs' recovery the way attorneys do under a contingent fee arrangement. Yet, they are nonrecourse loans because the plaintiff need only pay back the advance if the lawsuit succeeds. The cash advance firm accepts the risk that the lawsuit will result in a defense verdict or a recovery that is less than the amount owed by the plaintiff.

There are serious problems with this cash advance system. The problems stem from the very high interest rates charged by cash advance firms—typically 3% to 5% monthly interest, and often much higher. The high interest rate is a problem for two reasons. First, it strips the risk-transfer mechanism of much of its value for the plaintiff. If our goal is to ensure that plaintiffs receive what they are entitled to under substantive law, it does no good if the plaintiff must pay away much of that value in interest. Second, the rapid accumulation of interest undermines our goal of bolstering plaintiffs' bargaining position vis-à-vis repeat player defendants. A plaintiff whose net recovery declines the longer he or she goes without settling will have strong incentives to settle quickly, and have a much harder time rejecting low settlement offers and holding out for more. . . .

The high interest rates charged by cash advance firms are partly a product of the risk involved, but they are also partly a byproduct of government regulation. Cash advance firms structure their products to avoid two areas of government regulation. First, by charging a fixed interest rate, rather than taking a share of the plaintiffs' recovery, cash advance firms avoid prohibitions against champerty and maintenance that historically have prevented third parties from funding litigation in exchange for a share of the recovery. . . . To avoid usury restrictions imposed on traditional loans, the cash advance firms make repayment of the advances entirely conditional on success in the lawsuit. . . .

Rather than paying a high, compounding interest rate a plaintiff might be far better-off simply selling a percentage of his recovery to a cash advance firm, just as he does to his attorney. . . . Just as plaintiffs today can use contingent fee arrangements to protect themselves from the downside risk of losing and being on the hook for legal fees, so too could plaintiffs sell an interest in a third of their cases to cash advance firms, thereby protecting themselves from the risk of collecting nothing. . . .

There are two obstacles to this shift from charging high interest rates to taking a share of the recovery. The first is economic. The diligence required of a cash advance firm to ensure that a lawsuit is worth more than a fixed amount is not as great as the diligence required to put a precise value on the suit. . . .

State regulation is a second obstacle that prevents cash advance firms from charging a percentage of the recovery. . . . [A]lthough many states have done away with champerty and maintenance restrictions, others have not. Before cash advance firms could routinely take shares of recoveries from personal injury victims, they would need to seek clarification or reform of the law and would have to structure their transactions very carefully.

b. Investment in Commercial Litigation by Investment Funds. . . . Some investment funds and investment banks have begun to buy interests in commercial lawsuits. . . . Hedge funds, and some traders at investment banks, have long viewed litigation risk as attractive because it is uncorrelated with markets—the outcome of a lawsuit will not depend upon fluctuations in the stock or bond markets. . . . Even if a fund can accurately predict the outcome of a pending lawsuit, [however,] the stock price of the company that is a party to that lawsuit will depend upon many factors outside of the pending litigation. . . .

For a fund that wants to make a clean bet on a lawsuit—a bet that will expose it to pure litigation risk while neutralizing other factors that can affect a company's share price—the most attractive course is to make a direct investment in the lawsuit. The hedge fund can offer the plaintiff cash for a portion of the recovery where the plaintiff needs cash or simply wants to reduce his exposure to litigation risk. . . . By selling part of its claim, the plaintiff can both eliminate the cost of pursuing the claim and monetize a portion of the claim to fuel the company's growth. . . . By enlisting the help and cash of a third party, the plaintiff may be able to bolster its negotiating position vis-à-vis the defendant, thereby increasing its recovery. . . .

Where commercial claims are involved, rather than personal injury claims, it is easy to structure transactions so that the capital provider takes a percentage of the recovery without running afoul of any potentially applicable maintenance or champerty restrictions. Lawsuits that are held by corporate entities can be sold simply by selling ownership interests in the relevant corporate entities—ownership interests with returns that may be tied to the recovery in the relevant lawsuit. Indeed, complicated structuring may be entirely unnecessary because most champerty and maintenance laws are confined to "personal" actions, like personal injury suits, and do not restrict the sale of commercial claims. Moreover, the pricing problems that may get in the way of cash advance firms buying a percentage of a personal injury claim are less daunting in the commercial claim context. It is much less costly and time consuming to value one $50 million commercial suit than to value one-thousand different $50,000 lawsuits, provided that each suit has its own individual set of facts and legal issues. Expected returns can cover the diligence expenses associated with such a large investment. . . .

c. Law-Firm Finance. Investment-fund capital has been of some use not only to small companies with large commercial claims, but also, in some instances, to law firms that want to take in capital and off-load risk associated with contingent fee cases. Recall that one limitation of the contingent fee system is that it does not permit lawyers to share fees with nonlawyers. However, some of the same entities that buy interests in lawsuits from plaintiffs have recently found ways to make investments in litigation via law firms. These investments in law firms, like investments in personal injury claims, are structured as loans rather than as the sale of a portion of claims. Unlike maintenance and champerty restrictions that have been relaxed in many states to permit litigation plaintiffs to sell portions of their claims, the ethical prohibition against attorney fee sharing is uniform. Only the District of Columbia permits lawyers to share fees with nonlawyers, though this permission is limited to other professionals, like accountants or lobbyists, who work side-by-side with lawyers in partnerships and take a share of profits for their work. No state permits lawyers to give away a portion of their legal fees—whether contingent fees or hourly fees—in exchange for a capital infusion from an investment fund.

Lawyers are, however, permitted to borrow money. And, just as cash advance firms make nonrecourse loans to personal injury victims, so too might investors make loans to law firms that are recoverable only out of the law firms' revenues for legal services rendered. The interest rates for these law-firm loans might not be quite as high as for personal injury victims, but they would still be quite high — 25% per year or greater, depending upon the risk involved. . . .

Why, one might wonder, would a law firm ever agree to pay such a high rate of interest? Do law firms really need outside financing? Outside the U.S., the answer has been yes, and at least regulators in Australia have moved toward allowing lawyers to raise capital from outside investors and even toward offering shares to the public. . . . In the United States, where equity-based financing is prohibited, would lawyers similarly be inclined to resort to outside financing, even if it must be in the form of debt, rather than equity? Different law firms may have different reasons for raising capital from outside investors or lenders. A law firm that generally works for a contingent fee may find that it has taken on a large, potentially quite profitable case, but lacks the resources to litigate a large, drawnout battle with the defendant. . . . Conventional bank loans may not suffice given the extent of the risk involved. For lawyers unwilling or unable to guarantee their law firms' loans personally, borrowing money from an investment fund at a high rate of interest may make sense. If the cases are sufficiently large and promising, the lawyers may still hope to make a great deal of money after paying off loans at a 25% interest rate. . . . Outside financing might also be of value to a risk-averse law firm that generally bills by the hour and is presented with attractive contingent fee opportunities. . . .

Law-firm finance represents a way for attorneys to take on risk through contingent fee arrangements, and then spread that risk over a broader pool of investors who are better able to bear it. As with the cash advance industry, however, the high-interest loan structure is not ideal if the ultimate goal is to bolster the bargaining power of risk-averse plaintiffs pitted against repeat-player defendants. A law firm paying interest on an outstanding loan, like a plaintiff who has received a cash advance, will have a strong incentive to settle early and repay its debt from the proceeds.

QUESTIONS TO PONDER

1. Consider the three forms of litigation financing in light of the discussion in Chapter 1 about access to justice. Would these different types of litigation financing allow more access to the courts for the underserved, would they increase litigation needlessly, or would they have no effect? How would one go about finding out?

2. The Federal Rules of Civil Procedure do not apply differently to different types of litigation. Instead, the Rules are trans-substantive. Molot argues that different types of cases should be treated differently. What do you think of this argument? Should the Rules explicitly take into account the different types of financing available to different litigants?

PRACTICE EXERCISE NO. 6:
FEE ARRANGEMENTS IN *CARPENTER* AND *WARNER*

Return to the *Carpenter* and *Warner* cases. Assume that you have been approached by the plaintiff(s) in each case to represent them. Estimate the relief available and the statutory attorneys' fees (if any). Would these plaintiffs pay an hourly fee or would you need to take them on a contingency? (If on a contingent fee, how would you handle costs and disbursements?)

Consider also representing the defendants in these cases. Is there symmetry with respect to access to counsel for plaintiffs and defendants? How would you be paid if you represented Randall Dee, the driver in the *Carpenter* case? And what about the defendant City of New York in *Warner*: Who is paying its counsel, and on what basis?

F. CONTEMPT

A party or lawyer who disobeys a court order or court rule risks being found in contempt of court. A court's contempt power extends to both civil and criminal contempt, but the distinction between the two types of contempt has caused much confusion among courts and law students alike. In the leading case distinguishing the two types of contempt, the Supreme Court stated that "[c]ontempts are neither wholly civil nor altogether criminal. And it may not always be easy to classify a particular act as belonging to either one of these two classes. It may partake of the characteristics of both." *Gompers v. Buck's Stove & Range Co.*, 221 U.S. 418 (1911) (internal quotations omitted).

Generally speaking, civil contempt is tied up with ongoing litigation, and is meant to induce some sort of outcome or remedy. The punishment is remedial and thus can be indefinite; the contempt is alleviated when the individual in contempt acquiesces to the court's will. For example, a party may be found to be in civil contempt for refusing to provide requested documents. The party may be conditionally punished until such time that the party agrees to produce the required documents. In *Turner v. Rogers*, discussed in Chapter 1, a South Carolina court held a father who did not pay child support in civil contempt. By contrast, criminal contempt involves punishment for violating a court order or interfering with court power. While civil contempt is intended to compel, criminal contempt is expressly punitive. Thus, punishment of criminal contempt must be definite and in accordance with the rules and procedures of criminal law, including a higher burden of proof. Unlike civil contempt, criminal contempt is adjudicated independently from other litigation. Examples of acts giving rise to criminal contempt proceedings include threatening a judge and obstructing court proceedings. For a useful comparison of civil and criminal contempt, *see* Jennifer Fleischer, *In Defense of Civil Contempt Sanctions*, 36 Colum. J.L. & Soc. Probs. 35 (2002).

On occasion, individuals deliberately disobey court orders just as they may disobey a statute in order to protest or challenge a rule or norm they consider unjust. In recent years, protestors have violated rules governing access to abortion clinics and military settings. *See, e.g., Bray v. Alexandria Women's Health Clinic*, 506 U.S. 263 (1993) (pro-life protest); *United States and Connecticut v. Vasquez*, 145 F.3d 74 (2d Cir. 1998) (same); *United States v. Albertini*, 472 U.S. 676 (1985) (anti-nuclear protest); *United States v. Springer*, 51 F.3d 861 (9th Cir. 1995) (same). When someone disobeys a *statute* and faces criminal or civil consequences, there usually is a chance to offer a defense and a challenge to the law at issue in the course of a judicial hearing. After a court finds a party in contempt for violating its order, should that party be able to defend the noncompliance by arguing the order was itself unlawful? Would failing to give such an opportunity undermine due process or substantive justice? Or would giving such an opportunity invite further violations of court orders and disrespect for judicial power? The leading case on the subject grew out of the civil rights effort, led by the Reverend Martin Luther King, Jr., to challenge racial segregation in Birmingham, Alabama. David Luban described the historical context for the case in the following excerpt.

David Luban, Legal Modernism
218-220 (1994)

In January 1963, the Southern Christian Leadership Conference (SCLC) held a retreat in Georgia to discuss strategy for a concerted attack on segregation in Birmingham, Alabama. Project C for "confrontation"—would consist of demonstrations and boycotts of Birmingham's downtown businesses during the normally busy Easter shopping season.

Birmingham itself had recently begun to display some sentiment for change in its segregationist ways. A group of whites headed by the Chamber of Commerce president campaigned to alter Birmingham's municipal government by abolishing the offices of the three segregationist commissioners (including the notoriously racist commissioner of public safety, Theophilus Eugene "Bull" Connor) who then ran the city. The voters agreed to move to a mayoral system, and in a special election, Connor was defeated by a more moderate segregationist named Albert Boutwell. Connor went to court to demand that he be allowed to finish his term of office as commissioner of public safety and while this matter was pending, Birmingham was governed by what were in effect two city governments, each passing its own laws and conducting city business after its own fashion; municipal checks were signed by both Connor and Boutwell. Some Birmingham whites hoped that the SCLC would cancel the Easter demonstrations to give the new government a chance to show what it could do, but the SCLC leadership—which had previously canceled demonstrations to allow the run-off election between Connor and Boutwell to proceed without the pressure of demonstrations—went ahead with Project C.

A Birmingham city ordinance required the demonstrators to obtain a parade permit from the city commission. On April 3, Mrs. Lola Hendricks, representing the demonstrators, approached Connor to request a permit; Connor replied, "No, you will not get a permit in Birmingham, Alabama to picket. I will picket you over to the City Jail." On April 5—one week before Good Friday—Connor replied to a second, telegraphic, request for a parade permit with another refusal. The demonstrators proceeded with their protests.

Project C included plans for the Reverend Martin Luther King, Jr., to place himself in a position to be arrested on Good Friday, April 12.

Late Wednesday evening, April 10, Connor obtained an ex parte injunction from Alabama Circuit Court Judge W. A. Jenkins, Jr., forbidding civil rights leaders, including all the leaders of Project C, from taking part in or encouraging demonstrations. The injunction was served at 1:00 A.M. on Thursday, and the SCLC leadership debated how to respond to it. King feared that complying with the injunction would deflate the protest, as had happened the previous summer in Albany, Georgia. He went ahead with the planned demonstration the following day and was arrested; a second demonstration took place on Easter Sunday, April 14. Subsequently, Judge Jenkins found several of the demonstrators guilty of criminal contempt and sentenced each of them (including King) to five days in jail and a $50 fine. It is this conviction that the *Walker v. City of Birmingham* Court upheld.

This ends the sequence of events recounted in *Walker* and King's Letter. But the largest chronicle of the Birmingham campaign did not end with King's arrest. The demonstrators subsequently embarked on a strategy of marches by schoolchildren, leading to literally thousands of arrests. As the demonstrations continued, Bull Connor upped the level of official response, ordering that fire hoses and police dogs be turned on the demonstrators. Television news horrified its audiences with the spectacle of children bowled over by hoses that hit with enough force to rip the bark off trees. White moderates and the SCLC leadership undertook negotiations that led to a settlement announced on May 10. On May 11, the Ku Klux Klan staged a rally; after the meeting, the motel where King had been staying and the home of his brother were bombed. Crowds of angry blacks rioted, and President Kennedy eventually sent in federal troops. A month later, Alabama Governor George Wallace personally blocked the entrance of a University of Alabama building to prevent the entrance of two black students whose admission had been ordered by a federal court. Evidently this action was the last straw. The same day, President Kennedy spoke on national television to announce that he was seeking comprehensive civil rights legislation that eventually became the Civil Rights Act. This announcement and the march were the culminating events of Project C.

But let us return to King's original April arrest. While King was in jail, eight white clergymen—significantly, they were liberals who had publicly opposed Governor George Wallace's "Segregation Forever!" speech—took out a full-page advertisement in the Birmingham News denouncing the demonstrations. King responded from his cell, writing in the newspaper's margins until he was able to obtain paper; after he was permitted visitors, King's manuscript was typed by his friends and returned to him in jail for revisions. His Letter from Birmingham Jail attracted little attention at first. It was eventually printed by the American Friends Service Committee and reprinted in numerous periodicals; its fame and influence grew, and by now it is perhaps the most famous document to emerge from the civil rights movement. . . .

Point and counterpoint: King's Letter has become one of the great classics in the literature of civil disobedience, both for its philosophy and for the soul-stirring magnificence of its language. No one has called Potter Stewart's *Walker* opinion a classic (in what might be called the literature of civil obedience), but its status as a Supreme Court precedent makes it the functional equivalent of a classic. Both *Walker* and the *Letter* address an ancient question, a question that more than any other defines the very subject of legal philosophy: that, of course, is the question whether we lie under an obligation to obey unjust legal directives, including directives ordering our punishment for disobeying other unjust directives. All political philosophy, from Plato's *Apology* and *Crito* on, is driven by this question; all our political hopes and aspirations are contained in the descriptive and argumentative materials we use to answer it.

Walker v. City of Birmingham
388 U.S. 307 (1967)

Justice STEWART delivered the opinion of the Court:

On Wednesday, April 10, 1963, officials of Birmingham, Alabama, filed a bill of complaint in a state circuit court asking for injunctive relief against 139 individuals and two organizations. The bill and accompanying affidavits stated that during the preceding seven days:

> [R]espondents (had) sponsored and/or participated in and/or conspired to commit and/or to encourage and/or to participate in certain movements, plans or projects commonly called "sit-in" demonstrations, "kneel-in" demonstrations, mass street parades, trespasses on private property after being warned to leave the premises by the owners of said property, congregating in mobs upon the public streets and other public places, unlawfully picketing private places of business in the City of Birmingham, Alabama; violation of numerous ordinances and statutes of the City of Birmingham and State of Alabama. . . .

It was alleged that this conduct was "calculated to provoke breaches of the peace," threaten[ed] the safety, peace and tranquility of the City, and placed an undue burden and strain upon the manpower of the Police Department.

The bill stated that these infractions of the law were expected to continue and would "lead to further imminent danger to the lives, safety, peace, tranquility and general welfare of the people of the City of Birmingham," and that the "remedy by law [was] inadequate." The circuit judge granted a temporary injunction as prayed in the bill, enjoining the petitioners from, among other things, participating in or encouraging mass street parades or mass processions without a permit as required by a Birmingham ordinance.

Five of the eight petitioners were served with copies of the writ early the next morning. Several hours later four of them held a press conference. There a statement was distributed, declaring their intention to disobey the injunction because it was "raw tyranny under the guise of maintaining law and order." At this press conference one of the petitioners stated: "That they had respect for the Federal Courts, or Federal Injunctions, but in the past the State Courts had favored local law enforcement, and if the police couldn't handle it, the mob would."

That night a meeting took place at which one of the petitioners announced that "[i]njunction or no injunction we are going to march tomorrow." The next afternoon, Good Friday, a large crowd gathered in the vicinity of Sixteenth Street and Sixth Avenue North in Birmingham. A group of about 50 or 60 proceeded to parade along the sidewalk while a crowd of 1,000 to 1,500 onlookers stood by, "clapping, and hollering, and [w]hooping." Some of the crowd followed the marchers and spilled out into the street. At least three of the petitioners participated in this march.

Meetings sponsored by some of the petitioners were held that night and the following night, where calls for volunteers to "walk" and go to jail were made. On Easter Sunday, April 14, a crowd of between 1,500 and 2,000 people congregated in the midafternoon in the vicinity of Seventh Avenue and Eleventh Street North in Birmingham. One of the petitioners was seen organizing members of the crowd in formation. A group of about 50, headed by three other petitioners, started down the sidewalk two abreast. At least one other petitioner was among the marchers. Some 300 or 400 people from among the onlookers followed in a crowd that occupied the entire width of the street and overflowed onto the sidewalks. Violence occurred. Members of the crowd threw rocks that injured a newspaperman and damaged a police motorcycle.

The next day the city officials who had requested the injunction applied to the state circuit court for an order to show cause why the petitioners should not be held in contempt for violating it. At the ensuing hearing the petitioners sought to attack the constitutionality of the injunction on the ground that it was vague and overbroad, and restrained free speech. They also sought to attack the Birmingham parade ordinance upon similar grounds, and upon the further ground that the ordinance had previously been administered in an arbitrary and discriminatory manner.

The circuit judge refused to consider any of these contentions, pointing out that there had been neither a motion to dissolve the injunction, nor an effort to comply with it by applying for a permit from the city commission before engaging in the Good Friday and Easter Sunday parades. Consequently, the court held that the only issues before it were whether it had jurisdiction to issue the temporary injunction, and whether thereafter the petitioners had knowingly violated it. Upon these issues the court found against the petitioners, and imposed upon each of them a sentence of five days in jail and a $50 fine, in accord with an Alabama statute.

The Supreme Court of Alabama affirmed. That court, too, declined to consider the petitioners' constitutional attacks upon the injunction and the underlying Birmingham parade ordinance. . . .

Without question the state court that issued the injunction had, as a court of equity, jurisdiction over the petitioners and over the subject matter of the controversy. And this is not a case where the injunction was transparently invalid or had only a frivolous pretense to validity. We have consistently recognized the strong interest of state and local governments in regulating the use of their streets and other public places. . . . When protest takes the form of mass demonstrations, parades, or picketing on public streets and sidewalks, the free passage of traffic and the prevention of public disorder and violence become important objects of legitimate state concern. As the Court stated, in *Cox v. State of Louisiana*, "We emphatically reject the notion . . . that the First and Fourteenth Amendments afford the same kind of freedom to those who would communicate ideas by conduct such as patrolling, marching, and picketing on streets and highways, as these amendments afford to those who communicate ideas by pure speech." 379 U.S. 536, 555. . . .

The generality of the language contained in the Birmingham parade ordinance upon which the injunction was based would unquestionably raise substantial constitutional issues concerning some of its provisions. *Schneider v. State of New Jersey*, 308 U.S. 147; *Saia v. People of State of New York*, 334 U.S. 558; *Kunz v. People of State of New York*, 340 U.S. 290. The petitioners, however, did not even attempt to apply to the Alabama courts for an authoritative construction of the ordinance. Had they done so, those courts might have given the licensing authority granted in the ordinance a narrow and precise scope. . . . [Here] it could not be assumed that this ordinance was void on its face.

The breadth and vagueness of the injunction itself would also unquestionably be subject to substantial constitutional question. But the way to raise that question was to apply to the Alabama courts to have the injunction modified or dissolved. The injunction in all events clearly prohibited mass parading without a permit, and the evidence shows that the petitioners fully understood that prohibition when they violated it.

The petitioners also claim that they were free to disobey the injunction because the parade ordinance on which it was based had been administered in the past in an arbitrary and discriminatory fashion. In support of this claim they sought to introduce evidence that, a few days before the injunction issued, requests for permits to picket had been made to a member of the city commission. One request had been rudely rebuffed, and this same official had later made clear that he was without power to grant the permit alone, since the issuance of such permits was the responsibility of the entire city commission. Assuming the truth of this proffered evidence, it does not follow that the parade ordinance was void on its face. The petitioners, moreover, did not apply for a permit either to the commission itself or to any commissioner after the injunction issued. Had they done so, and had the permit been refused, it is clear that their claim of arbitrary or discriminatory administration of the ordinance would have been considered by the state circuit court upon a motion to dissolve the injunction.

This case would arise in quite a different constitutional posture if the petitioners, before disobeying the injunction, had challenged it in the Alabama courts, and had been met with delay or frustration of their constitutional claims. . . .

The rule of law that Alabama followed in this case reflects a belief that in the fair administration of justice no man can be judge in his own case, however exalted his station, however righteous his motives, and irrespective of his race, color, politics, or religion. This Court cannot hold that the petitioners were constitutionally free to ignore all the procedures of the law and carry their battle to the streets. . . .

Affirmed.

Appendix to Opinion of Court
[The Full Text of Dr. King's Speech]

In our struggle for freedom we have anchored our faith and hope in the rightness of the Constitution and the moral laws of the universe.

Again and again the Federal judiciary has made it clear that the privileges guaranteed under the First and the Fourteenth Amendments are too sacred to be trampled upon by the machinery of state government and police power. In the past we have abided by Federal injunctions out of respect for the forthright and consistent leadership that the Federal judiciary has given in establishing the principle of integration as the law of the land.

However we are now confronted with recalcitrant forces in the Deep South that will use the courts to perpetuate the unjust and illegal system of racial separation.

Alabama has made clear its determination to defy the law of the land. Most of its public officials, its legislative body and many of its law enforcement agents have openly defied the desegregation decision of the Supreme Court. We would feel morally and legally responsible to obey the injunction if the courts of Alabama applied equal justice to all of its citizens. This would be sameness made legal. However the issuance of this injunction is a blatant [example] of difference made legal.

Southern law enforcement agencies have demonstrated now and again that they will utilize the force of law to misuse the judicial process.

This is raw tyranny under the guise of maintaining law and order. We cannot in all good conscience obey such an injunction, which is an unjust, undemocratic and unconstitutional misuse of the legal process.

We do this not out of any disrespect for the law but out of the highest respect for the law. This is not an attempt to evade or defy the law or engage in chaotic anarchy. Just as in all good conscience we cannot obey unjust laws, neither can we respect the unjust use of the courts.

We believe in a system of law based on justice and morality. Out of our great love for the Constitution of the U.S. and our desire to purify the judicial system of the state of Alabama, we risk this critical move with an awareness of the possible consequences involved.

Chief Justice WARREN, with whom Justice BRENNAN and Justice FORTAS join, dissenting:

Petitioners in this case contend that they were convicted under an ordinance that is unconstitutional on its face because it submits their First and Fourteenth Amendment rights to free speech and peaceful assembly to the unfettered discretion of local officials. They further contend that the ordinance was unconstitutionally applied to them because the local officials used their discretion to prohibit peaceful demonstrations by a group whose political viewpoint the officials opposed. The Court does not dispute these contentions, but holds that petitioners may nonetheless be convicted and sent to jail because the patently unconstitutional ordinance was copied into an injunction—issued ex parte without prior notice or hearing on the request of the Commissioner of Public Safety—forbidding all persons having notice of the injunction to violate the ordinance without any limitation of time. I dissent because I do not believe that the fundamental protections of the Constitution were meant to be so easily evaded, or that "the civilizing hand of law" would be hampered in the slightest by enforcing the First Amendment in this case.

The salient facts can be stated very briefly. Petitioners are Negro ministers who sought to express their concern about racial discrimination in Birmingham, Alabama, by holding peaceful protest demonstrations in that city on Good Friday and Easter Sunday 1963. For obvious reasons, it was important for the significance of the demonstrations that they be held on those particular dates. A representative of petitioners' organization went to the City Hall and asked to see the person or persons in charge to issue permits, permits for parading, picketing, and demonstrating. She was directed to Public Safety Commissioner Connor, who denied her request for a permit in terms that left no doubt that petitioners were not going to be issued a permit under any circumstances. He said, "No you will not get a permit in Birmingham, Alabama to picket. I will picket you over to the City Jail," and he repeated that twice. A second, telegraphic request was also summarily denied, in a telegram signed by Eugene "Bull" Connor, with the added information that permits could be issued only by the full City Commission, a three-man body consisting of Commissioner Connor and two others. According to petitioners' offer of proof, the truth of which is assumed for purposes of this case, parade permits had uniformly been issued for all other groups by the city clerk on the request of the traffic bureau of the police department, which was under Commissioner Connor's direction. The requirement that the approval of the full Commission be obtained was applied only to this one group.

Understandably convinced that the City of Birmingham was not going to authorize their demonstrations under any circumstances, petitioners proceeded with their plans despite Commissioner Connor's orders. On Wednesday, April 10, at 9 in the evening, the city filed in a state circuit court a bill of complaint seeking an ex parte injunction. The complaint recited that petitioners were engaging in a series of demonstrations as "part of a massive effort . . . to forcibly integrate all business establishments, churches, and other institutions" in the city, with the result that the police department was strained in its resources and the safety, peace, and tranquility were threatened. It was alleged as particularly menacing that petitioners were planning to conduct "kneel-in" demonstrations at churches where their presence was not wanted. The city's police dogs were said to be in danger of their lives. Faced with these recitals, the Circuit Court issued the injunction in the form requested, and in effect ordered petitioners and all other persons having notice of the order to refrain for an unlimited time from carrying on any demonstrations without a permit. A permit, of course, was clearly unobtainable; the city would not have sought this injunction if it had any intention of issuing one.

Petitioners were served with copies of the injunction at various times on Thursday and on Good Friday. Unable to believe that such a blatant and broadly drawn prior restraint on their First Amendment rights could be valid, they announced their intention to defy it and went ahead with the planned peaceful demonstrations on Easter weekend. On the following Monday, when they promptly filed a motion to dissolve the injunction, the court found them in contempt, holding that they had waived all their First Amendment rights by disobeying the court order.

These facts lend no support to the court's charges that petitioners were presuming to act as judges in their own case, or that they had a disregard for the judicial process. They did not flee the jurisdiction or refuse to appear in the Alabama courts. Having violated the injunction, they promptly submitted themselves to the courts to test the constitutionality of the injunction and the ordinance it parroted. They were in essentially the same position as persons who challenge the constitutionality of a statute by violating it, and then defend the ensuing criminal prosecution on constitutional grounds. It has never been thought that violation of a statute indicated such a disrespect for the legislature that the violator always must be punished even if the statute was unconstitutional. On the contrary, some cases have required that persons seeking to challenge the constitutionality of a statute first violate it to establish their standing to sue. Indeed, it shows no disrespect for law to violate a statute on the ground that it is unconstitutional and then to submit one's case to the courts with the willingness to accept the penalty if the statute is held to be valid.

The Court concedes that "[t]he generality of the language contained in the Birmingham parade ordinance upon which the injunction was based would unquestionably raise substantial constitutional issues concerning some of its provisions." That concession is well-founded but minimal. I believe it is patently unconstitutional on its face. . . . When local officials are given totally unfettered discretion to decide whether a proposed demonstration is consistent with "public welfare, peace, safety, health, decency, good order, morals or convenience," as they were in this case, they are invited to act as censors over the views that may be presented to the public. The unconstitutionality of the ordinance is compounded, of course, when there is convincing evidence that the officials have in fact used their power to deny permits to organizations whose views they dislike. . . .

I do not believe that giving this Court's seal of approval to such a gross misuse of the judicial process is likely to lead to greater respect for the law any more than it is likely to lead to greater protection for First Amendment freedoms. The ex parte temporary injunction has a long and odious history in this country, and its susceptibility to misuse is all too apparent from the facts of the case. . . . Respect for the courts and for judicial process was not increased by the history of the labor injunction.

Justice DOUGLAS, with whom THE CHIEF JUSTICE, Justice BRENNAN, and Justice FORTAS concur, dissenting:

The record shows that petitioners did not deliberately attempt to circumvent the permit requirement. Rather they diligently attempted to obtain a permit and were rudely rebuffed and then reasonably concluded that any further attempts would be fruitless.

The right to defy an unconstitutional statute is basic in our scheme. Even when an ordinance requires a permit to make a speech, to deliver a sermon, to picket, to parade, or to assemble, it need not be honored when it is invalid on its face. . . .

Yet by some inscrutable legerdemain these constitutionally secured rights to challenge prior restraints invalid on their face are lost if the State takes the precaution to have some judge append his signature to an ex parte order which recites the words of the invalid statute. The State neatly insulates its legislation from challenge by mere incorporation of the identical stifling, overbroad, and vague restraints on exercise of the First Amendment freedoms into an even more vague and pervasive injunction obtained invisibly and upon a stage darkened lest it be open to scrutiny by those affected. . . .

The Court today lets loose a devastatingly destructive weapon for infringement of freedoms jealously safeguarded not so much for the benefit of any given group of any given persuasion as for the benefit of all of us. We cannot permit fears of "riots" and "civil disobedience" generated by slogans like "Black Power" to divert our attention from what is here at stake—not violence or the right of the State to control its streets and sidewalks, but the insulation from attack of ex parte orders and legislation upon which they are based even when patently impermissible prior restraints on the exercise of First Amendment rights, thus arming the state courts with the power to punish as a "contempt" what they otherwise could not punish at all. Constitutional restrictions against abridgments of First Amendment freedoms limit judicial equally with legislative and executive power. Convictions for contempt of court orders which invalidly abridge First Amendment freedoms must be condemned equally with convictions for violation of statutes which do the same thing. I respectfully dissent.

REVIEW QUESTIONS

1. What are the two cases involved in *Walker* and who are the plaintiffs/defendants in each case?
2. What is the "collateral bar rule"? Is it a part of federal or state law?
3. The rule requiring obedience to a court order even if it is later found to be unconstitutional forbids challenge by anyone who first disobeys the rule and then seeks to challenge it in court. In *Walker*, the U.S. Supreme Court defers to Alabama's collateral bar rule but also announces exceptions to that rule. What are those exceptions?
4. What is the dissent's response to the majority's argument that it must enforce the contempt order because no man can be judge in his own case?
5. How are violations of legislative action treated differently than violations of a court's injunction? Should they be treated differently?
6. The Alabama rule of procedure did not require the plaintiff (in this case the City's lawyers) to attempt to notify the defendants of the hearing. How is this different than the procedure in Rule 65? Can you articulate the argument that the Alabama rule in place at that time violated due process? Is there a counter-argument?

QUESTIONS TO PONDER

1. The majority opinion attached the following footnote, discussing *Kasper v. Brittain*, 245 F.2d 92 (6th Cir. 1957), to its statement that "in the fair administration of justice no man can be judge in his own case, however exalted his station, however righteous his motives, and irrespective of his race, color, politics, or religion":

   There, a federal court had ordered the public high school in Clinton, Tennessee, to desegregate. Kasper . . . organized a campaign "to run the Negroes out of the school." The federal court issued an ex parte restraining order enjoining Kasper from interfering with desegregation. Relying upon the First Amendment, Kasper harangued a crowd "to the effect that although he had been served with the restraining order, it did not mean anything. . . ." His conviction for criminal contempt was affirmed by the Court of Appeals for the Sixth Circuit. That court concluded that "'an injunctional order issued by a court must be obeyed,'" whatever its seeming invalidity, citing *Howat v. Kansas*, 258 U.S. 181 (1922). This Court denied certiorari.

Does this footnote affect your assessment of the collateral bar rule? Some state courts have rejected the collateral bar rule. *See In re Berry*, 68 Cal. 2d 137 (1968). What are the arguments for retaining and rejecting it? Further historical context can be found in Alan Westin and Barry Mahoney, *The Trial of Martin Luther King* (1974), Taylor Branch, *Parting the Waters* (1988), and the award-winning Public Broadcasting Service series, *Eyes on the Prize* (1987).

2. After its decision in *Walker*, the Supreme Court held that the Birmingham parade-permit ordinance violated the First Amendment because it gave unfettered discretion to city officials to restrict speech. *Shuttlesworth v. City of Birmingham*, 394 U.S. 147 (1967). The Court also ruled there that Reverend Shuttlesworth could overturn his conviction for parading without a permit. Why do you think the Supreme Court treated Reverend Shuttlesworth's action in violation of the law differently from Reverend King's violation of a court order predicated on the same law? Do you think there is a distinction here worth maintaining? For one effort to address these issues, *see* Alexander Bickel, *Civil Disobedience and the Duty to Obey*, 8 Gonz. L. Rev. 199 (1973).

3. Long before the Supreme Court's decision in *Walker*, back at the time of his arrest for violating the Alabama court order, Reverend Martin Luther King, Jr., wrote a response to a statement by eight Alabama clergymen urging him and others in the black community to stop their program of "direct action," including sit-ins, boycotts, and marches against racial segregation. King's direct-action approach pursued tenets of civil disobedience in response to the Southern resistance to integration, which had been mandated by the Supreme Court since its decision in *Brown v. Bd. of Educ. of Topeka, Shawnee County, Kan.*, 347 U.S. 483 (1954). King was awarded the Nobel Peace Prize for his struggle for civil rights. He was murdered in Memphis in April 1968. Following his assassination, major urban areas in the United States erupted in violence. As you read portions of Reverend King's letter, consider what you find persuasive, and why, and whether any of his arguments join issue with the majority opinion in *Walker*. You can also find the full text of King's letter in *Civil Disobedience: Theory and Practice* 72-89 (Hugo Bedav ed. 1969).

Martin Luther King, Jr., Letter from Birmingham Jail

A Testament of Hope: The Essential Writings and Speeches of Martin Luther King, Jr., 289
(James M. Washington ed. 1986)

The following is the public statement directed to Martin Luther King, Jr., by eight Alabama clergymen: *

We the undersigned clergymen are among those who, in January, issued "An Appeal for Law and Order and Common Sense," in dealing with racial problems in Alabama. We expressed understanding that honest convictions in racial matters could properly be pursued in the courts, but urged that decisions of those courts should in the meantime be peacefully obeyed.

Since that time there had been some evidence of increased forbearance and a willingness to face facts. Responsible citizens have undertaken to work on various problems which cause racial friction and unrest. In Birmingham, recent public events have given indication that we all have opportunity for a new constructive and realistic approach to racial problems.

However, we are now confronted by a series of demonstrations by some of our Negro citizens, directed and led in part by outsiders. We recognize the natural impatience of people who feel that their hopes are slow in being realized. But we are convinced that these demonstrations are unwise and untimely.

We agree rather with certain local Negro leadership which has called for honest and open negotiation of racial issues in our area. And we believe this kind of facing of issues can best be accomplished by citizens of our own metropolitan area, white and Negro, meeting with their knowledge and experience of the local situation. All of us need to face that responsibility and find proper channels for its accomplishment.

Just as we formerly pointed out that "hatred and violence have no sanction in our religious and political traditions," we also point out that such actions as incite to hatred and violence, however technically peaceful those actions may be, have not contributed to the resolution of our local problems. We do not believe that these days of new hope are days when extreme measures are justified in Birmingham.

We commend the community as a whole, and the local news media and law enforcement officials in particular, on the calm manner in which these demonstrations have been handled. We urge the public to continue to show restraint should the demonstrations continue, and the law enforcement officials to remain calm and continue to protect our city from violence.

We further strongly urge our own Negro community to withdraw support from these demonstrations, and to unite locally in working peacefully for a better Birmingham. When rights are consistently denied, a cause should be pressed in the courts and in negotiations among local leaders, and not in the streets. We

---

* Reprinted by arrangement with The Heirs to the Estate of Martin Luther King, Jr., c/o Writers House as agent for the proprietor New York, NY. Copyright 1963 Dr. Martin Luther King, Jr.; copyright renewed 1991 Coretta Scott King.

appeal to both our white and Negro citizenry to observe the principles of law and order and common sense.

Bishop C. C. J. Carpenter, Bishop Joseph A. Durick, Rabbi Milton L. Grafman, Bishop Paul Hardin, Bishop Nolan B. Harmon, Rev. George M. Murray, Rev. Edward V. Ramage, Rev. Earl Stallings

April 12, 1963

My dear Fellow Clergymen.

While confined here in the Birmingham City Jail, I came across your recent statement calling our present activities "unwise and untimely." Seldom, if ever, do I pause to answer criticism of my work and ideas. If I sought to answer all of the criticisms that cross my desk, my secretaries would be engaged in little else in the course of the day, and I would have no time for constructive work. But since I feel that you are men of genuine goodwill and your criticisms are sincerely set forth, I would like to answer your statement in what I hope will be patient and reasonable terms. . . .

Several months ago our local affiliate here in Birmingham invited us to be on call to engage in a nonviolent direct action program if such were deemed necessary. We readily consented and when the hour came we lived up to our promises. So I am here, along with several members of my staff, because we were invited here. I am here because I have basic organizational ties here.

Beyond this, I am in Birmingham because injustice is here. Just as the eighth century prophets left their little villages and carried their "thus saith the Lord" far beyond the boundaries of their home towns; and just as the Apostle Paul left his little village of Tarsus and carried the gospel of Jesus Christ to practically every hamlet and city of the Graeco-Roman world, I too am compelled to carry the gospel of freedom beyond my particular home town. Like Paul, I must constantly respond to the Macedonian call for aid.

Moreover, I am cognizant of the interrelatedness of all communities and states. I cannot sit idly by in Atlanta and not be concerned about what happens in Birmingham. Injustice anywhere is a threat to justice everywhere. We are caught in an inescapable network of mutuality, tied in a single garment of destiny. Whatever affects one directly affects all indirectly. Never again can we afford to live with the narrow, provincial "outside agitator" idea. Anyone who lives inside the United States can never be considered an outsider anywhere in this country.

You deplore the demonstrations that are presently taking place in Birmingham. But I am sorry that your statement did not express a similar concern for the conditions that brought the demonstrations into being. I am sure that each of you would want to go beyond the superficial social analyst who looks merely at effects, and does not grapple with underlying causes. I would not hesitate to say that it is unfortunate that so-called demonstrations are taking place in Birmingham at this time, but I would say in even more emphatic terms that it is even more unfortunate that the white power structure of this city left the Negro community with no other alternative.

In any nonviolent campaign there are four basic steps: 1) Collection of the facts to determine whether injustices are alive. 2) Negotiation. 3) Self-purification. and 4) Direct Action. We have gone through all of these steps in Birmingham. There can be no gainsaying of the fact that racial injustice engulfs this community.

Birmingham is probably the most thoroughly segregated city in the United States. Its ugly record of police brutality is known in every section of this country. Its unjust treatment of Negroes in the courts is a notorious reality. There have been more unsolved bombings of Negro homes and churches in Birmingham than any city in this nation. These are the hard, brutal and unbelievable facts. On the basis of these conditions Negro leaders sought to negotiate with the city fathers. But the political leaders consistently refused to engage in good faith negotiation. . . .

When we discovered that Mr. Connor was in [a run-off election], we decided again to postpone action so that the demonstrations could not be used to cloud the issues. At this time we agreed to begin our nonviolent witness the day after the run-off.

This reveals that we did not move irresponsibly into direct action. We too wanted to see Mr. Connor defeated; so we went through postponement after postponement to aid in this community need. After this we felt that direct action could be delayed no longer.

CREATIVE TENSION

You may well ask, "Why direct action? Why sit-ins, marches, etc.? Isn't negotiation a better path?" You are exactly right in your call for negotiation. Indeed, this is the purpose of direct action. Nonviolent direct action seeks to create such a crisis and establish such creative tension that a community that has constantly refused to negotiate is forced to confront the issue. It seeks so to dramatize the issue that it can no longer be ignored. I just referred to the creation of tension as a part of the work of the nonviolent resister. This may sound rather shocking. But I must confess that I am not afraid of the word tension. I have earnestly worked and preached against violent tension, but there is a type of construc-tive nonviolent tension that is necessary for growth. Just as Socrates felt that it was necessary to create a tension in the mind so that individuals could rise from the bondage of myths and half-truths to the unfettered realm of creative analysis and objective appraisal, we must see the need of having nonviolent gad-flies to create the kind of tension in society that will help men to rise from the dark depths of prejudice and racism to the majestic heights of understanding and brotherhood. So the purpose of the direct action is to create a situation so crisis-packed that it will inevitably open the door to negotiation. We, there-fore, concur with you in your call for negotiation. Too long has our beloved Southland been bogged down in the tragic attempt to live in monologue rather than dialogue.

One of the basic points in your statement is that our acts are untimely. Some have asked. "Why didn't you give the new administration time to act?" The only answer that I can give to this inquiry is that the new administration must be prodded about as much as the outgoing one before it acts. We will be sadly mistaken if we feel that the election of Mr. Boutwell will bring the millennium to Birmingham. While Mr. Boutwell is much more articulate and gentle than Mr. Connor, they are both segregationists, dedicated to the task of maintaining the status quo. The hope I see in Mr. Boutwell is that he will be reasonable enough to see the futility of massive resistance to desegregation. But he will not see this without pressure from the devotees of civil rights. My friends, I must say to you that we have not made a single gain in civil rights without determined legal and nonviolent pressure. History is the long and tragic story of the fact that privileged groups seldom give up their privileges voluntarily. Individuals may see the moral light and voluntarily give up their unjust posture; but as Reinhold Niebuhr has reminded us, groups are more immoral than individuals.

We know through painful experience that freedom is never voluntarily given by the oppressor; it must be demanded by the oppressed. Frankly, I have never yet engaged in a direct action movement that was "well timed," according to the timetable of those who have not suffered unduly from the disease of segregation. For years now I have heard the words "Wait!" It rings in the ear of every Negro with a piercing familiarity. This "Wait" has almost always meant "Never." It has been a tranquilizing thalidomide, relieving the emotional stress for a moment, only to give birth to an ill-formed infant of frustration. We must come to see with the distinguished jurist of yesterday that "justice too long delayed is justice denied." We have waited for more than three hundred and forty years for our constitutional and God-given rights. The nations of Asia and Africa are moving with jet-like speed toward the goal of political independence, and we still creep at horse and buggy pace toward the gaining of a cup of coffee at a lunch counter. I guess it is easy for those who have never felt the stinging darts of segregation to say, "Wait." But when you have seen vicious mobs lynch your mothers and fathers at will and drown your sisters and brothers at whim; when you have seen hate-filled policemen curse, kick, brutalize and even kill your black brothers and sisters with impunity; when you see the vast majority of your twenty million Negro brothers smothering in an airtight cage of poverty in the midst of an affluent society; when you suddenly find your tongue twisted and your speech stammering as you seek to explain to your six-year-old daughter why she can't go to the public amusement park that has just been advertised on television, and see tears welling up in her little eyes when she is told that Funtown is closed to colored children, and see the depressing clouds of inferiority begin to form in her little mental sky, and see her begin to distort her little personality to unconsciously developing a bitterness toward white people; when you have to concoct an answer for a five-year-old son asking in agonizing pathos: "Daddy, why do white people treat colored people so mean?"; when you take a cross country drive and find it necessary to sleep night after night in the uncomfortable corners of your automobile because no motel will accept you; when you are humiliated day in and day out by nagging signs reading "white" and "colored"; when your first name becomes "nigger" and your middle name becomes "boy" (however old you are) and your last name becomes "John," and when your wife and mother are never given the respected title "Mrs."; when you are harried by day and haunted at night by the fact that you are a Negro, living constantly at tip-toe stance never quite knowing what to expect next, and plagued with inner fears and outer resentments; when you are forever fighting a degenerating sense of "nobodiness"; then you will understand why we find it difficult to wait. There comes a time when the cup of endurance runs over, and men are no longer willing to be plunged into an abyss of injustice where they experience the blackness of corroding despair. I hope, sirs, you can understand our legitimate and unavoidable impatience.

BREAKING THE LAW

You express a great deal of anxiety over our willingness to break laws. This is certainly a legitimate concern. Since we so diligently urge people to obey the Supreme Court's decision of 1954 outlawing segregation in the public schools, it is rather strange and paradoxical to find us consciously breaking laws. One may well ask, "how can you advocate breaking some laws and obeying others?" The answer is found in the fact that there are two types of laws: There are *just* and there are *unjust* laws. I would agree with Saint Augustine that "An unjust law is no law at all."

Now what is the difference between the two? How does one determine when a law is just or unjust? A just law is a man-made code that squares with the moral law or the law of God. An unjust law is a code that is out of harmony with the moral law. To put it in the terms of Saint Thomas Aquinas, an unjust law is a human law that is not rooted in eternal and natural law. Any law that uplifts human personality is just. Any law that degrades human personality is unjust. All segregation statutes are unjust because segregation distorts the soul and damages the personality. It gives the segregator a false sense of superiority, and the segregated a false sense of inferiority. To use the words of Martin Buber, the great Jewish philosopher, segregation substitutes an "I-it" relationship for the "I-thou" relationship, and ends up relegating persons to the status of things. So segregation is not only politically, economically and sociologically unsound, but it is morally wrong and sinful. Paul Tillich has said that sin is separation. Isn't segregation an existential expression of man's tragic separation, an expression of his awful estrangement, his terrible sinfulness? So I can urge men to disobey segregation ordinances because they are morally wrong.

Let us turn to a more concrete example of just and unjust laws. An unjust law is a code that a majority inflicts on a minority that is not binding on itself. This is difference made legal. On the other hand a just law is a code that a majority compels a minority to follow that it is willing to follow itself. This is sameness made legal.

Let me give another explanation. An unjust law is a code inflicted upon a minority which that minority had no part in enacting or creating because they did not have the unhampered right to vote. Who can say that the legislature of Alabama which set up the segregation laws was democratically elected? Throughout the state of Alabama all types of conniving methods are used to prevent Negroes from becoming registered voters and there are some counties without a single Negro registered to vote despite the fact that the Negro constitutes a majority of the population. Can any law set up in such a state be considered democratically structured?

These are just a few examples of unjust and just laws. There are some instances when a law is just on its face and unjust in its application. For instance, I was arrested Friday on a charge of parading without a permit. Now there is nothing wrong with an ordinance which requires a permit for a parade, but when the ordinance is used to preserve segregation and to deny citizens the First Amendment privilege of peaceful assembly and peaceful protest, then it becomes unjust.

Walker v. Birmingham

I hope you can see the distinction I am trying to point out. In no sense do I advocate evading or defying the law as the rabid segregationist would do. This would lead to anarchy. One who breaks an unjust law must do it *openly, lovingly* (not hatefully as the white mothers did in New Orleans when they were seen on television screaming "nigger, nigger, nigger"), and with a willingness to accept the penalty. I submit that an individual who breaks a law that conscience tells him is unjust, and willingly accepts the penalty by staying in jail to arouse the conscience of the community over its injustice, is in reality expressing the very highest respect for law.

Of course, there is nothing new about this kind of civil disobedience. It was seen sublimely in the refusal of Shadrach, Meshach and Abednego to obey the laws of Nebuchadnezzar because a higher moral law was involved. It was practiced superbly by the early Christians who were willing to face hungry lions and the excruciating pain of chopping blocks, before submitting to certain unjust laws of the Roman empire. To a degree academic freedom is a reality today because Socrates practiced civil disobedience.

THE WHITE MODERATE

We can never forget that everything Hitler did in Germany was "legal" and everything the Hungarian freedom fighters did in Hungary was "illegal." It was "illegal" to aid and comfort a Jew in Hitler's Germany. But I am sure that if I had lived in Germany during that time I would have aided and comforted my Jewish brothers even though it was illegal. If I lived in a Communist country today where certain principles dear to the Christian faith are suppressed, I believe I would openly advocate disobeying these anti-religious laws. I must make two honest confessions to you, my Christian and Jewish brothers. First, I must confess that over the last few years I have been gravely disappointed with the white moderate. I have almost reached the regrettable conclusion that the Negro's great stumbling block in the stride toward freedom is not the White Citizen's Councilor or the Ku Klux Klanner, but the white moderate who is more devoted to "order" than to justice; who prefers a negative peace which is the absence of tension to a positive peace which is the presence of justice; who constantly says "I agree with you in the goal you seek, but I can't agree with your methods of direct action"; who paternalistically feels that he can set the timetable for another man's freedom; who lives by the myth of time and who constantly advises the Negro to wait until a "more convenient season." Shallow understanding from people of good will is more frustrating than absolute misunderstanding from people of ill will. Lukewarm acceptance is much more bewildering than outright rejection.

I had hoped that the white moderate would understand that law and order exist for the purpose of establishing justice, and that when they fail to do this they become dangerously structured dams that block the flow of social progress. . . .

You spoke of our activity in Birmingham as extreme. At first, I was rather disappointed that fellow clergymen would see my nonviolent efforts as those of the extremist. I started thinking about the fact that I stand in the middle of two opposing forces in the Negro community. One is a force of complacency made up of Negroes who, as a result of long years of oppression, have been so completely drained of self-respect and a sense of "somebodiness" that they have adjusted to segregation, and of a few Negroes in the middle class who, because of a degree of academic and economic security, and because at points they profit by segregation, have unconsciously become insensitive to the problems of the masses. The other force is one of bitterness and hatred and comes perilously close to advocating violence. It is expressed in the various black nationalist groups that are springing up over the nation, the largest and best known being Elijah Muhammad's Muslim movement. This movement is nourished by the contemporary frustration over the continued existence of racial discrimination. It is made up of people who have lost faith in America, who have absolutely repudiated Christianity, and who have concluded that the white man is an incurable "devil." I have tried to stand between these two forces saying that we need not follow the "do-nothingism" of the complacent or the hatred and despair of the black nationalist. There is the more excellent way of love and nonviolent protest. I'm grateful to God that, through the Negro church, the dimension of nonviolence entered our struggle. If this philosophy had not emerged, I am convinced that by now many streets of the South would be flowing with floods of blood. And I am further convinced that if our white brothers dismiss as "rabble rousers" and "outside agitators" those of us who are working through the channels of nonviolent direct action and refuse to support our nonviolent efforts, millions of Negroes, out of frustration and despair, will seek solace and security in black nationalist ideologies, a development that will lead inevitably to a frightening racial nightmare. . . .

EXTREMISTS FOR LOVE

. . . [A]s I continued to think about the matter, I gradually gain[ed] a bit of satisfaction from being considered an extremist. Was not Jesus an extremist in love—"Love your enemies, bless them that curse you, pray for them that despitefully use you." Was not Amos an extremist for justice—"Let justice roll down like waters and righteousness like a mighty stream." Was not Paul an extremist for the gospel of Jesus Christ—"I bear in my body the marks of the Lord Jesus." Was not Martin Luther an extremist—"Here I stand; I can do none other so help me God." Was not John Bunyan an extremist—"I will stay in jail to the end of my days before I make a butchery of my conscience." Was not Abraham Lincoln an extremist—"This nation cannot survive half slave and half free." Was not Thomas Jefferson an extremist—"We hold these truths to be self-evident, that all men are created equal." So the question is not whether we will be extremist but what kind of extremist will we be. Will we be extremists for hate or will we be extremists for love? Will we be extremists for the preservation of injustice—or will we be extremists for the cause of justice? In that dramatic scene on Calvary's hill, three men were crucified. We must not forget that all three were crucified for the same crime—the crime of extremism. Two were extremists for immorality, and thusly fell below their environment. The other, Jesus Christ, was an extremist for love, truth, and goodness, and thereby rose above his environment. So, after all, maybe the South, the nation and the world are in dire need of creative extremists. . . .

[In this portion of his letter, Doctor King criticizes white churches that "stand on the sideline and merely mouth pious irrelevancies and sanctimonious trivialities, and speak about obeying law, but neither about 'right' nor 'injustice.'" He also criticizes most moderate whites: "I guess I should have realized that few members of a race that has oppressed race can understand or appreciate the deep groans and passionate yearnings of those that have been oppressed and still fewer have the vision to see that injustice must be rooted out by strong, persistent and determined action."]

BULL CONNOR'S POLICE

I must close now. But before closing, I am impelled to mention one other point in your statement that troubled me profoundly. You warmly commended the Birmingham police force for keeping "order" and "preventing violence." I don't believe you would have so warmly commended the police force if you had seen its angry violent dogs literally biting six unarmed, nonviolent Negroes. I don't believe you would so quickly commend the policemen if you would observe their ugly and inhuman treatment of Negroes here in the city jail; if you would watch them push and curse old Negro women and young Negro girls; if you would see them slap and kick old Negro men and young boys; if you will observe them, as they did on two occasions, refuse to give us food because we wanted to sing our grace together. I'm sorry that I can't join you in your praise for the police department.

It is true that they have been rather disciplined in their public handling of the demonstrators. In this sense they have been rather publicly "nonviolent." But for what purpose? To preserve the evil system of segregation. Over the last few years I have consistently preached that nonviolence demands that the means we use must be as pure as the ends we seek. So, I have tried to make it clear that it is wrong to use immoral means to attain moral ends. But now I must affirm that it is just as wrong, or even more so, to use moral means to preserve immoral ends. Maybe Mr. Connor and his policemen have been rather publicly nonviolent, as Chief Pritchett was in Albany, Georgia, but they have used the moral means of nonviolence to maintain the immoral end of flagrant racial injustice. T. S. Eliot has said that there is no greater treason than to do the right deed for the wrong reason.

I wish you had commended the Negro sit-inners and demonstrators of Birmingham for their sublime courage, their willingness to suffer and their amazing discipline in the midst of the most inhuman provocation. One day the South will recognize its real heroes. They will be the James Merediths, courageously and with a majestic sense of purpose facing jeering and hostile mobs and the agonizing loneliness that characterizes the life of the pioneer. They will be old oppressed, battered Negro women, symbolized in a seventy-two year old woman of Montgomery, Alabama, who rose up with a sense of dignity and with her people decided not to ride the segregated buses, and responded to one who inquired about her tiredness with ungrammatical profundity: "My feet is tired, but my soul is rested." They will be the young high school and college students, young ministers of the gospel and a host of their elders courageously and non-violently sitting-in at lunch counters and willingly going to jail for conscience's sake. One day the South will know that when these disinherited children of God sat down at lunch counters they were in reality standing up for the best in the American dream and the most sacred values in our Judeo-Christian heritage, and thusly, carrying our whole nation back to those great wells of democracy which were dug deep by the founding fathers in the formulation of the Constitution and the Declaration of Independence.

Never before have I written a letter this long (or should I say a book?). I'm afraid that it is much too long to take your precious time. I can assure you that it would have been much shorter if I had been writing from a comfortable desk, but what else is there to do when you are alone for days in the dull monotony of a narrow jail cell other than write long letters, think strange thoughts, and pray long prayers?

If I have said anything in this letter that is an overstatement of the truth and is indicative of an unreasonable impatience, I beg you to forgive me. If I have said anything in this letter that is an understatement of the truth and is indicative of my having a patience that makes me patient with anything less than brother-hood, I beg God to forgive me.

I hope this letter finds you strong in the faith. I also hope that circumstances will soon make it possible for me to meet each of you, not as an integrationist or a civil rights leader, but as a fellow clergyman and a Christian brother. Let us all hope that the dark clouds of racial prejudice will soon pass away and the deep fog of misunderstanding will be lifted from our fear-drenched communities and in some not too distant tomorrow the radiant stars of love and brotherhood will shine over our great nation with all of their scintillating beauty.

Yours for the cause of Peace and Brotherhood
Martin Luther King, Jr.

QUESTIONS TO PONDER

1. If you represented Dr. King and his colleagues, how would you have advised them to act after they were served with the injunction? If they told you they did not believe they could get a fair hearing from the segregationist judge who had issued the injunction they were just served, what would you tell them?

2. A possible rejoinder to King's Letter from Birmingham City Jail follows the logic of civil disobedience: If a person or group wants to dramatize the injustice of a law by disobeying it, they should be willing to take the consequences of that disobedience. This would strengthen their impact, either by producing martyrs or by dramatizing the perceived injustice. It would also express ultimate respect for the rule of law and the law's rules for bringing about change. According to this view, we see the outer limit of judicial remedies for potential injustices when protestors take their claims to the streets rather than to the courts. How should defenders of Reverend King respond? How does this debate affect your view of the collateral bar rule? These issues are discussed in Abe Fortas, *Concerning Dissent and Civil Disobedience* (1968). Justice Fortas joined the dissenting opinion in *Walker*.

CHAPTER 3

Thinking Like a Trial Lawyer, Pleadings, and Joinder

A. INTRODUCTION

In Chapters 3, 4, and 5, we turn to the major steps in civil litigation. Chapter 3 covers the requirements for a complaint and also considers how many plaintiffs and defendants must, can, and should be joined, and what responses the defendant can and should make. Chapter 4 addresses the discovery process, which is central to the civil litigation process. Chapter 5 discusses the right of trial by jury and the many methods that have evolved to instruct and constrain juries.

It is important that you begin to internalize your own sense of the chronological flow of a civil lawsuit from the filing of the initial pleadings; through discovery and motions; through trial, verdict, and judgment; and then to the concept of finality. To this end, we have provided various ways in which you can gain perspective on the entire process. After this introduction, we provide a brief description of the major aspects of a case in the chronological order in which they typically take place. You may find it helpful to refer back to this section whenever you are learning a new topic, so that you can appreciate where the concept that you are studying fits into the larger picture.

B. THE STAGES AND ESSENTIAL CONCEPTS OF A CIVIL LITIGATION

Most civil cases are introduced to plaintiffs' lawyers when a client comes to the office and expresses dissatisfaction with the behavior of others. As the client describes what is wrong, the lawyer considers whether this is a situation for which the law gives any relief. Assume, for instance, the potential client, Joe, says, "I was in an elevator yesterday, and a passenger, Sally, didn't say hello to me." If this is the whole story, the lawyer would probably think that the law does not recognize snubbing as a wrong. In other words, the action of Sally the passenger was not legally "cognizable." Thus, whether the law will give relief is sometimes called a question of *cognizability*.

The underlying concept (or "unit of measurement" if you like scientific analogies) the lawyer would use in reaching this result is called the *cause of action* or *claim showing that the pleader is entitled to relief*. Causes of action are a shorthand for what events or circumstances must have taken place (or, in some instances, will take place) before a court will grant relief under some applicable substantive law.

Each cause of action or claim has components, called *elements*. Through your substantive law courses (torts, contracts, property, environmental law, employment discrimination, etc.) you will learn the elements of many different causes of action. So let us suppose Joe said instead: "I was walking down the street and I think Sally tripped me, or perhaps she was just careless in sticking out her leg." The attorney might now think about two potential causes of action: negligence and battery. The lawyer might say to herself: "Sally, as another pedestrian, had a 'duty' to Joe to refrain from unreasonable conduct, and perhaps she breached that duty by acting 'unreasonably' in tripping Joe, and that caused him harm ('cause in fact') which was foreseeable or within the risk Sally took ('proximate cause'), and since he broke his leg as a result of her action, he has suffered 'harm' or sustained 'damages.' So if the facts are true, there may be a cause of action for negligence because all five elements (of the negligence cause of action) are present: duty, unreasonable conduct (breach of duty), cause in fact, proximate cause, and harm or damages."

Perhaps Sally acted intentionally. If so, there may be a cause of action for battery with these elements: (1) an intentional act by defendant; (2) resulting in harmful or offensive contact; (3) without consent; and (4) causing injury. Of course, even within this single cause of action there may be multiple factual *theories* of the case. For instance, a battery could result from a punch in the face, pulling a chair out from underneath someone, creating an electric shock, tainting someone's food, and so forth. Multiple factual theories could arise even within a single case.

Throughout this course, we will deal with many causes of action from many different substantive areas of the law. This will require us to consider what are the elements of those causes of action. Please remember that different jurisdictions, lawyers, and law professors choose to treat or express the elements somewhat differently. So, do not be alarmed if in your torts class "negligence" and "battery" are explained a bit differently than in this rendition.

If, after talking to the potential client and possibly performing further investigation, a lawyer is satisfied that there is at least one provable cause of action, she will discuss fees and perhaps take the case. Joe's lawyer, at some point, will want to discuss with Joe whether commencing a lawsuit is the best way to begin. Perhaps a call to Sally, or to her insurance company or her lawyer, if they exist, makes more sense. A demand letter, and perhaps the suggestion of mediation or some other method of alternative dispute resolution (ADR), should be considered. We will discuss some specific ADR techniques later in the course, but understand that the parties will usually be negotiating a resolution of their dispute before, during, and even after the formal phases of litigation. The formal processes of litigation, however, will alter the parties' expectations and settlement positions.

If a lawsuit is to be filed, then the lawyer will have to decide in which states the defendant can be sued; this is a question of *personal jurisdiction*. Let's say you are an Oregon lawyer, and Sally, who lives in California, allegedly caused Joe to trip on a street in Oregon. He has come to discuss the case with you in Oregon. You would probably conclude quickly, since Oregon has typical personal jurisdiction statutes, that Sally could be sued on the facts of this case either in Oregon or in California. If you decide California is a better *forum* state — a state in which a court sits, and where a suit has been or will be brought — you would help Joe find a lawyer in California, since you have probably not been admitted to practice law there.

It probably makes sense to sue in Oregon, where your client lives and where the accident occurred; this would also mean that you could handle the case and earn a fee. Next, you would have to decide in which Oregon court to commence suit. Oregon, like all other states, has a state court system and at least one federal district court (remember, federal district courts are trial courts). The issue of "what court is empowered to hear this type of case" is called a question of *subject matter jurisdiction*. A combination of constitutional provisions and statutes grant different courts the right to hear different types of cases. For instance, in any given state, either the state constitution or statutes will give at least one trial court the authority to hear most types of cases. This broad grant of power to a trial court is called a grant of *general subject matter jurisdiction*.

Article III of the U.S. Constitution describes what cases Congress is permitted to authorize the federal district courts to hear. This grant of power is considerably narrower than the authorization provided in state constitutions and statutes. Thus, subject matter jurisdiction in the federal courts is commonly called *limited subject matter jurisdiction*. The limited subject matter jurisdiction for federal district courts can be found primarily in Title 28, in the "1330" sections of the U.S. Code. (After Congress passes a bill, it becomes an Act. Acts are assigned to a Title, by subject matter. Peruse these sections either in your rules supplement or in the U.S. Code volumes in the library or online.) The two major grants of limited subject matter jurisdiction to the federal district courts are called *federal question* and *diversity of citizenship*. See if you can find where these grants appear in your rules supplement. Sometimes, grants of limited subject matter jurisdiction to the federal district courts appear in various substantive statutes granting specific rights (scattered throughout the Code), so Title 28 is not the only title in which one can find such grants of federal subject matter jurisdiction.

Even after the lawyer decides in what court system and in what state to commence a suit (and please keep in mind that litigation is not the only rational alternative to resolve disputes), she must determine where—within the state or within the federal system—the case can be brought. This question is geographic, but it is different from personal jurisdiction or subject matter jurisdiction. This additional issue is called *venue*. For instance, if the suit of Joe against Sally is brought in an Oregon Circuit Court, a trial court of the Oregon state judicial system, one still must decide in which geographic section of the state to bring the case. Typical state venue statutes look to the county in which the cause of action arose (in this instance, it would be where Sally allegedly tripped Joe) or where the defendant resides. *See, e.g.,* Or. Rev. Stat. § 14.080. Congress has placed venue restrictions on where plaintiffs can commence cases in federal court. Try to find the relevant section(s) in your rules supplement.

The plaintiff must have not only personal jurisdiction over the defendant or defendants, subject matter jurisdiction in the appropriate court, and proper venue, but the defendants must also be appropriately notified of the commencement of suit. The "due process" requirements of notice and the right to be heard are explored at length in Chapter 1 and again in several cases concerning provisional relief in Chapter 2. These issues of personal jurisdiction, subject matter jurisdiction, venue, and notice raise fascinating and complex issues of federalism, separation of powers, and elemental fairness, and they occupy much of the second half of the materials in this book.

In the case of *Joe v. Sally*, as Joe's lawyer, you may have the opportunity to choose either a state court in Oregon or California, or a federal court in either state, if the potential damages were in excess of $75,000. Assuming Joe is a citizen of Oregon and Sally is a citizen of California, and the potential damages were sufficient, there would be diversity of citizenship within the meaning of Title 28, § 1332. Note that this would then be a case where there is *concurrent subject matter jurisdiction* among state courts and federal courts. Unless Congress makes a grant of *exclusive subject matter jurisdiction*, then a case that would have federal subject matter jurisdiction will also have state subject matter jurisdiction. On the other hand, if, for instance, Congress says that only federal courts can hear a certain type of case, such as actions alleging certain types of anti-competitive behavior specifically prescribed in the Sherman Anti-Trust Act (15 U.S.C. § 4), then the plaintiff's lawyer would be unable to bring that exact violation into a state trial court. Many first-year law students assume that if there is a federal question, such as a violation of a federal civil rights act, then the case can only be brought in federal court. But unless Congress grants exclusivity to the federal court system, there is concurrent subject matter jurisdiction and the plaintiff has the choice of state or federal courts. Under certain circumstances defendants may also *remove* cases from state to federal court.

Returning to the case of *Joe v. Sally*, let us assume as Joe's lawyer that you have decided to bring the case in the Circuit Court of Oregon (a state court with general subject matter jurisdiction) sitting in the County of Yamhill. You will have checked what is called the *long-arm statute* of Oregon to make sure that Sally, a California citizen, can be sued in Oregon for a tort she allegedly committed there

(Rule 4(c) of the Oregon Rules of Civil Procedure would indeed permit this exercise of personal jurisdiction). Also, you will have checked the applicable Oregon venue statute and complied with it in choosing the location of the court in Oregon in which to sue. You will then draft a *complaint* in accordance with Oregon's procedural rules. If the case were in a federal court, such pleading rules would appear in the Federal Rules of Civil Procedure. The pleading rules and cases interpreting them (as well as local culture, and in some instances, local rules) will tell you how precise you must be in your complaint about the facts and the specific relevant causes of action and their elements. You will have to check the applicable *statute of limitations* to make certain that the complaint has been filed within a statutorily prescribed time or, depending on the state law, that each defendant (in this case, "Sally") is "served" the complaint (*service of process*) or (again depending on statutes and their constitutionality) otherwise notified about the case. You will also have to decide whether you can and desire to demand a *jury* trial. This is usually a question of both constitutional right and trial strategy.

A plaintiff's lawyer also must consider *joinder* issues at the beginning of a case. If you choose to raise both negligence and battery causes of action against Sally, that would be called joinder of causes of action or, in the language of the Federal Rules, *joinder of claims*. If Joe tells you that the doctor who treated him for his broken leg after Sally tripped him did a bad job in setting the splint, then you will consider whether Joe has a negligence action against the doctor (often called a *medical malpractice* cause of action). Whether one can and should join Sally and the doctor as defendants in the same lawsuit is called a *joinder of parties* issue.

One reason that plaintiffs' lawyers begin their analysis of potential cases by considering causes of action is that the defendant, in answering the plaintiff, can promptly bring a *motion to dismiss* the case because of the plaintiff's failure to state a cause of action, or, in the words of Fed. R. Civ. P. 12(b)(6), "failure to state a claim upon which relief can be granted." This includes the concept of cognizability: A complaint may be dismissed for failure to state a claim when the circumstances alleged are not considered a wrong by the substantive law, even if everything that is alleged in the complaint actually happened exactly as plaintiff described it. Such a motion may also be brought on the basis that the plaintiff has alleged insufficient facts.

As you will find out, the defendant, either by motion or in its answer, has many options and many responsibilities. The defendant can challenge personal jurisdiction, subject matter jurisdiction, venue, and notice (service of process). The defendant, if filing an *answer*, must admit or deny the allegations. The defendant must state, or risk waiving by not stating, *affirmative defenses*. Affirmative defenses are defenses that the defendant has to the plaintiff's causes of action, even if the case is in an appropriate court and the plaintiff otherwise has a good cause of action. In the case of Joe against Sally, Sally might claim, for example, that Joe's own negligence contributed to the fall, or that he consented to contact, or that the applicable statute of limitations has already run. The defendant can also *counterclaim* against the plaintiff for damages or relief that the defendant seeks from the plaintiff. In some instances, such counterclaims are compulsory, in the sense that if the defendant does not bring the claim within the restricted period of time, it will be treated as waived and not permitted in the future. In federal court, for example, Fed. R. Civ. P. 13(a) mandates *compulsory counterclaims* if the defendant has a claim that "arises out of the transaction or occurrence that is the subject matter of the opposing party's claim" (although the rule is more complicated than this abbreviated statement of it). Perhaps Joe slandered Sally immediately after the incident. Lawyers might then debate whether this is a compulsory or *permissive counterclaim.*

Sally may have good reason to believe that if she is responsible to Joe, someone else is responsible to her for what she owes Joe. Let's say that Sally was acting as a messenger for a delivery company when the accident happened, and that the company had agreed to indemnify her for any harm caused while she made deliveries. Sally could bring a complaint for indemnification against the company, called an *impleader* or *third-party claim.* In federal court, impleader is covered by Fed. R. Civ. P. 14. If there are co-defendants, they may have claims against each other, which are called *cross-claims* in some states and in Fed. R. Civ. P. 13(g).

In some instances a plaintiff must join certain parties, or the case cannot go forward. These are called issues of *necessary and indispensable parties,* and are covered by Fed. R. Civ. P. 19. There are also more complex joinder issues, such as *intervention* (Fed. R. Civ. P. 24), *interpleader* (Fed. R. Civ. P. 22), and *class actions* (Fed. R. Civ. P. 23). These devices are introduced in this casebook but are explored more fully in a Complex Litigation course.

Assuming that the case survives preliminary motions that challenge the pleadings, the parties may then engage in *discovery.* Most states, as well as the federal courts, have a group of procedures whereby one party may gain information from the other parties, and, in some instances, even from nonparty witnesses. Fed. R. Civ. P. 26 through 37 cover the discovery provisions, and are drafted to permit quite liberal discovery. In federal courts and some state courts, selected information is subject to *mandatory disclosure* in the earliest stages of the litigation. Additional discovery is obtained by other methods, including written questions to opposing parties called *interrogatories,* written and oral *depositions,* requests to inspect *documents,* and motions to inspect real or personal property. In oral depositions, one party normally forces another and/or other witnesses to appear in person before a court reporter to answer a series of oral questions under oath. Court orders may limit the amount and scope of discovery; there are sanctions for interfering with legitimate discovery and for abuse of the discovery rules; and many district courts also have local rules that limit discovery. All ninety-four federal district courts, and many state trial courts, have *local rules* and *standing orders* of judges that supplement the rules found throughout the country or in a given state. Consequently, a lawyer in federal court, for example, must know not only the Federal Rules of Civil Procedure, but also the applicable local rules and standing orders of the individual judges.

To understand the procedure that logically likely comes next, you must understand the concepts of the *burden of production* and the *burden of persuasion*. At the trial of a case, the party with the burden of proof, usually the plaintiff, must have a sufficiency of evidence as to each element of at least one cause of action to permit a reasonable fact finder to find that each element is true. This is called the *burden of production*. Let's say that Joe in fact sued Sally for negligence, the case reached a jury trial, and Joe's lawyer examined the witnesses in court and offered whatever evidence she had in favor of Joe. Assume that she was done with her part of the case, which is called *resting*. If the defendant's lawyer does not think there was a sufficiency of evidence to permit reasonable juries to find that all of the elements are true, that lawyer can move for a *judgment as a matter of law* under Fed. R. Civ. P. 50(a). (This motion was once labeled and is still often referred to as a motion for a *directed verdict*.) For instance, in the case of Joe against Sally, if Joe's lawyer offered no evidence from which reasonable people could infer that Sally acted intentionally or unreasonably, then the trial judge, upon the defendant's motion, would grant a directed verdict, meaning that the jury would have to find for the defendant. This is because Joe would not have met his "production" burden.

But it is logical that even if Joe survives a motion for directed verdict, he may not ultimately win. Let's say that Joe describes in open court how Sally carelessly tripped him, and also presents other potentially believable evidence of each element of his negligence case. This would mean that he would survive a directed verdict motion because he has met his production burden, that is, produced a sufficiency of evidence to permit reasonable jurors to find that each element is true. But the jury may not actually believe all or part of Joe's testimony, or it may find that what he said to Sally did not in their minds add up to negligence or unreasonable conduct. Thus the jury might find for the defendant, because Joe did not persuade them that each element is true. In that instance, Joe did not meet the persuasion burden. In civil cases, the plaintiff must ordinarily persuade the fact finder by a *preponderance of the evidence* that each element is more likely than not to be true (or, as it is sometimes said, that the scale of justice tips at least a little bit in favor of the plaintiff as to each and every element of the plaintiff's cause of action). You can now see that in the normal case, the plaintiff has three burdens with respect to the merits of his or her case: He or she must plead correctly in the complaint, then meet the production burden, and then, in order to ultimately win, meet the persuasion burden.

If, after discovery, it appears that there is no way a plaintiff can win his or her case because it is predictable that at the trial the plaintiff will not have a sufficiency of evidence to meet the production burden, the defendant can then bring a motion for *summary judgment*. This will dispose of the case after (or during) discovery but before trial. This motion is described in Fed. R. Civ. P. 56.

A plaintiff can win a case at summary judgment or directed verdict, though this is far less common than a defendant prevailing on such motions. But let's say that the cause of action is nonpayment of a promissory note, and that it is undisputed after discovery that the plaintiff lent the defendant money, got a valid promissory note in return, and that the defendant, without any affirmative defense, has not paid. If the elements of a plaintiff's cause of action are self-evident, why have a trial? Put another way, if it is clear that every element of the plaintiff's claim *must be* true, then the plaintiff should win without the necessity of a trial. This plaintiff should win on a summary judgment motion. And if the plaintiff has not filed a summary judgment motion, she could still win this case, after defendant has rested, at the directed verdict stage.

There are other important motions, such as the motion for *renewed judgment as a matter of law* under Fed. R. Civ. P. 50(b). (This motion was once labeled and is still often referred to as a motion for a *judgment notwithstanding the verdict* or *JNOV*.) Other motions include new trial motions and motions to vacate judgment; we will tackle all of these in Chapter 5. The JNOV motion raises precisely the same question as a directed verdict motion, and requires the judge to apply exactly the same test, but the motion is brought *after* the jury has rendered its verdict. (The Federal Rules refer to both directed verdict and JNOV as motions for judgment as a matter of law, with the latter being a *renewed* form of the former.) Later in the course we will explore why a judge might deny a motion for directed verdict (thereby suggesting that the evidence was sufficient), and yet, after the jury has found for one party (usually the plaintiff), grant a JNOV on behalf of the opposing party (thereby suggesting that the evidence was insufficient).

Before you read what happens at trial, we want to caution that civil trials have become very rare. Only 1 to 2 percent of cases in state and federal courts are terminated by a trial. Many cases are disposed of through a dispositive motion, such as a motion to dismiss for failure to state a claim for which relief can be granted or a motion for summary judgment; some cases are dismissed because the plaintiff has failed to prosecute the claim for a prolonged period of time. A large percentage — maybe even 70 percent in some courts — of commenced cases are terminated by settlement. Most settlements are achieved solely by the lawyers or the parties — often at the express urging of judges. Further, mediators (professionals trained or experienced in resolving disputes) may assist the lawyers and the parties in their negotiations.

You should also be aware that in federal courts, and increasingly in state courts as well, the cases do not just go, unsupervised by the courts, from pleadings, discovery, and motions to settlement or trial. There are often several stages of *case management* in which the judges or other court personnel exercise control over the time sequence of the case and the amount and order of pretrial discovery. Especially in federal courts, much litigation time and expense is frequently spent on pretrial conferences and documents that are designed to focus the case, whittle it down to essentials, and provide the opposing lawyers and the judge with a description of the witnesses, evidence, and potential evidentiary problems that would be present in the unlikely event a trial actually occurs. You might wish to look at this time at Fed. R. Civ. P. 16 in order to get a preliminary sense of the ways in which case management has become an essential characteristic of much civil litigation.

That many, if not most, cases settle does not mean that litigators are not concerned about the facts that would likely come out, the law that would be applied, or the verdicts or orders that might be rendered after a full-scale trial. It is frequently said that settlement discussion is "in the shadow of the law,"* in an attempt to indicate how lawyers, and mediators or judges who assist them in helping to achieve settlement, tend to think and talk in terms of what the results might be if the case is ultimately decided by a judge or jury. Trials are important to the disposition of civil cases in several ways. A firm trial date is one of the strongest inducements to serious settlement talks. The costs of trial, and the uncertainty of trial results, also encourage settlement. What has happened in the trial of similar cases, and the potential verdicts in the case at hand, inform settlement discussion. That one is willing to try a case and is fully prepared for trial can influence settlement demands and offers. And sometimes, trials actually happen.

Trials usually begin with each side giving *opening statements*. The plaintiff's lawyer then introduces her case first, with *direct examination* of each witness. Then the defendant's lawyer will ordinarily *cross-examine* those witnesses. At the trial, as the parties introduce evidence, the attorneys may raise *objections* to some of the questions asked or exhibits offered. The judge will apply *rules of evidence* in assessing the validity of the counsel's objections. If the question is a proper one, the judge will *overrule* the objection, and the witness must answer the question. If the judge finds that the question is improperly framed by counsel or that counsel seeks *inadmissible* testimony, she will *sustain* the objection, which means that the lawyer will have to reframe the question or move on to another matter.

Assume this is a jury case (as opposed to a bench trial, where a judge is the fact-finder). Once both sides rest, assuming neither side wins on a motion for directed verdict, each side will give *closing arguments*. These will be preceded or followed by the judge's *instructing* the jury. The jury will render its *verdict*. The verdict will later become a *judgment*. If the plaintiff wins, they can use formal methods to *execute* on the judgment—that is, force the defendant to pay it. Bear in mind, though, that in some cases the plaintiff will be seeking injunctive relief. She may seek a *temporary restraining order* at the beginning of the case to stop the defendant from doing irreparable harm, and then seek to have that judgment become a *preliminary* injunction, stopping the defendant from doing something prior to trial. If the plaintiff wins, the injunction may become a *permanent injunction*.

---

* This expression comes from the oft-cited article *Bargaining in the Shadow of the Law: The Case of Divorce*, 88 Yale L.J. 950 (1979). The authors, Robert Mnookin and Lewis Kornhauser, discuss how divorce negotiations occur "in the shadow of the law" in the sense that they are shaped by what the parties suspect a court will do if no agreement is reached and they are forced instead to go to trial.

In most instances, in both state and federal courts, the losing party can appeal only from a *final judgment*. In the federal court system, the party that loses at the district court level has a right to appeal to the U.S. Court of Appeals. If the appeal is lost at this level, the losing party can apply to the U.S. Supreme Court for review. This is called a petition for a *writ of certiorari*. (Supreme Court review is governed by 28 U.S.C. §§ 1253-1258.)

If a party loses in the state trial court of general jurisdiction, then the party usually has the right to appeal to an intermediate appellate court. If the appeal is lost at this level, the losing party can appeal to the state's highest court, but that court usually has discretion over which cases it will hear. Some of the appellate decisions at the highest state court level can be reviewed by the U.S. Supreme Court, but only if that decision involved federal law. *See* 28 U.S.C. § 1257.

Generally, appellate courts insist that the party seeking review has objected to the decision or ruling it is appealing at the time the decision was originally made. Additionally, appellate courts usually require that the trial court's decision be based on the same point. Consequently, a good trial lawyer is always keeping a close eye on the proceedings, looking to object to questionable decisions so that she has a viable, appealable point in the event of a later unfavorable final judgment.

Can you imagine why appellate courts are reluctant to let a party who only loses on a preliminary matter appeal that point at that time to an appellate court? What if, for instance, Sally files a motion to dismiss for improper venue and loses. Why shouldn't she be permitted to appeal immediately on this matter? This would be called an *interlocutory appeal*. Appeals of interlocutory orders sometimes are allowed under 28 U.S.C. § 1292(b) if (i) the question involved is one of law; (ii) the question is controlling; (iii) there are substantial grounds for a difference of opinion; and (iv) immediate appeal materially advances the ultimate termination of litigation. For example, appeals from interlocutory orders of the district courts regarding injunctions are sometimes allowed because of the final and irreparable effect on the rights of the parties, and because the evaluation is completely separate from the merits of the case and is unreviewable on appeal. 28 U.S.C. § 1292(a).

Once a case reaches final judgment, the concept of *res judicata* (literally "a matter adjudged") applies. Let's say that a jury renders a defendant's verdict in the case of *Joe v. Sally*, which then becomes a judgment. A year later, Joe decides to go to another lawyer to try again. Intuitively, this would be both unfair to Sally and expensive for the court system. The defense to the second case would be *res judicata*, because plaintiffs are not permitted to bring the same case twice. Even if Joe decided to sue in case one alleging only battery, and now tries to bring a case for negligence arising from the same incident, *res judicata* would apply. In modern parlance, one would say that Joe is not permitted to split his claim, a concept also called *claim preclusion*.

Sometimes, an issue is decided in one case, and is relevant to a new claim between the same parties in a subsequent case. Assume that *A* sues *B* on a promissory note and wins a case for installments not paid up until the time of the verdict. (Assume further that the note does not have an "acceleration clause" making all of the installments due upon any single failure to pay.) Subsequently, *B* continues not to pay, and *A* sues for the subsequent installments owed. *A* will probably not have to reprove the validity of the promissory note, because that issue has already been litigated between the same parties. The second court would say that *A* can *collaterally estop B* from denying that the note was valid. In other words, the second fact finder, whether judge or jury, would summarily have to find that the note was a valid one. This concept is usually called *issue preclusion*.

Unfortunately some courts use the term *res judicata* to cover both claim preclusion and issue preclusion. In any event, the issues of *res judicata* and collateral estoppel are covered near the end of this book—appropriate, given their finality.

It is now time to explore more deeply the concepts of claims, causes of action, and elements as a prelude to lessons on pleading and the history of pleading.

C. CLAIMS, CAUSES OF ACTION, AND ELEMENTS

At the heart of a trial lawyer's thinking and strategy about civil litigation are the fundamental concepts of claims or causes of action (these terms frequently mean the same thing*) and elements. A lawsuit usually begins when there has been a dispute and a party or parties to that dispute, and their lawyers, believe that they are entitled to relief because the law recognizes the injury they have suffered, and permits the court to intervene and provide injunctive, monetary, or declaratory relief. A *cause of action* is one shorthand term for what the plaintiff must prove in order to win a lawsuit. The corresponding term used by the Federal Rules of Civil Procedure, however, is a *claim showing that the pleader is entitled to relief.* Why the Federal Rules use the phrase "claim showing that the pleader is entitled to relief" rather than the previously used term, "cause of action," is something you should consider throughout this chapter. (One relevant factor is the period during which the Federal Rules were drafted, 1935-1937. The New Deal, which enlarged the power of the federal government through a myriad of new agencies and programs, was in full swing.) Each cause of action or claim connotes a group of circumstances for which a court will grant relief. These circumstances, in turn, are divided into parts called elements. In this section, we will provide several examples of causes of action and their elements. In civil litigation, a judge often asks the plaintiff's lawyer what her *prima facie case* is. This can mean that the judge is asking either for an enumeration of the elements of the plaintiff's claim (or cause of action) or for a short description of the evidence as to each of those elements.

---

* The term "claim" is also often used to denote one transaction or occurrence that may permit multiple causes of action.

Putting aside for now jurisdictional and notice issues, we have seen that plaintiffs have three obligations in order to win in civil litigation. First, whether in state or federal court, plaintiffs must state in their initial pleading that they are entitled to relief. Depending on the court system, the procedural rules may also require a statement of the facts underlying the cause of action. Second, after satisfying their initial pleading obligation, plaintiffs must meet a production burden. This is shorthand for the idea that a plaintiff must present sufficient evidence to permit a reasonable person to find that each element of the claim (or cause of action) is true. Finally, in order to prevail, a plaintiff must meet a burden of persuasion by persuading the fact finder that each element is true. Although a lawyer must, when deciding whether to take a case, assess the likelihood of satisfying the pleading obligation, meeting the production burden, and persuading the fact finder, this chapter focuses on the pleading obligation. We will focus on burdens of production and burdens of persuasion in Chapter 5.

A lawyer cannot responsibly draft a complaint without analyzing her client's situation in order to see if there is a cognizable claim, a claim for which the law will give her client relief. In order to do this analysis, she will have to analyze the elements of her claim or claims. Indeed, much of your law school curriculum will deal with the exploration of causes of action and elements from a wide variety of fields. Causes of action and their elements constitute the substantive law that it is the responsibility of procedure to "process." Lawyers thus can spend much creative energy trying to convince courts to expand older causes of action and to create new ones. Lawyers, lobbyists, and legislators also may create new causes of action through statutes.

The library offers hundreds of places in which to research available causes of action and their elements (as well as the type of evidence one might find to meet both production and persuasion burdens). Each state, for instance, is likely to have at least one or more volumes in a "practice" series that explains causes of action in that state. Volumes in the library containing "pattern jury instructions" will also give you insight into how the substantive law is expressed through causes of action that, in turn, are composed of elements.

What follows is a summary of some popular causes of action. Please realize that this is a limited list with only a summary group of elements. Once you begin to prepare an actual case, you will gain sophistication in articulating the elements. It is also important to remember that different jurisdictions (and law school instructors) may teach the elements of a claim or cause of action in a different manner than you see them here.

Assault: (1) intent to cause harmful or offensive contact; and (2) imminent apprehension of such contact.

Battery: (1) intentional act; (2) resulting in harmful or offensive contact; (3) lack of consent; and (4) causing injury.

Breach of Contract: (1) valid contract; (2) breach; (3) performance by plaintiff; and (4) damage.

Conversion: (1) right to property; (2) right to possession; (3) demand for possession; and (4) wrongful possession or control by defendant.

Copyright Infringement: (1) ownership of valid copyright; and (2) copying of constituent elements of the work that are original.

Defamation (or Libel): (1) false and defamatory statement; (2) publication not privileged; (3) fault (ranging from negligence to malice, depending on the publisher); (4) harm (may be presumed); and (5) recipient understood communication refers to plaintiff.

Failure to Warn of a Product Defect: (1) danger existing with foreseeable use of product; (2) inadequate warning of the danger; (3) product was defective and unreasonably dangerous; (4) defect existed at the time it left the control of the manufacturer; (5) product reached user without substantial change; (6) causation; and (7) injury.

False Imprisonment: (1) deprivation of liberty; (2) lack of consent; and (3) no legal justification.

Fraud: (1) false representation; (2) knowledge of falsity; (3) intent to induce reliance; (4) reasonable reliance; and (5) damage.

Fraudulent Conveyance: (1) conveyance without fair consideration; (2) knowledge of an impending obligation; and (3) obligation not satisfied.

Intentional Infliction of Emotional Distress: (1) intent; (2) extreme and outrageous conduct; (3) causation; and (4) severe emotional distress.

Medical Malpractice: (1) professional standard of care in the community; (2) departure from the standard; (3) causation; and (4) injury.

Negligence: (1) duty; (2) breach; (3) cause-in-fact; (4) proximate cause; and (5) harm.

Negligent Entrustment of a Vehicle: (1) entrustment by the owner; (2) to a known unlicensed, incompetent, or reckless driver; (3) negligence by driver; and (4) driver's negligence proximately caused the accident.

Nuisance (Private): (1) substantial interference; (2) intentional act; (3) unreasonable interference with right to use and enjoy land; and (4) causation.

Patent Infringement: (1) unauthorized use or sale; (2) of a patented invention; (3) within or imported into the United States.

Spoliation of Evidence: (1) pending or probable litigation involving the plaintiff; (2) defendant's knowledge that litigation exists or is probable; (3) destruction of evidence; (4) disruption of plaintiff's case; (5) proximate cause; and (6) damages.

Strict Products Liability (Design Defect): (1) sale of a product by one engaged in the business of selling such products; (2) product reached consumer without substantial change in condition; (3) product was in a defective condition unreasonably dangerous to the user; (4) causation; and (5) injury.

Tortious Interference with Contractual Relations: (1) existing contract; (2) defendant aware of that contract; (3) defendant intentionally procured breach of that contract; (4) lack of justification; and (5) resulting damage.

Trademark Infringement: (1) plaintiff possessed a mark; (2) defendant used the mark; (3) use of mark occurred in commerce; and (4) use was likely to confuse customers.

Trespass: (1) unauthorized entry by defendant; (2) property possessed by plaintiff; and (3) damage.

Trespass to Chattel: (1) dispossession by defendant of plaintiff's chattel; and (2) impairment of chattel's condition, quality, or value, or deprivation of use for a substantial period of time.

Unjust Enrichment: (1) benefit conferred on defendant; (2) defendant appreciated or knew of benefit; and (3) circumstances would make it inequitable for the receiving party to benefit without paying for its value.

Wrongful Death: (1) tort; (2) resulting death; and (3) damages suffered by heirs. (This cause of action is usually statutory, as you will see later in the course.)

This list of causes of action and their elements primarily includes common law private causes of action. Claims of a more public nature often incorporate burden shift problems and more sophisticated issues of definition. For instance, much civil rights litigation is brought under 42 U.S.C. § 1983, the post-Civil War statute now utilized to enforce constitutional and other federal law violations committed by state actors. Much employment discrimination litigation is brought under "Title VII," which is a reference to Title VII of the Civil Rights Act of 1964; those provisions now appear at 42 U.S.C. §§ 2000e et seq.

PRACTICE EXERCISE NO. 7: INITIAL STRATEGY SESSION IN *CARPENTER*

Assume that you are an associate in a law firm and have received a memorandum in preparation for a strategy session. The memorandum on the potential client, which you should read for the exercise, is the first document in the Case Files for *Carpenter v. Dee*. (The documents relating to this case are printed at the end of your book in the section labeled Case Files.) Prepare to discuss with the senior partner the causes of action that may be available to Nancy Carpenter (and against whom) if the firm chooses to represent her. Consider each element of a potential claim and, using the facts of the case, note where you will need additional information. Of course, at this early stage in the litigation the memorandum is not a complete statement of the case; indeed, some important facts are missing. Although you do not know much about specific claims or causes of action yet, consider the sampling of causes of action and elements that you just read; also read the three brief Massachusetts statutes in the Case Files that follow the initial memorandum. Do you think the firm should take this case? Why?

D. PLEADINGS AND AMENDMENTS

Having considered how plaintiffs' lawyers think about potential litigation, we now address the documents and motions that parties draft in the beginning stages of a lawsuit. Although most cases are brought in state courts, we concentrate our inquiry on the Federal Rules of Civil Procedure that control litigation in the federal trial courts. These rules have been highly influential on state rules and practices, and provide a common reservoir of procedural learning for most law students in the United States. Fed. R. Civ. P. 7, 8, 9, and 10 lay out the requirements for a federal complaint, and 12(b)(6) describes the motion that a defendant may bring to challenge whether the plaintiff's complaint adequately describes a claim for which relief can be granted.

At this point in the course both you (the student) and your professor encounter a severe conceptual and practical problem. The Federal Rules of Civil Procedure were drafted from 1935 to 1937, and became law in 1938. The underlying assumptions that animated the Rules included the importance of simplicity and liberality in pleading. Later in this chapter we provide history about the evolution of different procedural regimes; you should recognize at the outset, however, that although the pleading rules have remained essentially the same since 1938, their interpretation has materially changed. Changes first occurred as a result of some federal district and circuit court judges acting on their own, and more recently endorsed by Supreme Court decisions. The trend has been in the direction of more rigorous pleading requirements, with plaintiffs obligated to provide more facts in the complaint, rather than waiting for the discovery stage for each side to explore in detail the underlying facts. As you will later study, other aspects of civil procedure, such as summary judgment, have moved in the same direction of requiring more of plaintiffs than was previously required. Again, this has been accomplished with only modest changes in the Rules themselves.

It is not your fault that the text (and history) of the Federal Rules suggest one interpretation, yet the Rules are construed to mean something else. We try to help you adjust to this predicament by providing three types of information: the Rules themselves and opinions interpreting them (doctrine), information about how and why the transformations have occurred (context), and practice exercises in which you make arguments in the course of applying the Rules to concrete situations. We think that you, as well as the accomplished lawyer, can act more successfully as advocates for clients and in policy arenas by studying how and why judges and others make their decisions. Your advocacy should be informed by knowledge of the political, social, and economic forces that influence those you are trying to persuade.

In any event, as you will see, the goal of simplicity and liberality in pleading has been the subject of recent, dramatic, and controversial reform. Of course, though, even with modest pleading requirements, there may be strategic reasons to plead with greater specificity than the Rules require. For instance, a more extensive story in a pleading may help educate the judge to see the case in a more favorable light, or it may lead to an earlier and more advantageous settlement.

In this section, you will also study the responses that a defendant must make, and may make, to a complaint. This will require particularly close attention to Rules 8 and 12. You will discover, for example, that the defendant will have the choice, if appropriate, of challenging, either through a motion or in an answer, whether the complaint sufficiently states a claim for which relief can be granted. This section will also expose you to the rules for amending pleadings. Indeed, a fundamental tenet of the simplicity theme of the drafters of the Federal Rules was ease of amendment. Amending complaints may have become a more frequent and necessary occurrence with the trend that requires more factual information in complaints.

By the end of this section, you should know the fundamental rules of pleading complaints and answers, as well as the rules governing amendments. You should also be thinking about pleadings from the points of view of a variety of essential actors and audiences in litigation: parties, lawyers, judges, the court system, and society.

1. The Purpose and Doctrine of Complaints

We now introduce the civil complaint and modern-day pleading standards. How much detail to require in pleadings raises a perplexing dilemma. If rules require too much specificity, some meritorious cases will either not be brought or will be terminated early in the process for failure to meet the standard. If rules require little precision, suits without merit will be more likely to be instituted. In a later section in this chapter, as mentioned previously, we provide some of the history behind attempts to improve this and other aspects of American procedure; we think, though, that the history and its importance will make more sense if you have some of the relevant rules and case law in mind before reading the history.

The Federal Rules of Civil Procedure became law in 1938. Their principal draftsman, Professor Charles E. Clark, subsequently became a judge on the U.S. Court of Appeals for the Second Circuit. In *Dioguardi v. Durning*, 139 F.2d 774 (2d Cir. 1944), Judge Clark had the opportunity to interpret the pleading rule that he had drafted. Read (or re-read) Federal Rules 1, 3, 8(a)(2), and 12(b)(6) in your rules supplement, and then consider the complaint that John Dioguardi filed in that case. (In fact, Mr. Dioguardi's initial complaint was dismissed, and the following is his *amended* complaint. It is reprinted here verbatim.)

> Plaintiff, as and for his bill of amended complaint the defendant, respectfully alleges:
>
> FIRST: I want justice done on the basis of my medicinal extracts which have disappeared saying that they had leaked, which could never be true in the manner they were bottled.
>
> SECOND: Mr. E.G. Collord Clerk in Charge, promised to give me my merchandise as soon as I paid for it. Then all of a sudden payments were stopped.
>
> THIRD: Then, he didn't want to sell me my merchandise at catalogue price with the 5% off, which was very important to me, after I had already paid $5,000 for them, beside a few other expenses.
>
> FOURTH: Why was the medicinaly given to the Springdale Distilling Co. with my betting price of $110; and not their price of $120.
>
> FIFTH: It isn't so easy to do away with two cases with 37 bottles of one quart. Being protected, they can take this chance.
>
> SIXTH: No one can stop my rights upon my merchandise, because of both the duly and the entry.
>
> WHEREFORE: Plaintiff demands judgment against the defendant, individually and as Collector of Customs at the Port of New York, in the sum of Five Thousand Dollars ($5,000) together with interest from the respective dates of payment as set forth herein, together with the costs and disbursements of this action.

The district judge dismissed this amended complaint for failure to state a claim. On appeal, Judge Clark described that dismissal as "another instance of judicial haste which in the long run makes waste." 139 F.2d at 775. Judge Clark reversed the lower court and found the claims, "however inartistically they may be stated," satisfactory under Federal Rule 8(a). *Id.* Thirteen years later, the U.S. Supreme Court confronted a similar situation and had the opportunity either to reinforce Judge Clark's vision or to outline a different course. Justice Black authored the opinion for a unanimous Court.

Conley v. Gibson
355 U.S. 41 (1957)

Justice BLACK delivered the opinion of the Court:

Once again Negro employees are here under the Railway Labor Act asking that their collective bargaining agent be compelled to represent them fairly. In a series of cases beginning with *Steele v. Louisville & Nashville R. Co.*, 323 U.S. 192, this Court has emphatically and repeatedly ruled that an exclusive bargaining agent under the Railway Labor Act is obligated to represent all employees in the bargaining unit fairly and without discrimination because of race and has held that the courts have power to protect employees against such invidious discrimination.

This class suit was brought in a Federal District Court in Texas by certain Negro members of the Brotherhood of Railway and Steamship Clerks, petitioners here, on behalf of themselves and other Negro employees similarly situated against the Brotherhood, its Local Union No. 28 and certain officers of both. In summary, the complaint made the following allegations relevant to our decision: Petitioners were employees of the Texas and New Orleans Railroad at its Houston Freight House. Local 28 of the Brotherhood was the designated bargaining agent under the Railway Labor Act for the bargaining unit to which petitioners belonged. A contract existed between the Union and the Railroad which gave the employees in the bargaining unit certain protection from discharge and loss of seniority. In May 1954, the Railroad purported to abolish 45 jobs held by petitioners or other Negroes all of whom were either discharged or demoted. In truth the 45 jobs were not abolished at all but instead filled by whites as the Negroes were ousted, except for a few instances where Negroes were rehired to fill their old jobs but with loss of seniority. Despite repeated pleas by petitioners, the Union, acting according to plan, did nothing to protect them against these discriminatory discharges and refused to give them protection comparable to that given to white employees. The complaint then went on to allege that the Union had failed in general to represent Negro employees equally and in good faith. It charged that such discrimination constituted a violation of petitioners' right under the Railway Labor Act to fair representation from their bargaining agent. And it concluded by asking for relief in the nature of declaratory judgment, injunction and damages.

The respondents appeared and moved to dismiss the complaint on several grounds: (1) the National Railroad Adjustment Board had exclusive jurisdiction over the controversy; (2) the Texas and New Orleans Railroad, which had not been joined, was an indispensable party defendant; and (3) the complaint failed to state a claim upon which relief could be given. The District Court granted the motion to dismiss holding that Congress had given the Adjustment Board exclusive jurisdiction over the controversy. The Court of Appeals for the Fifth Circuit, apparently relying on the same ground, affirmed. 229 F.2d 436. Since the case raised an important question concerning the protection of employee rights under the Railway Labor Act we granted certiorari.

[Justice Black then provided his rationale for overturning the district and circuit court determinations of the jurisdictional issue. Although "the District Court did not pass on the other reasons advanced for dismissal of the complaint," he thought it "timely and proper for" the Supreme Court to consider the other two arguments for dismissal. The "indispensable party" contention was swiftly rejected, and Black proceeded to address the 12(b)(6) motion.]

[W]e hold that . . . the complaint adequately set forth a claim upon which relief could be granted. In appraising the sufficiency of the complaint we follow, of course, the accepted rule that a complaint should not be dismissed for failure to state a claim unless it appears beyond doubt that the plaintiff can prove no set of facts in support of his claim which would entitle him to relief. Here, the complaint alleged, in part, that petitioners were discharged wrongfully by the Railroad and that the Union, acting according to plan, refused to protect their jobs as it did those of white employees or to help them with their grievances all because they were Negroes. If these allegations are proven there has been a manifest breach of the Union's statutory duty to represent fairly and without hostile discrimination all of the employees in the bargaining unit. This Court squarely held in *Steele* and subsequent cases that discrimination in representation because of race is prohibited by the Railway Labor Act. The bargaining representative's duty not to draw "irrelevant and invidious" distinctions among those it represents does not come to an abrupt end, as the respondents seem to contend, with the making of an agreement between union and employer. Collective bargaining is a continuing process. Among other things, it involves day-to-day adjustments in the contract and other working rules, resolution of new problems not covered by existing agreements, and the protection of employee rights already secured by contract. The bargaining representative can no more unfairly discriminate in carrying out these functions than it can in negotiating a collective agreement. A contract may be fair and impartial on its face yet administered in such a way, with the active or tacit consent of the union, as to be flagrantly discriminatory against some members of the bargaining unit.

The respondents point to the fact that under the Railway Labor Act aggrieved employees can file their own grievances with the Adjustment Board or sue the employer for breach of contract. Granting this, it still furnishes no sanction for the Union's alleged discrimination in refusing to represent petitioners. The Railway Labor Act, in an attempt to aid collective action by employees, conferred great power and protection on the bargaining agent chosen by a majority of them. As individuals or small groups the employees cannot begin to possess the bargaining power of their representative in negotiating with the employer or in presenting their grievances to him. Nor may a minority choose another agent to bargain in their behalf. We need not pass on the Union's claim that it was not obliged to handle any grievances at all because we are clear that once it undertook to bargain or present grievances for some of the employees it represented it could not refuse to take similar action in good faith for other employees just because they were Negroes.

The respondents also argue that the complaint failed to set forth specific facts to support its general allegations of discrimination and that its dismissal is therefore proper. The decisive answer to this is that the Federal Rules of Civil Procedure do not require a claimant to set out in detail the facts upon which he bases his claim. To the contrary, all the Rules require is "a short and plain statement of the claim" that will give the defendant fair notice of what the plaintiff's claim is and the grounds upon which it rests. . . . Such simplified "notice pleading" is made possible by the liberal opportunity for discovery and the other pretrial procedures established by the Rules to disclose more precisely the basis of both claim and defense and to define more narrowly the disputed facts and issues. Following the simple guide of Rule 8[e] that "all pleadings shall be so construed as to do substantial justice," we have no doubt that petitioners' complaint adequately set forth a claim and gave the respondents fair notice of its basis. The Federal Rules reject the approach that pleading is a game of skill in which one misstep by counsel may be decisive to the outcome and accept the principle that the purpose of pleading is to facilitate a proper decision on the merits.

The judgment is reversed and the cause is remanded to the District Court for further proceedings not inconsistent with this opinion. . . .

QUESTIONS TO PONDER

In order to defend or criticize a pleading standard one must consider the goals of a system of pleading. Is the goal to screen out claims that lack merit? If so, wouldn't a more rigorous pleading standard require plaintiffs to do their legal and factual homework prior to filing? Is that such a bad idea? What are the competing goals?

What might more specific factual allegations have described or addressed? Why didn't the lawyers include such particulars in their complaint? Is there a tactical reason to leave them out?

a. The Lower Courts' Response to Notice Pleading

Some lower federal courts reacted to the regime of "notice pleading" by requiring stricter pleading in some types of cases — most notably civil rights cases. Indeed, during the 1970s and 1980s all federal courts of appeals applied a standard demanding factual specificity of civil rights plaintiffs filing cases in federal courts. Moreover, in some of these cases, judges appeared almost mean-spirited. For example, in *Leatherman v. Tarrant County Narcotics Intelligence and Coordination Unit*, 954 F.2d 1054 (5th Cir. 1992), the Fifth Circuit reviewed the *sua sponte* dismissal of a complaint filed by a family against law enforcement officers who, while executing the search of a residence that yielded nothing for their investigation, callously shot the plaintiffs' two dogs and then lounged in the yard "for over an hour drinking, smoking, talking, and laughing, apparently celebrating their seemingly unbridled power." With opinions that featured such topical headings as "Dog Day Afternoon," "These Dogs Want Their Day," and "Let Sleeping Dogs Lie," the Fifth Circuit affirmed the dismissal, concluding that the plaintiff's complaint was "All Bark, No Bite."

The Supreme Court reversed the Fifth Circuit. Then-Chief Justice Rehnquist wrote a unanimous opinion for the Court: "We think that it is impossible to square the 'heightened pleading standard' applied by the Fifth Circuit in this case with the liberal system of 'notice pleading' set up by the Federal Rules. . . . Perhaps if Rules 8 and 9 were rewritten today, claims against municipalities under § 1983 might be subjected to the added specificity requirement of Rule 9(b). But that is a result which must be obtained by the process of amending the Federal Rules, and not by judicial interpretation." 507 U.S. 163, 168 (1992). Should Federal Rules 8(a) and/or 9(b) be amended to require a heightened degree of particularity when pleading claims against municipalities? Is it unrealistic to expect a single pleading standard to apply to all types of actions (other than fraud and mistake)?

Notwithstanding the Court's decision in *Leatherman*, lower courts persisted in imposing higher pleading standards for civil rights cases. This phenomenon led, in turn, to another Supreme Court decision. Reversing a decision of the U.S. Court of Appeals for the Second Circuit in an employment discrimination case, the Court, in another unanimous opinion, made clear that a plaintiff need not allege facts to support each element of its prima facie case: Justice Thomas wrote that a prima facie case is "an evidentiary standard, not a pleading requirement." *Swierkiewicz v. Sorema, N.A.* 534 U.S. 500, 510 (2002).

b. A New Pleading Standard: Plausibility

Although Rule 8(a) was never amended, the Supreme Court nevertheless launched a controversial new era of pleading in 2007. In *Bell Atlantic Corp v. Twombly*, a nationwide class of local telephone and high-speed internet users filed a class action against a group of regional telephone companies, alleging that the defendants had conspired to maintain monopolies in their respective regions. The defendants were the so-called "Baby Bells" that were formed in the mid-1980s when the U.S. Department of Justice brought an antitrust suit that led ultimately to an order that AT&T divest itself of certain of its operations. The Baby Bells were regional in scope (e.g. "Bell South" in the Southeast; "NYNEX" in New England). Also known as "Regional Bell Operating Companies" (RBOCs) and "Incumbent Local Exchange Carriers" (ILECs), they were somewhat constrained from competing with one another until Congress passed the 1996 Telecommunications Act. By design, the Telecommunications Act authorized the companies to offer local telephone and high-speed internet services in each other's territories. Yet that competition did not happen. The lack of competition led ultimately to the filing of the instant suit.

The complaint alleged a conspiracy on the part of the RBOCs, and alleged that the defendants' actions would be anomalous in the absence of an agreement among the RBOCs not to compete with one another. The complaint described, for example, that SBC Communications alone did business in Connecticut even though Verizon alone did business in the states that surrounded Connecticut. Other examples described similar geographic parsing and lack of competition in other states—islands of business conducted alone by one RBOC. Qwest, for example, did not compete for business in California and Nevada, notwithstanding the fact that its predominance in surrounding areas would have given it substantial competitive advantages. The plaintiffs alleged that "the failure of the RBOCs that serve the surrounding territories to make significant attempts to compete in the surrounded territories is strongly suggestive of conspiracy, since the service of such surrounded territories presents RBOC serving surrounded territories with an especially attractive business opportunity that such RBOCs have not meaningfully pursued."

The complaint also included factual details that could be suggestive of a conspiracy. For example, Paragraph 42 of the plaintiffs' 96-paragraph, 29-page Complaint described a 2002 Chicago Tribune article about Richard Notebaert, CEO of Qwest. Notebaert is characterized as saying that it would be fundamentally wrong for his company to compete in a neighboring territory, and is quoted as saying "it might be a good way to turn a quick dollar but that doesn't make it right."

Bell Atlantic Corp. v. Twombly
550 U.S. 544 (2007)

Justice SOUTER delivered the opinion of the Court, in which ROBERTS, C.J., and SCALIA, KENNEDY, THOMAS, BREYER, and ALITO joined:

Liability under § 1 of the Sherman Act, 15 U.S.C. § 1, requires a "contract, combination . . ., or conspiracy, in restraint of trade or commerce." The question in this putative class action is whether a § 1 complaint can survive a motion to dismiss when it alleges that major telecommunications providers engaged in certain parallel conduct unfavorable to competition, absent some factual context suggesting agreement, as distinct from identical, independent action. We hold that such a complaint should be dismissed.

I

. . . Respondents William Twombly and Lawrence Marcus (hereinafter plaintiffs) represent a putative class consisting of all "subscribers of local telephone and/or high speed internet services . . . from February 8, 1996 to present." In this action against petitioners . . . plaintiffs seek treble damages and declaratory and injunctive relief for claimed violations of § 1 of the Sherman Act, which prohibits "[e]very contract, combination in the form of trust or otherwise, or conspiracy, in restraint of trade or commerce among the several States, or with foreign nations.". . .

The complaint couches its ultimate allegations this way:

> In the absence of any meaningful competition between the [Baby Bells] in one another's markets, and in light of the parallel course of conduct that each engaged in to prevent competition . . . within their respective local telephone or high speed internet services markets and the other facts and market circumstances alleged above, Plaintiffs allege upon information and belief that [the defendants] have entered into a contract, combination or conspiracy to prevent competitive entry in their respective . . . markets and have agreed not to compete with one another and otherwise allocated customers and markets to one another.

The United States District Court for the Southern District of New York dismissed the complaint for failure to state a claim upon which relief can be granted. The District Court acknowledged that "plaintiffs may allege a conspiracy by citing instances of parallel business behavior that suggest an agreement," but emphasized that "while '[c]ircumstantial evidence of consciously parallel behavior may have made heavy inroads into the traditional judicial attitude toward conspiracy[, . . .] "conscious parallelism" has not yet read conspiracy out of the Sherman Act entirely.'" 313 F.Supp.2d 174, 179 (2003). Thus, the District Court understood that allegations of parallel business conduct, taken alone, do not state a claim under § 1; plaintiffs must allege additional facts that "ten[d] to exclude independent self-interested conduct as an explanation for defendants' parallel behavior." 313 F.Supp.2d at 179. The District Court found plaintiffs' allegations of parallel ILEC actions to discourage competition inadequate because "the behavior of each ILEC . . . is fully explained by the ILEC's own interests in defending its individual territory." As to the ILEC's supposed agreement against competing with each other, the District Court found that the complaint does not "alleg[e] facts . . . suggesting that refraining from competing in other territories . . . was contrary to the ILECs' apparent economic interests, and consequently [does] not rais[e] an inference that [the ILECs'] actions were the result of a conspiracy."

The Court of Appeals for the Second Circuit reversed, holding that the District Court tested the complaint by the wrong [pleading] standard. . .

We granted certirorari to address the proper standard for pleading an antitrust conspiracy through allegations of parallel conduct, and now reverse.

II

A

Because § 1 of the Sherman Act "does not prohibit [all] unreasonable restraints of trade . . . but only restraints effected by a contract, combination, or conspiracy," *Copperweld Corp. v. Independence Tube Corp.*, 467 U.S. 752, 775 (1984), "[t]he crucial question" is whether the challenged anticompetitive conduct "stem[s] from independent decision or from an agreement, tacit or express," *Theatre Enterprises, Inc. v. Paramount Film Distributing Corp.*, 346 U.S. 537, 540 (1954). While a showing of parallel "business behavior is admissible circumstantial evidence from which the fact finder may infer agreement," it falls short of "conclusively establish[ing] agreement or . . . itself constitut[ing] a Sherman Act offense." *Id.*, at 540-541. Even "conscious parallelism," a common reaction of "firms in a concentrated market [that] recogniz[e] their shared economic interests and their interdependence with respect to price and output decisions" is "not in itself unlawful." *Brooke Group Ltd. v. Brown & Williamson Tobacco Corp.*, 509 U.S. 209, 227 (1993).

The inadequacy of showing parallel conduct or interdependence, without more, mirrors the ambiguity of the behavior: consistent with conspiracy, but just as much in line with a wide swath of rational and competitive business strategy unilaterally prompted by common perceptions of the market. Accordingly, we have previously hedged against false inferences from identical behavior at a number of points in the trial sequence. An antitrust conspiracy plaintiff with evidence showing nothing beyond parallel conduct is not entitled to a directed verdict, *see Theatre Enterprises, supra*; proof of a § 1 conspiracy must include evidence tending to exclude the possibility of independent action, *see Monsanto Co. v. Spray-Rite Service Corp.*, 465 U.S. 752 (1984); and at the summary judgment stage a § 1 plaintiff's offer of conspiracy evidence must tend to rule out the possibility that the defendants were acting independently, *see Matsushita Elec. Industrial Co. v. Zenith Radio Corp.*, 475 U.S. 574 (1986).

B

This case presents the antecedent question of what a plaintiff must plead in order to state a claim under § 1 of the Sherman Act. Federal Rule of Civil Procedure 8(a)(2) requires only "a short and plain statement of the claim showing that the pleader is entitled to relief," in order to "give the defendant fair notice of what the . . . claim is and the grounds upon which it rests," *Conley v. Gibson*, 355 U.S. 41, 47 (1957). While a complaint attacked by a Rule 12(b)(6) motion to dismiss does not need detailed factual allegations, *ibid.*, a plaintiff's obligation to provide the "grounds" of his "entitle[ment] to relief" requires more than labels and conclusions, and a formulaic recitation of the elements of a cause of action will not do. Factual allegations must be enough to raise a right to relief above the speculative level, *see* 5 C. Wright & A. Miller, Federal Practice and Procedure § 1216, pp. 235-236 (3d ed.2004) (hereinafter Wright & Miller) ("[T]he pleading must contain something more . . . than . . . a statement of facts that merely creates a suspicion [of] a legally cognizable right of action"),[3] on the

---

3. The dissent greatly oversimplifies matters by suggesting that the Federal Rules somehow dispensed with the pleading of facts altogether. . . . While, for most types of cases, the Federal Rules eliminated the cumbersome requirement that a claimant "set out *in detail* the facts upon which he bases his claim," *Conley v. Gibson*, 355 U.S. 41, 47 (1957) (emphasis added), Rule 8(a)(2) still requires a "showing,"

assumption that all the allegations in the complaint are true (even if doubtful in fact), *see, e.g., Swierkiewicz v. Sorema N. A.*, 534 U.S. 506, 508, n. 1, (2002). . . .

In applying these general standards to a § 1 claim, we hold that stating such a claim requires a complaint with enough factual matter (taken as true) to suggest that an agreement was made. Asking for plausible grounds to infer an agreement does not impose a probability requirement at the pleading stage; it simply calls for enough fact to raise a reasonable expectation that discovery will reveal evidence of illegal agreement. And, of course, a well-pleaded complaint may proceed even if it strikes a savvy judge that actual proof of those facts is improbable, and "that a recovery is very remote and unlikely." *Ibid*. In identifying facts that are suggestive enough to render a § 1 conspiracy plausible, we have the benefit of the prior rulings and considered views of leading commentators, already quoted, that lawful parallel conduct fails to bespeak unlawful agreement. It makes sense to say, therefore, that an allegation of parallel conduct and a bare assertion of conspiracy will not suffice. Without more, parallel conduct does not suggest conspiracy, and a conclusory allegation of agreement at some unidentified point does not supply facts adequate to show illegality. Hence, when allegations of parallel conduct are set out in order to make a § 1 claim, they must be placed in a context that raises a suggestion of a preceding agreement, not merely parallel conduct that could just as well be independent action.

The need at the pleading stage for allegations plausibly suggesting (not merely consistent with) agreement reflects the threshold requirement of Rule 8(a)(2) that the "plain statement" possess enough heft to "sho[w] that the pleader is entitled to relief." A statement of parallel conduct, even conduct consciously undertaken, needs some setting suggesting the agreement necessary to make out a § 1 claim; without that further circumstance pointing toward a meeting of the minds, an account of a defendant's commercial efforts stays in neutral territory. An allegation of parallel conduct is thus much like a naked assertion of conspiracy in a § 1 complaint: it gets the complaint close to stating a claim, but without some further factual enhancement it stops short of the line between possibility and plausibility of "entitlement to relief.". . .

[I]t is one thing to be cautious before dismissing an antitrust complaint in advance of discovery, but quite another to forget that proceeding to antitrust discovery can be expensive. As we indicated over 20 years ago in *Associated Gen. Contractors of Cal., Inc. v. Carpenters*, 459 U.S. 519, 528, n. 17 (1983), "a district court must retain the power to insist upon some specificity in pleading before allowing a potentially massive factual controversy to proceed." *See also Car Carriers, Inc. v. Ford Motor Co.*, 745 F.2d 1101, 1106 (C.A.7 1984) ("[T]he costs of modern federal antitrust litigation and the increasing caseload of the federal courts counsel against sending the parties into discovery when there is no reasonable likelihood that the plaintiffs can construct a claim from the events

---

rather than a blanket assertion, of entitlement to relief. Without some factual allegation in the complaint, it is hard to see how a claimant could satisfy the requirement of providing not only "fair notice" of the nature of the claim, but also "grounds" on which the claim rests. . . .

related in the complaint") . . . That potential expense is obvious enough in the present case: plaintiffs represent a putative class of at least 90 percent of all subscribers to local telephone or high-speed Internet service in the continental United States, in an action against America's largest telecommunications firms (with many thousands of employees generating reams and gigabytes of business records) for unspecified (if any) instances of antitrust violations that allegedly occurred over a period of seven years.

It is no answer to say that a claim just shy of a plausible entitlement to relief can, if groundless, be weeded out early in the discovery process through careful case management . . . [I]t is only by taking care to require allegations that reach the level suggesting conspiracy that we can hope to avoid the potentially enormous expense of discovery in cases with no "reasonably founded hope that the [discovery] process will reveal relevant evidence" to support a § 1 claim. *Dura Pharms., Inc. v. Broudo,* 544 U.S. 336, 347 (2005).

Plaintiffs do not, of course, dispute the requirement of plausibility and the need for something more than merely parallel behavior. [T]heir main argument against the plausibility standard at the pleading stage is its ostensible conflict with an early statement of ours construing Rule 8. Justice Black's opinion for the Court in *Conley v. Gibson* spoke not only of the need for fair notice of the grounds for entitlement to relief but of "the accepted rule that a complaint should not be dismissed for failure to state a claim unless it appears beyond doubt that the plaintiff can prove no set of facts in support of his claim which would entitle him to relief." 355 U.S., at 45-46. This "no set of facts" language can be read in isolation as saying that any statement revealing the theory of the claim will suffice unless its factual impossibility may be shown from the face of the pleadings. . . .

On such a focused and literal reading of *Conley*'s "no set of facts," a wholly conclusory statement of claim would survive a motion to dismiss whenever the pleadings left open the possibility that a plaintiff might later establish some "set of [undisclosed] facts" to support recovery. . . .

Seeing this, a good many judges and commentators have balked at taking the literal terms of the *Conley* passage as a pleading standard [citing several courts of appeals opinions and law review articles]. We could go on, but there is no need to pile up further citations to show that *Conley*'s "no set of facts" language has been questioned, criticized, and explained away long enough. To be fair to the *Conley* Court, the passage should be understood in light of the opinion's preceding summary of the complaint's concrete allegations, which the Court quite reasonably understood as amply stating a claim for relief. But the passage so often quoted fails to mention this understanding on the part of the Court, and after puzzling the profession for 50 years, this famous observation has earned its retirement. The phrase is best forgotten as an incomplete, negative gloss on an accepted pleading standard: once a claim has been stated adequately, it may be supported by showing any set of facts consistent with the allegations in the complaint. . . . *Conley*, then, described the breadth of opportunity to prove what

Interpretation of Conley Standard

an adequate complaint claims, not the minimum standard of adequate pleading to govern a complaint's survival.

III

neplasability

When we look for plausibility in this complaint, we agree with the District Court that plaintiffs' claim of conspiracy in restraint of trade comes up short. To begin with, the complaint leaves no doubt that plaintiffs rest their § 1 claim on descriptions of parallel conduct and not on any independent allegation of actual agreement among the ILECs. Although in form a few stray statements speak directly of agreement, on fair reading these are merely legal conclusions resting on the prior allegations. Thus, the complaint first takes account of the alleged "absence of any meaningful competition between [the ILECs] in one another's markets," "the parallel course of conduct that each [ILEC] engaged in to prevent competition from CLECs," "and the other facts and market circumstances alleged [earlier]"; "in light of" these, the complaint concludes "that [the ILECs] have entered into a contract, combination or conspiracy to prevent competitive entry into their . . . markets and have agreed not to compete with one another." Complaint ¶ 51, App. 27.10 The nub of the complaint, then, is the ILECs' parallel behavior, consisting of steps to keep the CLECs out and manifest disinterest in becoming CLECs themselves, and its sufficiency turns on the suggestions raised by this conduct when viewed in light of common economic experience.

We think that nothing contained in the complaint invests either the action or inaction alleged with a plausible suggestion of conspiracy. As to the ILECs' supposed agreement to disobey the 1996 Act and thwart the CLECs' attempts to compete, we agree with the District Court that nothing in the complaint intimates that the resistance to the upstarts was anything more than the natural, unilateral reaction of each ILEC intent on keeping its regional dominance. The 1996 Act did more than just subject the ILECs to competition; it obliged them to subsidize their competitors with their own equipment at wholesale rates. The economic incentive to resist was powerful, but resisting competition is routine market conduct, and even if the ILECs flouted the 1996 Act in all the ways the plaintiffs allege, there is no reason to infer that the companies had agreed among themselves to do what was only natural anyway; so natural, in fact, that if alleging parallel decisions to resist competition were enough to imply an antitrust conspiracy, pleading a § 1 violation against almost any group of competing businesses would be a sure thing.

The complaint makes its closest pass at a predicate for conspiracy with the claim that collusion was necessary because success by even one CLEC in an ILEC's territory "would have revealed the degree to which competitive entry by CLECs would have been successful in the other territories." Id., ¶ 50. But, its logic aside, this general premise still fails to answer the point that there was just no need for joint encouragement to resist the 1996 Act; as the District Court said, "each ILEC has reason to want to avoid dealing with CLECs" and "each

ILEC would attempt to keep CLECs out, regardless of the actions of the other ILECs." . . .

Plaintiffs' second conspiracy theory rests on the competitive reticence among the ILECs themselves in the wake of the 1996 Act, which was supposedly passed in the " 'hop[e] that the large incumbent local monopoly companies . . . might attack their neighbors' service areas, as they are the best situated to do so.' " Complaint ¶ 38, App. 20 (quoting Consumer Federation of America, Lessons from 1996 Telecommunications Act: Deregulation Before Meaningful Competition Spells Consumer Disaster, p. 12 (Feb. 2000)). Contrary to hope, the ILECs declined " 'to enter each other's service territories in any significant way,' " Complaint ¶ 38, App. 20, and the local telephone and high-speed Internet market remains highly compartmentalized geographically, with minimal competition. Based on this state of affairs, and perceiving the ILECs to be blessed with "especially attractive business opportunities" in surrounding markets dominated by other ILECs, the plaintiffs assert that the ILECs' parallel conduct was "strongly suggestive of conspiracy." Id., ¶ 40, App. 21.

But it was not suggestive of conspiracy, not if history teaches anything. In a traditionally unregulated industry with low barriers to entry, sparse competition among large firms dominating separate geographical segments of the market could very well signify illegal agreement, but here we have an obvious alternative explanation. In the decade preceding the 1996 Act and well before that, monopoly was the norm in telecommunications, not the exception. The ILECs were born in that world, doubtless liked the world the way it was, and surely knew the adage about him who lives by the sword. Hence, a natural explanation for the noncompetition alleged is that the former Government-sanctioned monopolists were sitting tight, expecting their neighbors to do the same thing. . . .

Congress may have expected some ILECs to [compete] in the legacy territories of other ILECs, but the disappointment does not make conspiracy plausible. We agree with the District Court's assessment that antitrust conspiracy was not suggested by the facts adduced under either theory of the complaint, which thus fails to state a valid § 1 claim.[14]

Plaintiffs say that our analysis runs counter to *Swierkiewicz*, 534 U.S., at 508, which held that "a complaint in an employment discrimination lawsuit [need] not contain specific facts establishing a prima facie case of discrimination." [In that case, w]e reversed on the ground that the Court of Appeals had impermissibly applied what amounted to a heightened pleading requirement by insisting

---

14. In reaching this conclusion, we do not apply any "heightened" pleading standard, nor do we seek to broaden the scope of Federal Rule of Civil Procedure 9, which can only be accomplished "by the process of amending the Federal Rules, and not by judicial interpretation." *Swierkiewicz v. Sorema N. A.*, 534 U.S. 506, 515, 122 S.Ct. 992, 152 L.Ed.2d 1 (2002). On certain subjects understood to raise a high risk of abusive litigation, a plaintiff must state factual allegations with greater particularity than Rule 8 requires. Fed. Rules Civ. Proc. 9(b)-(c). Here, our concern is not that the allegations in the complaint were insufficiently "particular[ized]," *ibid.*; rather, the complaint warranted dismissal because it failed in toto to render plaintiffs' entitlement to relief plausible.

that Swierkiewicz allege "specific facts" beyond those necessary to state his claim and the grounds showing entitlement to relief. *Id.*, at 508. Here, in contrast, we do not require heightened fact pleading of specifics, but only enough facts to state a claim to relief that is plausible on its face. Because the plaintiffs here have not nudged their claims across the line from conceivable to plausible, their complaint must be dismissed.

The judgment of the Court of Appeals for the Second Circuit is reversed, and the case is remanded for further proceedings consistent with this opinion.

Justice STEVENS, with whom Justice GINSBURG joins except as to Part IV, dissenting.

In the first paragraph of its 23-page opinion the Court states that the question to be decided is whether allegations that "major telecommunications providers engaged in certain parallel conduct unfavorable to competition" suffice to state a violation of § 1 of the Sherman Act. The answer to that question has been settled for more than 50 years. If that were indeed the issue, a summary reversal citing *Theatre Enterprises, Inc. v. Paramount Film Distributing Corp.*, 346 U.S. 537 (1954), would adequately resolve this case. As *Theatre Enterprises* held, parallel conduct is circumstantial evidence admissible on the issue of conspiracy, but it is not itself illegal. Id., at 540-542.

Thus, this is a case in which there is no dispute about the substantive law. If the defendants acted independently, their conduct was perfectly lawful. If, however, that conduct is the product of a horizontal agreement among potential competitors, it was unlawful. The plaintiffs have alleged such an agreement and, because the complaint was dismissed in advance of answer, the allegation has not even been denied. Why, then, does the case not proceed? Does a judicial opinion that the charge is not "plausible" provide a legally acceptable reason for dismissing the complaint? I think not.

Respondents' amended complaint describes a variety of circumstantial evidence and makes the straightforward allegation that petitioners

> "entered into a contract, combination or conspiracy to prevent competitive entry in their respective local telephone and/or high speed internet services markets and have agreed not to compete with one another and otherwise allocated customers and markets to one another."

The complaint explains that, contrary to Congress' expectation when it enacted the 1996 Telecommunications Act, and consistent with their own economic self-interests, petitioner Incumbent Local Exchange Carriers (ILECs) have assiduously avoided infringing upon each other's markets and have refused to permit nonincumbent competitors to access their networks. The complaint quotes Richard Notebaert, the former chief executive officer of one such ILEC, as saying that competing in a neighboring ILEC's territory " 'might be a good way to turn a quick dollar but that doesn't make it right.' " Id., ¶ 42, App. 22. Moreover, respondents allege that petitioners "communicate amongst themselves" through numerous industry associations. Id., ¶ 46, App. 23. In sum, respondents allege that petitioners entered into an agreement that has long been recognized as a classic per se violation of the Sherman Act. *See* Report of the Attorney General's National Committee to Study the Antitrust Laws 26 (1955).

Under rules of procedure that have been well settled since well before our decision in *Theatre Enterprises*, a judge ruling on a defendant's motion to dismiss a complaint "must accept as true all of the factual allegations contained in the complaint." *Swierkiewicz v. Sorema N. A.*, 534 U.S. 506, 508, n. 1 (2002). . . . But instead of requiring knowledgeable executives such as Notebaert to respond to these allegations by way of sworn depositions or other limited discovery — and indeed without so much as requiring petitioners to file an answer denying that they entered into any agreement — the majority permits immediate dismissal based on the assurances of company lawyers that nothing untoward was afoot. The Court embraces the argument of those lawyers that "there is no reason to infer that the companies had agreed among themselves to do what was only natural anyway," that "there was just no need for joint encouragement to resist the 1996 Act," and that the "natural explanation for the noncompetition alleged is that the former Government-sanctioned monopolists were sitting tight, expecting their neighbors to do the same thing."

The Court and petitioners' legal team are no doubt correct that the parallel conduct alleged is consistent with the absence of any contract, combination, or conspiracy. But that conduct is also entirely consistent with the presence of the illegal agreement alleged in the complaint. And the charge that petitioners "agreed not to compete with one another" is not just one of "a few stray statements"; it is an allegation describing unlawful conduct. As such, the Federal Rules of Civil Procedure, our longstanding precedent, and sound practice mandate that the District Court at least require some sort of response from petitioners before dismissing the case.

Two practical concerns presumably explain the Court's dramatic departure from settled procedural law. Private antitrust litigation can be enormously expensive, and there is a risk that jurors may mistakenly conclude that evidence of parallel conduct has proved that the parties acted pursuant to an agreement when they in fact merely made similar independent decisions. Those concerns merit careful case management, including strict control of discovery, careful scrutiny of evidence at the summary judgment stage, and lucid instructions to juries; they do not, however, justify the dismissal of an adequately pleaded complaint without even requiring the defendants to file answers denying a charge that they in fact engaged in collective decisionmaking. More importantly, they do not justify an interpretation of Federal Rule of Civil Procedure 12(b)(6) that seems to be driven by the majority's appraisal of the plausibility of the ultimate factual allegation rather than its legal sufficiency.

I

Rule 8(a)(2) of the Federal Rules requires that a complaint contain "a short and plain statement of the claim showing that the pleader is entitled to relief." The Rule did not come about by happenstance, and its language is not inadvertent. The English experience with Byzantine special pleading rules—illustrated by the hypertechnical Hilary rules of 1834—made obvious the appeal of a pleading standard that was easy for the common litigant to understand and sufficed to put the defendant on notice as to the nature of the claim against him and the relief sought. Stateside, David Dudley Field developed the highly influential New York Code of 1848, which required "[a] statement of the facts constituting the cause of action, in ordinary and concise language, without repetition, and in such a manner as to enable a person of common understanding to know what is intended." An Act to Simplify and Abridge the Practice, Pleadings and Proceedings of the Courts of this State, ch. 379, § 120(2), 1848 N.Y. Laws pp. 497, 521. Substantially similar language appeared in the Federal Equity Rules adopted in 1912. *See* Fed. Equity Rule 25 (requiring "a short and simple statement of the ultimate facts upon which the plaintiff asks relief, omitting any mere statement of evidence").

A difficulty arose, however, in that the Field Code and its progeny required a plaintiff to plead "facts" rather than "conclusions," a distinction that proved far easier to say than to apply. As commentators have noted,

> "it is virtually impossible logically to distinguish among 'ultimate facts,' 'evidence,' and 'conclusions.' Essentially any allegation in a pleading must be an assertion that certain occurrences took place. The pleading spectrum, passing from evidence through ultimate facts to conclusions, is largely a continuum varying only in the degree of particularity with which the occurrences are described." Weinstein & Distler, Comments on Procedural Reform: Drafting Pleading Rules, 57 Colum. L.Rev. 518, 520-521 (1957).

Rule 8 was directly responsive to this difficulty. Its drafters intentionally avoided any reference to "facts" or "evidence" or "conclusions." *See* 5 C. Wright & A. Miller, Federal Practice and Procedure § 1216, p. 207 (3d ed.2004) (hereinafter Wright & Miller) ("The substitution of 'claim showing that the pleader is entitled to relief' for the code formulation of the 'facts' constituting a 'cause of action' was intended to avoid the distinctions drawn under the codes among 'evidentiary facts,' 'ultimate facts,' and 'conclusions' . . .").

Under the relaxed pleading standards of the Federal Rules, the idea was not to keep litigants out of court but rather to keep them in. The merits of a claim would be sorted out during a flexible pretrial process and, as appropriate, through the crucible of trial. *See Swierkiewicz*, 534 U.S., at 514 ("The liberal notice pleading of Rule 8(a) is the starting point of a simplified pleading system, which was adopted to focus litigation on the merits of a claim"). Charles E. Clark, the "principal draftsman" of the Federal Rules, put it thus:

> "Experience has shown . . . that we cannot expect the proof of the case to be made through the pleadings, and that such proof is really not their function. We can expect a general statement distinguishing the case from all others, so that the manner and form of trial and remedy expected are clear, and so that a permanent judgment will result." The New Federal Rules of Civil Procedure: The Last

Phase—Underlying Philosophy Embodied in Some of the Basic Provisions of the New Procedure, 23 A.B.A.J. 976, 977 (1937) (hereinafter Clark, New Federal Rules).

The pleading paradigm under the new Federal Rules was well illustrated by the inclusion in the appendix of Form 9, a complaint for negligence. As relevant, the Form 9 complaint states only: "On June 1, 1936, in a public highway called Boylston Street in Boston, Massachusetts, defendant negligently drove a motor vehicle against plaintiff who was then crossing said highway." Form 9, Complaint for Negligence, Forms App., Fed. Rules Civ. Proc., 28 U.S.C.App., p. 829 (hereinafter Form 9). The complaint then describes the plaintiff's injuries and demands judgment. The asserted ground for relief—namely, the defendant's negligent driving—would have been called a "'conclusion of law'" under the code pleading of old. But that bare allegation suffices under a system that "restrict[s] the pleadings to the task of general notice-giving and invest[s] the deposition-discovery process with a vital role in the preparation for trial."[3] *Hickman v. Taylor*, 329 U.S. 495, 501 (1947).

II

doctrinal

It is in the context of this history that *Conley v. Gibson*, 355 U.S. 41 (1957), must be understood. The *Conley* plaintiffs were black railroad workers who alleged that their union local had refused to protect them against discriminatory discharges, in violation of the National Railway Labor Act. The union sought to dismiss the complaint on the ground that its general allegations of discriminatory treatment by the defendants lacked sufficient specificity. Writing for a unanimous Court, Justice Black rejected the union's claim as foreclosed by the language of Rule 8. In the course of doing so, he articulated the formulation the Court rejects today: "In appraising the sufficiency of the complaint we follow, of course, the accepted rule that a complaint should not be dismissed for failure to state a claim unless it appears beyond doubt that the plaintiff can prove no set of facts in support of his claim which would entitle him to relief." *Id.*, at 45-46. Consistent with the design of the Federal Rules, *Conley*'s "no set of facts" formulation permits outright dismissal only when proceeding to discovery or beyond would be futile. Once it is clear that a plaintiff has stated a claim that, if true, would entitle him to relief, matters of proof are appropriately relegated to other stages of the trial process. Today, however, in its explanation of a decision to dismiss a complaint that it regards as a fishing expedition, the Court scraps *Conley*'s "no set of facts" language. Concluding that the phrase has been "questioned, criticized, and explained away long enough," the Court dismisses it as careless composition.

If *Conley*'s "no set of facts" language is to be interred, let it not be without a eulogy. That exact language, which the majority says has "puzzl[ed] the

---

3. The Federal Rules do impose a "particularity" requirement on "all averments of fraud or mistake," Fed. Rule Civ. Proc. 9(b), neither of which has been alleged in this case. We have recognized that the canon of *expressio unius est exclusio alterius* applies to Rule 9(b). *See Leatherman v. Tarrant Cty. Narcotics Intelligence and Coordination Unit*, 507 U.S. 163, 168 (1993).

profession for 50 years," has been cited as authority in a dozen opinions of this Court and four separate writings. [Citations.] In not one of those 16 opinions was the language "questioned," "criticized," or "explained away." Indeed, today's opinion is the first by any Member of this Court to express *any* doubt as to the adequacy of the *Conley* formulation. Taking their cues from the federal courts, 26 States and the District of Columbia utilize as their standard for dismissal of a complaint the very language the majority repudiates: whether it appears "beyond doubt" that "no set of facts" in support of the claim would entitle the plaintiff to relief.

Petitioners have not requested that the *Conley* formulation be retired, nor have any of the six amici who filed briefs in support of petitioners. I would not rewrite the Nation's civil procedure textbooks and call into doubt the pleading rules of most of its States without far more informed deliberation as to the costs of doing so. Congress has established a process—a rulemaking process—for revisions of that order. *See* 28 U.S.C. §§ 2072-2074 (2000 ed. and Supp. IV). . . .

We have consistently reaffirmed that basic understanding of the Federal Rules in the half century since *Conley*. For example, in *Scheuer v. Rhodes*, 416 U.S. 232 (1974), we reversed the Court of Appeals' dismissal on the pleadings when the respondents, the Governor and other officials of the State of Ohio, argued that the petitioners' claims were barred by sovereign immunity. In a unanimous opinion by then-Justice Rehnquist, we emphasized:

> "When a federal court reviews the sufficiency of a complaint, before the reception of any evidence either by affidavit or admissions, its task is necessarily a limited one. The issue is not whether a plaintiff will ultimately prevail but whether the claimant is entitled to offer evidence to support the claims. *Indeed it may appear on the face of the pleadings that a recovery is very remote and unlikely but that is not the test.*" *Id.*, at 236 (emphasis added).

The *Rhodes* plaintiffs had "alleged generally and in conclusory terms" that the defendants, by calling out the National Guard to suppress the Kent State University student protests, "were guilty of wanton, wilful and negligent conduct." *Krause v. Rhodes*, 471 F.2d 430, 433 (C.A.6 1972). We reversed the Court of Appeals on the ground that "[w]hatever the plaintiffs may or may not be able to establish as to the merits of their allegations, their claims, as stated in the complaints, given the favorable reading required by the Federal Rules of Civil Procedure," were not barred by the Eleventh Amendment because they were styled as suits against the defendants in their individual capacities. 416 U.S., at 238.

We again spoke with one voice against efforts to expand pleading requirements beyond their appointed limits in *Leatherman v. Tarrant County Narcotics Intelligence and Coordination Unit*, 507 U.S. 163 (1993). Writing for the unanimous Court, Chief Justice Rehnquist rebuffed the Fifth Circuit's effort to craft a standard for pleading municipal liability that accounted for "the enormous expense involved today in litigation," *Leatherman v. Tarrant County Narcotics Intelligence and Coordination Unit*, 954 F.2d 1054, 1057 (1992) (internal quotation marks omitted), by requiring a plaintiff to "state with factual detail and particularity the basis for the claim which necessarily includes why the defendant-official cannot successfully maintain the defense of immunity," 507 U.S., at 167. We found this language inconsistent with Rules 8(a)(2) and 9(b) and emphasized that motions to dismiss were not the place to combat discovery abuse: "In the absence of [an amendment to Rule 9(b)], federal courts and litigants must rely on summary judgment and control of discovery to weed out unmeritorious claims sooner rather than later." *Id.*, at 168-169.

Most recently, in *Swierkiewicz*, 534 U.S. 506, we were faced with a case more similar to the present one than the majority will allow. In discrimination cases, our precedents require a plaintiff at the summary judgment stage to produce either direct evidence of discrimination or, if the claim is based primarily on circumstantial evidence, to meet the shifting evidentiary burdens imposed under the framework articulated in *McDonnell Douglas Corp. v. Green*, 411 U.S. 792 (1973). Swierkiewicz alleged that he had been terminated on account of national origin in violation of Title VII of the Civil Rights Act of 1964. The Second Circuit dismissed the suit on the pleadings because he had not pleaded a prima facie case of discrimination under the *McDonnell Douglas* standard.

We reversed in another unanimous opinion, holding that "under a notice pleading system, it is not appropriate to require a plaintiff to plead facts establishing a prima facie case because the *McDonnell Douglas* framework does not apply in every employment discrimination case." *Swierkiewicz*, 534 U.S., at 511. We also observed that Rule 8(a)(2) does not contemplate a court's passing on the merits of a litigant's claim at the pleading stage. Rather, the "simplified notice pleading standard" of the Federal Rules "relies on liberal discovery rules and summary judgment motions to define disputed facts and issues and to dispose of unmeritorious claims." *Id.*, at 512.

As in the discrimination context, we have developed an evidentiary framework for evaluating claims under § 1 of the Sherman Act when those claims rest on entirely circumstantial evidence of conspiracy. *See Matsushita Elec. Industrial Co. v. Zenith Radio Corp.*, 475 U.S. 574 (1986). Under *Matsushita*, a plaintiff's allegations of an illegal conspiracy may not, at the summary judgment stage, rest solely on the inferences that may be drawn from the parallel conduct of the defendants. In order to survive a Rule 56 motion, a § 1 plaintiff "must present evidence 'that tends to exclude the possibility' that the alleged conspirators acted independently.'" *Id.*, at 588. That is, the plaintiff "must show that the inference of conspiracy is reasonable in light of the competing inferences of independent action or collusive action." 475 U.S., at 588.

Everything today's majority says would therefore make perfect sense if it were ruling on a Rule 56 motion for summary judgment and the evidence included nothing more than the Court has described. But it should go without saying in the wake of *Swierkiewicz* that a heightened production burden at the summary judgment stage does not translate into a heightened pleading burden at the complaint stage. The majority rejects the complaint in this case because—in light of the fact that the parallel conduct alleged is consistent with ordinary market behavior—the claimed conspiracy is "conceivable" but not "plausible." I have my doubts about the majority's assessment of the plausibility of this alleged conspiracy. *See* Part III, *infra*. But even if the majority's speculation is correct, its "plausibility" standard is irreconcilable with Rule 8 and with our governing precedents. As we made clear in *Swierkiewicz* and *Leatherman*, fear of the burdens of litigation does not justify factual conclusions supported only by lawyers' arguments rather than sworn denials or admissible evidence.

This case is a poor vehicle for the Court's new pleading rule, for we have observed that "in antitrust cases, where 'the proof is largely in the hands of the alleged conspirators,' . . . dismissals prior to giving the plaintiff ample opportunity for discovery should be granted very sparingly." *Hospital Building Co. v. Trustees of Rex Hospital*, 425 U.S. 738, 746 (1976). Moreover, the fact that the Sherman Act authorizes the recovery of treble damages and attorney's fees for successful plaintiffs indicates that Congress intended to encourage, rather than discourage, private enforcement of the law. *See Radovich v. National Football League*, 352 U.S. 445, 454 (1957) ("Congress itself has placed the private anti-trust litigant in a most favorable position. . . . In the face of such a policy this Court should not add requirements to burden the private litigant beyond what is specifically set forth by Congress in those laws"). It is therefore more, not less, important in antitrust cases to resist the urge to engage in armchair economics at the pleading stage.

The same year we decided *Conley*, Judge Clark wrote, presciently,

> "I fear that every age must learn its lesson that special pleading cannot be made to do the service of trial and that live issues between active litigants are not to be disposed of or evaded on the paper pleadings, i.e., the formalistic claims of the parties. Experience has found no quick and easy short cut for trials in cases generally and antitrust cases in particular." Special Pleading in the "Big Case"? in Procedure—The Handmaid of Justice 147, 148 (C. Wright & H. Reasoner eds.1965) (hereinafter Clark, Special Pleading in the Big Case) (emphasis added).

In this "Big Case," the Court succumbs to the temptation that previous Courts have steadfastly resisted. While the majority assures us that it is not applying any "'heightened'" pleading standard, *see ante*, at 1973, n. 14, I shall now explain why I have a difficult time understanding its opinion any other way.

III

. . . Even if I were inclined to accept the Court's anachronistic dichotomy and ignore the complaint's actual allegations, I would dispute the Court's suggestion that any inference of agreement from petitioners' parallel conduct is "implausi-ble." Many years ago a truly great economist perceptively observed that "[p]eo-ple of the same trade seldom meet together, even for merriment and diversion, but the conversation ends in a conspiracy against the public, or in some con-trivance to raise prices." A. Smith, An Inquiry Into the Nature and Causes of the

Wealth of Nations, in 39 Great Books of the Western World 55 (R. Hutchins & M. Adler eds. 1952). I am not so cynical as to accept that sentiment at face value, but I need not do so here. Respondents' complaint points not only to petitioners' numerous opportunities to meet with each other, Complaint ¶ 46, App. 23, but also to Notebaert's curious statement that encroaching on a fellow incumbent's territory "might be a good way to turn a quick dollar but that doesn't make it right," *id.*, ¶ 42, App. 22. What did he mean by that? One possible (indeed plausible) inference is that he meant that while it would be in his company's economic self-interest to compete with its brethren, he had agreed with his competitors not to do so. According to the complaint, that is how the Illinois Coalition for Competitive Telecom construed Notebaert's statement, *id.*, ¶ 44, App. 22 (calling the statement "evidence of potential collusion among regional Bell phone monopolies to not compete against one another and kill off potential competitors in local phone service"), and that is how Members of Congress construed his company's behavior, *id.*, ¶ 45, App. 23 (describing a letter to the Justice Department requesting an investigation into the possibility that the ILECs' " 'very apparent non-competition policy' " was coordinated).

Perhaps Notebaert meant instead that competition would be sensible in the short term but not in the long run. That's what his lawyers tell us anyway. *See* Brief for Petitioners 36. But I would think that no one would know better what Notebaert meant than Notebaert himself. Instead of permitting respondents to ask Notebaert, however, the Court looks to other quotes from that and other articles and decides that what he meant was that entering new markets as a competitive local exchange carrier would not be a " 'sustainable economic model.' " Never mind that—as anyone ever interviewed knows—a newspaper article is hardly a verbatim transcript; the writer selects quotes to package his story, not to record a subject's views for posterity. But more importantly the District Court was required at this stage of the proceedings to construe Notebaert's ambiguous statement in the plaintiffs' favor. The inference the statement supports—that simultaneous decisions by ILECs not even to attempt to poach customers from one another once the law authorized them to do so were the product of an agreement—sits comfortably within the realm of possibility. That is all the Rules require.

. . . To be clear, if I had been the trial judge in this case, I would not have permitted the plaintiffs to engage in massive discovery based solely on the allegations in this complaint. On the other hand, I surely would not have dismissed the complaint without requiring the defendants to answer the charge that they "have agreed not to compete with one another and otherwise allocated customers and markets to one another."12 Complaint, ¶ 51, App. 27. Even a sworn denial of that charge would not justify a summary dismissal without giving the plaintiffs the opportunity to take depositions from Notebaert and at least one responsible executive representing each of the other defendants. . . .

I fear that the unfortunate result of the majority's new pleading rule will be to invite lawyers' debates over economic theory to conclusively resolve antitrust suits in the absence of any evidence. It is no surprise that the antitrust defense bar—among whom "lament" as to inadequate judicial supervision of discovery is most "common," *see ante*, at 1967—should lobby for this state of affairs. But "we must recall that their primary responsibility is to win cases for their clients, not to improve law administration for the public." Clark, Special Pleading in the Big Case 152. As we did in our prior decisions, we should have instructed them that their remedy was to seek to amend the Federal Rules—not our interpretation of them. . . .

I respectfully dissent.

REVIEW QUESTIONS

1. What is the plaintiffs' cause(s) of action, and what are the elements? Where does "conscious parallelism" fit into this discussion?
2. Is the plaintiffs' claim a species of fraud? Does this case implicate the first sentence of Fed. R. Civ. P. 9(b)?
3. Is the second sentence of Fed. R. Civ. P. 9(b) relevant? Does the majority or dissent address this?
4. How does the majority distinguish *Leatherman* and *Swierkiewicz*? Does the majority say that it is overruling those cases? Are those two cases still good law?

c. The Aftermath of *Twombly*

After *Twombly*, it was not entirely clear to district judges, practitioners, or commentators exactly what a plausibility pleading standard entailed. On one hand, the *Twombly* Court demanded something more than notice pleading. Yet the Court emphasized in footnote 14 that it was not applying a heightened pleading standard. Moreover, it was unclear whether this new plausibility pleading standard applied across-the-board to all cases—or, instead, only to antitrust cases, class actions, and/or cases where it was obvious that discovery would be extensive, cumbersome, and costly. Two years later the Court took another pleading case, resolving this latter question about the broader applicability *vel non* of plausibility pleading. The former question—about exactly what plausibility pleading requires—is still debated.

In 2009, the Supreme Court decided *Ashcroft v. Iqbal*. *The New York Times* later described the Court's 5-4 decision as possibly "the most consequential ruling" in Chief Justice Robert's then-10-year tenure. The decision quickly became one of the five most-cited Supreme Court decisions of all time.

The case involved Javaid Iqbal, a New Yorker, Pakistani immigrant, Muslim, and cable repairman who challenged the conditions of his confinement in the wake of September 11, 2001. An extraordinary law review article by Professor Shirin Sinnar offers background information about Mr. Iqbal and this case that the Court's opinion does not. *See* Shirin Sinnar, *The Lost Story of* Iqbal, 105 Geo.

L.J. 379 (2017). Sinnar describes how Iqbal was an undocumented immigrant who arrived in New York City from Pakistan in 1992. He worked various odd jobs (using a false identity) before becoming a cable repair technician, a job that he held for five years prior to his arrest. Upon his arrival to the U.S., Iqbal met and married an American woman, moved in with her and her children, and applied for a green card based on his marriage. Four years later, the couple separated.

On the morning of September 11, Mr. Iqbal was headed for an appointment to renew his work authorization card with the U.S. Immigration & Naturalization Service (INS) in lower Manhattan. After the terrorist attack on the World Trade Center, he was stranded at Grand Central Station until police finally allowed people to use the subway. Eight weeks later, he was arrested. The arresting officers searched his studio apartment and were particularly interested in a letter from the INS informing Iqbal of his appointment in Lower Manhattan on the morning of September 11. The officers also noted that Iqbal had a copy of *Time* magazine that featured the burning World Trade Center on the cover, and also a Pakistani newspaper reporting on the attacks. When questioned, Iqbal admitted that he had used a false identity to obtain work, admitted that he did not have lawful immigrant status, and admitted that he entered the United States using another identity that smugglers had assigned him.

Mr. Iqbal was arraigned and housed with the general inmate population. Later that month, he was indicted on two counts of identity fraud. He soon fired his court-appointed attorney who, Iqbal describes, treated him like a terrorist. A friend paid for a private criminal defense attorney to represent him.

The government then labeled him as being of interest to its terrorism investigation. Mr. Iqbal's name was on a list with over one hundred others, even though the FBI's list of "Special Interest Cases" from that period includes Iqbal's name and a description only of the false identity case. The government ultimately obtained a superseding indictment charging Iqbal with conspiracy to utter counterfeited securities, uttering forged securities, and identity fraud, specifically accusing Iqbal of creating checks in the names of various financial institutions and depositing them in bank accounts in his name.

While incarcerated, Iqbal was abused and attacked, as you will read below in the Court's opinion. Iqbal ultimately pled guilty to two charges—conspiracy to make, utter, or possess counterfeited securities and fraud with identification documents. He was sentenced to sixteen months imprisonment and to three years of supervised release with the condition that he not return to the United States illegally. During his incarceration, his wife signed divorce papers, making him ineligible for legal status through marriage. After his sentence, he voluntarily deported to Pakistan. Iqbal believes that his experience as a post-9/11 detainee in the United States marked him publicly in Pakistan where he was branded an American agent. Among other tragedies since his return to Pakistan, Iqbal's teenage son was persecuted and disappeared.

Two organizations working with post-9/11 detainees — the Islamic Circle of North America and Amnesty International — discussed with Mr. Iqbal the possibility of filing a lawsuit. He decided to sue, notwithstanding the risks and his family's disapproval.

Ashcroft v. Iqbal
556 U.S. 662 (2009)

Justice KENNEDY delivered the opinion of the Court, in which Chief Justice ROBERTS, Justice SCALIA, Justice THOMAS, and Justice ALITO joined:

Respondent Javaid Iqbal is a citizen of Pakistan and a Muslim. In the wake of the September 11, 2001, terrorist attacks he was arrested in the United States on criminal charges and detained by federal officials. Respondent claims he was deprived of various constitutional protections while in federal custody. To redress the alleged deprivations, respondent filed a complaint against numerous federal officials, including John Ashcroft, the former Attorney General of the United States, and Robert Mueller, the Director of the Federal Bureau of Investigation (FBI). Ashcroft and Mueller are the petitioners in the case now before us. As to these two petitioners, the complaint alleges that they adopted an unconstitutional policy that subjected respondent to harsh conditions of confinement on account of his race, religion, or national origin.

In the District Court petitioners raised the defense of qualified immunity and moved to dismiss the suit, contending the complaint was not sufficient to state a claim against them. The District Court denied the motion to dismiss, concluding the complaint was sufficient to state a claim despite petitioners' official status at the times in question. Petitioners brought an interlocutory appeal in the Court of Appeals for the Second Circuit. The court, without discussion, assumed it had jurisdiction over the order denying the motion to dismiss; and it affirmed the District Court's decision.

Respondent's account of his prison ordeal could, if proved, demonstrate unconstitutional misconduct by some governmental actors. But the allegations and pleadings with respect to these actors are not before us here. This case instead turns on a narrower question: Did respondent, as the plaintiff in the District Court, plead factual matter that, if taken as true, states a claim that petitioners deprived him of his clearly established constitutional rights. We hold respondent's pleadings are insufficient.

I

Following the 2001 attacks, the FBI and other entities within the Department of Justice began an investigation of vast reach to identify the assailants and prevent them from attacking anew. . . .

In the ensuing months the FBI questioned more than 1,000 people with suspected links to the attacks in particular or to terrorism in general. Of those individuals, some 762 were held on immigration charges; and a 184-member subset of that group was deemed to be "of 'high interest'" to the investigation. The high-interest detainees were held under restrictive conditions designed to prevent them from communicating with the general prison population or the outside world.

Respondent was one of the detainees. According to his complaint, in November 2001 agents of the FBI and Immigration and Naturalization Service arrested him on charges of fraud in relation to identification documents and conspiracy to defraud the United States. *Iqbal v. Hasty*, 490 F.3d 143, 147-148 (2d Cir. 2007). Pending trial for those crimes, respondent was housed at the Metropolitan Detention Center (MDC) in Brooklyn, New York. Respondent was designated a person "of high interest" to the September 11 investigation and in January 2002 was placed in a section of the MDC known as the Administrative Maximum Special Housing Unit (ADMAX SHU). . . . ADMAX SHU detainees were kept in lockdown 23 hours a day, spending the remaining hour outside their cells in handcuffs and leg irons accompanied by a four-officer escort.

Respondent pleaded guilty to the criminal charges, served a term of imprisonment, and was removed to his native Pakistan. *Id.*, at 149. He then filed a *Bivens* action in the United States District Court for the Eastern District of New York against 34 current and former federal officials and 19 "John Doe" federal corrections officers. *See Bivens v. Six Unknown Fed. Narcotics Agents*, 403 U.S. 388 (1971). The defendants range from the correctional officers who had day-to-day contact with respondent during the term of his confinement, to the wardens of the MDC facility, all the way to petitioners—officials who were at the highest level of the federal law enforcement hierarchy. First Amended Complaint in No. 04-CV1809 (JG)(JA), ¶¶ 10-11 (hereinafter Complaint).

The 21-cause-of-action complaint does not challenge respondent's arrest or his confinement in the MDC's general prison population. Rather, it concentrates on his treatment while confined to the ADMAX SHU. The complaint sets forth various claims against defendants who are not before us. For instance, the complaint alleges that respondent's jailors "kicked him in the stomach, punched him in the face, and dragged him across" his cell without justification, *id.*, ¶ 113; subjected him to serial strip and body-cavity searches when he posed no safety risk to himself or others, *id.*, ¶¶ 143-145; and refused to let him and other Muslims pray because there would be "[n]o prayers for terrorists," *id.*, ¶ 154.

The allegations against petitioners are the only ones relevant here. The complaint contends that petitioners designated respondent a person of high interest on account of his race, religion, or national origin, in contravention of the First and Fifth Amendments to the Constitution. The complaint alleges that "the [FBI], under the direction of Defendant Mueller, arrested and detained thousands of Arab Muslim men . . . as part of its investigation of the events of September 11." *Id.*, ¶ 47. It further alleges that "[t]he policy of holding post-September-11th detainees in highly restrictive conditions of confinement until they were 'cleared' by the FBI was approved by Defendants Ashcroft and Mueller in discussions in the weeks after September 11, 2001." *Id.*, ¶ 69. Lastly, the complaint posits that petitioners "each knew of, condoned, and willfully and maliciously agreed to subject" respondent to harsh conditions of confinement "as a matter of policy, solely on account of [his] religion, race, and/or national origin and for no legitimate penological interest." *Id.*, ¶ 96. The pleading names Ashcroft as the "principal architect" of the policy, *id.*, ¶ 10, and identifies Mueller as "instrumental in [its] adoption, promulgation, and implementation." *Id.*, ¶ 11.

Petitioners moved to dismiss the complaint for failure to state sufficient allegations to show their own involvement in clearly established unconstitutional conduct. The District Court denied their motion. Accepting all of the allegations in respondent's complaint as true, the court held that "it cannot be said that there [is] no set of facts on which [respondent] would be entitled to relief as against" petitioners. Invoking the collateral-order doctrine petitioners filed an interlocutory appeal in the United States Court of Appeals for the Second Circuit. While that appeal was pending, this Court decided *Bell Atlantic Corp. v. Twombly*, 550 U.S. 544 (2007), which discussed the standard for evaluating whether a complaint is sufficient to survive a motion to dismiss.

The Court of Appeals considered *Twombly*'s applicability to this case. Acknowledging that *Twombly* retired the *Conley* [v. Gibson, 355 U.S. 41 (1957),] no set-of-facts test relied upon by the District Court, the Court of Appeals' opinion discussed at length how to apply this Court's "standard for assessing the adequacy of pleadings." 490 F.3d, at 155. It concluded that *Twombly* called for a "flexible 'plausibility standard,' which obliges a pleader to amplify a claim with some factual allegations in those contexts where such amplification is needed to render the claim plausible." *Id.*, at 157-158. The court found that petitioners' appeal did not present one of "those contexts" requiring amplification. As a consequence, it held respondent's pleading adequate to allege petitioners' personal involvement in discriminatory decisions which, if true, violated clearly established constitutional law. *Id.*, at 174.

Judge Cabranes concurred . . . [but] nonetheless expressed concern at the prospect of subjecting high-ranking Government officials — entitled to assert the defense of qualified immunity and charged with responding to "a national and international security emergency unprecedented in the history of the American Republic" — to the burdens of discovery on the basis of a complaint as nonspecific as respondent's. . . .

We granted certiorari, and now reverse.

II

[In this Part the Court concluded that the Court of Appeals had subject matter jurisdiction to affirm the District Court's denial of the motion to dismiss, and that an interlocutory appeal to the Supreme Court was permitted, even though there was not yet a final judgment.]

III

[In this Part the Court reviewed the elements of the cause of action for a *Bivens* claim. T]o state a claim based on a violation of a clearly established right, respondent must plead sufficient factual matter to show that petitioners adopted and implemented the detention policies at issue not for a neutral, investigative reason but for the purpose of discriminating on account of race, religion, or national origin. . . .

IV

A

We turn to respondent's complaint. Under Federal Rule of Civil Procedure 8(a)(2), a pleading must contain a "short and plain statement of the claim showing that the pleader is entitled to relief." As the Court held in *Twombly*, 550 U.S. 544, the pleading standard Rule 8 announces does not require "detailed factual allegations," but it demands more than an unadorned, the-defendant-unlawfully-harmed-me accusation. *Id.*, at 555.

A pleading that offers "labels and conclusions" or "a formulaic recitation of the elements of a cause of action will not do." 550 U.S., at 555. Nor does a complaint suffice if it tenders "naked assertion[s]" devoid of "further factual enhancement." *Id.*, at 557.

To survive a motion to dismiss, a complaint must contain sufficient factual matter, accepted as true, to "state a claim to relief that is plausible on its face." *Id.*, at 570. A claim has facial plausibility when the plaintiff pleads factual content that allows the court to draw the reasonable inference that the defendant is liable for the misconduct alleged. *Id.*, at 556. The plausibility standard is not akin to a "probability requirement," but it asks for more than a sheer possibility that a defendant has acted unlawfully. *Ibid.* Where a complaint pleads facts that are "merely consistent with" a defendant's liability, it "stops short of the line between possibility and plausibility of 'entitlement to relief.' " *Id.*, at 557 (brackets omitted).

Two working principles underlie our decision in *Twombly*. First, the tenet that a court must accept as true all of the allegations contained in a complaint is inapplicable to legal conclusions. Threadbare recitals of the elements of a cause of action, supported by mere conclusory statements, do not suffice. *Id.*, at 555 (although for the purposes of a motion to dismiss we must take all of the factual allegations in the complaint as true, we "are not bound to accept as true a legal conclusion couched as a factual allegation" (internal quotation marks omitted)). Rule 8 marks a notable and generous departure from the hyper-technical, code-pleading regime of a prior era, but it does not unlock the doors of discovery for a plaintiff armed with nothing more than conclusions. Second, only a complaint that states a plausible claim for relief survives a motion to dismiss. *Id.*, at 556. Determining whether a complaint states a plausible claim for relief will, as the Court of Appeals observed, be a context-specific task that requires the reviewing court to draw on its judicial experience and common sense. 490 F.3d, at 157-158. But where the well-pleaded facts do not permit the court to infer more than the mere possibility of misconduct, the complaint has alleged — but it has not "show[n]" — "that the pleader is entitled to relief." Fed. Rule Civ. Proc. 8(a)(2).

In keeping with these principles a court considering a motion to dismiss can choose to begin by identifying pleadings that, because they are no more than conclusions, are not entitled to the assumption of truth. While legal conclusions can provide the framework of a complaint, they must be supported by factual allegations. When there are well-pleaded factual allegations, a court should assume their veracity and then determine whether they plausibly give rise to an entitlement to relief.

Our decision in *Twombly* illustrates the two-pronged approach. There, we considered the sufficiency of a complaint alleging that incumbent telecommunications providers had entered an agreement not to compete and to forestall competitive entry, in violation of the Sherman Act, 15 U.S.C. § 1. Recognizing that § 1 enjoins only anticompetitive conduct "effected by a contract, combination, or conspiracy," the plaintiffs in *Twombly* flatly pleaded that the defendants "ha[d] entered into a contract, combination or conspiracy to prevent competitive entry . . . and ha[d] agreed not to compete with one another." 550 U.S., at 551 (internal quotation marks omitted). The complaint also alleged that the defendants' "parallel course of conduct . . . to prevent competition" and inflate prices was indicative of the unlawful agreement alleged. *Ibid.* (internal quotation marks omitted). . . . Because the well-pleaded fact of parallel conduct, accepted as true, did not plausibly suggest an unlawful agreement, the Court held the plaintiffs' complaint must be dismissed. *Id.*, at 570.

B

Under *Twombly*'s construction of Rule 8, we conclude that respondent's complaint has not "nudged [his] claims" of invidious discrimination "across the line from conceivable to plausible." *Ibid.*

We begin our analysis by identifying the allegations in the complaint that are not entitled to the assumption of truth. Respondent pleads that petitioners "knew of, condoned, and willfully and maliciously agreed to subject [him]" to harsh conditions of confinement "as a matter of policy, solely on account of [his] religion, race, and/or national origin and for no legitimate penological interest." Complaint ¶ 96. The complaint alleges that Ashcroft was the "principal architect" of this invidious policy, *id.*, ¶ 10, and that Mueller was "instrumental" in adopting and executing it, *id.*, ¶ 11. These bare assertions, much like the pleading of conspiracy in *Twombly*, amount to nothing more than a "formulaic recitation of the elements" of a constitutional discrimination claim, 550 U.S., at 555, namely, that petitioners adopted a policy " 'because of,' not merely 'in spite of,' its adverse effects upon an identifiable group." [*Personnel Adm'r of Mass. v. Feeney*, 442 U.S. 256, 279 (1979)]. As such, the allegations are conclusory and not entitled to be assumed true. *Twombly*, *supra*, 550 U.S., at 554-555. To be clear, we do not reject these bald allegations on the ground that they are unrealistic or nonsensical. We do not so characterize them any more than the Court in *Twombly* rejected the plaintiffs' express allegation of a " 'contract, combination or conspiracy to prevent competitive entry,' " *id.*, at 551, because it thought that claim too chimerical to be maintained. It is the conclusory nature of respondent's allegations, rather than their extravagantly fanciful nature, that disentitles them to the presumption of truth.

We next consider the factual allegations in respondent's complaint to determine if they plausibly suggest an entitlement to relief. The complaint alleges that "the [FBI], under the direction of Defendant Mueller, arrested and detained thousands of Arab Muslim men . . . as part of its investigation of the events of September 11." Complaint ¶ 47. It further claims that "[t]he policy of holding post-September-11th detainees in highly restrictive conditions of confinement until they were 'cleared' by the FBI was approved by Defendants Ashcroft and Mueller in discussions in the weeks after September 11, 2001." *Id.*, ¶ 69. Taken as true, these allegations are consistent with petitioners' purposefully designating detainees "of high interest" because of their race, religion, or national origin. But given more likely explanations, they do not plausibly establish this purpose. . . .

On the facts respondent alleges the arrests Mueller oversaw were likely lawful and justified by his nondiscriminatory intent to detain aliens who were illegally present in the United States and who had potential connections to those who committed terrorist acts. As between that "obvious alternative explanation" for the arrests, *Twombly*, *supra*, at 567, and the purposeful, invidious discrimination respondent asks us to infer, discrimination is not a plausible conclusion.

But even if the complaint's well-pleaded facts give rise to a plausible inference that respondent's arrest was the result of unconstitutional discrimination, that inference alone would not entitle respondent to relief. It is important to recall that respondent's complaint challenges neither the constitutionality of his arrest nor his initial detention in the MDC. Respondent's constitutional claims against petitioners rest solely on their ostensible "policy of holding post-September-11th detainees" in the ADMAX SHU once they were categorized as "of high interest." Complaint ¶ 69. To prevail on that theory, the complaint must contain facts plausibly showing that petitioners purposefully adopted a policy of classifying post-September-11 detainees as "of high interest" because of their race, religion, or national origin.

This the complaint fails to do. [T]he complaint does not show, or even intimate, that petitioners purposefully housed detainees in the ADMAX SHU due to their race, religion, or national origin. All it plausibly suggests is that the Nation's top law enforcement officers, in the aftermath of a devastating terrorist attack, sought to keep suspected terrorists in the most secure conditions available until the suspects could be cleared of terrorist activity. . . . [R]espondent's complaint does not contain any factual allegation sufficient to plausibly suggest petitioners' discriminatory state of mind. His pleadings thus do not meet the standard necessary to comply with Rule 8.

It is important to note, however, that we express no opinion concerning the sufficiency of respondent's complaint against the defendants who are not before us. . . .

C

Respondent offers three arguments that bear on our disposition of his case, but none is persuasive.

1

1. Respondent first says that our decision in *Twombly* should be limited to pleadings made in the context of an antitrust dispute. This argument is not supported by *Twombly* and is incompatible with the Federal Rules of Civil Procedure. . . . Our decision in *Twombly* expounded the pleading standard for "all civil actions," and it applies to antitrust and discrimination suits alike. *See* 550 U.S., at 555-556.

2

2. Respondent next implies that our construction of Rule 8 should be tempered where, as here, the Court of Appeals has "instructed the district court to cabin discovery in such a way as to preserve" petitioners' defense of qualified immunity "as much as possible in anticipation of a summary judgment motion." We have held, however, that the question presented by a motion to dismiss a complaint for insufficient pleadings does not turn on the controls placed upon the discovery process. *Twombly*, *supra*, at 559. . . .

We decline respondent's invitation to relax the pleading requirements on the ground that the Court of Appeals promises petitioners minimally intrusive discovery. That promise provides especially cold comfort in this pleading context, where we are impelled to give real content to the concept of qualified immunity for high-level officials who must be neither deterred nor detracted from the vigorous performance of their duties. Because respondent's complaint is deficient under Rule 8, he is not entitled to discovery, cabined or otherwise.

3

3. Respondent finally maintains that the Federal Rules expressly allow him to allege petitioners' discriminatory intent "generally," which he equates with a conclusory allegation. Iqbal Brief 32 (citing Fed. Rule Civ. Proc. 9). It follows, respondent says, that his complaint is sufficiently well pleaded because it claims that petitioners discriminated against him "on account of [his] religion, race, and/or national origin and for no legitimate penological interest." Complaint ¶ 96. Were we required to accept this allegation as true, respondent's complaint would survive petitioners' motion to dismiss. But the Federal Rules do not require courts to credit a complaint's conclusory statements without reference to its factual context.

It is true that Rule 9(b) requires particularity when pleading "fraud or mistake," while allowing "[m]alice, intent, knowledge, and other conditions of a person's mind [to] be alleged generally." But "generally" is a relative term. In the context of Rule 9, it is to be compared to the particularity requirement applicable to fraud or mistake. Rule 9 merely excuses a party from pleading discriminatory intent under an elevated pleading standard. . . .

V

We hold that respondent's complaint fails to plead sufficient facts to state a claim for purposeful and unlawful discrimination against petitioners. The Court of Appeals should decide in the first instance whether to remand to the District Court so that respondent can seek leave to amend his deficient complaint.

The judgment of the Court of Appeals is reversed, and the case is remanded for further proceedings consistent with this opinion. It is so ordered.

Justice SOUTER, with whom Justice STEVENS, Justice GINSBURG, and Justice BREYER join, dissenting.

[Justice Souter dissented on two grounds: First, that the Court erred in deciding the substantive scope of an action under *Bivens v. Six Unknown Fed. Narcotics Agents*, 403 U.S. 388 (1971); and second, that the Court misinterpreted his decision in *Twombly*. The second issue is more relevant to the focus of this chapter.]

II

. . .

Under *Twombly*, the relevant question is whether, assuming the factual allegations are true, the plaintiff has stated a ground for relief that is plausible. That is, in *Twombly*'s words, a plaintiff must "allege facts" that, taken as true, are "suggestive of illegal conduct." 550 U.S., at 564, n. 8. In *Twombly*, we were faced with allegations of a conspiracy to violate § 1 of the Sherman Act through parallel conduct. . . . Here, by contrast, the allegations in the complaint are neither confined to naked legal conclusions nor consistent with legal conduct. The complaint alleges that FBI officials discriminated against Iqbal solely on account of his race, religion, and national origin, and it alleges the knowledge and deliberate indifference that, by Ashcroft and Mueller's own admission, are sufficient to make them liable for the illegal action. Iqbal's complaint therefore contains "enough facts to state a claim to relief that is plausible on its face." *Id.*, at 570.

I do not understand the majority to disagree with this understanding of "plausibility" under *Twombly*. Rather, the majority discards the allegations discussed above with regard to Ashcroft and Mueller as conclusory, and is left considering only two statements in the complaint: that "the [FBI], under the direction of Defendant Mueller, arrested and detained thousands of Arab Muslim men . . . as part of its investigation of the events of September 11," Complaint ¶ 47, and that "[t]he policy of holding post-September-11th detainees in highly restrictive conditions of confinement until they were 'cleared' by the FBI was approved by Defendants Ashcroft and Mueller in discussions in the weeks after September 11, 2001," *id.*, ¶ 69. . . .

But these allegations do not stand alone as the only significant, nonconclusory statements in the complaint, for the complaint contains many allegations linking Ashcroft and Mueller to the discriminatory practices of their subordinates. *See* Complaint ¶ 10 (Ashcroft was the "principal architect" of the discriminatory policy); *id.*, ¶ 11 (Mueller was "instrumental" in adopting and executing the discriminatory policy); *id.*, ¶ 96 (Ashcroft and Mueller "knew of, condoned, and willfully and maliciously agreed to subject" Iqbal to harsh conditions "as a matter of policy, solely on account of [his] religion, race, and/or national origin and for no legitimate penological interest").

The majority says that these are "bare assertions" that, "much like the pleading of conspiracy in *Twombly*, amount to nothing more than a 'formulaic recitation of the elements' of a constitutional discrimination claim" and therefore are "not entitled to be assumed true." The fallacy of the majority's position, however, lies in looking at the relevant assertions in isolation. The complaint contains specific allegations that, in the aftermath of the September 11 attacks, the Chief of the FBI's International Terrorism Operations Section and the Assistant Special Agent in Charge for the FBI's New York Field Office implemented a policy that discriminated against Arab Muslim men, including Iqbal, solely on account of their race, religion, or national origin. *See* Complaint ¶ ¶ 47-53. Viewed in light of these subsidiary allegations, the allegations singled out by the majority as "conclusory" are no such thing. Iqbal's claim is not that Ashcroft and Mueller "knew of, condoned, and willfully and maliciously agreed to subject" him to a discriminatory practice that is left undefined; his allegation is that "they knew of, condoned, and willfully and maliciously agreed to subject" him to a particular, discrete, discriminatory policy detailed in the complaint. Iqbal does not say merely that Ashcroft was the architect of some amorphous discrimination, or that Mueller was instrumental in an ill-defined constitutional violation; he alleges that they helped to create the discriminatory policy he has described. Taking the complaint as a whole, it gives Ashcroft and Mueller " 'fair notice of what the . . . claim is and the grounds upon which it rests.' " *Twombly*, 550 U.S., at 555 (quoting *Conley v. Gibson*, 355 U.S. 41, 47 (1957) (omission in original)).

That aside, the majority's holding that the statements it selects are conclusory cannot be squared with its treatment of certain other allegations in the complaint as nonconclusory. For example, the majority takes as true the statement that "[t]he policy of holding post-September-11th detainees in highly restrictive conditions of confinement until they were 'cleared' by the FBI was approved by Defendants Ashcroft and Mueller in discussions in the weeks after September 11, 2001." Complaint ¶ 69. This statement makes two points: (1) after September 11, the FBI held certain detainees in highly restrictive conditions, and (2) Ashcroft and Mueller discussed and approved these conditions. If, as the majority says, these allegations are not conclusory, then I cannot see why the majority deems it merely conclusory when Iqbal alleges that (1) after September 11, the FBI designated Arab Muslim detainees as being of " 'high interest' " "because of the race, religion, and national origin of the detainees, and not because of any evidence of the detainees' involvement in supporting terrorist activity," Complaint ¶ ¶ 48-50, and (2) Ashcroft and Mueller "knew of, condoned, and willfully and maliciously agreed" to that discrimination, *id.*, ¶ 96. By my lights, there is no principled basis for the majority's disregard of the allegations linking Ashcroft and Mueller to their subordinates' discrimination.

Justice BREYER, dissenting.

I agree with Justice Souter and join his dissent. I write separately to point out that, like the Court, I believe it important to prevent unwarranted litigation from interfering with "the proper execution of the work of the Government." But I cannot find in that need adequate justification for the Court's interpretation of *Bell Atlantic Corp. v. Twombly*, 550 U.S. 544 (2007), and Federal Rule of Civil Procedure 8. The law, after all, provides trial courts with other legal weapons designed to prevent unwarranted interference. As the Second Circuit explained, where a Government defendant asserts a qualified immunity defense, a trial court, responsible for managing a case and "mindful of the need to vindicate the purpose of the qualified immunity defense," can structure discovery in ways that diminish the risk of imposing unwarranted burdens upon public officials. A district court, for example, can begin discovery with lower level government defendants before determining whether a case can be made to allow discovery related to higher level government officials. Neither the briefs nor the Court's opinion provides convincing grounds for finding these alternative case-management tools inadequate, either in general or in the case before us. For this reason, as well as for the independently sufficient reasons set forth in Justice Souter's opinion, I would affirm the Second Circuit.

REVIEW QUESTIONS

1. Re-read the second sentence of Federal Rule 9(b). How does the majority interpret this mandate? Does that interpretation make sense?
2. Much to the dismay of the dissenters in *Twombly* and *Iqbal,* the Court retired the "no set of facts" language from *Conley.* But how would the dissenters rule on a 12(b)(6) motion to dismiss if a complaint provided only: "Defendant, my former employer, discriminated against me on the basis of my race"?

d. What Happened Next?

Although the claims against Ashcroft and Mueller were dismissed, Mr. Iqbal's claims against the other defendants were viable. Iqbal ultimately settled his case for $265,000. Iqbal did not receive any official acknowledgment of wrongdoing by the federal government nor any assistance in resettlement to a third country where he and his family could feel safe. For more details about Iqbal, again, *see* Shirin Sinnar, *The Lost Story of* Iqbal, 105 Geo. L.J. 379 (2017).

e. Plausibility Pleading in Action

Often a plaintiff cannot plead with much specificity absent the opportunity to request documents or to ask the defendant some questions. This can be a problem even for a simple slip-and-fall case. Consider this action against a discount retail store where

> [t]he plaintiff alleged in her complaint that she "fell due to the negligence of the Defendants . . . who negligently failed to remove the liquid from the floor and had negligently failed to place warning signs to alert and warn the Plaintiff of the wet floor." The defendant moved to dismiss the complaint for failure to state a claim and the court granted the motion. In doing so, the court wrote:

>> In this case, the Plaintiff has failed to allege any facts that show how the liquid came to be on the floor, whether the Defendant knew or should have known of the presence of the liquid, or how the Plaintiff's accident occurred. Without such allegations, the Plaintiff cannot show that she has a "right to relief above the speculative level." While consistent with the possibility of the Defendant's liability, the Plaintiff's conclusory allegations that the Defendant was negligent because there was liquid on the flood [sic], but that the Defendant failed to remove the liquid or warn her of its presence are insufficient to state a plausible claim for relief.

> Two things are clear. First, prior to *Twombly*, not one single court would have treated this plaintiff's complaint as insufficient under the *Conley* interpretation of Rule 8(a). Second, even courts that had embraced heightened pleading previously would not have considered applying such a standard to a basic slip-and-fall negligence case. To the extent more stringent pleading now permeated across all case types, such is a change that will shift the pleading landscape among the lower courts beyond where they stood before *Twombly*.

A. Benjamin Spencer, *Pleading and Access to Civil Justice: A Response to* Twiqbal *Apologists,* 60 UCLA L. Rev. 1710, 1724-1725 (2013) (citing *Branham v. Dolgencorp, Inc.,* 2009 WL 2604447 (W.D. Va. Aug. 24, 2009)).

Some district judges have pushed back against this demand for heightened specificity. For example, in *DuRocher v. Riddell, Inc.,* 97 F. Supp. 3d 1006 (S.D. Ind. 2015), two former University of Washington football players filed a complaint seeking recovery for injuries associated with concussions and repeated traumatic head impacts. Their injuries included severe headaches, memory loss, inability to focus, anxiety, and depression. The complaint alleged "[u]pon information and belief," that the plaintiffs "wore Riddell helmets while playing and/or practicing during their collegiate football careers."

These plaintiffs pursued a claim for defective design of a product. Plaintiffs filed a robust 55-page, 194-paragraph complaint that detailed the dangers associated with head trauma; they offered a thick account of Riddell's helmet designs and protective features; and they provided a chronology of manufacturing dates of the corporation's helmets. However, the plaintiffs could not (at the time of the filing of complaint) identify the specific model of the helmets that they had worn years earlier — and therefore could not identify the *particular* design defect, nor the safer alternative design. And these were essential elements of their claim under the Washington product liability law. Yet the district court was forgiving:

> Plaintiffs have set forth basic identifying information regarding the product at issue — helmets manufactured and sold by the Defendants and worn by Plaintiffs at Washington University during a six-year time period. We expect discovery to expand the parties' knowledge as to the model and type of helmet worn by the Plaintiffs during their collegiate football career, or at least to narrow the possibilities. If not, Defendants will likely pursue summary judgment based on a lack of product identification. . . . Plaintiffs have satisfied the minimal pleading standard to assert a products liability claim for design defect. Given the nature of Plaintiffs' claims, the amount of detail set out in the second amended complaint, and in view of the well-established principles of law that disfavor motions to dismiss, Defendants' motion to dismiss Plaintiffs' design defect claim must be denied.

Id. at 1020, 1022. Is this opinion consistent with *Iqbal*? Does Justice Kennedy's opinion in *Iqbal* encourage district judges to take "the nature of Plaintiffs' claims" into account as this judge suggests? Is this judge following Justice Kennedy's invitation to invoke "judicial experience and common sense"? Does Justice Kennedy's opinion in *Iqbal* invoke "the well-established principles of law that disfavor motions to dismiss" that are invoked here?

The *TwIqbal* standard is especially problematic for plaintiffs who are pleading causes of actions where an essential element of the claim pertains to the defendant's subjective motivations or regards concealed conditions. This so-called information asymmetry is especially likely to affect civil rights, employment discrimination, and other cases where the defendant's intent is often an element of the prima facie case. *See, e.g.,* Suzette M. Malveaux, *Front Loading and Heavy Lifting: How Pre-Dismissal Discovery Can Address the Detrimental Effect of* Iqbal *on Civil Rights Cases,* 14 Lewis & Clark L. Rev. 65 (2010); Howard M. Wasserman, Iqbal, *Procedural Mismatches, and Civil Rights Litigation,* 14 Lewis & Clark L. Rev. 157 (2010).

A number of empirical studies have tried to measure the effect of *Twombly* and *Iqbal* on the rates at which motions to dismiss have been granted. *See* Benjamin Sunshine and Victor Abel Pereyra, *Access-to-Justice v. Efficiency: An Empirical Study of Settlement Rates After* Twombly *and* Iqbal, 2015 U. Ill. L. Rev. 357, 363 (2015) (summarizing nine studies of dismissal rates, with conflicting findings); David Freeman Engstrom, *The* Twiqbal *Puzzle and Empirical Study of Civil Procedure,* 65 Stan. L. Rev. 1203, 1248 n.7 (2013) (referencing twenty published and unpublished studies). The effect is difficult to measure because imposition of a heightened pleading standard also changed parties' behavior. For example, a plaintiff who, because of *TwIqbal*, does not even file a lawsuit will not register as a dismissed case. But a study that examined motions filed before, but decided after, *Twombly* arguably controlled even for this variable — and it found no change in the dismissal rate. *See* William H.J. Hubbard, *Testing for Change in Procedural Standards, with Application to* Bell Atlantic v. Twombly, 42 J. Legal Stud. 35 (2013).

> **WANT TO KNOW MORE?**
>
> The Court's *Twombly* and *Iqbal* decisions— sometimes collectively referred to as "TwIqbal" or "Twom-bal"—have generated a considerable amount of scholarly attention. Most of the literature is critical. *See, e.g.,* Kenneth S. Klein, Ashcroft v. Iqbal *Crashes Rule Pleading Standards on to Unconstitutional Shores*, 88 Neb. L. Rev. 261 (2009); Arthur R. Miller, *From* Conley *to* Twombly *to* Iqbal, 60 Duke L.J. 1 (2010); A. Benjamin Spencer, *Plausibility Pleading*, 49 B.C. L. Rev. 431, 433 (2008); Stephen N. Subrin, Ashcroft v. Iqbal: *Contempt for Rules, Statutes, the Constitution, and Elemental Fairness*, 12 Nev. L.J. 571 (2012). For more positive accounts of this reform, *see, e.g.,* Brian T. Fitzpatrick, Twombly *and* Iqbal *Reconsidered*, 87 Notre Dame L. Rev. 1621 (2012); Michelle Kallen, *Plausible Screening: A Defense of* Twombly *and* Iqbal's *Plausibility Pleading*, 14 Rich. J.L. & Pub. Int. 257 (2010); Mark Moller, *Procedure's Ambiguity*, 86 Ind. L.J. 645 (2011); Victor E. Schwartz and Christopher E. Appel, *Rational Pleading in the Modern World of Civil Litigation: The Lessons and Public Policy Benefits of* Twombly *and* Iqbal, 33 Harv. J.L. & Pub. Pol'y 1107 (2010).

f. Abrogating the Forms

In his dissent in *Twombly*, Justice Stevens invoked and quoted a Form to evince the drafters' vision of ease of pleading. On April 29, 2015, the Supreme Court prescribed a set of amendments that abrogated the Appendix of Forms. These Forms had, since 1938, offered guidance to practitioners and judges about the Rules' prescriptions. What is the significance of the abrogation? *See* Brooke D. Coleman, *Abrogation Magic: The Rules Enabling Act Process, Civil Rule 84, and the Forms,* 15 Nev. L.J. 1093 (2015); A. Benjamin Spencer, *The Forms Had a Function: Rule 84 and the Appendix of Forms as Guardians of the Liberal Ethos in Civil Procedure,* 15 Nev. L.J. 1113 (2015).

g. Frivolous Litigation

It is not easy to define what constitutes frivolous litigation, but whatever it is, there is the risk that a liberal pleading requirement will let such cases continue to the discovery stage of litigation, or will result in some defendants paying off the plaintiff through settlement in order to avoid litigation costs. On the other hand, a pleading rule that requires specificity before the plaintiff is entitled to discovery may deter the bringing of some meritorious suits or lead to the dismissal of meritorious suits. In order to make rational judgments about what type of rule makes sense for what types of cases, one has to factor in variables such as who is likely to have the required information prior to discovery and what are the costs to the parties, the lawyers, and the court system under different pleading regimes. To complicate even further the problem of designing desirable pleading rules, one should also consider the role that pleading rules play in deterring untoward pre-litigation conduct of defendants. *See* Robert Bone, *Modeling Frivolous Suits*, 145 U. Pa. L. Rev. 519 (1997); Avery Katz,

The Effect of Frivolous Lawsuits on the Settlement of Litigation, 10 Intl. Rev. L. & Econ. 3 (1990).

h. Congressional Legislation and Pleading

Congress, and some state legislatures, on occasion integrate specific pleading requirements into the substantive law. For instance, as a result of tort reforms, some states imposed stringent pleading requirements for medical malpractice cases. *See* Alex Stein, *Toward a Theory of Medical Malpractice,* 97 Iowa L. Rev. 1201, 1203, 1208 (2012). Congress, in order to deter allegedly frivolous or weak securities fraud class action cases, passed the Private Securities Litigation Reform Act (PSLRA), Pub. L. No. 104-67, 109 Stat. 737 (1995). These rules require that the complaint "specify each statement alleged to have been misleading [and] the reason or reasons why the statement is misleading." When liability depends on defendant's state of mind (such as intent or reckless disregard), the plaintiffs must "state with *particularity* the facts giving rise to a *strong inference* that the defendant acted with the required state of mind." 15 U.S.C. § 78u-4(b)(2) (emphasis added).

In the same term that it decided *Twombly,* the Court heard a case involving the pleading standard required under the PSLRA. In *Tellabs, Inc. v. Makor Issues & Rights, Ltd.,* 551 U.S. 308 (2007), the Court noted that "[e]xacting pleading requirements are among the control measures Congress included in the [Reform Act]" as a "check against abusive litigation." Because Congress left the term "strong inference" undefined, the Court articulated the standard: "To qualify as 'strong' within the intendment of [the PSLRA] an inference of scienter must be more than merely plausible or reasonable—it must be cogent and at least as compelling as any opposing inference of nonfraudulent intent." Justice Ginsburg explained that a "court must take into account plausible opposing inferences" because "[t]he strength of an inference cannot be decided in a vacuum." The Court further held that in assessing whether a plaintiff's allegations satisfy these standards, "omissions and ambiguities count against inferring scienter."

Some scholars suggest that, after *Twombly* and *Iqbal,* the pleading standard under Rule 8(a) may be more exacting and onerous than the *heightened* pleading standard under the PSLRA. *See, e.g.,* Marc I. Steinberg and Diego E. Gomez-Cornejo, *Blurring the Lines Between Pleading Doctrines: The Enhanced Rule 8(a)(2) Plausibility Pleading Standard Converges with the Heightened Fraud Pleading Standards Under Rule 9(b) and the PSLRA,* 30 Rev. Litig. 1 (2010); Marc I. Steinberg, *Pleading Securities Fraud Claims—Only Part of the Story,* 45 Loy. U. Chi. L.J. 603 (2014).

Legislators also proposed bills that would have reversed the *Twombly* and *Iqbal* decisions. *See* S.B. 1504, Notice Pleading Restoration Act of 2009 (July 22, 2009); H.R. 4115, Open Access to the Courts Act of 2009 (Nov. 19, 2009); S.B. 4054, Notice Pleading Restoration Act of 2010 (Dec. 22, 2010). Those efforts stalled.

QUESTIONS TO PONDER

1. In *Iqbal* Justice Kennedy observes that the amount of pleading specificity that is required is somewhat "context-specific." What does this suggest about the nature of trans-substantive rules of procedure?
2. Calibrating the pleading standard to weed out claims that *will be* meritless is a good idea. But that requires some element of speculation at the pleading stage. Is it defensible, as a policy matter, to err on the side of dismissing claims that only *might be* meritless? What do we know about the merits of the *Twombly* and *Iqbal* plaintiffs' claims?

i. Winning a 12(b)(6) Motion

We have now seen two different grounds for prevailing on a 12(b)(6) motion: (1) Plaintiff fails to state a cognizable claim—i.e., the substantive law offers no relief for this type of injury; and (2) plaintiff has failed to plead sufficient facts—i.e., such a cause of action exists, but the plaintiff does not provide sufficient allegations within the meaning of *Twombly* and *Iqbal*. *Bower v. Weisman* shows still a third way that a portion of a claim may be deficient. Focus in particular on how it is different from the other two. The case also illustrates a 12(e) motion.

Bower v. Weisman
639 F. Supp. 532 (S.D.N.Y. 1986)

SWEET, District Judge:

. . . [I]n July, 1985, Bower and Weisman terminated a fifteen-year close personal and business relationship. According to Bower, in exchange for valuable business and social assistance which Bower rendered to Weisman during their relationship, Weisman promised to provide Bower with an economic interest in his affairs and to provide Bower and her daughter with financial security. Bower contends that Weisman agreed to provide these benefits even after their relationship terminated, as long as Bower, a Japanese citizen, did not remarry or leave the United States and that Weisman breached a series of written and oral agreements, codifying Weisman's promise of financial security.

Bower asserts that in the final version of this agreement dated July 6, 1985, Weisman agreed (1) to purchase a house in California for Bower at a cost of $6.5 million; (2) to provide Bower with an irrevocable trust in the amount of $3.9 million and $100,000 in trust for Bower's daughter; (3) to pay Bower an annual sum of $120,000 for ten years over and above a promissory note held by Frederick Weisman Company (FWC) dated November 1, 1983; (4) to pay Bower's living expenses until her remarriage or departure from the United States;

(5) to provide rent-free possession of Weisman's New York townhouse until her remarriage or departure from the United States. Provision number (3) concerns a promissory note and consultant agreement executed on November 1, 1983 by FWC and Preferred Capital International Inc. (Preferred Capital), a corporation wholly owned by Bower.

In mid-July, 1985, the Bower-Weisman relationship terminated, and according to Bower, Weisman reneged on this agreement and attempted to coerce her to leave the townhouse, which she asserts was purchased with her own money but which she sold to Weisman in 1980 at his request to accommodate his tax needs in reliance on his promises of a rent-free tenancy. In September and November, 1985, Weisman instructed his agents to enter the apartment, to strip it of artwork and furniture which was purportedly the property of Weisman, to change the locks on Bower's door when she was at work and her daughter was home ill, and to station three armed guards in the townhouse lobby, with instructions to prevent the entry of "unauthorized" individuals. Furthermore, Bower claims that Weisman's real estate agents and attorneys made unauthorized visits to the apartment and disturbed her personal belongings.

The complaint alleges seven claims arising from the July 6, 1985 agreement outlined above, each of which is challenged in [defendant's] motion. Claim One asserts tort and contract claims for money damages arising from the "breach of express agreements"; Claim Two alleges fraud, misrepresentation and deceit in connection with the agreement; Claim Three is for "breach of contract and conversion" and concerns Weisman's attempt to remove Bower from the townhouse and his alleged conversion of art and furniture. Claims Four and Five charge the defendants with trespass and false imprisonment in connection with the townhouse, and Claims Six and Seven concern intentional infliction of emotional distress, and private nuisance, also in connection with Weisman's actions to recover the townhouse. . . .

MOTION FOR A MORE DEFINITE STATEMENT

Weisman [next] argues that pursuant to Fed. R. Civ. P. 12(e), he is entitled to a more definite statement with respect to two aspects of the complaint. First, Weisman asserts that the complaint fails to disclose the specific provisions of the alleged agreements upon which plaintiff relies. Moreover, he argues that the complaint fails to reveal which parts of the agreements have been modified and which provisions remain in effect after these modifications. Second, Weisman urges that the complaint fails to identify which of the three defendants is charged with each act and merely discusses all as "defendant.". . . For the following reasons, this motion for a more definite statement is granted.

A motion for a more definite statement may be granted if "a pleading . . . is so vague and ambiguous that a party cannot reasonably be required to frame a responsive pleading. . . ." Fed. R. Civ. P. 12(e). A motion pursuant to Rule 12(e) should not be granted "unless the complaint is so excessively vague and ambiguous as to be unintelligible and as to prejudice the defendant seriously in attempting to answer it." *Boothe v. TRW Credit Data*, 523 F. Supp. 631, 635

(S.D.N.Y. 1981). With respect to Weisman's first assertion, Bower's complaint is not so unintelligible as to preclude Weisman from drafting a responsive pleading. The essence of a complaint is to inform the defendant as to the general nature of the action and as to the incident out of which a cause of action arose. *Id.* Bower's complaint satisfies this requirement as it clearly identifies the offending acts. The complaint traced in detail the interactions of Bower and Weisman which led to the first written agreement of July, 1983, and the series of subsequent modifications that occurred in September through November of 1983, September, 1984, October, 1984, culminating in the final agreement of July 6, 1985, embodied in paragraph 25. Moreover, paragraph 26 describes the provisions of the agreement that were allegedly violated by Weisman. Weisman has been given fair notice of the claims against him, and nothing prevents him from formulating a responsive pleading.

Weisman seeks to remove the ambiguity that is present in paragraphs 36, 40, 43-47, 50 and 52-55. These paragraphs employ the term "defendant" without specifying which particular defendant is referred to. Obviously, Weisman cannot effectively respond to Bower's complaint until he knows which claims Bower is asserting against him in his individual capacity. Although Rare Properties is a wholly owned subsidiary of FWC, of which Weisman is the sole owner, Bower has not produced any evidence that the proper corporate forms have not been observed with respect to these corporations. The motion for a more particular statement will be granted on this ground. . . .

MOTION TO DISMISS FOR FAILURE TO STATE FRAUD WITH PARTICULARITY

Fed. R. Civ. P. 9(b) requires that: "In all averments of fraud or mistake, the circumstances constituting fraud or mistake shall be stated with particularity." There is tension between the specificity required under Rule 9(b) and the liberal pleading allowances of Fed. R. Civ. P. 8(a)(2) which requires only a "short and plain statement of the claim showing that the pleader is entitled to relief." However, Rule 9(b) does not render Rule 8 meaningless in fraud cases. The two rules must be read in conjunction with each other. Courts have not struck a balance between these rules by devising an easily applied test. Thus, the degree of specificity required will be dependent upon the facts of each case.

Bower's allegations do no more than state generally that all three defendants intentionally misrepresented and defrauded the plaintiff by making promises and representations. In paragraph 32, Bower alleges that "[t]hose representations of the defendants were false and deceitful at the time they were made to the plaintiff. . . ." Such sweeping statements fail to clarify which alleged agreements form the basis of Bower's claim for fraud. "[A well-pleaded claim of fraud] normally includes the time, place, and content of the false representations, the facts misrepresented, and the nature of the detrimental reliance. . . ." *Elster v. Alexander*, 75 F.R.D. 458, 461 (N.D. Ga. 1977). Bower's claim fails with respect to all of these particulars. Moreover, Bower's failure to separate Weisman from the two corporate defendants involved in this case makes it impossible for Weisman to frame an effective response.

Rule 9(b) seeks, in part, to assure that defendants ". . . are given notice of the exact nature of the fraud claimed, sufficient to permit responsive measures." *Todd v. Oppenheimmer & Co., Inc.*, 78 F.R.D. 415, 419 (S.D.N.Y. 1978). Here, Bower's pleadings are vague and fail to provide the specificity required by Rule 9(b). Therefore, Bower's second claim for misrepresentation, fraud and deceit is dismissed with leave to replead.

When determining whether to grant a Rule 12(b)(6) motion, the court must primarily consider allegations in the complaint. However, at this early stage of the proceedings, a court's review of the sufficiency of the complaint is a very limited one. The allegations are accepted as true, and the complaint is construed in a light most favorable to the pleader. . . .

MOTION TO DISMISS FOR FAILURE TO STATE A CLAIM UPON WHICH RELIEF CAN BE GRANTED

The motion to dismiss for failure to state a claim is disfavored and is seldom granted. The reason for such a policy is two-fold. First, "[t]he salvaged minutes that may accrue from circumventing these procedures can turn to wasted hours if the appellate court feels constrained to reverse the dismissal of the action." *Rennie & Laughlin, Inc. v. Chrysler Corporation*, 242 F.2d 208, 213 (9th Cir. 1957). Second, courts are wary of dismissal in view of the policy of the federal rules which seeks to have determinations reached on the merits. *Id.* The test that is in accord with these goals is that ". . . a complaint should not be dismissed for failure to state a claim unless it appears beyond doubt that the plaintiff can prove no set of facts in support of his claim which would entitle him to relief." *Conley v. Gibson*, 355 U.S. 41, 45-46 (1957). Thus, this court must determine in the light most favorable to the plaintiff whether the following claims state any basis for relief.

A. TRESPASS

Plaintiff has alleged the necessary elements to sustain a cause of action in trespass. From July, 1983 to July, 1985, the agreements between Bower and Weisman contained a provision that in the event of the breakup of the parties' relationship, Bower would be permitted to reside rent-free at the 73rd Street townhouse so long as she paid all maintenance expenses and did not remarry or move out of the country. Upon termination of the relationship in August, 1985, plaintiff alleges that she was in actual possession of the townhouse and that she shared this residence only with her daughter, Teru. "Trespass is an action for injury to possession for which an action may be maintained even against an owner by the one entitled to possession." *Meadow Point Properties v. Nick Mazzoferro & Sons*, 219 N.Y.S.2d 908, 909 (Sup. Ct. Suffolk Co. 1961). Because Bower alleges to have been in actual (and exclusive) possession of the townhouse, she may maintain an action for trespass. . . .

Considering the allegations in the light most favorable to the plaintiff, Bower's complaint asserts a possessory interest in the townhouse beyond a licensing arrangement. . . .

Bower has also successfully pleaded the other requisite elements of trespass. . . . Bower asserts that Weisman, through his agents, intentionally entered the townhouse property without her consent. She alleges that artwork was removed from the premises by defendant and/or his agents. Bower also states that defendant changed her apartment locks and placed three armed guards at the entrance of the property. . . .

Defendant's motion to dismiss the trespass claim is denied.

B. FALSE IMPRISONMENT

The action for the tort of false imprisonment seeks to protect an individual's freedom from restraint of movement. The Court of Appeals of New York has set forth the following elements as constituting a cause of action for false imprisonment: (1) defendant intended to confine the plaintiff; (2) plaintiff was conscious of the confinement; (3) plaintiff did not consent to the confinement, and (4) confinement was not otherwise privileged.

Plaintiff's fifth claim for false imprisonment fails to set forth any facts which would support the allegation that plaintiff was confined at the 73rd Street townhouse. Bower alleges that due to the posting of three armed guards at the townhouse entrance, she "has been unable to freely enter and exit her home in the unfettered manner to which she is accustomed and . . . has become a prisoner by virtue of the defendant's acts." However, other paragraphs of Bower's Second Amended Complaint are entirely at odds with the proposition set forth above. Paragraph 42 states that on November 5, 1985, plaintiff left her house to go to work. Paragraph 44 states that the three armed guards were instructed "not to permit access to anyone other than the plaintiff, her daughter, or a person seeking access for emergency and/or medical purposes." This indicates that plaintiff was permitted ingress and egress from the townhouse. Moreover, paragraph 47 alleges that unauthorized persons entered the townhouse while Bower was not home. Plaintiff's own allegations support the conclusion that her movement was unrestrained. . . . Plaintiff's fifth claim for false imprisonment is dismissed with leave to replead within twenty (20) days.

C. INTENTIONAL INFLICTION OF EMOTIONAL DISTRESS

The following components form a claim for intentional infliction of emotion distress: (1) an extreme and outrageous act by the defendant; (2) an intent to cause severe emotional distress; (3) resulting severe emotional distress; (4) caused by the defendant's conduct. Plaintiff's complaint pleads each of the necessary elements of this cause of action to survive a 12(b)(6) challenge.

Paragraph 63 sets forth the "outrageous" acts by defendant that were directed at the plaintiff. First, three armed guards were placed in the lobby of the townhouse to prevent all persons except Bower, her child and medical personnel from entering or exiting from the townhouse. Second, the locks to Bower's apartment were changed without her consent which caused her to become "frightened and distraught." Third, Weisman, through his agents, entered plaintiff's apartment without her permission and removed artwork without her consent. Bower contends that defendant intended that such acts would cause her severe emotional distress, and that she has, in fact, "suffered severe mental anguish, anxiety, and unwarranted pain and suffering."

These allegations demonstrate that defendant embarked upon a course of conduct that was designed to intimidate, threaten and humiliate the plaintiff and which resulted in emotional upset. It will be for the trier of fact to determine whether defendant's conduct went beyond all reasonable bounds of decency, and would arouse resentment against the defendant as to cause the trier of fact to exclaim that such conduct was "outrageous." Restatement (Second) of Torts § 46 comment (d) (1965).

D. PRIVATE NUISANCE

The elements of a private nuisance in New York are: (1) an interference substantial in nature, (2) intentional in origin, (3) unreasonable in character, (4) with a person's property right to use and enjoy land, (5) caused by another's conduct in acting or failure to act. Plaintiff's seventh claim for private nuisance must be dismissed since Bower has failed to allege an interference which is substantial in nature and unreasonable in character.

The "substantial" and "unreasonable" interference requirements distinguish an action for private nuisance from that of trespass. . . . The substantial interference requirement is to satisfy the need for a showing that the land is reduced in value because of the defendant's conduct. "The law does not concern itself with trifles and there must be a real and appreciable invasion of the plaintiff's interests before he can have an action for either a public or private nuisance." Restatement (Second) of Torts § 821F comment c.

In paragraph 68, Bower asserts that defendant trespassed upon the townhouse, removed articles from the premises, changed locks and positioned guards in the lobby. However, plaintiff failed to allege that these acts caused a reduction in the value of the property. . . . Plaintiff's failure to plead a substantial and unreasonable interference with the land is fatal to her claim for private nuisance. . . .

In summary, Weisman's motion for a more definite statement pursuant to Fed. R. Civ. P. 12(e) and motion to dismiss the second claim in the Complaint for failure to state fraud with particularity pursuant to Rule 9(b) is granted, and Bower has leave to replead within thirty (30) days of this opinion. In addition, Bower's Fifth Claim for false imprisonment, and Seventh Claim for private nuisance are dismissed, as they fail to state a claim upon which relief can be granted, Fed. R. Civ. P. 12(b)(6). All other motions are denied. . . .

REVIEW QUESTIONS

1. The last comment before the *Bower* opinion identified two different grounds for prevailing on a 12(b)(6) motion, and Judge Sweet's discussion

of the false imprisonment count gives us a third. In which of these three categories does the dismissal of the private nuisance count fall?

2. Rule 8(d)(3) provides: "[A] party may state as many separate claims or defenses as it has, *regardless of consistency*." (Emphasis added.) If inconsistency is tolerated, why did Judge Sweet grant the defendant's 12(b)(6) motion as to the false imprisonment count in *Bower v. Weisman*?

QUESTIONS TO PONDER

1. A dismissal without prejudice gives plaintiff the opportunity to refile the claim. Why would a court bother writing an opinion dismissing a count (or an entire complaint) and yet leave the door open for plaintiff to file again? Put another way: Has defendant accomplished anything by getting an action dismissed when the court orders that that dismissal is without prejudice?

2. Rule 9(b), which the court applied in *Bower v. Weisman*, requires "particularity" in the pleading of the "circumstances constituting fraud or mistake." What is unique about fraud and mistake claims that justify this special treatment?

   Note also that Rule 9(g) requires that "[i]f an item of special damage is claimed, it must be specifically stated." The purpose of the Rule is to notify the defendant when the type of loss is unusual for the type of claim being sued upon, so that the defendant is not unfairly surprised. For instance, the defendant might not know, absent specific pleading, that a plaintiff incurred expenses to minimize a loss.

j. The Four-Corners Rule

Judges ordinarily do not look beyond the "four corners" of the complaint when ruling on a 12(b)(6) motion. Fed. R. Civ. P. 10(c) states, however, that "[a] copy of a written instrument that is an exhibit to a pleading is a part of the pleading for all purposes." Professor Marcus observes that "[c]ourts have energetically seized this opportunity and permitted defendants to bring a range of materials to bear on the complaint in support of motions to dismiss, even where not attached as exhibits." (His footnote 57 gives examples of courts' taking consideration of unattached informational brochures, an unattached partnership agreement, and an EEOC charge that was not attached to the complaint.) Richard L. Marcus, *The Puzzling Persistence of Pleading Practice*, 76 Tex. L. Rev. 1749, 1757 (1998).

WANT TO KNOW MORE?

In the field of civil procedure we are fortunate to have the benefit of several exceptionally well written treatises, including Jack H. Friedenthal, Mary Kay Kane, and Arthur R. Miller, *Civil Procedure* (5th ed. 2015); Geoffrey C. Hazard, Jr., John Leubsdorf, and Debra Lyn Basset, *Civil Procedure* (6th ed. 2011); Charles A. Wright and Mary Kay Kane, *Law of Federal Courts* (7th ed. 2011); and Stephen S. Gensler, *Federal Rules of Civil Procedure: Rules and Commentary* (2 vols.) (published annually). The late Professor Wright also authored a multi-volume treatise entitled *Federal Practice and Procedure*. Many of the volumes of this treatise were co-authored with Arthur Miller, and the treatise thus is often referred to as *Wright & Miller*. The other most frequently cited multi-volume treatise in the federal procedure field is called *Moore's Federal Practice*, named after William Moore, who was its initial author. Find out where these books are in your law library or online databases. When you are stumped by a procedure question during this course, or want to know more about a given topic, act like a practitioner and consult one of these authoritative and comprehensive sources. Professor Richard Freer has also authored an excellent book that is tailored for students. *See* Richard D. Freer, *A Student Treatise for Civil Procedure* (2017).

PRACTICE EXERCISE NO. 8: ANALYZING 12(b)(6) AND 12(e) MOTIONS IN *CARPENTER*

After an initial client interview and strategy session, Attorney Carol Coblentz decided to represent Nancy Carpenter. Some legal research and factual investigation were done, and a complaint was filed. The defendants filed a 12(b)(6) motion to dismiss and a 12(e) motion for a more definite statement. You are a law clerk to a trial judge who soon will have to rule on the two motions. What rulings do you suggest and why? Assume that the pleading rules applicable in the state courts of the Commonwealth of Massachusetts are identical to the Federal Rules of Civil Procedure. The complaint, relevant statutes, and motions can be found (with the initial memorandum) in the *Carpenter v. Dee* Case Files. These motions were actually filed in this case. How would you assess their quality? Their likelihood of success?

2. Strategy Considerations

Many litigation decisions require the lawyer to consider three different questions: What must I do? What may I do? What should I do? As you have seen, the Federal Rules of Civil Procedure instruct the lawyer about the minimum requirements for a complaint. But lawyers can compose a much more comprehensive complaint if they choose, including even more facts than mandated by *Twombly* and *Iqbal*. In addition to drafting a complaint so that it will survive a 12(b)(6) motion, a plaintiff's lawyer will have a number of audiences she may wish to persuade or influence. The obvious ones are the judge and the opposing party and her lawyer. But who are other target audiences? Does the complaint in *Carpenter* adequately tell Nancy's *story*? Is it a sterile legal document? Could it be more literary—or a better advocacy document—without compromising (or perhaps even while advancing) its other important functions?

Importantly, pleadings within the formal system are not the only outlet for the skilled lawyer to advocate. Indeed, there is something of a parallel system that has no procedural rulebook, is largely ignored in law schools, and is seldom mentioned by judges. Yet it is a methodical and logical system that civil litigators are aware of and, increasingly, rely on as a necessary complement to the formal system:

> [M]any civil litigators, particularly those representing plaintiffs, seem to find it both desirable and necessary (in order to achieve optimum results for their clients) to prepare various written documents, notebooks, and even videos containing narratives that integrate the law and facts of their cases in ways that may persuade their relevant audiences — the opposing lawyer, the opposing lawyer's client, their own client, insurance companies, and mediators. These advocacy materials appear in myriad forms, including demand letters, other settlement correspondence, notebooks, mediation statements, edifying brochures, and documentary videos.

Stephen N. Subrin and Thomas O. Main, *The Integration of Law and Fact in an Uncharted Parallel Procedural Universe*, 79 Notre Dame L. Rev. 1981, 1983 (2004). Does the emergence of this parallel system suggest that the formal system does not adequately allow the expression of narrative and advocacy? Notice that, in the formal system, Fed. R. Civ. P. 12(f) authorizes a motion to strike material from a pleading that is "redundant, immaterial, impertinent, or scandalous." Is this mandate unduly restrictive? What is the danger of allowing extraneous matter in a pleading?

PRACTICE EXERCISE NO. 9: CONSIDERING THE *WARNER* COMPLAINT

Option A: As an associate in a law firm, you have received an initial memorandum introducing a case involving New York City's "stop and frisk" policy. Our clients (and many other New Yorkers like them) have, because of their race, been stopped and searched by city police officers. The memorandum is printed in the Case Files, under *Warner v. City of New York*. The senior partner in the firm wants you to read the memorandum in order to acquaint yourself with the facts and law in the case. The partner also wants you to review the draft of the complaint that is in the Case Files. Prepare for a strategy session at the law firm where you may be asked to (1) explain the relevant causes of action and the elements; (2) discuss the audiences for whom the complaint is (or should be) written; (3) advise on the appropriate tone for this complaint; and (4) evaluate the factual sufficiency of this draft. Consider also these questions: What do we want the newspapers to report the day after we file? Do we draft the complaint differently if we know that a majority of the public is in favor of the city's stop-and-frisk policy? Is it a better strategy to name more or fewer defendants? (Should we name the mayor? The police commissioner? The deputy police commissioner?)

Option B: Read Option A above. But instead of focusing primarily on the complaint, prepare a demand letter, on behalf of plaintiffs, addressed to the City of New York. Although we will talk more about the nonformal elements of dispute resolution in a later chapter, it is useful at this stage to consider why (and when) an attorney would send a demand letter. The main objectives in sending a demand letter include "(1) to show that your client is serious; (2) to spur the opposition into action; (3) to ultimately save money and time, and to avoid unintended costs, such as destroyed relationships, the loss of control, and the lack of creative solutions; (4) to reach a mutually beneficial outcome; and (5) to appear reasonable and willing to work with the opposition — for the benefit of the opposition initially and perhaps at court later on." Allison Martin, *Six Tips for Writing Effective Demand Letters,* Res Gestae, Oct. 2013, at 28. As you draft the demand letter for the *Warner* plaintiffs, compare the rhetoric and tone of the demand letter with the rhetoric and tone of a formal complaint. Why might they differ even though both documents are drawing from common facts and law?

3. Technical Pleading Requirements

In this part we emphasize some important, but more technical, pleading requirements. Technical requirements are traps for the unwary that can be costly and embarrassing if not followed. We will focus on the Federal Rules, but remember that the rules of practice and procedure in state court may differ.

First, re-read Rule 10. This rule addresses such matters as the contents of the "caption" (the introductory content that provides a heading for each pleading and motion) and the form of the allegations. These are important requirements, but should be self-explanatory. If the *Carpenter v. Dee* complaint in the Case Files were instead filed in *federal* court, would it comply with these mandates?

Second, re-read Rule 17(a). This rule requires that an action be prosecuted in the name of the *real party in interest*. The real party in interest is the person who has the right to come to court and seek the relief, as recognized by the law. Usually this is a matter of consulting the applicable substantive law to ascertain to whom the substantive law allows recovery for a particular cause of action. If your friend was damaged by the negligent conduct of x and you (rather than your friend) filed the lawsuit against x, the lawsuit would fail because the substantive law of negligence gives the cause of action to the injured party. Now consider a trickier problem: If Charlie Carpenter is deceased, to whom do his causes of action belong — his wife, his child, his parents? What if Charlie had a lover, or an ex-wife, or a child by another woman? The answer, again, would turn on the applicable substantive laws and to whom each of those laws gives the cause of action. We answer the *procedural* question as to the real party in interest by consulting the applicable *substantive* law.

Why doesn't the "real party in interest" Rule 17(a) cover defendants? Can you come up with a credible argument that such a rule is not needed for plaintiffs (either)?

Assume that an action is not brought by the real party in interest. What should you file? Similarly, by what motion (or otherwise) would you challenge the lack of capacity to sue or be sued?

Third, re-read Rule 17(b) and (c). Capacity to sue (or be sued) raises similar but different concerns than those implicated by Rule 17(a). With this part of the Rule we are concerned with the ability of certain entities to sue. For example, if a contractor performs faulty work on a church, can the church sue in its own name? What if this "church" is just a handful of folks who meet in someone's basement each Sunday morning? And now, what about the contractor? If the church's check was issued to "Dan's Construction Services," is that necessarily the right defendant? What if that business is not a corporation or otherwise registered? The Rule explains where you will look to answer these questions. Also, remember that a party may be the real party in interest yet lack the capacity to sue. For example, a minor or mentally incompetent person who is injured in a car wreck may be the real party in interest in the outcome of the litigation yet lack the capacity to sue. Such a party would need a surrogate to stand in for her/him and make the important decisions relating to the lawsuit.

If you wanted to sue your law school for a personal injury that occurred on campus, which of the following is the proper institutional defendant: The University? The Board of Regents of the University? The Law School? Or something (or someone) else?

4. Anonymous Plaintiffs

Occasionally parties want to initiate a lawsuit without disclosing their identity in court filings, which ordinarily are accessible to the press and to the public. It may be obvious to understand why someone would prefer not to disclose certain details about themselves, their past, prior jobs, business dealings, relationships, and so forth. These plaintiffs are willing to have their identities known to the defendant, but wish to remain anonymous in court filings. Should this be allowed under (some) circumstances? Or is disclosure part of the price a litigant must pay in litigation? What do the Federal Rules require?

Freedom From Religion Foundation, Inc. v. Emanuel County School System
109 F. Supp. 3d 1353 (S.D. Ga. 2015)

SMITH, G.R., Magistrate Judge:

[The Freedom From Religion Foundation and two of its members, Jane and John Doe] filed suit under 42 U.S.C. § 1983 alleging that defendants have violated the Establishment Clause of the First Amendment by endorsing prayer in a public school classroom located in Emanuel County, Georgia. Plaintiffs seek both declaratory and injunctive relief, as well as an award of compensatory and punitive damages, attorneys fees, and court costs.

Two days after filing their initial complaint, the four individual plaintiffs—the parents of children enrolled in kindergarten and the first grade at the Swainsboro Primary School, and the two students themselves—sought leave of court to proceed using pseudonyms rather than their actual names in this litigation. The plaintiffs contend that even though they informed the Superintendent of the Emanuel County School System ("ECS") that the prayer and proselytizing practices of certain teachers at the primary school violated the Constitution, the practices did not cease. Instead, the teachers not only continued to lead prayer in the classroom, they began to punish the "Doe" children for not participating by making them sit in the hallway while the rest of the class prayed, trying to persuade them to ignore their parents and join in the class prayers, and assuring one child that her mother was "a bad person for not believing in God." Given the "bullying and unwanted proselytization" of the Doe children, and the documented history of retaliation against those who challenge government-endorsed prayer in the public schools or other public institutions, plaintiffs contend that this is the type of exceptional case where they must remain anonymous or else suffer reprisal from the broader community, a reprisal that they fear will be far worse than what these young children have already experienced. Three of the five defendants oppose plaintiffs' motion. . . .

Lawsuits are public events and the public has a presumptive right to know the identity of the litigants who use the courts to resolve their disputes. The Federal Rules of Civil Procedure specifically provide that "the complaint must name all the parties" to the suit. Fed. R. Civ. P. 10(a). But "[p]ublic access to this information is more than a customary procedural formality; First Amendment guarantees are implicated when a court decides to restrict public scrutiny of judicial proceedings." *Doe v. Stegall,* 653 F.2d 180, 185 (5th Cir. Unit A 1981). Generally, therefore, a plaintiff may not remain anonymous and proceed under a fictitious name simply because the litigation may expose plaintiff to "some personal embarrassment." *Doe v. Frank*, 951 F.2d 320, 324 (11th Cir. 1992) (per curiam) (denying Doe status to a plaintiff alleging unlawful discrimination because of his handicap, alcoholism).

This general rule is not absolute, however. In some "exceptional" cases, the public interest in knowing the identity of all the parties must yield " 'to a policy of protecting privacy in a very private matter.' " *Stegall*, 653 F.2d at 185. There is "no hard and fast formula for ascertaining whether a party may sue anonymously." *Id.* at 186. "The ultimate test . . . is whether the plaintiff has a substantial privacy right which outweighs the 'customary and constitutionally-imbedded presumption of openness in judicial proceedings.' " *Frank*, 951 F.2d at 323. The Eleventh Circuit, like most federal courts, has developed "a multi-factor balancing test" for weighing these competing interests. . . . No one factor is "meant to be dispositive"; rather, it is the court's task to "review *all* the circumstances of a given case and then decide whether the customary practice of disclosing the plaintiff's identity should yield to the plaintiffs privacy concerns." *Plaintiff B. v. Francis*, 631 F.3d 1310, 1316 (11th Cir. 2011).

In this circuit, the "first step" in the analysis is to look at the three factors identified in the Fifth Circuit's seminal decision in *S. Methodist Univ. Ass'n of Women*

Law Students v. Wynne & Jaffe, 599 F.2d 707 (5th Cir. 1979) and restated in *Stegall*. The Court must ask (1) whether the plaintiffs who seek anonymity are challenging governmental activity; (2) whether the prosecution of their suit compels them to disclose information of the "utmost intimacy;" and (3) whether plaintiffs will be compelled to admit their intention to engage in illegal conduct, thus risking criminal prosecution. *Id.* The *SMU* factors are not "prerequisites to bringing an anonymous suit," *Stegall*, 653 F.2d at 185, for no rigid formula can hope to incorporate all the considerations that may inform the analysis of the individual case. *Id.* (noting that *SMU* was a "fact-sensitive holding"). Thus, the Eleventh Circuit has identified such additional factors "as whether the plaintiffs [are] minors, *Stegall*, 653 F.2d at 186, whether they [are] threatened with violence or physical harm by proceeding in their own names, *id.,* and whether their anonymity pose[s] a unique threat of fundamental unfairness to the defendant." *Francis*, 631 F.3d at 1316.

Two of the three factors identified in *SMU* and *Stegall* apply here. First, plaintiffs clearly challenge governmental activity—defendants' alleged policy of allowing teacher-led prayer in a public school classroom. "But of course, in only a very few cases challenging governmental activity can anonymity be justified." *Stegall*, 653 F.2d at 186. Indeed, the Eleventh Circuit has rejected the notion "that there is more reason to grant a plaintiff's request for anonymity if the plaintiff is suing the government." *Frank*, 951 F.2d at 324.

It is not that suing the government weighs in *favor* of granting a request for anonymity; rather, the operative principle is that a suit against a private party weighs *against* a plaintiff's request for anonymity. *Id.* (noting that in *SMU* it was "because the plaintiffs were suing private individuals rather than a government agency[, which can suffer no injury to its good name and reputation, that] the court found *more* reason *not* to grant the plaintiffs' request for anonymity"). Here, plaintiffs sue not only a governmental entity but also the individual administrators and teachers who allegedly punished their children for refusing to participate in classroom prayer. So, the fact that plaintiffs have named a governmental entity as a defendant does not establish their right to anonymity. Indeed, because plaintiffs are suing the school officials in their *individual* capacities, this factor weighs against their request for anonymity.

The second *SMU/Stegall* factor—whether plaintiffs will be compelled to disclose information of the "utmost intimacy"—also applies, for plaintiffs' suit touches upon their beliefs about religion, a topic deemed by this circuit to be "the quintessentially private matter." *Stegall*, 653 F.2d at 186. The fact that religion is an intensely private concern does not inevitably require that an Establishment Clause plaintiff be given Doe status, however. While religion is certainly an individual matter of conscience that is constitutionally shielded from government intervention, it is generally practiced openly and communally, and no court from this or any other circuit has considered a plaintiff's religious beliefs to be a matter of such sensitivity as to *automatically* entitle the plaintiff to Doe status. In Establishment Clause cases, therefore, something more is required than just an intrusion into a plaintiff's religious privacy before a court will allow the plaintiff to proceed using a pseudonym. Where the plaintiff is unable to make that additional showing, courts have denied anonymity. *See, e.g., Freedom From Religion Found., Inc. v. Cherry Creek Sch. Dist.*, 2009 WL 2176624 (D. Colo. July 22, 2009) (denying parties' unopposed motion to allow adult and minor plaintiffs to remain anonymous in a suit challenging public school district's listing of religious attendance as one of "forty developmental assets" that would reflect positively on a student's future success). . . .

In *Stegall,* the court granted anonymity to a mother and two children challenging the constitutionality of prayer and bible reading exercises in the Mississippi public schools. 653 F.2d at 181. In addition to noting the intensely private nature of religion, the court emphasized "the special vulnerability" of the child litigants and the fact that they might "expect extensive harassment or perhaps even violent reprisals if their identities are disclosed to a . . . community hostile to the viewpoint reflected in [their] complaint." *Id.* at 186. Although the court did not point to any compelling evidence of significant threats of violence or harassment, it emphasized that "[t]he gravity of the danger posed" by revealing plaintiffs' identities need not be as great where children are at risk. *Id.* (viewing "the youth of these plaintiffs as a significant factor in the matrix of considerations arguing for anonymity"). So, even where the evidence of retaliatory violence is not particularly strong, the balance can tip in favor of anonymity in a case involving child litigants seeking to prevent the state from intruding into a matter of the "utmost intimacy."

Defendants concede, as they must, that this case touches upon plaintiffs' intensely personal beliefs about religion, and that the law's special solicitude for children must be taken into account when assessing the seriousness of the risk posed by the denial of their motion to proceed pseudonymously. Defendants argue, however, that these critical factors do not weigh in favor of granting plaintiffs' motion under the particular circumstances of this case.

First, defendants note (and correctly) that plaintiffs have presented no evidence of any "concrete threats of physical harm or extreme harassment directed toward them . . . *in response to [the] filing of this lawsuit.*" Doc. 37 at 2, 9 (emphasis in original). Defendants argue that neither plaintiffs' "vague, unsubstantiated" fears of a hostile community reaction, *id.* at 11, nor their reference to "horror stories of harassment" in other Establishment Clause cases, *id.* at 15, overcomes the public's interest in open judicial proceedings. Second, defendants contend (again, correctly) that the mere fact that two of the individual plaintiffs are minors does not automatically entitle them to Doe status. *Id.* at 17-19. Finally, defendants claim that they will suffer "prejudicial and fundamental unfairness" if the plaintiffs are allowed to proceed anonymously. *Id.* at 21. The Court is not convinced by these arguments.

It is difficult, if not impossible, to quantify the risk of harm a plaintiff faces when litigating such a socially-charged issue as the constitutionality of teacher-led prayer in a public school setting. In this case, however, the Court does not have to speculate whether plaintiffs will suffer any harm, for they have stated in an unrebutted declaration that such harm has *already* occurred. According to Jane Doe's Declaration, the Doe children were pressured to ignore their parents and adopt a theistic belief system, and made to suffer when they failed to do so. Doc. 17-2. Defendants' assertion that this evidence is simply a "rehash" of the complaint's allegations, and therefore of little or no importance, is not persuasive. Doc. 37 at 9. Other courts have given great weight to plaintiff declarations about pre-filing reprisals resulting from "airing their views on religion." *Doe v. Elmbrook Sch. Dist.,* 658 F.3d 710, 723 (7th Cir. 2011), *rev'd in part on other grounds,* 687 F.3d 840 (7th Cir. 2012) (specifically adopting the panel opinion's anonymity analysis). That the evidence of retaliatory harm relates to defendants' own actions rather than the post-filing behavior of other members of the community does not diminish its significance. . . . If these defendants—who are educated professionals charged with the welfare and protection of very young children—are willing to pressure those children to ignore their parents and join in classroom prayer, and then ostracize them when they refuse to do so, it is permissible to infer that other, less responsible members of the local community (or the broader Internet community) might engage in even more extreme conduct if they learn the identities of the plaintiffs in this litigation. The Court, therefore, is not convinced by defendants' argument that plaintiffs' concern about their welfare is "unsubstantiated."

As this case unfolds the Court may be required to issue a ruling that is most unpopular in the small, mostly rural community where plaintiffs reside, and then the Furies may be unleashed. Many reported cases have described the most vicious, and sometimes criminal, acts committed against those who have commenced litigation under the Establishment Clause. *See* Benjamin P. Edwards, *When Fear Rules in Law's Place: Pseudonymous Litigation as a Response to Systematic Intimidation,* 20 Va. J. Soc. Pol'y & L. 437, 438, 455-67 (2013). The Court recognizes that what's past is not always prologue, and that many of the passions that were aroused when the prayer-in-school cases first began to wind their way through the federal courts may diminish over time. (This is true of many other civil rights litigation as well: One no longer sees mass public demonstrations because children of African American heritage are attending a public school or college from which they were once excluded.) But reprisals against plaintiffs litigating church-state issues are still commonplace. *Id.* . . .

Finally, defendants argue that it would be inherently unfair to allow plaintiffs to proceed anonymously in a suit that not only attacks their reputation and integrity but that seeks compensatory and punitive damages against them in their individual capacities. [But] the potential harm to defendants is not so great as to override plaintiffs' privacy interest or need to shield their children from any further harm. First, this case primarily concerns the resolution of a legal question—the constitutionality of allowing teacher-led prayer in a public school classroom—rather than a determination of plaintiffs' credibility regarding hotly disputed factual allegations. Thus there does not appear to be a compelling need for defendants to publicize plaintiffs' names in order to "shake out" information bearing on their credibility. Defendants do not state particularly *what* facts are in dispute, other than a statement in defendant Thompson's brief denying that she engaged in "bullying" or "prosyletizing" [sic] either Doe child. Defendants, however, do not dispute plaintiffs' central allegation that the Doe children were subjected to teacher-led classroom prayer. Nor do they specifically rebut plaintiffs' declaration that they were singled out for special treatment when they did not join in those prayers. Second, defendant Thompson concedes that she knows the identities of the Doe plaintiffs, and she assumes that this is true for "the other defendants as well." *Id.* "[W]here the defendants already know the plaintiffs' names . . . their interest in fairness is diminished because defendants may depose plaintiffs, request ordinary discovery, and otherwise litigate the case normally." Allowing plaintiffs to cloak their identities from the public will not pose that great a risk of unfairness to defendants, therefore. ["Nor will plaintiffs' use of fictitious names unduly prejudice the public interest. All of the pleadings and other filings in this case remain unsealed, and thus the public is well aware of the nature of the suit, the positions of the parties, and the issues at play. The public and the press will have full access to all court proceedings, including the trial itself."]. . .

REVIEW QUESTION

There are many cases where plaintiffs would prefer to sue with a pseudonym. In *Jane Roes 1-2 v. SFBSC Mgmt., LLC,* 77 F. Supp.3d 990 (N.D. Cal. 2015), two exotic dancers brought a claim under the Fair Labor Standards Act (FLSA), claiming that the nightclub wrongfully classified them as independent contractors and, thus, denied them the minimum wage and other benefits to which the FLSA entitled them. In *Plaintiffs #1-21 v. County of Suffolk,* 138 F.Supp.3d 264 (E.D.N.Y. 2015), Latino residents filed a claim under 42 U.S.C. § 1983 alleging that they were subjected to discriminatory policing, and theft of money by police officers during traffic stops, in violation of their Fourth, Fifth, and Fourteenth Amendment rights. In both of these cases, the plaintiffs moved to proceed anonymously, and both courts reached the same conclusion. Would you predict that these two sets of plaintiffs were or were not allowed to proceed anonymously?

QUESTIONS TO PONDER

1. Where does the court get the authority to alter the clear language of the Rules, for instance, Rule 10(a)? What about the Rules Enabling Act, 28 U.S.C. § 2072?
2. Based on the values inherent in our procedural system, under what circumstances does it make sense to permit plaintiffs to proceed anonymously? When should plaintiffs be obliged to disclose their identities in litigation and receive the same attention to which they have subjected the defendants that they have named in that litigation? (When should plaintiffs have to "pay to play"?)

Distinguishing Anonymous Plaintiffs from "John Doe" Defendants. You will find that "John Doe" parties appear in another context—where a plaintiff names an unidentified defendant in a complaint in an effort to avoid a statute of limitations bar. The John Doe pseudonym is a placeholder. But appreciate how *unknown* is different than *anonymous*. Once a plaintiff discovers the identity of defendants named fictitiously in the complaint, she will amend the complaint by naming the actual defendants in lieu of the John Doe defendants. We will address the subject of amendments later in this chapter.

5. Answers, Motions, and Affirmative Defenses

a. Preliminary Motions

Assume that you are an attorney with a client who has been served with a civil complaint. You will first note how much time is remaining in which you have to act, because you will not want your client to lose by *default* for failing to respond. If you were in federal district court, you would examine Rule 12(a) to determine the applicable time period. If you needed an extension, you would turn to Rule 6(b). You would also want to check the local rules of the court in question to determine if there were special rules for seeking an enlargement of time. Do not assume that you can deal with extensions by merely obtaining the consent of the plaintiff's lawyer, although such consent (in writing, when possible) is desirable. The safest course is to have the court grant a motion to extend time within the initial period allowed. Check with a knowledgeable person in your office or with a clerk at the court in question to determine how gaining an extension of time is correctly accomplished in the court in question. It makes sense to satisfy yourself that not only are you in tune with the court's customs, but that you can back up your behavior with the specific language in a rule.

What are your options when faced with a complaint, assuming that you have now solved the timing question? In federal court, a good place to begin is Fed. R. Civ. P. 12 and 8, probably in that order.

A motion for a more definite statement (Fed. R. Civ. P. 12(e)) is available if the complaint is so vague or ambiguous that your client cannot reasonably be required to formulate a response. The rule mandates that the motion include a description of the "defects complained of and the details required." This motion must be made, as Rule 12(e) states, "before interposing a responsive pleading." You cannot answer and *then* successfully bring the motion. (There was a 12(e) Motion in Practice Exercise No. 8; you can find the motion in the *Carpenter v. Dee* Case Files.) Given that *Twombly* and *Iqbal* seem to require a good deal more from the plaintiff than *Conley v. Gibson* had suggested, won't defendants now usually file a 12(b)(6) motion rather than a 12(e) motion?

The courts have tried to prevent the motion for a more definite statement from being used as a substitute for discovery. Previous language in Federal Rule 12(e) permitted motions for a bill of particulars, but this method was deleted in 1946 because, according to the Advisory Committee, "[w]ith respect to the preparations for trial, the party is properly relegated to the various methods of examination and discovery provided in the rules for that purpose."

A motion to strike (Fed. R. Civ. P. 12(f)) asks the court to delete from a pleading "any insufficient defense or any redundant, immaterial, impertinent, or scandalous matter." Note that Rule 12(f) also imposes time limits, although the court can act on its "own initiative at any time" to strike the matters described in the Rule. If a plaintiff lists several potential causes of action, and one of them "fails to state a claim upon which relief can be granted," the defendant can use Rule 12(f) on the ground that the particular count is "immaterial" or, more typically, can use a 12(b)(6) motion to seek the dismissal of that count. Where would you find examples of what courts have previously found to be insufficient defenses or "redundant, immaterial, impertinent, or scandalous" matters?

b. Motions to Dismiss

Re-read Federal Rule 12(b) to find the seven permitted motions to dismiss. Note that 12(b) gives you the choice of either raising these defenses as part of your answer, or by preliminary motions prior to filing an answer. You should consider as a matter of the defendant's strategy why you would choose to answer first, including your 12(b) defenses in the answer, rather than acting by motions and delaying your answer. One very practical consideration is whether defense counsel is prepared to file an answer. As you will see, an answer must contain the defendant's theories and contentions, and this research, investigation, and preparation may take time. The deadline for defendant's response is short: *see* Fed. R. Civ. P. 12(a)(1)(A). Can you come up with other strategic considerations for taking the answer or motion route?

You are already familiar with the *motion to dismiss for failure to state a claim* (12(b)(6)). Each of the other "12(b)'s" will be taken up when they are covered later in the course. For example, Chapters 7 and 8 deal with, among other things, jurisdictional issues and service of process. Consequently, the defenses (or motions to dismiss) based on *lack of jurisdiction over the subject matter* (12(b)(1)), *lack of jurisdiction over the person* (12(b)(2)), *improper venue* (12(b)(3)), *insufficiency of process* (12(b)(4)), and *insufficiency of service of process* (12(b)(5)) will be examined then. Perhaps you cannot wait to find out the difference between an "insufficiency of process" and an "insufficiency of service of process." In fact, lawyers often move under both subsections when they are challenging service of process. Technically, the former addresses a failure to conform the summons with the requirements of Rules 4(a) and 4(b), and the latter challenges a failure to properly serve the opponent. For instance, the form of a summons could be correct, but not served at all or not served correctly upon the defendant.

The final 12(b) defense, Fed. R. Civ. P. 12(b)(7), *failure to join a party under Rule 19*, refers to the failure to join an indispensable party in accordance with Rule 19. You will later learn the circumstances under which defendants can use Rule 19 strategically to insist that a necessary party be joined in a suit (even if the plaintiff doesn't want to include the party). In circumstances where such joinder is impossible—because it would destroy subject matter jurisdiction or because the court does not have personal jurisdiction over the omitted Rule 19 party—the court may dismiss the whole case.

Remember that although we are discussing the 12(b) defenses or motions in the context of a defendant's answering a plaintiff's complaint, such defenses or motions will also have to be considered in other situations, such as by a plaintiff when she faces a counterclaim or a co-defendant who faces a cross-claim. Rule 8(a) gives the requirements for all claims, whether an original claim, counterclaim, cross-claim, or third-party claim, and Rule 8(b) requires defenses and admissions or denials to allegations when one is faced with an adverse claim (such as a plaintiff faced with a counterclaim).

Before moving on to the drafting of an answer (with admissions and denials and affirmative defenses), you should consider Rules 12(g) and 12(h), which deal with consolidating defenses in a motion and the waiver or preserving certain defenses. There are several ways that by omission you can lose the right to bring four of the 12(b) defenses or motions. (We will explain in a moment the "favored" three defenses, which receive greater protection against waiver.) One way to lose 12(b) defenses is to bring only one 12(b) motion, and omit others. This is the purpose of 12(g). Let's say you, as defendant's counsel, bring a motion to dismiss for failure of personal jurisdiction (for instance, the defendant has never had any affiliation with the forum state and has not consented to be sued there), the motion is denied, and you then bring a motion to dismiss for lack of venue. Rule 12(h) forbids this, and you will have lost your challenge to venue by failure to consolidate the two motions.

Consider the same example, but this time you try to circumvent Rule 12(g) by filing an answer with your challenge to venue after losing the personal jurisdiction motion. Again, you will be stymied, but this time by Rule 12(h)(1); read it, and you will see why.

Or let's say that you do not raise any 12(b) defenses by motion, but instead put a 12(b)(2) defense—lack of jurisdiction over the person—in your answer. Later you try to add a challenge to venue. This is prohibited by Rule 12(h)(1). An amendment to add the defense will usually not save you from your waiver. Can you see why?

Another possibility is that you do not bring any 12(b) motions prior to answering, nor do you include any in your answer. You will have waived your personal jurisdiction (12(b)(2)), venue (12(b)(3)), and process (12(b)(4)) and (12(b)(5)) defenses—the nonfavored defenses—by your inaction.

The long and short of it is this: (1) If you file a 12(b) motion prior to your answer, include any plausible less-favored defenses in your motion at the same time; and (2) if you answer, without having first brought 12(b) motions, include plausible less-favored defenses in your answer. Do these rules regarding consolidation and waiver of 12(b) defenses make sense to you? Why or why not?

We have yet to discuss why the defenses of failure to state a claim upon which relief can be granted, failure to join an indispensable party under Rule 19, and lack of subject matter jurisdiction are not waived by a failure to consolidate them with other 12(b) motions nor by failing to include them in your answer. Notice that Rule 12(h)(3) goes even further.

We will discuss the sanctity of subject matter jurisdiction and indispensable party when we confront those concepts later. Similarly, we will discuss the common sense of having waiver provisions for personal jurisdiction, venue, and process issues when we reach those topics. But you are already equipped to figure out why 12(b)(6) is protected against waiver. Consider, for instance, what would happen at trial in a case where there was one alleged cause of action, but it was clear from the pleading that it did not cover the transaction in question. In other words, a 12(b)(6) motion would have been granted had it been filed or included in the answer as a defense. What if the court could not now consider the motion because of waiver? Would this make sense? Why or why not?

Rule 12(h)(2) further states that "failure . . . to state a legal defense to a claim may be raised (A) in any pleading allowed or ordered under Rule 7(a); (B) by a motion under Rule 12(c); or (C) at trial." Why is the plaintiff's objection—of failure to state a legal defense to a claim—also protected against waiver?

Although the favored 12(b) defenses relating to subject matter jurisdiction, Rule 19, and failure to state a claim are not waived by omission in the answer or failure to consolidate with other 12(b) motions, it is common practice for a defendant's lawyers to include them in their answer when applicable. Sometimes, however, defendants refrain from including such a defense. For example, defense counsel might want to see more of the plaintiff's case before getting the case dismissed. Or defense counsel might not want to draw attention to the deficiency: Filing a 12(b)(6) motion might motivate a plaintiff to more vigorously address some identified but curable weakness; because that same weakness might be incurable at a later stage of the proceeding, defendant might raise it only then.

There is one final matter on the 12(b) defenses. Whether they are raised by preliminary motion, or in the answer, or—in the case of the "favored" defenses—after the answer, Rule 12(i) states that such defenses "must be heard and decided before trial unless the court orders a deferral until trial." Why do the Rules encourage the early determination of the 12(b) defenses?

You should also be aware of the Rule 12(c) motion for judgment on the pleadings, although it is infrequently used. It is possible that upon considering all of the pleadings, which usually will be a complaint and an answer, it is clear that the plaintiff or defendant must win. An example of the latter would be a complaint in which the allegations, taken as true, show that the statute of limitations has run, coupled with an answer that raises the statute of limitations as an affirmative defense. An example of the former would be an answer that admits all of plaintiff's allegations and raises no applicable defenses. In this case, a plaintiff could win a motion for judgment on the pleadings.

c. Answers

It is now time to consider what you, as defense counsel, will put in your answer. Let us assume that you have decided not to bring 12(b) defenses by separate motion. Your answer will potentially contain at least four types of material: (1) *admissions* and *denials* to the averments in the plaintiff's complaint (Fed. R. Civ. P. 8(b)); (2) *12(b) defenses*; (3) *affirmative defenses* (Fed. R. Civ. P. 8(c)); and (4) *counterclaims* and *cross-claims* (Fed. R. Civ. P. 13). Recognizing that the answer is an advocacy document, defendants may also use the answer to assert their theory(ies) of their case; defendants often include as additional mislabeled "defenses," for example, that there was no negligence or that there is a lack of causation. The inclusion of a "defense" that is not a proper affirmative defense could be the target of a motion to strike. Review Fed. R. Civ. P. 12(f).

In addition, when filing their answer, defense counsels simultaneously consider whether they wish to *implead* a third party (Fed. R. Civ. P. 14) or *otherwise seek to add parties*. For instance, the defendant might consider adding an additional defendant to a counterclaim in accordance with Rule 13(h). Defense counsel might further attempt to enlarge the case through a motion to consolidate (Fed. R. Civ. P. 42(a)), or by encouraging someone else to intervene (Fed. R. Civ. P. 24). And defense counsel might seek to *reduce the number of parties* through a motion for misjoinder pursuant to Rule 21. Finally, defense counsel should also consider at the time of answering whether to *claim a jury trial*. The jury claim is often stated in the answer. We will discuss the topic of jury trials in Chapter 5.

d. Admissions and Denials

The doctrine on admissions and denials is fairly straightforward. Read Rule 8(b). The rule requires the admission or denial of each averment, except when a party "lacks knowledge or information sufficient to form a belief about the truth of an allegation," a topic we explore in greater detail in a moment. A pleader may deny specific allegations (or averments), whole paragraphs of the complaint, or even the entire complaint. But all pleadings are subject to Rule 11, a Rule that we will study later. It is typical to deny entire paragraphs, as you will note by looking at the answers in the *Carpenter v. Dee* case. Rule 8(b)(6) prescribes that if a responsive pleading is required, allegations not denied, except for the amount of damages, will be deemed admitted. When no responsive pleading is required, "an allegation is considered denied or avoided." *Id.*

Which pleadings require a response and which do not? When answering this question, first revisit the list of pleadings in Rule 7(a).

A major purpose of an answer is to narrow the issues and to apprise the parties of what is still in dispute. Defense lawyers are very careful not to admit anything that they in fact dispute, because once the defendant admits an averment, absent an amendment changing the admission to a denial, it will be taken as true for the remainder of the case. Consequently, admissions in pleadings are more binding than evidence given at a trial, which the fact finder can believe or disbelieve. Thus, it is very difficult to get a defendant to admit a legal conclusion, such as "duty" or "negligence," if there is *any* ground for denying the allegation. Sometimes, defense counsel states that the plaintiff has alleged a "legal conclusion" that does not require admission or denial, although the Rules do not specifically cover the situation. More frequently, the defendant will just deny the allegation. If a plaintiff desires to use the pleadings as a mechanism for reducing the legal battlefield, she is better off pleading very specific facts so that opposing counsel has more difficulty stating an unconditional denial.

Penalties exist for denying an entire group of averments when in fact the pleader denies only a portion (and could admit the remainder). Fed. R. Civ. P. 8(b)(4). A favorite example of casebooks is *Zielinski v. Philadelphia Piers, Inc.*, 139 F. Supp. 408 (D.C. Pa. 1956), where the plaintiff alleged in the complaint that a vehicle owned, operated, and controlled by the defendant, its agents, servants, and employees was managed so negligently and carelessly that it came into contact with the plaintiff and caused him injuries. The defendant denied the entire paragraph of averments in the complaint, but could have admitted that (1) the accident happened; (2) it owned the vehicle that came into contact with the plaintiff; and (3) there was some injury to plaintiff. The defendant denied the group of allegations, however, presumably because it had leased the vehicle to another entity, which, in turn, had hired the allegedly negligent driver. The plaintiff thus had sued the wrong defendant, and the statute of limitations on its claim (against the proper defendant) had expired sometime after the defendant answered but before the plaintiff ascertained the identity of the correct defendant. Although the named defendant arguably was responsible under certain theories of agency, the court ruled that the defendant should be treated as if it had admitted operation and control of the vehicle, in part because it had not more carefully admitted and denied specific averments in the complaint. This is an unusual case, and in fact the court thought the plaintiff had been misled in additional ways. Nonetheless, the case is a reminder to defendants not to be casual (nor overly aggressive) in their admissions and denials.

Frequently, a defense lawyer lacks the knowledge or information either to admit or to deny an allegation. The Rules permit a defendant to state exactly that when answering, and this has the effect of a denial. *See* Fed. R. Civ. P. 8(b)(5). Importantly, however, this is not a license for defendants to avoid making a reasonable inquiry prior to answering. Much like denying a factual allegation that should have been admitted, a court may later deem the defendant to have admitted that allegation. (*See also* Fed. R. Civ. P. 11(b)(4), which we will discuss later.) Consider the following excerpt from a district court opinion rebuking the defendant, the U.S. government, for its answer:

> The preparation of this case by the Government has been quite casual. There have been delays in service of third-party complaints and answers. . . . [F]ailure to make reasonable investigation of even Government files in the preparation of this case prevented defendant from actually responding to plaintiff's allegation that he was a business invitee. In answer to that averment in plaintiff's original and amended complaints defendant stated that it lacked sufficient knowledge or information to admit or deny, in accord with Fed. R. Civ. P. 8(b).
>
> An answer of lack of knowledge or information will usually be deemed a denial. A party, however, may be held to the duty to exert reasonable effort to obtain knowledge of a fact. . . . In the present case defendant failed to examine available, highly relevant Government documents which would have given a basis for the belief that plaintiff was not a business invitee and that the Court did not have jurisdiction under the FTCA. A fact which is denied for lack of knowledge or information may be deemed admitted if the matter is one to which the party does have knowledge or information. . . . The Government will be held to an admission that plaintiff was a business invitee at the time of the accident. . . .

Greenbaum v. United States, 360 F. Supp. 784 (E.D. Pa. 1973).

e. Affirmative Defenses

Affirmative defenses allow defendants to assert something to the effect of: "Even if you prove your cause of action, I still win because of some other doctrine." For instance, plaintiff might prove all of the elements of a negligence case, and yet lose because of the defense of statute of limitations. Usually, but not always, defendants have the burdens of pleading, production, and persuasion as to all elements of the affirmative defense, just as plaintiffs usually have the same burdens as to the elements of their causes of action.

Rule 8(c) lists eighteen affirmative defenses. Other affirmative defenses to be pled under certain circumstances and causes of action include comparative negligence, gift, truth, privilege, multiplicity of suits, rescission, election of remedies, and many others. In the same fashion that causes of action have elements, affirmative defenses likewise have constituent elements that defendant must plead and, ultimately, prove.

Does the heightened pleading standard of *TwIqbal* apply to affirmative defenses? The Supreme Court did not address that question in either *Twombly* or *Iqbal*. Yet the consequence of a heightened pleading standard for a defendant could be as significant as it is for a plaintiff. Review the textual standards for pleading claims and for pleading affirmative defenses: Do the Federal Rules prescribe one uniform standard or two different standards?

Are the textual differences important? Do the concerns that motivated the Court in the *TwIqbal* decisions also find traction with respect to the pleading of affirmative defenses? Does fairness suggest that "what's good for the goose is good for the gander"? Does the short time frame for filing an answer make it unrealistic for defendants to plead with heightened specificity? (How short is that time frame?) Although there is no consensus on the issue, a majority of district courts do not apply heightened pleading standards to affirmative defenses. *See* Brian Soucek and Remington B. Lamons, *Heightened Pleading Standards for Defendants: A Case Study of Court-Counting Precedent*, 70 Ala. L. Rev. 875 (2019).

Generally speaking, the failure to plead an affirmative defense as required by Federal Rule 8(c) results in the waiver of that defense and its exclusion from the case. "This is so well settled a principle under the Federal Rules of Civil Procedure that the very possibility of waiver makes it important (and certainly prudent) to plead all appropriate affirmative defenses." *Brown v. Herbert,* 43 F. Supp. 3d 1229, 1232 (D. Utah 2014). Courts have allowed defendants to raise the affirmative defense at some later point only in very limited circumstances. For example, on occasion, the availability of an affirmative defense may not be clear from the face of the complaint. Some courts have concluded that a defendant may raise that defense later provided the plaintiff is not prejudiced by the tardiness of its assertion.

Similarly, it is not always obvious what constitutes an affirmative defense; "the general rule of waiver is more easily applied when a party fails to set forth one of the . . . defenses specifically listed in Rule 8(c)." *Proctor v. Fluor Enterprises, Inc.,* 494 F.3d 1337, 1350-1351 (11th Cir. 2007). It might be hard to imagine how there could be any confusion about whether something is or isn't an affirmative defense. To be sure, in the ordinary situation, lawyers know or are able to find out in advance and with certainty the elements of causes of action and the applicable affirmative defenses. The same sources that describe causes of action also usually describe affirmative defenses. But occasionally a provision in a statute could be interpreted as either an element of the plaintiff's cause of action or as an affirmative defense.

Sometimes, a court or legislature will wish to place some burden on a defendant, but not a total affirmative defense. For instance, consider the case where a plaintiff takes a suit to the dry cleaners for cleaning (a bailment) and it is not returned in as good condition as when the cleaner received it or it is not returned at all. Who has the burden of showing negligence or lack thereof? Some courts put the burden of proving negligence on the plaintiff, but then say that if the fact finder believes that the plaintiff took the suit to the dry cleaner in good condition and the dry cleaner accepted it and did not return it in at least as good condition (the triggering facts), then negligence is presumed, unless the defendant produces enough evidence to permit a finding that it was not negligent (production burden) and then the burden of persuasion is again on the plaintiff. Some courts use such a presumption to shift the entire burden of proof to the defendant, thus effectively creating an affirmative defense, but only after the plaintiff proves the triggering facts.

Another device courts occasionally use is to place the pleading burden on the plaintiff, but to require the defendant to plead the nonexistence of the element as an affirmative defense and to prove it. For instance, usually the plaintiff must allege nonpayment in a promissory note case, but the defendant must allege payment as an affirmative defense and has both the production and persuasion burdens with respect to payment.

PRACTICE EXERCISE NO. 10: ANALYZING THE ANSWER IN *CARPENTER*

The purpose of this exercise is to help you learn the differences among 12(b)(6) defenses, denials, and affirmative defenses. The Answer of Randall Dee to the initial Complaint is in the Case Files. Analyze the Answer in *Carpenter* in light of the Complaint. (Assume that the pleading rules in Massachusetts are the same as the Federal Rules of Civil Procedure.)

1. What effect will the admissions in paragraphs four and five of Randall Dee's answer have on the trial?
2. Assuming that the defendant has reasonable knowledge, is the answer to paragraph six in compliance with the applicable rules?
3. What does the denial to the allegations in paragraph eleven put in issue? Assuming that further stages of this case (such as discovery, summary judgment, pretrial conference) do not bring closure to the issue and that it remains as defined by the pleadings, how will the judge instruct the jury on the question of conscious suffering, including instructions on burden of proof?
4. Examine each of Randall Dee's defenses, and explain what type of defense it is. Is it a defense at all or a mislabeled "denial"?
5. Should *Twombly* and *Iqbal* change the pleading standard for *defendants*? How would a more rigorous pleading standard for defendants change the content of Randall Dee's answer? Could Randall Dee plead with greater specificity? Who is in the better position to plead details about what happened and why: Nancy Carpenter or Randall Dee?
6. Notice that Randall Dee's counsel lumps different types of defenses together, rather than separating affirmative defenses from other types. This is common practice, although some lawyers divide their answer by making distinct categories, such as "12(b) defenses" and "affirmative defenses."
7. If you were a legislator or judge faced with the question, would you make the second defense an affirmative defense? Why or why not?

REVIEW EXERCISE NO. 1

The following question will help you review the material to ensure that you are integrating doctrine, practice, and context. Read the question and then answer all four questions. This Review Exercise should take you at least ninety minutes to complete.

When answering a question, understand that the quality of the answer is a function of, among other things, the precision, comprehensiveness, and persuasiveness of your writing. An answer that exhibits those characteristics is stronger than one that lacks them even when both answers reach the same basic conclusion. Your exam answer is assessed not based on *what* you think, but rather *how* you think. Show that you see how the details presented in the exam question are important. And show that you see all of the important counterarguments.

The following complaint is pending in a federal district court in Iowa.

1. [Assume a proper allegation of the court's subject matter jurisdiction.]
2. Plaintiff's intestate, Paula Pennsky, was a participant in a July 15, 2019, DangerMyn race in Ames, Iowa ("the Race"), that was managed by the Defendant, DangerMyn.
3. DangerMyn organizes triathlon races for male and female endurance athletes. These triathlons require competitors to swim for 2.4 miles, then bike for 112 miles, and then run for 26.2 miles—all in a single day. DangerMyn organized, promoted, and oversaw the Race, and drafted the rules governing the Race.
4. Pennsky is a world-class triathlete who was recruited by DangerMyn to participate in the Race in order to bring attention and news coverage to the event. DangerMyn waived the $750 registration fee for Pennsky, and provided her with a $2,500 stipend to cover her travel expenses.
5. The Race was scheduled to take place from 6 A.M. to 9 P.M., and for the duration of the race, security barriers filled with sand or water demarcated the race course and separated the competitors from observers and from users of other parts of the roadways.
6. Around 2:30 P.M., Paula Pennsky was struck by a 2006 Ford Taurus during the run portion of the Race, and was killed. The driver of that car was Drake Driver, a drunk driver who smashed through a security barrier at the intersection of Grassley and Harkin Streets, and struck Pennsky just six miles from the finish line. She was leading the Race at the time of the accident.
7. The intersection of Grassley and Harkin Streets was not adequately safe for Pennsky, as the Driver entered the race path and struck Pennsky. Installed security barriers and a security officer that was stationed at the intersection failed to stop Driver from entering the race course.
8. Pennsky received immediate medical attention from DangerMyn medical officials, but died at the scene of the accident from severe head trauma.

9. The fatal injury was a result of Defendant's failure to install security barricades adequate to prevent a driver from entering the race path. Plaintiff therefore seeks to recover under a theory of negligent wrongful death.

10. Plaintiff has suffered $4.5 million in damages.

Question No. 1. DangerMyn has moved to dismiss the complaint for failure to state a claim. You are a law clerk to a federal judge. The judge has informed the parties that she will hear oral argument on this motion, and she has asked you for a memo preparing her for that oral argument. What should she expect to hear in the oral argument, and how should she rule? You should assume that, under the applicable substantive law, a claim of negligent wrongful death requires proof of the following elements by the decedent's surviving spouse: (1) a duty or obligation recognized by law; (2) a breach of that duty; (3) a causal connection between the wrongful conduct and a resulting death; and (4) damages. The judge has told you that duty is a question of law, and there is no doubt here that DangerMyn owed Pennsky a duty to use reasonable care when operating a race.

Question No. 2. Again, you are the judge's law clerk. The judge approached you and said, "I don't know whether 'DangerMyn' is the proper defendant in this case. I don't think that DangerMyn is the name of any corporation. I think it's just a trade name for a race. Should I be worried about this?" What do the Federal Rules have to say about this?

Question No. 3. For this question, assume that your law firm represents the defendant. A senior partner has asked you to consider whether the defense should file a 12(f) motion to strike. What is your response?

Question No. 4. Again, you represent the defendant. Imagine that you are preparing a first draft of the answer for your supervising partner. With respect to paragraphs 6, 7, and 8 of the complaint, would you admit them, deny them, or something else? When you reviewed the complaint with your client, you asked them specifically about these paragraphs and the defendant's chief executive officer said to you, "Yes, tragically, that sounds right. That's how it happened."

6. Amendments

When judges and lawyers want a quick introduction to a civil lawsuit, they often first look at the complaint and answer in order to educate themselves on the factual background of the case and the claims and defenses. Unless altered by a pretrial conference order, the pleadings also set the boundaries for the trial, confining the parties to the alleged claims and defenses and instructing the judge and the lawyers as to what facts have been admitted. But much of modern civil litigation revolves around discovery, and during that stage new facts, and consequently previously unpleaded causes of action and defenses, often emerge. It is true that the most plaintiff-friendly reading of Rule 8(a)(2) would permit the plaintiff simply to state a claim showing one cause of action, and that the plaintiff would then be able to prove at trial any cause of action within the story told in the complaint. But lawyers are cautious and want to be certain that at trial they can introduce evidence on their entire case. Since the trial judge may tell them that they cannot introduce evidence of causes of action and defenses absent from their pleadings (or outside the limits of a pretrial order under Rule 16 or a similar state rule), lawyers frequently want to amend their pleadings. In federal court civil litigation, Rule 15 controls whether one can amend a pleading, although sometimes local rules provide further requirements and limitations.

Rule 15 has four subparagraphs. From a practice perspective, the most critical portions are (1) the sentence in 15(a)(2) stating that the "court should freely give leave when justice so requires"; and (2) 15(c), which describes when an amendment "relates back to the date of the original pleading."

You should be aware, though, of the situations covered by Fed. R. Civ. P. 15(b) and 15(d). Rule 15(b) is there to help solve the problem of proffered or admitted evidence that seems to go beyond the confines of the pleadings. The first sentence to Rule 15(b)(2) places trial lawyers in somewhat of a dilemma. It states: "When an issue not raised by the pleadings is tried by the parties' express or implied consent, it must be treated in all respects as if raised in the pleadings." Consider opposing counsel's options when the plaintiff introduces a cause of action that is slightly different from what is explicit in the complaint (or when the defendant raises an affirmative defense that was not pleaded). If one objects, the opponent will move to amend and leave is "freely given when justice so requires." (Fed. R. Civ. P. 15(a).) Yet if one doesn't object, the risk is that one has given "implied" consent.

In general, it is probably better to object when you think your opponent is introducing evidence beyond the pleadings. First, it is important to know whether a new issue has in fact been raised, so that you know whether you have to meet it through cross-examination or by introducing your own evidence. Sometimes it is not clear what your opponent is driving at when she introduces evidence, and you do not want to invite her to invent a new theory that perhaps she didn't see. So there may be occasions when you do not object because you do not want to educate the opposition. But the ambiguity may be resolved against you later (as a result of your "implied" consent by your not objecting to the admissibility of the evidence), so you are often better off knowing exactly where you and opposing counsel stand.

Second, you might win by your objection, and in fact keep a new cause of action, theory, or defense out of the case. Your arguments for keeping out evidence on a new theory will be similar to the arguments that you normally raise against an amendment. In other words, here are arguments that parties make as to why "justice" does not require granting the right to amend within the meaning of Rule 15(a). The stock ones (in addition to the argument that the statute of limitations has run, which we will take up later) are (1) the opponent has unreasonably delayed raising the issue, although this argument usually fails without an additional argument about prejudice; (2) you have been prejudiced in your preparation of the case by the delay; (3) the new issue is raised in bad faith, such as for the purpose of clouding real issues or confusing the fact finder or making the other side look "bad" on a largely irrelevant question; or (4) the new issue is "futile" in the sense that the party pressing it cannot win on it. The last sentence of 15(b)(1) permits the court to grant a continuance to the objecting party so she can prepare to meet the new issue without prejudice, but this option is particularly unappealing to judges in the middle of a jury trial or when the party introducing the new issue has had ample opportunity to raise the question by seeking a formal amendment.

Sometimes, events have happened since the date of the original pleading that are relevant to the case, but could not have been pleaded specifically at the time because they had not yet occurred. This is the reason for Fed. R. Civ. P. 15(d) on "Supplemental Pleadings." For instance, there may be subsequent breaches of the contract sued upon, or additional installment payments due, or patent, copyright, or trademark infringements that occurred after the initial complaint. A 1963 amendment to 15(d) makes clear that the trial court is empowered to grant a supplemental pleading even if the new material cures a defect in the original complaint. If a new claim is involved and the statute of limitations has now run, the pleader who seeks the supplemental pleading will have to rely on the provisions of 15(c) dealing with "relation back" of amendments.

Probably the most litigated provisions of Rule 15, or of any rules regarding amendments, concern statute of limitations problems and whether such a statute can be met by having the additional claim or defense relate back to the date of the original pleading. For example, if a plaintiff brought the initial cause of action within the statute of limitations, and the new claim or new cause of action to be "amended in" is now beyond the statutory period, the plaintiff will want the "amended in" claim or cause of action to "relate back" to the commencement date of the initial case. Can you see why it is the intersection of statutes of limitations and motions to amend that raises the most controversial amendment issues?

It is important to know clearly what a statute of limitations is. Most states have statutes requiring that certain causes of action be brought within a certain number of years from when the cause of action accrued. Some federal statutes provide limitations periods for specific federal claims. (*See, e.g.,* 28 U.S.C. § 1658.) Usually, the cause of action accrues when every element of the cause of action has taken place, and usually the last element to occur is the damage or harm. A typical statute of limitations for tort claims is three years. Consequently, if an automobile accident happened on Day One, and the plaintiff was therefore injured on Day One, the plaintiff would have to bring her lawsuit within three years from Day One. (A typical statute of limitations for contract claims is six years.)

Sometimes, potential parties will agree to stop the running of a statute of limitations. A defendant may not want a complaint to be filed and may be willing to agree to forestall the running of the period of time under the statute of limitations pending settlement negotiations. These are often called "tolling agreements."

Reasons for the existence of statutes of limitations include (1) giving potential parties a sense of repose or peace after time has expired (one shouldn't have to worry a lifetime about potential wrongdoing); (2) permitting accused parties to amass evidence while it is still fresh; (3) helping courts to avoid depleting their scarce resources on stale cases in which it will be difficult, if not impossible, to find out what happened. These rationales should help you see why the amendment doctrine becomes more complicated when amendments are sought after the expiration of a statute of limitations.

Consider the facts of *Carpenter v. Dee*. Let's say that *prior* to the running of the applicable statute of limitations, Nancy Carpenter's lawyer, who initially pleaded only a wrongful death count, decided that it was necessary to add a count for conscious suffering. Or assume that her lawyer, through discovery, found plausible defendants in addition to the Dee brothers, such as the retailer that sold the tires and the suspension lift kit. Such amendments normally will not cause parties or courts much trouble. Why? Then consider the same motions to amend *after* the applicable statute of limitations has expired. Why is it now more problematic?

Before reading an amendment/statute of limitations case, you should note two conceptual problems. One is whether the amendment concerns merely adding a claim or defense, as opposed to adding a party. Re-read Fed. R. Civ. P. 15(c). Assume a federal cause of action that does not have any special "relationship back" law attached to it. (If you were in federal court and there were a claim grounded in state law, the federal court, by virtue of 15(c)(1)(A), would apply the "relation back" doctrine of the state law if it were more lenient than the Federal Rules.) If you sought to add a second federal claim to your first, after the statute of limitations had run, "relation back" would be governed by 15(c)(1)(B). But if you sought to add a new *party* to your initial federal cause of action after the applicable statute of limitations had run, the more stringent provisions of 15(c)(1)(C) would apply. Why are the provisions different?

The second conceptual problem arises from the fact that Fed. R. Civ. P. 15(a) and 15(c) impose different tests. Justice may require adding a claim, defense, or a party within the meaning of 15(a), but if the applicable statute of limitations has already expired, there may be a sound affirmative defense, unless the 15(c) "relation back" provisions save the amending party. A court could first grant the amendment and then, after the affirmative defense of statute of limitations is raised in answer to the amended pleading, examine whether 15(c) permits the amending party to surmount the defense. Or a court could decide not to permit the amendment unless it first determines that the amending party will be able to bring the amendment within the contours of the applicable statute of limitations. Some judges prefer the first route (decide the issues of amendment and relation back separately) and some prefer the second (deny the amendment if there is no relation back).

A practical point: Careful lawyers often place the exact language to be amended (added or subtracted) within the motion to amend, and then attach the entire pleading in the form it would take if the amendment were granted. If you do this, the court can then merely ask the clerk to docket the amended pleading when the motion is granted. Often, local rules or special court rules will spell out the method you should use in seeking amendments.

In reading *Singletary*, make sure that you can articulate every portion of Rule 15(c) that must be met, and how the court handles each requirement. Unfortunately, the Third Circuit here was interpreting an earlier iteration of Federal Rule 15. We have changed the references within the text to correspond with the current numbering. Further, Federal Rule 15(c) then, as now, includes a cross-reference to the "period provided by Rule 4(m) for serving the summons and complaint." When *Singletary* was decided, Rule 4(m) prescribed a period of 120 days; since 2015, however, Rule 4(m) has prescribed a period of 90 days.

Singletary v. Pennsylvania Department of Corrections
266 F.3d 186 (3d Cir. 2001)

BECKER, Chief Judge:

This is an appeal from a grant of summary judgment for defendants Pennsylvania Department of Corrections (PADOC), State Correctional Institute at Rockview (SCI-Rockview), and former Superintendent of SCI-Rockview, Joseph Mazurkiewicz, in a 42 U.S.C. § 1983 civil rights lawsuit brought against them by Dorothy Singletary, the mother of Edward Singletary, a prisoner who committed suicide while incarcerated at Rockview. [The appeals court concluded that the entry of summary judgment in favor of all of these named defendants was proper.]

In her original complaint, the plaintiff also included as defendants "Unknown Corrections Officers." The only chance for the plaintiff to prevail depends on her ability to succeed in: (1) amending her original complaint to add as a defendant Robert Regan, a psychologist at SCI-Rockview, against whom the plaintiff has her only potentially viable case; and (2) having this amended complaint relate back to her original complaint under Federal Rule of Civil Procedure [15(c)(1)(C)] so that she overcomes the defense of the statute of limitations. Rule [15(c)(1)(C)] provides for the "relation back" of amended complaints that add or change parties if certain conditions are met, in which case the amended complaint is treated, for statute of limitations purposes, as if it had been filed at the time of the original complaint.

The District Court denied the plaintiff's motion for leave to amend because it concluded that the amended complaint would not meet the conditions required for relation back under [15(c)(1)(C)]. . . .

We conclude that the District Court was correct in ruling that the amended complaint did not meet the notice requirements of Rule [15(c)(1)(C)(i)]. . . .

I

Edward Singletary was serving a 6-12 year sentence at SCI-Rockview for his conviction of rape. In November 1995, Singletary was transferred to the maximum security restricted housing unit (MSRHU) of SCI-Rockview as a result of "threatening an employee or family with bodily harm." Over the next ten months, Singletary became increasingly agitated, acting hostilely to the staff and accusing them of tampering with his food and mail. During this period, Singletary was given chances to leave the MSRHU and re-enter the general population unit of SCI-Rockview, but he refused each time.

During his stay in the MSRHU, Singletary was seen weekly by a counselor, monthly by a three-person Program Review Committee, and by medical psychological staff as needed. A staff psychiatrist, Dr. Abdollah Nabavi, prescribed an anti-depressant to help Singletary with his sleeplessness and anxiety. Nabavi also offered Singletary Trilafon, an anti-psychotic drug, because he "felt [Singletary] was agitated, he was over suspicious, he was just very uncomfortable in the environment. . . . I think he was [psychotic]. If he was not, he was very close to being psychotic." Dep. of Dr. Nabavi at 31-32. Singletary, however, refused the Trilafon.

On October 3, 1996, Singletary became agitated when he was told to remove some magazines that had accumulated in his cell, and he threatened a prison officer. Because of the threat, the next day Singletary was transferred to a cell in the "Deputy Warden" (DW) building with the approval of the prison Superintendent, defendant Joseph Mazurkiewicz. After placement in a DW cell, Singletary was seen on October 4, 1996 by Kevin Burke, a psychiatrist consultant for SCI-Rockview, and by Robert Regan, a psychological services staff member and the person whom Dorothy Singletary seeks to add as a defendant. Regan was working as a "psychological service specialist" at SCI-Rockview at this time; his duties included the psychological testing and assessment of inmates, parole evaluations, group therapy, mental health intervention, and suicide risk evaluation and prevention. Regan did not have any administrative or supervisory duties at the prison. Beginning in late 1994, Regan had met with and evaluated Singletary on a weekly basis.

In their meetings with Singletary on October 4, Regan and Burke talked separately with him to assess his mental state. Singletary vehemently denied to both of them at that time that he was suicidal. On the basis of these examinations, neither Regan nor Burke saw any reason to take further precaution for Singletary. Just after midnight on October 6, 1996, Singletary committed suicide by hanging himself with a bedsheet.

On October 6, 1998, Dorothy Singletary filed in the District Court for the Eastern District of Pennsylvania a § 1983 deliberate indifference lawsuit alleging cruel and unusual punishment in violation of the Eighth Amendment along with pendent state law claims for wrongful death. Named as defendants were PADOC, SCI-Rockview, Mazurkiewicz, and "Unknown Corrections Officers.". . . On April 16, 1999, PADOC and SCI-Rockview moved for judgment on the pleadings pursuant to Federal Rule of Civil Procedure 12(c), and on May 28, 1999, the District Court granted this motion in part by dismissing Singletary's § 1983 claims against these defendants on Eleventh Amendment grounds, but denied their motion to dismiss the pendent state claims on sovereign immunity grounds.

The parties then conducted discovery, and on June 23, 2000, the defendants moved for summary judgment. On July 28, 2000, about a week after filing her response to the summary judgment motion, the plaintiff moved to amend her complaint to add Regan as a defendant. In two orders dated September 20, 2000, the District Court [(1) entered summary judgment for all of the named defendants and (2)] . . . denied the plaintiff leave to amend her complaint to add Regan as a defendant on the grounds that that claim would be barred by the statute of limitations because it did not meet the conditions for relation back in Federal Rule of Civil Procedure [15(c)(1)(C)]. This appeal followed.

II

. . . We . . . turn to Singletary's contention that the court erred by not granting her leave to amend her complaint to add Regan as a defendant.

A. RULE [15(C)(1)(C)]

The parties agree that the statute of limitations for this action is two years, which expired on October 6, 1998, the day that Singletary filed her original complaint. The plaintiff then moved to amend her complaint by adding Regan as a defendant on July 28, 2000, almost two years after the statute of limitations had run. The plaintiff argues that this proposed amendment did not violate the statute of limitations because the amendment would relate back to the original, timely filed complaint under Federal Rule of Civil Procedure [15(c)(1)(C)]. Rule 15(c) can ameliorate the running of the statute of limitations on a claim by making the amended claim relate back to the original, timely filed complaint. . . .

The issue in the case is whether the plaintiff can use [15(c)(1)(C)] to have her amended complaint substituting Regan as a defendant in place of "Unknown Corrections Officers" relate back to her original complaint. The Rule is written in the conjunctive, and courts interpret [15(c)(1)(C)] as imposing three conditions, all of which must be met for a successful relation back of an amended complaint that seeks to substitute newly named defendants. *See Urrutia v. Harriburg County Police Dept.*, 91 F.3d 451, 457 (3d Cir. 1996). The parties do not dispute that the first condition—that the claim against the newly named defendants must have arisen "out of the conduct, transaction, or occurrence set forth or attempted to be set forth in the original pleading"—is met. The second and third conditions are set out in [15(c)(1)(C)(i) & (ii)], respectively, and must be met "within the period provided by Rule 4(m) for service of the summons and complaint," Fed. R. Civ. P. [15(c)(1)(C)], which is "120 days after the filing of the complaint,"

Fed. R. Civ. P. 4(m). The second condition is that the newly named party must have "received such notice of the institution of the action [within the 120-day period] that the party will not be prejudiced in maintaining a defense on the merits." Fed. R. Civ. P. [15(c)(1)(C)(i)]. *Urrutia* states that this condition "has two requirements, notice and the absence of prejudice, each of which must be satisfied." 91 F.3d at 458. The third condition is that the newly named party must have known, or should have known, (again, within the 120 day period) that "but for a mistake" made by the plaintiff concerning the newly named party's identity, "the action would have been brought against" the newly named party in the first place. Fed. R. Civ. P. [15(c)(1)(C)(ii)].

Under these facts, we are concerned with three issues: (1) did Regan receive notice of the institution of the action before February 3, 1999 (which is 120 days after the complaint was filed); (2) was the notice that Regan received sufficient that he was not prejudiced in maintaining his defense; and (3) did Regan know (or should he have known) by February 3, 1999 that but for a mistake Singletary would have named him as a party in the original complaint? As explained above, the answers to all of these questions must be "Yes" for Singletary to prevail on her Rule [15(c)(1)(C)] argument. The District Court concluded that Regan did not receive any notice of the litigation or of his role in that litigation during the 120 day period. The court also concluded that Regan would be unfairly prejudiced by having to mount his defense at this late date, and that he neither knew nor should have known that, but for a mistake, he would have been named in the original complaint.

Notice is the main issue, and we will address that first. . . . [T]he unfair prejudice issue is closely dependent on the outcome of our notice inquiry; because we agree with the District Court that Regan did not receive notice within the 120 day period (and because the District Court based its decision on notice and mentioned prejudice only in passing), we will not address prejudice. ["Prejudice and notice are closely intertwined in the context of Rule [15(c)(1)(C)], as the amount of prejudice a defendant suffers under [15(c)(1)(C)] is a direct effect of the type of notice he receives. . . ."]

B. NOTICE

This court has seldom spoken on the meaning of "notice" in the context of Rule [15(c)(1)(C)]. Still, we can glean some general instruction from the few cases that address the issue. First, Rule [15(c)(1)(C)] notice does not require actual service of process on the party sought to be added; notice may be deemed to have occurred when a party who has some reason to expect his potential involvement as a defendant hears of the commencement of litigation through some informal means. *See Varlack v. SWC Caribbean, Inc.*, 550 F.2d 171, 175 (3d Cir. 1977) (holding that a person who the plaintiff sought to add as a defendant had adequate notice under [15(c)(1)(C)] when, within the relevant period, the person by happenstance saw a copy of the complaint naming both the place where he worked and an "unknown employee" as a defendant, which he knew referred to him). . . . At the same time, the notice received must be more than notice of the event that gave rise to the cause of action; it must be notice that the plaintiff has instituted the action.

The plaintiff does not argue that Regan received formal or even actual notice within the 120 day period; instead, she contends that Regan received "constructive or implied notice" of the institution of the action. . . .

1. Notice Via Sharing an Attorney with an Original Defendant

The "shared attorney" method of imputing Rule [15(c)(1)(C)] notice is based on the notion that, when an originally named party and the party who is sought to be added are represented by the same attorney, the attorney is likely to have communicated to the latter party that he may very well be joined in the action. This method has been accepted by other Courts of Appeals and by district courts within this Circuit. We endorse this method of imputing notice under Rule [15(c)(1)(C)].

The relevant inquiry under this method is whether notice of the institution of this action can be imputed to Regan within the relevant 120 day period, i.e., by February 3, 1999, by virtue of representation Regan shared with a defendant originally named in the lawsuit. The plaintiff contends that Regan shared an attorney with all of the originally named defendants; more precisely, she submits that appellee's attorney, Deputy (State) Attorney General Gregory R. Neuhauser, entered an appearance as "Counsel for Defendants" in the original lawsuit, and hence that Neuhauser represented the "several Unknown Corrections Officers" defendants, one of whom turned out to be Regan. The plaintiff submits that Neuhauser's investigation for this lawsuit, must have included interviewing Regan (as he was one of the last counselors to evaluate Edward Singletary's mental state), so that Regan would have gotten notice of the institution of the lawsuit at that time.

The plaintiff notes further that Neuhauser responded to all of the allegations in the complaint including those governing the unknown corrections officers; that Neuhauser defended at Regan's deposition; and that nothing in Neuhauser's Answer to the Complaint was inconsistent with jointly representing employees like Regan. The defendants counter that, even if Regan were made a defendant in this suit, Regan would not have to accept Neuhauser as his counsel: Pennsylvania law specifically allows state employees to engage their own counsel when sued for actions taken in the course of their employment.

The plaintiff's contentions raise an interesting issue: whether an attorney's original entry of appearance as "Counsel for Defendants" can be used to establish, at the time of that appearance, a sufficient relationship for Rule [15(c)(1)(C)] notice purposes with a party who is later substituted as a defendant for a "John Doe" (or its functional equivalent) named in the original complaint. Because we are concerned with the notice that the newly named defendant received, the fundamental issue here is whether the attorney's later relationship with the newly named defendant gives rise to the inference that the attorney, within the 120 day period, had some communication or relationship with, and thus gave notice of the action to, the newly named defendant.

In this case, however, the record is clear that Neuhauser did not become the attorney for the defendants until well after the relevant 120 day period had run. . . .

Furthermore, the plaintiff has not made a "shared attorney" argument regarding the original attorney Shellenberger (the defendants' attorney of record during the 120 day period), but even if she did, Shellenberger has not represented, and will never represent, Regan at any point in this action. . . .

2. Notice Via an Identity of Interest with an Originally Named Defendant

The "identity of interest" method of imputing Rule [15(c)(1)(C)] notice to a newly named party is closely related to the shared attorney method. Identity of interest is explained by one commentator as follows: "Identity of interest generally means that the parties are so closely related in their business operations or other activities that the institution of an action against one serves to provide notice of the litigation to the other.". . .

In *Schiavone v. Fortune*, 477 U.S. 21 (1986), the Supreme Court seemingly endorsed the identity of interest method of imputing notice for Rule [15(c)(1)(C)]: "Timely filing of a complaint, and notice within the limitations period to the party named in the complaint, permit imputation of notice to a subsequently named and sufficiently related party." *Id*. at 29. . . .

The plaintiff does not substantially develop her identity of interest argument (she concentrates mainly on the shared attorney method of imputing notice), but she does advance the argument that Regan shared an identity of interest with SCI-Rockview because he was employed by SCI-Rockview. The question before us is therefore whether an employee in Regan's position (staff psychologist) is so closely related to his employer for the purpose of this type of litigation that these two parties have a sufficient identity of interest so that the institution of litigation against the employer serves to provide notice of the litigation to the employee. . . .

We believe, however, that Regan does not share sufficient identity of interest with SCI-Rockview so that notice given to SCI-Rockview can be imputed to Regan for Rule [15(c)(1)(C)] purposes. Regan was a staff level employee at SCI-Rockview with no administrative or supervisory duties at the prison. Thus, Regan's position at SCI-Rockview cannot alone serve as a basis for finding an identity of interest, because Regan was clearly not highly enough placed in the prison hierarchy for us to conclude that his interests as an employee are identical to the prison's interests. That is, Regan and SCI-Rockview are not "so closely related in their business operations or other activities that the institution of an action against one serves to provide notice of the litigation to the other.". . .

[A]bsent other circumstances that permit the inference that notice was actually received, a non-management employee like Regan does not share a sufficient nexus of interests with his or her employer so that notice given to the employer can be imputed to the employee for Rule [15(c)(1)(C)] purposes. For this reason, we reject the plaintiff's identity of interest argument, and conclude that the District Court did not err in denying the plaintiff leave to amend her complaint to add Regan as a defendant.

C. BUT FOR A MISTAKE CONCERNING THE IDENTITY OF THE PROPER PARTY

Rule [15(c)(1)(C)(ii)] provides a further requirement for relating back an amended complaint that adds or changes a party; the newly added party knew or should have known that "but for a mistake concerning the identity of the proper party, the action would have been brought against the party." Fed. R. Civ. P. [15(c)(1)(C)(ii)]. The plaintiff argues that this condition is met in her proposed amended complaint, but the District Court found otherwise. The defendants also contend that (1) the plaintiff did not make a *mistake* as to Regan's identity, and (2) Regan did not know, nor should he have known, that the action would have been brought against him had his identity been known, because the original complaint named "Unknown Corrections Officers" and Regan is not a corrections officer but a staff psychologist.

The issue whether the requirements of Rule [15(c)(1)(C)(ii)] are met in this case is a close one. We begin by noting that the bulk of authority from other Courts of Appeals takes the position that the amendment of a "John Doe" complaint—i.e., the substituting of real names for "John Does" or "Unknown Persons" named in an original complaint—does not meet the "but for a mistake" requirement in [15(c)(1)(C)(ii)], because not knowing the identity of a defendant is not a mistake concerning the defendant's identity. This is, of course, a plausible theory, but in terms of both epistemology and semantics it is subject to challenge.

In *Varlack v. SWC Caribbean, Inc.*, 550 F.2d 171, 175 (3d Cir. 1977), this Court appeared to have reached the opposite conclusion insofar as we held that the amendment of a "John Doe" complaint met all of the conditions for Rule [15(c)(1)(C)] relation back, including the "but for a mistake" requirement. In *Varlack*, the plaintiff had filed a complaint against, *inter alia*, an "unknown employee" of a branch of the Orange Julius restaurant chain, alleging that this employee had hit him with a two-by-four in a fight, which caused him to fall through a plate glass window, injuring his arm so severely that it had to be amputated. After the statute of limitations had run, the plaintiff sought to amend his complaint to change "unknown employee" to the employee's real name, using Rule [15(c)(1)(C)] to have the amended complaint relate back to the original. The newly named defendant testified that he had coincidentally seen a copy of the complaint naming both Orange Julius and an "unknown employee" as defendants, and that he had known at that time that he was the "unknown employee" referred to. This Court affirmed the district court's grant of the [15(c)(1)(C)] motion, holding that the plaintiff met all the requirements of [15(c)(1)(C)], including the requirement that the newly named defendant "knew or should have known but for a mistake concerning the identity of the proper party." *See id.* at 175.

We are, of course, bound by *Varlack* insofar as it held that the plaintiff's lack of knowledge of a particular defendant's identity can be a mistake under Rule [15(c)(1)(C)(ii)]. *See* Internal Operating Procedures of the United States Court of Appeals for the Third Circuit 9.1 (2000). Moreover, as is also noted above, every other Court of Appeals that has considered this issue (specifically, the First, Second, Fourth, Fifth, Sixth, Seventh, and Eleventh Circuits) has come out contrary to *Varlack*, generally speaking, the analysis in these other cases centers on the linguistic argument that a lack of knowledge of a defendant's identity is not a "mistake" concerning that identity. However, even assuming that *Varlack* allows for amended "John Doe" complaints to meet Rule [15(c)(1)(C)(ii)]'s "mistake" requirement, it is questionable whether the other parts of [15(c)(1)(C)(ii)] are met in this case, namely, whether Regan knew or should have known that he would have been named in the complaint if his identity were known. Because the original complaint named "Unknown *Corrections Officers*," it is surely arguable that psychologist Regan would have no way of knowing that the plaintiff meant to name him.

These are sticky issues. Because, as we explained above, the plaintiff's argument on the applicability of Rule [15(c)(1)(C)] to her case fails on notice grounds, we do not need to decide these questions here. We do, however, take this opportunity to express . . . our concern over the state of the law on Rule [15(c)(1)(C)] (in particular the other Circuits' interpretation of the "mistake" requirement) and to recommend to the Advisory Rules Committee a modification of Rule [15(c)(1)(C)] to bring the Rule into accord with the weight of the commentary about it.[5]

---

5. As we note in the text, some Courts of Appeals have held that proposed amended complaints that seek to replace a "John Doe" or other placeholder name in an original complaint with a defendant's real name do not meet Rule [15(c)(1)(C)(ii)]'s "but for a mistake" requirement. We find this conclusion to be highly problematic. It is certainly not uncommon for victims of civil rights violations (e.g. an assault by police officers or prison guards) to be unaware of the identity of the person or persons who violated those rights. This information is in the possession of the defendants, and many plaintiffs cannot obtain this information until they have had a chance to undergo extensive discovery following institution of a civil action. If such plaintiffs are not allowed to relate back their amended "John Doe" complaints, then the statute of limitations period for these plaintiffs is effectively substantially shorter than it is for other plaintiffs who bring the exact same claim but who know the names of their assailants; the former group of plaintiffs would have to bring their lawsuits well before the end of the limitations period, immediately begin discovery and hope that they can determine the assailants' names before the statute of limitations expires. There seems to be no good reason to disadvantage plaintiffs in this way simply because for example, they were not able to see the name tag of the offending state actor.

The rejoinder to this argument is that allowing the relation back of amended "John Doe" complaints risks unfairness to defendants, who, under the countervailing *Varlack* interpretation of Rule [15(c)(1)(C)(ii)], may have a lawsuit sprung upon them well after the statute of limitations period has run. But fairness to the defendants is accommodated in the other requirements of Rule [15(c)(1)(C)], namely the requirements that (1) the newly named defendants had received "such notice of the institution of the action" during the relevant time period "that the party will not be prejudiced in the maintaining a defense on the merits"; and (2) the newly named defendants knew or should have known that the original complaint was directed towards them ("the action would have been brought against the party"). These requirements generally take care of the "springing a claim on an unsuspecting defendant" problem. . . .

III. CONCLUSION

For the above reasons, the District Court's grant of summary judgment for the defendants and the court's order denying the plaintiff's motion to amend her complaint will be affirmed. The Clerk is directed to send copies of this opinion to the Chairman and Reporter of the Judicial Conference Advisory Committee on Civil Rules and the Standing Committee on Practice and Procedure, calling attention to footnote 5.

REVIEW QUESTIONS

If all courts (other than the Third Circuit, that is) distinguish "lack of knowledge" from a "mistake," this becomes a very important distinction to master. Imagine that a complaint names the comedic actor "Will Farrell" as the defendant. When plaintiff realizes that the actor's name is instead spelled "Will Ferrell," is this a "mistake"? If the error in the original complaint was a typographical error (meaning that the typist meant to spell Ferrell with two *e*'s, but a rogue *a* nonetheless appeared), this would surely be a paradigmatic "mistake." But what if plaintiff spelled the last name with an ersatz *a* without thinking about it? Or included the *a* because she has known many folks named "Farrell"? Or included the *a* because she looked it up on the Internet and copied a misspelling that appeared there? Are these all "mistakes"? And/or do these cases involve *lack of knowledge* of the correct information? At the other extreme, a complaint that names "John Doe" as the defendant is surely the paradigmatic "lack of knowledge" that does *not* qualify as a mistake. In *Singletary*, Judge Becker referred to this distinction as a linguistic argument: The plaintiff is not *mistaken* in thinking that the defendant is actually named John Doe; hence, no relation back (outside the Third Circuit). Imagine a case like *Singletary* is pending in the Second Circuit. And rather than naming John Doe defendants in her complaint, imagine that Dorothy Singletary's counsel goes online and sees that someone named "Stuart Gardiner" is the "Director of Psychological Services" at the prison where Dorothy's son committed suicide. The complaint names Stuart Gardiner as the defendant even though, as it later turns out, the Web site is outdated and Stuart Gardiner has not worked there for years. Now aware that Joseph Regan is the name of the psychologist whose negligent treatment contributed to the death of her son, the plaintiff moves to amend her complaint, substituting Stuart Gardiner with Joseph Regan. When the analysis turns to Rule 15(c)(1)(C)(ii), was this a "mistake"? Would it be a mistake if,

---

All of the commentators who address this issue (at least those that we found in our research) call for Rule [15(c)(1)(C)] to allow relation back in cases in which a "John Doe" complaint is amended to substitute real defendants' names. . . . As the Supreme Court has said, "the requirements of the rules of procedure should be liberally construed and . . . 'mere technicalities' should not stand in the way of consideration of a case on its merits." *Torres v. Oakland Scavenger Co.*, 487 U.S. 312, 316 (1988). Rule [15(c)(1)(C)] is clearly meant to further the policy of considering claims on their merits rather than dismissing them on technicalities, and this policy is substantially furthered by the *Cooper* approach to Rule [15(c)(1)(C)(ii)].

prior to Dorothy's filing of the suit, prison officials had erroneously told her that "Stuart Gardiner" was the name of her son's psychologist? Or what if, prior to filing, she asked the prison for the name of her son's psychologist and they refused to tell her?

Notwithstanding Judge Becker's call for action, the rulemakers have neither amended nor clarified the "mistake" portion of Federal Rule 15.

In the next case we look at the "mistake" language of relation back from a very different perspective.

Krupski v. Costa Crociere S.p.A.
560 U.S. 538 (2010)

Justice SOTOMAYOR delivered the opinion of the Court.

Rule 15(c) of the Federal Rules of Civil Procedure governs when an amended pleading "relates back" to the date of a timely filed original pleading and is thus itself timely even though it was filed outside an applicable statute of limitations. Where an amended pleading changes a party or a party's name, the Rule requires, among other things, that "the party to be brought in by amendment . . . knew or should have known that the action would have been brought against it, but for a mistake concerning the proper party's identity." Rule 15(c)(1)(C). In this case, the Court of Appeals held that Rule 15(c) was not satisfied because the plaintiff knew or should have known of the proper defendant before filing her original complaint. The court also held that relation back was not appropriate because the plaintiff had unduly delayed in seeking to amend. We hold that relation back under Rule 15(c)(1)(C) depends on what the party to be added knew or should have known, not on the amending party's knowledge or its timeliness in seeking to amend the pleading. Accordingly, we reverse the judgment of the Court of Appeals.

I

On February 21, 2007, petitioner, Wanda Krupski, tripped over a cable and fractured her femur while she was on board the cruise ship Costa Magica. Upon her return home, she acquired counsel and began the process of seeking compensation for her injuries. Krupski's passenger ticket—which explained that it was the sole contract between each passenger and the carrier—included a variety of requirements for obtaining damages for an injury suffered on board one of the carrier's ships. The ticket identified the carrier as

> "Costa Crociere S.p.A., an Italian corporation, and all Vessels and other ships owned, chartered, operated, marketed or provided by Costa Crociere, S.p.A., and all officers, staff members, crew members, independent contractors, medical providers, concessionaires, pilots, suppliers, agents and assigns onboard said Vessels, and the manufacturers of said Vessels and all their component parts."

The ticket required an injured party to submit "written notice of the claim with full particulars . . . to the carrier or its duly authorized agent within 185 days after the date of injury." The ticket further required any lawsuit to be "filed within one year after the date of injury" and to be "served upon the carrier within 120 days after filing." For cases arising from voyages departing from or returning to a United States port in which the amount in controversy exceeded $75,000, the ticket designated the United States District Court for the Southern District of Florida in Broward County, Florida, as the exclusive forum for a lawsuit. The ticket extended the "defenses, limitations and exceptions . . . that may be invoked by the Carrier" to "all persons who may act on behalf of the Carrier or on whose behalf the Carrier may act," including "the Carrier's parents, subsidiaries, affiliates, successors, assigns, representatives, agents, employees, servants, concessionaires and contractors" as well as "Costa Cruise Lines N. V.," identified as the "sales and marketing agent for the Carrier and the issuer of this Passage Ticket Contract." The front of the ticket listed Costa Cruise Lines' address in Florida and stated that an entity called "Costa Cruises" was "the first cruise company in the world" to obtain a certain certification of quality.

On July 2, 2007, Krupski's counsel notified Costa Cruise Lines of Krupski's claims. On July 9, 2007, the claims administrator for Costa Cruise requested additional information from Krupski "[i]n order to facilitate our future attempts to achieve a pre-litigation settlement." The parties were unable to reach a settlement, however, and on February 1, 2008 — three weeks before the 1-year limitations period expired — Krupski filed a negligence action against Costa Cruise, invoking the diversity jurisdiction of the Federal District Court for the Southern District of Florida. The complaint alleged that Costa Cruise "owned, operated, managed, supervised and controlled" the ship on which Krupski had injured herself; that Costa Cruise had extended to its passengers an invitation to enter onto the ship; and that Costa Cruise owed Krupski a duty of care, which it breached by failing to take steps that would have prevented her accident. The complaint further stated that venue was proper under the passenger ticket's forum selection clause and averred that, by the July 2007 notice of her claims, Krupski had complied with the ticket's pre-suit requirements. *Id.*, at 23. Krupski served Costa Cruise on February 4, 2008.

Over the next several months — after the limitations period had expired — Costa Cruise brought Costa Crociere's existence to Krupski's attention three times. First, on February 25, 2008, Costa Cruise filed its answer, asserting that it was not the proper defendant, as it was merely the North American sales and marketing agent for Costa Crociere, which was the actual carrier and vessel operator. Second, on March 20, 2008, Costa Cruise listed Costa Crociere as an interested party in its corporate disclosure statement. Finally, on May 6, 2008, Costa Cruise moved for summary judgment, again stating that Costa Crociere was the proper defendant.

On June 13, 2008, Krupski responded to Costa Cruise's motion for summary judgment, arguing for limited discovery to determine whether Costa Cruise should be dismissed. According to Krupski, the following sources of information led her to believe Costa Cruise was the responsible party: The travel documents prominently identified Costa Cruise and gave its Florida address; Costa Cruise's Web site listed Costa Cruise in Florida as the United States office for the Italian company Costa Crociere; and the Web site of the Florida Department of State listed Costa Cruise as the only "Costa" company registered to do business in that State. Krupski also observed that Costa Cruise's claims administrator had responded to her claims notification without indicating that Costa Cruise was not a responsible party. With her response, Krupski simultaneously moved to amend her complaint to add Costa Crociere as a defendant.

On July 2, 2008, after oral argument, the District Court denied Costa Cruise's motion for summary judgment without prejudice and granted Krupski leave to amend, ordering that Krupski effect proper service on Costa Crociere by September 16, 2008. Complying with the court's deadline, Krupski filed an amended complaint on July 11, 2008, and served Costa Crociere on August 21, 2008. On that same date, the District Court issued an order dismissing Costa Cruise from the case pursuant to the parties' joint stipulation, Krupski apparently having concluded that Costa Cruise was correct that it bore no responsibility for her injuries.

Shortly thereafter, Costa Crociere—represented by the same counsel who had represented Costa Cruise—moved to dismiss, contending that the amended complaint did not relate back under Rule 15(c) and was therefore untimely. The District Court agreed. Rule 15(c), the court explained, imposes three requirements before an amended complaint against a newly named defendant can relate back to the original complaint. First, the claim against the newly named defendant must have arisen "out of the conduct, transaction, or occurrence set out—or attempted to be set out—in the original pleading." Fed. Rules Civ. Proc. 15(c)(1)(B), (C). Second, "within the period provided by Rule 4(m) for serving the summons and complaint" (which is ordinarily 120 days from when the complaint is filed, see Rule 4(m)), the newly named defendant must have "received such notice of the action that it will not be prejudiced in defending on the merits." Rule 15(c)(1)(C)(i). Finally, the plaintiff must show that, within the Rule 4(m) period, the newly named defendant "knew or should have known that the action would have been brought against it, but for a mistake concerning the proper party's identity." Rule 15(c)(1)(C)(ii).

The first two conditions posed no problem, the court explained: The claim against Costa Crociere clearly involved the same occurrence as the original claim against Costa Cruise, and Costa Crociere had constructive notice of the action and had not shown that any unfair prejudice would result from relation back. But the court found the third condition fatal to Krupski's attempt to relate back, concluding that Krupski had not made a mistake concerning the identity of the proper party. Relying on Eleventh Circuit precedent, the court explained that the word "mistake" should not be construed to encompass a deliberate decision not to sue a party whose identity the plaintiff knew before the statute of limitations had run. Because Costa Cruise informed Krupski that Costa Crociere was the proper defendant in its answer, corporate disclosure statement, and motion for summary judgment, and yet Krupski delayed for months in moving to amend and then in filing an amended complaint, the court concluded that Krupski knew of the proper defendant and made no mistake.

The Eleventh Circuit affirmed in an unpublished per curiam opinion. Rather than relying on the information contained in Costa Cruise's filings, all of which were made after the statute of limitations had expired, as evidence that Krupski did not make a mistake, the Court of Appeals noted that the relevant information was located within Krupski's passenger ticket, which she had furnished to her counsel well before the end of the limitations period. Because the ticket clearly identified Costa Crociere as the carrier, the court stated, Krupski either knew or should have known of Costa Crociere's identity as a potential party. It was therefore appropriate to treat Krupski as having chosen to sue one potential party over another. Alternatively, even assuming that she first learned of Costa Crociere's identity as the correct party from Costa Cruise's answer, the Court of Appeals observed that Krupski waited 133 days from the time she filed her original complaint to seek leave to amend and did not file an amended complaint for another month after that. In light of this delay, the Court of Appeals concluded that the District Court did not abuse its discretion in denying relation back.

We granted certiorari to resolve tension among the Circuits over the breadth of Rule 15(c)(1)(C)(ii), and we now reverse.

II

. . . In our view, neither of the Court of Appeals' reasons for denying relation back under Rule 15(c)(1)(C)(ii) finds support in the text of the Rule. We consider each reason in turn.

A

The Court of Appeals first decided that Krupski either knew or should have known of the proper party's identity and thus determined that she had made a deliberate choice instead of a mistake in not naming Costa Crociere as a party in her original pleading. By focusing on Krupski's knowledge, the Court of Appeals chose the wrong starting point. The question under Rule 15(c)(1)(C)(ii) is not whether Krupski knew or should have known the identity of Costa Crociere as the proper defendant, but whether Costa Crociere knew or should have known that it would have been named as a defendant but for an error. Rule 15(c)(1)(C)(ii) asks what the prospective defendant knew or should have known during the Rule 4(m) period, not what the plaintiff knew or should have known at the time of filing her original complaint.

Information in the plaintiff's possession is relevant only if it bears on the defendant's understanding of whether the plaintiff made a mistake regarding the proper party's identity. For purposes of that inquiry, it would be error to conflate knowledge of a party's existence with the absence of mistake. A mistake is "[a]n error, misconception, or misunderstanding; an erroneous belief." Black's Law Dictionary 1092 (9th ed. 2009); see also Webster's Third New International Dictionary 1446 (2002) (defining "mistake" as "a misunderstanding of the meaning or implication of something"; "a wrong action or statement proceeding from faulty judgment, inadequate knowledge, or inattention"; "an erroneous belief"; or "a state of mind not in accordance with the facts"). That a plaintiff knows of a party's existence does not preclude her from making a mistake with respect to that party's identity. A plaintiff may know that a prospective defendant—call him party A—exists, while erroneously believing him to have the status of party B. Similarly, a plaintiff may know generally what party A does while misunderstanding the roles that party A and party B played in the "conduct, transaction, or occurrence" giving rise to her claim. If the plaintiff sues party B instead of party A under these circumstances, she has made a "mistake concerning the proper party's identity" notwithstanding her knowledge of the existence of both parties. The only question under Rule 15(c)(1)(C)(ii), then, is whether party A knew or should have known that, absent some mistake, the action would have been brought against him.

Respondent urges that the key issue under Rule 15(c)(1)(C)(ii) is whether the plaintiff made a deliberate choice to sue one party over another. We agree that making a deliberate choice to sue one party instead of another while fully understanding the factual and legal differences between the two parties is the antithesis of making a mistake concerning the proper party's identity. We disagree, however, with respondent's position that any time a plaintiff is aware of the existence of two parties and chooses to sue the wrong one, the proper defendant could reasonably believe that the plaintiff made no mistake. The reasonableness of the mistake is not itself at issue. As noted, a plaintiff might know that the prospective defendant exists but nonetheless harbor a misunderstanding about his status or role in the events giving rise to the claim at issue, and she may mistakenly choose to sue a different defendant based on that misimpression. That kind of deliberate but mistaken choice does not foreclose a finding that Rule 15(c)(1)(C)(ii) has been satisfied.

This reading is consistent with the purpose of relation back: to balance the interests of the defendant protected by the statute of limitations with the preference expressed in the Federal Rules of Civil Procedure in general, and Rule 15 in particular, for resolving disputes on their merits. A prospective defendant who legitimately believed that the limitations period had passed without any attempt to sue him has a strong interest in repose. But repose would be a windfall for a prospective defendant who understood, or who should have understood, that he escaped suit during the limitations period only because the plaintiff misunderstood a crucial fact about his identity. Because a plaintiff's knowledge of the existence of a party does not foreclose the possibility that she has made a mistake of identity about which that party should have been aware, such knowledge does not support that party's interest in repose. . . .

B

The Court of Appeals offered a second reason why Krupski's amended complaint did not relate back: Krupski had unduly delayed in seeking to file, and in eventually filing, an amended complaint. The Court of Appeals offered no support for its view that a plaintiff's dilatory conduct can justify the denial of relation back under Rule 15(c)(1)(C), and we find none. The Rule plainly sets forth an exclusive list of requirements for relation back, and the amending party's diligence is not among them. Moreover, the Rule mandates relation back once the Rule's requirements are satisfied; it does not leave the decision whether to grant relation back to the district court's equitable discretion. *See* Rule 15(c)(1) ("An amendment . . . relates back . . . when" the three listed requirements are met (emphasis added)).

The mandatory nature of the inquiry for relation back under Rule 15(c) is particularly striking in contrast to the inquiry under Rule 15(a), which sets forth the circumstances in which a party may amend its pleading before trial. By its terms, Rule 15(a) gives discretion to the district court in deciding whether to grant a motion to amend a pleading to add a party or a claim. Following an initial period after filing a pleading during which a party may amend once "as a matter of course," "a party may amend its pleading only with the opposing party's written consent or the court's leave," which the court "should freely give . . . when justice so requires." Rules 15(a)(1)-(2). We have previously explained that a court may consider a movant's "undue delay" or "dilatory motive" in deciding whether to grant leave to amend under Rule 15(a). *Foman v. Davis*, 371 U.S. 178, 182 (1962). As the contrast between Rule 15(a) and Rule 15(c) makes clear, however, the speed with which a plaintiff moves to amend her complaint or files an amended complaint after obtaining leave to do so has no bearing on whether the amended complaint relates back.

C

Applying these principles to the facts of this case, we think it clear that the courts below erred in denying relation back under Rule 15(c)(1)(C)(ii). The District Court held that Costa Crociere had "constructive notice" of Krupski's complaint within the Rule 4(m) period. Costa Crociere has not challenged this finding. Because the complaint made clear that Krupski meant to sue the company that "owned, operated, managed, supervised and controlled" the ship on which she was injured, and also indicated (mistakenly) that Costa Cruise performed those roles, Costa Crociere should have known, within the Rule 4(m) period, that it was not named as a defendant in that complaint only because of Krupski's misunderstanding about which "Costa" entity was in charge of the ship—clearly a "mistake concerning the proper party's identity."

It is also worth noting that Costa Cruise and Costa Crociere are related corporate entities with very similar names; "crociera" even means "cruise" in Italian. Cassell's Italian Dictionary 137, 670 (1967). This interrelationship and similarity heighten the expectation that Costa Crociere should suspect a mistake has been made when Costa Cruise is named in a complaint that actually describes Costa Crociere's activities. . . . In addition, Costa Crociere's own actions contributed to passenger confusion over "the proper party" for a lawsuit. The front of the ticket advertises that "Costa Cruises" has achieved a certification of quality without clarifying whether "Costa Cruises" is Costa Cruise Lines, Costa Crociere, or some other related "Costa" company. . . .

In light of these facts, Costa Crociere should have known that Krupski's failure to name it as a defendant in her original complaint was due to a mistake concerning the proper party's identity. We therefore reverse the judgment of the Court of Appeals for the Eleventh Circuit and remand the case for further proceedings consistent with this opinion.

REVIEW QUESTIONS

1. Be prepared to explain with precision which provisions of Rule 15 the *Singletary* and *Krupski* decisions, respectively, are interpreting, and how and why each court decided the issues the way that they did.

2. Judge Becker's opinion in *Singletary* noted the controversy over the interpretation of the "mistake" requirement for relation back in the context of adding new parties. *See* Fed. R. Civ. P. 15(c)(1)(C)(ii). In *Krupski,* Justice Sotomayor recognizes that denying an amendment "would be a windfall for a prospective defendant who understood, or who should have understood, that he escaped suit during the limitations period only because the plaintiff misunderstood a crucial fact about his identity." Should this reasoning apply to defendants (like Dr. Regan in *Singletary*) who could not be identified because of the plaintiff's "lack of knowledge" or only to defendants (like Costa Crociere) who are not identified because of the plaintiff's "mistake"? *See generally Almazo v. M.A. Angeliades, Inc.,* 2015 WL 6965116, at *6 (S.D.N.Y. Nov. 10, 2015).

3. Remember that when a party seeks to amend a pleading she must meet the "justice so requires" language of 15(a), whether or not 15(c) is applicable. Review the types of arguments that should be relevant as to whether "justice so requires" which are given in our preliminary discussion of amendments. Also be prepared to discuss the policies behind statutes of limitations which are frequently relevant to arguments on whether to grant or deny a motion to amend.

a. State Procedural Rules

Singletary and *Krupski* are interpreting the Federal Rule on amendments. The practice and procedure for amendments is one of the rules where there can be significant variation between state and federal practice—even in those states that have largely replicated the Federal Rules. In some states, like Massachusetts, for example (remember this for Practice Exercise No. 11), the rule on relation back—whether adding parties or claims—provides "Whenever the claim or defense asserted in the amended pleading arose out of the conduct, transaction, or occurrence set forth or attempted to be set forth in the original pleading, the amendment (including an amendment changing a party) relates back to the original pleading." In fact, this is the old Federal Rule before it was amended in 1966.

b. Calculating the Statute of Limitations Period

Statutes of limitation, tolling, and the "discovery rule" (which states that a statute of limitations period should not commence until the cause of action is discovered) are creatures both of statute and of case law. For instance, a federal statute tolls the statute of limitations when a potential plaintiff is in the armed forces. *See* Soldiers and Sailors Relief Act, 50 App. U.S.C.A. § 525. Also, states often have statutes that toll the statute of limitations for minors, so that the limitations period begins when the minor reaches majority, such as eighteen or twenty-one, depending on the applicable law. You will discover in your torts course that the statutes of limitations may not begin to run in circumstances where a reasonable potential plaintiff would not know she has been harmed; this is the so-called Discovery Rule. For example, in the situation in which a surgeon leaves a sponge in the patient's stomach, the statute may not begin running until the plaintiff becomes aware that the sponge was left in her stomach. The following case excerpt should give you a sense of how these issues arise, and how each inquiry may be fact-specific:

> Equitable tolling applies only in the rare and exceptional circumstance. . . . The burden of demonstrating the appropriateness of equitable tolling lies with the party seeking to invoke it. . . . In order to avail himself of equitable tolling, [plaintiff] must demonstrate (1) the existence of the aforementioned rare and exceptional circumstances, and (2) that those circumstances prevented him from filing a timely petition despite the exercise of due diligence. . . . To merit application of equitable tolling, the petitioner must demonstrate that he acted with reasonable diligence during the period he wishes to have tolled, but that despite his efforts, extraordinary circumstances beyond his control prevented successful filing during that time. A petitioner must demonstrate a causal relationship between the extraordinary circumstances on which the claim for equitable tolling rests and the lateness of his filing, a demonstration that cannot be made if the petitioner, acting with reasonable diligence, could have filed on time notwithstanding the extraordinary circumstances.
>
> The district courts within this circuit have recognized that illness, including mental incapacity, can be an exceptional circumstance "for the purposes of equitable tolling. . . . Depending on the recency and severity of . . . mental conditions, they might well amount to an extraordinary circumstance that, in an appropriate case, would warrant equitable tolling."). However, the existence of a mental illness alone is insufficient to toll the statute of limitations. Rather, illness or mental incapacity will only constitute an exceptional circumstance if it rendered the petitioner unable to pursue his legal rights

during the relevant time period. . . . While mental illness can form the basis of an equitable tolling argument, without a particularized description of how his condition adversely affected his capacity to function generally or in relationship to the pursuit of his rights, defendant's claim is manifestly insufficient to justify equitable tolling. . . . To justify tolling, a petitioner must show that his mental health problems left him unable to pursue his legal rights during the relevant time period.

Stephenson v. Ercole, 2009 WL 3872358 (E.D.N.Y. 2009) (internal quotations and citations omitted).

PRACTICE EXERCISE NO. 11: ARGUMENT ON PLAINTIFF'S MOTION TO AMEND IN *CARPENTER*

Except as modified in this exercise, assume that the facts in the initial memo concerning *Carpenter v. Dee* are still the same (including that the plaintiff's lawyer did not know where Randall Dee bought the tires and suspension kit until she took Randall Dee's deposition). Assume that Nancy Carpenter's attorney did not file her suit until February 23, 2022, and that the Dees were served on April 30, 2022. Assume also that on February 19, 2020 (about six months after the accident), the plaintiff, through an attorney, gave written notice of her claim to the City of Lowell. After discovery, the plaintiff moved to file an amended complaint.

Assume the following timeline of relevant events: Randall Dee's deposition was first noticed by the plaintiff for June 30, 2022; that deposition was then delayed several times, usually to meet Randall's needs (to meet his work schedule, a death in his family, and, on one occasion, his illness). The deposition finally took place more than two months later, on September 6, 2022. At his deposition, Randall Dee stated that he purchased the oversized tires and suspension lift kit from Ultimate Auto. The following day, Carpenter's lawyer once again notified the city of Lowell of their responsibility. Of course, Lowell police knew of the accident at the time it occurred and, according to the plaintiff, knew or should have known of statutory violations even before the accident occurred.

Assume further that according to Dee's deposition, he told the owner of Ultimate Auto about the accident on or about September 3, 2019, a few days after the accident happened. Years later, and approximately one month after Dee had been served, Dee again mentioned the accident to him (Mr. Jenkins), and also told him that the Dees had been sued.

On October 4, 2022, Carpenter's counsel received the transcript from the deposition and, the following week, moved to amend the complaint by adding Ultimate Auto and the City of Lowell as defendants.

Assume that the applicable statute of limitations in this case is three years.

The motion to amend was first scheduled to be heard on December 14, 2022, but the judge then postponed the hearing for two weeks and asked Carpenter's lawyer to notify Ultimate Auto and the Legal Department of the City of Lowell, informing them of the pending motion and inviting them to participate in a hearing upon that motion. (Incidentally, note that notice to and the participation of putative parties is *not* required.) Assume that Carpenter's lawyers notified Ultimate Auto and the City, and lawyers for those parties are present at the hearing that is about to take place.

You should assume that the hearing on the motion to amend is taking place on December 28, 2022. You know that the judge hearing this motion usually calls first on the moving party. Think about what rule and, thus, what standards the court will apply in deciding this motion. (Except for the relation-back provision described above, the Massachusetts and Federal Rules on amendments are the same in all relevant respects.) Consider what each party would lose or gain if the motion is granted or denied. Attached to the motion to amend (in the Case Files) is the amended complaint that plaintiff seeks to file if the motion to amend is allowed. Reasonable inferences can be made about what records might be available to the City of Lowell and to Ultimate Auto.

The amended complaint, if allowed, mentions implied warranties and Mass. General Laws, chapter 90, § 7P. Massachusetts has adopted the Uniform Commercial Code provisions on implied warranties, and those provisions follow the amended complaint. You will also find other relevant Massachusetts law (statutory provisions relating to wrongful death, conscious suffering, and fraudulent conveyance) in the Case Files.

If your last name begins with a letter from A through H, you are plaintiff's counsel and thus should prepare arguments in favor of the motion to amend. Persons with last names beginning with the letters I and J will represent the defendants Randall and Peter Dee. Persons with last names beginning with the letters K through P will represent Ultimate Auto in opposition to the motion. Persons with last names beginning with a letter from Q through V will represent the City of Lowell in opposition to the motion. And persons with last names beginning with the letters W through Z will act as clerks to the judge. (Judicial clerks ordinarily help the judge prepare for a motion session by informing the judge about the legal standard, summarizing essential facts, and offering suggestions for questions to pose to the parties. Judges also will often ask their clerks how they would decide the motion, and why.)

For purposes of the discussion that may follow the motion session, please consider the following questions:

1. Would the issues be different had this been a (diversity) case brought in the federal district court for the U.S. District Court for the District of Massachusetts? Focus on Fed. R. Civ. P. 15(c)(1)(A).
2. Would the issues be different had Massachusetts adopted the current version of the Federal Rule?

c. Tips on Arguing Motions

It is not patronizing and, in fact, is prudent advocacy to assume that a judge in a motion session knows very little or even nothing about your case, the motion before the court, or even the controlling standard of law. Judges at motion sessions are often presiding over many cases and dozens of motions in any given day. Often the judges are looking at your motion papers for the first time the minute before argument begins.

First, state who you are and whom you represent. Then inform the judge of the precise thing that is before the court. (For example, "Your Honor, before this court is a motion brought pursuant to Fed. R. Civ. P. 12(b)(6) to dismiss the first count of the plaintiff's complaint for failure to state a claim for which relief may be granted.") If you are speaking first, tell the judge enough about the facts of the case and its procedural posture that she can easily follow your argument. As you introduce a rule or statute, tell the judge precisely which provisions and words are implicated, and why those provisions and words should lead the court to reach the conclusion you seek. Explain why what you seek is permitted, reasonable, and fair, or even compelled, given the facts of this case. If you rely on case law, you will probably need to tell the judge enough about the facts of the case upon which you rely so that she can understand its holding in context and can determine whether the case you rely upon is similar to the case then before her.

Listen to the judge's questions. Answer them directly, honestly, and forthrightly. Do not ignore your opponent's strong arguments or the judge's skepticism. Anticipate these statements and meet them head on. Throughout, be polite but not obsequious. Usually, common sense arguments in plain English work the best. Make sure the judge understands the impact (the unfairness, the inefficiency, etc.) if the judge were to rule against your client on this motion. (Of course, you will not want to be confrontational with the court, and thus, some subtlety may be necessary.) As you conclude your argument, make sure the judge knows exactly what you want her to do. (For example, "Therefore, we ask Your Honor to grant the motion for a more definite statement and require that plaintiffs include the specific dates of the publications that they claim were libelous.")

We wish to point out here that many, indeed most, pretrial motions are no longer heard at oral argument; rather they are decided on the basis of arguments made in written motions and memoranda. When oral arguments are allowed, judges may appear impatient or distracted, as they have much work to do. Nevertheless, assume that the judge is unfamiliar with your case, the motion before the court, and the controlling standard of law. Effective advocacy thus may require a *succinct* summary, overview, and introduction; take your cues from the judge to ascertain how much background she needs to decide the motion before her in favor of your client.

E. THE HISTORICAL BACKGROUND OF CIVIL PROCEDURE

We think it is important that you get a sense of historical context to help you understand both the current procedural debates and the tensions that appear in most procedural systems.* We hope that learning about the historical background of the Federal Rules and the systems that preceded them will help you make sense of the contradictions in, and problems confronting, current procedure. Appreciating historical context will also make you a better advocate: Understanding the history of a rule enhances your grasp of its content.

The history of American civil procedure divides rather naturally into three eras. The first era commenced with the founding of the United States. The second era began in the middle of the nineteenth century with the introduction of the Field Code. The third era commenced in 1938 with the promulgation of Federal Rules of Civil Procedure. We are now, at least arguably, in a fourth era. This fourth era is not defined, for the most part, by the introduction of a new set of formal procedural rules; indeed, the formal procedural rules of the third era are largely intact. Yet the cumulative effect of a number of judicial decisions in recent decades supports the notion that we are in a fourth era. Let's briefly consider each of these eras.

1. The First Era: Common Law and Equity

In the seventeenth and eighteenth centuries, English substantive and procedural laws were transplanted to the United States. Ironically, the reception of English law continued even after the Revolution. As a practical matter, however, this was all the colonists knew. The inherited characteristics of procedure included the divergent yet complementary systems of *common law* (or "law") and *equity*. Each of the two systems had their own procedural system, jurisprudence, and outlook; and it is impossible to fully understand the development of American procedure without first understanding their English antecedents.

a. Common Law Procedure

References to the "common law" can be confusing because the term has at least three meanings.

- Sometimes the term is used to refer to countries born of a tradition that emerged in England during the Middle Ages and spread to the colonies of the British Empire, including the United States, India, Canada, Australia,

---

* Some of the authors of this book have described the history of procedure in other publications, and the history reported here borrows verbatim some of that text. *See* Stephen N. Subrin and Thomas O. Main, *The Fourth Era of American Civil Procedure*, 162 U. Pa. L. Rev. 1839 (2014); Stephen N. Subrin, *How Equity Conquered Common Law: The Federal Rules of Civil Procedure in Historical Perspective*, 135 U. Pa. L. Rev. 909 (1987); Stephen N. Subrin, *David Dudley Field and the Field Code: An Historical Analysis of an Earlier Procedural Vision*, 6 Law & Hist. Rev. 311 (1988).

and South Africa. In this usage of the term, the Common Law tradition is distinguished from the Civil Law tradition (or neo-Roman law, Romano-Germanic law, or Continental law). The Civil Law tradition developed in continental Europe around the same time and spread to the colonies of European imperial powers, including much of Latin America and parts of Asia and Africa. The distinction between Common Law and Civil Law traditions, although important for students of comparative law, is not our focus here.

- Sometimes the term is used to refer to law that has developed through judicial opinions and the evolution of case precedent. In this usage of the term, common law is distinguished from statutory or codified law. Common law is law that is produced by judges through the issuance of opinions that have some precedential effect; statutes and codes are the binding product of legislators. Although a Civil Procedure course involves the mastery of both common law and statutes (and rules), this is not the Common Law to which the rest of this unit refers.

- Here the term is used to refer to one of the sets of courts in which formal litigation took place in England at least as early as the thirteenth century. This set of courts, which included the King's Bench, Exchequer, and Common Pleas, used common law procedures. In this usage of the term, common law is distinguished from equity or chancery, which was an alternative system for justice. Common Law is the system of law (or Law) courts.

The law courts had three major characteristics: writs, single-issue pleading, and juries. The writ system developed in Chancery, which (somewhat confusingly) later housed the equity court. As early as the thirteenth century, subjects of the King would bring grievances to the Chancellor, who served as the King's secretary, advisor, and agent. The Chancellor's staff sold writs, royal orders that authorized a court to hear a case and instructed a sheriff to secure the defendant's attendance. Over time, the writs became organized into categories of often-used complaints. They became formalized, so that a plaintiff could not get into court without fitting into a specific category, such as trespass, replevin, or covenant. Each writ implied a range of procedural, remedial, and evidentiary incidents, such as subject matter and personal jurisdiction, burden of proof, and method of execution. Writs began to connote what events would permit what remedy; a body of substantive law ultimately evolved.

Accompanying the writ system was a process that we would call "single-issue pleading." At an earlier time, pleading designed to reduce cases to a single issue took place orally before a judge in London. Later, this developed into exchanges of documents. A defendant could plead jurisdictional defenses, demur to test a legal question, or traverse to raise a factual dispute. Alternatively, the defendant could plead a "confession and avoidance," today's affirmative defense. Unless a jurisdictional plea was granted, the parties pleaded back and forth until one side either demurred, resulting in a legal issue, or traversed, requiring the resolution of a factual dispute.

A factual dispute would be brought to a jury. The jury replaced earlier common law trial methods by which the parties were tested before God through ordeal, battle, or the swearing of neighbors ("compurgators") that they believed the parties. Like the writ system and single-issue pleading, the jury evolved as an attempt to make the resolution of human disputes more rational and predictable. Because human beings, instead of God, were to hear and decide cases, it became advantageous for parties to present facts that could change the minds of conscious dispute resolvers.

The technicality and rigidity of the common law writ and single-issue system drew ridicule. To be called a "special pleader" was an insult. But given the complexity of many lawsuits today, with so many legal issues and so much discovery, one can perhaps sympathize with our procedural ancestors' attempts to reduce and focus cases, achieve a degree of predictability, and, through the writ system, use defined procedures to integrate the ends sought and means used. Moreover, today one can perhaps appreciate the historical development of the lay jury, for most current citizens have few opportunities other than jury service to partake in government.

WANT TO KNOW MORE?

This may be a good occasion for you to browse through the historical section of the law library. There exist several fine descriptions of the historical English bifurcated common law-equity system. The two courses of lectures of Frederick W. Maitland, *Equity and the Forms of Action at Common Law* (1913), and Stroud Francis Charles Milsom, *Historical Foundation of the Common Law* (1969), deserve special mention. The latter requires careful reading and re-reading. An easier and more comprehensive single volume is Theodore F.T. Plucknett, *A Concise History of the Common Law* 139-156 (5th ed. 1956). Two well-regarded multivolume histories of the law in England are William S. Holdsworth, *A History of the Common Law* (2d ed. 1937), and Frederick Pollock and Frederick W. Maitland, *History of English Law* (2d ed. 1905). For copies of common law documents (such as writs), see a set of volumes published through the years by the Selden Society. Perhaps the most engaging way to learn about the Chancery Court in England, however, is to read *Bleak House* (1853), a classic by Charles Dickens.

The most cited single-volume history of American law is the extremely readable *A History of American Law*, by Lawrence M. Friedman (rev. 3d ed. 2010). This is available in paperback and in electronic formats. A useful single volume on early American law is the compilation of essays reprinted in *Essays in the History of Early American Law* (David H. Flaherty ed. 1969). On the colonial experience, and the early faith in juries, William Nelson, *Americanization of the Common Law* (1975), is extremely useful. Morton J. Horwitz, *The Transformation of American Law 1780-1860* (1977), and Morton J. Horwitz, *The Transformation of American Law, 1870-1960: The Crisis of Legal Orthodoxy* (1993), invite one to think about the socioeconomic agendas of those who developed American law. Historical events and forces that we are about to tackle in this unit (and later in the course) are exquisitely put into their social-economic-political context in books authored by procedural historian Edward Purcell. *See* Edward A. Purcell, Jr., *Litigation and Inequality: Federal Diversity Litigation in Industrial America, 1870-1958* (1992); *Brandeis and the Progressive Constitution:* Erie, *the Judicial Power, and the Politics of the Federal Courts in Twentieth-Century America* (2000); *Originalism, Federalism, and the American Constitutional Enterprise: A Historic Inquiry* (2014).

For a light and very entertaining account of the evolution of American civil procedure, *see* Charles Rembar, *The Law of the Land: The Evolution of Our Legal System* (1980). It is available in paperback and will also provide context for other first-year courses.

Understanding history is not merely edifying. Advocates *use* history as a tool. Lawyers who understand the historical trend of a particular doctrine, for example, might use that trendline to argue for the natural extension of that trend. Imagine that the circumstances of your client's case do not fall within the scope of a particular doctrine. But if the scope of that doctrine has been consistently expanding for the past seventy-five years, it should be natural for the judge to continue expanding it so that it reaches the circumstances of your client's case. History is also a source of creative inspiration for policies, arguments, and counter-arguments. Understanding history (and theory and context) is not just about being well-read; it's about being a better advocate who can use that knowledge to win cases.

b. Equity Procedure

By the early sixteenth century it was apparent that the common law system was accompanied by a substantially different one called equity, probably based on the historical power of the Chancellor to fashion new writs. The formulary writ system's defined cubbyholes did not readily allow for individual assistance in unusual and unfair circumstances, such as a contract based on mistake or fraud, or a beneficiary's being deprived of the benefits of property where title was in the name of another. Bills in equity were written to persuade the Chancellor to relieve the petitioner from an alleged injustice that would result from the rigorous application of the common law. One could turn to equity only if there was no adequate remedy at law.

The equity court and its procedure were distinguishable from that of the common law courts in several ways. The bill in equity permitted, and often required, the joinder of multiple parties. While in the law courts the self-interest of the parties was thought too great to permit them to testify, the Chancellor in equity compelled the defendant personally to come before him to answer under oath each sentence of the petitioner's bill. As a precursor to modern pretrial discovery, a petitioner in equity could attach interrogatories to the petition, requiring answers from the defendant. The Chancellor did not take testimony in open court, but relied on documents to decide a case. The Chancellor, not juries, decided equity cases. The Chancellor was able to fashion injunctive relief, such as compelling a defendant to give the use and profit of a property to a beneficiary, rather than being limited to awarding a specific amount of damages, as in common law courts. Finally, a Chancellor was less bound by the rigidity of the common law writ and pleading system, and could exercise more discretion in an attempt to do justice in the particular case.

c. Coming to America

Just as the common law system provoked ridicule for injustice through technicality, the equity system brought complaints arising from the burdens of too many parties, issues, and papers. Many colonists in the New World brought with them a deep distrust of the royal Chancellor, who for them symbolized the unjust King. To them equity represented uncontrolled discretion, arbitrariness, and needless delay and expense.

Some of the earliest colonial courts had jurisdiction over disputes and lawmaking functions that in England would have fallen to several different courts and even to legislators. From 1680 to 1820, there was a gradual movement from the relatively unstructured, nontechnical procedural systems of the early colonists to a greater reliance on common law forms and procedures. Pleadings were usually limited to a few simple steps; joinder was restricted; and only a single form of action was allowed. After the Revolution brought victory over the British, many states more formally followed the British system not only in pleading requirements, but in establishing separate equity courts or permitting common law judges to hear equity cases and grant equitable remedies.

Through the entire colonial period, great confidence was reposed in juries. Upon attaining statehood, each of the thirteen original colonies, as well as the federal government, provided citizens with the right to a jury trial in both criminal and civil cases. The jury was viewed as a means of permitting laymen to partake in governing themselves, educating the citizenry, and controlling the discretion and possible arbitrariness of judges. But by the beginning of the nineteenth century, American judges had begun to fashion ways for constricting and controlling the role of juries. Over time, many lawyers and judges began to view the jury as a cumbersome and unreliable mode of dispute resolution, rather than as an integral part of democratic government.

QUESTIONS TO PONDER

Consider this paragraph from Frederick W. Maitland, *Selected Essays* 19 (H.D. Hazeltine et al. eds. 1936):

> We ought not to think of common law and equity as of two rival systems. Equity was not a self-sufficient system, at every point it presupposed the existence of common law. Common law was a self-sufficient system. I mean this: that if the legislature had passed a short act saying "Equity is hereby abolished," we might still have got on fairly well; in some respects our law would

have been barbarous, unjust, absurd, but still the great elementary rights, the right to immunity from violence, the right to one's good name, the rights of ownership and of possession would have been decently protected and contract would have been enforced. On the other hand had the legislature said, "Common Law is hereby abolished," this decree if obeyed would have meant anarchy. At every point equity presupposed the existence of common law. Take the case of the trust. It's of no use for Equity to say that A is a trustee of Blackacre for B, unless thereby some court that can say that A is the owner of Blackacre. Equity without common law would have been a castle in the air, an impossibility.

1. What is Maitland talking about? Could you explain to another person why he found equity standing alone "anarchy" or "a castle in the air"? Maitland is apparently talking about equity as a repository of substantive law. Would his insight retain force with respect to procedural law?
2. Maitland sees common law and equity as complementary. In terms of procedure, how do common law and equity perspectives relate to each other? What are the advantages and disadvantages of each?

2. The Second Era: The Field Code

During the first half of the nineteenth century, objections developed to the common law-equity system that the United States had inherited from the English. In 1846, a new constitution in the State of New York eliminated the chancery court and created a court "having general jurisdiction in law and equity." It also provided for the legislature to appoint a commission of three members to "revise, reform, simplify, and abridge the rules of practice, pleading, forms, and proceeding of the courts of record of this state, and to report thereon to the legislature." This commission became known as the Practice Commission.

David Dudley Field (1805-1894) was an enormously talented and successful trial lawyer in New York City who participated in some of the most important litigation of his day. For instance, he represented Jim Fisk and Jay Gould in their struggle for control of the Erie Railroad and also represented the notorious Boss Tweed. Later in his career, in unpublished notes for an autobiography he contemplated writing, he concluded, probably accurately: "My practice was the largest and my income from it the most that any lawyer had at the New York Bar, and probably at any Bar in the country." His firm, Field and Shearman, later became the prestigious firm of Shearman and Sterling.

Although not among the original members of the Practice Commission, Field was appointed to replace an original member in 1847 and became the most dominant and well-known commissioner. The New York procedural code, adopted in that state in 1848, became known as the Field Code. It eventually was adopted in twenty-seven states, including such populous states as California and Ohio. As of 1890, 38 million Americans out of 63 million (60 percent of the population) lived in Field Code states. Field also wrote codes for almost all substantive law, but those codes did not find traction like the procedural code.

The Field Code eliminated the forms of action and, for the most part, provided the same procedure for all types of cases. It reduced the number of pleadings to the complaint, answer, reply, and demurrer, and discarded the stylized search for a single issue. It required that complaints contain: "A statement of the facts constituting the cause of action in ordinary and concise language, without repetition, and in such a manner as to enable a person of common understanding to know what is intended." (N.Y. Laws 1848, c. 379, § 120(2).) In 1851, this was amended to read: "A plain and concise statement of the facts constituting a cause of action without unnecessary repetition." (N.Y. Laws 1851, c. 479, § 1.)

The Code liberalized a party's ability to amend pleadings and to enter evidence at variance with a pleading. It expanded—but not to the same degree as the Federal Rules later would—the number of potential parties, causes of action, and defenses that could be joined in one suit. The Field Code eliminated equitable bills of discovery and interrogatories, but provided for limited discovery through requests to inspect and copy "a paper" in the other's possession or control "relating to the merits of the action, or the defense therein" (§ 342), and for limited requests to admit the genuineness of writings (§ 341). The Code permitted oral depositions of the opposing party. But unlike the Federal Rules, the Code deposition was in lieu of calling the adverse party at the trial; the deposition was before a judge, who would rule on evidentiary objections (§ 345). The Code permitted the court to grant the plaintiff "any relief consistent with the case made by the complaint, and embraced within the issue" (§ 231).

Procedural reform has recurrent themes. To understand this better, isolate the rationales of the Field Code reformers and keep them in mind as you encounter other eras (and locales) of procedural reform. The following are portions of an essay on procedural reform written by David Dudley Field on January 1, 1847.

David Dudley Field, What Shall Be Done with the Practice of the Courts?

Speeches, Arguments, and Miscellaneous Papers of David Dudley Field
226-260 (A.P. Sprague ed., 1884)

The Constitution of this State, which goes into effect today, will render great changes necessary in our system of legal procedure. It remodels our Courts; unites the administration of law and equity in the same tribunal; directs testimony to be taken in like manner in both classes of cases; abolishes the offices of Master and Examiner in Chancery, hitherto important parts of our equity system; and, finally, directs that the next Legislature shall provide for the appointment of three commissioners, "whose duty it shall be to revise, reform, simplify, and abridge the rules and practice, pleadings, forms, and proceedings of the courts of record," and report thereon to the Legislature for its action. . . .

What I propose . . . in respect to cases of legal cognizance, is this: that the present forms of action be abolished, and in their stead a complaint and answer required, each setting forth the real claim and defense of the parties. Such pleadings would be precisely similar to those proposed for equity cases, *and we should thus have a uniform course of pleading for all cases, legal and equitable*. The distinction between the two classes of cases is now merely a distinction in the forms of proceeding. . . .

Let the plaintiff set forth his cause of action in his complaint briefly, in ordinary language, and without repetition; and let the defendant make his answer in the same way. Let each party verify his allegation by making oath that he believes it to be true. The complaint will then acquaint the defendant with the real charge, while the answer will inform the plaintiff of the real defense. The disputed facts will be sifted from the undisputed, and the parties will go to trial knowing what they have to answer. The plaintiff will state his case as he believes it, and as he expects to prove it. The defendant, on his part, will set forth what he believes and expects to establish, and he need set forth no more. He will not be likely to aver what he does not believe. His answer will disclose the whole of his defense, because he will not be allowed to prove anything which the answer does not contain. He will not be perplexed with questions of double pleading, nor shackled by ancient technical rules. . . .

The legitimate end of every administration of law is to do justice, with the least possible delay and expense. Every system of pleading is useful only as it tends to this end. This it can do but in one of two ways: *either by enabling the parties the better to prepare for trial, or by assisting the jury and the court in judging the cause*. Let us consider it, then, in these two aspects:

First, as it enables the parties to prepare for trial. This it can only do by informing them of each other's case. To make them settle beforehand wherein they disagree, so as to enable them to dispense with unnecessary proofs, and to be prepared with those which are necessary, is the legitimate end of pleadings, so far as the parties are concerned. Now, no system could accomplish this more effectually than the one proposed. The plaintiff's whole case is stated in his complaint, the defendant's whole case in his answer; and nothing beyond what is contained in one of these is to be received in evidence, except, perhaps, such rebutting proof as may have been specified in written points, filed a certain number of days before the trial. . . .

Second, as it assists the jury and the Court in performing their functions. An opinion prevails that nothing but common-law issues are fit for a jury. Many lawyers are wedded to the system of pleading according to the ancient rules, though they admit and deplore the imperfections of our present practice. It is said that the production of the issue disentangles the case, lessens the number of questions of fact, and separates them from the questions of law.

Now, I deny, in the first place, that the production of an issue, according to the course of the common law, does really lessen the number of questions of fact. The declaration may contain any number of counts, each setting forth different causes of action, or the same cause of action in different forms. If the same plea is put into all the counts, there will be as many issues as there are counts. But the defendant may plead as many pleas to each count as he likes; and the plaintiff, with leave of the Court, may put in as many replications to each plea as he may happen to have answers to it. Suppose, now, a declaration containing five counts—no uncommon thing—three pleas to each count, and a single replication to each plea. Here are fifteen issues; and, if there be two replications to each plea, there will be thirty. . . .

The attempt to reduce questions to all their elements before trial, must commonly fail. What subordinate ones may arise can scarcely be known till the evidence is all disclosed. The greatest diligence and skill will lead only to an approximation, greater or less according to the nature of the original questions. The first one is always this: Has the plaintiff the right, or the defendant? This depends upon others. You may go on, if you please, to reduce them as far as possible, but you will scarcely ever reach the elementary ones till the cause is brought to trial, and the evidence produced. Then, by a strict analysis, they are rapidly sifted; and the cause turns at last upon two or three. . . .

REVIEW QUESTION

Common law procedure emphasized pleading. What stage of the litigation was most important to Field?

a. The Field Family

The Field siblings may rank with the Adams and James families among the most productive and important in the early history of our country: Henry was the editor of a Presbyterian newspaper for forty-four years; Jonathan was a leader in the Massachusetts legislature; Matthew built the longest suspension bridge of his time; Cyrus laid the first transatlantic cable; and Stephen became a U.S. Supreme Court Justice. Not many women were allowed to progress in the legal profession (or any other) at the time, but Field's only sister, Emelia, gave birth to David Brewer, who joined his uncle on the Supreme Court.

b. The Politics of Procedure

Usually, sound procedural reasons support procedural reform. But procedural reform has many faces. Field and his reforms had several progressive elements. He wanted litigation to be less costly and more efficient, and strove to make law understandable and accessible to ordinary people. He fervently believed in equality of opportunity. One law professor summarized the progressive elements in Field and his work, concluding that Field had worked for "scientific law reform, international peace, feminism, and abolition of slavery." *See* Peggy A. Rabkin, *The Origins of Law Reform: The Social Significance of the Nineteenth Century Codification Movement and Its Early Contribution to the Passage of the Early Married Women's Property Acts*, 24 Buff. L. Rev. 683, 714 (1974). But at the same time, there were several less liberal aspects undergirding Field's reforms. At a time of mounting complaints about the technicality of law and a movement to eliminate the legal profession, Field stressed the need for well-trained legal experts both to represent clients and to "reform" the law. His reforms eliminated state regulation of lawyer's litigation fees and permitted Field and his extremely wealthy clients to make their own fee arrangements. At a time when a farmers' rebellion in the state of New York questioned the entire socioeconomic fabric of the country, Field emphasized a need to reform the judicial system and civil procedure. He wanted a well-defined substantive and procedural law that would both tie the hands of judges and permit clients to act freely, except where the law specifically prohibited such activity.

QUESTION TO PONDER

Most procedural reformers tend to ignore potential problems in their own proposals; consequently, most procedural reform inevitably charts the path for some successive reform. What miscalculations, if any, do you think Field made?

c. Transnational Civil Procedure

The American Law Institute and UNIDROIT, an international law-reform organization headquartered in Rome, have drafted Principles and Rules of Transnational Civil Procedure that a country could adopt for adjudication of disputes arising from international commercial transactions. And in these principles and rules, the influence of David Dudley Field is apparent — although it is perhaps more accurate to say that Field himself was largely influenced by European procedure and that most of the world requires more specificity in pleading than do the Federal Rules. The Transnational Rule Reporters have acknowledged that the pleading rule they have incorporated is essentially the Field Code standard. Transnational Rule 12, entitled "Statement of Claim (Complaint)," requires the plaintiff to "state the facts on which the claim is based, describe the evidence to support those statements, and refer to the legal grounds that support the claim, including foreign law, if applicable." Rule 12.1.

3. The Third Era: Federal Rules of Civil Procedure

The third era in the history of American civil procedure began in the early twentieth century. For this era, the engine for procedural reform was the federal government, rather than the states. The Field Code was enacted by the State of New York and was adopted by many other state legislatures for their courts. Yet it was never adopted by Congress for the federal courts. To understand the third era, we first must backfill more than a century's history of procedure in the *federal* courts. Thereafter we can focus on the pivotal legislation by Congress that launched the third era: the Rules Enabling Act of 1934.

a. The Rules of Decision Act, and the Process and Conformity Acts

When the United States Constitution established a new federal government, including a federal judiciary, it was unclear exactly what law(s) the federal courts would apply. In 1789, the same year as the first presidential election, the Federal Judiciary Act provided for the establishment of the Supreme Court, as well as thirteen district and three circuit courts. Section 34 of the Judiciary Act of 1789 provided "that the laws of the several states, except where the constitution, treaties, or statutes of the United States shall otherwise require or provide, shall be regarded as the rules of decision in trials at common law in the courts of the United States in cases where they apply." This section became known as the "Rules of Decision Act" and is now found, in slightly different form, in 28 U.S.C. § 1652. The exception clause in the Rules of Decision Act tracks the Supremacy Clause in Article VI of the Constitution.

It was unclear whether the Rules of Decision section of the Judiciary Act of 1789 covered procedural law, but the Process Act of the same year supplied the same basic formula: Apply state law in federal court, unless a federal law provides otherwise. Act of Sept. 29, 1789, ch. 21, § 2, 1 Stat. 93 (Process Act). Subsequent Process and Conformity Acts repeated the pattern of requiring federal trial courts, for the most part, to apply the procedure of the state in which the federal court sat. Therefore, absent applicable federal law, state substantive and procedural law applied in both state and federal courts. Put another way, there was substantial intrastate uniformity.

Until 1872, the Conformity Acts were what have been called "static conformity acts," for they required the federal courts to apply the state procedural law in existence at the time the federal act was passed. It was thought to be unwise, if not unconstitutional, to permit the states to effectively pass laws that would become federal laws of procedure. The problem was thought to be mitigated if Congress could look at the procedure of the states at the time of any one conformity act, and then vote to conform the federal procedure to the state procedure as of that date.

By 1872, it was clear that the static conformity acts presented some severe problems for practitioners. Most lawyers were applying procedural provisions similar to the Field Code in their state courts, but were required to apply out-moded state common law procedures in federal court. In the Conformity Act of 1872, Congress moved to what is called "dynamic conformity," requiring federal courts, for the most part, to apply the same procedural law of the state that the state courts would then apply, thus keeping the federal courts up to date—in a dynamic way—with the then-current state procedures. The same procedure would apply in suits at common law whether the matter was pending in a state or a federal court; this is referred to as intrastate procedural uniformity.

Yet for several practical reasons, lawyers in federal court in their own state could not just apply the state procedural law with which they were familiar. The Conformity Act of 1872 provided that the federal trial judges should conform the federal procedure to state procedure "as near as may be." Federal judges used this language to apply some *federal* procedures that they favored, such as rules permitting them to supervise, if not control, juries through instructions and the granting of new trial motions. The Conformity Act (along with the Supremacy Clause and the exception clause of the Rules of Decision Act) also obligated federal trial judges to apply any specific procedural laws that Congress had passed for the federal courts.

The potential for state-federal court procedural uniformity was further eroded by equity practice in the federal courts. In 1789, when the first process act was passed, equity jurisdiction, jurisprudence, and procedure either did not exist or were underdeveloped in many state courts. Therefore, in some states, there would be little or no distinct equity law to which the federal courts could conform. The solution in the succession of process and conformity acts was to have federal courts apply historical equity law, and not state law, in equity cases. The Supreme Court adopted specific procedural rules for equity cases to be applied in the federal trial courts. The Supreme Court adopted the Federal Equity Rules of 1912, which became effective in 1913, to replace the outdated Equity Rules of 1842, which had been drafted to operate in the context of historical equity practice. The opinion of most contemporaneous commentators was that the Equity Rules of 1912 were simple and efficient, and greatly improved equity practice by appropriately freeing judges from procedural technicalities. A system of procedural rules that applied to federal cases in equity created interdistrict uniformity (albeit at the expense of intrastate uniformity).

b. The Rules Enabling Act and the Drafting of the Federal Rules of Civil Procedure

After the turn of the twentieth century, reformers demanded a new procedure that would apply uniformly across all federal district courts. They premised their position on the failure of the conformity acts to provide intrastate procedural uniformity, and the efficacy of the Equity Rules of 1812 as a model for interdistrict procedural uniformity. Reformers also promised that federal rules of procedure would be so enlightened and simple that intra-state uniformity would follow naturally as states voluntarily adopted the federal model.

Starting in 1911, the American Bar Association (ABA), at the urging of a Virginia lawyer, Thomas Wall Shelton, lobbied in Congress for a bill that would enable the Supreme Court to promulgate uniform procedural rules for all district courts — an "Enabling Act." What Shelton's call for procedural uniformity lacked in modesty and nuance, it supplied in passion:

> [Uniformity is] so splendid, so beautiful and so beneficial in every respect, as to command unstintedly the loving labor, time and treasure of the best men of this marvelous age in which we live. There must be . . . uniformity of judicial procedure. . . . There are agencies at work too earnest and powerful to be thwarted by ignorance, pessimism or evil. . . . I have the most implicit faith in the Divine origin of the great basic principles, and fundamentals of the law that governed the Hebrews, were used by the Athenians, borrowed by the Romans, reluctantly absorbed by the English and are being adopted in America. And I believe they have existed since God said "Let there be light," coincident with the laws of nature and of the universe. . . . [Uniformity] symbolize[s] an unselfish love of country and a surrender of personal inclinations that will . . . solidify sentiment and reincarnate the old time respect and veneration for the courts.

Thomas Wall Shelton, *Uniformity of Judicial Procedure and Decision*, 22 Law Student's Helper 5, 9 (1914).

Many of the arguments for reform were based on the often cited, and little read, 1906 address of Roscoe Pound, then Dean of the Nebraska College of Law School, to the annual meeting of the ABA. In his historic address on *The Causes of Popular Dissatisfaction with the Administration of Justice*, 29 A.B.A. Rep. 395, 409-413 (1906), Pound — in addressing the topic suggested by the title of his speech — argued that the public was mistaken in its criticisms of the judiciary. The problem was not the power of judges under our constitutional system to hold legislative enactments unconstitutional, nor was it that judges were inevitably thrown into political controversy as a result of our tripartite government. According to Pound, much of the real fault was procedure, particularly "contentious procedure," and the "sporting theory of justice" whereby lawyers took advantage of procedural technicalities that stood in the way of justice. During the decade starting in 1905, he argued that it was the formalism of the common law writ system (which in his view survived the Field Code) and its rigid and inflexible procedural steps that hindered the just application of substantive law and the adjustment of law to modern circumstances. Pound complained that American judges were unduly constrained by procedural rules designed to control them and handicapped by their inability to "search independently for truth and justice." Pound thus turned to equity as a model for expanded judicial discretion and for more liberal principles of pleading and joinder in order to meet the needs of modern jurisprudence.

In almost every year between 1912 and 1932, the ABA proposed in Congress a bill for an Enabling Act that would authorize the Supreme Court to draft uniform federal rules. President and later Chief Justice William Howard Taft, presidential candidate and later Chief Justice Charles Evan Hughes, virtually every luminary in the American Bar Association, and legions of local bar leaders and law school scholars supported the ABA effort. But for twenty years the bill was usually held up in the Senate Judiciary Committee, and on one occasion killed on the floor, because of the determined opposition of Senator Thomas Walsh. Walsh was a Montana Progressive Democrat who was first elected to the Senate in 1912, at the same time Woodrow Wilson was elected President. Walsh famously led the Teapot Dome scandal investigation, and later chaired both the 1924 and 1932 Democratic National Conventions. Walsh was a brilliant constitutional and trial lawyer, who argued and wrote passionately for the confirmation of Louis D. Brandeis to the Supreme Court, for judicial recall, against judicial control of juries, and for enhancing jury power in labor disputes.

Walsh had many objections to proposals for an Enabling Act that would empower the Supreme Court to promulgate uniform federal procedural rules. A trip to England and its courts had convinced him that legal culture was considerably more influential than procedural rules on the professional conduct of lawyers. He thought, based on his own experience as a trial lawyer in Montana, that the Conformity Act rarely caused procedural uncertainty and that the Field Code, which had been adopted in his state, worked well. He argued that uniform federal rules, as opposed to conforming to state practice, would prejudice the vast majority of lawyers because, although they knew their state procedure, they rarely appeared in federal court. Walsh thought that Supreme Court members, far removed from the trial of cases, were ill-adapted for what he saw as the legislative function of procedural rule making. Finally, he urged that equity rules, which he correctly assumed would form the basis for new uniform federal rules, were complex in practice and would not lead to uniformity and simplicity as the Enabling Act proponents contended. Walsh's death on the way to President Franklin Roosevelt's inauguration in 1933, after which Walsh was to have been sworn in as Attorney General, removed the major opponent to uniform federal procedural rules. In 1932, the ABA gave up trying to get Congress to pass an Enabling Act. Homer Cummings, Franklin Roosevelt's first Attorney General, was perfectly typecast to resubmit the Enabling Act to Congress in 1934, after conservatives had failed to accomplish its passage for twenty years. This Democratic liberal spokesperson was, like Taft and Hughes, familiar with big cases and with clients that were major banks, corporations, and utilities. When he sponsored the Act in 1934, he invoked the then-familiar themes: Now was the time for lawyers to give up their technical rules and to aid the government in drafting and implementing new legislation to solve national problems.

In 1934, the Enabling Act was passed with only modest resistance. It is now found in 28 U.S.C. § 2072. At first, the Supreme Court seemed reluctant to centralize the drafting of uniform federal rules or to take advantage of a provision in the Enabling Act that permitted the Court to merge law and equity procedure. During the first six months of 1935, Charles E. Clark, professor and later the dean at Yale Law School, lobbied vigorously and effectively to have the Supreme Court exercise its authority under the Enabling Act to adopt the same procedural rules for both law and equity cases, to have those rules patterned on equity practice (particularly on the Federal Equity Rules of 1912), and to have a centralized drafting committee of experts to accomplish these aims. Later in 1935, the Supreme Court appointed a fourteen-person committee "to Draft Unified System of Equity and Law Rules," which became known as the Advisory Committee. 295 U.S. 774 (1935).

The composition of the Advisory Committee that drafted the Federal Rules of Civil Procedure reflected both the political conservatives and the academic liberals who had joined in supporting uniform federal rules. Clark and other legal academics were joined by nine lawyers, most of whom were in large firm practice or were active participants in the ABA—in most cases, both. The chairman of the committee, William D. Mitchell, had been Solicitor General under President Coolidge and Attorney General under President Hoover before setting up his partnership in New York.

The drafters of the Federal Rules wanted cases to be resolved on the merits. Yet it appears that the drafters had little faith in the ability of procedure to engineer that result. In the first and second eras, procedure was so rigid and technical that it led to dismissals based upon technicalities. In the third era, the drafters cast procedure more as a villain or a necessary evil, rather than as a solution or a savior. The Federal Rules, which became law in 1938, minimized judicial interference with the natural course of litigation as dictated by the attorneys, embracing notice pleading, broad discovery, broad joinder of parties and claims, and ease of amendment. Notice pleading eliminated the technical rigors of common law and code-pleading regimes that undermined substantive law. Broad discovery guaranteed that both parties would have full information. Broad joinder facilitated complete justice among all interested parties. And ease of amendment ensured a dynamism that would keep the focus on the merits.

WANT TO KNOW MORE?

The most comprehensive history of the Enabling Act is provided in Stephen Burbank, *The Rules Enabling Act of 1934*, 130 U. Pa. L. Rev. 1015 (1982). This meticulously researched and reasoned article also provides in its footnotes exhaustive cites to historical material on the Process and Conformity Acts. For a thorough exploration of the early process acts and the Rules of Decision Act, *see* J. Goebel, *History of the Supreme Court of the United States: Antecedents and Beginnings to 1801* (1971).

QUESTIONS TO PONDER

1. How is it that the combination of conservatives and liberals on the Advisory Committee agreed also with Pound, Taft, Shelton, and the ABA leadership on the trajectory of this procedural reform? Yet this

effort did not include Walsh, even though he and Clark would otherwise have been political allies. Were these Federal Rules not political? Or perhaps not obviously political? Or maybe the political consequences were not predictable?

2. In the debate over the Enabling Act and in discussions surrounding the drafting of the Federal Rules, there was very little explicit talk about the fact that the Rules (or procedural options within the Rules) were the same for all cases (trans-substantive civil procedure). There was, of course, a good deal of discussion concerning the merger of law and equity. How, then, did this procedural choice of trans-substantive rules come about? Was it inherent in the proponents' other assumptions about civil procedure?

c. Trans-Substantive Procedure and Politics

We saw in the context of motions to dismiss that asymmetries may deny certain types of plaintiffs the information that they may need to survive a (trans-substantive) pleading standard. Does (should) civil procedure knowingly favor some types of litigants or some types of cases? Is trans-substantive procedure a neutral and apolitical procedure? For a discussion of these issues on the occasion of the fiftieth anniversary of the Federal Rules of Civil Procedure, *see* Stephen N. Subrin, *Fireworks on the Fiftieth Anniversary of the Federal Rules of Civil Procedure*, 73 Judicature 4 (1989). *See also* 137 U. Pa. L. Rev. 1873-2257 (1989) (symposium issue); Stephen N. Subrin, *The Limitations of Transsubstantive Procedure: An Essay on Adjusting the "One Size Fits All" Assumption,* 87 Denv. U. L. Rev. 377 (2010). For a careful examination of a departure from the trans-substantive design of the Federal Rules by judicial decisions that create substance-specific procedure, *see* Margaret B. Kwoka, *Judicial Rejection of Trans-substantivity: the FOIA Example,* 15 Nev. L.J. 1493 (2015).

d. Procedural Rulemaking

The current procedural rulemaking provisions are contained in 28 U.S.C. §§ 2071-2072. A wonderful resource for understanding the rulemaking process is the United States Courts' Web site, *http://www.uscourts.gov/rules-policies* (last visited July 1, 2019). Proposals for amendments to the Federal Rules of Civil Procedure are first considered and drafted in the Advisory Committee on Civil Rules and are then reviewed, with the power to change them, in the Standing Committee on Rules of Practice and Procedure. There are also Advisory Committees on Criminal, Bankruptcy, Evidence, and Appellate Rules. The Chief Justice appoints members to the Advisory Committees and the Standing Committee.

The Standing Committee proposes rules to the Judicial Conference of the United States, which in turn proposes rules to the Supreme Court. The Judicial Conference of the United States is defined in 28 U.S.C. § 331. It begins:

> The Chief Justice of the United States shall summon annually the chief judge of each judicial circuit, the chief judge of the Court of International Trade and a district judge from each judicial circuit to a conference at such time and place in the United States as he may designate. He shall preside at such conference which shall be known as the Judicial Conference of the United States.

The Supreme Court decides what, if any, rules to present to Congress. In accordance with Title 28, § 2072, "[s]uch rules shall not take effect until they have been reported to Congress by the Chief Justice at or after the beginning of a regular session thereof but not later than the first day of May, and until the expiration of ninety days after they have been thus reported." Congress has specifically refused to allow some amendments to become law by this method of inaction, and, although infrequently, has even passed its own rule. Given these exceptions, Federal Rules of Civil Procedure are not actually statutes, for they have not gone through the normal congressional committee process, been voted on by both houses, or signed by the President. Section 2072, however, does state that "all laws in conflict with such rules shall be of no further force or effect after such rules have taken effect."

The politicization of the rulemaking process is explored in Jeffrey Stempel, *Ulysses Tied to the Generic Whipping Post: The Continuing Odyssey of Discovery "Reform,"* 64 Law & Contemp. Probs. 197 (2001) (using discovery "reform" in 2000 as his prime example). *See also* Martin H. Redish and Umu M. Amuluru, *The Supreme Court, The Rules Enabling Act, and the Politicization of the Federal Rules: Constitutional and Statutory Implications*, 90 Minn. L. Rev. 1303 (2006); Richard D. Freer, *The Continuing Gloom About Federal Judicial Rulemaking*, 107 Nw. U. L. Rev. 447 (2013).

4. Are We Now in a Fourth Era?

The set of procedural rules that launched the third era—the Federal Rules of Civil Procedure—are still formally intact. Yet waves of profound, correlated, and enduring reforms have engulfed the core values of those Rules, thereby establishing de facto what appears to be a new fourth era in the history of American civil procedure.

The third era was premised on the notion that, once the parties learned the relevant facts, cases would either settle or go to trial. Judges had a limited role in this process: (1) ensure that both parties had access to all relevant facts; and (2) for those cases that did not settle, preside over a trial. Judges had very limited authority to dismiss the case prior to the discovery of relevant facts, and judges would rarely enter a summary judgment. Judges tried cases. In 1951, the federal courts tried more than 5,000 civil cases—about 12.5 percent of the total number of terminated cases. Throughout the 1980s, federal courts tried more than 10,000 civil cases per year. Most cases settled.

A fourth era emerged through a number of reforms, most of which were initiated by judges through new interpretations of extant rules. Experiencing something of a role reversal, judges in the fourth era play a significant role at each stage of litigation except for trials. Indeed, trials have all but disappeared. Instead, in the fourth era: (1) as you have seen earlier in this chapter, the motion to dismiss has a screening function that terminates some cases (and chills others); (2) as you will see in Chapter 4, the discovery stage is harder to reach, and broad discovery harder to obtain; and (3) as you will see in Chapter 5, the summary judgment is the "focal point" of litigation. In this new, fourth era, fewer than 2,500 civil cases are tried in federal courts each year—an amount that is about 1 percent of the total number of terminated cases. As a point of reference, there are about 2,500 major league baseball games played each year. Major league baseball is played in only nineteen states (including Canada)—and it is a seasonal sport that is played about half the year. As in the third era, most cases in the fourth era settle; but the important difference is that rather than cases settling in the shadow of a trial, they now settle in the shadow of a sword of Damocles.

It is difficult to untangle the many forces that conspired to produce this fourth era. Also, conspicuously absent from the history of the fourth era is the policy debate that should occur when lawmakers and the public are presented with a choice between the competing visions of the third and fourth eras. Procedure is power, of course, so choosing one over the other means different winners and losers. In a debate, the trade-offs between the two visions would be explored, the empirical data gathered, and the interested constituencies consulted. Yet that debate never happened.

The absence of such a debate also makes a history of the fourth era more difficult to write: There was no specific moment when it was passed, no legislative history revealing its purpose, and no anointed leaders personifying it. Another barrier to a complete understanding of the historical origins of the fourth era is the fact that we are still in it. Accordingly, any description of it necessarily lacks the objectivity and distance that tend to improve historical accounts. Still, three strands seem demonstrably true. First, just as prior to the third era all signs pointed to liberal equity procedure for the new Federal Rules, as one looks back to the 1970s, most paths instead lead to a more constrictive procedure and a reduction of live, oral participation in the civil litigation process. Second, the very liberality of the original Federal Rules, accompanied by rights-granting federal legislation and the civil and consumer rights movements, provides one cluster of causal links to the intense backlash of constriction. And third, although conservative ideology and actors played a significant role in bringing this new era to fruition, conservatives did not act alone.

In the bullet points that follow, we identify some of the forces that powered the transition from the third era to the fourth.

- Between the 1960s and 1990s, Congress significantly expanded the scope of federal jurisdiction and created hundreds of new causes of action. In the three decades leading up to 1969, the civil caseloads of federal courts grew at a modest average annual rate of approximately 3.4 percent. But in the 1970s, the average annual rate of growth was 7.4 percent. And from 1980 to 1985, the average annual rate of growth was 10.1 percent. (Since 1985, there has been essentially no growth.) Of course, the number of federal judges has also increased over time. But between 1969 and 1983, the average federal judge doubled the number of cases she terminated each year.

- The increase in the number of filings was fueled in part by an increase in the number of lawyers. The number of lawyers nearly doubled between 1970 and 1984 — a growth rate three times faster than that of other professions and four times faster than the general population. An entrepreneurial plaintiffs' bar emerged. And as the size of law firms grew, an appetite and capacity for bigger and more complex cases followed. Moreover, technology was transforming litigation generally and discovery in particular.

- Judges were also experiencing an increase in the *criminal* docket. Between 1962 and 1975 (a period of time during which the civil docket doubled), the total number of criminal dispositions increased by a factor of 1.5. (Between 1975 and 1983, when the civil docket doubled again, the total number of dispositions in criminal cases actually decreased.) To be sure, however, the Speedy Trial Act of 1974, which required criminal cases to be terminated within sixty days of arraignment, added pressure on judges.

- The judges' reaction to the perception that things were "out of control" was to "take control." Case management became the norm for mega cases during the 1970s, and thereafter, for all cases. The federal judiciary taught effective case management to new federal judges who were brought to the Federal Judicial Center in Washington for an intensive indoctrination with experienced federal judges as their mentors. As one judge-instructor explained in 1971, the purpose of case management is to promote settlement: "[M]y goal is to settle all my cases. I don't subscribe to the theory at all that we should take hold of a case at its inception and labor mightily to bring it to trial only. . . . Most of the time when I try a case I consider that I have somehow failed. . . . [T]he judge must not only explore settlement but must actively pursue it with all the vigor at his command." Fred J. Cassibry, *The Role of the Judge in the Settlement Process, in* Seminars for Newly Appointed United States District Judges 271 (1971). By the mid-1990s, a host of statutory reforms and amendments to the Federal Rules institutionalized case management as a central feature of the federal civil pretrial process.

- For the past few decades, the business community has attacked the allegedly pro-plaintiff aspects of civil litigation. In the 1970s, for example, insurance companies spent millions of dollars in advertisements in national magazines attacking greedy plaintiffs and runaway juries. Reformers have painted a portrait of American civil litigation that is extrapolated from memorable anecdotes and isolated problems. For reasons other than its empirical foundation, an anti-litigation narrative found and still enjoys traction. Indeed, citizens, politicians, law students, lawyers, and judges have internalized the notion that civil litigation is expensive, anti-competitive, arbitrary, and out of control.

- Substantial segments of the population favor withdrawing parts of the social safety net installed by the New Deal and the Great Society. These individuals, who passionately believe in free market solutions, also lament the growth of tort law and the dozens of federal statutes granting private rights of action. Procedural reform can accomplish indirectly what may be harder to achieve through substantive reform.

That systems of civil procedure are influenced by political currents should not surprise us. The Common Law process in England was influenced by the King's desire to centralize the legal system in London. The Field Code was part of American nineteenth-century political maneuvering for a laissez-faire social-economic system. The Federal Rules became law as a New Deal reform. Moreover, in both the instances of the Field Code and the Federal Rule reforms, there was some coalescence of both liberal and conservative thought. In 1976, Chief Justice Burger convened what was called the Pound Conference on Civil Justice Reform, in part commemorating Roscoe Pound's famous procedural reform speech of 1906. In the following excerpts of speeches given at the Pound Conference, you will observe many of the themes that frame the contemporary discourse of civil procedure reform—alternative dispute resolution, discovery, pleading standards, and power. One might fairly suggest that 1976 is the year that the fourth era commenced.

Chief Justice Warren E. Burger, Agenda for 2000 A.D. — A Need for Systematic Anticipation

The Pound Conference: Perspectives on Justice in the Future 23, 29-32 (1979)

The conference we open tonight is significant because it is the first time that the chief justices of the highest state courts, the leaders of the federal courts, leaders of the organized Bar, legal scholars and thoughtful members of other disciplines have joined forces to take a hard look at how our system of justice is working. We will ask whether it can cope with the demands of the future, and being a process of inquiry into needed change. . . . We are not here to deal primarily with specifics and details but with fundamentals. . . .

Whatever risks may be involved in our probing and talking, we must be prepared to take them. There is nothing dangerous about studying and considering basic change, if the alterations will preserve old values and "deliver" justice at the lowest possible cost in the shortest feasible time. I do not, for example, think it subversive to ask why England, the source of all our legal institutions, found it prudent and helpful 40 years ago to abandon jury trials for most civil cases. . . .

[We should not] be surprised at the loss of public confidence caused by lawyers' using the courts for their own ends rather than with a consideration of the public interest. If Pound was correct in his analysis that excessive contentious-ness was an impediment to fair administration of justice in 1906, I doubt that anyone could prove it less so today. Correct or not, there is also a widespread feeling that the legal profession and judges are overly tolerant of lawyers who exploit the inherently contentious aspects of the adversary system to their own private advantage at public expense. The willingness of some of the participants to elevate procedural maneuvering above the search for truth, as Pound said, sends out "to the whole community a false notion of the purpose and end of law." And he saw this as a large factor in the American cynicism about the law and the urge to want to "beat the law.". . . I believe that American lawyers, by and large, are the equal of any in the world, but a handful of members of any profession can inflict harm out of proportion to their number, on both the pub-lic and on the image of their profession.

Other conditions that caused dissatisfaction in 1906 are still with us. Jurors, witnesses and litigants continue to have their time squandered. They are often shuffled about courthouses in confusion caused by poor manage-ment within the courts. The delays and high costs in resolving civil disputes continue to frighten away potential litigants, and those who persist and ulti-mately gain a verdict often see up to half of the recovery absorbed by fees and expenses. . . .

There is nothing incompatible between efficiency and justice. Inefficient courts cause delay and expense, and diminish the value of the judgment. . . . Efficiency—like the trial itself—is not an end in itself. It has as its objective the very purpose of the whole system—to do justice. Inefficiency drains the value of even a just result either by delay or excessive cost, or both.

It is time, therefore, to ask ourselves whether the tools of procedure, the methods of judicial process that developed slowly through the evolution of the common law, and were fitted to a rural, agrarian society, are entirely suited, without change, to the complex modern society of the late 20th and the 21st centuries.

Simon H. Rifkind, Are We Asking Too Much of Our Courts?
The Pound Conference: Perspectives on Justice in the Future 51-63 (1979)

The cause of dissatisfaction which is most important today is [a function] of the peculiarities of the Anglo-American legal system, as they find expression in the environment of our judicial administration.

It is quite easy to document support for the proposition that our courts have become the handymen of our society. The American public today perceives courts as jacks-of-all-trades, available to furnish the answer to whatever may trouble us: Shall we build nuclear plants, and if so, where? Shall the Concorde fly to our shores? How do we tailor dismissal and lay-off programs during the depression, without undoing all of the progress achieved during prosperity by anti-discrimination statutes? All these are now the continuous grist of the judicial mills. . . . Thus, it is not surprising to learn that a lawsuit was recently filed in the Southern District of New York seeking to prevent the United States Postal Service from issuing a commemorative stamp honoring Alexander Graham Bell—on the grounds that someone else invented the telephone.

It is equally easy to compile reports—both state and federal—attesting to the backbreaking burden which the courts are carrying. Students of the subject report that caseloads in both the federal and state courts are increasing at a pace far beyond the growth in population. . . .

It is clear to me that one item on our agenda for the future must include efforts to lighten the workload of the courts if we are to eliminate public dissatisfaction with the administration of justice.

At this point, allow me to lay to rest some apprehension that I have heard expressed about the investigation launched by this conference. A large percentage of the increase in the business which has come into our courts in recent years has related to the protection of civil rights. That circumstance has generated a fear that this conference is conspiring to promote a counterrevolution; in the guise of an inquiry into whether the courts are being asked to do too much, and to do that for which they are ill-equipped, it is suggested we are seeking to erect an impassible barrier against the growing recognition of the rights of the accused, the voter, the consumer, the stockholder, the victims of racial and sexual discrimination; and indeed to reverse the generation-long movement for expansion of their rights.

Let me at once disengage myself from any such enterprise. The exploration of the Constitution, and discovery therein, progressively, of more commands for the humanization of our society have by no means run their course. . . . However, new rights—newly acknowledged and only recently enjoyed—will inevitably supply the pressure for judicial innovation to continue. If that momentum is to proceed without the artificial impediment of overladen courts, we must relieve the courts of burdens that do not require their special expertise.

Innovations of the future, whether the work-product of judges or legislators, will inevitably have to pass through courthouse strainers and filters. If these are clogged and stuffed, the passage is bound to be more sluggish, less reflective, and probably less sagacious.

What I suggest is that the direction of our search should be guided by our view of our courts as institutions of last resort. We should require them to do nothing which other, less irreplaceable institutions can do as well, and, as far as possible, preserve the courts for doing that which cannot be done elsewhere.

There are two main routes we can take toward the goal of lightening the workload of the courts—substantive and procedural.

The most important method of proceeding along the substantive route is to address the question: Shall the courts continue to be not only the dispute-resolvers, but also the problem-solvers of our society?

Heretofore, the accepted model of an American court was that of an institution devoted to the resolution of disputes. . . . The adversary process is a well honed tool for use in such a contest. . . .

Problem-solving is an enterprise of a different sort altogether. The problem-solver finds no refuge in the burden of proof. He does not confine his edict to the parties before him. The consequences of his pronouncement of a solution cannot be confined to tile-sized changes. He frequently administers avulsive changes. Problem-solving is, thus, a chancy business requiring, in a democracy, not only wisdom and inventiveness but a keen perception of the political implications. Moreover, it imposes a duty upon the problem-solver to hear all those who have a significant interest in the problem. Very frequently the problem-solver tends to become a champion of a cause and not a neutral decider. . . .

If we remove problem-solving from the courts, we will improve the administration of the *courts*. To improve the administration of *justice*, we must, in addition, change the manner in which the legislatures and executives respond to difficult social and political problems, so that very few will need to bring them to the courthouse door. The courts should not be the only place in which justice is administered. . . .

We must also explore the procedural route to lessening the burdens on the courts. This route is, of course, one which has often been used both to keep certain business out of the courts and to guide other business through the courts. . . . What more can we do to keep out the worthless, the trivial, and those litigations which, by a definition not yet formulated, ought not to be in the courts? . . .

It would seem to me that the higher threshold in front of the courthouse door should be built on the probable merit of the claim. That suggests the question whether it would be prudent to borrow from our criminal practice and require a civil litigant to show "probable merit" before he cranks into action the prodigious machinery of the judicial process. . . . Further exploration might reveal whether the requirement for such a showing of merit would favorably affect the judicial burden.

Frank E.A. Sander, Varieties of Dispute Processing
The Pound Conference: Perspectives on Justice in the Future 65, 66, 83-84 (1979)

[One] way of reducing the judicial caseload is to explore alternative ways of resolving disputes outside the courts. . . . By and large we lawyers and law teachers have been far too single-minded when it comes to dispute resolution. Of course . . . good lawyers have always tried to prevent disputes from coming about, but when that was not possible, we have tended to assume that the courts are the natural and obvious dispute resolvers. In point of fact there is a rich variety of different processes, which I would submit, singly or in combination may provide far more "effective" conflict resolution. . . .

What I am . . . advocating is a flexible and diverse panoply of dispute resolution processes, with particular types of cases being assigned to differing processes (or combinations of processes). . . . Conceivably such allocation might be accomplished for a particular class of cases at the outset by the legislature; that in effect is what was done by the Massachusetts legislature for malpractice cases. Alternatively one might envision by the year 2000 not simply a courthouse but a Dispute Resolution Center, where the grievant would be channeled through a screening clerk who would then direct him to the process (or sequence of processes) most appropriate to his type of case. The room directory in the lobby of such a Center might look as follows:

Screening Clerk	Room 1
Mediation	Room 2
Arbitration	Room 3
Fact Finding	Room 4
Malpractice Screening Panel	Room 5
Superior Court	Room 6
Ombudsman	Room 7

. . . [One concern is] the need to retain the courts as the ultimate agency capable of effectively protecting the rights of the disadvantaged. This is a legitimate concern which I believe to be consistent with the goals I have advocated. I am not maintaining that cases asserting novel constitutional claims ought to be diverted to mediation or arbitration. On the contrary, the goal is to reserve the courts for those activities for which they are best suited and to avoid swamping and paralyzing them with cases that do not require their unique capabilities.

Laura Nader, Commentary

The Pound Conference: Perspectives on Justice in the Future 114 (1979)

I come to this conference as a citizen, an anthropologist, an outsider to your profession. And I would like to make comments as an outsider. . . . I've been struck by a number of observations here. . . .

One is the absence of data undergirding statements by several people here. Associated with the absence of data is the absence of detachment—the ability to step back and see the problem. Associated with that is the absence of thinking in a broader context. Associated with that is the absence of reality-testing. I also notice in the discussions thus far . . . that there is an absence of a discussion of power. And related to this is an absence of a serious discussion of block solutions. I also find that there is a total lack of self-consciousness in discussing judges as workers—workers who have all the alienation problems that are common to employees and the problems that relate alienation to questions having to do with empathy.

Justice Burger asked us yesterday, to take a hard look at our own system of justice, and how it is working. In fact, we can only take a soft look because of the absence of data. I am puzzled . . . that we really know more about the workings of justice in non-western legal systems than we know about the workings of justice in the United States. We have law trained personnel for whom data means cases. You can't take a serious hard look at the system of justice solely on the basis of cases, although cases are important. . . . [W]e need to understand some things—and basic data is a requirement: we need to know who uses the American legal system; we need to know what it costs to run the system; we need to know whether in fact litigation is increasing at a pace beyond the needs of an industrial society and the growth of population. Some people agree, some people disagree. . . . The first thing that struck me when I began the study of how Americans complain—all we had were anecdotes. We did not have any idea, systematic or unsystematic, about what Americans do with legal problems when they feel they can't take them to court for whatever reason. . . .

I refer here to a *set of mind* which insists that problems of justice be phrased in terms of court case load, and the like—most certainly a problem in developing a just legal system. This is, at the least, a limited technical view. . . .

The most dramatic changes in social relationship in the past hundred years, has to do with the fact that most people's potential disputes are between individuals or between parties who do not know each other and never will. When a complainant has a complaint about General Motors, or about the federal government, or Social Security, or any number of things, these are not problems that can be settled in neighborhood courts. . . .

What is important is that we get some sense of reality, if we're going to make policy. Reality-testing is the way a psychiatrist judges whether somebody's insane or not—to measure the gap between what an individual thinks he is and what he in fact is. We're here to solve problems, and I would say that the first step is to see them. You can't solve them until you see them. I'm concerned that nothing was said yesterday, specifically about alleviating peoples' ills, and I think we need to look at specific examples. . . . It is the details that we should pay attention to. Now we need to understand in this reality-testing, that for example, people are not always equal before the law. People will not always have access to law. People will be afraid to take cases to law, which should go to law, because of extra-legal retaliation. I think these observations need to be considered here. . . .

a. The Role of Procedural Rules

Procedure—in any era or system—mediates a tension between formalism, on one hand, and narrative on the other.

First, procedure is a means, along with substantive law, of reducing the number of variables that the decision maker will consider. Procedural rules provide necessary definition, focus, and constraints. Some would say that the very purpose of law is to provide such formalized definition and restraint. Justice Harlan put it this way in *Boddie v. Connecticut*, 401 U.S. 371, 374 (1971):

> Perhaps no characteristic of an organized and cohesive society is more fundamental than its erection and enforcement of a system of rules defining the various rights and duties of its members, enabling them to govern their affairs and definitively settle their differences in an orderly predictable manner. Without such a "legal system," social organization and cohesion are virtually impossible. . . . Put more succinctly, it is this injection of the rule of law that allows society to reap the benefits of rejecting what political theorists call "the state of nature."

Yet a goal of any system is to do justice based on the facts in each dispute. Human situations and particularly human disputes do not easily lend themselves to rigidity and formalism. The story, what many now call the "narrative," inevitably seeps beyond the narrowness of causes of actions and their elements. Indeed, it may be impossible to understand a claim without knowing the full story that gives rise to it; one meaning of "claim" under the federal rules is the entirety of a transaction or occurrence, and you will find out later in the course that principles of *res judicata* and preclusion law track this understanding. Professor James White, a professor of both law and English at the University of Michigan, has argued that the discipline of law is not unique in its inability to reduce life's circumstances to a selected set of variables captured in words that mean exactly what they say. *See* James B. White, *The Legal Imagination: Studies in the Nature of Legal Thought* (1973). Lawyers, like poets, novelists, and historians, are inevitably telling a story larger than the precise meaning of words. Trial lawyers know that the art of persuasion is in large measure the art of creating and telling stories. As you will soon see, this tension between, on the one hand, the narrowing focus of the story confined by substantive law and procedure and, on the other, the need to tell larger stories is played out in some measure in the history of the different procedures of law courts and equity courts dating back to the Middle Ages.

This tension between formalism and narrative does not take place in a human vacuum. Issues of power underlie many of the most perplexing questions of civil procedure. This is not a recent phenomenon. By establishing the jury in common law courts, for example, the King sought to gain the loyalty of the citizens of England. And by requiring that land disputes be resolved in his courts, rather than in those of barons or the county, the King sought to centralize his emerging nation and bring power to himself. The emerging power of the entrepreneurial class and the desire of lawyers to earn a better living (an issue of professional power) were important factors in the mid-nineteenth-century American procedural reform called the "Field Code."

The drafters of the Federal Rules avoided the "technicalities" that plagued common law and code pleading. Not burdened by rigid rules and strict protocols that would limit their options, judges enjoyed broad discretion. This discretion could be used to facilitate litigation — providing access to plaintiffs who could not afford lawyers, allowing the pursuit of novel causes of action, and tolerating fishing expeditions until the parties and court could determine whether the substantive law had been violated. But that discretion can also be used to deter litigation—requiring plaintiffs to stop and think before invoking the remedial machinery of the federal courts. The third and fourth eras of procedure are both interpreting the same discretionary mandates of the Federal Rules of Civil Procedure.

The Rules' embrace of broad judicial discretion also undermines one of the primary goals of the drafters of the Federal Rules, to wit: procedural uniformity. *See* Stephen B. Burbank, *The Costs of Complexity,* 85 Mich. L. Rev. 1463, 1474 (1987) ("Many of the Federal Rules authorize essentially ad hoc decisions and therefore are trans-substantive in only the most trivial sense."); Stephen B. Burbank, *Pleading and the Dilemmas of "General Rules,"* 2009 Wis. L. Rev. 535. The idea of procedural uniformity (inter-district uniformity) has also been eroded by the proliferation of local rules. *See* Fed. R. Civ. P. 83. The Local Rules Project of the Committee on Rules of Practice and Procedure collected the local rules of all district courts, and reported in 1988:

> The ninety-four district courts currently have an aggregate of approximately 5,000 local rules, not including many "sub-rules," standing orders and standard operating procedures. These rules are extraordinarily diverse and their numbers continue to grow rapidly. To give one stark example, the Central District of California, based in Los Angeles, has about thirty-one local rules with 434 "sub-rules," supplemented by approximately 275 standing orders. At the other extreme, the Middle District of Georgia has only one local rule and just one standing order. These local rules cover the entire spectrum of federal practice, from attorney admission and discipline, through the various stages of trial, including pleading and filing requirements, pre-trial discovery procedures, and taxation of costs.

Report of the Local Rules Project 1 (1989).

The Civil Justice Reform Act of 1990, Pub. L. No. 101-650, Title I, 28 U.S.C. §§ 471-482, virtually mandated procedural diversity from district court to district court, by obligating each district court to implement its own civil justice expense and delay reduction plan within three years after enactment of the legislation. A major purpose of the Act was to encourage courts to experiment with different types of case management systems and also to experiment with a variety of alternative dispute resolution (ADR) methods. The expiration of this Act has also caused a considerable lack of clarity. *See* Carl Tobias, *The Expiration of the Civil Justice Reform Act of 1990,* 59 Wash. & Lee L. Rev. 541 (2002).

F. SANCTIONS

You have now learned about the liberalizing aspects of the pleading rules, which were an important part of the 1938 Federal Rules of Civil Procedure. Yet you have seen that in procedure, revolutions can precipitate counterrevolutions—such as plausibility pleading. In the regime of plausibility pleading, "naked assertions devoid of further factual enhancement" are insufficient to survive a motion to dismiss for failure to state a claim. *Ashcroft v. Iqbal*, 556 U.S. 662, 678 (2009) (Kennedy, J.). Iqbal's allegation that Ashcroft was the "principal architect" of the invidious policy, for example, lacked sufficient factual enhancement and was therefore disregarded by the Court in determining the sufficiency of that complaint. Plaintiff's counsel might well have theories or speculations about additional facts to enhance that specific allegation, but Fed. R. Civ. P. 11 constrains what plaintiff can include.

Federal Rule 11 clarifies that it is the lawyer (not the client) who signs every pleading, motion, or other paper. That signature constitutes a certification to the court of the several representations outlined in Fed. R. Civ. P. 11(b). Carefully review each of the four representations. In its broadest sense, Rule 11 is targeted at frivolous litigation, and is intended to ensure that litigants "stop and think" before filing pleadings, motions, and other papers. Since its inception in 1938, Federal Rule 11 has been substantively changed twice—first in 1983, and then again in 1993. But the Rule continues to be the target of reformers. For a recent reform effort, *see, e.g.,* 2017 Lawsuit Abuse Reduction Act, S. 237, 115th Cong. (2017).

There are six parts of the current and prior versions of the Rule that have drawn (or draw) the most attention:

1. *The triggering conduct.* Reasonable minds disagree about whether a lawyer should be subject to sanctions if she violates the Rule even when acting in good faith. Does the current rule provide that good faith is an acceptable excuse for failing to do reasonable prefiling factual and legal inquiry?

2. *Judicial discretion to sanction.* Some argue that sanctions should be *mandatory* once there has been a violation of the Rule. Does the current Rule give the district court discretion to withhold a sanction notwithstanding a violation of the Rule?

3. *The nature of sanctions.* Sanctions can be monetary or nonmonetary, and the availability of or preference for monetary sanctions can alter litigation behavior by those with novel claims or by those who are risk-averse. When monetary sanctions are allowed, should they be based on the attorneys' fees incurred by the side seeking the sanctions? When monetary sanctions are allowed, another question arises: To whom should the sanction be paid—the court or the other party? What does the current rule provide as to the nature of sanctions?

4. *The timing of the compliance obligation.* A lawyer's signature on a pleading or motion constitutes a series of representations to the court. But are those representations static—meaning that the certifications are accurate (only) at the time the pleading or motion is filed (the "snap-shot" approach)—or are those representations dynamic and continuing thereafter? Again, review the current rule to understand the lawyer's obligation.

5. *The ability to avoid sanctions.* Reasonable minds differ on whether the lawyer should have notice and an opportunity to correct a sanctionable document before a sanction may be imposed. The current rule has what is referred to as a "safe harbor" provision. When does that safe harbor apply and what — exactly — does it require?

6. *The target of sanctions.* The current rule permits the court to impose a sanction on more than simply the attorney who signed the pleading or motion. Who or what else may be sanctioned?

The following case illustrates an application of Federal Rule 11. Use the case to focus, in particular, on exactly what a lawyer certifies to the court when she or he puts her or his signature on a pleading (or motion).

Chaplin v. DuPont Advance Fiber Systems
303 F. Supp. 2d 766 (E.D. Va. 2004), aff'd, 124 Fed. Appx. 771 (4th Cir. 2005)

HUDSON, District Judge:

[In September 2000, DuPont Advance Fiber Systems, DuPont Spruance, and DuPont Textiles & Interiors, Incorporated (collectively, "DuPont") instituted a policy banning the display of offensive symbols on DuPont property. Included in the policy is a ban on the display of the Confederate battle flag on DuPont's Spruance Plant in Richmond, Virginia. Each of the seven plaintiffs is an employee at DuPont's Spruance plant, and each professes to be a Caucasian, a Christian, and a Confederate Southern American. As a result of DuPont's policy, plaintiffs brought a Title VII action, 42 U.S.C.A. §§ 2000e et seq., alleging employment discrimination based upon their national origin (Count I), their religion (Count II), and their race (Count III).

[More specifically, the plaintiffs allege that DuPont committed a number of acts of direct and indirect discrimination against them. At the root of these, it appears, was DuPont's decision, in approximately September of 2000, to issue a ban on the wearing or displaying of Confederate symbols on clothing, newspapers, pictures, photographs, and bumper stickers. Am. Compl. ¶ 40. Thereafter, Jones was ordered to discontinue wearing clothing bearing Confederate symbols. *Id.* at ¶ 39. Lewis was told "it was not a good idea" to wear his Confederate belt buckle. *Id.* at ¶ 41. Oliver was ordered to remove a bumper sticker and window decal from his vehicle. *Id.* at ¶ 42. Ritenour was ordered to remove Confederate bumper stickers from his car "to avoid problems." *Id.* at ¶ 43. Rowlette was told to cease wearing a Confederate t-shirt or risk a reprimand, and he was ordered to sit in the back of the room during an off-site, DuPont-sponsored multi-cultural workshop because he wore such a shirt. *Id.* at ¶ 44. Of his own accord and as a result of the ban, Turley also ceased wearing his Confederate attire. *Id.* at ¶ 45.

[Since then, it appears that each of the plaintiffs has had some discussion with his supervisor about the ban. Defendants' Site Staff Manager, Mike

Mayberry ("Mayberry"), is said to have responded, at one time, with a declaration to Chaplin that, "I'm discriminating against you and there ain't nothing you can do about it. . ." Am. Compl. ¶ 40. On another occasion, Mayberry explained to Turley that the ban was imposed because "the Confederate flag has been declared a hate symbol, is used by the Klan, represents slavery and is offensive to some black employees." *Id.* at ¶ 45. Thereafter, Plaintiffs told their supervisors, managers, and/or co-workers that the DuPont ban discriminates against them based on their national origin, their religion, and their race. *Id.* at ¶ 46.

[Additionally, Plaintiffs Oliver, Lewis, and Jones aver that in July of 2001, the defendants denied their request for approval of a "Heritage Preservation Network," which was to be a network for Confederate Southern Americans. *Id.* at ¶ 38. DuPont apparently supports other such networks, similar in nature, for groups of women, African American, Asian American, Italian American, Greek American, Irish American, Native American, Hispanic, and gay and lesbian employees. *Id.* at ¶ ¶ 38, 48, 49.

[As a result of DuPont's actions, Plaintiffs contend that racial tensions have increased in the plant and that they fear the "potential and dangerous result of this tension." Am. Compl. ¶ 50. Further, DuPont has caused them to "fear the loss of their job and career opportunities," and to suffer from humiliation, embarrassment, and emotional distress. *Id.*

[The District Court for the Eastern District of Virginia dismissed plaintiffs' action as to all counts pursuant to Fed. R. Civ. P. 12(b)(6). Prior to the ruling of the court, DuPont served upon plaintiffs its Rule 11 motion for sanctions, along with a letter requesting that they voluntarily dismiss the action within twenty-one days. Thereafter, when plaintiffs failed to dismiss their claims, DuPont filed its sanctions motion with the district court.]

. . .

I. DEFENDANTS' MOTION FOR RULE 11 SANCTIONS

Within their Rule 11 motion, Defendants argued that Plaintiffs' counsel, Kirk Lyons, Esquire ("Lyons"), should be sanctioned (1) for filing an Amended Complaint that contains claims not warranted by existing law, by a non-frivolous extension, modification, or reversal thereof, or by the establishment of new law; and (2) for filing claims that contain allegations and other factual contentions without current or potential future evidentiary support. At an earlier stage, this Court reviewed Defendants' motion and deferred its ruling pending supplemental briefing on critical sub-issues. Additionally, at that time, the Court raised a third Rule 11 issue, which was whether Lyons's actions, in filing pleadings without having the sponsorship of an attorney admitted to practice in the Eastern District of Virginia, comported with Local Rule 83.1. Subsequently, the parties analyzed all three issues in light of the Rule 11 jurisprudence of the Fourth Circuit.

First, as it relates to pleadings in general, Federal Rule of Civil Procedure 11(b) states that:

By presenting to the court (whether by signing, filing, submitting, or later advocating) a pleading, written motion, or other paper, an attorney . . . is certifying that to the best of the person's knowledge, information, and belief, formed after an inquiry reasonable under the circumstances, —

(1) it is not being presented for any improper purpose, such as to harass or to cause unnecessary delay or needless increase in the cost of litigation;

(2) the claims, defenses, and other legal contentions therein are warranted by existing law or by a nonfrivolous argument for the extension, modification, or reversal of existing law or the establishment of new law; [and]

(3) the allegations and other factual contentions have evidentiary support or, if specifically so identified, are likely to have evidentiary support after a reasonable opportunity for further investigation or discovery. . . .

Fed. R. Civ. P. 11(b). In other words, whether a civil complaint satisfies the requirements of Rule 11 depends upon how it measures up against three criteria. First, the complaint must be filed for a proper purpose. Second, each count of the complaint must have a sufficient basis in law. And third, each of the claims must have a sufficient basis in fact.

With respect to the first factor, Defendants argue that Plaintiffs' "crusading," repeat litigation of identical claims and subject matter, in the face of a number of adverse rulings from various courts and circuits, supports an inference that the immediate litigation was meant to harass DuPont. Under the circumstances of this case, which emphasizes Plaintiffs' claim of national origin discrimination, the Court does not agree.

Rule 11 "is not intended to chill an attorney's enthusiasm or creativity in pursuing factual or legal theories." *See* Fed. R. Civ. P. 11 (notes of advisory committee on 1983 amendment). Likewise, Rule 11 "does not seek to stifle the exuberant spirit of skilled advocacy or to require that a claim be proven before a complaint can be filed." *Cleveland Demolition Co. v. Azcon Scrap Corp.*, 827 F.2d 984, 988 (4th Cir. 1987). "Creative claims, coupled even with ambiguous or inconsequential facts, may merit dismissal, but not punishment." *Davis v. Carl*, 906 F.2d 533, 538 (11th Cir. 1990).

Here, it is the opinion of the Court that, regardless of the merits of the claims, Lyons's purpose in filing the immediate lawsuit was not to harass DuPont but, rather, to create or expand Title VII jurisprudence. As the Fourth Circuit has said, "if a complaint is filed to vindicate rights in court, and for some other purpose, a court should not sanction counsel for an intention that the court does not approve, so long as the added purpose is not undertaken in bad faith and is not so excessive as to eliminate a proper purpose. Thus, the purpose to vindicate rights in court must be central and sincere." *In re Kunstler*, 914 F.2d 505, 518 (4th Cir. 1990), *cert. denied*, 499 U.S. 969 (1991). Whatever Lyons's collateral intentions were, this Court is convinced that he filed the immediate action, on behalf of the plaintiffs, primarily to broaden the Fourth Circuit's interpretation of "national origin" protection. Consequently, the Court finds no proof that Lyons filed this action for an improper purpose.

Second, Defendants request sanctions because Lyons filed the immediate case in spite of the contrary Fourth Circuit ruling in *Terrill v. Chao*, 31 Fed. Appx. 99, 2002 WL 376681 (4th Cir. 2002) (per curiam), *cert. denied*, 537 U.S. 823 (2002). In so arguing, Defendants remind this Court that, in *Terrill*, the Fourth Circuit ruled against Lyons when he argued that Title VII included "Confederate Southern American" as a protected class. In light of *Terrill*, it is Defendants' position that the immediate case "ha[d] absolutely no chance of success under the existing precedent." *Lewin v. Cooke*, 95 F. Supp. 2d 513, 527 (E.D. Va. 2000).

For his part, Lyons concedes that an argument that "has absolutely no chance of success under the existing precedent" may be sanctionable. *Hunter v. Earthgrains Co. Bakery*, 281 F.3d 144, 153 (4th Cir. 2002) (citation omitted). He insists, however, that the precedent precluding the claim must be authoritative. *See Goldstein v. Malcolm G. Fries & Assocs.*, 72 F. Supp. 2d 620, 628 (E.D. Va. 1999). The Fourth Circuit agrees. In *Hogan v. Carter*, 85 F.3d 1113 (4th Cir. 1996), the Fourth Circuit noted that:

> [S]ince unpublished opinions are not even regarded as binding precedent in our circuit, such opinions cannot be considered in deciding whether particular conduct violated clearly established law. . . . We could not allow liability to be imposed . . . based upon unpublished opinions that we ourselves have determined will be binding only upon the parties immediately before the court.

Id. at 1118 (refusing to reject qualified immunity based upon an unpublished opinion that was not directly on point). In this case, although the Court has found no authoritative case law anywhere in the nation to support Plaintiffs' claim of national origin discrimination, neither has it found a single, binding case to the contrary. Thus, this Court cannot say that the plaintiffs' claim is "[un]warranted by existing law or by a nonfrivolous argument for the extension, modification, or reversal of existing law or the establishment of new law." Fed. R. Civ. P. 11(b)(2). Thus, Defendants' motion for sanctions will not be granted on that basis.

On the other hand, when compared with the requirements of Rule 11(b)(3), Lyons's Amended Complaint gives this Court great pause. According to Rule 11(b)(3), before filing Plaintiffs' claims, Lyons was required to assure that "the allegations and other factual contentions [therein had] evidentiary support or, if specifically so identified, [were] likely to have evidentiary support. . . ." Fed. R. Civ. P. 11(b)(3). This means that Lyons was required to conduct a reasonable investigation of the factual bases underlying each of his clients' claims before filing them. *See Cleveland Demolition Co.*, 827 F.2d at 987. When there is no factual basis for a particular claim, that claim violates Rule 11(b)(3). *See In re Kunstler*, 914 F.2d at 516.

In this case, Plaintiffs' amended complaint included three allegations. In sum, it averred that DuPont's ban on the display of the Confederate flag discriminated against them based upon their national origin, their religion, and their race. With respect to Count I, Plaintiffs provided the Court with voluminous facts, both supported and unsupported, purporting to back their claim of national origin discrimination. Irrespective of the merits of that claim, it marginally satisfies Rule 11(b)(3).

[With regard to Count II,] however, the Court is convinced that Lyons had absolutely no factual foundation upon which to base a claim of religious discrimination. [N]owhere in the Amended Complaint did Plaintiffs allege that they had both requested and been denied a religious accommodation. Even Plaintiffs' belated letter-writing effort failed to support such a claim. Accordingly, it is the opinion of this Court that Count II is so lacking in reasonable evidentiary support that the Court must impose Rule 11 sanctions for the filing of that claim.

Likewise, the Court finds that Plaintiffs' Count III racial discrimination claim is neither factually supported nor supportable. The plaintiffs are all Caucasian, but never once did they suggest that DuPont's policy discriminates, directly or indirectly, against Caucasians. On the contrary, Plaintiffs' averred class, Southern Confederate Americans, is multiracial. This fact alone practically eviscerates Plaintiffs' claim that DuPont discriminated against them on the basis of race. Thus, Plaintiffs' amended complaint contains no factual basis whatsoever to support an allegation that DuPont's ban discriminates by race. Lyons's prefiling inquiry could not have revealed otherwise.

Consequently, . . . it is clear that Count III is both frivolous and unwarranted such that it fails to satisfy the requirements of Rule 11(b)(3). . . . [T]he Court . . . grants the Defendants' motion for sanctions on that count.

The purposes of Rule 11 are to compensate the victims of the violation, to punish present litigation abuse, to streamline court dockets, to facilitate court management, and to deter future litigation abuse. *In re Kunstler*, 914 F.2d at 522-23. Whether Counts II and III are the product of bad faith or just poor judgment, it is the opinion of the Court that each is so devoid of merit as to warrant Rule 11 sanctions. Consequently, although the Court denies Defendants' Rule 11 motion for sanctions with respect to Count I of the Amended Complaint, the motion is granted with respect to Counts II and III. Fed. R. Civ. P. 11(b)(3). . . .

[The Court sanctioned counsel for the plaintiffs in the amount of $10,000.]

REVIEW QUESTIONS

1. Rule 11 is not a pleading rule. But (how) does it affect the pleading requirements under Rule 8(a)? Focus, in particular, on 11(b)(3). What role does (and should) *evidence* play in determining the sufficiency of a pleading under Rule 12(b)(6)?

2. If a complaint contains factual allegations that are "specifically . . . identified" as allegations that are likely to "have evidentiary support after a reasonable opportunity for further investigation or discovery," are those allegations included or excluded from the threshold analysis to determine the sufficiency of a complaint under Rules 8(a) and 12(b)(6)?

3. Would Randall Dee's motion to dismiss for failure to state a claim be sanctionable under Rule 11?

4. Is the complaint in *Iqbal* sanctionable?

a. Safe Harbor

The safe harbor provision of the new Rule, albeit a procedural technicality of sorts, has generated a substantial amount of litigation. Review that procedure carefully now. *See* Fed. R. Civ. P. 11(c)(2). Most of these disputes regard circumstances where a litigant has won the case and, thereafter, pursues sanctions, seeking some sort of compensation (or retribution) for the expense and delay caused by the other party's baseless assertions and/or arguments. However, unless the moving party also complied with the safe harbor provisions — thereby giving the other party the opportunity to withdraw or otherwise cure — the court will typically deny the motion. *See, e.g., Penn, LLC v. Prosper Bus. Dev. Corp.*, 773 F.3d 764, 764-765 (6th Cir. 2014); *Islamic Shura Council of S. California v. F.B.I.*, 757 F.3d 870, 872 (9th Cir. 2014).

Importantly, the "safe harbor" does not apply when a court awards a sanction on its own initiative. Fed. R. Civ. P. 11(c)(3). However, "the power of the court under Rule 11 to issue sanctions *sua sponte* without affording the offender the opportunity to withdraw the challenged document in the manner provided in the 'safe harbor' provision Rule 11(c)(1)(A) is akin to the court's inherent power of contempt. . . . [S]*ua sponte* sanctions . . . should issue only upon a finding of subjective bad faith." *Muhammad v. Walmart Stores E., L.P.*, 732 F.3d 104, 108 (2d Cir. 2013).

The safe harbor provision was added by amendment in 1993. When the Supreme Court submitted the amendments (without change) to the Congress, it noted that the transmittal did not "necessarily indicate that the Court itself would have proposed these amendments in the form submitted." Letter from William H. Rehnquist, Chief Justice of the U.S. Supreme Court, to Thomas S. Foley, Speaker of the House of Representatives (April 22, 1993), *reprinted in* 146 F.R.D. 403 (1993). The transmittal of the Promulgated Rules was accompanied by a statement from Justice White challenging the wisdom of the current rule-making process, and a dissent from Justice Scalia (joined by Justice Thomas with respect to amendments to Rule 11) challenging the wisdom of the proposed amendments. *Id.* at 507. With regard to the safe-harbor provision, Justice Scalia wrote:

> It is undeniably important to the Rules' goal of "the just, speedy, and inexpensive determination of every action," Fed. R. Civ. P. 1, that frivolous pleadings and motions be deterred. . . .
>
> In my view, those who file frivolous suits and pleadings should have no "safe harbor." The Rules should be solicitous of the abused (the courts and the opposing party), and not of the abuser. Under the revised Rule, parties will be able to file thoughtless, reckless, and harassing pleadings, secure in the

knowledge that they have nothing to lose: If objection is raised, they can retreat without penalty. The proposed revision contradicts what this Court said only three years ago: "Baseless filing puts the machinery of justice in motion, burdening courts and individuals alike with needless expense and delay. Even if the careless litigant quickly dismisses the action, the harm triggering Rule 11's concerns has already occurred. Therefore a litigant who violates Rule 11 merits sanctions even after a dismissal." *Cooter & Gell v. Hartmarx Corp.*, 496 U.S. 384, 398 (1990).

The proposed Rule also decreases both the likelihood and the severity of punishment for those foolish enough not to seek refuge in the safe harbor after an objection is raised. Proposed subsection (c) makes the issuance of any sanction discretionary, whereas currently it is *required*. Judges, like other human beings, do not like imposing punishment when their duty does not require it, especially upon their own acquaintances and members of their own profession. They do not immediately see, moreover, the system-wide benefits of serious Rule 11 sanctions, though they are intensely aware of the amount of their own time it would take to consider and apply sanctions in the case before them. For these reasons, I think it important to the effectiveness of the scheme that the sanctions remain mandatory.

Finally, the likelihood that frivolousness will even be *challenged* is diminished by the proposed Rule, which restricts the award of compensation to "unusual circumstances," with monetary sanctions "ordinarily" to be payable to the court. . . . As seen from the viewpoint of the victim of an abusive litigator, these revisions convert Rule 11 from a means of obtaining compensation to an invitation to throw good money after bad. The net effect is to decrease the incentive on the part of the person best situated to alert the court to perversion of our civil justice system.

I would not have registered this dissent if there were convincing indication that the current Rule 11 regime is ineffective, or encourages excessive satellite litigation. . . . But the overwhelming approval of the Rule by the federal district judges who daily grapple with the problem of litigation abuse is enough to persuade me that it should not be gutted as the proposed revision suggests. . . .

b. "Bad Faith" Is Not a Necessary Condition

On motion of a party (in contrast to *sua sponte* sanctions), bad faith is ordinarily not a prerequisite to an award of sanctions. In *Chaplin, supra,* Judge Hudson was indifferent as to whether the plaintiffs were acting in bad faith or instead simply had poor judgment. *See also Jackson v. Hall Cnty. Govt., Georgia,* 568 Fed. Appx. 676, 679 (11th Cir. 2014) (holding that the court can impose sanctions for violations of Rule 11, even if the claims were brought in good faith, so long as the attorney failed to conduct a reasonable inquiry). The fact that an attorney has done a good deal of prefiling investigation (150 hours, for example) does not relieve her of potential sanctions when her client's own deposition shows that her case is without factual merit. *See Mercury Air Group, Inc. v. Mansour et al.,* 237 F.3d 542 (5th Cir. 2001).

MORE TO PONDER

The benefits of a sanctions rule must be weighed against its costs. Consider the cost and value of satellite litigation about a litigant's purpose (11(b)(1)), whether an argument to change the law is nonfrivolous (11(b)(2)), or whether an allegation is likely to have evidentiary support (11(b)(3)).

c. The Chilling Effect of Sanctions

The threat of sanctions can have a chilling effect. Indeed, the very purpose of the Rule is to encourage lawyers to stop and think before filing. But especially in prior iterations of this Rule, the concern was that it would be heavily pro-defendant and especially detrimental to plaintiffs (like civil rights plaintiffs) who may need discovery before they can evaluate the strength of their claim. *See, e.g.,* Melissa L. Nelkin, *Sanctions Under Amended Federal Rule 11—Some "Chilling" Problems in the Struggle Between Compensation and Punishment,* 74 Geo. L.J. 1313 (1986). The only thorough empirical analysis, which surveyed one year of practice (in 1987-1988) in the U.S. Court of Appeals for the Third Circuit (under an old version of Rule 11), revealed that (1) practitioners' behavior was affected by the Rule; (2) motions for sanctions were made in 0.5 percent of civil cases; (3) sanctions were imposed pursuant to 13.6 percent of motions; (4) plaintiffs were twice as likely as defendants to be the target of a motion; (5) plaintiffs were sanctioned in 15.9 percent of the motions in which they are targeted; and (6) defendants were sanctioned in 9.1 percent of the motions in which they are targeted. There was also evidence that in civil rights cases, plaintiff were more likely to be the targets, and much more likely to be sanctioned. *See* American Judicature Society, *Rule 11 in Transition: The Report of the Third Circuit Task Force on Federal Rule of Civil Procedure 11* (Stephen B. Burbank, Reporter, 1989). The 1993 amendment to Rule 11 that added the safe harbor provision was drafted to moderate the chilling effect. Even after 1993, some commentators expressed concern about the Rule's chilling effect. *See* Jeffrey W. Stempel, *Contracting Access to the Courts: Myth or Reality? Boon or Bane?,* 40 Ariz. L. Rev. 965, 994 (1998); Danielle Kie Hart, *Still Chilling After All These Years: Rule 11 of the Federal Rules of Civil Procedures and Its Impact on Civil Rights Plaintiffs After the 1993 Amendments,* 37 Val. U. L. Rev. 1 (2002). But those concerns are now wrapped inside the debate about the pleading standard.

d. Monetary and Nonmonetary Sanctions

The 1993 Advisory Committee Notes suggest the following nonmonetary sanctions: (1) striking the offending paper; (2) issuing an admonition; (3) requiring participation in seminars or other educational programs; and (4) referring the matter to disciplinary authorities. Some judges have been more creative. *See, e.g., Patsy's Brand, Inc. v. I.O.B. Realty, Inc.,* Misc. Action No. 02-194, 2002 WL 59434

(S.D.N.Y. Jan. 16, 2002) (requiring dissemination of the district court's opinion to each lawyer in the represented firm, accompanied by a memorandum regarding ethics); *Balthazar v. Atlantic City Med. Center*, 279 F. Supp. 2d 574, 595 (D.N.J. 2003) (ordering plaintiff's counsel to attend and complete two continuing legal education courses, one in court practice and procedure and one in attorney professionalism); *Curran v. Price*, 150 F.R.D. 85 (D. Md. 1993) (ordering counsel to copy, in his own handwriting, a chapter of a procedure treatise). Of course, there are limits on a trial judge's discretion to sanction. *See In re Tutu Wells Contamination Litig.*, 120 F.3d 368, 381-385 (3d Cir. 1997) (district court did not have power to require sanctioned party to contribute to halfway house, since sanction was legislative in nature); *Whelan v. Heffler, Radetich & Saitta, LLP*, No. 3:99-CV-0337-P, 1999 WL 818749, at *5 (N.D. Tex. Oct. 13, 1999) (lifetime permanent injunction enjoining attorney from local bankruptcy practice was excessive).

The emphasis on nonmonetary directives reflects the Advisory Committee's reluctance to see Rule 11 become a fee-shifting device. *See* Fed. R. Civ. P. 11(c)(4). What is wrong with the goal of compensation in addition to that of deterrence? Is the Committee afraid that attorneys will bring questionable Rule 11 motions? Wouldn't the threat of a countermotion under Rule 11 take care of that?

e. State Procedure

In 1982, Professor John Oakley of the University of California used a nine-variable test to determine which states had procedural rules that "replicated" the Federal Rules. He found that in 1975, Massachusetts became the last of twenty-two states plus the District of Columbia to conform its procedure substantially to the Federal Rules through judicially promulgated rules; if one included statutorily adopted versions of the Federal Rules, there were four additional states, making a total of twenty-six. However, of the ten most populous states, only Ohio was a replica state. John B. Oakley and Arthur F. Coon, *The Federal Rules in State Courts: A Survey of State Court Systems of Civil Procedure*, 61 Wash. L. Rev. 1367 (1986). *See also* John B. Oakley, *A Fresh Look at the Federal Rules in State Courts*, 3 Nev. L.J. 354 (Winter 2002/2003).

States that adopted the Federal Rules have not necessarily kept in lockstep with amendments to the federal model. As a result, navigating the procedure in the state courts can be like walking through a time machine that transports one to an earlier era of federal procedure. If one were to travel from Ohio to Kentucky to West Virginia, one could sample practice under the text of three different versions of Federal Rule 11, namely circa pre-1983, circa 1983-1993, and circa post-1993, respectively. Yet all three of these states are generally thought to be among the category of states that follow the federal model. State replication is also an issue with respect to federal court interpretations (and reinterpretations) of Federal Rules. Consider plausibility pleading, for example. *See, e.g., Walsh v. U.S. Bank, N.A.*, 851 N.W.2d 598, 603 (Minn. 2014) ("we . . . decline to engraft the plausibility standard from *Twombly* and *Iqbal*," notwithstanding a state rule that has identical text to the Federal Rule). *See generally* Zachary D. Clapton, *Procedural Retrenchment and the States*, 106 Cal. L. Rev. 411 (2018).

> ### QUESTIONS TO PONDER
>
> What are the advantages of uniform state and federal rules (and interpretations of those rules)? Does intrastate procedural uniformity compromise other procedural values?

f. Frivolous Litigation

The materials in this chapter lend the impression that there is an abundance of frivolous litigation in the present court system. This may or may not be true. Because there has been little data collected regarding the behavior of the court system, no one really knows. Michael Saks, a law professor at Arizona State University, summarized much of the literature on this subject in the seminal law review article, *Do We Really Know Anything About the Behavior of the Tort Litigation System — And Why Not?*, 140 U. Pa. L. Rev. 1147 (1992). His introductory words epitomize the article: "Much of what we know about the tort litigation system is untrue, unknown, or unknowable." *Id.*

In response to a 2011 version of a bill named the Lawsuit Abuse Reduction Act, which resembles the aforementioned 2017 iteration of the bill of the same name, Professor Lonny Hoffman wrote the following about the prevalence of frivolous litigation.

> There is an abundance of high-quality research, to which anyone interested in reliable data may turn, that shows the claims of [the Act's] supporters are, at the least, greatly exaggerated. The predominant view in the literature is that there is no credible evidence that has been presented that "frivolous" litigation poses a serious problem. Some of the best-known works exposing the absence of hard proof in the claims of tort reformers are by Marc Galanter, but there are quite a few other works to consult as well.
>
> Stephen Burbank, Sean Farhang, and Herbert Kritzer have concisely summed up the state of academic research on the problem of "frivolous" litigation in a recent paper discussing private law enforcement. As they observe, "[c]areful studies demonstrate that the 'litigation explosion' and 'liability crisis' are largely myths."
>
> The predominant academic view about the incidence of "frivolous" litigation is consistent with the views of a vast majority of federal judges. In 2005, in the same survey in which the FJC asked federal judges their views of current Rule 11, they also asked judges to assess how much of a problem "frivolous" cases were in the federal courts. What the FJC researchers found was the 85% of judges thought frivolous lawsuits were either "[n]o problem," a "[v]ery small problem," or a "[s]mall problem."

Lonny Hoffman, *The Case Against the Lawsuit Abuse Reduction Act of 2011,* 48 Hous. L. Rev. 545, 571-573 (2011) (citations and footnotes omitted).

g. Other Sources of Authority to Sanction

Rule 11 is not the only means to sanction improper conduct in the federal courts. Because Rule 11 is inapplicable to discovery disputes (*see* Rule 11(d)), courts use Rule 37 to enforce the discovery rules. (And remember that Federal Rule 26(g) is the analogue to Federal Rule 11 in the discovery context.) Further, 28 U.S.C. § 1927 permits the court to make attorneys liable for excessive "costs, expenses and attorneys fees reasonably incurred because of such unreasonable and vexatious conduct." *Id.* A court can also "rely on its inherent power" to impose appropriate sanctions to control its proceedings. *Chambers v. NASCO, Inc.*, 501 U.S. 32, 50 (1991). Awards of attorneys' fees pursuant to a court's inherent authority to sanction typically require a finding of bad faith.

PRACTICE EXERCISE NO. 12: REVIEWING THE *WARNER* ANSWER UNDER RULE 11

Re-read the introductory memorandum and the Complaint in the *Warner v. City of New York* Case Files. You are an intern in the law firm that represents the plaintiffs. Your supervising attorney has sent you a memo that contains the following text:

> We recently received Defendants' answer to our complaint. Defendants' answer denied sufficient knowledge or information on a few paragraphs of the complaint that we think they may have had an obligation to admit.
>
> Please review, in particular, paragraphs 52-57 of our Complaint and of the defendants' Answer. With respect to the statistics, remember that these data were gathered by NYPD officers and, pursuant to defendant's policies and a settlement in a prior case, were reported to Defendants City, Commissioner Kelly, and Mayor Bloomberg. In other words, we are quoting data that they gathered and reported.
>
> As the lawyers for plaintiffs, we are thinking about sending over a safe harbor warning to defendants regarding these specific paragraphs. What exactly must that notice include? Do you think that their responses to these paragraphs warrant a Rule 11 notice? If you were the defendants' lawyers, do you think that you would have had an obligation to admit these paragraphs? What is the strategic or tactical value of our sending them this notice?

G. SIMPLE JOINDER

When drafting a complaint, a lawyer must think not only about her causes of action or claims, but also about how many claims to join against the same defendant, and how many plaintiffs and defendants to include in one suit. As usual, there are three different types of questions: What must I do? What may I do? And what should I do?

In federal court, the breadth of permissible joinder of claims is fairly simple. Fed. R. Civ. P. 18 provides that a plaintiff can include as many claims against a defendant as she wants, even if they are totally unrelated. You can sue someone for breaching a contract with you, slandering you, defrauding you, and negligently running you over, even if these happened on different dates and are not connected in any way. Rule 42(b), however, allows a judge to separate claims for trial for reasons of convenience, avoiding prejudice, and economy. When you later study *res judicata* and claim preclusion, you will find that the joinder of claims is a bit less friendly than Rule 18 implies. If you do not bring all of your potential causes of action and remedies that arise from the same transaction at the same time (sometimes called "splitting your claim"), a final judgment will normally result in your not being able to bring those other causes of action or remedies later.

This concept of "transaction" pervades joinder issues, as well as other questions in federal procedure. At common law and under the Field Code, joinder of both claims and parties in law cases was severely limited. The joinder provisions, and the interpretation of those provisions by most courts, tended to prohibit joinder unless the writs or causes of action were the same and unless there were joint interests or joint ownership between the plaintiffs or defendants who were to be joined. In equity, the courts tended to permit, and often require, the joinder of all parties who played a part in the underlying factual situation giving rise to the litigation and of all equitable claims falling within that fact pattern. (In later equity practice, legal claims could be joined to equity claims in equity court.) Convenience was the key, rather than strict analytic cubbyholes such as provided by writs. Rule 26 of the Federal Equity Rules of 1912 had a catchall provision that permitted joinder of causes of action if "sufficient grounds . . . appear[ed] for uniting causes of action in order to promote the convenient administration of justice." The Rule ended with language familiar to the current federal court litigator: "If it appears that any such causes of action cannot be conveniently disposed of together, the court may order separate trials."

Rule 20, covering the permissive joinder of parties, is, like the pleading provisions and Rule 18, a further example of how Charles Clark and the others who drafted the Federal Rules attempted to liberalize litigation practice by making it more permissive, flexible, and inclusive. Once again, they turned to an idea prevalent in equity practice, the seeking of a convenient litigation package, rather than worrying whether the causes of action were identical. Rule 20 requires that the persons joining or joined in an action have rights "arising out of the same transaction, occurrence, or series of transactions or occurrences," and that there be a common "question of law or fact." Rule 20(b) permits the court to separate parties for purposes of trial or otherwise.

You have previously encountered the terms "transaction" and "occurrence" (along with "conduct") in Rule 15(c), with respect to whether an amendment subsequent to the expiration of the statute of limitations can "relate back" to the date of the original pleading. "Transaction" and "occurrence" appear again in Rule 13's definition of compulsory counterclaims, identifying claims that must be brought with an answer or otherwise be waived; in defining permissible "cross-claims" (claims between co-defendants) in Rule 13(g); and in portions of Rule 14, covering third-party practice. You have already read how this concept of the "same transaction" sets the contours for modern claim preclusion law. When you study subject matter jurisdiction, you will learn how the concept of pendent jurisdiction (now called supplemental jurisdiction) also looks to the underlying transaction in order to discern whether a state claim that lacks subject matter jurisdiction on its own can be constitutionally "appended" to a companion federal question claim; basically, if they arise from the same trans-action (for this purpose called "the same nucleus of operative facts," which may be somewhat different from the same transaction), the state claim can ride the back of the federal, and stay in federal court.

Consequently, it is important that you begin to learn to make arguments about what constitutes the same transaction or occurrence. The courts tend to look to whether there is a sufficient overlap of facts or evidence, and to whether claims are logically related to each other. You will want to emphasize different points dependent on the purpose of the Rule's use of the term "transaction." For exam-ple, is the Rule or concept that utilizes a transactional test in your case concerned with efficiency, fairness, convenience, or constitutional restraint? It is conclusory (which is bad in legal discourse) just to say that claims obviously arise from the same underlying transaction or obviously are related. You must learn to support this conclusion with analysis of exactly which facts and which evidence are the same for distinct claims or distinct parties. In close cases, trial judges will want to know why it will be convenient, efficient, or fair for the court or the parties to keep the claims joined: exactly which evidence will not have to be entered twice, pre-cisely which witnesses would otherwise have to be inconvenienced multiple times.

Another Rule associated with these Rules, Rule 21, permits the court to drop or add any dispensable party on its own initiative or as a result of a motion by any party. Because this Rule is very straightforward, this chapter does not pro-vide a case for illustration. Simply put, Rule 21 permits the court to drop or add any non-necessary party at any stage in the action on any terms "as are just." Further, the court may sever any claim against any party and proceed with the severed claim separately.

Cooper v. Fitzgerald
266 F.R.D. 86 (E.D. Pa. 2010)

KELLY, Senior District Judge:

Presently before the Court is the Motion to Sever filed by Defendants Karen Fitzgerald (District Director, United States Citizenship and Immigration Services ("USCIS"), Philadelphia District), Paul Novack (Director, USCIS, Vermont Service Center), Alejandro Mayorkas (Director, USCIS), Janet Napolitano (Secretary of

Homeland Security), Robert S. Mueller, III (Director of the Federal Bureau of Investigation ("FBI")), and Eric H. Holder Jr. (Attorney General of the United States) (collectively "Defendants"). . . .

I. BACKGROUND

The seven Plaintiffs in this lawsuit — Karpeh Cooper, Kelley Cooper, Afua Hammond, Anderson Knoble, Trudi Ann Brown-Cooper, Sabri Cooper, and Mamadou Sacko (collectively "Plaintiffs") — filed a single Complaint to compel action on their individual applications for immigration benefits pending before the USCIS. . . . Plaintiffs seek among other things, declaratory relief, injunctive relief, and a Writ in the Nature of Mandamus to compel action on the outstanding applications.

In the instant Motion, Defendants allege that because of the dissimilarity of Plaintiffs' claims, they do not satisfy the Federal Rule of Civil Procedure 20(a) test for permissive joinder. Specifically, Defendants contend that permissive joinder is inappropriate under Rule 20(a) because Plaintiffs' claims do not arise out of the same transaction or occurrence and lack a common question of law or fact. Pursuant to Federal Rule of Civil Procedure 21, the Defendants request that the Court sever the claims of Plaintiff Karpeh Cooper and dismiss without prejudice the remaining Plaintiffs' claims as a result of improper joinder.

The general background of the Plaintiffs, the types of immigration applications they have outstanding, and the status of those applications are described in the . . . Complaint and Declaration ("Bausman Declaration") of Kathleen Bausman ("Bausman") that is attached to Defendants' Motion. Bausman is the acting Field Office Director of the USCIS Philadelphia, Pennsylvania Field Office. As the Field Office Director, Bausman is "responsible for monitoring and ensuring the timely adjudication of all immigration applications being adjudicated in [the] field office." (Defs.' Mot. to Sever, Bausman Declar., Ex. A ¶ 1.) Bausman reviewed the agency's administrative files for each Plaintiff in preparing the Declaration. (*Id.* ¶ 2.)

The Court will not rehash all of the factual details of each Plaintiff's application for immigration benefits, or the status of those applications. For purposes of the instant Motion, however, it is important to note that there are different immigration applications at issue (I-130 Petitions for Alien Relative and I-485 Applications to Adjust Status) and that each application is at a different stage in the adjudication process. [Some of the Plaintiffs are U.S. citizens who have filed I-130 applications to have their spouses declared as immediate relatives, while others are aliens who have filed I-485 applications to adjust status. According to Bausman, "[i]nitial decisions were made on several of the Plaintiffs' applications and some of the final adjudication delays have been associated with different types of delays in the appellate process."]

II. STANDARD OF REVIEW AND GENERAL APPLICABLE LAW

A district court has broad discretion in deciding whether to sever a party pursuant to Federal Rules of Civil Procedure 21. Rule 21 states "Misjoinder of parties is not a ground for dismissing an action. On motion or on its own, the court may at any time, on just terms, add or drop a party." Fed. R. Civ. P. 21. The court may also sever any claim against a party. Fed. R. Civ. P. 21(a). Notably, Rule 21 is most commonly invoked to sever parties improperly joined under Rule 20.

As a threshold matter, joinder is strongly encouraged. However, joinder is only appropriate if both elements of Rule 20(a) are met. Specifically, Rule 20(a) permits the joinder of plaintiffs in a single action if: "(1) the plaintiffs have a right to relief arising out of the same transaction, occurrence, or series of transactions or occurrences; and (2) there exists some question of law or fact common to the plaintiffs." *Cumba v. Merck & Co., Inc.*, No. 08-2328, 2009 WL 1351462, at *1 (D.N.J. May 12, 2009); *see also* Fed. R. Civ. P. 20(a). Importantly, "Rule 20(a)'s purpose is to 'promote trial convenience and expedite the final determination of disputes, thereby preventing multiple law suits.' " *Al Daraji v. Monica*, No. 07-1749, 2007 WL 2994608, at *10 (E.D. Pa. Oct. 21, 2007) (citation omitted). The rule is designed " 'to promote judicial economy . . . [and] reduce inconvenience, delay, and added expense.' " Id. (citation omitted).

III. DISCUSSION

As discussed below, the Court finds that the Plaintiffs are improperly joined because they do not meet the elements of permissive joinder outlined in Rule 20(a). In addition, judicial economy would not be served by the joinder of these Plaintiffs. Further, Plaintiffs will not be prejudiced by severance. Thus, the Court finds that severance of the Plaintiffs is appropriate pursuant to Rule 21.

A. "SAME TRANSACTION" ELEMENT

The first element of Rule 20(a), the "same transaction" or transactional relatedness prong, refers to the similarity in the factual background of the relevant claims. *Coughlin v. Rogers*, 130 F.3d 1348, 1350 (9th Cir. 1997). Courts generally apply a case-by-case approach when considering whether the facts of several claims constitute a single transaction or occurrence, or a series of transactions or occurrences. Significantly, " '[t]ransaction' is a word of flexible meaning, which 'may comprehend a series of many occurrences, depending not so much upon the immediateness of their connection, as upon their logical relationship.' " *Al Daraji*, 2007 WL 2994608, at *8 (citation omitted).

In their . . . Complaint, Plaintiffs support their joinder under Rule 20(a) by alleging that they are:

> Persons who have submitted applications for adjustment of status or petitions for alien relative to CIS, and who have met all statutory requirements for adjustment of status or petitions for alien relative, and whose applications for

adjustment of status or petitions for alien relative *are not adjudicated within a reasonable period of time of their initial examination based on the lack of CIS and the FBI to clear background checks and other unknown checks.*

(emphasis added). Clearly, when the . . . Complaint was filed, Plaintiffs believed joinder was appropriate based on speculation that the adjudication of their applications was delayed because of pending FBI checks or other background checks. (Compl. ¶ 63 (referencing "delays in 'name checks' and other background checks").) These alleged checks were the related "transactions and occurrences" that they based joinder upon when the . . . Complaint was filed.

However, as evidenced in the Bausman Declaration, "background checks, including the FBI name check, have not delayed the adjudication of [the Plaintiffs'] applications for immigration benefits." (Defs.' Mot. to Sever, Bausman Declar., Ex. A ¶ 3.) In regard to the I-130 petitions, USCIS does not perform background checks on these applications. (*Id.* ¶ 2(a).) Moreover, in reference to the Plaintiffs who filed suit with respect to their I-485 applications, Bausman confirmed that USCIS completed all relevant background checks before the Plaintiffs filed their initial Complaint on November 4, 2009. (*Id.* ¶ ¶ 2(b), (c).) Thus, contrary to the allegations in the . . . Complaint, Plaintiffs cannot justify joinder based on a common delay caused by name checks, FBI checks, or other background checks. Further, Plaintiffs' references in the . . . Complaint to other "unknown checks" do not entitle them to joinder under Rule 20(a).

In response to Defendants' Motion to Sever and the Bausman Declaration, Plaintiffs change their argument in support of joinder. Specifically, in their brief, Plaintiffs argue that "[t]he basic common denominator is that all plaintiffs' cases involve an I-130, Petition for Alien Relative, filing with USCIS which USCIS refuses to adjudicate." (Pls.' Resp. to Mot. to Sever at 3.) This argument also does not satisfy the "same transaction" prong of Rule 20(a).

As an initial matter, there are two delayed immigration applications (i.e. I-130s and I-485s) at issue among the various Plaintiffs. This is made clear in both the . . . Complaint and the Bausman Declaration. (Compl. ¶ 2 ("Plaintiffs are all applicants for lawful permanent residence and/or U.S. Citizens filing for their spouse. Each of them has sought to seek an immigration benefit by becoming a lawful permanent resident by applying for adjustment of status or an immigrant visa.").) The fact that there are two separate immigration applications at issue in the case cuts against joinder under the "same transaction" prong of Rule 20(a).

Further, Plaintiffs' argument that they are entitled to joinder because they all filed I-130 and/or I-485 applications is without merit. Plaintiffs claim that these applications are companion filings, and that a common thread exists because each of the Plaintiffs' immigration files involves an I-130 petition. Even pursuant to Plaintiffs' line of reasoning, the Court cannot allow joinder merely because the various Plaintiffs are awaiting adjudication of similar immigration benefits. This is not the sufficient similarity needed to satisfy Rule 20(a). Plaintiffs' applications are at different stages in the agency decision process and have different reasons associated with delays in their final adjudication. Thus, permissive joinder is not appropriate. *See Cumba,* 2009 WL 1351462, at *1 ("Here, Plaintiffs have failed to demonstrate sufficient similarities among the personal injury plaintiffs to satisfy Rule 20(a)'s 'same transaction' requirement. It appears, for example, that the only unifying factors among the personal injury plaintiffs lie in the allegations that each took the drug Vytorin and that each sustained broadly similar injuries as a result thereof. As Defendants correctly point out, however, the personal injury plaintiffs are nonetheless 'different people with different medical histories who separately took a drug prescribed by different physicians under different circumstances, probably for different periods of time and at different points of time.' ").

This case is similar to the *Coughlin* case in the Ninth Circuit. In *Coughlin,* multiple plaintiff-applicants for USCIS immigration filed suit alleging delays in adjudicating their immigration applications. Subsequently, the government filed a motion to sever the forty-nine joined plaintiffs. The district court granted the motion to sever and the Ninth Circuit affirmed. The Ninth Circuit stated:

> In this case, the basic connection among all the claims is the alleged procedural problem of delay. However, the *mere allegation of general delay is not enough to create a common transaction or occurrence.* Each Plaintiff has waited a different length of time, suffering a different duration of alleged delay. Furthermore, the delay is disputed in some instances and varies from case to case. And, most importantly, there may be numerous reasons for the alleged delay. *Therefore, the existence of a common allegation of delay, in and of itself, does not suffice to create a common transaction or occurrence.*

Coughlin, 130 F.3d at 1350 (9th Cir. 1997) (emphasis added); *see also Abdelkarim v. Gonzales,* No. 06-14436, 2007 WL 1284924, at *4 (E.D. Mich. Apr. 30, 2007) (finding that plaintiff failed to satisfy "same transaction" prong of Rule 20(a) because "[a]lthough each of the approximately 59 Plaintiffs here alleges a delay in processing their individual applications for naturalization, the reasons for the delays vary and are dependent upon each Plaintiff's particular circumstances."). Significantly, similar to this case, the plaintiffs in *Coughlin* sought different types of immigration benefits and the adjudication of their applications was at different stages. Moreover, just like in *Coughlin,* Plaintiffs' critical and common factual allegation is that final adjudication of their applications has been delayed—even if for wide-ranging reasons. As the Ninth Circuit stated, a "common allegation of delay" does not meet the "same transaction" element of the Rule 20(a) test. *Coughlin,* 130 F.3d at 1350.

The facts of this case are significantly different from the *Al Daraji* case from this District. In *Al Daraji,* a case after *Coughlin,* the court permitted joinder where plaintiffs uniformly challenged "the allegedly delayed actions of USCIS in adjudicating their [immigration] applications due to the newly-required FBI name checks." *Al Daraji,* 2007 WL 2994608, at *8. Consistent with dicta from *Coughlin,* the court found that the plaintiffs' claims "arose from the same transaction or occurrence" because plaintiffs alleged a "pattern or policy" of delay on USCIS's part because of the FBI name check policy. *Id.* at *9. In the instant case, no similar "pattern or policy" is relevant to Plaintiffs' applications. As previously discussed, Bausman's Declaration makes clear that no FBI name checks or other background checks have delayed the final adjudication of Plaintiffs' petitions for immigration benefits. (Defs.' Mot. to Sever, Bausman Declar., Ex. A ¶ 3.) Further, as will be discussed below, the Bausman Declaration provides other specific reasons why each of the Plaintiffs' applications has been delayed based on the unique factual circumstances surrounding each application.

B. COMMONALITY ELEMENT

The Plaintiffs are improperly joined because they fail to meet the "same transaction" prong of the Rule 20(a) test. Nevertheless, the Court will address the second prong of the test, which requires courts to analyze whether "any question of law or fact common to all plaintiffs will arise in the action." Fed. R. Civ. P. 20(a). Notably, the "threshold for the commonality requirement is 'very low.'" *Al Daraji*, 2007 WL 2994608, at *9. Thus, the propriety of joinder under the commonality prong is a much closer call. However, the Court ultimately concludes that Plaintiffs have failed to satisfy this element as well.

The court in *Al Daraji* discussed the commonality prong in detail and specifically referenced the aforementioned *Abdelkarim* case where that court did not find that commonality existed under Rule 20(a). Specifically, the court in *Al Daraji* stated:

> In [*Abdelkarim*], *the parties provided the court with much more information regarding the reasons for the delays in USCIS adjudication, leading that court to determine that the facts of the plaintiffs' cases were disparate enough to destroy commonality. . . . A similar quantity of evidence pertaining to the particularized circumstances regarding USCIS's delays has not been provided to this Court at this stage in the litigation. Thus far, the government has not alleged any distinguishing reasons why the individual plaintiffs' applications have been delayed.* Further, in *Abdelkarim*, the FBI had completed some of the plaintiffs' name checks, whereas others were incomplete. In the instant case, all plaintiffs await the resolution of their name checks. Thus, the Court concludes that, at the present time, insufficient evidence of individual causes for delay has been presented to justify severance. Should such evidence be presented at a later date, the Court retains the option to sever under Federal Rule of Civil Procedure 21.

Id. At *10 (citations omitted).

In this case, through the Bausman Declaration, Defendants have provided the Plaintiffs and the Court with the background, and specific reasons, for any delay between each Plaintiff's initial immigration filing and final adjudication of that filing. Notably, none of Plaintiffs' applications have been delayed because of FBI name checks or other background checks. Thus, no factual commonality exists on these grounds. Unlike in *Al Daraji,* sufficient individualized causes for delay of final adjudication have been presented to justify severance under the commonality prong.

In addition, the Plaintiffs have not shown any questions of law common to all of them. In the . . . Complaint and briefing, they contend that there are common grounds for relief in this case including the United States Constitution, Administrative Procedures Act, Mandamus Act, and Declaratory Judgment Act. However, as stated in *Coughlin*, "the mere fact that all Plaintiffs' claims arise under the same general law does not necessarily establish a common question of law. . . ." *Coughlin*, 130 F.3d at 1351. As a result, Plaintiffs have not satisfied the Rule 20(a) commonality hurdle.

c. Judicial Economy and Prejudice

As previously mentioned, Rule 20 is designed " 'to promote judicial economy . . . [and] reduce inconvenience, delay, and added expense.' " *Al Daraji*, 2007 WL 2994608, at *10. Joinder in this case would not promote judicial economy or convenience. As in *Coughlin*, "trial efficiency will not be promoted by allowing all Plaintiffs to bring a single case. Each claim raises potentially different issues, and must be viewed in a separate and individual light by the Court." *Coughlin*, 130 F.3d at 1351. Specifically, if the Court permitted joinder of the seven Plaintiffs, each case would still need to be examined in light of their individualized circumstances and the unique reasons surrounding any final adjudication delay.

Finally, Plaintiffs will not be prejudiced by severance. Defendants have only requested that the Court dismiss, without prejudice, all of the Plaintiffs except the first-named Plaintiff—Karpeh Cooper. Significantly, any dismissed Plaintiffs would still have the ability to re-file complaints against Defendants for their individual claims.

For the reasons set forth above, the Court finds that severance of the parties pursuant to Rule 21 is appropriate in this matter. Accordingly, Defendants' Motion to Sever will be granted.

REVIEW QUESTIONS

1. Questions about Rule 20 and the joinder of parties present especially good opportunities to "get your hands dirty" with facts. Exactly why couldn't these plaintiffs be joined? A major difference between good and sloppy legal analysis is whether the lawyer is excruciatingly precise with what particular facts make the doctrine apply. For example, when making these arguments we cannot say only that it is (or isn't) the "same transaction, occurrence, or series of transactions or occurrences," or that there is (or isn't) a "question of law or fact common to all" the persons who have been joined. Prove your points to a skeptic by including the particular facts in the case. Much of civil procedure is proving the commonality of events that happened to different people. One way to focus your analysis is to ask which particular facts and legal questions are relevant to each element of each cause of action that applies to each party. For instance, think about the case of *Joe v. Sally* from the beginning of

this chapter. Assume that Sally allegedly tripped Mary the following day. It is difficult to come up with any overlapping questions of law or fact, or any commonality of transaction, without going to such a level of generality that a judge would dismiss the commonality out of hand. You could argue that a common question of law is whether tripping can ever be intentional (or an act of unreasonable care), but surely a more precise bit of commonality is required by either the same transaction test or the "common question of law or fact" test in Rule 20.

2. In *Cooper*, why doesn't the court tackle more directly the question whether the plaintiffs' claims arise out of a *series* of occurrences? And what *is* the relationship between these seven plaintiffs? If you were the plaintiffs' lawyer trying to argue that your clients' claims are related, what are the sort of facts that would help you argue that 20(a) is satisfied — even if it's also true, as the court emphasizes, that there are two types of applications, those applications are on different timetables, and there are different reasons that the applications are delayed? At the end of its analysis in Part III.A, the court distinguishes the *Al Daraji* case because, in that case, there was an allegation of a pattern or policy; why didn't the plaintiffs' lawyer include that allegation here? (Could it add that allegation now?)

3. One reason we have given you *Carpenter v. Dee* is to provide you a set of facts that you can return to in order to prove to yourself that you can apply procedural rules. Can Nancy Carpenter join the various causes of action and theories you came up with in former assignments? What if Randall Dee owed Charlie Carpenter $1,000 on a debt unrelated to the jeep or the accident? Could the plaintiff join that claim? What if Randall Dee had borrowed $1,000 from Nancy Carpenter after the accident and now refuses to repay that debt. Can she join that claim in her complaint? Can she join Randall Dee, his brother, Ultimate Auto (where Dee bought the oversized tires and suspension lift kit), McGill's Garage, Inc. (where the jeep passed inspection), the City of Lowell (whose police evidently let the infractions relating to height pass without comment), and the manufacturer of the tires (assuming you can come up with a cause of action) as defendants in the same case? Prove your conclusion — using specific facts! What if Scott was injured in a similar incident a week later by Keefe, who also bought tires and a suspension lift kit from Ultimate Auto and lifted his jeep in the same manner? Can Carpenter and Scott draft one complaint against Ultimate Auto — a joinder of plaintiffs? What if Randall Dee and Keefe were racing their jeeps against each other when each tipped, injuring Charlie Carpenter and Scott? Could Nancy Carpenter and Scott join in a suit against Dee, Keefe, and Ultimate Auto? At the beginning of the course, we wrote that learning procedure permits you to exercise a great deal of imagination by considering "what ifs." Get in the habit of constructing your own hypotheticals to analyze alone or

with your study group. The facts of the jeep case and the *City of New York* stop-and-frisk case are rich with potential hypotheticals.

4. How is the rule for consolidation (Fed. R. Civ. P. 42(a)) different from the rule for joinder of parties (Fed. R. Civ. P. 20(a))?

a. Joinder Is Only One Star in the Constellation of Procedure

Rules 18 and 20 do not mention other procedural rules, concepts, and laws that might impose their own restraints, but those restraints are present. For instance, the Advisory Committee Notes to Rule 18 remind lawyers that jurisdictional and venue requirements must still be met. Issues of subject matter jurisdiction, personal jurisdiction, venue, and notice would of course apply to each party joined under Rule 20 as well. These topics are covered elsewhere in the course. Moreover, although Rule 18 (joinder of claims) is permissive, you must consider another field of civil procedure to decide what causes of action or theories to join. For example, in the case of *Joe v. Sally*, what would happen if Joe sued for battery and omitted negligence? Let's say Sally wins, and the case goes to final judgment. Could Joe then sue Sally again in negligence for the same tripping? Maybe you should put *res judicata* or *preclusion* in the margin of Rule 18 to remind yourself that the law does not allow as much permissiveness as Rule 18 would lead you to believe.

b. The "Transaction or Occurrence" Test

As previously mentioned, throughout the course you should keep a very close watch on the expression "transaction or occurrence"—the phrase is a malleable guideline, but it is also a favorite of the drafters of the Federal Rules. Pay special attention to *which* rules use the phrase and notice *how* (as explained in the appellate holdings). Why did Charles Clark use a concept such as "transaction" as his unit of measure for the limits of joinder? What role does this "transactional" approach play in the overall philosophy of the Federal Rules? Why did the common law procedure inherently have much more limited joinder of claims and parties? Why would Field have wanted less joinder, particularly if he knew the types of cases brought today? When making arguments to courts, lawyers often go to the rationale of a rule in order to convince the court of the rule/application they want on the facts of the case. In *Cooper*, do the plaintiffs have policy arguments that would help them convince the court of a broad meaning for "transaction, occurrence, or series of transactions or occurrences"?

c. Litigation Strategy

Strategic considerations matter in deciding how many claims and parties to try to put in any one lawsuit. For example, the size of the lawsuit may have a tremendous impact on (1) discovery (e.g., interrogatories can only be sent to actual parties of the suit); (2) costs (e.g., the more parties and theories, the more discovery and the more costs to your client); (3) evidence (e.g., different hearsay restrictions and altering what is relevant evidence depend on what claims and parties you have joined); (4) the jury (e.g., you may or may not want several defendants all pointing at each other, or you may or may not want to associate yourself with another party whose case or personality may rub off on your client); (5) *res judicata* (e.g., you may not want all of your eggs in one basket, but you don't want to be barred from plausible claims); and (6) control (e.g., with more parties it may or may not be harder to settle, depending on how you assess the situation; more defendants mean more pockets from which to pay your client, but may also mean that no one of them will want to give very much; more parties may also mean more lawyers who want to control the litigation in various ways). Use *Cooper* and *Carpenter v. Dee* to assess some of the strategic concerns relating to joinder. What did the *Cooper* plaintiffs gain by joining as plaintiffs? What did the *Cooper* defendants achieve by challenging the joinder? Was it worth more than the time and expense of litigating the motion to sever that led to the opinion that you just read? The *Cooper* defendants were represented by attorneys for the federal government. Would defense counsel have pursued this strategy if a private client were paying the legal bill? How many hours of factual and legal research must it have taken for the defendants' attorneys to have prepared their motion?

QUESTIONS TO PONDER

Do the values "codified" in Rules 18 and 20 further the goal of making remedial justice more accessible? The goal of efficiency? Are these goals a zero-sum trade-off? For example, in *Cooper*, what do the plaintiffs and defendants gain or lose by broad joinder rules? What does society gain or lose? What about the values inherent in the tremendous discretion offered the trial judge by Rule 20(b) and Rule 42? If you were drafting the joinder provisions, would you grant this discretion to judges? In all cases?

H. COUNTERCLAIMS AND CROSS-CLAIMS

A counterclaim is a claim asserted against an opposing party, usually by a defendant against a plaintiff. A counterclaim may seek any kind of relief that the court is competent to give. The relief may or may not be related to the plaintiff's claim. A counterclaim may ask for relief that merely neutralizes or cancels out the plaintiff's claim, or it may seek relief that exceeds the plaintiff's desired relief. Under the Federal Rules, counterclaims can be either compulsory or permissive. *See* Fed. R. Civ. P. 13.

A cross-claim is a claim between co-parties, usually defendants. In contrast to the blanket permissiveness of the counterclaim, a cross-claim may not assert every claim that possibly exists between co-parties. Instead, a cross-claim must be closely related to the transaction of the original claim asserted by plaintiff. (However, once a cross-claim has been legitimately asserted, consider the expansiveness permitted by Rule 18(a).) Cross-claims are always permissive. A party who does not bring a claim under 13(g) will not be barred by *res judicata*, waiver, or estoppel from asserting the claim at another time.

Podhorn v. Paragon Group, Inc.
606 F. Supp. 185 (D. Mo. 1985)

HUNGATE, District Judge:

This matter is before the Court on defendants' joint motion to dismiss plaintiffs' complaint.

Plaintiffs [Paul E. Podhorn, Jr., Liana E. Podhorn, and Renata A. Podhorn] bring this civil action alleging constructive eviction, breach of implied warranty of habitability, false swearing, false credit report, breach of implied covenant of quiet enjoyment, negligence, abuse of process, prima facie tort, conversion, and initiation of malicious prosecution by defendants. Defendant Paragon Group, Inc., is the owner of defendant San Miguel Apartments. All of these claims arose out of plaintiffs' tenancy at defendants' apartment building from April 1 to July 31, 1983.

On or about November 17, 1983, defendant Paragon Group, Inc., filed a petition in the Circuit Court of St. Louis County against the plaintiffs in this case, Paul and Liana Podhorn, for rent due. The state court action arose out of the same tenancy that gives rise to this federal cause. The Podhorns did not file a counterclaim in the state court action, and on March 28, 1984, a judgment in default was entered against the Podhorns in the sum of $1,113.33, plus costs.

Defendants move to dismiss plaintiffs' claim in this case asserting that it should have been filed as a compulsory counterclaim in the state court action.

Missouri Supreme Court Rule 55.32(a) requires the filing of compulsory counterclaims:

> A pleading shall state as a counterclaim any claim which at the time of serving the pleading the pleader has against the opposing party, if it arises out of the transaction or occurrence that is the subject matter of the opposing party's claim and does not require for its adjudication the presence of third parties of whom the court cannot acquire jurisdiction. . . .

The Court finds plaintiffs' claims in this case arise out of the transaction or occurrence that gave rise to Paragon's rent action in the earlier state court case, namely plaintiffs' tenancy at defendants' apartment. Accordingly, plaintiffs were required to file the instant claims as compulsory counterclaims and their failure to do so bars them from having those claims heard.

Plaintiffs contend that associate circuit judges are granted limited authority and may not properly hear a civil case where the sum demanded, exclusive of interest and cost, exceeds $5,000. Mo. Rev. Stat. § 478.225.2(1). Plaintiffs argue that since their claims then and now exceed the statutory limit, the state court was without jurisdiction to hear their counterclaim if filed. Plaintiffs assert that the compulsory counterclaim rule does not apply in this action before an associate circuit judge.

Mo. Rev. Stat. § 517 governs the procedural dispute in this matter. The Supreme Court rule which requires the filing of compulsory counterclaims in the circuit court also applies to cases before an associate circuit judge. Mo. Rev. Stat. § 517.020.1(3). In the event the counterclaim is not triable before an associate circuit judge, as in this case where the counterclaim exceeds $5,000, the case is to be certified for assignment to a judge who may hear the claim. In short, although plaintiffs' counterclaim may not have been triable before the associate circuit judge, plaintiffs were not relieved of their obligation to file it.

Therefore, plaintiffs' claim is barred and this Court will grant defendants' motion to dismiss.

REVIEW QUESTIONS

1. A discussion of the important facts is conspicuously absent in the *Podhorn* opinion. Is this because there are *no* claims that could have arisen during the tenancy that would not also have been compulsory counterclaims in the first action? Revisit plaintiffs' causes of action and consider whether those causes of action would necessarily be part of the "transaction or occurrence" that was the subject of the previous suit. For example, imagine that when the Podhorns were moving into the apartment on April 1, 1983, Renata Podhorn suffered serious injuries because the landlord negligently failed to warn the family about some dangerous defect in the apartment. Would Renata's claim be a compulsory counterclaim in the nonpayment of rent action later filed against Paul and Liana? How about a conversion claim if the landlord had entered the Podhorns' apartment without their permission or knowledge on June 15, and confiscated and sold many of the family's valuables?

2. What does it mean to say that a counterclaim is "compulsory" or "permissive"? In what circumstances will the question of whether a potential counterclaim was compulsory normally be raised? For instance, assume that *A* and *B* are in a motor vehicle accident, each potentially having driven negligently into the other. *A* sues *B*. Will a court have to face the issue of whether *B* should have counterclaimed against *A* in the first suit, or in a later suit? As a defendant, how will you plead if you are in doubt as to whether a counterclaim is compulsory?

a. Revisiting Motions to Dismiss

Why is this case decided on a motion to dismiss? Is it obvious from the face of the complaint that defendant must win? Of what significance to these questions is the fact that *res judicata* is an affirmative defense?

QUESTIONS TO PONDER

1. What place would Rule 13(a) counterclaims play in the overall procedural philosophy of Charles Clark? If you were on a committee drafting procedural rules, would you consider that a compulsory counterclaim provision would lead to "efficiency" or "inefficiency" or both? Consider the viewpoints of the court system, litigants, and their attorneys.
2. What are the reasons for the two exceptions in Rule 13(a)(2)?

---

b. The "Transaction or Occurrence" Test, Again

Wright and Miller describe four tests for applying the words *"transaction or occurrence"* within the meaning of Rule 13(a):

a. Are the issues of fact and law raised by the claim and counterclaim largely the same?

b. Would *res judicata* bar a subsequent suit on defendant's claim absent the compulsory counterclaim rule?

c. Will substantially the same evidence support or refute plaintiff's claim as well as defendant's counterclaim?

d. Is there any logical relation between the claim and the counterclaim?

Charles A. Wright, Arthur R. Miller, and Mary Kay Kane, *Federal Practice and Procedure* § 1410.

You have now seen the terms "transaction" or "occurrence" as a portion of different rules: Fed. R. Civ. P. 20 (permissive joinder of parties); Fed. R. Civ. P. 15(c) (relation back of amendments); Fed. R. Civ. P. 13(a) (compulsory counterclaims); Fed. R. Civ. P. 13(g) (cross-claims against a co-party). Should the words be interpreted the same way, regardless of these different contexts, or might their interpretations take on slightly different shades of meaning? One way to approach such a question is to consider the purposes for using the terms in each context. Why are "transaction" and "occurrence" relevant to relationship back? Why are they relevant to joinder of parties or whether a counterclaim is compulsory? Would such a functional analysis lead one to different meanings? Professor Kane has explained how the term "transaction" has been used in the Federal Rules and elsewhere for differing purposes, and argues that those divergent purposes lead to different interpretations of the same word. Mary

Kay Kane, *Original Sin and the Transaction in Federal Civil Procedure*, 76 Tex. L. Rev. 1723 (1998).

c. Cross-claims

Cross-claims must be closely related to at least one claim in the action. Consider the purpose of this requirement:

> When plaintiff brings suit against defendant, he is not free to object at some later time if defendant utilizes the forum to assert some unrelated claim against him in the forum of his own choice. But plaintiff's suit could become unduly complicated and prejudice might result to him if defendant is allowed to raise a claim against a co-defendant in which the original plaintiff has no interest.

Charles A. Wright, Arthur R. Miller, and Mary Kay Kane, *Federal Practice and Procedure* § 1431.

Cross-claims are always permissive. Why aren't cross-claims compulsory?

PRACTICE EXERCISE NO. 13: CONSIDERING COUNTERCLAIMS, CROSS-CLAIMS, AND RULE 13(h) ADDITIONAL PARTIES IN *CARPENTER*

Counterclaims. Consider the following possible counterclaim in the *Carpenter* case. Shortly after the accident in which her husband was killed, Nancy Carpenter calls a friend of the family who works at Raytheon (where Randall Dee was and is employed) and tells her that Randall Dee is an alcoholic. Randall Dee is then fired from his job. Does Randall Dee have a defamation claim against Nancy Carpenter for slander? Would this be a compulsory counterclaim? A permissive counterclaim? Would you need to do some legal research before you could answer this question?

Cross-claims. Assume that the judge in the motions session in the previous class has granted the motion of Nancy Carpenter to add Ultimate Auto, Inc. and the City of Lowell as named defendants, and the complaint is now filed as amended. Assume further that you represent the defendant driver of the jeep in question, Randall Dee. Do you have a plausible cross-claim? Prove it. Focus on the language of Mass. R. Civ. P. 13(g), which is the same as Fed. R. Civ. P. 13(g). If you do have a plausible cross-claim, how many counts would it have? What are the strategic reasons for filing it or not filing it? Regardless, try your hand at drafting such a cross-claim. Will you draft *de novo*, or can you get some help from a form somewhere near at hand?

You should also now look at the Massachusetts Contribution Statute in the Case Files. Consider other possible cross-claims, as well as Mass. R. Civ. P. 13(h) (which is also the same as the Federal Rule). Are there parties you might wish to bring in through the 13(h) route? Would you be able to?

I. THIRD-PARTY PRACTICE

Rule 14 governs the procedure through which a defendant can bring a third party into the action. The rule permits the court to allow a defendant to *implead* a person not already a party to the action who is purportedly liable to the defendant for all or part of the defendant's liability to the plaintiff. In such an instance, the original defendant, now acting as a *third-party plaintiff*, impleads a *third-party defendant*. The case below illustrates.

Gross v. Hanover Insurance Co.
138 F.R.D. 53 (S.D.N.Y. 1991)

LEISURE, District Judge:

This is an action arising out of an insurance claim following the alleged loss of a substantial amount of jewelry. Defendant Hanover Insurance Company has now moved, pursuant to Federal Rule of Civil Procedure 14(a), to implead as third-party defendants Joseph Rizzo and Anthony Rizzo. For the reasons stated below, defendant's motion is granted.

BACKGROUND

The facts necessary to decide the instant motion are not complex. Plaintiff alleges that he suffered a loss consisting of approximately $217,800 worth of diamonds consigned to one "3-R Jewelers" ("3-R"), a retail jewelry store, and approximately $48,000 worth of diamonds and emeralds left by plaintiff at 3-R for safekeeping. 3-R was at the relevant time owned by one Anthony Rizzo ("Anthony"), who employed his brother Joseph Rizzo ("Joseph") at the store. Plaintiff thereafter made a claim under a jewelers' block insurance policy issued to him by defendant, seeking $50,000 for loss of consignment goods and $25,000 for loss of goods left for safekeeping. The parties agree that the loss of the jewels was the result of a theft that occurred at the 3-R store.

Defendant alleges, however, that on December 16, 1989, the evening of the theft, a witness observed a man enter the 3-R store and begin talking to Joseph. Shortly thereafter, the man talking with Joseph walked out, then returned with a paper bag and proceeded to walk behind the counter and into a back room. When the witness left 3-R, the man was still in the store. Affidavit of Stephen H. Marcus, Esq., sworn to on June 28, 1991 ("Marcus Aff."), Exhibit H. In a statement he gave to the police, Joseph stated that he was in the store preparing to close for the night when two men entered and asked to purchase a watch. Joseph stated that he left the two men in the front of the store and went to the back to get a warranty card for the watch. He stated that he then heard the front door slam. When he returned to the front of the store the men were gone and a box and case of jewels were missing from the safe, which he had left open. Marcus Aff., Exhibit G. Defendant also claims that Joseph was addicted to cocaine, and that Anthony was aware of this fact but nevertheless continued to employ Joseph at 3-R. The police report includes statements from Anthony that Joseph had a cocaine habit, that he thought the habit was under control, but "guess bigger problem than he [Anthony] thought," and that it "[l]ooked like Joey was setting place up." Marcus Aff., Exhibit F.

Defendant's proposed third-party complaint thus seeks to implead Joseph and Anthony on the ground that they will be liable to defendant, should defendant be found to be liable to plaintiff. Marcus Aff., Exhibit E. Specifically, the proposed third-party complaint asserts claims against Joseph for negligent handling of the jewels as plaintiff's consignee or bailee, or as the agent of 3-R; against Joseph for actual conversion of the jewels; and against Anthony for the negligent hiring, retention and supervision of Joseph.

DISCUSSION

Rule 14(a) provides in relevant part that "[a]t any time after commencement of the action a defending party, as a third-party plaintiff, may cause a summons and complaint to be served upon a person not a party to the action who is or may be liable to the third-party plaintiff for all or part of the plaintiff's claim against the third-party plaintiff." Fed. R. Civ. P. 14(a). Where, as here, the defendant seeks to file the third-party complaint more than ten days after serving its original answer, the defendant "must obtain leave on motion upon notice to all parties to the action." Fed. R. Civ. P. 14(a). "The purpose of this rule is to promote judicial efficiency by eliminating the necessity for the defendant to bring a separate action against a third individual who may be secondarily or derivatively liable to the defendant for all or part of the plaintiff's original claim." *McLaughlin v. Biasucci*, 688 F. Supp. 965, 967 (S.D.N.Y. 1988). Accordingly, the district court has considerable discretion in deciding whether to permit a third-party complaint. *See Consolidated Rail Corp. v. Metz*, 115 F.R.D. 216, 218 (S.D.N.Y. 1987); *Old Republic Insurance Co. v. Concast.*, 99 F.R.D. 566, 568 (S.D.N.Y. 1983). "The court must balance the benefits derived from impleader—that is, the benefits of settling related matters in one suit—against the potential prejudice to the plaintiff and third-party defendants." *Oliner v. McBride's Industries, Inc.*, 106 F.R.D. 14, 20 (S.D.N.Y. 1985).

In the case at bar, defendant's proposed third-party claims arise from " 'the same aggregate or core of facts which is determinative of the plaintiff's claim,' " and thus the interest in judicial economy would be served by permitting those claims to proceed in the instant action. *National Bank of Canada v. Artex Industries, Inc.*, 627 F. Supp. 610, 613 (S.D.N.Y. 1986) (quoting *Dery v. Wyer*, 265 F.2d 804, 807 (2d Cir. 1959)). Plaintiff argues, however, that the proposed third-party claims are "speculative," and thus the motion to implead should be denied. This argument fails for several reasons.

First, there is some question as to whether plaintiff may attack the merits of the proposed third-party claims at this stage of the proceedings. Second, it is well established that the words "is or may be liable" in Rule 14(a) make it clear that impleader is proper even though the third-party defendant's liability is not automatically established once the third-party plaintiff's liability to the original plaintiff has been determined. . . . Finally, the proposed third-party claims are sufficiently alleged, for Rule 14(a) purposes. "The federal and New York state court decisions hold that third-party impleader practice encompasses subrogation claims.". . .

Plaintiff's second argument in opposition to the instant motion consists of a claim that defendant has been dilatory in seeking to implead, and that plaintiff will suffer prejudice if discovery is expanded to include the third-party claims. There is, however, little evidence to suggest that defendant was so slow in bringing its Rule 14(a) motion that that motion should be denied. More importantly, the Court believes that the prejudice to be felt by plaintiff—if any—due to the need for additional discovery, is sufficiently outweighed by the benefits of more efficient litigation to be gained by permitting impleader. . . . If, in the future, plaintiff believes that defendant is using its third-party claims to delay the progress of the principal complaint in this action, he should so inform the Court. Needless to say, the Court would not countenance such tactics. . . .

CONCLUSION

For the reasons stated above, defendant's motion to implead Joseph Rizzo and Anthony Rizzo, pursuant to Federal Rule of Civil Procedure 14(a), is granted. SO ORDERED.

* * *

Perhaps the most difficult concept to grasp with impleaders is who can be brought in as a third-party defendant. Note the following words carefully: "[W]ho is or may be liable to it [the third-party plaintiff] for all or part of the claim against it." Fed. R. Civ. P. 14(a)(1). Consequently, in order for a defendant (third-party plaintiff) to implead a new party (the third-party defendant), three conditions must be met (leaving out for now jurisdiction and notice problems, which are addressed elsewhere in the course).

First, and easiest, impleader can be used only in order to bring in one who is not already a party.

Second, the defendant (third-party plaintiff) has to have a claim against the new party it is trying to implead (the third-party defendant). In other words, if *A* sues *B*, and *B* says, in effect, "It's not my fault, it is *C*'s fault," that alone does *not* a good impleader make. Instead, *B* needs a theory of liability *against* *C*. By the way, nothing prevents *B* from pointing the finger at *C* throughout the trial, or even subpoenaing *C* to testify at the trial. *C* doesn't have to be a party in order for one side to blame *C*, assuming the evidence is relevant.

Third, for *B* to have a valid impleader against *C*, *B* not only needs a theory of liability against *C*, but it has to be "for all or part of" *A*'s claim against *B*. Here is an example of a good impleader: *A* lent money to *C*, and *B* agreed to be *C*'s guarantor. Under guaranty or surety law, if the guarantor or surety has to pay the lender, then the guarantor ordinarily has a claim against the borrower for what the guarantor was forced to pay the lender because of the borrower's debt. Therefore, if *A* (lender) sues *B* (guarantor), then *B* could implead *C* (borrower) because *B* will have a claim against *C* for all of what *B* will have to pay *A*. Notice that *B* has a claim against *C* if, but *only* if, *A* prevails on *A*'s claim against *B*. If *B* has a claim regardless of the outcome of *A v. B*, then this is not a valid impleader.

As you read the following excerpt from *United States v. Olavarrieta*, 812 F.2d 640 (11th Cir. 1987), see if you agree with the court that it is an improper impleader, and consider the tactical issues facing a litigator who has the option of impleader versus separate trials. Assuming Olavarrieta's impleader against the Board of Regents was proper, could Olavarrieta claim more from the Board of Regents than the United States was claiming from him? Precisely where would you look to find an answer to this?

The United States, as guarantor of Jose Olavarrieta's federally insured student loans totaling $4,000, filed suit against Olavarrieta in order to collect the unpaid balance and interest on the loans. Inter-National Bank of Miami made the loans to Olavarrieta under the Federal Insured Student Loan Program, Title IV-B of the Higher Education Act of 1965, 20 U.S.C.A. §§ 1071-88. After Olavarrieta defaulted on the loans, the bank sought payment from the government. The government paid off Olavarrieta's liability to the bank and then sought reimbursement from Olavarrieta by filing this suit.

Olavarrieta filed a third party complaint against the University of Florida, claiming that it had violated the Higher Education Act of 1965 and had breached its contract with him by failing to award him a J.D. degree. Olavarrieta amended this complaint to add the Board of Regents of the Division of Universities of the Florida Department of Education as a third party defendant and to add a claim for indemnification by the third party defendants for any sums he was found to owe the government. The district court granted the University of Florida's motion to dismiss. . . .

[W]e hold that the district court properly dismissed the third party complaint against the University of Florida. The capacity to be sued is determined by state law. Fed. R. Civ. P. 17(b). Under Florida law, the University of Florida is not endowed with an independent corporate existence or the capacity to be sued in its own name. Rather, those characteristics are bestowed on the Board of Regents as the head of Florida's university system. Therefore, the University of Florida is not a proper party in this action, and the district court was correct in dismissing the third party complaint asserted against it.

The district court was also correct in dismissing the third party complaint against the Board of Regents. Olavarrieta simply has failed to state any legal or factual grounds for indemnification. Furthermore, to the extent the third party complaint seeks relief on account of the University's failure to award

Olavarrieta a J.D. degree as promised, it does not set forth proper grounds for a third party claim under Fed. R. Civ. P. 14(a). Rule 14(a) allows a defendant to assert a claim against any person not a party to the main action only if that third person's liability on that claim is in some way dependent upon the outcome of the main claim. Rule 14(a) does not allow the defendant to assert a separate and independent claim even though the claim arises out of the same general set of facts as the main claim. . . . Olavarrieta's third party claim alleging breach of contract or fraud on account of the University of Florida's failure to award him a J.D. degree as promised is a separate and independent action from the government's action against him. Whether Olavarrieta is entitled to any relief on this claim is wholly independent of his liability to the government for defaulting on his student loans. Therefore, Olavarrieta has failed to state any appropriate grounds for maintaining a third party complaint against the Board of Regents.

The Rule 8(a) pleading requirements explicitly apply to a Rule 14 third-party complaint. Rule 7 makes clear that a third-party complaint is ordinarily a "pleading" and that a third-party answer is required if a "third-party complaint is served." An answer by the third-party defendant should include Rule 8(b) admissions and denials and 8(c) affirmative defenses. Moreover, Rule 12(b) requires that all defenses to a "claim for relief in any pleading," explicitly including third-party claims, "shall be asserted in the responsive pleading thereto if one is required," and then excepts the 12(b) defenses that can be made by motion. Therefore, the third-party defendant should raise 12(b) defenses against the third-party plaintiff either by answer or motion. The third-party defendant may also, according to Rule 14(a)(2)(C), "assert against the plaintiff any defense that the third-party plaintiff has to the plaintiff's claim." Why should the third-party defendant be able to assert the initial defendant's defenses against the plaintiff?

Be sure to read all of Rule 14. It contains some details regarding transactions or occurrences that you should know. For instance, the third-party defendant may, but is not required to, assert any claims arising out of the same transaction or occurrence against the plaintiff. Also, the (original) plaintiff may assert a claim against the third-party defendant if the claim arises out of the same transaction or occurrence.

REVIEW QUESTION

Return to the *Carpenter* facts and assume that the only named parties in the suit are Nancy Carpenter (as administratrix), Ultimate Auto, and Randall Dee. List all the ways that another entity could be added to this suit — using only the Rules we have learned so far. For example, (1) plaintiff could move to amend pursuant to Rule 15 and add an additional defendant; (2) plaintiff could move to amend pursuant to Rule 15 and add an additional plaintiff. There are at least eight other possibilities to be added to this list.

PRACTICE EXERCISE NO. 14: CONSIDERING AN IMPLEADER IN *WARNER*

You are in your first week as a summer associate in the office that represents the City of New York in the *Warner* action. Imagine that the City of New York is the named insured on a public sector liability policy issued by Inspirada Insurance Company. The insurance policy provides coverage for "liability for bodily injury, personal injury, or property damage that results from law enforcement activities or operations and is caused by acts undertaken in the ordinary course of those activities or operations." This policy specifically excludes coverage for "intentionally perpetrated harms"; this is the so-called intentional acts exception. Your preliminary research suggests that courts tend to read these exceptions narrowly. Specifically, courts find the exceptions inapplicable unless the actor(s) covered by the policy specifically intended to cause the resulting harm. In other words, the court focuses on whether the insured intended the injury, not whether the insured intended the act.

Since *Warner* was filed, Inspirada has refused to provide the City and the named defendants with a defense and, invoking the intentional acts exclusion, has denied coverage. May the City implead Inspirada? Must the City implead Inspirada (lest it waive its right to challenge the scope of the insurance policy)? If it is an *option*, should the City implead Inspirada?

J. AN INTRODUCTION TO NECESSARY AND INDISPENSABLE PARTIES

Federal Rule 19 identifies persons who have not been named as parties but are necessary for a just adjudication of the underlying dispute. Such persons were not initially named as parties either because the plaintiff decided not to join the additional persons, or could not join them for jurisdictional reasons, or because the additional persons refused the plaintiff's invitation to join. Fed. R. Civ. P. 19(a) identifies three situations in which an absentee should be joined: where the plaintiff cannot get relief from the named party (read Rule 19(a)(1)(A)); where the absentee may be prejudiced by the failure to join (read Rule 19(a)(1)(B)(i)); and where the defendant may be prejudiced by the failure to join the absentee (read Rule 19(a)(1)(B)(ii)). Thus any party whose absence results in any of the problems identified in part (a) of the Rule is a party whose joinder is compulsory, if feasible.

For reasons that are explored elsewhere in the course, sometimes the absentee cannot be joined in this lawsuit. And when joinder is not feasible, the court must choose one of two difficult options: Either dismiss the plaintiff's case or proceed without a necessary party. The four factors enumerated in Rule 19(b) guide that inquiry. The labels "necessary" and "indispensable" are conclusory and inexact; they are simply vestiges of a prior version of Rule 19. Nevertheless, lawyers and judges use the terms frequently in the Rule 19 context, with "necessary" parties defined by Rule 19(a), and with those parties whose presence is deemed "indispensable" described by Rule 19(b).

We consider first the parameters of Rule 19(a).

Temple v. Synthes Corporation, Ltd.
498 U.S. 1042 (1991)

PER CURIAM:

Petitioner Temple, a Mississippi resident, underwent surgery in October 1986 in which a "plate and screw device" was implanted in his lower spine. The device was manufactured by respondent Synthes Corp., Ltd. ("Synthes"), a Pennsylvania corporation. Dr. S. Henry LaRocca performed the surgery at St. Charles General Hospital in New Orleans, Louisiana. Following surgery, the device's screws broke off inside Temple's back.

Temple filed suit against Synthes in the United States District Court for the Eastern District of Louisiana. The suit, which rested on diversity jurisdiction, alleged defective design and manufacture of the device. At the same time, Temple . . . filed suit against the doctor and the hospital in Louisiana state court.

Synthes did not attempt to bring the doctor and the hospital into the federal action by means of a third-party complaint, as provided in Federal Rule of Civil Procedure 14(a). Instead, Synthes filed a motion to dismiss Temple's federal suit for failure to join necessary parties pursuant to Federal Rule of Civil Procedure 19. Following a hearing, the District Court ordered Temple to join the doctor and the hospital as defendants within 20 days or risk dismissal of the lawsuit. According to the court, the most significant reason for requiring joinder was the interest of judicial economy. The court relied on this Court's decision in *Provident Tradesmens Bank & Trust Co. v. Patterson*, 390 U.S. 102 (1968), wherein we recognized that one focus of Rule 19 is "the interest of the courts and the public in complete, consistent, and efficient settlement of controversies." *Id.* at 111. When Temple failed to join the doctor and the hospital, the court dismissed the suit with prejudice.

Temple appealed, and the United States Court of Appeals for the Fifth Circuit affirmed. The court deemed it "obviously prejudicial to the defendants to have the separate litigations being carried on," because Synthes' defense might be that the plate was not defective but that the doctor and the hospital were negligent, while the doctor and the hospital, on the other hand, might claim that they were not negligent but that the plate was defective. The Court of Appeals found that the claims overlapped and that the District Court therefore had not abused its discretion in ordering joinder under Rule 19. A petition for rehearing was denied.

In his petition for certiorari to this Court, Temple contends that it was error to label joint tortfeasors as indispensable parties under Rule 19(b) and to dismiss the lawsuit with prejudice for failure to join those parties. We agree. Synthes does not deny that it, the doctor, and the hospital are potential joint tortfeasors. It has long been the rule that it is not necessary for all joint tortfeasors to be named as defendants in a single lawsuit. Nothing in the 1966 revision of Rule 19 changed that principle. The Advisory Committee Notes to Rule 19(a) explicitly state that "a tortfeasor with the usual 'joint-and-several' liability is merely a permissive party to an action against another with like liability." There is nothing in Louisiana tort law to the contrary. . . .

Here, no inquiry under Rule 19(b) is necessary, because the threshold requirements of Rule 19(a) have not been satisfied. As potential joint tortfeasors with Synthes, Dr. LaRocca and the hospital were merely permissive parties. The Court of Appeals erred by failing to hold that the District Court abused its discretion in ordering them joined as defendants and in dismissing the action when Temple failed to comply with the court's order. For these reasons, we grant the petition for certiorari, reverse the judgment of the Court of Appeals for the Fifth Circuit, and remand for further proceedings consistent with this opinion.

REVIEW QUESTIONS

1. Assuming that it would be more *efficient* to require the joinder of joint tortfeasors, what interests or policies are instead given priority here?
2. Given the narrow scope of Rule 19(a), the *Temple* Court seems to have found it unnecessary to parse the language of the three categories of "necessary party" status. Work carefully through the language of Rule 19(a) and be able to explain why a joint tortfeasor is not a necessary party.

* * *

Subtle issues of interpretation are presented in each of the provisions of part (a). Consider, first, the language of Fed. R. Civ. P. 19(a)(1)(A). This provision confers necessary status upon the absentee only if "in that person's absence, the court cannot accord complete relief among existing parties."

The 19(a)(1)(A) inquiry focuses on the relief that is sought and the ability of the named parties to render that relief, if so ordered by the court. If a plaintiff seeks equitable relief that the named defendant(s) cannot alone effect, then the additional parties needed to effect that relief could be necessary parties. For example, if a lawsuit seeking specific performance of the conveyance of land is filed against only one of two joint owners of the property, the single defendant could not alone effect the transfer even if so ordered by the court.

Temple makes clear that in damages cases, joint tortfeasors are not necessary parties. But what if the named defendant is judgment-proof? Can a plaintiff obtain "complete relief" from the named defendant if he is unable to collect on the judgment? Although, as a practical matter, he may not be able to obtain complete relief, the inability to collect on a judgment typically will *not* satisfy the "complete relief" criterion of 19(a)(1)(A).

Some commentators consider this first category of Rule 19(a) a "null set." *See, e.g.*, Richard D. Freer, *Rethinking Compulsory Joinder: A Proposal to Restructure Federal Rule 19*, 60 N.Y.U. L. Rev. 1061, 1062 (1985). Indeed, the Rule's narrow construction makes it applicable in very few cases, and Rule 19(a)(1)(A) may be misapplied more often than it is properly invoked. *Id.* At 1081-1082.

Next, Fed. R. Civ. P. 19(a)(1)(B)(i) confers necessary party status if the interests of the absentee would be prejudiced from the adverse effects of a judgment rendered in their absence. The challenge here is to determine which interests are protected and what quantum of impairment is required.

Courts typically recognize only "legally protected" interests. This interest must be more than a financial stake. One's family, for example, may be greatly affected by a judgment in one's favor or by a judgment against one, but this ordinarily would not make them necessary parties. These absentees would not have a direct stake or "interest relating to the subject matter of the action."

The joinder of an absent party is compulsory under Rule 19(a)(1)(B)(i) if the litigation would have a preclusive effect against the absent party in subsequent litigation. If collateral estoppel could be invoked against the absentee in other litigation, continuation of the federal action could "as a practical matter impair or impede" the absentee's interests and so Rule 19(a)(1)(B)(i) would require its joinder if joinder were feasible. One might expect the Due Process Clause to solve the problem, as no absentee can be bound unless it is named as a party in the litigation. The exception, of course, is for an absentee that is in privity with a named party; but, in that instance, the absent party will, in effect, have had its day in court by virtue of its privity with the named party. However, consider the facts of *Lopez v. Martin Luther King, Jr., Hospital*, 97 F.R.D. 24 (C.D. Cal. 1983). There the parents of a child sued the hospital and various doctors, alleging medical malpractice in the course of childbirth, for recovery of damages suffered by them (and not the child). (Under California law, the parents had a cause of action separate from the child's.) The child was not named as a plaintiff, because it would have destroyed the diversity jurisdiction of the federal court. (The Lopez parents were Mexican nationals; the child was a citizen of California.) The district court held that the child was a necessary party because the child might later have been precluded if a California court found privity. Importantly, however, courts disagree on the extent to which the likelihood of preclusion must be demonstrated. *See Janney Montgomery Scott, Inc. v. Shepard Niles, Inc.*, 11 F.3d 399 (3d Cir. 1993) (holding "[m]ere presentation of an argument that issue preclusion is possible is not enough to trigger Rule 19(a). . .").

A second classic example is the group of cases involving a limited pie. A fixed fund that a court is asked to allocate may create a protectable interest in putative beneficiaries of the fund. (Consider, for example, the proceeds of a trust account.) Allocation to the plaintiff could "as a practical matter" impair the absentee's interest therein. Similarly, a judgment decreeing that the plaintiff is the owner of land will not bind absentees who claim title; but the absentee may be a necessary party if it casts a cloud on their title.

Further, courts are disinclined to find necessary parties in litigation involving the vindication of public rights. *See National Licorice Co. v. NLRB*, 309 U.S. 350 (1940).

> In some cases, the courts have not insisted on Rule 19 joinder of those whose interests will "be impaired or impeded" by a litigation if their position is already advanced by another party. . . , if mandatory joinder would be unwieldy or impossible, and if there was a strong public interest that the case proceed. In an environmental suit brought by the Sierra Club, for example, the District Court for the Eastern District of California held that although miners' property rights would be affected, the miners were not necessary parties: "where what is at stake are essentially issues of public concern and the nature of the case would require joinder of a large number of persons, Rule 19's joinder requirements need not be satisfied." [*Sierra Club v. Watt*, 608 F. Supp. 305, 321-324 (E.D. Cal. 1985).] Also citing Federal Rule 1, the district court reasoned that "[s]urely justice cannot be done if public interest litigation is precluded by virtue of the requirements of joinder."

Phyllis Tropper Bauman et al., *Substance in the Shadow of Procedure: The Integration of Substantive and Procedural Law in Title VII Cases*, 33 B.C. L. Rev. 211, 281-282 (1992) (footnotes omitted).

Finally, consider Fed. R. Civ. P. 19(a)(1)(B)(ii) and the meaning of "inconsistent obligations." In *Carpenter*, assume that Nancy Carpenter sued (only) Randall Dee and, in that trial, a jury found for the plaintiff and awarded damages of $100,000. Assume, then, that Carpenter brought a second action against (only) Ultimate Auto and, in that second trial, a jury found for the plaintiff and awarded damages of $500,000. (And assume further that Ultimate Auto could not use nonmutual defensive collateral estoppel against Carpenter on the amount of her harm.) Would this constitute "inconsistent obligations" within the meaning of Fed. R. Civ. P. 19(a)(1)(B)(ii)? The answer is *no*, even though the verdicts certainly are inconsistent. Inconsistent verdicts are not uncommon. Frequently, when non-joined plaintiffs sue a defendant on the same theory (e.g., asbestos, tobacco, handguns, mass disaster), some plaintiffs win and others lose — even if the relevant facts are identical. An inconsistent *obligation* occurs if one court orders a party to do one thing (e.g., deed Blackacre to *A*) and another court orders the same party to perform an inconsistent act (e.g., deed Blackacre to *B*).

REVIEW QUESTIONS

1. In *Carpenter*, if two passengers were killed, would both of them be necessary parties who should be joined as plaintiffs, if feasible? Why or why not? (What else would you need to know?) Would Randall Dee and Ultimate Auto have to be joined as defendants? Were Twyla Burrell and/or Peter Dee necessary parties given the construction of the original complaint?

2. What if Randall Dee had a liability insurance policy on the jeep requiring the insurer to indemnify the insured (Dee) for liability as a result of driving the jeep, with certain exclusions that are not relevant here? You will find out when you study preclusion law in Chapter 10 that insurers are in privity with the insured when the insurer can control the litigation. A provision granting such control is typical in liability policies and so the insurer is normally bound by a judicial liability determination against the insured. Do you think that the insurer in the jeep case cannot only be *impleaded* by Randall Dee but is also a Rule 19(a) *necessary party*?

* * *

The next case reviews all of the Rule 19(a) categories of necessary party status and also introduces the indispensability analysis of Rule 19(b).

Daynard v. Ness, Motley, Loadholt, Richardson & Poole, P.A.
184 F. Supp. 2d 55 (D. Mass. 2001)

YOUNG, Chief Judge:

. . . The plaintiff, Professor Richard A. Daynard ("Daynard") of Northeastern University School of Law, has spent much of his academic career studying how to defeat the tobacco industry in court. The defendants—the Ness, Motley, Loadholt, Richardson & Poole, P.A. law firm and one of its partners, Mr. Motley (together "the South Carolina defendants"), and the Scruggs, Milette, Bozeman & Dent, P.A. law firm and one of its partners, Mr. Scruggs (together "the Mississippi defendants")—were among the many law firms representing state governments in the titanic battle against the tobacco industry ("the State Tobacco Litigation").

Between 1993 and 1997, Daynard provided advice to the defendants. No written contract detailed how Daynard would be compensated, but Daynard alleges that he and one of the Mississippi defendants shook hands in Chicago, Illinois in 1996 on an agreement whereby he would receive 5% of any attorneys' fees paid to the defendants as a result of the State Tobacco Litigation. In 1997 and 1998, the tobacco industry agreed to settle the State Tobacco Litigation for billions of dollars. Since then, the defendants have received millions of dollars in attorneys' fees and Daynard has received nothing.

[The plaintiff brought suit against both the South Carolina defendants and the Mississippi defendants. Upon a successful motion by the latter to dismiss for lack of personal jurisdiction, the South Carolina defendants then moved to dismiss the case under Fed. R. Civ. P. 12(b)(7) for failure to join an indispensable party. The dismissal on grounds of lack of personal jurisdiction was on appeal at the time of this opinion; the order of dismissal ultimately was reversed. *See Daynard v. Ness, Motley, Loadholt, Richardson & Poole, P.A.*, 290 F.3d 42 (1st Cir. 2002).]

The South Carolina defendants argue that the case should not proceed without the Mississippi defendants because it was Mr. Scruggs who allegedly shook hands with Daynard in Chicago, so any lawsuit without Mr. Scruggs would be incomplete and only spawn subsequent lawsuits that do include Mr. Scruggs. Daynard, in response, argues that the handshake in Chicago was merely the culmination of many assurances from both the South Carolina defendants and the Mississippi defendants that he would receive attorneys' fees. In other words, Daynard argues that the defendants together agreed to pay him 5% of their attorneys' fees from the State Tobacco Litigation, so under a theory of joint and several liability, only one defendant need be named in the complaint.

1. PROCEDURAL POSTURE

A defense of failure to join an indispensable party, Fed. R. Civ. P. 12(b)(7), may be made at any time before the end of trial. Fed. R. Civ. P. 12(h)(2). The defense turns on Rule 19, which implicitly distinguishes "necessary" parties from "indispensable" parties. A "necessary" party under Rule 19(a) is one that should be joined to effect a just adjudication, while an "indispensable" party under Rule 19(b) is simply a "necessary" party under Rule 19(a) who, for one reason or another, cannot be made a party and without whom the court determines the action cannot proceed. The important point to note is that "indispensable" is a subset of "necessary," not a mutually exclusive category.

Thus, determination of whether a party is "indispensable" requires two steps: First, is the party "necessary" under Rule 19(a)? Second, if the party is "necessary," is it also "indispensable" under Rule 19(b)?. . .

As the moving party, the South Carolina defendants bear the burden of showing why the Mississippi defendants are indispensable and dismissal is proper under Rule 12(b)(7). In meeting its burden, the moving party may present, and the court may consider, evidence outside of the pleadings. . . . Fed. R. Civ. P. 19 advisory committee's note (1966 amendment) (noting decision may "properly be deferred if adequate information is not available at the time").

2. DISCUSSION

A. RULE 19(a) — NECESSARY?

(1) Some Rules of Thumb

Over the years, several rules of thumb have developed under Rule 19:

- Joint tortfeasors are not necessary parties. Thus, by definition, they may not be indispensable.
- Co-obligors [to a contract] may be necessary parties, but generally are not indispensable.
- As a general rule, an action to set aside a contract requires the joinder of all parties to the contract.

Moore's Federal Practice § 19.06[1]. . . .

The South Carolina defendants cite several decisions for the proposition that, generally speaking, all parties to a contract must be joined. The South Carolina defendants apparently advocate a rule of thumb in contravention to the rules of thumb recognized by the Supreme Court and the commentators, but regardless, the proper approach today is to examine each case in light of the factors mentioned in Rules 19(a) and 19(b).

(2) First Circuit Caselaw

In *Acton* [*Co. v. Bachman Foods, Inc.*, 668 F.2d 76 (1st Cir. 1982)], the First Circuit affirmed the dismissal of a contract action for failure to join an indispensable party. The facts are as follows: A parent corporation and its subsidiary agreed to purchase the assets of another company. When the deal fell through, two lawsuits arose: (i) the seller sued both the parent and the sub in New York state court for breach of contract, and (ii) the sub — without joining the parent — sued the seller in the District of Massachusetts seeking a declaration that the contract was void as a result of the seller's misrepresentations. The district court dismissed the sub's lawsuit for failure to join the parent. The First Circuit affirmed:

> There is little doubt that [the parent], as a party to the letter of intent and to the purchase agreement, should be joined to this action if feasible. . . . To begin, [the parent] played a substantial role in negotiating both agreements; indeed, [the sub] did not even exist in April 1979 when the letter of intent was signed. Thus [the parent] may have rights under this preliminary agreement not shared by [the sub]. Moreover, according to the express terms of the purchase agreement, [the parent] and not [the sub] would be entitled to refund of the $250,000 deposit. Unless [the parent] were bound by the results of [the sub's] suit, it would remain free to commence a new action on its claims. [The parent's] presence is therefore desirable not only to avoid piecemeal and duplicative litigation, but also to provide complete relief to the [seller]. *See* Rule 19(a)(1).
>
> In addition, [the parent], as [the sub's] parent corporation and as [the sub's] guarantor, might be bound by [the sub's] suit under the doctrine that *res judicata* applies not only to the actual parties but also to those in privity with the parties. If so, to proceed in [the parent's] absence might impair [the parent's] interest in the controversy very significantly. Even if [the parent] would not be legally bound, an adverse ruling would be a persuasive precedent in a subsequent proceeding, and would weaken [the parent's] bargaining position for settlement purposes. In either case, to proceed without [the parent] might "as a practical matter impair or impede" [the parent's] ability to protect its interest in this matter. Rule 19(a)(2)(i).* [The parent] is therefore a ["necessary" party].

668 F.2d at 78-79 (citations omitted). The facts of *Acton* are distinguishable from the case at bar in two notable respects: (i) the absent party in *Acton* was

---

* *Eds.' Note:* This case is interpreting an earlier version of Fed. R. Civ. P. 19. The language that appeared at 19(a)(2)(i) at the time of this case now appears (with slightly different language) at Fed. R. Civ. P. 19(a)(1)(B)(i).

a co-obligee, not a co-obligor, and (ii) any judgment in *Acton* likely would have been binding against the absent defendant because it was in privity with the co-obligee.

In *H.D. Corp.* [*v. Ford Motor Co.*, 791 F.2d 987 (1st Cir. 1986)], several automobile dealerships brought a breach of contract action in the District of Puerto Rico against Ford Motor Company and its local subsidiary. The dealerships and Ford were all Delaware corporations, so the district court dismissed Ford from the action to preserve diversity, leaving only its local subsidiary as a defendant. The district court went on to dismiss the action entirely, however, because it concluded that Ford was an indispensable party. The First Circuit affirmed. The holding of *H.D. Corp.* is not instructive, though, for two reasons. First, the court held that Ford was "indispensable" without considering whether it was "necessary." Second, given the case-specific inquiry required by Rule 19(b), an opinion affirming a finding that a party is "indispensable" does not provide useful guidance far beyond its particular facts.

Finally, in *Pujol* [*v. Shearson/American Express, Inc.*, 877 F.2d 132 (1st Cir. 1989)], the First Circuit noted with approval the distinction traditionally drawn between joint tortfeasors and persons jointly liable on a contract:

> [I]f one thing is clear in respect to Rule 19, it is that, unlike a person vicariously liable in tort, a person potentially liable as a joint tortfeasor is not a necessary or indispensable party, but merely a permissive party subject to joinder under Rule 20. . . .
>
> Of course, one might wonder why Rule 19 would treat "joint tortfeasors" differently in this respect than, say, persons jointly liable under a contract. *See Acton*, 688 F.2d at 81-82 ("an action seeking rescission of a contract must be dismissed unless all parties to the contract, and others having a substantial interest in it, can be joined"); *see also H.D. Corp.*, 791 F.2d at 993. The reason for the difference may lie in the history of joinder doctrine, or it may reflect a compromise between the interests served by Rule 19 and the policies of tort law. But, regardless of the reasons, this case presents no basis for ignoring such well established precedent [concerning jointly and severally liable tortfeasors].

877 F.2d at 137 (citations omitted). The quotation above, however, is dictum and adds nothing to the holdings of *Acton* and *H.D. Corp.*

(3) *Janney*

In *Janney* [*Montgomery Scott, Inc. v. Shepard Niles, Inc.*, 11 F.3d 399 (3d Cir. 1993)], an investment bank agreed to be the exclusive advisor to a parent corporation and its subsidiaries. Later, the investment bank sued one of the subs — but not the parent — for failing to pay the fees contemplated by the agreement. Both the parent and the sub were co-obligors, but only the parent had signed the contract. The Third Circuit carefully analyzed each provision of Rule 19(a) and concluded that the parent was not a "necessary" party:

Rule 19(a)(1) — "in the person's absence complete relief cannot be accorded among those already parties." The court held that this factor did not apply because the defendants could be jointly and severally liable under the contract. The court noted that it was possible that the contract, in fact, did not impose joint and several liability on the defendants, but the court held that all inferences had to be drawn in the plaintiff's favor on a motion to dismiss, so the court assumed joint and several liability.

Rule 19(a)(2)(i) — "the person claims an interest relating to the subject of the action and is so situated that the disposition of the action in the person's absence may as a practical matter impair or impede the person's ability to protect that interest." The court held that this factor did not apply because any judgment against the defendants would not bind the absent defendant. The court also rejected the argument that any such judgment would nevertheless act as "persuasive precedent" and thus impair the absent defendant's ability to protect its interests:

> We are not sure what the district court means by the phrase "persuasive precedent." To the extent it involves the doctrine of *stare decisis*, we are not inclined to hold that any potential effect the doctrine may have on an absent party's rights makes the absent party's joinder compulsory under Rule 19(a) whenever "feasible." Such a holding would greatly expand the class of "necessary" or compulsory parties Rule 19(a) creates. Moreover, to whatever extent the rule's phrase "as a practical matter impair or impede" has broader meaning than that given by principles of issue preclusion, we think the effect of the federal decision must be more direct and immediate than the effect a judgment in [the defendant's] favor would have on [the absent defendant] here. They are, after all, separate corporate entities. In any event, we do not believe any possibility of a "persuasive precedent" requires joinder under subsection 19(a)(2)(i). . . .
>
> [The defendant] cites [*Acton Co. v. Bachman Foods, Inc.*, 668 F.2d 76 (1st Cir. 1982),] to support its argument that the potentially persuasive effect of the federal action on any related litigation justifies the district court's conclusion that the absent party's joinder is compulsory under Rule 19(a)(2)(i). That argument ignores the United States Court of Appeals for the First Circuit's refusal to adopt a persuasive precedent standard for a Rule 19(a) determination that all tortfeasors who could be jointly and severally liable should be joined if feasible. *See Pujol v. Shearson/American Express, Inc.*, 877 F.2d 132, 136 (1st Cir. 1989) ("The mere fact, however, that Party A, in a suit against Party B, intends to introduce evidence that will indicate that a non-party, C, behaved improperly does not, by itself, make C a necessary party."). Though we recognize that the *Pujol* court distinguished joint tortfeasors from joint obligors and stated that *Acton* was still good law as applied to contract liability, we see no logical distinction that would justify treating contract actions differently than tort actions for purposes of compulsory joinder. Instead, we believe the distinction made by the Court of Appeals for the First Circuit is based on authority, not logic. Thus, to the extent *Pujol* goes beyond a panel's recognition of the need to accept controlling circuit precedent, it does not persuade us. For the reasons already stated, we hold instead that [the absent defendant], a co-obligor, is not a party whose joinder Rule 19(a)(2)(i) requires because continuation of the federal litigation in

[a co-obligor's] absence will not create a precedent that might persuade another court to rule against [the co-obligor] on principles of *stare decisis*, or some other unidentified basis not encompassed by the rules of collateral estoppel or issue preclusion.

Id. at 407, 408-09 (citations and footnotes omitted).

Rule 19(a)(2)(ii)* — "the person claims an interest relating to the subject of the action and is so situated that the disposition of the action in the person's absence may leave any of the persons already parties subject to a substantial risk of incurring double, multiple, or otherwise inconsistent obligations by reason of the claimed interest." The court held that this factor did not apply because the risk of inconsistent *adjudications* is not the same thing as inconsistent *obligations*.

> The possibility that [the defendant] may bear the whole loss if it is found liable [and the absent defendant later is found not liable] is not the equivalent of double liability. It is instead a common result of joint and several liability and should not be equated with prejudice. Inherent in the concept of joint and several liability is the right of a plaintiff to satisfy its whole judgment by execution against any one of the multiple defendants who are liable to him, thereby forcing the debtor who has paid the whole debt to protect itself by an action for contribution against the other joint obligors.

Id. at 412.

Thus, the Court in *Janney* held that the absent co-obligor was not even a "necessary" party under Rule 19(a), let alone an "indispensable" party under Rule 19(b).

(4) The Parties' Arguments

First, pointing to subsection (a)(1), the South Carolina defendants argue that Daynard cannot get complete relief in this Court because he will not be able to recover the money owed by the Mississippi defendants. This argument assumes that Daynard entered into separate contracts with the South Carolina and Mississippi defendants, an assumption the Court cannot make on a motion to dismiss. To the contrary, the South Carolina defendants bear the burden of persuasion, so the Court must draw inferences in Daynard's favor and assume that the defendants are jointly and severally liable.

Second, pointing to subsection (a)(2)(i), the South Carolina defendants argue that because they likely will pursue the "empty chair" defense — in particular, that Daynard made a contract only with Mr. Scruggs — a judgment in favor of the South Carolina defendants would be "persuasive precedent" against the Mississippi defendants, thus impairing the Mississippi defendants' ability to defend themselves as a practical matter. As discussed above,

---

* *Eds.' Note:* The corresponding provision in the current rule appears at Fed. R. Civ. P. 19(a)(1)(B)(ii).

both the First Circuit and *Janney* have rejected this very argument, and so must this Court.[5]

Third, pointing to subsection (a)(2)(ii), the South Carolina defendants argue that there is the possibility that they alone will end up footing the entire bill when, in fact, the Mississippi defendants are entirely or partly responsible. As discussed above, both the First Circuit and *Janney* have rejected this very argument, and so must this Court.

Fourth, recognizing the traditional rule of thumb that co-obligees are "indispensable" parties while co-obligors might not even be "necessary," the South Carolina defendants try to cast themselves as co-obligees under the alleged contract. In other words, the South Carolina defendants argue that Daynard still owes legal research and advice to the defendants—even though the State Tobacco Litigation settled years ago. This argument is as silly as it is belated. The only question before the Court is whether the defendants owe Daynard money; there has never been any suggestion that Daynard still owes services to the defendants. The Court rejects the notion that the South Carolina defendants are co-obligees and instead recognizes them for what they really are—co-obligors.

Finally, recognizing the traditional rule of thumb that an action to set aside a contract requires the joinder of all parties to the contract, the South Carolina defendants argue that a mutual release to which Daynard allegedly agreed puts the validity and enforceability of the alleged contract into question and thus requires joinder of all parties to the alleged contract. This argument twists the traditional rule of thumb, which is that an action in equity to determine the rights under a contract requires joinder of all the parties to the contract. The case at bar concerns only money damages (legal relief) and does not concern rescission or specific performance (equitable relief). Accordingly, the traditional rule of thumb that rescission requires joinder of all parties must give way to the traditional rule of thumb that a plaintiff need not name all co-obligors as defendants.

In short, the Court holds that it is not necessary for Daynard to join the Mississippi defendants in this action because they are (or, drawing inferences in Daynard's favor, could be) jointly and severally liable co-obligors.

B. RULE 19(b)—INDISPENSABLE?

If the Mississippi defendants are not "necessary" under Rule 19(a), then by definition they cannot be "indispensable" under Rule 19(b). Nevertheless, the Court will consider the South Carolina defendants' arguments under Rule 19(b) for the sake of completeness.

---

5. Similarly, the Mississippi defendants cannot be "necessary" merely because the South Carolina defendants need to obtain evidence from them. *E.g., Johnson v. Smithsonian Inst.*, 189 F.3d 180, 188-89 (2d Cir. 1999) (citing *Costello Publ'g Co. v. Rotelle*, 670 F.2d 1035, 1044-45 (D.C. Cir. 1981)).

If a "necessary" party cannot be joined (*e.g.*, because of a lack of personal jurisdiction), "the court shall determine whether in equity and good conscience the action should proceed among the parties before it, or should be dismissed, the absent person being thus regarded as indispensable." Fed. R. Civ. P. 19(b). The factors to be considered by the court include:

> [F]irst, to what extent a judgment rendered in the person's absence might be prejudicial to the person or those already parties; second, the extent to which, by protective provisions in the judgment, by the shaping of relief, or other measures, the prejudice can be lessened or avoided; third, whether a judgment rendered in the person's absence will be adequate; fourth, whether the plaintiff will have an adequate remedy if the action is dismissed for nonjoinder.

Id. The Supreme Court has identified four corresponding interests a court might want to consider:

> (1) the interest of the outsider whom it would have been desirable to join; (2) the defendant's interest in avoiding multiple litigation, inconsistent relief, or sole responsibility for a liability it shares with another; (3) the interest of the courts and the public in complete, consistent, and efficient settlement of controversies; and (4) the plaintiff's interest in having a forum.

H.D. Corp., 791 F.2d at 992 (citing *Provident Tradesmens Bank & Trust Co. v. Patterson*, 390 U.S. 102, 108-111 (1968)).

. . . [T]he First Circuit will review this Court's determination under Rule 19(b) for an abuse of discretion. Accordingly, precedent provides little guidance. "Whether a person is 'indispensable,' that is, whether a particular lawsuit must be dismissed in the absence of that person, can only be determined in the context of particular litigation." *Provident Tradesmens*, 390 U.S. at 118. With this in mind, the Court turns to the four factors enumerated in Rule 19(b), which substantially overlap with the factors enumerated in Rule 19(a).

First, to what extent might a judgment rendered in the person's absence be prejudicial to the person or those already parties? This factor tends to favor Daynard. The South Carolina defendants argue that (i) there is the possibility that they alone will end up footing the entire bill, which would prejudice them; (ii) there is the possibility that a successful "empty chair" defense would result in "persuasive precedent," which would prejudice the Mississippi defendants; and (iii) there is the possibility of an inconsistent adjudication in a later lawsuit, which could prejudice any of the parties. The Court rejects these arguments for the same reasons given before, namely (i) joint and several liability by definition includes the possibility that one defendant ends up footing the entire bill, (ii) "persuasive precedent" alone cannot, as a practical matter, impair or impede the Mississippi defendants' ability to defend themselves, and (iii) Rule 19 is concerned with the risk of inconsistent obligations, not inconsistent adjudications.

Second, to what extent can the prejudice be lessened or avoided by protective provisions in the judgment, by the shaping of relief, or other measures? This factor does not seem relevant to this dispute. According to the advisory committee's note, "protective provisions" includes requiring a defendant to set aside money in case absent plaintiffs later obtain judgments, and the "shaping of relief" includes awarding money damages in lieu of specific performance where the latter might affect an absentee adversely.

Third, would a judgment rendered in the person's absence be adequate? This factor clearly favors Daynard. The South Carolina defendants are (or, drawing inferences in Daynard's favor, could be) jointly and severally liable. The South Carolina defendants complain that allowing Daynard to obtain complete relief from them will result in a second lawsuit between the defendants, but that is their problem, not Daynard's. Obviously a single lawsuit would be more efficient than multiple lawsuits, but this factor only concerns whether the judgment would be adequate to Daynard.

Fourth, would the plaintiff have an adequate remedy if the action is dismissed for nonjoinder? This factor clearly favors the South Carolina defendants. Daynard could bring suit against all the defendants in Mississippi.

In sum, the first and third factors favor Daynard, the second factor is not relevant, and the fourth factor favors the South Carolina defendants. The question is not simply how many factors point in one direction, of course, but "whether in equity and good conscience the action should proceed among the parties before [the court], or should be dismissed, the absent person being thus regarded as indispensable." Fed. R. Civ. P. 19(b). To this question the Court answers that it would allow the action to proceed against the South Carolina defendants even if the Mississippi defendants properly were regarded as "necessary" parties.

REVIEW QUESTIONS

1. Carefully consider each case that Judge Young describes (i.e., *Acton Co.*, *H.D. Corp.*, *Pujol*, and *Janney*), and be prepared to explain the result in each and why it is like or distinguishable from *Daynard*.

2. Put yourself in Judge Young's shoes. Why did he write "Part 2b" of his opinion regarding Rule 19(b)? Wasn't this unnecessary given his decision in "Part 2a"? Had the First Circuit decided, as it ultimately did, that the Mississippi defendants should not have been dismissed for lack of personal jurisdiction, what effect would that have had on the South Carolina defendants' Rule 12(b)(7) motion to dismiss?

3. There is considerable overlap between the four factors in parts (a) and (b) of Fed. R. Civ. P. 19. What is the difference, then, between "necessary" and "indispensable" parties?

a. Considering Strategy

What types of considerations might have convinced Professor Daynard and his lawyers not to file suit in Mississippi? What other techniques might these defendants have employed to get the case into Mississippi?

QUESTIONS TO PONDER

1. Is mandatory joinder disfavored? If so, why?
2. Why does Fed. R. Civ. P. 12(h)(2) add "a defense of failure to join a party indispensable under Rule 19" to those which can be made as late as "at the trial on the merits"?

K. INTERPLEADER

An individual or corporation who is or may be exposed to double or multiple liability may also initiate the joinder of the parties who have asserted or could assert such claims. This joinder device is called *interpleader*, and many of these cases involve insurance disputes. For example, a life insurance company may have issued a policy payable to the beneficiary "Roy Adams" upon the death of the insured. But when two persons named "Roy Adams" claim to be the beneficiaries entitled to the proceeds of the policy, the insurance company may be uncertain as to which of the two it should pay. Under these circumstances, the life insurance company can *interplead* those alleging rights to the proceeds. By doing so, the company seeks a determination of whom to pay and avoids the risk that it will have to pay the policy amount twice. Consequently, the insurance company, which ordinarily would be the defendant in a case in which a beneficiary makes a claim, becomes the plaintiff in an interpleader. In the terminology of interpleaders, the insurance company is the *stakeholder*. The *stake* is subject to the claims of the *adverse claimants*, who in this hypothetical would be the two persons named Roy Adams.

The words *stake* and *adverse claimants* convey an important restriction about the utility of the interpleader device: The claims must be demanding the same thing or obligation—that is, a piece of property, a prize, or, most commonly, the proceeds of an insurance policy. Importantly, Ultimate Auto could *not* interplead some other putative plaintiff who was injured by a suspension lift kit that Ultimate Auto sold; that putative plaintiff and Charles Carpenter's estate would not be asserting claims that compete for the same thing. Understand the important difference: The insurance company promised to pay one person named Roy Adams—the only question is *which* Roy Adams.

The Roy Adams hypothetical can be complicated still further if the insurance company is not only the stakeholder but also one of the adverse claimants. This could occur in our hypothetical if the insurance company claims that the premium was not timely paid and, thus, no payout is necessary. The insurance company would interplead both of the individuals named Roy Adams to avoid paying twice, but it would also be an adverse claimant and would argue that it should not have to pay even once.

Interpleader is also available to a stakeholder who is sued by one of the claimants, allowing it to interplead the other claimants by way of a third-party claim, cross-claim, or counterclaim. A trial court deciding an interpleader action first considers whether there is real potential for exposure to multiple liability for a single "claim." If so, then a court will proceed to address the merits of the interpleader action. Two types of interpleader are available in federal court: Rule 22 and 28 U.S.C. § 1335. (Regarding the latter, *see also* 28 U.S.C. §§ 1397 and 2361.) The major differences between the Rule and the statute pertain to jurisdictional and venue requirements, which are the subject of Chapter 7.

L. INTERVENTION

Federal Rule 24 allows nonparties to join ongoing litigation either as a matter of right or in the discretion of the court. Intervenors can protect their interests against the possible adverse effects of a judgment. The criteria for intervention as a matter of right differ in degree rather than in kind from those governing permissive or discretionary intervention.

United States v. Northern Indiana Public Service Co., et al.
100 F.R.D. 78 (N.D. Ind. 1983)

SHARP, Chief Judge:

I.

This case is presently before the court on the motion to intervene of the petitioner, Save the Dunes Council (Council) under Rule 24 Fed. R. Civ. P. The following facts are not disputed. On August 7, 1978, plaintiff, United States of America (United States) filed its "Notice of Condemnation" affecting 36.95 acres of land owned by Northern Indiana Public Service Company (NIPSCO) adjacent to its Michigan City Generating Station. NIPSCO filed its answer, objections to condemnation and motion to sustain objections on September 25, 1978. Subsequently, a request for a hearing on NIPSCO's legal objections was filed on October 26, 1981. A trial date of February 8, 1982 was set by order of the court October 9, 1981. That trial setting was vacated by order of January 22, 1982. On April 4, 1982, the Council filed a motion to intervene as a plaintiff under Rule 24. NIPSCO's response to the motion to intervene and a motion to strike were docketed April 8, 1982. Council then filed a memorandum in support of its motion to intervene and an answer to NIPSCO's motion to strike on April 20, 1982.

On September 7, 1983, the United States and NIPSCO entered into a stipulation and joint motion to dismiss. A pretrial conference was held in Lafayette, Indiana on October 20, 1983 where oral argument was heard on the intervention issue and the parties were instructed to file supplementary briefs by October 31, 1983. In addition, the Council filed, in open court, a copy of a pleading related to the subject matter of this case, a complaint for mandamus under 28 U.S.C. § 361, which had been filed on October 19, 1983 in the United States District Court for the District of Columbia. In compliance with this court's directive, supplemental briefs were filed by the Council on October 31, 1983 and by NIPSCO on November 1, 1983. To date, the United States had made no independent response to the Council's motion to intervene.

II.

To intervene as of right under Fed. R. Civ. P. 24(a)(2), a proposed intervenor must show: (1) timely application; (2) an interest relating to the property or transaction which is the subject of the action; (3) that the disposition of the action may as a practical matter impair or impede his ability to protect that interest; and (4) that the interest is not adequately represented by existing parties.

Timeliness is a threshold question in a Rule 24(a) application and is determined by the court from all the circumstances in the exercise of its sound discretion. As soon as a prospective intervenor knows or has reason to know his interest may be adversely affected by the outcome of the litigation, he must move promptly to intervene. NIPSCO contends that the Council should not be allowed to intervene at this time because the Council had ample opportunity to petition the court prior to the time of the original parties' settlement. A careful review of the court record in this action indicates that the first reference to a possible settlement was alluded to in the joint motion for extension of time filed by the United States and NIPSCO on January 12, 1982. The Council filed its motion to intervene on April 2, 1982 while the parties' joint motion for dismissal was not filed until more than a year later on September 7, 1983. From the commencement of this action to the early months of 1982, the Council had no reason to believe that intervention would be required to protect its alleged interest in the tract of land since condemnation of the NIPSCO property would seem to effectuate the intent of Congress as manifested in a series of National Lakeshore expansion bills, all of which included the area at issue in this case. Moreover, there has been neither a trial nor an extensive exchange of pleadings. Thus, the first requirement—timeliness—has been met by the Council.

The second test the Council must meet concerns a determination as to whether or not it has an interest relating to the property or transaction which is the subject of the action. Council alleges that it has an environmental interest in that for the past 30 years it has been actively engaged in, and, has been at the forefront of, the campaign to preserve and protect the Indiana Dunes for public use and enjoyment.

There is as yet no consensus of what constitutes a litigable interest for purposes of standing and intervention under Rule 24(a). C.A. Wright, *Law of Federal Courts*, at 503 (4th ed. 1983). The more liberal view is set forth in *Cascade Natural*

Gas Corp. v. El Paso Natural Gas Co., 386 U.S. 129 (1967). That case expanded the application of "interest" by holding that a state, a customer, and a competitor all have a sufficient interest to intervene in a government antitrust divestiture proceeding. Cascade gives a decidedly broad interpretation to Rule 24 while noting that intervention of right is:

> . . . a kind of counterpart to Rule 19(a)(2)(i) on joinder of persons needed for just adjudication: where, upon motion of a party in an action, an absentee should be joined so that he may protect his interest which as a practical matter may be substantially impaired by the disposition of the action, he ought to have a right to intervene in the action on his own motion.

Id. at 134 n.3.

However, the most recent interpretation of Rule 24(a)(2) by the Supreme Court has added a gloss that the rule is referring to a direct, "significantly protectable" interest in the property or transaction subject to the action. *Donaldson v. United States*, 400 U.S. 517, 531 (1971). Cases in this circuit construing a Rule 24(a) interest also emphasize an interest which is legally protectable. In *Wade v. Goldschmidt*, 673 F.2d 182 (7th Cir. 1982), the court relied on this definition of "interest":

> [A]n interest, to satisfy the requirements of Rule 24(a)(2) must be significant, must be direct rather than contingent, and must be based on a right which belongs to the proposed intervenor rather than to an existing party to the suit.

Id. at 185-86 n.5.

Clearly, the party with the paramount interest, indeed, the only legal interest, in the land at issue is NIPSCO. While the Council has played a laudatory role in the development of the Indiana Dunes National Lake Shore, with respect to this tract of land, it is essentially a private citizen with no interest in the property sought to be condemned to warrant intervention as a right.

Because the Council does not assert an interest in the property subject to this action, it has no protectable interest that can be impaired or impeded. Nor does it have the right to assert that its interest is being inadequately represented by the existing parties.

Moreover, the Council cannot avail itself of the permissive intervention allowed by Fed. R. Civ. P. 24(b). . . . While the Council's claim and this action center on the same factual basis, *i.e.*, the condemnation of the same tract of land, this court concludes that permissive intervention should be denied in order to avoid the likelihood of undue delay and prejudice to the rights of the original parties.

Four years have elapsed since the institution of this suit and the original parties have submitted a stipulated judgment for the court's approval. To allow intervention at this point in time to a party with no legal interest in the private property which is the subject of the proceeding and whose position is contrary to that of both the original parties, would serve no viable purpose except to prolong an already lengthy and tired lawsuit. Accordingly, it is ordered that the Council's motion for intervention under Rule 24 be and hereby is denied.

REVIEW QUESTIONS

What language do Fed. R. Civ. P. 19 and 24(a) have in common? What situation is each trying to address? Does it make sense to you that there would be two rules with such similar language? Consider that the Rules are not identical—either in language or in usage. Further, while Rule 19 typically is used by a defendant to force the plaintiff to add a party, Rule 24 is used by an absentee party to become a party. Also, Fed. R. Civ. P. 24(a) contains the additional clause, "unless existing parties adequately represent that interest." Moreover, since there is a more lenient test for intervention under Fed. R. Civ. P. 24(b), a judge may permit an absentee to intervene without having to justify fulfillment of the more stringent requirements of Fed. R. Civ. P. 24(a)(2). Some judges have been extremely lenient in permitting a wide range of intervening parties, yet have severely curtailed independent participation.

a. Statutory Authority to Intervene

Federal statutes may also grant absentees the right of intervention, and Federal Rule 24 contemplates these rights. The Clean Air Act, for example, provides that in any government action brought to enforce compliance with the Act's standards "any person may intervene *as a matter of right.*" 42 U.S.C. § 7064(b)(1)(B) (emphasis added).

REVIEW EXERCISE NO. 2

In this problem you must complete the opinion of the trial court. The factual background and procedural posture are already completed, and you are expected to write the portion that integrates the facts provided with the governing law.

Be a careful judge, who explains her or his actions. It should take you at least ninety minutes to answer this question fully.

JUSTICE, J.:

The facts that underlie this lawsuit for $2.8 million are traceable to a dispute over $12.00 between a customer and the management of a retail store. Ms. Flannel seeks to "make a federal case"—as certainly is her right under the existing statutes—out of the circumstances that befell her after she purchased a pair of blue jeans for $40.00 at the J.C. Penney store in Capital City, Northeastern. The following facts are alleged in her complaint filed in district court.

The day after she purchased the jeans, she discovered that the jeans were defective and returned them to the store. She requested that they give her a new pair or that they refund her the purchase price, which she had paid by personal check. The store refused. Ms. Flannel left the store with the jeans and then did two things: she stopped payment on her check and went and had the zipper replaced at the local cleaners at a cost of $12.00. With the repair bill in hand, she then returned to the store and demanded that the store pay her back for the cost of the repair. The customer-returns employee, Isabel Duffey, refused.

Instead she made an oral demand of Ms. Flannel for $65.00 representing the original purchase price and the bank service handling charge for the stopped check. Ms. Flannel refused to honor this demand for payment in rather colorful language. The next day, the store's assistant manager, Douglas A. Stauffer, filed a criminal complaint against her, charging her with a violation of the bad check statute. 18 N.G.L. § 4195.11.*

After the criminal complaint was filed, Ms. Flannel returned to the store and offered to pay the $40.00; the offer was refused. Ms. Flannel went to see the store manager, Robert Boyd, who told Ms. Flannel that he had authorized the complaint because "you attempted fraud on my store." He also stated that he would not drop the complaint because "then the store would have to pay court costs and we want to make an example of you so that people don't try to stop checks on us and keep the goods." These remarks were made in the presence of Ms. Flannel, her son, and other customers.

Ms. Flannel then wrote to the corporate president, Manfred Brecker, at the head office in New Jersey, explaining the history of the transaction and asking him to intervene and order his subordinates to drop the criminal complaint. She also told him that she was concerned about the defamation to her character and good standing in the community as she was the local PTA president and an elder in her church. His letter in response, as described in her complaint, shows that he was informed as to the facts of the transaction and that he supported the actions of his employees at the Capital City store in filing the criminal charges against her.

Ms. Flannel was tried and acquitted of the bad check charge and later voluntarily paid the Capital City store $28.00 "in full satisfaction and settlement of her debt."

Ms. Flannel then filed suit in this court for $2.8 million in damages for malicious prosecution. The elements of the relevant Northeastern law on malicious prosecution are: (1) the termination in the complainant's favor of the criminal proceedings; (2) want of probable cause for the criminal proceedings; and (3) malice. Probable cause has been defined as "a reasonable ground of suspicion supported by circumstances sufficiently strong in themselves as to make a cautious person believe that the person accused is guilty of the charged offense." Malice has been defined as "the intentional doing of a wrongful act

---

* 18 N.G.L., §4195.11 provides:

(a) Offense defined. A person commits an offense if s/he issues or passes a check or similar order for the payment of money, knowing that it will not be honored by the drawee.

(b) Presumption. For the purposes of this section as well as in any prosecution for theft committed by means of a bad check, an issuer is presumed to know that the check or order (other than a postdated check or order) would not be paid, if (1) the issuer had no account with the drawee at the time the check or order was issued; or (2) payment was refused by the drawee for lack of funds, upon presentation within thirty days after issue, and the issuer failed to make good within ten days after receiving notice of that refusal.

(c) Grading. An offense under this section is a misdemeanor of the second degree if the amount of the check or order exceeds $200.00; otherwise it is a summary offense.

without just cause or excuse, with an intent to inflict an injury or under circumstances that the law will imply an evil intent."

The defendants have filed a 12(b)(6) motion to dismiss, claiming that the allegations in the plaintiff's complaint fall short of making out a claim for relief under Northeastern law. We rule that. . .

[Students: Complete the opinion, giving your ruling and your reasoning.]

REVIEW EXERCISE NO. 3

You have ninety minutes to answer the following question. Your rules supplement is the only source you should require (though you may cite to cases we have studied).

> To: Judicial Clerk
> From: Judge Joakim Bergros, Central Superior Court
> Re: *Bentham et al. v. Delivery*
> Date: June 25, 2020

Assume that Central is a state that has adopted the Fed. R. Civ. P. in all relevant parts. There is a two-year statute of limitations for torts cases. I have four motions pending before me in the above entitled case. *Please help me anticipate arguments on all sides, to the extent there are any, and tell me how to rule and why. Please include as much of your reasoning processes as you are able.*

Robert and Elisabeth Bentham, and Sally Schoose (hereafter called "Benthams" and "Schoose" or "plaintiffs") served one complaint with a summons on Home Delivery, Inc. ("Delivery" or "defendant") on January 5, 2020. "Delivery," in the complaint, is defined to mean the "corporation, and its servants, agents, and employees." The plaintiffs allege that the Benthams at all relevant times have lived on Elm Street, Capitol, Central, on the same block and five doors away from Schoose, who has lived at her home on Elm Street at all relevant times; that the Benthams retained Delivery in January 2018 to deliver groceries to their house once a week under an agreement that the Benthams had with Delivery whereby the plaintiffs would order groceries by phone on or before Tuesday of each week, and Delivery would deliver them to the Bentham house on Friday. The Benthams provided Delivery with a key to their house. The complaint further alleges that Schoose had the same deal with Delivery, beginning in February 2018, and that Schoose gave Delivery a key to her house. The complaint further alleges that on Friday, March 8, 2018, the Bentham house was negligently left unlocked by Delivery, and that as a result thereof, their house was burglarized that day, and $15,000 worth of property was stolen. The complaint also alleges that on Friday, April 12, 2018, the Schoose house was negligently left unlocked by Delivery, and that as a result thereof, her house was burglarized that day, and $9,000 worth of property was stolen. The plaintiffs seek damages in these amounts, plus interest, and demand a jury trial.

Delivery, in its answer, adopted the plaintiffs' definition of "Delivery." It admitted all allegations but the following: It denied that Delivery left either house unlocked, it denied any negligence, and it said it was without knowledge or information sufficient to form a belief as to whether the burglaries took place or as to the value of what was allegedly stolen.

No discovery has taken place as yet. Under Central law, if an employer is held responsible because of an employee's negligence (*respondeat superior*), the employer has a cause of action for indemnification from the employee.

(1) Defendant has moved to dismiss or to sever on the grounds of misjoinder of plaintiffs.

(2) A week ago, the Benthams moved to amend the complaint to add a count against Delivery for negligently delivering rotten food. Robert Bentham claims that on March 8, 2018, he ate sliced turkey that had been delivered by Delivery on that same day and was supposed to be fresh; that he became extremely ill from the bad turkey; and that he told Delivery of his illness the next day, at the same time he told them they were liable for the burglary.

(3) Delivery moves to implead Worker, whom they allege was their driver at all times and places in question. They seek indemnification from him. Central has no joint tortfeasor contribution statute.

(4) Notwithstanding your answer to the previous question, assume that Worker was not added as a third party defendant. Is s/he a Rule 19 party? Also, if Schoose has a spouse, is she or he a Rule 19 party?

CHAPTER 4

Discovery

A. INTRODUCTION

As you saw in Chapter 3, the drafters of the original Federal Rules of Civil Procedure had a vision of what an enlightened procedural regime would look like. Eschewing the technicalities of previous systems, they would make procedure simpler yet also more comprehensive. More specifically, this meant simplified nontechnical pleadings and enlarged joinder. But this also meant that parties could exit the pleading stage without disclosing the particulars of their claims or defenses. The drafters imagined that the discovery stage could meet that need. The parties would share and gather the evidence that they needed — by producing and deposing witnesses, by producing and requesting documents, by answering and serving interrogatories. Once informed by all of the relevant evidence, the parties would either settle the case or proceed to trial to resolve disputed facts.

From the outset there was a lack of clarity about the scope of discovery. Although there was no question that the discovery rules revolutionized American procedure by establishing a broad scope for what may be obtained through discovery, just how broad was it? The most common disagreements involved plaintiffs who, defendants claimed, were using discovery as a "fishing expedition" to find a viable cause of action.

The Supreme Court's first major opinion about the discovery process occurred in 1947—about a decade after the 1938 enactment of the Federal Rules of Civil Procedure. The case, *Hickman v. Taylor,* involved a tug that sank while towing cargo across the Delaware River. Five crew members drowned, and four survived. Samuel Fortenbaugh, who was counsel for the tug owners, took statements privately from survivors and witnesses in anticipation of possible litigation from the families of the deceased. A lawsuit indeed followed, and during discovery, a plaintiff's lawyer sought Fortenbaugh's notes of those conversations. Fortenbaugh refused to deliver them and was held in contempt by the trial judge, who ordered Fortenbaugh to be jailed. The Court of Appeals reversed, and the U.S. Supreme Court ultimately took the case. The Supreme Court held that Fortenbaugh's notes were "work product" that Fortenbaugh was not obligated to disclose. (We will talk about work product later in this chapter.) But the Court's opinion is more frequently cited for its endorsement of the remarkable breadth of discovery under the Federal Rules. The Court viewed the work product doctrine and other privileges as very narrow exceptions to a revolutionary approach to information and evidence gathering.

> [The] discovery rules are to be accorded a broad and liberal treatment. No longer can the time-honored cry of "fishing expedition" serve to preclude a party from inquiring into the facts underlying his opponent's case. Mutual knowledge of all the relevant facts gathered by both parties is essential to proper litigation. To that end, either party may compel the other to disgorge whatever facts he has in his possession. [Discovery] simply advances the stage at which the disclosure can be compelled from the time of trial to the period preceding it, thus reducing the possibility of surprise.

Hickman v. Taylor, 329 U.S. 495, 507 (1947). (The *Hickman* opinion appears near the end of this chapter. Your professor may assign it here, may assign it at the end of the chapter as a way to review the topic of discovery, or may rely on the description of the opinion here and not assign it all.)

This was a substantial departure from practice prior to the Federal Rules. At common law, discovery was virtually nonexistent. The federal courts had no general inherent power to order discovery and were only invested with that power by two statutes allowing the taking of statements under oath under very limited conditions. Trial by surprise was the norm because at the time of trial many litigants did not know what their adversary's position or evidence would be.

By making discovery a vital part of the litigation process, the Federal Rules transformed the practice of law in the United States.

> Among the many benefits [the drafters] saw for expanded discovery were the following: the elimination of surprise; preserving testimony so it will be available in case of the death or other unavailability of witness; diminishing the importance of pleadings; increasing the effectiveness of the summary judgment; focusing the trial on the main points in controversy; and permitting each side to assess the strengths and weaknesses of their cases in advance, frequently making trials unnecessary because of informed settlement.

Stephen N. Subrin, *Fishing Expeditions Allowed: The Historical Background of the 1938 Federal Discovery Rules*, 39 B.C. L. Rev. 691, 716 (1998).

This regime of broad discovery is uniquely American. We have been criticized in many other countries for the delays and expense created by discovery, as well as the system's intrusions upon privacy. Yet it is important to appreciate the unique role that civil litigation plays in the fabric of American society. We rely heavily on private civil litigation to enforce our shared norms; these norms include laws regarding the environment, antitrust, banking, securities, consumer safety, employment discrimination, worker safety, civil rights, and so forth. Approximately 97 percent of the actions to enforce such laws are filed by private litigants, as opposed to enforcement agencies. This result is a product of several forces, including distrust of the government generally and the executive branch in particular, confidence in the private sector and market incentives, the bureaucratic cost of public enforcement, and lawyers' interest in the availability of profitable litigation. Sean Farhang, *The Litigation State* (Princeton Univ. Press 2010). In this vein, discovery "is the American alternative to the administrative state." Paul D. Carrington, *Renovating Discovery*, 49 Ala. L. Rev. 51, 54 (1997). If private litigants — as opposed to, say, government bureaucracies — are charged with enforcing these laws, then it follows that private litigants need tools that are associated with law enforcement.

But our system of broad discovery has also surfaced some pathologies. Judge Selya of the U.S. Court of Appeals for the First Circuit described the historical impact of liberal rules of discovery in very colorful terms: "A herd of bulls had been set loose in the decorous confines of the judge's lobby — and the china shop would never be the same." *In re San Juan Dupont Plaza Hotel Fire Litig.*, 859 F.2d 1007 (1st Cir. 1988). Indeed, the pretrial phase of litigation in some cases has taken on a nightmarish quality and has become prohibitively expensive. At the same time, however, in the majority of cases the amount of discovery is relatively modest. This dual reality has posed a serious challenge for rulemakers.

The evolution of civil litigation more generally in recent decades has also called discovery's role into question. The drafters of the original Federal Rules imagined that discovery would perform a function that the pleading stage would not, to wit: narrowing and clarifying the issues. But as you learned in Chapter 3, the pleading standard has changed. The original Federal Rules also imagined that discovery would allow the parties to prepare meaningfully for trial. However, only 1-2 percent of all civil cases ever reach the trial stage. In particular, a combination of emphasis on settlement and the summary judgment device now prevents many litigants from reaching trials. Accordingly, in contemporary litigation, discovery is principally about gathering sufficient evidence (1) to leverage a favorable settlement; and (2) to survive a summary judgment motion — which, from the plaintiff's perspective, requires *prima facie* evidence from which a reasonable fact finder could find in your favor. We will study summary judgments in Chapter 5.

In Part B of this chapter we will explore in greater depth the tensions that animate discovery, discovery abuse, and discovery reform. Then, in Part C, we turn to the mechanics of the discovery process: mandatory initial disclosure obligations; the formal techniques (depositions, interrogatories, requests for admissions, document requests, and physical and mental examinations); and the scope of permissible discovery. In this chapter you will find a number of practice exercises that challenge you to confront the ethical dilemmas and the practical applications of the subtleties of the rules. With this knowledge of the burdens and benefits of discovery, you will then be in a position to consider, in Part D, whether the current rulemaking process makes sense.

B. DISCOVERY AND ITS TENSIONS

Wayne Brazil, The Adversary Character of Civil Discovery
31 Vand. L. Rev. 1295 (1978)

. . . The literature that emanated from the academic and Judicial proponents of discovery during the decades surrounding the 1938 adoption of the Federal Rules of Civil Procedure is replete with optimistic forecasts about the beneficial changes discovery would bring to the adversary system. Edson R. Sunderland, who is credited with drafting the discovery components of the 1938 Federal Rules, wrote that the new procedural rules: "mark the highest point so far reached in the English speaking world in the elimination of secrecy in the preparation for trial. Each party may in effect be called upon by his adversary or by the judge to lay all his cards upon the table, the important consideration being who has the stronger hand, not who can play the cleverer game." . . .

The academic and judicial proponents of the modern rules of discovery apparently failed to appreciate how tenaciously litigators would hold to their adversarial ways and the magnitude of the antagonism between the principal purpose of discovery (the ascertainment of truth through disclosure) and the protective and competitive instincts that dominate adversary litigation. . . .

Instead of reducing the sway of adversary forces in litigation and confining them to the trial stage, discovery has greatly expanded the arenas in which those forces can operate. It also has provided attorneys with new weapons, devices, and incentives for the adversary gamesmanship that discovery was designed to curtail. Rather than discourage "the sporting or game theory of justice," discovery has expanded both the scope and the complexity of the sport. Modern discovery also has removed most of the decisive plays from the scrutiny of the court. Because so many civil cases are settled before trial and because the conduct of attorneys is subject only to fitful and superficial judicial review during the discovery stage, much of the decisive gamesmanship of modern litigation takes place in private settings.

Such factors as traditional professional loyalties, deeply ingrained lawyering instincts, and competitive economic pressures assured that the process of gathering and organizing evidence would not take place in an essentially nonadversarial context. Escape from this outcome would have required substantial changes in the institutional context within which discovery is conducted. However, no such changes have been made. Attorneys conducting discovery still are commanded by the rules of professional responsibility and by their own economic self-interest to commit their highest loyalty to their client's best interests. By contrast, there is generally no ethical pressure or financial incentive for attorneys voluntarily to disclose the fruits of their investigations or in any way make ascertainment of the truth easier for opposing counsel or the trier of fact. In short, all the well-established institutional pressures that for generations have operated to make attorneys partisan advocates and to make them view each other as committed adversaries have remained intact. In this context, it is indeed naive to expect that discovery, armed only with its own executional rules, could somehow resist the inroads of the adversarial and competitive pressures that dominate its surroundings. . . .

Attorneys in litigation have five primary objectives: (1) to win; (2) to make money; (3) to avoid being sued for malpractice; (4) to earn the admiration of the professional community; and (5) to develop self-esteem for the quality of their performances. These objectives are not born simply of cynicism and selfishness. They are institutionalized commands that emanate from a system of combat within a competitive economic structure. It is not difficult to perceive that these goals make the purposes of discovery for individual litigators quite different from the purposes which the architects of the discovery system contemplated. . . .

[A]dversary litigation and competitive economics offer no institutionalized rewards for disclosure of potentially relevant data. They instead offer many institutional deterrents to full disclosure. Review of the primary means by which litigators seek to earn the rewards of the legal system graphically illustrates this generalization. Litigators generally believe they will win the primary forms of recognition our system offers not through full disclosure, not through relentless efforts to secure just results, not through honesty, openness, and uncalculating cooperation, nor even necessarily through efficiency and superior work quality, but rather by tailoring the most clever package of tactics and stratagems to fit the needs of a given case.

The means employed by litigators to achieve victory for their clients regularly involve manipulating people and the flow of information in order to present their client's positions as persuasively and favorably as possible. This manipulation may involve any or all of the following general techniques: not disclosing evidence that could be damaging to the client or helpful to an opposing party; not disclosing persuasive legal precedents that could be damaging to the client; undermining or deflating persuasive evidence and precedents that are damaging to the client and are introduced by opposing counsel, by such means as upsetting or discrediting honest and reliable witnesses or by burying adverse evidence under mounds of obfuscating evidentiary debris; overemphasizing and presenting out of context evidence and precedents that appear favorable to the client; pressuring or cajoling witnesses, jurors, and judges into adopting views that support the client's position; deceiving opposing counsel and parties about the weaknesses of the client's case and the strengths of opposing cases; aggravating and exploiting to the fullest extent possible vulnerabilities of the opposing party and counsel that have nothing to do with the merits of a given dispute by such means as intimidating an anxious opponent, spending a poor opponent into submission, or "soaking" in settlement an opponent who has public image problems or who for other reasons cannot endure the risk and public exposure of a trial. . . .

Strategic Considerations in Discovery. One could expect strategic behavior to complicate matters, but appreciate the stakes. If, say, a plaintiff with a claim for employment discrimination needs to prove, as an element of her case, that her employer acted with a particular intent, the plaintiff needs evidence to prove the defendant's state of mind. And if, say, a defendant is defending against a negligence claim, she needs evidence to disprove the plaintiff's claim that they have experienced substantial pain and suffering. In other words, with strategic behavior in the context of discovery we are not only talking about the costs of litigation, but also the results. Or, put differently, another way of addressing discovery abuse would be to revisit the elements of substantive law so that the discovery inquiry could be more focused.

Scholars of the law and economics movement have described a basic incentive that can lead to discovery abuse: raising a rival's costs. Because it costs less to *prepare* a discovery request than to *answer* one, parties can inflict costs on their opponents with broad discovery requests, regardless of the value of the information to the requesting party. *See generally* Robert Bone, *Discovery,* in Procedural Law and Economics 16 (Edward Elgar ed. 2012); Frank Easterbrook, *Discovery as Abuse*, 69 B.U. L. Rev. 635, 644 (1989). In *Am. Bank v. City of Menasha,* 627 F.3d 261, 266 (7th Cir. 2010), as amended (Dec. 8, 2010), Judge Posner said that the animating force of plausibility pleading was "to prevent settlement extortion — using discovery to impose asymmetric costs on defendants in order to force a settlement advantageous to the plaintiff regardless of the merits of his suit." Appreciate how the phases of litigation are conceptually related and intertwined: Although the alleged problem is discovery, the solution was implemented instead in the pleading phase.

Could We Eliminate Discovery? Notwithstanding the patriotic talk in this chapter about the importance of discovery, some wonder whether we could skip the discovery phase altogether and proceed directly to trial. (To oversimplify, that is essentially what we do in criminal cases. It is also, in broad strokes, how civil cases are litigated in most of the rest of the world.) Of course, eliminating discovery would reverse what the drafters of the

Federal Rules hoped to achieve. But does the element of surprise at trial, for example, necessarily run counter to the pursuit of justice? As one federal judge put it, "A certain amount of surprise is often a catalyst which precipitates the truth." *Margeson v. Boston & Maine R.R.*, 16 F.R.D. 200, 201 (D. Mass. 1954). When does "surprise," which may not be problematic, become instead, "trial by ambush," which surely is problematic?

Further, the drafters of the Federal Rules designed a process of discovery that would help identify and frame issues for trial. But in order to satisfy Rule 11 and to survive a Rule 12(b)(6), most plaintiffs will—at the pleadings stage—have already done their legal and factual homework, articulated their causes of action, and gathered evidence to support their allegations. If a plaintiff has satisfied the plausibility pleading standard, do we need formal discovery in order to identify and frame the issues?

Even if we do not need discovery to fulfill the roles imagined by the drafters of the Federal Rules, it may have a new and essential role in the dispute resolution process. What is that role?

Professional Ethics in Discovery. You might be thinking that the ethical obligations of lawyers, if not the discovery rules themselves, would prevent abuse of the discovery process by lawyers. Currently in the United States, disciplinary rules are embodied in two "model" forms. The Model Code of Professional Responsibility and the Model Rules of Professional Conduct. The Model Code of Professional Responsibility was created in 1969, when the American Bar Association (ABA) grouped and adopted nearly fifty canons from various state bar associations. In 1983, the ABA adopted the Model Rules of Professional Conduct to replace the Model Code. In general, the Model Rules are more confining and less abstract than the Model Code. Nearly all of the states have moved from the Model Code to the Model Rules. We excerpt portions of the Model Code and the Model Rules here for you to consider the ethical obligations of lawyers in the context of discovery. Be prepared to answer these questions:

(a) On a scale of 1 (low) to 10 (high), to what extent do these rules offer clarity about what is ethical (and unethical) conduct in the context of discovery?

(b) Is it unethical to use discovery primarily for the purpose of increasing your opponent's litigation expenses?

(c) Is it unethical to use discovery primarily for the purpose of delay or to gain some tactical advantage?

(d) Is it unethical to seek, through discovery, information, or documents that are not necessary for the prosecution or defense of your action?

(e) Is it unethical to respond to inquiries for discovery in a very restrictive manner to avoid the disclosure of relevant nonprivileged information?

ABA Model Code of Professional Responsibility

CANON 7

A lawyer should represent a client zealously within the bounds of the law

Disciplinary Rule 7-101. Representing a Client Zealously

(A) A lawyer shall not intentionally:

(1) Fail to seek the lawful objectives of his client through reasonably available means permitted by law and the Disciplinary Rules, except as provided by DR 7-101(B). A lawyer does not violate this Disciplinary Rule, however, by acceding to reasonable requests of opposing counsel which do not prejudice the rights of his client, by being punctual to fulfilling all professional commitments, by avoiding offensive tactics, or by treating with courtesy and consideration all persons involved in the legal process.

(2) Fail to carry out a contract of employment entered into with a client for professional services, but he may withdraw as permitted under DR 2-110, DR 5-102, and DR 5-105.

(3) Prejudice or damage his client during the course of the professional relationship, except as required under DR 7-102(B).

(B) In his representation of a client, a lawyer may:

(1) Where permissible, exercise his professional judgment to waive or fail to assert a right or position of his client.

(2) Refuse to aid or participate in conduct that he believes to be unlawful, even though there is some support for an argument that the conduct is legal.

Disciplinary Rule 7-102. Representing a Client Within the Bounds of the Law

(A) In his representation of a client, a lawyer shall not:

(1) File a suit, assert a position, conduct a defense, delay a trial, or take other action on behalf of his client when he knows or when it is obvious that such action would serve merely to harass or maliciously injure another.

(2) Knowingly advance a claim or defense that is unwarranted under existing law, except that he may advance such claim or defense if it can be supported by good faith argument for an extension, modification, or reversal of existing law.

(3) Conceal or knowingly fail to disclose that which he is required by law to reveal.

(4) Knowingly use perjured testimony or false evidence.

(5) Knowingly make a false statement of law or fact.

(6) Participate in the creation or preservation of evidence when he knows or it is obvious that the evidence is false.

(7) Counsel or assist his client in conduct that the lawyer knows to be illegal or fraudulent.

(8) Knowingly engage in other illegal conduct or conduct contrary to a Disciplinary Rule.

(B) A lawyer who receives information clearly established that:

(1) His client has, in the course of the representation, perpetrated a fraud upon a person or tribunal shall promptly call upon his client to rectify the same, and if his client refuses or is unable to do so, he shall reveal the fraud to the affected person or tribunal, except when the information is protected as a privileged communication.

(2) A person other than his client has perpetrated a fraud upon a tribunal shall promptly reveal the fraud to the tribunal.

ABA Model Rules of Professional Conduct

RULE 1.1 COMPETENCE

A lawyer shall provide competent representation to a client. Competent representation requires the legal knowledge, skill, thoroughness and preparation reasonably necessary for the representation.

COMMENT:

Legal Knowledge and Skill. In determining whether a lawyer employs the requisite knowledge and skill in a particular matter, relevant factors include the relative complexity and specialized nature of the matter, the lawyer's general experience, the lawyer's training and experience in the field in question, the preparation and study the lawyer is able to give the matter and whether it is feasible to refer the matter to, or associate or consult with, a lawyer of established competence in the field in question. In many instances, the required proficiency is that of a general practitioner. Expertise in a particular field of law may be required in some circumstances. . . .

Thoroughness and Preparation. Competent handling of a particular matter includes inquiry into and analysis of the factual and legal elements of the problem, and use of methods and procedures meeting the standards of competent practitioners. It also includes adequate preparation. The required attention and preparation are determined in part by what is at stake; major litigation and complex transactions ordinarily require more extensive treatment than matters of lesser complexity and consequence. . . .

RULE 1.3 DILIGENCE

A lawyer shall act with reasonable diligence and promptness in representing a client.

COMMENT:

A lawyer should pursue a matter on behalf of a client despite opposition, obstruction or personal inconvenience to the lawyer, and take whatever lawful and ethical measures are required to vindicate a client's cause or endeavor. A lawyer must also act with commitment and dedication to the interests of the client and with zeal in advocacy upon the client's behalf. A lawyer is not bound, however, to press for every advantage that might be realized for a client. For example, a lawyer may have authority to exercise professional discretion in determining the means by which a matter should be pursued. *See* Rule 1.2. The lawyer's duty to act with reasonable diligence does not require the use of offensive tactics or preclude the treating of all persons involved in the legal process with courtesy and respect. . . .

RULE 3.2 EXPEDITING LITIGATION

A lawyer shall make reasonable efforts to expedite litigation consistent with the interests of the client.

COMMENT:

Dilatory practices bring the administration of justice into disrepute. Although there will be occasions when a lawyer may properly seek a postponement for personal reasons, it is not proper for a lawyer to routinely fail to expedite litigation solely for the convenience of the advocates. Nor will a failure to expedite be reasonable if done for the purpose of frustrating an opposing party's attempt to obtain rightful redress or repose. It is not a justification that similar conduct is often tolerated by the bench and bar. The question is whether a competent lawyer acting in good faith would regard the course of action as having some substantial purpose other than delay. Realizing financial or other benefit from otherwise improper delay in litigation is not a legitimate interest of the client.

* * *

Now read Federal Rule 26(g) carefully. An analog to Federal Rule 11, this rule requires the attorney (meaning you, not your client!) to sign every discovery request and response. With your signature you are certifying to the court that, to the best of your knowledge, information, and belief—formed after a reasonable inquiry—(1) your disclosures are complete and correct; (2) you have done your legal homework; (3) your request/response is not asserted for an improper purpose; and (4) your request is not unreasonable, not unduly burdensome or expensive, nor disproportionate.

Notwithstanding the constraints of the ethical rules and of Federal Rule 26(g), the **perception**—and to a limited extent the **reality**—is that discovery is overused, misused, and abused. To be sure, the discovery process can be lengthy and expensive. In recent litigation involving Actos (pioglitazone), a Type 2 diabetes drug, discovery involved 32 million pages of documents and 130 depositions. *See In re Actos (Pioglitazone) Prods. Lia. Litigation*, 273 F.Supp.3d 485 (W.D. La. 2017). And in litigation involving the sale of corn seeds, discovery involved 200 depositions and 19 expert witnesses. *In re Syngenta AG Mir162 Corn Litigation*, 2018 WL 7254709 (D. Kan. Nov. 21, 2018). But does extensive discovery necessarily mean that the discovery process was abused? The Actos drug was the best-selling Type 2 diabetes drug in the world, and persons who took it had a far higher rate of bladder cancer than patients on similar drugs; the company ultimately agreed to pay a $2.3 billion settlement. And the corn litigation involved the allegedly unlawful sale of genetically modified corn seeds—resulting in a $1.51 billion settlement. By contrast, most studies show that in ordinary litigation (as opposed to both *Actos* and *Syngenta,* which were complex cases) discovery use is very limited. *See* Emery G. Lee III & Thomas E. Willging, *Litigation Costs in Civil Cases: Multivariate Analysis* (Federal Judicial Center 2010).

Discovery is expensive because, as you will read later in this chapter, the lawyers for both sides must review—perhaps even scrutinize—every piece of paper. In an article recounting her role in the tobacco litigation that peaked in the 1990s, attorney Martha Wivell, then a partner in the law firm of Robins, Kaplan, Miller & Ciresi, L.L.P., answered the question of how her firm reviewed the 30 million documents that were produced in her case. Her answer: "One at a time." *See* Martha Wivell, *Key to the Tobacco Fortress*, 38 Trial 45, 45 (Dec. 2002). While some lawyers perceive of such a task as tedious and mind-numbing, the effective lawyer seizes the opportunity to get educated about their client, their adversary, and the case. This can be "the equivalent of poking around in a friend's medicine cabinet or closet. The rules of civil procedure are license to snoop. If you have an interest in people—and you must to be a good litigator—document review is an opportunity to find out the intimate thoughts of the people involved in your case. . . ." Janet S. Kole, *Why I Love Document Reviews*, 33 Litig. 53, 53 (Winter 2007).

The perception of laypersons and of many lawyers is that the discovery process is too expensive. "A . . . survey of parties in fifty-seven separate cases found that parties frequently spend millions of dollars simply preparing documents for production. In one case, the total cost of document production alone was $27 million. An average of 73% of the costs incurred during document production occurred during the document review phase. . . ." Robert Keeling et al., *Separating the Privilege Wheat from the Chaff—Using Text Analytics and Machine Learning to Protect Attorney-Client Privilege*, 25 Rich. J.L. & Tech. 2, 19 (2019). Yet when lawyers are asked about the costs of discovery in specific cases, the costs seem to be relatively low (under 4 percent) as a proportion of the value of the case. *See* Emery G. Lee III & Thomas E. Willging, *National, Case-Based Civil Rules Survey: Preliminary Report to the Judicial Conference Advisory Committee on Civil Rules* (Federal Judicial Center 2009).

Discovery can be either an essential element in the pursuit of justice or a crippling obstacle to it. As you proceed through this chapter, think about the incentives that lead discovery *use* to become discovery *abuse*. When does that happen, and why?

Although it is incontrovertible that discovery can be problematic, it would be useful to understand exactly where the problems surface. Strangely, however, there is very little empirical data to inform our conversations. Lawyers and parties are under no obligation to publicly report the amounts they have spent in preparation for trial or in relation to the discovery process. *See generally* Nicholas M. Pace and Laura Zakaras, *Where the Money Goes: Understanding Litigant Expenditures for Producing Electronic Discovery,* RAND Institute for Civil Justice 4 (2012). Accordingly, discussions about the cost of discovery are based principally on self-reported perceptions that might be (intentionally or unintentionally) wrong, and from certain types of practice that may not be representative of civil litigation generally. Commentators and practitioners generally agree that the following observations are true:

(1) In a minority of cases — usually cases involving a high degree of complexity, and/or substantial damages, and/or large law firms — there is a very large number of discovery events and massive discovery costs. Cases in this group are often referred to as the "mega cases."

(2) In the majority of cases there is no, very little, or only a reasonable amount of formal discovery.

Lawyers who litigate cases that fall in the first group tend to be especially vocal. And because most of these lawyers are members of large, prominent law firms, their voices tend to be heard. Indeed, these lawyers' voices are (disproportionately) heard by the media, who help frame the public's understanding of the cost-and-delay narrative. And these lawyers' voices are also (disproportionately) represented on the committees that review and amend the rules.

But because the second observation highlighted above is the reality for most litigation (i.e., no, very little, or only a reasonable amount of discovery), this creates a dissonant picture for rulemakers. The reforms that might be necessary and useful in the cases where there is massive discovery (including discovery abuse) are unnecessary and could even be counterproductive in cases where the amount of discovery is modest. For example, limiting the scope of discovery, limiting the tools of discovery, requiring the parties to confer about discovery, and requiring meetings with the judge about discovery could help streamline the discovery process in the mega-cases, but needlessly confine and complicate discovery in routine cases.

This is not to say, however, that discovery is not a problem also even in routine cases. Some argue that the relative absence of discovery in routine cases is evidence of the high costs and/or low benefits of discovery. If engaging in discovery only creates needless fights and rewards unethical behavior, why bother? In fact, because discovery can be weaponized by either side, there is an element of mutually assured destruction that keeps either side from engaging in a war that neither side will survive. This perspective—which undoubtedly explains behavior in some cases—is dramatically at odds with the more idealistic perspective that discovery is simply not a problem in most cases. Again, the lack of hard empirical data about discovery complicates policy-making in this area.

As you will observe later in this chapter, the past three decades have witnessed repeated attempts by the rulemakers to rein in discovery abuse. The Rules were amended to require lawyers to meet and confer, thereby leveraging the promise of dialogue. The Rules were amended to encourage judges to get involved in the discovery process—both to prevent abuse and to sanction it. To encourage the efficient use of discovery devices, the Rules were amended to limit the number of interrogatories and depositions available to each party. The rulemakers created a category of mandatory initial disclosures that they hoped would streamline the discovery process. The scope of discovery and the trigger for sanctions have been recalibrated. And most recently—and quite controversially—the rulemakers embedded the notion that discovery must be proportional. Notwithstanding the various efforts to reform the discovery process, the criticisms continue: Discovery costs too much; discovery takes too long; the parties don't comply with the discovery rules; and the judges don't enforce the rules. In the next part we will examine specific disputes.

Before we turn to the mechanics of discovery practice in the next part, we want to flag one more criticism about discovery for you to keep in mind. This criticism is not about the *amount* of discovery nor the *abuse* of discovery, but rather is about the fundamental nature of discovery itself. Because the scope of discovery is so broad, there is tension between the goal of seeking full disclosure and the importance in a democracy of protecting privacy.

> [D]iscovery of documents in American litigation often is wide-ranging, with intrusion on the discovered party and expense to both parties. . . . [Discovery of] documents goes after what public and private officials regard as their most private thoughts, such that this kind of discovery, to them, resembles self-incrimination. . . [T]he impression of American discovery in most foreign countries is that of an alien legal regime conducting a warrantless search in someone else's domestic territory. The scope the American system affords to private litigants for compulsory production of documents is ordinarily afforded in other countries only to prosecutorial criminal investigations by government agencies.

Geoffrey Hazard, *From Whom No Secrets Are Hid*, 76 Tex. L. Rev. 1665, 1675-1676 (1999). Why should a private individual and his or her lawyer be able to search the innermost thoughts of private and public officials? Such privacy invasions, when permitted at all, are usually thought to be the province of government—and are typically circumscribed by the protections of criminal procedure. Moreover, the government, unlike lawyers, can be held accountable for excesses through elections.

To be sure, the discovery rules can require parties to produce the "smoking gun" document that dooms their case. Discovery rules can require individuals to admit their failures, confront their misconduct, and otherwise tell the truth. Imagine, for example, someone reading your posts to social media accounts. Think about all of the emails and text messages that you have sent or received. Contemplate the data gathered by applications that track your location and workouts or that reveal your preferences, how you spend your free time, or how you spend your money. Some argue that technology has made it too easy for the techniques of discovery to invade another's privacy. Others contend that technology has fundamentally transformed our understanding of what information is private. The discovery rules are a platform where all of these policy matters surface. Effective litigators will invoke and leverage these policies — sometimes subtly, sometimes overtly — in an otherwise mundane discovery dispute.

C. THE MECHANICS OF DISCOVERY

Formal discovery is typically divided into two phases: (1) mandatory initial disclosures; and (2) party-controlled discovery. The scope of discovery is governed by Fed. R. Civ. P. 26(b).

1. Mandatory Initial Disclosures

Rule 26(a) requires that lawyers, at an early stage of litigation, exchange certain core information as part of a regime of mandatory initial disclosures. Parties must make these disclosures without awaiting a discovery request from any other party. The disclosures are made "based on the information then reasonably available to it." Fed. R. Civ. P. 26(a)(1)(E).

Rules 26(a)(1)(A) requires disclosure of the identities of witnesses and documents "that the disclosing party may use to support its claims or defenses." Notice that the disclosures need not include information that the *opposing* party might find useful. Additionally, the Rule requires plaintiffs to disclose a computation of each category of claimed damages, and requires defendants to disclose their insurance coverage.

Adding mandatory initial disclosures was one of many efforts by rulemakers to streamline the discovery process, to reduce discovery abuse, and to encourage settlements. Mandatory initial disclosures were introduced in 1993. And between the years 1993 and 2000, the Rules required parties to disclose favorable *and unfavorable* witnesses and documents; in 2000, the requirement was amended to require disclosure only of the witnesses and documents "that the disclosing party may use," which is to say the *favorable* evidence. The thinking behind mandatory initial disclosures is that there is no reason for either party to have to request, nor to wait for, nor to fight about entitlement to who the key witnesses are, what the key documents are, and what this evidence shows. Further, if plaintiffs are forced to articulate their damages, and defendants are forced to disclose their insurance coverage, then many cases might settle early based on this free flow of information.

According to Federal Rule 26(a)(1)(C), the initial disclosures should be made within fourteen days of the Rule 26(f) discovery conference. The Rule 26(f) conference should be at least twenty-one days before the Rule 16(b) scheduling order is due. *See* Fed. R. Civ. P. 26(f)(1). The Rule 16(b) scheduling order, in turn, should issue on the earlier of ninety days after the defendant has been served or sixty days after the defendant has appeared. *See* Fed. R. Civ. P. 16(b)(2). The chronological sequence of these three events, then, is: the Rule 26(f) discovery conference; the Rule 26 mandatory initial disclosures; and then the Rule 16(b) scheduling conference/order. (As you practice these rules remember also Rule 6, which governs calculating deadlines under the Rules.)

Importantly, the failure to disclose information in discovery is a basis for disallowing its use at some later stage of the litigation. Fed. R. Civ. P. 37(c)(1). Accordingly, one must be attentive to the mandate of 26(a)(1)(A) that applies to witnesses and documents "that the disclosing party may use." A lawyer may wish to *use* a witness or a document at a pretrial conference, or to support/oppose a motion, or at a trial. If the lawyer has not disclosed something, she presumptively may not use it at a deposition or otherwise.

Much to the consternation of the rulemakers, it is common for parties to opt out of the mandatory initial disclosure requirements. *See* Fed. R. Civ. P. 29(b).

Paragraph (a)(1)(B) of Federal Rule 26 exempts certain types of proceedings from the mandatory initial disclosure requirement. Whenever an exception is written into a rule (or regulation or statute), seize the opportunity to reverse-engineer the drafters' thought process. In this particular instance, to appreciate *why* certain types of proceedings are excluded is also to appreciate, by implication, why everything else was included. That implication may be wrong in a particular case, and the effective advocate will leverage that. This sort of implication may be wrong on the facts of a particular case, and an effective advocate may be able to win an otherwise counterintuitive argument.

As an important practice note, Fed. R. Civ. P. 26(e) requires *supplementation* of any information that would have been subject to the mandatory disclosure requirement. Further, that obligation to disclose information the party may use connects directly to the exclusion sanction of Fed. R. Civ. P. 37(c)(1). Rule 37(c) provides an almost automatic sanction for a failure to disclose under Rule 26(a). In this sense, one of the most important "rules of evidence" may not appear in the "Rules of Evidence."

You should also be familiar with two additional stages of mandatory disclosures. Fed. R. Civ. P. 26(a)(2)(D) requires certain disclosures of expert testimony at least ninety days before the trial date. A third stage requiring disclosures of the identities of witnesses and documents to be used at trial is to occur at least thirty days prior to trial. *See* Fed. R. Civ. P. 26(a)(3)(B).

2. Party-Controlled Discovery

The federal discovery rules outline the formal techniques by which parties may obtain discovery. These techniques include depositions (*see* Rules 27-32); interrogatories (*see* Rule 33); requests for production of documents (*see* Rule 34); physical and mental examinations (*see* Rule 35); and requests for admissions (*see* Rule 36). The permissible scope of discovery for all of these formal mechanisms, of course, is defined by Rule 26, which permits the discovery of any unprivileged matter that is relevant to the claim or defense of any party, and is proportional to the needs of the case. In this part we identify certain advantages and disadvantages of the various formal as well as informal discovery techniques. We also discuss the increasingly important role of experts.

a. Depositions

Depositions are used by attorneys to question potential witnesses (both parties and nonparties) under oath about their knowledge of and participation in certain events or circumstances concerning the underlying action. Depositions typically are conducted orally, and every word that is spoken is recorded *verbatim* by a court reporter (or by mechanical means) and is transcribed. The witness (called the *deponent*) is given an opportunity to review the transcript and make technical corrections. Fed. R. Civ. P. 30(e).

Depositions are widely thought to be the most important step of the formal discovery process. It is perhaps no surprise, then, that half of the twelve discovery rules pertain solely to deposition practice. Read Fed. R. Civ. P. 27 through 32, which address a range of technicalities, including how depositions should be noticed, under what circumstances a witness may be deposed, before whom a deposition may be taken, and how a deposition transcript may be used.

A deposition may be scheduled on "reasonable notice" in writing. The noticing party may ask the witness to bring documents along, but that invokes the time limits of Fed. R. Civ. P. 34. *See* Fed. R. Civ. P. 30(b)(2). If the deponent is a nonparty, the noticing party must also provide for the attendance of the witness, usually by serving him with a subpoena. *See* Fed. R. Civ. P. 45. If a witness (whether a party or nonparty) fails to show up for the deposition, she may be assessed to pay the expenses and fees of the noticing party under Rule 30(g).

The noticing party schedules the location of the deposition and usually identifies her own law office as the situs. Depositions typically resemble a business meeting, with the deponent and his counsel on one side of the table and opposing counsel on the other side. Parties are entitled to attend any depositions taken in their case, and it is often a matter of strategy who, from each side, appears to observe a given deposition. Deponent's counsel may object to questions during the deposition, but the only objections that may preclude the deponent from answering the question posed are an objection as to the form of the question and an objection that to answer would reveal privileged information. All other answers are required and recorded, but remain "subject to the objection." Fed. R. Civ. P. 30(c).

There are at least five fundamental advantages to oral depositions. First, an oral deposition gives an attorney a chance to question potential witnesses under oath, in a manner similar to trial. This may be particularly useful as a means of assessing the demeanor of a witness under a variety of questioning styles. Second, while it is true that nearly all deponents will have been coached by an attorney prior to a deposition, responses to questions will have a degree of spontaneity unavailable under other discovery methods. Third, in a deposition an attorney has the opportunity to follow up on information revealed in answers and to take the questioning in any new direction that may reveal itself. Fourth, subject to the rules of evidence, anything recorded in a deposition is available for use at trial. Portions of depositions are often used to impeach a witness's testimony and can sometimes substitute for live testimony in cases where a witness is unavailable for trial. Fifth, nonparties may be deposed. Indeed, nonparties may also be subpoenaed to bring documents or other tangible items to the deposition and, thus, otherwise undiscoverable evidence may be obtained through questioning regarding those documents or items.

The most significant disadvantage to taking depositions is the expense. The party requesting the deposition must spend a significant amount of time preparing for each deposition. And at hourly billing rates of several hundreds of dollars per hour, this adds up quickly. Moreover, the counsel that notices the deposition must also hire a court reporter. The bill for a court reporter is the sum of two numbers: (1) an appearance fee of approximately $250 plus an hourly rate of approximately $50, plus (2) a transcription fee of $3.50-$5.00 per page. Depending on the pace of the deposition, court reporters usually generate 45-55 pages per hour. Thus even excluding the expense associated with the lawyers' time, one deposition will typically cost the requesting party at least $2,000. In addition to these expenses, parties must also pay travel expenses when the deponent is not local. Deponents also suffer costs, including preparation time spent with their counsel and, often, lost time from work. Notice the numerical limitations in Fed. R. Civ. P. 30(a)(2)(A)(i) and Fed. R. Civ P. 30(d)(1). Courts may order even further limits (*see* Fed. R. Civ. P. 26(b)(2)). Lawyers, by agreement, can agree to waive the Federal Rules' numeric restrictions on depositions and other discovery mechanisms. (*See* Fed. R. Civ. P. 29.) Such stipulations are commonplace in complex matters.

Of course, in some cases, a lawyer contemplating the taking of a deposition may decide not to do so because she does not want the deponent (or the deponent's lawyer) to be able to infer anything about her theories of the case; similarly, she may not want the putative deponent to be confronted until the trial.

b. Written Interrogatories

Under Fed. R. Civ. P. 33, written questions may be submitted to an opposing party and must be answered in writing, under oath, and returned within the specified time period. Read Fed. R. Civ. P. 33. Notice that Rule 33(b) specifies agency concepts for interrogating corporations and partnerships. Questions may seek any information discoverable under the scope of discovery standard of Rule 26(b)(1).

There are at least three advantages to using written interrogatories. First, interrogatories are usually the most useful mechanism for obtaining detailed and/or noncontroversial information from an adversary. If served early in the case, interrogatories can be very useful in obtaining names, addresses, dates, employers, relationships, histories, lists, numbers, or other technical information that a party may be required to assemble. Second, interrogatories are inexpensive to prepare and serve (or "propound") upon the opposing party. In fact, most lawyers (and many practice books) have pattern interrogatories for specific types of cases. Third, interrogatories are available for use at trial. Interrogatory answers are statements of an opposing party, and thus may be admitted as an admission under the Rules of Evidence over a hearsay objection.

The unfortunate downside to interrogatories, however, is that the answers are almost always drafted by lawyers and, thus, typically are crafted to contain as little useful information as possible. The answers are not spontaneously offered, and there is no opportunity for a timely follow-up question for clarification. Moreover, some lawyers delay the answering of interrogatories until their client is compelled to answer by the judge or will make every conceivable objection to the wording and scope of the interrogatories. As with depositions, there is a limit on the numbers of interrogatories that parties may serve as a matter of right. *See* Fed. R. Civ. P. 33(a). Local rules may limit still further. *See* Fed. R. Civ. P. 26(b)(2).

A strategic consideration that is part of both drafting and answering interrogatories is the extent to which you choose to inform the party of your theories of the case. On the one hand, the interrogatory is a subtle rhetorical device, an opportunity for advocacy; on the other hand, detail sufficient to persuade will necessarily inform the other party of your line of thinking and may give your opponent ample time to formulate a responsive theory.

Importantly, Fed. R. Civ. P. 26(e) imposes a continuing duty to supplement your discovery responses.

c. Production of Documents (Including ESI) and Things

Under Fed. R. Civ. P. 34, any party may request another party to produce documents and things and may then inspect and copy those documents and things before returning them to the producing party. Read Fed. R. Civ. P. 34. "Production" can include turning over a copy of the requested information or making it available at a specified time and place. Parties who respond to requests for the production of documents typically produce those documents at the office of the responding party's attorney for inspection or copying. *See* Fed. R. Civ. P. 34(b). Occasionally, the responding party will simply make copies of the requested documents and serve that package of documents on the requesting party's counsel. This process is straightforward and simple in (the vast majority of) cases where there is a modest amount of discovery. When a large amount of documents needs to be produced, counsel for the requesting and the responding parties will make other arrangements.

Rule 34(b)(2)(E)(i) mandates that the responding party that is producing documents may either (1) organize and label the produced documents in a manner that corresponds to the request; or (2) produce those documents in the order in which they are kept in the usual course of business. Producing documents in the order in which they are kept does not, however, give a party *carte blanche* to produce documents in a completely disorganized condition even if that is how they are maintained. For example, the court in *SEC v. Collins & Aikman Corp.,* 256 F.R.D. 403, 413 (S.D.N.Y. 2009), stated that "[t]he purpose of the Rule is to facilitate the production of records in a useful manner and to minimize discovery costs; thus it is reasonable to require litigants who do not create and/or maintain records in a 'routine and repetitive' manner to organize the records in a usable fashion prior to producing them."

One advantage of what commonly is referred to as a *document request* is that the term "documents" is construed widely (as the listed items in the Rule itself imply) to mean almost any type of written or electronically stored item of information. A document request may also include a request for things, which may include the physical inspection of real or personal property, including equipment, devices, vehicles, and the like. The broad scope of the definition of *document* works in tandem with the broad scope of discovery under Fed. R. Civ. P. 26(b).

One primary disadvantage of a document request is that it is difficult to strike a balance between over- and under-inclusiveness. On the one hand, a certain level of specificity is required, because a requesting party must request with specificity sufficient to ensure that the opposing party will deliver the sought documents. However, casting the request too broadly can result in an avalanche of documents that are responsive to the request but will bury the desired document(s).

One historical disadvantage to use of a discovery request was that Rule 34 was limited to parties and, even as to parties, to items only within their "possession, custody, or control." Later amendments to the Federal Rules, however, relaxed the requirement that the request be directed to a party. Part (c) of Rule 34 permits a party to subpoena documents even from a nonparty in conformity with the requirements for a subpoena in Rule 45.

(Again, remember that Fed. R. Civ. P. 26(e) imposes a continuing duty to supplement your discovery responses.)

At least 90 percent of the documents generated today are electronic, and the vast majority of those are never printed. Electronic documents are also qualitatively different than traditional paper documents. Electronic files contain metadata about when a document was created and by whom, and who accessed it. Electronic documents introduce complexity about computer formats and encoding. Because of backups and servers and transmissions, electronic documents tend to be more durable — and less likely (or less able, as the case may be) to be destroyed; for these same reasons, there tends to be greater redundancy in electronic documents. Further, although most paper documents are written by human beings, some electronic documents are generated by electronic means. For all of these reasons, the discovery of electronic documents — "e-discovery" or "electronically stored information" (ESI) — has introduced new challenges for the judicial process and created a cottage industry to help businesses preserve ESI and, when litigation arises, to facilitate the production of it during discovery.

Rulemakers have responded to the unique challenges that electronically stored information presents.

First, Rule 26(b)(2)(B) protects a responding party from producing ESI that is relevant and otherwise discoverable when it is "not reasonably accessible because of undue burden or cost." In order to get that discovery, the judge must require its production.

Second, Rule 26(b)(2)(C) allows a party to resist producing otherwise relevant ESI (or traditional) discovery where (i) the information sought is unreasonably cumulative or duplicative; (ii) the information is available from another source; or (iii) the request is untimely.

Third, the mention of "conditions for . . . discovery" in Rule 26(b)(2)(B) is an invitation by the Advisory Committee for judges to consider requiring some requesting parties to pay part or all of the reasonable costs of obtaining ESI from sources that are not reasonably accessible. This is a departure from the American Rule on attorneys' fees that each side bears its own litigation expense, including the cost of responding to discovery requests.

Fourth, the possibility of inadvertent disclosures of ESI that is privileged led to so-called "claw-back" provisions in Rule 26(b)(5)(B) that enable the producing party to assert retroactively a protective claim to the information. (Ordinarily, the inadvertent production of a document constitutes a waiver of any privilege.)

In the typical case involving the production of ESI, at least as envisioned by the rulemakers and judges, the parties will meet in advance of e-discovery and reach some agreement as to what ESI will be produced, in what technological format it will be made available, and when. *See* Fed. R. Civ. P. 26(f)(3) (C). "Custodians" of the targeted ESI are identified; these are the individuals who have administrative control of the document or file. Accordingly, if you were suing your law school and/or university over a dispute regarding, say, an accommodation of a disability, the *custodians* would be the persons whose email accounts (text messages, Instagram posts, Facebook. . .) you would want to review — *e.g.,* your professor, the associate dean for academic affairs, the dean, etc. Naturally, the parties often disagree on the number and identity of custodians whose files will be searched.

Even once it is agreed upon or determined which custodians' files will be searched, the search of ESI poses unique challenges because of the quantity of electronic documents. Imagine a products liability action where the plaintiff is looking for, *inter alia*, evidence from the defendant-manufacturer of who knew what and when about a product's defect. To ask the defendant to review every byte of ESI in each custodian's possession or control could be time-consuming, expensive, and unreasonably burdensome. Accordingly, the parties (sometimes with the benefit of a judicial nudge) will agree on the parameters of a search of each custodian's ESI. In contemporary litigation, the most common method of searching involves using keywords or search terms. If the product at issue was a suspension lift kit, possible keywords might be "suspension," "center of gravity," "roll-over," "lift," "axle," and so forth. Plaintiff's counsel would want many search terms, and defense counsel fewer.

> In many cases, the way lawyers choose keywords is the equivalent of the child's game of "Go Fish." The requesting party guesses which keywords might produce evidence to support its case without having much, if any, knowledge of the responding party's "cards" (i.e., the terminology used by the responding party's custodians). Indeed, the responding party's counsel often does not know what is in its own client's "cards."

Monica McCarroll, *Discovery and the Duty of Competence*, 26 Regent U. L. Rev. 81, 104 (2014). This is a competency that lawyers need to master—especially in light of the fact that judges may not have the technological sophistication and, in any event, may be disinclined to help. *See, e.g., Thompson v. C&H Sugar Co., Inc.,* 2014 WL 595911, at *5 (N.D. Cal. Feb. 14, 2014) ("The court is not in the business of drafting e-discovery search terms. These types of decisions about minute discovery details are typically negotiated by the parties who are better equipped with knowledge of the needs of their case to make these choices."); *William A. Gross Constr. Assocs., Inc. v. American Mfrs. Mut. Ins. Co.,* 256 F.R.D. 134, 136 (S.D.N.Y. 2009) ("[W]here counsel are using keyword searches for retrieval of ESI, they at a minimum must carefully craft the appropriate keywords with input from the ESI's custodians as to the words and abbreviations they use, and the proposed methodology must be quality control tested to assure accuracy in retrieval and elimination of 'false positives.' It is time that the bar—even those lawyers who did not come of age in the computer era—understand this.")

Although technology is responsible for creating the unique challenges associated with ESI, technology is also a solution. As opposed to merely using a computer to search ESI for key terms, technology-assisted review (TAR), computer-assisted review (CAR), and other evolving forms of artificial intelligence (AI) can (and increasingly will) be used to search ESI faster and more accurately. Generally speaking, these technologies are trained with seed sets of documents—imagine one seed set prepared by the lawyers that is labeled "Produce—Responsive" and a second set labeled "Do Not Produce—Not Responsive." So trained, the computer can then march through millions of additional documents and predict which are likely to contain responsive content. Emerging technologies use continuous active learning to return more accurate and complete results than any human document review team. Interestingly, the improved accuracy and completeness of ESI review by AI tends to come at the expense of transparency. There is a lack of transparency because artificial intelligence operates as something of a black-box—even to its creators. We might know that an AI system is classifying documents with, say, 80% accuracy—which is better performance than human document review. But the AI cannot be interviewed or cross-examined to reveal its thought process.

The *preservation* of ESI poses special challenges for practitioners. Litigants have a common law duty to preserve discoverable material once a party knows or should know that litigation is reasonably foreseeable, and that the material is likely to be requested in discovery. Although reasonable minds differ on exactly when that moment occurs, it is very critical that you (and in-house counsel and outside counsel advising companies) appreciate that this is (usually) well before the lawsuit is filed. An organization's general counsel will typically issue a "litigation hold notice" to all of the custodians of the organization's records. This duty to preserve extends to both ESI and traditional discovery, and it is essential that clients know when they must suspend any ordinary or extraordinary practices that could destroy evidence. ESI is different from paper discovery, however, because doing "nothing" with regard to ESI may result in its destruction due to deletion, overwriting, upgrading, or recycling. The sanction for destroying ESI is more forgiving, however. When ESI that "should have been preserved" in anticipation of litigation is lost because of a failure to take "reasonable steps," and its loss "cannot be restored or replaced through additional discovery," then a court, upon a finding of prejudice to the requesting party, can determine a remedy "no greater than necessary to cure the prejudice." Fed. R. Civ. P. 37(e)(1). Only if the court finds intent to destroy ESI may the court impose the remedies of adverse inference, jury instruction, or dismissal. Fed. R. Civ. P. 37(e)(2).

d. Physical and Mental Examinations

Under Fed. R. Civ. P. 35, a physical and/or mental examination of a person may be requested when the person's condition is in controversy and the person to be examined is given proper notice. Read Fed. R. Civ. P. 35. Medical examinations are the only discovery tools for which advance court approval is required, and the court requires a showing of "good cause" for the examination.

This device applies only to a relatively narrow subset of cases, where the condition of the putative examinee is truly "in controversy." The Supreme Court has made clear that the Rule requires more than "mere conclusory allegations of the pleadings" or even "mere relevance to the case." Instead, there must be "an affirmative showing by the movant that each condition as to which examination is sought is really and genuinely in controversy." *Schlagenhauf v. Holder*, 379 U.S. 104 (1964).

When an examination is permitted, the court orders the time and place. Counsel for the party being examined typically is not permitted to attend. Re-read Fed. R. Civ. P. 35(b)(1), and you will see what, in addition to expense, may be viewed as a disadvantage of this device.

e. Requests for Admissions

Under Fed. R. Civ. P. 36, a party may serve upon any other party a request for admission of any matter within the scope of discovery. Read Fed. R. Civ. P. 36. Requests for admissions typically are "question and answer" statements that are used by either party to further explore specific contentions. The requesting party formulates a "question" in the form of a statement, which the answering party is requested to admit or deny. For example, a defense attorney may incorporate a request such as "Admit or deny: Charles Carpenter was not wearing a seat belt at the time of the fatal accident." This type of request may be intended to determine whether certain affirmative defenses will be available at trial.

The primary benefit of requests for admission is that they provide an opportunity to "lock in" particular admissions or denials of fact. Unlike evidence at trial, which may be rebutted and refuted, once admitted, the fact must be taken as true in the pending action, unless the court permits the admission to be "withdrawn or amended." Fed. R. Civ. P. 36(b). Importantly, under the Federal Rules, there is no limit on the number of allowable requests a party can make. Accordingly, the device may be especially helpful as a pretrial device to obviate the need for certain presentations of proof, including, for example, establishing the foundations for the admissibility of documents.

f. Informal Discovery

The Federal Rules do not discuss what are perhaps the most commonly used methods for discovering information. Informal discovery techniques include (1) nonparty interviews; (2) site visits; (3) exchange of information (for instance, cooperation with other attorneys who have handled cases against the same defendants or regarding similar events); (4) requests for information from government agencies (under the Freedom of Information Act, for example); (5) review of publicly available records; (6) private investigation; and (7) Internet research. Informal discovery thus refers to any form of extrajudicial research or inquiry that attempts to obtain facts relevant to the case.

There are two primary advantages to informal discovery techniques. First, informal discovery may cost less. Indeed, in certain circumstances the party may be able to perform the discovery for or in concert with the attorney, and thereby dramatically limit the fees incurred. Second, informal discovery often provides no notice to (nor requires any cooperation with) opposing parties. This may be particularly useful to an attorney who wishes to develop elements of her case without alerting her opponents to theories she may pursue (or to evidence that she already has).

It bears mentioning that informal discovery, such as information obtained from the Internet, may be inaccurate. Some informal discovery, such as the use of private investigators or the contact of nonparty witnesses, can—at some point—violate rules of professional ethics. And of course certain sources of informal discovery, such as hospitals or employers, will not release confidential information without the authorization of the party about whom information is sought. Nevertheless, informal discovery remains a valuable discovery tool for the effective litigator.

Informal discovery methods are especially important for gathering evidence prior to filing a case. Remember the demands of the plausibility pleading standard imposed at the Rule 12(b)(6) stage and also your obligation under Fed. R. Civ. P. 11(b)(3). Yet at this stage you do not have any authority to propound interrogatories, take depositions, or request documents until your case has survived the pleading stage. Some scholars have suggested that the new heightened pleading standard necessitates a mechanism for pre-filing discovery. *See, e.g.,* Scott Dodson, *New Pleading, New Discovery*, 109 Mich. L. Rev. 53 (2010). As logical as that may sound, remember that *avoiding* discovery was one of the Court's primary justifications for imposing plausibility pleading.

g. Experts

In the past two decades, expert witnesses have performed an increasingly important role in the process of developing and, ultimately, presenting a case. It is now generally accepted that expert testimony is necessary to aid a jury, especially when scientific, medical, technological, or statistical information is presented. A study conducted by the Federal Judicial Center, for example, suggests that tort plaintiffs will, on average, use at least three experts at trial, and defendants will use at least two. Yet experts typically are involved long before trial. Experts are routinely consulted to assist in the process of framing the pleadings, preparing discovery requests, responding to discovery, and when developing a strategy for pretrial motions.

The use of experts in presenting and interpreting evidence is not unique to the American system of jurisprudence. Civil law systems also use experts to aid in the interpretation of complicated evidence. However, where the American system allows the parties to choose, prepare, and groom their experts, most civil law systems put these decisions solely in the hands of the judge. That difference has a marked effect on the role of the expert in each instance. American experts are increasingly criticized for their biased opinions, offered as "expert testimony" to support the case for the hand that feeds them. In contrast, the judge-selected experts in the civil law system are viewed as neutral witnesses able to provide factual assertions regarding the evidence, not based upon the party that hired them.

Note that although there is not a specific discovery rule governing the involvement of experts, their participation is contemplated by the rules. When are you obliged to disclose the identity of your experts? Can experts be deposed?

h. A Brief Introduction to the Rules of Evidence

The scope of discovery is broader than the scope of evidence that would be admissible at trial. But some basics about the law of evidence may be helpful to you as you contemplate the mechanics of discovery. Evidence itself is a complex subject and will be covered in a separate course; this is but an overview.

As a threshold matter, it is important to realize, in the words of one trial lawyer, that "the courtroom is its own reality": If evidence is not admitted into the record of that case by one of the established techniques, then it cannot be considered by the fact finder. Put another way, the evidence necessary to support a verdict must be *on the record*; the attorney thus must ensure that all pieces of the evidence that she wants the fact finder to consider are properly admitted lest they be ignored. Importantly, facts alleged in a pleading, discovery materials produced or held, and statements or arguments made in pretrial proceedings are not evidence and cannot support a verdict. Evidence is only that information that was introduced by the parties at trial (whether through testimony or documents or things) and was admitted by the court onto the record.* The rules of evidence govern what evidence is admissible for parties to submit for the record.

Most cases are not proved with "the smoking gun," that is, *direct evidence* of an issue. Direct evidence is evidence that is precisely on point. For example, in *Carpenter*, a witness on the stand can testify that she saw the jeep tip over to prove that it, in fact, tipped over. Why it tipped will probably require *circumstantial evidence*, which is evidence relating to a series of facts other than those directly at issue in order to prove a fact at issue. An expert may take the stand in order to testify as to how raising a vehicle will alter its center of gravity and destabilize it when it turns a corner. This, along with other evidence, may permit an *inference* that the sale of the oversized tires and elevation kit without a warning was (1) negligent, (2) the cause in fact, and/or (3) the proximate cause of the death of Charlie Carpenter. A good deal of the civil litigator's skill and art relates to creatively getting facts into evidence that will later permit the drawing of desired inferences.

When one is in federal court, the admissibility of evidence is governed by the Federal Rules of Evidence. In state court, admissibility is governed by either a written code or statute of evidence rules, often patterned after the federal rules, or common law rules of evidence, often supplemented by statutes. The Federal Rules of Evidence are usually fairly representative of the common law of evidence, although in many instances they are more generous (than the common law rules) about admitting evidence.

Relevant evidence, according to Rule 401, "means evidence having any tendency to make the existence of any fact that is of consequence to the determination of the action more probable or less probable than it would be without

---

* There are a few methods of providing evidence that are often overlooked, such as asking the court to take judicial notice of a particular fact or by the submission of facts stipulated by the parties.

the evidence." Fed. R. Evid. 401. In order to make a relevancy argument, one must usually turn to the concepts that you learned early in the course: causes of action and elements. After all, how does one know whether a fact is "of consequence to the determination of the action" unless one knows the cause of action relied upon, its elements, defenses and their elements, and the theories propounded by each side?

Relevance is contextual. If the sole theory in a negligence case was that the driver failed to wear his prescription glasses and therefore didn't see the pedestrian whom he hit, then evidence of unusually large tires on the vehicle would probably be irrelevant. (We say "probably" because maybe the high tires are relevant to line of vision, and perhaps you can come up with another "relevancy" argument.) But when the theories against a driver are that it was negligent to alter a jeep by lifting it with unusually large tires and a suspension kit (plus hockey pucks!) and to drive the jeep in that condition, evidence that would be irrelevant in another context, is suddenly relevant.

The more remote the relationship between the proffered evidence and the issue in question, the less likely the judge will be to find it relevant. In *Carpenter,* the fact that Ultimate Auto recently laid off several workers is arguably relevant; but it seems quite remote from the issues in the case, and in all likelihood would be excluded on an evidence objection. In evidence parlance, the party trying to exclude evidence makes an *objection*. If the judge agrees with the objection, she *sustains* it. If the judge decides it's a bad objection, she *overrules* it. If the objection is overruled, that means that the witness at a trial will be ordered to answer the question or, if pertaining to physical evidence, the proffered exhibit will be admitted.

A witness's credibility is always relevant. The evidence rules permit a number of ways to *impeach* credibility, such as through *bias*, a *contradictory statement*, what is called *bad reputation for truth and veracity*, or documentation of a *conviction for a felony or for a crime involving dishonesty or false statement*. Occasionally, otherwise relevant evidence might be excluded because it is *prejudicial* (*see* Rule 403). For instance, if the deceased in the *Carpenter* case was under indictment for burglary at the time of the accident, one could argue that the deceased was distracted at the time, and therefore consented to accompany Randall Dee in the jeep when he should have refused because of its altered construction. One might also argue that this testimony is relevant to the deceased's earning capacity. Whether or not this information is slightly probative of comparative negligence (assuming Charles Carpenter's negligence is relevant in the wrongful death action brought by his widow) or somewhat relevant to damage issues, some judges would consider the relevancy of such information to be sufficiently attenuated and thus outweighed by the potential prejudice.

Hearsay according to Rule 801(c) is "a statement, other than one made by the declarant [the person who makes a statement] at the trial or hearing, offered in evidence to prove the truth of the matter asserted." Fed. R. Evid. 801(c). Hearsay includes both oral and written statements. In general, even if an out-of-court statement introduced to prove the truth of its contents is signed or under oath, it is still hearsay. Hearsay is perhaps the most elusive of evidentiary concepts and takes many forms. Hearsay is generally inadmissible, unless one can find an exception to the hearsay rule.

Some hearsay examples are relatively easy. In *Carpenter*, if Melissa takes the stand in order to testify to what Sherman told her about the jeep accident he witnessed, such testimony would ordinarily be hearsay. The fact finder would have to determine whether Sherman's rendition of the accident were true, yet Sherman would not be on the stand to be cross-examined. If Melissa were asked where Sherman was standing at the time he allegedly saw the accident, she would probably answer "I don't know." She might say, "Ask Sherman." That's the point; it is the person who actually witnessed the event who should testify, instead of the person to whom he or she told the story.

Sometimes an out-of-court statement is not being introduced for a hearsay purpose (that is, for the truth of the matter asserted), and therefore it is admissible. In an oral contract case in which *A* says that *B* made an oral promise, the words of the contract are themselves relevant and admissible over a hearsay objection. If *C* takes the stand and says that he heard "*A* tell *B* that he would take care of her mother for $500 a week, and *B* said she'd pay that amount," then that is not hearsay in a lawsuit based on that contract. The words spoken are themselves relevant, and one doesn't need to cross-examine the speakers (*A* and *B*). It is enough that *C* can be cross-examined about where *C* was standing, and about *C*'s ability to hear or *C*'s bias. Indeed, for the same reasons, *A* and *B* could also testify to the words of contract that were spoken between them. The concept of "nonhearsay purpose" is tricky, and it takes many students enrolled in an Evidence course (and many practicing attorneys) time to catch on.

Even if offered testimony is hearsay, it may be subject to an exception and thus admissible as evidence in court. Probably the most common way of getting around what would otherwise be hearsay is through what historically was called the *admissions* exception. Fed. R. Evid. 801(d)(2). For evidence purposes, an "admission" is any statement made by the party-opponent. It doesn't matter whether the opponent is in fact admitting anything. If your opponent said it or wrote it, it will not be excluded on hearsay grounds. In other words, if in a motor vehicle personal injury negligence case the defendant said that "the roads were slippery the night of the accident," the plaintiff could put a witness on the stand to testify she heard what the defendant had said. It will be admitted against the defendant without any analysis of whether defendant thought he was admitting anything. If your opponent (the opposing party) said it or wrote it, and it's relevant, it normally will be admitted. For a very sophisticated reason, which we won't consider here, the drafters of the federal rules made "admissions" nonhearsay, rather than an exception (*see* Rule 801(d)(2)). But the result is the same: Statements of a party-opponent will be admitted over a hearsay objection.

The many hearsay exceptions are divided among those in which it matters whether or not the out-of-court declarant is available to testify because of reasons such as death, illness, refusal, or memory problems. Rule 804 lists the exceptions that require the proponent of what would otherwise be hearsay to show that the declarant is unavailable.

The *opinion* rule normally makes opinions by laypersons inadmissible. *See* Fed. R. Evid. 701. In a discrimination case, the plaintiff could not ordinarily say that in her opinion she was discriminated against. She would be permitted to describe how she was treated by the defendant-employer so that the fact finder can conclude whether there was discrimination in violation of the law. If a witness is shown through questions (or by stipulation of the parties) to be an expert (this is often called *qualification*) and seeks to give an opinion in her field of expertise that will aid the fact finder on a relevant point, then such *expert opinion* is normally admissible (*see* Fed. R. Evid. 702). There are occasions when a party needs experts in order to meet the production burden. For example, in a medical malpractice case the plaintiff will usually have trouble surviving a directed verdict without evidence from at least one expert on the standard of medical care that was allegedly breached and on the question of whether the alleged negligence was the cause of the alleged injury.

Another group of evidence rules relates to *privileges*. You have probably heard of the Fifth Amendment constitutional privilege against "self-incrimination." But several other privileges identify and protect confidential communications between certain people. Perhaps the most frequently used in litigation is the *attorney-client* privilege, which was developed at common law, but is now statutory in many states. If a protected professional relationship exists, such as that between attorney and client, it is the client who controls the privilege. The lawyer may not provide any information she learned from her client. The client, not the attorney, can waive the right to exclude oral and written communications between them that are related to their professional relationship. The rationale here is that without such a privilege, clients would not reveal information that their lawyers need to know in order to give good sound legal advice. Another important privilege relating to lawyers, which we will discuss later in this chapter, is the work product doctrine, which protects the lawyers' own work, even when that information is not obtained directly from the client. In the aforementioned *Hickman v. Taylor,* attorney Fortenbaugh's informal interviews of survivors of the tug boat crash (and his notes from those interviews) are examples of work product.

Many states also have some combination of the following privileges: *priest-penitent, doctor-patient, spousal (husband-wife), psychotherapist-patient.* Various rationales support these and other privileges that you will read about in your Evidence class. The drafters of the Federal Rules were unable to reach agreement on privileges that would also satisfy Congress. This was particularly true with privileges relating to state secrets. Consequently, Fed. R. Evid. 501 is the only portion of the Federal Rules of Evidence on privileges in federal courts.

Thus, the federal courts look to other sources (such as the Constitution, congressional statutes, and the common law developed in the federal courts or state evidence law, especially in diversity of citizenship cases) for the applicable evidence rules.

When lawyers need more guidance in evidence matters, they often look to a treatise such as *McCormick on Evidence* or *The New Wigmore: A Treatise on Evidence*. Annotated versions of the Federal Rules of Evidence also provide relevant case law after every rule. Lawyers often use this case law to supplement their arguments regarding the admissibility of a particular piece of evidence. The Advisory Committee Notes to the Federal Rules of Evidence are also quite helpful in this respect. There also exist Uniform Rules of Evidence, which some states have adopted in whole or in part. Lawyers in state court often use a handbook on the rules of evidence in their state. For direction with respect to a particular state evidence issue, lawyers often refer to state treatises that specifically discuss the particular state's evidence law.

PRACTICE EXERCISE NO. 15: DISCOVERY PLANNING IN *CARPENTER*

Carol Coblentz is the senior partner in the plaintiff's firm that represents Nancy Carpenter. Your firm is small and does not have the luxury of endless resources. You have filed a strong complaint and served the defendants Randall Dee, Peter Dee, and Ultimate Auto. You have a good relationship with defense counsel, and you have agreed to opt out of the mandatory initial disclosure obligations.

The case is approaching the earliest stages of discovery. During class, you will engage in a strategy session with two of your colleagues to discuss a discovery plan. What *exactly* will be the first few acts of discovery that our firm should pursue, and why? After meeting with your colleagues for fifteen minutes, we will rejoin as a group. The instructor will call upon you to explain precisely what discovery you have in mind, the order of that discovery, and your reasons for that approach.

3. The Scope of Discovery

The scope of discovery is defined in Federal Rule 26(b). Generally speaking, a party is *entitled* to demand the discovery of any matter that:

- is relevant to the claim or defense of any party;
- is not privileged; and
- is proportional to the needs of the case.

Each of these three criteria must be satisfied. Or, put differently, one can resist a discovery request on the grounds that it exceeds the scope of discovery by demonstrating that the request seeks irrelevant evidence, seeks evidence that is privileged, *or* is a request that is disproportionate. We will consider each of these criteria in turn before reading cases where judges must define the scope of permissible discovery.

First, **relevance** for purposes of discovery is not the same as relevancy for purposes of trial; the last sentence of Rule 26(b)(1) confirms this. Historically, in the discovery context, relevancy has been broadly construed to encompass even the possibility that the information sought may bear upon, or reasonably could lead to other matters that could bear upon, any issue that is or likely may be raised in the case. "[D]iscovery should ordinarily be allowed under the concept of relevancy unless it is clear that the information sought has no possible bearing on claims and defenses of the parties." 6 *Moore's Federal Practice: Civil* § 26.42 (2019). One reason that some judges interpreted the relevancy criterion so broadly was that, for decades, the Rule provided that the request need only "appear[] reasonably calculated to lead to the discovery of admissible evidence." Because that language was eliminated by a 2015 amendment, we might expect at least some judges to be more stingy when exercising their broad discretion to define the parameters of relevance. Still, given the capacity of the human imagination, a good creative lawyer should be able to make an argument that anything potentially useful (or detrimental) to her case is relevant. Remember that Fed. R. Civ. P. 26(g) and the lawyer's ethical obligations loom for both the requesting and the responding party.

Second, with certain exceptions, a requesting party is not entitled to information that is **privileged** or is protected by the work product doctrine. To be sure, depriving parties of privileged information runs counter to the goals of full disclosure and arriving at the truth. Yet lawmakers and courts consider it a greater priority to facilitate and respect confidential communications between, for example, penitents and priests, doctors and patients, and attorneys and clients. Accordingly, in a jurisdiction that recognizes a doctor-patient privilege, it would be beyond the scope of discovery to ask a doctor or her patient about the content of their conversations. References to "privilege" typically also include the attorney work-product doctrine. The discussion of *Hickman v. Taylor* that opened this chapter involved a discovery request for the attorney's work product, to wit: his notes of conversations with witnesses who watched the tug sink. In *Hickman*, the Supreme Court specifically endorsed the new era of "fishing expeditions" authorized by broad discovery rules. But in doing so, it recognized some limit to discovery: you can't ask the other side's lawyer to disclose her thoughts and strategy — her "work product."

The Federal Rules of Civil Procedure require parties to explicitly assert privilege claims, usually by providing information about the privileged materials in the form of a "privilege log." *See* Fed. R. Civ. P. 26(b)(5)(A). The notion of a log clarifies the idea that while the content of privileged information is exempt from disclosure, the *existence* of that information is discoverable. A privilege log conveys that the document exists while also justifying its non-production. A privilege log will often include (i) a description of the document; (ii) the date of the document; (iii) the general subject matter of the document; (iv) the identities of the author and the recipients; (v) a description of where and how each document has been maintained; and (vi) the nature of the privilege claim. We encourage you to search "examples of privilege logs" in your web browser to appreciate the work involved with creating one. Logs are required so that the requesting party can contest the responding party's assertion of a privilege. And yet again, remember Federal Rule 26(g) and every lawyer's ethical obligations.

Third, discovery is limited to that which is **proportional** to the needs of the case. To evaluate proportionality, the Rule provides six illustrative factors for courts to consider: (i) the importance of the issues at stake in the actions; (ii) the amount in controversy; (iii) the parties' relative access to relevant information; (iv) the parties' resources; (v) the importance of the discovery in resolving the issues; and (vi) whether the burden or expense of the proposed discovery outweighs its likely benefit. Fed. R. Civ. P. 26(b)(1). Especially because this proportionality criterion is a relatively recent phenomenon ("proportionality" was elevated in significance by 2015 amendments to the rules), there is very little consensus about how it (and its six factors) should be applied.*

The emergence of the proportionality criterion is controversial because it has reframed the Federal Rules' approach to discovery from an approach that was generally focused on preventing abuse to an approach that applies a cost-benefit analysis filter to the scope of discovery. A document that a party requests in discovery may be relevant, not protected by any privilege, and in no sense an abuse of the discovery process, yet that document may, by virtue of the proportionality criterion, fall outside the scope of discovery. Further, according to Federal Rule 26(b)(2)(C), under certain circumstances "a court *must* limit the frequency or extent of discovery otherwise allowed" (emphasis added). And Federal Rule 26(c)(1)(B) permits "expense allocation," where a judge requires the responding party to produce the requested evidence provided the requesting party compensates the responding party for the expense occurred in producing it.

Discovery disputes arise when counsel disagree about the propriety of a question or request. Of course, even when a discovery request is beyond the scope of discovery, the responding party may nevertheless produce the requested document or answer the posed question. After all, if Randall Dee's attorneys want to serve interrogatories asking Nancy Carpenter about her favorite books and podcasts, her attorney might well be inclined to allow her (or even encourage her) to answer those "irrelevant" questions. Similarly, a document request by Nancy Carpenter that asks Randall Dee to produce a copy of his high school yearbook is at least arguably beyond the scope of discovery, yet his counsel might nevertheless choose to produce it.

---

* The Advisory Committee that amended Federal Rule 26 to more prominently feature the element of proportionality described the change as modest. In his 2015 Year-End Report, however, Chief Justice Roberts suggested that the 2015 amendments were "a big deal." John G. Roberts, Jr., *2015 Year-End Report on the Federal Judiciary 5 (2015), http://www.supremecourt.gov/publicinfo/year-end/2015year-endreport. pdf* (last visited July 1, 2019).

But when a party does not want to comply with a discovery request, she can either (1) object to that request and "wait and see" what happens next; or (2) bring the dispute to the attention of the court by filing a protective order under Fed. R. Civ. P. 26(c). If the responding party objects to the request per the "wait and see" option, then the requesting party, in turn, has at least two available courses of action: (1) abandon or reframe the discovery request; or (2) bring the dispute to the attention of the court by filing a motion to compel under Fed. R. Civ. P. 37(a).

Assume, then, that an interrogatory request arguably exceeds the permissible scope of discovery. From the perspective of the responding party, what is the *advantage* of objecting and following the "wait and see" option? What is the *advantage* of instead filing a motion for a protective order?

One disadvantage of filing motions and bringing discovery disputes to the attention of the court is that judges often regard discovery motions as nuisances. "[M]any judges loathe discovery disputes, and may view both sides as akin to bickering children." David F. Herr and Steven Baicker-McKee, *Deposition—Protective Order to Narrow or Strike Rule 30(b)(6) Deposition,* 29 Fed. Litigator 10 (Oct. 2014).

> We all know the pattern. You run into problems with your opposing counsel in getting compliance with discovery demands. You follow all the customary procedures, revising demands to make them specific, meeting and conferring to try to ensure the maximum compliance, filing a motion that is targeted and clear. And the result you get? Judges hate discovery disputes. So they instinctively blame you for having raised one. And their response is one of "a pox on both your houses," issuing vague orders telling both parties to behave themselves.

Robert E. Shapiro, *Conclusion Assumed,* Litigation 59, 62 (Spring 2010). Judges may have this reaction because discovery disputes are uninteresting. Or perhaps discovery disputes are especially difficult to resolve. To be sure, "adjudication of discovery motions takes time. The busier the court, the less time it has for such ancillary disputes." Hon. James G. Carr, *Fixing Discovery: The Judge's Job,* Litigation 6, 8 (Summer/Fall 2012). But just how ancillary or uninteresting is a dispute about whether or not a party is entitled to evidence that may be essential to proving its case?

A prerequisite for filing a motion to compel is a good faith effort to resolve the matter without court action. *See* Fed. R. Civ. P. 37(a)(1). To be sure, the discovery system presumes and requires cooperation between the parties. Lawyers may have very different impressions about the scope of permissible discovery under Rule 26(b)(1). But there are many other provisions in the discovery rules about which lawyers can disagree: What constitutes "reasonable . . . notice" for a deposition under Rule 30(b)(1)? When is a document request "describe[d] with reasonable particularity" according to Rule 34(b)(1)(A)? How does one count the number of interrogatories, given the limits of Rule 33(a)(1)? When is a mental or physical condition "in controversy" within the meaning of Rule 35(a)(1)? Seasoned practitioners advise young lawyers to work mightily to resolve the dispute with opposing counsel.

> Make a motion to compel discovery only when you have exhausted every other avenue, and the information is essential to the case. . . . When judges are forced to decide discovery disputes, they typically give both sides a hard time — the abuser for violating the rules, and the petitioner for wasting the court's time with annoying trivia.

James W. McElhaney, *Making the Most of Motions Purpose, Not Plenitude, Is What Matters in Pretrial Filings,* A.B.A. J. 74, 75 (1996) (quotation marks omitted). Unfortunately, judges' reluctance to resolve discovery disputes tends to compound the problem because lawyers who misbehave are less likely to have their conduct scrutinized.

Of course, many discovery disputes are brought to the attention of judges, and the following case excerpts will give you a better sense of what these disputes look like and how judges resolve them.

Oxbow Carbon & Minerals LLC v. Union Pacific R.R. Co.
322 F.R.D. 1 (D.D.C. 2017)

HARVEY, United States Magistrate Judge:

. . . BACKGROUND

Plaintiffs are five related companies (collectively, "Oxbow") that mine and sell coal and petroleum coke ("petcoke"). They allege in the Amended Complaint that Union Pacific ("UP") and BNSF Railway Company ("BNSF") — both railroad companies with which Oxbow contracts to ship coal and petcoke — conspired to engage in anticompetitive conduct from 2004 to 2012 in violation of the Sherman Antitrust Act, codified at 15 U.S.C. §§ 1 and 2, that forced Oxbow to pay higher prices to ship coal and petcoke. Specifically, Oxbow believes that UP and BNSF conspired to (1) fix fuel rates applied to commercial rail freight service above competitive levels through a uniform fuel surcharge and (2) allocate certain markets for coal shipment to each other, granting UP a monopoly in at least one region of the country. Oxbow claims it paid Defendants more than $50,000,000 in illegal fuel surcharges as a result of the conspiracy. Oxbow seeks to recover treble damages under 15 U.S.C. § 15, as well as its "lost business and profits" that proximately resulted from the conspiracy.

[Presently before this court is Defendants' motion to] compel Oxbow to add William I. Koch ("Koch"), Oxbow's founder, CEO, and principle [sic] owner as a document custodian whose records will be searched for material responsive to Plaintiffs' discovery requests. Defendants maintain that Koch indisputably possesses relevant, unique information responsive to their requests, and argue that Oxbow has improperly refused to produce this information based on the unsupported theory that production of his documents would be disproportionately burdensome and duplicative of the documents produced from the search of the nineteen other Oxbow document custodians' files. Based upon its review of the documents already produced from the other Oxbow custodians, Defendants believe that Koch's records contain information that would, among other things, reveal that market forces—as opposed to Defendants' alleged collusion—contributed to the increasing rail freight costs and any of Oxbow's lost profits. Relatedly, Defendants assert that their discovery request is proportionate and reasonable in light of the facts of this case, including that tens of millions of dollars that Oxbow seeks in damages.

In their opposition, Oxbow argues that Defendants have failed to satisfy their burden of demonstrating that the discovery they seek is responsive and not unduly burdensome. Based on their calculations, Oxbow estimated that adding Koch as a document custodian would result in roughly 130 gigabytes of additional documents to be filtered through the parties' previously-agreed-upon search terms, a process that Oxbow initially estimated would cost $250,000. Oxbow further contends that many of Koch's documents would likely be duplicative of the other custodians' documents or only marginally responsive given Koch's senior position over a conglomerate of Oxbow companies, only some of which are involved in the coal and petcoke businesses. Despite these arguments Oxbow represented at the first hearing on Defendants' motion that it was open to analyzing a random sample of Koch's records using the agreed-upon search terms to provide the parties with concrete numbers regarding the responsiveness of Koch's documents to the terms and with a basis to negotiate new search terms if necessary. Accordingly, the undersigned held Defendants' motion [to compel] in abeyance pending the analysis of a sample of Koch's documents and the parties' attempt to negotiate a resolution of the dispute themselves.

Following the hearing, Oxbow collected a total of 467,614 documents from Koch's electronic and physical files and provided them to a vendor for processing. After removing any duplicative records, the vendor searched Koch's documents using the previously-agreed-upon search terms, which yielded 45,639 document hits—82,600 documents in total when including "families" of documents. [If a search yields one email, an attachment to that email (regardless of whether the attachment is itself responsive to the search term) falls within the email-document's "family."] The vendor collected a random sample of ten percent of these hits and any associated families—12,074 documents in total—and provided them to Oxbow for review for privilege and responsiveness. Of these 12,074 documents, Oxbow determined that approximately 1,300 documents—11.67 percent of them—were actually responsive to the search terms and produced them to Defendants. In total, the initial processing of Koch's records and review of the sample documents cost Oxbow $57,197.95. Based on its experience reviewing the sample documents, Oxbow now estimates that it will cost approximately $85,000 to process, review, and produce the remainder of Koch's documents to the Defendants, bringing the total cost of the effort, including the review of the sample documents, to approximately $142,000—significantly less than Oxbow's original estimate of $250,000 [which was premised on reviewing an estimated 214,000 rather than 82,600 documents].

Unfortunately, the sampling effort did not result in the parties resolving the dispute without further intervention of the Court. . . . Oxbow believes that . . . a complete production of Koch's documents would be an unnecessary burden and expense, particularly in light of the documents' low responsiveness rate to the search terms. . . . Defendants, in turn, view the results of the sampling as proof of the existence of relevant and unique documents in Koch's records. . . .

LEGAL STANDARD

Rule 37 of the Federal Rules of Civil Procedure provides that, "[o]n notice to other parties and all affected persons, a party may move for an order compelling disclosure of discovery" from a party who fails to comply with its discovery obligations. The party that brings the motion to compel bears the initial burden of proving that the opposing party's answers were incomplete. If the movant satisfies this burden, the burden then shifts to the non-movant to explain why discovery should not be permitted.

[The sweep of discovery permitted by Federal Rule 26, although broad,] is not without limits. . . . [U]nder the amended Rule 26, discovery must be relevant *and* "proportional to the needs of the case." Fed. R. Civ. P. 26(b)(1). To determine whether a discovery request is proportional, courts weigh . . . six factors. . . . "No single factor is designed to outweigh the other factors in determining whether the discovery sought is proportional," and all proportionality determinations must be made on a case-by-case basis. *Williams v. BASF Catalysts, LLC*, 2017 WL 3317295, at *4 (D.N.J. Aug. 3, 2017). To be sure, however, "the amendments to Rule 26(b) do not alter the basic allocation of the burden on the party resisting discovery to — in order to successfully resist a motion to compel — specifically object and show that . . . a discovery request would impose an undue burden or expense or is otherwise objectionable." *Mir v. L-3 Commc'ns Integrated Sys., L.P.*, 319 F.R.D. 220, 226 (N.D. Tex. 2016).

DISCUSSION

Oxbow ultimately does not dispute that Koch's records contain documents that are responsive to the parties' negotiated search terms and relevant to this litigation. In fact, Oxbow has already produced approximately 1,300 such documents as a result of the sampling of Koch's records. Instead, Oxbow objects to Defendants' request that it be compelled to review and produce discovery from Koch's remaining documents because doing so would be unduly burdensome and because the benefit to Defendants would not justify that effort and expense. Indeed, Oxbow argues that the cost of complying with Defendants' request is so unreasonable that, if the undersigned is inclined to order such discovery, the Court should ignore the long-standing presumption that a "responding party must bear the expense of complying with discovery requests," and order Defendants to cover the costs of the production. *Oppenheimer Fund, Inc. v. Sanders*, 437 U.S. 340, 358 (1978).

The Court is unpersuaded by Oxbow's arguments. In its briefing, Oxbow declines to address any of the other proportionality factors highlighted in Rule 26—namely, the importance of the issues at stake in this action, the amount in controversy, the parties' relative access to relevant information, the parties' resources, or the importance of the discovery in resolving the issues in this case, *see* Fed. R. Civ. P. 26(b)(1)—stressing only that the burden and cost of complying with Defendants' request would outweigh its likely benefit. *Id.* Weighing the Rule 26 proportionality factors, however, demonstrates that adding Koch as a custodian of documents to be searched for material responsive to Defendants' discovery requests in this matter will be neither unduly burdensome nor unreasonably expensive in light of the facts of this case. Likewise, the Court finds that the instant circumstances do not warrant shifting the costs of doing so to Defendants. Accordingly, Defendants' motion to compel will be granted, and Plaintiffs shall be ordered to produce all remaining responsive documents from Koch's file, the cost of which Plaintiffs shall bear.

A. THE PROPORTIONALITY OF DEFENDANTS' DISCOVERY REQUEST

1. The Importance of the Issues at Stake

The first Rule 26 factor calls for the Court to "examine[] 'the significance of the substantive issues [at stake in the litigation], as measured in philosophic, social, or institutional terms.'" *Arrow Enter. Computing Solutions, Inc. v. BlueAlly, LLC,* 2017 WL 876266, at *4 (E.D.N.C. Mar. 3, 2017) (quoting Fed. R. Civ. P. 26 advisory committee's note). For example, courts should carefully scrutinize discovery requests in "cases in public policy spheres, such as employment practices, free speech, and other matters," which often "seek[] to vindicate vitally important personal and public values" and "may have importance far beyond the monetary amount involved." Fed. R. Civ. P. 26 advisory committee's note. By Oxbow's own suggestion, the instant case involves important issues and has the potential to broadly impact a wide range of third-parties not involved in the litigation. Oxbow has stated that a favorable ruling from this Court "could benefit all of America's shippers and consumers, saving billions of dollars a year in reduced rail freight charges in the United States." Def. Ex. 22 at 2. What is more, Koch himself has publicly accused Defendants of long relying on "overreaching and abusive behavior" to "shortchange[] the American consumer," and of "using aggressive tactics to prevent competition and intimidate customers," including "American farmers, miners[,] and shippers[.]" *Id.* at 3.

Defendants, for their part, do not disagree with Oxbow's estimation of the significance of this case, noting that Oxbow has made serious allegations against Defendants that have the potential to impact many people *See* Defendant's Motion at 12-13. Accordingly, the undersigned finds that the importance of the issues at stake here weighs in favor of granting Defendants' discovery request, which Oxbow concedes will produce documents that are relevant to the resolution of this case's claims. *See BlueAlly,* 2017 WL 876266, at *4 (finding that this factor weighs against allowing discovery where the issues at stake in the case would not "have an impact beyond the parties involved").

2. The Amount in Controversy

Under the second proportionality factor, courts should "compare[] the cost of discovery to the amount in controversy to determine [the proposed discovery's] proportionality." *Id.* Here, Oxbow seeks to recover the more than $50,000,000 in illegal fuel surcharges it alleges were the result of the Defendants' collusion. It also seeks recovery of its lost business and profits, and a trebling of its damages under 15 U.S.C. § 15. While Oxbow does not specifically quantify these damages in the Amended Complaint, Defendants have suggested that Oxbow seeks to recover over $150 million — a figure that Defendants do not appear to dispute. Meanwhile, Oxbow's estimated cost of complying with Defendants' proposed discovery is approximately $140,000, including the $57,197.95 that Oxbow has already spent on sampling Koch's documents. Given the very substantial amount of damages that Oxbow seeks to recover in this case, its cost of complying with the discovery request to produce information relevant to Defendants' defense of Oxbow's claims does not strike the undersigned as excessive. Accordingly, the Court finds that this factor, too, favors granting Defendants' discovery request.

3. The Parties' Relative Access to the Relevant Information

In considering this factor, courts look for "information asymmetry" — a circumstance in which one party has very little discoverable information while the other party has vast amounts of discoverable information. *See* Fed. R. Civ. P. 26 advisory committee's notes. In such a case, "the burden of responding to discovery lies heavier on the party who has more information, and properly so." *Id.* To the extent this factor is applicable here, any informational asymmetry favors Oxbow. Indeed, neither party disputes that Koch is in possession of relevant, unique information, and there appears to be no other way for Defendants to obtain this information than moving to compel Oxbow to produce it. Accordingly, the Court finds that this factor militates in favor of granting Defendant's request.

4. The Parties' Resources

Taking into account the parties' resources, the Court again concludes that this factor weighs in favor of granting Defendants' request. While discovery should not be used to "wage a war of attrition or as a device to coerce a party," regardless of whether the party is "financially weak or affluent," *see* Fed. R. Civ. P. 26 advisory committee's notes, Oxbow represented at the hearing in this matter that it does not object to Defendants' request based on an inability to pay for it. Accordingly, the undersigned sees no reason to deny Defendants' request on this basis.

5. The Importance of the Discovery in Resolving the Issues

This fifth factor requires courts to determine whether "[t]he issues at stake are at the very heart of [the] litigation." *LaBrier v. State Farm Fire and Casualty Co.*, 314 F.R.D. 637, 643 (W.D. Mo. 2016; *see also BlueAlly*, 2017 WL 876266, at *5 (looking at whether "this discovery request goes to a central issue or a side one"). Though Oxbow initially objected to the relevance of any documents in Koch's possession, it has since acknowledged that Koch's records contain relevant and unique documents, although not in the same ratio as other Oxbow custodians' records, and has produced a portion of these documents to Defendants. The Court appreciates that Koch's files do not appear to contain as high a proportion of responsive documents as the files of custodians who dealt exclusively with Oxbow's coal and petcoke business, but it strains reason to suggest that the principal owner and CEO of a company, who has publicly commented on the importance and magnitude of litigation to which his company is a party and in which the financial health of his company is at issue, would have no unique information relevant to that litigation in his possession. While it may be too early in the production process to determine exactly how significant Koch's records are, the categories of relevant documents identified by Defendants after reviewing the approximately 1,300 documents produced from Koch's files indicates to the Court that Defendants' discovery request has merit and is not intended to be the first strike in a war of attrition or a coercion tactic.[4] Accordingly, the Court concludes that this factor favors granting Defendants' proposed discovery.

6. Whether the Burden or Expense of the Proposed Discovery Outweighs Its Likely Benefit

Oxbow rests its argument on this final factor, asserting that it is the most important of the Rule 26 proportionality factors and counsels against granting Defendants' proposed discovery. In support of its argument, Oxbow contends that its random sampling analysis suggests that approximately half of the agreed-upon search terms' hits on Koch's documents are false positives with no or only marginal relevance to the litigation. To be sure, Oxbow also concedes that the cost of processing Koch's records for discovery is far less than it originally estimated and that the search terms narrowed the scope of Koch's responsive documents far more than it originally anticipated. Nevertheless, it asserts that the $85,000 that it estimates it will take to review and produce the remaining responsive documents from Koch's files is prohibitively burdensome.

The Court disagrees. The cost of reviewing and producing Koch's documents does not strike the undersigned as unduly burdensome or disproportionate,

---

4. After reviewing Oxbow's initial production of roughly 1,300 documents from Koch's files, Defendants believe that Koch is a unique source of documents regarding, among other things, Oxbow's finances and business strategies with respect to the coal and petcoke businesses at issue during the relevant time period. These sorts of documents would surely bear on Oxbow's claim that Defendants' conduct was the source of damage to those Oxbow businesses and resulted in lost profits, and thus strike the Court as critical in resolving the issues in this case.

especially given the discovery conducted to date and the damages that Oxbow seeks in this action. Plaintiffs' counsel explained at the second hearing in this matter that Oxbow has spent $1.391 million to date on reviewing and producing approximately 584,000 documents from its nineteen other custodians and Oxbow's email archive. And again, Oxbow seeks tens of millions of dollars from Defendants. Through that lens, the estimated cost of reviewing and producing Koch's responsive documents—even considering the total approximate cost of $142,000 for that effort, which includes the expense of the sampling effort—while certainly high, is not so unreasonably high as to warrant rejecting Defendants' request out of hand. *See Zubulake v. UBS Warburg, LLC,* 217 F.R.D. 309, 321 (S.D.N.Y. 2003) (explaining, in the context of a cost-shifting request, that "[a] response to a discovery request costing $100,000 sounds (and is) costly, but in a case potentially worth millions of dollars, the cost of responding may not be unduly burdensome"); *Xpedior Creditor Trust v. Credit Suisse First Boston (USA), Inc.,* 309 F.Supp.2d 459, 466 (S.D.N.Y. 2003) (finding no "undue burden or expense" to justify cost-shifting where the requested discovery cost approximately $400,000 but the litigation involved at least $68.7 million in damages). Moreover, based on the parties' representations at the second hearing in this matter, the projected number of responsive and unique documents in Koch's files—approximately 10,000—is largely consistent with the number of responsive and unique documents produced by the other Oxbow custodians, and the responsiveness rate of Koch's documents—11.67 percent—while low, is [more than the 3.03 percent responsiveness rate of another Oxbow custodian].

In light of the above analysis—including the undersigned's assessment of each of the Rule 26 proportionality factors, all of which weigh in favor of granting Defendants' motion—the Court is unwilling to find that the burden of reviewing the remaining 65,000 responsive documents for a fraction of the cost of discovery to date should preclude Defendants' proposed request. *See BlueAlly,* 2017 WL 876266, at *5 ("This [last Rule 26] factor may combine all the previous factors into a final analysis of burdens versus benefits.") (citing Fed. R. Civ. P. 26 advisory committee's notes)). For all of the reasons stated above, and absent any evidence establishing that Defendants are using the discovery of Koch's records to wage a war of attrition or as a device to coerce Oxbow, the Court finds that Defendants' motion must be granted.

B. OXBOW'S REQUEST TO SHIFT DISCOVERY COSTS TO DEFENDANTS

In the event that the Court grants Defendants' motion, Oxbow asks in the alternative that the Court direct Defendants to bear the costs of the production, either in whole or in part. The Court denies that request. "The presumption under the Federal Rules of Civil Procedure is that the producing party bears the costs of complying with a discovery request," but "the Court may shift a portion of the costs to the requesting party in the event that the discovery request would unduly burden the producing party." *D'Onofrio v. SFX Sports Group, Inc.,* 254 F.R.D. 129, 134 (D.D.C. 2008). . . .

Rule 26 was amended in 2015 to expressly recognize the courts' capacity to order cost-shifting in the hopes of forestalling "the temptation [that] some parties may feel to contest" the courts' authority to do. *See* Fed. R. Civ. P. 26 advisory committee's notes. Specifically the amendment added subsection 26(c)(1)(B), which permits a court to issue an order, for good cause, to protect a party from "annoyance, embarrassment, oppression, or undue burden or expense," by specifying the terms of discovery, "including time and place or the allocation of expenses[.]" *Id.* at 26(c)(1)(B). In considering this amendment, courts have found that determining whether a discovery request warrants cost-shifting based on its burdensomeness turns on: the needs of the case; the amount in controversy; the parties' resources; the importance of the issues at stake; and the importance of the proposed discovery in resolving these issues. *See McClurg v. Mallinckrodt, Inc.*, 2016 WL 7178745, at *3 (E.D. Mo. Dec. 9, 2016). . . . To be sure, however, this amendment does not "imply that cost-shifting should become a common practice," and "[c]ourts and parties should continue to assume that a responding party ordinarily bears the costs of responding." Fed. R. Civ. P. 26 advisory committee's note.

Oxbow has failed to rebut the presumption imposed by the Federal Rules of Civil Procedure that it should bear the cost of complying with Defendants' proposed discovery. The above analysis of the Rule 26(b) proportionality factors, which are essentially identical to the factors courts have considered in determining whether to shift discovery costs under Rule 26(c), confirms that Defendants' proposed discovery does not impose an undue burden or expense that warrants a reallocation of expenses. . . . Accordingly Oxbow's request to shift discovery fees to Defendants in whole or in part is denied.

CONCLUSION

For the foregoing reasons, Defendants' motion to compel the production of documents from Koch's records is granted. Oxbow shall produce all unique and relevant documents from Koch's records within 30 days of the entry of this Memorandum Opinion.

REVIEW QUESTIONS

1. In this case, the court concluded that *all* of the proportionality factors pointed in the same direction: in favor of requiring Oxbow/Koch to respond to the defendants' discovery request. You should imagine, however, that in practice or on an exam, some factors may point in one direction, and others in the opposite direction. Does *Oxbow* give you any insight about the hierarchy of these factors—which factor matters the most? The least?

2. The judge frequently cites the advisory committee's notes in his opinion. What is the precedential or persuasive value of these notes?

The Fact-Contingent Nature of Discovery Disputes. A common mistake by law students (and even young lawyers) is to assume that case law definitively resolves most disputes. The discovery dispute in *Oxbow* seems rather straightforward, after all—it's about access to the electronically-stored information of the CEO of the plaintiff; so surely, one might assume, there is controlling case law on point. Yet there isn't controlling case law. In fact, the cases cited by the magistrate judge even for relatively general propositions of law are from district (not appellate) courts in North Carolina, New York, Missouri, and other states. Moreover, the judge says that "all proportionality determinations must be made on a case-by-case basis." Effective lawyering is about advocacy, not merely pattern-matching.

QUESTION TO PONDER

Are the advisory committee's notes to a Federal Rule of Civil Procedure deserving of more or less weight than the legislative history of a Congressional statute?

More on Fee-Shifting. Oxbow refused to comply with the defendants' discovery request. Defendants moved to compel. And the defendants won that motion. Should the plaintiffs be obliged to pay the defendants' costs incurred in bringing this motion? Review Fed. R. Civ. P. 37(a)(5)(A). What incentives would be created if fee-shifting were mandatory in discovery disputes?

The Proportionality Factors in Oxbow. When the judge evaluated the first proportionality factor, he quoted many of the *plaintiff's* own words in finding against them. Did the plaintiff make a strategic mistake by saying these things (which proved harmful to them in the resolution of this discovery dispute)?

When the judge evaluated the first proportionality factor, he linked the notion of importance with the impact of this lawsuit to individuals other than the extant parties. Imagine, on an exam or in practice, a discovery dispute surfacing in a breach of contract action between a commercial landlord and a tenant. Does the resolution of *that* lawsuit have any impact beyond those parties? Does the resolution of a wrongful death action against the manufacturer of a suspension lift kit have any impact beyond the named parties? What does the first of the proportionality factors really mean when it suggests that some issues are important—which is to say by implication, then, that some issues in litigation are relatively unimportant?

The second proportionality factor focuses on the amount in controversy. And here the court looks to the plaintiff's claim for damages to frame the amount in controversy. But now imagine a case, whether on an exam or in practice, where the discovery dispute arises because the *plaintiff* has requested discovery and the *defendant* has resisted. Would we still look to the plaintiff's claim for damages to frame the amount in controversy? This creates problematic incentives, doesn't it?

When the judge evaluated the fifth proportionality factor, he observed that there was no evidence that the defendants' discovery request for Koch's ESI was a "first strike in a war of attrition or a coercion tactic." If such evidence *did* exist, what would it look like?

When the judge evaluated the sixth proportionality factor, he observed that the $1.391 million spent by Oxbow in responding to the defendant's discovery requests militated in favor of a finding that Oxbow should spend another $85,000/$142,000 to produce Koch's ESI. What incentives does this kind of reasoning create for litigants like Oxbow in future cases?

Oxbow resisted the discovery of Koch's documents, arguing that the additional expense of $85,000/$142,000 was unduly burdensome. Yet the attorney's fees incurred by Oxbow with respect to the dispute—which included multiple conferences, extensive briefing, two hearings, and other fanfare—may have exceeded that amount. And they incurred all of these litigation expenses knowing also that they might lose the discovery fight (which they, in fact, did). Why did Oxbow bother resisting the discovery of Koch's ESI?

Alley v. MTD Products, Inc.
__ F.Supp.3d __, 2018 WL 4689112 (E.D. Pa. Sept. 28, 2018)

GIBSON, United States District Judge:

. . . BACKGROUND

. . . [This is a products liability action where the Plaintiff, Reynolds Alley, alleges that he was injured by a defective snowblower—a 5.5 HP 22-inch Two Stage Snow Thrower—that Defendants MTD Products, Inc., and its affiliates manufactured and sold. In his suit, which was filed on January 10, 2017,] Mr. Alley alleges that he was inflating the tire of the snowblower using an air compressor when the tire's plastic rim burst, injuring Mr. Alley's hand. . . .

A discovery dispute arose regarding Plaintiff's Amended Rule 30(b)(6) Deposition Notice and a request for a production of documents. In the disputed deposition notice, Plaintiff lists nine topics regarding Defendants' methods for storing, creating, retrieving, and retaining electronically stored information that Plaintiff seeks in discovery.

The disputed request for production of documents, Request for Document No. 6, seeks:

> [a]ny document including Complaints and correspondence referencing any prior or subsequent claims against you which resulted from the same or similar circumstances as those set forth in the Complaint . . . [including] any instance where an individual claims he sustained an injury as a result of use of a similar product.

Plaintiff argues that this request for production of documents requires Defendants to produce all expert reports, deposition transcripts, and discovery responses generated in prior cases involving snowblowers that Defendants manufactured.

Defendants filed the Motion for Protective Order pending before this Court on May 4, 2018, and the Court held oral argument on August 27, 2018. In their Motion for Protective Order, Defendants argue: (1) that in his Rule 30(b)(6) deposition notice, Plaintiff seeks improper "discovery on discovery" by requesting information on Defendants' storage, creation, retrieval, and retention of documents that Plaintiff seeks in discovery; and (2) that Plaintiff's discovery requests for documents from prior litigation involving Defendants' snowblowers are not proportional to the needs of this case under Rule 26(b) of the Federal Rules of Civil Procedure.

. . . Legal Standard

"A party or any person from whom discovery is sought may move for a protective order in the court where the action is pending. . . . The court may, for good cause, issue an order to protect a party or person from annoyance, embarrassment, oppression, or undue burden or expense[.]" Fed. R. Civ. P. 26(c).

"Good cause is demonstrated by the party establishing a clearly defined and serious injury shown with specificity that will result without the protective order." *Spano v. CSX Transp., Inc.*, 2017 WL 3332246, at *3 (W.D. Pa. Aug. 3, 2017). "[T]he party seeking the protective order bears the burden of showing that it is particularly necessary to obviate a significant harm; broad allegations of harm will not suffice." *EEOC v. Grane Healthcare Co.*, 2013 WL 1102880, at *2 (W.D. Pa. Mar. 5, 2013).

. . . Discussion

A. The Court Will Grant Defendants' Motion with Respect to Topics in Plaintiff's 30(b)(6) Deposition Notice that Improperly Seek Discovery on Discovery

"Federal courts will not compel a party to disclose its discovery process as a result of the opponent's mere suspicion that the party's process has not produced adequate documents." *Brand Energy & Infrastr. Servs. v. Irex Corp.*, 2018 WL 806341, at *6 (E.D. Pa. Feb. 7, 2018) (quoting Sean Grammel, *Protecting Search Terms As Opinion Work Product: Applying the Work Product Doctrine to Electronic*

Discovery, 161 U. Pa. L. Rev. 2063, 2084 (2013)). A party cannot seek discovery of another party's discovery processes "[w]ithout any showing of bad faith or unlawful withholding of documents." *Ford Motor Co. v. Edgewood Properties, Inc.,* 257 F.R.D. 418, 428 (D.N.J. 2009).

Here, Plaintiff's Rule 30(b)(6) deposition notice lists topics regarding Defendants' systems for creating, storing, retrieving, and retaining documents. Plaintiff has not shown that Defendants have acted in bad faith or that they have unlawfully withheld documents.

Rather, Plaintiff argues that its deposition notice does not merely seek information on Defendants' discovery processes, i.e. "discovery on discovery," but rather that Plaintiff "seeks information relevant to Defendants' bald assertion of undue burden." However, it is clear that Plaintiff's deposition notice seeks discovery on discovery. Plaintiff seeks "identities of custodians of relevant evidence, the manner and location of storage of documents, the purpose for the creation of documents, how they are indexed, filed, and maintained, etc."

Despite Plaintiff's characterization of its deposition notice, the Court finds that it is an impermissible request for information on [Defendants'] discovery processes. Other courts faced with discovery disputes regarding requests for information on document storage and retention have found that these requests are impermissible. *See Edgewood,* 257 F.R.D. at 426-28 (holding that discovery requests regarding the servers that Defendants used to access and store digital information were impermissible). Therefore, the Court finds that topics one through nine in Plaintiff's Amended Rule 30(b)(6) Notice of Deposition seek improper discovery on discovery.

Accordingly, the Court will grant Defendants' Motion for Protective Order with respect to topics one through nine in Plaintiff's Amended Rule 30(b)(6) Notice of Deposition.

B. The Court Will Grant Defendants' Motion with Respect to Plaintiff's Requests for Discovery Documents from Prior Litigation Because These Requests Are Not Proportional to the Needs of This Case

In its discovery requests, Plaintiff seeks expert reports, deposition transcripts, and copies of all discovery requests and responses from prior litigation involving the snowblower model that injured Mr. Alley. The Court agrees with Defendants and finds that these requests are not proportional to the needs of this case.

Under Rule 26(b), "[p]arties may obtain discovery regarding any nonprivileged matter that is relevant to any party's claim or defense and proportional to the needs of the case considering [1] the importance of the issues at stake in the action, [2] the amount in controversy, [3] the parties' relative access to relevant information, [4] the parties' resources, [5] the importance of the discovery in resolving the issues, and [6] whether the burden or expense of the proposed discovery outweighs its likely benefit." Fed. R. Civ. P. 26(b). "Rulings regarding the proper scope of discovery . . . are matters consigned to the Court's discretion and judgment." *Johnson v. Johnson,* 2015 WL 9259405, at *1 (W.D. Pa. Dec. 18, 2015).

First, the issues in this action are important. This case involves an individual who sustained bodily injury due to an allegedly defective snowblower. The Court recognizes that Mr. Alley's alleged injuries are serious and that companies producing defective products must be held responsible for injuries caused by their products. However, when considering the other factors in Rule 26(b), the importance of the issues at stake in this case alone does not justify the extensive production of discovery materials from prior litigation.

Second, Plaintiff's request for production of documents from prior litigation are not proportional to the amount in controversy in this case. At the oral argument on this Motion, Defendants' Counsel stated that the total amount in controversy in this case is about $100,000, and stated that Mr. Alley incurred about $6,000 in medical bills. Plaintiff's counsel did not dispute either of these figures.

The total amount in controversy in this case is roughly equivalent to the cost for Defendants to comply with Plaintiff's discovery requests. Defendants submitted the affidavit of Angel Lavin, Defendants' national discovery counsel, which detailed the cost of producing discovery materials from prior lawsuits in which Defendants were involved. In her affidavit, Ms. Lavin states that it would likely cost Defendants more than $100,000 to produce the documents that Plaintiff seeks. This calculation is based on the costs of locating and storing the responsive documents, reviewing these documents for privileged information and HIPPA [sic] compliance, and complying with protective orders from the prior lawsuits.[2]

While Plaintiff disputes how much it would cost Defendants to comply with Plaintiff's discovery requests, the Court finds that a comparison of the amount in controversy to the cost of complying with Plaintiff's discovery requests weighs against production, and weighs in favor of granting Defendants' protective order. Even if Defendants overstated the cost of complying with Plaintiff's discovery request by several thousand dollars, the cost of producing these documents would still be disproportionately close to the amount in controversy in this case. Therefore, the Court finds that Plaintiff's request for the production of documents from prior cases is not proportional to the amount in controversy in this case.

Third, the Court recognizes that Defendants have greater access to the discovery documents that Plaintiff seeks. However, Defendants produced considerable information on prior cases involving the snowblower model that allegedly injured Mr. Alley. Defendants produced the names of the plaintiffs in prior cases, the courts where those cases were filed, and the names of the plaintiffs'

---

2. The Court appreciates that "the fact that these repositories [of electronically stored information] create complex mechanisms to store huge amounts of information cannot be used in and of itself as a shield to avoid discovery requests otherwise permitted under the Federal Rules of Civil Procedure." *EEOC v. FedEx Ground Package Sys., Inc.*, 2018 WL 1441426, at *3 (W.D. Pa. Mar. 21, 2018). But in this case, the Court has no reason to doubt the veracity of the information in Attorney Lavin's affidavit. Moreover, the Court finds that even if the cost of complying with the discovery requests in question were significantly lower than Attorney Lavin estimated, that burden is still not proportional to the needs of this case.

attorneys in those cases. Plaintiff's counsel admitted that he had not investigated state court dockets to determine if he could obtain the sought-after documents through online document-filing systems. Thus, Plaintiff's counsel has sufficient information to seek out discovery materials from those prior cases on his own.

Fourth, the Court also recognizes that the Defendant-corporations likely have more resources than Plaintiff, who is an individual. However, this factor is less important to the Court's proportionality analysis here because, as discussed more below, the Court does not find that discovery documents from prior litigation involving Defendants' snowblowers are crucial to the resolution of this this case.

Fifth, the documents Plaintiff requests are not vital to resolving the issues at stake in this action. Plaintiff argues that these documents are necessary to prove that Plaintiff is entitled to punitive damages, which requires a showing that "Defendants were aware of the risks of their defective product and consciously disregarded said risks." However, Plaintiff does not need discovery documents like expert reports, deposition transcripts, and responsive documents from prior cases to prove that Defendants were aware of defects in the snowblowers they produced. Defendants already provided Plaintiff with information on prior lawsuits involving the tire rims of the snowblower model that injured Mr. Alley, thereby admitting that Defendants were on notice of problems with the tire rims. Defendants' counsel stated that these prior lawsuits generally involved "some version of putting air in the tire rims and the rims exploded [resulting in] eye or face or hand injuries." Moreover, Defendants also provided Plaintiff with information on product recalls for the snowblower model that injured Mr. Alley, further acknowledging their knowledge of the defect. In sum, the Court finds that there is ample evidence that Defendants were on notice of the defective measure of the snowblower tires. Accordingly, discovery documents from prior litigation are not necessary for Plaintiff to pursue punitive damages or to resolve any other issues in the case.

Finally, the burden and expense of Defendants' production of these documents clearly outweighs the likely benefit. The Court finds that the estimated cost to Defendants of producing discovery documents from prior litigation is overly burdensome and unduly expensive, especially in light of the amount in controversy in this case. Similarly, the Court does not find that producing discovery documents from prior litigation will be beneficial to resolving the key issues in this case.

Therefore, Defendants have demonstrated that a protective order is necessary to protect them from unduly burdensome production of documents. . . . A corresponding order follows.

30(b)(6) Depositions. *Alley* involved a "30(b)(6) deposition." Re-read Fed. R. Civ. P. 30(b)(6). Since 1970, this device has existed to facilitate discovery against an entity when a discovering party does not know exactly whom to depose. Federal Rule 30(b)(6) allows a discovering party to specify topics on which testimony is sought, whereupon the responding entity is required to designate one or more witnesses to provide testimony on those topics. *See generally* Kelly Tenille Crouse, *An Unreasonable Scope: The Need for Clarity in Federal Rule 30(b)(6) Depositions,* 49 U. Louisville L. Rev. 133, 133 (2010).

Contrast Fed. R. Civ. P. 30(b)(6) with a 30(b)(1) deposition of a witness who happens to work for an organization. If Nancy Carpenter wants to learn about Ultimate Auto's policies with respect to the sale of suspension lift kits, she could find out that store manager's name and notice his or her deposition per Rule 30(b)(1). But when that person is deposed, Carpenter's lawyer might be frustrated to learn that (1) the deponent was not the store manager during the time in question; (2) the deponent has never worked the sales floor and thus has no firsthand knowledge about product sales or customer interactions; and (3) the deponent is not the person responsible for processing product warnings. The deposition transcription would involve a litany of responses where the deponent says, truthfully, "I don't know." A 30(b)(6) deposition, by contrast, allows Carpenter's lawyer to ask questions to witnesses who are commanded to be prepared to give answers on the noticed subjects.

Discovery on Discovery. In *Alley*, the court was reluctant to allow "discovery on discovery" absent some evidence of bad faith on the part of the responding party. But allowing the plaintiff to depose the defendants about their document storage could educate the plaintiff in a way that could narrow and streamline the discovery process. (Isn't that the logic also behind Fed. R. Civ. P. 26(f)?) So why the hesitation to allow "discovery on discovery"? Also, the court said that it would allow "discovery on discovery" on a showing of bad faith or unlawful withholding of documents. What would that evidence look like, and how one would obtain such evidence without "discovery on discovery"?

The Proportionality Factors in **Alley.** With respect to the second discovery dispute—the document request—the court quotes the six proportionality factors of Federal Rule 26(b). Revisit the court's analysis of each factor and create a scorecard of whether each factor favored production or not-production. You will learn in law school (and in law practice) that the law contains many multifactor tests where the test does not prescribe the outcome in the inevitable circumstance where the factors point in opposite directions. Every opinion that tackles a multifactor test (including this opinion) is another opportunity for you to draw a broader lesson about winning disputes that involve the application of multifactor tests. How would you describe Judge Gibson's approach here? Judge Gibson heard the parties' arguments on this motion. Imagine making those arguments to him; control the narrative and you control the result.

When applying the first proportionality factor, the court focused on the seriousness of the injury to plaintiff. How does this characterization and application of the first factor differ from Judge Harvey's characterization and application of this factor in *Oxbow*? Now with two distinct examples of how courts evaluate "the importance of issues at stake in the action," you are in a position to contemplate additional ways of conceptualizing this first factor. Indeed, you might fairly assume that your law professor is contemplating additional ways of conceptualizing this factor for hypos and exams. How, why, what, and when could *issues* be more or less *important*?

When applying the second proportionality factor, the court focused on the plaintiff's claim for damages. Because this case happened to reach a trial, we have the benefit of a jury verdict: Mr. Alley was awarded $15,532.74 in past medical expenses; $155,000 for past, present, and future noneconomic damages; and no punitive damages. Now with the benefit of hindsight, how should plaintiff's counsel have characterized "the amount in controversy"? What is the downside risk of plaintiff's counsel artificially inflating that amount in the complaint (or in oral argument)?

When applying the third proportionality factor, Judge Gibson criticizes the plaintiff's counsel for not investigating whether the sought-after documents were available through online document-filing systems. The judge's criticism may be fair, but you should understand that discovery is generally not filed with the court—and therefore would not be available through online document-filing systems. *See* Fed. R. Civ. P. 5(d)(1). (To that end, notice that Judge Gibson refers to "*state* court dockets" (emphasis added) in his opinion.) Judge Gibson also observes that plaintiff's counsel has been given the names of the plaintiffs' attorneys in the other actions involving this model of snowblower. Those other attorneys are not under any obligation to provide information to this plaintiff's counsel; would you expect them to help?

According to Federal Rule 26, the fifth proportionality factor is "the importance of the discovery in resolving the issues." Defense counsel would surely concede that the sought-after information would be *helpful* to plaintiff in proving their case. (Hence this dispute.) But notice instead how the court (presumably at defense counsel's urging) frames its inquiry into this factor: It asks whether the information is "vital" and "necessary" to the plaintiff's case. "Importance," by contrast, is a scalable concept; few items of evidence are truly "necessary" or "vital."

With regard to the sixth proportionality factor, Judge Gibson credits but also hedges (in a footnote) against defense counsel's affidavit that it would cost them approximately $100,000 to comply with the plaintiff's document request. Frankly, it is hard to imagine that producing discovery that the defendants have already produced in the other matters would be that burdensome and expensive. (And to the extent that it is burdensome because there are *so many other cases*, then this fact should militate in favor of finding this discovery important to the plaintiff's claim for punitive damages.) You should appreciate that the two disputed discovery issues — the 30(b)(6) deposition and the document request — are, in fact, related. If you, as plaintiff's counsel, were trying to figure out why it was supposedly so burdensome for defendants to produce this information, you would want to ask questions of someone at the company about how they maintain their records. So why does the court separate these issues in its opinion, rejecting plaintiff's argument?

Framing a Discovery Request. In *Alley*, the plaintiff's counsel limited his discovery request to documents and lawsuit regarding only the model of snowblower that injured the plaintiff. You might imagine a target of increasingly-larger concentric circles where the bullseye is the same model of snowblower that injured the plaintiff, the next larger circle a different but substantially-similar model, and the next larger circle a different model that is less similar, and so forth. The outer circles of the target might be *lawnmowers* manufactured by the defendant. But because even lawnmowers might use the same (or similar) tires and plastic rims, plaintiff's counsel might seek information about the lawnmowers and rototillers — and, naturally, the parties would disagree about the scope of discovery. It is probably obvious why defendants would (typically) prefer to keep the scope of discovery narrow. But why would plaintiffs ever voluntarily circumscribe the scope of their discovery request?

Seeking Discovery Produced in Other Lawsuits. Should courts ever tolerate a discovery request like the *Alley* plaintiff's that demands documents that the responding party produced in other cases? If the plaintiff's counsel here instead simply made the same requests as in those other cases, then the defendant would have answered and produced the same documents that it produced in those other cases. Was the plaintiff's counsel just being lazy then? Or was the plaintiff's counsel trying to streamline discovery — maybe even trying to do the defendants a favor — by simply asking them for everything that they produced in the other actions (rather than parsing and disputing hundreds of new document requests, that is)? Or was the plaintiff's counsel trying to get his hands on the discovery that was produced by the *plaintiffs* in those other actions?

Options for Responding to Overbroad or Objectionable Discovery Requests. In *Alley*, the responding party moved for a protective order under Federal Rule 26(c). By contrast, in *Oxbow*, *supra*, the responding party objected to the discovery request and the requesting party ultimately decided to bring a motion to compel. Revisit the strategic advantages and disadvantages of a responding party who (i) brings a motion for a protective order; or instead (ii) merely objects. Does this strategic decision help explain the different outcomes in *Alley* and *Oxbow*?

Career Opportunities. ESI's transformation of litigation includes the creation of new jobs and roles for lawyers and for litigation support professionals. The *Alley* Court refers to Angel Lavin as "Defendants' national discovery counsel."

Law Review Articles. In *Alley*, Judge Gibson cites a law review article by Sean Grammel. This article was a comment that Mr. Grammel wrote while he was a law student. Scholarship in law reviews is often described as the academy's conversation with the judiciary. Even as a law student you will have the opportunity to contribute to that conversation.

Freedom's Path at Dayton v. Dayton Metro. Hous. Auth.
__ F.Supp.3d __, 2018 WL 2948021 (S.D. Ohio, June 13, 2018)

OVINGTON, United States Magistrate Judge:

I. INTRODUCTION

Plaintiff Freedom's Path at Dayton brings this action alleging Defendant Dayton Metropolitan Housing Authority (DMHA) doing business as Greater Dayton Premier Management (GDPM) "blocked funding for and financing of 60 units of project-based funded affordable housing for veterans . . ." in violation of the Americans with Disabilities Act of 1990, as amended, 42 U.S.C. § 12101, and the Fair Housing Act of 1968, as amended, 42 U.S.C. § 3601.

This case is presently before the Court upon Defendant's Motion for Protective Orders . . . and Plaintiff's Motion to Compel. . . .

II. BACKGROUND

To understand the parties' discovery disputes requires a brief look into the history of the case. [The plaintiff, Freedom's Path at Dayton, is a private development company that builds and owns affordable housing projects for veterans. The plaintiff's business plan contemplated use of a federal program called Veterans Affairs Supportive Housing (VASH). The VASH program has two aspects: one provides individual *tenant*-based rental assistance, and the other funds development *projects*. Because only public housing authorities are eligible for VASH funds, Freedom's Path needed a public housing authority as a partner for its 60-unit development project known as Freedom Path-Dayton VA on the VA Medical Center's campus in Dayton, Ohio.

On April 9, 2013, DMHA's Interim Chief Executive Officer, Alphonzio Prude, confirmed in writing that DMHA would support Freedom Path's development project and would commit 33 project-based vouchers. Plaintiff understood this to be DMHA's initial affirmative commitment to support Plaintiff's efforts to obtain more VASH financing. But since this letter, GDPM has balked at providing support to Plaintiff and, in fact, has applied for VASH funding on behalf of itself. According to Freedom's Path, DMHA has given various inconsistent and legally-erroneous rationales for its actions.]

On September 2, 2016, Plaintiff's counsel sent a detailed letter to DMHA asking it to apply . . . on Plaintiff's behalf for 60 VASH vouchers before the impending September 9, 2016 deadline. Plaintiff asked Defendant to "[p]lease treat this as a request for reasonable accommodation under the Fair Housing Amendments Act of 1988 and the Americans with Disabilities Act, and take whatever steps necessary to accommodate our request." Plaintiff asserts that [DMHA] denied the requested accommodation. [Plaintiff claims that the Defendant's conduct violated the Fair Housing Act and the Americans with Disabilities Act because it made housing unavailable to the prospective residents, and the defendant's conduct was "undertaken with the intent to discriminate against, and had the effect of discriminating against, disabled veterans and those who provide services to them."]

Plaintiff seeks (1) declaratory relief concluding that DMHA violated the FHA and ADA; (2) an Order mandating DMHA to apply . . . on Plaintiff's behalf for VASH project-based rental assistance or, alternatively, to grant Plaintiff a reasonable accommodation; (3) preliminary and permanent injunctions prohibiting DMHA from violating the ADA and FHA; and [4] damages for the harm it experienced as a result of DMHA's discriminatory and dilatory practices. [Without the 60 VASH vouchers, Plaintiff claims that it has been damaged by having to pay case management services and other benefits to its residents that the vouchers would have covered. Plaintiff also claims damages for "frustration of mission, diversion of resources, [and] lost financing and funding in the form of credits."]

III. STANDARD OF REVIEW

Under the Federal Rules of Civil Procedure, the scope of discovery is traditionally quite broad. . . . But "this desire to allow broad discovery is not without limits and the trial court is given wide discretion in balancing the needs and rights of both plaintiff and defendant." *Scales v. J.C. Bradford & Co.*, 925 F.2d 901, 906 (6th Cir. 1991).

A party may file a motion to compel discovery when a deponent fails to answer a question under Rules 30 or 31. Fed. R. Civ. P. 37(a)(3)(B). "[T]he proponent of a motion to compel discovery bears the initial burden of proving that the information sought is relevant." *Mayer v. Allstate Vehicle & Prop. Ins. Co.*, 2016 WL 1632415, at *2 (S.D. Ohio Apr. 22, 2016). . . . If the proponent meets its initial burden, then "the party resisting production has the burden of establishing that the information is either not relevant or is so marginally relevant that the presumption of broad disclosure is outweighed by the potential for undue burden or harm." *Pillar Title Agency v. Pei*, 2015 WL 2238180, at *3 (S.D. Ohio May 12, 2015).

When a party seeks to limit discovery, it may file a motion for protective order. Federal Rule of Civil Procedure 26(c) provides that a "court may, for good cause, issue an order to protect a party or person from annoyance, embarrassment, oppression, or undue burden or expense. . . ." "To justify restricting discovery, the harassment or oppression should be unreasonable, but discovery has limits and . . . these limits grow more formidable as the showing of need decreases." *Serrano v. Cintas Corp.*, 699 F.3d 884, 901 (6th Cir. 2012). To prevail on a motion for protective order, the party must "show that the requested discovery does not fall within Rule 26(b)(1)'s scope of relevance (as now amended) or that a discovery request would impose an undue burden or expense or is otherwise objectionable." *Bros. Trading Co. v. Goodman Factors*, 2016 WL 9781140, at *2 (S.D. Ohio Mar. 2, 2016).

IV. DISCUSSION

A. PROTECTIVE ORDERS

Defendant DMHA filed two motions for protective orders barring the depositions of five individuals. In its first motion, Defendant DMHA sought a protective order barring the deposition of its former interim CEO, Jeff Rieck. District Judge Walter H. Rice overruled Defendant's Motion for Protective Order Barring the Deposition of Jeff Rieck as moot.

In its second motion for protective order, Defendant DMHA seeks to bar the depositions of third-party witnesses Alphonzio Prude, De Carol Smith, Phyllis Smelkinson, and Raymond Keyser. Defendant asserts that (1) the depositions are irrelevant to any claim or defense; (2) the depositions would subject DMHA to severe undue burden and expense; and (3) none of the depositions meet the proportionality requirement of Rule 26(b)(1).

(i) Relevance under Rule 26(b)(2)

Defendant asserts that the deposition of Mr. Prude—a former interim CEO of DMHA—is "largely irrelevant" because his "only involvement in the events giving rise to Plaintiff's lawsuit pertains to the letter that Prude authored in his capacity as interim CEO of DMHA in April 2013 expressing the agency's purported support for Plaintiff's request for vouchers for its housing project." Defendant claims to be "categorically barred [from] satisfying Plaintiff's reasonable accommodation request through use of the Prude letter as a matter of law." The law Defendant refers to is 24 C.F.R. § 983.51. And, this requires some additional information: Under 24 C.F.R. § 983.51(b), there are two methods by which a public housing authority (PHA) can select project-based voucher (PBV) proposals: (1) request PBV proposals; or (2) rely on previous competition. A public housing authority—such as Defendant in the present case—must have an administrative plan that describes "the procedures for owner submission of PBV proposals and for PHA selection of PBV proposals." *Id.* § 983.51(a).

Defendants asserts that its administrative plan indicates it may only select project-based vouchers using the *first* method. Thus, according to Defendant, because "Plaintiff's attempt to utilize Prude's letter to obtain vouchers for its housing project involved the issuance of vouchers through the second method . . . ," and "because awarding Plaintiff housing vouchers through the use of the Prude letter would have violated federal . . . regulations, it is beyond dispute that the letter is completely irrelevant to Plaintiff's sole claim in this case that DMHA improperly refused to satisfy Plaintiff's accommodation request."

Plaintiff asserts that this is merely one of Defendant's "various inconsistent, mistaken, or shifting rationales for its inactions." Plaintiff argues that, because Defendant's administrative plan requires Defendant to comply with all [federal] regulations and [federal] regulations allow two methods of selection of PBV proposals, Defendant could rely on the second method for selecting PBV proposals. And, because Plaintiff's previous competitive processes satisfy this second method, awarding Plaintiff housing vouchers through Mr. Prude's letter would not violate [federal] regulations.

Further, if Defendant could not — under its administrative plan at that time — select Plaintiff's PBV proposal, Defendant could amend its administrative plan. And, indeed, Defendant did. In October 2016, Defendant's Board approved changes to its administrative plan to include the second method for selecting PBV proposals. [The federal government] approved the changes in April 2017.

Plaintiff alleges that through Mr. Prude's letter, Defendant "extended its support for Plaintiff's new development on the campus of the VA Medical Center and committed thirty-three (33) project-based vouchers." This commitment is at the heart of Plaintiff's claims. And, Mr. Prude, as Defendant's interim CEO at the time of this commitment, likely has relevant and thus discoverable information about Plaintiff's claims.

[Next,] Defendant contends that the deposition of Ms. Smith — an Enhanced Use Lease Project Manager at the United States Department of Veterans Affairs — is "largely irrelevant." Ms. Smith's "involvement in the event giving rise to this lawsuit is limited to her correspondence with DMHA and Plaintiff's representatives regarding the status of DMHA's response to Plaintiff's accommodation request." But, Defendant argues, "any testimony provided by Smith regarding her conversations and interactions with DMHA would constitute inadmissible hearsay, and as such cannot . . . be used to support either of the causes of action asserted by Plaintiff against DMHA in this action."

Given Defendant's assertion that "Plaintiff's sole claim in this case" is "that DMHA improperly refused to satisfy Plaintiff's accommodation request," the deposition of Ms. Smith — who, as Defendant claims, was involved with Plaintiff's accommodation request — seeks information relevant to Plaintiff's claim. Defendant's argument that Ms. Smith's testimony is not relevant because it would constitute inadmissible hearsay lacks merit for discovery purposes: "Information within this scope of discovery need not be admissible in evidence to be discoverable." Fed. R. Civ. P. 26(b)(1).

[Next,] Defendant asserts that depositions of Ms. Smelkinson — a Housing Program Specialist at [the U.S. Department of Housing and Urban Development (HUD)] — and Mr. Keyser — General Counsel for HUD — "must be barred due to these two individuals' lack of personal knowledge regarding *any* facts underlying the [present] lawsuit." [VASH is a collaborative program between HUD and the Department of Veterans Affairs.] Defendant insists that neither was "involved in any of the events giving rise to Plaintiff's action relating to Plaintiff's accommodation request for an award of vouchers for Plaintiff's housing complex, or DMHA's handling of and response to Plaintiff's accommodation request."

Plaintiff alleges that Ms. Smith consulted Ms. Smelkinson on whether Plaintiff was disqualified from HUD VASH NOFA (notice of finding availability) process. And, Ms. Smelkinson "reportedly told the VA VASH person, De Carol Smith, that, contrary to Defendant's assertion, Plaintiff was eligible to partner with Defendant. . . ."

Likewise, Ms. Heapy—the current CEO of Defendant DMHA—stated that Mr. Keyser, HUD general counsel, agreed with the opinion of Gordon Black, a low-level HUD official, who said that she could not "'honor' the original commitment of 33 vouchers to Plaintiff 'without going through the necessary RFP [competitive] process.'" But, according to Plaintiff, its attorney, Orlando Cabrera, spoke to Mr. Keyser, and he "said that there were a number of ways that DMHA could partner with Plaintiff, including amending its Administrative Plan." As explained above, "DMHA's Administrative Plan was amended by its Board in October or early November of 2016, and approved by HUD in April 2017 to specifically include selection based on previous competition. . . ."

In other words, Ms. Smelkinson and Mr. Keyser were allegedly involved—to some degree—in the facts giving rise to the present lawsuit. And, Plaintiff asserts, Ms. Smith, Ms. Smelkinson, and Mr. Black all possess information regarding whether Defendant could lawfully honor its initial commitment of thirty-three project-based vouchers and/or whether Defendant could lawfully grant Plaintiff's request for reasonable accommodation. Therefore, their depositions search for relevant and discoverable information about Plaintiff's claims.

Further, Plaintiff alleges that "[t]he historical background of [Defendant's] actions, the sequence of events, [Defendant's] departures from the normal procedural sequence or substantive criteria all reflect intent to discriminate." Accordingly, the background—including Mr. Prude's initial commitment letter, Defendant's and Plaintiff's consultation with HUD employees, and HUD employees' discussions with VA employees—might or might not shed light on the merits of Plaintiff's claims. Consequently, the information Plaintiff seeks by deposing Mr. Prude, Ms. Smith, Ms. Smelkinson, and Mr. Keyser is discoverable.

(ii) Proportionality

Under Federal Rule of Civil Procedure 26(b)(1), discovery must be "proportional to the needs of the case, considering the importance of the issues at stake in the action, the amount in controversy, the parties' relative access to relevant information, the parties' resources, the importance of the discovery in resolving the issues, and whether the burden or expense of the proposed discovery outweighs its likely benefit."

Importance of the Issues at Stake

Plaintiff correctly asserts that the issues at stake in the present case are important: "They involve housing for homeless veterans, many of whom are disable due to their service to this country. This case implicates important national policies about eradicating homelessness, especially for veterans, and providing permanent housing for them as proposed by Plaintiff." Defendant does not argue to the contrary.

Amount in Controversy

Plaintiff validly contends that the amount-in-controversy factor weighs in its favor. "Plaintiff's damages expert opines that DMHA's actions caused Plaintiff, and more importantly the veterans, to lose more than $15,000,000 in lost housing and overlay services." Defendant does not suggest otherwise.

Parties' Relative Access to Relevant Information

It is likely that Defendant has, or has access to, most or all of the information Plaintiff seeks. Thus, this factor falls in Plaintiff's favor.

Parties' Resources

Defendant contends that the parties'-resources factor weighs in favor of barring the depositions. "DMHA is a public housing agency funded solely by taxpayer dollars. Thus, DMHA has limited resources as it relates to defendant against Plaintiff's claims in this case, as each dollar spent on defending this meritless action is a dollar that cannot be put toward providing affordable housing to the residents of Dayton."

Plaintiff contends that the parties' resources are the same. "Defendant is being defended by an insurance defense firm and has millions of dollars in potential coverage. Its annual budget is $45,000,000."

Without additional information about the parties' resources—which the record presently lacks—this factor favors neither party.

Importance of the Discovery in Resolving the Issues

[Defendant argues] that none of the depositions "are in any way necessary or otherwise important to resolving the sole dispute at issue in this lawsuit—whether DMHA improperly declined to satisfy Plaintiff's accommodation request regarding the issuance of vouchers for it housing complex."

Plaintiff disagrees, asserting "The discovery is necessary for Plaintiff's anticipated summary judgment motion. The witnesses all have important information that is directly relevant to whether Defendant improperly employed shifting rationales for denying Plaintiff's request for housing vouchers."

As explained in greater detail above, these four individuals were involved with the events underlying Plaintiff's claims and likely have information regarding whether Defendant improperly employed shifting rationales for denying Plaintiff's request for the housing vouchers.

Whether the Burden or Expense of the Proposed Discovery Outweighs Its Likely Benefit

Defendant argues that "all four depositions would subject DMHA to severe undue burden and expense." According to Defendant, the distant depositions of

Ms. Smith and Ms. Smelkinson (in Washington D.C.), Mr. Prude (in Michigan), and Mr. Keyser (in Cleveland) "would force [Defendant] to incur both air [or other] travel and overnight lodging expenses. . . ." In addition, Defendant "would incur substantial additional litigation expenses in having to prepare for and attend those depositions, none of which will produce any tangible benefit for either of the parties involved in this action." Defendant asserts that Plaintiff will receive "little — if any — benefit" because the witnesses "possess scant knowledge of facts or evidence that would assist Plaintiff. . . ."

Plaintiff insists, however, that Defendant's "counsel is located in Cincinnati, which has regular non-stop service to the Washington D.C. area where Smelkinson and Smith are located." It also has frequent non-stop flights to Cleveland, where Mr. Keyser is located, and to Chicago, near where Plaintiff intends to depose Mr. Prude.

Plaintiff notes that it scheduled the depositions of Mr. Keyser and Gordon Block, a low-level HUD official, on the same day in Cleveland. Defendant did not seek a protective order barring the deposition of Mr. Black. And, if Defendant had agreed to the deposition of Mr. Keyser on the same day as Mr. Black, Defendant would not have incurred significant additional expenses.

Defendant bears the burden of establishing good cause for a protective order. "To show good cause, a movant for a protective order must articulate specific facts showing clearly defined and serious injury resulting from the discovery sought and cannot rely on mere conclusory statements." *Nix v. Sword*, 11 Fed. Appx. 498, 500 (6th Cir. 2001); *see* Fed. R. Civ. P. 26(b)(1) advisory committee's note (2015) ("A party claiming undue burden or expense ordinarily has far better information — perhaps the only information — with respect to that part of the determination."). Defendant's broad allegations of "significant travel expenses" and "substantial additional litigation expenses" [do not] suffice to show it will suffer undue burden or expanse and do not establish good cause for a protective order.

In sum, the balancing of these factors weighs in favor of allowing the depositions of Mr. Prude, Ms. Smith, Ms. Smelkinson, and Mr. Keyser. Additionally, Plaintiff has shown that it seeks information from their depositions that is relevant to its claims and proportional to the needs of the case. Accordingly, Defendant's Motion for Protective Order is denied.

B. MOTION TO COMPEL

Plaintiff's Motion to Compel Discovery and Request for Attorneys' Fees and Expenses asks the Court for an order compelling Ms. Heapy's deposition testimony and admonishing defense counsel to refrain from speaking and coaching objections, instructing witnesses not to answer questions, and making baseless objections.

Under Federal Rule of Civil Procedure 30, "An objection at the time of the examination whether to evidence, to a party's conduct, to the officer's qualifications, to the manner of taking the deposition, or to any other aspect of the deposition — must be noted on the record, but the examination still proceeds;

the testimony is taken subject to any objection. An objection must be stated concisely in a nonargumentative and nonsuggestive manner. A person may instruct a deponent not to answer only when necessary to preserve a privilege, to enforce a limitation ordered by the court, or to present a motion under Rule 30(d)(3)."

(i) Mr. Freudiger's Objections

Plaintiff asserts, "Mr. Freudiger made at least 17 other speaking objections that suggested to his client how to answer questions." Further, "In 20+ instances, Mr. Freudiger instructed Ms. Heapy not to answer even though no claim of privilege had been raised or was implicated."

Plaintiff asserts that opposing counsel's statements such as "if you can" or "if you know" are suggestive and, therefore, in violation of Rule 30. For example, after noting his objection, Mr. Freudiger instructed Ms. Heapy to respond:

> *Q.* (Mr. Green) Does the Americans with Disabilities Act apply to your policies and actions?
> *Mr. Freudiger:* Objection. You can answer *if you know.*
> *The witness:* That's a legal determination. I don't know.

Defendant disagrees: "this statement merely patterns the extremely common principal [sic] followed almost uniformly by all litigants in both state and federal court that deponents should not guess or speculate as to their deposition answers."

This is why astute counsel prepares witnesses—before depositions begin—to testify about their personal knowledge rather than to guess or speculate. Defendant is correct that deponents should not guess or speculate as to their deposition answers. Nevertheless, assuming this practice is widespread in state and federal courts, there is no valid reason why Defendant's counsel would need to repeatedly interrupt the deposition questioning of any individual—here, Ms. Heapy—who has been an attorney for nearly fifteen years. Indeed, at a minimum, Defendant's "counsel would do well to avoid using this phrasing in the future, as it can plausibly be[] seen as coaching [the] witness. It is the attorney's job to make an objection and then stop talking. If the deponent does not know how to answer a question, he or she may state as much, but it is not appropriate for his or her attorney to push him or her in that direction." *Pogue v. NorthWestern Mut. Life Ins. Co.*, 2017 WL 3044763, at *11 (W.D. Ky. July 18, 2017).

Plaintiff also points to multiple instances where Mr. Freudiger objected and then suggested a response.

> *Q.* (Mr. Green) So would it be fair to say . . . that there would be minutes . . . of the meeting where Mr. Prude was terminated, but that those may or may not be available under the public record law depending upon whether the meeting was open or closed?
> *Mr. Freudiger:* Yeah, I have to object. *I don't think she's going to know that.*
> *Mr. Green:* Well, I'm asking her a question. It's not for you to testify.
> *Mr. Freudiger:* Well, it's beyond the purview of the topics. You're asking a question that probably needs to be asked of her general counsel. She

is hired by the board. You can answer if you know. If you do not know, then say you do not know.

The witness: Can you repeat the question?

(Record read.)

The witness: I do not know the answer to that.

Rather than allowing Ms. Heapy to respond to — or ask for clarification of — Mr. Green's questions, Mr. Freudiger expressed his own opinions:

> Q. (Mr. Green) What part of the regulations did Orlando Cabrera say that you could ignore?
>
> A. (The witness) He didn't specifically state which ones could be — what he said was as long as the administrative plan says just a blanket statement that you will comply with all HUD rules and regulations, that we didn't have to follow what was in our administrative plan.
>
> Q. Is that because the HUD regulations trumped your administrative plan?
>
> *Mr. Freudiger:* Objection.
>
> Q. Is that because the HUD regulations controlled your administrative plan?
>
> *Mr. Freudiger:* Objection, vague. *It's not clear whether you're talking about whether Cabrera said that or you're asking for her legal opinion.*

Mr. Freudiger's comments are improper under Rule 30(c)(2). *See Little Hocking Water Ass'n, Inc. v. E.I. DuPont de Nemours & Co.*, 2013 WL 6632678, at *15 (S.D. Ohio Dec. 17, 2013) ("The Court strongly disapproves of defense counsel's efforts to interject [defendant] positions into the course of plaintiff's deposition inquiry. Certainly, [defendant] has a right to attempt to clarify the witness' testimony, if it perceives a need to do so, but that attempt must await the completion of plaintiff's inquiry."); *Cullen v. Nissan N. Am., Inc.*, 2010 WL 11579750, at *6 (M.D. Tenn. Feb. 2, 2010) ("[I]t is not proper for counsel for the deponent to ask the deposing attorney to clarify the question; that is the responsibility of the deponent.").

Notably, during Ms. Heapy's deposition, Mr. Freudiger declared, "I can instruct my witness. Speaking objections — *we all know what the federal rules say.* I have been less vocal than you were. So I'm permitted to instruct the witness whether she can answer or not." And shortly thereafter, "I have a right to tell my witness that she can answer a question."

Mr. Freudiger's interpretation of "what the federal rules say" is incorrect. He does not have the right to tell his witness that she can answer a question. Indeed, all he can do is state a concise, nonargumentative, and nonsuggestive objection on the record and instruct his witness not to answer in the limited circumstances laid out in Rule 30(c)(2). *See Montiel v. Taylor*, 2011 WL 1532529, at *3 (E.D. Tenn. Apr. 21, 2011) ("Rule 30(c)(2) allows non-examining counsel at a deposition to do one of two things: (1) listen and (2) make objections.").

(ii) The CEOs Prior to Ms. Heapy

Plaintiff asserts that Defendant's counsel improperly instructed Ms. Heapy not to respond to questions about Mr. Prude's application for unemployment. On March 23, 2018 (after Ms. Heapy's deposition), at Plaintiff's request, the

Court held an informal telephone conference regarding, in part, the termination of Alphonzio Prude's employment with Defendant. Plaintiff reported that, although Defendant provided Mr. Prude's employment file, his file did not include Defendant's response to Mr. Prude's application for unemployment. This Court found that this evidence was relevant, therefore discoverable, and directed Defendant to investigate whether there was a response to Mr. Prude's application and, if there was, produce it. If Defendant could not produce the response, then Defendant must certify that it could not be located. It appears that Defendant failed to follow the Court's instruction.

Accordingly, Defendant must, within one week of this Order, produce its response to Mr. Prude's application for unemployment.

Plaintiff also notes that Mr. Freudiger—objecting on the basis of "pending litigation"—instructed Ms. Heapy not to answer questions about why Danielle Wright and Jeff Rieck, former CEOs, left DMHA.

Defendant does not suggest that "pending litigation" is a valid ground for instructing a deponent not to answer. Instead, Defendant insists that Plaintiff's questions were "wholly improper" because Ms. Wright and Mr. Rieck's prior employment are "wholly irrelevant" to the present case. Defendant's argument misses the mark: Rule 30(c)(2) requires a deponent to continue her testimony over objection unless she has asserted a privilege, is enforcing a limitation ordered by the court, or to present a motion under Rule 30(d)(3). Objecting on the basis of relevance does not constitute one of these exceptions.

Accordingly, Plaintiff is permitted to send written deposition questions to Ms. Heapy to which she must respond within two weeks after she receives them.

(iii) Defendant's Administrative Plan and HUD Regulations

Next, Plaintiff asserts that Defendant's counsel improperly objected to questions concerning Defendant's Administrative Plan and HUD regulations. On several occasions, Mr. Freudiger objected and instructed Ms. Heapy not to respond on the grounds that the question called for a legal conclusion or for her to interpret law.

> *Q.* (Mr. Green) Is there any HUD authority or rule that requires an expiration date for the . . . April 9th, 2013, commitment vouchers?
>
> *Mr. Freudiger:* Again, objection, legal conclusion, beyond the scope of the topic for the 30(b)(6). She can't answer that.
>
> *Q.* (Mr. Green) Are you aware of any HUD authority or HUD rule that requires an expiration date for Mr. Prude's 2013 letter committing to 33 units of PBRA?
>
> *Mr. Freudiger:* Same objection, same instruction.

Mr. Freudiger stopped her from answering questions as the Rule 30(b)(6) designee or as an individual.

> *Q.* (Mr. Green) Would you agree as CEO that your organization is required to interpret your administrative plan consistently with HUD regulations?

Mr. Freudiger: Objection, legal conclusion, beyond the scope of the notice of taking 30(b)(6).

Mr. Green: I'm asking her as an individual.

Mr. Freudiger: Well, she cannot give a legal opinion as an individual.

Q. As a member of management, do you agree that you need to interpret your administrative plan consistently with HUD regulations?

Mr. Freudiger: Objection.

Mr. Green: Go ahead and answer.

The witness: Can you repeat the question again?

(Record read.)

The witness: We have to write our administrative plan taking into consideration the regulations.

Q. Okay. I asked you the question are you required to interpret your administrative plan consistently with federal regulations?

Mr. Freudiger: Well, she answered to the best of her ability, and you're asking her if she is required to interpret—

Mr. Green: No.

Mr. Freudiger: —or if GDPM is required to interpret, so I don't think she can answer that question.

Mr. Green: She said she was required to write the administrative plan.

Mr. Freudiger: I know what she said, but she's not going to answer your next question.

Mr. Green: Okay. So you're directing her not to answer the last question about interpretation?

Mr. Freudiger: Yeah.

Mr. Green: Okay.

And he stopped some questions without providing a reason:

Q. (Mr. Green) Okay. As CEO of GDPM, is it your understanding that federal law trumps state and local law?

Mr. Freudiger: Objection. That is still a legal conclusion and beyond the scope of the 30(b)(6).

Mr. Green: It is entirely within the scope.

Mr. Freudiger: No, it's not.

Mr. Green: I asked her for the reasons, and she stated that the administrative plan did not provide for something that HUD regulations provided for, so I'm trying to explore that.

Mr. Freudiger: Your topic said the factual basis for the refusal. So obviously she can testify to the reasons that she gave your client as to her understanding. But you asked her a general question about whether federal law trumps state law. That's entirely outside the scope of your topic or the reasons that she has ever given.

Mr. Green: Okay.

Mr. Freudiger: So she can't answer that.

Mr. Green: She can answer that as an individual.

Q. (Mr. Green) You're a lawyer, correct?

Mr. Freudiger: No, we're not going there. We're not going there.

Mr. Green: So you're instructing her not to answer as an individual who is also a lawyer; is that correct?

Mr. Freudiger: Well, I'm instructing her to . . . not answer, period. I don't have to give you my reasons. She is not answering it.

Mr. Green: Okay.

On at least one occasion, Mr. Freudiger answered the question himself:

Q. (Mr. Green) And if HUD regulations specifically allow . . . that Freedom's Path could qualify for the PBV under (b)(2), that would allow your agency to . . . treat them as being qualified, correct?

Mr. Freudiger: No.

The witness: No.

Mr. Freudiger: Objection. *She cannot answer that question.* You're asking her to interpret the regulations.

The Rule is clear: "An objection . . . must be noted on the record, but the examination still proceeds; *the testimony is taken subject to any objection.* . . . A person may instruct a deponent not to answer only when necessary to preserve a privilege, to enforce a limitation ordered by the court, or to present a motion under Rule 30(d)(3)." Fed. R. Civ. P. 30. There is no indication from Defendant that any of the exceptions apply. Accordingly, it was improper for Mr. Freudiger to instruct Ms. Heapy not to answer questions on the ground that it called for a legal conclusion.

(iv) Ms. Heapy's Failure to Prepare as a Rule 30(b)(6) Designee

Under Federal Rule of Civil Procedure 30(b)(6), "a party may name as the deponent a . . . corporation . . . and must describe with reasonable particularity the matters for examination. The named organization must then designate one or more . . . persons who consent to testify on its behalf. . . . The persons designated must testify about information known or reasonably available to the organization." "A Rule 30(b)(6) deponent testifies as to the knowledge of the corporation and the corporations' subjective beliefs and opinions and interpretation of documents and events." *Buck v. Ford Motor Co.,* 2012 WL 601922, at *3 (N.D. Ohio Feb. 23, 2012). The corporation has a duty to prepare the witness to answer all questions about the designated topics fully and without evasion. *Great American Ins. Co. v. Vegas Constr. Co., Inc.,* 251 F.R.D. 534, 539 (D. Nev. March 24, 2008) ("Counsel has the responsibility to prepare its designee to the extent matters are reasonably available, whether from documents, past employees, or other sources.")

Plaintiff contends that Ms. Heapy failed to adequately prepare as the Rule 30(b)(6) designee. Specifically, she "failed to look for records concerning the reasons for terminating the employment of former Interim CEO, Alphonzio Prude. She conducted no written review of documentation as to the reasons for the termination. She spoke with only one member of her board."

Ms. Heapy testified that, in preparation for her deposition, she spoke to one board member about Mr. Prude's termination and reviewed Mr. Prude's personnel file. His file did not contain a record of the reasons for his termination. Ms. Heapy did not, however, review Mr. Prude's "benefits file" because she does not consider it to be part of a personnel matter.

When asked about "how Mr. Prude came to be terminated," she explained, "He was placed on administrative leave in November and was ultimately fired that following month." Ms. Heapy did not know if he was given reasons why he was placed on administrative leave and she did not ask anyone. She testified that she believed there was a board meeting when Mr. Prude was terminated but she was not at the meeting and she did not remember whether it was an open or closed meeting. Ms. Heapy knew, based on her previous discussions with the board of directors and general counsel, that Mr. Prude "was fired by our Board of Commissioners for his lack of ability to maintain compliance of the agency and to work within the rules and regulations laid out by HUD. He also settled a lawsuit without consulting the board." The areas of non-compliance included their public records policy and their violence against women policy. The lawsuit involved an employment issue brought by Karen Boneski. Ms. Heapy did not know "the specific allegations"; the settlement amount; or if Mr. Prude was named individually. She knew that there were no allegations of sexual harassment or issues with violence against women.

When asked if she knew that Mr. Prude applied for unemployment compensations, she replied, "I believe he did." However, Ms. Heapy did not know what position DMHA took regarding his application and stated that she did not ask anyone. At that point, Mr. Freudiger objected, contending

> That's beyond the scope of the topics. She was asked for the personnel and disciplinary reasons and the reasons for his separation discharge or termination. There's nothing in here about DMHA's position in his request for unemployment, and it's totally outside the bounds of any kind of relevancy whatsoever, so she won't be answering any questions on that.

Mr. Freudiger, however, is not correct on either assertion. Plaintiff's list of Rule 30(b)(6) topics includes "The personnel and disciplinary records of Alphonzio Prude." It is reasonable to think that his application for unemployment and any response by Defendant would be included in Mr. Prude's personnel file. Further, as explained above, DMHA's response is relevant and Defendant must produce a copy of its response to Mr. Prude's application for unemployment compensation or a sworn affidavit stating that it cannot be located.

Although Ms. Heapy could not answer every question concerning Mr. Prude's termination, "the inability of a designee to answer every question on a particular topic does not necessarily mean that the corporation has failed to comply with its obligations under the Rule." *Pogue, supra,* at *8. Ms. Heapy did adequately prepare for her deposition and was able to provide the reasons for Mr. Prude's termination.

Further, Defendant, in response to Plaintiff's Motion to Compel, provided a sworn affidavit from a Board member, Reverend Wilburt Shanklin. Rev. Shanklin indicated that the Board discussed Mr. Prude's employment issues during an executive session and no meeting minutes were generated. Ideally, Ms. Heapy would have known those details during her deposition. But a 30(b)(6) witness is not expected to perform with absolute perfection.

(v) Reasonable Attorney Fees and Costs

Under Rule 30(d)(2), a court "may impose an appropriate sanction—including the reasonable expenses and attorney's fees incurred by any party—on a person who impedes, delays, or frustrates the fair examination of the deponent."

Plaintiff asks the Court to award attorneys' fees—at an hourly rate of $500 per hour—for the time spent preparing the motion to compel. Plaintiff also asks the Court to order Ms. Heapy and Defendant's employees "to directly and fully respond to questions posed by Plaintiff's counsel unless subject to a valid exception under Rule 30(c)(2); and . . . order Mr. Freudiger, as counsel for Defendant, to refrain from making speaking objections and comments intended to influence the testimony, such as 'if you know.'"

Although Defendant's counsel's conduct during the deposition of Ms. Heapy was improper at times, the imposition of sanctions is presently unwarranted because Plaintiff was not ultimately prevented from conducting a "fair examination of the deponent." Fed. R. Civ. P. 30(d)(2).

In this contentious case, counsel for both parties "should strive to be cooperative, practical and sensible, and should turn to the courts (or take positions that force others to turn to the courts) only in extraordinary situations that implicate truly significant interests." *Cable & Computer Tech., Inc. v. Lockheed Saunders, Inc.*, 175 F.R.D. 646 (C.D. Cal. 1997); *see also Saria v. Mass. Mut. Life Ins. Co.*, 228 F.R.D. 536, 539 (S.D. W.Va. 2005) ("The integrity of the discovery process rests on the faithfulness of parties and counsel to the rules—both the spirit and the letter. [T]he discovery provisions of the Federal Rules are meant to function without the need for constant judicial intervention and . . . those Rules rely on the honesty and good faith of counsel in dealing with adversaries.").

It is therefore ordered that Defendant's Motion for Protective Order is denied; and Plaintiff's Motion to Compel Discovery and Request for Attorneys' Fees and Expenses is granted, in part, and denied, in part.

REVIEW QUESTION

This case involved two major discovery disputes—the defendant's motion for a protective order with respect to the noticed depositions, and the plaintiff's motion to compel testimony—and the Plaintiff Freedom's Path prevailed on both. So why didn't the court award plaintiff their attorneys' fees? (In answering that question, address the two disputes separately.)

The Proportionality Factors in Freedom's Path. When Judge Ovington analyzes the first two proportionality factors, she observes that the defendant did not contest either of them. Why would the defendant have conceded these? (What was the alternative?)

The third proportionality factor regards the parties' relative access to relevant information. The notion here is that, in some circumstances, the requesting party could obtain the information through means other than requesting it of the responding party. That is because sometimes the information is publicly available, or it is available from other sources, or even because the requesting party may already have it. How does the court here characterize this factor?

With respect to the fourth proportionality factor, what is the "additional information about the parties' resources" that the court finds conspicuously absent? It appears that one side or the other may have squandered the opportunity to prevail on this factor by failing to prove it. What might such evidence look like?

The fifth proportionality factor requires the court to evaluate the importance of the discovery in resolving the issues. When Judge Gibson engaged this factor in *Alley, supra*, he asked whether the sought discovery was "vital" and "necessary" to the plaintiff's case. How does Judge Ovington frame the inquiry?

Civility and Professionalism. Discovery disputes can get heated — especially in the context of a deposition where egos and personalities are on display and there is no judge to incentivize or to force good behavior. Accordingly, there are many instances demonstrating a lack of civility in the discovery process. In the following excerpt, Judge Marvin E. Aspen, a U.S. District Judge in the Northern District of Illinois, describes some of these problems:

> These are troubled times for lawyers. Not only is the practice of law suffering from the current economic malaise, but lawyer bashing has become our new national pastime. . . . Most of this public derision and media abuse is, of course, unjustified. But is some of it self-inflicted? Just how much has the legal profession contributed to the public's misperception of lawyers as heartless, self-interested parasites, flourishing only by virtue of others' misery and misfortune?
>
> Let us, for example, look at the following exchange during a deposition taken in Madison, Wisconsin, this year by two veteran Chicago trial lawyers. Attorney V had just asked Attorney A for a copy of a document he was using to question the witness:
>
> *Mr. V.:* Please don't throw it at me.
>
> *Mr. A.:* Take it.
>
> *Mr. V.:* Don't throw it at me.
>
> *Mr. A.:* Don't be a child, Mr. V. You look like a slob the way you're dressed, but you don't have to act like a slob.
>
> *Mr. V.:* Stop yelling at me. Let's get on with it.
>
> *Mr. A.:* Have you not? You deny I have given you a copy of every document?

Mr. V.:   You just refused to give it to me.

Mr. A.:   Do you deny it?

Mr. V.:   Eventually you threw it at me.

Mr. A.:   Oh, Mr. V., you're about as childish as you can get. You look like a slob, you act like a slob.

Mr. V.:   Keep it up.

Mr. A.:   Your mind belongs in the gutter.

> Although obviously an extreme incident of lawyer incivility, this interaction of attorneys during a multi-billion dollar case nonetheless exemplifies the erosion of professionalism in attorney relationships. . . .

Marvin E. Aspen, *The Search of Renewed Civility in Litigation*, 28 Val. U. L. Rev. 513, 513-514 (1994). Unfortunately, there are many additional examples of discovery squabbles that are viewable on the Internet. *See, e.g., http://www.youtube.com/watch?v=td-KKmcYtrM* (last visited July 29, 2019).

Do you have any suggestions for improving the civility of lawyers in the legal profession? What effect is your legal education having on your civility in law school or in daily life? What effect do you think your legal education will have on your civility in practicing law? What do you think the causes are of a lack of civility in litigation?

During a deposition, a lawyer who does not follow the rules will typically get away with such behavior unless her adversary brings a motion to the judge. If/when that happens, your reputation, sanctions, and perhaps even a suspension of your license to practice law hang in the balance. If you were Mr. Freudiger (in *Freedom's Path*), would you be embarrassed to read Judge Ovington's opinion? And if you were Mr. Green, how would you react to the first sentence of the penultimate paragraph of the opinion — specifically the quotes from *Cable & Computer Tech., Inc.* and *Saria*?

Magistrate Judges.   As in *Freedom's Path*, many discovery motions are referred by federal district judges to magistrate judges. Magistrate judges are appointed by judges of federal district courts and possess many, but not all, of the powers of a federal judge. *See* 28 U.S.C. §§ 631-639. *See generally* Symposium, *Magistrate Judges and the Transformation of the American Judiciary*, 16 Nev. L.J. 775 (2016).

Moreover, for most discovery issues, the ruling by the magistrate or district judge is the final word. Ordinarily, discovery rulings are reviewed only for an abuse of discretion. Appellate courts are understandably reluctant to interfere with district court decisions regarding their own day-to-day operations.

> [A]n appellate court will not interfere with the trial court's exercise of its discretion to control its docket and dispatch its business . . . except upon the clearest showing that the procedures have resulted in actual and substantial prejudice to the complaining litigant.

United States v. Microsoft Corp., 253 F.3d 34, 100 (D.C. Cir. 2001).

Discovery Abuse: The Avalanche and the Stonewall.   Some scholars have argued that discovery reforms are targeted almost exclusively at over-discovery—that is, parties trying to extract from their opponents more than that to which they are entitled (and more than a cost/benefit analysis could justify). Indeed, few proposals are instead targeted at abusive resistance to discovery. What are possible explanations for this difference? Consider also that empirical research commissioned by the Advisory Committee and done by the Federal Judicial Center suggests that the most common problems in document production are failure to respond adequately and failure to respond in a timely fashion. *See* Thomas E. Willging et al., *An Empirical Study of Discovery and Disclosure Practice Under the 1993 Federal Rule Amendments*, 39 B.C. L. Rev. 525, 540 (1998).

Start your own list of ways to defend against discovery. By creating such a list, neither you nor we are endorsing all of these techniques. Indeed, some lawyers engage in dubious behavior in discovery even though unethical methods should never be utilized. But here are some of the methods you might include in a list: objections to answering (such as objections to interrogatories or instructing a witness at a deposition not to answer); seeking continuances; restricting an answer or compliance with a request to the most narrow possible reading of the question or request; seeking a limiting order or a protective order; moving to quash; reading a request in the broadest possible light and thereby providing so much information that the most relevant information may become lost in the shuffle; claiming that the opponent has not complied with the required disclosure, meeting, planning, and certification requirements prior to commencing additional discovery. Find the corresponding Federal Rules that authorize each of these techniques (and for any additional techniques that you add to this list). When and how might a practice be authorized by rule yet unethical to use?

Start your own list of ways to compel discovery. Begin with the following and, again, find the corresponding Federal Rules that authorize them: seeking an order to compel; seeking the assistance of the court through case management; moving for sanctions; moving for a contempt order; defending and then trying to reach a voluntary and explicit agreement with opposing counsel on how discovery will be sensibly and fairly conducted, with very precise commitments. You can also move to force your opponent to comply with required disclosures, supplemental disclosures, or a discovery plan.

QUESTIONS TO PONDER

Now armed with a better understanding of the particulars of the discovery rules, you may wish to revisit the uneasy placement of discovery within the broader context of our adversarial system. Would more specific discovery rules solve the problems created by adversarialism? Would they create new problems?

PRACTICE EXERCISE NO. 16: ETHICAL ISSUES IN DISCOVERY

The following two fact patterns present issues that may arise in the context of discovery. We are interested in finding out how you would respond under each of these circumstances. (Assume that you are an attorney with the authority to make these choices.) Remember that you have a duty both to zealously (or "competently" and "diligently," under the Model Rules) represent your clients and to behave ethically. You may want to consider the potential effect your decision will have on your clients and their case, on the opposing party and its case, on your practice, and on the legal system generally. You may, of course, consider other factors as you see fit.

Scenario No. 1

Your clients, the City Police Department, its Chief, and members of the Department, are defendants in a civil rights case. Plaintiff claims that two policemen stood by and watched her husband brutally beat her, and that their failure to stop the beating was part of a pattern and practice of refusing to come to the aid of victims of domestic violence. Plaintiff is represented by a solo practitioner who recently graduated from law school and (you know from a friend) has lots of debt and almost no assets. She is representing the plaintiff on a pro bono basis and (you have heard) has volunteered to front the costs for her client, pending settlement or a favorable verdict. You are a third-year associate in a successful, respected firm. Defendants pay (through the City) $300 per hour for your services, plus costs.

Plaintiff has sent you a request for production of the following documents and things, *inter alia*:

1. Any and all records from the period commencing five (5) years prior to the date of the incidents giving rise to the lawsuit of or pertaining to any and all complaints, formal and/or informal, made by women to the City Police Department, regarding violence, abuse, forced sexual relations, and/or any other injury, act, or practice perpetrated upon them by a present or past husband, a present or past "boyfriend," and/or a present or past lover, and/or any other person known to them.

2. Any and all statements, memoranda, reports, or internal policy guidelines, pertaining to the period commencing five (5) years prior to the date of the incident giving rise to the lawsuit of or pertaining to the handling of complaints formal and/or informal, made by women to the City Police Department, regarding violence, abuse, forced sexual relations, and/or any other injury, act, or practice perpetrated upon them by a present or past husband, a present or past "boyfriend," and/or a present or past lover, and/or any other person known to them.

With no further investigation (based on conversations you have had with some of the defendants), you know that some items exist that arguably would fit into each category requested by the plaintiff. You also know that considerable time and expense (on the part of the Police Department) would be involved in fairly compiling all of the materials requested. From what you know so far, it could go a long way toward proving Plaintiff's claims if the request is read with any liberality. You also have reason to believe that there may even be some particularly damaging correspondence authored by the Chief and others in the department calling domestic violence cases "a real waste of time" and "none of our damn business."

You consider the following responses to the request (or any others that make sense to you):

(a) Produce nothing and respond that these "requests are overly broad, unduly burdensome, and request materials beyond the scope of discovery."

(b) File a motion for a protective order, arguing that the request seeks documents that are not within the scope of permissible discovery.

(c) Respond by producing all of the requested documents and records that are not privileged. This option would involve reviewing, for privileged documents, more than 3,000 boxes of stored complaints, memoranda, etc., in the City Police Department basement, and producing almost all of them.

(d) Respond by producing all of the requested documents and records that are, in your best estimation, within the broadest scope of permissible discovery (and objecting to the request to the extent that it extended beyond the scope of permissible discovery). This option would involve reviewing the 3,000 boxes and producing about 1,000 of them.

(e) Review all of your clients' files and produce what you understand to be the spirit of the request in as direct a manner as possible. (Will you include documents and records pertaining to complaints made by women regarding matters unrelated to domestic violence?) Assume that this option would involve producing about 60 boxes.

(f) Ask the Chief to provide you with whatever he thinks fits the request. With this approach you're pretty sure that his "eyesight is poor."

Prepare, first, to explain to the clients your strategic options and recommendation(s). How is he (and/or "the City") likely to respond to your recommendation? Then, assume that your clients have concurred with your decision, but the opposing counsel calls you to complain. How will you respond to this? And finally, assume that the opposing counsel brings this dispute before a judge, and you are called upon to explain your approach. Can you defend your tactics?

Scenario No. 2

Continuing with the same facts as in Scenario 1, the Chief comes to your office to prepare for his deposition, which is to occur next week. Upon his arrival, he says, "Hey, I know I told you I hadn't exactly established a firm policy for how to handle domestic violence cases, but you know what? I forgot about this memo I sent around a couple of years ago. One of my best officers just gave me his copy this morning. I'm sure you'll love it because I took all of the ideas from a great civil rights lawyer on how police departments ought to handle these cases. Before I left the station this morning, I talked with a bunch of my veteran cops, and they all said they had seen copies of this; they distinctly remember my long lecture to them on handling these cases seriously. I can't believe that this slipped my mind earlier, but I've been under a lot of pressure, you know. I'm really feeling better about my deposition testimony already."

What are you going to ask or say to the Chief? And what will you do at the deposition if he has the opportunity to testify according to what you have just heard?

PRACTICE EXERCISE NO. 17: ANALYZING THE SCOPE OF DISCOVERY

Your law firm has been hired to serve as appellate counsel for Wounded Warriors Family Support, Inc. (WWFS), a non-profit organization in Omaha, Nebraska. Several lawyers have been assigned to assess the strengths and weaknesses of the appeal, and your supervisor has asked you to focus exclusively on the discovery issue. Our firm is a boutique appellate practice that did not represent WWFS in the trial court.

In the trial court, Wounded Warrior Project, Inc. (WWP) sued WWFS for trademark infringement, unfair competition, and deceptive trade practices. Both organizations offer charitable services to wounded veterans and their families. WWP claimed that WWFS deceived donors into thinking that they were supporting the more established charity with the similar name. A jury found for WWP and awarded them a judgment for $1.7 million; the judge also issued a permanent injunction that forced the defendant to shut down its website. WWFS timely filed a notice of appeal. And hired us.

On the merits of their claim, WWP introduced persuasive evidence that WWFS was trying to leverage the plaintiff's notoriety and reputation. WWFS adopted a new name, featuring the words "wounded warrior." WWFS revamped its website with a look that closely resembled WWP's website. And with the WWP already located at woundedwarrior.org, the WWFS added only the letter "s", doing its business at woundedwarriors.org. (The WWFS site included an anemic disclaimer in a difficult-to-read typeface.) The damages award was based principally on the fact that, when WWFS launched its new website, WWFS's donations jumped from $1,300 per month to about $87,900 per month. Some of the donations received by WWFS were made by persons who used the words "Wounded Warrior Project" in their correspondence with WWFS. Both WWP and WWFS had received high ratings from Consumer Reports and other evaluators of charities for their low overhead, social impact, and financial performance.

The trial counsel timely filed a notice of appeal, and our firm is in the process of reviewing all possible bases for an appeal.

During discovery, WWFS requested that WWP produce "all documents relating to or evidencing any donations received by WWP since the date of WWFS's founding." WWP refused to produce information about its donors, and WWFS moved to compel. WWP had already produced its tax returns, audited financial statements, and monthly contribution summaries to WWFS, which showed the total donations to WWP for the relevant time periods. The district court denied WWFS's motion to compel, citing three reasons. The district court found, among other things, that WWFS's motion to compel was (1) "overbroad in scope" because WWFS was seeking donor information without regard to source or location; (2) "unduly burdensome" because WWFS was requesting production of all documents" relating to tens of thousands of donors and that this was "not proportionate discovery"; and (3) "not reasonably calculated to lead to the discovery of admissible evidence," because WWFS had not asserted a counterclaim for unjust enrichment seeking the return of any misdirected donations. The district court concluded "the discovery of some donations intended for WWFS but instead retained by WWP is not relevant to the calculation of damages here because WWP's damages were based on misdirected donations to WWFS."

Prepare for a meeting with the senior partner. She will be trying to make an initial determination about whether the trial judge's denial of the motion to compel may be an issue worth including in the appellate brief. Prepare to give her your assessment; your recommendation; and what, exactly, you would do as next steps if assigned to research this issue more thoroughly.

PRACTICE EXERCISE NO. 18: ANALYZING THE SCOPE OF THIRD-PARTY DISCOVERY

Rocky Callaskey moved to New Hampshire to be a yoga teacher at White Mountains Lodge. For nine months he received only rave reviews from his students. He also received only positive reports from the local operators of the Lodge — and even from the owners of the Lodge, a Colorado company that owns many ski resorts. But Callaskey was then abruptly terminated without notice or explanation. He came to your law firm for counsel. Callaskey owns a home in North Woodstock, New Hampshire that will not be easy to sell in the current market, and he doesn't have other good job prospects in the area.

Your firm filed a complaint against the owners of the Lodge, claiming race and sexual orientation discrimination. Callaskey was an at-will employee, but he is a member of these protected classes, and his termination occurred approximately one week after he was featured in a news story that went viral about a large, controversial political protest that he organized and led in nearby Boston, Massachusetts.

The complaint offers detailed allegations of each element of Callaskey's claim for employment discrimination, including the essential element that he was qualified for the position. To that end, the complaint details, *inter alia*, his professional training and certifications, his "nineteen years of experience as an exceptional yoga instructor," and his "unique ability to develop a community of students of all skill levels." A colleague of yours at the firm drafted these allegations of the complaint using a copy of the resume that Callaskey gave to the Lodge when he applied for the job. Callaskey has confirmed that all of that information is true to the best of his knowledge.

Early in discovery, the Lodge served interrogatories that asked about Callaskey's work history. With your assistance, Callaskey answered those interrogatories forthrightly, identifying the three yoga studios where Callaskey worked over the past twenty years. Yesterday, the Lodge served those three yoga studios (who, to be clear, are not parties to the suit) with *subpoenas duces tecum* seeking "all documents and communications, whether paper, electronic, or other media, referring or relating to Rocky Callaskey including but not limited to personnel files, disciplinary files, and any other employment documents or records." Your law firm was simultaneously served with copies of all three subpoenas.

Callaskey has told us that, although he has nothing to hide, it's embarrassing to have this lawsuit brought to the attention of his former employers — especially since he will soon be looking for work.

Aware that you've never handled a litigation matter by yourself, the senior partner of the firm has asked you to take the lead on this discovery matter. "This is a good introduction to discovery disputes. Get these third-party subpoenas quashed! The defendant didn't follow the proper procedure, and surely this information is not discoverable." Is she right? Develop the arguments that you would make to the court (and to defense counsel).

PRACTICE EXERCISE NO. 19: ANALYZING PROPORTIONALITY IN DISCOVERY

You are a law clerk to a federal judge. She describes the circumstances leading to a motion to compel that was just filed in her court. Although briefing on the motion is not yet complete, she would like to take a stab at solving this matter tomorrow morning at a discovery conference that was already scheduled in this case. "Sometimes with aggressive case management I can keep discovery disputes from finding any traction," she said. "Think about this dispute and give me your thoughts: What's your gut feeling about the proper scope of discovery here? Start there and work backwards to probe, challenge, or justify that intuition."

Pingree operates a restaurant called Birdland at 6 Russell Square in New Orleans, Louisiana. Russell Square is a massive multi-building, mixed-use development that includes restaurants, luxury apartments, a hotel, an office tower, retail space, and a minor-league baseball stadium. The Russell Square development is owned by Auerbach Associates. Pingree entered into a ten-year lease agreement with Auerbach Associates for a space of approximately 9,000 square feet in the first floor of building number 6, which is in the heart of Russell Square. Auerbach Associates' business offices occupy all of the other floors of this building. About two years into the term of the lease, the foundation of building number 6 shifted structurally, causing difficulties including plumbing problems, cracks in the floor and ceiling, and inoperable doors. Over the past six months Auerbach Associates has done very little to address the structural problems. Birdland has continued operations, but its business has suffered.

According to the terms of the Lease Agreement, the landlord has a continuing obligation to keep the structural components of the building in good condition and to repair any related defects. Pingree ultimately filed suit against Auerbach Associates in state court for breach of contract and other causes of action. Some discovery has taken place, but disputes about the scope of discovery have already arisen. The state court's rules of procedure are in lockstep with the Federal Rules of Civil Procedure.

The current discovery dispute involves the following discovery requests by Pingree:

> For the time period commencing with the execution of the Lease Agreement and continuing to the present, any and all of the following documents, including electronically stored information, within Auerbach Associates' possession, custody, or control relating to the leased premises at 6 Russell Square or to any other building in the Russell Square development:
>
> (1) lease agreements with tenants;
> (2) agreements or correspondence with tenants regarding rent reductions, financial assistance, rent concessions or modifications;
> (3) written estimates, contracts, offers, bids for construction or repairs relating to building structure or foundation sent, received, or entered into;
> (4) memoranda, reports, letters, correspondence, or studies to/from third parties that discuss the cause(s) of, the consequence(s) of, or the remediation of changes to building foundation(s); and
> (5) agreements or correspondence with realtors regarding future plans, proposals, uses, or development.

Auerbach Associates refused to produce any of these documents on the grounds that the requests sought "evidence that was irrelevant and beyond the scope of discovery, disproportionate, unduly burdensome to produce, and confidential."

PRACTICE EXERCISE NO. 20: FINDING AN EXPERT (AND EXPERTISE) IN *CARPENTER*

You are an associate in a law firm representing the plaintiffs in *Carpenter v. Dee*. As you develop your case against Randall Dee and other possible defendants, you will need to have a solid understanding of how and why the jeep rolled over.

This knowledge will help you prove responsibility and fault, and it will help you explain why and how Charlie suffered, and ultimately died, at the scene of the accident. Assume that you are in the early stages of this suit.

1. Go online (or to the library) and locate an expert who would likely be able to teach you what *you* want to know about the mechanics of this accident. As you narrow your search, consider these questions:
   - What makes one expert more attractive than another?
   - What would you ask/tell this person in your first telephone conversation?
   - Is your conversation with this person discoverable by opposing counsel?
   - Are you required to disclose this person as one of your experts? (When?)
2. As the case moves toward summary judgment or trial you may need an expert who will testify.
   - Can the expert who educated you also be your testifying expert?
   - When and how do you need to disclose the identity of this expert?
   - Are your conversations with this person discoverable by opposing counsel?

Hickman v. Taylor
329 U.S. 495 (1947)

Justice MURPHY delivered the opinion of the Court:

This case presents an important problem under the Federal Rules of Civil Procedure . . . the extent to which a party may inquire into oral and written statements of witnesses, or other information, secured by an adverse party's counsel in the course of preparation for possible litigation after a claim has arisen. Examination into a person's files and records, including those resulting from the professional activities of an attorney, must be judged with care. It is not without reason that various safeguards have been established to preclude unwarranted excursions into the privacy of a man's work. At the same time, public policy supports reasonable and necessary inquiries. Properly to balance these competing interests is a delicate and difficult task. . . .

[The facts of the case are summarized as follows: The *J. M. Taylor* tug sank while towing a Baltimore & Ohio Railroad car float across the Delaware River. Five crew members drowned; four survived. Two months after the accident, the United States Steamboat Inspectors held a public hearing in which the four survivors were examined. Shortly thereafter, counsel for the tug owners, Fortenbaugh, took statements privately from survivors and witnesses in anticipation of possible litigation from the families of the deceased. Eventually, families of each of the deceased brought claims against the tug owners. All but one of the claims settled without litigation. About nine months after the accident, the fifth claimant (Petitioner) brought suit in the federal district court suing the tug owners and the railroad (Defendants).]

One year later, petitioner filed 39 interrogatories directed to the tug owners. The 38th interrogatory read:

State whether any statements of the members of the crews of the Tugs *J. M. Taylor* and *Philadelphia* or of any other vessel were taken in connection with the towing of the car float and the sinking of the Tug *John M. Taylor*.

Attach hereto exact copies of all such statements if in writing, and if oral, set forth in detail the exact provisions of any such oral statements or reports.

Supplemental interrogatories asked whether any oral or written statements, records, reports or other memoranda had been made concerning any matter relative to the towing operation, the sinking of the tug, the salvaging and repair of the tug, and the death of the deceased. If the answer was in the affirmative, the tug owners were then requested to set forth the nature of all such records, reports, statements or other memoranda.

The tug owners, through Fortenbaugh, answered all of the interrogatories except No. 38 and the supplemental ones just described. While admitting that statements of the survivors had been taken, they declined to summarize or set forth the contents. They did so on the ground that such requests called "for privileged matter obtained in preparation for litigation" and constituted "an attempt to obtain indirectly counsel's private files." It was claimed that answering these requests "would involve practically turning over not only the complete files, but also the telephone records and, almost, the thoughts of counsel."

In connection with the hearing on these objections, Fortenbaugh made a written statement and gave an informal oral deposition explaining the circumstances under which he had taken the statements. But he was not expressly asked in the deposition to produce the statements. . . . [The District Court held that the subjects of the petitioner's requests were not privileged and ordered counsel to answer the interrogatory and the supplemental interrogatories, produce all of the witnesses' statements, and state any facts concerning the case that Defendants learned through the witnesses, and to] produce Mr. Fortenbaugh's memoranda containing statements of fact by witnesses or to submit these memoranda to the Court for determination of those portions which should be revealed to Plaintiff. Upon their refusal, the court adjudged them in contempt and ordered them imprisoned until they complied.

The Third Circuit Court of Appeals, also sitting *en banc*, reversed the judgment of the District Court. It held that the information here sought was part of the "work product of the lawyer" and hence privileged from discovery under the Federal Rules of Civil Procedure. The importance of the problem, which has engendered a great divergence of views among district courts, led us to grant certiorari. . . .

The pre-trial deposition-discovery mechanism established by Rules 26 to 37 is one of the most significant innovations of the Federal Rules of Civil Procedure. Under the prior federal practice, the pre-trial functions of notice-giving, issue-formulation, and fact-revelation were performed primarily and inadequately by the pleadings. Inquiry into the issues and the facts before trial was narrowly confined and was often cumbersome in method. The new rules, however, restrict the pleadings to the task of general notice-giving and invest the deposition-discovery process with a vital role in the preparation for trial. The various instruments of discovery now serve (1) as a device, along with the pre-trial hearing under Rule 16, to narrow and clarify the basic issues between the parties, and (2) as a device for ascertaining the facts, or information as to the existence or whereabouts of facts, relative to those issues. Thus civil trials in the federal courts no longer need be carried on in the dark. The way is now clear, consistent with recognized privileges, for the parties to obtain the fullest possible knowledge of the issues and facts before trial. . . .

[T]he basic question at stake is whether [discovery] may be used to inquire into materials collected by an adverse party's counsel in the course of preparing for possible litigation. . . .

In urging that he has a right to inquire into the materials secured and prepared by Fortenbaugh, petitioner emphasizes that the deposition-discovery portions of the Federal Rules of Civil Procedure are designed to enable the parties to discover the true facts and to compel their disclosure wherever they may be found. It is said that inquiry may be made under these rules, epitomized by Rule 26[b], as to any relevant matter which is not privileged; and since the discovery provisions are to be applied as broadly and liberally as possible, the privilege limitation must be restricted to its narrowest bounds. On the premise that the attorney-client privilege is the one involved in this case, petitioner argues that it must be strictly confined to confidential communications made by a client to his attorney. And since the materials here in issue were secured by Fortenbaugh from third persons rather than from his clients, the tug owners, the conclusion is reached that these materials are proper subjects for discovery under Rule 26[b].

As additional support for this result, petitioner claims that to prohibit discovery under these circumstances would give a corporate defendant a tremendous advantage in a suit by an individual plaintiff. Thus in a suit by an injured employee against a railroad or in a suit by an insured person against an insurance company the corporate defendant could pull a dark veil of secrecy over all the pertinent facts it can collect after the claim arises merely on the assertion that such facts were gathered by its large staff of attorneys and claim agents. At the same time, the individual plaintiff, who often has direct knowledge of the matter in issue and has no counsel until some time after his claim arises could be compelled to disclose all the intimate details of his case. By endowing with immunity from disclosure all that a lawyer discovers in the course of his duties, it is said, the rights of individual litigants in such cases are drained of vitality and the lawsuit becomes more of a battle of deception than a search for truth.

But framing the problem in terms of assisting individual plaintiffs in their suits against corporate defendants is unsatisfactory. Discovery concededly may work to the disadvantage as well as to the advantage of individual plaintiffs. Discovery, in other words, is not a one-way proposition. It is available in all types of cases at the behest of any party, individual or corporate, plaintiff or defendant. The problem thus far transcends the situation confronting this petitioner. And we must view that problem in light of the limitless situations where the particular kind of discovery sought by petitioner might be used.

We agree, of course, that the deposition-discovery rules are to be accorded a broad and liberal treatment. No longer can the time-honored cry of "fishing expedition" serve to preclude a party from inquiring into the facts underlying his opponent's case. Mutual knowledge of all the relevant facts gathered by both parties is essential to proper litigation. To that end, either party may compel the other to disgorge whatever facts he has in his possession. The deposition-discovery procedure simply advances the stage at which the disclosure can be compelled from the time of trial to the period preceding it, thus reducing the possibility of surprise. But discovery, like all matters of procedure, has ultimate and necessary boundaries. . . .

Petitioner has made more than an ordinary request for relevant, non-privileged facts in the possession of his adversaries or their counsel. He has sought discovery as of right of oral and written statements of witnesses whose identity is well known and whose availability to petitioner appears unimpaired. He has sought production of these matters after making the most searching inquiries of his opponents as to the circumstances surrounding the fatal accident, which inquiries were sworn to have been answered to the best of their information and belief. Interrogatories were directed toward all the events prior to, during and subsequent to the sinking of the tug. Full and honest answers to such broad inquiries would necessarily have included all pertinent information gleaned by Fortenbaugh through his interviews with the witnesses. Petitioner makes no suggestion, and we cannot assume, that the tug owners or Fortenbaugh were incomplete or dishonest in the framing of their answers. In addition, petitioner was free to examine the public testimony of the witnesses taken before the United States Steamboat Inspectors. We are thus dealing with an attempt to secure the production of written statements and mental impressions contained in the files and the mind of the attorney Fortenbaugh without any showing of necessity or any indication or claim that denial of such production would unduly prejudice the preparation of petitioner's case or cause him any hardship or injustice. For aught that appears, the essence of what petitioner seeks either has been revealed to him already through the interrogatories or is readily available to him direct from the witnesses for the asking. . . .

In our opinion, neither Rule 26 nor any other rule dealing with discovery contemplates production under such circumstances. That is not because the subject matter is privileged or irrelevant, as those concepts are used in these rules. Here is simply an attempt, without purported necessity or justification, to secure written statements, private memoranda and personal recollections prepared or formed by an adverse party's counsel in the course of his legal duties. As such, it falls outside the arena of discovery and contravenes the public policy underlying the orderly prosecution and defense of legal claims. Not even the most liberal of discovery theories can justify unwarranted inquiries into the files and the mental impressions of an attorney.

Historically, a lawyer is an officer of the court and is bound to work for the advancement of justice while faithfully protecting the rightful interests of his clients. In performing his various duties, however, it is essential that a lawyer work with a certain degree of privacy, free from unnecessary intrusion by opposing parties and their counsel. Proper preparation of a client's case demands that he assemble information, sift what he considers to be the relevant from the irrelevant facts, prepare his legal theories and plan his strategy without undue and needless interference. That is the historical and the necessary way in which lawyers act within the framework of our system of jurisprudence to promote justice and to protect their clients' interests. This work is reflected, of course, in interviews, statements, memoranda, correspondence, briefs, mental impressions, personal beliefs, and countless other tangible and intangible ways—aptly though roughly termed by the Circuit Court of Appeals in this case as the "Work product of the lawyer." Were such materials open to opposing counsel on mere demand, much of what is now put down in writing would remain unwritten. An attorney's thoughts, heretofore inviolate, would not be his own. Inefficiency, unfairness and sharp practices would inevitably develop in the giving of legal advice and in the preparation of cases for trial. The effect on the legal profession would be demoralizing. And the interests of the clients and the cause of justice would be poorly served.

We do not mean to say that all written materials obtained or prepared by an adversary's counsel with an eye toward litigation are necessarily free from discovery in all cases. Where relevant and non-privileged facts remain hidden in an attorney's file and where production of those facts is essential to the preparation of one's case, discovery may properly be had. Such written statements and documents might, under certain circumstances, be admissible in evidence or give clues as to the existence or location of relevant facts. Or they might be useful for purposes of impeachment or corroboration. And production might be justified where the witnesses are no longer available or can be reached only with difficulty. Were production of written statements and documents to be precluded under such circumstances, the liberal ideals of the deposition-discovery portions of the Federal Rules of Civil Procedure would be stripped of much of their meaning. But the general policy against invading the privacy of an attorney's course of preparation is so well recognized and so essential to an orderly working of our system of legal procedure that a burden rests on the one who would invade that privacy to establish adequate reasons to justify production through a subpoena or court order. That burden, we believe, is necessarily implicit in the rules as now constituted.

Rule 30(b), as presently written, gives the trial judge the requisite discretion to make a judgment as to whether discovery should be allowed as to written statements secured from witnesses. But in the instant case there was no room for that discretion to operate in favor of the petitioner. No attempt was made to establish any reason why Fortenbaugh should be forced to produce the written statements.

There was only a naked, general demand for these materials as of right and a finding by the District Court that no recognizable privilege was involved. That was insufficient to justify discovery under these circumstances and the court should have sustained the refusal of the tug owners and Fortenbaugh to produce.

But as to oral statements made by witnesses to Fortenbaugh, whether presently in the form of his mental impressions or memoranda, we do not believe that any showing of necessity can be made under the circumstances of this case so as to justify production. Under ordinary conditions, forcing an attorney to repeat or write out all that witnesses have told him and to deliver the account to his adversary gives rise to grave dangers of inaccuracy and untrustworthiness. No legitimate purpose is served by such production. The practice forces the attorney to testify as to what he remembers or what he saw fit to write down regarding witnesses' remarks. Such testimony could not qualify as evidence; and to use it for impeachment or corroborative purposes would make the attorney much less an officer of the court and much more an ordinary witness. The standards of the profession would thereby suffer.

Denial of production of this nature does not mean that any material, non-privileged facts can be hidden from the petitioner in this case. He need not be unduly hindered in the preparation of his case, in the discovery of facts or in his anticipation of his opponents' position. Searching interrogatories directed to Fortenbaugh and the tug owners, production of written documents and statements upon a proper showing and direct interviews with the witnesses themselves all serve to reveal the facts in Fortenbaugh's possession to the fullest possible extent consistent with public policy. Petitioner's counsel frankly admits that he wants the oral statements only to help prepare himself to examine witnesses and to make sure that he has overlooked nothing. That is insufficient under the circumstances to permit him an exception to the policy underlying the privacy of Fortenbaugh's professional activities. If there should be a rare situation justifying production of these matters, petitioner's case is not of that type.

We fully appreciate the widespread controversy among the members of the legal profession over the problem raised by this case. It is a problem that rests on what has been one of the most hazy frontiers of the discovery process. But until some rule or statute definitely prescribes otherwise, we are not justified in permitting discovery in a situation of this nature as a matter of unqualified right. When Rule 26 and the other discovery rules were adopted, this Court and the members of the bar in general certainly did not believe or contemplate that all the files and mental processes of lawyers were thereby opened to the free scrutiny of their adversaries. And we refuse to interpret the rules at this time so as to reach so harsh and unwarranted a result.

We therefore affirm the judgment of the Circuit Court of Appeals.

Justice JACKSON, concurring:

. . . Counsel for the petitioner candidly said on argument that he wanted this information to help prepare himself to examine witnesses, to make sure he overlooked nothing. He bases his claim to it in his brief on the view that the Rules were to do away with the old situation where a law suit developed into "a battle of wits between counsel." But a common law trial is and always should be an adversary proceeding. Discovery was hardly intended to enable a learned profession to perform its functions either without wits or on wits borrowed from the adversary.

The real purpose and the probable effect of the practice ordered by the district court would be to put trials on a level even lower than a "battle of wits." I can conceive of no practice more demoralizing to the Bar than to require a lawyer to write out and deliver to his adversary an account of what witnesses have told him. Even if his recollection were perfect, the statement would be his language permeated with his inferences. Every one who has tried it knows that it is almost impossible so fairly to record the expressions and emphasis of a witness that when he testifies in the environment of the court and under the influence of the leading question there will not be departures in some respects. Whenever the testimony of the witness would differ from the "exact" statement the lawyer had delivered, the lawyer's statement would be whipped out to impeach the witness. Counsel producing his adversary's "inexact" statement could lose nothing by saying, "Here is a contradiction, gentlemen of the jury. I do not know whether it is my adversary or his witness who is not telling the truth, but one is not." Of course, if this practice were adopted, that scene would be repeated over and over again. The lawyer who delivers such statements often would find himself branded a deceiver afraid to take the stand to support his own version of the witness' conversation with him, or else he will have to go on the stand to defend his own credibility—perhaps against that of his chief witness, or possibly even his client.

Every lawyer dislikes to take the witness stand and will do so only for grave reasons. This is partly because it is not his role; he is almost invariably a poor witness. But he steps out of professional character to do it. He regrets it; the profession discourages it. But the practice advocated here is one which would force him to be a witness, not as to what he has seen or done but as to other witnesses' stories, and not because he wants to do so but in self-defense. . . .

REVIEW QUESTIONS

1. An important theme in this case is contained in the Court's statement:

    > No longer can the time-honored cry of "fishing expedition" serve to preclude a party from inquiring into the facts underlying his opponent's case. Mutual knowledge of all the relevant facts gathered by both parties is essential to proper litigation. To that end, either party may compel the other to disgorge whatever facts he has in his possession.

    What exactly does Justice Murphy identify as the virtue of this full exchange of information? Is this for the benefit of the court? For the parties? For justice?

2. A discovery stage that promises a robust exchange of information is not meaningful if cases are resolved before they reach the discovery stage (when that exchange would happen). Reconcile the tolerance for "fishing

expeditions" in discovery with the demand for plausibility pleading and judicial pressure to settle.

3. The drafters of the Federal Rules thought that broad discovery would help get the relevant facts into the open before trial, thereby reducing the possibility of surprise and producing a more just result. Why, then, offer protection to an attorney's work product? Put another way, why preserve this particular element of surprise?

D. PROCEDURAL RULEMAKING

At this point in the course you should be able to form an opinion about the wisdom of the current procedural rulemaking process. All of the Federal Rules are, of course, a product of the Rules Enabling Act, and you will certainly want to re-read 28 U.S.C. §§ 2072 and 2074 in preparation for this part. For an overview of the rulemaking process and an up-to-date status report of all current rulemaking efforts, we highly recommend that you click on the rulemaking link at *www.uscourts.gov*.

The questions you must face are: Who should make the rules? And by what process? To help you answer these questions, you will gain some perspective by reading differing views of procedural rulemaking. Professor Struve articulates the tenuous relationship between the Supreme Court's dual roles as both the maker and the arbiter of procedural rules. Professor Burbank concludes that the rulemaking process, bereft of a strong empirical foundation for formulating new policies, should be reconsidered. And Professor Walker defends the judiciary as the most effective rulemaking body among available options. As you read these articles, remember that the Rules and the rulemaking process affect the work of practitioners and their clients on a daily basis, and that frequent changes to the Rules have become an increasingly common feature of the current rulemaking process. In light of these concerns, who should be making procedural rules? The Supreme Court? The judiciary? The legislative branch? Practitioners? Academics? We are also including with these readings an excerpt of the Supreme Court's transmittal letter to Congress of the 1993 amendments (as well as Justice White's statement). These materials will give you some perspective of how the Court views its role in the rulemaking process.

Catherine T. Struve, The Paradox of Delegation: Interpreting the Federal Rules of Civil Procedure
150 U. Pa. L. Rev. 1099, 1129-1131 (2002)

. . . Should the Court wish to alter a Rule already in force, the Enabling Act does not contemplate that the Court could do so outside the rulemaking structure. Though the Court, like other entities, can suggest changes for the rulemakers' consideration, it cannot promulgate such changes against the wishes of the other participants in the rulemaking process.

Accordingly, since the Enabling Act conditions the delegation of rulemaking power on the Court's use of the prescribed procedures, it appears to require the Court to resort to those procedures when seeking to change a Rule. The matter is rendered somewhat more complex, however, by the question of the Court's inherent procedural authority. The Supreme Court has asserted that "certain implied powers must necessarily result" to the federal courts "from the nature of their institution," powers "which cannot be dispensed with . . . because they are necessary to the exercise of all others."

Advocates of judicial discretion thus might argue that, to the extent the Enabling Act's delegation merely duplicates the courts' inherent powers, courts should have greater latitude to interpret freely the Rules promulgated under the Act. Under this view, the Court can weigh policy considerations when exercising its inherent authority, and it should be accorded the same latitude when interpreting the Rules. This argument, however, overlooks the limits of such inherent powers. Although the question is murky . . . it is not at all clear that the federal courts' inherent powers include authority to promulgate rules of procedure. Rather, such inherent authority may be limited to powers necessary to the fulfillment of the courts' Article III responsibilities—a far narrower range than is covered by the current Federal Rules. Moreover, the courts' inherent powers— whatever their initial extent—are subject to Congress's separate authority to regulate federal court procedure. As the Court observed soon after the promulgation of the original Rules, "Congress has undoubted power to regulate the practice and procedure of federal courts, and may exercise that power by delegating to this or other federal courts authority to make rules not inconsistent with the statutes or constitution of the United States." So long as Congress's regulation of federal procedure does not "prevent[] a court from discharging its Article III duties," Congress's directives trump contrary principles adopted by the Supreme Court pursuant to its inherent authority. . . .

Stephen B. Burbank, *Ignorance and Procedural Law Reform*
59 Brook. L. Rev. 841, 841-842, 847, 854-855 (1993)

In 1881, Oliver Wendell Holmes, Jr. observed that "ignorance is the best of law reformers. People are glad to discuss a question on general principles, when they have forgotten the special knowledge necessary for technical reasoning.". . .

I want to suggest that by failing to take seriously the task of defining limitations on the rulemaking power, the Supreme Court and those who assist it have encouraged Congress also to ignore the question of appropriate allocation rules. Similarly, by failing to seek empirical evidence on the operation of the Rules or proposed amendments, the rulemakers have both put their work product at risk of legislative override and encouraged Congress to initiate its own half-baked reforms. We need a moratorium on procedural law reform, whether by court rule or by statute, until such time as we know what we are doing. The knowledge needed concerns alternative reform strategies and their likely impacts, but we also need to know who is responsible for what.

If this sounds like crisis rhetoric . . . so be it. It is difficult, however, not to sense a crisis in federal procedural reform when the Chief Justice's letter transmitting the 1993 amendments to the Federal Rules disclaimed any implication "that the Court itself would have proposed these amendments in the form submitted," and when four other Justices indicated their agnosticism about, lack of competence to evaluate or disagreement with, one or more of the amendments. When a majority of the Supreme Court has washed its hands of proposed Federal Rules, and when some of the Justices have aired the dirty linen, what is it that should restrain Congress from responding to those who wish to do the same?. . .

If neutrality is not to be a prescription for ignorance, the rulemakers must have other sources of information about the likely impact of proposed Federal Rules or amendments that will serve as a surrogate for empirical work. Three possibilities come to mind: the collective experience and wisdom of the rulemakers, information provided through written comments and public hearings and the fruits of scholarly inquiry. It seems to me that the rulemakers' own knowledge base has been shrinking, or should I say narrowing, that their professed distaste for politics and unwillingness to share power have consequentially diminished the utility of public comment and that the nature of scholarship in the aid of legal reform has changed depressingly little since the days when Charles Clark was rewriting the Enabling Act as a scholar to suit his purposes as a rulemaker. . . .

It is time for a breather, for a group that includes rulemakers, members of Congress and members of the bar carefully to review where we have been, where we are going and where we should be going. It is time for a moratorium on ignorance and procedural law reform.

Laurens Walker, Federal Civil Rulemaking
61 Geo. Wash. L. Rev. 455, 459-460 (1993)

. . .The debate about the merits of judicial rulemaking is an old one, and I will not rehearse it, except to say that, in my view, the merits of judicial rulemaking far outweigh the demerits, largely because trial and appellate judges typically bring great expertise to the task. In the specific case of civil rulemaking, trial judges participate in far more trials than attorneys, and appellate judges review these same trials for error. This expertise is a sound starting point for the task of rulemaking. The chief alternative is legislative rulemaking, an alternative that diminishes the pertinent knowledge of the rulemaker. At best, the initial work might be done by legislators who are also attorneys, but enactment would almost certainly be left to a majority of legislators with no expertise at all. Executive participation in rulemaking has essentially the same shortcoming: Judicial expertise will be diminished or lost as an asset. By passing the Rules Enabling Act of 1934, Congress correctly determined that judicial expertise should be the foundation of civil rulemaking in federal courts.

Letter of Transmittal from Justice Rehnquist
Supreme Court of the United States Washington, D.C. 20543

Chambers of
THE CHIEF JUSTICE
April 22, 1993
Dear Mr. Speaker [of the House of Representatives]:

By direction of the Supreme Court of the United States, I have the honor to submit to the Congress amendments to the Federal Rules of Civil Procedure that have been adopted by the Supreme Court pursuant to Section 2072 of Title 28, United States Code. While the Court is satisfied that the required procedures have been observed, this transmittal does not necessarily indicate that the Court itself would have proposed these amendments in the form submitted.

Justice White has issued a separate statement. Justice Scalia has issued a dissenting statement, which Justice Thomas joins and Justice Souter joins in part. . . .

Sincerely,

/s/

William H. Rehnquist

[The Order transmitting the amendments has been omitted.]

SUPREME COURT OF THE UNITED STATES AMENDMENTS TO THE FEDERAL RULES OF CIVIL PROCEDURE [APRIL 22, 1993]

Statement of Justice WHITE.

28 U.S.C. § 2072 empowers the Supreme Court to prescribe general rules of practice and procedure and rules of evidence for cases in the federal courts, including proceedings before magistrates and courts of appeals. But the Court does not itself draft and initially propose these rules. Section 2073 directs the Judicial Conference to prescribe the procedures for proposing the rules mentioned in § 2072. The Conference is authorized to appoint committees to propose such rules. These rules advisory committees are to be made up of members of the professional bar and trial and appellate judges. The Conference is also to appoint a standing committee on rules of practice and evidence to review the recommendations of the advisory committees and to recommend to the Conference such rules and amendments to those rules "as may be necessary to maintain consistency and otherwise promote the interest of justice." § 2073(b). Any rules approved by the Conference are transmitted to the Supreme Court, which in turn transmits

any rules "prescribed" pursuant to § 2072 to the Congress. Except as provided in § 2074(b), such rules become effective at a specified time unless Congress otherwise provides.

The members of the advisory and standing committees are carefully named by The Chief Justice, and I am quite sure that these experienced judges and lawyers take their work very seriously. It is also quite evident that neither the standing committee nor the Judicial Conference merely rubber stamps the proposals recommended to it. It is not at all rare that advisory committee proposals are returned to the originating committee for further study.

During my 31 years on the Court, the number of advisory committees has grown as necessitated by statutory changes. During that time, by my count at least, on some 64 occasions we have "prescribed" and transmitted to Congress a new set of rules or amendments to certain rules. Some of the transmissions have been minor, but many of them have been extensive. Over this time, Justices Black and Douglas, either together or separately, dissented 13 times on the ground that it was inappropriate for the Court to pass on the merits of the rules before it. Aside from those two Justices, Justices Powell, Stewart and then Justice Rehnquist dissented on one occasion and Justice O'Connor on another as to the substance of proposed rules. . . . Only once in my memory did the court refuse to transmit some of the rule changes proposed by the Judicial Conference. . . .

That the Justices have hardly ever refused to transmit the rules submitted by the Judicial Conference and the fact that, aside from Justices Black and Douglas, it has been quite rare for any Justice to dissent from transmitting any such rule, suggest that a sizable majority of the 21 Justices who sat during this period concluded that Congress intended them to have a rather limited role in the rulemaking process. The vast majority (including myself) obviously have not explicitly subscribed to the Black-Douglas view that many of the rules proposed dealt with substantive matters that the Constitution reserved to Congress and that in any event were prohibited by § 2072's injunction against abridging, enlarging or modifying substantive rights.

Some of us, however, have silently shared Justice Black's and Justice Douglas's suggestion that the enabling statutes be amended

> to place the responsibility upon the Judicial Conference rather than upon this Court. Since the statute was first enacted in 1934, 48 Stat. 1064, the Judicial Conference has been enlarged and improved and is now very active in its surveillance of the work of the federal courts and in recommending appropriate legislation to Congress. The present rules produced under 28 U.S.C. § 2072 are not prepared by us but by Committees of the Judicial Conference designated by The Chief Justice, and before coming to us they are approved by the Judicial Conference pursuant to 28 U.S.C. § 331. The Committees and the Conference are composed of able and distinguished members and they render a high public service. It is they, however, who do the work, not we, and the rules have only our imprimatur. The only contribution that we actually make is an occasional exercise of a veto power. If the rule-making for Federal District Courts is to continue under the present plan, we believe that the Supreme Court should not have any

part in the task; rather, the statute should be amended to substitute the Judicial Conference. The Judicial Conference can participate more actively in fashioning the rules and affirmatively contribute to their content and design better than we can. Transfer of the function to the Judicial Conference would relieve us of the embarrassment of having to sit in judgment on the constitutionality of rules which we have approved and which as applied in given situations might have to be declared invalid.

374 U.S. 865, 869-870 (1963) (footnote omitted).

Despite the repeated protestations of both or one of those Justices, Congress did not eliminate our participation in the rulemaking process. Indeed, our statutory role was continued as the coverage of § 2072 was extended to the rules of evidence and to proceedings before magistrates. Congress clearly continued to direct us to "prescribe" specified rules. But most of us concluded that for at least two reasons Congress could not have intended us to provide another layer of review equivalent to that of the standing committee and the Judicial Conference. First, to perform such a function would take an inordinate amount of time, the expenditure of which would be inconsistent with the demands of a growing caseload. Second, some [of] us, and I remain of this view, were quite sure that the Judicial Conference and its committees, "being in large part judges of the lower courts and attorneys who are using the Rules day in and day out, are in a far better position to make a practical judgment upon their utility or inutility than we." 383 U.S. 1089, 1090 (1966) (Douglas, J., dissenting).

I did my share of litigating when in practice and once served on the Advisory Committee for the Civil Rules, but the trial practice is a dynamic profession, and the longer one is away from it the less likely it is that he or she should presume to second-guess the careful work of the active professionals manning the rulemaking committees, work that the Judicial Conference has approved. At the very least, we should not perform a de novo review and should defer to the Judicial Conference and its committees as long as they have some rational basis for their proposed amendments.

Hence, as I have seen the Court's role over the years, it is to transmit the Judicial Conference's recommendations without change and without careful study, as long as there is no suggestion that the committee system has not operated with integrity. If it has not, such a fact, or even such a claim, about a body so open to public inspection would inevitably surface. This has been my practice, even though on several occasions, based perhaps on out-of-date conceptions, I had serious questions about the wisdom of particular proposals to amend certain rules.

In connection with the proposed rule changes now before us, there is no suggestion that the rulemaking process has failed to function properly. No doubt the proposed changes do not please everyone, as letters I have received indicate. But I assume that such opposing views have been before the committees and have been rejected on the merits. That is enough for me.

Justice Douglas thought that the Court should be taken out of the rulemaking process entirely, but as long as Congress insisted on our "prescribing" rules, he refused to be a mere conduit and would dissent to forwarding rule changes with which he disagreed. I note that Justice Scalia seems to follow that example. But I also note that as time went on, Justice Douglas confessed to insufficient familiarity with the context in which new rules would operate to pass judgment on their merits.

In conclusion, I suggest that it would be a mistake for the bench, the bar, or the Congress to assume that we are duplicating the function performed by the standing committee or the Judicial Conference with respect to changes in the various rules which come to us for transmittal. As I have said, over the years our role has been a much more limited one.

PRACTICE EXERCISE NO. 21: ASSESSING THE RULEMAKING PROCESS

You have been asked to testify before the Senate Committee on the Judiciary regarding a proposal to revisit the rulemaking process contemplated by the current Rules Enabling Act. You may assume that Professors Struve, Burbank, and Walker have already testified before this Committee. The senators have asked you for your comments regarding the prior testimony. And they have identified several specific questions as possible lines of inquiry, including:

(1) Are there any separation of powers issues here? If there were no Rules Enabling Act, who would have the responsibility for drafting procedural rules—Congress or the Judiciary?

(2) We have seen throughout this chapter and others the politicization of procedure or, put another way, the ability of procedure to alter or mask substantive intentions. Does the Rules Enabling Act make sense in light of what we now know about the false dichotomy between substance and procedure?

(3) Constitutional issues aside, who is most competent to draft procedural rules? Lawyers? Judges? Academics? Congress? How should that process be designed?

(4) The shelf life of a Federal Rule of Civil Procedure seems to be on a steep decline. Where amendments to Federal Rules used to be relatively few and far between, they are now routine. Does a large number of amendments suggest that the rulemaking process is working or, rather, that it is not working?

(5) What rulemaking process would be called for if *efficiency* in the judicial system were the sole or at least a primary criterion?

Prepare to be called upon to share your thoughts with regard to the Federal Rules of Civil Procedure. Naturally, you should prepare to explain and defend any reforms suggested in your remarks.

CHAPTER 5

The Right to Jury Trial and Judicial Control of Results

T his chapter explores the debate over the civil jury, as well as the doctrine of the right to jury trial and the many methods for controlling the jury or preventing cases from reaching a trial, such as summary judgment, judgment as a matter of law (directed verdict and JNOV), jury instructions, motions for new trial, motions to vacate judgment, special verdicts, bifurcation, and remittitur and additur. The chapter ends with sections on closing arguments and appeals.

A. VALUES AND HISTORICAL BACKGROUND

1. Introduction

When the Federal Rules of Civil Procedure were enacted, about 18 percent of civil cases in federal court were resolved by trial.* That percentage eroded to about 12 percent in 1962 and is now just above 1 percent. Tort cases such as *Carpenter v. Dee* had a 1-in-4 chance of reaching trial in 1938, but today have approximately a 1-in-90 chance. And of that narrow slice of cases that reach a trial, approximately two-thirds of those will be tried to a jury. Why, then, would a course in Civil Procedure have a whole chapter on "The Right to Jury Trial and Judicial Control of Results"? Despite the relative paucity of actual civil jury trials, or of civil trials of any kind, the right to jury trial is claimed in a substantial percentage of cases, and the filing, preparation, and settlement of lawsuits is often done "in the shadow" of educated guesses about what a jury would ultimately decide if a jury trial did take place. Moreover, it is difficult to understand much of current civil procedure, and of the development of American law generally (and particularly in the field of evidence), without

---

* Marc Galanter, *A World Without Trials?*, 2006 J. Disp. Resol. 7, 12-13.

taking account of the historical ambivalence in our country about juries. You will see as this chapter unfolds, that there is a good deal of procedural doctrine defining and protecting the right to civil jury trial, accompanied by many different procedures to control juries and their verdicts, developed as a result of judicial distrust of laypeople's ability to act without prejudice and to deal with complexity.

Major tensions in American civil procedure emerge in debates about the civil jury and in the doctrine that has developed both to protect and to control the jury: formalism and definition versus narrative and less constraint; experts versus laypeople. Heated disputes in our society on issues of race and gender come to the fore in doctrinal battles about the selection and composition of juries. Political views influence whether one reads the right to jury trial more or less broadly and whether one would restrict or liberate the jury in the evidence they hear, the manner in which they are instructed, and the deference given to their decisions.

This chapter begins with two orientation sections, the first providing excerpts from the ongoing debate about the American civil jury and the second outlining a brief history of the development of the jury. You will then read about the constitutional right to trial by jury in civil cases and the quite complicated case law that has attempted to define that right. The Seventh Amendment to the U.S. Constitution states:

> In Suits at common law, where the value in controversy shall exceed twenty dollars, the right of trial by jury shall be preserved, and no fact tried by a jury shall be otherwise re-examined in any Court of the United States, than according to the rules of the common law.

The language "shall be preserved" has caused the Supreme Court to consider the extent to which one had the right to a civil jury as of 1791, when the Bill of Rights became part of the Constitution. Consequently, history is important not only to understand the context of another element of civil procedure, the jury, but also because courts turn to history in attempting to define the right.

Part C of this chapter covers the doctrine and practice that have developed around jury selection. You will see once again how a procedural issue becomes a lightning rod for ongoing cultural arguments about race and gender. The remainder of the chapter covers many different ways that have developed to influence, control, and overturn jury verdicts. Issues that you have previously heard about, such as summary judgment and directed verdict (now called judgment as a matter of law), will now be covered in more detail. And you will learn that some of this doctrine, such as ending a case early because there is insufficient evidence to permit the plaintiff to win, also governs cases in which the judge—not the jury—is the trier of fact, with permutations to take account of that difference.

As you read the following passages favoring or opposing the American civil jury, along with the remainder of the chapter, which explores jury composition and jury control, try to formulate and defend your own opinions about the continued utility (or lack thereof) of the civil jury. What are the most compelling arguments, pro and con?

2. The Debate over the American Civil Jury

What do modern juries do in the United States? In civil cases, they are instructed to impartially weigh the evidence, to decide what actually happened in the dispute ("the facts"), and to apply the law (as given by the judge) to those facts. The strategic importance of the jury in modern legal practice, then, is unquestioned, both in those cases actually decided by a jury and those settled in their "shadow." But the jury as an institution has been a target of sustained criticism for centuries. At the present time, about 80 percent of the jury trials in the world are conducted in the United States, a fact not lost on opponents of the jury concept: "Some opponents of the civil jury cite its abolition in other legal systems as evidence that civil juries are outmoded. Indeed, the use of civil juries has declined significantly in Canada and Australia and has effectively disappeared in England, their country of origin." *Developments in the Law—The Civil Jury*, 110 Harv. L. Rev. 1408, 1411 (1997). But the reforms are not unidirectional: There are also countries such as Japan, Russia, South Korea, and Spain that have introduced (or re-introduced) juries into their legal systems, although primarily for criminal cases. *See* Toby S. Gelbach et al., *The Movement of U.S. Criminal and Administrative Law: Processes of Transplanting and Translating*, 20 Ind. J. Global Legal. Stud. 141, 158 (2013) (recognizing that fifty-four countries now use jury trials "despite popular perceptions of the institution as a key source of the long delays and great costs associated with adversarial trials"); Nancy S. Marder, *An Introduction to Comparative Jury Systems*, 86 Chi.-Kent L. Rev. 453 (2011) (suggesting that the jury may be "experiencing a renaissance" worldwide).

Those who oppose the use of the civil jury usually make efficiency arguments, emphasize the amateurish nature of lay jurors, and aver that jurors are influenced by prejudice and passion. Supporters, increasingly relying on empirical data, dispute such assumptions about inefficiency and incompetence. Moreover, they argue that the civil jury plays critical roles in a democracy—legitimizing the process, curbing arbitrary judicial behavior, inculcating community values, and permitting citizen participation and education, in addition to providing neutral, fair, and accurate dispute resolution. Consider the following voices from the debate, past and present, and draw your own conclusions:

Mark Twain said, "The jury system puts a ban upon intelligence and honesty, and a premium upon ignorance, stupidity, and perjury. It is a shame that we must continue to use a worthless system because it was good a thousand years ago." Mark Twain, *Roughing It* 309 (1872).

Dean Erwin Griswold of Harvard Law School said, "Even in the best of cases trial by jury is the apotheosis of amateurs. How can anyone think that 12 people selected at random in twelve different ways with the only criterion being a complete lack of general qualification, would have special ability to decide on disputes between people?" Erwin N. Griswold, Harvard Law School, Dean's Report 5-6 (1962-1963).

And Edward J. Devitt, a statesman who served in the U.S. House of Representatives and was later appointed to the federal bench, wrote:

> [W]e live in a different age now and our society has grown increasingly complex, as has our legal system. In earlier times, a jury might have been called upon to sit for a day or two to consider a simple dispute between neighbors. Today, however, a jury often finds itself sitting for many months, attempting to assimilate mountains of evidence in controversies pitting large corporations against each other in complicated cases involving antitrust, securities, tax, patent, and similar business related issues. . . .
>
> A lengthy trial . . . may make it impossible to impanel a jury of impartial minds of diverse backgrounds. It is unrealistic to suppose that employed persons, who compose the group most likely to have any familiarity with business matters of the type frequently at issue in lengthy litigation, would be available for jury service in lengthy trials. Judge Charles L. Brieant of the Southern District of New York aptly put it: "[M]ust litigants be left with a panel consisting solely of retired people, the idle rich, those on welfare, and housewives whose children are grown? Hardly a 'fair cross section of the community wherein the court convenes.'" . . .
>
> Studies of this subject suggest that factual issues presented in a case can be considered complex, either when the facts needing resolution are conceptually difficult for a non-specialist to understand, or when the facts are made difficult by the volume of evidentiary material needed to establish them. It also has been suggested that legal issues can be considered complex when they are multiple, overlapping, ambiguous, or pose issues requiring instructions on close questions of statutory interpretation. Even with instructions carefully crafted with an eye toward clarity and simplicity, it is practically impossible in some specialized fields of law to guide a jury through the awesome job of rationally applying complex instructions to a huge volume of technical evidence.

Edward J. Devitt, *Should Jury Trial Be Required in Civil Cases? A Challenge to the Seventh Amendment*, 47 J. Air L. & Com. 495, 497, 498, 500 (1982).

Jerome T. Frank, Courts on Trial
110-111, 129-130 (1949)

. . . There are three theories of the jury's function:

(1) The naive theory is that the jury merely finds the facts; that it must not, and does not, concern itself with the legal rules, but faithfully accepts the rules as stated to them by the trial judge.

(2) A more sophisticated theory has it that the jury not only finds the facts but, in its deliberation in the jury-room, uses legal reasoning to apply to those facts the legal rules it learned from the judge. . . .

This theory ascribes to jurors a serpentine wisdom. It assumes that they thoroughly understand what the judge tells them about the rules, and that they circumvent the rules by falsely contriving—with consummate skill and cunning—the exact findings of fact which, correlated with those rules, will logically compel the result they desire.

(3) We come now to a third theory which may be called the "realistic" theory. It is based on what anyone can discover by questioning the average person who has served as a juror—namely that often the jury are neither able to, nor do they attempt to, apply the instructions of the court. The jury are more brutally direct. They determine that they want Jones to collect $5,000 from the railroad company, or that they don't want pretty Nellie Brown to go to jail for killing her husband; and they bring in their general verdict accordingly. Often, to all practical intents and purposes, the judge's statement of the legal rules might just as well never have been expressed. . . .

The "realistic" theory, then, is that, in many cases, the jury, often without heeding the legal rules, determine, not the "facts," but the respective legal rights and duties of the parties to the suit. For the judgment of the court usually follows the general verdict of the jury, so that the verdict results in a decision which determines those rights and duties. . . .

The [pro-jury] argument that juries make better rules than judges do has at least the virtue of honestly admitting the realities—of conceding that jurors often disregard what the trial judge tells the jurors about the [rules]. But as a rational defense of the jury system, it is surely curious. It asserts that, desirably, each jury is a twelve-man ephemeral legislature, not elected by the voters, but empowered to destroy what the elected legislators have enacted or authorized. Each jury is thus a legislative assembly, legislating independently of all others. For even if a jury does no more than nullify a legal rule by refusing to apply it in a particular lawsuit, yet it is legislating, since the power to destroy legal rules is legislative power. This argument for the jury should lead to a revised description of our legislative system to show that it consists, in the case of our federal government for instance, of (1) a Senate, (2) a House of Representatives, and (3) a multitude of juries.

I have one objection to such a description: I think it too sophisticated. It implies that the members of the ordinary jury say to themselves, "We don't like this legal rule of which the judge told us, and we won't apply it but will apply one of our own making." But when, as often happens, juries do not understand what the judge said to them about the applicable rule, it simply is not true that they refuse to follow it because they dislike it. Many juries in reaching their verdicts act on their emotional responses to the lawyers and the witnesses; they like or dislike, not any legal rule, but they do like an artful lawyer for the plaintiff, the poor widow, the brunette with the soulful eyes, and they do dislike the big corporation, the Italian with the thick, foreign accent. We do not have uniform jury nullification of harsh rules; we have juries avoiding—often in ignorance that they are so doing—excellent as well as bad rules, and in capricious fashion.

Harry Kalven, The Dignity of the Civil Jury
50 U. Va. L. Rev. 1055, 1059-1067 (1964)

How much longer is a jury trial than a bench trial? . . . By using a series of estimates, we reached the conclusion that on the average a bench trial would be 40 percent less time consuming than a jury trial of the same case. . . .

As we come to the merits of the institution, it may be useful to sketch three main heads under which criticism and defense of the jury have fallen.

First, there is a series of collateral advantages and disadvantages such as the fact that the jury provides an important civic experience for the citizen; that, because of popular participation the jury makes tolerable the stringency of certain decisions; or that because of its transient personnel the jury acts as a lightning rod for animosity and suspicion which might otherwise center on the more exposed judge; or that the jury is a guarantor of integrity since it is said to be more difficult to reach twelve men than one. On the negative side it is urged that jury fees are an added expense to the administration of justice; that jury service often imposes an unfair economic and social burden on those forced to serve; and that exposure to jury service disenchants the citizen and leads him to lose confidence in the administration of justice.

Although many of these considerations loom large in the tradition of jury debate, they are unamenable to research and will not concern us here. We have, however, collected considerable data bearing on the reaction of jurors to service. It will suffice for present purposes simply to state that there is much evidence that most people, once actually serving in a trial, become highly serious and responsible toward their task and toward the joint effort to deliberate to a verdict. . . . The heart of the matter, the trial itself and deliberation, is very often a major and moving experience in the life of the citizen-juror.

The second cluster of issues goes to the competence of the jury. Can it follow and remember the presentation of the facts and weigh the conflicting evidence? Can it follow and remember the law? Can it deliberate effectively?

The third cluster of issues goes to the adherence of the jury to the law, to what its admirers call its sense of equity and what its detractors view as its taste for anarchy.

The latter two issues go to the heart of the debate and have long been the occasion for a heated exchange of proverbs. Further, they may seem so heavily enmeshed in difficult value judgments as to make further discussion unpromising. Yet it is precisely here that our empirical studies can offer some insight, although they too cannot fully dispose of the issues.

When one asserts that jury adjudication is of low quality, he must be asserting that jury decisions vary in some significant degree from those a judge would have made in the same cases.

[The University of Chicago Jury Project found that, in a study of several thousand personal injury cases, judges and juries agreed on liability in 79 percent of cases. "The judge disagrees with the jury because he is more pro-plaintiff about as often as the jury disagrees with him because it is more pro-plaintiff." In awarding damages, there is more disagreement. Of the 44 percent of cases where both judge and jury agreed, the jury gave the higher award in 23 percent, the judge gave a higher award in 17 percent, and the awards were approximately equal in 4 percent of cases. Jury awards averaged about 20 percent higher than those of the judge.]

There are . . . some further observations about the issue of jury competence. We have been told often enough that the jury trial is a process whereby twelve inexperienced laymen, who are probably strangers to each other, are invited to apply law which they will not understand to facts which they will not get straight and by secret deliberation arrive at a group decision. We are told also that heroic feats of learning law, remembering facts, and running an orderly discussion as a group are called for in every jury trial. . . .

In the judge-jury survey the trial judge, among other things, classified each case as to whether it was "difficult to understand" or "easy." We can therefore spell out the following hypothesis to test against the judge-jury data. If the jury has a propensity not to understand, that propensity should be more evident in the cases rated by the judges as difficult than in those rated as easy. Further, disagreement should be higher in cases which the jury does not understand than in cases which they do understand since, where the jury misunderstands the case, it must be deciding on a different basis than the judge. We reach, then, the decisive hypothesis to test, namely, that the jury should disagree more often with the judges in difficult cases than in easy ones. However, when we compare the decision patterns in easy cases with those in difficult cases we find that the level of disagreement remains the same. . . .

Any mystery as to why the plausible *a priori* surmises of jury incompetence should prove so wrong is considerably reduced when we take a closer look at the dynamics of the jury process, a look we have been able to take as a result of intensive and extensive post-trial juror interviews in actual cases and as a result of complete observation of jury deliberations in mock experimental cases, a technique used widely in the project. We observed that the trial had structured the communication to the jury far more than the usual comment recognizes and had made certain points quite salient. A more important point is that the jury can operate by *collective* recall. Different jurors remember, and make available to all, different items of the trial so that the jury as a group remembers far more than most of its members could as individuals. It tends, in this connection, to be as strong as its strongest link. The conclusion, therefore, is that the jury understands well enough for its purposes and that its intellectual incompetence has been vastly exaggerated. . . .

Valerie P. Hans and Neil Vidmar, Judging the Jury
247-249 (1986)

In judging the jury there are some other issues to consider.* The first concerns the alternatives to the jury. In France, West Germany, and some other European countries, mixed tribunals composed of a judge and prominent laypersons decide legal cases. In Britain, minor crimes are tried in a magistrate's courts by tribunals of laypersons. However, in most instances those who advocate abolition of the jury propose that the jury's work should be done by a judge. The question then becomes, are judges really superior to juries? Unfortunately, we have little data about the competency of judges, though . . . we know that the jury would agree with their decisions in four cases out of five. To be sure, judges have training in law, and perhaps, as Judge Frank claimed, they attempt to be more scientific in their approach to the evidence. On the other hand, many knowledgeable legal commentators have argued that judges are not necessarily better triers of fact. A jury which contains one or more persons proficient in automobile repair might be far better at assessing evidence in a products liability case involving a car manufacturer than a judge whose experience with things mechanical is limited to changing a spare tire. Even if one argues that the average judge is smarter in discerning legal facts than the average juror, is the judge as smart as twelve jurors?

We must also consider the fact that trials are about justice as well as law. The inescapable fact is that despite attempts in recent years to recruit minority group members and women into the judiciary, the overwhelming majority of judges are still white males who come from a privileged sector of our society. Often their views of the world reflect their backgrounds. Some rather rigidly adhere to a narrow perspective of justice and fairness that is not consistent with that of the general community. . . .

There are two other aspects to the political side of the jury. One is its "legitimating" function. In a democracy the average citizen obeys the law not so much because of its threat but because he or she grants it legitimacy, that is, accepts it as a body of rules to be followed. It may be true that democracies can survive without juries. Many Western democracies do not have juries and seem to function quite well. Yet, in the United States, Canada and Great Britain, the jury is an important symbol that helps to confer legitimacy to law.

The remaining political aspect of the jury concerns its socializing function. Not only does the jury system allow the people to contribute to the legal system, but the legal system, through the jury, contributes to the education of the people.

* * *

There is widespread agreement that jury verdicts help lawyers and their clients assess the value of cases for settlement purposes. Moreover, jury verdicts influence behavior, particularly when the parties are informed professionals or employed in a business in which profit is influenced by financial losses, real or potential. Indeed, one purpose of the tort liability system is to deter unreasonable behavior, and the jury often determines what is reasonable.

Although trials (and especially civil trials) are vanishing, many Americans still participate each year in the jury process. According to the National Center for State Courts, approximately 15 percent of the adult American population is summoned to jury service each year in state and federal courts, and an estimated 8 to 10 million citizens report for jury service. *See* National Center for State Courts, *http://www.ncsc.org/Services-and-Experts/Areas-of-expertise/Jury-management.aspx* (last visited November 1, 2015). In a 2012 survey, researchers found that about 27 percent of the adult population (including 53 percent of senior citizens) report having served on a jury at some point in their lives. *See* DRI, The Voice of the Defense Bar, *The DRI National Poll on the Civil Jury System* 5-6 (Aug. 2012). Further, 75 percent of Americans view a jury summons more as "a civic duty to fulfill" rather than as "a burden to avoid." *Id.* at 5. For results of a fascinating study by social scientists who examined Americans' willingness to serve on juries, see Marc A. Musick et al., *Much Obliged: Volunteering, Normative Activities, and Willingness to Serve on Juries,* 40 Law & Soc. Inquiry 433 (2015) (advocating that the public service and duty-based nature of jury participation be emphasized).

> Americans might not always agree with the verdict that any given jury renders, but they continue to express their support for the jury system in poll after poll. If jury trials were to disappear altogether in the United States, many Americans would undoubtedly feel that they had lost an essential protection and an important tradition. They may experience dismay upon receiving a summons for jury duty, but those who actually serve on a jury usually view their experience favorably and form a positive view of the jury. Jury duty, though resisted initially, eventually inspires those who serve on a jury to participate more actively in their democracy, such as by voting.

Nancy S. Marder and Valerie P. Hans, *Introduction to Juries and Lay Participation: American Perspective and Global Trends,* 90 Chi.-Kent L. Rev. 789, 789 (2015) (footnotes and citations omitted).

Indeed, those who serve on juries usually find it a positive and important experience:

> Nearly every juror interviewed for this book is proud of the job he or she did, proud of the seriousness of deliberations, proud of having exercised power soberly, proud—rightly or wrongly—of the verdicts that were reached. More than when they vote, or pay taxes, or attend a parade, they are realizing the democratic vision that still sustains our nation: They are governing themselves. . . . There's disorder in the court but not despair. The jury system can be saved and is, for all our disappointments, well worth saving.

Stephen J. Adler, *Trial and Error in the American Courtroom* 242 (1994).

According to a survey conducted by the defense bar, "64 percent of Americans say they prefer to have juries rather than judges decide lawsuits, including 41 percent who feel that way 'strongly,' a high level of strong sentiment. Far fewer, 27 percent, prefer to have judges decide civil cases, and just 13 percent hold that view strongly." DRI, The Voice of the Defense Bar, *The DRI National Poll on the Civil Jury System* 4 (Aug. 2012).

You have read about the famous Kalven and Zeisel University of Chicago Jury Project, conducted in the 1950s, which found that judges and juries agreed on liability approximately 80 percent of the time in personal injury cases. More recently, scholars deploying an array of research methods, "including comparing jury verdicts with judicial evaluations, analysis of verdict patterns and trends, questionnaires and interviews with jurors and other trial participants, and mock jury studies," continue to find that by any measure, juries appear to act competently most of the time—regardless of the complexity of the issues raised. David A. Logan, *Juries, Judges, and the Politics of Tort Reform,* 83 U. Cin. L. Rev. 903, 923-924 (2015) (citing studies).

> On average, judges are far better educated than the average juror, for almost all judges have both a college and an advanced degree. But a jury is not composed of average jurors. They are an array of individuals, some of whom may be as well or better educated than the judge, while others, although poorly educated academically, may have case-relevant knowledge that a better educated judge lacks; for example, an auto mechanic with a tenth grade education in a case where an accident was allegedly due to faulty brakes. Moreover, juries deliberate, and most often, the collective judgments of diverse groups are superior to judgments reached by individuals.
>
> In many ways, however, it is a mistake to compare the fact-finding competency of juries and judges as separate entities. What is important is how they work together. Thus, some years ago when I reviewed a number of cases studies that examined jury performance in complex cases, I found that the jury did not always cover itself with glory. There were cases where it was clear the jury did not understand the evidence and reached verdicts that were questionable if not clearly wrong. But in almost every such case, either the judge or one or both lawyers performed poorly, sometimes indicating that they did not understand the case or making tactical decisions that came back to haunt them. When the trial judge was competent and in control of the proceedings, jury verdicts were invariably defensible, usually appeared correct and suggested a good understanding of the case. In another article, I had the occasion to look at how federal judges handled statistical evidence in Title VII employment discrimination cases. It was discouragingly easy to find cases where judges sitting alone, or sometimes as part of larger courts, misunderstood the import of statistical evidence and reached verdicts that seemed not to fairly reflect the evidence. So just as judges can ensure against jury verdicts reflecting bias or a poor understanding of the evidence, the jury can protect against decisions based on judicial biases or judicial mistakes in comprehension. The jury system is a system, and both the judge and jury are key components. When they both perform well, fair trials and accurate verdicts are the rule and not the exception.

Richard Lempert, *The American Jury System: A Synthetic Overview,* 90 Chi.-Kent L. Rev. 825, 838-840 (2015) (footnotes and citations omitted).

Punitive Damages. One of the major battlegrounds in the debate over the positive and negative aspects of the American jury is punitive damages. Probably the most notorious example of allegedly irresponsible or "runaway" jury behavior is the famous (or infamous) McDonald's coffee spill case.

> The story, as widely reported, involved an elderly woman who suffered serious burns when she spilled a cup of McDonald's coffee on herself. Later, she sued McDonald's and a jury awarded her $160,000 in actual damages and $2.9 million in punitive damages, amounts that strike people learning of the incident as outrageous. The fuller version, as reported in a detailed account in the Wall Street Journal, leaves a different impression. An eighty-one-year old woman, Stella Liebeck, spilled the coffee on herself while sitting in a parked car when she took the lid from a Styrofoam cup to add cream. Her burns were so severe that she needed skin grafts and was hospitalized for a week, and her daughter, a nurse, had to take time off from her job to care for her. Far from being a greedy plaintiff, which is how she was widely portrayed, Liebeck initially asked McDonald's for only a few thousand dollars to pay her hospital bills and to modestly compensate her for her pain. McDonald's offered eight hundred dollars, which did not begin to cover her expenses. Shortly before trial, in accord with local procedure, the case was brought before a mediator who found that an award of $225,000 was appropriate. McDonald's turned this down and chose to litigate. The evidence at trial revealed that McDonald's instructed its franchisees to serve its coffee at a temperature of 180 to 190 degrees, which was about twenty degrees higher than the temperature of the coffee served at other similar establishments; that it took only three seconds for coffee that hot to cause third degree burns; that McDonald's knew of more than seven hundred other instances when spilled coffee had caused burns, and that it had paid these victims a total of more than $500,000 to forestall or settle lawsuits. Despite this, McDonald's had neither changed its coffee temperature directive, nor taken adequate steps to warn customers of the harm that its coffee, if spilled, might cause. After hearing this and other evidence, the jury awarded Ms. Liebeck $160,000 for her actual damages, reduced from $200,000 because they found her twenty percent at fault, and awarded $2.9 million in punitive damages, later reduced by the trial judge to $480,000. Whether one agrees with the outcome or not, we do not have the horror story heard around the world. Nor is there any reason to think that the jury verdict was motivated by sympathy for the "little guy" or hostility toward big business. Indeed, one juror indicated that after learning what the suit was about, he wanted to be on the jury so that he could deny recovery and teach Ms. Liebeck a lesson. The facts of the case changed his mind and the views of other jurors. The result was a verdict within reason produced by a system in which a judge's judgment may temper that of a jury.

Lempert, *The American Jury System,* 90 Chi.-Kent L. Rev. at 840-841 (footnotes and citations omitted).

News stories about blockbuster punitive damages awards by juries lead many to conclude that juries are arbitrary, erratic, unpredictable, and unreliable. To be sure, blockbuster punitive damages almost always are the product of juries rather than judges. *See* Joni Hersch and W. Kip Viscusi, *Punitive Damages: How Judges and Juries Perform*, 33 J. Legal Stud. 1 (2004) (reporting that of the 63 punitive damage awards of at least $100 million, 95 percent were awarded by juries). But the story of blockbuster awards is not the whole story about punitive damages. Punitive damages in *any* amount are imposed in less than 1 percent of all civil cases, and blockbuster awards are almost anomalous. *See* Theodore Eisenberg and Michael Heise, *Judge-Jury Difference in Punitive Damages Awards: Who Listens to the Supreme Court?*, 8 J. Empirical Legal Stud. 325, 330 (2011).

> When they do award punitive damages, judges and juries do not differ significantly in their rates of awarding punitive damages. In fact, "the bulk of punitive damages awards have been reasonably sober, modest in size, and relatively stable over time." In trial cases where the plaintiff prevails, judges award punitive damages approximately 4.8% of the time, and juries award them approximately 3.4% of the time. In the unusual occurrence when a jury awards punitive damages, the awards are generally not in jaw-dropping amounts. More than half of punitive damages cases involve awards of less than $100,000; 86.6% involve awards of less than $1 million. In other words, juries who impose significant punitive damages are the relatively rare exception.
>
> Another factor in the perception that juries award outrageous punitive damages is the difference in the type of cases judges and juries hear. Juries hear most tort disputes, whereas judges hear most contract disputes. Punitive damages are generally not available in contract disputes, meaning juries decide most punitive damage awards. However, despite this finding, several studies show judges awarded a "surprisingly high fraction"—31.3%, according to one study—of the total number of punitive damages awards given. In fact, more than juries, judges tend to award punitive damages in cases with higher financial stakes, whether the defendant is an individual or a corporation.

Cortney E. Lollar, *Punitive Compensation*, 51 Tulsa L. Rev. 99, 123 (2015) (footnotes and citations omitted).

Although there are undoubtedly cases in which punitive damages awarded by juries are exorbitant and unfair (a topic discussed in Chapter 2), perhaps the *McDonald's* case and others like it show that the jury, the jury trial, and the punitive damages worked exactly as they should. One group of scholars, however, using simulations to discern how diverse groups of people would assess punitive damages, found that jurors were likely to be very predictable and sound in determining the degree of outrageousness in behavior, but that they would be highly arbitrary and unpredictable in placing a dollar amount on that behavior. Cass R. Sunstein, Daniel Kahneman, and David Schkade, *Assessing Punitive Damages (With Notes on Cognition and Valuation in Law)*, 107 Yale L.J. 2071 (1998).

The Competence of Juries. One consequence of the perception that juries are incompetent and/or unpredictable is the growth of a new profession of jury consultants. Many jury consultants emphasize the ways in which their services can leverage jurors' incompetence and/or predict jury trial outcomes.

The Arizona Jury Filming Project provides useful insight into the jury deliberation process. The Arizona Supreme Court, in conjunction with the American Bar Foundation (and with the consent of all of the participants), videotaped fifty actual civil jury deliberations. Results from this project paint a very positive picture of juries—suggesting that jurors are, on the whole, competent, unbiased, and diligent. American Bar Foundation, *How Civil Juries Really Decide Cases*, 18 Researching L., No. 2 (Spring 2007).

Policy Arguments in Favor of Juries. In thinking about the burdens and benefits of the American jury, punitive damages, and civil litigation in America generally, there is one other critical consideration. The United States relies less on government for the enforcement of social norms and also supplies less of a safety net for its citizens than many other countries. Much of the task of the enforcement of safety standards falls on the civil litigation system, and in turn on juries. One wanting to dramatically alter our heavy reliance on civil litigation and juries would, to act sensibly, have to consider whether to forgo whatever deterrence and compensation the current private civil litigation system provides or whether to replace it with governmental activity of a different and more substantial nature. *See generally* Sean Farhang, *The Litigation State* (Princeton 2010).

Detractors of the jury system must also defend the baggage that attends the alternative: judicial determination. Are judges immune from the criticism that, like juries, some may be ignorant, emotional, prejudiced, or unpredictable? In fact, judges are subject to many of the same psychological tendencies that influence laypeople. *See generally* Chris Guthrie et al., *Blinking on the Bench: How Judges Decide Cases*, 93 Cornell L. Rev. 1, 43 (2007); Jeffrey J. Rachlinski et al., *Does Unconscious Race Bias Affect Trial Judges?*, 84 Notre Dame L. Rev. 1195 (2008). *See also* Daniel Givelber and Amy Farrell, *Not Guilty: Are the Acquitted Innocent?* 134-136 (2012) (demonstrating how, in criminal cases, there is empirical evidence that when juries considered the case strong for defendants, judges would convict blacks at five times the rate of juries, and they appeared to be most satisfied with case outcomes when the composition of the jury was all white, as opposed to when at least one-third of the jury was black).

More than forty states rely upon some form of election to choose their judges. *See* Mark Walsh, *A Pragmatic Turn: Judges May Not Seek Campaign Cash, But They May Express Their Gratitude,* A.B.A. J. 19 (July 2015). For a discussion of the untoward effects that can result when judges are elected, see James Sample et al., *The New Politics of Judicial Elections 2000-2009: Decade of Change* 1-4 (2010) (finding that the consequences of judicial elections include a surge in campaign spending, a rise in attack ads, and the loss of public faith in the judiciary). *See also* Dmitry Bam, *Voter Ignorance and Judicial Elections,* 102 Ky. L.J. 553, 580 (2014); Hon. Raymond J. McKoski, *Living with Judicial Elections,* 39 U. Ark.-L.R. L. Rev. 491 (2017).

QUESTIONS TO PONDER

1. Consider again the tiny fraction of cases that reach a jury trial. Describe the profile of cases that are most likely to reach that stage of litigation. For example, would it be the cases where compensatory and punitive damages are high (or low)? Would it be cases where liability and/or damages are more ambiguous (or more certain)? Do you think that *Carpenter v. Dee* has characteristics that would make it a case likely to reach a trial?

2. Which pro-jury arguments do you find the strongest? Which anti-jury arguments are most persuasive? What other arguments can you imagine for and against the use of juries in particular cases?

3. Do *Twombly* and *Iqbal* offer any hint as to how the Court perceives the importance and centrality of juries?

Three Current Debates About Juries.

1. *Size.* "In a series of decisions in the 1970s [*Williams v. Florida*, 399 U.S. 78 (1970); *Colgrove v. Battin*, 413 U.S. 149 (1973); *Ballew v. Georgia*, 435 U.S. 223 (1978)], the U.S. Supreme Court set aside 600 years of settled common law tradition and two centuries of constitutional history, including the reversal of its own precedents to the contrary, in holding that both criminal and civil juries smaller than 12 do not violate constitutional requirements. Many states and federal districts took advantage of the permission that the Court, in effect, granted them to reduce the size of their juries. . . . [T]he majority of justices concluded that the size of the jury made no difference, at least down to sizes as small as six." Michael J. Saks, *The Smaller the Jury, the Greater the Unpredictability*, 79 Judicature 263 (Mar.-Apr. 1996).

   There is now a great deal of theory and empirical data suggesting that the Supreme Court was mistaken and that in fact twelve-person juries better represent the community, better recall trial details, deliberate longer, return better considered verdicts, and improve the collective experience of the group. Thomas Gilovich et al., Social Psychology 555-566 (2d ed. 2011); Valerie P. Hans, *The Power of Twelve: The Impact of Jury Size and Unanimity on Civil Jury Decision Making*, 4 Del. L. Rev. 1, 8 (2001); Shari Seidman Diamond et al., *Achieving Diversity on the Jury: Jury Size and the Peremptory Challenge*, 6 J. Empirical Legal Stud. 425 (2009); Samuel R. Somers, *On Racial Diversity and Group Decision Making: Identifying Multiple Effects of Racial Composition on Jury Deliberations*, 90 J. Personality & Soc. Psychol. 597 (2006). *See also In re Relafen Antitrust Litigation,* 231 F.R.D. 52 (D. Mass. 2005) (Young, J.); *EIU Group, Inc. v. Citibank Delaware, Inc.,* 429 F. Supp. 2d 367 (D. Mass. 2006) (Young, J.).

2. *Unanimity.* The Seventh Amendment preserves the essential elements of trial by jury, rather than particular details. Although it long had been

supposed that a unanimous verdict was, except as waived by the parties, an essential element of trial by jury, "whether it is constitutionally required is now a matter of doubt. . . . There are no recent opinions on the requirement of unanimity in civil cases, but if the issue should arise, it seems very likely that the Court would hold that unanimity is not required." Charles A. Wright and Mary Kay Kane, *Federal Practice & Procedure: Federal Practice Deskbook* § 100 at 670-671 n.5 (2d ed. 2019). Fed. R. Civ. P. 48 requires a unanimous verdict "[u]nless the parties otherwise stipulate." Some jury simulation studies suggest that moving to non-unanimity in jury verdicts may have some unfortunate consequences. For example, when unanimity, is required, deliberations may last longer, but evaluation of the evidence and the law may be more thorough, jurors in the minority may participate more actively in the discussion and be more listened to, and jurors may be more satisfied with the final verdict. Valerie P. Hans and Neil Vidmar, *Judging the Jury* 175 (1986). *See also* Shari Seidman Diamond, Mary R. Rose, and Beth Murphy, *Revisiting the Unanimity Requirement: The Behavior of the Non-Unanimous Civil Jury,* 100 Nw. U. L. Rev. 201, 229-230 (2006) (observing that individuals who hold minority positions are disempowered). Further, "[s]maller juries, and those that need only reach a majority decision, might be more unpredictable than larger unanimous decision-making bodies." Valerie P. Hans and Theodore Eisenberg, *The Predictability of Juries,* 60 DePaul L. Rev. 375, 378 (2011). Justice Douglas vigorously argued that "human experience teaches that polite and academic conversation is no substitute for the earnest and robust argument necessary to reach unanimity." *Johnson v. Louisiana,* 406 U.S. 380, 389 (1972) (Douglas, J.) (dissenting).

3. *Complexity.* Some argue that in complex civil cases that are apt to last a long time, the Constitution does not require a jury trial. In an enigmatic footnote in *Ross v. Bernhard*, 396 U.S. 531, 538 n.10 (1970), the Supreme Court mentioned a new factor, in addition to custom and remedy sought, as relevant to whether a party is entitled to a jury trial under the Seventh Amendment: "the practical abilities and limitations of juries." Some have also argued that there exist English precedents before 1791 for an exception to the Seventh Amendment for complex cases. Others have made a similar argument, relying on the Due Process Clause of the Fifth Amendment. These arguments "have been raised in a number of federal courts, but the question has not been resolved by the Supreme Court. . . . The Ninth Circuit rejected these arguments finding that there is no complexity exception to be found in the Seventh Amendment. *In re U.S. Financial Securities Litig.*, 609 F.2d 411 (9th Cir.), cert. denied, 446 U.S. 929 (1979). . . . One year later, in *In re Japanese Electronic Prods. Antitrust Litig.*, 631 F.2d 1069 (3rd Cir.), rev'd on other grounds, 475 U.S. 574 (1980), the Third Circuit also rejected the historical and the juror capacity arguments, but tentatively accepted the argument based on due process rights. . . . The court concluded that if a jury could not reach a verdict through a

rational process because of the complexity of a case, a jury trial would violate due process. In these instances, the Third Circuit held that a district court should balance the interests protected by the Fifth and Seventh Amendments [but deny a jury trial 'only in exceptional circumstances.'" Arthur R. Miller, 9 *Federal Practice and Procedure* § 2302.1 (3d ed. 2019). You may recall from the famous Kalven Chicago jury study that juries do not disagree with judges more in difficult cases than they do in easier ones.

Professor Graham Lilly of the University of Virginia Law School has argued that the increasing complexity of contemporary litigation, and particularly the central role played by expert testimony, science, and statistics in today's cases, make the jury—as currently selected—an inappropriate body to decide complex cases. One of his examples of how misguided it is to use jurors in complex cases is *Brooke Group Ltd. v. Brown & Williamson Tobacco Corp.*, 509 U.S. 209 (1993), a 115-day trial, which involved an alleged predatory pricing scheme in the domestic cigarette market. Lilly cites to two researchers who conducted post-trial juror interviews, and found that "the jurors were overwhelmed, frustrated, and confused by testimony well beyond their comprehension." In the article that Lilly relies upon for his information about jurors in the *Brooke Group* case (Arthur Austin, *The Jury System at Risk from Complexity, the New Media, and Deviancy*, 73 Denv. U. L. Rev. 51 (1995)), Austin concluded that "at no time did any juror grasp—even at the margins—the law, the economics, or any other testimony relating to the allegations or defense."

Professor Lilly urges the courts, including the Supreme Court, to revisit Justice White's suggestion in *Ross v. Bernhard* that "the practical abilities and limitations of juries" is one appropriate criterion for determining the scope of the right to a jury under the Seventh Amendment. He also suggests requiring jurors to have a certain level of formal education, or equivalent training or experience, for specific types of cases, and the use of expert jury panels depending on the type of case, as means of retaining the benefits of jury trial, while at the same time achieving more suitable jurors. Finally, he proposes the increased use of court-appointed experts to assist jurors in complex cases. Graham C. Lilly, *The Decline of the American Jury*, 72 U. Colo. L. Rev. 53 (2001). For a comprehensive account of questions and cases regarding the complexity exception, see James Oldham, *On the Question of a Complexity Exception to the Seventh Amendment Guarantee of Trial by Jury*, 71 Ohio St. L.J. 1031 (2010); Jay Tidmarsh, *The English Fire Courts and the American Right to Civil Jury Trial*, 83 U. Chi. L. Rev. 1893, 1901 n.33 (2016) (collecting articles debating the issue).

Reforming Juries. The modern jury debate has revolved less around abolishing the jury altogether than around possible modifications of the jury system. Consider the following proposed modifications in light of the values discussed in the preceding text, as well as the "notice and the right to be heard" values discussed earlier in the book:

- allowing jurors to take notes during all or parts of the trial;
- allowing jurors to ask questions of the witnesses;
- rewriting jury instructions in simpler language (jury instructions ordinarily are given only orally, can be several hours long, and are often complex);
- giving legal instructions to the jury before the evidence is heard;
- allowing interim summation by counsel and discussion by jurors;
- permitting jurors to have written copies of the instructions;
- increasing juror fees;
- reducing juror "down time" by scheduling attorney-judge conferences when jurors are not present; and/or
- special verdicts (which we will discuss later in this chapter).

Many of these modifications are already present in some jurisdictions, and researchers have assessed their impact. *See, e.g.,* Lynne Forster Lee and Irwin A. Horowitz, *The Effects of Jury-Aid Innovations on Juror Performance in Complex Civil Trials*, 86 Judicature 184 (2003). "Although justice and fairness cannot be measured by an objective standard, [there is evidence that such innovations can enhance] the jury trial process and jurors' understanding during the trials' various phases." James F. Holderman, *Trying the ABA's Principles for Juries and Jury Trial*, 33 A.B.A. Litig. No. 33, at 9 (Spring 2007).

3. The Historical Background of the Modern American Civil Jury

While some historians trace the modern American civil jury back to the ancient civilizations of Greece and Rome or to the Scandinavians who settled England before A.D. 1000, most modern scholars begin the story of the jury at the time of the Norman Conquest of England in 1066. Those early juries were committees assembled by William the Conqueror to determine who owned the various tracts of land in a given area. Later, trial by jury became an alternative to the other forms of trial available, which involved various forms of battle or ordeal, or compurgation, and in which each side would bring forth friends to swear to the truth of his position. Jurors were selected from the local community where the dispute arose and were required to have some familiarity with the facts of the case. In a sense, then, the earliest juries were groups of witnesses, who discussed the case among themselves and arrived at a verdict. The judge's role in such a case was to tell the jurors the law that applied to the dispute. *See* Lloyd E. Moore, *The Jury: Tool of Kings, Palladium of Liberty* (2d ed. 1985).

In the centuries that followed, the distinction between juror and witness became more pronounced. In one intermediary phase, jurors who had personal knowledge of the case were required to testify in open court as witnesses and then to return to the jury box. Gradually, courts recognized the need for jurors who based their verdict not on personal knowledge, but only on the evidence presented in court. Elaborate procedures developed to ensure that only disinterested persons sat on juries. *See* John Marshall Mitnick, *From Neighbor-Witness to Judge of Proofs: The Transformation of the English Civil Juror*, 32 Am. J. Legal Hist. 201 (1988).

When the first English colonists brought trial by jury to America, it was still in flux. As late as 1670, in *Bushell's Case*, 124 Eng. Rep. 1006 (C.P), an English judge declared that jurors had the right to use their personal knowledge to decide the verdict. In colonial America, jurors often heard three different versions of the law from three different judges. In such cases, the jury could decide both fact and law, a situation that prevailed in some colonies, such as Massachusetts, until the Revolution. *See* William E. Nelson, *Americanization of the Common Law* (1975).

During the colonial period, juries were perceived to be guardians of local community values against outsider judges appointed by the royal governor. They were also seen as bulwarks of integrity against corrupt public officials, and, finally, as revolution drew near, as wellsprings of patriotism in the fight against imperialist injustices. British attempts to constrain the use of jury trial were among the foremost complaints of the founders of the movement for American independence and were mentioned in the Declaration of Independence.

When the British presence was eradicated and American judges were placed at the head of the various courts, some leaders of the new nation sought to restrain the influence of juries, who, they believed, were thwarting creditors from collecting on their debts and jeopardizing the economic stability of the new nation. At the Constitutional Convention, which was dominated by pro-creditor Federalists, no provision for civil jury trial was adopted in the original document. Indeed, in Federalist No. 83, Alexander Hamilton argued that the right to civil jury trial was not fundamental to liberty and that, given the diversity of practice throughout the states, it would be impossible to draft a provision that would satisfy all factions.

The omission of a right to jury trial in civil cases, as well as a provision that would have allowed the Supreme Court to reconsider factual issues decided by a jury, were among the chief rallying cries of the pro-debtor Anti-Federalists, whose impassioned pleas in state legislatures' ratification debates called for a guarantee of civil jury trial in all common law cases. In the end, the Anti-Federalists won the debate. The Seventh Amendment to the Constitution, adopted in 1791, provides that "[i]n suits at common law, where the amount in controversy exceeds twenty dollars, the right to trial by jury shall be preserved. . . ." For a complete discussion of the Federalist/Anti-Federalist debate over the Seventh Amendment, see Charles W. Wolfram, *The Constitutional History of the Seventh Amendment*, 57 Minn. L. Rev. 639 (1973). When all thirteen colonies became states, they, too, ensured the right to trial by jury in both criminal and civil cases. *Id.* at 655-656.

B. THE RIGHT TO JURY TRIAL IN CIVIL CASES IN FEDERAL COURT

Read the language of the Seventh Amendment. In its earliest review of the Seventh Amendment, the Supreme Court, under Justice Story, declared that the "common law" referred to in the Constitution should be determined by looking at the common law of England. *United States v. Wonson*, 28 F. Cas. 745. Later courts refined the analysis, focusing on the historical implications of the word "preserved" to require looking at the common law of England in 1791—when the Seventh Amendment was adopted.

Two complications arose, one almost immediately and the other after the merger of law and equity in federal practice. First, what about civil causes of action created by statute after 1791? Were these actions automatically exempted from the Seventh Amendment because they were not part of the "common law"? Second, after the merger of law and equity, what are the rights of parties who raise both equitable and legal (or common law) claims? Justice Story began to answer these questions in the 1830 Supreme Court case *Parsons v. Bedford*, 28 U.S. 433, 447:

> By *common law*, [the framers of the Seventh Amendment] meant . . . not merely suits, which the *common* law recognized among its old and settled proceedings, but suits, in which *legal* rights were to be ascertained and determined, in contradistinction to those where equitable rights alone were recognized, and equitable remedies were administered.

In recent history, beginning with *Beacon Theaters v. Westover*, 359 U.S. 500 (1959), and continuing until the present day, the Supreme Court has continued to wrestle with the answers to these questions.

Chauffeurs, Teamsters and Helpers, Local No. 391 v. Terry
494 U.S. 558 (1990)

Justice MARSHALL delivered the opinion of the Court, except as to Part III-A:

This case presents the question whether an employee who seeks relief in the form of back pay for a union's alleged breach of its duty of fair representation has a right to trial by jury. We hold that the Seventh Amendment entitles such a plaintiff to a jury trial.

I

McLean Trucking Company and the Chauffeurs, Teamsters and Helpers Local Union No. 391 were parties to a collective-bargaining agreement that governed the terms and conditions of employment at McLean's terminals. The 27 respondents were employed by McLean as truckdrivers in bargaining units covered by the agreement, and all were members of the Union. In 1982 McLean implemented a change in operations that resulted in the elimination of some of its terminals and the reorganization of others. As part of that change, McLean transferred respondents to the terminal located in Winston-Salem and agreed to give them special seniority rights in relation to "inactive" employees in Winston-Salem who had been laid off temporarily.

After working in Winston-Salem for approximately six weeks, respondents were alternately laid off and recalled several times. Respondents filed a grievance with the Union, contesting the order of the layoffs and recalls. Respondents also challenged McLean's policy of stripping any driver who was laid off of his special seniority rights. Respondents claimed that McLean breached the collective-bargaining agreement by giving inactive drivers preference over respondents. After these proceedings, the grievance committee ordered McLean to recall any respondent who was then laid off and to lay off any inactive driver who had been recalled; in addition, the committee ordered McLean to recognize respondents' special seniority rights until the inactive employees were properly recalled.

On the basis of this decision, McLean recalled respondents and laid off the drivers who had been on the inactive list when respondents transferred to Winston-Salem. Soon after this, though, McLean recalled the inactive employees, thereby allowing them to regain seniority rights over respondents. In the next round of layoffs, then, respondents had lower priority than inactive drivers and were laid off first. Accordingly, respondents filed another grievance, alleging that McLean's actions were designed to circumvent the initial decision of the grievance committee. The Union representative appeared before the grievance committee and presented the contentions of respondents and those of the inactive truckdrivers. At the conclusion of the hearing, the committee held that McLean had not violated the committee's first decision.

McLean continued to engage in periodic layoffs and recalls of the workers at the Winston-Salem terminal. Respondents filed a third grievance with the Union, but the Union declined to refer the charges to a grievance committee on the ground that the relevant issues had been determined in the prior proceedings.

In July 1983, respondents filed an action in District Court, alleging that McLean had breached the collective-bargaining agreement in violation of § 301 of the Labor Management Relations Act, 1947, 61 Stat. 156, 29 U.S.C. § 185 (1982 ed.) and that the Union had violated its duty of fair representation. [Section 301(a) of the Labor Management Relations Act, 1947, provides for suits by and against labor unions: "Suits for violation of contracts between an employer and a labor organization representing employees in an industry affecting commerce as defined in this chapter, or between any such labor organizations, may be brought in any district court of the United States having jurisdiction of the parties, without respect to the amount in controversy or without regard to the citizenship of the parties." 61 Stat. 156, 29 U.S.C. § 185 (a) (1982).] Respondents requested a permanent injunction requiring the defendants to cease their illegal acts and to reinstate them to their proper seniority status; in addition, they sought, inter alia, compensatory damages for lost wages and health benefits. In 1986 McLean filed for bankruptcy; subsequently, the action against it was voluntarily dismissed, along with all claims for injunctive relief.

Respondents had requested a jury trial in their pleadings. The Union moved to strike the jury demand on the ground that no right to a jury trial exists in a duty of fair representation suit. The District Court denied the motion to strike. After an interlocutory appeal, the Fourth Circuit affirmed the trial court, holding that the Seventh Amendment entitled respondents to a jury trial of their claim for monetary relief. We granted the petition for certiorari to resolve a circuit conflict on this issue, and now affirm the judgment of the Fourth Circuit.

II

. . . [Employees] must prove the same two facts to recover money damages: that the employer's action violated the terms of the collective-bargaining agreement and that the union breached its duty of fair representation.

III

We turn now to the constitutional issue presented in this case—whether respondents are entitled to a jury trial. The Seventh Amendment provides that "[i]n Suits at common law, where the value in controversy shall exceed twenty dollars, the right of trial by jury shall be preserved." The right to a jury trial includes more than the common-law forms of action recognized in 1791; the phrase "Suits at common law" refers to "suits in which legal rights [are] to be ascertained and determined, in contradistinction to those where equitable rights alone [are] recognized, and equitable remedies [are] administered." *Parsons v. Bedford,* 3 Pet. 433, 447, 7 L. Ed. 732 (1830) ("[T]he amendment then may well be construed to embrace all suits which are not of equity and admiralty jurisdiction, whatever may be the peculiar form which they may assume to settle legal rights"). The right extends to causes of action created by Congress. Since the merger of the systems of law and equity, *see* Fed. R. Civ. P. 2, this Court has carefully preserved the right to trial by jury where legal rights are at stake. As the Court noted in *Beacon Theatres, Inc. v. Westover,* "Maintenance of the jury as a fact-finding body is of such importance and occupies so firm a place in our history and jurisprudence that any seeming curtailment of the right to a jury trial should be scrutinized with the utmost care." 359 U.S. 500, 501 (1959).

To determine whether a particular action will resolve legal rights, we examine both the nature of the issues involved and the remedy sought. "First, we compare the statutory action to 18th-century actions brought in the courts of England prior to the merger of the courts of law and equity. Second, we examine the remedy sought and determine whether it is legal or equitable in nature." 481 U.S., at 417-418. The second inquiry is the more important in our analysis.

A

An action for breach of a union's duty of fair representation was unknown in 18th-century England; in fact, collective-bargaining was unlawful. We must therefore look for an analogous cause of action that existed in the 18th century to determine whether the nature of this duty of fair representation suit is legal or equitable.

The Union contends that this duty of fair representation action resembles a suit brought to vacate an arbitration award because respondents seek to set aside the result of the grievance process. In the 18th century, an action to set aside an arbitration award was considered equitable. 2 Joseph Story, *Commentaries on*

Equity Jurisprudence § 1452, pp. 789-790 (13th ed. 1886) (equity courts had jurisdiction over claims that an award should be set aside on the ground of "mistake of the arbitrators"). . . .

The arbitration analogy is inapposite, however, to the Seventh Amendment question posed in this case. No grievance committee has considered respondents' claim that the Union violated its duty of fair representation; the grievance process was concerned only with the employer's alleged breach of the collective-bargaining agreement. Thus, respondents' claim against the Union cannot be characterized as an action to vacate an arbitration award. . . .

The Union next argues that respondents' duty of fair representation action is comparable to an action by a trust beneficiary against a trustee for breach of fiduciary duty. Such actions were within the exclusive jurisdiction of courts of equity. This analogy is far more persuasive than the arbitration analogy. Just as a trustee must act in the best interests of the beneficiaries, a union, as the exclusive representative of the workers, must exercise its power to act on behalf of the employees in good faith, *Vaca v. Sipes*, [386 U.S., 171, 177 (1967)]. Moreover, just as a beneficiary does not directly control the actions of a trustee, an individual employee lacks direct control over a union's actions taken on his behalf. . . .

Respondents contend that their duty of fair representation suit is less like a trust action than an attorney malpractice action, which was historically an action at law. . . . [W]e find that, in the context of the Seventh Amendment inquiry, the attorney malpractice analogy does not capture the relationship between the union and the represented employees as fully as the trust analogy does.

The attorney malpractice analogy is inadequate in several respects. Although an attorney malpractice suit is in some ways similar to a suit alleging a union's breach of its fiduciary duty, the two actions are fundamentally different. The nature of an action is in large part controlled by the nature of the underlying relationship between the parties. Unlike employees represented by a union, a client controls the significant decisions concerning his representation. Moreover, a client can fire his attorney if he is dissatisfied with his attorney's performance. . . . Thus, we find the malpractice analogy less convincing than the trust analogy.

Nevertheless, the trust analogy does not persuade us to characterize respondents' claim as wholly equitable. The Union's argument mischaracterizes the nature of our comparison of the action before us to 18th-century forms of action. As we observed in *Ross v. Bernhard*, 396 U.S. 531 (1970), "The Seventh Amendment question depends on the nature of the issue to be tried rather than the character of the overall action." *Id.*, at 538 (finding a right to jury trial in a shareholder's derivative suit, a type of suit traditionally brought in courts of equity, because plaintiffs' case presented legal issues of breach of contract and negligence). As discussed above, . . . to recover from the Union here, respondents must prove both that McLean violated § 301 by breaching the collective-bargaining agreement and that the Union breached its duty of fair representation. When viewed in isolation, the duty of fair representation issue is analogous to a claim against a trustee for breach of fiduciary duty. The § 301 issue, however, is comparable to a breach of contract claim—a legal issue.

Respondents' action against the Union thus encompasses both equitable and legal issues. The first part of our Seventh Amendment inquiry, then, leaves us in equipoise as to whether respondents are entitled to a jury trial.

B

Our determination under the first part of the Seventh Amendment analysis is only preliminary. In this case, the only remedy sought is a request for compensatory damages representing back pay and benefits. Generally, an action for money damages was "the traditional form of relief offered in the courts of law." *Curtis v. Loether*, 415 U.S. 189, 196 (1974). This Court has not, however, held that "any award of monetary relief must necessarily be 'legal' relief." *Ibid.* Nonetheless, because we conclude that the remedy respondents seek has none of the attributes that must be present before we will find an exception to the general rule and characterize damages as equitable, we find that the remedy sought by respondents is legal.

First, we have characterized damages as equitable where they are restitutionary, such as in "action[s] for disgorgement of improper profits," *Tull* [*v. United States*, 481 U.S. 412, 424 (1987)]. The back pay sought by respondents is not money wrongfully held by the Union, but wages and benefits they would have received from McLean had the Union processed the employees' grievances properly. Such relief is not restitutionary.

Second, a monetary award "incidental to or intertwined with injunctive relief" may be equitable. *Tull*, 481 U.S. at 424. *See, e.g., Mitchell v. DeMario Jewelry, Inc.*, 361 U.S. 288, 291-292 (1960) (district court had power, incident to its injunctive powers, to award back pay under the Fair Labor Standards Act; also back pay in that case was restitutionary). Because respondents seek only money damages, this characteristic is clearly absent from the case.

The Union argues that the back pay relief sought here must nonetheless be considered equitable because this Court has labeled back pay awarded under Title VII, 42 U.S.C. § 2000e et seq. (1982 ed.), as equitable. *See Albemarle Paper Co. v. Moody*, 422 U.S. 405, 415-418 (1975) (characterizing back pay awarded against employer under Title VII as equitable in context of assessing whether judge erred in refusing to award such relief). It contends that the Title VII analogy is compelling in the context of the duty of fair representation because its back pay provision was based on the NLRA provision governing back pay awards for unfair labor practices, 29 U.S.C. § 160(c) (1982 ed.). ("[W]here an order directs reinstatement of an employee, back pay may be required of the employer or labor organization"). We are not convinced.

The Court has never held that a plaintiff seeking back pay under Title VII has a right to a jury trial. *See Lorillard v. Pons*, 434 U.S. 575, 581-582 (1978). Assuming, without deciding, that such a Title VII plaintiff has no right to a jury trial, the Union's argument does not persuade us that respondents are not entitled to a jury trial here. Congress specifically characterized back pay under Title VII as a form of "equitable relief." 42 U.S.C. § 2000e-5(g) (1982 ed.). . . . Congress made no similar pronouncement regarding the duty of fair representation.

Furthermore, the Court has noted that back pay sought from an employer under Title VII would generally be restitutionary in nature, *see Curtis v. Loether*, at 197, in contrast to the damages sought here from the Union. Thus, the remedy sought in this duty of fair representation case is clearly different from back pay sought for violations of Title VII. . . .

We hold, then, that the remedy of back pay sought in this duty of fair representation action is legal in nature. Considering both parts of the Seventh Amendment inquiry, we find that respondents are entitled to a jury trial on all issues presented in their suit.

IV

On balance, our analysis of the nature of respondents' duty of fair representation action and the remedy they seek convinces us that this action is a legal one. Although the search for an adequate 18th-century analog revealed that the claim includes both legal and equitable issues, the money damages respondents seek are the type of relief traditionally awarded by courts of law. Thus, the Seventh Amendment entitles respondents to a jury trial, and we therefore affirm the judgment of the Court of Appeals.

Justice BRENNAN, concurring in part and concurring in the judgment:

I agree with the Court that respondents seek a remedy that is legal in nature and that the Seventh Amendment entitles respondents to a jury trial on their duty of fair representation claims. I therefore join Parts I, II, III-B, and IV of the Court's opinion. I do not join that part of the opinion which reprises the particular historical analysis this Court has employed to determine whether a claim is a "Suit at common law" under the Seventh Amendment, . . . because I believe the historical test can and should be simplified. . . .

I believe that our insistence that the jury trial right hinges in part on a comparison of the substantive right at issue to forms of action used in English courts 200 years ago needlessly convolutes our Seventh Amendment jurisprudence. For the past decade and a half, this Court has explained that the two parts of the historical test are not equal in weight, that the nature of the remedy is more important than the nature of the right. Since the existence of a right to jury trial therefore turns on the nature of the remedy, absent congressional delegation to a specialized decisionmaker, there remains little purpose to our rattling through dusty attics of ancient writs. The time has come to borrow William of Occam's razor and sever this portion of our analysis. . . .

Requiring judges, with neither the training nor time necessary for reputable historical scholarship, to root through the tangle of primary and secondary sources to determine which of a hundred or so writs is analogous to the right at issue has embroiled courts in recondite controversies better left to legal historians. . . .

Furthermore, inquiries into the appropriate historical analogs for the rights at issue are not necessarily susceptible of sound resolution under the best of circumstances. . . .

In addition, modern statutory rights did not exist in the 18th-century and even the most exacting historical research may not elicit a clear historical analog. The right at issue here, for example, is a creature of modern labor law quite foreign to Georgian England. . . .

To rest the historical test required by the Seventh Amendment solely on the nature of the relief sought would not, of course, offer the federal courts a rule that is in all cases self-executing. Courts will still be required to ask which remedies were traditionally available at law and which only in equity. But this inquiry involves fewer variables and simpler choices, on the whole, and is far more manageable than the scholasticist debates in which we have been engaged. Moreover, the rule I propose would remain true to the Seventh Amendment, as it is undisputed that, historically, "[j]urisdictional lines [between law and equity] were primarily a matter of remedy." John C. McCoid, II, *Procedural Reform and the Right to Jury Trial: A Study of Beacon Theatres, Inc. v. Westover*, 116 U. Pa. L. Rev. 1 (1967). . . .

The encroachment on civil jury trial by colonial administrators was a "deeply divisive issue in the years just preceding the outbreak of hostilities between the colonies and England," and all thirteen States reinstituted the right after hostilities ensued. Charles W. Wolfram, *The Constitutional History of the Seventh Amendment*, 57 Minn. L. Rev. 639, 654-655 (1973). . . .

We can guard this right and save our courts from needless and intractable excursions into increasingly unfamiliar territory simply by retiring that prong of our Seventh Amendment test which we have already cast into a certain doubt. If we are not prepared to accord the nature of the historical analog sufficient weight for this factor to affect the outcome of our inquiry, except in the rarest of hypothetical cases, what reason do we have for insisting that federal judges proceed with this arduous inquiry? It is time we read the writing on the wall, especially as we ourselves put it there.

[The opinion of Justice STEVENS, concurring in part and concurring in the judgment, is omitted.]

Justice KENNEDY, with whom Justice O'CONNOR and Justice SCALIA join, dissenting:

. . . To determine whether rights and remedies in a duty of fair representation action are legal in character, we must compare the action to the 18th-century cases permitted in the law courts of England, and we must examine the nature of the relief sought. I agree also with those Members of the Court who find that the duty of fair representation action resembles an equitable trust action more than a suit for malpractice.

I disagree with the analytic innovation of the Court that identification of the trust action as a model for modern duty of fair representation actions is insufficient to decide the case. The Seventh Amendment requires us to determine whether the duty of fair representation action "is more similar to cases that were tried in courts of law than to suits tried in courts of equity." *Tull v. United States*, 481 U.S. 412, 417 (1987). Having made this decision in favor of an equitable action, our inquiry should end. Because the Court disagrees with this proposition, I dissent.

I

[Justice Kennedy explains that he finds the analogy to an equitable suit by a beneficiary against a trustee more persuasive, largely because a trustee is required to serve all beneficiaries with impartiality and may not ordinarily be directed to act by a beneficiary. He notes that this is unlike an action by a client against an attorney because the attorney is entrusted with representing the sole interests of the client and acts as an agent on the client's behalf. Moreover, Justice Kennedy states that the remedies available to employees in claims for breach of the duty of fair representation are equitable in nature and are therefore more like the remedies available in an action against a trustee. On the other hand, in an action by a client against an attorney, compensatory damages are often the appropriate remedy.]

II

The Court relies on two lines of precedents to overcome the conclusion that the trust action should serve as the controlling model. The first consists of cases in which the Court has considered simplifications in litigation resulting from modern procedural reforms in the federal courts. Justice Marshall asserts that these cases show that the Court must look at the character of individual issues rather than claims as a whole. The second line addresses the significance of the remedy in determining the equitable or legal nature of an action for the purpose of choosing the most appropriate analogy. Under these cases, the Court decides that the respondents have a right to a jury because they seek money damages. These authorities do not support the Court's holding.

A

In three cases we have found a right to trial by jury where there are legal claims that, for procedural reasons, a plaintiff could have or must have raised in the courts of equity before the systems merged. In *Beacon Theatres, Inc. v. Westover*, 359 U.S. 500 (1959), Fox, a potential defendant threatened with legal antitrust claims, brought an action for declaratory and injunctive relief against Beacon, the likely plaintiff. Because only the courts of equity had offered such relief prior to the merger of the two court systems, Fox had thought that it could deprive Beacon of a jury trial. Beacon, however, raised the antitrust issues as counterclaims and sought a jury. We ruled that, because Beacon would have had a right to a jury trial on its antitrust claims, Fox could not deprive it of a jury merely by taking advantage of modern declaratory procedures to sue first. The result was consistent with the spirit of the Federal Rules of Civil Procedure, which allow liberal joinder of legal and equitable actions, and the Declaratory Judgment Act, 28 U.S.C. §§ 2201, 2202 (1982 ed.), which preserves the right to jury trial to both parties. *See* 359 U.S., at 509-510.

In *Dairy Queen, Inc. v. Wood*, 369 U.S. 469 (1962), we held, in a similar manner, that a plaintiff, by asking in his complaint for an equitable accounting for trademark infringement, could not deprive the defendant of a jury trial on contract claims subsumed within the accounting. Although a court of equity would have heard the contract claims as part of the accounting suit, we found them severable under modern procedure. *See id.*, at 477-479.

In *Ross v. Bernhard*, 396 U.S. 531 (1970), a shareholder-plaintiff demanded a jury trial in a derivative action asserting a legal claim on behalf of his corporation. The defendant opposed a jury trial. In deciding the case, we recognized that only the courts of equity had procedural devices allowing shareholders to raise a corporation's claims. We nonetheless again ruled that modern procedure allowed trial of the legal claim to a jury. *See id.* at 542.

These three cases responded to the difficulties created by a merged court system. *See* John C. McCoid, II, *Procedural Reform and the Right to Jury Trial: A Study of Beacon Theatres, Inc. v. Westover*, 116 U. Pa. L. Rev. 1 (1967). They stand for the proposition that, because distinct courts of equity no longer exist, the possibility or necessity of using former equitable procedures to press a legal claim no longer will determine the right to a jury. Justice Marshall reads these cases to require a jury trial whenever a cause of action contains legal issues and would require a jury trial in this case because the respondents must prove a breach of the collective-bargaining agreement as one element of their claim.

I disagree. The respondents, as shown above, are asserting an equitable claim. Having reached this conclusion, the *Beacon, Dairy Queen*, and *Ross* cases are inapplicable. . . .

B

The Court also rules that, despite the appropriateness of the trust analogy as a whole, the respondents have a right to a jury trial because they seek money damages. The nature of the remedy remains a factor of considerable importance in determining whether a statutory action had a legal or equitable analog in 1791, but we have not adopted a rule that a statutory action permitting damages is by definition more analogous to a legal action than to any equitable suit. In each case, we look to the remedy to determine whether, taken with other factors, it places an action within the definition of "suits at common law." . . .

III

The Court must adhere to the historical test in determining the right to a jury because the language of the Constitution requires it. The Seventh Amendment "preserves" the right to jury trial in civil cases. We cannot preserve a right existing in 1791 unless we look to history to identify it. Our precedents are in full agreement with this reasoning and insist on adherence to the historical test. No alternatives short of rewriting the Constitution exist. . . .

If Congress has not provided for a jury trial, we are confined to the Seventh Amendment to determine whether one is required. Our own views respecting the wisdom of using a jury should be put aside. Like Justice Brennan, I admire the jury process. Other judges have taken the opposite view. *See, e.g.,* Jerome Frank, *Law and the Modern Mind* 170-185 (1931). But the judgment of our own times is not always preferable to the lessons of history. Our whole constitutional experience teaches that history must inform the judicial inquiry. Our obligation to the Constitution and its Bill of Rights, no less than the compact we have with the generation that wrote them for us, do not permit us to disregard provisions that some may think to be mere matters of historical form. . . .

REVIEW QUESTIONS

1. Articulate the current test as interpreted by Justice Marshall writing for the majority. For an excellent example of a lower court applying this test, see *Goettsch v. Goettsch,* 29 F. Supp. 3d 1231 (N.D. Iowa 2014) (Strand, J.).
2. Justice Brennan and Justice Kennedy would each apply a different test. How do their approaches differ from each other, and from Justice Marshall's?

Markman *Hearings.*   Although the Supreme Court continues to apply the historical test, it made room for consideration of functional criteria and policy in a 1996 Seventh Amendment case. In *Markman v. Westview Instruments, Inc.,* 517 U.S. 370 (1996), a unanimous Court agreed that in a patent infringement claim the interpretation of terms in a patent is a matter of law to be decided by the court, not a jury. After finding the historical evidence equivocal, the Court took into consideration "the relative interpretive skills of judges and juries and the statutory policies that ought to be furthered" in allocating the interpretation to either judge or jury. Because this is the general type of factual inquiry ordinarily undertaken by juries, commentators who were protective of jury trials worried that this was a dangerous incursion by judges into the sphere of factual determinations. (After all, if one has little faith in juries, couldn't the relative interpretive skills of judges and juries justify taking many issues away from juries?) Defenders of juries now focus on the near-extinction of all trials.

Sequencing Jury and Judicial Determinations.   As you have learned, modern procedure has merged law and equity into one court. The merger of law and equity in federal courts has thus eliminated the distinction that the Seventh Amendment purports to "preserve[]." But sometimes a case presents both questions of law and of equity. For example, an employer who is suing a former employee for stealing and using trade secrets may seek—and ultimately be entitled to—both damages (for past harm) and a permanent injunction (preventing future harm). Under circumstances where there are issues for both a jury (i.e., the damages) and a judge (i.e., the injunction), the Supreme Court has held that the Seventh Amendment prohibits a court from deciding the equitable issues in a way that would interfere with the jury's resolution of the legal issues. In a series of opinions over the course of the past few decades, the Court has found a constitutional guarantee to have all legal matters tried to a jury first. *See Beacon Theatres, Inc. v. Westover*, 359 U.S. 500 (1959); *Dairy Queen, Inc. v. Wood*, 369 U.S. 469 (1962); *Ross v. Bernhard*, 396 U.S. 531 (1970). Accordingly, after the jury has rendered its verdict, the judge may resolve remaining equitable matters in a manner not inconsistent with the jury's verdict.

Statutes and the Right to a Jury Trial. Remember that the constitutional analysis is unnecessary if the statute itself provides litigants the right to jury trial. In these circumstances, the right to jury trial would be premised on the statute, regardless of whether the Constitution would also require a jury. When statutes are silent on the issue, the parties may argue about congressional intent. *See, e.g., NLRB v. Jones & Laughlin*, 301 U.S. 1 (1937) (jury trial would subvert purpose of Congress in creating separate administrative agency for labor disputes); *Katchen v. Landy*, 382 U.S. 323 (1966) (Bankruptcy Court is special, Chancery-like court for resolving complex disputes; jury trial would subvert Congress's intent as expressed by Bankruptcy Act).

Now consider one other possibility. Can a statute create a cause of action and expressly deny litigants the right to a jury trial thereunder? The quick answer would be no—because the Seventh Amendment is a *constitutional* right that no statute could abridge. But what is the counter-argument?

State Procedure. As you will learn in Constitutional Law, the Seventh Amendment is one of the few Bill of Rights guarantees that has not been applied to the states through the Fourteenth Amendment's Due Process Clause. Most state constitutions provide a right to trial by jury, although the form of the right varies from state to state. Some states provide a right to jury trial that is even broader than in the federal courts. In other states, "equitable clean-up" doctrines give state judges authority to resolve some legal questions alongside equitable ones—a practice that would be unconstitutional in federal court.

PRACTICE EXERCISE NO. 22: LEGISLATIVE EXERCISE REGARDING RIGHT TO JURY TRIAL

You are a politician assigned to a state legislative committee that is drafting legislation to create a new cause of action for educational malpractice. Supporters of the legislation argue that teachers and schools have a duty to exercise reasonable care as they educate their students. Although tort law widely recognizes a duty to provide for the physical safety of the students, there is no similar duty to ensure that students acquire academic skills. Efforts to hold teachers and schools accountable using the more traditional causes of action—intentional torts, breach of contract, fraud, and violations of constitutional rights—have largely failed. This legislation would create a cause of action for professional malpractice akin to doctors and lawyers. The drafting committee is considering various ways to articulate the appropriate standard of care and to calibrate the elements and procedures to ensure that the cause of action achieves its desired effect without creating a flood of litigation. One question presently before the committee is whether this cause of action should provide a jury trial right. Regardless of whether the relevant state constitution might require it, *should* the legislature provide for juries as a matter of right in these new educational malpractice cases?

PRACTICE EXERCISE NO. 23:
LAW FIRM STRATEGY SESSION REGARDING JURY TRIAL
IN *WARNER*

You are an associate at a staff meeting of the attorneys in *Warner v. City of New York*. The task of this meeting is limited to one question: whether or not to demand a jury trial. If your last name begins with the letters A-L, you are counsel for the plaintiffs; all others represent the defendants.

C. JURY SELECTION: TECHNIQUES AND PURPOSES, INCLUDING PEREMPTORY CHALLENGES

In this section, you will learn the basic premises and techniques of modern jury selection, explore the need for a fair representation of the community in the jury pool, and examine current attempts to curb discrimination in jury selection. You begin with an orientation essay, followed by the federal jury statutes and an overview of the case law.

1. Attorney Behavior

In most courts a "pool" or "panel" of potential jurors has been selected by lottery in advance. In some instances, prior to their encounter with any attorneys, the jurors are shown a film or are simply told about the duties of a juror. Prospective jurors are often given a pamphlet describing the obligations of jurors and detailing what will go on in the courtroom. In most courts, the lawyers are given a list of basic information about who is in the pool. In federal court, the lawyers are given a list that contains the pool members' names, addresses, occupations, and spouses' occupations. Normally, lawyers would not see the list of who is in the pool until right before the jury is selected.

Next, there is what is called a voir dire examination of the prospective jurors as part of the selection process. The stated purpose is to disqualify jurors who cannot be impartial and fair. For instance, a prospective juror may know one of the parties or lawyers, or have previous information about the lawsuit. But lawyers also use the process to begin establishing a rapport with the jury and advocating their view of the case through the questions that they ask.

Depending on the section of the country and the particular court, the voir dire is conducted in different ways. It used to be that the voir dire was conducted primarily by the lawyers, who asked the potential jurors a number of questions. It is probably more typical today, particularly in federal court, for the judge to do the bulk of the questioning. In some courts, the judge asks preliminary questions, and the attorneys are permitted to add a few questions of their own.

Of course, good lawyering calls for finding out in advance how the voir dire will be conducted in your particular case. In some courts, the entire panel is questioned. In others, a smaller number of potential jurors are randomly picked from the panel to be questioned. Sometimes, the whole panel gets general questions, with more particular questions reserved for the chosen portion of the pool.

Most young lawyers spend a lot of time seeking information about local practices and customs from older lawyers and clerks. One needs to know how many jurors will hear the case and how many alternates. Who asks the questions at voir dire? Who picks the jury foreperson, and where will she be seated? Must the jury return a unanimous vote? Can they ask questions or take notes? It may be important for the lawyers to read any pamphlet and view any instructional film that is given or shown to the jurors. The jurors are the audience, and it is crucial for the advocate to know the common information base.

Lawyers can challenge jurors either for cause or with peremptory challenges, for which a cause is not given. The number of challenges for cause is unlimited; sometimes statutes list the "for cause" reasons. Statutes normally also list the number of permitted peremptory challenges. Some statutes permit the judge to add to the number of peremptory challenges. You will also want to know in advance such things as whether you have a second chance to strike jurors once a full jury has been selected and whether you will have to state in open court the name of the juror you have challenged, as well as the reason for the strike.

Lawyers vary on their theories of jury selection; naturally, the court, locale, jury pool, type of case, local customs, and similar matters are relevant. For instance, in some courts the panel sits for an entire month. If it is nearer to the end of the month, some lawyers are reluctant to ever strike a potential juror, except for obvious and noncontroversial cause. The person one strikes may have become a luncheon companion of a juror—now resentful—who later sits on the jury. This concern is heightened if the lawyer has had to publicly challenge or strike a juror; but even if the process is secret, some lawyers are hesitant to have the jurors guessing about who made the challenge. Some lawyers, if permitted, like to say in open court: "No challenges; I am content." Perhaps they believe that this advertises that they have such a strong case that it does not matter which jurors are selected.

As you think about the jurors whom you would challenge or strike, probe your own reasoning and prejudices. Some lawyers seek jurors who have certain ethnic or professional characteristics. Some very good lawyers doubt their own ability—or anyone's ability—to strike jurors rationally, and they very rarely challenge a juror. For instance, it used to be folklore that employees of insurance companies were defense-prone in civil cases; some attorneys now think that it is equally likely that an employee of a large company could be hostile to other large entities. One's sense of such matters may change from decade to decade. It has remained a constant, however, that lawyers are reluctant to use up their peremptory challenges unless they absolutely have to; they are afraid that a subsequently selected juror may be worse than the one they already "bumped."

Regardless of the philosophy that you develop for jury selection, remember that every time you appear before a judge or jury, you too are on trial. The judge and jurors who will sit in your case are watching and listening. This does not mean that you should change your personality for the voir dire or trial; often who we really are comes out during the pressure of a trial anyway. It does mean you should consider how best to present the "you" who you are during each stage of litigation.

What assumptions, if any, do you have about potential jurors? How would you go about testing whether they are true or false?

How do attorneys know when their jury selection techniques have worked? How do they know if they have failed? What other factors might influence the outcome of a case? In Great Britain, attorneys have extremely limited rights to challenge jurors and have little or no opportunity to ask them questions. Are you inclined to think that their system is better or worse? In federal court, Fed. R. Civ. P. 47(a) leaves to the judge's discretion whether to conduct examination of potential jurors herself or permit the parties or their attorneys to conduct the examination. Consider the results of at least one study, which indicates that the verdicts of juries (for criminal matters) selected according to the current procedure and those selected at random with no attorney input do not differ significantly. Valerie P. Hans and Neil Vidmar, *Judging the Jury* 90 (1986) (citing Hans Zeisel and Shari S. Diamond, *The Effect of Peremptory Challenges on Jury and Verdict: An Experiment in a Federal District Court*, 30 Stan. L. Rev. 491 (1978)). *See also* Cathy Johnson and Craig Haney, *Felony Voir Dire: An Exploratory Study of Its Content and Effect*, 18 Law & Hum. Behav. 487, 498 (1994) (finding that jury composition varied only slightly between a carefully selected jury and a randomly selected jury); David Baldus et al., *The Use of Peremptory Challenges in Capital Murder Trials: A Legal and Empirical Analysis,* 3 U. Pa. J. Const. L. 3, 10, 122-128 (2001) (concluding that discriminatory use of peremptories had an effect on outcomes, increasing the likelihood of death verdicts for defendants); Roger Allen Ford, *Modeling the Effects of Peremptory Challenges on Jury Selection and Jury Verdicts,* 17 Geo. Mason L. Rev. 377 (2010) (describing the effects of uncertainty in different methods for challenging potential jurors).

Techniques for selecting jurors have become increasingly complex in the past decade or so, with an entire cottage industry of jury consultants available to clients with adequate means to pay for their services. Consider the following account, taken from Valerie P. Hans and Neil Vidmar's *Judging the Jury* and based on contemporary newspaper accounts. As you read it, think about the techniques M.C.I. used. Would justice be served by widespread use of such methods? What are the potential drawbacks, if any?

Valerie P. Hans and Neil Vidmar, Judging the Jury
79-80 (1986)

In June of 1980, after 15 weeks of testimony, a federal jury deciding an antitrust suit awarded M.C.I. Communications Corporation $600 million, to be paid by the American Telephone and Telegraph Company. Antitrust awards are automatically tripled for punitive purposes, which meant that M.C.I. was to receive the largest antitrust judgment ever—the stunning amount of $1.8 billion. Although the attorneys for the winning side were jubilant, they were not really surprised by the decision. Before the trial, they had engaged jury researchers who used sophisticated social science techniques to determine which jurors would be most favorable to M.C.I., and to predict how jurors would react to the evidence.

A Chicago research firm conducted a telephone poll of local residents and supplemented it by personal interviews. In their interview they asked questions designed to reveal whether the respondents, if they were jurors, would be likely to side with M.C.I. or AT&T. They also obtained the demographic characteristics of these individuals. With computer analyses of these responses, the researchers developed demographic profiles of people who were favorable and unfavorable to M.C.I.'s case, knowledge that would later be of benefit in selecting jurors for the trial.

Next, the firm paid individuals of varying sympathy toward M.C.I. to meet on three successive evenings. On each evening, a mock jury composed of eight of these individuals listened to M.C.I.'s attorneys present abbreviated versions of both M.C.I.'s and AT&T's sides of the dispute in a minitrial. The researchers and attorneys then watched the mock jurors deliberate on the case through a one-way mirror. What they learned from behind the one-way mirror affected how the attorneys presented their side before the real jury.

M.C.I. was suing AT&T for damages they alleged were due to AT&T's monopolistic practices. By law, AT&T was required to share its long lines with other communication companies, and this information was presented to the simulated juries. The first evening, from behind the one-way mirror, the observers watched while the mock jurors debated heatedly about the fairness of this law. After all, some jurors argued, why should AT&T have to share its lines with competitors if it owned the lines? The attorneys learned from their experiences. The next evening, they emphasized to the mock jury that they were to decide the M.C.I.-AT&T case according to the letter of the law, regardless of their personal views about its fairness. That night, the jurors did not have much trouble accepting the law.

Another lesson from the observations may have played a role in netting M.C.I. the largest antitrust award in history. In the first evening's presentation, the attorney representing M.C.I.'s side argued that M.C.I. had suffered $100 million in lost profit from AT&T's monopolistic behavior. The first mock jury decided in M.C.I.'s favor and awarded it exactly $100 million. Noting the similarity, the attorneys wondered what would happen if they avoided mentioning a specific figure. The next night they experimented, and left it to the jury's speculation how much AT&T had cost M.C.I. With no exact dollar amounts to guide or constrain them, the second mock jury's award was $900 million.

Thus, from the community surveys and the mock juries, the M.C.I. attorneys learned what kinds of jurors to look for and to eliminate during the selection process. They also obtained tactical clues about how to present their case to different types of individuals. Morton Hunt, a journalist who has written about the M.C.I. case, likened it to "putting juries on the couch." In a sense, though, in M.C.I.'s attempt to put its jury on the couch, the M.C.I. team was doing more precisely and with scientific assistance what lawyers have tried to do for centuries: stack the jury in their favor. The M.C.I. team may have been *too* successful. The jury award was judged to be excessive and on appeal it was overturned. A second jury evaluating the damages awarded M.C.I. only $37.8 million.

FEDERAL JURY SELECTION STATUTES

28 U.S.C. § 1861 Declaration of Policy

It is the policy of the United States that all litigants in Federal courts entitled to trial by jury shall have the right to grand and petit juries selected at random from a fair cross section of the community in the district or division wherein the court convenes. It is further the policy of the United States that all citizens shall have the opportunity to be considered for service on grand and petit juries in the district courts of the United States, and shall have an obligation to serve as jurors when summoned for that purpose.

28 U.S.C. § 1862 Exemptions

No citizen shall be excluded from service as a grand or petit juror in the district courts of the United States or in the Court of International Trade on account of race, color, religion, sex, national origin, or economic status.

28 U.S.C. § 1865 Qualification for Jury Service

(a) The chief judge of the district court, or such other district court judge as the plan may provide, on his initiative or upon recommendation of the clerk or jury commission, shall determine solely on the basis of information provided on the juror qualification form and other competent evidence whether a person is unqualified for, or exempt, or to be excused from jury service. The clerk shall enter such determination in the space provided on the juror qualification form and in any alphabetical list of names drawn from the master jury wheel. If a person did not appear in response to a summons, such fact shall be noted on said list.

(b) In making such determination the chief judge of the district court, or such other district court judge as the plan may provide, shall deem any person qualified to serve on grand and petit juries in the district court unless he—

(1) is not a citizen of the United States eighteen years old who has resided for a period of one year within the judicial district;

(2) is unable to read, write, and understand the English language with a degree of proficiency sufficient to fill out satisfactorily the juror qualification form;

(3) is unable to speak the English language;

(4) is incapable, by reason of mental or physical infirmity, to render satisfactory jury service; or

(5) has a charge pending against him for the commission of, or has been convicted in a State or Federal court of record of, a crime punishable by imprisonment for more than one year and his civil rights have not been restored.

QUESTIONS TO PONDER

1. What is a "fair cross section of the community"? Should diversity be based on race and ethnicity, religion, age, gender, political views, or some other criteria? The most common method of juror selection is the use of voter registration lists covering the district or division in which the court resides. Does a collection of registered voters represent a "fair cross section of the community"? What groups might be excluded or underrepresented when jurors are drawn solely from voter registration lists?

2. The Supreme Court has ruled that the requirement of a "fair cross section of the community" applies only to the jury pool or panel as a whole, not to any one particular jury. What are the practical and philosophical reasons for such a distinction? What are its likely results?

---

2. Peremptory Challenges and Discrimination

Traditionally, attorneys have used their peremptory challenges to remove jurors on grounds that did not amount to "cause." These grounds range from "gut" feelings to the systematic exclusion of certain types of people. Clarence Darrow advised criminal defense lawyers to exclude women from juries; Melvin Belli, in contrast, suggests in his books on trial technique that the defense should seek to include women, because of their alleged "sympathy" for defendants. The most notorious uses of peremptories—to exclude members of a single race, ethnic group, or gender on the basis of often unproved assumptions and beliefs—have been under attack in recent years.

In *Batson v. Kentucky*, 476 U.S. 79 (1986), a criminal case, the Supreme Court ruled that the use of peremptory challenges by the government to systematically exclude black jurors violated the Fourteenth Amendment Equal Protection rights of a black defendant. The Court established a three-part test to detect race-based uses of peremptory strikes; that test continues to be used today. First, the party opposing the strike must show that circumstances surrounding a particular strike permit an inference that the peremptory challenge was race-based. For instance, a party may satisfy the first part of the test by proving that the opposing party excluded all members of a cognizable racial group. Second, the burden shifts to the proponent of the challenge to provide a race-neutral reason for exercising the strike. If the prosecution satisfies this burden of production, third, it is then incumbent upon the party opposing the strike to prove to the court that use of the strike was motivated by purposeful discrimination. If the race-neutral reason for the striking of a juror applies equally to a juror who was impaneled, then this evidence of pretext can support a conclusion of purposeful discrimination. *See, e.g., Turner v. Marshall*, 121 F.3d 1248, 1251-1252 (9th Cir. 1997) (race-neutral reasons are pretextual when impaneled nonminority juror shared characteristics of struck minority juror).

In *Powers v. Ohio*, 499 U.S. 400 (1991), the Court extended the right to a white criminal defendant who protested the prosecution's exclusion of blacks from the jury. Several questions remained, however. One of the most pressing questions was, did the *Batson* rule apply to civil cases, where the government was not a litigant? The key doctrinal question revolved around the constitutional law concept of "state action." Under the Fourteenth Amendment, from which *Batson* and *Powers* rights are derived, only the government is prohibited from taking away an individual's equal protection of the law. Can private plaintiffs and defendants be characterized as "state actors" when they challenge jurors?

The *Batson* holding has been expanded by subsequent cases to include peremptory strikes in civil actions, *see, e.g., Edmonson v. Leesville Concrete Co., Inc.*, 500 U.S. 614, 616, 618 (1991), and peremptory challenges based on gender, *see, e.g., J.E.B. v. Alabama ex rel. T.B.*, 511 U.S. 127, 128-129 (1994). In *Edmonson*, the majority found "state action" because peremptory challenges are sanctioned and administered by the courts. And in *J.E.B.*, Justice Blackmun held that gender discrimination in jury selection violates the Fourteenth Amendment and "causes harm to litigants, the community, and the individual jurors who are wrongfully excluded from participation in the judicial process." *Id.*, 511 U.S. at 140. Thus, although the Court in *Batson* relied on the rights of the criminal defendant to forbid racially based challenges, the *Edmonson* Court located the rights in a different player. Whose rights are being protected in *Edmonson*? *See also Georgia v. McCollum*, 505 U.S. 42 (1992) (extending *Batson* to allow the prosecution to assert the equal protection rights of the jurors against a criminal defendant who has excluded black jurors).

In *Foster v. Chatman*, 136 S. Ct. 11737 (2016), the Supreme Court reaffirmed *Batson*. In this case, Mr. Foster was convicted of murder and was sentenced to die in 1987 by an entirely white jury. Prosecutors struck all four members of the jury pool who were African American. The case was a poignant illustration of how lawyers circumvent *Batson*. Using the State of Georgia's Open Records Act, Foster's attorneys obtained the prosecutors' notes; these notes provide compelling evidence "that the prosecutors in Foster's case were taking race into account at every step of jury selection. . . . The prosecutors' notes revealed the disjuncture between the proffered reasons and the motivating reasons." Nancy S. Marder, Foster v. Chatman: *A Missed Opportunity for* Batson *and the Peremptory*

Challenge, 49 Conn. L. Rev. 1137, 1141 (2017) (arguing for elimination of the peremptory challenge).

Should Peremptory Challenges Be Eliminated? In *Purkett v. Elem*, 514 U.S. 765 (1995), the majority held in a *per curiam* opinion (Justice Stevens, joined by Justice Breyer, dissenting) that a race-neutral explanation tendered by the proponent of a peremptory challenge need not be "persuasive, or even plausible." In this case, the prosecutor said that he challenged one black male because he "'had long curly hair, . . . the longest hair on anybody on the panel by far'" and "'he had a mustache and goatee type beard.'" He challenged a second black male because he "'also has a mustache and goatee type beard. Those are the only two people on the jury . . . with facial hair. . . . And I don't like the way they looked, with the way the hair is cut, both of them. And the mustaches and the beards look suspicious to me.'" He added that he feared that the second struck juror, who had had a sawed-off shotgun pointed at him during a supermarket robbery, would believe that "'to have a robbery you have to have a gun, and there is no gun in this case.'" The Supreme Court upheld the challenges, reversing the Court of Appeals for the Eighth Circuit, which had found that the prosecution's explanation for striking the first of the two black males was "pretextual." The Court stated that all that is required under the second step in *Batson* is a "legitimate reason . . . not a reason that makes sense, but a reason that does not deny equal protection."

Many have argued that *Batson*'s framework is fundamentally flawed— manifest in a lingering and tragic legacy that the courts almost never find purposeful discrimination. "[T]he *Batson* challenge process may allow the implicit biases of the judges and attorneys to go unchecked during jury selection. Thus, while judge-dominated voir dire may result in implicitly biased jurors deciding cases, the *Batson* challenge process may result in implicitly biased courtroom actors selecting jurors. In his concurring opinion in *Batson*, Justice Marshall foreshadowed the discovery of implicit bias, stating: 'A prosecutor's own conscious or unconscious racism may lead him easily to the conclusion that a prospective black juror is "sullen," or "distant," a characterization that would not have come to his mind if a white juror had acted identically. A judge's own conscious or unconscious racism may lead him to accept such an explanation as well supported. . . . Even if all parties approach the Court's mandate with the best of conscious intentions, that mandate requires them to confront and overcome their own racism on all levels—a challenge I doubt all of them can meet.' The promise of *Batson* remains illusory for two reasons in particular: trial judges are reluctant to doubt prosecutors' proffered reasons for their challenged strikes, and appellate courts are highly deferential to the trial courts' decisions on these matters. . . . *Batson* and its progeny appear to remain ineffective, despite the fact that other members of the Court have recognized the role of implicit bias in the legal system." Judge Mark W. Bennett, *Unraveling the Gordian Knot of Implicit Bias in Jury Selection: The Problems of Judge-Dominated Voir Dire, The Failed Promise of* Batson, *and Proposed*

Solutions, 4 Harv. L. & Pol'y Rev. 149 (2010). Put more bluntly, "*Batson* is either a disingenuous charade or an ill-conceived sinkhole." Anthony Page, Batson*'s Blind-Spot: Unconscious Stereotyping and the Peremptory Challenge*, 85 B.U. L. Rev. 155, 178-179 (2005).

Is the system of peremptory challenges worth preserving? Perhaps we should "invent ways to achieve governmental purposes that do not deploy the group-based identities yet again." Martha Minow, *Not Only for Myself—Identity, Politics and the Law* (1997).

> Several benefits could emerge from this elimination of the peremptory challenge. The messy administration of the Equal Protection challenges and the strategic gamesmanship surrounding jury selection would end, or at least be forced into the "for cause" exclusions, which require reasons and judicial approval. Eliminating peremptory challenges would reduce the parties' (and lawyers') abilities to shape the jury and seek to influence their results, which could both help but also significantly hurt members of disadvantaged groups. The very practice of trying to shape the jury through peremptory challenges has been deeply characterized by stereotypic predictions about how members of particular groups would respond to the topics on trial. Ending the peremptory challenge would, at least symbolically, rule all such thinking out of bounds, at least in this setting.
>
> Indeed, parties, and lawyers, commonly seek to remove jurors based on their group characteristics because they load many presumptions—and prejudices—onto those identities. The prosecution tries to exclude people who look like the defendant on the assumption of undue sympathy; the defense tries to exclude those whose racial and ethnic membership differs from that of the defendant. Why permit peremptory challenges that presume that people *cannot* empathize across lines of difference? Not only is such a rule untrue to human possibilities, it might also be a self-fulfilling prophecy.
>
> Eliminating peremptory challenges would not halt attention to group-based categories, for aggressive anti-discrimination enforcement would still be needed at the systemic levels defining the pool of available jurors and calling specific people to serve. Eliminating peremptory challenges would afford one way to restrict the use of governmentally imposed group-based categories while still achieving the underlying governmental purpose. It would send a signal that a practice must end if it plays into or reinforces group stereotyping.

Id. at 99-100.

QUESTION TO PONDER

What effect(s), if any, do you think the elimination of peremptory challenges would have on the behavior of lawyers, judges, and prospective jurors?

* * *

Notwithstanding the Supreme Court's holding that racially based challenges are unconstitutional, empirical data indicate that people of color are underrepresented in both the jury pool and in the jury as finally constituted. Professor Deborah Ramirez has summarized the data and explained why it is disturbing:

> In judicial districts in which minorities comprise a relatively small percentage of the population, even a jury venire that fairly reflects the population of the district would produce some juries that contain no minority jurors. Furthermore, jury venires often do not fairly reflect the percentage of minorities in the general population, thereby exacerbating the problem. In both federal and state courts, in cities and towns across the nation, the percentage of minority jurors remains significantly lower than the percentage of minority adults living in the communities from which these jurors are selected.
>
> When a jury that is not racially mixed must pass judgment in a case involving minority defendants or victims, the fairness of its judgment is often met with skepticism, rightly or wrongly. Both minority defendants and victims, having experienced prejudice among citizens outside the courts, fear that prejudice may be carried into the jury room. They believe that some minority representation on the jury is critical to a fair outcome. As a result, the failure to secure a multiracial jury may diminish the credibility and legitimacy of the jury's verdict and, in certain highly publicized cases, shatter the public confidence needed to preserve peace following the verdict [citations omitted].

Deborah Ramirez, *The Mixed Jury and the Ancient Custom of Trial by Jury de Linguae: A History and a Proposal for Change*, 74 B.U. L. Rev. 777, 780-781 (1994).

There are many reasons why minorities are frequently underrepresented in both the jury pool and the jury. Local residency requirements and standards requiring the ability to read, write, speak, and understand English, or excluding members of the court or a law enforcement agency, can all be factors. The source lists, often reliant on voting lists, tip prospective jurors to the elderly, the relatively affluent, the self-employed, and government workers, and away from minorities, including blacks, Hispanics, and women. Those who frequently change residence, who often happen to be citizens of color, are less likely to register to vote. Even when other lists are used, such as driver's registration lists, the manner in which duplicate names remain can lead to underrepresentation. Some states have subjective tests, such as "good character," "sound judgment," "mentally sound," and "intelligence," that can result in discriminatory exclusion. Language requirements, lack of follow-up of qualification questionnaires sent to prospective jurors, and excuses from jury duty based on travel difficulties and the loss of wages are additional factors. Hiroshi Fukurai and Edgar W. Butler, *Sources of Racial Disenfranchisement in the Jury and Jury Selection System*, 13 Natl. Black L.J. 238 (1994). The use of race-based peremptory challenges, hiding under the pretense of "neutral reasons," also may be a critical factor: "[A] statistical analysis of the results of federal lower court decisions . . . reveals that the federal courts rarely find *Batson* violations and overwhelmingly accept proffered 'neutral reasons.'" Jeffrey Brand, *The*

Supreme Court, Equal Protection, and Jury Selection: Denying That Race Still Matters, 1994 Wis. L. Rev. 511, 584.

Professor Ramirez has explained that the problem of achieving juries with a diverse mix of participants is by no means a new one, and that "for 600 years English law used quotas to create mixed juries. Beginning in the Twelfth Century, the legal principle called *de medietate linguae* or 'the jury of the half tongue' guaranteed Jewish civil and criminal defendants in England that one-half of their jurors would be fellow Jews." Deborah Ramirez, *Affirmative Jury Selection: A Proposal to Advance Both the Deliberative Ideal and Jury Diversity,* 1998 U. Chi. Legal F. 161, 167-168 (citations omitted). Later, the same right was extended to alien merchants, "eventually becoming a right enjoyed by all aliens to a jury divided equally between English nationals and fellow countrymen. When the English colonized the New World, they brought with them this principle." *Id.* (Ramirez does not, however, propose quotas as a solution for achieving more diverse juries.)

Some suggestions to achieve interracial juries, especially when people of color are parties, are to (1) eliminate peremptory challenges; (2) treat challenges differently when they operate to the detriment of a minority group; (3) affirmatively add a quota of minorities to the jury pool or the jury; and (4) allow peremptory additions of each party's choice to the qualified jury pool from which the ultimate jury will be picked. In addition to the previously cited articles by Jeffrey Brand and Deborah Ramirez, see Albert W. Alschuler, *Racial Quotas and the Jury,* 44 Duke L.J. 704 (1995).

Studies have shown that racially diverse juries reach better decision processes: They consider a broader set of information; they reach and resolve more complex and polarizing issues; they are less biased; and they make fewer factually inaccurate statements when discussing the evidence. *See* Samuel R. Sommers, *On Racial Diversity and Group Decision Making: Identifying Multiple Effects of Racial Composition on Jury Deliberations,* 90 J. Personality & Soc. Psychol. 597, 598-608 (2006).

As mentioned previously, judges can also have biases and prejudices that may be difficult or impossible to set aside. Justice Cardozo put it this way: "[E]very day there is borne in on me a new conviction of the inescapable relation between the truth without us and the truth within. The spirit of the age, as it is to each of us, is too often only the spirit of the group in which the accidents of birth or education or occupation or fellowship have given us a place. No effort or revolution of the mind will overthrow utterly and at all times the empire of these subconscious loyalties." Benjamin N. Cardozo, *The Nature of the Judicial Process* 174-175 (1921). Justice Holmes made a similar point: "What we most love and revere generally is determined by early associations. I love granite rocks and barberry bushes, no doubt because with them were my earliest joys that reach back through the past eternity of my life. But while one's experience thus makes certain preferences dogmatic for oneself, recognition of how they came to be so leaves one able to see that others, poor souls, may be equally dogmatic about something else. And this again means skepticism." Oliver Wendell Holmes, *Natural Law*, 32 Harv. L. Rev. 40, 41 (1918).

That judges and other court personnel, let alone other lawyers, may be unable to put aside their prejudices with respect to race and gender is the topic of numerous state and federal court race and gender bias studies. *See, e.g.*, Todd D. Peterson, *Studying the Impact of Race and Ethnicity in the Federal Courts*, 64 Geo. Wash. L. Rev. 173, 178 (1996): "Forty-three percent of minority lawyers reported that they had been ignored or not listened to by a federal judge because of gender, race, or ethnicity, while only seven percent of white lawyers reported such experiences. Female minority litigators reported such experiences in even higher numbers. . . . Forty percent of African American respondents believed that they were at a disadvantage compared to white attorneys in a bench trial, while only two percent of white attorneys believed that African American litigators suffer such a disadvantage." (Citations omitted.) (This article describes a Federal D.C. Circuit Study and Report on Race and Ethnicity (which is reprinted in the same issue of the George Washington Law Review), and in note 4, page 174, lists a number of other court bias studies.) Here are conclusions of Massachusetts state court studies: "Minority attorneys often receive poor treatment from other attorneys, court-room personnel and some judges because of their race and ethnicity. Such conduct ranges from a negative perception of the attorneys' professionalism to discourteous and discriminatory comments and actions." Commission to Study Racial and Ethnic Bias in the Courts, Massachusetts Supreme Judicial Court, Final Report, Equal Justice 117 (Sept. 1994): "Gender bias exists in many forms throughout the Massachusetts court system. Sexist language and behavior are still common. Beyond these overt signs of bias, many practices and procedures exist that may not appear motivated by bias but nonetheless produce biased results." *Report of the Gender Bias Study of the Supreme Judicial Court, Commonwealth of Massachusetts* 1 (1989). Reports of gender bias studies undertaken by the First, Tenth, and Eleventh Circuits are reprinted in volume 32 of the University of Richmond Law Review at pages 647, 745, and 751, respectively. *See also* John C. Coughenour et al., *The Effects of Gender in the Federal Courts: The Final Report of the Ninth Circuit Gender Bias Task Force*, 67 S. Cal. L. Rev. 745 (1994).

Extending **Batson.** *J.E.B. v. Alabama* (quoted above) prompts the question of what other groups should be entitled to *Batson* protection. In *Hernandez v. New York*, 500 U.S. 352 (1991), the Supreme Court found that peremptory challenges based on ethnic origin (the struck jurors were Hispanic) were illegal, but upheld challenges based on the prospective Spanish-speaking jurors' inability to reassure the prosecutor that they would rely solely on the English translations of testimony given in Spanish. Some courts have held that *Batson* extends to strikes based on religious affiliation. *See United States v. DeJesus*, 347 F.3d 500, 511 (3d Cir. 2003). Some commentators (and at least one court) have taken the position that peremptory challenges based on disability also are illegal. *See* Andrew Weis, *Peremptory Challenges: The Last Barrier to Jury Service for People* *with Disabilities*, 33 Willamette L. Rev. 1 (Winter 1997); and *People v. Green*, 561 N.Y.S.2d 130 (N.Y. Co. Ct. 1990) (involving challenges to deaf jurors). For contrary analyses, see *United States v. Watson,* 483 F.3d 828 (D.C. Cir. 2007) (*Batson* does not apply to use of peremptory challenges by government of blind jurors); *United States v. Harris*, 197 F.3d 870 (7th Cir. 1999) (peremptory challenge based on disability does not violate equal protection).

Waiving the Jury Trial Right. Even in cases where the Seventh Amendment (or a state constitution) guarantees the right to jury trial in a particular case, both parties may waive the right and choose instead to try the case before a single judge. Fed. R. Civ. P. 38(b) requires a party with the right to try an issue to a jury to serve upon the other parties a written jury demand "no later than 14 days after the last pleading directed to the issue is served," and to file the demand in court in accordance with Rule 5(d). Otherwise, the right is waived. Fed. R. Civ. P. 38(d). (Recall that many lawyers put their demand in their complaint or answer in order not to waive their right by inadvertence.) In other words, the Seventh Amendment does not *require* jury trial in any civil case. Should it? Why or why not? Put another way: Whose right is it?

* * *

Take a moment to assess your feelings about juries. The next subjects you will learn include the mechanisms by which a judge can take cases away from the jury at various points before, during, and after the trial. Try to evaluate these powerful jury-controlling tools in light of what you believe about the jury.

D. SUMMARY JUDGMENT

The discussion in this chapter thus far has been about the role and composition of the American jury. The remainder of the chapter covers several judicial methods for controlling and limiting the power of the jury. Throughout this chapter, you will want to consider the advantages and disadvantages of each method and the extent to which they improve or hinder the benefits of jury trial.

Although our focus will frequently be on the relationship of these procedural steps to the right and substance of jury trial, you should keep in mind that some of the procedural incidents we discuss also apply to nonjury cases. For instance, summary judgment applies both to jury and nonjury cases. A motion for summary judgment is typically made after discovery and before trial. It might be helpful for you to familiarize yourself now with the rule governing summary judgment. *See* Fed. R. Civ. P. 56.

You can probably figure out on your own why the drafters of the Federal Rules made available a motion for summary judgment at a point after discovery and before trial. Bear in mind that as originally construed, Rules 8(a) and 12(b)(6) made it relatively easy for a plaintiff to survive to the discovery stage. Charles Clark and his colleagues on the Advisory Committee did not think it made much sense to try to weed out many cases at the pleading stage. But since the pleadings alone would strain out few meritless cases, some mechanism was needed after discovery to weed out cases in which it was clear what the result at trial would be. It does not make sense to force the parties to try a case in which the result is a foregone conclusion. For instance, if you as a judge knew in a negligence case that the plaintiff was incapable of producing evidence at trial of unreasonable care, why put the parties and the court system to the expense of a trial?

A very similar version of that question can also present itself *during* a trial. Imagine that, at the trial of a negligence case, the plaintiff presents its full case yet introduced no evidence of unreasonable care. Why put the defendant and the court system through the ordeal of hearing the defendant's evidence when the result is a foregone conclusion? As a matter of fact, we generally do not put the defendant through that ordeal. Instead, we would grant the defendant a "judgment as a matter of law" under Federal Rule 50(a) (formerly known as a "directed verdict"). You will also study directed verdict motions in this chapter. But first, we are going to focus on the summary judgment, which, in an important sense, is a *prediction* of a directed verdict motion. If, in a particular case, a directed verdict motion would be granted in the middle of the trial, why not instead avoid the trial altogether? A summary judgment grants the prevailing party a judgment before (and without) a trial.

But, as is typical in devising and interpreting procedures, there are dangers in whatever tack one takes. If it is too easy for a moving party to gain a judgment on what, after all, is only a prediction of what the evidence will be at trial, then the right to jury trial can be seriously impaired. If, on the other hand, courts are too reluctant to grant a summary judgment in cases that will later be determined by the granting of a directed verdict, it is wasteful to the parties and the public, and unfair to the party who ultimately wins. Even when there will be no jury, the judge considering a summary judgment motion must be careful not to deprive a party of what might have been a different result if witnesses had to appear before the judge in person, with the added formality of a full trial, cross-examination, and opening and closing arguments.

Four additional points bear mention. First, keep in mind the differences that a judge must consider among a 12(b)(6) motion, a motion for summary judgment, and a motion for a directed verdict. In a 12(b)(6), there exist only the *allegations* in the complaint. In summary judgment, the judge, in trying to predict what the *evidence* will be at trial, can consider the pleadings, affidavits, and discovery. (The mention of pleadings in Rule 56(c) is a bit misleading. Since, as you will see, the judge is trying to predict at the summary judgment stage what evidence will have been admitted by the time of a motion for directed verdict, a mere allegation in an unverified pleading would not aid a party trying to show that she will adduce evidence at the trial.) Unlike the 12(b)(6) motion (based on allegations alone) or the summary judgment motion (primarily based on affidavits and discovery), the directed verdict motion will be based on the evidence actually admitted at the trial (plus evidence taken to be true by virtue of admissions, stipulations, or otherwise).

Second, most motions for summary judgment or directed verdict that result in a final judgment for the moving party are motions made by the defendant. Can you see why? For a plaintiff to win at summary judgment, she would have to convince the judge that she will have admissible, persuasive, uncontroverted evidence to prove every element of her cause of action. In a negligence case, for example, a plaintiff moving for a summary judgment would have to persuade the judge through affidavits and discovery (and facts admitted by the defendant to be true) that reasonable people would have to believe that there was a duty, a breach of duty or unreasonable care, cause in fact, proximate cause, and a certain amount of damages. The plaintiff moving for summary judgment would have to convince the judge that there was no credibility issue and no task to be performed by the jury on *any* of the elements. In short, the moving plaintiff would have to convince the judge that she has met both her production and persuasion burdens in a manner permitting no reasonable argument to the contrary. On the other hand, the defendant in a negligence case who seeks a summary judgment (or directed verdict) would have to poke a hole in only one of the elements, and as to that, she would have to show only that the plaintiff's production burden cannot be met. It is considerably easier to show a lack of potential evidence as to one element than to convince a judge that all elements must be taken as true.

Third, study the critical language in Rule 56(a), which states that the moving party is entitled to a summary judgment if the "movant shows that there is no genuine dispute as to any material fact and the movant is entitled to a judgment as a matter of law." The term *material fact* has a rather specialized meaning in this context—a meaning that embodies some notion of relevance, but goes beyond merely that. Let's say in the *Carpenter* case that genuine disputes exist as to unreasonable care, causation, and the amount of damages. But assume further that there is uncontroverted evidence leading to the inescapable conclusion that the statute of limitations has already run. If the defendant can persuade the judge at the summary judgment stage that, at a trial, it (the defendant) necessarily would win on this affirmative defense (in effect, a verdict would have to be directed on the statute of limitations in favor of the defendant), then this would render the issues of unreasonable care, causation, and the amount of damages "immaterial." Similarly, if a defendant convinces a judge that at trial the plaintiff will have no admissible evidence to permit a finding as to any one of the plaintiff's elements, that would render dispute as to facts with respect to any other element "immaterial."

Put another way, a judge could believe at the summary judgment stage that there are loads of disputed facts (as to the color of the jeep, the sobriety of the driver, the amount of damages), but if the plaintiff still will have to lose because of a failure of evidence as to one element (or if an affirmative defense must be taken as true), that renders all other disputes immaterial. In these instances, summary judgment should be granted even though there are disputes of fact; summary judgment would be appropriate because there is no genuine dispute as to any *material* fact.

Fourth, it is a bit awkward conceptually when the moving party at summary judgment is not the party with the burden of production and persuasion at the trial. Regrettably, this is in fact the typical situation: The defendant has the burden of convincing the judge to grant a summary judgment motion based on the argument that the plaintiff will have an insufficiency of evidence to meet its production burden on at least one element at the trial. In these cases, the moving party (the defendant) has a positive burden to do something to win on the motion, but it is with respect to a negative, to wit: that the plaintiff lacks the evidence to survive a directed verdict. What *exactly* the movant-defendant must show has been the subject of much litigation. For example, if there has been no discovery at all, can the defendant merely move for summary judgment (and do nothing more), thus forcing the plaintiff to reveal the supporting evidence for each element of plaintiff's case? Or, at the other extreme, must the defendant demonstrate not only that the plaintiff has no evidence of a particular element but also that such evidence could not exist? The significance of these two different interpretations is evident in the fact patterns of the *Adickes* and *Celotex* cases that follow: Does the absence of evidence to support one of the elements of the plaintiff's case necessarily mean that summary judgment should enter? Since *Adickes* and *Celotex*, Rule 56 was amended to address this issue—at least in part. Read 56(c)(1)(A) & (B).

1. An Extraordinary Remedy

The first case you will read is *Adickes v. S.H. Kress & Co.* Note that there is historical background on this case following the opinion. Some students may prefer to read the history first.

Adickes v. S.H. Kress & Co.
398 U.S. 144 (1970)

Justice HARLAN delivered the opinion of the Court:

Petitioner, Sandra Adickes, a white school teacher from New York, brought this suit in the United States District Court for the Southern District of New York against respondent S. H. Kress & Co. ("Kress") to recover damages under 42 U.S.C. § 1983 for an alleged violation of her constitutional rights under the Equal Protection Clause of the Fourteenth Amendment. The suit arises out of Kress' refusal to serve lunch to Miss Adickes at its restaurant facilities in its Hattiesburg, Mississippi, store on August 14, 1964, and Miss Adickes' subsequent arrest upon her departure from the store by the Hattiesburg police on a charge of vagrancy. At the time of both the refusal to serve and the arrest, Miss Adickes was with six young people, all Negroes, who were her students in a Mississippi "Freedom School" where she was teaching that summer. Unlike Miss Adickes, the students were offered service, and were not arrested.

Petitioner's complaint had two counts, each bottomed on § 1983, and each alleging that Kress had deprived her of the right under the Equal Protection Clause of the Fourteenth Amendment not to be discriminated against on the basis of race. The first count charged that Miss Adickes had been refused service by Kress because she was a "Caucasian in the company of Negroes." Petitioner sought, inter alia, to prove that the refusal to serve her was pursuant to a "custom of the community to segregate the races in public eating places." However, in a pretrial decision, 252 F. Supp. 140 (1966), the District Court ruled that to recover under this court, Miss Adickes would have to prove that at the time she was refused service, there was a specific "custom . . . of refusing service to whites in the company of Negroes" and that this custom was "enforced by the State" under Mississippi's criminal trespass statute. Because petitioner was unable to prove at the trial that there were other instances in Hattiesburg of a white person having been refused service while in the company of Negroes, the District Court directed a verdict in favor of respondent. A divided panel of the Court of Appeals affirmed on this ground, also holding that § 1983 "requires that the discriminatory custom or usage be proved to exist in the locale where the discrimination took place, and in the State generally," and that petitioner's "proof on both points was deficient."

The second count of her complaint, alleging that both the refusal of service and her subsequent arrest were the product of a conspiracy between Kress and the Hattiesburg police, was dismissed before trial on a motion for summary judgment. The District Court ruled that petitioner had "failed to allege any facts from which a conspiracy might be inferred." 252 F. Supp., at 144. This determination was unanimously affirmed by the Court of Appeals, 409 F.2d, at 126-127.

Miss Adickes, in seeking review here, claims that the District Court erred both in directing a verdict on the substantive count, and in granting summary judgment on the conspiracy count. Last Term we granted certiorari, 394 U.S. 1011 (1969), and we now reverse and remand for further proceedings on each of the two counts.

As explained in Part I, because the respondent failed to show the absence of any disputed material fact, we think the District Court erred in granting summary judgment. With respect to the substantive count, for reasons explained in Part II, we think petitioner will have made out a claim under § 1983 for violation of her equal protection rights if she proves that she was refused service by Kress because of a state-enforced custom requiring racial segregation in Hattiesburg restaurants. We think the courts below erred (1) in assuming that the only proof relevant to showing that a custom was state-enforced related to the Mississippi criminal trespass statute; (2) in defining the relevant state-enforced custom as requiring proof of a practice both in Hattiesburg and throughout Mississippi, of refusing to serve white persons in the company of Negroes rather than simply proof of state-enforced segregation of the races in Hattiesburg restaurants.

I

Briefly stated, the conspiracy count of petitioner's complaint made the following allegations: While serving as a volunteer teacher at a "Freedom School" for Negro children in Hattiesburg, Mississippi, petitioner went with six of her students to the Hattiesburg Public Library at about noon on August 14, 1964. The librarian refused to allow the Negro students to use the library, and asked them to leave. Because they did not leave, the librarian called the Hattiesburg chief of police who told petitioner and her students that the library was closed, and ordered them to leave. From the library, petitioner and the students proceeded to respondent's store where they wished to eat lunch. According to the complaint, after the group sat down to eat, a policeman came into the store "and observed [Miss Adickes] in the company of the Negro students." A waitress then came to the booth where petitioner was sitting, took the orders of the Negro students, but refused to serve petitioner because she was a white person "in the company of Negroes." The complaint goes on to allege that after this refusal of service, petitioner and her students left the Kress store. When the group reached the sidewalk outside the store, "the Officer of the Law who had previously entered [the] store" arrested petitioner on a groundless charge of vagrancy and took her into custody.

On the basis of these underlying facts petitioner alleged that Kress and the Hattiesburg police had conspired (1) "to deprive [her] of her right to enjoy equal treatment and service in a place of public accommodation"; and (2) to cause her arrest "on the false charge of vagrancy."

A. Conspiracies Between Public Officials and Private Persons—Governing Principles

The terms of § 1983 make plain two elements that are necessary for recovery. First, the plaintiff must prove that the defendant has deprived him of a right secured by the "Constitution and laws" of the United States. Second, the plaintiff must show that the defendant deprived him of this constitutional right "under color of any statute, ordinance, regulation, custom, or usage, of any State or Territory." This second element requires that the plaintiff show that the defendant acted "under color of law."

As noted earlier we read both counts of petitioner's complaint to allege discrimination based on race in violation of petitioner's equal protection rights. Few principles of law are more firmly stitched into our constitutional fabric than the proposition that a State must not discriminate against a person because of his race or the race of his companions, or in any way act to compel or encourage racial segregation. Although this is a lawsuit against a private party, not the State or one of its officials, our cases make clear that petitioner will have made out a violation of her Fourteenth Amendment rights and will be entitled to relief under § 1983 if she can prove that a Kress employee, in the course of employment, and a Hattiesburg policeman somehow reached an understanding to deny Miss Adickes service in the Kress store, or to cause her subsequent arrest because she was a white person in the company of Negroes.

The involvement of a state official in such a conspiracy plainly provides the state action essential to show a direct violation of petitioner's Fourteenth Amendment equal protection rights, whether or not the actions of the police were officially authorized, or lawful; [citations omitted]. Moreover, a private party involved in such a conspiracy, even though not an official of the State, can be liable under § 1983. "Private persons, jointly engaged with state officials in the prohibited action, are acting 'under color' of law for purposes of the statute. To act 'under color' of law does not require that the accused be an officer of the State. It is enough that he is a willful participant in joint activity with the State or its agents," *United States v. Price*, 383 U.S. 787, 794 (1966).

B. SUMMARY JUDGMENT

We now proceed to consider whether the District Court erred in granting summary judgment on the conspiracy count. In granting respondent's motion, the District Court simply stated that there was "no evidence in the complaint or in the affidavits and other papers from which a 'reasonably-minded person' might draw an inference of conspiracy," 252 F. Supp., at 144, *aff'd*, 409 F.2d at 126-127. Our own scrutiny of the factual allegations of petitioner's complaint, as well as the material found in the affidavits and depositions presented by Kress to the District Court, however, convinces us that summary judgment was improper here, for we think respondent failed to carry its burden of showing the absence of any genuine issue of fact. Before explaining why this is so, it is useful to state the factual arguments, made by the parties concerning summary judgment, and the reasoning of the courts below.

In moving for summary judgment, Kress argued that "uncontested facts" established that no conspiracy existed between any Kress employee and the police. To support this assertion, Kress pointed first to the statements in the deposition of the store manager (Mr. Powell) that (a) he had not communicated with the police,[8] and that (b) he had, by a prearranged tacit signal,[9] ordered the food counter supervisor to see that Miss Adickes was refused service only

---

8. In his deposition, Powell admitted knowing Hugh Herring, chief of police of Hattiesburg, and said that he had seen and talked to him on two occasions in 1964 prior to the incident with Miss Adickes. (App. 123-126.) When asked how often the arresting officer, Ralph Hillman, came into the store, Powell stated that he didn't know precisely but "Maybe every day." However, Powell said that on August 14 he didn't recall seeing any policemen either inside or outside the store (App. 136), and he denied (1) that he had called the police, (2) that he had agreed with any public official to deny Miss Adickes the use of the library, (3) that he had agreed with any public official to refuse Miss Adickes service in the Kress store on the day in question, or (4) that he had asked any public official to have Miss Adickes arrested. App. 154-155.

9. The signal, according to Powell, was a nod of his head. Powell claimed that at a meeting about a month earlier with Miss Baggett, the food counter supervisor, he "told her not to serve the white person in the group if I . . . shook my head no. But, if I didn't give her any sign, to go ahead and serve anybody." App. 135. Powell stated that he had prearranged this tacit signal with Miss Baggett because "there was quite a lot of violence . . . in Hattiesburg" directed towards whites "with colored people, in what you call a mixed group." App. 131.

because he was fearful of a riot in the store by customers angered at seeing a "mixed group" of whites and blacks eating together.[10] Kress also relied on affidavits from the Hattiesburg chief of police,[11] and the two arresting officers,[12] to the effect that store manager Powell had not requested that petitioner be arrested. Finally, Kress pointed to the statements in petitioner's own deposition that she had no knowledge of any communication between any Kress employee and any member of the Hattiesburg police, and was relying on circumstantial evidence to support her contention that there was an arrangement between Kress and the police.

Petitioner, in opposing summary judgment, pointed out that respondent had failed in its moving papers to dispute the allegation in petitioner's complaint, a statement at her deposition,[13] and an unsworn statement by a Kress

10. Powell described the circumstances of his refusal as follows: "On this particular day, just shortly after 12 o'clock, I estimate there was 75 to 100 people in the store, and the lunch counter was pretty—was pretty well to capacity there, full, and I was going up towards the front of the store in one of the aisles, and looking towards the front of the store, and there was a group of colored girls, and a white woman who came into the north door, which was next to the lunch counter. And the one thing that really stopped me and called my attention to this group, was the fact that they were dressed alike. They all had on, what looked like a light blue denim skirt. And the best I can remember is that they were— they were almost identical, all of them. And they came into the door, and people coming in stopped to look, and they went on to the booths. And there happened to be two empty there. And one group of them and the white woman sat down in one, and the rest of them sat in the second group. And, almost immediately there—I mean this, it didn't take just a few seconds from the time they came into the door to sit down, but, already the people began to mill around the store and started coming over towards the lunch counter. And, by that time I was up close to the candy counter, and I had a wide open view there. And the people had real sour looks on their faces, nobody was joking, or being corny, or carrying on. They looked like a frightened mob. They really did. I have seen mobs before. I was in Korea during the riots in 1954 and 1955. And I know what they are. And this actually got me. I looked out towards the front, and we have what they call see-through windows. There is no backs to them. You can look out of the store right into the street. And the north window, it looks right into the lunch counter. 25 or 30 people were standing there looking in, and across the street even, in a jewelry store, people were standing there, and it looked really bad to me. It looked like one person could have yelled 'Let's get them,' which has happened before, and cause this group to turn into a mob. And, so, quickly I just made up my mind to avoid the riot, and protect the people that were in the store, and my employees, as far as the people in the mob who were going to get hurt themselves. I just knew that something was going to break loose there." App. 133-134.

11. The affidavit of the chief of police, who it appears was not present at the arrest, states in relevant part: "Mr. Powell had made no request of me to arrest Miss Sandra Adickes or any other person, in fact, I did not know Mr. Powell personally until the day of this statement. (*But cf.* Powell's statement at his deposition, n.8, *supra.*) Mr. Powell and I had not discussed the arrest of this person until the day of this statement and we had never previously discussed her in any way." (App. 107.)

12. The affidavits of Sergeant Boone and Officer Hillman each state, in identical language: "I was contacted on this date by Mr. John H. Williams, Jr., a representative of Genesco, owners of S. H. Kress and Company, who requested that I make a statement concerning alleged conspiracy in connection with the aforesaid arrest. This arrest was made on the public streets of Hattiesburg, Mississippi, and was an officers discretion arrest. I had not consulted with Mr. G. T. Powell, Manager of S. H. Kress and Company in Hattiesburg, and did not know his name until this date. No one at the Kress store asked that the arrest be made and I did not consult with anyone prior to the arrest." (App. 110, 112.)

13. When asked whether she saw any policeman in the store up to the time of the refusal of service, Miss Adickes answered: "My back was to the door, but one of my students saw a policeman come in." (App. 75.) She went on to identify the student as "Carolyn." At the trial, Carolyn Moncure, one of the students who was with petitioner, testified that "about five minutes" after the group had sat down and while they were still waiting for service, she saw a policeman come in the store. She stated: "[H]e came in the store, my face was facing the front of the store, and he came in the store and he passed, and he stopped right at the end of our booth, and he stood up and he looked around and he smiled, and

employee,[14] all to the effect that there was a policeman in the store at the time of the refusal to serve her, and that this was the policeman who subsequently arrested her. Petitioner argued that although she had no knowledge of an agreement between Kress and the police, the sequence of events created a substantial enough possibility of a conspiracy to allow her to proceed to trial, especially given the fact that the noncircumstantial evidence of the conspiracy could only come from adverse witnesses. Further, she submitted an affidavit specifically disputing the manager's assertion that the situation in the store at the time of the refusal was "explosive," thus creating an issue of fact as to what his motives might have been in ordering the refusal of service.

We think that on the basis of this record, it was error to grant summary judgment. As the moving party, respondent had the burden of showing the absence of a genuine issue as to any material fact, and for these purposes the material it lodged must be viewed in the light most favorable to the opposing party. Respondent here did not carry its burden because of its failure to foreclose the possibility that there was a policeman in the Kress store while petitioner was awaiting service, and that this policeman reached an understanding with some Kress employee that petitioner not be served.

It is true that Mr. Powell, the store manager, claimed in his deposition that he had not seen or communicated with a policeman prior to his tacit signal to Miss Baggett, the supervisor of the food counter. But respondent did not submit any affidavits from Miss Baggett,[16] or from Miss Freeman,[17] the waitress who actually refused petitioner service, either of whom might well have seen and communicated with a policeman in the store. Further, we find it particularly

---

he went to the back of the store, he came right back and he left out." (App. 302.) This testimony was corroborated by that of Dianne Moncure, Carolyn's sister, who was also part of the group. She testified that while the group was waiting for service, a policeman entered the store, stood "for awhile" looking at the group, and then "walked to the back of the store." (App. 291.)

14. During discovery, respondent gave to petitioner an unsworn statement by Miss Irene Sullivan, a check-out girl. In this statement Miss Sullivan said that she had seen Patrolman Hillman come into the store "[s]hortly after 12:00 noon," while petitioner's group was in the store. She said that he had traded a "hello greeting" with her, and then walked past her check-out counter toward the back of the store "out of (her) line of vision." She went on: "A few minutes later Patrolman Hillman left our store by the northerly front door just slightly ahead of a group composed of several Negroes accompanied by a white woman. As Hillman stepped onto the sidewalk outside our store the police car pulled across the street and into an alley that is alongside our store. The police car stopped and Patrolman Hillman escorted the white woman away from the Negroes and into the police car." (App. 178.)

16. In a supplemental brief filed in this Court respondent lodged a copy of an unsworn statement by Miss Baggett denying any contact with the police on the day in question. Apart from the fact that the statement is unsworn, see Fed. R. Civ. P. 56(e), the statement itself is not in the record of the proceedings below and therefore could not have been considered by the trial court. Manifestly, it cannot be properly considered by us in the disposition of the case. During discovery, petitioner attempted to depose Miss Baggett. However, Kress successfully resisted this by convincing the District Court that Miss Baggett was not a "managing agent," and "was without power to make managerial decisions."

17. The record does contain an unsworn statement by Miss Freeman in which she states that she "did not contact the police or ask anyone else to contact the police to make the arrest which subsequently occurred." (App. 177.) (Emphasis added.) This statement, being unsworn, does not meet the requirements of Fed. R. Civ. P. 56(e), and was not relied on by respondent in moving for summary judgment. Moreover, it does not foreclose the possibility that Miss Freeman was influenced in her refusal to serve Miss Adickes by some contact with a policeman present in the store.

noteworthy that the two officers involved in the arrest each failed in his affidavit to foreclose the possibility (1) that he was in the store while petitioner was there; and (2) that, upon seeing petitioner with Negroes, he communicated his disapproval to a Kress employee, thereby influencing the decision not to serve petitioner.

Given these unexplained gaps in the materials submitted by respondent, we conclude that respondent failed to fulfill its initial burden of demonstrating what is a critical element in this aspect of the case—that there was no policeman in the store. If a policeman were present, we think it would be open to a jury, in light of the sequence that followed, to infer from the circumstances that the policeman and a Kress employee had a "meeting of the minds" and thus reached an understanding that petitioner should be refused service. Because "[o]n summary judgment the inferences to be drawn from the underlying facts contained in [the moving party's] materials must be viewed in the light most favorable to the party opposing the motion," *United States v. Diebold, Inc.*, 369 U.S. 654, 655 (1962), we think respondent's failure to show there was no policeman in the store requires reversal.

Pointing to Rule 56(e),* as amended in 1963,[18] respondent argues that it was incumbent on petitioner to come forward with an affidavit properly asserting the presence of the policeman in the store, if she were to rely on that fact to avoid summary judgment. Respondent notes in this regard that none of the materials upon which petitioner relied met the requirements of Rule 56(e).

This argument does not withstand scrutiny, however, for both the commentary on and background of the 1963 amendment conclusively show that it was not intended to modify the burden of the moving party under Rule 56(c) to show initially the absence of a genuine issue concerning any material fact. The Advisory Committee note on the amendment states that the changes were not designed to "affect the ordinary standards applicable to the summary judgment." And, in a comment directed specifically to a contention like respondent's, the Committee stated that "[w]here the evidentiary matter in support of the motion does not establish the absence of a genuine issue, summary judgment must be denied even if no opposing evidentiary matter is presented." Because respondent did not meet its initial burden of establishing the absence of a policeman in the store, petitioner here was not required to come forward with suitable opposing affidavits.

If respondent had met its initial burden by, for example, submitting affidavits from the policemen denying their presence in the store at the time in question,

---

Eds.' Note: Rule 56 has been amended slightly and restyled considerably since 1970. Much of what was once in 56(c) and (e) is in the contemporary 56(a) and (c). And the contemporary 56(d) includes much of the prior 56(f).

18. The amendment added the following to Rule 56(e): "When a motion for summary judgment is made and supported as provided in this rule, an adverse party may not rest upon the mere allegations or denials of his pleading, but his response, by affidavits or as otherwise provided in this rule, must set forth specific facts showing that there is a genuine issue for trial. If he does not so respond, summary judgment, if appropriate, shall be entered against him."

Rule 56(e) would then have required petitioner to have done more than simply rely on the contrary allegation in her complaint. To have avoided conceding this fact for purposes of summary judgment, petitioner would have had to come forward with either (1) the affidavit of someone who saw the policeman in the store or (2) an affidavit under Rule 56(f) explaining why at that time it was impractical to do so. Even though not essential here to defeat respondent's motion, the submission of such an affidavit would have been the preferable course for petitioner's counsel to have followed. As one commentator has said: "It has always been perilous for the opposing party neither to proffer any countering evidentiary materials nor file a 56(f) affidavit. And the peril rightly continues (after the amendment to Rule 56(e)). Yet the party moving for summary judgment has the burden to show that he is entitled to judgment under established principles; and if he does not discharge that burden then he is not entitled to judgment. No defense to an insufficient showing is required." 6 James Moore, *Federal Practice*, 6.22(2), pp. 2824-2825 (2d ed. 1966). . . .

[We have omitted Part II of Justice Harlan's opinion, which addresses the meaning of "custom" for purposes of § 1983 and the substance of the alleged Fourteenth Amendment violation. We also have omitted Justice Black's concurring opinion; the opinion of Justice Douglas, dissenting in part; and the opinion of Justice Brennan, concurring in part and dissenting in part.]

* * *

As you read the historical background that follows, consider whether it helps explain this case. This background may also be relevant in helping you reconcile *Adickes* with *Celotex*, which follows this historical account.

Background of Adickes v. S.H. Kress & Co. In Mississippi in 1964, no one could have foreseen that this story—among all that was happening—would have such a profound effect.* Mississippi was a state at war with itself. In the four months after Sandra Adickes arrived in Mississippi, three persons would be killed, "80 beaten, three wounded by gunfire in 35 shootings, more than 1,000 arrested, 35 Negro churches burned . . . and 31 homes and other buildings bombed. In addition [there would be] several unsolved murders of Negroes that may have been connected with the racial conflict." John Herbers, *Communique from the Mississippi Front*, N.Y. Times Mag., Oct. 8, 1964, at 34.

Barely a year before, federal troops had faced down a mob of armed whites as James Meredith became the first black to register at the University of Mississippi. In the ensuing disturbance, two journalists were killed.

Black rhetoric, though mild compared to what would follow in the late 1960s, had taken on an undertone of violence. Pulitzer Prize winner Hodding

---

* Thanks to Joel Rosen, then a student of Northeastern University School of Law, for research and writing. Mr. Rosen was an editor at *Boston Magazine* and a columnist for the *Lawrence Eagle Tribune* before attending law school. Mr. Rosen was a partner at Metaxas, Norman & Pidgeon, before starting his own firm in 2007, Rosen Law Office, in Andover, Massachusetts.

Carter wrote, "Attitudes on both sides have been hardening. A fatalistic belief in an eventual and inevitable showdown has animated many members of both races. . . . The hatred of the Negro for the white man is stark, naked and openly expressed to anyone to whom a Negro is willing to talk." Hodding Carter, *Mississippi Now—Hate and Fear*, N.Y. Times Mag., June 23, 1963, at 11, 24. Mississippians feared race riots like those that had occurred in Washington, New York, Chicago, and Detroit.

Frightened by unprecedented black militancy, whites girded themselves for war. Rumors flew. It was said that black men, designated with white Band-Aids on their throats, had been assigned to rape white women; black cooks were poisoning the food at local restaurants; black maids had been instructed to harass their white mistresses by hiding valuables so that their owners would briefly be terrified that they had been stolen.

The whites' response was terrible. Medgar Evers, the Mississippi-born field secretary for the National Association for the Advancement of Colored People (NAACP), was shot to death in an ambush. The Ku Klux Klan "airforce" used light planes to drop bombs on black churches and meeting places. Others drove by in cars, spraying community centers with hails of bullets. In the arrest of men accused of bombing black homes in southwestern Mississippi, police uncovered a cache of high-powered rifles, carbines, pistols, dynamite bombs, several thousand rounds of ammunition, hand grenades, clubs, and blackjacks.

Northern liberals, seeking to help African Americans join the mainstream of the country, concentrated on two areas. One was the overthrow of segregation imposed by Mississippi law. The other was to get blacks to vote.

Voter registration was the most obvious and immediate means of power sharing. The 900,000 blacks in Mississippi made up 42 percent of the state's population; their potential political power was enormous. Getting them to seize that power, however, was difficult in the face of white resistance. Blacks, dependent on whites for jobs, were afraid to risk their survival by antagonizing the power structure. Behind the threat of starvation loomed that of violence.

As if these barriers to participation were not enough, the state required that prospective voters be of "good moral character," pass a literacy test, and interpret two sections of the state constitution. Robert Kennedy's Justice Department challenged these arbitrary testing procedures as discriminatory, particularly as applied to uneducated blacks. But in March 1964, a federal court upheld the constitutionality of those laws. Clearly, then, if black voters were to be registered, they must first be educated.

The two-tiered program of education and registration was the goal of the Freedom Schools, a project underwritten by the Council of Federated Organizations (COFO) and run by a Yale historian named Staughton Lynd. COFO set up forty-seven schools throughout Mississippi in churches, dance halls, and panel trucks. They were a welcome supplement to the sixth-grade education of the average Mississippi black. The black schools were typically underfunded, and black children were expected to help pay for their education by spending one day a year picking cotton.

The Freedom Schools were ad hoc gatherings that specialized in African-American history and American government. They allowed a free range of ideas, and classes discussed topics like skepticism, power sharing, and the right to vote. Teachers and students canvassed the black neighborhoods, signing up voters and talking about new ideas. Predictably, the white reaction to these schools was sometimes deprecatory, sometimes violent. *See* Pat Waters, *Their Text Is a Civil Rights Primer*, N.Y. Times Mag., Dec. 20, 1964, at 44.

In the early months of 1964, Sandra Adickes was in New York, training for her work at the Freedom Schools. She learned that she would not be merely making lesson plans and teaching classes. Rather, she would live among the poor blacks and participate in the life of their community. "If we were called upon to chop cotton, if that is the thing people did in the community, and we wanted to be good Freedom School teachers, that . . . is what we would do." Brief for Petitioner (*Adickes v. Kress*) at 44. The trainees were instructed never to resist arrest, never to provoke incidents. "If we were insulted we were . . . not to respond to abuse. . . .We were advised not to travel alone, so in case one of us is arrested, the other could at least report, or if we were both arrested . . . we would offer some sort of comfort to each other." *Id.* at 50. Adickes had no illusions about how white Mississippians would see the Freedom School teachers. "They think of themselves as God-fearing, law-abiding, good citizens, and you are atheists and communists, and you are there to . . . destroy their way of life." *Id.* at 51.

On July 4, two days after Congress passed the Civil Rights Act of 1964, Sandra Adickes left New York for a Freedom School in Hattiesburg, Mississippi.

Hattiesburg, the seat of Forrest County, was a city of 35,000, largely black. Civil rights leaders had targeted the city for voter-registration efforts. The city stepped up harassment of the Northern agitators. In March, ten clergymen were arrested and fined in the registration drive. In May, another seven demonstrators were arrested for unlawful picketing. On July 10, a rabbi and two other whites were beaten by segregationists. By then, Sandra Adickes had finished her orientation and begun teaching at the local Freedom School.

Adickes lived with a black family in Palmer's Crossing, a rural, black community on the outskirts of Hattiesburg. She joined approximately seven other teachers at the Priest Creek Baptist Church, instructing eighty African-American students in The History of the American Negro, American Social Ideals, and Current Events, including the passage of the 1964 Civil Rights Act.

In early August, the class was discussing what new freedoms the Civil Rights Act provided. The conversation turned to immediate, simple freedoms. What the students really wanted was to go to the Holiday Inn, the white schools, the public library, and the movies. Only one movie theater had admitted blacks until that time, and that was in a small roped-off section. Some of the students said that since the Civil Rights Act had passed, they had eaten at lunch counters at local Woolworth and Kress department stores but that service had been deliberately slow and other customers had insulted them while they were eating. The class was determined to go on a simple field trip, to a place to which they had never been admitted, although their parents paid taxes to support it: the Hattiesburg Public Library. Then they would have lunch.

Adickes, along with five black girls and one boy, took the bus from Palmer's Crossing into the white section of town and walked to the library. A young woman at the desk was on the phone when the group walked in. She hung up, buzzed her supervisor, and then turned to the members of the group, who were asking for library cards. "We are not giving any cards right now," she said.

The supervisor arrived and suggested that the children try a branch of the library that served blacks. The students replied that they had been there, but the branch did not have the books they wanted. The supervisor told the students that she was a Yankee and was sympathetic to their cause; in fact she had tried to get the trustees to integrate the library. The trustees, she said, had told her they would close the library if that were to happen. Didn't the students agree that a segregated library was better than no library at all?

When it turned out that the students did not agree, the librarian said, "Close your mouths and open your minds." Finally, this sympathetic Yankee threw up her hands. "I can't make you go," she said, "but if you insist on staying, I will have to close the library and call the police."

The party refused. In several minutes the chief of police arrived and closed the library.

Following this object lesson on the effect of federal law on their everyday civil rights, the party decided to have lunch. They started for the lunch counter at Woolworth's, but when that was crowded, they decided on the nearby S.H. Kress store. While the group waited for a table, Hattiesburg patrolman Ralph Hillman entered the store and then left. A waitress then took the students' orders for hamburgers and Cokes. Adickes asked if the waitress had forgotten about her.

"No," the waitress said, "I am not serving you."

Adickes asked why.

"We have to serve Negroes," the waitress said, "but we are not serving whites who come in with them."

"Do you realize," asked Adickes, continuing the civics lesson, "this is a violation of the Civil Rights Bill [sic]?"

The waitress said she was acting under orders from her manager, Mr. G.T. Powell, who later testified that he gave those orders because he feared the "explosive situation" in the store.

The group left without eating. As Adickes stepped out onto the sidewalk, a police car pulled out of an alley and stopped on the street in front of her. In it were patrolman Hillman and a sergeant. They arrested her on a charge of vagrancy. Adickes had over fifty dollars with her and had a job making $2,200 a year as a New York City schoolteacher. She did not fit the definition of a vagrant who is "without regular employment or any visible means of support," and told the officers so. One replied, "We have orders to pick you up." Then he took her arm, saying, "Don't resist," and she got into the back of the cruiser.

On the way down, one of the officers taunted her, asking repeatedly, "Are you a nigger? You with the Liberace glasses, are you a nigger?"

The ride took five minutes, after which she was booked, fingerprinted, and placed in a cell. After about an hour, three lawyers came down to bail her out.

Adickes did not take the case to trial again after the Supreme Court decision in her favor.

Sandra Adickes did not drop out of the legal limelight, though. She turned up again in federal court against New York City in 1969. The suit involved a scuffle during a teachers' strike in which she allegedly kicked a policeman in the groin. When she was arrested for interfering with the arrest of another teacher, she sued the city, also under 42 U.S.C. § 1983, for depriving her of her constitutional provision for such a right. Adickes did not win.

The Original Conception of Summary Judgment. During the era of *Adickes*, summary judgment was often referred to as an "extraordinary remedy"—one that should be granted only when there was not the "slightest doubt" as to the actual facts. *See, e.g., Tomalewski v. State Farm Life Ins. Co.*, 494 F.2d 882 (3d Cir. 1974); *Clausen & Sons, Inc. v. Hamm Brewing Co.*, 395 F.2d 388 (8th Cir. 1968). It was extraordinary because the court was taking a case away from the jury.

The drafters probably did not think that summary judgment would be used frequently and in all types of cases. They were thinking in terms of the English experience in which summary judgment was used, in the words of Charles Clark, "as a simple and quick way of disposing of routine matters. Typically these are cases of debts or liquidated demands." *See* Stephen B. Burbank, *Vanishing Trials and Summary Judgment in Federal Civil Cases: Drifting Toward Bethlehem or Gomorrah*, 1 J. Empirical Legal Stud. 591, 602 n.48 (2004). For example, if a defendant has not repaid a loan and has no affirmative defenses to the creditor's action for breach, there is no reason for this case to go to trial; a summary judgment for the *plaintiff* would be appropriate.

REVIEW QUESTION

Assume that all of the evidence in the *Adickes* case was presented in the form of factual allegations in Adickes's complaint. Would that complaint survive a 12(b)(6) motion to dismiss for failure to state a claim after *Twombly* and *Iqbal*, which likewise involved elements of conspiracy or agreement?

QUESTIONS TO PONDER

Consider the questions presented in *Adickes* from a normative perspective. *Should* Adickes be able to present her claim to a jury? *Should* a jury be able to find that there existed a conspiracy based upon the evidence described?

More About the Case. Look up "Sandra Adickes" for an oral history and other accounts of her work as a Freedom School teacher and a veteran of the civil rights movement. She also wrote a book, *The Legacy of a Freedom School* (Palgrave Macmillan 2005). In public remarks she has lauded the role of courageous lawyers, such as Eleanor Jackson Piel, who were willing to offer legal representation in cases like hers.

2. A Focal Point of Litigation

As you have seen, by the mid-1980s there had been a good deal of criticism about alleged abuses of the wide-open, permissive Federal Rules. Amendments to the discovery rules and Rule 11 were one reaction. *Twombly* and *Iqbal* are more recent reactions in the pleading arena. Allegations about frivolous lawsuits also brought demands for more judicial responsiveness to summary judgment motions. *Celotex* and two other cases decided in the same term (combined, "the summary judgment trilogy cases") were read by most commentators as an attempt to dissuade and terminate what the majority of the Supreme Court thought was a growing number of meritless lawsuits.

Celotex Corp. v. Catrett
477 U.S. 317 (1986)

Justice REHNQUIST delivered the opinion of the Court:

The United States District Court for the District of Columbia granted the motion of petitioner Celotex Corporation for summary judgment against respondent Catrett because the latter was unable to produce evidence in support of her allegation in her wrongful-death complaint that the decedent had been exposed to petitioner's asbestos products. A divided panel of the Court of Appeals for the District of Columbia Circuit reversed, however, holding that petitioner's failure to support its motion with evidence tending to negate such exposure precluded the entry of summary judgment in its favor. *Catrett v. Johns-Manville Sales Corp.*, 244 U.S. App. D.C. 160, 756 F.2d 181 (1985). This view conflicted with that of the Third Circuit in *In re Japanese Electronic Products*, 723 F.2d 238 (1983), *rev'd on other grounds sub nom. Matsushita Electric Industrial Co. v. Zenith Radio Corp.*, 475 U.S. 574 (1986). We granted certiorari to resolve the conflict, and now reverse the decision of the District of Columbia Circuit.

Respondent commenced this lawsuit in September 1980, alleging that the death in 1979 of her husband, Louis H. Catrett, resulted from his exposure to products containing asbestos manufactured or distributed by 15 named corporations. Respondent's complaint sounded in negligence, breach of warranty, and strict liability. Two of the defendants filed motions challenging the District Court's in personam jurisdiction, and the remaining 13, including petitioner, filed motions for summary judgment. Petitioner's motion, which was first filed in September 1981, argued that summary judgment was proper because respondent had "failed to produce evidence that any [Celotex] product . . . was the proximate cause of the injuries alleged within the jurisdictional limits of [the

District] Court." In particular, petitioner noted that respondent had failed to identify, in answering interrogatories specifically requesting such information, any witnesses who could testify about the decedent's exposure to petitioner's asbestos products. In response to petitioner's summary judgment motion, respondent then produced three documents which she claimed "demonstrate that there is a genuine material factual dispute" as to whether the decedent had ever been exposed to petitioner's asbestos products. The three documents included a transcript of a deposition of the decedent, a letter from an official of one of the decedent's former employers whom petitioner planned to call as a trial witness, and a letter from an insurance company to respondent's attorney, all tending to establish that the decedent had been exposed to petitioner's asbestos products in Chicago during 1970-1971. Petitioner, in turn, argued that the three documents were inadmissible hearsay and thus could not be considered in opposition to the summary judgment motion.

In July 1982, almost two years after the commencement of the lawsuit, the District Court granted all of the motions filed by the various defendants. The court explained that it was granting petitioner's summary judgment motion because "there [was] no showing that the plaintiff was exposed to the defendant Celotex's product in the District of Columbia or elsewhere within the statutory period." Respondent appealed only the grant of summary judgment in favor of petitioner, and a divided panel of the District of Columbia Circuit reversed. The majority of the Court of Appeals held that petitioner's summary judgment motion was rendered "fatally defective" by the fact that petitioner "made no effort to adduce *any evidence*, in the form of affidavits or otherwise, to support its motion." 244 U.S. App. D.C., at 163, 756 F.2d, at 184 (emphasis in original). According to the majority, Rule 56(e) of the Federal Rules of Civil Procedure, and this Court's decision in *Adickes v. S. H. Kress & Co.*, 398 U.S. 144, 159 (1970), establish that "the party opposing the motion for summary judgment bears the burden of responding only after the moving party has met its burden of coming forward with proof of the absence of any genuine issues of material fact." The majority therefore declined to consider petitioner's argument that none of the evidence produced by respondent in opposition to the motion for summary judgment would have been admissible at trial. *Ibid*. The dissenting judge argued that "[t]he majority errs in supposing that a party seeking summary judgment must always make an affirmative evidentiary showing, even in cases where there is not a triable, factual dispute." According to the dissenting judge, the majority's decision "undermines the traditional authority of trial judges to grant summary judgment in meritless cases."

We think that the position taken by the majority of the Court of Appeals is inconsistent with the standard for summary judgment set forth in Rule 56(c) of the Federal Rules of Civil Procedure. Under Rule 56(c), summary judgment is proper "if the pleadings, depositions, answers to interrogatories, and admissions on file, together with the affidavits, if any, show that there is no genuine issue as any material fact and that the moving party is entitled to a judgment as a matter of law." In our view, the plain language of Rule 56(c) mandates the entry of summary judgment, after adequate time for discovery and upon motion, against a party who fails to make a showing sufficient to establish the existence of an element essential to that party's case, and on which that party will bear the burden of proof at trial. In such a situation, there can be "no genuine issue as to any material fact," since a complete failure of proof concerning an essential element of the nonmoving party's case necessarily renders all other facts immaterial. The moving party is "entitled to a judgment as a matter of law" because the nonmoving party has failed to make a sufficient showing on an essential element of her case with respect to which she has the burden of proof. "[T]h[e] standard [for granting summary judgment] mirrors the standard for a directed verdict under Federal Rule of Civil Procedure 50(a). . . ." *Anderson v. Liberty Lobby, Inc.*, 477 U.S. 242, 250 (1986).

Of course, a party seeking summary judgment always bears the initial responsibility of informing the district court of the basis for its motion, and identifying those portions of "the pleadings, depositions, answers to interrogatories, and admissions on file, together with the affidavits, if any," which it believes demonstrate the absence of a genuine issue of material fact. But unlike the Court of Appeals, we find no express or implied requirement in Rule 56 that the moving party support its motion with affidavits or other similar materials negating the opponent's claim. On the contrary, Rule 56(c), which refers to "*the affidavits, if any . . .*" (emphasis added), suggests the absence of such a requirement. And if there were any doubt about the meaning of Rule 56(c) in this regard, such doubt is clearly removed by Rules 56(a) and (b), which provide that claimants and defendants, respectively, may move for summary judgment "with or without supporting affidavits." . . .

Respondent argues, however, that Rule 56(e), by its terms, places on the nonmoving party the burden of coming forward with rebuttal affidavits, or other specified kinds of materials, only in response to a motion for summary judgment "made and supported as provided in this rule." According to respondent's argument, since petitioner did not "support" its motion with affidavits, summary judgment was improper in this case. But as we have already explained, a motion for summary judgment may be made pursuant to Rule 56 "with or without supporting affidavits." In cases like the instant one, where the nonmoving party will bear the burden of proof at trial on a dispositive issue, a summary judgment motion may properly be made in reliance solely on the "pleadings, depositions, answers to interrogatories, and admissions on file." Such a motion, whether or not accompanied by affidavits, will be "made and supported as provided in this rule," and Rule 56(e) therefore requires the nonmoving party to go beyond the pleadings and by her own affidavits, or by the "depositions, answers to interrogatories, and admissions on file," designate "specific facts showing that there is a genuine issue for trial."

We do not mean that the nonmoving party must produce evidence in a form that would be admissible at trial in order to avoid summary judgment. Obviously, Rule 56 does not require the nonmoving party to depose her own witnesses. Rule 56(e) permits a proper summary judgment motion to be opposed by any of the kinds of evidentiary materials listed in Rule 56(c), except the mere pleadings themselves, and it is from this list that one would normally expect the nonmoving party to make the showing to which we have referred.

The Court of Appeals in this case felt itself constrained, however, by language in our decision in *Adickes v. S. H. Kress & Co.*, 398 U.S. 144 (1970). There we held that summary judgment had been improperly entered in favor of the defendant restaurant in an action brought under 42 U.S.C. § 1983. In the course of its opinion, the *Adickes* Court said that "both the commentary on and the background of the 1963 amendment conclusively show that it was not intended to modify the burden of the moving party . . . to show initially the absence of a genuine issue concerning any material fact." *Id.* at 159. We think that this statement is accurate in a literal sense, since we fully agree with the *Adickes* Court that the 1963 amendment to Rule 56(e) was not designed to modify the burden of making the showing generally required by Rule 56(c). It also appears to us that, on the basis of the showing before the Court in *Adickes*, the motion for summary judgment in that case should have been denied. But we do not think the *Adickes* language quoted above should be construed to mean that the burden is on the party moving for summary judgment to produce evidence showing the absence of a genuine issue of material fact, even with respect to an issue on which the nonmoving party bears the burden of proof. Instead, as we have explained, the burden on the moving party may be discharged by "showing"—that is, pointing out to the district court—that there is an absence of evidence to support the non-moving party's case.

The last two sentences of Rule 56(e) were added, as this Court indicated in *Adickes*, to disapprove a line of cases allowing a party opposing summary judgment to resist a properly made motion by reference only to its pleadings. While the *Adickes* Court was undoubtedly correct in concluding that these two sentences were not intended to reduce the burden of the moving party, it is also obvious that they were not adopted to add to that burden. . . .

In this Court, respondent's brief and oral argument have been devoted as much to the proposition that an adequate showing of exposure to petitioner's asbestos products was made as to the proposition that no such showing should have been required. But the Court of Appeals declined to address either the adequacy of the showing made by respondent in opposition to petitioner's motion for summary judgment, or the question whether such a showing, if reduced to admissible evidence, would be sufficient to carry respondent's burden of proof at trial. We think the Court of Appeals with its superior knowledge of local law is better suited than we are to make these determinations in the first instance.

The Federal Rules of Civil Procedure have for almost 50 years authorized motions for summary judgment upon proper showings of the lack of a genuine, triable issue of material fact. Summary judgment procedure is properly regarded not as a disfavored procedural shortcut, but rather as an integral part of the Federal Rules as a whole, which are designed "to secure the just, speedy and inexpensive determination of every action." Fed. R. Civ. Proc. 1; *see* William Schwarzer, *Summary Judgment Under the Federal Rules: Defining Genuine Issues of Material Fact*, 99 F.R.D. 465, 467

(1984). Before the shift to "notice pleading" accomplished by the Federal Rules, motions to dismiss a complaint or to strike a defense were the principal tools by which factually insufficient claims or defenses could be isolated and prevented from going to trial with the attendant unwarranted consumption of public and private resources. But with the advent of "notice pleading," the motion to dismiss seldom fulfills this function anymore, and its place has been taken by the motion for summary judgment. Rule 56 must be construed with due regard not only for the rights of persons asserting claims and defenses that are adequately based in fact to have those claims and defenses tried to a jury, but also for the rights of persons opposing such claims and defenses to demonstrate in the manner provided by the Rule, prior to trial, that the claims and defenses have no factual basis.

The judgment of the Court of Appeals is accordingly reversed, and the case is remanded for further proceedings consistent with this opinion.

Justice WHITE, concurring:

I agree that the Court of Appeals was wrong in holding that the moving defendant must always support his motion with evidence or affidavits showing the absence of a genuine dispute about a material fact. I also agree that the movant may rely on depositions, answers to interrogatories, and the like, to demonstrate that the plaintiff has no evidence to prove his case and hence that there can be no factual dispute. But the movant must discharge the burden the Rules place upon him: It is not enough to move for summary judgment without supporting the motion in any way or with a conclusory assertion that the plaintiff has no evidence to prove his case.

A plaintiff need not initiate any discovery or reveal his witnesses or evidence unless required to do so under the discovery Rules or by court order. Of course, he must respond if required to do so; but he need not also depose his witnesses or obtain their affidavits to defeat a summary judgment motion asserting only that he has failed to produce any support for his case. It is the defendant's task to negate, if he can, the claimed basis for the suit. . . .

Justice BRENNAN, with whom THE CHIEF JUSTICE and Justice BLACKMUN join, dissenting:

This case requires the Court to determine whether Celotex satisfied its initial burden of production in moving for summary judgment on the ground that the plaintiff lacked evidence to establish an essential element of her case at trial. I do not disagree with the Court's legal analysis. The Court clearly rejects the ruling of the Court of Appeals that the defendant must provide affirmative evidence disproving the plaintiff's case. Beyond this, however, the Court has not clearly explained what is required of a moving party seeking summary judgment on the ground that the nonmoving party cannot prove its case. This lack of clarity is unfortunate: district courts must routinely decide summary judgment motions, and the Court's opinion will very likely create confusion. For this reason, even if I agreed with the Court's result, I would have written separately to explain more clearly the law in this area. However, because I believe that Celotex did not meet its burden of production under Federal Rule of Civil Procedure 56, I respectfully dissent from the Court's judgment.

I

Summary judgment is appropriate where the Court is satisfied "that there is no genuine issue as to any material fact and that the moving party is entitled to a judgment as a matter of law." Fed. R. Civ. P. 56(c). The burden of establishing the nonexistence of a "genuine issue" is on the party moving for summary judgment. This burden has two distinct components: an initial burden of production, which shifts to the nonmoving party if satisfied by the moving party; and an ultimate burden of persuasion, which always remains on the moving party. The court need not decide whether the moving party has satisfied its ultimate burden of persuasion unless and until the Court finds that the moving party has discharged its initial burden of production. *Adickes v. S. H. Kress & Co.*, 398 U.S. 144, 157-161 (1970); 1963 Advisory Committee's Notes on Fed. R. Civ. P. 56(e).

The burden of production imposed by Rule 56 requires the moving party to make a prima facie showing that it is entitled to summary judgment. The manner in which this showing can be made depends upon which party will bear the burden of persuasion on the challenged claim at trial. If the moving party will bear the burden of persuasion at trial, that party must support its motion with credible evidence—using any of the materials specified in Rule 56(c)—that would entitle it to a directed verdict if not controverted at trial. *Ibid.* Such an affirmative showing shifts the burden of production to the party opposing the motion and requires that party either to produce evidentiary materials that demonstrate the existence of a "genuine issue" for trial or to submit an affidavit requesting additional time for discovery. *Ibid.*; Fed. R. Civ. P. 56(e), (f).

If the burden of persuasion at trial would be on the nonmoving party, the party moving for summary judgment may satisfy Rule 56's burden of production in either of two ways. First, the moving party may submit affirmative evidence that negates an essential element of the nonmoving party's claim. Second, the moving party may demonstrate to the Court that the nonmoving party's evidence is insufficient to establish an essential element of the nonmoving party's claim. If the nonmoving party cannot muster sufficient evidence to make out its claim, a trial would be useless and the moving party is entitled to summary judgment as a matter of law. *Anderson v. Liberty Lobby, Inc.*, 477 U.S. 242, 249 (1986).

Where the moving party adopts this second option and seeks summary judgment on the ground that the nonmoving party—who will bear the burden of persuasion at trial—has no evidence, the mechanics of discharging Rule 56's burden of production are somewhat trickier. Plainly, a conclusory assertion that the nonmoving party has no evidence is insufficient. Such a "burden" of production is no burden at all and would simply permit summary judgment procedure to be converted into a tool for harassment. Rather, as the Court confirms, a party who moves for summary judgment on the ground that the nonmoving party has no evidence must affirmatively show the absence of evidence in the record. This may require the moving party to depose the nonmoving party's witnesses or to establish the inadequacy of documentary evidence. If there is literally no evidence in the record, the moving party may demonstrate this by reviewing for the court the admissions, interrogatories, and other exchanges between the parties that are in the record. Either way, however, the moving party must affirmatively demonstrate that there is no evidence in the record to support a judgment for the nonmoving party.

If the moving party has not fully discharged this initial burden of production, its motion for summary judgment must be denied, and the Court need not consider whether the moving party has met its ultimate burden of persuasion. Accordingly, the nonmoving party may defeat a motion for summary judgment that asserts that the nonmoving party has no evidence by calling the Court's attention to supporting evidence already in the record that was overlooked or ignored by the moving party. In that event, the moving party must respond by making an attempt to demonstrate the inadequacy of this evidence, for it is only by attacking all the record evidence allegedly supporting the nonmoving party that a party seeking summary judgment satisfies Rule 56's burden of production. Thus, if the record disclosed that the moving party had overlooked a witness who would provide relevant testimony for the nonmoving party at trial, the Court could not find that the moving party had discharged its initial burden of production unless the moving party sought to demonstrate the inadequacy of this witness' testimony. Absent such a demonstration, summary judgment would have to be denied on the ground that the moving party had failed to meet its burden of production under Rule 56.

The result in *Adickes v. S. H. Kress & Co., supra*, is fully consistent with these principles. In that case, petitioner was refused service in respondent's lunchroom and then was arrested for vagrancy by a local policeman as she left. Petitioner brought an action under 42 U.S.C. § 1983 claiming that the refusal of service and subsequent arrest were the product of a conspiracy between respondent and the police; as proof of this conspiracy, petitioner's complaint alleged that the arresting officer was in respondent's store at the time service was refused. Respondent subsequently moved for summary judgment on the ground that there was no actual evidence in the record from which a jury could draw an inference of conspiracy. In response, petitioner pointed to a statement from her own deposition and an unsworn statement by a Kress employee, both already in the record and both ignored by respondent, that the policeman who arrested petitioner was in the store at the time she was refused service. We agreed that "[i]f a policeman were present, . . . it would be open to a jury, in light of the sequence that followed, to infer from the circumstances that the policeman and Kress employee had a 'meeting of the minds' and thus reached an understanding that petitioner should be refused service." 398 U.S., at 158. Consequently, we held that it was error to grant summary judgment "on the basis of this record" because respondent had "failed to fulfill its initial burden" of demonstrating that there was no evidence that there was a policeman in the store. *Id.*, at 157-158.

The opinion in *Adickes* has sometimes been read to hold that summary judgment was inappropriate because the respondent had not submitted affirmative evidence to negate the possibility that there was a policeman in the store. The Court of Appeals apparently read *Adickes* this way and therefore required Celotex to submit evidence establishing that plaintiff's decedent had not been exposed to Celotex asbestos. I agree with the Court that this reading of *Adickes* was erroneous and that Celotex could seek summary judgment on the ground that plaintiff could not prove exposure to Celotex asbestos at trial. However, Celotex was still required to satisfy its initial burden of production.

II

I do not read the Court's opinion to say anything inconsistent with or different than the preceding discussion. My disagreement with the Court concerns the application of these principles to the facts of this case.

Defendant Celotex sought summary judgment on the ground that plaintiff had "failed to produce" any evidence that her decedent had ever been exposed to Celotex asbestos. Celotex supported this motion with a two-page "Statement of Material Facts as to Which There is No Genuine Issue" and a three-page "Memorandum of Points and Authorities" which asserted that the plaintiff had failed to identify any evidence in responding to two sets of interrogatories propounded by Celotex and that therefore the record was "totally devoid" of evidence to support plaintiff's claim.

Approximately three months earlier, Celotex had filed an essentially identical motion. Plaintiff responded to this earlier motion by producing three pieces of evidence which she claimed "[a]t the very least . . . demonstrate that there is a genuine factual dispute for trial": (1) a letter from an insurance representative of another defendant describing asbestos products to which plaintiff's decedent had been exposed; (2) a letter from T. R. Hoff, a former supervisor of decedent, describing asbestos products to which decedent had been exposed; and (3) a copy of decedent's deposition from earlier workmen's compensation proceedings. Plaintiff also apparently indicated at that time that she intended to call Mr. Hoff as a witness at trial.

Celotex subsequently withdrew its first motion for summary judgment. However, as a result of this motion, when Celotex filed its second summary judgment motion, the record did contain evidence—including at least one witness—supporting plaintiff's claim. Indeed, counsel for Celotex admitted to this Court at oral argument that Celotex was aware of this evidence and of plaintiff's intention to call Mr. Hoff as a witness at trial when the second summary judgment motion was filed. Moreover, plaintiff's response to Celotex' second motion pointed to this evidence—noting that it had already been provided to counsel for Celotex in connection with the first motion—and argued that Celotex had failed to "meet its burden of proving that there is no genuine factual dispute for trial."

On these facts, there is simply no question that Celotex failed to discharge its initial burden of production. Having chosen to base its motion on the argument that there was no evidence in the record to support plaintiff's claim, Celotex was not free to ignore supporting evidence that the record clearly contained. Rather, Celotex was required, as an initial matter, to attack the adequacy of this evidence. Celotex' failure to fulfill this simple requirement constituted a failure to discharge its initial burden of production under Rule 56, and thereby rendered summary judgment improper.

This case [therefore] is indistinguishable from *Adickes*. . . .

[The dissenting opinion of Justice STEVENS is omitted.]

REVIEW QUESTION

Do you agree with Justice Brennan that *Adickes* and *Celotex* are reconcilable? Be able to state the arguments for and against the proposition that the cases are reconcilable.

After* Celotex *Was Remanded. On remand to the appeals court that had earlier heard the case. Judge Kenneth Starr, a judge on that appeals court, wrote an opinion denying the defendant's summary judgment motion. *Catrett v. Johns-Mansville*, 826 F.2d 33 (D.C. Cir. 1987).

The Trilogy of Cases. The Supreme Court ruled on two other summary judgment cases during the same term as *Celotex*; the three cases (all three among the ten most-cited of all Supreme Court opinions) are frequently referred to as the "trilogy" of summary judgment cases. Most commentators at the time read the trilogy as signaling that the federal courts would be more favorably disposed to summary judgment motions than before. For instance, a partner at Skadden, Arps, Slate, Meagher & Flom, a large New York City law firm, already noted this tendency a year after the trilogy: "There is no question that the courts are more hospitable toward summary judgment. The attitude throughout the country has been changing toward them. Judges want more than ever to dispose of cases if they can at an early stage." Stephen Labaton, *The Summary Judgment Rule*, N.Y. Times, Aug. 17, 1987, at 22.

Another case in the trilogy was *Anderson v. Liberty Lobby, Inc.*, 477 U.S. 242 (1986). In *Liberty Lobby*, libel was the plaintiff's cause of action, and according to the substantive law, one of the elements of that cause of action—malice—needed to be proven by *clear and convincing evidence*. The issue in this case was whether that higher burden of proof at trial affected how the sufficiency of evidence was evaluated at the summary judgment stage. Justice White, writing for the majority in this 6-3 split, emphasized that the standard for summary judgment "mirrors the standard for a direct verdict under Fed. R. Civ. P. 50(a)." *Id.* at 250. Accordingly, when the standard of proof on an element would be higher at trial, the judge should incorporate that into the summary judgment inquiry, to wit: whether a reasonable jury could find the evidence of *x* to be clear and convincing?

Justice Brennan argued in dissent that when trial judges apply a "clear-and-convincing" standard at the summary judgment stage, they cannot avoid weighing evidence. Accordingly, they are improperly infringing on the province of the jury. Justice Brennan complained that the Court's opinion did not explain how a judge should "assess how one-sided evidence is, or what a 'fair-minded' jury could 'reasonably' decide. . . . I simply cannot square the direction that the judge 'is not himself to weigh the evidence' with the direction that the judge also bear in mind the 'quantum' of proof required and consider whether the evidence is of sufficient 'caliber or quantity' to meet that 'quantum.' I would have thought that a determination of the 'caliber and quantity,' i.e., the importance and value, of the evidence in light of the 'quantum,' i.e., amount 'required,' could *only* be performed by weighing the evidence." *Id.* at 265, 266 (emphasis in original).

Justice Rehnquist, joined by Chief Justice Burger, argued in a separate dissent that the majority's test would be difficult to apply. If the plaintiff could show that it had evidence of malice at the summary judgment stage, Justice Rehnquist did not see how a judge ruling on a summary judgment motion could determine that it would be insufficient evidence for the jury to find malice at the trial itself, unless the judge made a credibility determination. Justice Rehnquist concluded: "The primary effect of the Court's opinion today will likely be to cause the decisions of trial judges on summary judgment motions in libel cases to be more erratic and inconsistent than before. This is largely because the Court has created a standard that is different from the standard traditionally applied in summary judgment motions without even hinting as to how its new standard will be applied to particular cases." *Id.* at 272-273.

On remand, the federal district court applied the "clear and convincing evidence of actual malice" standard and granted summary judgment on seven of the nine counts remanded. *Liberty Lobby v. Anderson*, 1991 WL 186998 (D.D.C. May 1, 1991).

The third case of the trilogy, *Matsushita Elec. Industrial Co. v. Zenith Radio Corp.*, 475 U.S. 574 (1986), dealt with a claim by Zenith Co. against twenty-one Japanese companies that manufactured or sold consumer electronics products in America. Zenith alleged that the Japanese companies had conspired, in violation of the Sherman Antitrust Act and other statutes, to keep prices artificially high in Japan in order to subsidize artificially low prices in the United States, in order to push American companies out of the market. The district court granted summary judgment because "the alleged price-cutting conspiracy did not rebut the more plausible inference that petitioners were cutting prices to compete in the American market and not to monopolize it." The Court of Appeals reversed, concluding that "a reasonable factfinder could find a conspiracy to depress prices in the American market."

Limiting its review to the proper standard in evaluating the district court's decision, Justice Powell, writing for a five-member majority, held that "if the factual context renders [plaintiffs'] claim implausible—if the claim is one that simply makes no economic sense—[plaintiffs] must come forward with more persuasive evidence to support their claim than would otherwise be necessary."

Id. at 583. Engaging the academic literature on the subject, the Court observed that because predatory pricing is expensive and uncertain, it is rarely tried and even more rarely successful. Moreover, the predatory pricing alleged by the plaintiffs here "is incalculably more difficult to execute than an analogous plan undertaken by a single predator." *Id.* at 595.

The Court ruled that "where the record taken as a whole could not lead a rational trier of fact to find for the nonmoving party, there is no genuine issue for trial." *Id.* at 587. On the facts of the *Matsushita* case, the Court held that Zenith, the nonmover with the burden of proof at trial, had failed to present evidence at the summary judgment stage that "tends to exclude the possibility that the alleged conspirators acted independently." *Id.* at 588. The Court was unmoved by the proposed testimony of plaintiff's expert that there was a conspiracy; the Court found that the expert's opinion was "implausible" and inconsistent with other evidence in the record.

Justice White, joined by Justices Brennan, Blackmun, and Stevens, dissented, arguing that the majority had disregarded traditional summary judgment doctrine. They found the majority's disregard for the expert's proposed testimony a clear violation of the judicial obligation not to weigh evidence and assess credibility when ruling on a summary judgment motion: "If the Court intends to give every judge hearing a motion for summary judgment in an antitrust case the job of determining if the evidence makes the inference of conspiracy more probable than not, it is overturning settled law. If the Court does not intend such a pronouncement, it should refrain from using unnecessarily broad and confusing language." *Id.* at 598, 601. With respect to the majority's rejection of the opinion of the plaintiff's proposed expert, the dissent concluded: "No doubt the Court prefers its own economic theorizing to Dr. DePodwin's, but that is not a reason to deny the fact finder an opportunity to consider Dr. DePodwin's views on how petitioners' alleged collusion harmed respondents." *Id.* at 598, 603. Indeed, from our current knowledge of how electronics firms have employed long-term pricing strategies to maximize efficiency, we may wonder whether DePodwin's testimony would have struck fact finders as unbelievable. Isn't a court's judgment that there is no evidence different from its refusal to believe evidence that will be presented?

Summary judgment became the "focal point" of litigation. This shift was a revolutionary departure from prior practice—a shift that has been labeled "inefficient," and "unfair." *See, e.g.,* Ann C. McGinley, *Credulous Courts and the Tortured Trilogy, The Improper Use of Summary Judgment in Title VII and ADEA Cases,* 34 B.C. L. Rev. 203, 208 (1993) (recognizing unfairness); John Broonsteen, *Against Summary Judgment,* 75 Geo. Wash. L. Rev. 522 (2007) (recognizing inefficiency); Jeffrey W. Stempel, *Taking Cognitive Illiberalism Seriously: Judicial Humility, Aggregate Efficiency, and Acceptable Justice,* 43 Loy. U. Chi. L.J. 627, 680 (2012) (noting inefficiency). An interesting historical side note: The trilogy cases "ratified" more than "charted" the transformation of this device. The effect of summary judgment on the decline of trials likely began in the lower courts in the 1970s. Stephen B. Burbank, *Vanishing Trials and Summary Judgment in Federal*

Civil Cases: Drifting Toward Bethlehem or Gomorrah?, 1 J. Empirical Legal Stud. 591 (2004).

Summary Judgment as Terminus. Summary judgment is the focal point of litigation because it is, increasingly, the endpoint of litigation. Even though a relatively small percentage of cases are terminated by summary judgments (approximately 7.7 percent in 2000, an increase from 1.8 percent in 1960, according to one careful scholar's conservative estimate), less than half of the cases that encounter a summary judgment motion will survive it. Some surveys suggest that movants win 55 percent to 68 percent of their summary judgment motions. Some district courts granted summary judgment motions in employment discrimination cases as much as 95 percent of the time. *See* Brooke D. Coleman, *Summary Judgment: What We Think We Know Versus What We Ought to Know*, 43 Loy. U. Chi. L.J. 705, 710 (2012) (citing studies); Stephen N. Subrin and Thomas O. Main, *The Fourth Era of American Civil Procedure*, 162 U. Pa. L. Rev. 1839, 1852-1853 (2014); Stephen B. Burbank, *Vanishing Trials and Summary Judgment in Federal Civil Cases: Drifting Toward Bethlehem or Gomorrah?*, 1 J. Empirical Legal Stud. 591 (2004).

Since a summary judgment motion can dispose of an entire case (or an important issue in a case) without there being a trial, the courts have developed a number of means to protect the parties, particularly the nonmoving party. For example, even courts that normally do not permit oral argument on motions often permit such argument on summary judgment motions. You have already read how the trial court is to give the nonmoving party the benefit of accepting its potential admissible evidence as true at the summary judgment stage, and also to give the nonmoving party the benefit of permissible inferences.

Further, you will recall from the opinion in *Adickes* that the Rules allow a nonmovant to postpone consideration of a summary judgment motion when it is impractical for them to present facts to defeat that motion. *See* Rule 56(d). Although the nonmovant is by no means entitled to additional time, this is the Rule and tack you should consider as a plaintiff whenever a defendant moves for summary judgment while discovery is still underway.

Historical Context. With the judicial reinterpretation of the summary judgment standard, some experts have questioned the "legislative history" behind Rule 56. To be sure, Charles Clark (one of the drafters of the Federal Rules) and Jerome Frank, another famous judge on the U.S. Court of Appeals for the Second Circuit, famously disagreed about the proper standard for summary judgment, with Judge Clark advocating for the more aggressive use. *See Arnstein v. Porter*, 154 F.2d 464, 480 (2d Cir. 1946) (Clark, J., dissenting). Judge Frank thought that the "slightest doubt" about an issue of fact should defeat the motion. *Id.* at 468. Clark worried that such a liberal standard would facilitate the use of litigation as a tool for plaintiffs to harass defendants and to extract extortionate settlements. *See* Charles E. Clark, *The Summary Judgment*, 36 Minn. L. Rev. 567, 579 (1952). But one should not overstate Clark's enthusiasm for summary judgment; he envisioned a more active role for the motion only in cases where the material facts were not contested by either party. *See generally* Stephen N. Subrin and Thomas O. Main, *The Fourth Era of American Civil Procedure*, 162 U. Pa. L. Rev. 1839, 1844 n.24 (2014).

Rule 56(a) contemplates that a summary judgment may be entered on "part of [a] claim or defense." This is commonly referred to as a *partial* summary judgment. After a partial summary judgment, some facts or some elements will be treated as true at trial, leaving the fact finder with only the remaining facts and elements to consider. Understand, then, that a summary judgment could resolve just one element of a cause of action, or a whole cause of action, or even an entire case.

Constitutionality. The Supreme Court found summary adjudication to be constitutional in *Fidelity & Deposit Co. v. United States*, 187 U.S. 315, 318-322 (1902). But the transformation of the summary judgment device over the course of the past century may raise new problems with the Seventh Amendment. *See* Suja Thomas, *Why Summary Judgment Is Unconstitutional*, 93 Va. L. Rev. 139, 144 (2007). Professor Thomas has also discussed how the *Twombly* and *Iqbal* decisions have, in certain respects, moved the summary judgment standard into the pleading phase. *See* Suja A. Thomas, *The New Summary Judgment Motion: The Motion to Dismiss Under* Iqbal *and* Twombly, 14 Lewis & Clark L. Rev. 15 (2010).

Genuine Disputes of Material Fact—and Video Evidence. It is often debatable whether there is a genuine dispute of material fact—or, put another way, it is often debatable whether a reasonable fact finder *could* find the proffered evidence sufficient. One of the interesting developments in this area of the law is the role that videotapes of key events can (and should) play in applying the summary judgment standard. In *Scott v. Harris*, 550 U.S. 372 (2007), Victor Harris alleged an excessive force violation (of his constitutional rights) when police officer Timothy Scott, who was pursuing Harris's vehicle, hit Harris's car from behind in an effort to terminate a high-speed car chase. The impact caused Harris to lose control of car, which flipped off the road, rendering him a quadriplegic.

Harris's cause of action required that he ultimately prove that Scott used "excessive force." Harris assembled evidence from which, he claimed, a reasonable fact finder could determine that it was unreasonable for Scott to believe that Harris posed a threat to others and that it was unreasonable for Scott to pursue Harris in a high-speed chase and to bump Harris off the road. Harris proffered evidence that he posed no threat to pedestrians or other motorists—first, because the roads were mostly empty; and second, because he remained in control of his vehicle, slowed for turns and intersections, and typically used his signal lights. Further, Harris demonstrated that at the time he was bumped off of the road, the motorway had been cleared of motorists and pedestrians by police blockades at nearby intersections. Both the trial court and the appeals court found Harris's evidence sufficient to defeat the defendant's motion for summary judgment.

The Supreme Court acknowledged that on a motion for summary judgment the evidence must be viewed in the light most favorable to the nonmoving party. However, the Court also recognized an important "wrinkle" in this case: There was a videotape of the car chase. Indeed, this wrinkle received much attention at the oral argument of this case, as reflected in this account of the Court's exchange with Harris's counsel, Mr. Jones.

> Justice Alito started, "I looked at the videotape on this. It seemed to me that [Harris] created a tremendous risk [to] drivers on that road." "He created the scariest chase I ever saw since 'The French Connection,'" Justice Scalia immediately chimed in, provoking laughter throughout the courtroom.
>
> Probably even more dispiriting was the exchange that came next with Justice Breyer, whose vote Jones had likely been counting on for affirmance. "I was with you when I read . . . the opinion of the court below," Justice Breyer related. "Then I look at that tape, and I have to say that when I looked at the tape, my reaction was somewhat similar to Justice Alito's." As Jones attempted to offer a less damaging interpretation of the tape's contents, reinforced by an invocation of the jury's prerogatives as factfinder, Justice Breyer sharply retorted:
>
> JUSTICE BREYER: . . . What am I supposed to assume? . . . I mean, I looked at the tape and the tape shows he is weaving on both sides of the lane, swerving around automobiles that are coming in the opposite direction with their lights on, goes through a red light where there are several cars that are right there, weaves around them, and there are cars coming the other way, weaves back, goes down the road. . . . [A]m I supposed to pretend I haven't seen that? . . .
> MR. JONES: Well, I didn't see that.
> JUSTICE BREYER: You didn't see that?
> . . .
> MR. JONES: But those are not the facts that were found by the court below in this—
> JUSTICE BREYER: Well that's, that's what I wonder. If the court says that isn't what happened, and I see with my eyes that is what happened, what am I supposed to do?
>
> Later, during the rebuttal argument of opposing counsel (at which point a helpless Jones was reduced to watching mute), Justice Breyer continued, "I look at the tape and I end up with Chico Marx's old question with respect to the Court of Appeals: Who do you believe, me or your own eyes?"

Dan M. Kahan et al., *Whose Eyes Are You Going to Believe?* Scott v. Harris *and the Perils of Cognitive Illiberalism,* 122 Harv. L. Rev. 837, 839-840 (2009).

The Court's opinion, authored by Justice Scalia, described the videotape as showing Harris's car "racing" down the road in "the dead of night," driving "shockingly fast" and resembling "a Hollywood-style car chase of the most frightening sort." 550 U.S. at 380. Addressing the question whether Scott used excessive force, the Court held that "it is clear from the videotape that [Harris] posed an actual and imminent threat to the lives of any pedestrians who might have been present, to other civilian motorists, and to the officers involved in the chase." *Id.* at 384. The Court held that Harris's "version of events is so utterly discredited by the record that no reasonable jury could have believed him." *Id.* at 380. Accordingly, Scott was entitled to a summary judgment.

Justice Stevens was the lone dissenter. He characterized the conduct on the videotape much differently, noting that pedestrians and other drivers

> were exposed to no greater risk than persons who take the same action in response to a speeding ambulance. . . . Rather than supporting the conclusion that what we see on the video "resembles a Hollywood-style car chase of the most frightening sort," the tape actually confirms, rather than contradicts, the lower courts' appraisal of the factual questions at issue. More important, it surely does not provide a principled basis for depriving the respondent of his right to have a jury evaluate the question whether the police officers' decision to use deadly force to bring the chase to an end was reasonable.

Links to the video appear in the Court's opinion, in the Wikipedia page dedicated to this case, and on YouTube. Please find it and watch it for yourself.

In posting the videotape to the Court's Web site, Justice Scalia noted in his opinion that "[w]e are happy to allow the videotape to speak for itself." *Scott v. Harris*, 550 U.S. at 378 n.5. A team of scholars then asked: "[D]oes the *Scott v. Harris* tape speak for itself? If so, what does it say?" Dan M. Kahan et al., *Whose Eyes Are You Going to Believe? Scott v. Harris and the Perils of Cognitive Illiberalism*, 122 Harv. L. Rev. 837, 841 (2009).

As part of their study, these professors showed the video to more than 1,000 viewers who, unlike the Court, haled from various backgrounds. A substantial majority of the participants who watched the video agreed with the majority of the Court—concluding that, under the circumstances, Scott did not use excessive force. Yet many viewers concluded instead that the amount of force was excessive. Importantly, the clustering within each of the two groups reflect "core[s] of identity-defining characteristics"; put another way, backgrounds and experiences inform what one sees in this video. Kahan and his coauthors invoke the substantial social science literature about cognitive bias. "[O]ur power to perceive it in ourselves tends to be quite poor. We thus simultaneously experience overconfidence in the unassailable correctness of the factual perceptions we hold in common with our confederates and unwarranted contempt for the perceptions associated with our opposites." Kahan et al., 122 Harv. L. Rev. at 842-843.

What should we make of the Court's conclusion that the viewers who see excessive force in this video hold unreasonable views?

Since *Scott v. Harris*, there have been other summary judgment cases involving similar fact patterns that have been decided by the Supreme Court. For example, *Tolan v. Cotton*, 572 U.S. 650 (2014), involved a case that arose from a police mistake. As a car stopped in front of a house, a police officer mistyped the license plate number of that car into the database, and received a report that

that car was stolen. The officer drew his weapon and ordered the driver (Tolan) and his passenger to lie on the ground on the front porch of the house. Tolan's parents came outside and attempted to explain that there was some mistake because they owned both the house and the car. A second officer (Cotton) arrived on the scene, and ordered Tolan's mother to stand by the garage door and used a disputed amount of force to accomplish that. At that point Tolan rose either to his knees or his feet (another disputed fact) and said, "[G]et your fucking hands off my mom." Cotton then shot Tolan three times in the chest, causing serious although ultimately not fatal injury.

Tolan filed a suit much like Harris's, and the district and appellate courts entered summary judgment for the defendants. Although there was no video, the "context" in this case, according to the lower courts, precluded any reasonable jury from concluding that Cotton used excessive force. That context included: (1) the area was dimly lit; (2) Tolan's mother refused repeated orders; (3) Tolan was shouting and threatening; and (4) Tolan had risen to his feet.

The Supreme Court reversed. Addressing each of the four enumerated items above, the Court recognized competing evidence that, on a motion for summary judgment, must be viewed in the light most favorable to the nonmoving party. Specifically, Tolan and his parents testified that the premises were not dimly lit; Tolan's mother testified that she was insistent, but not agitated; Tolan testified that he was not screaming; and Tolan testified that he was on his knees, not his feet, and wasn't going anywhere. This contradictory testimony created factual disputes that made summary judgment inappropriate. *See generally* Howard M. Wasserman, *Mixed Signals on Summary Judgment*, 2014 Mich. St. L. Rev. 1331, 1341-1342.

About three weeks after *Tolan*, the Court issued its opinion in *Plumhoff v. Rickard*, 572 U.S. 765 (2014). Like *Scott v. Harris*, this case arose from the use of deadly force by police officers to end a car chase. After a traffic stop for a broken light, Rickard tried to evade the police on interstate and city streets. Rickard was eventually cornered by the police in a parking lot, thereby (and this was disputed) pausing or perhaps ending the pursuit. When Rickard did not exit the vehicle, police fired fifteen shots at the vehicle to prevent any further escape. Rickard then drove out of the lot and back onto the street before crashing the car into a building. Rickard and his daughter (his passenger) died from some combination of gunshot wounds and injuries from the crash. Dashboard cameras in the police cars captured video of the events. This video is also available from various online resources; view it before you come to class.

The district court denied Plumhoff's motion for summary judgment, identifying a number of disputed facts and analyzing the evidence in the light most favorable to Rickard, the nonmoving party. According to that district judge, the undisputed facts did not support a finding that it was objectively reasonable for the officers to use deadly force where a broken light precipitated this event, where none of the officers were in danger of being hit by Rickard's vehicle, and where no one believed or suspected that Rickard was armed. Although noting the similarity to *Scott v. Harris*, the Sixth Circuit affirmed because it could not conclude that the officers' conduct was reasonable as a matter of law. The Supreme Court reversed with a decision that is described and criticized in an article by Professor Howard Wasserman that is excerpted below.

The Court held in fairly short order (and without dissent) that the defendant officers were entitled to summary judgment. The officers did not violate the plaintiff's constitutional rights by firing fifteen shots at the car because (1) the chase was ongoing, meaning deadly force was justified to end it, and (2) having (properly) decided to use deadly force, the officers were entitled to use however much force was necessary to end the chase. In any event, the officers were entitled to qualified immunity because even if they used excessive force, it was not clearly established that such force violated the Fourth Amendment, given the absence of nondistinguishable case law finding a violation in using deadly force in similar circumstances. . . .

[*Plumhoff* is troubling because of its] over-reliance on video at summary judgment. The Court described at length what "happened" in the chase based solely on its review and interpretation of the video—it characterized the victim's driving as "outrageously reckless"; spoke of cars on the road "forced to alter course" to avoid the cars involved in the pursuit; saw the trapped driver in the parking lot "obviously pushing down on the accelerator because the car's wheels were spinning" while his car's bumper was flush against a police cruiser; and described the fleeing suspect as making "an attempt to escape." From this, the Court insisted that the "record conclusively disproves respondent's claims that the chase in the present case was already over when [the officers] began shooting."

The Court conspicuously and explicitly grounded its analysis in *Scott*. While it did not insist that the video can "speak for itself" and did not include a URL link to the video in the opinion—in fact, the Court never mentioned the video at all—it insisted that there was no reason to reach a different result. As in *Scott*, the Court drew conclusions and inferences about what the video showed. The Justices understood the video as necessarily and unavoidably onesided, capable of only one meaning and telling only one unquestionable and unambiguous story—the chase remained ongoing in the parking lot because the driver was still maneuvering his car, meaning he was trying to escape capture. Police thus did not act unreasonably in using deadly force at that point, because the video established that the chase, and thus the ongoing threat to public safety, was not at an end. . . .

[One problem with this approach to video evidence on summary judgment] is that video cannot, as *Scott* insisted and *Plumhoff* assumed, speak for itself. What video actually says depends on a number of different considerations—who and what is depicted, who created the images, and details of the images themselves (such as length, clarity, lighting, distance, angle, scope, steadiness, quality). These all affect the inferences that can and will be drawn from the video, allowing for many different possible conclusions. But that uncertainty is precisely why summary judgment is inappropriate in a case such as this, which requires that a fact finder view the video and draw those inferences for itself.

Second, as Dan Kahan and his co-authors famously showed, what a viewer "sees"—and the inferences and conclusions a viewer draws—from video are affected by cultural, demographic, social, political, and ideological characteristics. Video speaks "only against the background of preexisting understandings of social reality that invest[ed] those facts with meaning." It thus becomes more essential that the broader range of community voices that comprise a jury be given an opportunity to review and draw inferences from the video.

Unfortunately, *Plumhoff* demonstrates that the Court has not taken those lessons to heart. Nor have lower courts, which routinely grant summary judgment for defendants, and sometimes even for plaintiffs, solely on judicial conclusions about video. *Plumhoff* validates and sanctions what courts have been doing, reaffirming this erroneous approach to video evidence and to summary judgment. Indeed, *Plumhoff* goes one step further in that the Court never mentioned the video as part of the record, even as it relied on it almost exclusively; we know there was video in the record only from the lower court opinion and because the attorneys referred to it during oral argument.

Howard M. Wasserman, *Mixed Signals on Summary Judgment*, 2014 Mich. St. L. Rev. 1331, 1335-1338 (footnotes and citations omitted).

QUESTIONS TO PONDER

The purpose of the doctrine of qualified immunity is to ensure that insubstantial lawsuits against certain types of defendants are terminated quickly. Is this best achieved by modifying the pleading standard, the summary judgment standard, or both? Whether for cases filed against government officials or other defendants, is there some new, third way of filtering out unmeritorious claims in the pretrial stage?

3. The Fact-Law Distinction

During your law career, you will hear many times that issues of fact are for the jury and issues of law are for the judge. A paradigmatic question of fact asks the jury to find what an objective on-the-scene observer would have witnessed; for example, was the traffic light green (or red or yellow)? By contrast, a paradigmatic question of law asks the judge to resolve an issue of more generalized applicability, such as whether a particular cause of action does or does not require proof of the defendant's intent. In between those two paradigmatic extremes, however, are much more complicated questions, including so-called mixed questions of law and fact, some of which are resolved by judges and others by juries. Negligence, for example, is a mixed question of law and fact that is a jury question. In these circumstances, juries are not simply determining the historical fact (e.g., what happened?) but are also determining the legal effect of that finding (e.g., was that conduct unreasonable?).

[T]he decision to label an issue a "question of law," a "question of fact," or a "mixed question of law and fact" is sometimes as much a matter of allocation as it is of analysis. At least in those instances in which Congress has not spoken and in which the issue falls somewhere between a pristine legal standard and a simple historical fact, the fact/law distinction at times has turned on a determination that, as a matter of the sound administration of justice, one judicial actor is better positioned than another to decide the issue in question.

Miller v. Fenton, 474 U.S. 104, 113-114 (1985).

The delineation of questions of fact from questions of law matters at the summary judgment stage because only disputed questions of *fact* need to be presented to a jury. (Questions of *law* can be resolved by the judge at the summary judgment stage.) But this can be confusing when a court says, at the summary judgment stage, that as a matter of *law* there is no dispute as to a particular *fact*. Indeed, the very notion of summary judgment presupposes that judges are permitted to enter the domain of factual issues. In order to ensure that juries do not act irrationally, the theory goes, judges must be certain that before the jury can decide a factual issue on behalf of the party with the burden of production, there is sufficient evidence to permit reasonable people to make such a finding. Thus, the judiciary has created a threshold legal issue in order to decide the factual issue: It is deemed a legal question whether there is sufficient evidence to make a rational factual determination.

William Schwarzer, Summary Judgment Under the Federal Rules: Defining Genuine Issues of Material Fact
99 F.R.D. 465, 471-474 (1984)

Thus the court should first consider whether the disputed issue, as a matter of precedent or policy, should be decided by the jury or by the court. That approach should present no difficulty with respect to a large category of issues traditionally tried to juries. Whether a defendant has failed to use due care in the operation of his vehicle, whether he was driving in the course of his employment, and whether the injuries suffered by plaintiff were proximately caused by the defendant's operation of the vehicle are issues of ultimate fact for the jury. Similarly, whether a person had reasonable cause, acted within a reasonable time or can be charged with notice are jury issues. All are ultimate facts turning on examination and assessment of human behavior within the common experience of jurors. Concerning issues of this sort, "[i]t is assumed that twelve men know more of the common affairs of life than does one man, that they can draw wiser and safer conclusions from admitted facts thus occurring than can a single judge." Decisions of such issues, moreover, are generally ad hoc, with little resort to policy, with precedent playing a minor part, and with no compelling need for uniform or predictable outcomes. Of such mixed issues of fact and law, one can say that their law content is relatively low.

This does not mean that every such issue must be submitted to the jury, i.e. that summary judgment is precluded. That will turn on the second prong of the test—whether the motion or the opposition is sufficient to establish that the proponent of the issue could survive a motion for directed verdict or for judgment n.o.v. . . .

A second category of ultimate fact issues consists of those which involve the application of predominantly legal standards to undisputed historical facts. The decision here turns not so much on factors within the common experience of jurors as on matters of law and policy and on technical questions underlying the particular legal scheme. It should not be made ad hoc; consistency, uniformity and predictability here are important to the administration of the underlying laws. Issues of this sort arise most frequently in the application of legislation or of public policies. Examples include whether a union breached its duty of fair representation, whether a controlling person acted in good faith within the meaning of the securities laws, whether location restrictions in a dealer agreement were an unreasonable restraint in violation of the antitrust laws. . . . Of mixed questions such as these, it is fair to say that their law content predominates.

Ultimate fact issues of this sort are properly decided by the court and are therefore appropriate for summary judgment if the underlying historical facts are not disputed. That is true even though the process of decision requires the trial court to "weigh the evidence" on both sides of the argument in deciding what ultimate fact to derive. . . .

A third category consists of those issues of ultimate fact which may be appropriate for jury determination in some cases but not in others. One example of such a variable issue is the existence of a conspiracy under the antitrust laws. In certain conspiracy cases the lawfulness of joint conduct of defendants can turn on their purpose and intent, a question of fact usually disputed and well within the conventional sphere of the jury. In other cases, the conspiracy issue may turn on whether, as a matter of law and policy, a particular relationship among parties, the historical facts of which are not disputed, should be treated as an unlawful conspiracy. . . .

4. Strategic Considerations

Like all motions, there are strategic matters to consider before filing a summary judgment motion. This is not just a matter of avoiding sanctions or avoiding a likely waste of time and money, although these are important considerations. To file a summary judgment motion and memorandum or brief in support thereof means educating opposing counsel about your view of their case and, in some instances, of your own case. On the other hand, it may be a way of smoking out opposing counsel's best case in advance of trial. But even this is more complicated. If a party against whom the motion is brought thinks she can easily defeat it without revealing all of her cards, she may do so. For instance, a plaintiff may have many theories of recovery or cumulative potential evidence, but reveal at the summary judgment stage only enough to survive the motion. This, too, is complex. It would be embarrassing—if not malpractice—for counsel defending against a summary judgment to hold back in order not to educate an opponent, only to find out that her client loses at the summary judgment stage.

Bear in mind that winning or losing the motion is not the only issue and that there are audiences other than opposing counsel. One must consider who the judge is likely to be and whether the summary judgment motion is a good means of early education for the judge. Will the judge who hears the motion be the same judge who sits at trial? There also looms the question of settlement. Will it be easier or harder to settle the case once the motion is filed and after each side files memoranda in support of or opposing the motion, or once the outcome of your motion is known? Do you want to run that risk?

Some cases look stronger or weaker depending on whether they are decided on a written record or with live testimony. Some cases simply look different when you consider whether a judge or a jury will be the fact finder. Even though a summary judgment motion is in large measure a prediction of what would happen at the directed verdict stage at trial, the situations are different psychologically. Many cases demand the drawing of inferences, for example, and sympathetic testimony for one side or another may contract or expand the inferences that a judge is willing to draw or to permit a jury to draw.

Finally, consider these questions. Will the filing of a summary judgment motion delay your trial date? Is delay good or bad for your client? Is a swift decision—even if it is a negative one—a priority for your client? Perhaps you and your client are trying to establish a new cause of action in your jurisdiction, and you want an appellate court to hear the question as soon as possible. But, then again, you may want to attempt to convince appellate judges to stretch current precedent with the aid of an entire trial record.

Litigation is a human enterprise in which experience means a great deal; lawyers tend to become more valuable with age and practice. If you choose to do trial work, over time you will work out your own sense of litigation strategy. You will become more skilled at deciding which variables are most important to you and your client—and, if your client is lucky, your mind will remain open to new variables and new assessments of the old variables.

PRACTICE EXERCISE NO. 24: SUMMARY JUDGMENT MOTION SESSION IN *CARPENTER*

This practice exercise has two parts. You may be assigned either or both. For each part, read the summary judgment motion of the third-party defendants, the memorandum in support of the motion, the Regulations, the stipulation of all parties, and the Restatement excerpts, which are in the Case Files, as well as any other materials in the *Carpenter v. Dee* case that you feel are relevant to the exercise. (Assume that the Massachusetts summary judgment rule is identical to Fed. R. Civ. P. 56. Moreover, in recent years, the Massachusetts Supreme Judicial Court, when interpreting Mass. R. Civ. P. 56, has cited and followed the reasoning of the U.S. Supreme Court's trilogy cases. There is absolutely no need to go beyond the pages of this textbook, including the Case Files, in order to do a first-rate job on these exercises.) As you read the materials, consider how, if you represented Dale McGill and McGill's Garage, you would attempt to convince a judge that there is no material issue of fact for the jury to decide and that this is a case that can be decided at summary judgment as a matter of law. Is it your position that the issue to be decided at summary judgment is for the court and not the jury or that, as to one or more elements, Ultimate Auto will have insufficient evidence for the court to find for it—or that both are true?

For purposes of both the written and oral portion of the exercise, assume that this is the structure of the case. Nancy Carpenter sued the Dees. She then amended to add Ultimate Auto and the City as defendants. Through Rule 14, Ultimate Auto impleaded McGill and his Garage. The Dees, Ultimate Auto, and the City each filed cross-claims against each other. After discovery, and before any amendment by Carpenter to claim against McGill and his Garage, McGill and his Garage moved for summary judgment against Ultimate Auto, and Ultimate Auto opposed this motion. It is the McGill and McGill Garage summary judgment motion against Ultimate Auto that you will address in both the written and oral portions of the exercise.

In the actual case, the City also moved for summary judgment, and that motion was denied. As a matter of trial strategy, however, the plaintiff's counsel later dropped the allegations against the City, because of (a) concern for the feelings a jury might have about blaming police officers for failing to get the jeep off the road (or otherwise warn), which might in turn prejudice a jury against the plaintiff's strong claim against Ultimate Auto; (b) concern about the reaction of jurors as taxpayers who might not want to cost the City money which, in turn, might somehow poison them against the plaintiff generally; (c) concern that juries think a plaintiff's case is weaker when a shotgun approach is used of suing everyone in sight; (d) belief that the City was largely judgment-proof; and (e) belief that the case against the City was not very strong anyway. In fact, after the actual lawsuit, the Massachusetts legislature passed a statute making it very unlikely that a case such as this could be successfully sustained against a Massachusetts municipality.

A. Written Exercise. *As counsel for Ultimate Auto, prepare a Memorandum for the Court in Opposition to the Third-Party Motion for Summary Judgment.* The memorandum cannot exceed four double-spaced pages (including the caption). The memoranda will be collected at the end of class. Before you prepare your memorandum, make sure you are clear on how many arguments you have. You may wish first to make an outline. For instance, are you arguing that the law requires a broader duty than the third-party defendants suggest, or that there are underlying factual disputes, or both? Or do you have other arguments? As to each argument, make sub-arguments or a list of reasons. Definition and clarity are essential in constructing effective legal arguments.

B. Oral Exercise. *As counsel for Ultimate Auto or the Garage, prepare an oral argument for or against the summary judgment motion.* A motion session judge will hear argument from both sides on the summary judgment motion of McGill and the Garage against Ultimate Auto. If your last name begins with any letter from H through T, be prepared to argue orally on behalf of Ultimate Auto. If your last name begins with any other letter, be prepared to argue for Dale McGill and McGill's Garage in favor of the summary judgment motion. Assume that the judge will ask to hear first from the moving party. Also assume that the judge was recently appointed to the bench, and is unfamiliar with the details of your case.

PRACTICE EXERCISE NO. 25: SUMMARY JUDGMENT MOTION SESSION IN *WARNER*

Defendants filed a motion for partial summary judgment on all of the claims brought by Plaintiff Jacob Warner, with respect to the stop in February 2012. The United States Supreme Court has held that "the police can stop and briefly detain a person for investigative purposes if the officer has reasonable suspicion supported by articulable facts that criminal activity may be afoot," even if the officer lacks probable cause. *Terry v. Ohio*, 292 U.S. 1 (1968). There must be a "minimal level of objective justification for making the stop." *Illinois v. Wardlow*, 528 U.S. 119, 123 (2000) (quotation omitted). The officer making a *Terry* stop "must be able to articulate something more than an inchoate and unparticularized suspicion or hunch." *Alabama v. White*, 496 U.S. 325, 329 (1990). The question is whether "all the facts taken together support a reasonable suspicion of wrongdoing" and the fact that the stop occurs in a high-crime area, while not by itself sufficient, may be "among the relevant contextual considerations[.]" *Wardlow*, 528 U.S. at 124. You may also wish to review the initial memorandum in this case.

This exercise is an oral argument. As a part of this exercise, the following prospective evidence is available in the Case Files: (1) Deposition of Jacob Warner; (2) Deposition of Officer Richard Cannon; (3) Affidavit of Lauren Cassidy; and (4) Affidavit of Detective Susan Stephens.

Student-lawyers with last names starting with the letters A through M will represent the defendants, and will argue in favor of defendants' motion for summary judgment. Student-lawyers with last names starting with the letters N through Z will represent the plaintiffs, and will argue in opposition to defendants' motion for summary judgment.

E. DISMISSAL, DIRECTED VERDICTS, JUDGMENTS NOTWITHSTANDING THE VERDICT, NEW TRIAL MOTIONS, AND MOTIONS TO VACATE JUDGMENT

You have now studied summary judgment, which takes place prior to trials. We next want to teach you about three jury-control mechanisms—directed verdict, judgment notwithstanding the verdict (JNOV), and new trial motions—and about methods for dismissing cases and having judgments vacated. If we were going in chronological order, a timeline for a typical federal jury case might look something like the following. Don't take the timeline too literally; not every step must take place, and many steps overlap or could happen in a different order for any of a number of good reasons.

> Complaint
> 12(b) motions
> Answer
> Motions for voluntary or involuntary dismissal
> Rule 16 scheduling conference and order (*see* Chapter 6)
> Discovery
> Motions to amend
> Settlement discussion
> Motions for summary judgment
> Rule 16 pretrial conference
> Trial
> Motions for directed verdict/judgment as a matter of law
> Verdict
> Entry of judgment
> Motions for JNOV/judgment as a matter of law
> Motions for new trial
> Appeals
> Motions to vacate judgment
> Execution of judgment

You should also have some picture in your mind of what goes on at a trial. A jury trial begins with impaneling a jury, including voir dire and challenges of jurors for cause and peremptory challenges, topics that we have already covered. Whether there is a jury or not, the next stage is for the plaintiff and the defendant to give opening statements, with the plaintiff ordinarily going first. The parties then present their evidence through witnesses and exhibits. As each party presents its evidence, the opposing parties may object on the grounds that the evidence is inadmissible. The defendant's lawyer has an opportunity to cross-examine each of the plaintiff's witnesses, usually followed by re-direct and re-cross. After the plaintiff rests, and assuming that there is not a directed verdict motion or that such a motion has been denied, the defendant presents its case in the same manner that the plaintiff did (with direct and cross-examination). The plaintiff can then present rebuttal evidence, and then the defendant can do the same. Assuming that the case is not disposed of by directed verdict motions after all parties have rested, there are then final arguments by each side. In many courts, the defendant closes first, followed by the plaintiff. In others, the plaintiff is permitted to have the first and final closing arguments, with the defendant's closing argument in between. If there is a jury, the judge will usually instruct it on the law after all of the closing arguments. Some judges choose to instruct at the beginning of the case and at the end, while others instruct the jury immediately before the lawyers give their closing arguments. The jury then deliberates and returns a verdict, filling in the verdict slip or answering the questions presented by the judge, sometimes both. (*See* Fed. R. Civ. P. 49.)

We next discuss the current ground rules on dismissals, directed verdict motions, judgment notwithstanding the verdict, and motions for new trial.

1. Voluntary Dismissal

Fed. R. Civ. P. 41(a)(1) prescribes when a plaintiff has a right to dismiss a case voluntarily, and 41(a)(2) describes the court's power to permit a plaintiff to dismiss a case voluntarily. Note that in the normal case, the plaintiff has an absolute right to dismiss voluntarily prior to the adverse party's filing an answer or a motion for summary judgment. Unless otherwise stated in the court's notice of dismissal or in a stipulation of dismissal signed by all parties who have appeared in the action, or unless the plaintiff has previously filed and dismissed the same claim in a state or federal court, then such voluntary dismissal will be *without prejudice*. That means the plaintiff can bring the claim again; put another way, it means the dismissal will *not* have a *res judicata* effect.

Under Fed. R. Civ. P. 41(a)(2), the plaintiff, in situations not covered by 41(a)(1), can apply to the court for a voluntary dismissal, and the court, upon "terms that the court considers proper," has the power to grant it. Unless the court otherwise states, this dismissal will also be "without prejudice." The reference to "terms" is an invitation to the court to condition the dismissal on the plaintiff's paying all or part of the defendant's expenses to date in defending the suit. The court can also decide to permit the voluntary dismissal only with prejudice. If the case has proceeded very far, and the court and the other party have already expended significant resources and time on the case, the court will likely dismiss with prejudice or dismiss without prejudice on the condition that plaintiff pay defendant's expenses to defend to date. Fed. R. Civ. P. 41(d) covers a lacuna in 41(a)(1), to wit: situations in which the plaintiff has an absolute right to voluntarily dismiss "without prejudice," but this is not the first time the plaintiff has had the same claim dismissed. In this situation, the court can award the costs of the action previously dismissed to the opposing party and "may stay the proceedings until the plaintiff has complied." There is a circuit conflict over whether federal district courts may award attorneys' fees under Rule 41(d)'s use of the word "costs" of the previously dismissed claim, and if so, whether the district court must first give notice of the approximate costs and/or an opportunity to withdraw the motion to dismiss. *See* Michael E. Solimine and Amy E. Lippert, *Deregulating Voluntary Dismissals*, 36 U. Mich. J.L. Reform 367 (2003).

Notice that Fed. R. Civ. P. 41(c) permits claimants other than plaintiffs to seek voluntary dismissals. This is because counterclaims, cross-claims, and third-party claims put the defendant in a plaintiff's posture for those aspects of the case.

2. Involuntary Dismissal

Often a court orders a case dismissed even though the plaintiff would very much like it to continue. For instance, you have already seen dismissals for failure to state a claim or for failure to survive a summary judgment motion. Pursuant to Fed. R. Civ. P. 41(b), unless the court otherwise orders, these and other involuntary dismissals "operate[] as an adjudication on the merits," which is another way of saying the dismissal has a *res judicata* effect. When we reach Chapters 7 and 8 we will consider in more detail why dismissals for lack of subject matter jurisdiction, personal jurisdiction, and venue do not have *res judicata* effect; a 12(b)(7) dismissal for failure to join a Rule 19 (necessary and indispensable) party also does not have *res judicata* effect. Involuntary dismissals for failing to comply with a court order operate "as an adjudication on the merits." It would be a very inefficient system, if not an unfair one, that permitted a plaintiff or its attorney to fail to comply with a discovery order, an order relating to pre-trial conferences, or other orders of the court, without the ultimate available sanction of dismissal with prejudice.

3. Directed Verdict (Judgment as a Matter of Law)

We have been anticipating this device ever since Chapter 3, when you were first exposed to the burden of production, and you have met the concept again in our classes on summary judgment. To refresh your recollection, the party with the burden of production on an issue (we have been using the word *element* previously, instead of *issue*, for that is usually what is at stake) has the obligation to enter sufficient evidence on that issue to permit a reasonable fact finder to find for that party. Otherwise, as to that issue, and upon proper motion by the opposition, the party with the production burden will lose. If losing on that issue means the party cannot win on the claim, it will lose the case.

Just as in summary judgment, the judge deciding a directed verdict motion is obligated to consider the evidence of the nonmoving party in the light most favorable to that party, taking the nonmover's conceivably believable evidence as true and giving the nonmover the benefit of all reasonable inferences. This procedural mechanism is usually used by a defendant to defeat a plaintiff, before the fact finder even deliberates on the evidence, on the ground that, on at least one element of the plaintiff's cause of action, no reasonable fact finder could find for the plaintiff. We will consider after *Galloway* the less typical situation of a plaintiff's seeking and receiving a directed verdict or "judgment as a matter of law."

As Fed. R. Civ. P. 50 now puts it, in cases tried before a jury, if a claim cannot be maintained without a party's having "a legally sufficient evidentiary basis to find for the party on that issue," and if such evidence was not presented—and if the party has been fully heard with respect to that issue—then the court "may . . . grant a motion for judgment as a matter of law" on that claim. Fed. R. Civ. P. 50(a)(1)(B). Read Federal Rule 50 with particular care, as it contains complexity and nuance.

A party may move for judgment as a matter of law at any time before submission to the jury. Fed. R. Civ. P. 50(a)(2). According to the Advisory Committee Notes on the amendment, this means that a judge could, for instance, require a plaintiff to introduce all of her evidence on a necessary element early in a case (such as duty or unreasonable care in a negligence case) and then, prior to the plaintiff's resting on the entire case, permit the defendant to move for judgment as a matter of law on the grounds of insufficient evidence on the one element. You can read the Advisory Committee Notes on the 1991 amendments to the Federal Rules to discover why the language was changed from "directed verdict" to "judgment as a matter of law," even though the Advisory Committee hastened to add that the new rule "effects no change in the existing standard" that has been "articulated in long-standing case law."

The concept of "sufficiency of evidence to permit a finding on an element of the case" (put another way, the idea of a "production burden") is also applicable in cases without a jury. For instance, if in a Title VII case without a jury the plaintiff had no evidence of discrimination (either through adverse impact or adverse treatment), then it would not make sense to force the defendant to present evidence or for the judge to hear it. Rule 52(c) covers this situation, and permits the judge to enter judgment as a matter of law against a party on a claim that the party cannot win, so long as that party "has been fully heard on an issue," the court finds against the party on that issue, and it is dispositive of the case.

Notice that Rule 52(c), which deals with actions without a jury, does not use the Rule 50(a) language about "legally sufficient evidentiary basis." Assume in *Carpenter*, for example, that the parties chose to try the case on a jury-waived basis. Assume further that the plaintiff introduced evidence that would be sufficient to permit a finding of unreasonable care against Ultimate Auto, the retailer, but that the judge does not believe the plaintiff's evidence, and the judge knows this even before the defendant has put on any evidence of its own. Could the judge enter judgment as a matter of law against the plaintiff, even though she could not have done so had there been a jury? Does the difference in language between Rules 50(a) and 52(c) make sense? In both jury cases and nonjury cases, could the plaintiff achieve a judgment as a matter of law prior to the defendant's having an opportunity to put on its case?

4. Judgment Notwithstanding the Verdict (JNOV/Renewed Judgment as a Matter of Law)

Even after the jury has rendered a verdict, a judge—having previously denied a directed verdict motion on the same grounds—can grant the party against whom the judgment was rendered a judgment notwithstanding the verdict. The test is identical to that of directed verdict (or the test for judgment as a matter of law, under Fed. R. Civ. P. 50(a)). For the federal rendition of this concept, see Fed. R. Civ. P. 50(b)—the *renewed* motion for judgment as a matter of law.

Consider a simple motor vehicle negligence case. Assume the plaintiff, a pedestrian, has introduced its evidence, and rested. The defendant, driver of a car, moves for directed verdict on the ground that there is insufficient evidence for the jury to find for the plaintiff on the element of unreasonable care. The judge may think the defendant is correct about the insufficiency of evidence, and be tempted to grant the motion, but remain uncertain. Since it is a close question—for example, one based on the inferences that can be drawn from a skid mark—the judge thinks that an appellate court may disagree. Can you see two reasons why it may make sense for the judge to deny the initial motion for directed verdict, and then, if the jury finds for the plaintiff, grant the motion for JNOV? If you need help, or just want to check your instincts, the Advisory Committee Notes to the 1991 amendments to Fed. R. Civ. P. 50(b) discuss this issue.

Re-read the Seventh Amendment to the U.S. Constitution carefully, concentrating on the language about "no fact tried by a jury," and you will see why JNOV was constitutionally problematic. (*JNOV* is shorthand for a somewhat different common law motion which, using Latin, was called *judgment non obstante veredicto*.) The motion was held unconstitutional by a bare majority in *Slocum v. New York Life Insurance Co.*, 228 U.S. 364 (1913). In *Baltimore & Carolina Line, Inc. v. Redman*, 295 U.S. 654 (1935), the Court allowed such a motion in a case in which the trial judge had reserved decision on the directed verdict motion until after the verdict was rendered. The Court seized upon the "reservation" to distinguish *Slocum*. The original drafters of the Federal Rules went one step further in Fed. R. Civ. P. 50(b) and said that if a party seeks directed verdict at the close of *all* of the evidence and it is denied or not granted, "the court is deemed to have submitted the action to the jury subject to a later determination of the legal questions raised by the motion." This fiction, which also remains in the current version of Rule 50(b), has been held sufficient to render the Rule and the practice constitutional. *Neely v. Martin K. Eby Construction Co.*, 386 U.S. 317, 321 (1967).

Courts have affirmed the requirement that a party move for directed verdict (now: judgment as a matter of law) at the close of all of the evidence in order to bring a motion for JNOV. One of the virtues of the modern terminology is its clarity on this point: The JNOV is now referred to as a *renewed* motion for judgment as a matter of law under Fed. R. Civ. P. 50(b). When such motions are made, defense counsel normally moves for directed verdict or judgment as a matter of law after the plaintiff rests, and then, if denied, again after all parties rest. In all motions under Fed. R. Civ. P. 50, Rule 50(a)(2) requires the moving party to "specify the judgment sought and the law and facts that entitle the movant to the judgment." (Does Federal Rule 7(b)(1)(A) require that this motion be made in writing? And because Rule 11 applies to all motions, what constraints does this impose on making Federal Rule 50(a) and 50(b) motions?)

The failure to file a renewed motion for judgment as a matter of law may constitute a waiver of the opportunity to challenge the sufficiency of the evidence on appeal. In *Unitherm Food Systems, Inc. v. Swift-Eckrich, Inc.*, 546 U.S. 394 (2006), the defendant properly filed its Rule 50(a) motion, and this motion was denied by the court. After the jury returned a verdict for plaintiff, the defendant neglected to file its renewed motion under Rule 50(b). On appeal, defendant argued the insufficiency of plaintiff's evidence and sought a *new trial*. Importantly, the defendant did not argue on the appeal that it was entitled to judgment as a matter of law. To be sure, defendant inadvertently waived the ability to challenge the sufficiency of evidence under Rule 50(b) by failing to raise that motion. But the Court also would not allow defendant to challenge the sufficiency of evidence under Rule 50(a)—even though defendant had properly asserted it. Compare the options available to the district judge under Rule 50(a)(1) and under Rule 50(b). Can you explain why the Court concluded that neither the district court nor the appellate courts would have the authority to grant a new trial under these circumstances?

5. Motions for New Trial

Even after the jury renders its verdict (or a judge without a jury, for that matter), the losing side can still move for a new trial. *See* Fed. R. Civ. P. 59(a)(1) and (a)(2). In fact, in federal court, pursuant to Rule 59(d), the judge is explicitly empowered to grant a new trial on the judge's own initiative. Students often find the notion of new trial motions the "straw that breaks the camel's back" when it comes to judicial control of juries. But before you draw that conclusion, give it some thought.

Consider first the language of the Rule itself, which says that a new trial may be granted in jury cases "for any reason for which a new trial has heretofore been granted in an action at law in federal court." Fed. R. Civ. P. 59(a)(1)(A). Many states have similar language, although the state rule would instead look to the historical practice in the courts of the state in question. Other states, by statute or rule, list the grounds for new trial motions, but these are often quite similar to the grounds that would be permissible in federal court or in a state that merely looks to precedents.

One type of new trial motion should not be problematic at all. Assume that after the jury has rendered its verdict (or even during a case), a judge becomes convinced that she has made a mistake that would be reversible error if considered by an appellate court, and that there is no way to correct the error. Say, for instance, the judge realizes after the jury has rendered its verdict and has been released that she mistakenly admitted evidence over correct objection, and that this was not "harmless" within the meaning of Fed. R. Civ. P. 61. Or assume that she was incorrect in her charge to the jury in a material way, even though the losing party had tried to save the court from error by complying with Fed. R. Civ. P. 51 ("Instructions to the Jury; Objections"). If the losing party moves for a new trial on grounds for which an appellate court would grant a new trial on appeal, then surely it makes sense for the new trial to be granted by the trial judge if she is now aware of the reversible error. Would not any other solution be wasteful, if not cruel, because it would force parties into the time, expense, and anxiety of an appeal in which the result is known? It is rare that a trial judge will be sure she has committed reversible error; but, nonetheless, trial judges should (and thus likely do) try to do justice by granting new trials when they are fairly certain an appellate court would do the same.

Perhaps a bit more problematic, but nonetheless well-established law in many jurisdictions, is the granting of new trial motions on grounds that the jury verdict is so excessive or inadequate as to demonstrate that the jury has misunderstood its duty or acted with extreme prejudice. The situation is most clear when the damages are liquidated, as in a written contract case with a specified monetary amount, and the jury finds for the plaintiff in an amount unrelated to the contractual provision. A tort verdict that contains an amount for "pain and suffering" or "disfigurement" is by its very nature discretionary. Consequently, the grant of a new trial because of the excessiveness or inadequacy of the award has a discretionary element. But even here, some awards would to most reasonable people seem "unsupported by the evidence." Consider a negligently caused scratch, without any sign of malice or realistically increased risk to the plaintiff, which results in a multimillion dollar award. Shouldn't a trial judge, who, like the jury, has taken an oath to do justice, grant a new trial? The courts are not in agreement on how far appellate courts should exercise authority over trial courts in granting or denying motions for a new trial based on the amount of damages.

Later, we will take up other questions related to damages and jury control, such as whether a judge can threaten to grant a new trial unless the plaintiff agrees to take less money (*remittitur*) or unless the defendant agrees to pay more (*additur*). Also can a trial, or a new trial, appropriately be held on only damages, if the judge believes the jury was right on liability but wrong on damages? We will also consider new trial motions on the grounds of "jury misconduct." Here again, even the most enthusiastic proponent of civil juries would want some judicial control. If a member of the jury had received a bribe, or the judge's law clerk made improper remarks to the jury, or a juror posted a live feed of the jury's deliberations online for viewers' input, these could be sufficient grounds for ordering a new trial.

Difficult questions arise when the alleged jury misconduct relates to the deliberative process of the jury. For example, should a verdict be set aside because a juror incorrectly remembered the testimony of a witness or misinterpreted the judge's instructions, although one could not infer these mistakes by examining the verdict? Such examples, which reflect the imperfection of human beings and social structures rather than perversion of the entire process, are usually handled by evidentiary rules that protect against intrusion into the jury's deliberations while at the same time admitting evidence of gross misconduct.

Let's consider several compelling policy issues. If lawyers, and then judges, were permitted to delve frequently and deeply into the deliberation of jurors, then perhaps few jury verdicts could stand. It is unlikely that twelve or six people could behave perfectly, hard as they might try. (Of course, the same could be said of a judge acting alone.) Indeed, if it were easy to attack jury verdicts because of faults in the deliberations, and if all that is said in the jury room were made admissible through the testimony of jurors, then (1) an attorney who has lost a case would feel obligated to question each juror at length, and (2) some jurors would not want to speak (or at least not say what they think) during deliberations. This would create real potential for juror silence during deliberations, and for juror harassment after verdict. (This leaves aside those intrusions on the jury, such as bribery or private conversations with one of the parties, that already are clearly forbidden and certainly should be.)

The Federal Rules of Evidence provide one attempt to find a healthy balance on this issue. This federal solution incorporates much of the common law rule that a jury verdict cannot be impeached by the testimony of the jurors themselves, but tries to draw a line between the normal deliberative process and unfair external intrusions upon it:

> Fed. R. Evid. 606(b) *Inquiry into the validity of verdict or indictment.* Upon an inquiry into the validity of a verdict or indictment, a juror may not testify as to any matter or statement occurring during the course of the jury's deliberations or to the effect of anything upon that or any other juror's mind or emotions as influencing the juror to assent to or dissent from the verdict or indictment or concerning the juror's mental processes in connection therewith, except that a juror may testify on the question whether extraneous prejudicial information was improperly brought to the jury's attention or whether any outside influence was improperly brought to bear upon any juror. Nor may a juror's affidavit or evidence of any statement by the juror concerning a matter about which the juror be precluded from testifying be received for these purposes.

Sometimes, behavior by the jury as a whole seems reprehensible but does not involve external influence. For example, what if the members of the jury agree to resolve the case with the flip of a coin? Or what if a jury that is evenly split on the question of liability agrees to resolve the case with a verdict for the plaintiff but with an award of damages that simply averages the sums that each of the jurors would award (also known as a "quotient verdict")? Courts disagree about how to handle these improprieties. One solution is to treat the behavior as substantive grounds for a new trial, but, in keeping with Fed. R. Evid. 606(b), to permit the behavior to be proved only by competent evidence other than the testimony of the jurors themselves. Such testimony might be given by an eavesdropper or a court official who finds a document in the jury room that indicates a quotient verdict.

Finally, we have arrived at the motion for new trial that you may find the most problematic: a motion for a new trial on the grounds that the verdict "is against the weight of the evidence." In federal courts, and in most state courts, the losing attorney can appeal to the discretion of the trial judge to grant a new trial motion, *not* because there is insufficient evidence to support the jury verdict (that is, the directed verdict or JNOV standard), but because the verdict is clearly wrong: The jury made a horrible mistake; there has been a gross miscarriage of justice. We will later raise issues about this motion after you have read *Galloway*, but before forming your opinion, consider the words of one state supreme court judge:

> The authority of the common pleas in the control and revision of excessive verdicts through the means of new trials was firmly settled in England before the foundation of this colony, and has always existed here without challenge under

any of our constitutions. It is a power to examine the whole case on the law and the evidence, with a view to securing a result, not merely legal, but also not manifestly against justice, without which the jury system would be a capricious and intolerable tyranny, which no people could long endure. This court has had occasion more than once recently to say that it was a power the courts ought to exercise unflinchingly.

Smith v. Times Publishing Co., 178 Pa. 481 (1897).

In *Aetna Casualty & Surety Co. v. Yeatts*, 122 F.2d 350 (4th Cir. 1941), which relies on the above quote, Judge Parker stated the position of most state and federal courts on the motion for a new trial on the ground that the verdict is *against the weight of the evidence*:

> On such a motion it is the duty of the trial judge to set aside the verdict and grant a new trial, if he is of the opinion that the verdict is against the clear weight of the evidence, or is based upon evidence that is false, or will result in a miscarriage of justice, even though there may be substantial evidence which would prevent the direction of a verdict.

Most appellate courts, including the federal, tend to leave this motion to the discretion of the trial judge, and almost always refuse to upset either the grant or the denial of the motion. It seems clear that the motion is brought far more often than it is granted. Moreover, it is rare that a party loses the same jury case twice and is granted yet a third jury trial on successive motions that call upon the judge to exercise this discretionary power.

If you were a judge, under what circumstances would you grant a motion for a new trial on the ground that the verdict is against the weight of the evidence? Do you think the judge should be required to state the reasons for granting such a motion? When denying such a motion? (Judges frequently deny or grant these motions, like other motions, without explanation.)

This would be a logical place to introduce you to motions to *vacate judgment* (Fed. R. Civ. P. 60), for such motions permit the correction of error in much the same way as motions for a new trial, except they usually are filed later. For pedagogical reasons, however, it makes more sense for you to now read *Galloway*, which is more directly related to directed verdict and the common law motion for a new trial. We will cover Rule 60 thereafter.

6. Judgments as a Matter of Law and New Trial Motions in More Detail

Galloway v. United States
319 U.S. 372 (1943)

Justice RUTLEDGE delivered the opinion of the Court:

Petitioner seeks benefits for total and permanent disability by reason of insanity he claims existed May 31, 1919. On that day his policy of yearly renewable term insurance lapsed for nonpayment of premium.

The suit was filed June 15, 1938. At the close of all the evidence the District Court granted the Government's motion for a directed verdict. Judgment was entered accordingly. The Circuit Court of Appeals affirmed. Both courts held the evidence legally insufficient to sustain a verdict for petitioner. He says this was erroneous and, in effect, deprived him of trial by jury, contrary to the Seventh Amendment.

The constitutional argument, as petitioner has made it, does not challenge generally the power of federal courts to withhold or withdraw from the jury cases in which the claimant puts forward insufficient evidence to support a verdict. The contention is merely that his case as made was substantial, the courts' decisions to the contrary were wrong, and therefore their effect has been to deprive him of a jury trial. . . . [T]he only question is whether the evidence was sufficient to sustain a verdict for petitioner. On that basis, we think the judgments must be affirmed.

I

Certain facts are undisputed. Petitioner worked as a longshoreman in Philadelphia and elsewhere prior to enlistment in the Army November 1, 1917. [The record does not show whether this employment was steady and continuous or was spotty and erratic. But there is no contention that petitioner's behavior was abnormal before he arrived in France in April, 1918.] He became a cook in a machine gun battalion. His unit arrived in France in April, 1918. He served actively until September 24. From then to the following January he was in a hospital with influenza. He then returned to active duty. He came back to the United States, and received honorable discharge April 29, 1919. He enlisted in the Navy January 15, 1920, and was discharged for bad conduct in July. The following December he again enlisted in the Army and served until May, 1922, when he deserted. Thereafter he was carried on the Army records as a deserter.

In 1930 began a series of medical examinations by Veterans' Bureau physicians. On May 19 that year his condition was diagnosed as "Moron, low grade; observation, dementia praecox, simple type." In November, 1931, further examination gave the diagnosis, "Psychosis with other diseases or conditions (organic disease of the central nervous system—type undetermined)." In July, 1934, still another examination was made, with diagnosis: "Psychosis manic and depressive insanity incompetent; hypertension, moderate; otitis media, chronic, left; varicose veins left, mild; abscessed teeth roots; myocarditis, mild."

Petitioner's wife, the nominal party in this suit, was appointed guardian of his person and estate in February, 1932. Claim for insurance benefits was made in June, 1934, and was finally denied by the Board of Veterans' Appeals in January, 1936. This suit followed two and a half years later.

Petitioner concededly is now totally and permanently disabled by reason of insanity and has been for some time prior to institution of this suit. It is conceded also that he was sound in mind and body until he arrived in France in April, 1918.

The theory of his case is that the strain of active service abroad brought on an immediate change, which was the beginning of a mental breakdown that has grown worse continuously through all the later years. Essential in this is the view it had become a total and permanent disability not later than May 31, 1919.

The evidence to support this theory falls naturally into three periods, namely, that prior to 1923; the interval from then to 1930; and that following 1930. It consists in proof of incidents occurring in France to show the beginnings of change; testimony of changed appearance and behavior in the years immediately following petitioner's return to the United States as compared with those prior to his departure; the medical evidence of insanity accumulated in the years following 1930; and finally the evidence of a physician, given largely as medical opinion, which seeks to tie all the other evidence together as foundation for the conclusion, expressed as of 1941, that petitioner's disability was total and permanent as of a time not later than May of 1919.

Documentary exhibits included military, naval and Veterans' Bureau records. Testimony was given by deposition or at the trial chiefly by five witnesses. One, O'Neill, was a fellow worker and friend from boyhood; two, Wells and Tanikawa, served with petitioner overseas; Lt. Col. Albert K. Mathews, who was an Army chaplain, observed him or another person of the same name at an Army hospital in California during early 1920; and Dr. Wilder, a physician, examined him shortly before the trial and supplied the only expert testimony in his behalf. The petitioner also put into evidence the depositions of Commander Platt and Lt. Col. James E. Matthews, his superior officers in the Navy and the Army, respectively, during 1920-22.

What happened in France during 1918-19 is shown chiefly by Wells and Tanikawa. Wells testified to an incident at Aisonville, where the unit was billeted shortly after reaching France and before going into action. Late at night petitioner created a disturbance, "hollering, screeching, swearing. . . . The men poured out from the whole section." Wells did not see the incident, but heard petitioner swearing at his superior officers and saw "the result, a black eye for Lt. Warner." However, he did not see "who gave it to him." Wells personally observed no infraction of discipline except this incident, and did not know what brought it on. Petitioner's physical appearance was good, he "carried on his duties as a cook all right," and the witness did not see him after June 1, except for about three days in July when he observed petitioner several times at work feeding stragglers.

Tanikawa, Hawaiian-born citizen, served with petitioner from the latter's enlistment until September, 1918, when Galloway was hospitalized, although the witness thought they had fought together and petitioner was "acting queer" at the Battle of the Argonne in October. At Camp Greene, North Carolina, petitioner was "just a regular soldier, very normal, . . . pretty neat." After reaching France "he was getting nervous . . . , kind of irritable, always picking a fight with other soldier." This began at Aisonville. Tanikawa saw Galloway in jail, apparently before June. It is not clear whether these are references to the incident Wells described.

Tanikawa described another incident in June "when we were on the Marne," the Germans "were on the other side and we were on this side." It was a new front, without trenches. The witness and petitioner were on guard duty with others. Tanikawa understood the Germans were getting ready for a big drive. "One night he (petitioner) screamed. He said, 'The Germans are coming' and we all gagged him." There was no shooting, the Germans were not coming, and there was nothing to lead the witness to believe they were. Petitioner was court martialed for the matter, but Tanikawa did not know "what they did with him." He did not talk with Galloway that night, because "he was out of his mind" and appeared insane. Tanikawa did not know when petitioner left the battalion or what happened to him after (as the witness put it) the Argonne fight, but heard he went to the hospital, "just dressing station I guess." The witness next saw Galloway in 1936, at a disabled veterans' post meeting in Sacramento, California. Petitioner then "looked to me like he wasn't all there. Insane. About the same . . . as compared to the way he acted in France, particularly when they gagged him. . . ."

O'Neill was "born and raised with" petitioner, worked with him as a longshoreman, and knew him "from when he come out of the army for seven years, . . . I would say five or six years." When petitioner returned in April or May, 1919, "he was a wreck compared to what he was when he went away. The fellow's mind was evidently unbalanced." Symptoms specified were withdrawing to himself; crying spells; alternate periods of normal behavior and nonsensical talk; expression of fears that good friends wanted "to beat him up"; spitting blood and remarking about it in vulgar terms. Once petitioner said, "G—d—it, I must be a Doctor Jekyll and Mr. Hyde."

O'Neill testified these symptoms and this condition continued practically the same for about five years. In his opinion petitioner was "competent at times and others was incompetent." The intervals might be "a couple of days, a couple of months." In his normal periods Galloway "would be his old self . . . absolutely O.K."

O'Neill was definite in recalling petitioner's condition and having seen him frequently in 1919, chiefly however, and briefly, on the street during lunch hour. He was not sure Galloway was working and was "surprised he got in the Navy, I think in the Navy or in the Government service."

O'Neill maintained he saw petitioner "right on from that (1920) at times." But his recollection of dates, number of opportunities for observation, and concrete events was wholly indefinite. He would fix no estimate for the number of times he had seen petitioner: "In 1920 I couldn't recall whether it was one or a thousand." For later years he would not say whether it was "five times or more or less." When he was pinned down by cross-examination, the effect of his testimony was that he recalled petitioner clearly in 1919 "because there was such a vast contrast in the man," but for later years he could give little or no definite information.

[The Court reprinted the following excerpt from the testimony in a footnote:

"**X** Can you tell us approximately how many times you saw him in 1919?"
"**A.** No; I seen him so often that it would be hard to give any estimate."
"**X** And the same goes for 1920?"

"**A.** I wouldn't be sure about 1920. I remember him more when he first came home because there was such a vast contrast in the man. Otherwise, if nothing unusual happened, I wouldn't probably recall him at all, you know, that is, recall the particular time and all."

"**X** Well, do you recall him at all in 1920?"

"**A.** I can't say."

"**X** And could you swear whether or not you ever saw him in 1921?"

"**A.** I think I seen him both in 1921 and 1920 and 1921 and right on. I might not see him for a few weeks or months at a time, but I think I saw him a few times in all the years right up to, as I say, at least five years after."

"**X** Can you give us an estimate as to the number of times you saw him in 1920?"

"**A.** No, I would not."

"**X** Was it more than five times or less?"

"**A.** In 1920 I couldn't recall whether it was one or a thousand. The time I recall him well is when he first come home, but I know that I seen him right on from that at times."

"**X** And the same goes for 1921, 1922, 1923 and 1924?"

"**A.** I would say for five years afterwards, but I don't know just when or how often I seen him except when he first come home for the first couple of months."

"**X** But for years after his return you couldn't say definitely whether you saw him five times or more or less, could you?"

"**A.** No, because it was a thing that there was a vast contrast when he first come home and everybody noticed it and remarked about it and it was more liable to be remembered. You could ask me about some more friends I knew during those years and I wouldn't know except there was something unusual."

The Court further noted that "[p]etitioner's own evidence shows without dispute he was on active duty in the Navy from January 15, 1920, to July of that year and in the Army from December, 1920, to May 6, 1922. As is noted in the text, O'neill was not sure he was working and 'was surprised he got in the Navy, I think in the Navy or in the Government service.' He only 'heard some talk' of petitioner's having reenlisted in the Army, but 'if it was the fact, I would be surprised that he could do it owing to his mental condition.' O'neill was not certain that he saw Galloway in uniform after the first week of his return to Philadelphia from overseas, although he said he saw petitioner during 'the periods of those reenlistments . . . but I can't recall about it.'"]

O'neill recalled one specific occasion after 1919 when petitioner returned to Philadelphia, "around 1920 or 1921, but I couldn't be sure," to testify in a criminal proceeding. He also said, "After he was away for five or six years, he came back to Philadelphia, but I wouldn't know nothing about dates on that. He was back in Philadelphia for five or six months or so, and he was still just evidently all right, and then he would be off."

Lt. Col. (Chaplain) Mathews said he observed a Private Joseph Galloway, who was a prisoner for desertion and a patient in the mental ward at Fort MacArthur Station Hospital, California, during a six weeks period early in 1920. The chaplain's testimony gives strong evidence the man he observed was insane. However, there is a fatal weakness in this evidence. In his direct testimony, which was taken by deposition, the chaplain said he was certain that the soldier was petitioner. When confronted with the undisputed fact that petitioner was on active duty in the Navy during the first half of 1920, the witness at first stated that he might have been mistaken as to the time of his observation. Subsequently he reasserted the accuracy of his original statement as to the time of observation, but admitted that he might have been mistaken in believing that the patient-prisoner was petitioner. In this connection he volunteered the statement, "Might I add, sir, that I could not now identify that soldier if I were to meet him face to face, and that is because of the long lapse of time." The patient whom the witness saw was confined to his bed. The record is barren of other evidence, whether by the hospital's or the Army's records or otherwise, to show that petitioner was either patient or prisoner at Fort MacArthur in 1920 or at any other time.

Commander Platt testified that petitioner caused considerable trouble by disobedience and leaving ship without permission during his naval service in the first half of 1920. After "repeated warnings and punishments, leading to court martials," he was sentenced to a bad conduct discharge.

Lt. Col. James E. Matthews (not the chaplain) testified by deposition which petitioner's attorney interrupted Dr. Wilder's testimony to read into evidence. The witness was Galloway's commanding officer from early 1921 to the summer of that year, when petitioner was transferred with other soldiers to another unit. At first Colonel Matthews considered making petitioner a corporal, but found him unreliable and had to discipline him. Petitioner "drank considerably," was "what we called a bolshevik," did not seem loyal, and "acted as if he was not getting a square deal." The officer concluded "he was a moral pervert and probably used narcotics," but could not secure proof of this. Galloway was court martialed for public drunkenness and disorderly conduct, served a month at hard labor, and returned to active duty. At times he "was one of the very best soldiers I had," at others undependable. He was physically sound, able to do his work, perform close order drill, etc., "very well." He had alternate periods of gaiety and depression, talked incoherently at times, gave the impression he would fight readily, but did not resent orders and seemed to get along well with other soldiers. The officer attributed petitioner's behavior to alcohol and narcotics and it occurred to him at no time to question his sanity.

Dr. Wilder was the key witness. He disclaimed specializing in mental disease, but qualified as having given it "special attention." He first saw petitioner shortly before the trial, examined him "several times." He concluded petitioner's ailment "is a schizophrenic branch or form of praecox." Dr. Wilder heard the testimony and read the depositions of the other witnesses, and examined the documentary evidence. Basing his judgment upon this material, with inferences drawn from it, he concluded petitioner was born with "an inherent instability," though he remained normal until he went to France; began there "to be subjected to the strain of military life, then he began to go to pieces." In May, 1919, petitioner "was still suffering from the acuteness of the breakdown. . . . He is going down hill still, but the thing began with the breakdown. . . ." Petitioner was "definitely insane, yes, sir," in 1920 and "has been insane at all times, at least since July, 1918, the time of this episode on the Marne"; that is, "to the point that he was unable to adapt himself. I don't mean he has not had moments when he could not perform some routine tasks," but "from an occupational standpoint . . . he has been insane." He could follow "a mere matter of routine," but would have no incentive, would not keep a steady job, come to work on time, or do anything he didn't want to do. Dr. Wilder pointed to petitioner's work record before he entered the service and observed: "At no time after he went into the war do we find him able to hold any kind of a job. He broke right down." He explained petitioner's enlistment in the Navy and later in the Army by saying, "It would have been no trick at all *for a man who was reasonably conforming* to get into the Service." (Emphasis added.)

However, the witness knew "nothing whatever except his getting married" about petitioner's activities between 1925 and 1930, and what he knew of them between 1922 and 1925 was based entirely on O'neill's testimony and a paper not of record here. Dr. Wilder at first regarded knowledge concerning what petitioner was doing between 1925 and 1930 as not essential. "We have a continuing disease, quite obviously beginning during his military service, and quite obviously continuing in 1930, and the minor incidents don't seem to me. . . ." Counsel for the government interrupted to inquire, "Well, if he was continuously employed for eight hours a day from 1925 to 1930 would that have any bearing?" The witness replied, "It would have a great deal." Upon further questioning, however, he reverted to his first position, stating it would not be necessary or helpful for him to know what petitioner was doing from 1925 to 1930: "I testified from the information I had."

II

This, we think, is the crux of the case and distinguishes it from the cases on which petitioner has relied. His burden was to prove total and permanent disability as of a date not later than May 31, 1919. He has undertaken to do this by showing incipience of mental disability shortly before that time and its continuance and progression throughout the succeeding years. He has clearly established incidence of total and permanent disability as of some period prior to 1938, when he began this suit. For our purposes this may be taken as medically established by the Veterans' Bureau examination and diagnosis of July, 1934.

But if the record is taken to show that some form of mental disability existed in 1930, which later became total and permanent, petitioner's problem remains to demonstrate by more than speculative inference that this condition itself began on or before May 31, 1919 and continuously existed or progressed through the intervening years to 1930.

To show origin before the crucial date, he gives evidence of two abnormal incidents occurring while he was in France, one creating the disturbance before he came near the fighting front, the other yelling that the Germans were coming when he was on guard duty at the Marne. There is no other evidence of abnormal behavior during his entire service of more than a year abroad.

That he was court martialed for these sporadic acts and bound and gagged for one does not prove he was insane or had then a general breakdown in "an already fragile mental constitution," which the vicissitudes of a longshoreman's life had not been able to crack.

To these two incidents petitioner adds the testimony of O'neill that he looked and acted like a wreck, compared with his former self, when he returned from France about a month before the crucial date, and O'neill's vague recollections that this condition continued through the next two, three, four or five years.

O'neill's testimony apparently takes no account of petitioner's having spent 101 days in a hospital in France with influenza just before he came home. But, given the utmost credence, as is required, it does no more than show that petitioner was subject to alternating periods of gaiety and depression for some indefinite period after his return, extending perhaps as late as 1922. But because of its vagueness as to time, dates, frequency of opportunity for observation, and specific incident, O'neill's testimony concerning the period from 1922 to 1925 is hardly more than speculative.

We have then the two incidents in France followed by O'neill's testimony of petitioner's changed condition in 1919 and its continuance to 1922. There is also the testimony of Commander Platt and Lt. Col. James E. Matthews as to his service in the Navy and the Army, respectively, during 1920-1922. Neither thought petitioner was insane or that his conduct indicated insanity. Then follows a chasm of eight years. The only evidence we have concerning this period is the fact that petitioner married his present guardian at some time within it, an act from which in the legal sense no inference of insanity can be drawn.

This period was eight years of continuous insanity, according to the inference petitioner would be allowed to have drawn. If so, he should have no need of inference. Insanity so long and continuously sustained does not hide itself from the eyes and ears of witnesses. The assiduity which produced the evidence of two "crazy" incidents during a year and a half in France should produce one during eight years or, for that matter, five years in the United States.

Inference is capable of bridging many gaps. But not, in these circumstances, one so wide and deep as this. Knowledge of petitioner's activities and behavior from 1922 or 1925 to 1930 was peculiarly within his ken and that of his wife, who has litigated this cause in his and presumably, though indirectly, in her own behalf. His was the burden to show continuous disability. What he did in this time, or did not do, was vital to his case. Apart from the mere fact of his marriage, the record is blank for five years and almost blank for eight. For all that appears, he may have worked full time and continuously for five and perhaps for eight, with only a possible single interruption.

No favorable inference can be drawn from the omission. It was not one of oversight or inability to secure proof. That is shown by the thoroughness with which the record was prepared for all other periods, before and after this one, and by the fact petitioner's wife, though she married him during the period and was available, did not testify. The only reasonable conclusion is that petitioner, or those who acted for him, deliberately chose, for reasons no doubt considered sufficient (and which we do not criticize, since such matters including tactical ones, are for the judgment of counsel) to present no evidence or perhaps to withhold evidence readily available concerning this long interval, and to trust to the genius of expert medical inference and judicial laxity to bridge this canyon.

In the circumstances exhibited, the former is not equal to the feat, and the latter will not permit it. No case has been cited and none has been found in which inference, however expert, has been permitted to make so broad a leap and take the place of evidence which, according to all reason, must have been at hand. To allow this would permit the substitution of inference, tenuous at best, not merely for evidence absent because impossible or difficult to secure, but for evidence disclosed to be available and not produced. This would substitute speculation for proof. Furthermore, the inference would be more plausible perhaps if the evidence of insanity as of May, 1919, were stronger than it is, such for instance as Chaplain Mathews' testimony would have furnished if it could be taken as applying to petitioner. But, on this record, the evidence of insanity as of that time is thin at best, if it can be regarded as at all more than speculative.

Beyond this, there is nothing to show totality or permanence. These come only by what the Circuit Court of Appeals rightly characterized as "long-range retroactive diagnosis." That might suffice, notwithstanding this crucial inference was a matter of opinion, if there were factual evidence over which the medical eye could travel and find continuity through the intervening years. . . . But eight years are too many to permit it to skip, when the bridgeheads (if the figure may be changed) at each end are no stronger than they are here, and when the seer first denies, then admits, then denies again, that what took place in this time would make "a great deal" of difference in what he saw. Expert medical inference rightly can do much. But we think the feat attempted here too large for its accomplishment. . . .

III

What has been said disposes of the case as the parties have made it. For that reason perhaps nothing more need be said. But objection has been advanced that, in some manner not wholly clear, the directed verdict practice offends the Seventh Amendment.

It may be noted, first, that the Amendment has no application of its own force to this case. The suit is one to enforce a monetary claim against the United States. It hardly can be maintained that under the common law in 1791 jury trial was a matter of right for persons asserting claims against the sovereign. Whatever force the Amendment has therefore is derived because Congress in the legislation cited, has made it applicable. Even so, the objection made on the score of its requirements is untenable.

If the intention is to claim generally that the Amendment deprives the federal courts of power to direct a verdict for insufficiency of evidence, the short answer is the contention has been foreclosed by repeated decisions made here consistently for nearly a century. More recently the practice has been approved explicitly in the promulgation of the Federal Rules of Civil Procedure. *Cf.* Rule 50. The objection therefore comes too late.

Furthermore, the argument from history is not convincing. It is not that "the rules of the common law" in 1791 deprived trial courts of power to withdraw cases from the jury, because not made out, or appellate courts of power to review such determinations. The jury was not absolute master of fact in 1791. Then as now courts excluded evidence for irrelevancy and relevant proof for other reasons. The argument concedes they weighed the evidence, not only piecemeal but in toto for submission to the jury, by at least two procedures, the demurrer to the evidence and the motion for a new trial. The objection is not therefore to the basic thing, which is the power of the court to withhold cases from the jury or set aside the verdict for insufficiency of the evidence. It is rather to incidental or collateral effects, namely, that the directed verdict as now administered differs from both those procedures because, on the one hand, allegedly higher standards of proof are required and, on the other, different consequences follow as to further maintenance of the litigation. Apart from the standards of proof, the argument appears to urge that in 1791, a litigant could challenge his opponent's evidence, either by the demurrer, which when determined ended the litigation, or by motion for a new trial which if successful, gave the adversary another chance to prove his case; and therefore the Amendment excluded any challenge to which one or the other of these consequences does not attach.

The Amendment did not bind the federal courts to the exact procedural incidents or details of jury trial according to the common law in 1791, any more than it tied them to the common-law system of pleading or the specific rules of evidence then prevailing. . . .

Each of the classical modes of challenge [that is, demurrer to the evidence and new trial motions] disproves the notion that the characteristic feature of the other, for effect upon continuing the litigation, became a part of the Seventh Amendment's guaranty to the exclusion of all others. That guaranty did not incorporate conflicting constitutional policies, that challenge to an opposing case must be made with the effect of terminating the litigation finally and, at the same time, with the opposite effect of requiring another trial. Alternatives so contradictory give room, not for the inference that one or the other is required, but rather for the view that neither is essential.

Finally, the objection appears to be directed generally at the standards of proof judges have required for submission of evidence to the jury. . . . Whatever may be the general formulation, the essential requirement is that mere speculation be not allowed to do duty for probative facts, after making due allowance for all reasonably possible inferences favoring the party whose case is attacked. . . .

Judged by this requirement, or by any standard other than sheer speculation, we are unable to conclude that one whose burden, by the nature of his claim, is to show continuing and total disability for nearly twenty years supplies the essential proof of continuity when he wholly omits to show his whereabouts, activities or condition for five years, although the record discloses evidence must have been available, and, further, throws no light upon three additional years, except for one vaguely described and dated visit to his former home. . . . The words "total and permanent" are the statute's, not our own. They mean something more than incipient or occasional disability. We hardly need add that we give full credence to all of the testimony. But that cannot cure its inherent vagueness or supply essential elements omitted or withheld.

Accordingly, the judgment is Affirmed.

Justice BLACK, with whom Justice DOUGLAS and Justice MURPHY concur, dissenting:

The Seventh Amendment to the Constitution provides:

> In suits at common law, where the value in controversy shall exceed twenty dollars, the right of trial by jury shall be preserved, and no fact tried by a jury shall be otherwise re-examined in any Court of the United States, than according to the rules of the common law.

The Court here reexamines testimony offered in a common law suit, weighs conflicting evidence, and holds that the litigant may never take this case to a jury. The founders of our government thought that trial of fact by juries rather than by judges was an essential bulwark of civil liberty. For this reason, among others, they adopted Article III, § 2 of the Constitution, and the Sixth and Seventh Amendments. Today's decision marks a continuation of the gradual process of judicial erosion which in one hundred fifty years has slowly worn away a major portion of the essential guarantee of the Seventh Amendment.

I

. . . In 1789, juries occupied the principal place in the administration of justice. They were frequently in both criminal and civil cases the arbiters not only of fact but of law. Less than three years after the ratification of the Seventh Amendment, this Court called a jury in a civil case brought under our original jurisdiction. There was no disagreement as to the facts of the case. Chief Justice Jay, charging the jury for a unanimous Court, three of whose members had sat in the Constitutional Convention, said: "For as, on the one hand, it is presumed, that juries are the best judges of facts; it is, on the other hand, presumable, that the court[s] are the best judges of law. But still, both objects are lawfully within your power of decision." *State of Georgia v. Brailsford*, 3 Dall. 1, 4, 1 L. Ed. 483. Similar views were held by state courts in Connecticut, Massachusetts, Illinois, Louisiana and presumably elsewhere. . . .

As Hamilton had declared in The Federalist, the basic judicial control of the jury function was in the court's power to order a new trial. In 1830, this Court said: "The only modes known to the common law to re-examine such facts, are the granting of a new trial by the court where the issue was tried, or to which the record was properly returnable; or the award of a venire facias de novo, by an appellate court, for some error of law which intervened in the proceedings." *Parsons v. Bedford*, [4 Pet. 433, 448 (1830)]. That retrial by a new jury rather than factual reevaluation by a court is a constitutional right of genuine value was restated as recently as *Slocum v. New York Life Insurance Co.*, 228 U.S. 364.

A long step toward the determination of fact by judges instead of by juries was the invention of the directed verdict. In 1850, what seems to have been the first directed verdict case considered by this Court, *Parks v. Ross*, 11 How. 362, 374, was presented for decision. The Court held that the directed verdict serves the same purpose as the demurrer to the evidence, and that since there was "no evidence whatever" on the critical issue in the case, the directed verdict was approved. The decision was an innovation, a departure from the traditional rule restated only fifteen years before in *Greenleaf v. Birth*, 1835, 9 Pet. 292, 299, in which this Court had said: "Where there is no evidence tending to prove a particular fact, the court[s] are bound so to instruct the jury, when requested; but they cannot legally give any instruction which shall take from the jury the right of weighing the evidence and determining what effect it shall have."

This new device contained potentialities for judicial control of the jury which had not existed in the demurrer to the evidence. In the first place, demurring to the evidence was risky business, for in so doing the party not only admitted the truth of all the testimony against him but also all reasonable inferences which might be drawn from it; and upon joinder in demurrer the case was withdrawn from the jury while the court proceeded to give final judgment either for or against the demurrant. Imposition of this risk was no mere technicality; for by making withdrawal of a case from the jury dangerous to the moving litigant's cause, the early law went far to assure that facts would never be examined except by a jury. Under the directed verdict practice the moving party takes no such chance, for if his motion is denied, instead of suffering a directed verdict against him, his case merely continues into the hands of the jury. The litigant not only takes no risk by a motion for a directed verdict, but in making such a motion gives himself two opportunities to avoid the jury's decision; for under the federal variant of judgment notwithstanding the verdict, the judge may reserve opinion on the motion for a directed verdict and then give judgment for the moving party after the jury was formally found against him. In the second place, under the directed verdict practice the courts soon abandoned the "admission of all facts and reasonable inferences" standard referred to, and created the so-called "substantial evidence" rule which permitted directed verdicts even though there was far more evidence in the case than a plaintiff would have needed to withstand a demurrer.

The substantial evidence rule did not spring into existence immediately upon the adoption of the directed verdict device. For a few more years federal judges held to the traditional rule that juries might pass finally on facts if there was "any evidence" to support a party's contention. The rule that a case must go to the jury unless there was "no evidence" was completely repudiated in *Schuylkill and Dauphin Improvement Co. v. Munson*, 14 Wall. 442, 447, 448 (1871), upon which the Court today relies in part. There the Court declared that "some" evidence was not enough—there must be evidence sufficiently persuasive to the judge so that he thinks "a jury can properly proceed." The traditional rule was given an ugly name, "the scintilla rule," to hasten its demise.

Later cases permitted the development of added judicial control. New and totally unwarranted formulas, which should surely be eradicated from the law at the first opportunity, were added as recently as 1929 in *Gunning v. Cooley*, 281 U.S. 90, which, by sheerest dictum, made new encroachments on the jury's constitutional functions. There it was announced that a judge might weigh the evidence to determine whether he, and not the jury, thought it was "overwhelming" for either party, and then direct a verdict. [The case] also suggests quite unnecessarily for its decision, that "When a plaintiff produces evidence that is consistent with an hypothesis that the defendant is not negligent, and also with one that he is, his proof tends to establish neither." This dictum . . . assumes that a judge can weigh conflicting evidence with mathematical precision and which wholly deprives the jury of the right to resolve that conflict. . . . With it, and other tools, jury verdicts on disputed facts have been set aside or directed verdicts authorized so regularly as to make the practice commonplace while the motion for directed verdict itself has become routine. . . .

Even *Gunning v. Cooley*, 281 U.S. at page 94, acknowledged that "issues that depend on the credibility of witnesses . . . are to be decided by the jury." Today the Court comes dangerously close to weighing the credibility of a witness and rejecting his testimony because the majority do not believe it.

The story thus briefly told depicts the constriction of a constitutional civil right and should not be continued. . . .

The language of the Seventh Amendment cannot easily be improved by formulas. The statement of a district judge in *Tarter v. United States*, D.C., 17 F. Supp. 691, 692, 693, represents, in my opinion, the minimum meaning of the Seventh Amendment:

> The Seventh Amendment to the Constitution guarantees a jury trial in law cases, where there is substantial evidence to support the claim of the plaintiff in an action. If a single witness testifies to a fact sustaining the issue between the parties, or if reasoning minds might reach different conclusions from the testimony of a single witness, one of which would substantially support the issue of the contending party, the issue must be left to the jury. Trial by jury is a fundamental guaranty of the rights of the people, and judges should not search the evidence with meticulous care to deprive litigants of jury trials.

The call for the true application of the Seventh Amendment is not to words, but to the spirit of honest desire to see that Constitutional right preserved. Either the judge or the jury must decide facts and to the extent that we take this responsibility, we lessen the jury function. Our duty to preserve this one of the Bill of Rights may be peculiarly difficult, for here it is our own power which we must restrain. . . . As for myself, I believe that a verdict should be directed, if at all, only when, without weighing the credibility of the witnesses, there is in the evidence no room whatever for honest difference of opinion over the factual issue in controversy. . . .

II

The factual issue for determination here is whether the petitioner incurred a total and permanent disability not later than May 31, 1919. It is undisputed that the petitioner's health was sound in 1918, and it is evidently conceded that he was disabled at least since 1930. When in the intervening period, did the disability take place?

A doctor who testified diagnosed the petitioner's case as a schizophrenic form of dementia praecox. He declared it to be sound medical theory that while a normal man can retain his sanity in the face of severe mental or physical shock, some persons are born with an inherent instability so that they are mentally unable to stand sudden and severe strain. The medical testimony was that this petitioner belongs to the latter class and that the shock of actual conflict on the battle front brought on the incurable affliction from which he now suffers. The medical witness testified that the dominant symptoms of the condition are extreme introversion and preoccupation with personal interests, a persecution complex, and an emotional instability which may be manifested by extreme exhilaration alternating with unusual depression or irrational outbursts. Persons suffering from this disease are therefore unable to engage in continuous employment.

The petitioner relies on the testimony of wartime and post war companions and superiors to show that his present mental condition existed on the crucial date. There is substantial testimony from which reasonable men might conclude that the petitioner was insane from the date claimed. [Justice Black then summarized that testimony.]

. . . All of this evidence, if believed, showed a man healthy and normal before he went to the war suffering for several years after he came back from a disease which had the symptoms attributed to schizophrenia and who was insane from 1930 until his trial. Under these circumstances, I think that the physician's testimony of total and permanent disability by reason of continuous insanity from 1918 to 1938 was reasonable. The fact that there was no direct testimony for a period of five years, while it might be the basis of fair argument to the jury by the government, does not, as the Court seems to believe, create a presumption against the petitioner so strong that his case must be excluded from the jury entirely. Even if during these five years the petitioner was spasmodically employed, we could not conclude that he was not totally and permanently disabled. . . . It is not doubted that schizophrenia is permanent even though there may be a momentary appearance of recovery. . . .

This case graphically illustrates the injustice resulting from permitting judges to direct verdicts instead of requiring them to await a jury decision and then, if necessary, allow a new trial. The chief reason given for approving a directed verdict against this petitioner is that no evidence except expert medical testimony was offered for a five to eight year period. Perhaps, now that the petitioner knows he has insufficient evidence to satisfy a judge even though he may have enough to satisfy a jury, he would be able to fill this time gap to meet any judge's demand. If a court would point out on a motion for new trial that the evidence as to this particular period was too weak, the petitioner would be given an opportunity to buttress the physician's evidence. If, as the Court believes, insufficient evidence has been offered to sustain a jury verdict for the petitioner, we should at least authorize a new trial. . . .

I believe that there is a reasonable difference of opinion as to whether the petitioner was totally and permanently disabled by reason of insanity on May 31, 1919, and that his case therefore should have been allowed to go to the jury. The testimony of fellow soldiers, friends, supervisors, and of a medical expert whose integrity and ability is not challenged cannot be rejected by any process available to me as a judge.

REVIEW QUESTIONS

1. What is the plaintiff's cause of action and what are its elements? One cannot meaningfully tackle a Rule 50 or 56 analysis without using this information to focus that analysis.

2. Which of the elements are not disputed? Explain how you know this.

3. In advance of trial, what methods could Galloway's lawyer have used to make certain that the points of common agreement were taken as true at the trial? (Do not yet consider Rule 16 or case management. We will do that later.) Could either side have gained a victory using Fed. R. Civ. P. 12(b)(6) or 12(c)?

4. Assume that you are Galloway's lawyer and that after you, representing the plaintiff, have rested, defense counsel moves for directed verdict (or "judgment as a matter of law" under Rule 50). The judge will call on you to explain precisely how you have met your production burden as to each disputed element. Be precise with the evidence. The judge will also ask you: "To what extent can I use the fact that you did not put plaintiff's wife on the stand? Do you have any reasons for not doing so other than the risk that her evidence would destroy your case? Tell me honestly, do I have a right to ask you that question?"

5. Assume that you represent the government. Explain the failure of evidence as to any element for which you think there is an insufficiency of evidence to permit a plaintiff's verdict. Among other questions, the trial judge will ask you: "Are you not asking me to engage in assessing credibility and weighing the evidence? I'm not allowed to do that, am I?"

6. Assume now that you are a clerk to the trial judge, who turns to you: "Clerk, I think the plaintiff's evidence is extremely weak and perhaps even nonexistent as to one element. Would this be a good case for me to let the case go to the jury, and then to grant a JNOV, rather than granting the directed verdict motion?" Why and why not? Consider the strategic considerations for the lawyers, their clients, the jurors, and the court system. What are the consequences if the judge goes the JNOV route as

opposed to the directed verdict? Which method is more efficient? Are you sure? Explain.

7. You represent the defendant. Assume that on February 1, a Thursday, the jury comes in with a plaintiff's verdict in *Galloway* and judgment is entered the same day. You wish to move for a JNOV and a new trial. You are awaiting a copy of the transcript, and therefore want the most time possible. Absent a snowstorm, when is the latest you can file your motions? Can you get an enlargement of time under Rule 6? Do the lengths of time for the making of such motions make sense?

8. You are a member of a new organization ("S.A.J."—Save American Juries—pronounced "sage") of lawyers, judges, and legal scholars who have organized to find ways to engender new respect for the right to jury trial in civil cases and to lobby state and federal legislators to invigorate that right. Take realistic positions on the motions for directed verdict, for JNOV, and for a new trial because the verdict is against the weight of the evidence, and be prepared to defend those positions. You should know that not everyone agrees with the history given in Justice Black's dissent about the modern instruments of control over juries. In Woolhandler and Collins, *The Article III Jury*, 87 Va. L. Rev. 587, at 591-592 (2001), the authors argue that premodern federal control of juries "likely exceeded the level of modern judicial controls."

Strategic Approaches. Defendants make motions for directed verdict based on many different theories. Many of the arguments overlap. Here are some:

There is insufficient evidence of one or more elements to permit reasonable people to find that it is true. This is often a matter of arguing that inferences do not stretch so far as the plaintiff claims. You have seen the argument in *Galloway*.

The facts are in a "fog." No one knows what happened. Therefore, the plaintiff cannot make out a prima facie case. Sometimes, this is a literal argument, as in the motor vehicle accident in which both drivers are killed, no witnesses exist because it happened in a fog, and no reconstruction is possible, based on the remaining physical evidence. In these and similar circumstances, defendants argue that a jury would have to engage in "mere speculation" or that a plaintiff's finding would be only "guesswork."

We know what happened, but reasonable people cannot find that it meets the legal standard. For instance, the plaintiff might describe the defendant's activity in great detail, but as a matter of law there was "no duty" or the activity does not add up to negligence or whatever wrongdoing is alleged. In a contract case, the defendant may ask the court to interpret a written contract such that the plaintiff's rendition of factual events, even if believed, cannot rationally be found to be a breach of anything the defendant promised to do.

The defendant may concede that the plaintiff has presented evidence of an element, but argues that no reasonable person could believe that evidence because it is not credible on its face. This is one way to read *Galloway* (and also the *Matsushita* and *Scott v. Harris* cases, which we addressed in our discussion of summary judgment).

There may be another kind of case in which the evidence seems to permit two *equal* but inconsistent inferences. The thinking here is that if the facts give *equal* support to alternative inferences, then neither of those alternatives is established and the judgment would have to go against the party with the burden of proof. The classic example of this in federal court is *Pennsylvania Railroad Co. v. Chamberlain*, 288 U.S. 333 (1933), but that case is probably no longer the rule in federal court. The more contemporary thinking is that the judge is not in a position to say that two inferences are "equal." *See* 9A Charles A. Wright, Arthur R. Miller, and Mary Kay Kane, *Federal Practice and Procedure* § 2528 (citation omitted).

Sometimes plaintiffs try to survive a directed verdict motion by arguing that the evidence is in the defendant's hands and that the jury, in judging the demeanor of the defendant or another witness, should find that the defendant or the witness is so unbelievable that the opposite is true: "Since the defendant denies he did it, and you can see what a rascal and liar he is, you should believe the opposite." This argument usually fails. If this sort of argument worked, then it would be difficult for defendants ever to win a directed verdict or for appellate courts to know whether a motion for directed verdict was incorrectly denied, for the jury might always believe the opposite of what they heard. If you want to research this issue, find where *Dyer v. MacDougall*, 201 F.2d 265 (2d Cir. 1952), is included in the procedural treatise or hornbook of your choice, for that is the opinion (rendered by Justice Learned Hand) that scholars frequently invoke when discussing this topic. We put the issue here because once a defendant defeats the plaintiff's argument to draw the positive inference from disbelief of a denial, the plaintiff may be left with no evidence of a particular element.

A defendant can seek a directed verdict by using evidence that must be believed. This could help a defendant in two ways. Perhaps evidence that must be believed will defeat one of plaintiff's necessary elements. Or perhaps an affirmative defense that must be taken as true will defeat the plaintiff "as a matter of law." Some courts say that whenever the testimony of a witness is involved, the issue must go to the jury, for the jury might disbelieve the testimony based on credibility. The prevailing view, however, regards the clear, uncontradicted, consistent, unimpeached testimony of even interested witnesses as evidence that must be taken as true, and therefore as sufficient basis for a directed verdict in favor of the party having the persuasion burden as well as the initial production burden. This amounts to a holding that reasonable people could not disbelieve such testimony on the basis of demeanor evidence.

The Role of Evidentiary Rules. The Federal Rules of Evidence play an important role in directed verdict, and consequently, in summary judgment. As the federal courts have taken a more active role in excluding expert testimony that they believe is unreliable (*see Daubert v. Merrell Dow Pharmaceuticals, Inc.*, 509 U.S.

579 (1993), and *Kumho Tire Co. Ltd. v. Carmichael*, 526 U.S. 137 (1999)), this in turn has led to increased restriction of what cases are permitted to reach a jury, and, if they do survive a directed verdict motion, what testimony the jury can consider.

Directed Verdict Motions by Plaintiffs. Plaintiffs do, on occasion, win directed verdicts, even though they have the burden of both production and persuasion. We have discussed this possibility previously, and it should now be clear to you why it is usually more unlikely for a plaintiff to win a directed verdict than for a defendant. Still, some cases are ripe for a plaintiff's directed verdict, such as a promissory note case in which the defendant has no defense and the damages are liquidated. Bear in mind also that a plaintiff can frequently win on some of its elements "as a matter of law." For example, if a defendant admits an element in the pleading, or through answering positively or neglecting to answer a request for an admission (Fed. R. Civ. P. 36), or through stipulation or a blanket admission on the stand, the judge can instruct the jury that the element must be believed. In the alternative, the judge can just omit such an element from those that the jury is instructed to consider.

A Question of Law (About the Sufficiency of Evidence/Facts!). You should understand that it is a question of law whether or not to grant a directed verdict—even though that determination necessarily involves factual issues. Another way to think of this is that a judge must decide the legal question of whether or not there are facts sufficient to let the jury deliberate on the matter.

The Supreme Court continues to try to clarify what the trial court should examine in deciding motions for judgment as a matter of law. In a unanimous opinion, the Supreme Court dealt with what constitutes a sufficiency of evidence to permit a plaintiff to survive a directed verdict motion in a disparate treatment age discrimination case in which the discharged plaintiff employee put in evidence of a prima facie case (he was a member of a protected class—over forty years of age, qualified for the position in question, discharged by the employer, and replaced by younger people), and also put in evidence refuting the nondiscriminatory reason proffered for his discharge. *Reeves v. Sanderson Plumbing Products, Inc.*, 530 U.S. 133 (2000). The plaintiff also had evidence of some discriminatory statements made by a supervisor concerning his age. Justice O'Connor, writing for the court, explained that although *St. Mary's Honor Center v. Hicks*, 509 U.S. 502 (1993), held that the fact finder's disbelief of the nondiscriminatory reason put forth by the employer-defendant, coupled with the plaintiff's initial prima facie case, did not mean automatic victory for the plaintiff, for the fact finder must still find discriminatory intent in order for the plaintiff to win, "[i]n appropriate circumstances, the trier of fact can reasonably infer from the falsity of the explanation that the employer is dissembling to cover up the discriminatory purpose." The Supreme Court reversed the Fifth Circuit's reversal of the jury verdict because the Circuit Court "misapplied the standard of review dictated by Rule 50. The court disregarded evidence favorable to Reeves [the plaintiff]—the evidence supporting his prima facie case and undermining respondent's nondiscriminatory explanation—and failed to draw all reasonable inferences in his favor." In a concurring opinion, Justice Ginsburg reiterated the principle of evidence law stated by Justice O'Connor, that "the jury is entitled to treat a party's dishonesty about a material fact as evidence of culpability," and expressed her opinion that when a plaintiff in a disparate treatment discrimination suit introduces both types of evidence—a prima facie case and a sufficiency of evidence to permit the fact finder to "conclude that the employer's proffered explanation for its actions was false"—this will typically permit the case to go to the jury in order to decide whether it draws the permissible inference of discriminatory intent. In her view, the permissible inference remains unless the defendant can "conclusively" demonstrate (which she suspects is atypical) "that discrimination could not have been the defendant's true motivation"; under those circumstances, according to Justice Ginsburg, the defendant would be entitled to judgment as a matter of law.

JNOV Motions and New Trial Motions. Shortly after the Federal Rules of Civil Procedure became law, the Supreme Court, in *Montgomery Ward & Co. v. Duncan*, 311 U.S. 243 (1940), was called upon to interpret the relationship between a motion for JNOV and a motion for new trial (Fed. R. Civ. P. 59). An amendment to Rule 50 in 1963 sought to clarify what a trial judge should do when confronted with both motions, and subsequent amendments have attempted to give further guidance. What is the trial judge now obligated to do when she grants a JNOV and has also been requested to grant a new trial? Consider why, from the defendant's point of view, it may be important to have an opportunity to argue the JNOV motion for a new trial in front of the same judge who heard argument for the motion for JNOV. Under what circumstances would it become relevant whether the trial judge decides both the JNOV and new trial motions? Does this suggest potential unfairness to the nonmoving party, normally the plaintiff?

The Supreme Court has interpreted Rule 50 to allow a circuit court, upon finding some of plaintiff's evidence admitted at the trial to be inadmissible, and further finding that the defendant, absent that evidence, was entitled to judgment as a matter of law, to enter final judgment for the defendant. Although this denies the plaintiff the opportunity to now present its new trial motion to the trial judge, the court thought it was not unfair because the plaintiff has had a full opportunity to enter its best case. *Weisgram v. Marley Co.*, 528 U.S. 440 (2000).

REVIEW EXERCISE NO. 4

You will benefit most from the quiz if you follow the directions: Set aside at least ninety minutes to answer this question; if you finish early this is an indication that you are not wrestling sufficiently with the facts. Use only your Rule Book. Answer the question yourself before discussing it with your study group.

The question involves a one-count complaint for injurious falsehood, and the elements of that cause of action appear at the end of the question.

Pristine Linear Technologies ("PLT") is the United States' largest manufacturer and seller of automatic car wash systems. Theresa Dupont ("Dupont") owns several gas stations in the Sacramento, California area. On August 1, 2017, Dupont ordered three automatic car wash systems from PLT. Dupont informed PLT that she planned to install these car wash systems in three of her new Sacramento area gas stations. Dupont promptly paid $500,000 for the three systems, and PLT shipped the systems from their facility in Miami, Florida. Because construction of the three gas stations was not completed at the time that Dupont ordered the car wash systems, she requested that delivery of those systems be delayed until the construction projects were completed; and PLT agreed to do so. PLT then contacted a business associate in Sacramento named Stan Pembroke, and paid him to store the three car wash systems in one of his warehouses. Pembroke owns dozens of gas stations and related enterprises throughout the Sacramento area and is a competitor of Dupont's.

On February 1, 2018, Dupont called PLT to arrange for the delivery of two of the three car wash systems. Two of the systems were delivered as requested; the third system remained in storage with Pembroke.

On May 1, 2018, Dupont contacted the Sacramento Police Department and told them that Pembroke possessed and was attempting to sell an automatic car wash system that belonged to her (Dupont). Dupont supplied the police with documentation that she had ordered and paid PLT for the automatic car wash system. Pembroke was immediately arrested and indicted on charges of theft. On July 1, 2018, the prosecutors abandoned the prosecution and dropped all of the charges. Around this same time, upon Dupont's request, the third car wash system was delivered to her.

On November 24, 2018, lawyers for PLT and Pembroke filed a lawsuit against Dupont in a federal district court in California. Dupont was properly served with a summons and a copy of the complaint later that same day. The complaint alleged each of the factual details specified in the preceding paragraphs, and claimed that "as a result of Dupont's unsubstantiated accusation of theft, the plaintiffs incurred substantial damages." The defendant moved to dismiss for failure to state a claim; that motion was denied. After discovery, defendant's motion for summary judgment also was denied.

At trial, a jury found in favor of Pembroke (but not in favor of PLT), and awarded Pembroke $250,000 in damages. The defendant's timely motion for a directed verdict (judgment as a matter of law) was denied. Now pending before the judge is Dupont's renewed motion for judgment as a matter of law (JNOV). The evidence of record includes the facts that are reported in this question, all of which were supported by evidence presented at trial. Additional evidence offered by the parties during the trial is included below:

Winkler, a gas station owner unaffiliated with the parties, testified that he had been asked by Pembroke on March 30, 2018, whether he (Winkler) wanted to buy a car wash system "quickly and discreetly." Winkler declined the offer and knew none of the details about which car system Pembroke was offering to sell. Winkler testified that he immediately made Dupont aware of this conversation because he knew that Dupont had been adding car wash systems to some of her gas stations.

Whitford, another gas station owner unaffiliated with the parties, testified that he had been asked by Pembroke in the middle of March 2018 whether he (Whitford) was in the market for a car wash system. When Whitford declined, Pembroke said that that was unfortunate since he had a "freebie that he needed to unload." Whitford further testified that he told Dupont about this conversation a week or so later because he had heard from someone else that Pembroke had been storing Dupont's car wash systems as a favor to Dupont.

Dupont testified that a few days after she had heard from both Winkler and Whitford she called Pembroke to ask whether and why he had her car wash system. Dupont testified that Pembroke denied storing or even knowing anything about her car wash systems. According to Dupont, in that telephone conversation Pembroke denied that he had even spoken with the folks at PLT within the last couple of years.

Dupont testified that she called PLT the same day that she called Pembroke, and that when she didn't hear back from the PLT folks within twenty-four hours, she "panicked." That's why she called the police the very next day.

Dupont testified that in early 2018 her businesses were in financial crisis, and that her competitors were well aware of her tenuous situation. "I had to fend off the vultures," she said.

Dupont testified that the first two car wash systems were delivered promptly after she had requested delivery. Dupont admitted that she had not asked PLT to deliver the third car wash system before she called the police.

Dupont testified that she was not ready for the third car wash system to be delivered because the gas station had not been constructed, and delivery of the system would have interfered with that construction. Dupont testified that when she ultimately asked for the car wash system to be delivered, she received it the next day.

Pembroke testified that he never offered to sell Dupont's car wash system to anyone. He testified: "How could I sell it when she had already paid PLT for it?"

Pembroke admitted that he knew Dupont was financially vulnerable and had joked to Dupont and to others that he would be buying her assets in a "ladies-only garage sale" sometime very soon.

Pembroke testified that he used an independent trucking company to deliver the first two car wash systems to Dupont. His own employees delivered the third system.

The chief executive officer of PLT testified that he never instructed Pembroke to do anything with Dupont's car wash systems other than to store them and to send him the bill for storage. He testified: "Of course, we weren't trying to sell that car wash system. I don't need to sell the same machine twice when I have others in manufacture."

The chief executive officer of PLT also testified that he never told Dupont that he was using Pembroke to store her car wash systems because he knew that would make her nervous since he was a competitor. "But it was just storage. There was no reason for her to worry about it, so I didn't tell her."

The police and prosecutor testified that, after Dupont notified the police department that her property was in Pembroke's possession, she did not "push the case." Dupont played no role in the decision to indict. They called Dupont from time to time, and she simply answered their questions. When asked whether she ever made any false statements to them, the police and the prosecutor both testified "No. It was her property, not Pembroke's."

PLT submitted legal bills indicating an expense of $85,000 attributable to the criminal investigation into the theft. Someone from the PLT public relations department testified that PLT also suffered "serious reputational harm from this. A conservative estimate would put that loss at $150,000."

Pembroke submitted bills from a criminal lawyer indicating a balance owing in the amount of $115,000 for legal services associated with the theft indictment. A local business school professor who had reviewed Pembroke's business records testified that Pembroke had suffered lost wages and lost profits because of the distraction and reputational loss associated with the theft charges that had damaged Pembroke in amounts that exceeded $550,000.

Assume that the only law under which PLT and Pembroke could possibly recover in this jurisdiction is a claim for injurious falsehood, which provides that one who (i) makes a false statement (ii) with intent to harm the interests of another (iii) is liable for any provable loss.

What arguments will the defendant make to support her renewed motion for judgment as a matter of law (JNOV)? What will Pembroke argue? And how should the court rule?

7. Motion to Vacate Judgment

Re-read Fed. R. Civ. P. 60, which gives the ground rules for moving to vacate a judgment in federal court. These rules are typical of what applies in most states as well. Rule 60 is mostly used subsequent to the time period that is permitted for making motions for JNOV or for new trial motions, but nothing prevents a losing party from making all three motions together if the time periods permit.

Fed. R. Civ. P. 60 requires the lawyer to do additional research before relying upon it. For example, many of the categories in Rule 60(b) have been interpreted in ways that one would be unlikely to infer by only reading the Rule; the interpretations generally narrow the application of the Rule. The following list of examples is by no means exhaustive:

(1) The "mistake, inadvertence, surprise, or excusable neglect" language in Rule 60(b)(1) has been severely limited by case law. In most of the cases in which a judgment is vacated under this provision, the losing party is unable to have any trial because of a default judgment or similar reason.

(2) The "newly discovered evidence" cases (60(b)(2)) tend to tack on a number of additional requirements. Some cases say, for example, that the evidence must not be merely cumulative or impeaching, and that such evidence must relate to facts that were in existence at the time of trial. The provision itself requires that the matter could not have been discovered "by reasonable diligence" in time to move for a Rule 59(b) new trial, which is a difficult condition to meet, given the many discovery devices.

(3) Cases applying the "fraud . . . , misrepresentation, or misconduct by an opposing party" category in Rule 60(b)(3) tend to consider a number of factors, such as the opportunities for detection of the misconduct, before or during trial, and the strength of the proof of the misconduct. These interpretive factors are complicated by the fact that fraud can also be a reason for voiding a judgment under 60(b)(4) and that the Rule explicitly "does not limit a court's power to . . . set aside a judgment for fraud on the court" through an independent action. Fed. R. Civ. P. 60(d). That there are several subcategories of fraud cases under Rule 60(b) is not merely a matter of academic concern, for the motions under 60(b)(1), (2), and (3) must be made within a year, and other motions must be made "within a reasonable time." Since the independent action is not a motion, it may have a different time period.

(4) Rule 60(b)(6) establishes the category "any other reason that justifies relief." Since this category is not subject to the one-year limitation set forth in Fed. R. Civ. P. 60(c)(1), lawyers frequently try to recast a motion that would ordinarily be brought under (b)(1), (2), and (3) into a reason not covered by those provisions. The courts tend to rule, however, that if the case could have been covered by the 60(b)(1) through (3) categories, then litigants cannot avoid the one-year limitation by seeking refuge in the catchall language of 60(b)(6).

The following case considers the application of the language of Fed. R. Civ. P. 60(a), (b)(1), and (b)(6). As you read the case, ask yourself how you would have decided it. Are you surprised by the court's result? Be prepared to explain the court's reasoning as to all three applicable provisions. Could you write an equally persuasive opinion reaching a different conclusion?

Brandon v. Chicago Board of Education
143 F.3d 293 (7th Cir. 1998)

ROVNER, Circuit Judge:

Lorenzo Brandon sought Rule 60 relief from a judgment entered against him for failure to prosecute his case. The district court denied relief and Brandon now appeals. The facts are unusual. Indeed, Brandon claims they are unique. Brandon filed his Americans with Disabilities action against the Chicago Board of Education on August 2, 1995. His attorneys, Paul F. Peters and James C. Reho, entered appearances in the case, listing as their address the Law Offices of Paul F. Peters, One North LaSalle Street, Chicago. It is undisputed that in docketing the case, the Clerk of the United States District Court erroneously entered, Paul A. Peters, another Chicago attorney, who is located at 10 South LaSalle Street, Chicago, as attorney for the plaintiff. As a result of this error, subsequent mailings from the court were directed to the wrong attorney at the wrong address. Admirably, Paul A. Peters actually took the time to write to the Clerk of the district court, informing the Clerk that he was not counsel of record in the case, had no connection to the case, and was returning any materials sent to him.

Unfortunately, the Clerk's office still did not understand the nature of its error, and continued to send all minute orders and other mailings to the wrong address. As a result, Brandon's counsel never received notice of two different status hearings, and failed to appear. After failing to appear for the second status hearing, the court dismissed the case for want of prosecution on December 13, 1995. The order dismissing the case was also sent to the wrong address. A little more than a year passed before plaintiff's counsel began to wonder what happened to the case. Upon visiting the Clerk's office in late 1996, he discovered his case had been quite active without him. Included in the court's file was the letter from Paul A. Peters, orders setting status hearings, and the order dismissing the case for want of prosecution.[1]

On December 16, 1996, one year and three days after the dismissal, Paul F. Peters filed a Rule 60 motion to vacate the judgment. Astonishingly, yet another clerical error, this one caused by plaintiff's counsel, caused the motion to be spindled under the wrong case number. When plaintiff's counsel noticed this error on the day the motion was to be heard, he pointed it out to the Clerk's office. The Clerk's office told him the motion would not be heard that day, and would have to be re-noticed. Plaintiff's counsel then refiled the motion under the correct case number. Before the new date for the hearing, however, plaintiff's counsel received a minute order from the court, granting the motion. As a courtesy, plaintiff's counsel sent a letter to defendant's counsel, stating that the motion had been granted and no appearance was necessary on the date set for hearing the motion. Nevertheless, defendant's counsel appeared in court on the day of the hearing and persuaded the court to vacate its order granting Rule 60 relief. After briefing on the motion, the court ultimately denied Rule 60 relief.

On appeal, Brandon argues that he cannot be faulted for a lack of diligence when he was never notified by the court that there was anything he was supposed to be doing. He never ignored a court order, he contends, because he never knew about any orders. Rather, the clerical error in the Clerk's office was the source of the problem, and the district court abused its discretion in refusing

---

1. The Board of Education filed two motions early in the case, one to extend the time to answer, and the other to file the answer *instanter*. Brandon received a notice for each of these motions, and opposed neither. The court entered minute orders granting the motions and, as before, the Clerk mailed the minute orders to the wrong attorney. The Board rightly points out that Brandon should have known something was amiss when he failed to receive either order.

to grant Rule 60 relief. Although Brandon initially moved for relief under Rule 60(a), he subsequently argued (and argues on appeal) that he is entitled to relief under Rule 60(b)(6). He admitted at oral argument that he is abandoning any claim to relief under Rule 60(a), which by its own terms applies only to clerical mistakes in "judgments, orders or other parts of the record and errors therein arising from oversight or omission."[2] The Chicago Board of Education focuses its response on Brandon's lack of entitlement to relief under Rule 60(b)(1), stating that it is the only conceivably relevant subsection.

We begin by examining, Rule 60(b), which provides, in relevant part, as follows:

> On motion and upon such terms as are just, the court may relieve a party or a party's legal representative from a final judgment, order, or proceeding for the following reasons: (1) mistake, inadvertence, surprise, or excusable neglect; (2) newly discovered evidence which by due diligence could not have been discovered in time to move for a new trial under Rule 59(b); (3) fraud (whether heretofore denominated intrinsic or extrinsic), misrepresentation, or other misconduct of an adverse party; (4) the judgment is void; (5) the judgment has been satisfied, released, or discharged, or a prior judgment upon which it is based has been reversed or otherwise vacated, or it is no longer equitable that the judgment should have prospective application; or (6) any other reason justifying relief from the operation of the judgment. The motion shall be made within a reasonable time, and for reasons (1), (2), and (3) not more than one year after the judgment, order, or proceeding was entered or taken.

Neither side argues that subsections (2) through (5) are applicable. Instead, Brandon argues that he is entitled to relief under subsection (b)(6), the catchall section. The Board contends that subsection (b)(1) is the only applicable section. The parties agree that we may not reverse a trial court's denial of a Rule 60(b) motion absent an abuse of discretion. *See Dickerson v. Board of Education of Ford Heights, Illinois*, 32 F.3d 1114, 1116 (7th Cir. 1994) (trial court's denial of Rule 60(b) motion reviewed under a highly deferential standard, and reversed only for abuse of discretion). Moreover, because a court's dismissal for failure to prosecute is itself reviewed only for abuse of discretion, "a court's decision under Rule 60(b) not to reinstate a case dismissed for want of prosecution has been described as 'discretion piled on discretion.'" *Id.*, 32 F.3d at 1117.

---

2. Brandon is correct to abandon his Rule 60(a) argument. *See Wesco Products Co. v. Alloy Automotive Co.*, 880 F.2d 981, 984 (7th Cir. 1989). We noted there that district courts often have difficulty determining whether motions are brought to correct a clerical error (as opposed to some other kind of error). "In this circuit, we have identified the relevant distinction as being between changes that implement the result intended by the court at the time the order was entered and changes that alter the original meaning to correct a legal or factual error. Thus, '[i]f the flaw lies in the translation of the original meaning to the judgement, then Rule 60(a) allows a correction; if the judgement captures the original meaning but is infected by error, [] the parties must seek another source of authority to correct the mistake.'" *Id.* (citing *United States v. Griffin*, 782 F.2d 1393, 1396-97 (7th Cir. 1986)) (internal citations omitted). In the instant case, as in *Wesco*, the dismissal for want of prosecution accurately reflected the court's intention at the time it was entered. Thus, the error, to the extent there was one, was not in the transcription, but in the court's decision, a ground for relief not contained in Rule 60(a).

"Inherent in the structure of Rule 60(b) is the principle that the first three clauses and the catchall clause are mutually exclusive. Thus, if the asserted grounds for relief fall within the terms of the first three clauses of Rule 60(b), relief under the catchall provision is not available." *Wesco Products Co. v. Alloy Automotive Co.*, 880 F.2d 981, 983 (7th Cir. 1989) (internal citations omitted). Therefore, we must first determine if the relief sought falls within Rule 60(b)(1). We noted in *Wesco* that Rule 60(b)(1) applies to errors by judicial officers as well as parties. 880 F.2d at 984-985. The district court here appeared to be analyzing the motion pursuant to Rule 60(b)(1), finding that "[t]here was a lack of diligence," and that this was "certainly not excusable neglect." *See* Transcript of Proceedings before the Honorable George W. Lindberg, Feb. 11, 1997, at p. 8. The district court also acknowledged that Rule 60(b)(1) applies to errors by the court, stating that "if the rules mean anything, and the Seventh Circuit jurisprudence means anything, it means that lawyers must follow their cases. They cannot rely on the Judge, the law clerks or the courtroom deputies or the Clerk's office. They must follow their case." *Id.*

We agree with the district court that Rule 60(b)(1) is the appropriate mechanism for analyzing Brandon's request for relief. Indeed, the facts here demonstrate an unusual combination of error by the Clerk's office and neglect by the attorney. Rule 60(b)(1) covers both. Having found that Rule 60(b)(1) applies, we must necessarily find that Rule 60(b)(6) does not apply. *Wesco*, 880 F.2d at 983. By its own terms, a motion brought pursuant to Rule 60(b)(1) must be made within one year of the date the judgment was entered. "[T]he one year time limit is jurisdictional and may not be extended in any event. . . ." *Wesco*, 880 F.2d at 985. No one disputes that Brandon brought his motion one year and three days after judgment was entered against him. We therefore conclude that the district court did not abuse its discretion in denying relief.

F. TYPES OF VERDICTS, BIFURCATION, TRIFURCATION, INSTRUCTIONS, REMITTITUR, AND ADDITUR

In this section we introduce the rationale, doctrine, and strategic concerns of jury instructions, bifurcation and trifurcation, types of verdict, and remittitur and additur. Are these ways of helping the jury to be just and rational, or do they invade the jury's fact-finding province?

1. Types of Verdicts

Traditionally, juries rendered general verdicts. In civil cases, juries were asked only to find for the plaintiff or for the defendant, and if for the plaintiff, to state the amount of monetary damages. One procedural device already available in federal and state courts is the *special verdict*, which provides means by which trial judges can structure a jury's reasoning process. Under the Federal

Rules of Civil Procedure, the trial judge can submit written questions to the jury, and the jury returns a special verdict in the form of written findings of fact. Alternatively, the judge can have the jury return a general verdict, but answer interrogatories that have been posed to it by the judge. With either method, the judge is outlining the way the jury should approach the issue, step by step. Read Fed. R. Civ. P. 49.

Some of the traditional arguments for special verdicts are that restricting the decision-making functions of the jury would "improve the deliberation process by packaging the dispute in distinct, manageable components," "concentrat[e] juror attention on certain matters," "aid the jurors in sorting out the facts and avoiding confusion," "ensure a truly unanimous decision," "facilitate the appellate process by spelling out the premises underlying the jury's ultimate conclusions," and "[be] extremely helpful in the application of collateral estoppel (issue preclusion)." *See* Mark Brodin, *Accuracy, Efficiency, and Accountability in the Litigation Process—The Case for the Fact Verdict*, 59 U. Cin. L. Rev. 15 (1990). These arguments all imply that the jury could use some help in structuring their deliberations and decisions. What do you think?

2. Bifurcation and Trifurcation

Another reform is splitting trials into stages. "Bifurcation" typically separates a case into two potential trials, usually liability and causation first. If the defendant wins, that ends the matter. If the plaintiff wins on liability and causation, and the case does not settle at that point, there is then a trial on damages. Of course, judicial separation can happen in many ways, although the term "bifurcation" is usually used to denote the separation of elements into two trials. A judge can also try parties separately or separate out different causes of action for trial. Fed. R. Civ. P. 42(b) is usually the authorization relied upon in federal court for such judicial dividing. "Trifurcation" divides a case into three parts for purposes of trial, usually separating out causation, liability (fault), and damages. Once again, if the plaintiff loses on one element, like causation, that obviates the need for a trial on the other elements. If the plaintiff wins on the first element, that may well lead to settlement.

The arguments in favor of bifurcation and trifurcation fall into three spheres. First, there is efficiency. You have already read how the determination of one portion of a case for the defendant will eliminate the need to go further. What is perhaps less obvious is that even if the plaintiff wins the first portion, say on liability, this will frequently lead to settlement, resulting in further efficiency and money-saving for the court and the parties. Second, by severing damages from liability, or causation from both, this eliminates some of the emotional element from jury consideration. For instance, if the injuries to the plaintiff are extensive and heart-rending, and those injuries are tried as part of a unitary case, this may cause a jury to find for the plaintiff on liability when otherwise they might not find the defendant at fault. Similarly, if causation is tried first in a trifurcated case, this can decrease the possibility that the horrendous injuries or untoward conduct of the defendant will magnetically draw a jury to a jury verdict on all elements, even though the conduct has not caused the harm.

In an interesting article in the *Columbia Business Law Review,* Meiring de Villiers analyzes experimental and trial data, as well as relying on theories of group deliberation, and makes comparisons between unitary trials in product liability cases and bifurcated trials, with liability being tried prior to damages. His conclusions seem very plausible: (1) When all elements are tried together, there will be some cases in which the jury might not have otherwise found liability, but instead will compromise by giving diminished damages; (2) when cases are bifurcated, there will be some cases in which the jury will not find liability, because they are unable to achieve a compromise verdict on the damage portion, which is not before them, and yet do not want to be a hung jury; and (3) once the plaintiff in a bifurcated case wins on the first stage, liability, there will be instances when the plaintiff achieves a higher damage settlement or a higher jury verdict than he or she would have had the case been tried in a unitary fashion (once again, this is because the jury cannot readily make the compromise they sometimes made in example (1) of finding liability, but giving lesser damages, because liability has already been found).

This leads de Villiers to a third sphere of argument in favor of bifurcation in products liability cases. Here is his conclusion:

> The theoretical analysis presented in the article has important public policy implications. Trial bifurcation will encourage plaintiffs to file suit in cases where evidence of liability is strong, and discourage marginal cases. Bifurcated litigation will provide clearer guidance to manufacturers of the product safety standard they will be expected to achieve, promote the achievement of deterrence, compensation and product safety, and reduce the likelihood that a high-risk/high-utility product, that is valued by consumers, will be driven out of the market on the whim of a minority of extremely risk-averse jurors [i.e., jurors who force the majority of jurors in a given case to find liability in exchange for reduced damages].

Meiring de Villiers, *A Legal and Policy Analysis of Bifurcated Litigation,* 2000 Colum. Bus. L. Rev. 153, 197. Other articles support the de Villiers pro-bifurcation view. *See, e.g.,* Steven S. Gensler, *Bifurcation Unbound,* 75 Wash. L. Rev. 705 (2000) (arguing that if trials were bifurcated between liability and damages stages, perhaps 70 percent would end without reaching the damages phase).

As you might expect, there are a group of counterarguments made by those who prefer a unitary, nonsplit trial. Throughout this book, we have presented the position that litigation generally, and jury trials in particular, are by no means merely a mechanical method of applying law to facts. Rather, we have suggested that there is a lot more going on, and that concepts of citizen participation, legitimization of results, community values, and the importance and power of narrative are critical parts of the mix.

> There is little doubt that the separation of liability from damages in personal injury cases may save time. A competent study concludes that cases handled

in this fashion take twenty percent less time than do cases tried routinely, with the liability and damage issues submitted simultaneously to the jury. The same data show, however, that although defendants win in forty-two percent of the cases tried routinely, they win in seventy-nine percent of the cases in which the liability issue is submitted alone. These figures suggest that juries are moved by sympathy when they have heard evidence of the extent of the plaintiff's injuries and that this influences their decision on the liability issue. The orthodox theory of the role of the jury, particularly its role in tort litigation, regards this as quite undesirable. But when it is seen that the split trial reduces by more than half the cases in which personal injury plaintiffs are successful, it is apparent that bifurcation makes a substantial change in the nature of the jury trial itself. . . .

[A] number of courts have indicated that separation of this kind should be used sparingly. Although recognizing the right of the courts to experiment with devices such as Rule 42(b) to minimize jury discretion and to present evidence more clearly to the jury, Judge Weinstein has indicated that the district court "ought not force substantive changes on the parties merely on the justification of existing delays in the courts."

Charles A. Wright and Arthur R. Miller, *Federal Practice and Procedure* § 2390 (citations omitted). Understand that there are fairness and efficiency arguments on both sides of the debate about the wisdom of bifurcation.

One of the more famous instances of bifurcation appeared in the *Bendectin* case, where many deformed children were among the plaintiffs. Not only was causation tried first (resulting in a defense verdict that ended the case), but "[f]earing undue prejudice to the defendant, the trial court also excluded from the courtroom all visibly deformed plaintiffs and all plaintiffs under the age of ten." *In re Bendectin Litigation*, 857 F.2d 290 (6th Cir. 1988). Presumably, the order excluding some of the plaintiffs was part of defendant's motivation for seeking to bifurcate. Was this a positive or negative consequence of bifurcation?

Although defendants are typically the party that can most benefit from bifurcation, aren't there circumstances where it would be in the plaintiff's interest to bifurcate?

3. Jury Instructions

Judges also give instructions to juries about the verdict form, the meaning of words on that form, the legal terminology at issue, and the task of deliberation that awaits them. Someone who is especially wary of the court's control of and interference with juries might question whether juries need any instructions. Yet surely even the most pro-jury among us would concede that instructions of some kind are necessary. The question, then, is what should these instructions include?

The most useful starting point for understanding jury instructions is to look at some of them. In your law library you will find volumes of books with "pattern" or "model" jury instructions. Pattern jury instructions can be the product of commercial publishers, of advocacy groups, or of governmental commissions or councils. There are also many pattern jury instructions available online. When you practice in a state that has officially endorsed a set of pattern jury instructions, those instructions enjoy preferential status. In a few states, a particular set of jury instructions can be mandatory. Whether a set of instructions is mandatory or just preferred or purely optional, counsel must exercise independent thought in tailoring the instructions to the particular facts in evidence and the law applicable to the case.

Federal Rule 51 emphasizes that the trial judge is authorized to require attorneys to submit proposed jury instructions prior to trial. The Rule also requires the judge, before instructing the jury and before closing arguments, to inform the attorneys of the jury instructions that will be given. If a judge definitively decides on the record to not read a proposed jury instruction, the proposing party need not make a later objection in order to preserve the issue for appeal; otherwise, both the initial request and the objection are needed to preserve the point on appeal.

As you continue to consider your views about the civil jury and about the many methods that have developed both to guide and control it, consider an example of what we know about an actual case. Our sources are an article by Steven Brill, the editor-in-chief of *American Lawyer* (Steven Brill, *Inside the Jury Room at the Washington Post Libel Trial*, Am. Law., 937 (Nov. 1982)), and the Order and Memorandum dated May 2, 1983, of Judge Oliver Gasch of the U.S. District Court, District of Columbia, in *Tavoulareas v. The Washington Post Company, et al.*, C.A. No. 80-3032. The additional defendants included *Post* editors Ben Bradlee and Bob Woodward. Tavoulareas was the president of Mobil Oil, and his son, Peter, was in the oil tanker business. In 1979, the *Post* published two articles about the father, a famous self-made man, and his son. The headline of the story, which appeared on the front page, was "Mobil Chief Sets Up Son in Venture." The lead paragraph stated: "Mobil Oil Corp. president William P. Tavoulareas set up his son five years ago as a partner in a London-based shipping management firm that has since done millions of dollars in business operating Mobil-owned ships under exclusive, no-bid contracts." The father, who claimed that he helped his son only when an opportunity arose, was upset that his "unblemished reputation" (Brill's words) had been sullied. He talked with Ben Bradlee four days after the first story, seeking a retraction, and only got a brief subsequent story adding a little information.

Tavoulareas said he tried to get the *Post* to admit its mistakes for a year, "[b]ut they're so damn arrogant. I kept telling them I'd sue." The lawsuit alleged libel. The plaintiffs were represented by John Walsh, a trial lawyer at the well-known Wall Street firm of Cadwalader, Wickersham & Taft (Taft was President William Howard Taft's brother and Wickersham was appointed to the initial Advisory Committee that drafted the Federal Rules of Civil Procedure). The *Post* and its staff were represented by the legendary Washington, D.C., firm of Williams & Connolly (the Williams, of course, was Edward Bennett Williams).

Irving Younger, who at the time was probably the country's most famous lecturer on evidence and jury strategy (although he "insists he always prefers a judge to a jury"), was chosen to be lead counsel for the *Post*. Prior to Younger's involvement, Williams & Connolly insisted on a jury trial.

The trial lasted nineteen days. The judge instructed the jury:

> It is not the defendants' burden to prove that the articles are true. The burden is upon the plaintiffs to prove to you that they are substantially false. . . . It is not enough for William Tavoulareas to prove the defendants did not conduct a thorough investigation of the facts or that they were negligent in the way they wrote or edited the articles. To recover, William Tavoulareas must prove the defendants had a high degree of awareness that the articles were false or probably false and that they were recklessly disregarded, whether the articles were false or not. If you find the defendants believed the sources of information in the story to be reliable and believed the story to be accurate when published, you must find the defendants have not acted with actual malice as to William Tavoulareas.

Brill reports that the jury foreman, who was going to attend law school the next fall, and the five other jurors, under his insistent lead, "operated as if these instructions had not been given." The jury foreman insisted that it was the obligation of the *Post* to prove in the article itself that the headline that the father had "set up his son" was accurate. In fact, Irving Younger had pitched his defense, which Brill thought was a mistake, on the ground that the article was accurate. Younger's experience had taught him that stressing burden of proof was not a good way to argue or win a lawsuit when one's client is accused of wrongdoing; instead, you should argue and prove that your client is in the right.

One of the jurors told the judge that a written copy of the instructions would be helpful, but the judge, with the agreement of counsel, did not allow that out of fear that "the instructions might be read piecemeal instead of taken as a whole." Brill reports: "[F]our jurors would later volunteer to me that, as one put it, 'we never understood the instructions and never pretended to.'" Although the first vote of the jury was 4-2 in favor of the *Post* on all counts, the young jury foreman kept "yelling," according to one juror, "where's the set-up?" By the third day of deliberations, the last of the six jurors gave in and compromised on a $250,000 verdict for compensatory damages for the father, William Tavoulareas, against the *Post*, an investigative reporter, and a freelance reporter. After a brief trial for the jury to consider punitive damages, at which the *Post* conceded its healthy financial condition and William Tavoulareas testified to a legal bill of about $1.8 million, the jury awarded the father an additional $1.8 million in punitive damages.

In later discussing the case and what prompted their decision, "[s]everal jurors . . . mentioned the judge's vacation plans and the humiliation of a hung jury." The final juror to relent, several recalled, told the others "that the pressure was too much for her, that she felt sick, and that this case was why, in her view, that there should be 12 jurors as there had been when [she had] served on jury panels in the past." When asked what would have happened if the jury had just been asked to decide "whether the *Post* had been recklessly or deliberately inaccurate or unfair," a juror answered: "Oh, in that case, there's no way the plaintiff would have won. We all, even . . . [the foreman], I think, conceded they hadn't done anything careless or on purpose."

Both sides appealed, the plaintiffs' counsel arguing that if the *Post* was liable to the father, then the son should have also won, and the defendants' counsel continuing to insist that there was no evidence to support the verdict, and seeking a JNOV or a reduction of damages. Months later, in a nine-page single-spaced memorandum opinion, the bulk of which meticulously reviewed the evidence in the light most favorable to plaintiff, the judge concluded: "Under the standards enunciated by the Supreme Court, . . . the jury verdict in this case will withstand the motions for JNOV only if there is sufficient evidence in the record from which a jury could reasonably find, by clear and convincing proof,* that the defendants published the November 30 article with actual malice. The article in question falls far short of being a model of fair, unbiased, investigative journalism. There is no evidence in the record, however, to show that it contained knowing lies or statements made in reckless disregard of the truth. Reviewed under the stringent test set forth by the Supreme Court in *New York Times Co. v. Sullivan*, the verdict in plaintiff's favor must be set aside." Consequently, the judge granted the defendants' motions for JNOV.

So, that's the story. Does this change your mind about jury cases? What lessons about civil litigation and jury trials do you draw from it?

PRACTICE EXERCISE NO. 26: JURY INSTRUCTIONS IN *CARPENTER*

You are an associate in the law firm that represents Nancy Carpenter. The trial date is approaching in Massachusetts state court, and the supervising partner has asked you to prepare the draft of our proposed jury instructions. For purposes of this exercise, *focus exclusively on Count IV* (wrongful death) of the Amended Complaint, and assume that the only remaining defendant is Ultimate Auto. Using resources available to you online and/or in the library, assemble a packet of proposed jury instructions. Be thoughtful when choosing one alternative construction of an instruction over its alternatives, and be prepared to demonstrate, explain, and justify some of those choices.

4. Remittitur and Additur

We have now considered bifurcation, different types of jury verdicts, and jury instructions. The remaining "jury control" doctrine relates to what are called

---

Eds.' Note: This is not the burden in the ordinary civil case; in the typical case, the plaintiff does not have to adduce "clear and convincing proof," but must merely convince the jury on the evidence (including all reasonable inferences) that it is more likely than not that all elements of the prima facie case are true.

remittitur and *additur.* To understand these concepts, you will have to recall what you learned about motions for a new trial based on the contention, in whole or in part, that the monetary amount of the jury verdict was too large or too small "as a matter of law." Given the time and expense to society and the parties resulting from the grant of a new trial, some courts devised the practice of conditioning the grant of a new trial (when damages were excessive) on the plaintiff's refusal to consent to a reduction of damages to a specific amount (called *nisi remittitur damna*). Put another way, the judge is either explicitly or implicitly saying to plaintiff's counsel: "I agree with the defendant that the damages are excessive, and will grant defendant's motion for a new trial, unless your client agrees to reduce the verdict by X amount of dollars."

There are additional, longer-standing precedents for the remittitur, which reduces damages, than for the additur, which increases them. In the additur situation, the judge is either explicitly or implicitly saying to the defendant's counsel: "The plaintiff, although winning the case, has moved for a new trial on the grounds that the damages given in the verdict are inadequate. I agree with the plaintiff, and intend to grant the plaintiff's motion for a new trial unless your client agrees to increase the damages by X dollars. It is your client's choice."

Before considering what you think of these devices, you should be aware of both constitutional and practical considerations. In *Dimick v. Schiedt*, 293 U.S. 474 (1935), the Supreme Court considered the constitutionality of additur and, in a 5-4 decision, found it unconstitutional for federal courts to use the device. The Court distinguished remittitur and implied, in dicta, that it would permit that device to stand. The points of distinction, according to the majority, were some evidence of the practice of remittitur in England prior to 1791 and that in the case of remittitur "what remains is included in the verdict along with the unlawful excess—in that sense it has been found by the jury—and the remittitur has the effect of merely lopping off the excrescence." The additur, according to the majority, is a "bald addition of something which in no sense can be said to be included in the verdict." *Id.* at 486. The Supreme Court has since given mixed signals about whether it would continue to hold additur unconstitutional. In *Tull v. United States*, 481 U.S. 412, 533 n.16 (1996), the Court implied that *Dimick* was an anomaly and hinted that the Court may "rethink" the additur question "on a later day." But more recently, in *Feltner v. Columbia Pictures Television, Inc.*, 523 U.S. 340 (1998), the Supreme Court found a jury trial right in assessing damages under the federal copyright statute and suggested that *Tull* was "at least in tension with" prior Supreme Court precedent, including *Dimick*, 523 U.S. at 355 n.9. Additur, and more frequently remittitur, have been permitted by the highest court of some states. State courts have been more willing to permit additur in cases where the amount to be added is a liquidated amount, such as a fixed financial amount in a contract, or readily calculable interest.

Assuming that a court is permitted to grant the motion for a new trial unless the nonmoving party agrees to lesser or greater damages, the question remains how a court should set the amount to be remitted or added. Consider these three possibilities in remittitur. The judge will grant defendant's motion for a new trial unless the plaintiff agrees to (1) remit the least amount possible that will bring the verdict into the range of what the judge believes is a permissible verdict; (2) remit the amount that will make the verdict what the judge believes a reasonable jury should have awarded; (3) remit the greatest amount possible that will bring the verdict to the smallest award that the judge believes to be rational, given the evidence.

If the plaintiff refuses to remit (or the defendant refuses to add) and the judge, therefore, decides to grant the motion for a new trial, the judge may also consider whether to grant a total new trial, or only a new trial on damages. To grant a new trial only on damages, of course, raises many of the same issues as bifurcation.

Some evidence suggests that plaintiffs in the United States often collect considerably less than the total amounts of their verdicts and the accrued interest. The widespread use of remittitur is one reason; another is settlement pending new trials or appeals, or during the period that plaintiffs try to collect on their judgments. Perhaps most important, the financial straits of defendants (such as bankruptcy or a lack of funds or property to pay the award) may result in plaintiffs taking a good deal less than the damages award plus interest. As a practical matter, the limit of the defendant's insurance policy often determines the extent to which the plaintiff will collect. Although there are few empirical studies on the collection of jury awards, we do know that the larger the verdict, the more likely and larger the unpaid portion or "haircut." The size of the haircut also varies dramatically by subject area. *See generally* David A. Hyman, Bernard Black, Kathryn Zeiler, Charles Silver, and William Sage, *Do Defendants Pay What Juries Award?: Post-Verdict Haircuts in Texas Medical Malpractice Cases, 1988-2003,* 4 J. Empirical Legal Stud. (2007).

REVIEW QUESTIONS

1. What is the specific constitutional problem raised by remittitur or additur? Scrutinize the language of the Seventh Amendment to the U.S. Constitution. Does the majority's constitutional distinction in *Dimick* make sense to you?

2. Why might a state constitutional decision on additur come out differently from the *Dimick* case?

QUESTIONS TO PONDER

1. When a defendant in federal court moves for a new trial based on excessive damages and the plaintiff remits the amount suggested by the judge so that the new trial motion is denied, should the defendant still be able to appeal the case? Can the defendant's appeal, if allowed at all, include the excessiveness of damages even after the remittitur? Can it include the excessiveness of damages before the remittitur?

When a remittitur has been made, what risks does the defendant's counsel run if he or she decides to appeal the verdict? In addition to checking the Seventh Amendment, please apply your common sense to all of these questions. There is no need for you to do additional research on them at this time, but when you determine where you are going to practice, you will want to acquaint yourself with both the law and the custom.

2. How should a judge determine the *amount* of remittitur?

Jury Controls. Review the methods of jury control we have considered: rules of evidence, summary judgment, directed verdict, JNOV, instructions, new-trial motions because the verdict is against the weight of the evidence, new-trial motions based on excessive or inadequate damages, specialized types of verdicts or interrogatories for the jury, bifurcation and trifurcation, and remittitur and additur and judicial control of punitive damages.

QUESTIONS TO PONDER

Which of the jury controls offend your sense of how juries should work? Which methods seem most sensible and fair to you?

PRACTICE EXERCISE NO. 27: MOTIONS TO CHALLENGE A JURY VERDICT

John Dinkins, a successful 32-year-old black male, has just won a malpractice claim against Forsyth Laboratories in state court in the State of Crabtree. The jury came in with a general verdict for Mr. Dinkins for $100,000. Forsyth Laboratories misread a laboratory test that would have diagnosed stomach cancer in its early stages. As a result of the lab's error, Mr. Dinkins's cancer was not detected until it had spread to other organs. Had the test been read accurately by the lab, Mr. Dinkins would have had a 90-95 percent survival chance after prompt removal of the cancer. Because of the delayed diagnosis, Mr. Dinkins had to endure two major operations, and is currently undergoing chemotherapy. His likelihood of survival has decreased to 50-60 percent.

In the past eighteen months in the State of Crabtree, four similar cases have been successfully tried by plaintiffs similarly situated as to age (pre- and post-incident), earning capacity, estimated life expectancy prior to the cancer, and survival rate after the misdiagnosis. These four jury verdicts averaged exactly $400,000. All plaintiffs in these four cases were white males.

The plaintiff believes that the low jury verdict was due to racial prejudice and stereotyping by jurors, as well as social devaluation of black males generally. During the trial, the defendants introduced medical evidence that black males have a higher rate of heart disease—because of genetics and as a result of their dietary and lifestyle choices—than males of other races. The defendants also introduced evidence that Mr. Dinkins, although financially stable, chose to live in the inner city and to drive a fast, fancy sports car.

Question: If you represented Dinkins, what motions would you bring to challenge this verdict? What arguments would you make? Anticipate Forsyth's justifications and strategies.

G. CLOSING ARGUMENTS

One of the most exciting moments in a trial lawyer's life is standing up to give a closing argument. Some lawyers start thinking about their closing arguments early in their analysis and preparation of a case, as a means of focusing their case preparation on what aspects of the case will eventually provide their most persuasive advocacy. Before moving on to other aspects of procedure, we want you to read about some of that sense of exhilaration.

Lloyd Paul Stryker, The Art of Advocacy
111-112, 125-129 (1954)

. . . The summation is the high point in the art of advocacy; it is the combination and the culmination of all of its many elements. It is the climax of the case. It is the opportunity to rescue a cause until that time perhaps seemingly lost. It calls for every skill the advocate possesses. It calls for more than skill—it is a summons to his courage, a testing ground of his character, a trial of his logic and reasoning powers, his memory, his patience and his tact, his ability to express himself in convincing words; in short, it is an assay of every power of persuasion he possesses. Small wonder, then, that there have been few great summations. . . .

An advocate is one who has been called to the aid of a fellow citizen in deep trouble. You are that advocate, and your one, sole and single aim is to aid that fellow citizen with all your heart and soul and mind.

The jury is watching you with an even greater scrutiny than that with which they looked at you while you were making, now so long ago, your opening address. They remember what you promised them; they have a good recollection of the evidence that followed and they are challenging you to persuade them that you have proved all that you promised them you would prove.

But if they have been studying you, your scrutiny of them has been no less intense. You will remember how they looked when certain evidence was introduced, how they reacted to your cross-examinations. Some one or more of them may have asked questions of a witness on the stand, and you will be thinking now, as you thought then, of the significance of those questions and the way in which the questioner received the answers. If you have succeeded thus far in the trial in establishing some credit with the jury, if your firmness, your good manners, and your complete integrity have won you some measure of approval in the jury box, you will strain now to avoid everything that may forfeit that good will and you will do all within your power to strengthen it. . . .

For each new case the lawyer has a special problem. He alone has seen and heard the witnesses. He, not some master of the past, has divined the feeling of his judge and jury; he alone has felt the atmosphere of his own courtroom and is, therefore, in a better position to decide upon his course of action than all the silent mentors of the printed page.

Imagination is of incalculable aid. An illustration of how it can be used was once given by a great Chicago lawyer, Weymouth Kirkland. He had been called upon to defend a group of insurance companies which were resisting claims based on the alleged death of an engineer named Peck. The plaintiff contended that Peck had fallen overboard from a steamer while crossing Lake Michigan. The defendants, on the other hand, were seeking to establish that Peck had never fallen overboard, that he had left his coat in his stateroom as a ruse, and that when the boat docked in the early morning, he had quietly slipped down the gangplank.

Much evidence was adduced by the plaintiff for the purpose of establishing that if Peck had in fact fallen overboard, the current and the prevailing winds would have carried his body to a particular spot. One of the plaintiff's witnesses was a cook on another steamer whose ship, three days after Peck's disappearance, sailed past the exact spot where other witnesses had said the currents would have carried Peck's body. On his direct examination, the cook said that exactly at that spot he happened to glance out from his locker, saw the body, and recognized it as that of his old friend, Peck.

It was a nice opportunity for cross-examination, and Mr. Kirkland used it in this way:

Q. How long had you known Peck?
A. Fifteen years.
Q. You knew him well?
A. Yes, sir.
Q. How did you happen to see his body?
A. I looked out of the porthole.
Q. You recognized it beyond doubt as the body of Peck?
A. Yes, sir.
Q. Did you make any outcry when you saw the body?
A. No, sir.
Q. Did you ask the captain to stop the ship?
A. No, sir.
Q. What were you doing when you happened to look out of the window and saw the body?

A. I was peeling potatoes.

Q. And when the body of your old friend, Peck, floated by, you just kept on peeling potatoes?

A. Yes, sir.

It was a bit of cross-examination well done. And how was it used in the summing up? Did Mr. Kirkland tell the jury that the cook's testimony was palpably untrue? Did he denounce the absurdity of the answers? He handled it far more adroitly. As he stood before the jury for his final appeal, he produced a potato from one pocket and a knife from another. Thus equipped, he rested one foot on a chair and proceeded to peel the potato, saying: "What ho? What have we here? Who is this floating past? As I live and breathe, if it isn't my old friend Peck! I shall tell the captain about this in the morning. In the meantime, I must go right on peeling my potatoes."

By innuendo he had destroyed all the cook's testimony. A little wit had accomplished far more than the finest rhetoric or the fiercest denunciation of this perjurer.

If I were asked to name the prerequisites of an advocate, I would mention imagination among the first. One seeking to persuade a court or jury which does not possess that quality would be a man impervious to all the overtones and subtle possibilities presented by the facts. Imagination for the trial lawyer is as essential as for the novelist, the artist, or the poet. Poetry and literature and painting are the products of a mental synthesis of ideas fused from many elements; and so it is that by the formation and expression of mental images that your true advocate brings before the jury [the] essence of his contention. In a single flood he dramatizes the real point and makes his hearers see a picture which their untrained senses had not yet dismissed.

Whatever means you employ, you must lift your jury from mere logic to the springs of action that transcend cold reasoning, to the feelings and the emotions that govern, inspire, and produce the verdict. Never for an instant forget that it is a favorable verdict you are seeking.

The most impregnable of syllogisms will not secure it for you. Nothing will do it but the hearts and wills of twelve men whom you must capture. You must find a way to reach those hearts. How better can you do this than by such a systematic arrangement and presentation of the facts that each bit of evidence fits into the pattern of your theory and every circumstance advances your contention. But persuasion is far more than that—persuasion is effected only when you make those who hear you want to follow you, only when you have, as it were, so proselytized your listeners as to turn them into zealots for your cause.

If you had the Stradivarius, you would not possess a more glorious instrument than the hearts and souls of twelve men. And if you had all the skill of Paganini, Ysaye, or Zimbalist, if you had all of Mischa Elman's magic, you would not have too much with which to make your jurors' heartstrings vibrate. There ranged before you they court the inspired touch of a master's hand.

And yet all your artistry will fail if your listeners who hear and feel your art suspect that it is nothing else. Plain men like to think themselves above emotion, impervious to rhetoric and susceptible only to cold reason. Knowing this, it will be yours somehow to disguise your highest flights so that Pegasus seems only a rather well-built and serviceable draft horse.

You must not be only a musician but an actor. You must have studied your client so perceptively that you can understudy him. You must be him. You must not merely play Hamlet, you must be Hamlet himself. More than a musician or an actor, you must be a soldier and a leader. You must be a general and a humble platoon leader who knows how to gain compliance with the most potent of all military orders: "Follow me!" You must make your jury follow you even as they follow your eyes that search them through and through. The true advocate is even more than that; he is a conqueror whose will has brought about subjection and surrender. Is advocacy an art? Is there anywhere a greater one? . . .

PRACTICE EXERCISE NO. 28:
CLOSING ARGUMENT IN *CARPENTER*

With this exercise, we hope to provide you with an opportunity to (1) prepare and present a closing argument in a case that you know in great detail; (2) help you experience how the formal litigation process (elements, causes of action, burdens of proof) and the passion, morality, and common sense of a real life story come together in creative advocacy; and (3) better understand the relationships among several parts of the process (complaint, discovery, motions, trial).

Accordingly, prepare a closing argument to a jury for one of the parties in *Carpenter v. Dee*. You may assume that Ultimate Auto is the only remaining defendant. Prepare a typed outline of your closing argument (not more than three pages double-spaced) that you will hand in. Notice that an essay with tips follows this exercise. Feel free to consult anyone. You may use the library, but you need not. Regardless of what help you get, your written outline should be your own. And, of course, your oral argument, if you are called upon, should be your own.

You may assume that anything that is in the Case Files has been properly entered into the trial record. Your argument may also include facts, witnesses, and details that are not in the Case Files, provided those additions are consistent with the information that you have been given and are likely to have been introduced in the trial. For example, to craft the arc of your closing argument, you might want to invent names for witnesses, add details about the content of expert testimony, and the like. Persons with last names that begin with the letters A-L represent the plaintiffs; others represent Ultimate Auto.

Expect your professor to ask you and your colleagues for the "first few minutes" of your closing argument. This will include an introduction of you, the party you represent, and the narrative of your case. As you prepare, think about where you will start your argument, whether you will have an express "theme," and how your personality and views of the litigation process inform your approach.

Expect your professor to ask you and your colleagues for "a few minutes from the middle" of your closing argument. In this segment of the argument, you will be summarizing and/or arguing about the evidence with respect to one or more of the elements of the cause of action. As you prepare, think about the approach and the arguments that would be most persuasive to your audience. Think about whether the theory or theme of your case is apparent even in this excerpt from the middle of your closing argument.

Expect your professor to ask you and your colleagues for the "last few minutes" of your closing argument. This will include your final words to the jury. As you prepare, think about your theme and your audience. Consider the relative importance of facts, law, emotions, and morality.

Tips on Making a Closing Argument. Most lawyers making a closing argument have a very good idea of what they are going to say; they have an outline, but they do not read the argument. They want to make eye contact with the judge or jury, and, if they are not arguing first, they want to adjust their argument to what the other lawyers have already argued.

Closing arguments to a jury usually state in general form the major instructions that the judge will give (if she hasn't already given them). The lawyer wants the jury to consider the law that they have to apply as they listen to the closing argument. Closing arguments usually rely heavily on the evidence that has come in during the trial, and they suggest how that evidence and natural inferences drawn therefrom support the conclusion. A good closing is not simply a summary of the testimony of the witnesses and other evidence; instead, a good argument uses select pieces to advance an argument. Often, closing arguments will address the motivation of important parties and witnesses, focusing on the credibility of certain so-called evidence. Closing arguments try to tell a story—to give a picture in words—that draws the jury to the desired conclusion and leaves a mark that jurors will remember throughout their deliberations.

Closing arguments may not include references to evidence that is not in the record. Also, as in most legal arguments, it is important not to ignore your opponents' strongest points. Rather, you must address them and undermine them—whether through evidence, logic, legal doctrine, morality, or otherwise. Explain to the jury why the picture painted by the opponent is inaccurate or at least incomplete.

If there are important exhibits, remember that the jury will usually have them in the jury room during their deliberations. Some lawyers like to weave the exhibits into their closing argument, so that the jury will be reminded of their argument as they review the exhibits.

It is unethical for a lawyer to say who or what they believe during a closing argument. Instead, you will use phrases like "The evidence suggests . . ." or "The evidence permits only one sound conclusion. . . ." Be sure to tell the fact finder exactly what you want them to do. For example, it is not patronizing and, in fact, is helpful to be as direct as, "If you agree with me, ladies and gentlemen of the jury, you should put an 'x' on the line on the jury slip that says 'for the defendant.'" When damages are involved in a matter, you will need to check with local law and custom to ascertain to what extent you may discuss particular sums of money. In many, if not most, jurisdictions you are not allowed in closing argument to ask the jury to "be in the plaintiff's shoes," nor are you allowed to suggest that they consider the value of having one day without the plaintiff's injury and multiplying that by life expectancy.

Most important, realize that there is no single right—or even best—way to make a closing. The effectiveness of the closing arguments depends on your personality, the type of case, the evidence, your witnesses, the jury, the judge, the ambience of the courtroom, and your ability to process each of these influences. Rhetoric—the art of persuasion—is an ancient and admirable enterprise. Enjoy.

H. APPEALS

The value of a favorable trial verdict is materially diminished if it cannot survive appellate review. Winners can quickly become losers, and losers have a second chance to convince the court that a verdict in their favor is the just result or that a new trial is necessary.

The appellate process differs from the trial proceedings in the lower courts in both its procedure and its purpose. The attorneys do not try their case as if the first trial had never happened, but rather present alleged errors of the trial judge for the appellate court to review. The appellate court serves the purpose of supervising the trial judge's decisions and establishing uniformity of the law within its jurisdiction. During the proceedings below, the trial judge may not have the time to consider the issues with the care and reflection afforded to appellate judges. Further, the perspective of the appellate court offers a check on the potential arbitrariness of the trial judge and may instill confidence in the trial process by reaffirming the judge's decisions.

Unlike a trial court, an appellate court looks somewhat beyond the rights of the parties in the specific case before them. The appellate courts are the voice of authority on the law in their jurisdiction and thus attempt to create a uniform body of law for predicting the outcome of future cases. Procedures for achieving these goals may vary, but the Federal Rules of Appellate Procedure establish mechanisms for the federal courts, and substantially similar rules have been adopted in many state courts.

The Judiciary Act of 1789 established three levels of courts in the federal system: the Supreme Court, circuit courts, and district courts. There are currently thirteen courts of appeals—eleven for numbered circuits, one for the District of Columbia, and the Court of Appeals for the Federal Circuit, established in 1982. The U.S. Courts of Appeals may hear the decisions of the federal district courts of the states and territories in their regions. For practical purposes, the right to appeal is statutory, not constitutional.

The appellate courts will hear only alleged errors that are revealed in the trial record, and ordinarily no new factual findings will be taken into consideration.

The trial record must also reveal that the aggrieved party made a timely objection to the alleged error. The alleged error must have materially affected the outcome of the case and must be necessary to the decree in order to be reviewable. If the party does not raise an error that is found in the trial record, the appellate court will usually consider it waived.

Federal courts and most state courts require finality in the trial court as a basis for appellate jurisdiction. This requirement, known as the final judgment rule, ensures that the proceedings below are completed before the review process begins. The timing of an appeal usually requires notice within thirty days after the final judgment is rendered.

The main principle behind this final judgment rule is the conservation of judicial resources. Finality requires that the trial below end on the merits and "leave nothing for the court to do but execute the judgment." *Catlin v. United States*, 324 U.S. 229, 233 (1945). If finality is not present, the appeal may be unnecessary. The pending proceedings may settle, or the issue may have become moot as a result of the trial. Also, denying immediate review prevents the use of expensive delaying tactics and harassment of opposing parties.

Not all requests for immediate appeal are denied. Immediate review can be important in providing guidance to the trial court and in preventing hardship. Exceptions to the final judgment rule include the collateral order doctrine, interlocutory appeals, and writs of mandamus and prohibition.

The collateral order doctrine is a judicial exception to the final judgment rule and exempts only a small number of cases—those in which there is an order that is an offshoot of the principal litigation, and where the appeal does not require delving into the merits of the case: "[T]he order must conclusively determine the disputed question, resolve an important issue completely separate from the merits of the action, and be effectively unreviewable on appeal from a final judgment." *Coopers & Lybrand v. Livesay*, 437 U.S. 463, 468 (1978).

An interlocutory decision is made while the case is pending in the trial court, but prior to the final determination of the merits. Under 28 U.S.C. § 1292, an interlocutory appeal may be taken from interlocutory orders with respect to injunctions, receiverships, and the rights and liabilities of parties to admiralty cases. Also, district court judges can, under limited circumstances, state in an interlocutory order that they think an immediate appeal would "materially advance the ultimate termination of the litigation," and the court of appeals, upon application, has discretion to permit such on appeal. Similarly, Federal Rule 23(f) states that "[a] court of appeals may permit an appeal from an order granting or denying class-action certification under this rule if a petition for permission to appeal is filed with the circuit clerk within fourteen days after the order is entered."

Writs of mandamus and prohibition seek an order from the appellate court to order a requirement or a prohibition of a certain action by a public official. The public official may be a judge of a lower court, making the procedure similar to interlocutory orders. In *Kerr v. United States District Court*, 426 U.S. 394 (1976), the U.S. Supreme Court stated, "[T]he remedy of mandamus is a drastic one" and "only exceptional circumstances amounting to judicial 'usurpation of power' will justify the invocation of this extraordinary remedy." *Kerr* also set forth various conditions for which the court would issue a writ, including if the party seeking the writ has no other adequate means to attain the desired relief, and if the party is able to establish that the need for the issuance is "clear and indisputable."

In the courts of appeals, ordinarily a panel of three judges reaches its decision by a majority vote. (On occasion, all of the judges of a court of appeals will hear an appeal.) Even though the panel may decide that the trial court erred in its decision, not all errors at trial are grounds for reversal. The likelihood of reversal depends on the standard of review. In reviewing the district court's finding of fact, the appellate court normally will defer to the authority of the trial judge, who has greater familiarity with the entire case and has observed the demeanor evidence at trial. Under Fed. R. Civ. P. 52(a), the appellate court will set aside findings of fact only if they are "clearly erroneous." In *United States v. U.S. Gypsum Co.*, 333 U.S. 364, 395 (1948), the Court defined the clearly erroneous standard as "when the reviewing court on the entire evidence is left with definite and firm conviction that a mistake has been committed." The trial judge must have misunderstood the law or made a finding without adequate evidentiary support. However, if the case below was a jury trial, the appellate court gives even greater deference to the findings of fact.

In *Cooper Indus., Inc. v. Leatherman Tool Group, Inc.*, 532 U.S. 424 (2001), the court held that while a jury's determination of compensatory damages is "essentially a factual determination," and thus reviewed only for clear error, a jury's award of punitive damages should be reviewed *de novo* since it is but "an expression of [the jury's] moral condemnation."

Fed. R. App. P. 52(a) does not require a "clearly erroneous" standard for reviewing conclusions of law. The absence of a standard for conclusions of law in the Federal Rules of Appellate Procedure has left the appellate courts with complete authority to freely consider conclusions of law. However, the appellate court will reverse only if it thinks it is more likely than not that the trial court erred in its decision. The standard to be applied in cases of mixed fact and law is generally the same standard as that applied to questions of pure law, although the courts have determined which standard to use in certain cases, like contract cases. Where a trial court judge makes a conclusion of law based on the four corners of the document, the appellate court will review the appeal *de novo*. But where the trial court considers extrinsic evidence to make a conclusion, the conclusion rests on findings of fact and, therefore, may be reviewable by the "clearly erroneous" standard.

Finally, when a trial judge makes a discretionary ruling, the standard for review is "abuse of discretion." Since the trial judge is in the best position to make discretionary rulings, the ruling will be overturned only if the appellate court is convinced that the judge was clearly wrong.

After a court of appeals renders its decision, an aggrieved party may seek an appeal at the next level of review. Seeking review from a U.S. Court of Appeals to the Supreme Court of the United States is almost always done through the discretionary writ of certiorari. Whether the Supreme Court grants the writ depends on such criteria as conflicts among circuits, the general importance of the legal questions involved, and the public importance of the case.

If the case originated in a state court, the party ordinarily has the right of appeal to the state's intermediate appellate court. As in the federal court system, most states require a petition to the state's highest court, which is granted only by the discretion of that court. Under 28 U.S.C. §1257, if a question of federal law exists, and a final judgment or decree has been "rendered by the highest court of a State in which a decision could be had . . ." then the decision "may be reviewed by the [United States] Supreme Court by writ of certiorari. . . ."

Only a small percentage of the cases in which review is sought by the Supreme Court of the United States are granted certiorari and disposed of by a written opinion. In fact, the number of Supreme Court written opinions has steadily declined. For example, in 1980, 4,174 cases were docketed and 159 were disposed of by written opinion. While the number of docketed cases each year now typically exceeds 10,000 cases, the number of cases disposed by written opinion is consistently fewer than 100—recently as few as 68.

REVIEW EXERCISE NO. 5

This question is designed to help you determine how much you have learned in the course to date, to help you review and learn some more, and to practice tackling typical law school exam questions.

You will benefit most from the quiz if you follow the directions: Put aside at least two hours to take this quiz; if you finish early, you should assume that you did not use sufficient precision and detail in your answer. Use only your rule book. Try the exam on your own before discussing it with your study group.

> *Memorandum*
> To: Summer Judicial Intern
> From: Zico Torre, State Trial Court Judge
> Date: November 10, 2020

In March 2020 Wayne Earnest and Cleveland Grover (hereafter, "Earnest" and "Grover," respectively) filed one complaint in my trial court and requested a jury. The statute of limitations for all cases in this jurisdiction is two years. Our state has adopted the Federal Rules of Civil Procedure in all relevant respects.* Our state does not have a contribution statute.

The complaint alleges: the plaintiffs' names and the names of Jill Joke and Sally Sales, as defendants (hereafter, "Joke" and "Sales," respectively); that on Halloween, October 31, 2018, at 9:15 A.M., Earnest entered The Joke Shop, owned and managed by Joke; at 3:30 P.M. Grover did the same; at about the

---

* In this state, however, the complaint does not have to allege subject matter jurisdiction because the trial courts are courts of general jurisdiction and can hear almost all types of cases.

time each opened the door, a ghost suddenly appeared, and then there was the sound of a loud explosion; as a result, each plaintiff was greatly scared; Earnest required seven weeks of medical care for his resulting fright, and Grover, as a result, did and still does require and receive medical care for his resulting fright; as a result each has incurred large medical expenses, missed several months of work, has severe anxiety and headaches, and has difficulty sleeping; wherefore each demands $200,000 in damages. The complaint is signed by a lawyer.

Joke filed a timely answer, in which she (1) admitted ownership and general management of The Joke Shop, denied all other allegations, and alleged that on October 31, 2018, she was not working in The Joke Shop; nor was it supposed to be open; nor was Sales an employee of hers at the time; (2) raised a 12(b)(6) defense; and (3) counterclaimed against Grover for failing to pay for $2,500 of goods purchased from The Joke Shop between January 1 and October 31, 2018, under terms that the price of each purchase was due at the time of purchase. Joke also filed an impleader claim against Sales stating that "Sales had been fired on October 15, 2018, and had no right being in The Joke Shop on October 31, 2018; that she, Joke, had intended and ordered that the Shop be closed that day; and that if she, Joke, is held liable, it would be as a result of Sales' negligence and trespass, and that Sales should therefore indemnify her." Joke also filed an impleader claim against Carl Cap alleging that if "on October 31, 2018, Carl Cap caused an explosion, I had nothing to do with it, since I was not there and knew nothing about it; that Grover alleges said explosion scared him; if it did, and if I am held liable, then Cap must indemnify me."

After discovery, Joke filed an affidavit that restates under oath everything alleged in her answer, counterclaim, and two impleaders. Joke also submitted a portion of deposition taken of Grover's doctor, which says "Grover was anxious and had all the same symptoms before October 31, 2018, as he had after. I do not believe that the October 31st incident, if it happened at all, caused him any harm." Joke also filed interrogatory answers of Sales in which she states, among other things, that "I was working in The Joke Shop with permission on October 31, 2018, but by noon I had discontinued all pranks. Carl Cap, whom both Joke and I had forbidden to come in the store, played a loud recording of an explosion outside the store window, which may have surprised Earnest. I only saw Cap after it happened." Grover filed an affidavit that states "Although I was anxious before the October 31, 2018, negligence of Joke and Sales, I felt much worse afterwards and probably would have gone back to work sooner and required less medical help, had the ghost and loud explosion noise not frightened me."

Although there was extensive discovery in which every party sought all relevant information, I have provided you (in this memo) all relevant portions of pleadings, affidavits, and discovery that you need to help me decide the motions before me.

I have to rule on:

1. Joke's 12(b)(6);
2. A motion for summary judgment by Joke against Grover;

3. A motion by Joke to dismiss against Grover for misjoinder, or, in the alternative, to sever the two plaintiffs' cases;

4. Motions by Sales and Cap to dismiss each respective impleader as improper;

5. A motion by Grover to dismiss Joke's counterclaim against him as improper;

6. A motion filed two weeks ago by Grover to amend his complaint by adding: "In addition, when I came back the next day to complain to Joke, Joke intentionally punched me in the nose, broke it, and caused me to incur headaches, medical expense, and lose additional work."

How should I rule on each of the above motions? (*Notice the date of this memorandum and assume that you are responding on this date.*) Please give me your analysis and reasons. Rule on all of the motions, even if one or more rulings might render others moot. There are, of course, additional pleadings and motions in the Earnest and Sales portions of the case, but I do not have to decide those yet.

You may assume that premises liability and intentional infliction of emotional distress (IIED) are the causes of action that give rise to the claims by Earnest and Grover. The elements of a premises liability claim are (1) a legal right to be on the property (e.g., as an invitee); (2) failure on the part of the property owner to use reasonable care in keeping visitors safe; (3) causation; and (4) injury. The elements of a claim for IIED are (1) intent; (2) extreme and outrageous conduct; (3) causation; and (4) severe emotional distress.

CHAPTER 6

Alternative Dispute Resolution

So far you have learned about the life of the lawsuit, from the filing of the complaint and motions to dismiss, through the process of obtaining discovery to pursue the claim, summary judgment, and the jury trial. One of the things you might have noticed about this process is that it is very complex and expensive. Anything that requires lawyer time (such as to review discovery requests and produce documents, to write motions and respond to them, and to argue in court) is costly, and the strategic lawyer must continuously consider the costs of financing litigation. Going through the litigation process also takes time, which can also impose costs on either party. At each stage of the litigation, the lawyer and her client will reevaluate whether continuing is worth it in light of the remedy the client is seeking. Most cases filed in court do not go through this entire process. Only about 2 percent of cases actually go to trial. Somewhere between 60 and 40 percent of cases are resolved by a motion, such as a motion to dismiss or a motion for summary judgment. The remainder settle.

To get a sense of how many cases are not resolved through judicial decision making, consider the litigation pyramid:*

---

* You may be wondering how many cases are resolved on motion versus in a settlement versus through a trial. About 1-2% of cases filed in federal court end in a trial. But there is not good data on the proportion of cases that settle as compared with cases being terminated by motion. And there is not good data on what proportion of disputes actually result in a lawsuit being filed at all.

Policymakers and judges have put a lot of thought into how the process of resolving disputes could be sped up, improved, and streamlined using mechanisms other than litigation. This chapter is about the mechanisms inside and outside the courtroom that can be used as alternatives to litigation and the arguments for and against them. These mechanisms are generally called *Alternative Dispute Resolution*, or ADR systems, and they come in as many forms as you can imagine. The main types of ADR are arbitration, mediation, and negotiation.

The chapter will begin with a history of alternative dispute resolution in the federal courts. We then turn to the debate over ADR, evaluating the costs and benefits of these methods to parties and the legal system. After that, we will explain the rules for judicial review of arbitral awards, the Federal Arbitration Act, and recent developments in arbitration. We close with a practice exercise that puts together the various forms of ADR you have learned about in this chapter.

As you read the materials below, keep in mind that how people react to alternative dispute resolution often depends on their understanding of the purpose of the court system. Is the primary purpose of the courts to resolve disputes or to declare the law? If the primary purpose of the courts is to resolve disputes, and ADR can achieve this goal faster and better, then it is clearly preferable. But if the primary purpose or even substantial purpose of the courts is to declare the law, then resolving cases through private means, whether arbitration, settlement, or otherwise, is suspect because in those cases, no law will be made. One important thing to note about any ADR system is that it does not require that the decisionmaker follow the law. Indeed, an arbitrator, mediator, or parties in a negotiation can reach an outcome that is not permitted under the law. Nor is a decision by an arbitrator treated as precedent or even publicly reported.

Arbitration is a formalized dispute resolution procedure involving a third-party decisionmaker, called a "neutral," such as a retired judge. Depending on the terms of the agreement, it can be binding or non-binding. Of the forms of ADR, arbitration is the most adversarial and formal. As we shall see, arbitration has been increasingly controversial as it has moved from a form of resolution mostly used in the context of large commercial dealings and organized labor to a form of resolution binding consumers in everyday service and consumer contracts.

Mediation is a slightly less formal system which uses a professionally trained and impartial third party to facilitate resolution of the dispute. In mediation, each party makes their case under supervision and in a controlled environment. It is often non-binding, is relatively informal and inexpensive, and it can be much less adversarial than either litigation or arbitration.

Negotiation is the least formal system for dispute resolution. This is the process that lawyers engage in when they settle lawsuits, for example. Negotiation can be as adversarial as the parties want it to be and different lawyers have different negotiation styles. Some are cooperative, trying to maximize value for both parties by sharing information and being forthright. Others are adversarial, seeing the negotiation as a zero-sum game in which their goal is to reach the best outcome for their client and avoid being taken advantage of.

A. HISTORY OF ADR IN THE FEDERAL COURTS

Arbitration has its roots in two distinctive areas. The first is commercial disputes, especially international disputes where the parties prefer to create their own forum rather than resolve their dispute in one side's country. Private dispute resolution has been used in commerce since the eighteenth century. Traditionally, contracting parties in commercial deals contracted to arbitrate as part of their larger negotiation over the terms of the contract. The second area where arbitration has been used is in resolving disputes between organized labor and management. This was a twentieth century development.

In the early twentieth century, some courts rejected arbitration agreements in favor of court-centered dispute resolution. In response, Congress adopted the Federal Arbitration Act of 1925 (FAA). Since then, courts continuously and routinely enforce agreements to arbitrate and the results of arbitration. However, some state courts were skeptical of arbitration in consumer contracts. As a result, more recently the question has arisen whether the FAA preempts state contract laws limiting enforceability of some contracts diverting suits to arbitration. For the most part, and with very rare exceptions, the Supreme Court has held that state contract law limiting arbitration agreements is preempted by the FAA and therefore unenforceable.

Another trend that has contributed to the rise in ADR and the preference of the Supreme Court (among others) for arbitration is the concern about an overly litigious society and delay in the courts. In the 1980s, policymakers became increasingly worried about the number of cases being filed and the speed of resolution of those cases. This led to a preference for ADR, which many saw as faster, simpler, and less adversarial as compared with litigation.

As one judicial decision explained, it is a "familiar axiom that a bad settlement is almost always better than a good trial." *In re Warner Commc'ns Sec. Litig.,* 618 F. Supp. 735, 740 (S.D.N.Y. 1985). The rulemakers responded to this preference for settlement by enacting a number of reforms aimed at enabling ADR in the courts. For example, in 1983, Rule 16 was amended to encourage judges to promote settlement. *See* Fed. R. Civ. P. 16(a)(5). The Advisory Committee Notes explain that the amended rule:

> . . . explicitly recognizes that it has become commonplace to discuss settlement at pretrial conferences. Since it obviously eases crowded court dockets and results in savings to the litigants and the judicial system, settlement should be facilitated at as early a stage of the litigation as possible. Although it is not the purpose of [the Rule] to impose settlement negotiations on unwilling litigants, it is believed that providing a neutral forum for discussing the subject might foster it. . . . In addition to settlement, Rule [16(c)(2)(I)] refers to exploring the use of procedures other than litigation to resolve the dispute. This includes urging the litigants to employ adjudicatory techniques outside the courthouse.

In 1990, Congress passed the Civil Justice Reform Act of 1990 (CJRA), Pub. L. No. 101-650, 104 Stat. 5089 (Title I of the Judicial Improvements Act of 1990), which included a number of provisions to promote ADR in federal courthouses. Academics debated whether ADR was a good addition to the judge's arsenal of ways to resolve lawsuits or instead a development that undermined basic principles of justice.

B. THE DEBATE OVER ADR

ADR takes many forms, and although it is often discussed as a unitary idea, in fact one might favor some forms of ADR but disfavor others and still be consistent as a matter of principle. The basic arguments in favor of ADR are that it is more informal, less adversarial, and therefore quicker and less contentious than litigation. But this is not true of all forms of ADR. The rules used in arbitration can be quite formal and the proceeding very adversarial, for example. But it is true that other forms of ADR, particularly mediation, are more informal. The basic arguments against ADR are that it is private and that it may reinforce existing power imbalances. While all forms of ADR are private, some may lead to greater power imbalances between litigants than others. In earlier chapters, we saw how difficult it is for some people to obtain legal representation. ADR could offer ways to increase access to justice by creating fair systems of dispute resolution that do not require legal representation. It is best not to paint all of ADR with a broad brush but instead to consider each form and each context separately based on your assessment of the values courts ought to promote. Nevertheless, here is a summary of the main arguments for and against resolving disputes outside the civil justice system:

BENEFITS	COSTS
Can enhance privacy for both litigants.	Does not produce public legal rulings.
Provides flexibility to both litigants to choose arbiter and procedural rules.	Coercive since usually imposed on at least one of the parties.
Less expensive and can be adjudicated more quickly.	Unstructured or potentially unfriendly procedural rules.
Possible alternative to corrupt or developing court system.	More informal than a traditional court proceeding.
Less adversarial nature can allow for enhanced focus on problem solving.	More prone to the repeat player effect, potential for bias among decisionmakers.

QUESTIONS TO PONDER

When thinking about particular forms of ADR, and as you read more about the debate over the imposition of arbitration in consumer contracts later in this chapter, it is useful to think about the following questions. There is no right answer to any of these questions, but knowing what you think about them helps to frame why you might favor or disfavor forms of ADR.

1. What should the role of the court system be when parties choose or have imposed onto them an alternative dispute resolution process? For example, should the court be ever be permitted to void an arbitrator's decision? If so, when?
2. Should there be a minimum standard of procedure in any dispute resolution system? What should that minimum be?
3. What role should expediency and cost savings have in justifying the alternative dispute resolution system? How should cost or time savings be weighed against other interests, such as creating precedent?
4. Do you think more formal or more informal proceedings lead to fairer outcomes for people? Why?

WANT TO KNOW MORE?

The forms that ADR can take and the benefits and costs of various approaches are worthy of an entire course, one that is taught at many schools. If you are interested in this topic, there is a great deal of existing scholarship in this area. Here are some places you might start your research.

For a defense of mediation and cooperation, *see* Carrie J. Menkel-Meadow, *When Winning Isn't Everything: The Lawyer as Problem Solver*, 28 Hofstra L. Rev. 905 (2000). For a counterpoint, raising concerns about fairness and bias in ADR, *see* Richard Delgado et al., *Fairness and Formality: Minimizing the Risk of Prejudice in Alternative Dispute Resolution*, Wis. L. Rev. 1359 (1985). For a critique of privacy in arbitration in particular and an explanation of why diverting disputes to ADR may impact rule of law values, *see* Myriam Gilles, *The Day Doctrine Died: Private Arbitration and the End of Law*, 2016 U. Ill. L. Rev. 371 (2016). And for a counterpoint on less developed legal systems, *see* Jean R. Sternlight, *Is Alternative Dispute Resolution Consistent with the Rule of Law? Lessons from Abroad*, 56 DePaul L. Rev. 569 (2007).

There are a number of interesting studies of specific communities that use ADR. It has long been used in religious communities, such as rabbinical or Islamic arbitration courts. Michael A. Helfand, *Religious Arbitration and the New Multiculturalism: Negotiating Conflicting Legal Orders*, 86 N.Y.U. L. Rev. 1231 (2011). It has also been used in small business communities, such as among diamond merchants as described in a famous study by Lisa Bernstein. *See* Lisa Bernstein, *Opting Out of the Legal System: Extralegal Contractual Relations in the Diamond Industry*, 21 J. Legal Stud. 115 (1992). For how manufacturers use alternative dispute resolution, *see* Shauhin A. Talesh, *The Privatization of Public Rights: How Manufacturers Construct the Meaning of Consumer Protection Law*, 43 Law & Soc'y Rev. 527 (2009).

If you are interested in history, consider Amalia Kessler's *The Invention of American Exceptionalism: The Origins of American Adversarial Legal Culture, 1800-1877* (Yale 2017) in which she describes many court alternatives that have been developed over the years and critiques the dominance of the adversarial system today. For the more recent history of the preference for settlement in the federal courts, *see* Judith Resnik, *Trial As Error, Jurisdiction As Injury: Transforming the Meaning of Article III*, 113 Harv. L. Rev. 924, 926 (2000). There are also some very good histories of the Federal Arbitration Act, such as Hiro N. Aragaki, *The Federal Arbitration Act as Procedural Reform*, 89 N.Y.U. L. Rev. 1939 (2014); Luke P. Norris, *The Parity Principle*, 93 N.Y.U. L. Rev. 249 (2018).

C. ARBITRATION AND JUDICIAL REVIEW

Arguably the most consequential and controversial form of ADR is arbitration. It has become almost ubiquitous in many areas of our lives. From credit card agreements to big international commercial transactions, arbitration is the dominant mode of dispute resolution. Some judges have expressed concern that arbitration is siphoning off disputes from the courts. Others are happy to see disputes handled privately. The debate often comes down to a preference for private ordering or public decision making, which in turn raises a fundamental question of the purpose of litigation: to resolve disputes or to declare the law?

Consider the following key differences between arbitration and litigation:

1. Decisionmakers

In arbitration, the "neutrals" are picked by the parties, whereas in litigation the judge is randomly assigned to the case. The parties pay the arbitrators, whereas the public pays the judge's salary. One reason people are sometimes concerned that arbitrators favor repeat players is that companies often use the same arbitration company and may systematically prefer arbitrators who have favored them in the past. Knowing this, arbitrators might rule in favor of these repeat players in order to get more business.

But arbitration need not be purely private. If the state statute or courts' local rules authorize it, arbitration can also be imposed by a court. This is called court-annexed arbitration or judicial arbitration. Courts use arbitration to relieve themselves of overcrowded dockets and to expedite proceedings. Unlike arbitration imposed by contract, court-annexed arbitration is not binding and the types of cases that are eligible are determined by the court system or legislature. For a description of various forms of court-annexed ADR, *see* Donna J. Stienstra, *ADR in the Federal Courts: An Initial Report* (Federal Judicial Center 2011).

2. Source of Law

Arbitration is grounded in contract law. *See First Options of Chicago v. Kaplan*, 514 U.S. 938 (1995). The contract can be as detailed as the drafter wants it to be as to nearly every aspect of the arbitration proceeding. Personal jurisdiction, the subject matter exposed to litigation, the scope of discovery, the availability of pretrial motions, which laws apply, the rules of evidence, the admission of experts, the burden of proof, and the scope of the award are all subject customization.

Unlike the court system, the arbitrator need not provide a reasoned opinion for her decision or even follow the law. *See, e.g., Baravati v. Josephthal, Lyon & Ross, Inc.*, 28 F.3d 704, 710 (7th Cir. 1994). This gives the arbitrators a great deal of flexibility to compromise. Indeed, one associate general counsel told an author of this casebook that he finds commercial arbitration to be more predictable than court because arbitrators routinely "split the baby." A judicial decision, by contrast, is usually all or nothing. That said, there is some empirical evidence that arbitrators mostly act like judges. *See* W. Mark C. Weidemaier, *Judging-Lite: How Arbitrators Use and Create Precedent*, 90 N.C. L. Rev. 1091, 1092 (2012).

3. Procedural Rules

Just as the federal and state courts have the rules of civil procedure as the foundational structure of litigation, arbitration has sets of rules that can be adopted by the drafter of the arbitration agreement. In a way, arbitration is an alternative private court system where the parties pick the rules and the judge. The most popular sets of arbitration rules are those published by the American Arbitration Association and the JAMS Comprehensive Arbitration Rules and Procedures. These organizations can also provide arbitration services. Other groups have created specific sets of arbitration procedures for particular areas of the law such as patents, international transactions, and commercial arbitration.

One area of contention has been the relationship between arbitration and class actions. The Supreme Court has held that absent clear agreement, an arbitration may not proceed as a class action. *Lamps Plus, Inc. v. Varela*, 139 S. Ct. 1407 (2019). When some state courts attempted to strike down arbitration clauses that forbade class actions on unconscionability grounds, the Supreme Court ruled that consumer contracts with arbitration agreements barring class actions and requiring individual arbitration must be permitted under the FAA. *AT&T Mobility LLC v. Concepcion*, 563 U.S. 333 (2011). The fact that class actions are not permitted in arbitration has been a source of significant concern because in many consumer cases the amount at stake is too small to bring individual arbitrations. The Supreme Court's response to this was to note that the arbitration agreement in *AT&T Mobility* included a provision that the company would pay the costs of arbitration. We will see the relevance of this later in this chapter.

In addition to either choosing a set of rules or defining them in the contract, there are some procedures embedded in the FAA. For example, Section 7 of the FAA gives arbitrators limited power to issue subpoenas to compel the attendance of witnesses, the production of documents, and even hold witnesses in contempt. 9 U.S.C. § 7.

Although the proposition hasn't been much tested, it is also true that parties can contract around procedures in the courts as well. One interesting question to think about is what a court would do in a contract action if the parties agreed not to engage in civil discovery. Can such a contract bind a court, as it would bind an arbitrator? Should it?

4. Appealing an Arbitration Award

When an arbitration agreement or result is challenged in court, the first question the court will ask is whether the contract imposing arbitration is valid. If it is, the court will generally impose arbitration as part of the contract, even if the plaintiff alleges that the contract was the result of unequal bargaining power or was a take-it-or-leave it consumer contract. *Concepcion*, 563 U.S. at 346-347 (rejecting the claim that a clause in a non-negotiated consumer contract required heightened scrutiny because "the times in which consumer contracts were anything other than adhesive are long past[.]").

Second, the court will ask whether there is a showing of fraud, misrepresentation, arbitrariness, capriciousness, evident partiality, corruption, or "manifest disregard of the law" by the arbitrator. Typically, an arbitrator's decision is binding. Courts are generally deferential to arbitrators, so overturning an arbitrator's decision is very unlikely. *Mitsubishi Motors Corp. v. Soler Chrysler-Plymouth, Inc.*, 473 U.S. 614, 656 (1985).

These are the only bases for appealing an award. The Supreme Court has held that under the FAA, parties cannot contract for judicial review for errors of law or fact by the arbitrator. The Court explained that the FAA embodied "a national policy favoring arbitration with just the limited review needed to maintain arbitration's essential virtue of resolving disputes straightaway." *Hall St. Assocs. L.L.C. v. Mattel, Inc.*, 552 U.S. 576, 588 (2008).

5. Policy Issues in Arbitration

Consider the questions below as you review the materials on arbitration that follow. These are the big questions at the heart of the debate over arbitration.

1. Should arbitrators be permitted to issue decisions that do not comply with the law, or should they have to follow the same rules as judges? Why?
2. If a private party writes a contract permitting judicial appeals from an arbitration, why should the courts not accept that agreement?

3. What are the reasons that the Supreme Court might be right in applying the same standard to arbitration provisions entered into by sophisticated business actors as those entered into by ordinary consumers? What are the counterarguments?

PRACTICE EXERCISE NO. 29: APPLYING THE FEDERAL ARBITRATION ACT

Read the following provisions of the Federal Arbitration Act and the credit card agreement that follows. Try to answer the following questions:

1. How is each section of the FAA reflected in the agreement?
2. How is jurisdiction determined under this agreement?
3. How are costs divided amongst the parties?
4. How is discovery to take place?
5. What confidentiality provisions are made in the agreement, and how is any award distributed?
6. What procedure is provided in the event of a class action?
7. If you were negotiating on equal footing with a vendor, would you negotiate these terms? How would you change them?

9 U.S. Code § 2—Validity, irrevocability, and enforcement of agreements to arbitrate

A written provision in any maritime transaction or a contract evidencing a transaction involving commerce to settle by arbitration a controversy thereafter arising out of such contract or transaction, or the refusal to perform the whole or any part thereof, or an agreement in writing to submit to arbitration an existing controversy arising out of such a contract, transaction, or refusal, shall be valid, irrevocable, and enforceable, save upon such grounds as exist at law or in equity for the revocation of any contract.

9 U.S. Code § 7—Witnesses before arbitrators; fees; compelling attendance

The arbitrators selected either as prescribed in this title or otherwise, or a majority of them, may summon in writing any person to attend before them or any of them as a witness and in a proper case to bring with him or them any book, record, document, or paper which may be deemed material as evidence in the case. The fees for such attendance shall be the same as the fees of witnesses before masters of the United States courts. Said summons shall issue in the name of the arbitrator or arbitrators, or a majority of them, and shall be signed by the arbitrators, or a majority of them, and shall be directed to the said person and shall be served in the same manner as subpoenas to appear and testify before the court; if any person or persons so summoned to testify shall refuse or neglect to obey said summons, upon petition the United States district court for the district in which such arbitrators, or a majority of them, are sitting may compel the attendance of such person or persons before said arbitrator or arbitrators, or punish said person or persons for contempt in the same manner provided by law for securing the attendance of witnesses or their punishment for neglect or refusal to attend in the courts of the United States.

9 U.S. Code § 9—Award of arbitrators; confirmation; jurisdiction; procedure
If the parties in their agreement have agreed that a judgment of the court shall be entered upon the award made pursuant to the arbitration, and shall specify the court, then at any time within one year after the award is made any party to the arbitration may apply to the court so specified for an order confirming the award, and thereupon the court must grant such an order unless the award is vacated, modified, or corrected as prescribed in sections 10 and 11 of this title. If no court is specified in the agreement of the parties, then such application may be made to the United States court in and for the district within which such award was made. Notice of the application shall be served upon the adverse party, and thereupon the court shall have jurisdiction of such party as though he had appeared generally in the proceeding. If the adverse party is a resident of the district within which the award was made, such service shall be made upon the adverse party or his attorney as prescribed by law for service of notice of motion in an action in the same court. If the adverse party shall be a nonresident, then the notice of the application shall be served by the marshal of any district within which the adverse party may be found in like manner as other process of the court.

9 U.S. Code § 10—Same; vacation; grounds; rehearing
(a) In any of the following cases the United States court in and for the district wherein the award was made may make an order vacating the award upon the application of any party to the arbitration—

(i) where the award was procured by corruption, fraud, or undue means;

(ii) where there was evident partiality or corruption in the arbitrators, or either of them;

(iii) where the arbitrators were guilty of misconduct in refusing to postpone the hearing, upon sufficient cause shown, or in refusing to hear evidence pertinent and material to the controversy; or of any other misbehavior by which the rights of any party have been prejudiced; or

(iv) where the arbitrators exceeded their powers, or so imperfectly executed them that a mutual, final, and definite award upon the subject matter submitted was not made.

(b) If an award is vacated and the time within which the agreement required the award to be made has not expired, the court may, in its discretion, direct a rehearing by the arbitrators.

Sample Cardmember Agreement
American Express GreenCard® member agreement (excerpts) as of June 30, 2017. (*https://www.americanexpress.com/us/content/cardmember-agreements/all-us.html*)

Arbitration
You or we may elect to resolve any claim by individual arbitration. Claims are decided by a neutral arbitrator. If arbitration is chosen by any party, neither you nor we will have the right to litigate that claim in court or have a jury trial on that claim. Further, you and we will not have the right to participate in a representative capacity or as a member of any class pertaining to any claim subject to arbitration. Arbitration procedures are generally simpler than the rules that apply in court, and discovery is more limited. The arbitrator's decisions are as enforceable as any court order and are subject to very

limited review by a court. Except as set forth below, the arbitrator's decision will be final and binding. Other rights you or we would have in court may also not be available in arbitration.

Initiating Arbitration

Before beginning arbitration, you or we must first send a claim notice. Claims will be referred to either JAMS or AAA, as selected by the party electing arbitration. Claims will be resolved pursuant to this Arbitration provision and the selected organization's rules in effect when the claim is filed, except where those rules conflict with this Agreement. If we choose the organization, you may select the other within 30 days after receiving notice of our selection. Contact JAMS or AAA to begin an arbitration or for other information. Claims also may be referred to another arbitration organization if you and we agree in writing or to an arbitrator appointed pursuant to section 5 of the Federal Arbitration Act, 9 U.S.C. sec. 1-16 (FAA). We will not elect arbitration for any claim you file in small claims court, so long as the claim is individual and pending only in that court. You or we may otherwise elect to arbitrate any claim at any time unless it has been filed in court and trial has begun or final judgment has been entered. Either you or we may delay enforcing or not exercise rights under this Arbitration provision, including the right to arbitrate a claim, without waiving the right to exercise or enforce those rights.

Limitations on Arbitration

If either party elects to resolve a claim by arbitration, that claim will be arbitrated on an individual basis. There will be no right or authority for any claims to be arbitrated on a class action basis or on bases involving claims brought in a purported representative capacity on behalf of the general public, other cardmembers or other persons similarly situated. The arbitrator's authority is limited to claims between you and us alone. Claims may not be joined or consolidated unless you and we agree in writing. An arbitration award and any judgment confirming it will apply only to the specific case and cannot be used in any other case except to enforce the award.

Notwithstanding any other provision and without waiving the right to appeal such decision, if any portion of these Limitations on Arbitration is deemed invalid or unenforceable, then the entire Arbitration provision (other than this sentence) will not apply.

Arbitration Procedures

This Arbitration provision is governed by the FAA. The arbitrator will apply applicable substantive law, statutes of limitations and privileges. The arbitrator will not apply any federal or state rules of civil procedure or evidence in matters relating to evidence or discovery. Subject to the Limitations on Arbitration, the arbitrator may otherwise award any relief available in court. The arbitration will be confidential, but you may notify any government authority of your claim. If your claim is for $10,000 or less, you may choose whether the arbitration will be conducted solely on the basis of documents, through a telephonic hearing, or by an in person hearing. At any party's request, the arbitrator will provide a brief written explanation of the award. The arbitrator's award will be final and binding, except for any right of appeal provided by the FAA; however, any party will have 30 days to appeal the award by notifying the arbitration organization and all parties in writing. The organization will appoint a three-arbitrator panel to decide anew, by majority vote based on written submissions, any aspect of the decision objected to. Judgment upon any award may be entered in any court having jurisdiction. At your election, arbitration hearings will take place in the federal judicial district of your residence.

Arbitration Fees and Costs

You will be responsible for paying your share of any arbitration fees (including filing, administrative, hearing or other fees), but only up to the amount of the filing fees you would have incurred if you had brought a claim in court. We will be responsible for any additional arbitration fees. At your written request, we will consider in good faith making a temporary advance of your share of any arbitration fees, or paying for the reasonable fees of an expert appointed by the arbitrator for good cause.

Additional Arbitration Awards

If the arbitrator rules in your favor for an amount greater than any final offer we made before arbitration, the arbitrator's award will include: (1) any money to which you are entitled, but in no case less than $5,000; and (2) any reasonable attorneys' fees, costs and expert and other witness fees.

Your Right to Reject Arbitration

You may reject this Arbitration provision by sending a written rejection notice to us at: American Express, P.O. Box 981556, El Paso, TX 79998. Go to americanexpress.com/reject for a sample rejection notice. Your rejection notice must be mailed within 45 days after your first card purchase. Your rejection notice must state that you reject the Arbitration provision and include your name, address, Account number and personal signature. No one else may sign the rejection notice. If your rejection notice complies with these requirements, this Arbitration provision and any other arbitration provisions in the cardmember agreements for any other currently open American Express accounts you have will not apply to you, except for Corporate Card accounts and any claims subject to pending litigation or arbitration at the time you send your rejection notice. Rejection of this Arbitration provision will not affect your other rights or responsibilities under this Claims Resolution section or the Agreement. Rejecting this Arbitration provision will not affect your ability to use your card or any other benefit, product or service you may have with your account.

Continuation

This section will survive termination of your Account, voluntary payment of your Account balance, any legal proceeding to collect a debt, any bankruptcy and any sale of your Account (in the case of a sale, its terms will apply to the buyer of your Account). If any portion of this Claims Resolution section, except as otherwise provided in the Limitations on Arbitration subsection, is deemed invalid or unenforceable, it will not invalidate the remaining portions of this Claims Resolution section.

D. THE FAA AND STATE LAW

The preeminent concern of Congress in passing the [Federal Arbitration] Act was to enforce private agreements into which parties had entered, and that concern requires that we rigorously enforce agreements to arbitrate, even if the result is "piecemeal" litigation, at least absent a countervailing policy manifested in another federal statute.

Dean Witter Reynolds, Inc. v. Byrd, 470 U.S. 213, 221 (1985).

When consumers opposing arbitration agreements have argued that these agreements violate state contract law, they have largely lost in federal court. This is because of the doctrine of preemption. The doctrine itself is complicated and beyond the scope of this course, but its premise is simple. Under the supremacy clause of the Constitution, federal law will displace state law that conflicts with it. Because often state and federal law operate on parallel tracks (for example, there are both state and federal securities laws, antitrust laws, etc.), it is sometimes difficult to tell whether a federal law displaces a state law or can be read to be consistent with state law. Sometimes Congress expressly preempts state law in a statute, but in other instances a statute appears to conflict with state law, and it is the job of the courts to determine whether that statute preempts state law entirely.

In cases involving the FAA, the Supreme Court has consistently held that state contract laws that conflict with the arbitration mandate of the FAA are expressly preempted by the language of the statute, despite the savings clause in that statute, which states that arbitration agreements are valid "save upon such grounds as exist at law or in equity for the revocation of any contract." 9 U.S.C. § 2. Only one member of the Supreme Court, Justice Thomas, has objected to the Court's arbitration decisions on federalism grounds based on this savings clause.

Recently, the Supreme Court was asked to decide whether provisions in a contract that waived arbitration where the governing state law prohibits it were preempted by the Federal Arbitration Act.

Kindred Nursing Centers Limited Partnership v. Clark
137 S. Ct. 1421 (2017)

Justice KAGAN delivered the opinion of the Court.

The Federal Arbitration Act (FAA or Act) requires courts to place arbitration agreements "on equal footing with all other contracts." In the decision below, the Kentucky Supreme Court declined to give effect to two arbitration agreements executed by individuals holding "powers of attorney"—that is, authorizations to act on behalf of others. According to the court, a general grant of power (even if seemingly comprehensive) does not permit a legal representative to enter into an arbitration agreement for someone else; to form such a contract, the representative must possess specific authority to "waive his principal's funda-mental constitutional rights to access the courts [and] to trial by jury." Because that rule singles out arbitration agreements for disfavored treatment, we hold that it violates the FAA.

I

Petitioner Kindred Nursing Centers L.P. operates nursing homes and reha-bilitation centers. Respondents Beverly Wellner and Janis Clark are the wife and daughter, respectively, of Joe Wellner and Olive Clark, two now-deceased resi-dents of a Kindred nursing home called the Winchester Centre.

At all times relevant to this case, Beverly and Janis each held a power of attorney, designating her as an "attorney-in-fact" (the one for Joe, the other for Olive) and affording her broad authority to manage her family member's affairs. . . .

Joe and Olive moved into the Winchester Centre in 2008, with Beverly and Janis using their powers of attorney to complete all necessary paperwork. As part of that process, Beverly and Janis each signed an arbitration agreement with Kindred on behalf of her relative. The two contracts, worded identically, provided that "[a]ny and all claims or controversies arising out of or in any way relating to . . . the Resident's stay at the Facility" would be resolved through "binding arbitration" rather than a lawsuit.

When Joe and Olive died the next year, their estates (represented again by Beverly and Janis) brought separate suits against Kindred in Kentucky state court. The complaints alleged that Kindred had delivered substandard care to Joe and Olive, causing their deaths. Kindred moved to dismiss the cases, argu-ing that the arbitration agreements Beverly and Janis had signed prohibited bringing their disputes to court. But the trial court denied Kindred's motions, and the Kentucky Court of Appeals agreed that the estates' suits could go forward.

The Kentucky Supreme Court, after consolidating the cases, affirmed those decisions by a divided vote. The court began with the language of the two pow-ers of attorney. [It found that one power of attorney did not authorize signing an arbitration agreement, whereas the other so authorized.] . . .

And yet, the court went on, both arbitration agreements . . . were invalid. That was because a power of attorney could not entitle a representative to enter into an arbitration agreement without *specifically* saying so. The Kentucky Constitution, the court explained, protects the rights of access to the courts and trial by jury; indeed, the jury guarantee is the sole right the Constitution declares "sacred" and "inviolate." Accordingly, the court held, an agent could deprive her principal of an "adjudication by judge or jury" only if the power of attorney "expressly so provide[d]." And that clear-statement rule—so said the court—complied with the FAA's demands. . . .

We granted certiorari.

II

A

The FAA makes arbitration agreements "valid, irrevocable, and enforceable, save upon such grounds as exist at law or in equity for the revocation of any contract." 9 U.S.C. § 2. That statutory provision establishes an equal-treatment principle: A court may invalidate an arbitration agreement based on "generally applicable contract defenses" like fraud or unconscionability, but not on legal rules that "apply only to arbitration or that derive their meaning from the fact that an agreement to arbitrate is at issue." *AT & T Mobility LLC v. Concepcion,* 563 U.S. 333, 339 (2011). The FAA thus preempts any state rule discriminating on its face against arbitration—for example, a "law prohibit[ing] outright the arbitration of a particular type of claim." And not only that: The Act also displaces any rule that covertly accomplishes the same objective by disfavoring contracts that (oh so coincidentally) have the defining features of arbitration agreements. In *Concepcion,* for example, we described a hypothetical state law declaring unenforceable any contract that "disallow[ed] an ultimate disposition [of a dispute] by a jury." *Id.,* at 342. Such a law might avoid referring to arbitration by name; but still, we explained, it would "rely on the uniqueness of an agreement to arbitrate as [its] basis"—and thereby violate the FAA.

The Kentucky Supreme Court's clear-statement rule, in just that way, fails to put arbitration agreements on an equal plane with other contracts. By the court's own account, that rule (like the one *Concepcion* posited) serves to safeguard a person's "right to access the courts and to trial by jury." In ringing terms, the court affirmed the jury right's unsurpassed standing in the State Constitution: The framers, the court explained, recognized "that right and that right alone as a divine God-given right" when they made it "the *only* thing" that must be "'held sacred'" and "'inviolate.'" So it was that the court required an explicit statement before an attorney-in-fact, even if possessing broad delegated powers, could relinquish that right on another's behalf. . . . Such a rule is too tailor-made to arbitration agreements—subjecting them, by virtue of their defining trait, to uncommon barriers—to survive the FAA's edict against singling out those contracts for disfavored treatment

And the state court's sometime-attempt to cast the rule in broader terms cannot salvage its decision. The clear-statement requirement, the court suggested, could also apply when an agent endeavored to waive other "fundamental constitutional rights" held by a principal. But what other rights, really? . . . [T]he court hypothesized a slim set of both patently objectionable and utterly fanciful contracts that would be subject to its rule: No longer could a representative lacking explicit authorization waive her "principal's right to worship freely" or "consent to an arranged marriage" or "bind [her] principal to personal servitude." Placing arbitration agreements within that class reveals the kind of "hostility to arbitration" that led Congress to enact the FAA. And doing so only makes clear the arbitration-specific character of the rule, much as if it were made applicable to arbitration agreements and black swans.

B

The respondents, Janis and Beverly, primarily advance a different argument—based on the distinction between contract formation and contract enforcement—to support the decision below. Kentucky's clear-statement rule, they begin, affects only contract formation, because it bars agents without explicit authority from entering into arbitration agreements. And in their view, the FAA has "no application" to "contract formation issues." The Act, to be sure, requires a State to enforce all arbitration agreements (save on generally applicable grounds) once they have come into being. But, the respondents claim, States have free rein to decide—irrespective of the FAA's equal-footing principle—whether such contracts are validly created in the first instance.

Both the FAA's text and our case law interpreting it say otherwise. The Act's key provision, once again, states that an arbitration agreement must ordinarily be treated as "valid, irrevocable, and enforceable." 9 U.S.C. § 2. By its terms, then, the Act cares not only about the "enforce[ment]" of arbitration agreements, but also about their initial "valid[ity]"—that is, about what it takes to enter into them. Or said otherwise: A rule selectively finding arbitration contracts invalid because improperly formed fares no better under the Act than a rule selectively refusing to enforce those agreements once properly made. Precedent confirms that point. In *Concepcion,* we noted the impermissibility of applying a contract defense like duress "in a fashion that disfavors arbitration." But the doctrine of duress . . . involves "unfair dealing at the contract formation stage." Our discussion of duress would have made no sense if the FAA, as the respondents contend, had nothing to say about contract formation.

III

. . . Our decision requires reversing the Kentucky Supreme Court's judgment in favor of the Clark estate. . . . [T]the decision below was based exclusively on the clear-statement rule that we have held violates the FAA. So the court must now enforce the Clark–Kindred arbitration agreement.

It is so ordered.

[Dissenting opinion of Justice THOMAS omitted.]

REVIEW QUESTIONS

1. What is Kentucky's clear statement rule, and why does the Court hold that it violates the FAA in this context?
2. The Kentucky courts' position was that the clear statement rule governs powers of attorney generally, not only with respect to arbitration agreements. The Court held that this does not save the rule as applied to arbitration agreements. Why not?

3. What does the Court make of the respondent's argument that the Court should distinguish between rules about the formation of contract and the terms of the contract once formed? Is this a viable distinction?

4. Rereading the Federal Arbitration Act, especially section 2, can you construct the argument that the Act was only intended to apply to the Federal Courts? Justice Thomas has made this argument in his dissent in every FAA preemption case. His position rests on the history of the FAA, its plain text, and principles of federalism. Here is his explanation from an earlier dissenting opinion:

> At the time of the FAA's passage in 1925, laws governing the enforceability of arbitration agreements were generally thought to deal purely with matters of procedure rather than substance, because they were directed solely to the mechanisms for resolving the underlying disputes. As then-Judge Cardozo explained: "Arbitration is a form of procedure whereby differences may be settled. It is not a definition of the rights and wrongs out of which differences grow." . . . And because the FAA was enacted against this general background, no one read it as such an attempt. . . . Indeed, to judge from the reported cases, it appears that no state court was even *asked* to enforce the statute for many years after the passage of the FAA. . . .
>
> It is easy to understand why lawyers in 1925 classified arbitration statutes as procedural. An arbitration agreement is a species of forum-selection clause: Without laying down any rules of decision, it identifies the adjudicator of disputes. A strong argument can be made that such forum-selection clauses concern procedure rather than substance. And if a contractual provision deals purely with matters of judicial procedure, one might well conclude that questions about whether and how it will be enforced also relate to procedure.
>
> The context of § 2 confirms this understanding of the FAA's original meaning. Most sections of the statute plainly have no application in state courts, but rather prescribe rules either for federal courts or for arbitration proceedings themselves. . . .
>
> Despite the FAA's general focus on the federal courts, of course, § 2 itself contains no such explicit limitation. But the text of the statute nonetheless makes clear that § 2 was not meant as a statement of substantive law binding on the States. After all, if § 2 really was understood to "creat[e] federal substantive law requiring the parties to honor arbitration agreements," . . . then the breach of an arbitration agreement covered by § 2 would give rise to a federal question within the subject-matter jurisdiction of the federal district courts. *See* 28 U.S.C. § 1331. Yet the ensuing provisions of the Act, without expressly taking away this jurisdiction, clearly rest on the assumption that federal courts have jurisdiction to enforce arbitration agreements only when they would have had jurisdiction over the underlying dispute. *See* 9 U.S.C. §§ 3, 4, 8. In other words, the FAA treats arbitration simply as one means of resolving disputes that lie within the jurisdiction of the federal courts; it makes clear that the breach of a covered arbitration agreement does not itself provide any independent basis for such jurisdiction. . .

While "Congress may legislate in areas traditionally regulated by the States" as long as it "is acting within the powers granted it under the Constitution," we assume that "Congress does not exercise [this power] lightly." *Gregory v. Ashcroft,* 501 U.S. 452, 460 (1991). To the extent that federal statutes are ambiguous, we do not read them to displace state law. Rather, we must be "absolutely certain" that Congress intended such displacement before we give preemptive effect to a federal statute. . . . Far from being "absolutely certain" that Congress swept aside these state rules, I am quite sure that it did not.

Allied-Bruce Terminix Cos. v. Dobson, 513 U.S. 265, 286-293 (1995) (Thomas, J., dissenting).

QUESTION TO PONDER

There have been a large number of documented instances where nursing homes have mistreated residents, especially those who have disorders such as Alzheimer's disease or dementia who cannot advocate on their own behalf. Indeed, the plaintiffs in *Kindred Nursing* were granted power of attorney because their parents were unable to make decisions for themselves. Patient and consumer advocates have raised concerns that arbitration will not adequately enforce the law to protect patients. On the other hand, nursing homes have argued that reducing litigation costs is important to their viability. In 2018, the Centers for Medicare and Medicaid Services considered an administrative rule prohibiting arbitration agreements in long term care contracts. If you were making the rule for that agency, what would you choose to do and why?

E. RECENT DEVELOPMENTS

In some recent cases, companies with consumer arbitration contracts have tried to escape or alter the terms of those contracts in court. So far, the courts have been reticent to do so, applying the same rules to both sides of these contracts of adhesion. Consider the policy issues as you read the examples below.

Arbitration is regulated at the state level. Sometimes arbitrators have been found to be biased and subsequently shut down. For example, in 2009, an arbitration provider called the National Arbitration Forum (NAF) entered into a consent decree with the Attorney General of Missouri to resolve allegations that it had been biased against consumers. As a result, it shut down operations nationwide. An arbitration agreement with King of Kash—a high-cost, short-term lender—required that any dispute with borrowers be resolved by arbitration exclusively with NAF. The Supreme Court of Missouri ruled that since the agreement specified arbitration exclusively before NAF, it could not bind the plaintiff once NAF was out of business. King of Kash argued that, under the FAA, the Court should rewrite the arbitration agreement to pick a different arbitrator, but the Court rejected this argument, stating: "The unequivocal, plain and clear terms of this Agreement establish that A-1 and Hunter agreed only to arbitrate before NAF. A-1 drafted this provision and it freely chose to require such an agreement from Hunter (and other borrowers) as a condition of obtaining loans from A-1. Having made the choice to insist upon NAF—and only NAF—as the arbitration forum, A-1 cannot now look to section 5 of the FAA to expand the arbitration promise it extracted from Hunter in the Agreement." *A-1 Premium Acceptance, Inc. v. Hunter*, 557 S.W.3d 923, 928 (Mo. 2018), *cert. denied,* 139 S. Ct. 1340 (2019). If you were deciding the case, how would you have decided it?

Do companies really want to arbitrate? In a recent case in San Francisco between consumers and Fitbit, the company argued that a class action of consumers could not proceed because the user agreements contained arbitration clauses forbidding class actions. The judge agreed. A consumer in that case then filed an arbitration proceeding with the American Arbitration Association (AAA), the provider in the user agreement, at a cost of $750. She wanted to test the validity of the arbitration provision, a decision that rested with the arbitrator. The AAA determined that her case was worth $200, and Fitbit offered her $2,800 to drop her claim. When she refused, Fitbit nevertheless communicated to the arbitrator that the case was over, preventing her from testing the validity arbitration provision. At a hearing following these events, Fitbit's lawyers admitted that arbitration was not feasible for most consumers because the filing fee far exceeded their likely recoveries: "A claim that is $162—an individual claim—is not one that any rational litigant would litigate." The judge threatened to hold Fitbit's lawyers in contempt for attempting to take away the consumer's right to arbitrate with these tactics. At a follow-up hearing, Fitbit's lawyers backed off their earlier statements, emphasizing that it was not rational for Fitbit to arbitrate a $162 claim and that the company would allow the arbitration to go forward. Alison Frankel, *Fitbit in "Ugly Truth" Case: We Meant to Say Arbitration Is Irrational for Us, Not Consumers,* Reuters (July 3, 2018). If you were the judge who had ordered arbitration in that case, enforcing the consumer's contract with Fitbit under the FAA, what would you have done?

As mentioned earlier, one way to pressure companies is to file large numbers of individual arbitration claims. Uber drivers who are subject to arbitration agreements have begun filing arbitration actions. As of May 2019, there were approximately 60,000 such individual arbitrations pending. The approximate cost of each arbitration for Uber ranges from $10,000 to $20,000. The drivers sued Uber in court, claiming that it was refusing to pay the obligatory filing fees to commence arbitration, but Uber argued that the drivers themselves were not paying their $400 fee. If Uber were to arbitrate all these cases, the cost of arbitration would very likely be higher for Uber than allowing the case to proceed as a class action in federal court. What do you think Uber's best course of action is in this scenario?

REVIEW EXERCISE NO. 6: ALTERNATIVE DISPUTE RESOLUTION UNDER LOCAL RULE

The Alternative Dispute Resolution Act of 1998, 28 U.S.C. § 651, requires that each district court authorize some form of ADR through local rule. The procedures can be voluntary, and the programs vary significantly across federal district courts.

Reprinted below is a local rule for the U.S. District Court for the District of Massachusetts and a letter that one judge in the district requires lawyers to mail to their clients. Assume that an identical local rule is in effect for the *Warner* case. Your clients have received a form letter identical to the one that follows, and you have told them that you will discuss the letter with them. (If your last name begins with letter *A* through *J*, you represent the defendant City, and if your last name begins with letter *K* through *Z*, you represent the plaintiffs.) In class, you will engage in a strategy session discussing what you should recommend to your client about ADR and the letter's options in their case. Your instructor is an older lawyer in your office. Most people use the terms "mediation" and "conciliation" interchangeably. This technique employs a third party to help the litigants reach a resolution of the dispute on their own agreed-upon terms. In arbitration, a third party (or group of people) hears evidence, usually at a formal hearing, and gives a formal decision, in much the same way a judge would. The litigants can agree, or a previous contract can compel, that the arbitration decision be binding, enforceable, and have a claim-preclusion effect. Many, if not most, arbitrators would say that they are applying the applicable law to the facts that they believe to be true after hearing and weighing the evidence.

The descriptions of mini-trial, summary jury trial, and early neutral evaluation in the Local Rule and judge's letter are rather straightforward.

> **Rule 16.4 Alternative Dispute Resolution**
>
> (a) The judicial officer shall encourage the resolution of disputes by settlement or other alternative dispute resolution programs.
>
> (b) **Settlement.** At every conference conducted under these rules, the judicial officer shall inquire as to the utility of the parties conducting settlement negotiations, explore means of facilitating those negotiations, and offer whatever assistance may be appropriate in the circumstances. Assistance may include a reference of the case to another judicial officer for settlement purposes. Whenever a settlement conference is held, a representative of each party who has settlement authority shall attend or be available by telephone.
>
> (c) **Other Alternative Dispute Resolution Programs.**
>
> (1) Discretion of Judicial Officer. The judicial officer, following an exploration of the matter with all counsel, may refer appropriate cases to alternative dispute resolution programs that have been designated for use in the district court or that the judicial officer may make available. The dispute resolution programs described in subdivisions (2) through (4) are illustrative, not exclusive.
>
> (2) Mini-trial.

(a) The judicial officer may convene a mini-trial upon the agreement of all parties, either by written motion or their oral motion in open court entered upon the record.

(b) Each party, with or without the assistance of counsel, shall present his or her position before:

(1) selected representatives for each party, or

(2) an impartial third party, or

(3) both selected representatives for each party and an impartial third party.

(c) An impartial third party may issue an advisory opinion regarding the merits of the case.

(d) Unless the parties agree otherwise, the advisory opinion of the impartial third party is not binding.

(e) The impartial third party's advisory opinion is not appealable.

(f) Neither the advisory opinion of an impartial third party nor the presentations of the parties shall be admissible as evidence in any subsequent proceeding, unless otherwise admissible under the rules of evidence. Also, the occurrence of the mini-trial shall not be admissible.

(3) Summary jury trial.

(a) The judicial officer may convene a summary jury trial:

(1) with the agreement of all parties, either by written motion or their oral motion in court entered upon the record, or

(2) upon the judicial officer's determination that a summary jury trial would be appropriate, even in the absence of the agreement of all the parties.

(b) There shall be six (6) jurors on the panel, unless the parties agree otherwise.

(c) The panel may issue an advisory opinion regarding:

(1) the respective liability of the parties, or

(2) the damages of the parties, or

(3) both the respective liability and the damages of the parties.

(d) Unless the parties agree otherwise, the advisory opinion is not binding and it shall not be appealable.

(e) Neither the panel's advisory opinion nor its verdict, nor the presentations of the parties shall be admissible as evidence in any subsequent proceeding, unless otherwise admissible under the rules of evidence. Also, the occurrence of the summary jury trial shall not be admissible.

(4) Mediation.

(a) The judicial officer may grant mediation upon the agreement of all parties.

(b) The mediator selected may be an individual, group of individuals or institution. The mediator shall be compensated as agreed by the parties.

(c) The mediator shall meet, either jointly or separately, with each party and counsel for each party and shall take any steps that may appear appropriate in order to assist the parties to resolve the impasse or controversy.

(d) If mediation does not result in a resolution of the dispute, the parties shall promptly report the termination of mediation to the judicial officer.

(e) If an agreement is reached between the parties on any issues, the mediator shall make appropriate note of that agreement and shall refer the parties to the judicial officer for entry of a court order.

(f) Any communication related to the subject matter of the dispute made during the mediation by any participant, mediator, or any other person present at the mediation shall be a confidential communication to the full extent contemplated by Fed. R. Evid. 408. No admission, representation, statement, or other confidential communication made in setting up or conducting the proceedings not otherwise discoverable or obtainable shall be admissible as evidence or subject to discovery.

Adopted effective, October 1, 1992.

UNITED STATES DISTRICT COURT
DISTRICT OF MASSACHUSETTS, BOSTON, 02109

William G. Young
District Judge
Date: /d/

Dear Litigant:

Your case has been assigned to this session of the U.S. District Court for all pretrial proceedings and trial. I assure you that our goal is to give your case a fair, impartial, and just trial as soon as possible. To that end, I have today met with the attorneys and placed your case on the running trial list in this session as of /date/.

As you may appreciate, full-scale trials are expensive, and the time spent awaiting trial is frequently lengthy. Therefore, I want you to be aware of various other programs we offer that may possibly resolve your case to your satisfaction with less expense and delay. Each of these programs is voluntary, and all parties to the lawsuit must agree before implementing any such program in your case. I list these programs in the order that they most resemble a trial in this Court.

1. *Trial before a Magistrate Judge:* You may agree to try your case, with or without a jury, before a U.S. Magistrate Judge. A Magistrate Judge is a judicial officer appointed by the judges of this Court for this purpose. The trial takes place in this courthouse and, if a jury has been claimed, before a federal jury. The advantage of this program is its speed—cases can usually be reached for trial before a Magistrate Judge within a few months. Moreover, the parties can usually agree with the Magistrate Judge upon a specific day to begin the trial. There is no charge for this service.

2. *Trial before a retired Superior Court Justice:* You may agree to try your case to a federal jury before a distinguished retired justice of the Massachusetts Superior Court. The Superior Court is "the great trial court of the Commonwealth," and

its justices are experts on jury trials and issues of Massachusetts law. The advantages are the same as for trials before Magistrate Judges—a speedy hearing and definite trial date. The cost of this program to you will be $250 per trial day plus sharing the per trial day cost of a court reporter. The trial will take place in this courthouse before a federal jury.

3. *Arbitration:* You may agree to resolve your case by submitting it to a skilled neutral arbitrator or group of arbitrators. You will have a chance to participate in the choice of arbitrators. Advantages of this program are that prompt arbitration hearings may be scheduled and the arbitrators may be technically skilled in the issues raised in this lawsuit. You and the other parties will share the costs of the arbitrators and the administration of the arbitration program.

4. *Summary jury trial:* You may agree to a summary jury trial. This is an advisory one-day proceeding before a federal jury. Each party will have the chance to make a brief presentation of its position, and, properly charged as to the law, the jury will render a nonbinding advisory verdict. I will meet with the attorneys that same day to discuss whether a settlement of the case is possible and proper. It may be helpful to you and the other parties to obtain the views of the summary jury in order to better evaluate your position. There is no cost for this program.

5. *Mediation:* You may agree to voluntary mediation. If you agree, I will appoint a skilled, neutral, and experienced mediator promptly to explore with all parties and their attorneys whether a settlement of this case may be reached that will satisfy your basic concerns. Unlike the previous options, mediation never imposes a result on the parties. Rather, it seeks to reach agreement. Prompt mediation may minimize your overall litigation costs.

6. *Early neutral evaluation:* You may agree to have your case evaluated by a neutral attorney skilled in the issues raised in this case. This may assist you in evaluating your position and may aid you in deciding whether to settle, press on to trial, or avail yourself of one or more of these other options.

Your attorney is familiar with each of these options and can advise you in detail concerning what advantages they may offer you. If the parties can agree, you may pursue variations on these options with the support of this Court.

Should you wish further information on any of these points or should all parties agree to pursue any one or a variant of any of them, your attorney should feel free to consult with Courtroom Deputy Clerk Kate Myrick, Esq., or Docket Clerk Elizabeth Smith.

PRACTICE EXERCISE NO. 30: ALTERNATIVE DISPUTE RESOLUTION IN *CARPENTER*

For the purpose of this exercise (only), assume the following facts and circumstances for the *Carpenter* case. A firm trial date has been set for the case, and that date is exactly two months away. Ultimate Auto, which is represented by a lawyer from its insurance company ("Commercial"), and the lawyer for Nancy Carpenter have agreed to attempt to settle the case through a facilitated (and nonbinding) mediation. A second insurance company, the insurer of the jeep, has already offered $10,000 (the maximum payable under the policy) to Carpenter; the Dees, however, are still in the case. The Dees' lawyer has declined the invitation to mediate. Assume that summary judgment was entered in favor of McGill and McGill's Garage, and thus they are out of the case. Assume that the City is still in the case, but the City has recently filed for bankruptcy and is judgment-proof. The City's general counsel refuses to show up for the mediation; she insists that the case against the City is spurious.

Ultimate Auto had a liability insurance policy with Commercial. Under these liability policies, insurance companies will typically assume the obligation of defending the insured. Naturally, this makes the insured somewhat dependent on the acts of the insurers, because the insurers typically have the power to settle the case up to the policy limit (and thereby foreclose an insured's exposure) or may instead refuse to settle the case and expose the insured to liability for any amounts in excess of the "policy limit." State laws typically impose some obligation on insurers to make good-faith efforts to compromise claims where the recovery may exceed the policy limits of the insured's protections. The policy issued by Commercial to Ultimate Auto has a policy limit of $500,000.

The mediator in this case insists that clients attend with their attorneys. The mediator's general practice is to first meet with the parties and their counsel together and to tell them his or her ground rules for the mediation. Often, the mediator will give a short speech about the importance of civility, the advantages of a mediated settlement (including cost savings and the possibility of creative solutions), the cloak of confidentiality, and some insight into the mediator's views about his or her role in the process of the mediation. The mediator then typically asks the parties to sign various documents including, among other things, confidentiality agreements and promises to pay the mediator's fees. The cost of a mediator varies from as low as nothing for a pro bono mediator to as much as $10,000 per day for an experienced mediator (or even $20,000 per day for a superstar mediator). In a case like ours, a typical mediator might cost $2,000 per day, or $1,000 for any portion up to a half-day. The parties typically share the expense equally.

The mediation in this case is scheduled for four hours. The mediator will answer any questions about the mediation process, and will then ask to hear opening statements from the lawyers about their views of the case and about previous negotiations, if any. The mediator is usually also very willing to hear any statements that the clients may wish to make. Most mediators will also ask for a written statement from each side; the mediator may even ask for a submission in advance of the mediation session. (The mediator will usually ask for you to identify any information that you expect the mediator to keep confidential.)

After both sides have had the opportunity to make their opening statements, the mediator typically will separate the parties, with the plaintiff's team in one conference room and the defendant's team in another. The mediator then performs a sort of "shuttle diplomacy" going back and forth between the two rooms with demands and counter-offers. Occasionally the mediator may bring everyone back together; and if there is a settlement, the mediator will meet with everyone to summarize and, ultimately, to memorialize the settlement in writing.

Assume in this case that Carpenter's lawyer and Commercial's lawyer have met briefly previously. Plaintiff's lawyer made a demand of $1.5 million and the defendant's lawyer offered $25,000. In this brief negotiation, plaintiff's lawyer shared with defense counsel the major economic information contained in the letter from Economics Specialists of Boston, Inc. that is in the Case Files. Defense counsel was (or at least appeared) unimpressed. The parties were so far apart that they then thought that an exchange of further offers and counter-offers was unlikely to lead to an agreement. Commercial's lawyer then wrote the president of Ultimate Auto that he should consider getting his own lawyer in order to protect Ultimate Auto against a judgment that could be greater than the policy limit. Ultimate Auto has declined to retain an additional lawyer. Assume that the plaintiff's lawyer has taken the case on a contingency basis: one-third of the recovery, plus out-of-pocket disbursements. The defense's lawyer is paid a relatively modest $250 per hour by Commercial. Discovery has been completed. The lawyers agree that it would probably take between three and five days to try the case.

This practice has four potential parts. Your professor may wish to assign one or more of them.

A. *Demand Letter.* Write a three-page double-spaced demand letter, on behalf of Nancy Carpenter, addressed to Ultimate Auto. You may wish to review the essentials of writing a demand letter, introduced in Practice Exercise No. 9, in Chapter 3.

B. *Writing Assignment.* Write a three-page, double-spaced opening statement to the mediator. If your last name begins with the letter A through M, you represent Nancy Carpenter and her son; if N through Z, you are the lawyer representing Ultimate Auto (and Commercial).

C. *Oral Statement.* Prepare an opening statement to the mediator of approximately five to ten minutes in length. If your last name begins with the letter A through M, you represent Nancy Carpenter and her son; if N through Z, you are the lawyer representing Ultimate Auto (and Commercial).

D. *Mediation.* Prepare to participate in a mediation session. If your last name begins with the letter A through C, you should prepare to play the role of Nancy Carpenter. The *lawyer* for Nancy Carpenter will be selected from persons with last names beginning with the letters H through L. If your last name begins with the letter D through G, you should prepare to play the role of Adam Jenkins, the president of Ultimate Auto. The *lawyer* for Ultimate Auto (selected and paid for by Commercial) will be selected from persons with last names beginning with the letters M through Q. Persons with last names beginning with the letters R and S should prepare to serve as the mediator. And persons with last names beginning with the letters T through Z should prepare to play the role of an assistant vice president of Commercial with authority to settle the case. The mediation may be conducted inside or outside the class. There may also be individual instructions for particular roles to accompany these general instructions.

CHAPTER 7

The Choice of an Appropriate Court: Personal Jurisdiction, Notice, and Venue

A. INTRODUCTION AND OVERVIEW

In addition to the issues we have already explored concerning the viability of the claim for relief and the availability of a meaningful remedy, a lawyer contemplating a lawsuit on behalf of a client must choose an appropriate court to hear the case. In order to entertain an action and enter a constitutionally valid and enforceable judgment, that court must have adjudicatory power consisting of (1) *personal jurisdiction* over the defendant, and (2) *subject matter jurisdiction* over the case. Adequate *notice* apprising the defendant of the action (in the form of service of process) is a third requirement. Mastering the law of jurisdiction is essential to effective lawyering, as invoking proper adjudicatory power is "the gateway to the judicial system."*

Personal (sometimes referred to as *territorial*) *jurisdiction* is a reflection of the geographic limitations on the judicial power of the sovereign states within our federal system. Assume that Nancy Carpenter had moved to Florida following her husband's tragic death and decided to bring suit against Randall Dee in the courts of that state. Intuitively it seems unfair to require Dee to defend a lawsuit in a distant state when all the events giving rise to the claim occurred in Massachusetts. We may also question the authority of a Florida court to adjudicate a matter when that state has no connection to the lawsuit other than fortuitously being the newly adopted residence of the plaintiff. Both concerns—fairness and power—play a role in the doctrine of personal jurisdiction. Over time (and what could fairly be called a long and winding road), the Supreme Court has developed an elaborate constitutional calculus for determining when a court has power to summon a defendant from beyond its borders.

While the concept of personal jurisdiction allocates judicial power among the states, *subject matter jurisdiction* (the topic of Chapter 8) allocates power

---

* Richard D. Freer, *Personal Jurisdiction: The Walls Blocking an Appeal to Rationality*, 72 Vand. L. Rev. En Banc 99 (2019).

between the federal and state court systems. Federal courts have *limited subject matter jurisdiction*. Constitutional and statutory provisions restrict their adjudicatory authority to certain types of cases, mainly disputes between citizens of different states ("diversity" cases) and disputes arising under federal law ("federal question" cases), such as patent, antitrust, and civil rights cases. In contrast, state courts have *general subject matter jurisdiction*—that is, they can hear and decide most categories of cases, including those that can be heard in federal court over which there is *concurrent jurisdiction*.

Once the principles of *personal* and *subject matter jurisdiction* identify those courts that have authority over both the defendant and the controversy, the administrative concept of *venue* further restricts the location of the lawsuit. Within the federal system, venue determines the appropriate judicial district(s) in which the case may be filed. The federal trial courts in New York State, for example, are divided into four districts: Eastern, Western, Northern, and Southern. Statutory provisions in the Judicial Code assign cases to particular districts based primarily on the residence of the parties, or the location of the events upon which the claim is based. Proper venue, unlike the three requirements set out above, is not a requisite for a constitutionally valid judgment, as discussed below.

B. JURISDICTION OVER THE PERSON OR PROPERTY OF THE DEFENDANT

Perhaps the most familiar evolution of American case law (certainly to first-year law students) has occurred in the area of personal jurisdiction. Since the decision in *Pennoyer v. Neff* in 1877, the courts have struggled with the task of defining the conditions that must be met before a court may require a nonresident to appear and defend. The complexity of the problem stems in part from the very nature of our federal system of government.

Each state retains its own sovereignty, a significant aspect of which is the power to adjudicate disputes. Because a judgment may have consequences beyond the borders of the state that renders it, the adjudication of disputes unavoidably implicates the conflicting authorities of the separate sovereigns. A valid judgment entered by a court in State A is entitled under our Constitution (Art. IV, § 1) to "full faith and credit" in all other states. If the judgment is against a citizen of State B, that state must (when requested by the plaintiff) recognize and enforce it against the defendant and any assets found within State B. The Supreme Court has made clear that the full faith and credit command is "exacting," not discretionary, with respect to a judgment rendered by a court possessing adjudicatory authority over the subject matter and the persons governed by the judgment. *Franchise Tax Board of California v. Hyatt*, 538 U.S. 488, 494 (2003).*

---

* Foreign judgments are not covered by the full faith and credit clause, and the United States is not a party to any international treaty providing for their enforcement. Recognition is governed by the laws of the several states, either by common law or the Uniform Foreign Judgment Recognition Act. *See generally* Gary Born and Peter Rutledge, *International Civil Litigation in United States Courts*, 1079–1081 (5th ed. 2011).

Pennoyer's traditional conception of jurisdiction required the physical presence of the defendant or his property within the adjudicating state. In the years immediately following that decision in 1877—a time of tremendous expansion of interstate industry and commerce—the *Pennoyer* scheme proved too confining, as it frustrated the ability of states to offer a judicial forum to residents who had claims against nonresidents. Its demise, in that sense, was inevitable.

The reworking began subtly, with resort to legal fictions such as "constructive presence" and "implied consent" to be sued, but in 1945 gave way to a new framework for the analysis of personal jurisdiction—*International Shoe Co. v. Washington*'s concept of "minimum contacts." Informed by notions of fair play as much as sovereign power, the modern formulation is highly contextual, and weighs many factors and policy concerns.

A word of warning about this chapter and the three that follow: We are leaving our focus on promulgated rules of procedure and entering an area of high-density, judge-made, legal doctrine.

C. THE TRADITIONAL CONCEPTION OF PERSONAL JURISDICTION

A Glossary of Terms. Before turning to the *Pennoyer* opinion (which generations of law students have insisted is not written in the English language), it is helpful to define certain terms central to the traditional conception of jurisdiction.

In personam jurisdiction is the power of a court to enter a money judgment against the defendant; the judgment may, if necessary, be satisfied by seizing and liquidating the defendant's assets. An in personam judgment (rendered, for example, in a personal injury tort action) is said to follow the defendant, meaning that it must be given "full faith and credit" and be enforced by any state in which the defendant or his assets are found.

In rem jurisdiction is the power of a court to act with regard to property (such as real estate) within its borders. An in rem judgment affects only the interests of persons in the property (and may indeed extinguish those interests) but, unlike an in personam judgment, does not create an obligation on the defendant's part to pay money to the plaintiff. An action to determine title to a parcel of land among opposing claimants is an example of in rem jurisdiction.

Quasi in rem jurisdiction is a hybrid of the other two forms of adjudicatory power. It is based on the presence of the defendant's property (either real or personal) within the forum state, and it permits the court to enter a judgment for an amount of money (not exceeding the value of the property) that may be satisfied from the forced sale of the property. Unlike the "true" in rem action, the claim for relief in a quasi in rem action is *unrelated to the property*, which merely serves as the basis for jurisdiction.

* * *

An example of litigation breeding litigation, *Pennoyer v. Neff* actually involved two successive lawsuits. Oregon attorney Mitchell sued nonresident Neff in state court in Oregon seeking $300 in legal fees allegedly due him. Neff's failure to appear led to a default judgment, which resulted in the forced sale of Neff's land in Oregon in order to satisfy the judgment. In the second suit, filed in federal court, Neff sought to recover his land from Pennoyer, who had purchased it at a sheriff's sale. The outcome of the second action turned upon the jurisdictional validity of the judgment entered in the first.

Pennoyer v. Neff
95 U.S. 714 (1877)

Justice FIELD delivered the opinion of the Court:

This is an action to recover the possession of a tract of land, of the alleged value of $15,000, situated in the State of Oregon. The plaintiff asserts title to the premises by a patent of the United States issued to him in 1866, under the act of Congress of Sept. 27, 1850, usually known as the Donation Law of Oregon. The defendant claims to have acquired the premises under a sheriff's deed, made upon a sale of the property on execution issued upon a judgment recovered against the plaintiff in one of the circuit courts of the State. The case turns upon the validity of this judgment.

It appears from the record that the judgment was rendered in February, 1866, in favor of J. H. Mitchell, for less than $300, including costs, in an action brought by him upon a demand for services as an attorney; that, at the time the action was commenced and the judgment rendered, the defendant therein, the plaintiff here, was a non-resident of the State that he was not personally served with process, and did not appear therein; and that the judgment was entered upon his default in not answering the complaint, upon a constructive service of summons by publication.

The Code of Oregon provides for such service when an action is brought against a non-resident and absent defendant, who has property within the State. It also provides, where the action is for the recovery of money or damages, for the attachment of the property of the non-resident. And it also declares that no natural person is subject to the jurisdiction of a court of the State, "unless he appear in the court, or be found within the State, or be a resident thereof, or have property therein; and, in the last case, only to the extent of such property at the time the jurisdiction attached." Construing this latter provision to mean, that, in an action for money or damages where a defendant does not appear in the court, and is not found within the State, and is not a resident thereof, but has property therein, the jurisdiction of the court extends only over such property, the declaration expresses a principle of general, if not universal, law. The authority of every tribunal is necessarily restricted by the territorial limits of the State in which it is established. Any attempt to exercise authority beyond those limits would be deemed in every other forum, as has been said by this court, an illegitimate assumption of power, and be resisted as mere abuse. In the case against the plaintiff, the property here in controversy sold under the judgment rendered was not attached, nor in any way brought under the jurisdiction of the court. Its first connection with the case was caused by a levy of the execution. It was not, therefore, disposed of pursuant to any adjudication, but only in enforcement of a personal judgment, having no relation to the property, rendered against a non-resident without service of process upon him in the action, or his appearance therein. The court below did not consider that an attachment of the property was essential to its jurisdiction or to the validity of the sale, but held that the judgment was invalid from defects in the affidavit upon which the order of publication was obtained, and in the affidavit by which the publication was proved.

. . .

If we were confined to the rulings of the court below upon the defects in the affidavits mentioned, we should be unable to uphold its decision [because we disagree as to the alleged defects]. But it was also contended in that court, and is insisted upon here, that the judgment in the State court against the plaintiff was void for want of personal service of process on him, or of his appearance in the action in which it was rendered and that the premises in controversy could not be subjected to the payment of the demand of a resident creditor except by a proceeding in rem; that is, by a direct proceeding against the property for that purpose. If these positions are sound, the ruling of the Circuit Court as to the invalidity of that judgment must be sustained, notwithstanding our dissent from the reasons upon which it was made. And that they are sound would seem to follow from two well-established principles of public law respecting the jurisdiction of an independent State over persons and property. . . . One of these principles is, that every State possesses exclusive jurisdiction and sovereignty over persons and property within its territory. . . . The other principle of public law referred to follows from the one mentioned; that is, that no State can exercise direct jurisdiction and authority over persons or property without its territory. The several States are of equal dignity and authority, and the independence of one implies the exclusion of power from all others. And so it is laid down by jurists, as an elementary principle, that the laws of one State have no operation outside of its territory, except so far as is allowed by comity; and that no tribunal established by it can extend its process beyond that territory so as to subject either persons or property to its decisions. "Any exertion of authority of this sort beyond this limit," says Story, "is a mere nullity, and incapable of binding such persons or property in any other tribunals."

But as contracts made in one State may be enforceable only in another State, and property may be held by non-residents, the exercise of the jurisdiction which every State is admitted to possess over persons and property within its own territory will often affect persons and property without it. To any influence exerted in this way by a State affecting persons resident or property situated elsewhere, no objection can be justly taken; while any direct exertion of authority upon them, in an attempt to give ex-territorial operation to its laws, or to enforce an ex-territorial jurisdiction by its tribunals, would be deemed an encroachment upon the independence of the State in which the persons are domiciled or the property is situated, and be resisted as usurpation. . . .

So the State, through its tribunals, may subject property situated within its limits owned by non-residents to the payment of the demand of its own citizens against them; and the exercise of this jurisdiction in no respect infringes upon the sovereignty of the State where the owners are domiciled. Every State owes protection to its own citizens; and, when non-residents deal with them, it is a legitimate and just exercise of authority to hold and appropriate any property owned by such non-residents to satisfy the claims of its citizens. It is in virtue of the State's jurisdiction over the property of the non-resident situated within its limits that its tribunals can inquire into that non-resident's obligations to its own citizens, and the inquiry can then be carried only to the extent necessary to control the disposition of the property. If the non-resident have no property in the State, there is nothing upon which the tribunals can adjudicate. . . .

Jurisdiction is acquired in one of two modes: first, as against the person of the defendant by the service of process [*in personam*]; or, secondly, by a procedure against the property of the defendant within the jurisdiction of the court [*in rem*]. In the latter case, the defendant is not personally bound by the judgment beyond the property in question. . . .

If, without personal service, judgments in personam, obtained ex parte against non-residents and absent parties, upon mere publication of process, which, in the great majority of cases, would never be seen by the parties interested, could be upheld and enforced, they would be the constant instruments of fraud and oppression. Judgments for all sorts of claims upon contracts and for torts, real or pretended, would be thus obtained, under which property would be seized, when the evidence of the transactions upon which they were founded, if they ever had any existence, had perished.

Substituted service by publication may be sufficient to inform parties of the object of proceedings taken where property is once brought under the control of the court by seizure. The law assumes that property is always in the possession of its owner, in person or by agent; and it proceeds upon the theory that its seizure will inform him, not only that it is taken into the custody of the court, but that he must look to any proceedings authorized by law upon such seizure for its condemnation and sale. Such service may also be sufficient in cases where the object of the action is to reach and dispose of property in the State, or of some interest therein, by enforcing a contract or a lien respecting the same, or to partition it among different owners, or, when the public is a party, to condemn and appropriate it for a public purpose. In other words, such service may answer in all actions which are substantially proceedings in rem. But where the entire object of the action is to determine the personal rights and obligations of the defendants, that is, where the suit is merely in personam, constructive service in this form upon a non-resident is ineffectual for any purpose. Process from the tribunals of one State cannot run into another State, and summon parties there domiciled to leave its territory and respond to proceedings against them. Publication of process or notice within the State where the tribunal sits cannot create any greater obligation upon the non-resident to appear. Process sent to him out of the State, and process published within it, are equally unavailing in proceedings to establish his personal liability.

The want of authority of the tribunals of a State to adjudicate upon the obligations of non-residents, where they have no property within its limits, is not denied by the court below: but the position is assumed, that, where they have property within the State, it is immaterial whether the property is in the first instance brought under the control of the court by attachment or some other equivalent act, and afterwards applied by its judgment to the satisfaction of demands against its owner; or such demands be first established in a personal action, and the property of the nonresident be afterwards seized and sold on execution. But the jurisdiction of the court to inquire into and determine his obligations at all is only incidental to its jurisdiction over the property. Its jurisdiction in that respect cannot be made to depend upon facts to be ascertained after it has tried the cause and rendered the judgment. If the judgment be previously void, it will not become valid by the subsequent discovery of property of the defendant, or by his subsequent acquisition of it. The judgment, if void when rendered, will always remain void: it cannot occupy the doubtful position of being valid if property be found, and void if there be none. Even if the position assumed were confined to cases where the non-resident defendant possessed property in the State at the commencement of the action, it would still make the validity of the proceedings and judgment depend upon the question whether, before the levy of the execution, the defendant had or had not disposed of the property. If before the levy the property should be sold, then, according to this position, the judgment would not be binding. This doctrine would introduce a new element of uncertainty in judicial proceedings. The contrary is the law: the validity of every judgment depends upon the jurisdiction of the court before it is rendered, not upon what may occur subsequently. . . .

Attempts have been made to enforce such judgments in States other than those in which they were rendered, under the provision of the Constitution requiring that "full faith and credit shall be given in each State to the public acts, records, and judicial proceedings of every other State"; "they shall have such faith and credit given to them in every court within the United States as they have by law or usage in the courts of the State from which they are or shall or taken." [But this provision is] applicable only when the court rendering the judgment had jurisdiction of the parties and of the subject-matter, and [does] not preclude an inquiry into the jurisdiction of the court in which the judgment was rendered, or the right of the State itself to exercise authority over the person or the subject-matter. . . .

[T]he courts of the United States are not required to give effect to judgments of this character [but] are bound to give to the judgments of the State courts only the same faith and credit which the courts of another State are bound to give to them.

Since the adoption of the Fourteenth Amendment to the Federal Constitution, the validity of such judgments may be directly questioned, and their enforcement in the State resisted, on the ground that proceedings in a court of justice to determine the personal rights and obligations of parties over whom that court has no jurisdiction do not constitute due process of law. . . . To give such proceedings any validity, there must be a tribunal competent by its constitution— that is, by the law of its creation—to pass upon the subject-matter of the suit; and, if that involves merely a determination of the personal liability of the defendant, he must be brought within its jurisdiction by service of process within the State, or his voluntary appearance.

Except in cases affecting the personal status of the plaintiff, the substituted service of process by publication, allowed by the law of Oregon and by similar laws in other States, where actions are brought against non-residents, is effectual only where [the action is in the nature of a proceeding in rem, and the] property in the State is brought under the control of the court. [F]or any other purpose than to subject the property of a non-resident to valid claims against him in the State, "due process of law would require appearance or personal service before the defendant could be personally bound by any judgment rendered."

It is true that, in a strict sense, a proceeding in rem is one taken directly against property, and has for its object the disposition of the property, [but] the terms are applied to actions between parties, where the direct object is to reach and dispose of property owned by them, or of some interest therein. Such are cases commenced by attachment against the property of debtors . . .

It follows from the views expressed that the personal judgment recovered in the State court of Oregon against the plaintiff herein, then a non-resident of the State, was without any validity, and did not authorize a sale of the property in controversy.

To prevent any misapplication of the views expressed in this opinion, it is proper to observe that we do not mean to assert, by anything we have said, that a State may not authorize proceedings to determine the status of one of its citizens towards a non-resident, which would be binding within the State, though made without service of process or personal notice to the non-resident. The jurisdiction which every State possesses to determine the civil status and capacities of all its inhabitants involves authority to prescribe the conditions on which proceedings affecting them may be commenced and carried on within its territory. The State, for example, has absolute right to prescribe the conditions upon which the marriage relation between its own citizens shall be created, and the causes for which it may be dissolved. One of the parties guilty of acts for which, by the law of the State, a dissolution may be granted, may have removed to a State where no dissolution is permitted. The complaining party would, therefore, fail if a divorce were sought in the State of the defendant; and if application could not be made to the tribunals of the complainant's domicile in such case, and proceedings be there instituted without personal service of process or personal notice to the offending party, the injured citizen would be without redress.

Neither do we mean to assert that a State may not require a non-resident entering into a partnership or association within its limits, or making contracts enforceable there, to appoint an agent or representative in the State to receive service of process and notice in legal proceedings instituted with respect to such partnership, association, or contracts, or to designate a place where such service may be made and notice given, and provide, upon their failure, to make such appointment or to designate such place that service may be made upon a public officer designated for that purpose, [nor do we assert] that judgments rendered upon such service may not be binding upon the non-residents both within and without the State. . . .

In the present case, there is no feature of this kind, and, consequently, no consideration of what would be the effect of such legislation in enforcing the contract of a non-resident can arise. The question here respects only the validity of a money judgment rendered in one State, in an action upon a simple contract against the resident of another, without service of process upon him, or his appearance therein.

Judgment affirmed.

[The dissenting opinion of Justice HUNT is omitted.]

YOUR TAKEAWAY

Pennoyer's conception of adjudicatory authority is based on the *physical presence* of defendant (in personam), or land claimed by defendant (in rem), within the borders of the adjudicating state—over which the state has obvious sovereign control. Persons or property beyond the borders are beyond the grasp of the state's judicial authority. Adjudicatory authority must be established at the outset of the litigation, thus the emphasis on the necessity for attachment of Neff's property before the case proceeded. A judgment entered without proper jurisdiction was now null and void by virtue of the newly adopted Due Process Clause of the Fourteenth Amendment, and could be challenged in a subsequent proceeding seeking to enforce the judgment as not entitled to full faith and credit.

REVIEW QUESTIONS

1. What exactly does *Pennoyer v. Neff* hold? Contrast the Supreme Court decision with the narrower ruling of the lower court, which reached the same result—invalidating the sheriff's deed that conveyed Neff's land to

Pennoyer—but on the basis of defects in the affidavit submitted for the publication service.

2. In his advice to entering law school students, Professor James B. White recommends thinking of the judicial opinions you read as the last stage of the dispute resolution process, the "artifact left behind." *The Study of Law as an Intellectual Activity*, 32 J. Legal Educ. 1 (1982). Your understanding of each case, and the legal process, will be enhanced if you invoke your imagination to reconstruct the events leading up to it—the factual context of the dispute, the steps taken by each of the opposing lawyers to set up the contested issues, and the legal arguments that are answered in the final decision. Try to reconstruct the opposing arguments that were presented to the Supreme Court in *Pennoyer v. Neff.*

3. What were the several bases for the exercise of jurisdiction provided for in the Code of Oregon? Which one did the Supreme Court think applicable in *Mitchell v. Neff*? Why did that not provide a valid basis for the judgment against Neff? What was the basis for jurisdiction in the second case, *Neff v. Pennoyer*?

4. What part did *notice* play in *Pennoyer*? Do we know from the opinion whether Neff had *actual* notice of the pendency of *Mitchell v. Neff*? If not, why was the absence of notice not itself a constitutional defect in the prior proceedings? What is the "substituted service by publication" referred to by the Court, and how could such dubious notice possibly be deemed constitutionally sufficient?

5. What openings in the confining *jurisdiction = physical presence* equation are suggested in the last three paragraphs of *Pennoyer*? How could compelling a nonresident corporation to appoint an agent to receive process within the forum state, as a condition of conducting business there, be deemed valid *consent* to jurisdiction?

   Note the reference to a type of jurisdiction that permits a court to adjudicate the *civil status* of the litigants regarding marriage or custody of children. A court may, for example, entertain a divorce action brought by a forum resident even though the defending spouse is now beyond the reach of in personam power. "This authority stems from a State's 'rightful and legitimate concern' in the status of 'persons domiciled within its borders,' a concern that is no less legitimate because that status might also affect a person outside of the State." *Caplan v. Donovan*, 450 Mass. 463, 468, 879 N.E.2d 117, 122 (2008). Entry of an order to pay alimony or child support, however, may require in personam power over the spouse. *Compare* NY CPLR § 302(b) *with Burnett v. Burnett*, 208 W. Va. 748, 755 (2000).

6. If you were representing Mitchell in a replay of *Mitchell v. Neff* after the Supreme Court's decision, what procedural steps would you follow to ensure proper adjudicatory power over defendant Neff? Would bringing the suit in federal court overcome the personal jurisdiction problem? The answer, we will see in Part G later in this chapter, is no.

QUESTIONS TO PONDER

1. For the fascinating story behind the story in *Pennoyer,* as well as its colorful cast of characters, *see* Wendy Collins Perdue, *Sin, Scandal, and Substantive Due Process: Personal Jurisdiction and* Pennoyer *Reconsidered,* 62 Wash. L. Rev. 479 (1987).

2. How do the Due Process and Full Faith and Credit Clauses interact on the matter of adjudicatory power?

3. Why should the then newly adopted Due Process Clause of the Fourteenth Amendment set the outer limits of state court power? What values are protected by the clause in this context? Professor Wendy Collins Perdue writes:

   > [Justice] Field's final and most startling step was to introduce the due process clause of the fourteenth amendment into his jurisdictional analysis. This step was unnecessary and surprising for several reasons. First, that clause had not been raised or argued by either party or by the court below. Second, Field had already concluded that the federal courts were not required to (and hence would not) enforce the prior Oregon judgment. Third, the due process discussion was dictum for the additional reason that the fourteenth amendment did not exist at the relevant time. Finally, the specific due process "holding" of the case—that a judgment rendered without personal jurisdiction is unenforceable even in the rendering forum—has been viewed by at least some courts and commentators as itself quite novel.

   Perdue, *supra,* 62 Wash. L. Rev. at 499-500.

4. As you read the post-*Pennoyer* cases that follow, consider Professor Perdue's further observation: "[Justice] Field's approach to personal jurisdiction continues to dominate modern personal jurisdiction doctrine. His opinion in *Pennoyer* not only laid the foundation for treating personal jurisdiction as a substantive liberty interest, but also established that geographic boundaries are central in the protection of that interest." 62 Wash. L. Rev. at 480.

5. Why are state borders so critical to the conception of adjudicatory authority? What underlying political theory of our federal republic is reflected?

6. ***When and how should the issue of personal jurisdiction be raised?*** How did Neff procedurally challenge the exercise of jurisdiction over him in *Mitchell v. Neff*? Why is this approach called a *collateral attack*? (Hint: Did Neff raise his objection in the original proceeding, or later in a *different proceeding*?)

   A more typical collateral challenge occurs when a nonresident defendant who is aware of the lawsuit fails to show up in court, deliberately suffering a default judgment with the intention of challenging jurisdiction when the plaintiff later sues to enforce the judgment in the defendant's home state. The risk of this approach is that the only basis left for opposing the judgment, once it becomes final in the original lawsuit, is the jurisdictional challenge—the defendant can no longer defend on the merits in the subsequent enforcement suit. This strategy places all of the defendant's eggs in the jurisdictional basket. If the court rejects the challenge, the judgment will be enforced no matter the merits of the claim. Under what circumstances might such a risky defense strategy make sense? What if the defendant has no real defense on the merits?

Assuming that Neff had been aware of Mitchell's lawsuit against him at the time it was still pending, what other options would have been available to challenge the court's power? In a *direct attack*, defendant files a motion to dismiss for lack of personal jurisdiction in the original proceeding (pursuant to Fed. R. Civ. P. 12(b)(2) in modern practice). If the court rules against the defendant and a final judgment is ultimately entered upholding jurisdiction, that determination is binding and forecloses any collateral challenge to jurisdiction. *See Baldwin v. Iowa State Traveling Men's Assn.*, 283 U.S. 522 (1931). (We will return to this topic in Chapter 10.)

Could Neff have appeared in the Oregon state court action and successfully argued that the court had no adjudicatory power over him? Note that appearance in court is itself one of the traditional bases for exercising power over the defendant, as expressly set out in the Code of Oregon. The modern device of a "special appearance" now saves the objecting defendant from this Catch-22 dilemma, as we will see in the cases that follow.

If Neff appeared today in a federal action brought against him by Mitchell and filed an answer merely denying that he owed Mitchell any legal fees, could he assert the lack of personal jurisdiction later in the proceeding? Look at Fed. R. Civ. P. 12(h)(1). The so-called fragile defenses, including lack of personal jurisdiction, are waived if not raised at the outset of the proceeding. Lack of subject matter jurisdiction is not among them, and can be asserted for the first time later in the litigation. Indeed, the judge is required to raise it even if no party does: "If the court determines at any time that it lacks subject matter jurisdiction, the court must dismiss the action." Fed. R. Civ. P. 12(h)(3). Why is the objection to subject matter jurisdiction treated so favorably? We will come back to this point in the next chapter.

Could Neff join his objection to personal jurisdiction in his first filing together with a 12(b)(6) motion to dismiss for failure to state a claim without waiving it? *See* Fed. R. Civ. P. 12(b) and (g).

7. ***Why do litigants and their lawyers care so much about personal jurisdiction?*** By the end of this chapter, we will have read more than a dozen cases in which the parties fight vigorously—all the way to the Supreme Court—over the issue of personal jurisdiction. Like all such

procedural disputes, these are not philosophical debates but, rather, are firmly rooted in the competing strategic and practical concerns of the litigants.

Plaintiffs choose the forum in which the lawsuit is initially filed, usually their home state for reasons of convenience and familiarity with the local courts, as well as in the hope that they will somehow benefit from a home court advantage. When the defendant is from a distant state, the inconvenience and expense of litigation may also translate into a more favorable settlement for plaintiffs.

The nonresident defendant can (and often does) challenge the plaintiff's choice of forum with a motion to dismiss for lack of personal jurisdiction, which, if successful, usually means the plaintiff will have to bear the expense and inconvenience of pursuing the litigation in the defendant's home state. In certain situations (discussed in Chapter 9), a litigant's choice of forum may also reflect an effort to shop for more favorable law.

Would strict application of *Pennoyer*'s conception of adjudicatory authority permit the exercise of jurisdiction over the defendants in our next two cases?

Harris v. Balk
198 U.S. 215 (1905)

Statement by Justice PECKHAM:

The plaintiff in error brings the case here in order to review the judgment of the supreme court of North Carolina, affirming a judgment of a lower court against him for $180, with interest, as stated therein. . . .

The facts are as follows: Harris was a resident of North Carolina at the time of the commencement of this action, in 1896, and prior to that time was indebted to Balk, also a resident of North Carolina, in the sum of $180, for money borrowed from Balk by Harris during the year 1896, which Harris verbally promised to repay, but there was no written evidence of the obligation. During the year above mentioned one Jacob Epstein, a resident of Baltimore, in the state of Maryland, asserted that Balk was indebted to him in the sum of over $300. In August, 1896, Harris visited Baltimore for the purpose of purchasing merchandise, and while he was in that city temporarily on August 6, 1896, Epstein caused to be issued out of a proper court in Baltimore a foreign or nonresident writ of attachment against Balk, attaching the debt due Balk from Harris, which writ the sheriff at Baltimore laid in the hands of Harris, with a summons to appear in the court at a day named. With that attachment, a writ of summons and a short declaration against Balk (as provided by the Maryland statute) were also delivered to the sheriff, and by him set up at the courthouse door, as required by the law of Maryland. Before the return day of the attachment writ Harris left Baltimore, and returned to his home in North Carolina. He did not contest the garnishee process, which was issued to garnish the debt which Harris owed Balk. After his return Harris made an affidavit on August 11, 1896, that he owed Balk $180, and stated that the amount had been attached by Epstein, of Baltimore, and by his counsel in the Maryland proceeding Harris consented therein to an order of condemnation against him as such garnishee for $180, the amount of his debt to Balk, [and] Harris paid the amount of the judgment to one Warren, an attorney of Epstein, residing in North Carolina. On August 11, 1896, Balk commenced an action against Harris in North Carolina to recover the $180 which he averred Harris owed him. Harris pleaded in bar the recovery of the Maryland judgment and his payment thereof, and contended that judgment was a valid judgment in Maryland, and was therefore entitled to full faith and credit in the courts of North Carolina. This contention was not allowed by the trial court, and judgment was accordingly entered against Harris for the amount of his indebtedness to Balk, and that judgment was affirmed by the supreme court of North Carolina. The ground of such judgment was that the Maryland court obtained no jurisdiction to attach the debt due from Harris to Balk, because Harris was but temporarily in the state, and the situs of the debt was in North Carolina.

Justice PECKHAM delivered the opinion of the Court:

The state court of North Carolina has refused to give any effect in this action to the Maryland judgment; and the Federal question is whether it did not thereby refuse the full faith and credit to such judgment which is required by the Federal Constitution. If the Maryland court had jurisdiction to award it, the judgment is valid and entitled to the same full faith and credit in North Carolina that it has in Maryland as a valid domestic judgment.

Balk contends that the Maryland court obtained no jurisdiction to award the judgment of condemnation, because the garnishee Harris, although at the time in the state of Maryland, and personally served with process therein, was a nonresident of that state, only casually or temporarily within its boundaries; that the situs of the debt due from Harris to Balk was in North Carolina, and did not accompany Harris to Maryland; that, consequently, Harris, though within the state of Maryland, had not possession of any property of Balk, and the Maryland state court therefore obtained no jurisdiction over any property of Balk in the attachment proceedings. Harris, on the contrary, insists that, though [he was only] temporarily in Maryland, the laws of that state provide for an attachment of this nature, and the court obtains jurisdiction over him by the service of process therein; that the judgment, condemning the debt from Harris to Balk, was a valid judgment, provided Balk could himself have sued Harris for the debt in Maryland. This, it is asserted, he could have done, and the judgment was therefore entitled to full faith and credit in the courts of North Carolina.

* * *

We regard the contention of Harris as the correct one.

There can be no doubt that Balk, as a citizen of the state of North Carolina, had the right to sue Harris in Maryland to recover the debt which Harris owed him. Being a citizen of North Carolina, he was entitled to all the privileges and immunities of citizens of the several states, one of which is the right to institute actions in the courts of another state. The law of Maryland provides for the attachment of credits in a case like this. . . .

It thus appears that Balk could have sued Harris in Maryland to recover his debt, notwithstanding the temporary character of Harris' stay there; it also appears that the municipal law of Maryland permits the debtor of the principal debtor to be garnished, and therefore if the court of the state where the garnishee is found obtains jurisdiction over him, through the service of process upon him within the state, then the judgment entered is a valid judgment. . . .

It seems to us, therefore, that the judgment against Harris in Maryland, condemning the $180 which he owed to Balk, was a valid judgment, because the court had jurisdiction over the garnishee by personal service of process within the state of Maryland. . . . Balk had notice of this attachment, certainly within a few days after the issuing thereof and the entry of judgment thereon, because he sued Harris to recover his debt within a few days after Harris' return to North Carolina, in which suit the judgment in Maryland was set up by Harris as a plea in bar to Balk's claim. . . .

The judgment of the Supreme Court of North Carolina must be reversed, and the cause remanded for further proceedings not inconsistent with the opinion of this court.

Reversed.

[Justice HARLAN and Justice DAY dissented.]

REVIEW QUESTIONS

1. What was the basis for the exercise of jurisdiction by the Maryland court over Balk in *Epstein v. Balk*? Is this consistent with *Pennoyer*? What language in *Pennoyer* permits this exercise of judicial power? What type of jurisdiction is this?

2. Why would the Supreme Court uphold a procedure as dubious as this: basing jurisdiction over a creditor on "attachment" of the debt owed *by seizing the debtor*? Can you think of other intangibles that might serve this function in future cases?

QUESTIONS TO PONDER

Did Balk have notice of the proceeding in Maryland during its pendency? If not, why wasn't this a due process violation?

Hess v. Pawloski
274 U.S. 352 (1927)

Justice BUTLER delivered the opinion of the Court:

This action was brought by Pawloski to recover damages for personal injuries. The declaration alleged that Hess negligently and wantonly drove a motor vehicle on a public highway in Massachusetts, and that by reason thereof the vehicle struck and injured Pawloski. Hess is a resident of Pennsylvania. No personal service was made on him, and no property belonging to him was attached. The service of process was made in compliance with chapter 90, General Laws of Massachusetts the material parts of which follow:

> The acceptance by a nonresident of the rights and privileges of the operation of a motor vehicle on a public way in the commonwealth shall be deemed equivalent to an appointment by such nonresident of the registrar to be his true and lawful attorney upon whom may be served all lawful processes in any action or proceeding against him, growing out of any accident or collision in which said nonresident may be involved while operating a motor vehicle on such a way, and said acceptance or operation shall be a signification of his agreement that any such process against him which is so served shall be of the same legal force and validity as if served on him personally. Service of such process shall be made by leaving a copy of the process with a fee of two dollars in the hands of the registrar, or in his office, and such service shall be sufficient service upon the said nonresident: Provided, that notice of such service and a copy of the process are forthwith sent by registered mail by the plaintiff to the defendant, and the defendant's return receipt and the plaintiff's affidavit of compliance herewith are appended to the writ and entered with the declaration. The court in which the action is pending may order such continuances as may be necessary to afford the defendant reasonable opportunity to defend the action.

Hess appeared specially for the purpose of contesting jurisdiction, and moved to dismiss on the ground that the service of process, if sustained, would deprive him of his property without due process of law, in violation of the Fourteenth Amendment. The court denied the motion. The Supreme Judicial Court held the statute to be a valid exercise of the police power, and affirmed the order. . . .

The question is whether the Massachusetts enactment contravenes the due process clause of the Fourteenth Amendment.

The process of a court of one state cannot run into another and summon a party there domiciled to respond to proceedings against him. Notice sent outside the state to a nonresident is unavailing to give jurisdiction in an action against him personally for money recovery. *Pennoyer v. Neff*, 95 U.S. 741. There must be actual service within the state of notice upon him or upon someone authorized to accept service for him. A personal judgment rendered against a nonresident, who has neither been served with process nor appeared in the suit, is without validity. . . .

Motor vehicles are dangerous machines, and, even when skillfully and carefully operated, their use is attended by serious dangers to persons and property.

In the public interest the state may make and enforce regulations reasonably calculated to promote care on the part of all, residents and nonresidents alike, who use its highways. The measure in question operates to require a nonresident to answer for his conduct in the state where arise causes of action alleged against him, as well as to provide for a claimant a convenient method by which he may sue to enforce his rights. Under the statute the implied consent is limited to proceedings growing out of accidents or collisions on a highway in which the nonresident may be involved. It is required that he shall actually receive and receipt for notice of the service and a copy of the process. . . .

The state's power to regulate the use of its highways extends to their use by nonresidents as well as by residents. And, in advance of the operation of a motor vehicle on its highway by a nonresident, the state may require him to appoint one of its officials as his agent on whom process may be served in proceedings growing out of such use. . . . [H]aving the power so to exclude, the state may declare that the use of the highway by the nonresident is the equivalent of the appointment of the registrar as agent on whom process may be served. The difference between the formal and implied appointment is not substantial, so far as concerns the application of the due process clause of the Fourteenth Amendment.

Judgment affirmed.

REVIEW QUESTIONS

1. What is the basis for the exercise of jurisdiction over the nonresident motorist? Is this consistent with *Pennoyer*? What language in *Pennoyer* permits this?

2. Why would the Supreme Court condone so dubious a fiction as *implied* consent to suit? What is the relevance of the Court's assertion that "motor vehicles are dangerous machines" to the issue of jurisdiction? What policy concerns are beginning to enter into jurisdictional analysis?

3. Note that both the Massachusetts statute and the Supreme Court decision upholding it treat the matter of notice (the statute requires registered mail to the nonresident motorist) as separate and apart from the issue of adjudicatory power, which is based on service of process in Massachusetts on Hess's "appointed" representative, the Registrar of Motor Vehicles. The Court recognizes that the "process of one state cannot run into another and summon a party there domiciled to respond to proceedings against him. Notice sent outside the state to a nonresident is unavailing to give jurisdiction in an action against him personally for money recovery. There must be actual service within the state of notice upon him or upon someone authorized to accept service for him."

    Within the traditional *Pennoyer* scheme, notice and jurisdiction were virtually inseparable because the primary basis for establishing in personam jurisdiction, namely, service of process (complaint and summons) on defendant within the state, simultaneously provided notice of the lawsuit. Now, with the change in focus from in-state service on defendant to in-state *activities* by the defendant (a move finally accomplished in *International Shoe, below*), jurisdiction and notice travel divergent paths.

4. Contrast the direct attack mounted by Hess, who "appeared specially for the purpose of contesting jurisdiction," with Balk's challenge to jurisdiction in the previous case, a collateral attack in a subsequent proceeding.

5. Lest you think implied consent statutes are a relic of a distant past, Massachusetts still has a nonresident motorist statute, Mass. Gen. Laws ch. 90, § 3A; Florida has one for out-of-state operators of aircraft and watercraft, Fla. Stat. Ann. § 48.19; but South Dakota, a favorite of pheasant hunters, may take the prize:

> The hunting of game birds or animals in this state by a nonresident shall be deemed an appointment by such nonresident of the secretary of state of South Dakota to be his true and lawful attorney upon whom may be served legal process in any action or proceeding against such nonresident or his personal representative growing out of such hunting which results in damages or loss to person or property, and said hunting shall be a signification of such nonresident's agreement that any such process in any action against him or his personal representative which is so served shall be of the same legal force and validity as if served upon him, or his personal representative, personally.

S.D. Cod. Laws § 15-7-13.

D. THE MODERN CONCEPTION OF PERSONAL JURISDICTION

Under pressure from an ever-expanding interstate economy, the rigid *Pennoyer* framework was stretched to the breaking point to accommodate the aggressive reach of states seeking to provide local forums for citizens litigating claims against nonresident persons and corporations. In 1945, the Supreme Court finally replaced the outdated structure and discarded such fictions as implied consent in favor of a new formulation premised on actual connections between the defendant and forum state. (But as we will see, *Pennoyer* is not quite dead.) The vehicle was the following landmark case.

International Shoe Co. v. State of Washington
326 U.S. 310 (1945)

Chief Justice STONE delivered the opinion of the Court:

[We must decide] whether, within the limitations of the due process clause of the Fourteenth Amendment, appellant, a Delaware corporation, has by its activities in the State of Washington rendered itself amenable to proceedings in the courts of that state to recover unpaid contributions to the state unemployment compensation fund exacted by [the] Washington Unemployment Compensation Act.

The statutes in question set up a comprehensive scheme of unemployment compensation, the costs of which are defrayed by contributions required to be made by employers to a state unemployment compensation fund. . . . Section 14(c) of the Act authorizes respondent Commissioner to issue an order and notice of assessment of delinquent contributions upon prescribed personal service of the notice upon the employer if found within the state, or, if not so found, by mailing the notice to the employer by registered mail at his last known address. . . .

In this case notice of assessment for the years in question was personally served upon a sales solicitor employed by appellant in the State of Washington, and a copy of the notice was mailed by registered mail to appellant at its address in St. Louis, Missouri. Appellant appeared specially . . . and moved to set aside the order and notice of assessment on the ground that the service upon appellant's salesman was not proper service upon appellant; that appellant was not a corporation of the State of Washington and was not doing business within the state; that it had no agent within the state upon whom service could be made. . . .

[The state courts ruled against the Company.]

Appellant is a Delaware corporation, having its principal place of business in St. Louis, Missouri, and is engaged in the manufacture and sale of shoes and other footwear. It maintains places of business in several states, other than Washington, at which its manufacturing is carried on and from which its merchandise is distributed interstate through several sales units or branches located outside the State of Washington.

Appellant has no office in Washington and makes no contracts either for sale or purchase of merchandise there. It maintains no stock of merchandise in that state and makes there no deliveries of goods in intrastate commerce. During the years from 1937 to 1940, now in question, appellant employed eleven to thirteen salesmen under direct supervision and control of sales managers located in St. Louis. These salesmen resided in Washington; their principal activities were confined to that state; and they were compensated by commissions based upon the amount of their sales. The commissions for each year totaled more than $31,000. Appellant supplies its salesmen with a line of samples, each consisting of one shoe of a pair, which they display to prospective purchasers. On occasion they rent permanent sample rooms, for exhibiting samples, in business buildings, or rent rooms in hotels or business buildings temporarily for that purpose. The cost of such rentals is reimbursed by appellant.

The authority of the salesmen is limited to exhibiting their samples and soliciting orders from prospective buyers, at prices and on terms fixed by appellant. The salesmen transmit the orders to appellant's office in St. Louis for acceptance or rejection, and when accepted the merchandise for filling the orders is shipped f.o.b. from points outside Washington to the purchasers within the state. All the merchandise shipped into Washington is invoiced at the place of shipment from which collections are made. No salesman has authority to enter into contracts or to make collections. . . .

Appellant . . . insists that its activities within the state were not sufficient to manifest its "presence" there and that in its absence the state courts were without jurisdiction, that consequently it was a denial of due process for the state to subject appellant to suit. . . .

Historically the jurisdiction of courts to render judgment in personam is grounded on their de facto power over the defendant's person. Hence his presence within the territorial jurisdiction of the court was prerequisite to its rendition of a judgment personally binding him. *Pennoyer v. Neff*, 95 U.S. 714, 733. But now due process requires only that in order to subject a defendant to a judgment in personam, if he be not present within the territory of the forum, he have certain minimum contacts with it such that the maintenance of the suit does not offend "traditional notions of fair play and substantial justice." Those activities of the corporation's agent within the state which courts will deem to be sufficient to satisfy the demands of due process [are] such contacts of the corporation with the state of the forum as make it reasonable, in the context of our federal system of government, to require the corporation to defend the particular suit which is brought there. An "estimate of the inconveniences" which would result to the corporation from a trial away from its "home" or principal place of business is relevant in this connection.

[Jurisdiction] has never been doubted when the activities of the corporation there have not only been continuous and systematic, but also give rise to the liabilities sued on, even though no consent to be sued or authorization to an agent to accept service of process has been given. Conversely it has been generally recognized that the casual presence of the corporate agent or even his conduct of single or isolated items of activities in a state in the corporation's behalf are not enough to subject it to suit on causes of action unconnected with the activities there. To require the corporation in such circumstances to defend the suit away from its home or other jurisdiction where it carries on more substantial activities has been thought to lay too great and unreasonable a burden on the corporation to comport with due process. [And] there have been instances in which the continuous corporate operations within a state were thought so substantial and of such a nature as to justify suit against it on causes of action arising from dealings entirely distinct from those activities.

True, some of the decisions holding the corporation amenable to suit have been supported by resort to the legal fiction that it has given its consent to service and suit, consent being implied from its presence in the state through the acts of its authorized agents. But more realistically it may be said that those authorized acts were of such a nature as to justify the fiction.

It is evident that the criteria by which we mark the boundary line between those activities which justify the subjection of a corporation to suit, and those which do not, cannot be simply mechanical or quantitative. Whether due process is satisfied must depend rather upon the quality and nature of the activity in relation to the fair and orderly administration of the laws which it was the purpose of the due process clause to insure. That clause does not contemplate that a state may make binding a judgment in personam against an individual or corporate defendant with which the state has no contacts, ties, or relations.

But to the extent that a corporation exercises the privilege of conducting activities within a state, it enjoys the benefits and protection of the laws of that state. The exercise of that privilege may give rise to obligations; and, so far as those obligations arise out of or are connected with the activities within the state, a procedure which requires the corporation to respond to a suit brought to enforce them can, in most instances, hardly be said to be undue.

Applying these standards, the activities carried on in behalf of appellant in the State of Washington were neither irregular nor casual. They were systematic and continuous throughout the years in question. They resulted in a large volume of interstate business, in the course of which appellant received the benefits and protection of the laws of the state, including the right to resort to the courts for the enforcement of its rights. The obligation which is here sued upon arose out of those very activities. It is evident that these operations establish sufficient contacts or ties with the state of the forum to make it reasonable and just according to our traditional conception of fair play and substantial justice to permit the state to enforce the obligations which appellant has incurred there. Hence we cannot say that the maintenance of the present suit in the State of Washington involves an unreasonable or undue procedure. . . . Nor can we say that the mailing of the notice of suit to appellant by registered mail at its home office was not reasonably calculated to apprise appellant of the suit. . . .

Appellant having rendered itself amenable to suit upon obligations arising out of the activities of its salesmen in Washington, the state may maintain the present suit in personam to collect the tax laid upon the exercise of the privilege of employing appellant's salesmen within the state. . . .

Affirmed.

Justice JACKSON took no part in the consideration of the case.

Justice BLACK delivered the following opinion:

. . . I believe that the Federal Constitution leaves to each State, without any "ifs" or "buts," a power to open the doors of its courts for its citizens to sue corporations whose agents do business in those States. Believing that the Constitution gave the States that power, I think it a judicial deprivation to condition its exercise upon this Court's notion of "fair play," however appealing that term may be. Nor can I stretch the meaning of due process so far as to authorize this Court to deprive a State of the right to afford judicial protection to its citizens on the ground that it would be more "convenient" for the corporation to be sued somewhere else.

There is a strong emotional appeal in the words "fair play," "justice," and "reasonableness." But they were not chosen by those who wrote the original Constitution or the Fourteenth Amendment as a measuring rod for this Court to use in invalidating State or Federal laws passed by elected legislative representatives. No one, not even those who most feared a democratic government, ever formally proposed that courts should be given power to invalidate legislation under any such elastic standards. . . . For application of this natural law concept, whether under the terms "reasonableness," "justice," or "fair play," makes judges the supreme arbiters of the country's laws and practices. This result, I believe, alters the form of government our Constitution provides. I cannot agree.

YOUR TAKEAWAY

Recognizing that the *Pennoyer* conception of adjudicatory power (premised on physical presence of the defendant in the forum) had outlived its utility, and unwilling to resort to the workarounds that had kept it in place, Chief Justice Harlan Fisk Stone led the Court into the modern era. Now it would be the forum activities of nonresidents that would be the hook to subject them to lawsuits arising from those activities. A corporation that benefits from conducting business in a state must carry the burden of defending related suits there.

The new challenge for the courts was to define the "minimum contacts" necessary to satisfy the due process standard of "fair play and substantial justice."

REVIEW QUESTIONS

1. Consider how International Shoe Co. had structured its business practices. No offices or inventory were maintained outside its home state of Missouri. Sales representatives had no authority to enter into contracts in the states in which they worked—they merely solicited orders and transmitted them back to headquarters in St. Louis. Product was sent "F.O.B. St. Louis," which meant that customers legally took possession at the point of shipment, thus avoiding the appearance that deliveries were being made beyond the borders of Missouri. The only items belonging to International Shoe that could be found in Washington were the single-shoe samples that the sales representatives could display to potential purchasers, obviously lacking market value that could be attached. Can you see why the company did business in this very strange way, seemingly limiting its potential sales and profits? Would you also have advised them to choose another name that didn't include the word "international"?

2. Reconstruct the opposing arguments presented by the parties before the Supreme Court in *International Shoe.*

3. What is the new basis for the exercise of jurisdiction over a nonresident corporation? How would you articulate this framework of personal jurisdiction?

4. Chief Justice Stone observes that the "obligation which is here sued upon [contributions to the unemployment compensation fund] arose out of [International Shoe's] very activities [in Washington]." What is the significance of the link between (1) the nonresident's *level of activity* in the forum state; and (2) the *relation of the plaintiff's claim to that activity*? What considerations would draw the Court to focus on these two variables? Can you articulate the benefit/burden rationale that underlies Stone's theory of personal jurisdiction?

5. Where on the activity spectrum (high level of contacts in the state, mid-level, single act) did Chief Justice Stone place International Shoe Co.? Was it necessary to decide, given that the claim clearly arose out of the company's activities in Washington? Where would you place the defendant in *Hess v. Pawloski*? What about the defendant in *Harris v. Balk*? Or does that latter exercise of jurisdiction fall outside of Stone's in personam categories?

6. If the claim asserted against International Shoe had arisen from a collision between a company truck and a citizen of Washington vacationing in San Diego, California, would the state court in Washington have jurisdiction over International Shoe when the plaintiff returned home and filed a tort suit? (Assume the company has the same contacts with Washington as in the original case.) If not, where could plaintiff obtain adjudicatory power over International Shoe?

7. Employing between eleven and thirteen sales representatives who together generated total commissions of $31,000 per year was deemed sufficient "minimum contacts" with the state for suit against International Shoe on the related unemployment fund claim. Would six sales reps have sufficed? Three? What if there were *no* reps, but instead a catalogue or Internet operation run completely out-of-state, and a dissatisfied Seattle customer sued for breach of contract after delivery of the wrong items?

8. Whether constitutional standards are met, *International Shoe* teaches, depends "upon the quality and nature of the [defendant's] activity in relation to the fair and orderly administration of the laws which it was the purpose of the due process clause to insure." What kind of "test" is this? Note the Court's admonition that minimum contacts analysis "cannot be simply mechanical or quantitative." As Justice Thurgood Marshall later put it, the jurisdictional determination "is one in which few answers will be written in black and white. The greys are dominant and even among them the shades are innumerable." *Kulko v. Superior Court*, 436 U.S. 84, 92 (1978). On a similar note:

> The idea of black letter law seduces us. We crave coherence and certainty in the law as we do in many areas of our lives. We know better, of course. We know that legal doctrine is often indeterminate—that in a particular case, perfectly convincing arguments supporting one conclusion can often be countered by perfectly convincing arguments supporting the opposite conclusion. Yet we continue to search for rules, principles, tests, approaches—anything that will impose order on doctrine. Nowhere is

the inherent frustration of this quest more vividly illustrated than in the debates concerning the due process limitations on the assertion of personal jurisdiction by state courts.

Richard K. Greenstein, *The Nature of Legal Argument: The Personal Jurisdiction Paradigm*, 38 Hastings L.J. 855 (1987).

9. One court has warned about misreading the *International Shoe* standard:

> This rule of law has been truncated in the minds and jargon of lawyers to "minimum contact"; however, minimum contact does not mean "minimum" or "slight" contact. Minimum contact requires that a foreign defendant have at least enough contact with [the forum] to satisfy minimum standards of due process.

Leonard v. USA Petroleum Corp., 829 F. Supp. 882 (S.D. Tex. 1993).

QUESTIONS TO PONDER

1. What is left of *Pennoyer*? *International Shoe* presumably leaves intact the traditional bases for the exercise of jurisdiction: residence/domicile in the forum state, appearance in the action, service on defendant within the forum state, in rem power over claimants in a dispute over land, and quasi in rem power over nonresidents who have property in the state (but any judgment is limited to the value of the property). The decision supplements, but does not supplant, these time-honored avenues of obtaining adjudicatory power.

2. What does Justice Hugo Black think of terms like "fair play" and "reasonableness" as the measuring rods for adjudicatory power? What standard would he substitute?

3. Note Justice Black's originalist perspective in the last paragraph of his separate opinion. You'll encounter more about this in your Constitutional Law course, and in the current debate about constitutional interpretation.

E. NOTE ON LONG-ARM STATUTES

International Shoe established a constitutional basis for the exercise of personal jurisdiction that focused on the nonresident's* activities or contacts within the forum state. Constitutional power is not, however, self-executing. A court must first be authorized by appropriate legislation or otherwise to assert jurisdiction (look back at the Code of Oregon in *Pennoyer*, at Mass. Gen. Laws ch. 90 in *Hess*,

---

* Although *International Shoe* involved a corporate defendant, we will see that the minimum contacts analysis was soon applied to individual defendants as well.

and at § 14(c) of the Washington Statutes in *International Shoe*). Only then is the minimum-contacts analysis employed to determine whether the particular assertion is within the permissible boundaries of due process.

In the years following *International Shoe*, states enacted "long-arm" statutes that authorized their courts to exercise jurisdiction over nonresidents who engaged in certain enumerated acts within the state. Typical among them is New York's CPLR § 302:

> Personal jurisdiction by acts of non-domiciliaries.
>
> (a) Acts which are the basis of jurisdiction. As to a cause of action arising from any of the acts enumerated in this section, a court may exercise personal jurisdiction over any non-domiciliary, or his executor or administrator, who in person or through an agent:
>
> (1) transacts any business within the state or contracts anywhere to supply goods or services in the state; or
>
> (2) commits a tortious act within the state, except as to a cause of action for defamation of character arising from the act; or
>
> (3) commits a tortious act without the state causing injury to person or property within the state, except as to a cause of action for defamation of character arising from the act, if he
>
>> (i) regularly does or solicits business, or engages in any other persistent course of conduct, or derives substantial revenue from goods used or consumed or services rendered, in the state, or
>>
>> (ii) expects or should reasonably expect the act to have consequences in the state and derives substantial revenue from interstate or international commerce; or
>
> (4) owns, uses or possesses any real property situated within the state. . . .

Examples of other state long-arm statutes appear in your rules supplement.

The Nexus Requirement. Note that the jurisdiction authorized by this long-arm statute is typically limited to claims *"arising from"* the enumerated act. Chief Justice Stone's constitutional analysis in *International Shoe* makes clear that such "specific jurisdiction" can extend only to claims *related to* the in-state activities. The Supreme Court has provided little guidance on what exactly satisfies this nexus requirement, leaving lower courts to formulate their own tests to determine whether a claim sufficiently "arises from" or "relates to" the defendant's contacts with the forum state.

In *Crocker v. Hilton International Barbados, Ltd.*, 976 F.2d 797 (1st Cir. 1992), for example, where the Massachusetts plaintiff alleged that her rape resulted from lax hotel security, the court affirmed dismissal for lack of personal jurisdiction in her home state. She asserted jurisdiction based on the facts that she had booked the room through a travel agency in Massachusetts, and that Hilton had advertised the Barbados hotel there as well. But it is not enough that a defendant "transact business" in the forum state within the meaning of the long-arm statute, the Court concluded—the crucial question is whether plaintiff's claim *arose out of* this activity. Here it did not—the booking and advertising were deemed too remote from the events on the island to satisfy the nexus requirement.

A similar result followed in *Bell v. Imperial Palace Hotel/Casino, Inc.*, 200 F. Supp. 2d 1082 (E.D. Mo. 2001), where plaintiffs sought damages for personal injuries suffered at the defendant hotel in Las Vegas, Nevada. The Bells' effort to base jurisdiction in their home state solely on a website maintained by Imperial Palace, and accessible to residents in Missouri, failed because neither plaintiffs nor their travel agent booked the reservation on the website, or even claimed to have ever viewed it. "The Court can see no causal link or relationship between Mr. Bell's accident and the sole forum contact by Imperial Palace, its website. Without such a connection, specific personal jurisdiction does not exist." 200 F. Supp. 2d at 1088.

Some courts have applied a more relaxed standard. The Ninth Circuit uses a broad "but for" test (e.g., "but-for" defendants' distribution of the software in California, plaintiffs' copyright infringement claims would not have arisen. *Metro-Goldwyn-Mayer Studios, Inc. v. Grokster, Ltd.*, 243 F.Supp.2d 1073 (9th Cir. 2003)). Others ask whether a plaintiff's claim is a foreseeable result of the defendant's contacts with the forum, borrowing from the tort concept of *proximate cause. See Pizarro v. Hoteles Concorde Int'l, C.A.*, 907 F.2d 1256 (1st Cir.1990).

The California Supreme Court requires only that there be "a substantial nexus"—a claim need not arise directly from the defendant's forum contacts in order to be sufficiently related to the contact to warrant the exercise of specific jurisdiction." *Snowney v. Harrah's Entertainment, Inc.*, 35 Cal. 4th 1054, 1068, 112 P.3d 28, 43 (2005). The California resident's class action alleged the Nevada hotel had failed to notify guests that an energy surcharge would be imposed at checkout. The hotel advertised heavily in California and maintained a website that permitted visitors to make reservations by credit card. Although plaintiff had made his reservations by phone, and there was no indication he had ever accessed the website or been induced by the ads, the Court applied a "sliding scale" approach (which we will see again later on in *Bristol-Myers Squibb Co. v. Superior Court*, 137 S. Ct. 1773 (2017)) and affirmed the exercise of specific jurisdiction over the hotel "because the harm alleged by plaintiff relate[d] directly to the content of defendants' promotional activities in California, an inherent relationship between plaintiff's claims and defendants' contacts with California exists." *Id.* at 1069.

And in *Shoppers Food Warehouse v. Moreno*, 746 A.2d 320, 332-336 (D.C. Ct. App. 2000), the District of Columbia Court of Appeals applied a "related to or discernible relationship" standard, which permitted the exercise of jurisdiction over the Maryland supermarket in a slip and fall case brought by a District resident injured there, based on defendant's weekly ads in District newspapers, even though plaintiff did not contend that the ads had brought her to the store.

For more on the concept of "relatedness" between the claim and defendant's activities, *see* Lea Brilmayer, *Related Contacts and Personal Jurisdiction*, 101 Harv. L. Rev. 1444 (1988), and Mary Twitchell, *A Rejoinder to Professor Brilmayer*, 101 Harv. L. Rev. 1465 (1988); Charles W. Rhodes and Cassandra Burke Robertson, *Toward a New Equilibrium in Personal Jurisdiction*, 48 U.C. Davis L. Rev. 207 (2014).

Long-Arm Statute Analysis. Determining whether a court may assert jurisdiction over a nonresident pursuant to a long-arm statute requires a two-step inquiry:

1. Does the plaintiff's claim *arise from* activity of the defendant that fits within *an enumerated category?*
2. If so, would application of the statute nonetheless reach beyond the constitutional constraints of *International Shoe*'s minimum-contacts test?

The first question is one of statutory construction; the second involves the substantial body of constitutional case law that has developed since 1945, to be explored in the pages that follow.

Rather than spelling out specific acts, as New York's CPLR § 302 does, some states have opted for an open-ended approach. California, for example, provides: "A court of this state may exercise jurisdiction on any basis not inconsistent with the Constitution of this state or of the United States." Cal. Code Civ. Proc. § 410.10. This scheme collapses the usual two-step inquiry (statutory authority and constitutionality of application) into one.

MORE TO PONDER

For a history of long-arm legislation and a survey of the state statutes, *see* Douglas D. McFarland, *Dictum Run Wild: How Long-Arm Statutes Extended to the Limits of Due Process*, 84 B. U. L. Rev. 491 (2004).

F. NOTE ON SPECIFIC AS COMPARED TO GENERAL JURISDICTION

As previously noted, long-arm statutes do not replace the traditional grounds for in personam jurisdiction, namely domicile, citizenship, incorporation, service of process in the forum state, appearance in court, and consent. Rather, they implement the constitutional authority at the lower end of the activity spectrum to reach nonresidents who engage in *particular* activities in the forum that give rise to the plaintiff's claim.

The *specific jurisdiction* authorized by long-arm statutes must be compared with *general jurisdiction*, which is power over *all* claims, whether related to defendant's activities within the forum state or not. General jurisdiction flows from the traditional bases of jurisdiction listed above. Thus, for example, an individual or corporate citizen may be sued in its home state on claims arising there *or elsewhere.*

International Shoe held that a corporate nonresident's conduct of continuous, systematic, and substantial business in the forum would also subject it to general jurisdiction over any claim, regardless of where it arose. *Perkins v. Benguet Consolidated Mining Co.*, 342 U.S. 437 (1952) held that an Ohio state court could properly exercise jurisdiction over a Philippine corporation on a stockholder's claim even though it did not arise from anything defendant did in Ohio. The mining company had relocated its president to Ohio for the duration of the Japanese military occupation of the Philippine Islands. At his new office there, he kept the company files, carried on correspondence, drew salary checks, maintained a bank account, and held directors' meetings—in other words, he carried on "a continuous and systematic supervision of the necessarily limited wartime activities of the company." Given this level of activity, it would not (the Court held) violate due process for Ohio to assert jurisdiction on the plaintiff's claim for dividends despite the fact that it arose from transactions conducted entirely outside the forum state.

We will have more to say about general jurisdiction, and some recent Supreme Court pronouncements limiting its reach, in Part M of this chapter.

In contrast, at the low end of the activity spectrum is *McGee v. International Life Insurance Co.*, 355 U.S. 220 (1957), a suit by the beneficiary of her deceased son's life insurance policy. International Life had no office or agent in the forum state of California and had not, as far as the record indicated, ever solicited or conducted any business there except for the *one* policy sued upon that was sold through the mail. The California court nonetheless exercised specific jurisdiction based on a statute subjecting nonresident insurance companies to suit on policies entered into with residents.

When the company failed to appear, McGee recovered a default judgment for the death benefit, which she then sought to enforce in defendant's home state of Texas. The courts there refused, holding that the judgment was not entitled to full faith and credit because the California court lacked jurisdiction over International Life.

The Supreme Court reversed in a landmark decision authored by Justice Black, who noted a "clearly discernible trend" toward expanding the scope of jurisdiction over nonresidents. Given "the fundamental transformation of our national economy over the years," he wrote, "today many commercial transactions touch two or more States and may involve parties separated by the full continent. With this increasing nationalization of commerce has come a great increase in the amount of business conducted by mail across state lines. At the same time modern transportation and communication have made it much less burdensome for a party sued to defend himself in a State where he engages in economic activity." 355 U.S. at 222-223.

Reflecting the high-water mark of specific jurisdiction, *McGee* concluded that the Due Process Clause allowed the California court to enter a judgment binding on the Texas company, notwithstanding its scant contact with the forum state:

> It is sufficient for purposes of due process that the suit was based on a contract that had substantial connection with that state. The contract was delivered

in California, the premiums were mailed from there, and the insured was a resident of that state when he died. It cannot be denied that California has a manifest interest in providing effective means of redress for its residents when their insurers refuse to pay claims. These residents would be at a severe disadvantage if they were forced to follow the insurance company to a distant state in order to hold it legally accountable. When claims were small or moderate, individual claimants frequently could not afford the cost of bringing an action in a foreign forum—thus in effect making the company judgment-proof. Often the crucial witnesses—as here on the company's defense of suicide—will be found in the insured's locality. Of course, there may be inconvenience to the insurer if it is held amenable to suit in California, where it had this contract, but certainly nothing that amounts to a denial of due process. There is no contention that respondent did not have adequate notice or sufficient time to prepare its defenses and appear.

355 U.S. at 222-224.

QUESTIONS TO PONDER

Can you detect a foreshadowing of this expansive approach in Justice Black's separate opinion in *International Shoe*? What social policy considerations entered into his elaboration of due process doctrine? As you read the cases to follow, consider the accuracy of Hugo Black's perception of a "clearly discernible trend" toward expanding specific jurisdiction.

G. NOTE ON PERSONAL JURISDICTION IN FEDERAL COURT

A common source of confusion for students is the matter of personal jurisdiction in federal court. Given the focus on *state* sovereignty and *state* boundaries in *Pennoyer* and *International Shoe*, together with the fact that the Fourteenth Amendment Due Process Clause limits only *state* power, one might assume that a *federal* trial court would not be limited by state geography in its jurisdictional reach. This assumption would, however, be only partially correct. Although the constitutional constraints on a federal court's exercise of jurisdiction (found in the Fifth Amendment's Due Process Clause) are defined by the *national* boundaries of the United States, the federal courts have not been afforded the full extent of their potential adjudicatory power.

The vehicle controlling personal jurisdiction in federal court is Fed. R. Civ. P. 4, which on its face seems only to deal with service of process. But look at 4(k)(1)(A), which incorporates the local state long-arm statute as a constraint on federal court jurisdiction. The jurisdictional reach of a federal district court in Illinois is consequently determined by, and equivalent to, the reach of the state trial courts there. If federal courts offered plaintiffs a longer reach than state courts, consider the considerable incentive for forum shopping (to be discussed in Chapter 9) that would be created.

There are some notable exceptions to the equation of federal and state long-arm jurisdiction. Fed. R. Civ. P. 4(k)(1)(B), the so-called 100-mile bulge rule, authorizes jurisdiction over an impleaded party not otherwise within the district court's reach if service is effected within 100 miles of the court. Subsection (C) provides for nationwide service when authorized by a federal statute—an interpleader action under 28 U.S.C. § 1335, for example, would implicate this provision. And, more dramatically, Fed. R. Civ. P. 4(k)(2) extends federal power to its outermost constitutional limits in federal question cases (28 U.S.C. § 1331).

Fed. R. Civ. P. 4(k)(2)—The "Federal Long-Arm Statute" and Jurisdiction over Foreign Corporations

With an increasingly global economy, it becomes more and more common for plaintiffs in U.S. courts to seek recovery against foreign corporate defendants. As we will see, the constraints of minimum-contacts analysis can make obtaining personal jurisdiction over such entities in state courts quite difficult.

It was in this context that Fed. R. Civ. P. 4(k)(2) was added in 1993 to allow federal courts to exercise personal jurisdiction "over the person of any defendant who is not subject to the jurisdiction of the courts of general jurisdiction of any state" when sued on claims arising under federal law, and where "the exercise of jurisdiction is consistent with the Constitution and laws of the United States." The Advisory Committee Note explains:

> The paragraph corrects a gap in the enforcement of federal law. Under the former rule, a problem was presented when the defendant was a non-resident of the United States having contacts with the United States sufficient to justify the application of United States law and to satisfy federal standards for forum selection, but having insufficient contact with any single state to support jurisdiction under state long-arm legislation or meet the requirements of the Fourteenth Amendment limitation on state court territorial jurisdiction. In such cases, the defendant was shielded from the enforcement of federal law by the fortuity of a favorable limitation on the power of state courts, which was incorporated into federal practice by the former rule.

Three elements are required for the exercise of jurisdiction under 4(k)(2): (1) the claim must arise under federal law; (2) the defendant must be beyond the jurisdictional reach of any state court; and (3) the exercise of jurisdiction must not violate the defendant's rights under the Constitution, meaning that even though defendant's contacts are so scattered that no one state has jurisdiction, there are *sufficient aggregate contacts* with the United States as a whole to satisfy the Fifth Amendment's Due Process Clause.

The first two elements were made out in *United States v. Swiss American Bank, Ltd.*, 274 F.3d 610 (1st Cir. 2001), in which the government sued under the RICO (Racketeer Influenced and Corrupt Organizations) Act to recover illegal drug proceeds that had been forfeited by a depositor in the foreign bank incorporated and located in Antigua. But the third requirement was held lacking, the Court of Appeals finding insufficient ties to the United States because the Bank had no physical presence and only intermittent contacts (such as the placing of advertisements in an airline magazine). Moreover, the Bank had not solicited the depositor's business in the United States; rather, he had opened the accounts in Antigua with moneys from outside the United States. *See also BP Chemicals Ltd. v. Formosa Chemical & Fibre Corp.*, 229 F.3d 254 (3d Cir. 2000) (defendant had insufficient purposeful contacts with United States).

For cases that did exercise jurisdiction over foreign defendants pursuant to 4(k)(2), *see ISI International, Inc. v. Borden Ladner Gervais LLP*, 256 F.3d 548 (7th Cir. 2001) (Canadian law firm, sued under federal law that forbids making false or deceptive statements in connection with commercial activities in interstate commerce, had sufficient aggregate contacts with several states to be sued in federal court in Illinois) and *Graduate Management Admission Council v. Raju*, 241 F. Supp. 2d 589 (E.D. Va. 2003) (Indian Internet website operator who specifically targeted U.S. customers was suable for copyright and trademark infringement). In *Mwani v. Osama bin Laden*, 417 F.3d 1 (D.C. Cir. 2005), the provision was invoked to assert jurisdiction over bin Laden in an Alien Tort Claims action, finding he had "engaged in unabashedly malignant actions directed at and felt in this forum" by directing his terror at the United States.

MORE TO PONDER

We will revisit the topic of personal jurisdiction in the context of international claims later on in this chapter. For further discussion of Fed. R. Civ. P. 4(k)(2) as well as other bases of federal adjudicatory authority in international disputes, *see* Stephen B. Burbank, *The United States' Approach to International Civil Litigation: Recent Developments in Forum Selection*, 19 U. Pa. J. Intl. Econ. L. 1 (1998); Thomas Main, *Global Issues in Civil Procedure*, 63-74 (2006).

H. MINIMUM-CONTACTS ANALYSIS IN OPERATION

Like much legal doctrine in its initial stages, *International Shoe*'s minimum contacts formulation left many unanswered questions, and considerable room for analytical development by courts in the face of live cases.

One of the most important elaborations came in *Hanson v. Denckla*, 357 U.S. 235 (1958). While residing in Pennsylvania, Dora Donner established a trust with the Wilmington Trust Co. of Delaware as trustee. She retained the right to receive the income until her death and to designate the beneficiaries who would ultimately get her substantial assets. Donner later moved to Florida, where before her death she designated the children of one of her three daughters to receive the payouts from the trust. She died a resident of Florida.

The two daughters whose children were not provided for filed suit in Florida state court challenging the disposition of the trust. The court exercised jurisdiction over the Delaware trustee, and invalidated the trust on technical grounds. When the daughters sought to enforce the decree against the trustee in its home state of Delaware, however, the courts there ruled that it was not entitled to full faith and credit because the Florida court possessed neither in personam jurisdiction over the Wilmington Trust Co., nor in rem jurisdiction over the assets of the trust located in Delaware. The U.S. Supreme Court agreed:

> [The parties seeking to enforce the Florida decree] urge that the circumstances of this case amount to sufficient affiliation with the State of Florida to empower its courts to exercise personal jurisdiction over this nonresident defendant. Principal reliance is placed upon *McGee v. International Life Ins. Co.* In *McGee* the Court noted the trend of expanding personal jurisdiction over nonresidents. . . .
>
> But it is a mistake to assume that this trend heralds the eventual demise of all restrictions on the personal jurisdiction of state courts. Those restrictions are more than a guarantee of immunity from inconvenient or distant litigation. They are a consequence of territorial limitations on the power of the respective States. However minimal the burden of defending in a foreign tribunal, a defendant may not be called upon to do so unless he has had the "minimal contacts" with that State that are a prerequisite to its exercise of power over him.
>
> We fail to find such contacts in the circumstances of this case. The defendant trust company has no office in Florida, and transacts no business there. None of the trust assets has ever been held or administered in Florida, and the record discloses no solicitation of business in that State either in person or by mail.
>
> The cause of action in this case is not one that arises out of an act done or transaction consummated in the forum State. In that respect, it differs from *McGee v. International Life Ins. Co.* In *McGee*, the nonresident defendant solicited a reinsurance agreement with a resident of California. The offer was accepted in that State, and the insurance premiums were mailed from there until the insured's death. Noting the interest California has in providing effective redress for its residents when nonresident insurers refuse to pay claims on insurance they have solicited in that State, the Court upheld jurisdiction because the suit was based on a contract which had substantial connection with that State. In contrast, this action involves the validity of an agreement that was entered without any connection with the forum State. The agreement was executed in Delaware by a trust company incorporated in that State and a settlor domiciled in Pennsylvania. The first relationship Florida had to the agreement was years later when the settlor became domiciled there, and the trustee remitted the trust income to her in that State. From Florida Mrs. Donner carried on several bits of trust administration that may be compared to the mailing of premiums in *McGee.* But the record discloses no instance in which the trustee performed any acts in Florida that bear the same relationship to the agreement as the solicitation in *McGee.* Consequently, this suit cannot be said to be one to enforce an obligation that arose from a privilege the defendant exercised in Florida.

357 U.S. at 250-252.

The Court went on to emphasize that the "unilateral activity of those who claim some relationship with a nonresident defendant cannot satisfy the requirement of contact with the forum State. It is essential in each case that

there be *some act by which the defendant purposefully avails itself of the privilege of con-*
ducting activities within the forum State, thus invoking the benefits and protections
of its laws." 357 U.S. at 253 (emphasis added). The trust company was connected to Florida only because its client chose to relocate there.

So much for the trend observed by Justice Black, just one year before *Hanson*,
toward liberalizing the restrictions on personal jurisdiction. The "purposeful
availment" gloss on the minimum contacts test has proven to be a substantial
constraint on the exercise of adjudicatory power, as we will see in our next case.

World-Wide Volkswagen Corp. v. Woodson
444 U.S. 286 (1980)

Justice WHITE delivered the opinion of the Court:

The issue before us is whether, consistently with the Due Process Clause of
the Fourteenth Amendment, an Oklahoma court may exercise in personam jurisdiction over a nonresident automobile retailer and its wholesale distributor in a
products-liability action, when the defendants' only connection with Oklahoma
is the fact that an automobile sold in New York to New York residents became
involved in an accident in Oklahoma.

I

Respondents Harry and Kay Robinson purchased a new Audi automo-
bile from petitioner Seaway in Massena, N.Y., in 1976. The following year the
Robinson family, who resided in New York, left that State for a new home in
Arizona. As they passed through the State of Oklahoma, another car struck their
Audi in the rear, causing a fire which severely burned Kay Robinson and her two
children.[1]

The Robinsons subsequently brought a products-liability action in the District
Court for Creek County, Okla., claiming that their injuries resulted from defective design and placement of the Audi's gas tank and fuel system. They joined
as defendants the automobile's manufacturer, Audi; its importer, Volkswagen;
its regional distributor, petitioner World-Wide; and its retail dealer, petitioner
Seaway. Seaway and World-Wide entered special appearances,[3] claiming that
Oklahoma's exercise of jurisdiction over them would offend the limitations on
the State's jurisdiction imposed by the Due Process Clause of the Fourteenth
Amendment.

The facts presented to the District Court showed that World-Wide is
incorporated and has its business office in New York. It distributes vehicles,

---

1. The driver of the other automobile does not figure in the present litigation.

3. Volkswagen also entered a special appearance in the District Court, but unlike World-Wide
and Seaway did not seek review in the Supreme Court of Oklahoma and is not a petitioner here. Both
Volkswagen and Audi remain as defendants in the litigation pending before the District Court in
Oklahoma.

parts, and accessories, under contract with Volkswagen, to retail dealers in New York, New Jersey, and Connecticut. Seaway, one of these retail dealers, is incorporated and has its place of business in New York. Insofar as the record reveals, Seaway and World-Wide are fully independent corporations whose relations with each other and with Volkswagen and Audi are contractual only. Respondents adduced no evidence that either World-Wide or Seaway does any business in Oklahoma, ships or sells any products to or in that State, has an agent to receive process there, or purchases advertisements in any media calculated to reach Oklahoma. In fact, as respondents' counsel conceded at oral argument, there was no showing that any automobile sold by World-Wide or Seaway has ever entered Oklahoma with the single exception of the vehicle involved in the present case.

Despite the apparent paucity of contacts between petitioners and Oklahoma, the District Court rejected their constitutional claim. Petitioners then sought a writ of prohibition* in the Supreme Court of Oklahoma to restrain the District Judge, respondent Charles S. Woodson, from exercising in personam jurisdiction over them. They renewed their contention that, because they had no "minimal contacts," with the State of Oklahoma, the actions of the District Judge were in violation of their rights under the Due Process Clause.

The Supreme Court of Oklahoma denied the writ, holding that personal jurisdiction over petitioners was authorized by Oklahoma's "long-arm" statute, Okla. Stat., Tit. 12, § 1701.03(a)(4).[7] Although the court noted that the proper approach was to test jurisdiction against both statutory and constitutional standards, its analysis did not distinguish these questions, probably because § 1701.03(a)(4) has been interpreted as conferring jurisdiction to the limits permitted by the U.S. Constitution. The court's rationale was contained in the following paragraph:

> In the case before us, the product being sold and distributed by the petitioners is by its very design and purpose so mobile that petitioners can foresee its possible use in Oklahoma. This is especially true of the distributor, who has the exclusive right to distribute such automobile in New York, New Jersey and Connecticut. The evidence presented below demonstrated that goods sold and distributed by the petitioners were used in the State of Oklahoma, and under the facts we believe it reasonable to infer, given the retail value of the automobile, that the petitioners derive substantial income from automobiles which from time to time are used in the State of Oklahoma. This being the case, we hold that under the facts presented, the trial court was justified in concluding that the petitioners derive substantial revenue from goods used or consumed in this State.

---

* *Eds.' Note:* This writ was the best available means for an immediate appeal of the trial judge's ruling refusing to dismiss the action.

7. This subsection provides: "A court may exercise personal jurisdiction over a person, who acts directly or by an agent, as to a cause of action or claim for relief arising from the person's . . . causing tortious injury in this state by act or omission outside this state if he regularly does or solicits business or engages in any other persistent course of conduct, or derives substantial revenue from goods used or consumed or services rendered, in this state. . . ."

We granted certiorari to consider an important constitutional question with respect to state-court jurisdiction and to resolve a conflict between the Supreme Court of Oklahoma and the highest courts of at least four other States. We reverse.

II

The Due Process Clause of the Fourteenth Amendment limits the power of a state court to render a valid personal judgment against a nonresident defendant. A judgment rendered in violation of due process is void in the rendering State and is not entitled to full faith and credit elsewhere. *Pennoyer v. Neff*, 95 U.S. 714, 732-733 (1877). Due process requires that the defendant be given adequate notice of the suit, and be subject to the personal jurisdiction of the court. In the present case, it is not contended that notice was inadequate; the only question is whether these particular petitioners were subject to the jurisdiction of the Oklahoma courts.

As has long been settled, and as we reaffirm today, a state court may exercise personal jurisdiction over a nonresident defendant only so long as there exist "minimum contacts" between the defendant and the forum State. *International Shoe Co. v. Washington*. The concept of minimum contacts, in turn, can be seen to perform two related, but distinguishable, functions. It protects the defendant against the burdens of litigating in a distant or inconvenient forum. And it acts to ensure that the States through their courts, do not reach out beyond the limits imposed on them by their status as coequal sovereigns in a federal system.

The protection against inconvenient litigation is typically described in terms of "reasonableness" or "fairness." We have said that the defendant's contacts with the forum State must be such that maintenance of the suit "does not offend 'traditional notions of fair play and substantial justice.'" *International Shoe Co. v. Washington*. The relationship between the defendant and the forum must be such that it is "reasonable . . . to require the corporation to defend the particular suit which is brought there." Implicit in this emphasis on reasonableness is the understanding that the burden on the defendant, while always a primary concern, will in an appropriate case be considered in light of other relevant factors, including the forum State's interest in adjudicating the dispute; the plaintiff's interest in obtaining convenient and effective relief, at least when that interest is not adequately protected by the plaintiff's power to choose the forum; the interstate judicial system's interest in obtaining the most efficient resolution of controversies; and the shared interest of the several States in furthering fundamental substantive social policies.

The limits imposed on state jurisdiction by the Due Process Clause, in its role as a guarantor against inconvenient litigation, have been substantially relaxed over the years. As we noted in *McGee v. International Life Ins. Co.*, this trend is largely attributable to a fundamental transformation in the American economy: "Today many commercial transactions touch two or more States and may involve parties separated by the full continent. With this increasing nationalization of commerce has come a great increase in the amount of business conducted by mail across state lines. At the same time modern transportation and communication have made it much less burdensome for a party sued to defend himself in a State where he engages in economic activity." The historical developments noted in *McGee*, of course, have only accelerated in the generation since that case was decided.

Nevertheless, we have never accepted the proposition that state lines are irrelevant for jurisdictional purposes, nor could we, and remain faithful to the principles of interstate federalism embodied in the Constitution. The economic interdependence of the States was foreseen and desired by the Framers. In the Commerce Clause, they provided that the Nation was to be a common market, a "free trade unit" in which the States are debarred from acting as separable economic entities. But the Framers also intended that the States retain many essential attributes of sovereignty, including, in particular, the sovereign power to try causes in their courts. The sovereignty of each State, in turn, implied a limitation on the sovereignty of all of its sister States—a limitation express or implicit in both the original scheme of the Constitution and the Fourteenth Amendment.

Hence, even while abandoning the shibboleth that "[t]he authority of every tribunal is necessarily restricted by the territorial limits of the State in which it is established," *Pennoyer v. Neff*, we emphasized that the reasonableness of asserting jurisdiction over the defendant must be assessed "in the context of our federal system of government."

[T]he Due Process Clause "does not contemplate that a state may make binding a judgment in personam against an individual or corporate defendant with which the state has no contacts, ties, or relations." *International Shoe Co. v. Washington*. Even if the defendant would suffer minimal or no inconvenience from being forced to litigate before the tribunals of another State; even if the forum State has a strong interest in applying its law to the controversy; even if the forum State is the most convenient location for litigation, the Due Process Clause, acting as an instrument of interstate federalism, may sometimes act to divest the State of its power to render a valid judgment. *Hanson v. Denckla*, 357 U.S. 235.

III

Applying these principles to the case at hand, we find in the record before us a total absence of those affiliating circumstances that are a necessary predicate to any exercise of state-court jurisdiction. Petitioners carry on no activity whatsoever in Oklahoma. They close no sales and perform no services there. They avail themselves of none of the privileges and benefits of Oklahoma law. They solicit no business there either through salespersons or through advertising reasonably calculated to reach the State. Nor does the record show that they regularly sell cars at wholesale or retail to Oklahoma customers or residents or that they indirectly, through others, serve or seek to serve the Oklahoma market.

In short, respondents seek to base jurisdiction on one, isolated occurrence and whatever inferences can be drawn therefrom: the fortuitous circumstance that a single Audi automobile, sold in New York to New York residents, happened to suffer an accident while passing through Oklahoma.

It is argued, however, that because an automobile is mobile by its very design and purpose it was "foreseeable" that the Robinsons' Audi would cause injury in Oklahoma. Yet "foreseeability" alone has never been a sufficient benchmark for personal jurisdiction under the Due Process Clause. . . .

If foreseeability were the criterion, a local California tire retailer could be forced to defend in Pennsylvania when a blowout occurs there, *see Erlanger Mills, Inc. v. Cohoes Fibre Mills, Inc.*, 239 F.2d 502, 507 (4th Cir. 1956); a Wisconsin seller of a defective automobile jack could be haled before a distant court for damage caused in New Jersey, *Reilly v. Phil Tolkan Pontiac, Inc.*, 372 F. Supp. 1205 (N.J. 1974); or a Florida soft-drink concessionaire could be summoned to Alaska to account for injuries happening there. Every seller of chattels would in effect appoint the chattel his agent for service of process. His amenability to suit would travel with the chattel. We recently abandoned the outworn rule of *Harris v. Balk*, that the interest of a creditor in a debt could be extinguished or otherwise affected by any State having transitory jurisdiction over the debtor. *Shaffer v. Heitner*, 433 U.S. 186 (1977) [see Part J, below]. Having [interred] the mechanical rule that a creditor's amenability to a *quasi in rem* action travels with his debtor, we are unwilling to endorse an analogous principle in the present case.

This is not to say, of course, that foreseeability is wholly irrelevant. But the foreseeability that is critical to due process analysis is not the mere likelihood that a product will find its way into the forum State. Rather, it is that the defendant's conduct and connection with the forum State are such that he should reasonably anticipate being haled into court there. The Due Process Clause, by ensuring the "orderly administration of the laws," *International Shoe Co. v. Washington*, gives a degree of predictability to the legal system that allows potential defendants to structure their primary conduct with some minimum assurance as to where that conduct will and will not render them liable to suit.

When a corporation "purposefully avails itself of the privilege of conducting activities within the forum State," it has clear notice that it is subject to suit there, and can act to alleviate the risk of burdensome litigation by procuring insurance, passing the expected costs on to customers, or, if the risks are too great, severing its connection with the State. Hence if the sale of a product of a manufacturer or distributor such as Audi or Volkswagen is not simply an isolated occurrence, but arises from the efforts of the manufacturer or distributor to serve directly or indirectly, the market for its product in other States, it is not unreasonable to subject it to suit in one of those States if its allegedly defective merchandise has there been the source of injury to its owner or to others. The forum State does not exceed its powers under the Due Process Clause if it asserts personal jurisdiction over a corporation that delivers its products into the stream of commerce with the expectation that they will be purchased by consumers in the forum State. *Cf. Gray v. American Radiator & Standard Sanitary Corp.*, 22 Ill. 2d 432 (1961).

But there is no such or similar basis for Oklahoma jurisdiction over World-Wide or Seaway in this case. Seaway's sales are made in Massena, N.Y. World-Wide's market, although substantially larger, is limited to dealers in New York, New Jersey, and Connecticut. There is no evidence of record that any automobiles distributed by World-Wide are sold to retail customers outside this tristate area. It is foreseeable that the purchasers of automobiles sold by World-Wide and Seaway may take them to Oklahoma. But the mere "unilateral activity of those who claim some relationship with a nonresident defendant cannot satisfy the requirement of contact with the forum State." *Hanson v. Denckla*, 357 U.S. 235.

. . . Respondents observe that the very purpose of an automobile is to travel, and that travel of automobiles sold by petitioners is facilitated by an extensive chain of Volkswagen service centers throughout the country, including some in Oklahoma. However, financial benefits accruing to the defendant from a collateral relation to the forum State will not support jurisdiction if they do not stem from a constitutionally cognizable contact with that State. In our view, whatever marginal revenues petitioners may receive by virtue of the fact that their products are capable of use in Oklahoma is far too attenuated a contact to justify that State's exercise of in personam jurisdiction over them.

Because we find that petitioners have no "contacts, ties, or relations" with the State of Oklahoma, the judgment of the Supreme Court of Oklahoma is Reversed.

Justice BRENNAN, dissenting:
. . . Because I believe that the Court reads *International Shoe* and its progeny too narrowly, and because I believe that the standards enunciated by those cases may already be obsolete as constitutional boundaries, I dissent. I would find that the forum State has an interest in permitting the litigation to go forward, the litigation is connected to the forum, the defendant is linked to the forum, and the burden of defending is not unreasonable. Accordingly, I would hold that it is neither unfair nor unreasonable to require these defendants to defend in the forum State. . . .

The interest of the forum State and its connection to the litigation is strong. The automobile accident underlying the litigation occurred in Oklahoma. The plaintiffs were hospitalized in Oklahoma when they brought suit. Essential witnesses and evidence were in Oklahoma. The State has a legitimate interest in enforcing its laws designed to keep its highway system safe, and the trial can proceed at least as efficiently in Oklahoma as anywhere else.

The petitioners are not unconnected with the forum. Although both sell automobiles within limited sales territories, each sold the automobile which in fact was driven to Oklahoma where it was involved in an accident. It may be true, as the Court suggests, that each sincerely intended to limit its commercial impact to the limited territory, and that each intended to accept the benefits and protection of the laws only of those States within the territory. But obviously these were unrealistic hopes that cannot be treated as an automatic constitutional shield. . . .

The sale of an automobile does purposefully inject the vehicle into the stream of interstate commerce so that it can travel to distant States. It is difficult to see why the Constitution should distinguish between a case involving goods which reach a distant State through a chain of distribution and a case involving goods which reach the same State because a consumer, using them as the dealer knew the customer would, took them there. In each case the seller purposefully injects the goods into the stream of commerce and those goods predictably are used in the forum State.

Furthermore, an automobile seller derives substantial benefits from States other than its own. A large part of the value of automobiles is the extensive, nationwide network of highways. Significant portions of that network have been constructed by and are maintained by the individual States, including Oklahoma. The States, through their highway programs, contribute in a very direct and important way to the value of petitioners' businesses. Additionally, a network of other related dealerships with their service departments operates throughout the country under the protection of the laws of the various States, including Oklahoma, and enhances the value of petitioners' businesses by facilitating their customers' traveling.

Thus, the Court errs in its conclusion that "petitioners have no 'contacts, ties, or relations'" with Oklahoma. There obviously are contacts, and, given Oklahoma's connection to the litigation, the contacts are sufficiently significant to make it fair and reasonable for the petitioners to submit to Oklahoma's jurisdiction. . . .

The plaintiffs in [this] case brought suit in a forum with which they had significant contacts and which had significant contacts with the litigation. I am not convinced that the defendants would suffer any "heavy and disproportionate burden" in defending the suits. Accordingly, I would hold that the Constitution should not shield the defendants from appearing and defending in the plaintiffs' chosen fora.

Justice MARSHALL, with whom Justice BLACKMUN joins, dissenting:
. . . This is a difficult case, and reasonable minds may differ as to whether respondents have alleged a sufficient "relationship among the defendant[s], the forum, and the litigation," to satisfy the requirements of *International Shoe*. I am concerned, however, that the majority has reached its result by taking an unnecessarily narrow view of petitioners' forum-related conduct. The majority asserts that "respondents seek to base jurisdiction on one, isolated occurrence and whatever inferences can be drawn therefrom: the fortuitous circumstance that a single Audi automobile, sold in New York to New York residents, happened to suffer an accident while passing through Oklahoma." If that were the case, I would readily agree that the minimum contacts necessary to sustain

jurisdiction are not present. But the basis for the assertion of jurisdiction is not the happenstance that an individual over whom petitioner had no control made a unilateral decision to take a chattel with him to a distant State. Rather, jurisdiction is premised on the deliberate and purposeful actions of the defendants themselves in choosing to become part of a nationwide, indeed a global, network for marketing and servicing automobiles.

. . . [P]etitioners could not know in advance that this particular automobile would be driven to Oklahoma. They must have anticipated, however, that a substantial portion of the cars they sold would travel out of New York. Seaway, a local dealer in the second most populous State, and World-Wide, one of only seven regional Audi distributors in the entire country, would scarcely have been surprised to learn that a car sold by them had been driven in Oklahoma on Interstate 44, a heavily traveled transcontinental highway. In the case of the distributor, in particular, the probability that some of the cars it sells will be driven in every one of the contiguous States must amount to a virtual certainty. This knowledge should alert a reasonable businessman to the likelihood that a defect in the product might manifest itself in the forum State—not because of some unpredictable, aberrant, unilateral action by a single buyer, but in the normal course of the operation of the vehicles for their intended purpose. . . .

I sympathize with the majority's concern that the persons ought to be able to structure their conduct so as not to be subject to suit in distant forums. But that may not always be possible. Some activities by their very nature may foreclose the option of conducting them in such a way as to avoid subjecting oneself to jurisdiction in multiple forums. This is by no means to say that all sellers of automobiles should be subject to suit everywhere; but a distributor of automobiles to a multistate market and a local automobile dealer who makes himself part of a nationwide network of dealerships can fairly expect that the cars they sell may cause injury in distant States and that they may be called on to defend a resulting lawsuit there.

Accordingly, I dissent.

Justice BLACKMUN, dissenting:

I confess that I am somewhat puzzled why the plaintiffs in this litigation are so insistent that the regional distributor and the retail dealer, the petitioners here, who handled the ill-fated Audi automobile involved in this litigation, be named defendants. It would appear that the manufacturer and the importer, whose subjectability to Oklahoma jurisdiction is not challenged before this Court, ought not to be judgment-proof. It may, of course, ultimately amount to a contest between insurance companies that, once begun, is not easily brought to a termination. Having made this much of an observation, I pursue it no further.

For me, a critical factor in the disposition of the litigation is the nature of the instrumentality under consideration. It has been said that we are a nation on wheels. What we are concerned with here is the automobile and its peripatetic character. One need only examine our national network of interstate highways, or make an appearance on one of them, or observe the variety of license plates present not only on those highways but in any metropolitan area, to realize that any automobile is likely to wander far from its place of licensure or from its place of distribution and retail sale. . . .

It therefore seems to me not unreasonable—and certainly not unconstitutional and beyond the reach of the principles laid down in *International Shoe Co. v. Washington*, and its progeny—to uphold Oklahoma jurisdiction over this New York distributor and this New York dealer when the accident happened in Oklahoma. I see nothing more unfair for them than for the manufacturer and the importer. All are in the business of providing vehicles that spread out over the highways of our several States. It is not too much to anticipate at the time of distribution and at the time of retail sale that this Audi would be in Oklahoma. . . .

My position need not now take me beyond the automobile and the professional who does business by way of distributing and retailing automobiles. Cases concerning other instrumentalities will be dealt with as they arise and in their own contexts.

I would affirm the judgment of the Supreme Court of Oklahoma. Because the Court reverses that judgment, it will now be about parsing every variant in the myriad of motor vehicles fact situations that present themselves. Some will justify jurisdiction and others will not. All will depend on the "contact" that the Court sees fit to perceive in the individual case.

YOUR TAKEAWAY

By the time *World-Wide Volkswagen* was decided, it was well-settled that the commission of a tort *within* a state established jurisdiction over the nonresident tortfeasor for a claim arising from the conduct. Had the Robinsons collided on the Oklahoma highway with a car driven by a Texas citizen, for example, that person could have been sued in Oklahoma on a negligence claim even if he had left the state (as in *Hess v. Pawloski, supra*). Their actual lawsuit fell in a murkier area, as the Robinsons were seeking recovery for something that happened *outside* Oklahoma—the allegedly dangerous design and manufacture of the Audi's gas tank—that caused *effects*, the explosion and injuries, *within* the forum state.

The issue of whether the manufacturer or retailer is amenable to suit merely because its product winds up in the state, through no deliberate act of its own, has sharply divided the Supreme Court since *World-Wide Volkswagen,* as we will see in the following line of cases. The prevailing view is that *purposeful action* (*à la Hanson v. Denckla*) on the part of the defendant, such as directing the product to the state, is the prerequisite for adjudicatory power. Unlike the bigger players, Volkswagen and Audi, who had dealerships and advertised in Oklahoma, World-Wide and Seaway were connected to Oklahoma only through the unilateral act of the Robinsons, much as the Delaware trust company was connected to Florida solely by virtue of Mrs. Donner's decision to move there. For the majority, this was a reach too far. Because these little guys lacked "contacts, ties, or relations" with the State of Oklahoma, the due process clause foreclosed Oklahoma from applying its long-arm statute and entering a valid judgment against them.

REVIEW QUESTIONS

1. The Justices in *World-Wide Volkswagen* all agree that *foreseeability of suit* is an important ingredient of due process analysis, as it allows potential defendants to predict where they are subject to suit and thus structure their business accordingly. But they disagree about what *foreseeability* means. Justice White concludes for the Court: "[T]he foreseeability that is critical to due process analysis is not the mere likelihood that a product will find its way into the forum State. Rather, it is that the defendant's conduct and connection with the forum State are such that he should reasonably anticipate being haled into court there."

   Is White suggesting that a defendant can reasonably foresee suit *only where* it has established minimum contacts? When foreseeability is equated with the existence of minimum contacts, does it not wash out as an independent factor in the analysis? Do you sense some circular reasoning here? Justice Brennan, in an omitted section of his dissent, complains: "A defendant cannot know if his actions will subject him to jurisdiction in another State until we have declared what the law of jurisdiction is." 444 U.S. at 311 n.18.

   How do the dissenters define *foreseeability*? What is the significance to them of the fact that defendants' product is highly mobile, and could foreseeably travel to *any* state?

2. On the issue of foreseeability of suit in Oklahoma, would it have made a difference if the Robinsons had *actually told* their salesperson at the Seaway dealership that they would be taking their Audi through Oklahoma on their way to Arizona? What might the dissenters have done with this information? Should amenability to suit turn on the fortuitous nature of such conversations?

3. Justice Blackmun appears to be arguing for a categorical rule permitting dealers to be sued wherever their defective automobiles allegedly cause injury, so as to avoid "parsing every variant in the myriad of motor vehicles fact situations that present themselves." We will see that to date, the Court has resisted such an approach, and has opted for case-by-case analysis of personal jurisdiction.

4. What role should geographic proximity play in the analysis of jurisdiction? What if the Robinsons' accident had occurred in Connecticut, within an hour's drive of the dealership? Shouldn't Seaway have reasonably anticipated the Audi ending up there? Justice Brennan is troubled because he reads the majority opinion as "[excluding] jurisdiction in a contiguous State such as Pennsylvania as surely as in more distant States such as Oklahoma." 444 U.S. at 306 n.10.

5. For the majority, it is the crossing of state boundaries, not distance, that counts, because in their view personal jurisdiction is a matter of state sovereign power and borders. Thus Justice White asserts that "the Due Process Clause, acting as an instrument of interstate federalism, may

sometimes act to divest the State of its power to render a valid judgment" even if the defendant would suffer "minimal or no inconvenience."

In sharp contrast, the dissenters treat the matter of personal jurisdiction as one of convenience to the parties and interest of the forum state in litigating the case. Brennan (in an omitted section of his dissent) observes ironically that "a courtroom just across the state line from a defendant may often be far more convenient for the defendant than a court-room in a distant corner of his own State." 444 U.S. at 301 n.1.

6. Justice White concedes that a "forum State does not exceed its powers under the Due Process Clause if it asserts personal jurisdiction over a corporation that delivers its products into the stream of commerce with the expectation that they will be purchased by consumers in the forum State." The disagreement on the Court seems to focus on the nature and extent of the *expectation*, which gets us back to the split on the "foreseeability" issue. The Court will further elaborate (and divide) on this "stream of commerce" concept in *Asahi Metal Industry Co.* and *J. McIntyre Machinery, Ltd. v. Nicastro*, set out below.

7. The Court clearly resists an interpretation of "minimum contacts" that would subject retailers to suit in any distant location where their product happens to end up. Can you see why this conjures up the ghost of *Harris v. Balk* (the debt travels with the debtor)?

8. If you think *World-Wide Volkswagen* was wrongly decided, how would you feel if the Robinsons filed suit in Oklahoma against Mom & Pop's grocery store in Brooklyn when a can of cola they had purchased for their trip exploded in Oklahoma? Should amenability to suit follow that soda can? Are there sufficient distinctions between the two scenarios that should make a difference on the jurisdictional question?

9. In what ways does Justice Brennan's dissent reflect the same expansive philosophy of personal jurisdiction expressed by Justice Black in *International Shoe* and *McGee*? Note Brennan's explicit reliance on the *McGee* factors: the forum state's interest; the plaintiff's interest; the actual burden on defendant; the location of witnesses and evidence.

QUESTIONS TO PONDER

1. Are you as "puzzled" as Justice Blackmun about why the Robinsons were so intent on keeping World-Wide and Seaway in the lawsuit when "deep pockets" Audi and Volkswagen were no longer contesting jurisdiction (probably because they were conducting a substantial level of activities in Oklahoma) and could certainly pay any judgment rendered?

In *World-Wide Volkswagen v. Woodson—The Rest of the Story*, 72 Neb. L. Rev. 1122 (1993), Professor Charles W. Adams reveals that the Robinsons' lawyer, believing a state court jury would be more generous to his clients than a federal jury, sought to prevent removal of the case to federal court. (We will explore removal procedure in Chapter 8.) It was therefore necessary to maintain non-diverse parties on each side of the litigation to defeat § 1332 diversity jurisdiction. Since the Robinsons were still citizens of New York, maintaining World-Wide and Seaway (also New York entities) as defendants would block removal.

Following the Supreme Court decision releasing these defendants, complete diversity of citizenship existed, and the case was removed and tried in federal district court. The federal jury rendered a verdict for the defendants, as the Robinson's lawyer had feared. *Jurisdiction matters*, as the Robinsons discovered the hard way.

2. If personal jurisdiction is a function of state sovereignty, how can it be that a defendant may *consent to* jurisdiction, or inadvertently *waive* the objection? *See* Fed. R. Civ. P. 12(h)(1). As we have seen, the lack of subject matter jurisdiction in contrast *cannot* be cured by consent or waiver of the parties, and must even be raised by the court on its own initiative, because it goes to the core authority of the court to proceed with the case. *See* Fed. R. Civ. P. 12(h)(3) and Advisory Committee Note.

3. Only two years after *World-Wide Volkswagen Corp. v. Woodson*, the Court shifted its emphasis away from the state sovereignty rationale of personal jurisdiction. *Insurance Corp. of Ireland, Ltd. v. Compagnie des Bauxites de Guinee*, 456 U.S. 694 (1982) explained: "The personal jurisdiction requirement recognizes and protects an individual liberty interest. It represents a restriction on judicial power not as a matter of sovereignty, but as a matter of individual liberty."

If the Justices cannot even agree on the rationale underlying the concept of personal jurisdiction, is it any wonder the doctrine invariably divides the Court? For a fundamental reconceptualization of adjudicatory power that rejects the *International Shoe* focus on fairness to the parties in favor of an approach founded on a state's "legitimate interest in the dispute," *see* A. Benjamin Spencer, *Jurisdiction to Adjudicate: A Revised Analysis*, 73 U. Chi. L. Rev. 617 (2006).

4. *World-Wide Volkswagen* roundly rejects the assertion that merely causing *an effect or injury* in a state is a sufficient basis for the exercise of jurisdiction over the actor. How then to explain the result in the next case?

Calder v. Jones
465 U.S. 783 (1984)

Justice REHNQUIST delivered the opinion of the Court:

Respondent Shirley Jones brought suit in California Superior Court claiming that she had been libeled in an article written and edited by petitioners in Florida. The article was published in a national magazine with a large circulation in California. Petitioners were served with process by mail in Florida and caused special appearances to be entered on their behalf, moving to quash the service of process for lack of personal jurisdiction. . . .

Respondent lives and works in California. She and her husband brought this suit against the National Enquirer, Inc., its local distributing company, and petitioners for libel, invasion of privacy, and intentional infliction of emotional harm. The Enquirer is a Florida corporation with its principal place of business in Florida. It publishes a national weekly newspaper with a total circulation of over 5 million. About 600,000 of those copies, almost twice the level of the next highest State, are sold in California. Respondent's and her husband's claims were based on an article that appeared in the Enquirer's October 9, 1979 issue. Both the Enquirer and the distributing company answered the complaint and made no objection to the jurisdiction of the California court.

Petitioner South is a reporter employed by the Enquirer. He is a resident of Florida, though he frequently travels to California on business. South wrote the first draft of the challenged article, and his byline appeared on it. He did most of his research in Florida, relying on phone calls to sources in California for the information contained in the article.[4] Shortly before publication, South called respondent's home and read to her husband a draft of the article so as to elicit his comments upon it. Aside from his frequent trips and phone calls, South has no other relevant contacts with California.

Petitioner Calder is also a Florida resident. He has been to California only twice—once, on a pleasure trip, prior to the publication of the article and once after to testify in an unrelated trial. Calder is president and editor of the Enquirer. He "oversee[s] just about every function of the Enquirer." He reviewed and approved the initial evaluation of the subject of the article and edited it in its final form. He also declined to print a retraction requested by respondent. Calder has no other relevant contacts with California. . . .

The Due Process Clause of the Fourteenth Amendment to the United States Constitution permits personal jurisdiction over a defendant in any State with which the defendant has "certain minimum contacts . . . such that the maintenance of the suit does not offend 'traditional notions of fair play and substantial justice.'" In judging minimum contacts, a court properly focuses on "the relationship among the defendant, the forum, and the litigation." The plaintiff's lack of "contacts" will not defeat otherwise proper jurisdiction, but they may be so manifold as to permit jurisdiction when it would not exist in their absence. Here, the plaintiff is the focus of the activities of the defendants out of which the suit arises.

The allegedly libelous story concerned the California activities of a California resident. It impugned the professionalism of an entertainer whose television career was centered in California. [The article alleged that respondent drank so heavily as to prevent her from fulfilling her professional obligations.] The article

---

4. The superior court found that South made at least one trip to California in connection with the article. South hotly disputes this finding, claiming that an uncontroverted affidavit shows that he never visited California to research the article. Since we do not rely for our holding on the alleged visit, . . . we find it unnecessary to consider the contention.

was drawn from California sources, and the brunt of the harm, in terms both of respondent's emotional distress and the injury to her professional reputation, was suffered in California. In sum, California is the focal point both of the story and of the harm suffered. Jurisdiction over petitioners is therefore proper in California based on the "effects" of their Florida conduct in California. *World-Wide Volkswagen Corp. v. Woodson*, 444 U.S. 286, 297-298 (1980).

Petitioners argue that they are not responsible for the circulation of the article in California. [But] petitioners are not charged with mere untargeted negligence. Rather, their intentional, and allegedly tortious, actions were expressly aimed at California. Petitioner South wrote and petitioner Calder edited an article that they knew would have a potentially devastating impact upon respondent. And they knew that the brunt of that injury would be felt by respondent in the State in which she lives and works and in which the National Enquirer has its largest circulation. Under the circumstances, petitioners must "reasonably anticipate being haled into court there" to answer for the truth of the statements made in their article. An individual injured in California need not go to Florida to seek redress from persons who, though remaining in Florida, knowingly cause the injury in California.

Petitioners are correct that their contacts with California are not to be judged according to their employer's activities there. On the other hand, their status as employees does not somehow insulate them from jurisdiction. Each defendant's contacts with the forum State must be assessed individually. In this case, petitioners are primary participants in an alleged wrongdoing intentionally directed at a California resident, and jurisdiction over them is proper on that basis. . . .

We hold that jurisdiction over petitioners in California is proper because of their intentional conduct in Florida calculated to cause injury to respondent in California. The judgment of the California Court of Appeal is affirmed.

YOUR TAKEAWAY

Calder splits the universe of tort claims into two categories for purposes of personal jurisdiction. "Mere untargeted negligence" claims, like *Volkswagen*, cannot take advantage of the broader reach of "effects jurisdiction," whereas courts entertaining intentional tort claims like defamation may tag defendants if the effects of their allegedly tortious conduct are felt in a significant way in the forum state, i.e., the latter is the "focal point of the harm suffered." In the narrative since *International Shoe*, intentional, purposeful, and directed conduct becomes the key to long-arm reach beyond the borders of the forum state.

REVIEW QUESTIONS

1. Why do you think the *National Enquirer* filed an answer without raising an objection to personal jurisdiction, as Calder and South did? (Hint: There are many inquiring minds in the Golden State.)
2. In *Keeton v. Hustler Magazine, Inc.*, 465 U.S. 770 (1984), decided the same day as *Calder*, a New York resident brought a defamation suit in the corporate defendant's home state of Ohio. When the case was dismissed because

that state's statute of limitations had run, she filed in New Hampshire, which had a longer limitations period. *Hustler* objected that jurisdiction was lacking. The Court ultimately ruled that the sale in New Hampshire of 10,000 to 15,000 copies of the magazine each month, even though its only contact with the forum, was sufficient to justify the exercise of jurisdiction. "Where *Hustler Magazine* has continuously and deliberately exploited the New Hampshire market, it must reasonably anticipate being haled into court there in a libel action based on the contents of its magazine."

Neither the transparent forum shopping by Keeton, nor her total lack of connection to, or reputation in, New Hampshire, nor the absence of any contacts (as there were in *Calder*) between the writers and the forum, deterred Justice Rehnquist and the unanimous Court from reversing dismissal of the case below. Do you think the writer and editor of the *Hustler* article themselves would also have been held subject to jurisdiction, as they were in *Calder*? Did they aim their article at New Hampshire?

MATTERS TO PONDER

1. Two critics of *Calder* observe:

> The key to the case—and the reason for the controversy—is that it required departing from the familiar physical-world framework that courts had so laboriously worked out for personal jurisdiction. Jones resided in California, and a sizeable percentage of the magazines wound up in California. But none of that really mattered: The critical factor was that Jones's *reputation* resided there. Reputations are intangible and can have multiple homes. Jones, a Broadway actress as well as a Hollywood one, doubtless had a reputation capable of injury in New York as well. The problem easily multiplies. Imagine Jones spent summers acting in traveling productions in Boston and annually appeared in a widely-loved version of *A Christmas Story* in Chicago. The *Enquirer* would arguably be subject to suit in Massachusetts and Illinois as well. Personal jurisdiction becomes coterminous with the plaintiff's reputation, which the defendant may or may not easily discover. And while the printed copies of the *Enquirer* physically landed on newsstands in Los Angeles, the harm came not from their weight or newsprint, but from the information contained therein.
>
> Thus, the *Calder* Court faced a situation with three intangible factors: the scope of the plaintiff's reputation, the spread of the allegedly defamatory information, and the extent of the defendant's knowledge about the plaintiff's reputation. While the *Calder* opinion portrays the contest as a choice between California and Florida, that bifurcation is a convenient fiction that overlooks important differences between physical and intangible effects. The Court pigeonholed the case into a familiar framework of intentional torts. For example, if someone aims a gun from a high-rise in Manhattan at a person just across the Hudson River in New Jersey, it makes sense that the gunman should be subject to jurisdiction in New Jersey, where he intended to cause physical harm. *Calder* treated

the *National Enquirer* and the hypothetical gunman as identical for jurisdictional purposes. The *National Enquirer* story effectively was a defamation bomb, armed in Florida and detonated in California that damaged Jones's reputation. . . .

Put simply, the *Calder* Court overlooked the most difficult aspect of the case: All of the relevant factors in the jurisdictional analysis were intangible and presented the usual problems of intangible goods. Yet the decision applied physical precedent without taking account of those conceptual differences.

Alan M. Trammell and Derek E. Bambauer, *Personal Jurisdiction and the "Interwebs,"* 100 Cornell L. Rev. 1129, 1140-1142 (2015).

2. What if the alleged defamatory material appears on the Internet rather than in print? Katherine Griffis brought a defamation action against Marianne Luban based on messages Luban posted on *sci.archaeology*, an Internet newsgroup, challenging Griffis's credentials as an Egyptologist, and accusing her of getting her degree from a "box of Cracker Jacks." Griffis, who taught at the University of Alabama, filed suit in Alabama state court. Luban, a Minnesota resident, defaulted on advice of counsel, who believed the Alabama courts did not have jurisdiction over her.

Griffis then sued to enforce the Alabama judgment in Minnesota. The defendant contended it was not entitled to full faith and credit because the Alabama court lacked personal jurisdiction over her. The Minnesota Supreme Court agreed: The mere fact that Luban had known that the subject of her criticisms lived in Alabama and that the Internet postings would affect her there was not sufficient to establish jurisdiction in that state, given the universal reach of the Internet. *Griffis v. Luban*, 646 N.W.2d 527 (Minn. 2002):

> While the record supports the conclusion that Luban's statements were intentionally directed at Griffis, whom she knew to be an Alabama resident, we conclude that the evidence does not demonstrate that Luban's statements were "expressly aimed" at the state of Alabama. Luban published the allegedly defamatory statements on an internet newsgroup accessible to the public, but nothing in the record indicates that the statements were targeted at the state of Alabama or at an Alabama audience beyond Griffis herself. . . . Griffis has not presented evidence that any other person in Alabama read the statements. Nor has she asserted that Alabama has a unique relationship with the field of Egyptology, like the close relationship between the plaintiff's profession and the forum state that the Supreme Court found relevant in *Calder*. Therefore, even if we assume Luban's statements were widely read by followers of the *sci.archaeology* newsgroup, the readers most likely would be spread all around the country—maybe even around the world—and not necessarily in the Alabama forum. The fact that messages posted to the newsgroup *could* have been read in Alabama, just as they *could* have been read anywhere in the world, cannot suffice to establish Alabama as the focal point of the defendant's conduct.

646 N.W.2d 536. We will return to the intriguing question of jurisdiction based on Internet connections, and particularly defamation on the Internet, in Part K, later in this chapter.

What does the next case do to *Calder*'s special treatment of intentional torts?

Walden v. Fiore
134 S. Ct. 1115 (2014)

Justice THOMAS delivered the opinion for a unanimous Court.

This case asks us to decide whether a court in Nevada may exercise personal jurisdiction over a defendant on the basis that he knew his allegedly tortious conduct in Georgia would delay the return of funds to plaintiffs with connections to Nevada. Because the defendant had no other contacts with Nevada, and because a plaintiff's contacts with the forum State cannot be "decisive in determining whether the defendant's due process rights are violated," we hold that the court in Nevada may not exercise personal jurisdiction under these circumstances.

I

Petitioner Anthony Walden serves as a police officer for the city of Covington, Georgia. In August 2006, petitioner was working at the Atlanta Hartsfield-Jackson Airport as a deputized agent of the Drug Enforcement Administration (DEA). As part of a task force, petitioner conducted investigative stops and other law enforcement functions in support of the DEA's airport drug interdiction program.

On August 8, 2006, TSA agents searched respondents Gina Fiore and Keith Gipson and their carry-on bags at the San Juan airport in Puerto Rico. They found almost $97,000 in cash. Fiore explained that she and Gipson had been gambling at a casino. After respondents were cleared for departure, a law enforcement official at the San Juan airport notified petitioner's task force in Atlanta that respondents had boarded a plane for Atlanta, where they planned to catch a connecting flight to Las Vegas, Nevada.

When respondents arrived in Atlanta, petitioner and another DEA agent approached them at the departure gate for their flight to Las Vegas. In response to petitioner's questioning, Fiore explained that the cash they were carrying was their gambling winnings. After using a drug-sniffing dog to perform a sniff test, petitioner seized the cash.[1] Petitioner advised respondents that their funds would be returned if they later proved a legitimate source for the cash. Respondents then boarded their plane.

---

1. Respondents allege that the sniff test was "at best, inconclusive," and there is no indication in the pleadings that drugs or drug residue were ever found on or with the cash.

The next day, petitioner received a phone call from respondents' attorney in Nevada seeking return of the funds. On two occasions over the next month, petitioner also received documentation from the attorney regarding the legitimacy of the funds.

At some point after petitioner seized the cash, he helped draft an affidavit to show probable cause for forfeiture of the funds and forwarded that affidavit to a United States Attorney's Office in Georgia. . . . According to respondents, the affidavit was false and misleading because petitioner misrepresented the encounter at the airport and omitted exculpatory information regarding the lack of drug evidence and the legitimate source of the funds. In the end, no forfeiture complaint was filed, and the DEA returned the funds to respondents in March 2007.

Respondents filed suit against petitioner in the United States District Court for the District of Nevada, seeking money damages under *Bivens v. Six Unknown Fed. Narcotics Agents*, 403 U.S. 388 (1971). Respondents alleged that petitioner violated their Fourth Amendment rights by (1) seizing the cash without probable cause; (2) keeping the money after concluding it did not come from drug-related activity; (3) drafting and forwarding a probable cause affidavit to support a forfeiture action while knowing the affidavit contained false statements; (4) willfully seeking forfeiture while withholding exculpatory information; and (5) withholding that exculpatory information from the United States Attorney's Office.

The District Court granted petitioner's motion to dismiss. Relying on this Court's decision in *Calder v. Jones*, 465 U.S. 783 (1984), the court determined that petitioner's search of respondents and his seizure of the cash in Georgia did not establish a basis to exercise personal jurisdiction in Nevada. The court concluded that even if petitioner caused harm to respondents in Nevada while knowing they lived in Nevada, that fact alone did not confer jurisdiction.

On appeal, a divided panel of the United States Court of Appeals for the Ninth Circuit reversed. The Court of Appeals assumed the District Court had correctly determined that petitioner's search and seizure in Georgia could not support exercise of jurisdiction in Nevada. The court held, however, that the District Court could properly exercise jurisdiction over "the false probable cause affidavit aspect of the case," [as] petitioner "expressly aimed" his submission of the allegedly false affidavit at Nevada by submitting the affidavit with knowledge that it would affect persons with a "significant connection" to Nevada. After determining that the delay in returning the funds to respondents caused them "foreseeable harm" in Nevada and that the exercise of personal jurisdiction over petitioner was otherwise reasonable, the court found the District Court's exercise of personal jurisdiction to be proper. . . .

We granted certiorari to decide whether due process permits a Nevada court to exercise jurisdiction over petitioner. We hold that it does not and therefore reverse.

II

A

"Federal courts ordinarily follow state law in determining the bounds of their jurisdiction over persons." This is because a federal district court's authority to assert personal jurisdiction in most cases is linked to service of process on a defendant "who is subject to the jurisdiction of a court of general jurisdiction in the state where the district court is located." Fed. Rule of Civ. Proc. 4(k)(1)(A). Here, Nevada has authorized its courts to exercise jurisdiction over persons "on any basis not inconsistent with . . . the Constitution of the United States." Nev. Rev. Stat. § 14.065 (2011). Thus, in order to determine whether the Federal District Court in this case was authorized to exercise jurisdiction over petitioner, we ask whether the exercise of jurisdiction "comports with the limits imposed by federal due process" on the State of Nevada.

B

1

. . . This case addresses the "minimum contacts" necessary to create specific jurisdiction. The inquiry whether a forum State may assert specific jurisdiction over a nonresident defendant "focuses on 'the relationship among the defendant, the forum, and the litigation.'" For a State to exercise jurisdiction consistent with due process, the defendant's suit-related conduct must create a substantial connection with the forum State. Two related aspects of this necessary relationship are relevant in this case.

First, the relationship must arise out of contacts that the "defendant himself" creates with the forum State. Due process limits on the State's adjudicative authority principally protect the liberty of the nonresident defendant—not the convenience of plaintiffs or third parties. We have consistently rejected attempts to satisfy the defendant-focused "minimum contacts" inquiry by demonstrating contacts between the plaintiff (or third parties) and the forum State. We have thus rejected a plaintiff's argument that a Florida court could exercise personal jurisdiction over a trustee in Delaware based solely on the contacts of the trust's settlor, who was domiciled in Florida and had executed powers of appointment there. *Hanson v. Denckla*, 357 U.S. 235, 253-254 (1958). We have likewise held that Oklahoma courts could not exercise personal jurisdiction over an automobile distributor that supplies New York, New Jersey, and Connecticut dealers based only on an automobile purchaser's act of driving it on Oklahoma highways. *World-Wide Volkswagen Corp*. Put simply, however significant the plaintiff's contacts with the forum may be, those contacts cannot be "decisive in determining whether the defendant' s due process rights are violated."

Second, our "minimum contacts" analysis looks to the defendant's contacts with the forum State itself, not the defendant's contacts with persons who reside there. Accordingly, we have upheld the assertion of jurisdiction over defendants who have purposefully "reach[ed] out beyond" their State and into another by, for example, entering a contractual relationship that "envisioned continuing and wide-reaching contacts" in the forum State, *Burger King, supra*, at 479-480, or by circulating magazines to "deliberately exploi[t]" a market in the forum State, *Keeton, supra,* at 781. And although physical presence in the forum is not a prerequisite to jurisdiction, physical entry into the State—either by the defendant in person or through an agent, goods, mail, or some other means—is certainly a relevant contact. *See, e.g., Keeton, supra,* at 773-774.

But the plaintiff cannot be the only link between the defendant and the forum. Rather, it is the defendant's conduct that must form the necessary connection with the forum State that is the basis for its jurisdiction over him. Due process requires that a defendant be haled into court in a forum State based on his own affiliation with the State, not based on the "random, fortuitous, or attenuated" contacts he makes by interacting with other persons affiliated with the State.

2

These same principles apply when intentional torts are involved. In that context, it is likewise insufficient to rely on a defendant's "random, fortuitous, or attenuated contacts" or on the "unilateral activity" of a plaintiff. A forum State's exercise of jurisdiction over an out-of-state intentional tortfeasor must be based on intentional conduct by the defendant that creates the necessary contacts with the forum.

Calder v. Jones illustrates the application of these principles. In *Calder*, a California actress brought a libel suit in California state court against a reporter and an editor, both of whom worked for the National Enquirer at its headquarters in Florida. The plaintiff's libel claims were based on an article written and edited by the defendants in Florida for publication in the National Enquirer, a national weekly newspaper with a California circulation of roughly 600,000.

We held that California's assertion of jurisdiction over the defendants was consistent with due process. Although we recognized that the defendants' activities "focus[ed]" on the plaintiff, our jurisdictional inquiry "focuse[d] on 'the relationship among the defendant, the forum, and the litigation.'" Specifically, we examined the various contacts the defendants had created with California (and not just with the plaintiff) by writing the allegedly libelous story.

We found those forum contacts to be ample: The defendants relied on phone calls to "California sources" for the information in their article; they wrote the story about the plaintiff's activities in California; they caused reputational injury in California by writing an allegedly libelous article that was widely circulated in the State; and the "brunt" of that injury was suffered by the plaintiff in that State. "In sum, California [wa]s the focal point both of the story and of the harm suffered." Jurisdiction over the defendants was "therefore proper in California based on the 'effects' of their Florida conduct in California."

The crux of *Calder* was that the reputation-based "effects" of the alleged libel connected the defendants to California, not just to the plaintiff. The strength of that connection was largely a function of the nature of the libel tort. However scandalous a newspaper article might be, it can lead to a loss of reputation only if communicated to (and read and understood by) third persons. Accordingly, the reputational injury caused by the defendants' story would not have occurred but for the fact that the defendants wrote an article for publication in California that was read by a large number of California citizens. Indeed, because publication to third persons is a necessary element of libel, the defendants' intentional tort actually occurred in California. In this way, the "effects" caused by the defendants' article—i.e., the injury to the plaintiff's reputation in the estimation of the California public—connected the defendants' conduct to California, not just to a plaintiff who lived there. That connection, combined with the various facts that gave the article a California focus, sufficed to authorize the California court's exercise of jurisdiction.

III

Applying the foregoing principles, we conclude that petitioner lacks the "minimal contacts" with Nevada that are a prerequisite to the exercise of jurisdiction over him. It is undisputed that no part of petitioner's course of conduct occurred in Nevada. Petitioner approached, questioned, and searched respondents, and seized the cash at issue, in the Atlanta airport. It is alleged that petitioner later helped draft a "false probable cause affidavit" in Georgia and forwarded that affidavit to a United States Attorney's Office in Georgia to support a potential action for forfeiture of the seized funds. Petitioner never traveled to, conducted activities within, contacted anyone in, or sent anything or anyone to Nevada. In short, when viewed through the proper lens—whether the *defendant's* actions connect him to the *forum*—petitioner formed no jurisdictionally relevant contacts with Nevada.

Petitioner's actions in Georgia did not create sufficient contacts with Nevada simply because he allegedly directed his conduct at plaintiffs whom he knew had Nevada connections. Such reasoning improperly attributes a plaintiff's forum connections to the defendant and makes those connections "decisive" in the jurisdictional analysis. It also obscures the reality that none of petitioner's challenged conduct had anything to do with Nevada itself.

Calder made clear that mere injury to a forum resident is not a sufficient connection to the forum. Regardless of where a plaintiff lives or works, an injury is jurisdictionally relevant only insofar as it shows that the defendant has formed a contact with the forum State. The proper question is not where the plaintiff experienced a particular injury or effect but whether the defendant's conduct connects him to the forum in a meaningful way.

Unlike the broad publication of the forum-focused story in *Calder*, the effects of petitioner's conduct on respondents are not connected to the forum State in a way that makes those effects a proper basis for jurisdiction.[4] Petitioner's

---

4. Respondents warn that if we decide petitioner lacks minimum contacts in this case, it will bring about unfairness in cases where intentional torts are committed via the Internet or other electronic means (e.g., fraudulent access of financial accounts or "phishing" schemes). [T]his case does not present the very different questions whether and how a defendant's virtual "presence" and conduct translate into "contacts" with a particular State. . . . We leave questions about virtual contacts for another day.

relevant conduct occurred entirely in Georgia, and the mere fact that his conduct affected plaintiffs with connections to the forum State does not suffice to authorize jurisdiction. We therefore reverse the judgment of the Court of Appeals. It is so ordered.

REVIEW QUESTIONS

1. Can you see how the Ninth Circuit would have read *Calder* as supporting the exercise of jurisdiction here? Does the Supreme Court's reversal confirm the suspicion among some that *Calder* may be limited to defamation cases, and that those plaintiffs have an easier time establishing jurisdiction?

   Wouldn't it have been a surprise, though, if the Court had signed off on the long jurisdictional reach of the Nevada federal court, dragging a Georgia citizen in to defend a claim arising at the Atlanta airport?

2. Note the Court's passing for another day (in footnote 4) the issue of torts committed over the Internet: How long can the nation's highest court dodge this recurring question? See Part J, later in this chapter.

* * *

We now return to the product liability area, where harms to the plaintiff are all too tangible. What do the next two cases teach us about the outer boundaries of personal jurisdiction based on the global commerce in goods, and the viability of the "stream of commerce" theory that divided the Court in *World-Wide Volkswagen*?

Asahi Metal Industry Co., Ltd. v. Superior Court of California, Solano County
480 U.S. 102 (1987)

Justice O'CONNOR announced the judgment of the Court and delivered the unanimous opinion of the Court with respect to Part I, the opinion of the Court with respect to Part II-B, in which THE CHIEF JUSTICE, Justice BRENNAN, Justice WHITE, Justice MARSHALL, Justice BLACKMUN, Justice POWELL, and Justice STEVENS join, and an opinion with respect to Parts II-A and III, in which THE CHIEF JUSTICE, Justice POWELL, and Justice SCALIA join:

This case presents the question whether the mere awareness on the part of a foreign defendant that the components it manufactured, sold, and delivered outside the United States would reach the forum State in the stream of commerce constitutes "minimum contacts" between the defendant and the forum State such that the exercise of jurisdiction "does not offend 'traditional notions of fair play and substantial justice.'" *International Shoe Co. v. Washington*, 326 U.S. 310, 316 (1945).

I

On September 23, 1978, on Interstate Highway 80 in Solano County, California, Gary Zurcher lost control of his Honda motorcycle and collided with a tractor. Zurcher was severely injured, and his passenger and wife, Ruth Ann Moreno, was killed. In September 1979, Zurcher filed a product liability action in the Superior Court of the State of California in and for the County of Solano. Zurcher alleged that the 1978 accident was caused by a sudden loss of air and an explosion in the rear tire of the motorcycle, and alleged that the motorcycle tire, tube, and sealant were defective. Zurcher's complaint named, inter alia, Cheng Shin, the Taiwanese manufacturer of the tube. Cheng Shin in turn filed a cross-complaint seeking indemnification from its codefendants and from petitioner, Asahi, the manufacturer of the tube's valve assembly. Zurcher's claims against Cheng Shin and the other defendants were eventually settled and dismissed, leaving only Cheng Shin's indemnity action against Asahi.

California's long-arm statute authorizes the exercise of jurisdiction "on any basis not inconsistent with the Constitution of this state or of the United States." Asahi moved to quash Cheng Shin's service of summons, arguing the State could not exert jurisdiction over it consistent with the Due Process Clause of the Fourteenth Amendment.

In relation to the motion, the following information was submitted by Asahi and Cheng Shin. Asahi is a Japanese corporation. It manufactures tire valve assemblies in Japan and sells the assemblies to Cheng Shin, and to several other tire manufacturers, for use as components in finished tire tubes. Asahi's sales to Cheng Shin took place in Taiwan. The shipments from Asahi to Cheng Shin were sent from Japan to Taiwan. Cheng Shin bought and incorporated into its tire tubes 150,000 Asahi valve assemblies in 1978; 500,000 in 1979; 500,000 in 1980; 100,000 in 1981; and 100,000 in 1982. Sales to Cheng Shin accounted for 1.24 percent of Asahi's income in 1981 and 0.44 percent in 1982. Cheng Shin alleged that approximately 20 percent of its sales in the United States are in California. Cheng Shin purchases valve assemblies from other suppliers as well, and sells finished tubes throughout the world.

In 1983 an attorney for Cheng Shin conducted an informal examination of the valve stems of the tire tubes sold in one cycle store in Solano County. The attorney declared that of the approximately 115 tire tubes in the store, 97 were purportedly manufactured in Japan or Taiwan, and of those 97, 21 valve stems were marked with the circled letter "A", apparently Asahi's trademark. Of the 21 Asahi valve stems, 12 were incorporated into Cheng Shin tire tubes. The store contained 41 other Cheng Shin tubes that incorporated the valve assemblies of other manufacturers. An affidavit of a manager of Cheng Shin whose duties included the purchasing of component parts stated: " 'In discussions with Asahi regarding the purchase of valve stem assemblies the fact that my Company sells tubes throughout the world and specifically the United States has been discussed. I am informed and believe that Asahi was fully aware that valve stem assemblies sold to my Company and to others would end up throughout the

United States and in California.'" An affidavit of the president of Asahi, on the other hand, declared that Asahi "'has never contemplated that its limited sales of tire valves to Cheng Shin in Taiwan would subject it to lawsuits in California.'" The record does not include any contract between Cheng Shin and Asahi.

Primarily on the basis of the above information, the Superior Court denied the motion to quash summons, stating: "Asahi obviously does business on an international scale. It is not unreasonable that they defend claims of defect in their product on an international scale."

The Supreme Court of California [agreed, observing]: "Asahi has no offices, property or agents in California. It solicits no business in California and has made no direct sales [in California]." Moreover, "Asahi did not design or control the system of distribution that carried its valve assemblies into California." Nevertheless, the court found the exercise of jurisdiction over Asahi to be consistent with the Due Process Clause. It concluded that Asahi knew that some of the valve assemblies sold to Cheng Shin would be incorporated into tire tubes sold in California, and that Asahi benefited indirectly from the sale in California of products incorporating its components. The court considered Asahi's intentional act of placing its components into the stream of commerce—that is, by delivering the components to Cheng Shin in Taiwan—coupled with Asahi's awareness that some of the components would eventually find their way into California, sufficient to form the basis for state court jurisdiction under the Due Process Clause.

We granted certiorari, and now reverse.

II

A

The Due Process Clause of the Fourteenth Amendment limits the power of a state court to exert personal jurisdiction over a nonresident defendant. "[T]he constitutional touchstone" of the determination whether an exercise of personal jurisdiction comports with due process "remains whether the defendant purposefully established 'minimum contacts' in the forum State." *Burger King Corp. v. Rudzewicz*, 471 U.S. 462, 474 (1985). Most recently we have reaffirmed the oft-quoted reasoning of *Hanson v. Denckla* that minimum contacts must have a basis in "some act by which the defendant purposefully avails itself of the privilege of conducting activities within the forum State, thus invoking the benefits and protections of its laws." *Burger King*, 471 U.S. at 475. "Jurisdiction is proper . . . where the contacts proximately result from actions by the defendant himself that create a 'substantial connection' with the forum State."

. . . Some courts have understood the Due Process Clause, as interpreted in *World-Wide Volkswagen*, to allow an exercise of personal jurisdiction to be based on no more than the defendant's act of placing the product in the stream of commerce. Other courts have understood the Due Process Clause to require the action of the defendant to be more purposefully directed at the forum State than the mere act of placing a product in the stream of commerce.

The reasoning of the Supreme Court of California in the present case illustrates the former interpretation of *World-Wide Volkswagen*. It held that, because the stream of commerce eventually brought some valves Asahi sold Cheng Shin into California, Asahi's awareness that its valves would be sold in California was sufficient to permit California to exercise jurisdiction over Asahi consistent with the requirements of the Due Process Clause. The Supreme Court of California's position was consistent with those courts that have held that mere foreseeability or awareness was a constitutionally sufficient basis for personal jurisdiction if the defendant's product made its way into the forum State while still in the stream of commerce.

Other courts, however, have understood the Due Process Clause to require something more than that the defendant was aware of its product's entry into the forum State through the stream of commerce in order for the State to exert jurisdiction over the defendant.

We now find this latter position to be consonant with the requirements of due process. The "substantial connection" between the defendant and the forum State necessary for a finding of minimum contacts must come about by an action of the defendant purposefully directed toward the forum State. The placement of a product into the stream of commerce, without more, is not an act of the defendant purposefully directed toward the forum State. Additional conduct of the defendant may indicate an intent or purpose to serve the market in the forum State, for example, designing the product for the market in the forum State, advertising in the forum State, establishing channels for providing regular advice to customers in the forum State, or marketing the product through a distributor who has agreed to serve as the sales agent in the forum State. But a defendant's awareness that the stream of commerce may or will sweep the product into the forum State does not convert the mere act of placing the product into the stream into an act purposefully directed toward the forum State.

Assuming, *arguendo*, that respondents have established Asahi's awareness that some of the valves sold to Cheng Shin would be incorporated into tire tubes sold in California, respondents have not demonstrated any action by Asahi to purposefully avail itself of the California market. Asahi does not do business in California. It has no office, agents, employees, or property in California. It does not advertise or otherwise solicit business in California. It did not create, control, or employ the distribution system that brought its valves to California. There is no evidence that Asahi designed its product in anticipation of sales in California. On the basis of these facts, the exertion of personal jurisdiction over Asahi by the Superior Court of California* exceeds the limits of due process.

---

* We have no occasion here to determine whether Congress could, consistent with the Due Process Clause of the Fifth Amendment, authorize federal court personal jurisdiction over alien defendants based on the aggregate of national contacts, rather than on the contacts between the defendant and the State in which the federal court sits. [*Eds.' Note:* Six years later, Fed. R. Civ. P. 4(k)(2) was adopted.]

B

The strictures of the Due Process Clause forbid a state court to exercise personal jurisdiction over Asahi under circumstances that would offend " 'traditional notions of fair play and substantial justice.' " *International Shoe Co. v. Washington.*

We have previously explained that the determination of the reasonableness of the exercise of jurisdiction in each case will depend on an evaluation of several factors. A court must consider the burden on the defendant, the interests of the forum State, and the plaintiff's interest in obtaining relief. It must also weigh in its determination "the interstate judicial system's interest in obtaining the most efficient resolution of controversies; and the shared interest of the several States in furthering fundamental substantive social policies."

A consideration of these factors in the present case clearly reveals the unreasonableness of the assertion of jurisdiction over Asahi, even apart from the question of the placement of goods in the stream of commerce.

Certainly the burden on the defendant in this case is severe. Asahi has been commanded by the Supreme Court of California not only to traverse the distance between Asahi's headquarters in Japan and the Superior Court of California in and for the County of Solano, but also to submit its dispute with Cheng Shin to a foreign nation's judicial system. The unique burdens placed upon one who must defend oneself in a foreign legal system should have significant weight in assessing the reasonableness of stretching the long arm of personal jurisdiction over national borders.

When minimum contacts have been established, often the interests of the plaintiff and the forum in the exercise of jurisdiction will justify even the serious burdens placed on the alien defendant. In the present case, however, the interests of the plaintiff and the forum in California's assertion of jurisdiction over Asahi are slight. All that remains is a claim for indemnification asserted by Cheng Shin, a Taiwanese corporation, against Asahi. The transaction on which the indemnification claim is based took place in Taiwan; Asahi's components were shipped from Japan to Taiwan. Cheng Shin has not demonstrated that it is more convenient for it to litigate its indemnification claim against Asahi in California rather than in Taiwan or Japan.

Because the plaintiff is not a California resident, California's legitimate interests in the dispute have considerably diminished. The Supreme Court of California argued that the State had an interest in "protecting its consumers by ensuring that foreign manufacturers comply with the state's safety standards." The Court's definition of California's interest, however, was overly broad. The dispute between Cheng Shin and Asahi is primarily about indemnification rather than safety standards. Moreover, it is not at all clear at this point that California law should govern the question whether a Japanese corporation should indemnify a Taiwanese corporation on the basis of a sale made in Taiwan and a shipment of goods from Japan to Taiwan. The possibility of being haled into a California court as a result of an accident involving Asahi's components undoubtedly creates an additional deterrent to the manufacture of unsafe components; however, similar pressures will be placed on Asahi by the purchasers of its components as long as those who use Asahi components in their final products, and sell those products in California, are subject to the application of California tort law. . . .

"Great care and reserve should be exercised when extending our notions of personal jurisdiction into the international field." Considering the international context, the heavy burden on the alien defendant, and the slight interests of the plaintiff and the forum State, the exercise of personal jurisdiction by a California court over Asahi in this instance would be unreasonable and unfair.

III

Because the facts of this case do not establish minimum contacts such that the exercise of personal jurisdiction is consistent with fair play and substantial justice, the judgment of the Supreme Court of California is reversed, and the case is remanded for further proceedings not inconsistent with this opinion.

It is so ordered.

Justice BRENNAN, with whom Justice WHITE, Justice MARSHALL, and Justice BLACKMUN join, concurring in part and concurring in the judgment:

I do not agree with the interpretation in Part II-A of the stream-of-commerce theory, nor with the conclusion that Asahi did not "purposely avail itself of the California market." I do agree, however, with the Court's conclusion in Part II-B that the exercise of personal jurisdiction over Asahi in this case would not comport with "fair play and substantial justice," *International Shoe Co. v. Washington*. This is one of those rare cases in which "minimum requirements inherent in the concept of 'fair play and substantial justice' . . . defeat the reasonableness of jurisdiction even [though] the defendant has purposefully engaged in forum activities." *Burger King Corp. v. Rudzewicz*, 471 U.S. 462, 477-478 (1985). I therefore join Parts I and II-B of the Court's opinion, and write separately to explain my disagreement with Part II-A.

Part II-A states that "a defendant's awareness that the stream of commerce may or will sweep the product into the forum State does not convert the mere act of placing the product into the stream into an act purposefully directed toward the forum State." Under this view, a plaintiff would be required to show "[a]dditional conduct" directed toward the forum before finding the exercise of jurisdiction over the defendant to be consistent with the Due Process Clause. I see no need for such a showing, however. The stream of commerce refers not to unpredictable currents or eddies, but to the regular and anticipated flow of products from manufacture to distribution to retail sale. As long as a participant in this process is aware that the final product is being marketed in the forum State, the possibility of a lawsuit there cannot come as a surprise. Nor will the litigation present a burden for which there is no corresponding benefit. A defendant who has placed goods in the stream of commerce benefits economically from the retail sale of the final product in the forum State, and indirectly benefits from the State's laws that regulate and facilitate commercial activity. These benefits accrue regardless of whether that participant directly conducts business in the forum State, or engages in additional conduct directed toward that State. Accordingly, most courts and commentators have found that jurisdiction premised on the placement of a product into the stream of commerce is consistent with the Due Process Clause, and have not required a showing of additional conduct.

In this case, the facts found by the California Supreme Court support its finding of minimum contacts. The court found that "[a]lthough Asahi did not design or control the system of distribution that carried its valve assemblies into California, Asahi was aware of the distribution system's operation, and it knew that it would benefit economically from the sale in California of products incorporating its components."[4] Accordingly, I cannot join the determination in Part II-A that Asahi's regular and extensive sales of component parts to a manufacturer it knew was making regular sales of the final product in California is insufficient to establish minimum contacts with California.

Justice STEVENS, with whom Justice WHITE and Justice BLACKMUN join, concurring in part and concurring in the judgment:

The judgment of the Supreme Court of California should be reversed for the reasons stated in Part II-B of the Court's opinion. While I join Parts I and II-B, I do not join Part II-A for two reasons. First, it is not necessary to the Court's decision. An examination of minimum contacts is not always necessary to determine whether a state court's assertion of personal jurisdiction is constitutional. Part II-B establishes, after considering the factors set forth in *World-Wide Volkswagen Corp. v. Woodson*, that California's exercise of jurisdiction over Asahi in this case would be "unreasonable and unfair." This finding alone requires reversal; this case fits within the rule that "minimum requirements inherent in the concept of 'fair play and substantial justice' may defeat the reasonableness of jurisdiction even if the defendant has purposefully engaged in forum activities." *Burger King*, 471 U.S. at 477-478. Accordingly, I see no reason in this case for the plurality to articulate "purposeful direction" or any other test as the nexus between an act of a defendant and the forum State that is necessary to establish minimum contacts.

Second, even assuming that the test ought to be formulated here, Part II-A misapplies it to the facts of this case. The plurality seems to assume that an unwavering line can be drawn between "mere awareness" that a component will find its way into the forum State and "purposeful availment" of the forum's market. Over the course of its dealings with Cheng Shin, Asahi has arguably engaged in a higher quantum of conduct than "[t]he placement of a product into the stream of commerce, without more. . . ." Whether or not this conduct rises to the level of purposeful availment requires a constitutional determination that is affected by the volume, the value, and the hazardous character of the components. In most circumstances I would be inclined to conclude that a regular course of dealing that results in deliveries of over 100,000 units annually over a period of several years would constitute "purposeful availment" even though the item delivered to the forum State was a standard product marketed throughout the world.

---

4. Moreover, the Court found that "at least 18 percent of the tubes sold in a particular California motorcycle supply shop contained Asahi valve assemblies," and that Asahi had an ongoing business relationship with Cheng Shin involving average annual sales of hundreds of thousands of valve assemblies.

YOUR TAKEAWAY

The Court reaches a unanimous result—jurisdiction cannot be constitutionally exercised over the Japanese valve manufacturer—yet divides on the reasoning. The prevailing view, represented by Justice O'Connor, follows the decision in *World-Wide Volkswagen v. Woodson* in applying a narrow view of "stream of commerce theory" that insists on purposeful conduct by the defendant directed to the forum state. The Brennan group would find the requisite minimum contacts where, as here, the defendant is aware that the flow of commerce is bringing its product (or its component part) into the state. All agree, including Justice Stevens, that the "fair play and substantial justice" factors—now raised to coequal status with minimum contacts in the due process analysis—point against the exercise of adjudicatory power.

REVIEW QUESTIONS

1. What does *Asahi* hold? Answering this question requires a close reading of Justice O'Connor's opinion of the Court (the critical Part II-A of which is joined only by Rehnquist, Powell, and Scalia) as well as the opinions of Justice Brennan (joined by White, Marshall, and Blackmun) and Justice Stevens. Sketch out the areas of agreement and disagreement among the O'Connor group, the Brennan group, and Justice Stevens. Which group is Stevens closest to?

2. How is the issue of foreseeability raised by the conflicting affidavits submitted by Cheng Shin and Asahi? What does *Asahi* add to our understanding of the interplay among the concepts of foreseeability, purposeful availment, and minimum contacts?

3. Note the determinative role the "fair play and substantial justice" factors play in the *Asahi* decision: (1) Asahi, a foreign corporation, would have been subjected to the unfamiliar American legal system if compelled to defend in California; (2) the only remaining claim against Asahi was one for indemnification (in the nature of an impleader) asserted by another foreign corporation (the original plaintiff Zurcher having settled and left the litigation); (3) the valves in question traveled a circuitous route—manufactured by Asahi in Japan, shipped to Taiwan for assembly into Cheng Shin's tubes, and ending up in a tire on a motorcycle in California.

5. What is the relationship between the "fair play" factors and the "minimum-contacts" test after *Asahi*? This is explored in more depth in *Burger King Corp. v. Rudzewicz*, set out later in this chapter.

6. Note Justice O'Connor's heavy emphasis on the new factor of "additional conduct" directed at the forum. Such conduct was found in the case of the French corporation Perrier, sued on claims arising from its startling admission that benzene was found in its "naturally pure" water. *In re Perrier Bottled Water Litigation*, 754 F. Supp. 264 (D. Conn. 1990). The district court found that Perrier had designed its containers specifically for U.S. markets, as its bottles were labeled in ounces rather than metric

measures. Similarly, in *Vermeulen v. Renault*, 985 F.2d 1534, 1550 (11th Cir. 1993), the court found jurisdiction over the French auto manufacturer in a design defect action brought by an accident victim in Georgia. The Eleventh Circuit concluded that Renault had delivered its cars into the stream of commerce with the expectation that they would be purchased by consumers in the United States, and found "additional conduct" of the type Justice O'Connor referred to in *Asahi*: "Defendant designed the Renault LeCar for the American market, advertised the LeCar in the United States, established channels for customers in the United States to seek advice about the LeCar, and maintained a distribution network by which LeCars were imported into the United States." 985 F.2d at 1550. *See also State of New Hampshire v. North Atlantic Refining Ltd.*, 160 N.H. 275, 284-285 (2010) (groundwater contamination defendant formulated its gasoline specifically for the Northeastern U.S. market, including New Hampshire).

QUESTIONS TO PONDER

1. What result if the tire valve had been manufactured by an Ohio corporation at a factory in Cleveland, shipped to a Pennsylvania company for assembly into a tube in Pittsburgh, and then ended up in a tire that exploded in California? (In other words, remove the international dimension.) Jurisdiction over the domestic company in an action brought by the accident victim in California?

2. The issues raised by *Asahi* divided the business community as sharply as the Court. The Chamber of Commerce of the United Kingdom submitted an *amicus* brief in support of Asahi, arguing that "a rule of U.S. law that a foreign component part manufacturer is subject to the personal jurisdiction of any U.S. court in the territory in which it may be aware its foreign customer's products might come to rest, would substantially increase the costs and uncertainties of international trade for British manufacturers," and could lead to retaliatory measures adversely affecting free trade.

   The California Manufacturers Association countered in its *amicus* brief that the assertion of jurisdiction in such cases would protect California consumers from "duplicative and costly litigation which would otherwise be made necessary but for the granting of jurisdiction; and the manufacturer doing business in California, subjected to the sword of myriad state laws, rules and regulations, should be entitled to seek a shield of protection from those same laws when faced with defending an action in court commenced as a result of the use of a faulty foreign or alien component." The CMA further asserted that a "reversal of the California court's holding [asserting jurisdiction] may jeopardize the lives, safety and health of California consumers, businesses and manufacturers, by providing another barrier which increases the difficulty an individual or company presently confronts when seeking a legitimate and lawful solution to the assignment of responsibility (i.e., through impleader of the third party)."

To read more about the application of stream-of-commerce theory in international product liability cases in the years following *Asahi*, *see* Gary Born and Peter Rutledge, *International Civil Litigation in United States Courts*, 137-162 (5th ed. 2011).

3. Does *Asahi* permit a component manufacturer to insulate itself from suit merely by using an intermediary distributor, even when it is aware that its products are being continuously sold and used in the forum state? If so, isn't this a big "escape clause" for corporate wrongdoers? We'll come back to this matter again in our next case.

4. If you are frustrated by *Asahi*'s divided-decision lack of clarity, you are not alone. The Fifth Circuit Court of Appeals expressed it this way: "Because the Court's splintered view of minimum contacts in *Asahi* provides no clear guidance on this issue, we continue to gauge [the nonresident defendant's] contacts with Texas by the stream of commerce standard as described in *World-Wide Volkswagen* and embraced in this circuit." *Ruston Gas Turbines, Inc. v. Donaldson Company, Inc.*, 9 F.3d 415, 420 (5th Cir. 1993).

The federal circuits were understandably split on the proper reading of *Asahi*. For a case siding with the Brennan group, *see Barone v. Rich Bros. Interstate Display Fireworks Co.*, 25 F.3d 610 (8th Cir. 1994), holding a Japanese manufacturer subject to jurisdiction in a personal injury action in Nebraska pursuant to a liberal stream-of-commerce analysis. The Eighth Circuit noted that "a plurality of the Court in *Asahi* indicated its desire to limit this line of cases, but Justice O'Connor failed to muster a majority on that issue. . . . Five justices [the Brennan Four plus Stevens] agreed that continuous placement of a significant number of products into the stream of commerce with knowledge that the product would be distributed into the forum state represents sufficient minimum contacts to satisfy due process."

Compare *Bridgeport Music, Inc. v. Still N The Water Pub*, 327 F.3d 472 (6th Cir. 2003), dismissing a copyright infringement action against a music publisher based on Justice O'Connor's narrower "stream of commerce *plus*" approach: "The placement of a product into the stream of commerce, without more, is *not* an act of the defendant purposefully directed toward the forum State."

Given the importance of the jurisdictional issue in the global litigation context, and the inconclusiveness of *Asahi*'s guidance, it was inevitable that the matter would be revisited. It just took the Court twenty-four years.

J. McIntyre Machinery, Ltd. V. Nicastro
131 S. Ct. 2780 (2011)

JUSTICE KENNEDY announced the judgment of the Court and delivered an opinion, in which THE CHIEF JUSTICE, Justice SCALIA, and Justice THOMAS join.

Whether a person or entity is subject to the jurisdiction of a state court despite not having been present in the State either at the time of suit or at the time of the alleged injury, and despite not having consented to the exercise of jurisdiction, is a question that arises with great frequency in the routine course of litigation. The rules and standards for determining when a State does or does not have jurisdiction over an absent party have been unclear because of decades-old questions left open in *Asahi Metal Industry Co. v. Superior Court of Cal., Solano Cty.*, 480 U.S. 102 (1987).

Here, the Supreme Court of New Jersey, relying in part on *Asahi*, held that New Jersey's courts can exercise jurisdiction over a foreign manufacturer of a product so long as the manufacturer "knows or reasonably should know that its products are distributed through a nationwide distribution system that might lead to those products being sold in any of the fifty states." *Nicastro v. McIntyre Machinery America, Ltd.*, 201 N.J. 48, 76, 77, 987 A.2d 575, 591, 592 (2010). Applying that test, the court concluded that a British manufacturer of scrap metal machines was subject to jurisdiction in New Jersey, even though at no time had it advertised in, sent goods to, or in any relevant sense targeted the State.

That decision cannot be sustained. Although the New Jersey Supreme Court issued an extensive opinion with careful attention to this Court's cases and to its own precedent, the "stream of commerce" metaphor carried the decision far afield. Due process protects the defendant's right not to be coerced except by lawful judicial power. As a general rule, the exercise of judicial power is not lawful unless the defendant "purposefully avails itself of the privilege of conducting activities within the forum State, thus invoking the benefits and protections of its laws." *Hanson v. Denckla*. There may be exceptions, say, for instance, in cases involving an intentional tort. But the general rule is applicable in this products-liability case, and the so-called "stream-of-commerce" doctrine cannot displace it.

I

This case arises from a products-liability suit filed in New Jersey state court. Robert Nicastro seriously injured his hand while using a metal-shearing machine manufactured by J. McIntyre Machinery, Ltd. (J. McIntyre). The accident occurred in New Jersey, but the machine was manufactured in England, where J. McIntyre is incorporated and operates. The question here is whether the New Jersey courts have jurisdiction over J. McIntyre, notwithstanding the fact that the company at no time either marketed goods in the State or shipped them there. Nicastro was a plaintiff in the New Jersey trial court and is the respondent here; J. McIntyre was a defendant and is now the petitioner.

At oral argument in this Court, Nicastro's counsel stressed three primary facts in defense of New Jersey's assertion of jurisdiction over J. McIntyre.

First, an independent company agreed to sell J. McIntyre's machines in the United States. J. McIntyre itself did not sell its machines to buyers in this country beyond the U.S. distributor, and there is no allegation that the distributor was under J. McIntyre's control.

Second, J. McIntyre officials attended annual conventions for the scrap recycling industry to advertise J. McIntyre's machines alongside the distributor. The conventions took place in various States, but never in New Jersey.

Third, no more than four machines (the record suggests only one), including the machine that caused the injuries that are the basis for this suit, ended up in New Jersey.

In addition to these facts emphasized by respondent, the New Jersey Supreme Court noted that J. McIntyre held both United States and European patents on its recycling technology. It also noted that the U.S. distributor "structured [its] advertising and sales efforts in accordance with" J. McIntyre's "direction and guidance whenever possible," and that "at least some of the machines were sold on consignment to" the distributor.

In light of these facts, the New Jersey Supreme Court concluded that New Jersey courts could exercise jurisdiction over petitioner without contravention of the Due Process Clause. Jurisdiction was proper, in that court's view, because the injury occurred in New Jersey; because petitioner knew or reasonably should have known "that its products are distributed through a nationwide distribution system that might lead to those products being sold in any of the fifty states"; and because petitioner failed to "take some reasonable step to prevent the distribution of its products in this State."

Both the New Jersey Supreme Court's holding and its account of what it called "[t]he stream-of-commerce doctrine of jurisdiction" were incorrect, however. This Court's *Asahi* decision may be responsible in part for that court's error regarding the stream of commerce, and this case presents an opportunity to provide greater clarity.

II

The Due Process Clause protects an individual's right to be deprived of life, liberty, or property only by the exercise of lawful power. . . . A court may subject a defendant to judgment only when the defendant has sufficient contacts with the sovereign "such that the maintenance of the suit does not offend 'traditional notions of fair play and substantial justice.'" *International Shoe Co. v. Washington*. As a general rule, the sovereign's exercise of power requires some act by which the defendant "purposefully avails itself of the privilege of conducting activities within the forum State, thus invoking the benefits and protections of its laws," *Hanson*, though in some cases, as with an intentional tort, the defendant might well fall within the State's authority by reason of his attempt to obstruct its laws. In products-liability cases like this one, it is the defendant's purposeful availment that makes jurisdiction consistent with "traditional notions of fair play and substantial justice."

A person may submit to a State's authority in a number of ways. There is, of course, explicit consent. Presence within a State at the time suit commences through service of process is another example. Citizenship or domicile—or, by analogy, incorporation or principal place of business for corporations—also indicates general submission to a State's powers. Each of these examples reveals circumstances, or a course of conduct, from which it is proper to infer an intention to benefit from and thus an intention to submit to the laws of the forum State. These examples support exercise of the general jurisdiction of the State's courts and allow the State to resolve both matters that originate within the State and those based on activities and events elsewhere. By contrast, those who live or operate primarily outside a State have a due process right not to be subjected to judgment in its courts as a general matter.

There is also a more limited form of submission to a State's authority for disputes that "arise out of or are connected with the activities within the state." Where a defendant "purposefully avails itself of the privilege of conducting activities within the forum State, thus invoking the benefits and protections of its laws," *Hanson*, it submits to the judicial power of an otherwise foreign sovereign to the extent that power is exercised in connection with the defendant's activities touching on the State. In other words, submission through contact with and activity directed at a sovereign may justify specific jurisdiction "in a suit arising out of or related to the defendant's contacts with the forum."

The imprecision arising from *Asahi*, for the most part, results from its statement of the relation between jurisdiction and the "stream of commerce." The stream of commerce, like other metaphors, has its deficiencies as well as its utility. It refers to the movement of goods from manufacturers through distributors to consumers, yet beyond that descriptive purpose its meaning is far from exact. This Court has stated that a defendant's placing goods into the stream of commerce "with the expectation that they will be purchased by consumers within the forum State" may indicate purposeful availment. *World-Wide Volkswagen Corp. v. Woodson* (finding that expectation lacking). But that statement does not amend the general rule of personal jurisdiction. It merely observes that a defendant may in an appropriate case be subject to jurisdiction without entering the forum—itself an unexceptional proposition—as where manufacturers or distributors "seek to serve" a given State's market. The principal inquiry in cases of this sort is whether the defendant's activities manifest an intention to submit to the power of a sovereign. In other words, the defendant must "purposefully avai[l] itself of the privilege of conducting activities within the forum State, thus invoking the benefits and protections of its laws." *Hanson*. Sometimes a defendant does so by sending its goods rather than its agents. The defendant's transmission of goods permits the exercise of jurisdiction only where the defendant can be said to have targeted the forum; as a general rule, it is not enough that the defendant might have predicted that its goods will reach the forum State.

In *Asahi*, an opinion by Justice Brennan for four Justices outlined a different approach. It discarded the central concept of sovereign authority in favor of considerations of fairness and foreseeability. As that concurrence contended, "jurisdiction premised on the placement of a product into the stream of commerce [without more] is consistent with the Due Process Clause," for "[a]s long as a participant in this process is aware that the final product is being marketed in the forum State, the possibility of a lawsuit there cannot come as a surprise" (opinion concurring in part and concurring in judgment). It was the premise of the concurring opinion that the defendant's ability to anticipate suit renders the assertion of jurisdiction fair. In this way, the opinion made foreseeability the touchstone of jurisdiction.

The standard set forth in Justice Brennan's concurrence was rejected in an opinion written by Justice O'Connor; but the relevant part of that opinion, too, commanded the assent of only four Justices, not a majority of the Court. That opinion stated: "The 'substantial connection' between the defendant and the forum State necessary for a finding of minimum contacts must come about by an action of the defendant purposefully directed toward the forum State. The placement of a product into the stream of commerce, without more, is not an act of the defendant purposefully directed toward the forum State."

Since *Asahi* was decided, the courts have sought to reconcile the competing opinions. But Justice Brennan's concurrence, advocating a rule based on general notions of fairness and foreseeability, is inconsistent with the premises of lawful judicial power. This Court's precedents make clear that it is the defendant's actions, not his expectations, that empower a State's courts to subject him to judgment.

The conclusion that jurisdiction is in the first instance a question of authority rather than fairness explains, for example, why the principal opinion in *Burnham* "conducted no independent inquiry into the desirability or fairness" of the rule that service of process within a State suffices to establish jurisdiction over an otherwise foreign defendant. 495 U.S., at 621, 110 S.Ct. 2105 (opinion of Scalia, J.). As that opinion explained, "[t]he view developed early that each State had the power to hale before its courts any individual who could be found within its borders." *Id.,* at 610, 110 S.Ct. 2105. Furthermore, were general fairness considerations the touchstone of jurisdiction, a lack of purposeful availment might be excused where carefully crafted judicial procedures could otherwise protect the defendant's interests, or where the plaintiff would suffer substantial hardship if forced to litigate in a foreign forum. That such considerations have not been deemed controlling is instructive. See, *e.g., World-Wide Volkswagen, supra,* at 294, 100 S.Ct. 559.

Two principles are implicit in the foregoing. First, personal jurisdiction requires a forum-by-forum, or sovereign-by-sovereign, analysis. The question is whether a defendant has followed a course of conduct directed at the society or economy existing within the jurisdiction of a given sovereign, so that the sovereign has the power to subject the defendant to judgment concerning that conduct. Personal jurisdiction, of course, restricts "judicial power not as a matter of sovereignty, but as a matter of individual liberty," for due process protects the individual's right to be subject only to lawful power. *Insurance Corp.*, 456 U.S., at 702, 102 S.Ct. 2099. But whether a judicial judgment is lawful depends on whether the sovereign has authority to render it.

The second principle is a corollary of the first. Because the United States is a distinct sovereign, a defendant may in principle be subject to the jurisdiction of the courts of the United States but not of any particular State. This is consistent with the premises and unique genius of our Constitution. Ours is "a legal system unprecedented in form and design, establishing two orders of government, each with its own direct relationship, its own privity, its own set of mutual rights and obligations to the people who sustain it and are governed by it." *U.S. Term Limits, Inc. v. Thornton,* 514 U.S. 779, 838, 115 S.Ct. 1842, 131 L.Ed.2d 881 (1995) (KENNEDY, J., concurring). For jurisdiction, a litigant may have the requisite relationship with the United States Government but not with the government of any individual State. That would be an exceptional case, however. If the defendant is a domestic domiciliary, the courts of its home State are available and can exercise general jurisdiction. And if another State were to assert jurisdiction in an inappropriate case, it would upset the federal balance, which posits that each State has a sovereignty that is not subject to unlawful intrusion by other States. Furthermore, foreign corporations will often target or concentrate on particular States, subjecting them to specific jurisdiction in those forums.

It must be remembered, however, that although this case and *Asahi* both involve foreign manufacturers, the undesirable consequences of Justice Brennan's approach are no less significant for domestic producers. The owner of a small Florida farm might sell crops to a large nearby distributor, for example, who might then distribute them to grocers across the country. If foreseeability were the controlling criterion, the farmer could be sued in Alaska or any number of other States' courts without ever leaving town. And the issue of foreseeability may itself be contested so that significant expenses are incurred just on the preliminary issue of jurisdiction. Jurisdictional rules should avoid these costs whenever possible.

The conclusion that the authority to subject a defendant to judgment depends on purposeful availment, consistent with Justice O'Connor's opinion in *Asahi,* does not by itself resolve many difficult questions of jurisdiction that will arise in particular cases. The defendant's conduct and the economic realities of the market the defendant seeks to serve will differ across cases, and judicial exposition will, in common-law fashion, clarify the contours of that principle.

III

In this case, petitioner directed marketing and sales efforts at the United States. . . . Here the question concerns the authority of a New Jersey state court to exercise jurisdiction, so it is petitioner's purposeful contacts with New Jersey, not with the United States, that alone are relevant.

Respondent has not established that J. McIntyre engaged in conduct purposefully directed at New Jersey. . . .The British manufacturer had no office in New Jersey; it neither paid taxes nor owned property there; and it neither advertised in, nor sent any employees to, the State. Indeed, after discovery the trial court found that the "defendant does not have a single contact with New Jersey short of the machine in question ending up in this state." These facts may reveal an intent to serve the U.S. market, but they do not show that J. McIntyre purposefully availed itself of the New Jersey market.

[T]he New Jersey Supreme Court . . . nonetheless held that petitioner could be sued in New Jersey based on a "stream-of-commerce theory of jurisdiction." As discussed, however, the stream-of-commerce metaphor cannot supersede either the mandate of the Due Process Clause or the limits on judicial authority that Clause ensures. The New Jersey Supreme Court also cited "significant policy reasons" to justify its holding, including the State's "strong interest in protecting its citizens from defective products." That interest is doubtless strong, but the Constitution commands restraint before discarding liberty in the name of expediency. . . .

Due process protects petitioner's right to be subject only to lawful authority. At no time did petitioner engage in any activities in New Jersey that reveal an intent to invoke or benefit from the protection of its laws. New Jersey is without power to adjudge the rights and liabilities of J. McIntyre, and its exercise of jurisdiction would violate due process. The contrary judgment of the New Jersey Supreme Court is reversed.

Justice BREYER, with whom Justice ALITO joins, concurring in the judgment.

The Supreme Court of New Jersey adopted a broad understanding of the scope of personal jurisdiction based on its view that "[t]he increasingly fast-paced globalization of the world economy has removed national borders as barriers to trade." I do not doubt that there have been many recent changes in commerce and communication, many of which are not anticipated by our precedents. But this case does not present any of those issues. So I think it unwise to announce a rule of broad applicability without full consideration of the modern-day consequences.

In my view, the outcome of this case is determined by our precedents. Based on the facts found by the New Jersey courts, respondent Robert Nicastro failed to meet his burden to demonstrate that it was constitutionally proper to exercise jurisdiction over petitioner J. McIntyre Machinery, Ltd., a British firm that manufactures scrap-metal machines in Great Britain and sells them through an independent distributor in the United States. On that basis, I agree with the plurality that the contrary judgment of the Supreme Court of New Jersey should be reversed. . . .

None of our precedents finds that a single isolated sale, even if accompanied by the kind of sales effort indicated here, is sufficient. Rather, this Court's previous holdings suggest the contrary. The Court has held that a single sale to a customer who takes an accident-causing product to a different State (where the accident takes place) is not a sufficient basis for asserting jurisdiction. See *World-Wide Volkswagen Corp. v. Woodson*, 444 U.S. 286 (1980). And the Court, in separate opinions, has strongly suggested that a single sale of a product in a State does not constitute an adequate basis for asserting jurisdiction over an out-of-state defendant, even if that defendant places his goods in the stream of commerce, fully aware (and hoping) that such a sale will take place. See *Asahi Metal Industry Co. v. Superior Court of Cal., Solano Cty.*, 480 U.S. 102, 111 (1987) (opinion of O'Connor, J.) (requiring "something more" than simply placing "a product into the stream of commerce," even if defendant is "awar[e]" that the stream "may or will sweep the product into the forum State"); (Brennan, J., concurring in part and concurring in judgment) (jurisdiction should lie where a sale in a State is part of "the regular and anticipated flow" of commerce into the State, but not where that sale is only an "edd[y]," *i.e.*, an isolated occurrence); (Stevens, J., concurring in part and concurring in judgment) (indicating that "the volume, the value, and the hazardous character" of a good may affect the jurisdictional inquiry and emphasizing Asahi's "regular course of dealing").

Here, the relevant facts found by the New Jersey Supreme Court show no "regular . . . flow" or "regular course" of sales in New Jersey; and there is no "something more," such as special state-related design, advertising, advice, marketing, or anything else. Mr. Nicastro, who here bears the burden of proving jurisdiction, has shown no specific effort by the British Manufacturer to sell in New Jersey. He has introduced no list of potential New Jersey customers who might, for example, have regularly attended trade shows. And he has not otherwise shown that the British Manufacturer "purposefully avail[ed] itself of the privilege of conducting activities" within New Jersey, or that it delivered its goods in the stream of commerce "with the expectation that they will be purchased" by New Jersey users. *World-Wide Volkswagen*.

Accordingly, on the record present here, resolving this case requires no more than adhering to our precedents. . . .

II

B

But though I do not agree with the plurality's seemingly strict no-jurisdiction rule, I am not persuaded by the absolute approach adopted by the New Jersey Supreme Court and urged by respondent and his amici. Under that view, a producer is subject to jurisdiction for a products-liability action so long as it "knows or reasonably should know that its products are distributed through a nation-wide distribution system that might lead to those products being sold in any of the fifty states." In the context of this case, I cannot agree.

For one thing, to adopt this view would abandon the heretofore accepted inquiry of whether, focusing upon the relationship between "the defendant, the *forum,* and the litigation," it is fair, in light of the defendant's contacts *with that forum,* to subject the defendant to suit there. It would ordinarily rest jurisdiction instead upon no more than the occurrence of a product-based accident in the forum State. But this Court has rejected the notion that a defendant's amenability to suit "travel[s] with the chattel." *World-Wide Volkswagen*.

For another, I cannot reconcile so automatic a rule with the constitutional demand for "minimum contacts" and "purposefu[l] avail[ment]," each of which rest upon a particular notion of defendant-focused fairness. A rule like the New Jersey Supreme Court's would permit every State to assert jurisdiction in a products-liability suit against any domestic manufacturer who sells its products (made anywhere in the United States) to a national distributor, no matter how large or small the manufacturer, no matter how distant the forum, and no matter how few the number of items that end up in the particular forum at issue. What might appear fair in the case of a large manufacturer which specifically seeks, or expects, an equal-sized distributor to sell its product in a distant State might seem unfair in the case of a small manufacturer (say, an Appalachian potter) who sells his product (cups and saucers) exclusively to a large distributor, who resells a single item (a coffee mug) to a buyer from a distant State (Hawaii). I know too little about the range of these or in-between possibilities to abandon in favor of the more absolute rule what has previously been this Court's less absolute approach.

Further, the fact that the defendant is a foreign, rather than a domestic, manufacturer makes the basic fairness of an absolute rule yet more uncertain. I am again less certain than is the New Jersey Supreme Court that the nature of international commerce has changed so significantly as to require a new approach to personal jurisdiction. . . .

[M]anufacturers come in many shapes and sizes. It may be fundamentally unfair to require a small Egyptian shirt maker, a Brazilian manufacturing cooperative, or a Kenyan coffee farmer, selling its products through international distributors, to respond to products-liability tort suits in virtually every State in the United States, even those in respect to which the foreign firm has no connection at all but the sale of a single (allegedly defective) good. . . .

I do not think we can find jurisdiction in this case. Accordingly, though I agree with the plurality as to the outcome of this case, I concur only in the judgment of that opinion and not its reasoning.

Justice GINSBURG, with whom Justice SOTOMAYOR and Justice KAGAN join, dissenting.

A foreign industrialist seeks to develop a market in the United States for machines it manufactures. It hopes to derive substantial revenue from sales it makes to United States purchasers. Where in the United States buyers reside does not matter to this manufacturer. Its goal is simply to sell as much as it can, wherever it can. It excludes no region or State from the market it wishes to reach. But, all things considered, it prefers to avoid products liability litigation in the United States. To that end, it engages a U.S. distributor to ship its machines state-side. Has it succeeded in escaping personal jurisdiction in a State where one of its products is sold and causes injury or even death to a local user?

Under this Court's pathmarking precedent in *International Shoe Co. v. Washington*, and subsequent decisions, one would expect the answer to be unequivocally, "No." But instead, six Justices of this Court, in divergent opinions, tell us that the manufacturer has avoided the jurisdiction of our state courts, except perhaps in States where its products are sold in sizeable quantities. Inconceivable as it may have seemed yesterday, the splintered majority today "turn[s] the clock back to the days before modern long-arm statutes when a manufacturer, to avoid being haled into court where a user is injured, need only Pilate-like wash its hands of a product by having independent distributors market it."

I

On October 11, 2001, a three-ton metal shearing machine severed four fingers on Robert Nicastro's right hand. Alleging that the machine was a dangerous product defectively made, Nicastro sought compensation from the machine's manufacturer, McIntyre UK. Established in 1872 as a United Kingdom corporation, and headquartered in Nottingham, England, McIntyre UK "designs, develops and manufactures a complete range of equipment for metal recycling." The company's product line, as advertised on McIntyre UK's Web site, includes "metal shears, balers, cable and can recycling equipment, furnaces, casting equipment and . . . the world's best aluminium dross processing and cooling system." McIntyre UK holds both United States and European patents on its technology.

The machine that injured Nicastro, a "McIntyre Model 640 Shear," sold in the United States for $24,900 in 1995, and features a "massive cutting capacity." According to McIntyre UK's product brochure, the machine is "use[d] throughout the [w]orld." McIntyre UK represented in the brochure that, by "incorporat[ing] off-the-shelf hydraulic parts from suppliers with international sales outlets," the 640 Shear's design guarantees serviceability "wherever [its customers] may be based." The instruction manual advises "owner[s] and operators of a 640 Shear [to] make themselves aware of [applicable health and safety regulations]," including "the American National Standards Institute Regulations (USA) for the use of Scrap Metal Processing Equipment."

Nicastro operated the 640 Shear in the course of his employment at Curcio Scrap Metal (CSM) in Saddle Brook, New Jersey. "New Jersey has long been a hotbed of scrap-metal businesses. . . ." New Jersey recycling facilities processed 2,013,730 tons of scrap iron, steel, aluminum, and other metals—more than any other State—outpacing Kentucky, its nearest competitor, by nearly 30 percent.

CSM's owner, Frank Curcio, "first heard of [McIntyre UK's] machine while attending an Institute of Scrap Metal Industries [(ISRI)] convention in Las Vegas in 1994 or 1995, where McIntyre UK was an exhibitor." ISRI "presents the world's largest scrap recycling industry trade show each year." The event attracts "owners [and] managers of scrap processing companies" and others "interested in seeing—and purchasing—new equipment." According to ISRI, more than 3,000 potential buyers of scrap processing and recycling equipment attend its annual conventions, "primarily because th[e] exposition provides them with the most comprehensive industry-related shopping experience concentrated in a single, convenient location." Exhibitors who are ISRI members pay $3,000 for 10′ × 10′ booth space.

McIntyre UK representatives attended every ISRI convention from 1990 through 2005. . . .

Although McIntyre UK's U.S. sales figures are not in the record, it appears that for several years in the 1990's, earnings from sales of McIntyre UK products in the United States "ha[d] been good" in comparison to "the rest of the world." . . .

From at least 1995 until 2001, McIntyre UK retained an Ohio-based company, McIntyre Machinery America, Ltd. (McIntyre America), "as its exclusive distributor for the entire United States." Though similarly named, the two companies were separate and independent entities with "no commonality of ownership or management." In invoices and other written communications, McIntyre America described itself as McIntyre UK's national distributor, "America's Link" to "Quality Metal Processing Equipment" from England.

In a November 23, 1999 letter to McIntyre America, McIntyre UK's president spoke plainly about the manufacturer's objective in authorizing the exclusive distributorship: "All we wish to do is sell our products in the [United] States—and get paid!" Notably, McIntyre America was concerned about U.S. litigation involving McIntyre UK products, in which the distributor had been named as a defendant. McIntyre UK counseled McIntyre America to respond personally to the litigation, but reassured its distributor that "the product was built and designed by McIntyre Machinery in the UK and the buck stops here—if there's something wrong with the machine." Answering jurisdictional interrogatories, McIntyre UK stated that it had been named as a defendant in lawsuits in Illinois, Kentucky, Massachusetts, and West Virginia. And in correspondence with McIntyre America, McIntyre UK noted that the manufacturer had products liability insurance coverage.

Over the years, McIntyre America distributed several McIntyre UK products to U.S. customers. . . . To achieve McIntyre UK's objective, i.e., "to sell [its] machines to customers throughout the United States, the two companies were acting closely in concert with each other." McIntyre UK never instructed its distributor to avoid certain States or regions of the country; rather, as just noted, the manufacturer engaged McIntyre America to attract customers "from anywhere in the United States."

In sum, McIntyre UK's regular attendance and exhibitions at ISRI conventions was surely a purposeful step to reach customers for its products "anywhere in the United States." At least as purposeful was McIntyre UK's engagement of McIntyre America as the conduit for sales of McIntyre UK's machines to buyers "throughout the United States." Given McIntyre UK's endeavors to reach and profit from the United States market as a whole, Nicastro's suit, I would hold, has been brought in a forum entirely appropriate for the adjudication of his claim. He alleges that McIntyre UK's shear machine was defectively designed or manufactured and, as a result, caused injury to him at his workplace. The machine arrived in Nicastro's New Jersey workplace not randomly or fortuitously, but as a result of the U.S. connections and distribution system that McIntyre UK deliberately arranged.[5] On what sensible view of the allocation of adjudicatory authority could the place of Nicastro's injury within the United States be deemed off limits for his products liability claim against a foreign manufacturer who targeted the United States (including all the States that constitute the Nation) as the territory it sought to develop?

II

[T]he constitutional limits on a state court's adjudicatory authority derive from considerations of due process, not state sovereignty. . . . "The restriction on state sovereign power described in *World-Wide Volkswagen Corp.* must be seen as ultimately a function of the individual liberty interest preserved by the Due Process Clause. That Clause is the only source of the personal jurisdiction requirement and the Clause itself makes no mention of federalism concerns. Furthermore, if the federalism concept operated as an independent restriction on the sovereign power of the court, it would not be possible to waive the personal jurisdiction requirement: Individual actions cannot change the powers of sovereignty, although the individual can subject himself to powers from which he may otherwise be protected.". . .

Whatever the state of academic debate over the role of consent in modern jurisdictional doctrines, the plurality's notion that consent is the animating concept draws no support from controlling decisions of this Court. Quite the contrary, the Court has explained, a forum can exercise jurisdiction when its contacts with the controversy are sufficient; invocation of a fictitious consent, the Court has repeatedly said, is unnecessary and unhelpful. See, e.g., *Burger King Corp. v. Rudzewicz* , 471 U.S. 462, 472 (1985) (Due Process Clause permits "forum . . . to assert specific jurisdiction over an out-of-state defendant who has not consented to suit there"); *McGee v. International Life Ins. Co.*, 355 U.S. 220, 222 (1957) ("[T]his Court [has] abandoned 'consent,' 'doing business,' and 'presence' as the standard for measuring the extent of state judicial power over [out-of-state] corporations.").[6]

---

5. McIntyre UK resisted Nicastro's efforts to determine whether other McIntyre machines had been sold to New Jersey customers. McIntyre did allow that McIntyre America "may have resold products it purchased from McIntyre UK to a buyer in New Jersey," but said it kept no record of the ultimate destination of machines it shipped to its distributor. A private investigator engaged by Nicastro found at least one McIntyre UK machine, of unspecified type, in use in New Jersey. But McIntyre UK objected that the investigator's report was "unsworn and based upon hearsay." Moreover, McIntyre UK maintained, no evidence showed that the machine the investigator found in New Jersey had been "sold into that State."

6. But see ante, at 4-8 (plurality opinion) (maintaining that a forum may be fair and reasonable, based on its links to the episode in suit, yet off limits because the defendant has not submitted to the State's authority). The plurality's notion that jurisdiction over foreign corporations depends upon the defendant's "submission," ante, at 6, seems scarcely different from the long-discredited fiction of implied consent. It bears emphasis that a majority of this Court's members do not share the plurality's view.

III

This case is illustrative of marketing arrangements for sales in the United States common in today's commercial world. A foreign-country manufacturer engages a U.S. company to promote and distribute the manufacturer's products, not in any particular State, but anywhere and everywhere in the United States the distributor can attract purchasers. The product proves defective and injures a user in the State where the user lives or works. Often, as here, the manufacturer will have liability insurance covering personal injuries caused by its products.

When industrial accidents happen, a long-arm statute in the State where the injury occurs generally permits assertion of jurisdiction, upon giving proper notice, over the foreign manufacturer. For example, the State's statute might provide, as does New York's long-arm statute, for the "exercise [of] personal jurisdiction over any nondomiciliary . . . who . . . "commits a tortious act without the state causing injury to person or property within the state, . . . if he . . . expects or should reasonably expect the act to have consequences in the state and derives substantial revenue from interstate or international commerce." N.Y. Civ. Prac. Law Ann. § 302(a)(3)(ii) (West 2008). Or, the State might simply provide, as New Jersey does, for the exercise of jurisdiction "consistent with due process of law." N.J. Ct. Rule 4:4-4(b)(1) (2011).

The modern approach to jurisdiction over corporations and other legal entities, ushered in by *International Shoe*, gave prime place to reason and fairness. Is it not fair and reasonable, given the mode of trading of which this case is an example, to require the international seller to defend at the place its products cause injury? Do not litigational convenience and choice-of-law considerations point in that direction? On what measure of reason and fairness can it be considered undue to require McIntyre UK to defend in New Jersey as an incident of its efforts to develop a market for its industrial machines anywhere and everywhere in the United States? Is not the burden on McIntyre UK to defend in New Jersey fair, i.e., a reasonable cost of transacting business internationally, in comparison to the burden on Nicastro to go to Nottingham, England to gain recompense for an injury he sustained using McIntyre's product at his workplace in Saddle Brook, New Jersey? . . .

Adjudicatory authority is appropriately exercised where "actions by the defendant himself" give rise to the affiliation with the forum. How could McIntyre UK not have intended, by its actions targeting a national market, to sell products in the fourth largest destination for imports among all States of the United States and the largest scrap metal market? . . .

IV

A

While this Court has not considered in any prior case the now-prevalent pattern presented here—a foreign-country manufacturer enlisting a U.S. distributor to develop a market in the United States for the manufacturer's products—none of the Court's decisions tug against the judgment made by the New Jersey Supreme Court. McIntyre contends otherwise, citing *World-Wide Volkswagen*, and *Asahi Metal Industry Co. v. Superior Court of Cal., Solano Cty.*

World-Wide Volkswagen concerned a New York car dealership that sold solely in the New York market, and a New York distributor who supplied retailers in three States only: New York, Connecticut, and New Jersey. New York residents had purchased an Audi from the New York dealer and were driving the new vehicle through Oklahoma en route to Arizona. On the road in Oklahoma, another car struck the Audi in the rear, causing a fire which severely burned the Audi's occupants. Rejecting the Oklahoma courts' assertion of jurisdiction over the New York dealer and distributor, this Court observed that the defendants had done nothing to serve the market for cars in Oklahoma. Jurisdiction, the Court held, could not be based on the customer's unilateral act of driving the vehicle to Oklahoma.

Notably, the foreign manufacturer of the Audi in *World-Wide Volkswagen* did not object to the jurisdiction of the Oklahoma courts and the U.S. importer abandoned its initially stated objection. And most relevant here, the Court's opinion indicates that an objection to jurisdiction by the manufacturer or national distributor would have been unavailing. To reiterate, the Court said in *World-Wide Volkswagen* that, when a manufacturer or distributor aims to sell its product to customers in several States, it is reasonable "to subject it to suit in [any] one of those States if its allegedly defective [product] has there been the source of injury."

Asahi arose out of a motorcycle accident in California. Plaintiff, a California resident injured in the accident, sued the Taiwanese manufacturer of the motorcycle's tire tubes, claiming that defects in its product caused the accident. The tube manufacturer cross-claimed against Asahi, the Japanese maker of the valve assembly, and Asahi contested the California courts' jurisdiction. By the time the case reached this Court, the injured plaintiff had settled his case and only the indemnity claim by the Taiwanese company against the Japanese valve-assembly manufacturer remained.

The decision was not a close call. The Court had before it a foreign plaintiff, the Taiwanese manufacturer, and a foreign defendant, the Japanese valve-assembly maker, and the indemnification dispute concerned a transaction between those parties that occurred abroad. All agreed on the bottom line: The Japanese valve-assembly manufacturer was not reasonably brought into the California courts to litigate a dispute with another foreign party over a transaction that took place outside the United States.

Given the confines of the controversy, the dueling opinions of Justice Brennan and Justice O'Connor were hardly necessary. How the Court would have "estimate[d] . . . the inconveniences," see *International Shoe*, had the injured Californian originally sued Asahi is a debatable question. Would this Court have given the same weight to the burdens on the foreign defendant had those been counterbalanced by the burdens litigating in Japan imposed on the local California plaintiff? Cf. *Calder v. Jones*, 465 U.S. 783, 788 (1984) (a plaintiff's contacts with the forum "may be so manifold as to permit jurisdiction when it would not exist in their absence").

In any event, Asahi, unlike McIntyre UK, did not itself seek out customers in the United States, it engaged no distributor to promote its wares here, it appeared at no tradeshows in the United States, and, of course, it had no Web site advertising its products to the world. Moreover, Asahi was a component-part manufacturer with "little control over the final destination of its products once they were delivered into the stream of commerce." It was important to the Court in *Asahi* that "those who use Asahi components in their final products, and sell those products in California, [would be] subject to the application of California tort law." To hold that *Asahi* controls this case would, to put it bluntly, be dead wrong.[9]

B

The Court's judgment also puts United States plaintiffs at a disadvantage in comparison to similarly situated complainants elsewhere in the world. Of particular note, within the European Union, in which the United Kingdom is a participant, the jurisdiction New Jersey would have exercised is not at all exceptional. The European Regulation on Jurisdiction and the Recognition and Enforcement of Judgments provides for the exercise of specific jurisdiction "in matters relating to tort . . . in the courts for the place where the harmful event occurred." The European Court of Justice has interpreted this prescription to authorize jurisdiction either where the harmful act occurred or at the place of injury.

V

. . . For the reasons stated, I would hold McIntyre UK answerable in New Jersey for the harm Nicastro suffered at his workplace in that State using McIntyre UK's shearing machine. While I dissent from the Court's judgment, I take heart that the plurality opinion does not speak for the Court, for that opinion would take a giant step away from the "notions of fair play and substantial justice" underlying *International Shoe*.

YOUR TAKEAWAY

The Court's third shot at defining the circumstances in which a distant manufacturer or retailer may be held amenable to suit in the state of injury reveals the familiar split between a plurality looking for (and not finding) evidence of a clear intent to directly serve the market in the forum, and dissenters who would find jurisdiction where the defendant *indirectly* connects itself to the forum, i.e., by setting up a distribution system through an intermediary. What's new is Justice Kennedy's premising jurisdiction on submission to the forum's authority.

---

9. The plurality notes the low volume of sales in New Jersey. A $24,900 shearing machine, however, is unlikely to sell in bulk worldwide, much less in any given State. By dollar value, the price of a single machine represents a significant sale. Had a manufacturer sold in New Jersey $24,900 worth of flannel shirts, cigarette lighters, or wire-rope splices, the Court would presumably find the defendant amenable to suit in that State.

To Justice Ginsburg, this turns the clock back to the long discredited fiction of implied consent, and permits easy circumvention of suit by interposing a distributor who, while ostensibly independent, acts at the direction of the defendant.

REVIEW QUESTIONS

1. Having stated the obvious, that "[t]he rules and standards for determining when a State does or does not have jurisdiction over an absent party have been unclear because of decades-old questions left open in *Asahi Metal Industry Co. v. Superior Court of Cal., Solano Cty.*," Justice Kennedy sees *Nicastro* as "an opportunity to provide greater clarity." Has he achieved that objective? Does the Court adopt a form of Justice O'Connor's "additional conduct" test, or something even stricter? Have we merely moved from the murkiness of *Asahi*'s 4-4-1 split to the ambiguity of *Nicastro*'s 4-2-3?

2. In the continuing debate about whether personal jurisdiction is a matter of sovereign power *or* individual liberty, Justice Kennedy makes no secret about where he comes out. Note Justice Ginsburg's (joined by Sotomayor and Kagan) response in her dissent: "The constitutional limits on a state court's adjudicatory authority derive from considerations of due process, not state sovereignty." Can there be "greater clarity" on the matter of personal jurisdiction absent agreement on the Court about its fundamental premise?

3. Were you surprised to see Justice Kennedy transform *International Shoe* into the power-based question of whether the defendant exhibited an "intention to submit to the laws of the forum State"? (How many times does Kennedy use the word "submit" or "submission"?) For Justice Ginsburg "the plurality's notion that consent is the animating concept draws no support from controlling decisions of this Court. Quite the contrary, the Court has explained, a forum can exercise jurisdiction when its contacts with the controversy are sufficient; invocation of a fictitious consent, the Court has repeatedly said, is unnecessary and unhelpful." 131 S. Ct. at 2799.

4. What has happened to the fair play/reasonableness prong of due process analysis?

5. Throughout the oral argument, Justice Breyer expressed concern for any rule that would subject a small business like a women's pottery cooperative in India or goat herders in Ethiopia or an Appalachian potter to suit wherever its product lands, by its direction or otherwise. Transcript, Oral Argument, pp. 30-34, 50-51. And Kennedy was worried about the "owner of a small Florida farm [who] might sell crops to a large nearby distributor, who might then distribute them to grocers across the country. If foreseeability were the controlling criterion, the farmer could be sued in Alaska or any number of other States' courts without ever leaving town." 564 U.S. at 885.

Are those scenarios really analogous to *Nicastro*? Could the little-guy defendant not be protected in such cases through the traditional fair play factors—weighing the interests of the litigants, the forum state, and the location of witnesses and evidence? What about use of a forum selection clause (discussed in Part N, later in this chapter)?

6. What do you make of the unlikely pairing of Justices Breyer and Alito, concurring? What is their position?

7. Had you been an observer in court during the first minutes of the oral argument in *Nicastro*, could you have predicted where at least two of the Justices would come out?

> *Mr. Fergenson:* Mr. Chief Justice, and may it please the Court: Because J. McIntyre did not direct any activity at residents of New Jersey either itself or by directing its distributor MMA to do so and had no awareness or knowledge that the distributor took the action that it did toward New Jersey, New Jersey lacked adjudicative jurisdiction.
>
> *Justice Scalia:* When you say "its distributor," was this distributor at all controlled by the defendant?
>
> *Mr. Fergenson:* No, Your Honor. It was not. And both under Ohio law and under the Restatement (Second) Agency, section 1-1, the right to control is essential to ascribe actions to create an agency, and it's on a per-purpose basis.
>
> *Justice Scalia [apparently offering legal assistance to defendant's counsel]:* It might be better to refer to it as the company that distributed its product, rather than calling it "its distributor."
>
> *Mr. Fergenson:* Very good, Your Honor.
>
> *Justice Scalia:* It's loaded, it seems to me.
>
> *Justice Kagan [tying down a key point for plaintiff's case]:* Mr. Fergenson, in your question presented to this court, you asked whether there's personal jurisdiction—and I'm quoting here—"solely because the manufacturer targets the United States market for the sale of the product." So I'm taking from that, that you acknowledge that this manufacturer, McIntyre, a British manufacturer, targeted the United States market for the sale of its product. That's correct, yes?
>
> *Mr. Fergenson:* Yes.

Transcript, Oral Argument, pp. 3-5.

8. The U.S. Chamber of Commerce filed an *amicus* brief in support of petitioner J. McIntyre Machinery, Ltd., citing the "vital concerns" for the nation's business community that were at stake. An *amicus* brief filed by a group of law professors (and who know more about personal jurisdiction?) in support of Nicastro urged the Court to adopt "a clear rule that a manufacturer establishes minimum contacts with the forum state when it purposefully endeavors to access the U.S. market generally and its product is thereby distributed to and causes injury in the forum state." Whose advice did the Court follow?

9. Where next for Mr. Nicastro? Either sue McIntyre in the UK, or forego his claim. (The Ohio distributor was bankrupt.) Trial in the UK would be before a judge rather than a jury, damages would be less generous than in the States, discovery more limited, and McIntyre would be in its home arena.

QUESTIONS TO PONDER

1. *Nicastro* allows a foreign manufacturer to insulate itself from suit in any state by careful arrangement through an independent distributor, *even as it directs the latter to sell anywhere it can*. J. McIntyre's stated objective was: "All we wish to do is sell our products in the States and get paid." But it also wanted to avoid being subject to U.S. litigation— as a McIntyre UK officer said in an e-mail to the American distributor: "American law—who needs it?" 131 S. Ct. at 2801 (Ginsburg, J., dissenting). Have we come full circle back to International Shoe's clever way of selling nationwide but trying to avoid suits that might follow? (But this time, J. McIntyre's scheme worked.) Should adjudicatory power be so easily avoided? Note that J. McIntyre didn't even change its name when it arranged for its American distributor.

2. J. McIntyre Machinery, Ltd. beat down another product liability suit filed by another New Jersey worker seriously injured by another of its shearing machines. By this time, the company had morphed into JMC Recycling Systems, Ltd., and arranged with Strip Technology, located in Texas, to be its exclusive distributor in the States, purchasing the machines from JMC in the U.K. and selling them in the U.S.. The district court dismissed for lack of personal jurisdiction without even allowing plaintiff discovery into the jurisdictional facts. *Benitez v. JMC Recycling Systems, Ltd.*, 97 F. Supp. 3d 576 (D.N.J. 2015).

3. Could a domestic corporation follow the same game plan of using an intermediary and thus avoid suit in any state where its product injures someone (except its home states)? *See* Alan B. Morrison, *The Impacts of* McIntyre *on Minimum Contacts*, 80 Geo. Wash. L. Rev. Arguendo 1 (2011).

4. Would plaintiffs be better off with *Pennoyer*'s "strict" regime for personal jurisdiction than *International Shoe*'s modern approach as it has evolved (regressed?) in recent years? At least one academic thinks so:

> As the story is traditionally told, the minimum contacts test introduced in International Shoe v Washington freed personal jurisdiction from the dark age of territorialism and gave courts the flexibility to expand the scope of personal jurisdiction to keep pace with modern society. While scholars have critiqued the minimum contacts test on a number of grounds, the narrative that the Territorial Model was inherently problematic—and that Shoe was a step in the right direction—has gone largely unchallenged.
>
> This Article challenges that narrative and argues for a return to the Territorial Model. While Shoe is traditionally cast as a step toward

expanding personal jurisdiction, the minimum contacts test has now become a greater restraint on state power than the territorial regime that preceded it. This constriction of state power has been coupled with a doctrine that has become increasingly confusing and malleable, unmoored from coherent constitutional and theoretical foundations, and unable to respond to economic and technological changes. The Territorial Model, by contrast, gave states numerous tools to assert jurisdiction over out-of-state defendants, including quasi in rem jurisdiction, consent statutes, and constructive presence. The rules governing personal jurisdiction were relatively straightforward and relied on objective criteria that were easily ascertainable with minimal litigation costs. Once the mythology surrounding personal jurisdiction doctrine is dismantled, the original wisdom of the Territorial Model, and the benefits of returning to it, are clear.

Cody J. Jacobs, *In Defense of Territorial Jurisdiction*, 85 U. Chi. L. Rev. 1589 (2018).

How would you describe the current state of "stream of commerce" theory after *Nicastro*? Test your understanding in the practice exercise that follows.

PRACTICE EXERCISE NO. 31: APPLYING A LONG-ARM STATUTE IN *CARPENTER V. DEE*

Memorandum

To: Associates

From: Carol Coblentz

Re: Jurisdiction Issue in *Carpenter v. Dee*

(a) As you know, this case is pending in Massachusetts Superior Court, and we have been permitted to amend to join Ultimate Auto, Inc. as a party defendant. Our theory is that Dee should have been warned about the dangers of installing the oversized tires and suspension kit he purchased there. Ultimate is incorporated in New Hampshire and has its only place of business (the retail parts store) in Nashua, New Hampshire. Not surprisingly, Ultimate has moved to dismiss for lack of personal jurisdiction, and I would like some help preparing for the hearing.

I sent an initial set of interrogatories to Ultimate Auto and gained the following pertinent information. Its corporate officers all live in Nashua, NH (approximately ten miles from the Massachusetts border), except for the vice president, William Q. Manconi, who lives in Lawrence, MA. Manconi commutes to work, but sometimes does paperwork for the company in his office at home.

Ultimate Auto advertises in several southern New Hampshire newspapers and on two Nashua radio stations. The advertising copy reads: "Buy Ultimate, the ultimate in tires. Our tires will take you safely from the streets of Nashua through the White and Green Mountains, to the Berkshires and the Alleghenies, to cities as tough on tires as Boston, New York, and Chicago. Our expertise, commitment to your safety, and prices cannot be beat." When I drive in Lawrence, Massachusetts, which is about thirty miles from Nashua, I can pick up one of the radio stations that Ultimate Auto advertises on. And a Nashua newspaper that carries the Ultimate ads can be purchased at some newsstands in Lawrence.

Ultimate Auto keeps no records of what percentage of its sales are to people who, like Randall Dee, reside outside New Hampshire. Its manager testified at his deposition that "lots of people come from Massachusetts to buy from us. We are particularly well known by hunters, sportsmen, and car buffs. And there's no sales tax." Most years Ultimate sets up a booth to promote its store at the Auto Show in Boston.

I'd like you to brief me on the current state of personal jurisdiction law in a situation like this. Regarding the significance of Ultimate's advertising, take a look at a case I came across, *Shoppers Food Warehouse v. Moreno*, 746 A.2d 320 (D.C. App. Ct. 2000), where the District of Columbia court placed great stock in the fact that the Maryland defendant placed ads in the *Washington Post* soliciting customers in bold letters: "No Matter Where You Live, It's Worth the Drive!" 746 A.2d at 330-331.

Please think about what further factual information we need to get, and how we should structure our legal argument. You will need the Massachusetts Long-Arm statute, which I have attached below.

(b) ***Now assume the following different scenario.*** Carpenter's attorney has identified the suspension lift kit as the culprit in causing the Jeep CJ7 to roll over. Discovery has revealed that the kit was manufactured by China Specialty Auto-Parts, Ltd. at its plant in Wuhan. China Specialty uses a number of distributors to sell its products in the United States, and the one covering the eastern states is USA Specialty Auto-Parts, Inc., a Maryland corporation wholly separate from China Specialty. USA Specialty sells hundreds of China Specialty lift kits per year to Massachusetts retailers, including the one in Lowell where Randall bought the kit he installed in the Jeep CJ7.

USA Specialty Auto-Parts has just declared bankruptcy, leaving China Specialty Auto-Parts, Ltd. as Nancy Carpenter's only hope for recovery. Construct an argument that the Massachusetts Superior Court can assert adjudicatory power over the Chinese corporation. How do you assess your chances of success after *Nicastro*?

Note: Justice Ginsburg posed a similar scenario at the oral argument in *Nicastro*, and raised the question of whether a plaintiff should be forced to sue a manufacturer in its home country if that venue does not provide "a trusted legal system." Transcript, Oral Argument, pp. 24-25.

Massachusetts General Laws: Jurisdiction of Courts over Persons in Other States and Countries
Mass. Gen. Laws ch. 223A § 3. Transactions or conduct for personal jurisdiction
A court may exercise personal jurisdiction over a person, who acts directly or by an agent, as to a cause of action in law or equity arising from the person's

(a) transacting any business in this commonwealth;

(b) contracting to supply services or things in this commonwealth;

(c) causing tortious injury by an act or omission in this commonwealth;

(d) causing tortious injury in this commonwealth by an act or omission outside this commonwealth if he regularly does or solicits business, or engages in any other persistent course of conduct, or derives substantial revenue from goods used or consumed or services rendered, in this commonwealth;

(e) having an interest in, using or possessing real property in this commonwealth;

(f) contracting to insure any person, property or risk located within this commonwealth at the time of contracting;

(g) maintaining a domicile in this commonwealth while a party to a personal or marital relationship out of which arises a claim for divorce, alimony, property settlement, parentage of a child, child support or child custody; or the commission of any act giving rise to such a claim; or

(h) having been subject to the exercise of personal jurisdiction of a court of the commonwealth which has resulted in an order of alimony, custody, child support or property settlement, notwithstanding the subsequent departure of one of the original parties from the commonwealth, if the action involves modification of such order or orders and the moving party resides in the commonwealth, or if the action involves enforcement of such order notwithstanding the domicile of the moving party.

* * *

Do the restraints on the exercise of personal jurisdiction inhibit the ability of plaintiffs from various states to pursue a single nationwide action against a Fortune 500 pharmaceutical company?

Bristol-Myers Squibb Co. v. Superior Court of California
137 S. Ct. 1773 (2017)

Justice ALITO delivered the opinion of the Court in which Chief Justice ROBERTS, Justice KENNEDY, Justice THOMAS, Justice GINSBURG, Justice BREYER, Justice KAGAN, and Justice GORSUCH joined.

More than 600 plaintiffs, most of whom are not California residents, filed this civil action in a California state court against Bristol-Myers Squibb Company (BMS), asserting a variety of state-law claims based on injuries allegedly caused by a BMS drug called Plavix. The California Supreme Court held that the California courts have specific jurisdiction to entertain the nonresidents' claims. We now reverse.

I

A

BMS, a large pharmaceutical company, is incorporated in Delaware and headquartered in New York, and it maintains substantial operations in both

New York and New Jersey. Over 50 percent of BMS's work force in the United States is employed in those two States.

BMS also engages in business activities in other jurisdictions, including California. Five of the company's research and laboratory facilities, which employ a total of around 160 employees, are located there. BMS also employs about 250 sales representatives in California and maintains a small state-government advocacy office in Sacramento.

One of the pharmaceuticals that BMS manufactures and sells is Plavix, a prescription drug that thins the blood and inhibits blood clotting. BMS did not develop Plavix in California, did not create a marketing strategy for Plavix in California, and did not manufacture, label, package, or work on the regulatory approval of the product in California. BMS instead engaged in all of these activities in either New York or New Jersey. But BMS does sell Plavix in California. Between 2006 and 2012, it sold almost 187 million Plavix pills in the State and took in more than $900 million from those sales. This amounts to a little over one percent of the company's nationwide sales revenue.

B

A group of plaintiffs—consisting of 86 California residents and 592 residents from 33 other States—filed eight separate complaints in California Superior Court, alleging that Plavix had damaged their health. All the complaints asserted 13 claims under California law, including products liability, negligent misrepresentation, and misleading advertising claims. The nonresident plaintiffs did not allege that they obtained Plavix through California physicians or from any other California source; nor did they claim that they were injured by Plavix or were treated for their injuries in California.

Asserting lack of personal jurisdiction, BMS moved to quash service of summons on the nonresidents' claims, but the California Superior Court denied this motion, finding that the California courts had general jurisdiction over BMS "[b]ecause [it] engages in extensive activities in California." [After the decision in *Daimler AG v. Bauman,* see Part L, below, indicating that general jurisdiction was lacking here, the California courts ruled nonetheless that there was specific jurisdiction over the nonresidents' claims against BMS. California law provides that its courts may exercise jurisdiction "on any basis not inconsistent with the Constitution . . . of the United States."]

The California Supreme Court majority applied a "sliding scale approach to specific jurisdiction." Under this approach, "the more wide ranging the defendant's forum contacts, the more readily is shown a connection between the forum contacts and the claim." Applying this test, the majority concluded that "BMS's extensive contacts with California" permitted the exercise of specific jurisdiction "based on a less direct connection between BMS's forum activities and plaintiffs' claims than might otherwise be required." This attenuated requirement was met, the majority found, because the claims of the nonresidents were similar in several ways to the claims of the California residents (as to which specific jurisdiction was uncontested). The court noted that "[b]oth the resident and nonresident plaintiffs' claims are based on the same allegedly defective product and the assertedly misleading marketing and promotion of that product." And while acknowledging that "there is no claim that Plavix itself was designed and developed in [BMS's California research facilities]," the court thought it significant that other research was done in the State.

Three justices dissented. "The claims of . . . nonresidents injured by their use of Plavix they purchased and used in other states," they wrote, "in no sense arise from BMS's marketing and sales of Plavix in California," and they found that the "mere similarity" of the residents' and nonresidents' claims was not enough. The dissent accused the majority of "expand[ing] specific jurisdiction to the point that, for a large category of defendants, it becomes indistinguishable from general jurisdiction."

We granted certiorari to decide whether the California courts' exercise of jurisdiction in this case violates the Due Process Clause of the Fourteenth Amendment.

II

A

It has long been established that the Fourteenth Amendment limits the personal jurisdiction of state courts. Because "[a] state court's assertion of jurisdiction exposes defendants to the State's coercive power," it is "subject to review for compatibility with the Fourteenth Amendment's Due Process Clause," which "limits the power of a state court to render a valid personal judgment against a nonresident defendant," The primary focus of our personal jurisdiction inquiry is the defendant's relationship to the forum State.

Since our seminal decision in *International Shoe*, our decisions have recognized two types of personal jurisdiction: "general" (sometimes called "all-purpose") jurisdiction and "specific" (sometimes called "case-linked") jurisdiction. "For an individual, the paradigm forum for the exercise of general jurisdiction is the individual's domicile; for a corporation, it is an equivalent place, one in which the corporation is fairly regarded as at home." A court with general jurisdiction may hear any claim against that defendant, even if all the incidents underlying the claim occurred in a different State. But "only a limited set of affiliations with a forum will render a defendant amenable to" general jurisdiction in that State. [To be discussed in Part L, below.]

Specific jurisdiction is very different. In order for a state court to exercise specific jurisdiction, "the suit " must "aris[e] out of or relat[e] to the defendant's contacts with the forum." In other words, there must be "an affiliation between the forum and the underlying controversy, principally, [an] activity or an occurrence that takes place in the forum State and is therefore subject to the State's regulation." For this reason, "specific jurisdiction is confined to adjudication of issues deriving from, or connected with, the very controversy that establishes jurisdiction."

B

In determining whether personal jurisdiction is present, a court must consider a variety of interests. These include "the interests of the forum State and of the plaintiff in proceeding with the cause in the plaintiff's forum of choice." But the "primary concern" is "the burden on the defendant." Assessing this burden obviously requires a court to consider the practical problems resulting from litigating in the forum, but it also encompasses the more abstract matter of submitting to the coercive power of a State that may have little legitimate interest in the claims in question. As we have put it, restrictions on personal jurisdiction "are more than a guarantee of immunity from inconvenient or distant litigation. They are a consequence of territorial limitations on the power of the respective States." "[T]he States retain many essential attributes of sovereignty, including, in particular, the sovereign power to try causes in their courts. The sovereignty of each State . . . implie[s] a limitation on the sovereignty of all its sister States." And at times, this federalism interest may be decisive. As we explained in *World-Wide Volkswagen*, "[e]ven if the defendant would suffer minimal or no inconvenience from being forced to litigate before the tribunals of another State; even if the forum State has a strong interest in applying its law to the controversy; even if the forum State is the most convenient location for litigation, the Due Process Clause, acting as an instrument of interstate federalism, may sometimes act to divest the State of its power to render a valid judgment."

III

A

Our settled principles regarding specific jurisdiction control this case. In order for a court to exercise specific jurisdiction over a claim, there must be an "affiliation between the forum and the underlying controversy, principally, [an] activity or an occurrence that takes place in the forum State." When there is no such connection, specific jurisdiction is lacking regardless of the extent of a defendant's unconnected activities in the State ("[E]ven regularly occurring sales of a product in a State do not justify the exercise of jurisdiction over a claim unrelated to those sales").

For this reason, the California Supreme Court's "sliding scale approach" is difficult to square with our precedents. Under the California approach, the strength of the requisite connection between the forum and the specific claims at issue is relaxed if the defendant has extensive forum contacts that are unrelated to those claims. Our cases provide no support for this approach, which resembles a loose and spurious form of general jurisdiction. For specific jurisdiction, a defendant's general connections with the forum are not enough. As we have said, "[a] corporation's 'continuous activity of some sorts within a state . . . is not enough to support the demand that the corporation be amenable to suits unrelated to that activity.'"

The present case illustrates the danger of the California approach. The State Supreme Court found that specific jurisdiction was present without identifying any adequate link between the State and the nonresidents' claims. As noted, the nonresidents were not prescribed Plavix in California, did not purchase Plavix in California, did not ingest Plavix in California, and were not injured by Plavix in California. The mere fact that other plaintiffs were prescribed, obtained, and ingested Plavix in California—and allegedly sustained the same injuries as did the nonresidents—does not allow the State to assert specific jurisdiction over the nonresidents' claims. As we have explained, "a defendant's relationship with a . . . third party, standing alone, is an insufficient basis for jurisdiction." This remains true even when third parties (here, the plaintiffs who reside in California) can bring claims similar to those brought by the nonresidents. Nor is it sufficient—or even relevant—that BMS conducted research in California on matters unrelated to Plavix. What is needed—and what is missing here—is a connection between the forum and the specific claims at issue.

Our decision in *Walden v. Fiore* (2014) illustrates this requirement. In that case, Nevada plaintiffs sued an out-of-state defendant for conducting an allegedly unlawful search of the plaintiffs while they were in Georgia preparing to board a plane bound for Nevada. We held that the Nevada courts lacked specific jurisdiction even though the plaintiffs were Nevada residents and "suffered foreseeable harm in Nevada." Because the "relevant conduct occurred entirely in Georgi[a] . . . the mere fact that [this] conduct affected plaintiffs with connections to the forum State d[id] not suffice to authorize jurisdiction."

In today's case, the connection between the nonresidents' claims and the forum is even weaker. The relevant plaintiffs are not California residents and do not claim to have suffered harm in that State. In addition, as in *Walden,* all the conduct giving rise to the nonresidents' claims occurred elsewhere. It follows that the California courts cannot claim specific jurisdiction. See *World-Wide Volkswagen* (finding no personal jurisdiction in Oklahoma because the defendant "carr[ied] on no activity whatsoever in Oklahoma" and dismissing "the fortuitous circumstance that a single Audi automobile, sold [by defendants] in New York to New York residents, happened to suffer an accident while passing through Oklahoma" as an "isolated occurrence").

. . .

C

In a last ditch contention, respondents contend that BMS's "decision to contract with a California company [McKesson] to distribute [Plavix] nationally" provides a sufficient basis for personal jurisdiction. But as we have explained, "[t]he requirements of *International Shoe* . . . must be met as to each defendant over whom a state court exercises jurisdiction." In this case, it is not alleged that BMS engaged in relevant acts together with McKesson in California. Nor is it alleged that BMS is derivatively liable for McKesson's conduct in California. And the nonresidents "have adduced no evidence to show how or by whom the Plavix they took was distributed to the pharmacies that dispensed it to them." The bare fact that BMS contracted with a California distributor is not enough to establish personal jurisdiction in the State.

IV

Our straightforward application in this case of settled principles of personal jurisdiction will not result in the parade of horribles that respondents conjure up. Our decision does not prevent the California and out-of-state plaintiffs from joining together in a consolidated action in the States that have general jurisdiction over BMS. BMS concedes that such suits could be brought in either New York or Delaware. Alternatively, the plaintiffs who are residents of a particular State—for example, the 92 plaintiffs from Texas and the 71 from Ohio—could probably sue together in their home States. In addition, since our decision concerns the due process limits on the exercise of specific jurisdiction by a State, we leave open the question whether the Fifth Amendment imposes the same restrictions on the exercise of personal jurisdiction by a federal court.

The judgment of the California Supreme Court is reversed, and the case is remanded for further proceedings not inconsistent with this opinion.

Justice SOTOMAYOR, dissenting.

Three years ago, the Court imposed substantial curbs on the exercise of general jurisdiction in its decision in *Daimler AG v. Bauman* (2014). Today, the Court takes its first step toward a similar contraction of specific jurisdiction by holding that a corporation that engages in a nationwide course of conduct cannot be held accountable in a state court by a group of injured people unless all of those people were injured in the forum State.

I fear the consequences of the Court's decision today will be substantial. The majority's rule will make it difficult to aggregate the claims of plaintiffs across the country whose claims may be worth little alone. It will make it impossible to bring a nationwide mass action in state court against defendants who are "at home" in different States. And it will result in piecemeal litigation and the bifurcation of claims. None of this is necessary. A core concern in this Court's personal jurisdiction cases is fairness. And there is nothing unfair about subjecting a massive corporation to suit in a State for a nationwide course of conduct that injures both forum residents and nonresidents alike.

I

Bristol-Myers Squibb is a Fortune 500 pharmaceutical company incorporated in Delaware and headquartered in New York. It employs approximately 25,000 people worldwide and earns annual revenues of over $15 billion. In the late 1990's, Bristol-Myers began to market and sell a prescription blood thinner called Plavix. Plavix was advertised as an effective tool for reducing the risk of blood clotting for those vulnerable to heart attacks and to strokes. The ads worked: At the height of its popularity, Plavix was a blockbuster, earning Bristol-Myers billions of dollars in annual revenues.

Bristol-Myers' advertising and distribution efforts were national in scope. It conducted a single nationwide advertising campaign for Plavix, using television, magazine, and Internet ads to broadcast its message. A consumer in California heard the same advertisement as a consumer in Maine about the benefits of Plavix. Bristol-Myers' distribution of Plavix also proceeded through nationwide channels: Consistent with its usual practice, it relied on a small number of wholesalers to distribute Plavix throughout the country. One of those distributors, McKesson Corporation, was named as a defendant below; during the relevant time period, McKesson was responsible for almost a quarter of Bristol-Myers' revenue worldwide.

The 2005 publication of an article in the New England Journal of Medicine questioning the efficacy and safety of Plavix put Bristol-Myers on the defensive, as consumers around the country began to claim that they were injured by the drug. The plaintiffs in these consolidated cases are 86 people who allege they were injured by Plavix in California and several hundred others who say they were injured by the drug in other States. They filed their suits in California Superior Court, raising product-liability claims against Bristol-Myers and McKesson. Their claims are "materially identical," as Bristol-Myers concedes. Bristol-Myers acknowledged it was subject to suit in California state court by the residents of that State. But it moved to dismiss the claims brought by the nonresident plaintiffs—respondents here—for lack of jurisdiction. The question here, accordingly, is not whether Bristol-Myers is subject to suit in California on claims that arise out of the design, development, manufacture, marketing, and distribution of Plavix—it is. The question is whether Bristol-Myers is subject to suit in California only on the residents' claims, or whether a state court may also hear the nonresidents' "identical" claims.

II

A

As the majority explains, since our pathmarking opinion in *International Shoe Co. v. Washington*, the touchstone of the personal-jurisdiction analysis has been the question whether a defendant has "certain minimum contacts with [the State] such that the maintenance of the suit does not offend 'traditional notions of fair play and substantial justice.' " For decades this Court has considered that question through two different jurisdictional frames: "general" and "specific" jurisdiction. Under our current case law, a state court may exercise general, or all-purpose, jurisdiction over a defendant corporation only if its "affiliations with the State are so 'continuous and systematic' as to render [it] essentially at home in the forum State." *Goodyear Dunlop Tires Operations, S.A. v. Brown.*

If general jurisdiction is not appropriate, however, a state court can exercise only specific, or case-linked, jurisdiction over a dispute. Our cases have set out three conditions for the exercise of specific jurisdiction over a nonresident defendant. First, the defendant must have " 'purposefully avail[ed] itself of the privilege of conducting activities within the forum State' " or have purposefully directed its conduct into the forum State. Second, the plaintiff's claim must "arise out of or relate to" the defendant's forum conduct. Finally, the exercise of jurisdiction must be reasonable under the circumstances. The factors relevant to such an analysis include "the burden on the defendant, the forum State's interest in adjudicating the dispute, the plaintiff's interest in obtaining convenient and effective relief, the interstate judicial system's interest in obtaining the most efficient resolution of controversies, and the shared interest of the several States in furthering fundamental substantive social policies."

B

Viewed through this framework, the California courts appropriately exercised specific jurisdiction over respondents' claims.

First, there is no dispute that Bristol-Myers "purposefully avail[ed] itself," of California and its substantial pharmaceutical market. Bristol-Myers employs over 400 people in California and maintains half a dozen facilities in the State engaged in research, development, and policymaking. It contracts with a California-based distributor, McKesson, whose sales account for a significant portion of its revenue. And it markets and sells its drugs, including Plavix, in California, resulting in total Plavix sales in that State of nearly $1 billion during the period relevant to this suit.

Second, respondents' claims "relate to" Bristol-Myers' in-state conduct. A claim "relates to" a defendant's forum conduct if it has a "connect[ion] with" that conduct. So respondents could not, for instance, hale Bristol-Myers into court in California for negligently maintaining the sidewalk outside its New York headquarters—a claim that has no connection to acts Bristol-Myers took in California. But respondents' claims against Bristol-Myers look nothing like such a claim. Respondents' claims against Bristol-Myers concern conduct materially identical to acts the company took in California: its marketing and distribution of Plavix, which it undertook on a nationwide basis in all 50 States. That respondents were allegedly injured by this nationwide course of conduct in Indiana, Oklahoma, and Texas, and not California, does not mean that their claims do not "relate to" the advertising and distribution efforts that Bristol-Myers undertook in that State. All of the plaintiffs—residents and nonresidents alike—allege that they were injured by the same essential acts. Our cases require no connection more direct than that.

Finally, and importantly, there is no serious doubt that the exercise of jurisdiction over the nonresidents' claims is reasonable. Because Bristol-Myers already faces claims that are identical to the nonresidents' claims in this suit, it will not be harmed by having to defend against respondents' claims: Indeed, the alternative approach—litigating those claims in separate suits in as many as 34 different States—would prove far more burdensome. By contrast, the plaintiffs' "interest in obtaining convenient and effective relief" is obviously furthered by participating in a consolidated proceeding in one State under shared counsel, which allows them to minimize costs, share discovery, and maximize recoveries on claims that may be too small to bring on their own. California, too, has an interest in providing a forum for mass actions like this one: Permitting the nonresidents to bring suit in California alongside the residents facilitates the efficient adjudication of the residents' claims and allows it to regulate more effectively the conduct of both nonresident corporations like Bristol-Myers and resident ones like McKesson.

Nothing in the Due Process Clause prohibits a California court from hearing respondents' claims—at least not in a case where they are joined to identical claims brought by California residents.

III

Bristol-Myers does not dispute that it has purposefully availed itself of California's markets, nor—remarkably—did it argue below that it would be "unreasonable" for a California court to hear respondents' claims. Instead, Bristol-Myers contends that respondents' claims do not "arise out of or relate to" its California conduct. The majority agrees, explaining that no "adequate link" exists "between the State and the nonresidents' claims," a result that it says follows from "settled principles [of] specific jurisdiction." But our precedents do not require this result, and common sense says that it cannot be correct.

A

The majority casts its decision today as compelled by precedent. But our cases point in the other direction.

The majority argues at length that the exercise of specific jurisdiction in this case would conflict with our decision in *Walden v. Fiore* (2014). That is plainly not true. Walden concerned the requirement that a defendant "purposefully avail" himself of a forum State or "purposefully direc[t]" his conduct toward that State, not the separate requirement that a plaintiff's claim "arise out of or relate to" a defendant's forum contacts. *Walden* teaches only that a defendant must have purposefully availed itself of the forum, and that a plaintiff cannot rely solely on a defendant's contacts with a forum resident to establish the necessary relationship. But that holding has nothing to do with the dispute between the parties: Bristol-Myers has purposefully availed itself of California—to the tune of millions of dollars in annual revenue. Only if its language is taken out of context, can *Walden* be made to seem relevant to the case at hand.

. . .

The majority's animating concern, in the end, appears to be federalism: "[T]erritorial limitations on the power of the respective States," we are informed, may—and today do—trump even concerns about fairness to the parties. Indeed, the majority appears to concede that this is not, at bottom, a case about fairness but instead a case about power: one in which "'the defendant would suffer minimal or no inconvenience from being forced to litigate before the tribunals of another State; . . . the forum State has a strong interest in applying its law to the controversy; [and] the forum State is the most convenient location for litigation'" but personal jurisdiction still will not lie. But I see little reason to apply such a principle in a case brought against a large corporate defendant arising out of its nationwide conduct. What interest could any single State have in adjudicating respondents' claims that the other States do not share? I would measure jurisdiction first and foremost by the yardstick set out in *International Shoe*—"fair play and substantial justice," The majority's opinion casts that settled principle aside.

B

I fear the consequences of the majority's decision today will be substantial. Even absent a rigid requirement that a defendant's in-state conduct must actually cause a plaintiff's claim, the upshot of today's opinion is that plaintiffs cannot join their claims together and sue a defendant in a State in which only some of them have been injured. That rule is likely to have consequences far beyond this case.

First, and most prominently, the Court's opinion in this case will make it profoundly difficult for plaintiffs who are injured in different States by a defendant's nationwide course of conduct to sue that defendant in a single, consolidated action. The holding of today's opinion is that such an action cannot be brought in a State in which only some plaintiffs were injured. Not to worry, says the majority: The plaintiffs here could have sued Bristol-Myers in New York or Delaware; could "probably" have subdivided their separate claims into 34 lawsuits in the States in which they were injured; and might have been able to bring a single suit in federal court (an "open . . . question"). Even setting aside the majority's caveats, what is the purpose of such limitations? What interests are served by preventing the consolidation of claims and limiting the forums in which they can be consolidated? The effect of the Court's opinion today is to eliminate nationwide mass actions in any State other than those in which a defendant is " 'essentially at home.' " Such a rule hands one more tool to corporate defendants determined to prevent the aggregation of individual claims, and forces injured plaintiffs to bear the burden of bringing suit in what will often be far flung jurisdictions.

Second, the Court's opinion today may make it impossible to bring certain mass actions at all. After this case, it is difficult to imagine where it might be possible to bring a nationwide mass action against two or more defendants headquartered and incorporated in different States. There will be no State where both defendants are "at home," and so no State in which the suit can proceed. What about a nationwide mass action brought against a defendant not headquartered or incorporated in the United States? Such a defendant is not "at home" in any State. Especially in a world in which defendants are subject to general jurisdiction in only a handful of States, see ibid., the effect of today's opinion will be to curtail—and in some cases eliminate—plaintiffs' ability to hold corporations fully accountable for their nationwide conduct.

The majority chides respondents for conjuring a "parade of horribles," but says nothing about how suits like those described here will survive its opinion in this case. The answer is simple: They will not.

It "does not offend 'traditional notions of fair play and substantial justice'" to permit plaintiffs to aggregate claims arising out of a single nationwide course of conduct in a single suit in a single State where some, but not all, were injured. But that is exactly what the Court holds today is barred by the Due Process Clause.

This is not a rule the Constitution has required before. I respectfully dissent.

YOUR TAKEAWAY

Despite the very considerable ties BMS had with California, what was missing in the Court's view was a direct relation between the nonresidents' claims and those activities, as these plaintiffs neither purchased Plavix in the state nor suffered their injuries there. This increased emphasis on relatedness further narrows the gateway into the courts, and bodes poorly for mass tort cases like this one.

REVIEW NOTES & QUESTIONS

1. How would you summarize *Bristol-Myers's* holding? Note that this is the only eight-to-one decision we have seen in the area of jurisdiction.

2. Justice Alito twice refers to the decision as narrowly governed by "settled principles." What principles do you think he is referring to? What is well-settled in this most murky area? Is there really consensus on the Court on matters of stream of commerce, foreseeability, relatedness, and sovereignty versus fairness?

    And what about *Asahi*'s settled principle (signed on to by the entire Court) that the reasonableness of the exercise of jurisdiction in each case must weigh the burden on the defendant, the interests of the forum state, the plaintiff's interest in obtaining relief, and the interstate judicial system's interest in obtaining the most efficient resolution of controversies? Has Alito engaged in this balancing?

3. Does disaggregating the 592 nonresident plaintiffs, forcing them to sue individually in their 33 states, serve a useful purpose? "Piecemeal litigation," as Justice Sotomayor views it, thwarts the plaintiffs' prospects for recovery and leaves defendant open to potentially hundreds of suits instead of one and the courts in 33 states to entertain those separate but repetitious litigations. Moreover, multiple litigation runs the risk of inconsistent results around the nation, as well as the prospect of the early-bird plaintiffs sending BMS into bankruptcy and depriving later plaintiffs of recovery.

    Note: We will see that issue preclusion (Chapter 10, Part C) may reduce the considerable inefficiency of trying so many similar actions.

    "A consolidated proceeding in one state under shared counsel," Justice Sotomayor observes, would "minimize costs" and "maximize recoveries on claims that may be too small to bring on their own." *Bristol-Myers,* she adds, "will make it profoundly difficult for plaintiffs who are injured in different States by a defendant's nationwide course of conduct to sue that defendant in a single, consolidated action," and "may make it impossible to bring certain mass actions at all." For Sotomayor, the Court has handed "one more tool to corporate defendants determined to prevent the aggregation of individual claims," forcing "injured plaintiffs to bear the burden of bringing suit in what will often be far flung jurisdictions."

Is Justice Alito's invocation of "interstate federalism" ("the majority's animating concern," as Justice Sotomayor identifies it) a satisfactory justification for such a troublesome result?

4. Consider this assessment: "Although it is destined for the personal jurisdiction canon, the Supreme Court's eight-to-one decision in *Bristol-Myers Squibb Co. v. Superior Court* does little to clarify that notoriously hazy doctrine. It does, however, significantly alter the balance of power in complex litigation. *Bristol-Myers* is a landmark case because it makes both mass-tort class actions and mass joinders impracticable in almost any state court outside of the defendant's home states. With federal courts already hostile to class actions, plaintiffs who want to aggregate their claims will have to do so on the defendant's terms [presumably] on the defendant's home turf." Andrew D. Bradt and D. Theodore Rave, *Aggregation on Defendants' Terms:* Bristol-Myers Squibb *and the Federalization of Mass-Tort Litigation*, 59 B.C. L. Rev. 1251 (2018).

5. Before the Court severely curtailed the exercise of general jurisdiction in *Goodyear* and *Daimler* (discussed in Part L, below), California would likely have been permitted to assert jurisdiction on that basis, given Bristol-Myers's substantial activities within the state: 400 employees, half a dozen research facilities, a California distributor, $1 billion in sales. Now specific jurisdiction must perform all this work, but it too has been severely curtailed.

6. *Nexus Redux.* Recall our discussion in Part E, above.

For Justice Alito, the lack of relationship between BMS's activity in California and the nonresidents' claims were a deal-breaker for specific jurisdiction. The California Supreme Court's "sliding scale approach," which finessed this by concluding that BMS's very substantial marketing, promotion, and distribution of Plavix in California allowed for less of a direct connection for the nonresidents' similar claims, was for Alito "difficult to square with our precedents. What is needed—and what is missing here—is a connection between the forum and the specific claims at issue."

But isn't the sliding-scale approach consistent with Chief Justice Stone's original formulation in *International Shoe*, i.e., the higher the defendant's level of activity, the less the requisite connection to plaintiff's claim? On this view, specific and general jurisdiction are not such different creatures, but simply located on opposite sides of the activity spectrum.

Arguing for a more relaxed standard of relatedness between the plaintiff's claim and defendant's forum activities, Justice Sotomayor asserts: "That respondents were allegedly injured by this nationwide course of conduct in Indiana, Oklahoma, and Texas, and not California, does not mean that their claims do not 'relate to' the advertising and distribution efforts that Bristol-Myers undertook in that State. All of the plaintiffs—residents and nonresidents alike—allege that they were injured by the same essential acts. Our cases require no connection more direct than that." Is she right about that last assertion?

Academics have weighed in against the insistence that "the very product that causes harm must have some connection to the forum." *See* Richard Freer, *Personal Jurisdiction: The Walls Blocking an Appeal to Rationality*, 72 Vand. L. Rev. En Banc 99, 113 (2019). "In the wake of the Court's restriction of general jurisdiction, the Court is putting up a second wall [for plaintiffs to traverse]; a strict requirement, set out in *Bristol-Myers Squibb,* that the plaintiff's claim be closely related to the defendant's contacts with the forum." *Id.* at 101. *See also* Michael H. Hoffheimer, *The Stealth Revolution in Personal Jurisdiction*, 70 Fla L. Rev. 499 (2018).

QUESTIONS TO PONDER

1. In his *Stealth Revolution* article noted above, Professor Hoffheimer asserts the following thesis: Since 2011 the Roberts Court has decided six personal jurisdiction cases that impose significant new constitutional restrictions on the power of courts and limit plaintiffs' access to justice. But the Court's opinions explaining those decisions have repeatedly denied that the Court is altering settled law. The Court is engaged in a stealth revolution, a process of radically changing existing law while claiming to follow controlling precedent. By claiming to rely on precedent, the Court avoids the need to offer a clear rule of decision, fails to explain the policies that motivate its changing approach to personal jurisdiction, and fosters a narrative of lower court lawlessness that both devalues the work of the lower courts and erodes public confidence in the judiciary. Professor Freer (see above) would agree.

2. Professor Hoffheimer raises an interesting question about *Bristol-Myers Squibb*'s potential implications for joinder: Does a plaintiff who has established personal jurisdiction over a defendant need to separately establish jurisdiction for each additional claim? "If so, the opinion marks a radical break with the traditional understanding of personal jurisdiction as a doctrine that restricted the power of courts over parties, not claims." 70 Fla L. Rev. at 526.

3. Does *BMS*, a mass tort action brought by multiple named plaintiffs, apply equally to class actions (discussed in Chapter 11), in which named plaintiffs represent a class of unnamed persons? *See* Justin A. Stone, *Totally Class-Less?: Examining* Bristol-Myers's *Applicability to Class Actions*, 87 Fordham L. Rev. 807, 818 (2018).

We now shift our focus from the tort to the commercial context, where the parties have *chosen* to enter into structured relationships. How does this change the personal jurisdiction calculus?

Burger King Corp. v. Rudzewicz
471 U.S. 462 (1985)

Justice BRENNAN delivered the opinion of the Court:

The State of Florida's long-arm statute extends jurisdiction to "[a]ny person, whether or not a citizen or resident of this state," who, *inter alia*, "[b]reach[es] a contract in this state by failing to perform acts required by the contract to be performed in this state," so long as the cause of action arises from the alleged contractual breach. Fla. Stat. § 48.193(1)(g) (Supp. 1984). The United States District Court for the Southern District of Florida, sitting in diversity, relied on this provision in exercising personal jurisdiction over a Michigan resident who allegedly had breached a franchise agreement with a Florida corporation by failing to make required payments in Florida. The question presented is whether this exercise of longarm jurisdiction offended "traditional conception[s] of fair play and substantial justice" embodied in the Due Process Clause of the Fourteenth Amendment. *International Shoe Co. v. Washington*, 326 U.S. 310, 320 (1945).

I

A

Burger King Corporation is a Florida corporation whose principal offices are in Miami. It is one of the world's largest restaurant organizations, with over 3,000 outlets in the 50 States, the Commonwealth of Puerto Rico, and 8 foreign nations. Burger King conducts approximately 80% of its business through a franchise operation that the company styles the "Burger King System"—"a comprehensive restaurant format and operating system for the sale of uniform and quality food products." Burger King licenses its franchisees to use its trademarks and service marks for a period of 20 years and leases standardized restaurant facilities to them for the same term. In addition, franchisees acquire a variety of proprietary information concerning the "standards, specifications, procedures and methods for operating a Burger King Restaurant." They also receive market research and advertising assistance; ongoing training in restaurant management;[2] and accounting, cost-control, and inventory-control guidance. By

---

2. Mandatory training seminars are conducted at Burger King University in Miami and at Whopper College Regional Training Centers around the country.

permitting franchisees to tap into Burger King's established national reputation and to benefit from proven procedures for dispensing standardized fare, this system enables them to go into the restaurant business with significantly lowered barriers to entry.

In exchange for these benefits, franchisees pay Burger King an initial $40,000 franchise fee and commit themselves to payment of monthly royalties, advertising and sales promotion fees, and rent computed in part from monthly gross sales. Franchisees also agree to submit to the national organization's exacting regulation of virtually every conceivable aspect of their operations. Burger King imposes these standards and undertakes its rigid regulation out of conviction that "[u]niformity of service, appearance, and quality of product is essential to the preservation of the Burger King image and the benefits accruing therefrom to both Franchisee and Franchisor."

Burger King oversees its franchise system through a two-tiered administrative structure. The governing contracts provide that the franchise relationship is established in Miami and governed by Florida law, and call for payment of all required fees and forwarding of all relevant notices to the Miami headquarters. The Miami headquarters sets policy and works directly with its franchisees in attempting to resolve major problems. Day-to-day monitoring of franchisees, however, is conducted through a network of 10 district offices which in turn report to the Miami headquarters.

The instant litigation grows out of Burger King's termination of one of its franchisees, and is aptly described by the franchisee as "a divorce proceeding among commercial partners." The appellee John Rudzewicz, a Michigan citizen and resident, is the senior partner in a Detroit accounting firm. In 1978, he was approached by Brian MacShara, the son of a business acquaintance, who suggested that they jointly apply to Burger King for a franchise in the Detroit area. MacShara proposed to serve as the manager of the restaurant if Rudzewicz would put up the investment capital; in exchange, the two would evenly share the profits. Believing that MacShara's idea offered attractive investment and tax-deferral opportunities, Rudzewicz agreed to the venture.

Rudzewicz and MacShara jointly applied for a franchise to Burger King's Birmingham, Michigan, district office in the autumn of 1978. Their application was forwarded to Burger King's Miami headquarters, which entered into a preliminary agreement with them in February 1979. During the ensuing four months it was agreed that Rudzewicz and MacShara would assume operation of an existing facility in Drayton Plains, Michigan. MacShara attended the prescribed management courses in Miami during this period, and the franchisees purchased $165,000 worth of restaurant equipment from Burger King's Davmor Industries division in Miami. Even before the final agreements were signed, however, the parties began to disagree over site-development fees, building design, computation of monthly rent, and whether the franchisees would be able to assign their liabilities to a corporation they had formed. During these disputes Rudzewicz and MacShara negotiated both with the Birmingham district office and with the Miami headquarters.[7] With some misgivings, Rudzewicz and MacShara finally obtained limited concessions from the Miami headquarters, signed the final agreements, and commenced operations in June 1979. By signing the final agreements, Rudzewicz obligated himself personally to payments exceeding $1 million over the 20-year franchise relationship.

The Drayton Plains facility apparently enjoyed steady business during the summer of 1979, but patronage declined after a recession began later that year. Rudzewicz and MacShara soon fell far behind in their monthly payments to Miami. Headquarters sent notices of default, and an extended period of negotiations began among the franchisees, the Birmingham district office, and the Miami headquarters. After several Burger King officials in Miami had engaged in prolonged but ultimately unsuccessful negotiations with the franchisees by mail and by telephone,[9] headquarters terminated the franchise and ordered Rudzewicz and MacShara to vacate the premises. They refused and continued to occupy and operate the facility as a Burger King restaurant.

B

Burger King commenced the instant action in the United States District Court for the Southern District of Florida in May 1981, invoking that court's diversity jurisdiction pursuant to 28 U.S.C. § 1332(a).[10] Burger King alleged that Rudzewicz and MacShara had breached their franchise obligations "within [the jurisdiction of] this district court" by failing to make the required payments "at plaintiff's place of business in Miami, Dade County, Florida," and also charged that they were tortiously infringing its trademarks and service marks through their continued, unauthorized operation as a Burger King restaurant. Burger King sought damages, injunctive relief, and costs and attorney's fees. Rudzewicz and MacShara entered special appearances and argued, inter alia, that because they were Michigan residents and because Burger King's claim did not "arise" within the Southern District of Florida, the District Court lacked personal jurisdiction over them. The District Court denied their motions after a hearing, holding that, pursuant to Florida's long-arm statute, "a non-resident Burger King franchisee is subject to the personal jurisdiction of this Court in actions arising out of its franchise agreements." Rudzewicz and MacShara then filed an answer and a counterclaim seeking damages for alleged violations by Burger King of Michigan's Franchise Investment Law.

---

7. Although Rudzewicz and MacShara dealt with the Birmingham district office on a regular basis, they communicated directly with the Miami headquarters in forming the contracts; moreover, they learned that the district office had "very little" decisionmaking authority and accordingly turned directly to headquarters in seeking to resolve their disputes.

9. Miami's policy was to "deal directly" with franchisees when they began to encounter financial difficulties, and to involve district office personnel only when necessary. In the instant case, for example, the Miami office handled all credit problems, ordered cost-cutting measures, negotiated for a partial refinancing of the franchisees' debts, communicated directly with the franchisees in attempting to resolve the dispute, and was responsible for all termination matters.

10. Rudzewicz and MacShara were served in Michigan with summonses and copies of the complaint pursuant to Federal Rule of Civil Procedure 4.

After a 3-day bench trial, the court again concluded that it had "jurisdiction over the subject matter and the parties to this cause." Finding that Rudzewicz and MacShara had breached their franchise agreements with Burger King and had infringed Burger King's trademarks and service marks, the court entered judgment against them, jointly and severally, for $228,875 in contract damages. The court also ordered them "to immediately close Burger King Restaurant Number 775 from continued operation or to immediately give the keys and possession of said restaurant to Burger King Corporation," found that they had failed to prove any of the required elements of their counterclaim, and awarded costs and attorney's fees to Burger King.

Rudzewicz appealed to the Court of Appeals for the Eleventh Circuit. A divided panel of that Circuit reversed the judgment, concluding that the District Court could not properly exercise personal jurisdiction over Rudzewicz because "the circumstances of the Drayton Plains franchise and the negotiations which led to it left Rudzewicz bereft of reasonable notice and financially unprepared for the prospect of franchise litigation in Florida." *Burger King Corp. v. MacShara*, 724 F.2d 1505, 1513 (1984). Accordingly, the panel majority concluded that "[j]urisdiction under these circumstances would offend the fundamental fairness which is the touchstone of due process." Burger King appealed the Eleventh Circuit's judgment to this Court. . . . We now reverse.

II

A

The Due Process Clause protects an individual's liberty interest in not being subject to the binding judgments of a forum with which he has established no meaningful "contacts, ties, or relations." *International Shoe Co. v. Washington*, 326 U.S. at 319. By requiring that individuals have "fair warning that a particular activity may subject [them] to the jurisdiction of a foreign sovereign," the Due Process Clause "gives a degree of predictability to the legal system that allows potential defendants to structure their primary conduct with some minimum assurance as to where that conduct will and will not render them liable to suit."

Where a forum seeks to assert specific jurisdiction over an out-of-state defendant who has not consented to suit there,[14] this "fair warning" requirement is satisfied if the defendant has "purposefully directed" his activities at residents of the forum, and the litigation results from alleged injuries that "arise out of or relate to" those activities. . . . [W]ith respect to interstate contractual obligations, we have emphasized that parties who "reach out beyond one state and create continuing relationships and obligations with citizens of another state"

---

14. We have noted that, because the personal jurisdiction requirement is a waivable right, there are a "variety of legal arrangements" by which a litigant may give "express or implied consent to the personal jurisdiction of the court." For example, particularly in the commercial context, parties frequently stipulate in advance to submit their controversies for resolution within a particular jurisdiction. Where such forum-selection provisions have been obtained through "freely negotiated" agreements and are not "unreasonable and unjust." [*Eds.' Note:* We will take up the topic of forum selection clauses in Part L.]

are subject to regulation and sanctions in the other State for the consequences of their activities.

We have noted several reasons why a forum legitimately may exercise personal jurisdiction over a nonresident who "purposefully directs" his activities toward forum residents. A State generally has a "manifest interest" in providing its residents with a convenient forum for redressing injuries inflicted by out-of-state actors. Moreover, where individuals "purposefully derive benefit" from their interstate activities, it may well be unfair to allow them to escape having to account in other States for consequences that arise proximately from such activities; the Due Process Clause may not readily be wielded as a territorial shield to avoid interstate obligations that have been voluntarily assumed. And because "modern transportation and communications have made it much less burdensome for a party sued to defend himself in a State where he engages in economic activity," it usually will not be unfair to subject him to the burdens of litigating in another forum for disputes relating to such activity.

Notwithstanding these considerations, the constitutional touchstone remains whether the defendant purposefully established "minimum contacts" in the forum State. . . . This "purposeful availment" requirement ensures that a defendant will not be haled into a jurisdiction solely as a result of "random," "fortuitous," or "attenuated" contacts, or of the "unilateral activity of another party or a third person," Jurisdiction is proper, however, where the contacts proximately result from actions by the defendant himself that create a "substantial connection" with the forum State.[18] Thus where the defendant "deliberately" has engaged in significant activities within a State, or has created "continuing obligations" between himself and residents of the forum, he manifestly has availed himself of the privilege of conducting business there, and because his activities are shielded by "the benefits and protections" of the forum's laws it is presumptively not unreasonable to require him to submit to the burdens of litigation in that forum as well.

Jurisdiction in these circumstances may not be avoided merely because the defendant did not physically enter the forum State. Although territorial presence frequently will enhance a potential defendant's affiliation with a State and reinforce the reasonable foreseeability of suit there, it is an inescapable fact of modern commercial life that a substantial amount of business is transacted solely by mail and wire communications across state lines, thus obviating the need for physical presence within a State in which business is conducted. So long as a commercial actor's efforts are "purposefully directed" toward residents of

---

18. So long as it creates a "substantial connection" with the forum, even a single act can support jurisdiction. *McGee v. International Life Insurance Co.*, 355 U.S. at 223. The Court has noted, however, that "some single or occasional acts" related to the forum may not be sufficient to establish jurisdiction if "their nature and quality and the circumstances of their commission" create only an "attenuated" affiliation with the forum. *International Shoe Co. v. Washington*, 326 U.S. 310, 318 (1945); *World-Wide Volkswagen Corp. v. Woodson*, 444 U.S. at 299. This distinction derives from the belief that, with respect to this category of "isolated" acts, the reasonable foreseeability of litigation in the forum is substantially diminished.

another State, we have consistently rejected the notion that an absence of physical contacts can defeat personal jurisdiction there.

Once it has been decided that a defendant purposefully established minimum contacts within the forum State, these contacts may be considered in light of other factors to determine whether the assertion of personal jurisdiction would comport with "fair play and substantial justice." *International Shoe Co. v. Washington*, 326 U.S. at 320. Thus courts in "appropriate case[s]" may evaluate "the burden on the defendant," "the forum State's interest in adjudicating the dispute," "the plaintiff's interest in obtaining convenient and effective relief," "the interstate judicial system's interest in obtaining the most efficient resolution of controversies," and the "shared interest of the several States in furthering fundamental substantive social policies." These considerations sometimes serve to establish the reasonableness of jurisdiction upon a lesser showing of minimum contacts than would otherwise be required. *See, e.g., Keeton v. Hustler Magazine, Inc.*, *supra*, 465 U.S. at 780; *Calder v. Jones*, *supra*, 465 U.S. at 788-789; *McGee v. International Life Insurance Co.*, *supra*, 355 U.S. at 223-224. On the other hand, where a defendant who purposefully has directed his activities at forum residents seeks to defeat jurisdiction, he must present a compelling case that the presence of some other considerations would render jurisdiction unreasonable. . . . Nevertheless, minimum requirements inherent in the concept of "fair play and substantial justice" may defeat the reasonableness of jurisdiction even if the defendant has purposefully engaged in forum activities. [J]urisdictional rules may not be employed in such a way as to make litigation "so gravely difficult and inconvenient" that a party unfairly is at a "severe disadvantage" in comparison to his opponent.

B

(1)

Applying these principles to the case at hand, we believe there is substantial record evidence supporting the District Court's conclusion that the assertion of personal jurisdiction over Rudzewicz in Florida for the alleged breach of his franchise agreement did not offend due process. At the outset, we note a continued division among lower courts respecting whether and to what extent a contract can constitute a "contact" for purposes of due process analysis. If the question is whether an individual's contract with an out-of-state party alone can automatically establish sufficient minimum contacts in the other party's home forum, we believe the answer clearly is that it cannot. The Court long ago rejected the notion that personal jurisdiction might turn on "mechanical" tests, *International Shoe Co. v. Washington*, *supra*, 326 U.S. at 319, or on "conceptualistic . . . theories of the place of contracting or of performance." Instead, we have emphasized the need for a "highly realistic" approach that recognizes that a "contract" is "ordinarily but an intermediate step serving to tie up prior business negotiations with future consequences which themselves are the real object of the business transaction." It is these factors—prior negotiations and contemplated future consequences, along with the terms of the contract and the parties' actual course of dealing—that must be evaluated in determining whether the defendant purposefully established minimum contacts within the forum.

In this case, no physical ties to Florida can be attributed to Rudzewicz other than MacShara's brief training course in Miami. Rudzewicz did not maintain offices in Florida and, for all that appears from the record, has never even visited there. Yet this franchise dispute grew directly out of "a contract which had a substantial connection with that State." *McGee v. International Life Insurance Co.* Eschewing the option of operating an independent local enterprise, Rudzewicz deliberately "reach[ed] out beyond" Michigan and negotiated with a Florida corporation for the purchase of a long-term franchise and the manifold benefits that would derive from affiliation with a nationwide organization. Upon approval, he entered into a carefully structured 20-year relationship that envisioned continuing and wide-reaching contacts with Burger King in Florida. In light of Rudzewicz' voluntary acceptance of the long-term and exacting regulation of his business from Burger King's Miami headquarters, the "quality and nature" of his relationship to the company in Florida can in no sense be viewed as "random," "fortuitous," or "attenuated." Rudzewicz' refusal to make the contractually required payments in Miami, and his continued use of Burger King's trademarks and confidential business information after his termination, caused foreseeable injuries to the corporation in Florida. For these reasons it was, at the very least, presumptively reasonable for Rudzewicz to be called to account there for such injuries.

The Court of Appeals concluded, however, that in light of the supervision emanating from Burger King's district office in Birmingham, Rudzewicz reasonably believed that "the Michigan office was for all intents and purposes the embodiment of Burger King" and that he therefore had no "reason to anticipate a Burger King suit outside of Michigan." This reasoning overlooks substantial record evidence indicating that Rudzewicz most certainly knew that he was affiliating himself with an enterprise based primarily in Florida. The contract documents themselves emphasize that Burger King's operations are conducted and supervised from the Miami headquarters, that all relevant notices and payments must be sent there, and that the agreements were made in and enforced from Miami. Moreover, the parties' actual course of dealing repeatedly confirmed that decisionmaking authority was vested in the Miami headquarters and that the district office served largely as an intermediate link between the headquarters and the franchisees. When problems arose over building design, site-development fees, rent computation, and the defaulted payments, Rudzewicz and MacShara learned that the Michigan office was powerless to resolve their disputes and could only channel their communications to Miami. Throughout these disputes, the Miami headquarters and the Michigan franchisees carried on a continuous course of direct communications by mail and by telephone, and it was the Miami headquarters that made the key negotiating decisions out of which the instant litigation arose.

Moreover, we believe the Court of Appeals gave insufficient weight to provisions in the various franchise documents providing that all disputes would be governed by Florida law. The franchise agreement, for example, stated: "This Agreement shall become valid when executed and accepted by BKC at Miami, Florida; it shall be deemed made and entered into in the State of Florida and shall be governed and construed under and in accordance with the laws of the State of Florida. The choice of law designation does not require that all suits concerning this Agreement be filed in Florida." . . . Although such a provision standing alone would be insufficient to confer jurisdiction, we believe that, when combined with the 20-year interdependent relationship Rudzewicz established with Burger King's Miami headquarters, it reinforced his deliberate affiliation with the forum State and the reasonable foreseeability of possible litigation there. As Judge Johnson argued in his dissent below, Rudzewicz "purposefully availed himself of the benefits and protections of Florida's laws" by entering into contracts expressly providing that those laws would govern franchise disputes.

(2)

Nor has Rudzewicz pointed to other factors that can be said persuasively to outweigh the considerations discussed above and to establish the unconstitutionality of Florida's assertion of jurisdiction. We cannot conclude that Florida had no "legitimate interest in holding [Rudzewicz] answerable on a claim related to" the contacts he had established in that State.[25] Moreover . . . the Court of Appeals' assertion that the Florida litigation "severely impaired [Rudzewicz'] ability to call Michigan witnesses who might be essential to his defense and counterclaim," is wholly without support in the record. And even to the extent that it is inconvenient for a party who has minimum contacts with a forum to litigate there, such considerations most frequently can be accommodated through a change of venue. Although the Court has suggested that inconvenience may at some point become so substantial as to achieve constitutional magnitude, *McGee v. International Life Insurance Co.*, *supra*, 355 U.S. at 223, this is not such a case.

The Court of Appeals also concluded, however, that the parties' dealings involved "a characteristic disparity of bargaining power" and "elements of surprise," and that Rudzewicz "lacked fair notice" of the potential for litigation in Florida because the contractual provisions suggesting to the contrary were merely "boilerplate declarations in a lengthy printed contract." . . . To the contrary, Rudzewicz was represented by counsel throughout these complex transactions

---

25. Complaining that "when Burger King is the plaintiff, you won't 'have it your way' because it sues all franchisees in Miami," Brief for Appellee 19, Rudzewicz contends that Florida's interest in providing a convenient forum is negligible given the company's size and ability to conduct litigation anywhere in the country. We disagree. Absent compelling considerations, *cf. McGee v. International Life Insurance Co.*, 355 U.S. at 223, a defendant who has purposefully derived commercial benefit from his affiliations in a forum may not defeat jurisdiction there simply because of his adversary's greater net wealth.

and, as Judge Johnson observed in dissent below, was himself an experienced accountant "who for five months conducted negotiations with Burger King over the terms of the franchise and lease agreements, and who obligated himself personally to contracts requiring over time payments that exceeded $1 million." Rudzewicz was able to secure a modest reduction in rent and other concessions from Miami headquarters; moreover, to the extent that Burger King's terms were inflexible, Rudzewicz presumably decided that the advantages of affiliating with a national organization provided sufficient commercial benefits to offset the detriments.[28]

III

Notwithstanding these considerations, the Court of Appeals apparently believed that it was necessary to reject jurisdiction in this case as a prophylactic measure, reasoning that an affirmance of the District Court's judgment would result in the exercise of jurisdiction over "out-of-state consumers to collect payments due on modest personal purchases" and would "sow the seeds of default judgments against franchisees owing smaller debts." We share the Court of Appeals' broader concerns and therefore reject any talismanic jurisdictional formulas; "the facts of each case must [always] be weighed" in determining whether personal jurisdiction would comport with "fair play and substantial justice."[29] The "quality and nature" of an interstate transaction may sometimes be so "random," "fortuitous," or "attenuated" that it cannot fairly be said that the potential defendant "should reasonably anticipate being haled into court" in another jurisdiction. We also have emphasized that jurisdiction may not be grounded on a contract whose terms have been obtained through "fraud, undue influence, or overweening bargaining power" and whose application would render litigation "so gravely difficult and inconvenient that [a party] will for all practical purposes be deprived of his day in court." Just as the Due Process Clause allows flexibility in ensuring that commercial actors are not effectively "judgment proof" for the consequences of obligations they voluntarily assume in other States, so too does it prevent rules that would unfairly enable them to obtain default judgments against unwitting customers.

For the reasons set forth above, however, these dangers are not present in the instant case. Because Rudzewicz established a substantial and continuing relationship with Burger King's Miami headquarters, received fair notice from the

---

28. We do not mean to suggest that the jurisdictional outcome will always be the same in franchise cases. Some franchises may be primarily intrastate in character or involve different decisionmaking structures, such that a franchisee should not reasonably anticipate out-of-state litigation. . . . For these reasons, we reject Burger King's suggestion for "a general rule, or at least a presumption, that participation in an interstate franchise relationship" represents consent to the jurisdiction of the franchisor's principal place of business.

29. This approach does, of course, preclude clear-cut jurisdictional rules. But any inquiry into "fair play and substantial justice" necessarily requires determinations "in which few answers will be written 'in black and white. The greys are dominant and even among them the shades are innumerable.'" *Kulko v. California Superior Court*, 436 U.S. at 92.

contract documents and the course of dealing that he might be subject to suit in Florida, and has failed to demonstrate how jurisdiction in that forum would otherwise be fundamentally unfair, we conclude that the District Court's exercise of jurisdiction pursuant to Fla. Stat. § 48.193(1)(g) (Supp. 1984) did not offend due process. The judgment of the Court of Appeals is accordingly reversed, and the case is remanded for further proceedings consistent with this opinion.

Justice POWELL took no part in the consideration or decision of this case.

Justice STEVENS, with whom Justice WHITE joins, dissenting:

In my opinion there is a significant element of unfairness in requiring a franchisee to defend a case of this kind in the forum chosen by the franchisor. It is undisputed that appellee maintained no place of business in Florida, that he had no employees in that State, and that he was not licensed to do business there. Appellee did not prepare his French fries, shakes, and hamburgers in Michigan, and then deliver them into the stream of commerce "with the expectation that they [would] be purchased by consumers in" Florida. To the contrary, appellee did business only in Michigan, his business, property, and payroll taxes were payable in that State, and he sold all of his products there.

Throughout the business relationship, appellee's principal contacts with appellant were with its Michigan office. Notwithstanding its disclaimer, the Court seems ultimately to rely on nothing more than standard boilerplate language contained in various documents to establish that appellee "'purposefully availed himself of the benefits and protections of Florida's laws.'" Such superficial analysis creates a potential for unfairness not only in negotiations between franchisors and their franchisees but, more significantly, in the resolution of the disputes that inevitably arise from time to time in such relationships. . . .

YOUR TAKEAWAY

A party who enters into a contract, especially after extensive negotiations and for a span of years, has engaged in purposeful conduct and should foresee that consequences may flow from the arrangement. If that party has reached across state lines, one of those consequences is likely to be amenability to suit in the other party's state.

REVIEW QUESTIONS

1. Note that in its first paragraph, the Court confirms that Fed. R. Civ. P. 4(k)(1)(A) ties the jurisdictional reach of the federal district courts to that of the local state courts. Here that means the Florida long-arm statute, measured against the due process standards of *International Shoe* and its progeny.
2. For the dissenting Justice Stevens, there is no jurisdiction because Rudzewicz "did not prepare his French fries, shakes and hamburgers in Michigan, and then deliver them into the stream of commerce with the

expectation that they would be purchased by customers in Florida." But does Brennan's opinion treat this as a "stream of commerce" case?

3. What does *Burger King* teach us about the relationship between the "fair play" factors and the "minimum-contacts" test? Look at the final paragraph of section II-A in the decision. The First Circuit has summed up the three questions that now must be asked to determine whether jurisdiction exists:

> (1) whether the state long-arm statute authorizes jurisdiction; (2) whether defendant has sufficient minimum contacts so that exercise of jurisdiction does not offend due process; and (3) whether exercise of jurisdiction is reasonable, and therefore does not offend due process.

Noonan v. Winston Company, 135 F.3d 85, 89 (1st Cir. 1998).

4. Consider the significance of the provision in the franchise agreement quoted by the Court in section II-B(1): "This agreement shall become valid when executed and accepted by BKC at Miami, Florida; it shall be deemed made and entered into in the State of Florida and shall be governed and construed under and in accordance with the laws of the State of Florida. The choice of law designation does not require that all suits concerning this Agreement be filed in Florida." In Part M later in this chapter, we will explore forum selection clauses that go the next step—that actually designate a particular forum before any dispute arises.

5. Suppose:
    A) Rudzewicz had been a management consultant retained by Burger King to evaluate its operations in Michigan. After a brief phone conversation, his contract for the project was sent from the Miami headquarters to his office in Michigan, where he signed and returned it by mail. The contract called for the work to be completed within two months. Dissatisfied with his work product, Burger King files a breach of contract action in Florida. Is there jurisdiction over Rudzewicz for this claim? What distinguishes this case from the actual *Burger King Corp. v. Rudzewicz*?

    B) Rudzewicz had clipped a mail order form from a magazine and sent it to the Sunshine Fitness Company in Miami, and the company in response shipped its Sweat-Your-Pounds-Away Exerciser to his home in Michigan. If Rudzewicz fails to pay the bill, can Sunshine sue him in Florida? What distinguishes this case from the actual *Burger King Corp. v. Rudzewicz*? Note Justice Brennan's reference at the beginning of section III to the concern the Eleventh Circuit had about jurisdiction over "out-of-state consumers to collect payments due on modest personal purchases," which would "sow the seeds of default judgments." How does Justice Brennan attempt to alleviate this concern?

    C) Rudzewicz is injured in his den on the Exerciser and files a product liability action against Sunshine in his home state of Michigan. Is there jurisdiction over the Florida company on his tort claim? What distinguishes this case from the actual *Burger King Corp. v. Rudzewicz*?

QUESTIONS TO PONDER

1. Although Burger King prevailed, the Court declined its request to adopt a general rule that participation in an interstate franchise relationship would *always* constitute consent to jurisdiction in the state of the franchiser's principal place of business, opting instead for an *ad hoc* approach. See the Court's footnote 28. Was counsel for Burger King wise in basing the proposed rule on a *consent* theory? Ironically, such a theory appears back in vogue after *Nicastro*, above.

2. Why do you think the Court is so hesitant to adopt categorical rules (e.g., for automobile product defect cases, for franchise arrangements) in the area of personal jurisdiction? Wouldn't it save a lot of time and energy for judges and litigants (and law students)?

PRACTICE EXERCISE NO. 32: RULING ON A RULE 12(b)(2) MOTION TO DISMISS IN A CONTRACT ACTION

Memorandum

To: Law Clerk

From: U.S. District Judge, District of Massachusetts

Re: Recommendation on 12(b)(2) Motion in *Shaw v. Northern Law School*

Norris Shaw, a Massachusetts citizen, has filed a diversity action against Northern Law School of Vermont (NLS) and one of its faculty, Albert Gloss. In a two-count complaint, Shaw seeks damages against the school for breach of contract, and against Gloss for intentional infliction of emotional distress.

After reading an article about NLS in the *Boston Globe*'s Education Section (and intrigued by the prospect of learning law amidst the beauty of the Green Mountains and Ben & Jerry's Ice Cream), Shaw wrote the school and expressed interest. NLS responded by mailing its catalogue and application form to Shaw's home in Boston. He filled out the application, mailed it back to NLS, and in the spring received an acceptance letter. Shaw sent in his $500 deposit and enrolled as a law student in the fall.

In his second year at NLS, Shaw took "Extremely Complex Litigation" from Professor Gloss (a lifelong Vermonter). Although he thought he had mastered the materials, Shaw received a failing grade and as a result was dismissed from the school. After attempting unsuccessfully to have the grade changed through the school's appeals procedure, he returned to Massachusetts and filed the instant lawsuit in federal court in Boston.

In his complaint, Shaw alleges that he regularly argued with Professor Gloss in class and that Gloss failed him in retaliation, thus intentionally inflicting emotional distress upon him. In the second count, he asserts that the school's refusal to reverse the failing grade constitutes a breach of its implied contractual obligation to deal fairly with him.

Defendants NLS and Gloss have both moved to dismiss the complaint pursuant to Fed. R. Civ. P. 12(b)(2). The school has filed an affidavit asserting that its only place of business is in Vermont, that it has never maintained any office, mailing address, or telephone listing in Massachusetts, and that it has never done business or advertised there. The affidavit does concede that NLS regularly sends recruiters to Massachusetts to inform pre-law advisors and undergraduates about the school. Gloss has submitted an affidavit asserting that he has never set foot in Massachusetts, and has no connection whatever with the state.

I need a memorandum from you recommending how I should rule on these two motions. (The Massachusetts long-arm statute is reprinted in an earlier Practice Exercise.)

I. PERSONAL JURISDICTION IN CYBERSPACE

How can a theory of jurisdiction so rooted in territorial notions and land borders adapt itself to a world where business and communication are regularly conducted in cyberspace? Consider the following case.

Rao v. Era Alaska Airlines
22 F. Supp. 3d 529 (D. Md. 2014)

GRIMM, District Judge:

Maryland Plaintiffs sue an Alaska-based airline and other Alaska Defendants for torts arising out of the loss of personal property on or shortly after a flight operated by Defendant airline. Defendants have moved to dismiss for lack of personal jurisdiction on the grounds that Plaintiffs' claims arise out of a flight within Alaska operated by an airline that transacts business only within Alaska. Plaintiffs respond by arguing that jurisdiction in Maryland is proper because Plaintiffs purchased the tickets for their intra-Alaska flight over the internet, which is sufficient to give Maryland personal jurisdiction over Defendants. Because I disagree with Plaintiffs, I find that Maryland cannot exercise personal jurisdiction over Defendants but that the interests of justice require me to transfer the case to the U.S. District Court for the District of Alaska.

I. BACKGROUND

In their Complaint, Plaintiffs Vijai Rao and Sumathi Mathur allege that, on August 22, 2010, they boarded a flight operated by Defendant Era Alaska Airlines ("Era") from Kodiak, Alaska to Anchorage, Alaska. "Plaintiffs carried with them personal items in a carrying case [(the "Case")] on board the airline operated by the Defendants including several items of valuable jewelry and cash. Plaintiff checked that these items were in their possession prior to boarding the airplane for the flight from Kodiak to Anchorage." After arriving in Anchorage and debarking from the airplane on August 23, 2010, Plaintiffs determined that the Case was missing. . . .

On August 23, 2012, Plaintiffs filed their complaint in this Court against Era alleging negligence [and other claims]. Defendant Era moved to dismiss for lack of personal jurisdiction. I denied the motion without prejudice and allowed the parties to undertake limited discovery to determine "if Defendants have sufficient connection with the State of Maryland such that the Court has personal jurisdiction over Defendants." Plaintiffs seek to amend the Complaint to include facts supporting personal jurisdiction in Maryland over the Defendants. The proposed amended complaint seeks to add new factual allegations, including that:

> In Maryland, the Defendants utilize the online service Sabre, a Global Distribution System, which allows bookings, reservations, itineraries, and ticketing by travel agencies and individual customers. Sabre (Sabre Travel Network) is held by Sabre Holdings a travel technology company which includes Travelocity and Expedia and has an office in Bethesda, MD. . . . In 2010, Plaintiffs reserved, booked, and paid for services offered by the Defendants using the internet travel site expedia.com "Expedia" in Maryland.

Defendant Era opposed the Motion to Amend. In addition to opposing the motion to amend, Defendants have renewed their motion to dismiss this case for lack of personal jurisdiction. Both the motion for leave to amend and the motion to dismiss are ripe and now are before me. Having reviewed the filings, I find a hearing is not necessary.

II. PERSONAL JURISDICTION

In determining whether the exercise of specific jurisdiction comports with due process, a court considers: "(1) the extent to which the defendant has purposefully availed itself of the privilege of conducting activities in the state; (2) whether the plaintiff['s] claims arise out of those activities directed at the state; and (3) whether the exercise of personal jurisdiction would be constitutionally reasonable."

A. Long-Arm Jurisdiction

For this Court to exercise jurisdiction, Plaintiffs' claims must "aris[e] from an[ ] act enumerated in" the Maryland long-arm jurisdiction statute. Md. Code Ann., Cts. & Jud. Proc. § 6-103(a). Maryland's statute provides:

A court may exercise personal jurisdiction over a person, who directly or by an agent:

> (1) Transacts any business or performs any character of work or service in the State;

(2) Contracts to supply goods, food, services, or manufactured products in the State;

(3) Causes tortious injury in the State by an act or omission in the State;

(4) Causes tortious injury in the State or outside of the State by an act or omission outside the State if he regularly does or solicits business, engages in any other persistent course of conduct in the State or derives substantial revenue from goods, food, services, or manufactured products used or consumed in the State;

(5) Has an interest in, uses, or possesses real property in the State; or

(6) Contracts to insure or act as surety for, or on, any person, property, risk, contract, obligation, or agreement located, executed, or to be performed within the State at the time the contract is made, unless the parties otherwise provide in writing.

Plaintiffs rely upon § 6-103(b)(1), which applies to a defendant who "[t]ransacts any business or performs any character of work or service in the State," and § 6-103(b)(2), which applies to a defendant who "[c]ontracts to supply goods, food, services, or manufactured products in the State." According to Plaintiffs, Era has conducted business in Maryland even though its flights operate only in Alaska because it sells tickets through the Sabre distribution system, which has "offices in Maryland," and because Plaintiffs themselves purchased their tickets in Maryland, via the website expedia.com ("Expedia").

At the outset, it is apparent that personal jurisdiction cannot rest on § 6-103(b)(2), because Era never contracted to supply any goods or services "in the State." Assuming, without deciding, that by purchasing tickets in Maryland, Plaintiffs entered into a contract with Era in Maryland, "the language of section 6-103(b)(2) cannot be read as extending to any contract negotiated in Maryland." It covers only contracts to supply goods and services in Maryland, irrespective of where the contract was negotiated. Here, there is no question that the only services provided by Era were in Alaska, not in Maryland, and irrespective of where Plaintiffs actually purchased their tickets, long-arm jurisdiction simply does not arise under § 6-103(b)(2).

The application of § 6-103(b)(1), however, presents a much thornier question. Here, Plaintiff argues that business transactions over the Internet are "mainstays of the modern tourism business," and that "[t]he Defendants utilize its [sic] membership in Sabre to locate customers, communicate with customers and confirm customer itineraries, make reservations and issue tickets for travel." Plaintiffs' cause of action does not arise out of the ticket sale itself, but out of events that took place in Alaska. Thus it is not entirely clear, and the parties do not address, whether the actions of Era employees in Alaska constitute "transact[ing] any business . . . in the State" merely by virtue of the fact that the tickets were purchased here. But assuming that they are, "[t]he Maryland courts have consistently held that the state's long-arm statute is coextensive with the limits of personal jurisdiction set by the due process clause of the Constitution." So if the contacts alleged by Plaintiffs are sufficient to satisfy the dictates of due process, they likely will satisfy the Maryland long-arm statute as well, insofar as the loss of Plaintiffs' Case can be seen to arise out of the purchase of tickets in Maryland.

To satisfy the constitutional due process requirement, a defendant must have sufficient "minimum contacts" with the forum state such that "the maintenance of the suit does not offend traditional notions of fair play and substantial justice." *International Shoe Co. v. Washington*, 326 U.S. 310, 316 (1945). The minimum contacts test requires the plaintiff to show that the defendant "purposely directed his activities at the residents of the forum" and that the plaintiff's cause of action "arise[s] out of" those activities. *Burger King Corp. v. Rudzewicz*, 471 U.S. 462, 472 (1985). This test is designed to ensure that the defendant is not "haled into a jurisdiction solely as a result of random, fortuitous, or attenuated contacts." It protects a defendant from having to defend himself in a forum where he should not have anticipated being sued. *See World-Wide Volkswagen Corp. v. Woodson*, 444 U.S. 286, 297 (1980).

Plaintiffs do not dispute that Era offers flights only within Alaska or that Plaintiffs, in fact, came to Alaska to fly on a flight operated by Era. Era maintains an Internet presence that includes a website, a Facebook account, and a Twitter account, as well as placing advertisements on the websites for the Anchorage Daily News and the Fairbanks Daily News-Miner, all of which can be viewed from anywhere with Internet access. With those exceptions, Era advertises only in Alaska-based sources that it believes "are primarily read and accessed by individual[s] residing in the State of Alaska." Era operates no flights that originate or terminate in Maryland or, indeed, anywhere outside of Alaska.

However, Plaintiffs note that they were able to purchase tickets to travel on an Era flight from within Maryland, through a somewhat attenuated set of relationships. To allow for tickets to be sold online, Era offers its flights through "a global distribution system ('GDS') called 'Sabre.' Sabre is one of three main GDS used in the travel industry. As a member of Sabre, Era Alaska makes its flights searchable by other Sabre members, who are then able to book flights on Era Alaska through Sabre." Plaintiffs have stated that they used the website Expedia to purchase tickets for their Era flight, through the Sabre system. They also assert that Sabre has offices in Maryland. Plaintiffs do not allege any other facts to justify Maryland's exercise of personal jurisdiction over Defendants.

The Fourth Circuit outlined the circumstances under which activity over the Internet can subject a defendant to long-arm jurisdiction in *ALS Scan, Inc. v. Digital Service Consultants, Inc.*, 293 F.3d 707 (4th Cir. 2002), which adopted the reasoning of the Western District of Pennsylvania in *Zippo Manufacturing Co. v. Zippo Dot Com, Inc.*, 952 F. Supp. 1119 (W.D. Pa. 1997). As the Fourth Circuit explained:

> In *Zippo*, the court concluded that "the likelihood that personal jurisdiction can be constitutionally exercised is directly proportionate to the nature and quality of commercial activity that an entity conducts over the Internet." 952 F. Supp. at 1124. Recognizing a "sliding scale" for defining when electronic contacts with a State are sufficient, the court elaborated:

At one end of the spectrum are situations where a defendant clearly does business over the Internet. If the defendant enters into contracts with residents of a foreign jurisdiction that involve the knowing and repeated transmission of computer files over the Internet, personal jurisdiction is proper. At the opposite end are situations where a defendant has simply posted information on an Internet web site which is accessible to users in foreign jurisdictions. A passive Web site that does little more than make information available to those who are interested in it is not grounds for the exercise [of] personal jurisdiction. The middle ground is occupied by interactive Web sites where a user can exchange information with the host computer. In these cases, the exercise of jurisdiction is determined by examining the level of interactivity and commercial nature of the exchange of information that occurs on the Web site.

ALS Scan, 293 F.3d at 713-14 (quoting *Zippo*, 952 F. Supp. at 1124).

Under this framework,

a State may, consistent with due process, exercise judicial power over a person outside of the state when that person (1) directs electronic activity into the State, (2) with the manifested intent of engaging in business or other interactions within the state, and (3) that activity creates, in a person within the State, a potential cause of action cognizable in the State's courts.

Id. at 714. For example, in *ALS Scan* itself, the Fourth Circuit held that the mere fact that a website containing copyrighted material is accessible in Maryland does not create personal jurisdiction over the website's out-of-state internet service provider ("ISP"). "Other than maintain its website on the Internet, [the ISP] has engaged in no activity in Maryland, and its only contacts with the State occur when persons in Maryland access Digital's website." The Fourth Circuit recognized:

If we were to conclude as a general principle that a person's act of placing information on the Internet subjects that person to personal jurisdiction in each State in which the information is accessed, then the defense of personal jurisdiction, in the sense that a State has geographically limited judicial power, would no longer exist. The person placing information on the Internet would be subject to personal jurisdiction in every state.

ALS Scan, 293 F.3d at 712.

In contrast, *Zippo* presented a scenario in which the out-of-state defendant itself had contracted with ISPs in Pennsylvania to provide access to a subscription news service. The court held that because the defendant "repeatedly and consciously chose to process Pennsylvania residents' applications and to assign them passwords," it had made "a conscious choice to conduct business with the residents of" Pennsylvania and was on notice that it could be subject to suit there. Importantly, the Western District of Pennsylvania discussed the degree of choice available to the defendant in determining where it would be subject to jurisdiction. It "was under no obligation to sell its services to Pennsylvania residents. . . . If [the defendant] had not wanted to be amenable to jurisdiction in Pennsylvania, the solution would have been simple—it could have chosen not to sell its services to Pennsylvania residents." As the Fourth Circuit later explained, "[w]hen a defendant runs an interactive site, through which he 'enters into contracts with residents of a foreign jurisdiction that involve the knowing and repeated transmission of computer files over the internet,' he can properly be haled into the courts of that foreign jurisdiction." *Carefirst of Md., Inc. v. Carefirst Pregnancy Ctrs., Inc.,* 334 F.3d 390, 399 (4th Cir. 2003).

In *Young v. New Haven Advocate,* the Fourth Circuit considered whether newspapers based in Connecticut could be subject to jurisdiction in the Commonwealth of Virginia for a defamation suit arising out of statements made about a Virginia prison warden in the context of a Connecticut policy transferring prisoners to Virginia. 315 F.3d 256 (4th Cir. 2002). The only basis for jurisdiction advanced by the plaintiff was that:

> (1) the newspapers, knowing that [the warden] was a Virginia resident, intentionally discussed and defamed him in their articles, (2) the newspapers posted the articles on their websites, which were accessible in Virginia, and (3) the primary effects of the defamatory statements on [the warden's] reputation were felt in Virginia.

The Fourth Circuit "ask[ed] whether the newspapers manifested an intent to direct their website content—which included certain articles discussing conditions in a Virginia prison—to a Virginia audience." Finding that the articles were not directed towards Virginia, the Fourth Circuit unequivocally rejected the notion that jurisdiction could be premised on such a thin foundation because otherwise "the traditional due process principles governing a State's jurisdiction over persons outside of its borders would be subverted." *But see Calder v. Jones,* 465 U.S. 783, 786-87 (1984) (reaching a contrary conclusion where the defendants knew that the publication containing their allegedly libelous article had its greatest circulation in the state seeking to exercise jurisdiction).

More recently, in *Carefirst of Maryland, Inc. v. Carefirst Pregnancy Centers, Inc.,* a regional licensee of BlueCross BlueShield incorporated in Maryland ("Carefirst") brought a trademark suit in Maryland against a similarly named "non-profit, evangelical, pro-life advocacy organization" incorporated in Illinois and working almost exclusively in the Chicago area ("CPC"). CPC's only ties with Maryland were a website accessible in Maryland and that was hosted and developed by company headquartered in Maryland, and a small number of donations to CPC by Marylanders, of which only one was shown to have been made through the CPC website. Although the CPC website was "'semi-interactive,' in that [it] contain[ed] features that ma[d]e it possible for a user to exchange information with the host computer," the Fourth Circuit noted that there was only a single instance of a donation by a Maryland resident in the record. Moreover, "the overall content of CPC's website has a strongly local character," emphasizing its work in Chicago specifically, "[r]ather than target[ing] a Maryland audience." "In fact, the only respect in which CPC even arguably reaches out to Marylanders via its Internet website is in its generalized request that anyone, anywhere make a donation to support CPC's Chicago-based mission. Such a generalized request is . . . an insufficient Maryland contact to sustain jurisdiction in that forum."

These cases demonstrate that the Fourth Circuit has been notably reluctant to extend personal jurisdiction to out-of-state defendants based on little more than their presence on the Internet. The mere fact that information can be accessed from within the forum state does [sic—not] subject the defendant to that state's jurisdiction, even when that information specifically relates to persons or events in the forum state, so long as it was not intentionally directed there. Nor does the mere fact that Marylanders may have engaged in transactions with an out-of-state defendant who did not deliberately direct its activities into the State.

Plaintiffs, citing to virtually no relevant authority, seek to distinguish this case from *Carefirst* on the basis that Era "utilize[s] its membership in Sabre to locate customers, communicate with customers and confirm customer itineraries, make reservations and issue tickets for travel. In this way, the Defendants are present in Maryland and doing business in Maryland." However, Plaintiffs' view of the facts is not supported by the record. First, it is not clear whether Era itself ever had any direct communications with Plaintiffs at all, or whether Sabre and Expedia effectively purchased the tickets from Era in Alaska and then resold them in Maryland. Second, and perhaps more importantly, Era did not "manifest[ ] intent of engaging in business or other interactions within" Maryland. Era was not "locat[ing] customers" in Maryland as Plaintiffs suggest; rather, Era was advertising exclusively in Alaska for flights wholly within Alaska, and was making tickets on those flights available on the Internet in a manner that could be accessed by potential passengers anywhere, but used by those passengers only if they first came to Alaska to board their flight. Rather, it was Plaintiffs who sought out Era, using the Internet to reach into Alaska from Maryland, not the other way around. It is not apparent that Era did anything affirmatively to reach into this jurisdiction; as in *Carefirst*, a single Maryland transaction reflected nothing more than the "generalized" possibility that "anyone, anywhere" may buy a ticket and was, "under the circumstances, an insufficient Maryland contact to sustain jurisdiction" here. Finally, even if there may be circumstances in which a defendant in Era's position could be subject to jurisdiction in Maryland, Plaintiff has failed to satisfy its burden to show or allege sufficient facts here. This Court lacks personal jurisdiction over Era.

III. CONCLUSION

[Although the court agreed it lacked jurisdiction, it chose to transfer the case to the United States District Court in Alaska pursuant to 28 U.S.C. § 1406. We address such transfers later in this chapter.]

YOUR TAKEAWAY

These Internet cases raise what Justice Breyer refers to in *Nicastro* as the "many recent changes in commerce and communication, many of which are not anticipated by our precedents." The U.S. Chamber of Commerce urged the Court in *Nicastro* to "make clear that certain forms of internet advertising do not satisfy the 'additional conduct' requirement of *Asahi*." *See* Brief of the Chamber of Commerce of the USA as *Amicus Curiae* in Support of Petitioner, pp. 24-25. But the Court has yet to tackle the issue—in *Walden v. Fiore*, 134 S. Ct. 1115, 1125 n.9 (2014), it expressly "le[ft] questions about virtual contacts for another day"

In the absence of Supreme Court guidance, the lower courts have adopted various approaches, the predominant one being the *Zippo Manufacturing Co. v. Zippo Dot Com, Inc.*, referenced in *Rao*, which envisions a sliding scale to determine whether the actor is purposefully transacting business over the Internet. (More to say below.)

REVIEW QUESTIONS

1. How does the *Rao* opinion attempt to translate past precedent into the digital age?

2. Unlike Era Alaska Airlines, which was one step removed from plaintiffs who booked through the third party Expedia, Harrah's Hotel in Las Vegas maintained an interactive website that permitted visitors to directly make reservations. And "by touting the proximity of their hotels to California and providing driving directions from that state to their hotels, Harrah's website specifically targeted residents of California." *See Snowney v. Harrah's Entertainment, Inc.*, 35 Cal. 4th 1054, 1068, 112 P.3d 28, 43 (2005). This purposeful availment rendered the Nevada hotel subject to specific jurisdiction in an action in California by a resident unhappy about an energy surcharge imposed by the hotel when he checked out.

   Other courts have insisted on "something more" in the way of targeting the forum state, examining for example the number of hits and actual transactions consummated from residents. *See, e.g., iAccess, Inc. v. Webcard Technologies, Inc.*, 182 F. Supp. 1183 (D. Utah 2002).

3. What is clear is that "the mere existence of a website that is visible in a forum and that gives information about a company and its products is not enough, by itself, to subject a defendant to personal jurisdiction in that forum." *Cossaboon v. Me. Med. Ctr.*, 600 F.3d 25, 35 (1st Cir. 2010). *See also Bensusan Restaurant Corp. v. King*, 126 F.3d 25 (2d Cir. 1997) (rejecting jurisdiction over The Blue Note jazz club in Columbia, Missouri, sued in New York by the iconic Blue Note jazz venue in lower Manhattan for trademark infringement based on the defendant's expropriation of the famous name on its website); *Roberts v. Legendary Marine Sales*, 447 Mass. 860, 864-865 (2006) (rejecting argument that defendant's advertisement on its passive website, which induced plaintiff to purchase an allegedly defective boat, was sufficient to establish jurisdiction).

QUESTIONS TO PONDER

Does the use of a third party like Expedia function in erecting the same kind of shield against personal jurisdiction that its distributor provided J. McIntyre Machinery, Ltd. in *Nicastro*? Should it? Can a seller insulate itself from amenability merely by using an e-commerce intermediary like Amazon.com? Compare *Standard Process, Inc. v. KDealz Ltd. Co.*, 2018 WL 3059673 (W.D. Wisc. 2018) ("The fact that [defendant] conducts that business through Amazon doesn't shield it from personal jurisdiction any more than shipping products via FedEx would.") with *Wireless Environment, LLC v. HooToo.com, Inc.*, 2016 WL 4530617 (N.D. Ohio 2016) ("Sales, marketing and advertising conduct aimed, through the services of a third party like Amazon, to the United States market in general is insufficient to satisfy Due Process requirements under the Sixth Circuit's "stream of commerce plus" approach.").

Note on Internet Jurisdiction Today. While still widely followed, *Zippo*'s sliding-scale analysis, referenced in *Rao*, has not met with universal approval. One court has observed:

> [I]t is not clear why a website's level of interactivity should be determinative on the issue of personal jurisdiction. As even courts adopting the *Zippo* test have recognized, a court cannot determine whether personal jurisdiction is appropriate simply by deciding whether a website is "passive" or "interactive" (assuming that websites can be readily classified into one category or the other). Even a "passive" website may support a finding of jurisdiction if the defendant used its website intentionally to harm the plaintiff in the forum state. *See Panavision International, LP v. Toeppen*, 141 F.3d 1316, 1322 (9th Cir. 1998). Similarly, an "interactive" or commercial website may not be sufficient to support jurisdiction if it is not aimed at residents in the forum state. *See GTE New Media Services, Inc. v. BellSouth Corp.*, 199 F.3d 1343, 1349-1350 (D.C. Cir. 2000). Moreover, regardless how interactive a website is, it cannot form the basis for personal jurisdiction unless a nexus exists between the website and the cause of action or unless the contacts through the website are so substantial that they may be considered "systematic and continuous" for the purpose of general jurisdiction. Thus, a rigid adherence to the *Zippo* test is likely to lead to erroneous results.

Hy Cite Corp. v. Badbusinessbureau.com. LLC, 297 F. Supp. 2d 1154, 1169 (W.D. Wis. 2004).

The Seventh Circuit has similarly cautioned that "the interactivity of a website is also a poor proxy for adequate in-state contacts. [C]ourts should be careful in resolving questions about personal jurisdiction involving online contacts to ensure that a defendant is not haled into court simply because the defendant owns or operates a website that is accessible in the forum state, even if that site is 'interactive.'" *Advanced Tactical Ordnance Systems, LLC v. Real Action Paintball, Inc.*, 751 F.3d at 803. For more, *see* Alan M. Trammell and Derek E. Bambauer, *Personal Jurisdiction and the "Interwebs."* 100 Cornell L. Rev. 1129 (2015).

Like other early cases, *Zippo*'s framework is largely "based on technology from the 1990s and do[es] not account for the rise of new web platforms and applications such as social media, targeted advertising, artificial intelligence, and bots, among other things." Zoe Niesel, *#Personaljurisdiction: A New Age Of Internet Contacts*, 94 Ind. L.J. 103, 104 (2019). E-commerce was, of course, in its infancy; Facebook and Instagram were yet to appear. "The Zippo test," in short, "is ultimately problematic because it is the product of an internet that no longer exists." *Id.* at 126. Professor Niesel proposes

> that courts should move away from interactivity-based analyses [where courts have to struggle to categorize a site as interactive or passive] to a more holistic analysis that examines the defendant's expectations based on the increased global presence of the internet and traditional notions of fairness [the burden on the defendant, the forum State's interest in adjudicating the dispute, the plaintiff's interest in obtaining convenient and effective relief, the interstate judicial system's interest in obtaining the most efficient resolution of controversies, and the shared interest of the several States in furthering fundamental substantive social policies].
>
> Instead of a tortured interpretation of purposeful availment, minimum contacts through website activity should be achieved when a defendant utilizes the internet knowing that the information could reach the forum state. The remaining aspects of the specific jurisdiction analysis—the requirement that the contact give rise to the claim and the application of reasonableness factors—provide a sufficient check on excessive exercises of jurisdiction. Such an approach should provide clarity, and certainty, as web platforms continue to develop.

Id. at 144.

Does such an approach strike you as leading to more "certainty" in the results?

The debate pits scholars Damon Andrews and John Newman (*Personal Jurisdiction and Choice of Law in the Cloud*, 73 Md. L. Rev. 313, 365 (2013)), suggesting that defendants in cases involving torts in "the cloud" should simply "take [their] plaintiff where [they] find him" and face suit wherever the plaintiff resides," against Alan Trammel and Derek Bambauer (*Personal Jurisdiction and the "Interwebs,"* 100 Cornell L. Rev. 1129, 1167 (2015)), who contend that "[i]nternet based contacts should rarely, if ever, suffice for personal jurisdiction," and that "courts should dispense with the fiction that purely virtual conduct creates any meaningful contact with a particular forum."

The Supreme Court has stayed out of this debate thus far.

Defamation over the Internet. Look back at *Griffis v. Luban*, discussed following *Calder v. Jones*, above. What about an allegedly defamatory statement posted on Facebook? Suppose Jane, residing in New York, posts on her Facebook page a rant against her former med school roommate Helen, now a practicing doctor in California, that asserts Helen "cheated her way through NYU" and showed up drunk at morning rounds. Can Helen file a defamation action in California, or must she travel to New York to litigate? *See Burdick v. Superior Court*, 233 Cal. App. 4th 8 (2015); *Farquharson v. Metz*, 2013 WL 3968018 (D. Mass. 2013).

Zidon v. Pickrell, 344 F. Supp. 2d 624 (D.N.D. 2004) held plaintiff's former girlfriend in Colorado subject to jurisdiction in North Dakota for allegedly defamatory postings on her website because they made specific references to plaintiff's professional and personal life in North Dakota, and thus were "directed uniquely toward the State of North Dakota."

Internet defamation cases raise at least two thorny issues: (1) where does an injury to one's reputation occur *geographically*? and (2) where does the defamatory statement exist *geographically*? Can either question be answered meaningfully, or do we need an entirely new *non-geographic* theory of personal jurisdiction?

Recognizing that defamation is different than other intentional torts like assault, some long-arm statutes exclude it from the "effects" provision. *See, e.g.,* NY CPLR 302(a):

> **Acts which are the basis of jurisdiction. As to a cause of action arising from any of the acts enumerated in this section, a court may exercise personal jurisdiction over any non-domiciliary who in person or through an agent:**
>
> (3) commits a tortious act without the state causing injury to person or property within the state, ***except as to a cause of action for defamation of character arising from the act*** . . .

Why do you think defamation is left out?

What about defamatory statements made in an "e-mail blast" read by many subscribers? The Seventh Circuit has ruled that a nonresident sender is not sufficiently connected to a forum state by the mere fact that that blast included some forum residents:

> As a practical matter, email does not exist in any location at all; it bounces from one server to another, it starts wherever the account-holder is sitting when she clicks the "send" button, and it winds up wherever the recipient happens to be at that instant. The connection between the place where an email is opened and a lawsuit is entirely fortuitous. We note as well that it is exceedingly common in today's world for a company to allow consumers to sign up for an email list. We are not prepared to hold that this alone demonstrates that a defendant made a substantial connection to each state (or country) associated with those persons' "snail mail" addresses. It may be different if there were evidence that a defendant in some way targeted residents of a specific state, perhaps through geographically-restricted online ads. But in such a case the focus would not be on the users who signed up, but instead on the deliberate actions by the defendant to target or direct itself toward the forum state.

Advanced Tactical Ordnance Systems, LLC v. Real Action Paintball, Inc., 751 F.3d 796, 803 (7th Cir. 2014).

For a particularly thoughtful analysis of this issue, *see Shrader v. Biddinger*, 633 F.3d 1235 (2011), recognizing that "a distinguishing characteristic of email that must be taken into account [is that] although email is directed to particular recipients, email addresses typically do not reveal anything about the geographic location of the addressee. Thus, if the plaintiff does not show that the defendant otherwise knew where the recipient was located, the email itself does not demonstrate purposeful direction of the message to the forum state, even if that happens to be where the recipient lived." 633 F.3d at 1247-1248.

MORE TO PONDER

The Communications Decency Act, 47 U.S.C. § 230, shields Internet service providers from defamation liability for merely conveying content obtained from a third party. § 230(c)(1) provides that "[n]o provider or user of an interactive computer service shall be treated as the publisher or speaker of any information provided by another information content provider." And "[n]o cause of action may be brought and no liability imposed under any State or local law that is inconsistent with this section." § 230(e)(3). *See Doe v. Friendfinder Network, Inc.*, 540 F. Supp. 2d 288 (D.N.H. 2008) (and cases cited). The Act does not, however, affect claims pertaining to intellectual property or privacy, § 230(e)(2), (4), and thus is not applicable in cases such as *ALS Scan*.

PRACTICE EXERCISE NO. 33: ELECTRONIC CONTACTS AND VIRTUAL PRESENCE

Memorandum

To: Associate
From: Partner
Re: Advice on *DermDocs v. Ad Space*

a) Our client DermDocs, a California based company, manufactures a skincare product known as RetinX® which it sells through its website under the domain name RetinX.com. A few years ago, DermDocs entered into a contract with an affiliate marketing network company, Ad Space, Inc., to help drum up more business for RetinX®. Under the agreement, Ad Space advertised RetinX® on its many websites, providing visitors with direct links to RetinX.com.

The contract has since expired, but Ad Space has not taken down the RetinX® advertisements. When visitors click on the advertisements, they are linked to the webpage *http://redirect.to* which displays a message stating, "This link is no longer available. We will redirect you to another in five seconds. If you do not wish to be redirected, click here."

After five seconds visitors are redirected to a site owned by SkinDocs, Inc. selling similar skincare products called RetX® and RetinAid® that are branded and packaged nearly identical to our client's product. SkinDocs pays Ad Space a commission based on the number of visitors redirected to its site through the advertisements. We have obtained data showing that a significant number of California residents have been redirected by *http://redirect.to*, many of whom have purchased RetX® and RetinAid®.

Our client seeks to bring suit in the District of California against Ad Space and SkinDocs for trademark infringement. I do not think we will have trouble establishing jurisdiction over SkinDocs, but Ad Space may prove more difficult. Its only contact with California is its webpage, *http://redirect.to*.

The California long-arm statute allows state courts to exercise jurisdiction on any basis not inconsistent with the Constitution. On its face, *http://redirect.to* appears to fall into the least "interactive" category of the *Zippo* test because it (1) does not provide the user with any information; (2) does not display any advertising; and (3) only interacts with a user for a maximum of five seconds. However, it strikes me that the act of redirecting users to websites selling RetX® and RetinAid® is itself interactive because Ad Space is attempting to influence users to buy these alternative products.

I need you to analyze whether Ad Space's contacts with California are sufficient to subject it to personal jurisdiction within the State.

PRACTICE EXERCISE NO. 34: A TWENTY-FIRST-CENTURY FISH STORY

You are a law clerk to U.S. District Judge Julie Roberts in the District of Maine. She has started a draft opinion that resolves a motion to dismiss in *Thomas v. Mobile Apps, Inc.* Your task is (1) to complete the first draft of the opinion; and (2) prepare a separate memo for the judge with any comments, questions, or concerns that you have about your portion of the draft opinion. In preparing the draft opinion, please be sure to address the best arguments and counterarguments that you would expect the parties to make, and direct the judge's attention to any additional information that you may need.

Draft Memorandum and Order

Plaintiff Joseph Thomas brings this action alleging claims for copyright infringement against Defendant Mobile Apps, Inc. ("MA"). MA has filed a Motion to Dismiss for Lack of Personal Jurisdiction. The Court takes the following facts from Plaintiff's Complaint and the affidavits and exhibits submitted by both parties. Plaintiff Thomas, a Maine resident, is an illustrator of various North American fish species. He has registered copyrights on forty-one fish illustrations, which he makes available for reproduction by purchase and download from his website, *www.americanfishes.com*.

Defendant MA is a California corporation that develops software applications ("apps") for smart phones. Its only office is in Fountain Valley, California; it does not have a local agent or bank account or own any property in the State of Maine; and its employees have never traveled to Maine for business purposes. MA does, however, maintain a website that is accessible to users worldwide. That website presents information about the company and its products and contains hyperlinks to the online stores of third-party app providers, like iTunes and Google Play, where its apps are offered for sale.

In late 2014, Connecticut resident Jason Stevens, a co-defendant in this case, approached MA with an idea for an app that would catalogue information about various fish species located in the United States. MA agreed to develop and launch the app with Mr. Stevens's help. The result of this partnership was "FishID," a mobile app billed as "a flexible tackle box of tools for identifying any catch, finding fishing spots, [and] reading up on local regulations." FishID provides detailed profiles of each fish species as well as range maps allowing users to identify species that can be found in particular locations, including bodies of water within the State of Maine. The app also links to each state's fishing regulations.

Mr. Stevens supplied MA with the pictures used in the app's fish species profiles. Plaintiff alleges that some of those pictures are direct copies of Plaintiff's copyrighted fish illustrations and that Mr. Stevens and MA incorporated those illustrations into the app without Plaintiff's permission, thus violating Plaintiff's copyrights. According to the affidavit of MA's CEO Andrew Maltin, Mr. Stevens indicated during the app's development phase that the fish species illustrations came "almost exclusively from government websites (i.e., the public domain)." Thus, Mr. Maltin declares, MA was unaware during the development and launch of the FishID app that any of the pictures supplied by Mr. Stevens was a copyrighted work.

MA later became aware of "potential copyright issues" when Plaintiff's attorney sent a letter informing it that some of the pictures infringed on Plaintiff's copyrights. The letter demanded that MA cease and desist from further distribution of the cited pictures. MA did not respond to the letter, and has since refused other similar demands.

Plaintiff does not allege that the FishID app has ever been purchased or used by a person located in Maine. He argues, however, that specific jurisdiction exists in this case based on MA's efforts in developing and marketing the FishID app. In addition, Plaintiff submits an exhibit tabulating the number of times MA's "other products" have been installed on mobile devices in each state. That spreadsheet shows that users in Maine have installed MA's apps on at least 6,663 occasions—a showing, Plaintiff contends, sufficient to establish specific jurisdiction.

Ruling on Defendant's Motion to Dismiss for Lack of Personal Jurisdiction

[to be completed by law clerk]

* * *

J. JURISDICTION BASED ON THE PRESENCE OF DEFENDANT'S PROPERTY

Would it have made any difference on the issue of adjudicatory power over Professor Gloss in Practice Exercise 31 if he owned a vacation home in Massachusetts? If Gloss had graded Shaw's examination there, arguably that might provide specific jurisdiction over Shaw's claim for intentional infliction of emotional distress. Ownership of the home in the forum state also raises two other possible bases of jurisdiction that go back to the original *Pennoyer* formulation. First, Shaw could try to have the professor served with process at or en route to the home—service within the state constitutes physical "presence." We will have more to say about so-called tag jurisdiction in the next section. Second, Shaw could cause the home to be attached and assert quasi in rem jurisdiction—under the *Pennoyer* scheme the presence of Gloss's property in Massachusetts creates jurisdiction on the unrelated tort claim, permitting entry of a judgment up to the value of the property. The Court's 1977 decision in the case that follows, however, radically altered (and indeed virtually abolishes) this category of adjudicatory power.

Shaffer v. Heitner involved a type of lawsuit we have not yet encountered. In a shareholder derivative action, stockholders sue on behalf of the corporation to enforce rights and obligations that the corporation itself has failed to act upon. Defendants are the officers and directors accused of mismanagement, or worse. Any recovery is (at least theoretically) for the benefit of the corporation.

Shaffer v. Heitner
433 U.S. 186 (1977)

Justice MARSHALL delivered the opinion of the Court:

The controversy in this case concerns the constitutionality of a Delaware statute that allows a court of that State to take jurisdiction of a lawsuit by sequestering any property of the defendant that happens to be located in Delaware. Appellants contend that the sequestration statute as applied in this case violates the Due Process Clause of the Fourteenth Amendment because it permits the state courts to exercise jurisdiction despite the absence of sufficient contacts among the defendants, the litigation, and the State of Delaware.

I

Appellee Heitner, a nonresident of Delaware, is the owner of one share of stock in the Greyhound Corp., a business incorporated under the laws of Delaware with its principal place of business in Phoenix, Ariz. On May 22, 1974, he filed a shareholder's derivative suit in the Court of Chancery for New Castle County, Del., in which he named as defendants Greyhound, its wholly owned subsidiary Greyhound Lines, Inc.,[1] and 28 present or former officers or directors of one or both of the corporations. In essence, Heitner alleged that the individual defendants had violated their duties to Greyhound by causing it and its subsidiary to engage in actions that resulted in the corporation's being held

---

1. Greyhound Lines, Inc., is incorporated in California and has its principal place of business in Phoenix, Ariz.

liable for substantial damages in a private antitrust suit[2] and a large fine in a criminal contempt action.[3] The activities which led to these penalties took place in Oregon.

Simultaneously with his complaint, Heitner filed a motion for an order of sequestration of the Delaware property of the individual defendants pursuant to Del. Code Ann., Tit. 10, § 366 (1975).[4] This motion was accompanied by a supporting affidavit of counsel which stated that the individual defendants were nonresidents of Delaware. The affidavit identified the property to be sequestered as common stock of the Defendant Greyhound Corporation, a Delaware corporation, [owned by the individual Defendants].

The requested sequestration order was signed the day the motion was filed. Pursuant to that order, the sequestrator "seized" approximately 82,000 shares of Greyhound common stock belonging to 19 of the defendants,[7] and options belonging to another 2 defendants. These seizures were accomplished by placing "stop transfer" orders or their equivalents on the books of the Greyhound Corp. So far as the record shows, none of the certificates representing the seized property was physically present in Delaware. The stock was considered to be in Delaware, and so subject to seizure, by virtue of Del. Code Ann., Tit. 8, § 169 (1975), which makes Delaware the situs of ownership of all stock in Delaware corporations.[9]

All 28 defendants were notified of the initiation of the suit by certified mail directed to their last known addresses and by publication in a New Castle County newspaper. The 21 defendants whose property was seized (hereafter referred to

---

2. A judgment of $13,146,090 plus attorneys' fees was entered against Greyhound in *Mt. Hood Stages, Inc. v. Greyhound Corp.*, 1972-3 Trade Cas. P 74,824, *aff'd*, 555 F.2d 687 (9th Cir. 1977).

3. *See United States v. Greyhound Corp.*, 363 F. Supp. 525 (N.D. Ill. 1973) and 370 F. Supp. 881 (N.D. Ill.), *aff'd*, 508 F.2d 529 (7th Cir. 1974). Greyhound was fined $100,000 and Greyhound Lines $500,000.

4. Section 366 provides:

(a) If it appears in any complaint filed in the Court of Chancery that the defendant or any one or more of the defendants is a nonresident of the State, the Court may make an order directing such nonresident defendant or defendants to appear by a day certain to be designated. Such order shall be served on such nonresident defendant or defendants by mail or otherwise, if practicable, and shall be published in such manner as the Court directs, not less than once a week for 3 consecutive weeks. The Court may compel the appearance of the defendant by the seizure of all or any part of his property, which property may be sold under the order of the Court to pay the demand of the plaintiff, if the defendant does not appear, or otherwise defaults. Any defendant whose property shall have been so seized and who shall have entered a general appearance in the cause may, upon notice to the plaintiff, petition the Court for an order releasing such property or any part thereof from the seizure. The Court shall release such property unless the plaintiff shall satisfy the Court that because of other circumstances there is a reasonable possibility that such release may render it substantially less likely that plaintiff will obtain satisfaction of any judgment secured. If such petition shall not be granted, or if no such petition shall be filed, such property shall remain subject to seizure and may be sold to satisfy any judgment entered in the case. The Court may at any time release such property or any part thereof upon the giving of sufficient security.

7. The closing price of Greyhound stock on the day the sequestration order was issued was $14⅜. New York Times, May 23, 1974, p. 62. Thus, the value of the sequestered stock was approximately $1.2 million.

9. Section 169 provides: "For all purposes of title, action, attachment, garnishment and jurisdiction of all courts held in this State, but not for the purpose of taxation, the situs of the ownership of the capital stock of all corporations existing under the laws of this State, whether organized under this chapter or otherwise, shall be regarded as in this State."

as appellants) responded by entering a special appearance for the purpose of moving to quash service of process and to vacate the sequestration order. They contended that the ex parte sequestration procedure did not accord them due process of law and that the property seized was not capable of attachment in Delaware. In addition, appellants asserted that under the rule of *International Shoe Co. v. Washington*, 326 U.S. 310 (1945), they did not have sufficient contacts with Delaware to sustain the jurisdiction of that State's courts.

The Court of Chancery rejected these arguments in a letter opinion which emphasized the purpose of the Delaware sequestration procedure:

> The primary purpose of "sequestration" as authorized by 10 Del. C. § 366 is not to secure possession of property pending a trial between resident debtors and creditors on the issue of who has the right to retain it. On the contrary, as here employed, "sequestration" is a process used to compel the personal appearance of a nonresident defendant to answer and defend a suit brought against him in a court of equity. It is accomplished by the appointment of a sequestrator by this Court to seize and hold property of the nonresident located in this State subject to further Court order. If the defendant enters a general appearance, the sequestered property is routinely released, unless the plaintiff makes special application to continue its seizure, in which event the plaintiff has the burden of proof and persuasion.

[T]he court held that the statutory Delaware situs of the stock provided a sufficient basis for the exercise of quasi in rem jurisdiction by a Delaware court.

On appeal, the Delaware Supreme Court affirmed the judgment of the Court of Chancery. . . . Appellants' claim that the Delaware courts did not have jurisdiction to adjudicate this action received cursory treatment. The court's analysis of the jurisdictional issue is contained in two paragraphs: "There are significant constitutional questions at issue here but we say at once that we do not deem the rule of *International Shoe* to be one of them. . . . The reason of course, is that jurisdiction under § 366 remains . . . *quasi in rem* founded on the presence of capital stock here, not on prior contact by defendants with this forum. Under 8 Del. C. § 169 the " 'situs of the ownership of the capital stock of all corporations existing under the laws of this State . . . [is] in this State,' and that provides the initial basis for jurisdiction. Delaware may constitutionally establish situs of such shares here, . . . it has done so and the presence thereof provides the foundation for § 366 in this case. . . ."

We reverse.

II

The Delaware courts rejected appellants' jurisdictional challenge by noting that this suit was brought as a quasi in rem proceeding. Since quasi in rem jurisdiction is traditionally based on attachment or seizure of property present in the jurisdiction, not on contacts between the defendant and the State, the courts considered appellants' claimed lack of contacts with Delaware to be unimportant.

This categorical analysis assumes the continued soundness of the conceptual structure founded on the century-old case of *Pennoyer v. Neff*, 95 U.S. 714 (1878).

[U]nder *Pennoyer* state authority to adjudicate was based on the jurisdiction's power over either persons or property. This fundamental concept is embodied in the very vocabulary which we use to describe judgments. If a court's jurisdiction is based on its authority over the defendant's person, the action and judgment are denominated "in personam" and can impose a personal obligation on the defendant in favor of the plaintiff. If jurisdiction is based on the court's power over property within its territory, the action is called "in rem" or "quasi in rem." The effect of a judgment in such a case is limited to the property that supports jurisdiction and does not impose a personal liability on the property owner, since he is not before the court. In *Pennoyer*'s terms, the owner is affected only "indirectly" by an in rem judgment adverse to his interest in the property subject to the court's disposition.

By concluding that "[t]he authority of every tribunal is necessarily restricted by the territorial limits of the State in which it is established," *Pennoyer* sharply limited the availability of in personam jurisdiction over defendants not resident in the forum State. If a nonresident defendant could not be found in a State, he could not be sued there. On the other hand, since the State in which property was located was considered to have exclusive sovereignty over that property, in rem actions could proceed regardless of the owner's location.

The *Pennoyer* rules generally favored nonresident defendants by making them harder to sue. This advantage was reduced, however, by the ability of a resident plaintiff to satisfy a claim against a nonresident defendant by bringing into court any property of the defendant located in the plaintiff's State.

In *International Shoe* the relationship among the defendant, the forum, and the litigation, rather than the mutually exclusive sovereignty of the States on which the rules of *Pennoyer* rest, became the central concern of the inquiry into personal jurisdiction. The immediate effect of this departure from *Pennoyer*'s conceptual apparatus was to increase the ability of the state courts to obtain personal jurisdiction over nonresident defendants.

We think that the time is ripe to consider whether the standard of fairness and substantial justice set forth in *International Shoe* should be held to govern actions in rem as well as in personam.

III

The case for applying to jurisdiction *in rem* the same test of "fair play and substantial justice" as governs assertions of jurisdiction in personam is simple and straightforward. It is premised on recognition that "[t]he phrase, 'judicial jurisdiction over a thing,' is a customary elliptical way of referring to jurisdiction over the interests of persons in a thing." *Restatement (Second) of Conflict of Laws* § 56, This recognition leads to the conclusion that in order to justify an exercise of jurisdiction *in rem*, the basis for jurisdiction must be sufficient to justify exercising "jurisdiction over the interests of persons in a thing."[23] The standard for determining whether an exercise of jurisdiction over the interests of persons is consistent with the Due Process Clause is the minimum-contacts standard elucidated in *International Shoe*.

This argument, of course, does not ignore the fact that the presence of property in a State may bear on the existence of jurisdiction by providing contacts among the forum State, the defendant, and the litigation. For example, when claims to the property itself are the source of the underlying controversy between the plaintiff and the defendant, it would be unusual for the State where the property is located not to have jurisdiction. In such cases, the defendant's claim to property located in the State would normally indicate that he expected to benefit from the State's protection of his interest. The State's strong interests in assuring the marketability of property within its borders and in providing a procedure for peaceful resolution of disputes about the possession of that property would also support jurisdiction, as would the likelihood that important records and witnesses will be found in the State. The presence of property may also favor jurisdiction in cases such as suits for injury suffered on the land of an absentee owner, where the defendant's ownership of the property is conceded but the cause of action is otherwise related to rights and duties growing out of that ownership.[29]

It appears, therefore, that jurisdiction over many types of actions which now are or might be brought *in rem* would not be affected by a holding that any assertion of state-court jurisdiction must satisfy the *International Shoe* standard. For the type of *quasi in rem* action typified by *Harris v. Balk* and the present case, however, accepting the proposed analysis would result in significant change. These are cases where the property which now serves as the basis for state-court jurisdiction is completely unrelated to the plaintiff's cause of action. Thus, although the presence of the defendant's property in a State might suggest the existence of other ties among the defendant, the State, and the litigation, the presence of the property alone would not support the State's jurisdiction. If those other ties did not exist, cases over which the State is now thought to have jurisdiction could not be brought in that forum.

Since acceptance of the *International Shoe* test would most affect this class of cases, we examine the arguments against adopting that standard as they relate to this category of litigation. Before doing so, however, we note that this type of case also presents the clearest illustration of the argument in favor of assessing assertions of jurisdiction by a single standard. For in cases such as *Harris* and this one, the only role played by the property is to provide the basis for bringing the defendant into court. Indeed, the express purpose of the Delaware sequestration procedure is to compel the defendant to enter a personal appearance.[33]

---

23. It is true that the potential liability of a defendant in an *in rem* action is limited by the value of the property, but that limitation does not affect the argument. The fairness of subjecting a defendant to state-court jurisdiction does not depend on the size of the claim being litigated.

29. If such an action were brought under the *in rem* jurisdiction rather than under a long-arm statute, it would be a *quasi in rem* action. . . .

33. This purpose is emphasized by Delaware's refusal to allow any defense on the merits unless the defendant enters a general appearance, thus submitting to full in personam liability.

In such cases, if a direct assertion of personal jurisdiction over the defendant would violate the Constitution, it would seem that an indirect assertion of that jurisdiction should be equally impermissible. . . .

We are left, then, to consider the significance of the long history of jurisdiction based solely on the presence of property in a State. . . . [But] "traditional notions of fair play and substantial justice" can be as readily offended by the perpetuation of ancient forms that are no longer justified as by the adoption of new procedures that are inconsistent with the basic values of our constitutional heritage. The fiction that an assertion of jurisdiction over property is anything but an assertion of jurisdiction over the owner of the property supports an ancient form without substantial modern justification. Its continued acceptance would serve only to allow state-court jurisdiction that is fundamentally unfair to the defendant.

We therefore conclude that all assertions of state-court jurisdiction must be evaluated according to the standards set forth in *International Shoe* and its progeny.[39]

IV

The Delaware courts based their assertion of jurisdiction in this case solely on the statutory presence of appellants' property in Delaware. Yet that property is not the subject matter of this litigation, nor is the underlying cause of action related to the property. Appellants' holdings in Greyhound do not, therefore, provide contacts with Delaware sufficient to support the jurisdiction of that State's courts over appellants. If it exists, that jurisdiction must have some other foundation.

Appellee Heitner did not allege and does not now claim that appellants have ever set foot in Delaware. Nor does he identify any act related to his cause of action as having taken place in Delaware. Nevertheless, he contends that appellants' positions as directors and officers of a corporation chartered in Delaware provide sufficient "contacts, ties, or relations" *International Shoe Co. v. Washington*, 326 U.S. at 319, with that State to give its courts jurisdiction over appellants in this stockholder's derivative action. This argument is based primarily on what Heitner asserts to be the strong interest of Delaware in supervising the management of a Delaware corporation. That interest is said to derive from the role of Delaware law in establishing the corporation and defining the obligations owed to it by its officers and directors. In order to protect this interest, appellee concludes, Delaware's courts must have jurisdiction over corporate fiduciaries such as appellants.

This argument is undercut by the failure of the Delaware Legislature to assert the state interest appellee finds so compelling. Delaware law bases jurisdiction, not on appellants' status as corporate fiduciaries, but rather on the presence of their property in the State. Although the sequestration procedure used here

---

39. It would not be fruitful for us to re-examine the facts of cases decided on the rationales of *Pennoyer* and *Harris* to determine whether jurisdiction might have been sustained under the standard we adopt today. To the extent that prior decisions are inconsistent with this standard, they are overruled.

may be most frequently used in derivative suits against officers and directors, the authorizing statute evinces no specific concern with such actions. Sequestration can be used in any suit against a nonresident, and reaches corporate fiduciaries only if they happen to own interests in a Delaware corporation, or other property in the State. But as Heitner's failure to secure jurisdiction over seven of the defendants named in his complaint demonstrates, there is no necessary relationship between holding a position as a corporate fiduciary and owning stock or other interests in the corporation. If Delaware perceived its interest in securing jurisdiction over corporate fiduciaries to be as great as Heitner suggests, we would expect it to have enacted a statute more clearly designed to protect that interest. . . .

Appellants have simply had nothing to do with the State of Delaware. Moreover, appellants had no reason to expect to be haled before a Delaware court. Delaware, unlike some States, has not enacted a statute that treats acceptance of a directorship as consent to jurisdiction in the State. And "[i]t strains reason . . . to suggest that anyone buying securities in a corporation formed in Delaware 'impliedly consents' to subject himself to Delaware's . . . jurisdiction on any cause of action." Appellants, who were not required to acquire interests in Greyhound in order to hold their positions, did not by acquiring those interests surrender their right to be brought to judgment only in States with which they had had "minimum contacts."

Delaware's assertion of jurisdiction over appellants in this case is inconsistent with that constitutional limitation on state power. The judgment of the Delaware Supreme Court must, therefore, be reversed. It is so ordered.

Justice REHNQUIST took no part in the consideration or decision of this case.

Justice POWELL, concurring:
I agree that the principles of *International Shoe Co. v. Washington* should be extended to govern assertions of in rem as well as in personam jurisdiction in a state court. I also agree that neither the statutory presence of appellants' stock in Delaware nor their positions as directors and officers of a Delaware corporation can provide sufficient contacts to support the Delaware courts' assertion of jurisdiction in this case.

I would explicitly reserve judgment, however, on whether the ownership of some forms of property whose situs is indisputably and permanently located within a State may, without more, provide the contacts necessary to subject a defendant to jurisdiction within the State to the extent of the value of the property. In the case of real property, in particular, preservation of the common-law concept of *quasi in rem* jurisdiction arguably would avoid the uncertainty of the general *International Shoe* standard without significant cost to " 'traditional notions of fair play and substantial justice.' "

Subject to the foregoing reservation, I join the opinion of the Court.

Justice STEVENS, concurring in the judgment:
The Due Process Clause affords protection against "judgments without notice." *International Shoe Co. v. Washington* , 326 U.S. 310, 324 (opinion of Black, J.). . . .

The requirement of fair notice also, I believe, includes fair warning that a particular activity may subject a person to the jurisdiction of a foreign sovereign. If I visit another State, or acquire real estate or open a bank account in it, I knowingly assume some risk that the State will exercise its power over my property or my person while there. My contact with the State, though minimal, gives rise to predictable risks. . . .

One who purchases shares of stock on the open market can hardly be expected to know that he has thereby become subject to suit in a forum remote from his residence and unrelated to the transaction. . . .

How the Court's opinion may be applied in other contexts is not entirely clear to me. I agree with Mr. Justice Powell that it should not be read to invalidate quasi in rem jurisdiction where real estate is involved. . . .

Justice BRENNAN, concurring in part and dissenting in part:

I join Parts I-III of the Court's opinion. I fully agree that the minimum-contacts analysis developed in *International Shoe Co. v. Washington* represents a far more sensible construct for the exercise of state-court jurisdiction than the patchwork of legal and factual fictions that has been generated from the decision in *Pennoyer v. Neff.* It is precisely because the inquiry into minimum contacts is now of such overriding importance, however, that I must respectfully dissent from Part IV of the Court's opinion.

I

The primary teaching of Parts I-III of today's decision is that a State, in seeking to assert jurisdiction over a person located outside its borders, may only do so on the basis of minimum contacts among the parties, the contested transaction, and the forum State. The Delaware Supreme Court could not have made plainer, however, that its sequestration statute, Del. Code Ann., Tit. 10, § 366 (1975), does not operate on this basis, but instead is strictly an embodiment of quasi in rem jurisdiction, a jurisdictional predicate no longer constitutionally viable: "[J]urisdiction under § 366 remains . . . *quasi in rem* founded on the presence of capital stock here, not on prior contact by defendants with this forum." *Greyhound Corp. v. Heitner*, 361 A.2d 225, 229 (1976). This state-court ruling obviously comports with the understanding of the parties, for the issue of the existence of minimum contacts was never pleaded by appellee, made the subject of discovery, or ruled upon by the Delaware courts. These facts notwithstanding, the Court in Part IV reaches the minimum contacts question and finds such contacts lacking as applied to appellants. Succinctly stated, once having properly and persuasively decided that the quasi in rem statute that Delaware admits to having enacted is invalid, the Court then proceeds to find that a minimum-contacts law that Delaware expressly denies having enacted also could not be constitutionally applied in this case.

In my view, a purer example of an advisory opinion is not to be found.

My concern with the inappropriateness of the Court's action is highlighted by two other considerations. First, an inquiry into minimum contacts inevitably is highly dependent on creating a proper factual foundation detailing the contacts between the forum State and the controversy in question. Because neither the plaintiff-appellee nor the state courts viewed such an inquiry as germane in this instance, the Court today is unable to draw upon a proper factual record in reaching its conclusion; moreover, its disposition denies appellee the normal opportunity to seek discovery on the contacts issue. Second, it must be remembered that the Court's ruling is a constitutional one and necessarily will affect the reach of the jurisdictional laws of all 50 States. Ordinarily this would counsel restraint in constitutional pronouncements. Certainly it should have cautioned the Court against reaching out to decide a question that, as here, has yet to emerge from the state courts ripened for review on the federal issue.

II

Nonetheless, because the Court rules on the minimum-contacts question, I feel impelled to express my view. While evidence derived through discovery might satisfy me that minimum contacts are lacking in a given case, I am convinced that as a general rule a state forum has jurisdiction to adjudicate a shareholder derivative action centering on the conduct and policies of the directors and officers of a corporation chartered by that State. Unlike the Court, I therefore would not foreclose Delaware from asserting jurisdiction over appellants were it persuaded to do so on the basis of minimum contacts. . . .

I, therefore, would approach the minimum-contacts analysis differently than does the Court. Crucial to me is the fact that appellants voluntarily associated themselves with the State of Delaware, "invoking the benefits and protections of its laws," by entering into a long-term and fragile relationship with one of its domestic corporations. They thereby elected to assume powers and to undertake responsibilities wholly derived from that State's rules and regulations, and to become eligible for those benefits that Delaware law makes available to its corporations' officials. While it is possible that countervailing issues of judicial efficiency and the like might clearly favor a different forum, they do not appear on the meager record before us and, of course, we are concerned solely with "minimum" contacts, not the "best" contacts. I thus do not believe that it is unfair to insist that appellants make themselves available to suit in a competent forum that Delaware might create for vindication of its important public policies directly pertaining to appellants' fiduciary associations with the State.

REVIEW QUESTIONS

1. What does *Shaffer* hold? How would you state the broadest version of the holding? The narrowest?
2. What property-based assertions of jurisdiction remain viable after *Shaffer*? Does Professor Gloss's vacation home in Practice Exercise 31 provide a basis for exercising jurisdiction over him after this decision? What if Gloss is an absentee owner, who never comes to Massachusetts, and the claim is for an injury suffered by a passerby who falls into a hole negligently left in the sidewalk? What if an adjacent neighbor seeks to legally settle the boundary between her property and Gloss's? Is there adjudicatory power over Gloss on her claim?

3. What are the points of disagreement that Justices Powell and Stevens have with the Court's opinion? How would they treat Professor Gloss's vacation home as an asserted basis for adjudicatory power over him? What role does predictability of outcomes (as compared to the uncertainty of minimum-contacts analysis) play in their reasoning?

4. What is the basis for Justice Brennan's accusation that the Court overstepped its authority by rendering "an advisory opinion" on the minimum-contacts issue?

5. Trace Justice Brennan's argument that, measured against the *International Shoe* standard, the Delaware courts *did have* constitutional power over the defendants? Does Brennan anticipate the importance the "fair play" factors would assume a decade later in *Burger King* and *Asahi*?

6. If Delaware had had an open-ended long-arm statute like California's (e.g., "A court of this state may exercise jurisdiction on any basis not inconsistent with the Constitution of this state or of the United States"), would *Shaffer* have come out differently? Was the Court's problem with Delaware's exercise of jurisdiction prompted by constitutional concerns, or by the *particular statutory basis* asserted? It did not help Heitner's case that the Delaware scheme allowed its courts to hold a nonresident's property hostage unless and until the defendant entered a general appearance. *See* § 366(a), set out in the Court's footnote 4.

7. In response to *Shaffer*, Delaware expanded its long-arm reach when it enacted Del. Code Ann. tit. 10, § 3114:

> Every nonresident of this State who . . . accepts election or appointment as a director, trustee or member of the governing body of a corporation organized under the laws of this State . . . shall, by such acceptance or by such service, be deemed thereby to have consented to the appointment of the registered agent of such corporation (or, if there is none, the Secretary of State) as an agent upon whom service of process may be made in all civil actions or proceedings brought in this State, by or on behalf of, or against such corporation, in which such director, trustee or member is a necessary or proper party, or in any action or proceeding against such director, trustee or member for violation of a duty in such capacity. . . .

The Delaware Supreme Court upheld the statute in *Armstrong v. Pomerance*, 423 A.2d 174 (1980), ruling that the state has a substantial interest in overseeing the conduct of those owing fiduciary duties to shareholders of Delaware corporations. The court reasoned that such interest far outweighs any burden to defendants (who have voluntarily associated themselves with such corporations by accepting directorships) in being required to submit to the jurisdiction of the courts. As a legislator in 1980, would you have drafted § 3114 as an implied consent law?

8. In footnote 36 (not reproduced above), the Court drew a distinction between a state's power to attach property located within its borders to satisfy a valid judgment entered in another state, and jurisdiction to adjudicate the underlying claim:

Once it has been determined by a court of competent jurisdiction that the defendant is a debtor of the plaintiff, there would seem to be no unfairness in allowing an action to realize on that debt in a State where the defendant has property, whether or not that State would have jurisdiction to determine the existence of the debt as an original matter.

QUESTIONS TO PONDER

1. The Federal Rules of Civil Procedure limit the use of attachment jurisdiction to situations where the defendant cannot be reached through other means. *See* Fed. R. Civ. P. 4(n). The Advisory Committee Note to the 1993 amendment explains: "Given the liberal availability of long-arm jurisdiction, the exercise of power *quasi-in-rem* has become almost an anachronism. Circumstances too spare to affiliate the defendant to the forum state sufficiently to support long-arm jurisdiction over the defendant's person are also inadequate to support seizure of the defendant's assets fortuitously found within the state (citing *Shaffer*)." Would Justices Powell and Stevens agree with that statement?

2. In 1999 Congress passed the Anti-Cybersquatting Consumer Protection Act (ACPA), 15 U.S.C. § 1125(d), to address situations in which someone would register a domain name (such as Coke.com) that included a trademark (such as "Coke") held by another person. A domain name is the device allowing a person to use their computer to locate an Internet website. A portion of the ACPA provides that a person claiming that their trademark is being violated as part of a domain name may, so long as the person claimed to have violated the trademark is not subject to personal jurisdiction anywhere in the United States, bring an in rem action directly against the domain name "in the judicial district in which the . . . domain name registry . . . is located." 15 U.S.C. § 1125(d)(2). The registry is the entity that maintains the computer equipment on which domain names are listed, thus enabling the Internet to function. Thus, in simple terms, the ACPA operates on the principle that a domain name is property that is located where the registry is located. For all names ending in .com and .net the location of the registry is in the Eastern District of Virginia.

   Are the ACPA's in rem provisions consistent with the Court's decision in *Shaffer v. Heitner*? Consider the case of a person from Germany, with no contacts to the United States, who registers a .com domain name in Germany. That name is then entered on a computer in Virginia where all .com names are entered. Assuming that line of computer code is property and that the German registrant is not subject to personal jurisdiction anywhere in the United States, is the ACPA constitutional in its attempt to obtain jurisdiction over the absent registrant solely by attaching the domain name?

The Fourth Circuit Court of Appeals has held that the ACPA's in rem provisions are constitutional. In a pair of decisions issued on the same day, two different panels of the court sustained the ACPA on two quite different, and inconsistent, grounds. First, in *Porsche Cars N. Am. Inc. v. Porsche.net*, 302 F.3d 248, 259-260 (4th Cir. 2003), the court held that *Shaffer* did not even apply to the ACPA because the domain name situation involved a true in rem action. *Shaffer*, the court reasoned, dealt only with quasi in rem cases and had no application to true in rem cases. Thus, the court upheld the in rem provisions under the logic of *Pennoyer*.

In the second case, *Harrods Ltd. v. Sixty Internet Domain Names*, 302 F.3d 214, 224 (4th Cir. 2003), a separate panel of the court held that *Shaffer* did require that a minimum-contacts analysis apply to every assertion of personal jurisdiction whether denominated as true in rem or not. However, the court held that one was to judge the minimum contacts not in terms of the absent defendant, but rather in terms of the property at issue. Thus, because the domain name had minimum contacts with the location of the registry (regardless of the situation with the absent citizen of Germany), the ACPA passed muster.

Which of the Fourth Circuit cases is a better reading of *Shaffer*? Are they both wrong? For a thorough and insightful discussion of the ACPA arguing that the in rem provisions are in fact unconstitutional under *Shaffer* and that the Fourth Circuit is incorrect in both *Harrods* and *Porsche*, *see* Michael P. Allen, *In Rem Jurisdiction from* Pennoyer *to* Shaffer *to the Anti-Cybersquatting Consumer Protection Act*, 11 Geo. Mason L. Rev. 245 (2002).

Justice Marshall's opinion for the Court in *Shaffer* holds that "*all* assertions of state-court jurisdiction must be evaluated according to the standards set forth in *International Shoe* and its progeny." As you read the next case, consider the limits of such broad categorical pronouncements.

K. JURISDICTION BASED SOLELY ON PERSONAL SERVICE WITHIN THE FORUM STATE

Burnham v. Superior Court of California
495 U.S. 604 (1990)

Justice SCALIA announced the judgment of the Court and delivered an opinion in which THE CHIEF JUSTICE and Justice KENNEDY join, and in which Justice WHITE joins with respect to Parts I, II-A, II-B, and II-C:

The question presented is whether the Due Process Clause of the Fourteenth Amendment denies California courts jurisdiction over a nonresident, who was personally served with process while temporarily in that State, in a suit unrelated to his activities in the State.

I

Petitioner Dennis Burnham married Francie Burnham in 1976 in West Virginia. In 1977 the couple moved to New Jersey, where their two children were born. In July 1987 the Burnhams decided to separate. They agreed that Mrs. Burnham, who intended to move [and did] to California, would take custody of the children. Mrs. Burnham brought suit for divorce in California state court in early January 1988.

In late January, petitioner visited southern California on business, after which he went north to visit his children in the San Francisco Bay area, where his wife resided. He took the older child to San Francisco for the weekend. Upon returning the child to Mrs. Burnham's home on January 24, 1988, petitioner was served with a California court summons and a copy of Mrs. Burnham's divorce petition. He then returned to New Jersey.

Later that year, petitioner made a special appearance in the California Superior Court, moving to quash the service of process on the ground that the court lacked personal jurisdiction over him because his only contacts with California were a few short visits to the State for the purposes of conducting business and visiting his children. The Superior Court denied the motion, and the California Court of Appeal denied mandamus relief, rejecting petitioner's contention that the Due Process Clause prohibited California courts from asserting jurisdiction over him because he lacked "minimum contacts" with the State. The court held it to be "a valid jurisdictional predicate for in personam jurisdiction" that the "defendant [was] present in the forum state and personally served with process." We granted certiorari.

II

A

To determine whether the assertion of personal jurisdiction is consistent with due process, we have long relied on the principles traditionally followed by American courts in marking out the territorial limits of each State's authority. That criterion was first announced in *Pennoyer v. Neff, supra*, in which we stated that due process "mean[s] a course of legal proceedings according to those rules and principles which have been established in our systems of jurisprudence for the protection and enforcement of private rights," including the "well-established principles of public law respecting the jurisdiction of an independent State over persons and property." In what has become the classic expression of the criterion, we said in *International Shoe Co. v. Washington* that a state court's assertion of personal jurisdiction satisfies the Due Process Clause if it does not violate "'traditional notions of fair play and substantial justice.'" Since *International Shoe*, we have only been called upon to decide whether these "traditional notions" permit States to exercise jurisdiction over absent defendants in a manner that deviates from the rules of jurisdiction applied in the 19th century. We have held such deviations permissible, but only with respect to suits arising out of the absent defendant's contacts with the State.

The question we must decide today is whether due process requires a similar connection between the litigation and the defendant's contacts with the State in cases where the defendant is physically present in the State at the time process is served upon him.

B

Among the most firmly established principles of personal jurisdiction in American tradition is that the courts of a State have jurisdiction over nonresidents who are physically present in the State.

Decisions in the courts of many States in the 19th and early 20th centuries held that personal service upon a physically present defendant sufficed to confer jurisdiction, without regard to whether the defendant was only briefly in the State or whether the cause of action was related to his activities there. . . . Most States, moreover, had statutes or common-law rules that exempted from service of process individuals who were brought into the forum by force or fraud, or who were there as a party or witness in unrelated judicial proceedings. These exceptions obviously rested upon the premise that service of process conferred jurisdiction. Particularly striking is the fact that, as far as we have been able to determine, not one American case from the period (or, for that matter, not one American case until 1978) held, or even suggested, that in-state personal service on an individual was insufficient to confer personal jurisdiction.

This American jurisdictional practice is, moreover, not merely old; it is continuing. We do not know of a single state or federal statute, or a single judicial decision resting upon state law, that has abandoned in-state service as a basis of jurisdiction. Many recent cases reaffirm it.

C

Despite this formidable body of precedent, petitioner contends, in reliance on our decisions applying the *International Shoe* standard, that in the absence of "continuous and systematic" contacts with the forum, a nonresident defendant can be subjected to judgment only as to matters that arise out of or relate to his contacts with the forum. This argument rests on a thorough misunderstanding of our cases.

As *International Shoe* suggests, the defendant's litigation-related "minimum contacts" may take the place of physical presence as the basis for jurisdiction. . . . Nothing in *International Shoe* or the cases that have followed it, however, offers support for the very different proposition petitioner seeks to establish today: that a defendant's presence in the forum is not only unnecessary to validate novel, nontraditional assertions of jurisdiction, but is itself no longer sufficient to establish jurisdiction. That proposition is unfaithful to both elementary logic and the foundations of our due process jurisprudence. The distinction between what is needed to support novel procedures and what is needed to sustain traditional ones is fundamental.

The short of the matter is that jurisdiction based on physical presence alone constitutes due process because it is one of the continuing traditions of our legal system that define the due process standard of "traditional notions of fair play and substantial justice." That standard was developed by analogy to "physical presence," and it would be perverse to say it could now be turned against that touchstone of jurisdiction.

D

Petitioner's strongest argument, though we ultimately reject it, relies upon our decision in *Shaffer v. Heitner*. In that case, a Delaware court hearing a shareholder's derivative suit against a corporation's directors secured jurisdiction quasi in rem by sequestering the out-of-state defendants' stock in the company, the situs of which was Delaware under Delaware law. Reasoning that Delaware's sequestration procedure was simply a mechanism to compel the absent defendants to appear in a suit to determine their personal rights and obligations, we concluded that the normal rules we had developed under *International Shoe* for jurisdiction over suits against absent defendants should apply—*viz.*, Delaware could not hear the suit because the defendants' sole contact with the State (ownership of property there) was unrelated to the lawsuit.

It goes too far to say, as petitioner contends, that *Shaffer* compels the conclusion that a State lacks jurisdiction over an individual unless the litigation arises out of his activities in the State. *Shaffer*, like *International Shoe*, involved jurisdiction over an absent defendant, and it stands for nothing more than the proposition that when the "minimum contact" that is a substitute for physical presence consists of property ownership it must, like other minimum contacts, be related to the litigation. Petitioner wrenches out of its context our statement in *Shaffer* that "all assertions of state-court jurisdiction must be evaluated according to the standards set forth in *International Shoe* and its progeny." . . .

Shaffer was saying, in other words, not that all bases for the assertion of *in personam* jurisdiction (including, presumably, in-state service) must be treated alike and subjected to the "minimum contacts" analysis of *International Shoe*, but rather that *quasi in rem* jurisdiction, that fictional "ancient form," and *in personam* jurisdiction, are really one and the same and must be treated alike—leading to the conclusion that *quasi in rem* jurisdiction, i.e., that form of in personam jurisdiction based upon a "property ownership" contact and by definition unaccompanied by personal, instate service, must satisfy the litigation-relatedness requirement of *International Shoe*. The logic of *Shaffer's* holding—which places all suits against absent nonresidents on the same constitutional footing, regardless of whether a separate Latin label is attached to one particular basis of contact—does not compel the conclusion that physically present defendants must be treated identically to absent ones. As we have demonstrated at length, our tradition has treated the two classes of defendants quite differently, and it is unreasonable to read *Shaffer* as casually obliterating that distinction. *International Shoe* confined its "minimum contacts" requirement to situations in which the defendant "be not present within the territory of the forum," and nothing in *Shaffer* expands that requirement beyond that.

It is fair to say, however, that while our holding today does not contradict *Shaffer*, our basic approach to the due process question is different. We have conducted no independent inquiry into the desirability or fairness of the prevailing in-state service rule, leaving that judgment to the legislatures that are free to amend it; for our purposes, its validation is its pedigree, as the phrase "traditional notions of fair play and substantial justice" makes clear. *Shaffer* did conduct such an independent inquiry, asserting that "'traditional notions of fair play and substantial justice' can be as readily offended by the perpetuation of ancient forms that are no longer justified as by the adoption of new procedures that are inconsistent with the basic values of our constitutional heritage." . . . But a doctrine of personal jurisdiction that dates back to the adoption of the Fourteenth Amendment and is still generally observed unquestionably meets that standard.

III

A few words in response to Justice Brennan's opinion concurring in the judgment: It insists that we apply "contemporary notions of due process" to determine the constitutionality of California's assertion of jurisdiction. But our analysis today comports with that prescription, at least if we give it the only sense allowed by our precedents. The "contemporary notions of due process" applicable to personal jurisdiction are the enduring "traditional notions of fair play and substantial justice" established as the test by *International Shoe*. By its very language, that test is satisfied if a state court adheres to jurisdictional rules that are generally applied and have always been applied in the United States.

But the concurrence's proposed standard of "contemporary notions of due process" requires more: It measures state-court jurisdiction not only against traditional doctrines in this country, including current state-court practice, but also against each Justice's subjective assessment of what is fair and just.

The subjectivity, and hence inadequacy, of this approach becomes apparent when the concurrence tries to explain why the assertion of jurisdiction in the present case meets its standard of continuing-American-tradition-plus-innate-fairness. Justice Brennan lists the "benefits" Mr. Burnham derived from the State of California—the fact that, during the few days he was there, "[h]is health and safety [were] guaranteed by the State's police, fire, and emergency medical services; he [was] free to travel on the State's roads and waterways; he likely enjoy[ed] the fruits of the State's economy." Three days' worth of these benefits strike us as powerfully inadequate to establish, as an abstract matter, that it is "fair" for California to decree the ownership of all Mr. Burnham's worldly goods acquired during the 10 years of his marriage, and the custody over his children. . . .

[The] continuing tradition, which anyone entering California should have known about, renders it "fair" for Mr. Burnham, who voluntarily entered California, to be sued there for divorce—at least "fair" in the limited sense that he has no one but himself to blame. Justice Brennan's long journey is a circular one, leaving him, at the end of the day, in complete reliance upon the very factor he sought to avoid: The existence of a continuing tradition is not enough, fairness also must be considered; fairness exists here because there is a continuing tradition.

Justice Brennan says that as a rule the exercise of personal jurisdiction over a defendant based on his voluntary presence in the forum will satisfy the requirements of due process." The use of the word "rule" conveys the reassuring feeling that he is establishing a principle of law one can rely upon—but of course he is not. Since Justice Brennan's only criterion of constitutionality is "fairness," the phrase "as a rule" represents nothing more than his estimation that, usually, all the elements of "fairness" he discusses in the present case will exist. But what if they do not? Suppose, for example, that a defendant in Mr. Burnham's situation enjoys not three days worth of California's "benefits," but 15 minutes' worth. Or suppose we remove one of those "benefits"—"enjoy[ment of] the fruits of the State's economy"—by positing that Mr. Burnham had not come to California on business, but only to visit his children. Or suppose that Mr. Burnham were demonstrably so impecunious as to be unable to take advantage of the modern means of transportation and communication that Justice Brennan finds so relevant. Or suppose, finally, that the California courts lacked the "variety of procedural devices" that Justice Brennan says can reduce the burden upon out-of-state litigants. One may also make additional suppositions, relating not to the absence of the factors that Justice Brennan discusses, but to the presence of additional factors bearing upon the ultimate criterion of "fairness." What if, for example, Mr. Burnham were visiting a sick child? Or a dying child? *Cf. Kulko v. Superior Court of California, City and County of San Francisco*, 436 U.S. 84, 93 (1978) (finding the exercise of long-arm jurisdiction over an absent parent unreasonable because it would "discourage parents from entering into reasonable visitation agreements"). Since, so far as one can tell, Justice Brennan's approval of applying the in-state service rule in the present case rests on the presence of all the factors he lists, and on the absence of any others, every different case will present a different litigable issue. Thus, despite the fact that he manages to work the word "rule" into his formulation, Justice Brennan's approach does not establish a rule of law at all, but only a "totality of the circumstances" test, guaranteeing what traditional territorial rules of jurisdiction were designed precisely to avoid: uncertainty and litigation over the preliminary issue of the forum's competence. It may be that those evils, necessarily accompanying a freestanding "reasonableness" inquiry, must be accepted at the margins, when we evaluate nontraditional forms of jurisdiction newly adopted by the States, *see, e.g., Asahi Metal Industry Co. v. Superior Court of California, Solano County*, 480 U.S. 102, 115 (1987). But that is no reason for injecting them into the core of our American practice, exposing to such a "reasonableness" inquiry the ground of jurisdiction that has hitherto been considered the very baseline of reasonableness, physical presence.

Nothing we say today prevents individual States from limiting or entirely abandoning the in-state-service basis of jurisdiction. And nothing prevents an overwhelming majority of them from doing so, with the consequence that the "traditional notions of fairness" that this Court applies may change. But the States have overwhelmingly declined to adopt such limitation or abandonment, evidently not considering it to be progress. The question is whether, armed with no authority other than individual Justices' perceptions of fairness that conflict with both past and current practice, this Court can compel the States to make such a change on the ground that "due process" requires it. We hold that it cannot.

Because the Due Process Clause does not prohibit the California courts from exercising jurisdiction over petitioner based on the fact of in-state service of process, the judgment is Affirmed.

Justice WHITE, concurring in part and concurring in the judgment:

I join Parts I, II-A, II-B, and II-C of Justice Scalia's opinion and concur in the judgment of affirmance. The rule allowing jurisdiction to be obtained over a nonresident by personal service in the forum State, without more, has been and is so widely accepted throughout this country that I could not possibly strike it down, either on its face or as applied in this case, on the ground that it denies due process of law guaranteed by the Fourteenth Amendment. Although the Court has the authority under the Amendment to examine even traditionally accepted procedures and declare them invalid, *e.g., Shaffer v. Heitner*, there has been no showing here or elsewhere that as a general proposition the rule is so arbitrary and lacking in common sense in so many instances that it should be held violative of due process in every case. Furthermore, until such a showing is made, which would be difficult indeed, claims in individual cases that the rule would operate unfairly as applied to the particular nonresident involved need not be entertained. At least this would be the case where presence in the forum State is intentional, which would almost always be the fact. Otherwise, there would be endless, fact-specific litigation in the trial and appellate courts, including this one. Here, personal service in California, without more, is enough, and I agree that the judgment should be affirmed.

Justice BRENNAN, with whom Justice MARSHALL, Justice BLACKMUN, and Justice O'CONNOR join, concurring in the judgment:

I agree with Justice Scalia that the Due Process Clause of the Fourteenth Amendment generally permits a state court to exercise jurisdiction over a defendant if he is served with process while voluntarily present in the forum

State.[1] I do not perceive the need, however, to decide that a jurisdictional rule that " 'has been immemorially the actual law of the land,' " automatically comports with due process simply by virtue of its "pedigree." Although I agree that history is an important factor in establishing whether a jurisdictional rule satisfies due process requirements, I cannot agree that it is the only factor such that all traditional rules of jurisdiction are, ipso facto, forever constitutional. Unlike Justice Scalia, I would undertake an "independent inquiry into the fairness of the prevailing in-state service rule." I therefore concur only in the judgment.

I

I believe that the approach adopted by Justice Scalia's opinion today—reliance solely on historical pedigree—is foreclosed by our decisions in *International Shoe Co. v. Washington*, and *Shaffer v. Heitner*. In *International Shoe*, we held that a state court's assertion of personal jurisdiction does not violate the Due Process Clause if it is consistent with " 'traditional notions of fair play and substantial justice.' "[2] In *Shaffer*, we stated that "all assertions of state-court jurisdiction must be evaluated according to the standards set forth in *International Shoe* and its progeny." 433 U.S. at 212 (emphasis added).

While our holding in *Shaffer* may have been limited to quasi in rem jurisdiction, our mode of analysis was not. Indeed, that we were willing in *Shaffer* to examine anew the appropriateness of the quasi in rem rule—until that time dutifully accepted by American courts for at least a century—demonstrates that we did not believe that the "pedigree" of a jurisdictional practice was dispositive in deciding whether it was consistent with due process. Notwithstanding the nimble gymnastics of Justice Scalia's opinion today, it is not faithful to our decision in *Shaffer*.

II

Tradition, though alone not dispositive, is of course relevant to the question whether the rule of transient jurisdiction is consistent with due process.[7] . . .

---

1. I use the term "transient jurisdiction" to refer to jurisdiction premised solely on the fact that a person is served with process while physically present in the forum State.

2. Our reference in *International Shoe* to " 'traditional notions of fair play and substantial justice,' " meant simply that those concepts are indeed traditional ones, not that, as Justice Scalia's opinion suggests, their specific content was to be determined by tradition alone. We recognized that contemporary societal norms must play a role in our analysis.

7. I do not propose that the "contemporary notions of due process" to be applied are no more than "each Justice's subjective assessment of what is fair and just." Rather, the inquiry is guided by our decisions beginning with *International Shoe Co. v. Washington*, and the specific factors that we have developed to ascertain whether a jurisdictional rule comports with "traditional notions of fair play and substantial justice." *See, e.g., Asahi Metal Industry Co. v. Superior Court of California, Solano County* (noting "several factors," including "the burden on the defendant, the interests of the forum State, and the plaintiff's interest in obtaining relief"). This analysis may not be "mechanical or quantitative," *International Shoe*, but neither is it "freestanding" or dependent on personal whim. Our experience with this approach demonstrates that it is well within our competence to employ.

Rather, I find the historical background relevant because, however murky the jurisprudential origins of transient jurisdiction, the fact that American courts have announced the rule for perhaps a century (first in dicta, more recently in holdings) provides a defendant voluntarily present in a particular State today "clear notice that [he] is subject to suit" in the forum. . . . The transient rule is consistent with reasonable expectations and is entitled to a strong presumption that it comports with due process. "If I visit another State, . . . I knowingly assume some risk that the State will exercise its power over my property or my person while there. My contact with the State, though minimal, gives rise to predictable risks."

By visiting the forum State, a transient defendant actually "avail[s]" himself of significant benefits provided by the State. His health and safety are guaranteed by the State's police, fire, and emergency medical services; he is free to travel on the State's roads and waterways; he likely enjoys the fruits of the State's economy as well.

The potential burdens on a transient defendant are slight. "[M]odern transportation and communications have made it much less burdensome for a party sued to defend himself" in a State outside his place of residence. That the defendant has already journeyed at least once before to the forum—as evidenced by the fact that he was served with process there—is an indication that suit in the forum likely would not be prohibitively inconvenient. Finally, any burdens that do arise can be ameliorated by a variety of procedural devices.[13] For these reasons, as a rule the exercise of personal jurisdiction over a defendant based on his voluntary presence in the forum will satisfy the requirements of due process.[14]

In this case, it is undisputed that petitioner was served with process while voluntarily and knowingly in the State of California. I therefore concur in the judgment.

---

13. For example, in the federal system, a transient defendant can avoid protracted litigation of a spurious suit through a motion to dismiss for failure to state a claim or through a motion for summary judgment. Fed. Rules Civ. Proc. 12(b)(6) and 56. He can use relatively inexpensive methods of discovery, such as oral deposition by telephone (Rule 30(b)(7)), deposition upon written questions (Rule 31), interrogatories (Rule 33), and requests for admission (Rule 36), while enjoying protection from harassment (Rule 26(c)), and possibly obtaining costs and attorney's fees for some of the work involved (Rules 37(a)(4), (b)-(d)). Moreover, a change of venue may be possible. 28 U.S.C. § 1404. In state court, many of the same procedural protections are available, as is the doctrine of *forum non conveniens*, under which the suit may be dismissed.

14. . . . Justice Scalia suggests that when and if a jurisdictional rule becomes substantively unfair or even "unconscionable," this Court is powerless to alter it. Instead, he is willing to rely on individual States to limit or abandon bases of jurisdiction that have become obsolete. This reliance is misplaced, for States have little incentive to limit rules such as transient jurisdiction that make it easier for their own citizens to sue out-of-state defendants. That States are more likely to expand their jurisdiction is illustrated by the adoption by many States of long-arm statutes extending the reach of personal jurisdiction to the limits established by the Federal Constitution. Out-of-staters do not vote in state elections or have a voice in state government. We should not assume, therefore, that States will be motivated by "notions of fairness" to curb jurisdictional rules like the one at issue here. The reasoning of Justice Scalia's opinion today is strikingly oblivious to the raison d'être of various constitutional doctrines designed to protect out-of-staters, such as the Art. IV Privileges and Immunities Clause and the Commerce Clause.

Justice STEVENS, concurring in the judgment:

As I explained in my separate writing, I did not join the Court's opinion in *Shaffer v. Heitner*, because I was concerned by its unnecessarily broad reach. The same concern prevents me from joining either Justice Scalia's or Justice Brennan's opinion in this case. For me, it is sufficient to note that the historical evidence and consensus identified by Justice Scalia, the considerations of fairness identified by Justice Brennan, and the common sense displayed by Justice White, all combine to demonstrate that this is, indeed, a very easy case. Accordingly, I agree that the judgment should be affirmed.

REVIEW QUESTIONS

1. Keep in mind that the controversy in *Burnham* concerns whether personal service within the forum is *itself* sufficient to establish jurisdiction over a nonresident. In such situations, service of process serves the dual purpose of establishing adjudicatory power *and* providing notice of the litigation, just as in the good old days of *Pennoyer*.

2. As in *Asahi*, the Justices in *Burnham* agree on the end result, but not on the path leading to it. What does *Burnham* actually hold? After *Burnham*, would service on Professor Gloss in Massachusetts in our Practice Exercise 31 establish adjudicatory power over him, even absent any other connection to the forum? Or would we need to know more about his relationship to the state?

3. Contrast the very different readings of the same short phrase: "traditional notions of fair play and substantial justice." For Scalia, the operative word is *traditional*. For Brennan, the emphasis is on *fair play and substantial justice*.

4. Note Justice White's condemnation of the ad hoc approach to in-state service that Brennan advocates in his concurrence because it would require "endless, fact-specific litigation." Can you sympathize with White's frustration regarding the elaborate minimum-contacts/fundamental fairness calculus?

5. Does Brennan make a persuasive case that Mr. Burnham had sufficient minimum contacts by virtue of his three days in the Golden State?

6. In the legendary case of *Grace v. MacArthur*, 170 F. Supp. 442 (E.D. Ark. 1959), a citizen of Tennessee contested the exercise of jurisdiction over him in Arkansas. A U.S. Marshal had personally served defendant while he was a passenger on a nonstop flight from Memphis to Dallas, when "said airplane was in the Eastern District of Arkansas and directly above Pine Bluff, Arkansas, in said District." Without addressing the *International Shoe* issue, the court upheld jurisdiction based solely on service at 35,000 feet altitude. Do you see why some have dubbed this "tag jurisdiction"? Same result after *Burnham*?

7. Does in-state service work on corporate defendants? *Wenche Siemer v. Learjet Acquisition Corp.*, 966 F.2d 179 (5th Cir. 1992), held that service

in Texas on the designated corporate agent of Learjet did not satisfy the requirements of due process so as to permit suit in Texas. The air crash out of which the lawsuit arose occurred in Egypt on a flight from Greece to Saudi Arabia. Decedents and the plaintiff-survivors were all residents of Greece or other European countries. The plane had been based in Greece and operated by a Greek company. It was not designed, manufactured, or serviced in Texas; nor had it ever been owned by a Texas resident. For more on this topic, *see* 4A Charles A. Wright, Arthur R. Miller, Mary Kay Kane, and R. Marcus, *Federal Practice and Procedure* § 1069.5 (4th ed. 2013).

8. What if a defendant is served after being lured or tricked into visiting the state, or while there to testify as a witness or appear as a party in another matter? A generally recognized immunity protects nonresidents in such situations. *See* Geoffrey C. Hazard, Jr., John Leubsdorf, and Debra Lyn Bassett, *Civil Procedure* §§ 3.17, 3.18, at 146-147, 149 (6th ed. 2011); 4A Wright & Miller, *Federal Practice and Procedure* § 1076 (4th ed. 2013).

9. The Massachusetts Supreme Judicial Court has recently followed *Burnham* and upheld in-state service as a proper basis for jurisdiction in the Commonwealth. *Roch v. Mollica*, 113 N.E.3d 820 (2019) (nonresident defendants served with process in Worcester on a claim arising from plaintiff's injury in Florida).

QUESTIONS TO PONDER

1. Justice Marshall's opinion in *Shaffer*, which invalidated quasi in rem jurisdiction despite its "long history," observed that due process "can be as readily offended by the perpetuation of ancient forms that are no longer justified as by the adoption of new procedures." Contrast Justice Scalia's virtual equation of tradition with due process in upholding transient jurisdiction in *Burnham*. What arguments favor each position? How should one weigh predictability and certainty against flexibility and discretion regarding legal standards?

2. *A Domestic Forum for International Human Rights Cases*. Transient jurisdiction has played a critical role in civil actions against high-ranking foreign nationals accused in the U.S. of violations of international law. *Xuncax v. Gramajo*, 886 F. Supp. 162 (D. Mass. 1995), for example, was brought by nine expatriate citizens of Guatemala against its former defense minister seeking damages under the Torture Victim Protection Act for acts committed against them in Guatemala. Gramajo was served with process while attending his commencement at Harvard's Kennedy School of Government in Cambridge, thus establishing adjudicatory power over him. A default judgment for $47 million was entered after he returned to Guatemala.

Bosnian leader Radovan Karadzic was similarly held subject to personal jurisdiction in an action brought by victims of alleged atrocities in the Balkans, based on service of process in a Manhattan hotel. *Kadic v. Karadzic*, 70 F.3d 232 (2d Cir. 1995). When Karadzic was approached by process servers in the hotel lobby, his security guards knocked the papers to the floor. The court nonetheless ruled that the service was effective, and rejected Karadzic's argument that he was immune from service because he was in New York on official United Nations business.

An earlier influential decision by the Second Circuit Court of Appeals had established that the federal courts have jurisdiction in such cases whenever the alleged torturer is found and served within the United States. The defendant in *Filartiga v. Pena-Irala*, 630 F.2d 876 (2d Cir. 1980), was served while being detained at the Brooklyn Navy Yard pending deportation back to Paraguay, where as Inspector General of the Police he allegedly had plaintiff's son kidnapped and tortured to death in retaliation for his father's political activities.

Subject matter jurisdiction (see Chapter 8) in these international human rights cases is based upon the Alien Tort Statute (ATS), which was part of the first Judiciary Act of 1789, and is now codified at 28 U.S.C. § 1350. It provides federal district courts with jurisdiction over civil actions brought by aliens alleging torts committed in violation of the "law of nations or a treaty of the United States." In 2004, the U.S. Supreme Court gave the ATS a narrow reading, granting the federal courts subject matter jurisdiction only over cases asserting violations of norms of customary international law of the type recognized in 1789. *Sosa v. Alvarez-Machain*, 542 U.S. 692 (2004). Subsequent cases have excluded most ATS claims occurring abroad, *Kiobel v. Royal Dutch Petroleum Co.*, 569 U.S. 108 (2013), as well as claims against corporate defendants. *Jesner v. Arab Bank, PLC*, 138 S. Ct. 1386 (2018).

L. GENERAL JURISDICTION

It has long been recognized that a state has general jurisdiction over its natural and corporate citizens—they are subject to suit on *any claim*, whether arising from events that occurred in the state or not. A state may enter a personal judgment against a domiciliary even if she is absent from the state and cannot be personally served with process there. General jurisdiction exists over a corporation that is incorporated in the forum state, or whose headquarters or principal place of business is located there. Thus there will always be at least one forum in which a defendant may be sued.

Chief Justice Stone described another form of general jurisdiction as well in *International Shoe*: When the forum activities of a corporate defendant are sufficiently continuous, systematic, and substantial, it may be sued there even on claims unrelated to those activities, as in *Perkins v. Benguet Consolidated Mining Co.*, 342 U.S. 437 (1957) (see Part F, above). But the Supreme Court has recently sharply curtailed this form of adjudicatory power.

Goodyear Dunlop Tires Operations, S.A., et al. v. Brown et ux., Co-Administrators of the Estate of Brown, et al.
564 U.S. 915 (2011)

Justice GINSBURG delivered the opinion of the Court.

This case concerns the jurisdiction of state courts over corporations organized and operating abroad. We address, in particular, this question: Are foreign subsidiaries of a United States parent corporation amenable to suit in state court on claims unrelated to any activity of the subsidiaries in the forum State?

A bus accident outside Paris that took the lives of two 13-year-old boys from North Carolina gave rise to the litigation we here consider. Attributing the accident to a defective tire manufactured in Turkey at the plant of a foreign subsidiary of The Goodyear Tire and Rubber Company (Goodyear USA), the boys' parents commenced an action for damages in a North Carolina state court; they named as defendants Goodyear USA, an Ohio corporation, and three of its subsidiaries, organized and operating, respectively, in Turkey, France, and Luxembourg. Goodyear USA, which had plants in North Carolina and regularly engaged in commercial activity there, did not contest the North Carolina court's jurisdiction over it; Goodyear USA's foreign subsidiaries, however, maintained that North Carolina lacked adjudicatory authority over them.

A state court's assertion of jurisdiction exposes defendants to the State's coercive power, and is therefore subject to review for compatibility with the Fourteenth Amendment's Due Process Clause. Opinions in the wake of the path-marking *International Shoe* decision have differentiated between general or all-purpose jurisdiction, and specific or case-linked jurisdiction. A court may assert general jurisdiction over foreign (sister-state or foreign-country) corporations to hear any and all claims against them when their affiliations with the State are so "continuous and systematic" as to render them essentially at home in the forum State. Specific jurisdiction, on the other hand, depends on an "affiliatio[n] between the forum and the underlying controversy," principally, activity or an occurrence that takes place in the forum State and is therefore subject to the State's regulation. In contrast to general, all-purpose jurisdiction, specific jurisdiction is confined to adjudication of "issues deriving from, or connected with, the very controversy that establishes jurisdiction."

Because the episode-in-suit, the bus accident, occurred in France, and the tire alleged to have caused the accident was manufactured and sold abroad, North Carolina courts lacked specific jurisdiction to adjudicate the controversy. Were the foreign subsidiaries nonetheless amenable to general jurisdiction in

North Carolina courts? Confusing or blending general and specific jurisdictional inquiries, the North Carolina courts answered yes. Some of the tires made abroad by Goodyear's foreign subsidiaries, the North Carolina Court of Appeals stressed, had reached North Carolina through "the stream of commerce"; that connection, the Court of Appeals believed, gave North Carolina courts the handle needed for the exercise of general jurisdiction over the foreign corporations.

A connection so limited between the forum and the foreign corporation, we hold, is an inadequate basis for the exercise of general jurisdiction. Such a connection does not establish the "continuous and systematic" affiliation necessary to empower North Carolina courts to entertain claims unrelated to the foreign corporation's contacts with the State.

I

On April 18, 2004, a bus destined for Charles de Gaulle Airport overturned on a road outside Paris, France. Passengers on the bus were young soccer players from North Carolina beginning their journey home. Two 13-year-olds, Julian Brown and Matthew Helms, sustained fatal injuries. The boys' parents, respondents in this Court, filed a suit for wrongful-death damages in the Superior Court of Onslow County, North Carolina, in their capacity as administrators of the boys' estates. Attributing the accident to a tire that failed when its plies separated, the parents alleged negligence in the "design, construction, testing, and inspection" of the tire.

Goodyear Luxembourg Tires, SA (Goodyear Luxembourg), Goodyear Lastikleri T. A. S. (Goodyear Turkey), and Goodyear Dunlop Tires France, SA (Goodyear France), petitioners here, were named as defendants. Incorporated in Luxembourg, Turkey, and France, respectively, petitioners are indirect subsidiaries of Goodyear USA, an Ohio corporation also named as a defendant in the suit. Petitioners manufacture tires primarily for sale in European and Asian markets. Their tires differ in size and construction from tires ordinarily sold in the United States. They are designed to carry significantly heavier loads, and to serve under road conditions and speed limits in the manufacturers' primary markets.

In contrast to the parent company, Goodyear USA, which does not contest the North Carolina courts' personal jurisdiction over it, petitioners are not registered to do business in North Carolina. They have no place of business, employees, or bank accounts in North Carolina. They do not design, manufacture, or advertise their products in North Carolina. And they do not solicit business in North Carolina or themselves sell or ship tires to North Carolina customers. Even so, a small percentage of petitioners' tires (tens of thousands out of tens of millions manufactured between 2004 and 2007) were distributed within North Carolina by other Goodyear USA affiliates. These tires were typically custom ordered to equip specialized vehicles such as cement mixers, waste haulers, and boat and horse trailers. Petitioners state, and respondents do not here deny, that the type of tire involved in the accident, a Goodyear Regional RHS tire manufactured by Goodyear Turkey, was never distributed in North Carolina.

Petitioners moved to dismiss the claims against them for want of personal jurisdiction. The trial court denied the motion, and the North Carolina Court of Appeals affirmed. Acknowledging that the claims neither "related to, nor . . . ar[o]se from, [petitioners'] contacts with North Carolina," the Court of Appeals confined its analysis to "general rather than specific jurisdiction," which the court recognized required a "higher threshold" showing: A defendant must have "continuous and systematic contacts" with the forum. That threshold was crossed, the court determined, when petitioners placed their tires "in the stream of interstate commerce without any limitation on the extent to which those tires could be sold in North Carolina."

Nothing in the record, the court observed, indicated that petitioners "took any affirmative action to cause tires which they had manufactured to be shipped into North Carolina." The court found, however, that tires made by petitioners reached North Carolina as a consequence of a "highly-organized distribution process" involving other Goodyear USA subsidiaries. Petitioners, the court noted, made "no attempt to keep these tires from reaching the North Carolina market." Indeed, the very tire involved in the accident, the court observed, conformed to tire standards established by the U.S. Department of Transportation and bore markings required for sale in the United States. As further support, the court invoked North Carolina's "interest in providing a forum in which its citizens are able to seek redress for [their] injuries," and noted the hardship North Carolina plaintiffs would experience "[were they] required to litigate their claims in France," a country to which they have no ties. The North Carolina Supreme Court denied discretionary review.

We granted certiorari to decide whether the general jurisdiction the North Carolina courts asserted over petitioners is consistent with the Due Process Clause of the Fourteenth Amendment.

II

A

International Shoe distinguished from cases that fit within the "specific jurisdiction" categories, "instances in which the continuous corporate operations within a state [are] so substantial and of such a nature as to justify suit against it on causes of action arising from dealings entirely distinct from those activities." Adjudicatory authority so grounded is today called "general jurisdiction." For an individual, the paradigm forum for the exercise of general jurisdiction is the individual's domicile; for a corporation, it is an equivalent place, one in which the corporation is fairly regarded as at home (domicile, place of incorporation, and principal place of business are paradigm bases for the exercise of general jurisdiction).

Since *International Shoe*, this Court's decisions have elaborated primarily on circumstances that warrant the exercise of specific jurisdiction, particularly in cases involving "single or occasional acts" occurring or having their impact within the forum State. . . . In only two decisions postdating *International Shoe* has this Court considered whether an out-of-state corporate defendant's in-state contacts were sufficiently "continuous and systematic" to justify the exercise of general jurisdiction over claims unrelated to those contacts: *Perkins v. Benguet Consol. Mining Co.*, 342 U.S. 437 (1952) (general jurisdiction appropriately exercised over Philippine corporation sued in Ohio, where the company's affairs were overseen during World War II); and *Helicopteros*, 466 U.S. 408 (helicopter owned by Colombian corporation crashed in Peru; survivors of U.S. citizens who died in the crash, the Court held, could not maintain wrongful-death actions against the Colombian corporation in Texas, for the corporation's helicopter purchases and purchase-linked activity in Texas were insufficient to subject it to Texas court's general jurisdiction).

B

To justify the exercise of general jurisdiction over petitioners, the North Carolina courts relied on the petitioners' placement of their tires in the "stream of commerce." The stream-of-commerce metaphor has been invoked frequently in lower court decisions permitting "jurisdiction in products liability cases in which the product has traveled through an extensive chain of distribution before reaching the ultimate consumer." Typically, in such cases, a nonresident defendant, acting outside the forum, places in the stream of commerce a product that ultimately causes harm inside the forum.

The North Carolina court's stream-of-commerce analysis elided the essential difference between case-specific and all-purpose (general) jurisdiction. Flow of a manufacturer's products into the forum, we have explained, may bolster an affiliation germane to specific jurisdiction. See, e.g., *World-Wide Volkswagen* (where "the sale of a product . . . is not simply an isolated occurrence, but arises from the efforts of the manufacturer or distributor to serve . . . the market for its product in [several] States, it is not unreasonable to subject it to suit in one of those States if its allegedly defective merchandise *has there been the source of injury to its owner or to others*" (emphasis added)). But ties serving to bolster the exercise of specific jurisdiction do not warrant a determination that, based on those ties, the forum has general jurisdiction over a defendant.

Our 1952 decision in *Perkins v. Benguet Consol. Mining Co.* remains "[t]he textbook case of general jurisdiction appropriately exercised over a foreign corporation that has not consented to suit in the forum." Sued in Ohio, the defendant in *Perkins* was a Philippine mining corporation that had ceased activities in the Philippines during World War II. To the extent that the company was conducting any business during and immediately after the Japanese occupation of the Philippines, it was doing so in Ohio: the corporation's president maintained his office there, kept the company files in that office, and supervised from the Ohio office "the necessarily limited wartime activities of the company." Although the claim-in-suit did not arise in Ohio, this Court ruled that it would not violate due process for Ohio to adjudicate the controversy.

We next addressed the exercise of general jurisdiction over an out-of-state corporation over three decades later, in *Helicopteros*. In that case, survivors of United States citizens who died in a helicopter crash in Peru instituted wrongful-death actions in a Texas state court against the owner and operator of the helicopter, a Colombian corporation. The Colombian corporation had no place of business in Texas and was not licensed to do business there. "Basically, [the company's] contacts with Texas consisted of sending its chief executive officer to Houston for a contract-negotiation session; accepting into its New York bank account checks drawn on a Houston bank; purchasing helicopters, equipment, and training services from [a Texas enterprise] for substantial sums; and sending personnel to [Texas] for training." These links to Texas, we determined, did not "constitute the kind of continuous and systematic general business contacts . . . found to exist in Perkins," and were insufficient to support the exercise of jurisdiction over a claim that neither "ar[o]se out of . . . no[r] related to" the defendant's activities in Texas.

Helicopteros concluded that "mere purchases [made in the forum State], even if occurring at regular intervals, are not enough to warrant a State's assertion of [general] jurisdiction over a nonresident corporation in a cause of action not related to those purchase transactions." We see no reason to differentiate from the ties to Texas held insufficient in *Helicopteros*, the sales of petitioners' tires sporadically made in North Carolina through intermediaries. Under the sprawling view of general jurisdiction urged by respondents and embraced by the North Carolina Court of Appeals, any substantial manufacturer or seller of goods would be amenable to suit, on any claim for relief, wherever its products are distributed. But cf. *World-Wide Volkswagen*, 444 U.S., at 296 (every seller of chattels does not, by virtue of the sale, "appoint the chattel his agent for service of process").

Measured against *Helicopteros* and *Perkins*, North Carolina is not a forum in which it would be permissible to subject petitioners to general jurisdiction. Unlike the defendant in *Perkins*, whose sole wartime business activity was conducted in Ohio, petitioners are in no sense at home in North Carolina. Their attenuated connections to the State fall far short of "the continuous and systematic general business contacts" necessary to empower North Carolina to entertain suit against them on claims unrelated to anything that connects them to the State.[10]

For the reasons stated, the judgment of the North Carolina Court of Appeals is reversed.

---

10. The North Carolina Court of Appeals invoked the State's "well-recognized interest in providing a forum in which its citizens are able to seek redress for injuries that they have sustained." But "[g]eneral jurisdiction to adjudicate has in [United States] practice never been based on the plaintiff's relationship to the forum. There is nothing in [our] law comparable to . . . article 14 of the Civil Code of France (1804) under which the French nationality of the plaintiff is a sufficient ground for jurisdiction." (French law permitting plaintiff-based jurisdiction is rarely invoked in the absence of other supporting factors). When a defendant's act outside the forum causes injury in the forum, by contrast, a plaintiff's residence in the forum may strengthen the case for the exercise of specific jurisdiction. See *Calder v. Jones*, 465 U.S. 783, 788 (1984).

YOUR TAKEAWAY

North Carolina's long reach of adjudicatory power here is clearly beyond the margins—a "sprawling view of general jurisdiction" that would subject "any substantial manufacturer or seller" to suit "on any claim for relief, wherever its products are distributed," Similarly, its "mix and match" of specific jurisdiction's stream of commerce theory and general jurisdiction's licence to entertain a non-forum claim allowed plaintiffs to assert their claim despite the fact that it arose in France and the foreign subsidiary defendants had virtually no ties to the state. In this sense, Justice Ginsburg's *unanimous* decision isn't much of a surprise.

"Domicile, place of incorporation, and principal place of business are," we are reminded, the "paradigm bases for the exercise of general jurisdiction." But beyond that, and the new and more descriptive vocabulary ("case specific" vs. "all purpose" jurisdiction, a corporation being "at home"), we learn little about the status (or contours) of Justice Stone's "continuous, systematic, and substantial" activities that render a corporate defendant amenable to suit on claims unrelated to forum activities.

REVIEW QUESTIONS

1. One court has proposed the following factors to determine whether a corporation is "at home" in the forum state:

   > (1) whether the corporation solicits business in the state through a local office or agents; (2) whether the corporation sends agents into the state on a regular basis to solicit business; (3) the extent to which the corporation holds itself out as doing business in the forum state, through advertisements, listings or bank accounts; and (4) the volume of business conducted in the state by the corporation.

   Tomelleri v. MEDL Mobile, Inc., 2015 WL 1957801, at *4 (D. Kan. Apr. 29, 2015), *aff'd* 657 Fed. Appx. 793 (10th Cir. 2016).

   The last factor, volume of business, is now (after the *Daimler* case that follows) subject to the caveat that volume must be weighed against defendant's *total business,* and not in isolation.

2. The Court's two earlier precedents on this topic were seemingly easy cases. Dislocated by the war from the Philippines, the Benguet Consolidated Mining Co. conducted its only wartime activities from its relocated office in Ohio. Had the Court not rendered the company subject to general jurisdiction, one wonders where else Perkins could have brought her suit. *Perkins v. Benguet Consolidated Mining Co.*, 342 U.S. 437 (1952). In *Helicopteros Nacionales de Colombia v. Hall*, 466 U.S. 408 (1984), on the other hand, defendant's ties to Texas were far too tenuous, as described by Justice Ginsburg in *Goodyear.* Where would you place the Goodyear European subsidiaries on the activity spectrum calibrated by these two cases?

3. Note Justice Ginsburg's dismissal of the lower court's hybrid of general and specific jurisdiction. She similarly rejects basing general jurisdiction on the forum's interest in providing a convenient venue to its citizen: "General jurisdiction to adjudicate has in [United States] practice never been based on the plaintiff's relationship to the forum. There is

nothing in [our] law comparable to article 14 of the Civil Code of France (1804) under which the French nationality of the plaintiff is a sufficient ground for jurisdiction." See footnote 10.

4. *The Timing of Contacts.* Should a corporation's contacts with the forum be measured at the time the claim arose, or when the complaint is filed? Courts have distinguished between assertions of general jurisdiction, in which contacts are measured up to the time the complaint is filed, and specific jurisdiction, in which the focus is limited to contacts leading up to the claimed injury. The First Circuit has explained:

> The reason for this approach stems from the basic distinction between specific and general jurisdiction. Unlike the specific jurisdiction analysis, which focuses on the cause of action, the defendant and the forum, a general jurisdiction inquiry is dispute blind, the sole focus being on whether there are continuous and systematic contacts between the defendant and the forum. Accordingly, for general jurisdiction a court should consider all of a defendant's contacts with the forum state prior to the filing of the lawsuit, rather than just those contacts that are related to the particular cause of action the plaintiff asserts.

Harlow v. Children's Hospital, 432 F.3d 50, 65 (1st Cir. 2005).

Contacts arising *after* the filing of the complaint are irrelevant to either inquiry. *See generally* Todd David Peterson, *The Timing of Minimum Contacts*, 79 Geo. Wash. L. Rev. 101 (2010).

QUESTIONS TO PONDER

For a case asserting general jurisdiction over two foreign multinational corporations on international human rights claims, *see Wiwa v. Royal Dutch Petroleum Co.*, 226 F.3d 88 (2d Cir. 2000), *cert. denied*, 532 U.S. 941 (2001). Nigerian émigrés sued under the Alien Tort Statute, alleging that the defendant companies (one incorporated in the Netherlands and the other in the United Kingdom) had participated in human rights abuses against them in Nigeria because of their opposition to oil exploration there. The Second Circuit concluded that defendants were subject to general jurisdiction because they were "doing business" in New York through a small investor-relations office operated by a subsidiary in Manhattan. Thus, even though plaintiffs' claims did not arise in or relate to activities in New York, they could be heard in federal district court in New York. Despite arguments from *amici curiae* (including the New York Stock Exchange) contending that the ruling could damage American business interests abroad, the Supreme Court refused to review the decision.

Is this decision still good law after *Goodyear* and *Daimler*, which follows? For a negative answer, *see* Gwynne L. Skinner, *Expanding General Personal Jurisdiction over Transnational Corporations for Federal Causes of Action*, 121 Penn St. L. Rev. 617, 653-654 (2017).

Daimler AG v. Bauman
134 S. Ct. 746 (2014)

Justice GINSBURG delivered the opinion of the Court in which Chief Justice ROBERTS, Justice SCALIA, Justice KENNEDY, Justice THOMAS, Justice BREYER, Justice ALITO, and Justice KAGAN joined.

This case concerns the authority of a court in the United States to entertain a claim brought by foreign plaintiffs against a foreign defendant based on events occurring entirely outside the United States. The litigation commenced in 2004, when twenty-two Argentinian residents filed a complaint in the United States District Court for the Northern District of California against DaimlerChrysler Aktiengesellschaft (Daimler), a German public stock company, headquartered in Stuttgart, that manufactures Mercedes-Benz vehicles in Germany. The complaint alleged that during Argentina's 1976-1983 "Dirty War," Daimler's Argentinian subsidiary, Mercedes-Benz Argentina (MB Argentina) collaborated with state security forces to kidnap, detain, torture, and kill certain MB Argentina workers, among them, plaintiffs or persons closely related to plaintiffs. Damages for the alleged human-rights violations were sought from Daimler under the laws of the United States, California, and Argentina. Jurisdiction over the lawsuit was predicated on the California contacts of Mercedes-Benz USA, LLC (MBUSA), a subsidiary of Daimler incorporated in Delaware with its principal place of business in New Jersey. MBUSA distributes Daimler-manufactured vehicles to independent dealerships throughout the United States, including California.

The question presented is whether the Due Process Clause of the Fourteenth Amendment precludes the District Court from exercising jurisdiction over Daimler in this case, given the absence of any California connection to the atrocities, perpetrators, or victims described in the complaint. Plaintiffs invoked the court's general or all-purpose jurisdiction. California, they urge, is a place where Daimler may be sued on any and all claims against it, wherever in the world the claims may arise. For example, as plaintiffs' counsel affirmed, under the proffered jurisdictional theory, if a Daimler-manufactured vehicle overturned in Poland, injuring a Polish driver and passenger, the injured parties could maintain a design defect suit in California. Exercises of personal jurisdiction so exorbitant, we hold, are barred by due process constraints on the assertion of adjudicatory authority.

In *Goodyear Dunlop Tires Operations, S.A. v. Brown,* 564 U.S. ___, 131 S. Ct. 2846 (2011), we addressed the distinction between general or all-purpose jurisdiction, and specific or conduct-linked jurisdiction. As to the former, we held that a court may assert jurisdiction over a foreign corporation "to hear any and all claims against [it]" only when the corporation's affiliations with the State in which suit is brought are so constant and pervasive "as to render [it] essentially at home in the forum State." Instructed by *Goodyear,* we conclude Daimler is not "at home" in California, and cannot be sued there for injuries plaintiffs attribute to MB Argentina's conduct in Argentina.

I

In 2004, plaintiffs (respondents here) filed suit in the United States District Court for the Northern District of California, alleging that MB Argentina collaborated with Argentinian state security forces to kidnap, detain, torture, and kill plaintiffs and their relatives during the military dictatorship in place there from 1976 through 1983, a period known as Argentina's "Dirty War." Based on those allegations, plaintiffs asserted claims under the Alien Tort Statute, 28 U.S.C. § 1350, and the Torture Victim Protection Act of 1991, 106 Stat. 73, note following 28 U.S.C. § 1350, as well as claims for wrongful death and intentional infliction of emotional distress under the laws of California and Argentina. The incidents recounted in the complaint center on MB Argentina's plant in Gonzalez Catan, Argentina; no part of MB Argentina's alleged collaboration with Argentinian authorities took place in California or anywhere else in the United States.

Plaintiffs' operative complaint names only one corporate defendant: Daimler, the petitioner here. Plaintiffs seek to hold Daimler vicariously liable for MB Argentina's alleged malfeasance. Daimler is a German *Aktiengesellschaft* (public stock company) that manufactures Mercedes-Benz vehicles in Germany and has its headquarters in Stuttgart. At times relevant to this case, MB Argentina was a subsidiary wholly owned by Daimler's predecessor in interest.

Daimler moved to dismiss the action for want of personal jurisdiction. Opposing the motion, plaintiffs submitted declarations and exhibits purporting to demonstrate the presence of Daimler itself in California. Alternatively, plaintiffs maintained that jurisdiction over Daimler could be founded on the California contacts of MBUSA, a distinct corporate entity that, according to plaintiffs, should be treated as Daimler's agent for jurisdictional purposes.

MBUSA, an indirect subsidiary of Daimler, is a Delaware limited liability corporation. MBUSA serves as Daimler's exclusive importer and distributor in the United States, purchasing Mercedes-Benz automobiles from Daimler in Germany, then importing those vehicles, and ultimately distributing them to independent dealerships located throughout the Nation. Although MBUSA's principal place of business is in New Jersey, MBUSA has multiple California-based facilities, including a regional office in Costa Mesa, a Vehicle Preparation Center in Carson, and a Classic Center in Irvine. According to the record developed below, MBUSA is the largest supplier of luxury vehicles to the California market. In particular, over 10% of all sales of new vehicles in the United States take place in California, and MBUSA's California sales account for 2.4% of Daimler's worldwide sales.

The relationship between Daimler and MBUSA is delineated in a General Distributor Agreement, which sets forth requirements for MBUSA's distribution of Mercedes-Benz vehicles in the United States. That agreement established MBUSA as an "independent contracto[r]" that "buy[s] and sell[s] [vehicles] . . . as an independent business for [its] own account." The agreement "does not make [MBUSA] . . . a general or special agent, partner, joint venturer or employee of DAIMLERCHRYSLER or any DaimlerChrysler Group Company"; MBUSA "ha[s] no authority to make binding obligations for or act on behalf of DAIMLERCHRYSLER or any DaimlerChrysler Group Company."

After allowing jurisdictional discovery on plaintiffs' agency allegations, the District Court granted Daimler's motion to dismiss. Daimler's own affiliations with California, the court first determined, were insufficient to support the exercise of all-purpose jurisdiction over the corporation. Next, the court declined to attribute MBUSA's California contacts to Daimler on an agency theory, concluding that plaintiffs failed to demonstrate that MBUSA acted as Daimler's agent.

The Ninth Circuit at first affirmed the District Court's judgment. Addressing solely the question of agency, the Court of Appeals held that plaintiffs had not shown the existence of an agency relationship of the kind that might warrant attribution of MBUSA's contacts to *Daimler. Bauman v. DaimlerChrysler Corp.*, 579 F.3d 1088, 1096-1097 (2009). Judge Reinhardt dissented. In his view, the agency test was satisfied and considerations of "reasonableness" did not bar the exercise of jurisdiction. Granting plaintiffs' petition for rehearing, the panel withdrew its initial opinion and replaced it with one authored by Judge Reinhardt, which elaborated on reasoning he initially expressed in dissent. *Bauman v. DaimlerChrysler Corp.*, 644 F.3d 909 (C.A.9 2011). . . .

We granted certiorari to decide whether, consistent with the Due Process Clause of the Fourteenth Amendment, Daimler is amenable to suit in California courts for claims involving only foreign plaintiffs and conduct occurring entirely abroad.

II

Federal courts ordinarily follow state law in determining the bounds of their jurisdiction over persons. See Fed. Rule Civ. Proc. 4(k)(1)(A) (service of process is effective to establish personal jurisdiction over a defendant "who is subject to the jurisdiction of a court of general jurisdiction in the state where the district court is located"). Under California's long-arm statute, California state courts may exercise personal jurisdiction "on any basis not inconsistent with the Constitution of this state or of the United States." Cal. Civ. Proc. Code Ann. § 410.10 (West 2004). California's long-arm statute allows the exercise of personal jurisdiction to the full extent permissible under the U.S. Constitution. We therefore inquire whether the Ninth Circuit's holding comports with the limits imposed by federal due process. *See, e.g., Burger King Corp. v. Rudzewicz*, 471 U.S. 462, 464 (1985).

III

. . . "The canonical opinion in this area remains *International Shoe*, in which we held that a State may authorize its courts to exercise personal jurisdiction over an out-of-state defendant if the defendant has "certain minimum contacts with [the State] such that the maintenance of the suit does not offend traditional notions of fair play and substantial justice."

International Shoe distinguished between, on the one hand, exercises of specific jurisdiction, and on the other, situations where a foreign corporation's "continuous corporate operations within a state [are] so substantial and of such a nature as to justify suit against it on causes of action arising from dealings entirely distinct from those activities." As we have since explained, "[a] court may assert general jurisdiction over foreign (sister-state or foreign-country) corporations to hear any and all claims against them when their affiliations with the State are so 'continuous and systematic' as to render them essentially at home in the forum State." *Goodyear*, 564 U.S., at ___, 131 S. Ct., at 2851.[5]

Since *International Shoe*, "specific jurisdiction has become the centerpiece of modern jurisdiction theory, while general jurisdiction [has played] a reduced role." *Goodyear*, 564 U.S., at ___, 131 S. Ct., at 2854. *International Shoe*'s momentous departure from *Pennoyer*'s rigidly territorial focus, we have noted, unleashed a rapid expansion of tribunals' ability to hear claims against out-of-state defendants when the episode-in-suit occurred in the forum or the defendant purposefully availed itself of the forum. Our subsequent decisions have continued to bear out the prediction that "specific jurisdiction will come into sharper relief and form a considerably more significant part of the scene."

Our post-*International Shoe* opinions on general jurisdiction, by comparison, are few. "[The Court's] 1952 decision in *Perkins v. Benguet Consol. Mining Co.* remains the textbook case of general jurisdiction appropriately exercised over a foreign corporation that has not consented to suit in the forum." The defendant in *Perkins*, Benguet, was a company incorporated under the laws of the Philippines, where it operated gold and silver mines. Benguet ceased its mining operations during the Japanese occupation of the Philippines in World War II; its president moved to Ohio, where he kept an office, maintained the company's files, and oversaw the company's activities. *Perkins v. Benguet Consol. Mining Co.*, 342 U.S. 437, 448 (1952). The plaintiff, an Ohio resident, sued Benguet on a claim that neither arose in Ohio nor related to the corporation's activities in that State. We held that the Ohio courts could exercise general jurisdiction over Benguet without offending due process. That was so, we later noted, because "Ohio was the corporation's principal, if temporary, place of business." *Keeton v. Hustler Magazine, Inc.*, 465 U.S. 770, 780 n.11 (1984).

---

5. Colloquy at oral argument illustrated the respective provinces of general and specific jurisdiction over persons. Two hypothetical scenarios were posed: *First*, if a California plaintiff, injured in a California accident involving a Daimler-manufactured vehicle, sued Daimler in California court alleging that the vehicle was defectively designed, that court's adjudicatory authority would be premised on specific jurisdiction. (Daimler's counsel acknowledged that specific jurisdiction "may well be . . . available" in such a case, depending on whether Daimler purposefully availed itself of the forum). *Second*, if a similar accident took place in Poland and injured Polish plaintiffs sued Daimler in California court, the question would be one of general jurisdiction.

Most recently, in *Goodyear*, we answered the question: "Are foreign subsidiaries of a United States parent corporation amenable to suit in state court on claims unrelated to any activity of the subsidiaries in the forum State?" That case arose from a bus accident outside Paris that killed two boys from North Carolina. The boys' parents brought a wrongful-death suit in North Carolina state court alleging that the bus's tire was defectively manufactured. The complaint named as defendants not only The Goodyear Tire and Rubber Company (Goodyear), an Ohio corporation, but also Goodyear's Turkish, French, and Luxembourgian subsidiaries. Those foreign subsidiaries, which manufactured tires for sale in Europe and Asia, lacked any affiliation with North Carolina. A small percentage of tires manufactured by the foreign subsidiaries were distributed in North Carolina, however, and on that ground, the North Carolina Court of Appeals held the subsidiaries amenable to the general jurisdiction of North Carolina courts.

We reversed, observing that the North Carolina court's analysis "elided the essential difference between case-specific and all-purpose (general) jurisdiction." Although the placement of a product into the stream of commerce "may bolster an affiliation germane to specific jurisdiction," we explained, such contacts "do not warrant a determination that, based on those ties, the forum has general jurisdiction over a defendant." As *International Shoe* itself teaches, a corporation's "continuous activity of some sorts within a state is not enough to support the demand that the corporation be amenable to suits unrelated to that activity." Because Goodyear's foreign subsidiaries were "in no sense at home in North Carolina," we held, those subsidiaries could not be required to submit to the general jurisdiction of that State's courts. . . .

As this Court has increasingly trained on the "relationship among the defendant, the forum, and the litigation," *Shaffer*, 433 U.S., at 204, i.e., specific jurisdiction, general jurisdiction has come to occupy a less dominant place in the contemporary scheme.

IV

With this background, we turn directly to the question whether Daimler's affiliations with California are sufficient to subject it to the general (all-purpose) personal jurisdiction of that State's courts. . . .

Daimler failed to object below to plaintiffs' assertion that the California courts could exercise all-purpose jurisdiction over MBUSA. We will assume then, for purposes of this decision only, that MBUSA qualifies as at home in California.

A

In sustaining the exercise of general jurisdiction over Daimler, the Ninth Circuit relied on an agency theory, determining that MBUSA acted as Daimler's agent for jurisdictional purposes and then attributing MBUSA's California contacts to

Daimler. The Ninth Circuit's agency theory appears to subject foreign corporations to general jurisdiction whenever they have an in-state subsidiary or affiliate, an outcome that would sweep beyond even the "sprawling view of general jurisdiction" we rejected in *Goodyear*. 564 U.S., at ___, 131 S. Ct., at 2856.

B

Even if we were to assume that MBUSA is at home in California, and further to assume MBUSA's contacts are imputable to Daimler, there would still be no basis to subject Daimler to general jurisdiction in California, for Daimler's slim contacts with the State hardly render it at home there.

Goodyear made clear that only a limited set of affiliations with a forum will render a defendant amenable to all-purpose jurisdiction there. "For an individual, the paradigm forum for the exercise of general jurisdiction is the individual's domicile; for a corporation, it is an equivalent place, one in which the corporation is fairly regarded as at home." With respect to a corporation, the place of incorporation and principal place of business are "paradig[m] . . . bases for general jurisdiction." Those affiliations have the virtue of being unique—that is, each ordinarily indicates only one place—as well as easily ascertainable. These bases afford plaintiffs recourse to at least one clear and certain forum in which a corporate defendant may be sued on any and all claims. . . .

The inquiry under *Goodyear* is not whether a foreign corporation's in-forum contacts can be said to be in some sense "continuous and systematic," it is whether that corporation's "affiliations with the State are so 'continuous and systematic' as to render [it] essentially at home in the forum State."[6]

Here, neither Daimler nor MBUSA is incorporated in California, nor does either entity have its principal place of business there. If Daimler's California activities sufficed to allow adjudication of this Argentina-rooted case in California, the same global reach would presumably be available in every other State in which MBUSA's sales are sizable. Such exorbitant exercises of all-purpose jurisdiction would scarcely permit out-of-state defendants "to structure their primary conduct with some minimum assurance as to where that conduct will and will not render them liable to suit." *Burger King Corp.*, 471 U.S., at 472.

It was therefore error for the Ninth Circuit to conclude that Daimler, even with MBUSA's contacts attributed to it, was at home in California, and hence

---

6. We do not foreclose the possibility that in an exceptional case, see, *e.g.*, *Perkins*, described *supra*, at 755-757, and n.8, a corporation's operations in a forum other than its formal place of incorporation or principal place of business may be so substantial and of such a nature as to render the corporation at home in that State. But this case presents no occasion to explore that question, because Daimler's activities in California plainly do not approach that level. It is one thing to hold a corporation answerable for operations in the forum State, quite another to expose it to suit on claims having no connection whatever to the forum State.

subject to suit there on claims by foreign plaintiffs having nothing to do with anything that occurred or had its principal impact in California.[7]

C

Finally, the transnational context of this dispute bears attention. The Court of Appeals emphasized, as supportive of the exercise of general jurisdiction, plaintiffs' assertion of claims under the Alien Tort Statute (ATS), 28 U.S.C. § 1350, and the Torture Victim Protection Act of 1991 (TVPA), 106 Stat. 73, note following 28 U.S.C. § 1350. *See* 644 F.3d, at 927 ("American federal courts, be they in California or any other state, have a strong interest in adjudicating and redressing international human rights abuses."). Recent decisions of this Court, however, have rendered plaintiffs' ATS and TVPA claims infirm. *See Kiobel v. Royal Dutch Petroleum Co.*, 569 U.S. ___, ___, 133 S. Ct. 1659, 1669 (2013) (presumption against extraterritorial application controls claims under the ATS); *Mohamad v. Palestinian Authority*, 566 U.S. ___, ___, 132 S. Ct. 1702, 1705 (2012) (only natural persons are subject to liability under the TVPA).

The Ninth Circuit, moreover, paid little heed to the risks to international comity its expansive view of general jurisdiction posed. Other nations do not share the uninhibited approach to personal jurisdiction advanced by the Court of Appeals in this case. In the European Union, for example, a corporation may generally be sued in the nation in which it is "domiciled," a term defined to

---

7. To clarify in light of Justice Sotomayor's opinion concurring in the judgment, the general jurisdiction inquiry does not "focu[s] solely on the magnitude of the defendant's in-state contacts." General jurisdiction instead calls for an appraisal of a corporation's activities in their entirety, nationwide and worldwide. A corporation that operates in many places can scarcely be deemed at home in all of them. Otherwise, "at home" would be synonymous with "doing business" tests framed before specific jurisdiction evolved in the United States. Nothing in *International Shoe* and its progeny suggests that "a particular quantum of local activity" should give a State authority over a "far larger quantum of . . . activity" having no connection to any in-state activity. Feder, Goodyear, *"Home," and the Uncertain Future of Doing Business Jurisdiction*, 63 S.C. L. Rev. 671, 694 (2012)].

Justice Sotomayor would reach the same result, but for a different reason. Rather than concluding that Daimler is not at home in California, Justice Sotomayor would hold that the exercise of general jurisdiction over Daimler would be unreasonable "in the unique circumstances of this case." In other words, she favors a resolution fit for this day and case only. True, a multipronged reasonableness check was articulated in *Asahi*, but not as a free-floating test. Instead, the check was to be essayed when *specific* jurisdiction is at issue. First, a court is to determine whether the connection between the forum and the episode-in-suit could justify the exercise of specific jurisdiction. Then, in a second step, the court is to consider several additional factors to assess the reasonableness of entertaining the case. When a corporation is genuinely at home in the forum State, however, any second-step inquiry would be superfluous.

Justice Sotomayor fears that our holding will "lead to greater unpredictability by radically expanding the scope of jurisdictional discovery." But it is hard to see why much in the way of discovery would be needed to determine where a corporation is at home. Justice Sotomayor's proposal to import *Asahi*'s "reasonableness" check into the general jurisdiction determination, on the other hand, would indeed compound the jurisdictional inquiry. The reasonableness factors identified in *Asahi* include "the burden on the defendant," "the interests of the forum State," "the plaintiff's interest in obtaining relief," "the interstate judicial system's interest in obtaining the most efficient resolution of controversies," "the shared interest of the several States in furthering fundamental substantive social policies," and, in the international context, "the procedural and substantive policies of other *nations* whose interests are affected by the assertion of jurisdiction." Imposing such a checklist in cases of general jurisdiction would hardly promote the efficient disposition of an issue that should be resolved expeditiously at the outset of litigation.

refer only to the location of the corporation's "statutory seat," "central administration," or "principal place of business." The Solicitor General informs us, in this regard, that "foreign governments' objections to some domestic courts' expansive views of general jurisdiction have in the past impeded negotiations of international agreements on the reciprocal recognition and enforcement of judgments." Considerations of international rapport thus reinforce our determination that subjecting Daimler to the general jurisdiction of courts in California would not accord with the "fair play and substantial justice" due process demands.

For the reasons stated, the judgment of the United States Court of Appeals for the Ninth Circuit is reversed.

Justice SOTOMAYOR, concurring in the judgment.

I agree with the Court's conclusion that the Due Process Clause prohibits the exercise of personal jurisdiction over Daimler in light of the unique circumstances of this case. I concur only in the judgment, however, because I cannot agree with the path the Court takes to arrive at that result.

The Court acknowledges that Mercedes-Benz USA, LLC (MBUSA), Daimler's wholly owned subsidiary, has considerable contacts with California. It has multiple facilities in the State, including a regional headquarters. Each year, it distributes in California tens of thousands of cars, the sale of which generated billions of dollars in the year this suit was brought. And it provides service and sales support to customers throughout the State. Daimler has conceded that California courts may exercise general jurisdiction over MBUSA on the basis of these contacts, and the Court assumes that MBUSA's contacts may be attributed to Daimler for the purpose of deciding whether Daimler is also subject to general jurisdiction.

Are these contacts sufficient to permit the exercise of general jurisdiction over Daimler? The Court holds that they are not, for a reason wholly foreign to our due process jurisprudence. The problem, the Court says, is not that Daimler's contacts with California are too few, but that its contacts with other forums are too many. In other words, the Court does not dispute that the presence of multiple offices, the direct distribution of thousands of products accounting for billions of dollars in sales, and continuous interaction with customers throughout a State would be enough to support the exercise of general jurisdiction over some businesses. Daimler is just not one of those businesses, the Court concludes, because its California contacts must be viewed in the context of its extensive "nationwide and worldwide" operations. In recent years, Americans have grown accustomed to the concept of multinational corporations that are supposedly "too big to fail"; today the Court deems Daimler "too big for general jurisdiction."

The Court's conclusion is wrong as a matter of both process and substance. As to process, the Court decides this case on a ground that was neither argued nor passed on below, and that Daimler raised for the first time in a footnote to its brief. As to substance, the Court's focus on Daimler's operations outside of California ignores the lodestar of our personal jurisdiction jurisprudence: A State may subject a defendant to the burden of suit if the defendant has sufficiently taken advantage of the State's laws and protections through its contacts in the State; whether the defendant has contacts elsewhere is immaterial.

Regrettably, these errors are unforced. The Court can and should decide this case on the far simpler ground that, no matter how extensive Daimler's contacts with California, that State's exercise of jurisdiction would be unreasonable given that the case involves foreign plaintiffs suing a foreign defendant based on foreign conduct, and given that a more appropriate forum is available. Because I would reverse the judgment below on this ground, I concur in the judgment only.

I

We identified the factors that bear on reasonableness in *Asahi Metal Industry Co. v. Superior Court of Cal., Solano Cty.*, 480 U.S. 102 (1987): "the burden on the defendant, the interests of the forum State," "the plaintiff's interest in obtaining relief" in the forum State, and the interests of other sovereigns in resolving the dispute. We held in *Asahi* that it would be "unreasonable and unfair" for a California court to exercise jurisdiction over a claim between a Taiwanese plaintiff and a Japanese defendant that arose out of a transaction in Taiwan, particularly where the Taiwanese plaintiff had not shown that it would be more convenient to litigate in California than in Taiwan or Japan.

The same considerations resolve this case. It involves Argentine plaintiffs suing a German defendant for conduct that took place in Argentina. Like the plaintiffs in *Asahi*, respondents have failed to show that it would be more convenient to litigate in California than in Germany, a sovereign with a far greater interest in resolving the dispute. *Asahi* thus makes clear that it would be unreasonable for a court in California to subject Daimler to its jurisdiction. . . .

A

The majority today announces the new rule that in order for a foreign defendant to be subject to general jurisdiction, it must not only possess continuous and systematic contacts with a forum State, but those contacts must also surpass some unspecified level when viewed in comparison to the company's "nationwide and worldwide" activities. The majority's approach unduly curtails the States' sovereign authority to adjudicate disputes against corporate defendants who have engaged in continuous and substantial business operations within their boundaries.

Second, the proportionality approach will treat small businesses unfairly in comparison to national and multinational conglomerates. Whereas a larger company will often be immunized from general jurisdiction in a State on account of its extensive contacts outside the forum, a small business will not be. For instance, the majority holds today that Daimler is not subject to general jurisdiction in California despite its multiple offices, continuous operations, and billions of dollars' worth of sales there. But imagine a small business that manufactures luxury vehicles principally targeting the California market and that has substantially all of its sales and operations in the State—even though those sales and operations may amount to one-thousandth of Daimler's. Under the majority's rule, that small business will be subject to suit in California on any cause of action involving any of its activities anywhere in the world, while its far more pervasive competitor, Daimler, will not be. . . .

Third, the majority's approach creates the incongruous result that an individual defendant whose only contact with a forum State is a one-time visit will be subject to general jurisdiction if served with process during that visit, *Burnham v. Superior Court of Cal., County of Marin*, 495 U.S. 604 (1990), but a large corporation that owns property, employs workers, and does billions of dollars' worth of business in the State will not be, simply because the corporation has similar contacts elsewhere (though the visiting individual surely does as well).

Finally, it should be obvious that the ultimate effect of the majority's approach will be to shift the risk of loss from multinational corporations to the individuals harmed by their actions. Under the majority's rule, for example, a parent whose child is maimed due to the negligence of a foreign hotel owned by a multinational conglomerate will be unable to hold the hotel to account in a single U.S. court, even if the hotel company has a massive presence in multiple States. Similarly, a U.S. business that enters into a contract in a foreign country to sell its products to a multinational company there may be unable to seek relief in any U.S. court if the multinational company breaches the contract, even if that company has considerable operations in numerous U.S. forums.[8] Indeed, the majority's approach would preclude the plaintiffs in these examples from seeking recourse anywhere in the United States even if no other judicial system was available to provide relief. I cannot agree with the majority's conclusion that the Due Process Clause requires these results. . . .

The Court rules against respondents today on a ground that no court has considered in the history of this case, that this Court did not grant certiorari to decide, and that Daimler raised only in a footnote of its brief. In doing so, the Court adopts a new rule of constitutional law that is unmoored from decades of precedent. Because I would reverse the Ninth Circuit's decision on the narrower ground that the exercise of jurisdiction over Daimler would be unreasonable in any event, I respectfully concur in the judgment only.

YOUR TAKEAWAY

Once again, through Justice Ginsburg, the Court unanimously retreats from an exercise of general jurisdiction in a so-called *F-Cubed* case (foreign plaintiffs,

---

8. The present case and the examples posited involve foreign corporate defendants, but the principle announced by the majority would apply equally to preclude general jurisdiction over a U.S. company that is incorporated and has its principal place of business in another U.S. State. Under the majority's rule, for example, a General Motors autoworker who retires to Florida would be unable to sue GM in that State for disabilities that develop from the retiree's labor at a Michigan parts plant, even though GM undertakes considerable business operations in Florida.

foreign defendant, foreign claim), concluding Daimler is not "at home" in California. Both *Daimler* and *Goodyear* make clear that even "substantial, continuous, and systematic" conduct does not equate with general jurisdiction (as we had previously thought)—rather the defendant's activities must be "so continuous and systematic as to render it essentially *at home* in the forum State." In footnote 6 (in our version), the *Daimler* Court refers to such a defendant as "an exceptional case." Thus, short of the defendant being incorporated or headquartered (or principal place of business) in the forum state, general jurisdiction is unlikely to exist.

REVIEW QUESTIONS

1. Clearly the Court is shifting *International Shoe*'s weight away from general and onto specific jurisdiction. But with the stingy view of specific jurisdiction that now prevails in the era of *Nicastro*, the bottom line is a continued narrowing of forum options for plaintiffs. *See generally* Bernadette Bollas Genetin, *The Supreme Court's New Approach to Personal Jurisdiction*, 68 SMU L. Rev. 107 (2015); Donald L. Doernberg, *Resolving* International Shoe, 2 Tex. A&M L. Rev. 247 (2014).

2. Are you troubled, as Justice Sotomayor is, by the disparity in standards for general jurisdiction between an individual and a corporation? "[T]he majority's approach creates the incongruous result that an individual defendant whose only contact with a forum State is a one-time visit will be subject to general jurisdiction if served with process during that visit, *Burnham v. Superior Court of Cal., County of Marin*, but a large corporation that owns property, employs workers, and does billions of dollars' worth of business in the State will not be, simply because the corporation has similar contacts elsewhere (though the visiting individual surely does as well)." Was Dennis Burnham "at home" in California? *See generally* Jeffrey W. Stempel, *The Irrepressible Myth of* Burnham *and Its Increasing Indefensibility After* Goodyear *and* Daimler, 15 Nev. L.J. 1203 (2015).

3. What about Justice Sotomayor's novel invocation of the reasonableness analysis in the context of general jurisdiction? Why do her fellow Justices resist this? (*See* footnote 7.)

4. Justice Ginsburg concludes: "The Ninth Circuit's agency theory thus appears to subject foreign corporations to general jurisdiction whenever they have an in-state subsidiary or affiliate, an outcome that would sweep beyond even the 'sprawling view of general jurisdiction' we rejected in *Goodyear*." 571 U.S. at 136. Does that leave any room for jurisdiction based on an agency relationship between parent and subsidiary?

QUESTIONS TO PONDER

How much of *Goodyear* and *Daimler* do you think is a reaction against U.S. courts entertaining foreign disputes against foreign actors (and, in *Daimler*, on behalf of foreign plaintiffs)—"F-Cubed litigations"? *See* Danielle Kantor, *The Limits of Federal Jurisdiction and the F-Cubed Case: Adjudicating Transnational Securities Disputes in Federal Courts*, 65 N.Y.U. Ann. Surv. Am. L. 839 (2010). Is this what Justice Ginsburg means when she describes the exercise of personal jurisdiction below as "exorbitant?" Could this not have been dealt with by the doctrine of *forum non conveniens* (discussed below)? *See generally* Judy M. Cornett and Michael H. Hoffheimer, *Good-Bye Significant Contacts: General Personal Jurisdiction After* Daimler v. Bauman, 76 Ohio St. L.J. 101 (2015).

What about *a domestic* corporation like McDonald's, with 36,000 restaurants worldwide, most in the United States? Is McDonald's Corporation, whose iconic yellow arches pervade every state (there's even one in Versailles next to the Palace!), suable in each of those states on claims arising elsewhere? Could a patron injured at a McDonald's while vacationing in Miami sue when she returns to her home state of New York, which has nearly 800 of its restaurants? What if she were injured at a hotel in Miami run by one of the largest chains in the world, like Hilton? Could she sue upon returning to the New York City area, where Hilton owns more than 50 hotels?

The answers used to be affirmative, as courts read *International Shoe* to permit the assertion of general jurisdiction over corporate entities "doing substantial and continuous" business within the state. That is probably why defendants like Volkswagen and Audi and the National Enquirer did not pursue their objections to jurisdiction in *World-Wide Volkswagen v. Woodson* and *Calder v. Jones*.

Daimler suggests a very different answer—a corporation that operates extensively in many states is not deemed "at home" in any one. Where does the Court get this novel "proportionality" analysis from, and what is its logic? Is it a function of *International Shoe*'s benefit/burden analysis? What would Chief Justice Harlan Fiske Stone, author of *International Shoe*, think about this?

Can you understand why Justice Sotomayor trounces this analysis so forcefully? Does it not give an undue advantage to the largest corporations to avoid inconvenient suits? How can the Court justify the disparity in treatment between a smaller corporation (suable) and one "too big for general jurisdiction"?

The third case in Ruth Bader Ginsburg's general jurisdiction trilogy:

BNSF Railway Co. v. Tyrrell
137 S. Ct. 1549 (2017)

Justice GINSBURG delivered the opinion of the Court in which Chief Justice ROBERTS, Justice KENNEDY, Justice THOMAS, Justice BREYER, Justice ALITO, JUSTICE KAGAN and Justice GORSUCH joined.

The two cases we decide today arise under the Federal Employers' Liability Act (FELA), 35 Stat. 65, as amended, 45 U.S.C. § 51 et seq., which makes railroads liable in money damages to their employees for on-the-job injuries. Both suits were pursued in Montana state courts although the injured workers did not reside in Montana, nor were they injured there. The defendant railroad, BNSF Railway Company (BNSF), although "doing business" in Montana when the litigation commenced, was not incorporated in Montana, nor did it maintain its principal place of business in that State. To justify the exercise of personal jurisdiction over BNSF, the Montana Supreme Court relied on § 56, which provides in relevant part:

"Under this chapter an action may be brought in a district court of the United States, in the district of the residence of the defendant, or in which the cause of action arose, or in which the defendant shall be doing business at the time of commencing such action. The jurisdiction of the courts of the United States under this chapter shall be concurrent with that of the courts of the several States."

We hold that § 56 does not address personal jurisdiction over railroads. Its first relevant sentence is a venue prescription governing proper locations for FELA suits filed in federal court. The provision's second relevant sentence, using the term "concurrent" jurisdiction, refers to subject-matter jurisdiction, not personal jurisdiction. It simply clarifies that the federal courts do not have exclusive subject-matter jurisdiction over FELA suits; state courts can hear them, too.

Montana's Supreme Court, in the alternative, relied on state law, under which personal jurisdiction could be asserted over "persons found within . . . Montana." Mont. Rule Civ. Proc. 4(b)(1) (2015). BNSF fit that bill, the court stated, because it has over 2,000 miles of railroad track and employs more than 2,000 workers in Montana. Our precedent, however, explains that the Fourteenth Amendment's Due Process Clause does not permit a State to hale an out-of-state corporation before its courts when the corporation is not "at home" in the State and the episode-in-suit occurred elsewhere. Daimler AG v. Bauman. We therefore reverse the judgment of the Montana Supreme Court.

I

In March 2011, respondent Robert Nelson, a North Dakota resident, brought a FELA suit against BNSF in a Montana state court to recover damages for knee injuries Nelson allegedly sustained while working for BNSF as a fuel-truck driver. In May 2014, respondent Kelli Tyrrell, appointed in South Dakota as the administrator of her husband Brent Tyrrell's estate, similarly sued BNSF under FELA in a Montana state court. Brent Tyrrell, his widow alleged, had developed a fatal kidney cancer from his exposure to carcinogenic chemicals while working for BNSF. Neither plaintiff alleged injuries arising from or related to work performed in Montana; indeed, neither Nelson nor Brent Tyrrell appears ever to have worked for BNSF in Montana.

BNSF is incorporated in Delaware and has its principal place of business in Texas. It operates railroad lines in 28 States. BNSF has 2,061 miles of railroad track in Montana (about 6% of its total track mileage of 32,500), employs some 2,100 workers there (less than 5% of its total work force of 43,000), generates less than 10% of its total revenue in the State, and maintains only one of its 24 automotive facilities in Montana (4%). Contending that it is not "at home" in Montana, BNSF moved to dismiss both suits for lack of personal jurisdiction. Its motion was granted in Nelson's case and denied in Tyrrell's.

After consolidating the two cases, the Montana Supreme Court held that Montana courts could exercise general personal jurisdiction over BNSF. Section 56, the court determined, authorizes state courts to exercise personal jurisdiction over railroads "doing business" in the State.

We granted certiorari to resolve whether § 56 authorizes state courts to exercise personal jurisdiction over railroads doing business in their States but not incorporated or headquartered there, and whether the Montana courts' exercise of personal jurisdiction in these cases comports with due process.

II

Nelson and Tyrrell contend that § 56's first relevant sentence confers personal jurisdiction on federal courts, and that the section's second relevant sentence extends that grant of jurisdiction to state courts. Neither contention is tenable. Section 56's first relevant sentence concerns venue; its next sentence speaks to subject-matter jurisdiction.

A

The first sentence of § 56 states that "an action may be brought in a district court of the United States," in, among other places, the district "in which the defendant shall be doing business at the time of commencing such action." Congress generally uses the expression, where suit "may be brought," to indicate the federal districts in which venue is proper. In contrast, Congress' typical mode of providing for the exercise of personal jurisdiction has been to authorize service of process.

B

The second § 56 sentence in point provides that "[t]he jurisdiction of the courts of the United States under this chapter shall be concurrent with that of the courts of the several States." Nelson and Tyrrell argue that this sentence extends to state courts the first sentence's alleged conferral of personal jurisdiction on federal courts. But, as just discussed, the first sentence concerns federal-court venue and confers no personal jurisdiction on any court.

III

Because FELA does not authorize state courts to exercise personal jurisdiction over a railroad solely on the ground that the railroad does some business in their States, the Montana courts' assertion of personal jurisdiction over BNSF here must rest on Mont. Rule Civ. Proc. 4(b)(1), the State's provision for the exercise of personal jurisdiction over "persons found" in Montana. Because neither Nelson nor Tyrrell alleges any injury from work in or related to Montana, only the propriety of general jurisdiction is at issue here.

Goodyear Dunlop Tires Operations, S.A. v. Brown clarified that "[a] court may assert general jurisdiction over foreign (sister-state or foreign-country) corporations to hear any and all claims against them when their affiliation with the State are so "continuous and systematic" as to render them essentially at home in the forum State." The "paradigm" forums in which a corporate defendant is "at home," we explained, are the corporation's place of incorporation and its principal place of business. The exercise of general jurisdiction is not limited to these forums; in an "exceptional case," a corporate defendant's operations in another forum "may be so substantial and of such a nature as to render the corporation at home in that State." Daimler, 134 S. Ct. at 7611 n. 19. . . .

BNSF, we repeat, is not incorporated in Montana and does not maintain its principal place of business there. Nor is BNSF so heavily engaged in activity in Montana "as to render [it] essentially at home" in that State. The business BNSF does in Montana is sufficient to subject the railroad to specific personal jurisdiction in that State on claims related to the business it does in Montana. But in-state business does not suffice to permit the assertion of general jurisdiction over claims like Nelson's and Tyrrell's that are unrelated to any activity occurring in Montana.

Justice SOTOMAYOR, concurring in part and dissenting in part.

I concur in the Court's conclusion that the Federal Employers' Liability Act (FELA) does not confer personal jurisdiction over railroads on state courts. I also agree that the Montana Supreme Court erred when it concluded that the nature of the claim here—a FELA claim against a railroad—answers the question whether the Due Process Clause allows the exercise of personal jurisdiction over BNSF. But my agreement with the majority ends there. I continue to disagree with the path the Court struck in Daimler AG v. Bauman, which limits general jurisdiction over a corporate defendant only to those States where it is "essentially at home." And even if the Court insists on adhering to that standard, I dissent from its decision to apply it here in the first instance rather than remanding to the Montana Supreme Court for it to conduct what should be a fact-intensive analysis under the proper legal framework. Accordingly, I join Parts I and II of the Court's opinion, but dissent from Part III and the judgment.

The Court would do well to adhere more faithfully to the direction from International Shoe Co. v. Washington, which instructed that general jurisdiction is proper when a corporation's "continuous corporate operations within a state

[are] so substantial and of such a nature as to justify suit against it on causes of action arising from dealings entirely distinct from those activities." Under International Shoe, in other words, courts were to ask whether the benefits a defendant attained in the forum State warranted the burdens associated with general personal jurisdiction."

The majority's approach grants a jurisdictional windfall to large multistate or multinational corporations that operate across many jurisdictions. Under its reasoning, it is virtually inconceivable that such corporations will ever be subject to general jurisdiction in any location other than their principal places of business or of incorporation. Foreign businesses with principal places of business outside the United States may never be subject to general jurisdiction in this country even though they have continuous and systematic contacts within the United States. What was once a holistic, nuanced contacts analysis backed by considerations of fairness and reasonableness has now effectively been replaced by the rote identification of a corporation's principal place of business or place of incorporation. The result? It is individual plaintiffs, harmed by the actions of a farflung foreign corporation, who will bear the brunt of the majority's approach and be forced to sue in distant jurisdictions with which they have no contacts or connection. . . .

The majority makes much of the fact that BNSF's contacts in Montana are only a percentage of its contacts with other jurisdictions. But International Shoe, which the majority agrees is the springboard for our modern personal jurisdiction jurisprudence, applied no comparative contacts test. There the Court analyzed whether the Delaware corporation had "by its activities in the State of Washington rendered itself amenable to proceeding" in the State. The Court evaluated whether the corporation had offices in the forum State, made contracts there, delivered goods there, or employed salesmen there. Despite acknowledging that the corporation maintained places of business in several States, the Court did not engage in a comparison between International Shoe's contacts within the State of Washington and the other States in which it operated. The Court noted that the corporation employed 11 to 13 salesmen in Washington but did not query how that number compared to the number of salesmen in other States. As well it should not have; the relative percentage of contacts is irrelevant. The focus should be on the quality and quantity of the defendant's contacts in the forum State.

The majority does even Daimler a disservice, paying only lipservice to the question the Court purported to reserve there—the possibility of an "exceptional case" in which general jurisdiction would be proper in a forum State that is neither a corporate defendant's place of incorporation nor its principal place of business. Its opinion here could be understood to limit that exception to the exact facts of Perkins v. Benguet Consol. Mining Co., 342 U.S. 437 (1952). That reading is so narrow as to read the exception out of existence entirely; certainly a defendant with significant contacts with more than one State falls outside its ambit. And so it is inevitable under its own reasoning that the majority would conclude that BNSF's contacts with Montana are insufficient to justify the exercise of personal jurisdiction here. This result is perverse. Despite having reserved the possibility of an "exceptional case" in Daimler, the majority here has rejected that possibility out of hand.

Worse, the majority reaches its conclusion only by departing from the Court's normal practice. Had it remanded to the Montana Supreme court to reevaluate the due process question under the correct legal standard, that court could have examined whether this is such an "exceptional case." Instead, with its ruling today, the Court unnecessarily sends a signal to the lower courts that the exceptional-circumstances inquiry is all form, no substance.

YOUR TAKEAWAY

Goodyear and *Daimler*'s "essentially at home" test strikes again against general jurisdiction. This notwithstanding that the defendant railroad is a *domestic* corporation with over 2,000 employees and over 2,000 miles of track *within* Montana, allowing it to reap upwards of $1.75 billion in annual revenue from the State. Justice Ginsburg's opinion for the Court discounts these figures by noting they amount to only about 6 percent of its total track mileage, less than 5 percent of its total work force, and less than 10 percent of its total revenue. Over Justice Sotomayor's objection, it would appear that proportionality analysis is here to stay, and the "exceptional case" in which general jurisdiction would be proper in a forum state that is neither a corporate defendant's place of incorporation nor its principal place of business has yet to appear.

REVIEW QUESTIONS

1. Note how easy a case this would be for assertion of specific jurisdiction if the plaintiffs had been injured in Montana.

2. Why do you think the Justices would, as Sonia Sotomayor complains, relegate "individual plaintiffs, harmed by the actions of a far-flung foreign corporation," to be "forced to sue in distant jurisdictions with which they have no contacts or connection?" Note that Sotomayor's use of the term *foreign* is applied to BNSF, a *domestic* corporation (incorporated in Delaware, PPB in Texas). No F-Cubed situation here. Would the result be the same for McDonalds and Hilton Hotels in our previous hypotheticals?

3. One critical review of *BNSF* observes:

   > *Goodyear* and *Daimler* were easy cases because they involved foreign defendants whose few forum contacts would not have sufficed for general jurisdiction under the Court's prior doctrine. But *BNSF* was not so easy because it denied jurisdiction over a domestic defendant with active operations, thousands of workers, and hundreds of millions of dollars in property in the forum state. By providing a bulletproof citation that the at-home test applies even when a defendant has substantial forum contacts, *BNSF* highlights, and will likely exacerbate, the costs of narrowing general jurisdiction: the at-home test creates tension with transient jurisdiction doctrine, confusingly draws attention to

forum shopping concerns, and undermines federal statutes by placing litigation-discouraging burdens on plaintiffs.

The Supreme Court 2016 Term, 131 Harv. L. Rev. 333, 337 (2017).

4. On the other hand, the "at home" test is a quick and efficient way to resolve threshold jurisdiction issues, and

> by making general jurisdiction available in just one or two states, the test also limits forum shopping and the cross-border effect of outlier laws. If general jurisdiction applied broadly, plaintiffs could strategically choose among numerous possible forums, and corporations doing a high volume of business in many states could be subject to the most plaintiff-friendly version of every law in the country whenever they injure someone anywhere in the world. This reality could hinder economic growth if corporations found the benefits of doing nationwide business did not outweigh these risks.

131 Harv. L. Rev. at 338.

On the forum shopping point, "the *Daimler* and *Goodyear* plaintiffs sued foreign defendants in states where the defendants did virtually no business, presumably to litigate in favorable or convenient forums," and Montana (venue of *BNSF*) was alleged to be "a haven for FELA plaintiffs. These accounts prompted the Justices [in the *BNSF* oral argument] to spend nearly four minutes engaging with the [Tyrell's] counsel about forum shopping." *Id.* at 341.

5. Justice Sotomayor continues her case against comparative contacts analysis and the "jurisdictional windfall" it brings the largest domestic and foreign corporations. Does her dissent hew closer to *International Shoe*'s conception of general jurisdiction than the Court's?

QUESTIONS TO PONDER

1. As a result of the three decisions just studied, claimants can no longer assert general jurisdiction over a nonresident corporation absent a showing that the corporation is essentially "at home" in the forum, which to date has meant incorporated or headquartered there. In conjunction with the severe limits now in place for specific jurisdiction, many plaintiffs thus face the choice of chasing defendants to their home states, foreign or domestic (with all the attendant expense and inconvenience), or simply abandoning their claims.

   As to foreign defendants, Professor Gwynne L. Skinner argues for legislative intervention, calling upon Congress to adopt laws that require all transnational entities doing substantial business in the United States to consent to general jurisdiction nationwide (remember the last paragraphs of *Pennoyer*?). *See Expanding General Personal Jurisdiction over Transnational Corporations for Federal Causes of Action*, 121 Penn St. L. Rev. 617 (2017).

Do you think a consent requirement would inhibit businesses from entering the U.S. market? Professors William Dodge and Scott Dodson offer another solution: broadening the geographic range for contacts of foreign defendants from a single state to the entire nation. *See Personal Jurisdiction and Aliens,* 116 Mich. L. Rev. 1205, 1224 (2018). This would mean essentially expanding Fed. R. Civ. P. 4(k)(2) to diversity as well as federal question cases. *See* Patrick J. Borchers, *Extending Federal Rule of Civil Procedure 4(k)(2): A Way to (Partially) Clean Up the Personal Jurisdiction Mess,* 67 Am. U. L. Rev. 412 (2017).

2. State sovereignty has been crucial to personal jurisdiction doctrine. Is it thought that because a domestic defendant's home state has plenary authority over any and all claims against it, that unless there is significant contact connecting the defendant's actions to a different state, it would be an intrusion for that state to assert personal jurisdiction?

   But how would this apply to foreign actors who do not have a home state? Does the "essentially at home" requirement give transnational corporations an unfair advantage when operating in the U.S. marketplace? Professor Skinner thinks so:

   > Allowing for personal jurisdiction over foreign corporations that conduct substantial and continuous business in the United States could actually be good for U.S. corporations, because it would create an even playing field. [F]oreign corporations not only have less exposure from lawsuits but will have to expend less and invest less money in compliance than U.S. corporations. This puts those foreign corporations that otherwise do business in the United States at a competitive edge.

   Skinner, *supra*, 121 Penn St. L. Rev. at 678.

M. CONSENT

As we have seen, consent is one of the traditional bases for the exercise of adjudicatory power. A defendant can voluntarily appear in court and thereby submit to jurisdiction. A defendant who appears and fails to assert a timely objection to personal jurisdiction thereby waives that objection—a form of involuntary consent. *See* Fed. R. Civ. P. 12(h)(1).

Pennoyer also suggested that states could require nonresidents conducting certain activities within the state to "consent" to the appointment of an agent to receive service of process for actions arising out of those activities. In the post-*Pennoyer* years, courts even resorted to the fiction of *implied* consent to justify the exercise of jurisdiction over nonresidents, as in *Hess v. Pawloski, supra,* the nonresident motorist case.

By operation of a "forum-selection clause," consent to jurisdiction can take place *before* the dispute even arises, as illustrated by the next case.

Carnival Cruise Lines, Inc. v. Shute
499 U.S. 585 (1991)

Justice BLACKMUN delivered the opinion of the Court:

In this admiralty case we primarily consider whether the United States Court of Appeals for the Ninth Circuit correctly refused to enforce a forum-selection clause contained in tickets issued by petitioner Carnival Cruise Lines, Inc., to respondents Eulala and Russel Shute.

I

The Shutes, through an Arlington, Wash., travel agent, purchased passage for a 7-day cruise on petitioner's ship, the Tropicale. Respondents paid the fare to the agent who forwarded the payment to petitioner's headquarters in Miami, Fla. Petitioner then prepared the tickets and sent them to respondents in the State of Washington. The face of each ticket, at its left-hand lower corner, contained this admonition: "SUBJECT TO CONDITIONS OF CONTRACT ON LAST PAGES IMPORTANT! PLEASE READ CONTRACT—ON LAST PAGES 1, 2, 3" App. 15.

The following appeared on "contract page 1" of each ticket:

TERMS AND CONDITIONS OF PASSAGE CONTRACT TICKET

. . . 3. (a) The acceptance of this ticket by the person or persons named hereon as passengers shall be deemed to be an acceptance and agreement by each of them of all of the terms and conditions of this Passage Contract Ticket.

. . . 8. It is agreed by and between the passenger and the Carrier that all disputes and matters whatsoever arising under, in connection with or incident to this Contract shall be litigated, if at all, in and before a Court located in the State of Florida, U.S.A., to the exclusion of the Courts of any other state or country.

The last quoted paragraph is the forum-selection clause at issue.

II

Respondents boarded the *Tropicale* in Los Angeles, Cal. The ship sailed to Puerto Vallarta, Mexico, and then returned to Los Angeles. While the ship was in international waters off the Mexican coast, respondent Eulala Shute was injured when she slipped on a deck mat during a guided tour of the ship's galley. Respondents filed suit against petitioner in the United States District Court for the Western District of Washington, claiming that Mrs. Shute's injuries had been caused by the negligence of Carnival Cruise Lines and its employees.

[Carnival Cruise Lines sought dismissal based on the forum selection clause in paragraph 8, requiring any action to be filed in Florida, its home state. Ultimately when the issue reached the Ninth Circuit Court of Appeals, it ruled that the forum clause should not be enforced because it "was not freely bargained for"; and as an "independent justification" for refusing to enforce it, there was evidence in the record to indicate that "the Shutes are physically and financially incapable of pursuing this litigation in Florida" and that the enforcement of the clause would operate to deprive them of their day in court.]

In evaluating the reasonableness of the forum clause at issue in this case, [a]s an initial matter, we do not adopt the Court of Appeals' determination that a nonnegotiated forum-selection clause in a form ticket contract is never enforceable simply because it is not the subject of bargaining. Including a reasonable forum clause in a form contract of this kind well may be permissible for several reasons: First, a cruise line has a special interest in limiting the fora in which it potentially could be subject to suit. Because a cruise ship typically carries passengers from many locales, it is not unlikely that a mishap on a cruise could subject the cruise line to litigation in several different fora. Additionally, a clause establishing ex ante the forum for dispute resolution has the salutary effect of dispelling any confusion about where suits arising from the contract must be brought and defended, sparing litigants the time and expense of pre-trial motions to determine the correct forum and conserving judicial resources that otherwise would be devoted to deciding those motions. Finally, it stands to reason that passengers who purchase tickets containing a forum clause like that at issue in this case benefit in the form of reduced fares reflecting the savings that the cruise line enjoys by limiting the fora in which it may be sued.

We also do not accept the Court of Appeals' "independent justification" for its conclusion that . . . the clause should not be enforced because "[t]here is evidence in the record to indicate that the Shutes are physically and financially incapable of pursuing this litigation in Florida." . . . The District Court made no finding regarding the physical and financial impediments to the Shutes' pursuing their case in Florida and we conclude that they have not satisfied the "heavy burden of proof" required to set aside the clause on grounds of inconvenience.

It bears emphasis that forum-selection clauses contained in form passage contracts are subject to judicial scrutiny for fundamental fairness. In this case, there is no indication that petitioner set Florida as the forum in which disputes were to be resolved as a means of discouraging cruise passengers from pursuing legitimate claims. Any suggestion of such a bad-faith motive is belied by two facts: Petitioner has its principal place of business in Florida, and many of its cruises depart from and return to Florida ports. Similarly, there is no evidence that petitioner obtained respondents' accession to the forum clause by fraud or overreaching. Finally, respondents have conceded that they were given notice of the forum provision and, therefore, presumably retained the option of rejecting the contract with impunity. In the case before us, therefore, we conclude that the Court of Appeals erred in refusing to enforce the forum-selection clause.

The judgment of the Court of Appeals is reversed. It is so ordered.

Justice STEVENS, with whom Justice MARSHALL joins, dissenting:

The Court prefaces its legal analysis with a factual statement that implies that a purchaser of a Carnival Cruise Lines passenger ticket is fully and fairly notified about the existence of the choice of forum clause in the fine print on the back of the ticket. Even if this implication were accurate, I would disagree with the Court's analysis. But, given the Court's preface, I begin my dissent by noting that only the most meticulous passenger is likely to become aware of the forum-selection provision. I have therefore appended to this opinion a facsimile of the relevant text, using the type size that actually appears in the ticket itself. A careful reader will find the forum-selection clause in the 8th of the 25 numbered paragraphs. [See Figure 7.1.]

Of course, many passengers, like the respondents in this case, will not have an opportunity to read paragraph 8 until they have actually purchased their tickets. By this point, the passengers will already have accepted the condition set forth in paragraph 16(a), which provides that "[t]he Carrier shall not be liable to make any refund to passengers in respect of . . . tickets wholly or partly not used by a passenger." Not knowing whether or not that provision is legally enforceable, I assume that the average passenger would accept the risk of having to file suit in Florida in the event of an injury, rather than canceling—without a refund— a planned vacation at the last minute. The fact that the cruise line can reduce its litigation costs, and therefore its liability insurance premiums, by forcing this choice on its passengers does not, in my opinion, suffice to render the provision reasonable.

Even if passengers received prominent notice of the forum-selection clause before they committed the cost of the cruise, I would remain persuaded that the clause was unenforceable. . . . These clauses are typically the product of disparate bargaining power between the carrier and the passenger, and they undermine the strong public interest in deterring negligent conduct. . . .

Forum-selection clauses in passenger tickets involve the intersection of two strands of traditional contract law that qualify the general rule that courts will enforce the terms of a contract as written. Pursuant to the first strand, courts traditionally have reviewed with heightened scrutiny the terms of contracts of adhesion, form contracts offered on a take-or-leave basis by a party with stronger bargaining power to a party with weaker power. Some commentators have questioned whether contracts of adhesion can justifiably be enforced at all under traditional contract theory because the adhering party generally enters into them without manifesting knowing and voluntary consent to all their terms.

The common law, recognizing that standardized form contracts account for a significant portion of all commercial agreements, has taken a less extreme position and instead subjects terms in contracts of adhesion to scrutiny for reasonableness. . . .

The stipulation in the ticket that Carnival Cruise sold to respondents certainly lessens or weakens their ability to recover for the slip and fall incident that occurred off the west coast of Mexico during the cruise that originated and terminated in Los Angeles, California. It is safe to assume that the witnesses— whether other passengers or members of the crew—can be assembled with less expense and inconvenience at a west coast forum than in a Florida court several thousand miles from the scene of the accident. . . .

I respectfully dissent.

TERMS AND CONDITIONS OF PASSAGE CONTRACT TICKET

1. (a) Whenever the word "Carrier" is used in this Contract it shall mean and include, jointly and severally, the Vessel, its owners, operators, characters and lenders. The term "Passenger" shall include, the plural where appropriate, and all persons engaging to and/or traveling under this Contract the masculine includes the feminine.

(b) The Master, Officers and Crew of the Vessel shall have the benefit of all of the terms and conditions of this contract.

2. This ticket is valid only for the person or persons named hereon as the passenger or passengers and cannot be transferred without the Carrier's consent written hereon. Passage money shall be deemed to be earned when paid and not refundable.

3. (a) The acceptance of this ticket by the person or persons named hereon as passengers shall be deemed to be an acceptance and agreement by each of them of all of the terms and conditions of this Passage Contract Ticket.

(b) The passenger admits a full understanding of the character of the Vessel and assumes all risk incident to travel and transportation and handling of passengers and cargo. The Vessel may or may not carry a ship's physician at the election of the Carrier. The fare includes full board, ordinary ship's food during the voyage, but no spirits, wine, beer or mineral waters.

4. The Carrier shall not be liable for any loss of life or personal injury or delay whatsoever wheresoever arising and howsoever caused even though the same may have been caused by the negligence or default of the Carrier or its servants or agents. No undertaking or warranty is given or shall be implied respecting the seaworthiness, fitness or condition of the Vessel. This exemption from liability shall extend to the employees, servants and agents of the Carrier and for this purpose this exemption shall be deemed to constitute a Contract entered into between the passenger and the Carrier on behalf of all persons who are or become from time to time its employees servants or agents and all such persons shall to this extent be deemed to be parties to this Contract.

5. The Carrier shall not be liable for losses of valuables unless stored in the Vessel's safety depository and then not exceeding $500 in any event.

6. If the Vessel carries a surgeon, physician, masseuse, barber, hair dresser or manicurist, it is done solely for the convenience of the passenger and any such person in dealing with the passenger is not and shall not be considered in any respect whatsoever, as the employee, servant or agent of the Carrier and the Carrier shall not be liable for any act or omission of such person or those under his orders or assisting him with respect to treatment, advice or care of any kind given to any passenger.

The surgeon, physician, masseuse, barber, hair dresser or manicurist shall be entitled to make a proper charge for any service performed with respect to a passenger and the Carrier shall not be concerned in any way whatsoever in any such arrangement.

7. The Carrier shall not be liable for any claims whatsoever of the passenger unless full particulars thereof in writing be given to the Carrier of their agents within 185 days after the passenger shall be landed from the Vessel or in the case the voyage is abandoned within 185 days thereafter. Suit to recover any claim shall not be maintainable in any event unless commenced within one year after the date of the loss, injury or death.

8. It is agreed by and between the passenger and the Carrier that all disputes and matters whatsoever arising under, in connection with or incident to this Contract shall be litigated, if at all, in and before a Court located in the State of Florida , U.S.A. to the exclusion of the Courts of any other state or country.

9. The Carrier in arranging for the service called for by all shore feature coupons or shore excursion tickets, acts only as agent for the holder thereof and assumes no responsibility and in no event shall be liable for any loss, damage, injury or delay to or of said person and/or baggage: property or effects in connection with said services, nor does Carrier guarantee the performance of any such service.

CONTRACT PAGE 1

Figure 7.1

YOUR TAKEAWAY

Carnival Cruise Lines dramatically illustrates the strategic importance of the issue of personal jurisdiction. The Ninth Circuit, in refusing to enforce the clause, had concluded that "the Shutes are physically and financially incapable of pursuing this litigation in Florida" and that the enforcement of the clause would operate to deprive them of their day in court. The Supreme Court found the evidentiary basis for this finding lacking. But what if their inability had been sufficiently established?

In an article critical of the Court's decision, Professor Linda Mullenix writes that "[a]s a practical matter, these [forum selection] clauses cause unwitting plaintiffs to forfeit legitimate legal claims due to the plaintiff's frequent inability to mount a case in a distant, inconvenient forum," and tip "the procedural balance in favor of well-heeled, savvy defendants." She accuses the Court of "tacitly encouraging highly-skilled, high-stakes forum shopping." Linda Mullenix, *Another Easy Case, Some More Bad Law:* Carnival Cruise Lines *and Contractual Personal Jurisdiction*, 27 Tex. Intl. L.J. 323 (1992). Yet these pervasive clauses remain presumptively enforceable.

REVIEW QUESTIONS

1. Would the Court have enforced a "no-liability clause" disclaiming any responsibility for injuries suffered during the cruise if one had been inserted into the passage contract? Such clauses are generally disfavored as against public policy. *See, e.g., Roberts v. T.H.E. Ins. Co.*, 367 Wis. 2d 386 (Sup. Ct. Wisc. 2016), where the Court refused to enforce a waiver releasing the operator of all potential claims that plaintiffs were required to sign prior to riding in its hot air balloon. Does the forum selection clause amount to the same thing for passengers like the Shutes who lack the wherewithal to litigate in the distant forum?

2. Should there be different rules regarding enforcement of these clauses for consumers and commercial actors? For plaintiffs and defendants?

3. Justice Blackmun asserts that "forum-selection clauses contained in form passage contracts are subject to judicial scrutiny for fundamental fairness." How strict is the Court's scrutiny here? What would "a bad-faith motive" look like?

4. Under what circumstances would a court refuse to enforce a forum selection clause? In *Walker v. Carnival Cruise Lines*, 107 F. Supp. 2d 1135 (N.D. Cal. 2000), plaintiffs were severely disabled passengers suing for violations of the Americans with Disabilities Act. The court declined to hold the plaintiffs to the forum selection clause in their ticket requiring suit in Florida because "plaintiffs' physical disabilities and economic constraints are so severe that, in combination, they would preclude plaintiffs

from having their day in court and, second, the fact that plaintiffs are seeking to vindicate important civil rights." 107 F. Supp. 2d at 1138.

Casavant v. Norwegian Cruise Line, Ltd., 63 Mass. App. 785 (2005), *cert. denied*, 546 U.S. 1173 (2006), similarly declined to enforce a forum selection clause because the cruise passengers were not afforded a reasonable time to reject the contract without incurring unfair penalties. The plaintiffs were scheduled to depart Boston on September 16, 2001, but in the aftermath of the terrorist attacks days before, they sought to reschedule. The cruise line refused to refund their money and the plaintiffs brought suit in the Massachusetts Superior Court, which dismissed based on the forum selection clause requiring that all litigation be filed in Florida. The Appeals Court reversed, noting that the contract had not been sent to the Casavants until they had paid in full, and only two weeks before the sail date. "Because the manner and means of the delivery of the terms of the contract for passage did not fairly allow the Casavants the option of rejecting with impunity, the Florida-dictated forum selection clause is not enforceable." 63 Mass. App. at 788-789. The plaintiffs went on to prevail in their action at trial and on appeal. *Casavant v. Norwegian Cruise Line Ltd.*, 460 Mass. 500 (2011).

In the typical personal injury case, however, forum selection clauses have been enforced against cruise passengers even where they require suit in a foreign country. *See, e.g., Effron v. Sun Line Cruises, Inc.*, 67 F.3d 7 (2d Cir. 1995) (clause requiring suit in Athens, Greece, enforced against Florida resident in case arising out of South American cruise).

5. What if the forum selection clause appears, not in the contract, but in the invoice sent to the buyer along with the shipment? The federal court in Massachusetts refused to enforce one against a commercial buyer. *See Duro Textiles, LLC v. Sunbelt Corp.*, 12 F. Supp. 3d 221 (D. Mass. 2014):

> Duro's principal place of business is in Fall River, Massachusetts, and Sunbelt's principal place of business is in Rock Hill, South Carolina. The forum selection clause in question would require Duro to litigate any disputes in Sunbelt's home state, in a forum far from Duro's own principal place of business and state of incorporation. Enforcement of the forum selection clause would entail "[s]ubtle differences in courts, jurors and law and considerations of litigation expense that most merchants would consider important." The court, therefore, finds that Sunbelt's forum selection clause is a material alteration to the contract. Consequently, this provision is not part of the contract between the parties.

6. Congress overruled *Carnival Cruise Lines* by amending an admiralty statute in 1992 to provide that a vessel passenger leaving from or returning to a U.S. port has a statutory right to bring an action for personal injury in *any* court of competent jurisdiction, and that the right could not be limited by a forum selection clause in a passenger ticket. Subsequent changes to the statutory language, however, appear to have restored the *Carnival Cruise Lines* result. *See Smith v. Doe*, 991 F. Supp. 781 (E.D. La. 1998) (and citations). For a discussion of the unusual legislative route

followed here, *see* Michael F. Sturley, *Congressional Action "Overruling" the Supreme Court*, 24 J. Mar. L. & Com. 399 (1993); *note Dark of the Night Legislation Takes Aim at Forum Selection Clauses: Statutory Revision to* Carnival Cruise Lines, Inc. v. Shute, 6 U.S.F. Mar. L.J. 259 (1993).

7. Does it make a difference when the forum selection clause forces a consumer to *defend* in a distant forum? What if Carnival Cruise Lines had sued the Shutes in Florida because the check they used to pay for the cruise was returned unpaid? Look back at clause 8 of the contract. Consider the following article that appeared in the *Massachusetts Lawyers Weekly*, April 14, 2003:

> **Forum Selection Clause Upheld**
>
> The Appellate Division of the District Court recently reinstated three collection claims brought by Leasecomm Corp. that had previously been dismissed for lack of personal jurisdiction. The Appellate Division opinions are the latest in a series of decisions upholding the forum selection clause used by Leasecomm in its contracts, which requires that all legal disputes be settled in Massachusetts.
>
> Leasecomm, an out-of-state financing company that lends money to small business owners, has come under fire for bringing thousands of claims in Massachusetts every year even though most of the claims are against non-Massachusetts defendants. The company receives thousands of default judgments each year as many of the out-of-state defendants cannot afford to travel to Massachusetts for their hearings.
>
> The out-of-state defendants in each of the recent cases had argued that Massachusetts did not have any personal jurisdiction over them, or alternatively, that Massachusetts was forum non conveniens. While the District Court judges agreed in each case and granted the defendants' motions to dismiss, the Appellate Division panel reversed their decisions and upheld the forum selection clause in the Leasecomm contracts.
>
> "A forum selection clause will be enforced by Massachusetts courts 'if it is fair and reasonable to do so,'" said Judge Brian R. Merrick, writing the majority opinion in *Leasecomm Corp. v. Crawford*. "We emphasize that economic hardship or geographical inconvenience are considered to have been contemplated by the parties when they entered into the contract with a forum selection clause and are not generally a reason to disregard a forum selection clause."
>
> Similarly, the majority opinion rejected the challenges based on forum non conveniens.
>
> One Appellate Division judge dissented, however, and said that the number of cases brought and the number of default judgments received by Leasecomm pointed to some unfairness. "Undoubtedly, there exists a risk in the extension of credit," said Judge Mark S. Coven. "But where a party's extension of credit results in the breach rate admitted herein, a judicial system cannot narrowly limit its focus by proceeding on a case-by-case basis, thereby overlooking the larger picture, the larger problem and the real issues of fairness and reasonableness." Coven added: "It is a perversion to say that the adjudication by default of nearly [55,000] cases

through the use of a forum selection clause somehow measures up to the spirit and substance of fairness and reasonableness envisioned by the United States Supreme Court and our Supreme Judicial Court."

8. The following has appeared on the back of the monthly telephone bill from Sprint Communications: "Pursuant to K.S.A. 60-308(b)(11), as a business customer, you may be subject to jurisdiction in Kansas for any dispute relating to your telephone service with Sprint. This is because you have arranged for or continued to receive phone service managed, operated or monitored in the State of Kansas." Is this a forum selection clause?

9. What about "click-wrap" and "browse-wrap" forum selection clauses, common when an Internet user clicks the "I agree" button? *See generally* Greg Lastowka, *Virtual Justice: The New Laws of Online Worlds* 92-96 (2010). The following is typical:

END USER LICENSE AGREEMENT
PLEASE READ THIS AGREEMENT CAREFULLY. BY CLICKING THE "I AGREE" BUTTON AT THE TOP OF THIS PAGE, YOU AGREE TO BE BOUND BY THE TERMS AND CONDITIONS OF THIS AGREEMENT. THIS AGREEMENT IS ENFORCEABLE LIKE ANY WRITTEN NEGOTIATED AGREEMENT SIGNED BY YOU.

* * *

11. Governing Law. This Agreement will be governed by and construed in accordance with the substantive laws in force in the State of [X], and any disputes shall be subject to the exclusive jurisdiction of the courts of the State of [X].

"Click-wrap" forum selection clauses have met with mixed results in the courts. More often than not, the clauses are enforced. *See, e.g., Bagg v. HighBeam Research, Inc.,* 862 F. Supp. 2d 41 (D. Mass. 2012) (upholding clause); *Evans v. Linden Research, Inc.,* 763 F. Supp. 2d 735 (E.D. Pa. 2011). *But see Specht v. Netscape Communications Corp.,* 306 F.3d 17 (2d Cir. 2002) (plaintiffs' downloading of software did not constitute acceptance of defendants' license terms).

10. For the appropriate procedural means of enforcing a forum selection clause, *see Atlantic Marine Construction Co., Inc.,* 571 U.S. 49 (2013), holding that defendant should file a motion to transfer to the particular designated federal district pursuant to 28 U.S.C. § 1404, or if a state or foreign forum is designated, pursuant to the doctrine of *forum non conveniens* (discussed in Part O, below). Only under extraordinary circumstances

unrelated to the convenience of the parties, which the parties are thought to have already bargained for, should the motion be denied.

For examples of enforcement, *see Detroit Coke Corp. v. NKK Chemical USA, Inc.*, 794 F. Supp. 214 (E.D. Mich. 1992) (granting defendants' motion to transfer pursuant to a forum selection clause in the purchase agreement); *Flake v. Medline Industries, Inc.*, 882 F. Supp. 947 (E.D. Cal. 1995) (age discrimination case transferred pursuant to a forum selection clause in the employment contract).

QUESTIONS TO PONDER

1. Why would the highest court in the land "sell out" consumers in these situations with such apparent indifference? Did Justice Blackmun really believe Carnival would pass its savings in litigation costs along to its passengers? Is *Carnival Cruise Lines* simply a reflection of pro-business bias, or a preference for private ordering? Or might it reflect a desire (as in *Burnham*) to preserve some basis for adjudicatory authority that is free from the complexity of due process analysis?

   One commentator complains that "by neglecting contract law dealing with adhesion and ignoring principles of due process, the *Shute* Court abandoned the consumer's rights in an age of form contracts and in a legal system that prefers the efficiency of justice rather than its equity." John McKinley Kirby, *Consumer's Right to Sue at Home Jeopardized Through Forum Selection Clause in* Carnival Cruise Lines v. Shute, 70 N.C. L. Rev. 888 (1992). The author fears that

   > a patron who slips and falls in a movie theater may be required to litigate her claim, if at all, in the home forum of the corporation due to a clause on her ticket. A consumer injured by a defective automobile could be limited to filing suit in the remote forum of the manufacturer due to a forum clause on the sales form, while the dealer that sold the automobile might be protected from suit in the purchaser's forum by notice on the doors that entering the premises signifies acceptance of a specified forum for all claims. The gains that *International Shoe* and its progeny made toward allowing plaintiffs to sue in their home jurisdictions will be largely recaptured by corporations in a frenzy to lower legal costs.

   Id. at 914-915.

2. Contractual provisions can not only dictate the forum for any lawsuit, but also take such suits out of the court system altogether by mandating arbitration. As you have seen in Chapter 6, agreements to arbitrate in consumer and employment contracts have largely been upheld by the Supreme Court. The matter remains quite controversial. *See, e.g., Note, Overcoming the Achilles' Heel of Consumer Protection: Limiting Mandatory Arbitration Clauses in Consumer Contracts*, 46 Hofstra L. Rev. 363 (2017).

N. NOTICE

You will recall that within the *Pennoyer* framework, dominated by the concept of "presence," notice of the lawsuit occurred simultaneously with the act that gave rise to jurisdiction, namely personal service or attachment of property within the state. ("Substituted service by publication" was held to be inadequate, you will recall, absent attachment of Neff's land.) As the basis for adjudicatory power became divorced from service, notifying a defendant had to be accomplished through other means. In *Hess v. Pawloski*, for example, the Massachusetts nonresident motorist statute required that notice be sent by registered mail to the defendant's residence in his home state. The following case defined the constitutional parameters of adequate notice.

Mullane v. Central Hanover Bank & Trust Co.
339 U.S. 306 (1950)

Justice JACKSON delivered the opinion of the Court:

This controversy questions the constitutional sufficiency of notice to beneficiaries on judicial settlement of accounts by the trustee of a common trust fund established under the New York Banking Law, Consol. Laws, c. 2. The New York Court of Appeals considered and overruled objections that the statutory notice contravenes requirements of the Fourteenth Amendment and that by allowance of the account beneficiaries were deprived of property without due process of law. The case is here on appeal.

New York law permits the pooling of small trust estates into one fund for investment administration. The income, capital gains, losses and expenses of the collective trust are shared by the constituent trusts in proportion to their contribution. By this plan, diversification of risk and economy of management can be extended to those whose capital standing alone would not obtain such advantage.

Statutory authorization for the establishment of such common trust funds is provided in the New York Banking Law. Under this Act a trust company may, with approval of the State Banking Board, establish a common fund and, within prescribed limits, invest therein the assets of an unlimited number of estates, trusts or other funds of which it is trustee. . . . Provisions are made for accountings twelve to fifteen months after the establishment of a fund and triennially thereafter. The decree in each such judicial settlement of accounts is made binding and conclusive as to any matter set forth in the account upon everyone having any interest in the common fund or in any participating estate, trust or fund.

In January, 1946, Central Hanover Bank and Trust Company established a common trust fund in accordance with these provisions, and in March, 1947, it petitioned the Surrogate's Court for settlement of its first account as common trustee. During the accounting period a total of 113 trusts, approximately half inter vivos and half testamentary, participated in the common trust fund, the gross capital of which was nearly three million dollars. The record does not show the number or residence of the beneficiaries, but they were many and it is clear that some of them were not residents of the State of New York.

The only notice given beneficiaries of this specific application was by publication in a local newspaper. Thus the only notice required, and the only one given, was by newspaper publication setting forth merely the name and address of the trust company, the name and the date of establishment of the common trust fund, and a list of all participating estates, trusts or funds.

At the time the first investment in the common fund was made on behalf of each participating estate, however, the trust company, pursuant to the requirements of the Banking Law, had notified by mail each person of full age and sound mind whose name and address was then known to it and who was "entitled to share in the income therefrom."

Upon the filing of the petition for the settlement of accounts, appellant was, by order of the court pursuant to the Banking Law, appointed special guardian and attorney for all persons known or unknown not otherwise appearing who had or might thereafter have any interest in the income of the common trust fund. Appellant appeared specially, objecting that notice and the statutory provisions for notice to beneficiaries were inadequate to afford due process under the Fourteenth Amendment, and therefore that the court was without jurisdiction to render a final and binding decree. Appellant's objections were entertained and overruled, the Surrogate holding that the notice required and given was sufficient. A final decree accepting the accounts has been entered, affirmed by the Appellate Division of the Supreme Court.

The effect of this decree, as held below, is to settle "all questions respecting the management of the common fund." We understand that every right which beneficiaries would otherwise have against the trust company for improper management of the common trust fund during the period covered by the accounting is sealed and wholly terminated by the decree.

We are met at the outset with a challenge to the power of the State—the right of its courts to adjudicate at all as against those beneficiaries who reside without the State of New York. It is contended that the proceeding is one *in personam* in that the decree affects neither title to nor possession of any *res*, but adjudges only personal rights of the beneficiaries to surcharge their trustee for negligence or breach of trust. Accordingly, it is said, under the strict doctrine of *Pennoyer v. Neff*, the Surrogate is without jurisdiction as to nonresidents upon whom personal service of process was not made.

We think that the requirements of the Fourteenth Amendment to the Federal Constitution do not depend upon a classification for which the standards are so elusive and confused generally and which, being primarily for state courts to define, may and do vary from state to state. We do not rest the power of the State to resort to constructive service in this proceeding upon how its courts or this Court may regard this historic antithesis. It is sufficient to observe that, whatever the technical definition of its chosen procedure, the interest of each state in providing means to close trusts that exist by the grace of its laws and are administered under the supervision of its courts is so insistent and rooted in custom as to establish beyond doubt the right of its courts to determine the interests of all claimants, resident or nonresident, provided its procedure accords full opportunity to appear and be heard.

Quite different from the question of a state's power [to hear the case] is that of the opportunity it must give beneficiaries to contest. Many controversies have raged about the cryptic and abstract words of the Due Process Clause but there can be no doubt that at a minimum they require that deprivation of life, liberty or property by adjudication be preceded by notice and opportunity for hearing appropriate to the nature of the case.

This proceeding does or may deprive beneficiaries of property. It may cut off their rights to have the trustee answer for negligent or illegal impairments of their interests. Certainly the proceeding is one in which they may be deprived of property rights and hence notice and hearing must measure up to the standards of due process.

Personal service of written notice within the jurisdiction is the classic form of notice always adequate in any type of proceeding. But the vital interest of the State in bringing any issues as to its fiduciaries to a final settlement can be served only if interests or claims of individuals who are outside of the State can somehow be determined. A construction of the Due Process Clause which would place impossible or impractical obstacles in the way could not be justified.

Against this interest of the State we must balance the individual interest sought to be protected by the Fourteenth Amendment. This is defined by our holding that "the fundamental requisite of due process of law is the opportunity to be heard." This right to be heard has little reality or worth unless one is informed that the matter is pending and can choose for himself whether to appear or default, acquiesce or contest.

The Court has not committed itself to any formula achieving a balance between these interests in a particular proceeding or determining when constructive notice may be utilized or what test it must meet. Personal service has not in all circumstances been regarded as indispensable to the process due to residents, and it has more often been held unnecessary as to nonresidents. [A] few general principles stand out in the books.

An elementary and fundamental requirement of due process in any proceeding which is to be accorded finality is notice reasonably calculated, under all the circumstances, to apprise interested parties of the pendency of the action and afford them an opportunity to present their objections. The notice must be of such nature as reasonably to convey the required information, and it must afford a reasonable time for those interested to make their appearance. But if with due regard for the practicalities and peculiarities of the case these conditions are reasonably met the constitutional requirements are satisfied.

But when notice is a person's due, process which is a mere gesture is not due process. The means employed must be such as one desirous of actually informing the absentee might reasonably adopt to accomplish it. The reasonableness and hence the constitutional validity of any chosen method may be defended on the ground that it is in itself reasonably certain to inform those affected, or, where conditions do not reasonably permit such notice, that the form chosen is not substantially less likely to bring home notice than other of the feasible and customary substitutes.

It would be idle to pretend that publication alone, as prescribed here, is a reliable means of acquainting interested parties of the fact that their rights are before the courts. It is not an accident that the greater number of cases reaching this Court on the question of adequacy of notice have been concerned with actions founded on process constructively served through local newspapers. Chance alone brings to the attention of even a local resident an advertisement in small type inserted in the back pages of a newspaper, and if he makes his home outside the area of the newspaper's normal circulation the odds that the information will never reach him are large indeed. The chance of actual notice is further reduced when as here the notice required does not even name those whose attention it is supposed to attract, and does not inform acquaintances who might call it to attention. In weighing its sufficiency on the basis of equivalence with actual notice we are unable to regard this as more than a feint.

Nor is publication here reinforced by steps likely to attract the parties' attention to the proceeding. It is true that publication traditionally has been acceptable as notification supplemental to other action which in itself may reasonably be expected to convey a warning. The ways of an owner with tangible property are such that he usually arranges means to learn of any direct attack upon his possessory or proprietary rights. Hence, [seizure] of a ship, attachment of a chattel or entry upon real estate in the name of law may reasonably be expected to come promptly to the owner's attention. When the state within which the owner has located such property seizes it for some reason, publication or posting affords an additional measure of notification. A state may indulge the assumption that one who has left tangible property in the state either has abandoned it, in which case proceedings against it deprive him of nothing, or that he has left some caretaker under a duty to let him know that it is being jeopardized.

This Court has not hesitated to approve of resort to publication as a customary substitute in another class of cases where it is not reasonably possible or practicable to give more adequate warning. Thus it has been recognized that, in the case of persons missing or unknown, employment of an indirect and even a probably futile means of notification is all that the situation permits and creates no constitutional bar to a final decree foreclosing their rights.

Those beneficiaries represented by appellant whose interests or whereabouts could not with due diligence be ascertained come clearly within this category. As to them the statutory notice is sufficient. However great the odds that publication will never reach the eyes of such unknown parties, it is not in the typical case much more likely to fail than any of the choices open to legislators endeavoring to prescribe the best notice practicable.

Accordingly we overrule appellant's constitutional objections to published notice insofar as they are urged on behalf of any beneficiaries whose interests or addresses are unknown to the trustee.

As to known present beneficiaries of known place of residence, however, notice by publication stands on a different footing. Exceptions in the name of necessity do not sweep away the rule that within the limits of practicability notice must be such as is reasonably calculated to reach interested parties. Where the names and post office addresses of those affected by a proceeding are at hand, the reasons disappear for resort to means less likely than the mails to apprise them of its pendency. The trustee has on its books the names and addresses of the income beneficiaries represented by appellant, and we find no tenable ground for dispensing with a serious effort to inform them personally of the accounting, at least by ordinary mail to the record addresses.

This type of trust presupposes a large number of small interests. The individual interest does not stand alone but is identical with that of a class. The rights of each in the integrity of the fund and the fidelity of the trustee are shared by many other beneficiaries. Therefore notice reasonably certain to reach most of those interested in objecting is likely to safeguard the interests of all, since any objections sustained would inure to the benefit of all.

The statutory notice to known beneficiaries is inadequate, not because in fact it fails to reach everyone, but because under the circumstances it is not reasonably calculated to reach those who could easily be informed by other means at hand.

Certainly it is instructive, in determining the reasonableness of the impersonal broadcast notification here used, to ask whether it would satisfy a prudent man of business, counting his pennies but finding it in his interest to convey information to many persons whose names and addresses are in his files. We are not satisfied that it would.

We hold the notice of judicial settlement of accounts required by the New York Banking Law is incompatible with the requirements of the Fourteenth Amendment as a basis for adjudication depriving known persons whose whereabouts are also known of substantial property rights. Accordingly the judgment is reversed and the cause remanded for further proceedings not inconsistent with this opinion.

YOUR TAKEAWAY

You'll recall that the cornerstones of due process are notice and an opportunity to be heard. The trust beneficiaries in *Mullane* were foreclosed from complaining about the management of their funds once the periodic accountings were settled, but their participation in the process was of course dependent on their knowing it was taking place. Justice Jackson (who had recently returned to the

Court after his stint as chief U.S. prosecutor at the Nuremberg Trials following World War II) defines the constitutional standard as "notice reasonably calculated, under all the circumstances (and with due regard for the practicalities and peculiarities of the case), to apprise interested parties of the pendency of the action and afford them an opportunity to present their objections." While such elasticity could potentially lead to endless litigation on the adequacy of notice in particular cases, the definition had to be fashioned to fit a wide variety of situations, such as *Mullane* itself, with interested parties whose identities were both known and unknown, as were their addresses.

REVIEW QUESTIONS

1. Note how Justice Jackson anticipates *Shaffer v. Heitner*'s later repudiation of the distinction between in rem and in personam power for purposes of due process analysis.

2. What is the basis for jurisdiction over the nonresident beneficiaries? If neither in rem nor in personam, what type of jurisdiction is this? Can you see why it has been dubbed "jurisdiction by necessity"? *See* George B. Fraser, Jr., *Jurisdiction by Necessity—An Analysis of the* Mullane *Case*, 100 U. Pa. L. Rev. 305 (1951).

3. Note how pragmatic Justice Jackson is in distinguishing between beneficiaries whose interests or addresses are unknown, and those for whom the bank has addresses. Each is entitled to the "best notice practicable" under the circumstances. That means the latter group must receive mail notice; the former have to settle for the "chance notice" of publication in a local newspaper. Neither gets personal in-hand service, the cost of which would significantly exhaust the trust funds.

4. Decisions since *Mullane* have set notice by U.S. mail as the constitutional minimum for defendants whose addresses can be ascertained by reasonably diligent efforts. *See Walker v. City of Hutchinson*, 352 U.S. 112 (1956) (where landowner's name was known to City, newspaper publication was inadequate notice of condemnation proceedings); *Greene v. Lindsey*, 456 U.S. 444 (1982) (posting notices of eviction proceedings on doors of public housing tenants violated due process where evidence indicated notices were often removed); *Mennonite Board of Missions v. Adams*, 462 U.S. 791 (1983) (notice by publication and posting was inadequate to notify a mortgagee of a pending tax sale).

5. Where defendant's whereabouts are unknown, publication notice may be permitted. Plaintiffs in *Mwani v. Osama bin Laden*, 417 F.3d 1 (D.C. Cir. 2005), victims of the 1998 bombing of the American embassy in Kenya, were granted leave by the district court to serve fugitive bin Laden by publication in three newspapers, including the *International Herald Tribune* and *Al-Quds Al-Arabi*, an Arabic publication in which bin Laden had himself published at least one *fatwa* threatening the United States.

6. Where defendant deliberately evades service of process, and his present location is unknown, the court may order service by publication. *See, e.g., American Indoor Football Assn., Inc. v. Lockwood*, 267 F.R.D. 663 (M.D. Ala. 2010); *BP Products v. Dagra*, 236 F.R.D. 270 (E.D. Va. 2006). *Compare Grove v. Guilfoyle*, 222 F.R.D. 255 (E.D. Pa. 2004) (plaintiff failed to exhaust all reasonable methods to locate and serve defendant). *See generally* Jennifer Lee Case, *Extra! Read All About It: Why Notice by Newspaper Publication Fails to Meet* Mullane'*s Desire-to-Inform Standard and How Modern Technology Provides a Viable Alternative*, 45 Ga. L. Rev. 1095 (2011).

7. In *Dusenbery v. United States*, 534 U.S. 161 (2002), the Court emphasized that due process requires a reasonably calculated *attempt* to provide actual notice, *not actual notice itself*. The Court concluded that certified mail addressed to Dusenbery at the prison where he was incarcerated on federal drug charges was adequate notice of a procedure to forfeit the $22,000 in cash found at the time of his arrest, even though the authorities could not document that he had actually received the notice.

   The means employed, *Mullane* teaches, "must be such as one desirous of actually informing the absentee might reasonably adopt to accomplish it." So when certified mail notice of an upcoming tax sale was returned marked "unclaimed," the state was constitutionally required to take additional practicable steps, such as resending the notice by regular mail, which requires no signature at time of delivery. *Jones v. Flowers*, 547 U.S. 220 (2006). "We do not think that a person who actually desired to inform a real property owner of an impending tax sale of a house he owns would do nothing when a certified letter sent to the owner is returned unclaimed."

Note on Fed. R. Civ. P. 4. Service of the summons to appear in court, together with a copy of the complaint, is the responsibility of the plaintiff. Fed. R. Civ. P. 4(c)(1). The provisions for service have been liberalized by amendments over the years designed to facilitate the initiation of litigation and reduce costs. Service can be effected by "any person who is at least 18 years old and not a party," Fed. R. Civ. P. 4(c)(2), and process can be left at the defendant's "dwelling or usual place of abode with someone of suitable age and discretion who resides there." Fed. R. Civ. P. 4(e)(2)(B). In the alternative, state rules for process may be followed. Fed. R. Civ. P. 4(e)(1).

Most significantly, service by mail has been incorporated and expanded through provisions providing for waiver of service. *See* Fed. R. Civ. P. 4(d). The plaintiff simply mails the complaint and request for waiver to defendant, who may sign and return it, thus accomplishing notice.

The waiver provisions are designed to enforce the defendant's "duty to avoid unnecessary expenses of serving the summons." Fed. R. Civ. P. 4(d)(1). What is the incentive for defendant to sign and return the waiver of service? Look at Fed. R. Civ. P. 4(d)(3). What is the penalty for not waiving? Fed. R. Civ. P. 4(d)(2). What is meant by "without good cause" in this provision? *See* Advisory Committee Note to the 1993 Amendment.

Note as well the provisions for serving individuals in foreign countries, Fed. R. Civ. P. 4(f) (incorporating the Hague Convention on Service Abroad); for corporations, Fed. R. Civ. P. 4(h); and for the federal government and its officials, Fed. R. Civ. P. 4(i). Where a plaintiff is suing a foreign state, may the plaintiff simply serve notice on the foreign state's embassy within the United States? In *Republic of Sudan v. Harrison*, 139 S. Ct. 1048 (2019), an action by Navy servicemembers seeking recovery for injuries sustained in a terrorist attack, the Supreme Court answered no, holding that serving notice on a foreign state requires mailing the service directly to the appropriate minister's office within the foreign state. Allowing a plaintiff to serve process on a foreign state's embassy within the United States would, the Court observed, lead to an "odd state of affairs" in which it would be easier to serve process on a foreign state than to serve a person within that foreign state.

For the emerging use of e-mail service of process, *see JBR, Inc. v. Café Don Paco, Inc.*, 2013 WL 1891386, at *1 (N.D. Cal. May 6, 2003) (reviewing case law and allowing service by e-mail); *First Time Videos, LLC v. FTV Programmgesellschaft MHB*, 2015 WL 5474650 (D. Nev. Sept. 16, 2015) (denying permission to serve by e-mail service because of uncertainty about whether e-mail address was current and valid). *See also* William Wagner and Joshua R. Castillo, *Friending Due Process: Facebook as a Fair Method of Alternative Service*, 19 Widener L. Rev. 259 (2013).

O. VENUE AND *FORUM NON CONVENIENS*

Beyond the constraints of personal jurisdiction, venue requirements operate as a further geographical limitation on the plaintiff's choice of court. Venue serves as an administrative funnel to direct cases to those locales, within the states that have jurisdiction, that have a connection to either the parties or the events that gave rise to the litigation. State venue rules identify the counties in which an action may be brought,* while federal venue provisions identify particular federal judicial districts (e.g., Southern District of New York, Northern District of Michigan).

28 U.S.C. § 1391, the general federal venue statute, provides for both party-based and claim-based venue. Venue is proper in either (1) "a judicial district in which any defendant resides, if all defendants are residents of the state in which the district is located" [note that a corporate defendant is deemed to reside in any district where it is "subject to the court's personal jurisdiction with respect to the civil action in question," § 1391(c)(2)], or (2) "a judicial district in which a substantial part of the events or omissions giving rise to the claim occurred, or a substantial part of property that is the subject of the action is situated." (For a

---

* The Massachusetts venue statute applicable in *Carpenter v. Dee*, for example, provides generally that a civil action shall be brought in the county where any resident party lives or has a usual place of business. Mass. Gen. Laws ch. 223, § 1. For other state venue statutes, see the Federal Rules Supplement to this book.

generous interpretation of this latter provision, *see Uffner v. La Reunion Francaise, S.A.,* 244 F.3d 38 (1st Cir. 2001).)

Under the so-called fallback provision, which is triggered only if neither the party-based nor claim-based provisions identify an appropriate district (as where, for example, the defendants are from different states and the events giving rise to the claim occurred in a foreign country), the action may be brought in any judicial district "in which any defendant is subject to the court's personal jurisdiction with respect to such action."

The federal venue provisions apply to the original parties to the action, and are not affected by third parties added by impleader or otherwise. *See* Wright & Miller, *Federal Practice and Procedure* § 3808 (4th ed. 2013).

Like personal jurisdiction, an objection to venue must be raised in a timely manner or it is waived. Fed. R. Civ. P. 12(h)(1). But unlike personal jurisdiction, proper venue is *not* a constitutional requirement for a valid judgment, and thus cannot be raised by way of collateral attack.

If a case is filed in a district in which venue does not properly lie, the court may, as an alternative to dismissal pursuant to Fed. R. Civ. P. 12(b)(3), transfer the case "in the interest of justice" to a district "in which it could have been brought," i.e., in which the requirements of jurisdiction and venue are met. *See* 28 U.S.C. § 1406. A second transfer provision applies where venue is proper, but the district court determines that "[f]or the convenience of the parties and witnesses, in the interest of justice," the case should be heard in another federal district "where it might have been brought" or "any district or division to which all parties have consented." 28 U.S.C. § 1404. This provision codifies, but does not displace, the common law doctrine of *forum non conveniens,* discussed in the next case.

Piper Aircraft Co. v. Reyno
454 U.S. 235 (1981)

Justice MARSHALL delivered the opinion of the Court:

These cases arise out of an air crash that took place in Scotland. Respondent, acting as representative of the estates of several Scottish citizens killed in the accident, brought wrongful-death actions against petitioners that were ultimately transferred to the United States District Court for the Middle District of Pennsylvania. Petitioners moved to dismiss on the ground of *forum non conveniens.* After noting that an alternative forum existed in Scotland, the District Court granted their motions. The United States Court of Appeals for the Third Circuit reversed. The Court of Appeals based its decision, at least in part, on the ground that dismissal is automatically barred where the law of the alternative forum is less favorable to the plaintiff than the law of the forum chosen by the plaintiff. Because we conclude that the possibility of an unfavorable change in law should not, by itself, bar dismissal, and because we conclude that the District Court did not otherwise abuse its discretion, we reverse.

I

A

In July 1976, a small commercial aircraft crashed in the Scottish highlands during the course of a charter flight from Blackpool to Perth. The pilot and five passengers were killed instantly. The decedents were all Scottish subjects and residents, as are their heirs and next of kin. There were no eyewitnesses to the accident. At the time of the crash the plane was subject to Scottish air traffic control.

The aircraft, a twin-engine Piper Aztec, was manufactured in Pennsylvania by petitioner Piper Aircraft Co. (Piper). The propellers were manufactured in Ohio by petitioner Hartzell Propeller, Inc. (Hartzell). At the time of the crash the aircraft was registered in Great Britain and was owned and maintained by Air Navigation and Trading Co., Ltd. (Air Navigation). It was operated by McDonald Aviation, Ltd. (McDonald), a Scottish air taxi service. Both Air Navigation and McDonald were organized in the United Kingdom. The wreckage of the plane is now in a hangar in Farnborough, England.

The British Department of Trade investigated the accident shortly after it occurred. A preliminary report found that the plane crashed after developing a spin, and suggested that mechanical failure in the plane or the propeller was responsible. At Hartzell's request, this report was reviewed by a three-member Review Board, which held a 9-day adversary hearing attended by all interested parties. The Review Board found no evidence of defective equipment and indicated that pilot error may have contributed to the accident. The pilot, who had obtained his commercial pilot's license only three months earlier, was flying over high ground at an altitude considerably lower than the minimum height required by his company's operations manual.

In July 1977, a California probate court appointed respondent Gaynell Reyno administratrix of the estates of the five passengers. Reyno is not related to and does not know any of the decedents or their survivors; she was a legal secretary to the attorney who filed this lawsuit. Several days after her appointment, Reyno commenced separate wrongful-death actions against Piper and Hartzell in the Superior Court of California, claiming negligence and strict liability. Air Navigation, McDonald, and the estate of the pilot are not parties to this litigation. The survivors of the five passengers whose estates are represented by Reyno filed a separate action in the United Kingdom against Air Navigation, McDonald, and the pilot's estate. Reyno candidly admits that the action against Piper and Hartzell was filed in the United States because its laws regarding liability, capacity to sue, and damages are more favorable to her position than are those of Scotland. Scottish law does not recognize strict liability in tort.

Moreover, it permits wrongful-death actions only when brought by a decedent's relatives. The relatives may sue only for "loss of support and society."

On petitioners' motion, the suit was removed to the United States District Court for the Central District of California. Piper then moved for transfer to the United States District Court for the Middle District of Pennsylvania, pursuant to 28 U.S.C. § 1404(a).[4] Hartzell moved to dismiss for lack of personal jurisdiction, or in the alternative, to transfer.[5] In December 1977, the District Court quashed service on Hartzell and transferred the case to the Middle District of Pennsylvania. Respondent then properly served process on Hartzell.

B

In May 1978, after the suit had been transferred, both Hartzell and Piper moved to dismiss the action on the ground of *forum non conveniens*. The District Court granted these motions in October 1979. It relied on the balancing test set forth by this Court in *Gulf Oil Corp. v. Gilbert*, 330 U.S. 501 (1947), and its companion case, *Koster v. Lumbermen's, Mut. Cas. Co.*, 330 U.S. 518 (1947). In those decisions, the Court stated that a plaintiff's choice of forum should rarely be disturbed. However, when an alternative forum has jurisdiction to hear the case, and when trial in the chosen forum would "establish . . . oppressiveness and vexation to a defendant . . . out of all proportion to plaintiff's convenience," or when the "chosen forum [is] inappropriate because of considerations affecting the court's own administrative and legal problems," the court may, in the exercise of its sound discretion, dismiss the case. To guide trial court discretion, the Court provided a list of "private interest factors" affecting the convenience of the litigants, and a list of "public interest factors" affecting the convenience of the forum. *Gilbert, supra*, 330 U.S. at 508-509.[6]

After describing our decisions in *Gilbert* and *Koster*, the District Court analyzed the facts of these cases. It began by observing that an alternative forum existed in Scotland; Piper and Hartzell had agreed to submit to the jurisdiction of the Scottish courts and to waive any statute of limitations defense that might be available. It then stated that plaintiff's choice of forum was entitled to little weight. The court recognized that a plaintiff's choice ordinarily deserves

---

4. Section 1404(a) provides: "For the convenience of parties and witnesses, in the interest of justice, a district court may transfer any civil action to any other district or division where it might have been brought."

5. The District Court concluded that it could not assert personal jurisdiction over Hartzell consistent with due process. However, it decided not to dismiss Hartzell because the corporation would be amenable to process in Pennsylvania.

6. The factors pertaining to the private interests of the litigants included the "relative ease of access to sources of proof; availability of compulsory process for attendance of unwilling, and the cost of obtaining attendance of willing, witnesses; possibility of view of premises, if view would be appropriate to the action; and all other practical problems that make trial of a case easy, expeditious and inexpensive." The public factors bearing on the question included the administrative difficulties flowing from court congestion; the "local interest in having localized controversies decided at home"; the interest in having the trial of a diversity case in a forum that is at home with the law that must govern the action; the avoidance of unnecessary problems in conflict of laws, or in the application of foreign law; and the unfairness of burdening citizens in an unrelated forum with jury duty.

substantial deference. It noted, however, that Reyno "is a representative of foreign citizens and residents seeking a forum in the United States because of the more liberal rules concerning products liability law," and that "the courts have been less solicitous when the plaintiff is not an American citizen or resident, and particularly when the foreign citizens seek to benefit from the more liberal tort rules provided for the protection of citizens and residents of the United States."

The District Court next examined several factors relating to the private interests of the litigants, and determined that these factors strongly pointed towards Scotland as the appropriate forum. Although evidence concerning the design, manufacture, and testing of the plane and propeller is located in the United States, the connections with Scotland are otherwise "overwhelming." The real parties in interest are citizens of Scotland, as were all the decedents. Witnesses who could testify regarding the maintenance of the aircraft, the training of the pilot, and the investigation of the accident—all essential to the defense—are in Great Britain. Moreover, all witnesses to damages are located in Scotland. Trial would be aided by familiarity with Scottish topography, and by easy access to the wreckage.

The District Court reasoned that because crucial witnesses and evidence were beyond the reach of compulsory process, and because the defendants would not be able to implead potential Scottish third-party defendants, it would be "unfair to make Piper and Hartzell proceed to trial in this forum." . . .

In opposing the motions to dismiss, respondent contended that dismissal would be unfair because Scottish law was less favorable. The District Court explicitly rejected this claim. It reasoned that the possibility that dismissal might lead to an unfavorable change in the law did not deserve significant weight; any deficiency in the foreign law was a "matter to be dealt with in the foreign forum."

C

On appeal, the United States Court of Appeals for the Third Circuit reversed and remanded for trial. [T]he Court held that dismissal is never appropriate where the law of the alternative forum is less favorable to the plaintiff.

We granted certiorari in these cases to consider the questions they raise concerning the proper application of the doctrine of *forum non conveniens.*

II

The Court of Appeals erred in holding that plaintiffs may defeat a motion to dismiss on the ground of *forum non conveniens* merely by showing that the substantive law that would be applied in the alternative forum is less favorable to the plaintiffs than that of the present forum. The possibility of a change in substantive law should ordinarily not be given conclusive or even substantial weight in the *forum non conveniens* inquiry. . . .

[B]y holding that the central focus of the *forum non conveniens* inquiry is convenience, *Gilbert* implicitly recognized that dismissal may not be barred solely because of the possibility of an unfavorable change in law. Under *Gilbert*, dismissal will ordinarily be appropriate where trial in the plaintiff's chosen forum imposes a heavy burden on the defendant or the court, and where the plaintiff is unable to offer any specific reasons of convenience supporting his choice. If substantial weight were given to the possibility of an unfavorable change in law, however, dismissal might be barred even where trial in the chosen forum was plainly inconvenient.

In fact, if conclusive or substantial weight were given to the possibility of a change in law, the *forum non conveniens* doctrine would become virtually useless. Jurisdiction and venue requirements are often easily satisfied. As a result, many plaintiffs are able to choose from among several forums. Ordinarily, these plaintiffs will select that forum whose choice-of-law rules are most advantageous. Thus, if the possibility of an unfavorable change in substantive law is given substantial weight in the *forum non conveniens* inquiry, dismissal would rarely be proper. . . .

We do not hold that the possibility of an unfavorable change in law should never be a relevant consideration in a *forum non conveniens* inquiry. Of course, if the remedy provided by the alternative forum is so clearly inadequate or unsatisfactory that it is no remedy at all, the unfavorable change in law may be given substantial weight; the district court may conclude that dismissal would not be in the interests of justice. In these cases, however, the remedies that would be provided by the Scottish courts do not fall within this category. Although the relatives of the decedents may not be able to rely on a strict liability theory, and although their potential damages award may be smaller, there is no danger that they will be deprived of any remedy or treated unfairly. . . .

Scotland has a very strong interest in this litigation. The accident occurred in its airspace. All of the decedents were Scottish. Apart from Piper and Hartzell, all potential plaintiffs and defendants are either Scottish or English. As we stated in *Gilbert*, there is "a local interest in having localized controversies decided at home." Respondent argues that American citizens have an interest in ensuring that American manufacturers are deterred from producing defective products, and that additional deterrence might be obtained if Piper and Hartzell were tried in the United States, where they could be sued on the basis of both negligence and strict liability. However, the incremental deterrence that would be gained if this trial were held in an American court is likely to be insignificant. The American interest in this accident is simply not sufficient to justify the enormous commitment of judicial time and resources that would inevitably be required if the case were to be tried here.

IV

The Court of Appeals erred in holding that the possibility of an unfavorable change in law bars dismissal on the ground of *forum non conveniens*. It also erred in rejecting the District Court's *Gilbert* analysis. The District Court properly decided that the presumption in favor of the respondent's forum choice applied with less than maximum force because the real parties in interest are foreign. It did not act unreasonably in deciding that the private interests pointed towards trial in

Scotland. Nor did it act unreasonably in deciding that the public interests favored trial in Scotland. Thus, the judgment of the Court of Appeals is [r]eversed.

[The opinion of Justice WHITE, concurring in part and dissenting in part, has been omitted. The dissenting opinion of Justice STEVENS, joined by Justice BRENNAN, likewise has been omitted.]

YOUR TAKEAWAY

We have seen in our cases so far that fights about personal jurisdiction and venue are driven by strategic goals of the opposing parties. Plaintiffs usually prefer their home courts, as do defendants, and their motions and oppositions around jurisdiction and venue reflect that. The Robinsons chose to sue in Oklahoma, where they were recovering from their injuries, rather than chase the defendants to New York, home state of the World-Wide and Seaway (but no longer their home state). Shirley Jones no doubt assessed her chances of recovery to be better in California than Florida, home base of the *National Enquirer*. And Rudzewicz wisely, though unsuccessfully, resisted suit in Burger King's home base, Miami, Florida.

Piper Cub and Hartzell Propeller managed to maneuver this case from California to home territory (for Piper at least) in Pennsylvania. Yet their push westward didn't stop there, but eyed Scotland as the end goal. Why? American tort law—strict liability for defective products and generous damages—was far more plaintiff-friendly than Scottish law.

Forum non conveniens was the tool to achieve this final move across the Atlantic. But it is was designed to accommodate defendants sued in inconvenient forums—not to give them a choice of more attractive law. So ruled the Third Circuit. Justice Marshall recognized, however, that "if conclusive or substantial weight were given to the possibility of a change in law, the *forum non conveniens* doctrine would become virtually useless. Jurisdiction and venue requirements are often easily satisfied. As a result, many plaintiffs are able to choose from among several forums. Ordinarily, these plaintiffs will select that forum whose choice-of-law rules are most advantageous. Thus, if the possibility of an unfavorable change in substantive law is given substantial weight in the *forum non conveniens* inquiry, dismissal would rarely be proper." A refreshingly candid acknowledgment of the reality of forum shopping.

REVIEW QUESTIONS

1. Be prepared to explain the procedural moves of the parties in this case. How did the case make the reverse "Manifest Destiny" journey from the superior court in California to the federal district court in Pennsylvania, and then on to Scotland?

2. What are the differences between a change of venue under § 1404, a transfer under § 1406, and a dismissal for *forum non conveniens*? Given these two statutory provisions, "the common-law doctrine of *forum non conveniens* has

continuing application [in federal courts] only in cases where the alternative forum is abroad." *Sinochem International Co. Ltd. v. Malaysia International Shipping Co.*, 549 U.S. 422, 430 (2007). *See also* 28 U.S.C. § 1407, providing for transfer of actions raising common questions and pending in different districts to a single district for purposes of "coordinated or consolidated pretrial proceedings"—the multidistrict litigation procedure used in mass tort cases (e.g., asbestos, tobacco, and breast implant litigation).

3. With the vitality of transient presence as a basis for personal jurisdiction (*see Burnham v. Superior Court, supra*), *forum non conveniens* gives courts a discretionary fail-safe for avoiding litigation in a forum both inconvenient to defendants and far removed from the witnesses and evidence. In *MacLeod v. MacLeod*, 383 A.2d 39 (Me. 1978), for example, a Virginia resident sued her former husband in a Maine court for breach of a French divorce decree. The couple having married in New York, the only basis for jurisdiction in Maine was service of process upon defendant—a CIA employee who lived abroad and had no permanent residence—while he happened to be in Maine to attend his parents' golden wedding anniversary party.

   The Supreme Judicial Court of Maine affirmed the trial court's dismissal of the action: "The present action concerns a nonresident plaintiff suing a nonresident defendant upon transitory causes of action which did not arise in the State of Maine. Given those facts, the trial court could rightly consider exercising its discretionary power, notwithstanding the existence of both subject matter and personal jurisdiction, to decline jurisdiction over the action." Noting that there can be no dismissal under *forum non conveniens* without an assurance that there is an alternative forum for plaintiff's action, the trial court's order was modified to condition dismissal on defendant's acceptance of service in Virginia, where plaintiff was residing and defendant held a driver's license.

4. When a multinational chemical company headquartered in New York was sued in federal district court there by victims of a devastating gas plant disaster in Bhopal, India, the Second Circuit Court of Appeals affirmed dismissal on grounds of *forum non conveniens* (conditioned upon defendant's agreement to submit to jurisdiction in India and to waive the statute of limitations defense). *See In re Union Carbide Corporation Gas Plant Disaster*, 809 F.2d 195 (2d Cir. 1984), *cert. denied*, 484 U.S. 871:

   > The vast majority of material witnesses and documentary proof bearing on causation of and liability for the accident is located in India, not the United States, and would be more accessible to an Indian court than to a United States court. The records are almost entirely in Hindi or other Indian languages, understandable to an Indian court without translation. The witnesses for the most part do not speak English but Indian languages understood by an Indian court but not by an American court. These witnesses could be required to appear in an Indian court but not in a court of the United States. Although witnesses in the United States could not be subpoenaed to appear in India, they are comparatively few in number and most are employed by UCC which, as a party, would

produce them in India, with lower overall transportation costs than if the parties were to attempt to bring hundreds of Indian witnesses to the United States. Lastly, Judge Keenan properly concluded that an Indian court would be in a better position to direct and supervise a viewing of the Bhopal plant, which was sealed after the accident. Such a viewing could be of help to a court in determining liability issues.

809 F.2d at 201.

5. The Second Circuit reached the opposite conclusion in *Wiwa v. Royal Dutch Petroleum Co.*, 226 F.3d 88 (2d Cir. 2000), *cert. denied*, 532 U.S. 941 (2001), where Nigerian émigrés sought to hold two foreign corporations accountable for human rights abuses committed upon them in Nigeria. Reversing the district court's dismissal on *forum non conveniens* grounds, the court noted the strong policy in favor of an American forum in actions brought under the Alien Tort Statute, which "convey[s] the message that torture committed under color of law of a foreign nation in violation of international law is 'our business,' as such conduct not only violates the standards of international law but also as a consequence violates our domestic law." 226 F.3d at 106. *See also* Kathryn Lee Boyd, *The Inconvenience of Victims: Abolishing* Forum Non Conveniens *in U.S. Human Rights Litigation*, 39 Va. J. Intl. L. 41 (1998) (expressing concern that dismissal in favor of a foreign forum could result in the suit not being brought at all, or at least lead to a reduced recovery by plaintiffs due to the barriers preventing plaintiffs from accessing justice in foreign courts). Note that the severe limitations the Supreme Court has placed on the ATS referenced above—excluding corporate liability—would preclude such a suit today.

6. Some states have a legislative formulation of *forum non conveniens* written into their long-arm statute. *See, e.g.*, Mass. Gen. Laws ch. 223A, § 5: "When the court finds that in the interest of substantial justice the action should be heard in another forum, the court may stay or dismiss the action in whole or in part on any conditions that may be just." A negligence action filed in Massachusetts against a New York college alleging that plaintiff was beaten by fellow students there was dismissed pursuant to this provision, conditioned on the school waiving the statute of limitations defense in New York. *Green v. Manhattanville College*, 40 Mass. App. 76, 661 N.E.2d 123 (1996). Similarly, a former employee of a Massachusetts multinational company who had worked as a consultant in California prevailed in his motion to dismiss a noncompete claim filed against him in Massachusetts, relying on ch. 223A, § 5 and finding California a more convenient forum. *Oxford Global Resources, LLC v. Hernandez*, 480 Mass. 462 (2018).

7. The Supreme Court has held (unanimously) that a district court has discretion to dismiss on *forum non conveniens* grounds even without resolving whether it has subject matter or personal jurisdiction (which, in that case, would have required considerable time and expense), if it determines that a foreign tribunal is a more suitable forum. *Sinochem International Co. Ltd. v. Malaysia International Shipping Co.*, 549 U.S. 422 (2007).

8. The presence of a forum selection clause is an important, usually conclusive, factor to be weighed when a court rules on a motion for transfer of venue under § 1404. *See Stewart Organization, Inc. v. Ricoh Corp.*, 487 U.S. 22 (1988), discussed in Chapter 9. A forum selection clause does not foreclose dismissal of the case from the designated venue pursuant to *forum non conveniens*. *See Oxford Global Resources, LLC v. Hernandez, supra.*

PRACTICE EXERCISE NO. 35: LOCATION, LOCATION, LOCATION

Las Vegas resident and small-time talent agent Danny Rose finally realized his lifelong dream of attending the Academy Awards ceremony at the Hollywood Bowl. But when the award for best actress in a low-budget horror movie went to Becky Roland, a former client who had rudely fired Rose some years before, he jumped from his seat in protest, ran wildly toward the stage screaming, "She's a no-talent hack!!!" and, in front of 5,000 live witnesses and 50 million TV viewers, was physically removed by security. While being dragged out by LAPD officer Clint Westwood, moonlighting at the event, Rose allegedly suffered permanent and disabling injuries, as well as irreparable harm to his reputation.

Seeking legal advice, Rose was told no jury in LA would ever find against a member of its police force in such circumstances. But by luck, Rose found out that Westwood was flying to New York in a week to attend a family wedding. As Westwood walked through the terminal at LaGuardia Airport, a process server hired by Danny's lawyer handed him a summons and complaint in a civil action filed that day in the United States District Court for the Eastern District of New York (where the airport is located) seeking $150,000 in damages.

As an associate with the firm Westwood has retained to represent him, your supervising partner has asked you to prepare a memo discussing all the options, and chances of success, for getting the case out of New York (with its notoriously generous juries). Please advise her as well as to any other information you might need.

REVIEW EXERCISE NO. 7

To: Summer Associate
From: Senior Partner
Re: Request for Memorandum in Monarch Insurance Matter

We represent Monarch Insurance Corp. ("Monarch"), a Maine corporation whose only place of business is in Portland, Maine. Monarch has been impleaded by its insured Dr. Sean Moran, an employment test consultant from New York who prepared a personality assessment device for Head Hunters Inc. to be used to screen applicants for managerial positions. Head Hunters operates in California.

A lawsuit was filed in the U.S. District Court for the Central District of California by three unsuccessful female applicants claiming that Head Hunters and Dr. Moran violated California's Employment Non-Discrimination Act prohibiting discrimination on grounds of gender. The complaint alleges Moran devised, and Head Hunters used, the evaluation device with the intent to exclude qualified female applicants.

The third-party impleader alleges that Monarch issued a policy to Moran providing him with $5 million of liability coverage for "claims made during the policy period against the insured arising from the insured's preparation of employment tests." The policy excludes coverage for intentional wrongful acts, and Monarch sent Moran a letter denying coverage based on this exclusion. Moran's impleader challenges the scope of the exclusion, and seeks indemnification for any judgment that may result against him.

I have interviewed Michelle Camden, the president of Monarch. She tells me that Dr. Moran came to her several years ago while he was vacationing in Maine. Moran was looking for professional liability coverage for his consulting practice. He told Michelle that he prepared personality tests for employer-clients up and down the East Coast, and had recently received feelers from other parts of the country. Moran was very excited about his expanding business, and thus eager to protect himself in the event of litigation arising from this work.

Dr. Moran's policy includes the following provision, standard in Monarch contracts: "Suits arising from this policy must be filed in a court within the State of Maine." Moran's attorney has informed us that they will contest this provision on the grounds that Moran never saw it when he signed up for the insurance coverage. He claims Michelle Camden told him at the time "not to be concerned about all that small print stuff—it's just for the lawyers. We'll take good care of you, you'll see. Just sign on the bottom line."

Ms. Camden believes that as a small insurance company, Monarch should not have to defend a suit like this so far from Maine, and expects us to vigorously contest the impleader in California.

Please advise me on: (1) how Monarch's objection to personal jurisdiction should be raised; (2) the arguments in favor of dismissal; (3) the opposing arguments you anticipate from Moran; and (4) our chances for dismissal. If you think that further legal or factual research is needed, please let me know what you need and how you would use it.

P. NOTE ON PERSONAL JURISDICTION UNDER INTERNATIONAL LAW

The *Restatement (Third) of Foreign Relations Law*, which purports to set forth the general consensus on principles of international law, provides in § 421:

> (1) A state may exercise jurisdiction through its courts to adjudicate with respect to a person or thing if the relationship of the state to the person or thing is such as to make the exercise of jurisdiction reasonable.

(2) In general, a state's exercise of jurisdiction to adjudicate with respect to a person or thing is reasonable if, at the time jurisdiction is asserted:

(a) the person or thing is present in the territory of the state, other than transitorily;

(b) the person, if a natural person, is domiciled in the state;

(c) the person, if a natural person, is resident in the state;

(d) the person, if a natural person, is a national of the state;

(e) the person, if a corporation or comparable juridical person, is organized pursuant to the law of the state;

(f) a ship, aircraft or other vehicle to which the adjudication relates is registered under the laws of the state;

(g) the person, whether natural or juridical, has consented to the exercise of jurisdiction;

(h) the person, whether natural or juridical, regularly carries on business in the state;

(i) the person, whether natural or juridical, had carried on activity in the state, but only in respect of such activity;

(j) the person, whether natural or juridical, had carried on outside the state an activity having a substantial, direct, and foreseeable effect within the state, but only in respect of such activity; or

(k) the thing that is the subject of adjudication is owned, possessed, or used in the state, but only in respect of a claim reasonably connected with that thing.

(3) A defense of lack of jurisdiction is generally waived by any appearance by or on behalf of a person or thing (whether as plaintiff, defendant, or third party), if the appearance is for a purpose that does not include a challenge to the exercise of jurisdiction.

* * *

Does this elaborate formulation sound familiar? Compare the expansively simple authority asserted in the French Civil Code, Article 14:

> An alien, even not residing in France, may be summoned before the French courts for fulfillment of obligations contracted by him in France toward a French person; he may be brought before French courts for obligations contracted by him in a foreign country toward French persons.

Now that's *long-arm* jurisdiction.

CHAPTER 8

The Choice of an Appropriate Court: Subject Matter Jurisdiction and Removal

A. INTRODUCTION TO SUBJECT MATTER JURISDICTION

The doctrine of subject matter jurisdiction focuses our attention on the choice between state courts, on one hand, and federal courts, on the other. Subject matter jurisdiction means that a court has power over the subject matter at issue in the suit. A court's subject matter jurisdiction may be determined by a constitution (state or federal) or by legislation. For example, Article III of the Constitution gives the federal courts *limited* subject matter jurisdiction. In theory, this means that the federal courts have the power to hear only a subset of cases. By contrast, state courts have broad subject matter jurisdiction. They can hear almost *any* lawsuit.

As illustrated in the Venn diagram to the left, most cases are filed in state court—as many as eighteen million per year according to the National Center for State Courts. In many of the cases where there is federal jurisdiction, there is also concurrent state court jurisdiction. The federal courts have *exclusive* jurisdiction over a very small set of subject areas (which we discuss below).

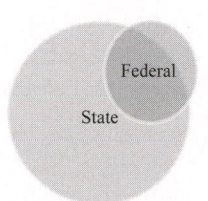

Understanding how subject matter jurisdiction works conceptually is easiest at the state court level. For example, many states have specialized courts for certain subject matters, such as probate courts for dealing with the administration of estates, family courts, and commercial courts. Cases about other areas of the law may not be brought in such specialized courts. States may also have multiple layers of trial courts, allocating their judicial business to one layer or another based upon the amount of money in controversy. You may have been familiar with small claims courts before law school, and we were introduced to the concept of the limited jurisdiction of small claims courts in *Podhorn v. Paragon Group* in Chapter 3. You may recall the Podhorns argued that they could not bring their claim against their landlord in the small claims court because the claim exceeded the jurisdictional threshold. In other words, the small claims court lacked subject matter jurisdiction.

Lawyers routinely refer to state courts as having *general subject matter jurisdiction*. This terminology can be confusing. As an initial matter, notwithstanding use of the words *general* and *jurisdiction*, this term has nothing to do with the concept of general jurisdiction in personal jurisdiction. While personal jurisdiction concerns *where* a suit might be brought geographically, subject matter jurisdiction asks *what* the lawsuit is about (a will, for example, or a commercial transaction gone wrong). Next, understand that within a particular state court system, the courts that are not specialized courts are often referred to as courts of *general jurisdiction*. These courts might have different names in different states. For example, in the State of Ohio the court of general jurisdiction is the Court of Common Pleas; in Massachusetts, the Superior Court; in New York, the Supreme Court; in Texas, the District Court. What all these state courts share is that they are ordinary or general trial courts with power over the run of cases; this is what it means to say they are courts of general jurisdiction.

References to state courts in the aggregate as courts of *general subject matter jurisdiction*, convey the idea that state court systems can (with only a few exceptions) hear *all type*s of cases. You might think of these as residual courts where most cases can always be brought. This includes cases arising under federal, state, or foreign laws; cases where in-state citizens, out-of-state citizens, or foreigners are parties; and many other cases, no matter the complexity, the number of parties involved, or the small/large amount in controversy. Most importantly, the phrase *general* subject matter jurisdiction is intended to mark the contrast to federal courts, which are courts of *limited* subject matter jurisdiction.

A plaintiff may file in a federal court only if the case falls within the limited parameters of federal subject matter authority—mainly the authority extends to cases between citizens of different states and to cases in which the claim arises from federal law. That is what most of this chapter is about. As you will see later in this chapter, a defendant can also exercise the federal option when a case filed in state court falls within the scope of federal subject matter jurisdiction; such a case may be "removed" to federal court by the defendant.

The purpose of this chapter is twofold. First, it introduces you to the sources of law and doctrines that govern the choice between federal and state courts for both sides and how these doctrines have evolved over time. Second, it gives you an opportunity to think about the relationship between court systems in the United States. Why do we have a federal system at all? What might be different if all cases were only adjudicated in the state courts? What is at stake for litigants in choosing one court over another? Why is it commonly assumed that plaintiffs prefer state courts while defendants prefer federal courts?

Sources of the Federal Courts' Subject Matter Jurisdiction. The subject matter jurisdiction of federal courts is limited by the U.S. Constitution. Article III, § 2, sets the constitutional parameters of federal judicial power. For our purposes, the most important extension of federal judicial power is to:

- "all Cases . . . arising under this Constitution, the Laws of the United States, and Treaties made," and
- "all Cases . . . between citizens of different States."

You should know that federal judicial authority also includes admiralty cases, controversies in which the United States is a party, and controversies between two or more states (such as border disputes); these subjects are usually addressed at greater length in a federal courts class.

It was left to Congress to effectuate this grant of power, which it has done in the Judicial Code provisions 28 U.S.C. §§ 1331 and 1332 (among others) empowering the federal courts to hear "all civil actions arising under the Constitution, laws or treaties of the United States" and cases "between citizens of different States," but in the latter category, only where the amount in controversy exceeds $75,000.

In a very narrow subset of these cases where the federal courts have subject matter jurisdiction, the federal courts have *exclusive jurisdiction*. In these cases (which include patent, copyright, admiralty, and bankruptcy, for example), only the federal courts—and not the state courts—may assert jurisdiction. In all other cases that fall within the federal courts' limited subject matter jurisdiction, the matter could be heard in either federal or state courts. This is usually described as the *concurrent subject matter jurisdiction* of federal and state courts.

In practice, where both the federal and state courts have authority to hear a case (i.e., where there is concurrent subject matter jurisdiction), the litigants' choice is usually dictated by strategic and pragmatic concerns. Familiarity with the processes and rules of a particular system may incline lawyers to select one over the other. Different rules of pleading or different discovery mechanisms might be attractive. A plaintiff in a civil rights action may prefer a federal court judge to a state court judge in the belief that the former is more experienced in such matters. *See* Burt Neuborne, *The Myth of Parity*, 90 Harv. L. Rev. 1105 (1977). During the 1950s and 60s, many civil rights activists believed that segregationist state court judges would not give them a fair hearing. *Walker v. City of Birmingham*, reproduced in Chapter 2, is one example. The prospect of more generous juries may, on the other hand, lead lawyers to file in state rather than federal court, as was apparently the case in *World-Wide Volkswagen Corp. v. Woodson*, reproduced in Chapter 7.

While some commentators have viewed the parallel state and federal court systems as an historical anachronism and dysfunctional redundancy, the late Professor Robert Cover discerned distinct advantages, such as permitting jurisdictional choice (and thus a kind of fairness) to litigants while encouraging innovation among competing courts. *See* Robert Cover, *The Uses of Jurisdictional Redundancy: Interest, Ideology and Innovation*, 22 Wm. & Mary L. Rev. 639 (1981). The coexistence of the two sets of courts has also been the subject of intense political battles by those interests that have a stake in expanding or denying access to federal courts. Indeed, when the ideological inclination of one system of courts is different (or is perceived as different) than the other, pressures to expand or to constrict the scope of federal subject matter jurisdiction invariably follow.

Many of the arguments about choosing between state and federal courts assume that all state courts are similar and that all federal courts are alike. It is very common, for example, to hear that [x] courts are pro-plaintiff or pro-defendant. One question to think about as you read on is whether all federal courts really are alike, such that it makes sense to contrast the federal courts with state courts. Few could disagree with the proposition that there are probably significant differences among the state courts of various states. Federal judges are part of a unified system of courts but they, too, are drawn from the bars of their respective state (often from the state judiciary). Accordingly, in many respects, a federal judge sitting in New Jersey may have more in common with state court judges from her home state than with other federal judges from Louisiana.

This chapter will first address the federal courts' power over questions involving federal law, then we will turn to the more controversial issue of the federal courts power over disputes between citizens of different states known as diversity jurisdiction, and finally to the ability of defendants to remove cases to federal courts where there is concurrent jurisdiction.

B. FEDERAL QUESTION JURISDICTION

Consider, first, why the framers of the U.S. Constitution would include within the limited subject matter jurisdiction of federal courts "all Cases . . . arising under this Constitution, the Laws of the United States, and Treaties made." Art. III, § 2. Three arguments are usually offered for this provision: first, that the federal courts have relative expertise in federal law; second, that the framers expected state courts to be hostile to federal rights; and third, that federal jurisdiction would insulate state courts from the consequences of unpopular decisions.

The Constitution defines the permissible scope of the judicial Power (notice that the Constitution defines the term Power with a capital "P"), but it does not provide federal district courts with subject matter jurisdiction to hear these cases. Indeed, the Constitution does not even require that federal district courts exist. But the Constitution provides that Congress *may* ordain and establish inferior courts—such as federal district courts— to hear cases that fall within the scope of the judicial Power. Most of our attention in this unit will focus on 28 U.S.C. § 1331, the federal question statute. Read that code section now and notice the similarity of language between it and the corresponding language in Art. III, § 2. But as we will see later, these common words have different meanings.

To the extent that the federal question statute extends to "*all* civil actions arising under," it is a general provision. 28 U.S.C. § 1331 (emphasis added).

For contrast, review a few code provisions that give the federal courts subject matter jurisdiction over specialized matters. See, *e.g.*, 28 U.S.C. §§ 1333-1340, 1343-1351, 1361-1364. Many of these specialized federal question statutes have been part of the federal courts' jurisdiction from the outset. It was not until 1875, however, that Congress passed the generalized provision in § 1331. "In the early days of our republic, Congress was content to leave the task of interpreting and applying federal laws in the first instance to the state courts." *Merrell Dow Pharmaceuticals, Inc. v. Thompson*, 478 U.S. 804, 826 (1986) (Brennan, J., dissenting).

Section 1331 is brief yet opaque. Case law has exposed and explored the ambiguity of the words "civil actions arising under." It is not altogether obvious whether a civil action does or does not *arise under* federal law. For example, does a civil action arise under federal law if the defendant's affirmative defense (rather than the plaintiff's cause of action) invokes federal law? Do claims that are a product of state law, yet will be resolved based upon an interpretation or application of federal law, arise under federal law? We begin with the most influential case on the scope of federal question jurisdiction.

Louisville & Nashville Railroad Co. v. Mottley
211 U.S. 149 (1908)

Statement by Justice MOODY:

The appellees (husband and wife), being residents and citizens of Kentucky, brought this suit in equity in the circuit court of the United States for the western district of Kentucky against the appellant, a railroad company and a citizen of the same state. The object of the suit was to compel the specific performance of the following contract:

> Louisville, Ky., Oct. 2d, 1871. The Louisville & Nashville Railroad Company, in consideration that E. L. Mottley and wife, Annie E. Mottley, have this day released company from all damages or claims for damages for injuries received by them on the 7th of September, 1871, in consequence of a collision of trains on the railroad of said company at Randolph's Station, Jefferson County, Kentucky, hereby agrees to issue free passes on said railroad and branches now existing or to exist, to said E. L. & Annie E. Mottley for the remainder of the present year, and thereafter to renew said passes annually during the lives of said Mottley and wife or either of them.

The bill alleged that in September, 1871, plaintiffs, while passengers upon the defendant railroad, were injured by the defendant's negligence, and released their respective claims for damages in consideration of the agreement for transportation during their lives, expressed in the contract. It is alleged that the contract was performed by the defendant up to January 1, 1907, when the defendant declined to renew the passes. The bill then alleges that the refusal to comply with the contract was based solely upon that part of the act of Congress of June 29, 1906 which forbids the giving of free passes or free transportation. The bill further alleges: First, that the act of Congress referred to does not prohibit the giving of passes under the circumstances of this case; and, second, that, if the law is to be construed as prohibiting such passes, it is in conflict with the 5th Amendment of the Constitution, because it deprives the plaintiffs of their property without due process of law. The defendant demurred to the bill. The judge of the circuit court overruled the demurrer, entered a decree for the relief prayed for, and the defendant appealed directly to this court.

Justice MOODY, after making the foregoing statement, delivered the opinion of the Court:

Two questions of law were raised by the demurrer to the bill, were brought here by appeal, and have been argued before us. They are, first, whether that part of the act of Congress of June 29, 1906 which forbids the giving of free passes or the collection of any different compensation for transportation of passengers than that specified in the tariff filed, makes it unlawful to perform a contract for transportation of persons who, in good faith, before the passage of the act, had accepted such contract in satisfaction of a valid cause of action against the railroad; and, second, whether the statute, if it should be construed to render such a contract unlawful, is in violation of the 5th Amendment of the Constitution of the United States. We do not deem it necessary, however, to consider either of these questions, because, in our opinion, the court below was without jurisdiction of the cause. Neither party has questioned that jurisdiction, but it is the duty of this court to see to it that the jurisdiction of the circuit court, which is defined and limited by statute, is not exceeded. This duty we have frequently performed of our own motion.

There was no diversity of citizenship, and it is not and cannot be suggested that there was any ground of jurisdiction, except that the case was a "suit . . . arising under the Constitution or laws of the United States." It is the settled interpretation of these words, as used in this statute, conferring jurisdiction, that a suit arises under the Constitution and laws of the United States only when the plaintiff's statement of his own cause of action shows that it is based upon those laws or that Constitution. It is not enough that the plaintiff alleges some anticipated defense to his cause of action, and asserts that the defense is invalidated by some provision of the Constitution of the United States. Although such allegations show that very likely, in the course of the litigation, a question under the Constitution would arise, they do not show that the suit, that is, the plaintiff's original cause of action, arises under the Constitution. In *Tennessee v. Union & Planters' Bank*, 152 U.S. 454, the plaintiff, the state of Tennessee, brought suit in the circuit court of the United States to recover from the defendant certain taxes alleged to be due under the laws of the state. The plaintiff alleged that the defendant claimed an immunity from the taxation by virtue of its charter, and that therefore the tax was void, because in violation of the provision of the Constitution of the United States, which forbids any state from passing a law impairing the obligation of contracts. The cause was held to be beyond the jurisdiction of the circuit court, the court saying, by Mr. Justice Gray (p. 464): "A suggestion of one party, that the other will or may set up a claim under the Constitution or laws of the United States, does not make the suit one arising under that Constitution or those laws." Again, in *Boston & M. Consol. Copper & S. Min. Co. v. Montana Ore Purchasing Co.*, 188 U.S. 632, the plaintiff brought suit in the circuit court of the United States for the conversion of copper ore and for an injunction against its continuance. The plaintiff then alleged, for the purpose of showing jurisdiction, in substance, that the defendant would set up in defense certain laws of the United States. The cause was held to be beyond the jurisdiction of the circuit court, the court saying, by Mr. Justice Peckham (pp. 638, 639):

> It would be wholly unnecessary and improper, in order to prove complainant's cause of action, to go into any matters of defense which the defendants might possibly set up, and then attempt to reply to such defense, and thus, if possible, to show that a Federal question might or probably would arise in the course of the trial of the case. To allege such defense and then make an answer to it before the defendant has the opportunity to itself plead or prove its own defense is inconsistent with any known rule of pleading, so far as we are aware, and is improper. The rule is a reasonable and just one that the complainant in the first instance shall be confined to a statement of its cause of action, leaving to the defendant to set up in his answer what his defense is, and, if anything more than a denial of complainant's cause of action, imposing upon the defendant the burden of proving such defense. Conforming itself to that rule, the complainant would not, in the assertion or proof of its cause of action, bring up a single Federal question. The presentation of its cause of action would not show that it was one arising under the Constitution or laws of the United States. The only way in which it might be claimed that a Federal question was presented would be in the complainant's statement of what the defense of defendants would be, and complainant's answer to such defense. Under these circumstances the case is brought within the rule laid down in *Tennessee v. Union & Planters' Bank, supra*. That case has been cited and approved many times since. . . . The application of this rule to the case at bar is decisive against the jurisdiction of the circuit court.

It is ordered that the judgment be reversed and the case remitted to the circuit court with instructions to dismiss the suit for want of jurisdiction.

REVIEW QUESTIONS

1. What was the lawsuit brought by the Mottleys? How did the defendant railroad respond? What was the railroad's argument that the case should be in federal court?

2. Re-read the excerpt of the case below articulating a standard for when a case "arises under" the Constitution or laws of the United States.

> It is the settled interpretation of these words, as used in this statute, conferring jurisdiction, that a suit arises under the Constitution and laws of the United States only when the plaintiff's statement of his own cause of action shows that it is based upon those laws or that Constitution. It is not enough that the plaintiff alleges some anticipated defense to his

cause of action, and asserts that the defense is invalidated by some provision of the Constitution of the United States. Although such allegations show that very likely, in the course of the litigation, a question under the Constitution would arise, they do not show that the suit, that is, the plaintiff's original cause of action, arises under the Constitution.

This test for original subject matter jurisdiction under § 1331 is often referred to as the "well-pleaded complaint" rule. That term is awkwardly phrased because this "rule" has nothing to do with the clarity or precision of the complaint or whether it complies with Rule 8. Instead, a "well-pleaded complaint" simply refers to a complaint that contains the allegations essential to stating the plaintiff's claim without any surplusage such as anticipated defenses. Put another way, the plaintiff's statement of his or her own claim determines whether the suit arises under federal law. Try to apply this standard to the Mottleys' complaint.

3. Think about this case from the perspective of the railroad. The railroad has a defense that is based upon an interpretation of federal law. In much the same way that plaintiffs with federal claims might wish to litigate those claims in federal court, defendants with federal defenses might wish to litigate those defenses in federal court. Yet plaintiff's claim, which does not arise under federal law (and the railroad's defense, which does arise under federal law) must be litigated in a state court. Can you think of a policy justification for this different treatment?

4. Although neither party questioned subject matter jurisdiction, the Supreme Court was able to—and, in fact was obligated to—raise the issue on its own initiative. This is true both at the trial and appellate levels. Does the court have an obligation to raise defects in *personal* jurisdiction? Look back at Fed. R. Civ. P. 12(h) and contrast subdivisions (1) and (3). Why the different treatment? Where defense counsel picks up on the issue of lack of subject matter jurisdiction in the district court, a Fed. R. Civ. P. 12(b)(1) motion to dismiss is the device for challenging the court's authority to hear the case. That motion can be brought at any time, or raised by the judge herself. Lack of subject matter jurisdiction is a defense that cannot be waived, and subject matter jurisdiction is also something that cannot be created by the parties' consent. *See* 28 U.S.C. § 1359.

5. One corollary of the limited nature of federal subject matter jurisdiction is that there is something of a presumption against its existence that plaintiff must overcome. Re-read Fed. R. Civ. P. 8(a)(1). If the defendant challenges subject matter jurisdiction by filing a motion to dismiss under Rule 12(b)(1), the plaintiff shoulders the burden of proving that the court has subject matter jurisdiction.

6. You should know that there is an important exception to the well-pleaded complaint rule, but it arises in the context of plaintiffs who are trying to *avoid* stating a claim that arises under federal law. We will address this situation later in this chapter when we study the doctrine of removal.

* * *

After their case was dismissed by the federal courts for lack of subject matter jurisdiction, the Mottleys refiled their action in a Kentucky state court (since the federal court's dismissal for want of jurisdiction had no *res judicata* effect, as we will see in Chapter 10). The case proceeded through the state court system, where the Mottleys prevailed. But the Railroad appealed to the U.S. Supreme Court, which again denied the Mottleys recovery. On this second appeal, the Supreme Court addressed the constitutionality of the statute upon which the Railroad relied to defend against the breach of contract claim. In an opinion by the first Justice Harlan, the Court seemed to be begging the Mottleys' forgiveness for depriving them of a recovery of at least some free train rides from the railroad that nearly killed them:

> It may be, as suggested, that a refusal to enforce the agreement of 1871 will operate as a great hardship upon the defendants in error. But that consideration cannot control the determination of this controversy. Our duty is to ascertain the intention of Congress in passing the statute upon which the railroad company relies as prohibitive of the further enforcement of the agreement in suit. That intention is to be gathered from the words of the act, interpreted according to their ordinary acceptation, and, when it becomes necessary to do so, in the light of the circumstances as they existed when the statute was passed. The court cannot mold a statute simply to meet its views of justice in a particular case.

Louisville & N.R. Co. v. Mottley, 219 U.S. 467, 474 (1911). The Mottleys thus secured their place of prominence in the Litigation Losers Hall of Fame.

Notice that the *Supreme Court* had subject matter jurisdiction over the appeal even though that same case was beyond the subject matter jurisdiction of the federal *district* courts. This is because the appellate jurisdiction of the U.S. Supreme Court is determined by the scope of the judicial Power outlined in Art. III, § 2, while the original jurisdiction of the district courts is determined by the scope of 28 U.S.C. § 1331. But compare yet again those two provisions.

> *U.S. Const. Art. III, § 2*: The judicial Power shall extend to all Cases . . . arising under this Constitution, the Laws of the United States, and Treaties made, or which shall be made. . . .

> *28 U.S.C. § 1331*: The district courts shall have original jurisdiction of all civil actions arising under the Constitution, laws, or treaties of the United States.

You can imagine an alternate universe in which the federal district courts would have original jurisdiction over cases such as that brought by the Mottleys. This is not that universe: The case *arises under* for purposes of Article III but not for § 1331.

This raises the question of why the Court construed § 1331 so narrowly. If the result in *Mottley* is not dictated by the language of the statute, there must be policy reasons for the strict construction. Acknowledging that the *Mottley* rule "may produce awkward results," the Supreme Court has concluded that it generally "makes sense as a quick rule of thumb," and continues to apply it. *See Franchise Tax Board v. Construction Laborers Vacation Trust*, 463 U.S. 1, 11 (1983). Why would the subject matter jurisdiction of federal courts be reduced to a test whose principal virtue is that it is a "quick rule of thumb"? Does subject matter jurisdiction *need* to be resolved "quick[ly]"? (Is this an area of the law that *should* be reduced to a "rule of thumb"?) Compare the tests for personal and subject matter jurisdiction. Is deciding personal jurisdiction quickly less important than subject matter jurisdiction?

Declaratory Judgments. What would happen if the litigation roles of the Mottleys and the Railroad were reversed? *Assume* that the Railroad had seized the initiative and brought a declaratory judgment action (now possible under 28 U.S.C. §§ 2201-2202, the Federal Declaratory Judgment Act) in federal court claiming that the Act of Congress invalidated the Mottleys' free pass and seeking a ruling that the consequent termination of the agreement was not in conflict with the Due Process Clause of the Fifth Amendment. Wouldn't the Railroad's complaint "arise under" the Constitution and laws of the United States—whether because the Due Process Clause is essentially the "cause of action" or because the suit arises under the Federal Declaratory Judgment Act, a federal law? Is the "well-pleaded complaint" rule so easily circumvented?

The answer is "no." In the context of a declaratory judgment action, courts essentially hypothesize the substance of the action that would be filed but for the availability of declaratory judgments. In other words, who would have brought a suit, and alleging what? If that hypothetical action could properly be filed in federal court, then the declaratory judgment action likewise falls within the scope of the court's subject matter jurisdiction. *See, e.g., Franchise Tax Board v. Construction Laborers Vacation Trust*, 463 U.S. 1 (1983), and *Skelly Oil Co. v. Phillips Petroleum Co.*, 339 U.S. 667 (1950). "To sanction suits for declaratory relief as within the jurisdiction of the District Courts merely because, as in this case, artful pleading anticipates a defense based on federal law would contravene the whole trend of jurisdictional legislation by Congress, disregard the effective functioning of the federal judicial system, and distort the limited procedural purpose of the Declaratory Judgment Act." *Skelly Oil Co.*, 339 U.S. at 673-674.

Counterclaims. *Counterclaims* have fared no better than anticipated defenses under the *Mottley* rule. Federal jurisdiction cannot be created by a defendant's pleading of a counterclaim arising under federal law. *See The Holmes Group, Inc. v. Vornado Air Circulation Systems, Inc.*, 535 U.S. 826 (2002); *Home Depot U.S.A., Inc. v. Jackson*, 139 S. Ct. 1743 (2019).

Although a defendant's counterclaim does not affect the analysis of whether the plaintiff's claim falls within the scope of federal subject matter jurisdiction, you should remember that counterclaims, third-party claims, and cross-claims each will require their own independent basis for federal subject matter jurisdiction if a party wishes to assert them in a pending federal court action. Indeed, federal subject matter jurisdiction is an inquiry that federal courts will entertain as to each and every claim against each and every defendant.

Exceptions to the Well-Pleaded Complaint Rule. The well-pleaded complaint rule of *Mottley* presents as a "quick rule of thumb" test that is simple to apply. Yet in fact there can be some nuance in its application.

First, there are the truly easy cases. In 1916, Justice Holmes proclaimed that "[a] suit *arises under* the law that creates the cause of action." *Am. Well Works Co. v. Layne & Bowler Co.,* 241 U.S. 257, 260 (1916) (emphasis added). Accordingly, when, for example, the *Warner* plaintiffs in the stop-and-frisk case (included in the Case Files) seek recovery under 42 U.S.C. § 1983 (a federal statute), this cause of action unquestionably arises under federal law. Causes of action that are created by federal law satisfy the arising under test of § 1331.

Yet when a cause of action is created by *state* law, the reverse is not always true. Indeed, sometimes, though rarely, a cause of action that is created by state law may nevertheless satisfy the arising under test of § 1331. In a special and small category of cases, federal question jurisdiction will lie over state-law claims that implicate "significant federal issues." *Grable & Sons Metal Prods., Inc. v. Darue Eng. & Mfg.,* 545 U.S. 308, 312 (2005).

The paradigmatic example of a state-law claim that implicates a federal issue (although not necessarily a *significant* federal issue) is a common law claim for negligence per se that is based on the violation of a federal duty. For example, in *Merrell Dow Pharmaceuticals Inc. v. Thompson,* 478 U.S. 804 (1986), the plaintiffs alleged that the defendant misbranded a drug in violation of the federal Food, Drug, and Cosmetic Act (FDCA), and that that violation constituted a rebuttable presumption of negligence, which caused injury to the plaintiffs. Although leaving open the possibility that such a circumstance might constitute a significant federal issue sufficient to trigger arising under jurisdiction, the Court held that this was not that case. The Court was influenced by the fact that the FDCA did not itself provide a remedy; "the congressional determination that there should be no federal remedy for the violation of [the FDCA] is tantamount to a congressional conclusion that the presence of a claimed violation of the [FDCA] is an element of a state cause of action is insufficiently 'substantial' to confer federal-question jurisdiction." *Id.* at 810-811.

More recently, the Court provided us with an example of a state-law claim that did implicate a significant federal issue. *See Grable & Sons Metal Prods., Inc. v. Darue Eng. & Mfg.,* 545 U.S. 308, 312 (2005). In *Grable,* the plaintiff filed a quiet title action (arising under state law). The plaintiff (Grable & Sons) once owned a parcel of property that, years earlier, had been seized and sold by the Internal Revenue Service (IRS) to satisfy tax obligations. The defendant (Darue Engineering) purchased the property at the tax sale and received a deed from the IRS. In the subsequent quiet title action, the plaintiff Grable contended that the defendant's title was invalid because the IRS failed to follow the proper procedures: The statute required notice of the tax sale by personal service, and Grable was instead notified by certified mail.

> [F]ederal jurisdiction demands not only a contested federal issue, but a substantial one, indicating a serious federal interest in claiming the advantages thought to be inherent in a federal forum.

But even when the state action discloses a contested and substantial federal question, the exercise of federal jurisdiction is subject to a possible veto. For the federal issue will ultimately qualify for a federal forum only if federal jurisdiction is consistent with congressional judgment about the sound division of labor between state and federal courts governing the application of § 1331. . . . Because arising-under jurisdiction to hear a state-law claim always raises the possibility of upsetting the state-federal line drawn (or at least assumed) by Congress, the presence of a disputed federal issue and the ostensible importance of a federal forum are never necessarily dispositive; there must always be an assessment of any disruptive portent in exercising federal jurisdiction.

These considerations have kept us from stating a "single, precise, all-embracing" test for jurisdiction over federal issues embedded in state-law claims between nondiverse parties. . . . Instead, the question is, does a state-law claim necessarily raise a stated federal issue, actually disputed and substantial, which a federal forum may entertain without disturbing any congressionally approved balance of federal and state judicial responsibilities. . . .

Whether Grable was given notice within the meaning of [26 U.S.C. § 6335(a)] is thus an essential element of its quiet title claim, and the meaning of the federal statute is actually in dispute; it appears to be the only legal or factual issue contested in the case. The meaning of the federal tax provision is an important issue of federal law that sensibly belongs in a federal court. The Government has a strong interest in the "prompt and certain collection of delinquent taxes[ ]" [through the seizure and sale of property]. The Government thus has a direct interest in the availability of a federal forum to vindicate its own administrative action, and buyers (as well as tax delinquents) may find it valuable to come before judges used to federal tax matters. Finally, because it will be the rare state title case that raises a contested matter of federal law, federal jurisdiction to resolve genuine disagreement over federal tax title provisions will portend only a microscopic effect on the federal-state division of labor. . . .

Given the absence of threatening structural consequences and the clear interest the Government, its buyers, and its delinquents have in the availability of a federal forum, there is no good reason to shirk from federal jurisdiction over the dispositive and contested federal issue at the heart of the state-law title claim.

Id. at 313-320. The *Grable* Court distinguished this case from *Merrell Dow*, stating:

[In *Merrell Dow*,] if the federal labeling standard without a federal cause of action could get a state claim into federal court, so could any other federal standard without a cause of action. And that would have meant a tremendous number of cases [in federal courts].

Id. at 318. An important characteristic of *Grable* that is worth emphasizing is that it involved "a nearly pure issue of law [to wit, defining "notice" under 26 U.S.C. § 6335(a)], one that could be settled once and for all and thereafter would govern numerous tax sale cases." *Empire Healthchoice Assurance v. McVeigh*, 547 U.S. 677, 699, 701 (2006). It was also the only disputed legal or factual issue in the case.

In the following case, the Court applied what is now characterized as *Grable*'s four-part test. One point of context may be helpful before you read *Gunn*. You will remember from the opening paragraphs of this chapter that there is a narrow subset of cases where the federal courts have exclusive jurisdiction. In this subset of cases, which include patent cases, only the federal courts—and not the state courts—may assert jurisdiction. Section 1338(a), the statute that creates exclusive jurisdiction over patents cases, uses the familiar "arising under" language to define its scope.

Gunn v. Minton
133 S. Ct. 1059 (2013)

Chief Justice ROBERTS delivered the opinion for a unanimous Court:

Federal courts have exclusive jurisdiction over cases "arising under any Act of Congress relating to patents." 28 U.S.C. § 1338(a). The question presented is whether a state law claim alleging legal malpractice in the handling of a patent case must be brought in federal court.

I

In the early 1990s, respondent Vernon Minton developed a computer program and telecommunications network designed to facilitate securities trading. In March 1995, he leased the system—known as the Texas Computer Exchange Network, or TEXCEN—to R.M. Stark & Co., a securities brokerage. A little over a year later, he applied for a patent for an interactive securities trading system that was based substantially on TEXCEN. The U.S. Patent and Trademark Office issued the patent in January 2000.

Patent in hand, Minton filed a patent infringement suit in Federal District Court against the National Association of Securities Dealers, Inc. (NASD) and the NASDAQ Stock Market, Inc. He was represented by Jerry Gunn and the other petitioners. NASD and NASDAQ moved for summary judgment on the ground that Minton's patent was invalid under the "on sale" bar, 35 U.S.C. § 102(b). That provision specifies that an inventor is not entitled to a patent if "the invention was . . . on sale in [the United States], more than one year prior to the date of the application," and Minton had leased TEXCEN to Stark more than one year prior to filing his patent application. Rejecting Minton's argument that there were differences between TEXCEN and the patented system that precluded application of the on-sale bar, the District Court granted the summary judgment motion and declared Minton's patent invalid.

Minton then filed a motion for reconsideration in the District Court, arguing for the first time that the lease agreement with Stark was part of ongoing testing of TEXCEN and therefore fell within the "experimental use" exception to the on-sale bar. The District Court denied the motion.

Minton appealed to the U.S. Court of Appeals for the Federal Circuit. That court affirmed, concluding that the District Court had appropriately held Minton's experimental-use argument waived.

Minton, convinced that his attorneys' failure to raise the experimental-use argument earlier had cost him the lawsuit and led to invalidation of his patent, brought this malpractice action in Texas state court. His former lawyers defended on the ground that the lease to Stark was not, in fact, for an experimental use, and that therefore Minton's patent infringement claims would have failed even if the experimental-use argument had been timely raised. The trial court agreed, holding that Minton had put forward "less than a scintilla of proof" that the lease had been for an experimental purpose. It accordingly granted summary judgment to Gunn and the other lawyer defendants.

On appeal, Minton raised a new argument: Because his legal malpractice claim was based on an alleged error in a patent case, it "aris[es] under" federal patent law for purposes of 28 U.S.C. § 1338(a). And because, under § 1338(a), "[n]o State court shall have jurisdiction over any claim for relief arising under any Act of Congress relating to patents," the Texas court— where Minton had originally brought his malpractice claim—lacked subject matter jurisdiction to decide the case. Accordingly, Minton argued, the trial court's order should be vacated and the case dismissed, leaving Minton free to start over in the Federal District Court.

A divided panel of the Court of Appeals of Texas rejected Minton's argument. . . .

The Supreme Court of Texas reversed, relying heavily on a pair of cases from the U.S. Court of Appeals for the Federal Circuit. The Court concluded that Minton's claim involved "a substantial federal issue" within the meaning of *Grable* [& *Sons Metal Prods., Inc. v. Darue Eng. & Mfg.*, 545 U.S. 308 (2005)] "because the success of Minton's malpractice claim is reliant upon the viability of the experimental use exception as a defense to the on-sale bar." 355 S.W.3d, 634, 644 (2011). Adjudication of Minton's claim in federal court was consistent with the appropriate balance between federal and state judicial responsibilities, it held, because "the federal government and patent litigants have an interest in the uniform application of patent law by courts well-versed in that subject matter." *Id.*, at 646. . . .

We granted certiorari.

II

"Federal courts are courts of limited jurisdiction," possessing "only that power authorized by Constitution and statute." *Kokkonen v. Guardian Life Ins. Co. of America*, 511 U.S. 375, 377 (1994). There is no dispute that the Constitution permits Congress to extend federal court jurisdiction to a case such as this one, see *Osborn v. Bank of United States*, 9 Wheat. 738, 823-824 (1824); the question is whether Congress has done so, see *Powell v. McCormack*, 395 U.S. 486, 515-516 (1969).

As relevant here, Congress has authorized the federal district courts to exercise original jurisdiction in "all civil actions arising under the Constitution, laws, or treaties of the United States," 28 U.S.C. § 1331, and, more particularly, over "any civil action arising under any Act of Congress relating to patents,"

§ 1338(a). Adhering to the demands of "[l]inguistic consistency," we have interpreted the phrase "arising under" in both sections identically, applying our § 1331 and § 1338(a) precedents interchangeably. *See Christianson v. Colt Industries Operating Corp.*, 486 U.S. 800, 808-809 (1988). For cases falling within the patent-specific arising under jurisdiction of § 1338(a), however, Congress has not only provided for federal jurisdiction but also eliminated state jurisdiction, decreeing that "[n]o State court shall have jurisdiction over any claim for relief arising under any Act of Congress relating to patents." § 1338(a) (2006 ed., Supp. V). To determine whether jurisdiction was proper in the Texas courts, therefore, we must determine whether it would have been proper in a federal district court—whether, that is, the case "aris[es] under any Act of Congress relating to patents."

For statutory purposes, a case can "aris[e] under" federal law in two ways. Most directly, a case arises under federal law when federal law creates the cause of action asserted. *See American Well Works Co. v. Layne & Bowler Co.*, 241 U.S. 257, 260 (1916) ("A suit arises under the law that creates the cause of action"). As a rule of inclusion, this "creation" test admits of only extremely rare exceptions, *see, e.g., Shoshone Mining Co. v. Rutter*, 177 U.S. 505 (1900), and accounts for the vast bulk of suits that arise under federal law, *see Franchise Tax Bd. of Cal. v. Construction Laborers Vacation Trust for Southern Cal.*, 463 U.S. 1, 9 (1983). Minton's original patent infringement suit against NASD and NASDAQ, for example, arose under federal law in this manner because it was authorized by 35 U.S.C. §§ 271, 281.

But even where a claim finds its origins in state rather than federal law— as Minton's legal malpractice claim indisputably does—we have identified a "special and small category" of cases in which arising under jurisdiction still lies. *Empire Healthchoice Assurance, Inc. v. McVeigh*, 547 U.S. 677, 699 (2006). In outlining the contours of this slim category, we do not paint on a blank canvas. Unfortunately, the canvas looks like one that Jackson Pollock got to first. *See* 13D C. Wright, A. Miller, E. Cooper, & R. Freer, Federal Practice and Procedure § 3562, pp. 175-176 (3d ed. 2008) (reviewing general confusion on question).

In an effort to bring some order to this unruly doctrine several Terms ago, we condensed our prior cases into the following inquiry: Does the "state-law claim necessarily raise a stated federal issue, actually disputed and substantial, which a federal forum may entertain without disturbing any congressionally approved balance of federal and state judicial responsibilities"? *Grable*, 545 U.S., at 314. That is, federal jurisdiction over a state law claim will lie if a federal issue is: (1) necessarily raised, (2) actually disputed, (3) substantial, and (4) capable of resolution in federal court without disrupting the federal-state balance approved by Congress. Where all four of these requirements are met, we held, jurisdiction is proper because there is a "serious federal interest in claiming the advantages thought to be inherent in a federal forum," which can be vindicated without disrupting Congress's intended division of labor between state and federal courts. *Id.*, at 313-314.

III

Applying *Grable*'s inquiry here, it is clear that Minton's legal malpractice claim does not arise under federal patent law. Indeed, for the reasons we discuss, we are comfortable concluding that state legal malpractice claims based on underlying patent matters will rarely, if ever, arise under federal patent law for purposes of § 1338(a). Although such cases may necessarily raise disputed questions of patent law, those cases are by their nature unlikely to have the sort of significance for the federal system necessary to establish jurisdiction.

A

To begin, we acknowledge that resolution of a federal patent question is "necessary" to Minton's case. Under Texas law, a plaintiff alleging legal malpractice must establish four elements: (1) that the defendant attorney owed the plaintiff a duty; (2) that the attorney breached that duty; (3) that the breach was the proximate cause of the plaintiff's injury; and (4) that damages occurred. *See Alexander v. Turtur & Associates, Inc.,* 146 S.W.3d 113, 117 (Tex. 2004). In cases like this one, in which the attorney's alleged error came in failing to make a particular argument, the causation element requires a "case within a case" analysis of whether, had the argument been made, the outcome of the earlier litigation would have been different. 355 S.W.3d, at 639 (2012). To prevail on his legal malpractice claim, therefore, Minton must show that he would have prevailed in his federal patent infringement case if only petitioners had timely made an experimental-use argument on his behalf. 355 S.W.3d, at 644. That will necessarily require application of patent law to the facts of Minton's case.

B

The federal issue is also "actually disputed" here—indeed, on the merits, it is the central point of dispute. Minton argues that the experimental-use exception properly applied to his lease to Stark, saving his patent from the on-sale bar; petitioners argue that it did not. This is just the sort of " 'dispute . . . respecting the . . . effect of [federal] law' " that *Grable* envisioned. 545 U.S., at 313.

C

Minton's argument founders on *Grable*'s next requirement, however, for the federal issue in this case is not substantial in the relevant sense. In reaching the opposite conclusion, the Supreme Court of Texas focused on the importance of the issue to the plaintiff's case and to the parties before it. 355 S.W.3d, at 644 ("because the success of Minton's malpractice claim is reliant upon the viability of the experimental use exception as a defense to the on-sale bar, we hold that it is a substantial federal issue"). As our past cases show, however, it is not enough that the federal issue be significant to the particular parties in the immediate suit; that will always be true when the state claim "necessarily raise[s]" a disputed federal issue, as *Grable* separately requires. The substantiality inquiry under *Grable* looks instead to the importance of the issue to the federal system as a whole.

In *Grable* itself, for example, the Internal Revenue Service had seized property from the plaintiff and sold it to satisfy the plaintiff's federal tax delinquency. 545 U.S., at 310-31. Five years later, the plaintiff filed a state law quiet title action against the third party that had purchased the property, alleging that the IRS had failed to comply with certain federally imposed notice requirements, so that the seizure and sale were invalid. In holding that the case arose under federal law, we primarily focused not on the interests of the litigants themselves, but rather on the broader significance of the notice question for the Federal Government. We emphasized the Government's "strong interest" in being able to recover delinquent taxes through seizure and sale of property, which in turn "require[d] clear terms of notice to allow buyers . . . to satisfy themselves that the Service has touched the bases necessary for good title." *Id.*, at 315. The Government's "direct interest in the availability of a federal forum to vindicate its own administrative action" made the question "an important issue of federal law that sensibly belong[ed] in a federal court." *Ibid.*

A second illustration of the sort of substantiality we require comes from *Smith v. Kansas City Title & Trust Co.*, 255 U.S. 180 (1921), which *Grable* described as "[t]he classic example" of a state claim arising under federal law. 545 U.S., at 312. In *Smith*, the plaintiff argued that the defendant bank could not purchase certain bonds issued by the Federal Government because the Government had acted unconstitutionally in issuing them. 255 U.S., at 198. We held that the case arose under federal law, because the "decision depends upon the determination" of "the constitutional validity of an act of Congress which is directly drawn in question." *Id.*, at 201. Again, the relevant point was not the importance of the question to the parties alone but rather the importance more generally of a determination that the Government "securities were issued under an unconstitutional law, and hence of no validity." *Ibid.*

Here, the federal issue carries no such significance. Because of the backward-looking nature of a legal malpractice claim, the question is posed in a merely hypothetical sense: If Minton's lawyers had raised a timely experimental-use argument, would the result in the patent infringement proceeding have been different? No matter how the state courts resolve that hypothetical "case within a case," it will not change the real-world result of the prior federal patent litigation. Minton's patent will remain invalid.

Nor will allowing state courts to resolve these cases undermine "the development of a uniform body of [patent] law." *Bonito Boats, Inc. v. Thunder Craft Boats, Inc.*, 489 U.S. 141, 162 (1989). Congress ensured such uniformity by vesting exclusive jurisdiction over actual patent cases in the federal district courts and exclusive appellate jurisdiction in the Federal Circuit. *See* 28 U.S.C. §§ 1338(a), 1295(a)(1). In resolving the nonhypothetical patent questions those cases present, the federal courts are of course not bound by state court case-within-a-case patent rulings. In any event, the state court case-within-a-case inquiry asks what would have happened in the prior federal proceeding if a particular argument had been made. In answering that question, state courts can be expected to hew closely to the pertinent federal precedents. It is those precedents, after all, that would have applied had the argument been made.

As for more novel questions of patent law that may arise for the first time in a state court "case within a case," they will at some point be decided by a federal court in the context of an actual patent case, with review in the Federal Circuit. If the question arises frequently, it will soon be resolved within the federal system, laying to rest any contrary state court precedent; if it does not arise frequently, it is unlikely to implicate substantial federal interests. The present case is "poles apart from *Grable*," in which a state court's resolution of the federal question "would be controlling in numerous other cases." *Empire Healthchoice Assurance, Inc.*, 547 U.S., at 700.

Minton also suggests that state courts' answers to hypothetical patent questions can sometimes have real-world effect on other patents through issue preclusion. Minton, for example, has filed what is known as a "continuation patent" application related to his original patent. *See* 35 U.S.C. § 120; 4A D. Chisum, Patents § 13.03 (2005) (describing continuation applications). He argues that, in evaluating this separate application, the patent examiner could be bound by the Texas trial court's interpretation of the scope of Minton's original patent. It is unclear whether this is true. The Patent and Trademark Office's Manual of Patent Examining Procedure provides that res judicata is a proper ground for rejecting a patent "only when the earlier decision was a decision of the Board of Appeals" or certain federal reviewing courts, giving no indication that state court decisions would have preclusive effect. *See* Dept. of Commerce, Patent and Trademark Office, Manual of Patent Examining Procedure § 706.03(w), p. 700-79 (rev. 8th ed. 2012); 35 U.S.C. §§ 134(a), 141, 145; Reply Brief 9-10. In fact, Minton has not identified any case finding such preclusive effect based on a state court decision. But even assuming that a state court's case-within-a-case adjudication may be preclusive under some circumstances, the result would be limited to the parties and patents that had been before the state court. Such "fact-bound and situation-specific" effects are not sufficient to establish federal arising under jurisdiction. *Empire Healthchoice Assurance, Inc., supra*, at 701.

Nor can we accept the suggestion that the federal courts' greater familiarity with patent law means that legal malpractice cases like this one belong in federal court. . . . It is true that a similar interest was among those we considered in *Grable*, 545 U.S., at 314. But the possibility that a state court will incorrectly resolve a state claim is not, by itself, enough to trigger the federal courts' exclusive patent jurisdiction, even if the potential error finds its root in a misunderstanding of patent law.

There is no doubt that resolution of a patent issue in the context of a state legal malpractice action can be vitally important to the particular parties in that case. But something more, demonstrating that the question is significant to the federal system as a whole, is needed. That is missing here.

D

It follows from the foregoing that *Grable*'s fourth requirement is also not met. That requirement is concerned with the appropriate "balance of federal and state judicial responsibilities." *Ibid.* We have already explained the absence of a substantial federal issue within the meaning of *Grable*. The States, on the other hand, have "a special responsibility for maintaining standards among members of the licensed professions." *Ohralik v. Ohio State Bar Assn.*, 436 U.S. 447, 460 (1978). Their "interest . . . in regulating lawyers is especially great since lawyers are essential to the primary governmental function of administering justice, and have historically been officers of the courts." *Goldfarb v. Virginia State Bar*, 421 U.S. 773, 792 (1975) (internal quotation marks omitted). We have no reason to suppose that Congress— in establishing exclusive federal jurisdiction over patent cases—meant to bar from state courts state legal malpractice claims simply because they require resolution of a hypothetical patent issue.

. . .

As we recognized a century ago, "[t]he Federal courts have exclusive jurisdiction of all cases arising under the patent laws, but not of all questions in which a patent may be the subject-matter of the controversy." *New Marshall Engine Co. v. Marshall Engine Co.*, 223 U.S. 473, 478 (1912). In this case, although the state courts must answer a question of patent law to resolve Minton's legal malpractice claim, their answer will have no broader effects. It will not stand as binding precedent for any future patent claim; it will not even affect the validity of Minton's patent. Accordingly, there is no "serious federal interest in claiming the advantages thought to be inherent in a federal forum," *Grable, supra*, at 313. Section 1338(a) does not deprive the state courts of subject matter jurisdiction.

The judgment of the Supreme Court of Texas is reversed, and the case is remanded for further proceedings not inconsistent with this opinion.

REVIEW QUESTIONS

1. What is the four-part test for determining whether there is an embedded federal question permitting the exercise of the federal courts' jurisdiction? What part of the test is likely to be hardest for parties seeking federal jurisdiction to meet?

2. The Supreme Court emphasizes that the embedded federal question doctrine will rarely be applied. If so, why have this exception at all? Is this test consistent with the idea discussed earlier that subject matter jurisdiction is important to determine quickly and therefore a rule of thumb is appropriate?

3. Try to answer the following hypothetical questions based on the readings so far:
   - A federal law requires that drinking water provided by states and local governments must comply with safety regulations, including limits on the level of contaminants in the water. The statute also provides that

"any person may commence a civil action on his own behalf against any person (including the United States, and any other governmental instrumentality or agency to the extent permitted by the Eleventh Amendment to the Constitution) who is alleged to be in violation of any requirement prescribed by or under this subchapter." A plaintiff has evidence that drinking water in her town does not comply with the federal regulation. Can the plaintiff file suit in federal court? Under what authority? Can the plaintiff sue in state court?

- A Buyer bought bottled water labeled "spring water" only to learn that the water did not in fact come from a spring, but from the defendant bottling company's tap water. She sued the company in federal court under her state consumer protection statute, claiming that the company misrepresented the tap water as spring water. The defendant company argued in its Answer that its product complies with the definition of "spring water" contained in the Federal Food, Drug, and Cosmetic Act. Assume that the Answer concedes that the court has subject matter jurisdiction. Do the federal courts have jurisdiction over this case?

- A client sued his lawyer, alleging that the lawyer's negligence resulted in his losing his case in bankruptcy. He wants to file his legal malpractice case in federal court; can he? (Federal courts have exclusive subject matter jurisdiction over bankruptcy matters.)

- The director of a community college was fired for testifying at a federal criminal trial of a local politician who was accused of fraud. The director wants to sue the college for breach of her employment contract. Based on these facts, can she sue in federal court on that claim? What if the director claims that the college violated her First Amendment right to freedom of speech by retaliating at her for testifying?

C. DIVERSITY JURISDICTION

While it is understandable that the Framers would grant the federal courts authority to hear cases arising under federal law, it is harder to explain the provision of diversity jurisdiction, which provides for the adjudication of some *state law* claims in federal court.

No doubt a major impetus for diversity jurisdiction was the concern in 1789 (when persons identified more with their locality than with the new national entity) that the state courts might not be level playing fields in cases pitting nonresident litigants against forum residents.

But the provision was controversial, and, as Judge Henry Friendly pointed out in his foundational article on the history of diversity jurisdiction, the defense of the provision was lackluster. Henry Friendly, *The Historic Basis of Diversity Jurisdiction*, 41 Harv. L. Rev. 483, 493 (1928). While the argument in its favor was concern about prejudice against out-of-state litigants, James Madison and other proponents offered no examples of such bias. This is likely because the real reason for the grant of jurisdiction was tied up with the development of American monetary policy. The federalist assumption (one that turns out to have been correct) seems to have been that the federal courts would favor creditors over debtors. By contrast, the Antifederalists feared that federal jurisdiction would make it difficult for people (i.e. debtors) to defend suits in distant and expensive federal forums. *Id.* at 491-492. The state courts, they argued, were expert enough and a known quantity. A secondary concern was that the federal courts would make state law with respect to property and contract. (We will see later how the federal judiciary evolved from imposing its own vision of law over diversity cases to applying state law.)

In the end, as the federalists expected, access to the federal courts promoted the national economy by providing a forum for commercial and property disputes among citizens of different states. President and Chief Justice William Howard Taft said that diversity jurisdiction "was the single most important element in securing capital for the development of the southern and western United States." William Howard Taft, *Possible and Needed Reforms in Administration of Justice in Federal Courts*, 8 A.B.A. J. 601, 604 (1922).

Over the years there have been unsuccessful legislative efforts to curtail or eliminate diversity jurisdiction. In the beginning, Congress debated limiting diversity jurisdiction by imposing an amount in controversy requirement to favor poorer debtors. The Judiciary Act of 1789 set the amount in controversy for federal diversity jurisdiction at $500, and this amount has been periodically increased, albeit not frequently. A 1982 Report of the House Judiciary Committee submitted in support of one attempt to eliminate diversity jurisdiction altogether observed: "[T]he abolition of diversity jurisdiction is an important step in reducing endemic court congestion and its insidious effects on litigants. . . . [T]he original reasons for diversity jurisdiction have long since disappeared." In addition to concerns about court congestion, other arguments against diversity jurisdiction are that (1) it is inconsistent with principles of federalism and respect for states; (2) it retards the development of state law (by state courts); and (3) it diminishes incentives for state court reform by influential professional groups who, by virtue of diversity jurisdiction, seldom litigate in state courts.

Of course, others disagree about the need for federal courts to exercise diversity jurisdiction. With regard to the need for a federal forum for some state law claims, consider these comments from a Justice of the West Virginia Supreme Court: "As long as I am allowed to redistribute wealth from out-of-state companies to injured in-state plaintiffs, I shall continue to do so. Not only is my sleep enhanced when I give someone else's money away, but so is my job security, because the in-state plaintiffs, their families and their friends will re-elect me." Hon. Richard Neely, *The Product Liability Mess: How Business Can Be Rescued from the Politics of State Courts* 4 (1988).

Arguments in favor of broader diversity jurisdiction have been dominant in recent years. Congress expanded the federal court's diversity jurisdiction at the start of the twenty-first century in two ways: first, by not raising the amount in controversy (as a result of inflation, cases of lower and lower value may be brought in the federal courts); and second, by statutorily expanding federal jurisdiction for controversial categories of cases, such as class actions and mass torts. You will learn more about this in Chapter 11.

The vast majority of cases in federal court on diversity jurisdiction are based upon 28 U.S.C. § 1332(a)(1), which regards actions between and among U.S. citizens (including U.S. corporations). That section provides that "[t]he district courts shall have original jurisdiction of all civil actions where the matter in controversy exceeds the sum or value of $75,000, exclusive of interest and costs, and is between . . . citizens of different States." There are two essential prerequisites for this species of diversity jurisdiction: (1) complete diversity and (2) a sufficient amount in controversy. We will consider each of these issues separately.

1. Complete Diversity

Section 1332 creates access to federal court for certain disputes "between . . . citizens of different States." This is referred to as a *diversity* requirement. A very early Supreme Court opinion, *Strawbridge v. Curtiss*, 7 U.S. (3 Cranch) 267 (1806), imposed a significant limitation on diversity jurisdiction under 28 U.S.C. § 1332(a)(1) by requiring *complete* diversity. In *Strawbridge*, there were citizens from different states on both sides of the "v.," but there were also citizens from the same state on both sides of the "v." (e.g., Plaintiff from Massachusetts v. Defendant 1 from Vermont and Defendant 2 from Massachusetts). The Court required—and § 1332 still requires—"complete diversity," meaning every plaintiff must be a citizen of a different state than every defendant in the action. Shared citizenship between any two parties across the "v." destroys diversity jurisdiction.

> [We] have adhered to the complete diversity rule in light of the purpose of the diversity requirement, which is to provide a federal forum for important disputes where state courts might favor, or be perceived as favoring, home-state litigants. The presence of parties from the same State on both sides of a case dispels this concern, eliminating a principal reason for conferring § 1332 jurisdiction over any of the claims in the action.

Exxon Mobil Corp. v. Allapattah Services, Inc., 545 U.S. 546, 553 (2005).

Especially because of the requirement of complete diversity, determining the citizenship of a party is critical. Is a student from Florida who is going to law school in Georgia a citizen of Florida or Georgia? What is the citizenship of a corporation that is incorporated in Delaware, has a principal place of business in Illinois, and does substantial business in all fifty states? And what is the citizenship of a partnership whose partners all work in New York, but who live in New Jersey, Connecticut, and New York? How does one determine the citizenship of a party—whether that party is a person, a corporation, or something else?

Corporations. For diversity purposes, a U.S. corporation is deemed a citizen of both its state of incorporation and the state where it has its principal place of business. Read 28 U.S.C. § 1332(c)(1). Unlike a natural person, a corporation may thus be a citizen of more than one state if incorporated in a state different from where its principal place of business is located. If a corporation that is incorporated in Delaware with a principal place of business in Texas files a lawsuit against a corporation that is incorporated in Delaware with a principal place of business in Virginia, complete diversity is absent and 1332(a)(1) does not authorize jurisdiction. A corporation's principal place of business is determined by the location of its "nerve center," meaning where the corporation has its headquarters—its "center of overall direction, control, and coordination." *Hertz Corp. v. Friend*, 559 U.S. 77 (2010).

Unincorporated Associations. An unincorporated association (e.g., a limited liability company (LLC), a partnership, labor union, the governing board of an institution) usually is a citizen of the states of each of its members. *See Americold Realty Trust v. ConAgra Foods, Inc.,* U.S., 136 S. Ct. 1012 (2016). Thus if a partnership wants to sue a California corporation that has its principal place of business in Nevada, there is no diversity jurisdiction if *any* member of the partnership: plaintiff is a citizen of either California or Nevada. (The citizenship of unincorporated associations is treated differently in the context of class actions. *See* 28 U.S.C. § 1332(d)(10).)

Natural Persons. The citizenship of a natural person is modified for diversity purposes by the concept of *domicile. Mas v. Perry*, 489 F.2d 1396, 1399 (5th Cir. 1974). One's domicile is determined by the last place where she was both present and intending to remain indefinitely. In other words, if a person's current residence is a place where she intends to remain indefinitely, the current residence would be her domicile—and, therefore, her state of citizenship for purposes of the diversity analysis. But if a person's current residence is not a place where she intends to remain indefinitely, then her domicile would be the place where she was last both present and intending to remain indefinitely. An individual always has only one domicile, and she keeps that domicile until she or he assumes a new domicile.

Whether one intends to remain somewhere indefinitely is a highly fact-specific inquiry. Sometimes people move to a different state without intending to remain there indefinitely (in which case, they maintain their previous domicile). Sometimes a person is displaced from a domicile by a natural disaster. It is sometimes hard to determine where someone intends to live indefinitely. Should an affidavit, signed after litigation has commenced, be sufficient to establish domicile? In the next case we see that courts consider a number of factors to determine whether an individual possesses the intent to remain somewhere indefinitely.

Many of you will already be familiar with the life story of at least one of the players in this case. Mark Zuckerberg is the founder of the social media company Facebook and was a billionaire by the age of 23. In 2010, Paul Ceglia filed a lawsuit claiming substantial ownership of that company based on an interaction he had with Zuckerberg in 2003. Ceglia wanted to keep his case in New York State Court, where he was domiciled and where Zuckerberg grew up. At the time that the lawsuit was brought, Zuckerberg was 26 years old.

Ceglia v. Zuckerberg
772 F. Supp. 2d 453 (W.D.N.Y. 2011)

RICHARD J. ARCARA, District Judge.

Plaintiff Paul Ceglia commenced this action in New York State Supreme Court asserting a breach of contract claim against defendants Mark Elliot Zuckerberg and Facebook, Inc. ("Facebook"). Defendants removed to federal court based upon diversity jurisdiction. Plaintiff moves to remand claiming that diversity is lacking because he and defendant Zuckerberg are both domiciled in New York. Zuckerberg opposes the motion and claims that his domicile is California. For the reasons stated, the Court finds that diversity jurisdiction exists because Zuckerberg is domiciled in California. Accordingly, the motion to remand is denied.

In this action, plaintiff claims that, pursuant to the terms of a 2003 contract between Zuckerberg and himself, he (plaintiff) owns an eighty-four percent interest in defendant Facebook. Facebook is a social media company that was founded by Zuckerberg in 2004. It has since grown into a highly successful company employing over 1,600 employees with more than 500 million active users. Zuckerberg is the founder, Chairman and CEO of Facebook, a Delaware corporation with its principal place of business in Palo Alto, California.

At issue in this motion is defendant Zuckerberg's domicile. Zuckerberg's domicile was also the subject of a prior unrelated federal proceeding. *See ConnectU LLC v. Zuckerberg, et al.,* 482 F.Supp.2d 3 (D. Mass. 2007), *rev'd,* 522 F.3d 82 (2008). In that case, Zuckerberg asserted New York domicile as of September 2004, the date on which that case had been filed. At the time, Zuckerberg had just completed his sophomore year at Harvard University, had spent the summer of 2004 in California, and had decided to take a temporary leave of absence from Harvard. Zuckerberg represented to the ConnectU court that, despite his temporary residency in California, he intended to return to New York after graduating from Harvard. Based upon those representations, the court determined that Zuckerberg's domicile as of September 2, 2004, was New York.

As it turns out, Zuckerberg never did return to Harvard or to New York. Instead, he remained in California where he continues to live today. Zuckerberg explains that certain events occurred in the fall of 2004 that caused him to alter his original plans and remain in California permanently. From 2004 to the present, Facebook grew from a small startup internet company with only a handful of employees to an international social media company with a global presence. Zuckerberg is the Chairman and CEO of the company and runs its day-to-day operations. He rents an apartment in Palo Alto, California, that is within walking distance to Facebook headquarters. Zuckerberg has provided a sworn affidavit stating that he intends to live in California indefinitely.

According to plaintiff, Zuckerberg's actual domicile remains New York where his parents still reside. Plaintiff claims that Zuckerberg has failed to demonstrate his intent to remain in California indefinitely and, as such, the law presumes that his prior New York domicile remains. Alternatively, plaintiff argues that jurisdictional discovery and a hearing are necessary to ascertain Zuckerberg's true domicile.

DISCUSSION

. . . Diversity jurisdiction exists where the parties are citizens of different states and the amount in controversy exceeds $75,000. *Hallingby v. Hallingby*, 574 F.3d 51, 56 (2d Cir.2009). "'[C]itizens of different States' means that there must be complete diversity, i.e., that each plaintiff's citizenship must be different from the citizenship of each defendant." *Id*. If Zuckerberg is a citizen of New York, as plaintiff contends, then diversity would be lacking because both the plaintiff and one of the defendants would be from the same state.

A person's citizenship for purposes of diversity is based upon his domicile. Domicile is "the place where a person has 'his true fixed home and principal establishment, and to which, whenever he is absent, he has the intention of returning.'" *Linardos v. Fortuna*, 157 F.3d 945, 948 (2d Cir.1998). A person can have multiple residences, but only one domicile. Domicile is determined as of the date the complaint is filed.

A person's domicile, once established, is presumed to continue absent evidence that it has been changed. To effect a change in domicile, two elements are required: (1) residence in a new domicile; and (2) the intention to remain there indefinitely. A person asserting a change in domicile bears the burden of proving it by clear and convincing evidence.

. . . Courts consider the following objective indicators to ascertain domiciliary intent: current residence; voting registration and voting practices; location of personal and real property; location of brokerage and bank accounts; membership in unions, fraternal organizations, churches, clubs, and other associations; place of employment or business; driver's license and automobile registration [and] payment of taxes. No single factor is conclusive and the determination is made based upon the totality of the circumstances.

Those objective indicators support Zuckerberg's claim of California domicile. He currently resides in California and has done so continuously since the summer of 2004. He has no other residences. He does not own real property in New York, California or elsewhere. In 2007, he purchased and registered a vehicle in California. He does not own or lease any other vehicles. Zuckerberg has paid California resident income taxes since 2004. He lists his California residence on his federal income tax returns. He has not filed taxes in any state other than California since 2004. Since at least 2007, he has been registered to vote in California and has voted in California. He possesses a valid California driver's license issued in 2006. His bank and brokerage accounts list his California residence and his investment advisors are located in California. Zuckerberg receives his mail at a California post office box and at his Facebook office. Most significantly, however, he is the owner, founder and CEO of a multi-billion dollar corporation with over 1,600 employees and a principal place of business within walking distance to his current residence in Palo Alto, California. Together, these facts overwhelmingly show that as of June 2010, Zuckerberg had changed his domicile to California and intends to remain there indefinitely.

Plaintiff cites what he perceives as a "dizzying array of zip codes" used by Zuckerberg to support his claim that Zuckerberg has no fixed roots in California. That Zuckerberg may use different addresses for different purposes provides no support for plaintiff's position where, as here, each zip code begins with a Northern California ("94") prefix.

Plaintiff also claims that Zuckerberg's assertion of California domicile is not credible in light of his prior claim of New York domicile. The fact that Zuckerberg was domiciled in New York in September 2004 does not preclude a finding of California domicile as of June 2010. In 2004, Zuckerberg was a 20-year old college student from New York who had decided to spend the summer of his sophomore year in California. Although he had originally intended to return to Harvard at the end of that summer, events occurred causing him to alter that plan. By August 2004, Facebook experienced significant growth and a $500,000 investment. At that point, Zuckerberg decided to take a temporary leave of absence from Harvard. Even then, however, he ultimately intended to return to Harvard to obtain his undergraduate degree. Over the next year, Facebook grew rapidly and by 2005, it had received $12.7 million in funding and had over 5 million users. That growth continued. In 2006, it had grown to 12 million users and had raised $27.5 million. Zuckerberg claims that at some point in 2006, he decided not to return to Harvard or to New York. Instead, he decided to remain in California to run Facebook. By 2007, Facebook had grown to over 50 million users. As of 2010, when this lawsuit was filed, Facebook had over 500 million active users and employed over 1,600 people. It is simply incomprehensible to believe that Zuckerberg intends to abandon his life, friends and daily management of his multi-billion dollar company to return to New York and live near his parents.

Although the law presumes that a prior domicile will continue until a change has occurred, there is ample evidence of Zuckerberg's change in domicile. The evidence of this change is so overwhelming that this Court finds a hearing on the issue to be unnecessary. . . .

Exceptions to the Complete Diversity Requirement. Even when the parties are completely diverse, matters of domestic relations (divorce, alimony, and custody) and probate (wills, trusts, and estates) have long been considered outside the realm of diversity jurisdiction by virtue of judicially created exceptions. *See generally Marshall v. Marshall*, 547 U.S. 293 (2006) (Anna Nicole Smith's dispute with her stepson over her husband's estate), and *Ankenbrandt v. Richards*, 504 U.S. 689 (1992). What explains this carve-out? Are these matters more "local" than other matters of state law (such as malpractice, fraud, battery, trespass)? Do they require expertise that only state judges possess? Is it sexism? *See* Judith Resnik, *"Naturally" Without Gender: Women, Jurisdiction, and the Federal Courts,* 66 N.Y.U. L. Rev. 1682 (1991).

For other subject areas, the complete diversity requirement is recognized as subject to Congressional alteration. For certain disputes, Congress has created original jurisdiction that requires only *minimal* diversity. Minimal diversity requires some diversity (as opposed to complete diversity) between the parties. For example, under the Class Action Fairness Act, the district courts have original jurisdiction over class actions in which the matter in controversy exceeds the sum of $5 million provided "any member of a class of plaintiff is a citizen of a State different from any defendant." 28 U.S.C. § 1332(d)(2)(A). Similarly, under the Federal Interpleader Act, the district courts have original jurisdiction over some interpleaders, provided any two rival claimants are diverse. 28 U.S.C. § 1335(a)(1). Remember that Congress cannot create original jurisdiction for the district courts that is not also authorized by the judicial Power outlined in Art. III, § 2 of the U.S. Constitution. To create federal subject matter jurisdiction over state law clams, one of those constitutional bases is "Controversies . . . between Citizens of different States." *See State Farm Fire & Cas. Co. v. Tashire,* 386 U.S. 523 (1967).

Alienage Jurisdiction. Actions that involve foreign citizens (or foreign corporations) do not fall within the scope of 28 U.S.C. § 1332(a)(1), which is limited to actions between "citizens of different States." The word "citizen" in that subsection means U.S. citizen. And use of the capital letter S on the word "State" means one of the United States. Accordingly, if the action involves a foreign citizen or a foreign corporation, diversity jurisdiction must be founded on one of the other subsections of § 1332.

Sections 1332(a)(2) and (a)(3) are often referred to as "alienage jurisdiction." These sections authorize another type of diversity jurisdiction. If a California plaintiff wants to sue a Panamanian defendant, she would invoke § 1332(a)(2), which (assuming the requisite amount in controversy) extends jurisdiction to actions between "citizens of a State and citizens or subjects of a foreign state." A "citizen[ ] or subject[ ] of a foreign state" refers to an alien citizen or alien corporation. In the hypothetical, this is the "Panamanian defendant." Notice, however, that if the Panamanian defendant has been admitted to the United States for permanent residence and is domiciled in California, the action no longer falls within the scope of § 1332(a)(2). In that circumstance, the Panamanian citizen is deemed a citizen of California, destroying diversity jurisdiction.

Section 1332(a)(3), in turn, provides jurisdiction when aliens are joined as additional parties in a lawsuit that would otherwise fall within the scope of § 1332(a)(1). If the California plaintiff wants to sue the Panamanian defendant *and a second defendant*, a U.S. citizen domiciled in Texas, this scenario is covered by § 1332(a)(3). This would be an action between "citizens of different states" (to wit, the California plaintiff and the Texas defendant) "in which citizens or subjects of a foreign state are additional parties" (to wit, the Panamanian defendant).

Citizens Without a Domicile. Generally speaking, jurisdictional statutes are construed narrowly. Such an approach can lead to unusual results. Consider the following fact pattern, which is based on a real case.

In a highly publicized contract dispute arising from the epic film *Cleopatra*, the motion picture studio sought to recover $25 million in damages from Richard Burton and Elizabeth Taylor. These two great actors from Hollywood's Golden Age met on the set of *Cleopatra* and eventually married. Burton was a British subject. Elizabeth Taylor was a citizen of the United States who, at the relevant time, lived abroad and intended to remain there indefinitely. The plaintiff, the motion picture studio, was a Delaware corporation with a principal place of business in California. Is there diversity jurisdiction? Try to answer this question yourself before reading any further.

Section 1332(a)(1) would not authorize jurisdiction because Burton was a foreign citizen. Section 1332(a)(1) does not include foreigners within its scope.

Section 1332(a)(2) would not authorize jurisdiction because although Burton was a "citizen[ ] or subject[ ] of a foreign state," the other defendant, Taylor, was not. Indeed, Taylor was an American citizen.

Section 1332(a)(3) would not authorize jurisdiction because, as to the first part of this subsection, this was not an action between "citizens of different States." Although the plaintiff was a citizen of a state (two states, actually), neither of the defendants was a "citizen of [a] State." Burton was not a U.S. citizen. And Taylor, although a U.S. citizen, was not a citizen *of a State*. Instead she was a citizen domiciled abroad. Without a (United) "State" to which she could be attributed, the statute did not authorize diversity jurisdiction. This phenomenon is often referred to as "the Stateless citizen." *See Twentieth Century-Fox Film Corporation v. Taylor and Burton*, 239 F. Supp. 913 (S.D.N.Y. 1965).

REVIEW QUESTIONS

Use the readings so far on citizenship in diversity jurisdiction to answer the following questions. Assume in each case the amount in controversy requirement is met.

1. Patty was raised in Alabama. After graduating high school she joined the military and served for two years in Florida. She then attended a Florida state school and paid in-state tuition. When she graduated from college she remained in Florida for several years, before returning to Alabama for one year, and then moving back to Florida last year. She has continued to see the same doctor in Alabama all this time, is registered to vote in

Alabama (although she has never voted), and visits frequently. She briefly attended law school at a public university in Florida last year, where she paid in-state tuition. She is currently staying with friends in Florida. If she wants to file a suit against an Alabama hospital for medical malpractice (a tort claim), is there federal jurisdiction over the suit?

2. The Flying Scooter Company is incorporated in Delaware and has its manufacturing plant and conducts research and development of new scooters in Stonington, Connecticut. The offices of the company's chief executive, chief operations officer, chief financial officer, and marketing director are all over the state line, less than twenty miles away in Westerly, Rhode Island. Of what states is Flying Scooter a citizen? If Peter, who is domiciled in Connecticut, wants to sue them for $100,000 for selling a defective scooter, can he sue in federal court?

3. A national law firm, Ward & Cho LLC, has offices in California, Illinois, Massachusetts, New York, and Washington. A client, who is domiciled in California, wants to sue the firm based on work Cho did for him in Illinois. Does the federal court have jurisdiction over the client's claim?

4. Paz, who was born, raised, and has always lived in New Hampshire, sues Dietz, who was born and raised in Connecticut but recently moved to Paris with the dream of becoming a fashion designer there. Assuming an amount in controversy of $250,000 on a state-law claim, would a U.S. district court in New Hampshire have diversity jurisdiction over the suit? How about a U.S. district court in Connecticut?

5. Pierre is a citizen of France. He wants to sue Julian, a citizen of Belize, in federal court. Can he? Under what authority?
   • Now assume that Pierre, still a citizen of France, has lived in New Mexico for the last seven years and is permanent resident alien. He wants to sue the New Mexico Light and Power Co., incorporated and doing business in New Mexico, in federal court. Can he? Under what authority?
   • If Joe, a citizen of California, joins Pierre's suit against New Mexico Light and Power, is there federal jurisdiction?

6. A plaintiff with a $100,000 state-law claim against a citizen of the same state moves to a neighboring state for the purpose of establishing diversity jurisdiction in federal court. Consider two possibilities: (1) What if the plaintiff "moved" to the neighboring state only for the day, and "moved" back the day after filing the suit? (2) What if the plaintiff "moved" to the neighboring state, genuinely intends to remain there indefinitely, but admits that the move was *solely* to establish diversity jurisdiction and not for any other reason?

2. Amount in Controversy

The amount in controversy for purposes of diversity jurisdiction is determined by the sum claimed by the plaintiff in good faith, and the standard for dismissal for lack of the jurisdictional minimum is quite high: "It must appear to a legal certainty that the claim is really for less than the jurisdictional amount to justify dismissal." *St. Paul Mercury Indemnity Co. v. Red Cab Co.*, 303 U.S. 283 (1938). *See, e.g., Sellers v. O'Connell*, 701 F.2d 575 (6th Cir. 1983) (complaint dismissed where plaintiff was only entitled to recover maximum of $9,875 in pension benefits). Since January 1997, in order to assert jurisdiction the matter in controversy must "exceed[ ] the sum or value of $75,000, exclusive of interest and costs." 28 U.S.C. § 1332.

Federal jurisdiction is not lost retroactively because a judgment is ultimately entered for less than the jurisdictional minimum. *See Mas v. Perry, supra*, 489 F.2d at 1400 (the fact that plaintiff husband recovered only $5,000 does not deprive federal court of jurisdiction, as his claim was made in good faith based on the evidence presented). Federal judges do, however, have the authority to impose court costs on a plaintiff who recovers less than the requisite minimum. 28 U.S.C. § 1332(b).

Like the "well-pleaded complaint" rule for § 1331 jurisdiction, the aim here is to be able to determine § 1332 jurisdiction early in the litigation on the basis of the complaint. Once jurisdiction "attaches," subsequent events (like the award of less than the jurisdictional minimum or the relocation of a diverse party to a non-diverse state) do not deprive the court of power. Do you see how the interests of efficiency and certainty dictate this approach? What would happen if subject matter jurisdiction were contingent on the ultimate award of damages?

In order to reach the requisite amount in controversy, a plaintiff may aggregate all claims (related or not, *see* Fed. R. Civ. P. 18) brought against a single defendant in the complaint. For example, a plaintiff may join a $50,000 tort claim and a (related or unrelated) $40,000 contract claim against a diverse defendant, and fall within the scope of the court's diversity subject matter jurisdiction.

A plaintiff may not, however, join *parties* to reach the amount in controversy. In other words, a plaintiff cannot satisfy the amount in controversy by joining a $50,000 claim against one defendant with a $40,000 (related or unrelated) claim against a second defendant.

What if one plaintiff has a claim that meets the amount in controversy and wants to join with a second plaintiff who does not? Section 1332 alone does not permit them to join; there would be no subject matter jurisdiction over the second plaintiff's claim. But a related statute discussed in Part D does allow the second plaintiff into the suit. That statute permits supplemental jurisdiction— that is, it allows a plaintiff to add a supplemental claim to a case that already meets the federal subject matter jurisdiction requirements. In *Exxon Mobil Corp. v. Allapattah Services, Inc.*, 545 U.S. 546 (2005), the Court held that the supplemental jurisdiction statute permits the exercise of diversity jurisdiction even where some plaintiffs fail to satisfy the minimum amount in controversy, as long as (1) at least one plaintiff does meet it, (2) complete diversity exists among the parties, and (3) all the claims are part of the same case or controversy.

In actions seeking declaratory or injunctive relief, the general rule is that courts weigh the value of the right sought to be enforced (as, for example, the value to plaintiff of preventing infringement of its trade name) or the cost of compliance to the defendant. Arthur R. Miller, 14AA Federal Prac. & Proc. Juris. § 3708 (4th ed. 2019).

As you read the following case, consider whether the court's reasoning is convincing to you, based on the information above as well as the general principle that jurisdictional statutes should be construed narrowly.

Hackman v. One Brands, LLC
No. CV 18-2101 (CKK) (D.D.C. APR. 1, 2019)

Colleen Kollar-Kotelly, United States District Judge.

Plaintiff Gloria Hackman filed suit against Defendant One Brands LLC, producer of One Bars, in the Superior Court of the District of Columbia ("Superior Court"), alleging that Defendant violated the District of Columbia Consumer Protection Procedures Act ("DCCPPA") by misleading consumers about the amount of sugar in One Bars. In short, Plaintiff's Complaint claims that One Bars contain far more sugar than is reported on labels and in advertising. . . .

. . . The Court concludes that . . . [it] lacks subject matter jurisdiction. First, the Court lacks class action jurisdiction under CAFA because this case is not a class action. Second, the Court lacks traditional diversity jurisdiction because, due to the non-aggregation principle, Defendant has not demonstrated that $75,000 or more is in controversy in this case.

I. BACKGROUND

Plaintiff is a resident of the District of Columbia who is a nurse as well as a public health and consumer watchdog. . . . As relief, Plaintiff seeks on behalf of the general public "[a]n injunction against Defendant, including that Defendant be barred from selling OneBars in the District of Columbia until the front of OneBar labels give truthful information about the sugar content of the bars." She also seeks attorneys' fees and costs and punitive damages. Finally, Plaintiff seeks statutory damages on her own behalf. She does not make a class action claim. . . .

III. DISCUSSION

. . .

B. TRADITIONAL DIVERSITY JURISDICTION

1. The Cost of Complying with the Requested Injunction

. . . Federal courts have diversity jurisdiction if the parties are citizens of different states and the amount in controversy exceeds $75,000. 28 U.S.C. § 1332(a). Plaintiff does not dispute that the parties are diverse. . . . Defendant is incorporated in Delaware and has its principal place of business in North Carolina, and Plaintiff resides in the District of Columbia. However, Plaintiff does dispute whether the amount in controversy exceeds $75,000. Defendant presents three grounds as to why the amount in controversy exceeds $75,000: the cost of complying with an injunction, punitive damages, and attorneys' fees. Addressing each argument in turn, the Court concludes that Defendant has failed to establish that Plaintiff's amount in controversy exceeds $75,000.

First, Defendant argues that the cost of complying with Plaintiff's requested injunction will exceed $75,000. In order to comply with the requested injunction, Defendant claims that it would need to "(1) recall[ ] the One Bars currently for sale in the District of Columbia; and either (2) redesign[ ] the packaging and marketing of One Bars to remove references to the bars' low sugar status; or (3) reformulat[e] One Bars." Defendant contends that recalling the One Bars currently on the market and redesigning and remarketing the bars would cost approximately $1,082,500. And, according to Defendant, recalling the One Bars currently on the market and reformulating future bars would cost approximately $130,000. Accordingly, Defendant argues that either method by which it would comply with the injunction exceeds the $75,000 threshold.

But, Defendant ignores the non-aggregation principle. Under the non-aggregation principle, "the separate and distinct claims of two or more plaintiffs cannot be aggregated in order to satisfy the jurisdictional amount requirement." *Snyder v. Harris*, 394 U.S. 332, 335 (1969). When a plaintiff seeks injunctive relief under the DCCPPA, courts in this Circuit have regularly held that the amount in controversy for purposes of jurisdiction is the total cost of the injunction divided by the number of beneficiaries in the general public.

. . . [T]he D.C. Circuit expressly recognized the "possible conflict" between the non-aggregation principle and "the rule which allows the jurisdictional amount to be based on the cost to the defendant of proposed relief," but explained that the Court has "not attempt[ed] to resolve" the possible conflict. *Fenster v. Schneider*, 636 F.2d 765, 767 n.1 (D.C. Cir. 1980). Lacking precedent from the D.C. Circuit, this Court is "persuaded by several district court opinions from this Circuit that have considered this conflict in the context of cases brought under the DCCPPA on behalf of the general public seeking injunctive relief and have determined that considering the *total* cost to the Defendant of complying with that relief would violate the non-aggregation principle."

The Court also considers and rejects Defendant's warning that plaintiffs may attempt to avoid federal jurisdiction through the non-aggregation principle by making a request for injunctive relief on behalf of many people. The Court finds that this risk of jurisdictional "gamesmanship" flows both ways. If the Court refused to apply the non-aggregation principle to the cost of complying with an injunction, then a plaintiff who was unable to meet the amount in controversy through damages could simply request injunctive relief in order to gain unmerited access to federal court. . . . The Court concludes that allowing unmerited access to federal courts in this way is the more serious risk because it is "contrary to the longstanding directive that federal jurisdiction should be strictly interpreted." Accordingly, the Court follows the vast weight of authority in this Circuit and concludes that the non-aggregation principle should be applied to the cost of Defendant's compliance with an injunction.

Assuming that Defendant's estimates of either $1,082,500 or $130,000 are accurate costs of compliance, Defendant has failed to establish that it meets the amount in controversy requirement. Defendant contends that 100 consumers in the District of Columbia have purchased One Bars. Accordingly, the apportioned cost of compliance would be either $10,825 for rebranding or $1,300 for reformulation, both of which fall below the diversity jurisdiction requirement of $75,000 dollars.

2. Punitive Damages

. . . Punitive damages are considered in determining the amount in controversy for purposes of diversity jurisdiction. . . . . For purposes of this Memorandum Opinion, the Court will assume that punitive damages could be as high as $900,000. However, the Court concludes that the non-aggregation principle also applies to punitive damages. As a result, Plaintiff's claim for punitive damages does not meet the amount in controversy.

. . . While the D.C. Circuit has not addressed this question, appellate courts in other circuits have similarly concluded that the non-aggregation principle applies to punitive damages. As the Ninth Circuit explained, "[i]t is undisputed that the plaintiffs in this case could sue [the defendant] individually on all the causes of action alleged in the current complaint. If they did so, nothing would preclude them from seeking and recovering punitive damages individually. This potential for multiple liability directly refutes the argument that there is some unitary res to which the plaintiffs jointly claim a right." *Gibson v. Chrysler Corp.*, 261 F.3d 927, 946 (9th Cir. 2001). Lacking a common and undivided interest in the punitive damages, the Ninth Circuit determined that the non-aggregation principle applies. Similarly, the Fifth Circuit and the Eleventh Circuit have both concluded that punitive damages are subject to the non-aggregation principle. . . .

. . . The Court also notes that the conclusion that punitive damages cannot be aggregated comports with practice of strictly interpreting federal jurisdiction. Accordingly, the estimated $900,000 in punitive damages must be divided by the approximately 100 similarly situated consumers. This division results in a total punitive damage amount of $9,000, well below the amount in controversy requirement of $75,000.

3. Attorneys' Fees

Third, Defendant claims that the value of the attorneys' fees attributable to Plaintiff exceeds $75,000. Defendant estimates that Plaintiff's attorneys' fees will total at least $500,000 if the case is litigated through trial. . . . Even accepting Defendant's estimate, the Court concludes that the attorneys' fees attributable to Plaintiff do not meet the amount in controversy requirement as attorneys' fees are not subject to aggregation.

"Attorney fees are part of the amount in controversy if they are provided for by statute or contract." And, the DCCPPA undisputedly does provide for attorneys' fees. D.C. Code § 28-3905(k)(2)(B). Nonetheless, the Court determines that potential attorneys' fees in this case are not sufficient to establish jurisdiction.

. . . Plaintiff argues that considering the total amount of attorneys' fees in a DCCPPA case brought on behalf of the general public would not comport with the non-aggregation principle. . . . The Court finds that the decision not to aggregate attorneys' fees is prudent given that this court, like others in this Circuit, "is not entirely comfortable with the premise that an action should be retained in federal court where satisfaction of the amount in controversy requirement depends upon a lump sum award of attorneys' fees," given its duty to "strictly construe[ ] the scope of its removal jurisdiction." . . .

. . . However, Defendant does cite one case . . . in which a district court in this Circuit took a slightly novel approach. In [that case] the court concluded that dividing the estimated attorneys' fees equally among all individuals who would benefit from the judgment "may underestimate the portion of fees properly attributed to [the plaintiff] in his role as the initial plaintiff." Instead of dividing the projected attorneys' fees equally among the plaintiff and the other beneficiaries, the court determined the plaintiff's portion of attorneys' fees "by calculating a reasonable contingency fee—say 33%—that would accompany a full judgment in [the plaintiff's] favor."

. . . [T]he Court concludes that . . . approach is not applicable to this case. . . . In determining the plaintiff's share of attorneys' fees, the . . . court calculated the plaintiff's statutory damages and divided that amount by 33% "because [the plaintiff's] lawyers [we]re working on a contingency fee basis, and hence any recoverable attorney fees [we]re inherently connected to the monetary value of the claims." . . . In this case, Plaintiff seeks, on behalf of the general public, only an injunction, not statutory damages. . . .

Here, Defendant estimates that attorneys' fees may total $500,000. Applying the non-aggregation principle, the Court will divide the total estimated attorneys' fees by the estimated number of Defendant's customers in the District of Columbia, 100. Accordingly, Plaintiffs' attorneys' fees total $5,000, far below the amount in controversy requirement.

REVIEW QUESTIONS

1. What is the best counterargument to the judge's conclusion that punitive damages should be divided among the beneficiaries of the lawsuit?

2. Do you see why the defendant tried to argue that jurisdiction was proper under the provision of 1332 that sets the amount in controversy for class actions at $5,000,000? You will learn more about this expansion of subject matter jurisdiction later in the course, but for now note the court's emphasis on dividing the benefits of the lawsuit among all persons affected rather than attributing them to the plaintiff herself. As a functional matter, is the plaintiff here really bringing an action on behalf of others as well as herself?

3. What is the possible conflict that the court describes between the non-aggregation rule and the rule allowing courts to value an injunction at

the cost of compliance to the defendant? Do you think the district court adequately resolves this contradiction?

4. Try to answer the following questions based on the reading above:
   - Buyer wants to sue Seller for a breach of contract claiming $50,000 in damages. She also has a $30,000 claim against Seller for stealing her grandfather's antique pocket watch. Can she combine both claims to meet the amount in controversy?
   - Two tenants who are domiciled in New York want to sue their landlord, who is domiciled in New Jersey, for damage to their baseball card collection when their apartment flooded. Each lost $50,000 worth of baseball cards. Can they meet the amount in controversy by joining in one lawsuit?
   - Buyer sued Seller for breach of contract, claiming $200,000 in damages. However, at trial she was only awarded $25,000 in damages. Can the case be dismissed for lack of federal jurisdiction? Under what authority? (Hint: check section 1332.)
   - An organic farmer brought an action under state law against Big Agra seeking an injunction preventing Big Agra from spraying pesticides in the fields abutting her farm when the wind blows westward. She claims that the pesticides travel onto her fields, putting her in danger of losing organic certification. The cost of delaying the spray of pesticides is $10,000 per day. The cost of damage to the crops by pests could rise as high as $500,000. Is the amount in controversy met?

QUESTIONS TO PONDER

1. You are now familiar with both federal question and diversity jurisdiction. In cases where the requirements of one or both of these jurisdictional bases are met, consider again how counsel chooses between federal or state court. Would you expect judges of the two systems to share the same sympathies, practice backgrounds, and philosophies? Do state judges and federal judges attend the same law schools, work at the same law firms, and navigate the same social circles? The fraternity of federal district judges is rather small (about 700)—smaller than the size of many law firms; what effect does that have? What are the relative abilities of federal and state judges?

2. State court judges are elected in most states, while federal judges are appointed for life. Would you expect the relative accountability of state judges to have a discernible effect on the outcome of judicial rulings? Time-to-trial and backlogs are likely to differ in particular localities. Might the location of the court influence your decision, as between, for example, a federal court that will draw a mostly suburban jury and a state court in the inner city? What about cost differentials of maintaining a suit? Discovery rules? Another question, which we will address in

Chapter 9, is whether the same substantive laws and procedures would be applied in the state and federal courts in a diversity action.

3. Many of the restrictions on federal question and diversity jurisdiction are designed to ensure that federal courts are put to their best use. After all, the dispute resolution provided by federal courts is a limited, shared, public resource. How should this resource be allocated for maximum effect? Which cases that arise under federal law "belong" in federal court, and which may be filed there? Which counterclaims that arise under federal law belong in federal court, and which may be filed there? Which cases that arise under state law whose outcomes will turn on a controlling issue of federal law belong in federal court, and which may be filed there?

4. Diversity jurisdiction accounts for about one-third to one-half of the cases in federal court. Do you find concerns about provincial bias persuasive? Should a resident plaintiff suing a nonresident defendant have the choice to file in her own state or federal court? (Does she have that choice, assuming the requisite amount in controversy?)

5. Although lawyers talk of separate state and federal court systems—and of cases arising under "federal law" or "state law"—it is important for you to appreciate the magnitude of "state law" that would apply in federal courts, and vice versa. We refer here not just to the law that gives rise to the cause of action, but also to hundreds of matters that arise throughout the course of litigation—in federal court, for example, statutes and rules of procedure often incorporate state law by reference. Similarly, in state court, the U.S. Constitution and the preemptive reach of federal statutes apply even if the cause of action arises under state law. Bottom line: Federal courts are routinely considering and applying state law; and state courts are routinely considering and applying federal law.

REVIEW EXERCISE NO. 8

Prem, a resident of California for the past twelve years, seeks your assistance. She has asked you to represent her in a lawsuit against her former employer, Def Engineering, Inc. (Def). Def is a Delaware corporation with a principal place of business in New York, NY. For many years, Def has maintained a large operation in Los Angeles, CA; the Los Angeles branch generates, on average, $55 million in annual revenues. Prem worked primarily with the Los Angeles branch, but also worked closely with the company's activities throughout the western United States.

Prem has shown you a copy of her contract with Def, and it appears that she has a strong claim for breach. The contract provides that during the term of the contract she can only be terminated for cause, and there is little or no evidence of a for-cause termination. Indeed, her letter of termination explains that the company is terminating her "with great regret" and the letter identifies the economic downturn as the reason for their decision. She was terminated one month ago, and she still has twenty-four months remaining on the consulting agreement, which pays her $40,000 per year.

Prem is despondent about the loss of her job even though she already has another job offer for similar work and for substantially the same salary in New York City. Prem lived in New York all her life before moving to California. She says she always planned to retire back in New York, but may need to move back there sooner than she had initially planned.

1   Assume a one-count complaint for breach of contract under state law. Would a federal court in California or in New York have subject matter jurisdiction? To the extent your answers are "it depends," identify the additional facts that you need, describe how you will obtain those facts, and explain how those facts would resolve the matter of federal subject matter jurisdiction.

2   As a matter of good public policy, does this case belong in federal court or state court? Explain your answer.

3   Prem is a 57-year-old woman and, therefore, a member of a protected class under the Age Discrimination in Employment Act (ADEA). Prem does not, however, believe that she was terminated because of her age. (Prem says, "Definitely not. They cut everyone in my job group, both young and old.") Preliminary research also suggests that Prem may have been an independent contractor (rather than an employee), and therefore would not covered by the ADEA. Would the court have subject matter jurisdiction over an ADEA claim? (Adding this ADEA claim could change the analysis about whether the court would have subject matter jurisdiction over the breach of contract claim. But don't worry about that yet; that's the subject of Part D.)

D. SUPPLEMENTAL JURISDICTION

Although the federal courts possess only limited subject matter jurisdiction, a small margin of "supplemental" jurisdiction has been recognized to encompass claims that do not fall within either the federal question or diversity categories but are closely connected to such claims already being entertained by the court. This grant of jurisdiction began as an interpretation of Article III, but has now been codified in the Supplemental Jurisdiction Statute, 28 U.S.C. § 1367. As you will see below, that statute was meant to codify the caselaw and the cases are helpful in parsing the statute.

As you read the next cases, consider the policy and pragmatic considerations underlying this "stretch" jurisdiction.

United Mine Workers of America v. Gibbs
383 U.S. 715 (1966)

Justice BRENNAN delivered the opinion of the Court:

Respondent Paul Gibbs was awarded compensatory and punitive damages in this action against petitioner United Mine Workers of America (UMW) for alleged violations of § 303 of the Labor Management Relations Act, 1947, 61 Stat. 158, as amended, and of the common law of Tennessee. The case grew out of the rivalry between the United Mine Workers and the Southern Labor Union over representation of workers in the southern Appalachian coal fields. Tennessee Consolidated Coal Company, not a party here, laid off 100 miners of the UMW's Local 5881 when it closed one of its mines in southern Tennessee during the spring of 1960. Late that summer, Grundy Company, a wholly-owned subsidiary of Consolidated, hired respondent as mine superintendent to attempt to open a new mine on Consolidated's property at nearby Gray's Creek through use of members of the Southern Labor Union. As part of the arrangement, Grundy also gave respondent a contract to haul the mine's coal to the nearest railroad loading point.

On August 15 and 16, 1960, armed members of Local 5881 forcibly prevented the opening of the mine, threatening respondent and beating an organizer for the rival union. . . . [A] picket line was maintained there for nine months; and no further attempts were made to open the mine during that period.

Respondent lost his job as superintendent, and never entered into performance of his haulage contract. He testified that he soon began to lose other trucking contracts and mine leases he held in nearby areas. Claiming these effects to be the result of a concerted union plan against him, he sought recovery not against Local 5881 or its members, but only against petitioner, the international union. The suit was brought in the United States District Court for the Eastern District of Tennessee, and jurisdiction was premised on allegations of secondary boycotts under § 303. The state law claim, for which jurisdiction was based upon the doctrine of pendent jurisdiction, asserted "an unlawful conspiracy and an unlawful boycott aimed at him and (Grundy) to maliciously, wantonly and willfully interfere with his contract of employment and with his contract of haulage."

. . . The jury's verdict was that the UMW had violated both § 303 and state law. Gibbs was awarded $60,000 as damages under the employment contract and $14,500 under the haulage contract; he was also awarded $100,000 punitive damages. On motion, the trial court set aside the award of damages with respect to the haulage contract on the ground that damage was unproved. It also held that union pressure on Grundy to discharge respondent as supervisor would constitute only a primary dispute with Grundy, as respondent's employer, and hence was not cognizable as a claim under § 303. Interference with the employment relationship was cognizable as a state claim, however, and a remitted award was sustained on the state law claim.

The Court of Appeals for the Sixth Circuit affirmed. We granted *certiorari*. We reverse.

I

. . . With the adoption of the Federal Rules of Civil Procedure . . . the impulse is toward entertaining the broadest possible scope of action consistent with fairness to the parties; joinder of claims, parties and remedies is strongly encouraged. [*See, e.g.*, Fed. R. Civ. Proc. 2, 18-20, 42.] . . . Pendent jurisdiction, in the sense of judicial power, exists whenever there is a claim "arising under [the] Constitution, the Laws of the United States, and Treaties made, or which shall be made, under their Authority . . .," U.S. Const., Art. III, § 2, and the relationship between that claim and the state claim permits the conclusion that the entire action before the court comprises but one constitutional "case." The federal claim must have substance sufficient to confer subject matter jurisdiction on the court. The state and federal claims must derive from a common nucleus of operative fact. But if, considered without regard to their federal or state character, a plaintiff's claims are such that he would ordinarily be expected to try them all in one judicial proceeding, then, assuming substantiality of the federal issues, there is power in federal courts to hear the whole.

That power need not be exercised in every case in which it is found to exist. It has consistently been recognized that pendent jurisdiction is a doctrine of discretion, not of plaintiff's right. Its justification lies in considerations of judicial economy, convenience and fairness to litigants; if these are not present a federal court should hesitate to exercise jurisdiction over state claims, even though bound to apply state law to them, *Erie R. Co. v. Tompkins*, 304 U.S. 64. Needless decisions of state law should be avoided both as a matter of comity and to promote justice between the parties, by procuring for them a surer-footed reading of applicable law. Certainly, if the federal claims are dismissed before trial, even though not insubstantial in a jurisdictional sense, the state claims should be dismissed as well. Similarly, if it appears that the state issues substantially predominate, whether in terms of proof, of the scope of the issues raised, or of the comprehensiveness of the remedy sought, the state claims may be dismissed without prejudice and left for resolution to state tribunals. There may, on the other hand, be situations in which the state claim is so closely tied to questions of federal policy that the argument for exercise of pendent jurisdiction is particularly strong. In the present case, for example, the allowable scope of the state claim implicates the federal doctrine of pre-emption; while this interrelationship does not create statutory federal question jurisdiction, *Louisville & N. R. Co. v. Mottley*, 211 U.S. 149, its existence is relevant to the exercise of discretion. Finally, there may be reasons independent of jurisdictional considerations, such as the likelihood of jury confusion in treating divergent legal theories of relief, that would justify separating state and federal claims for trial, Fed. Rule Civ. Proc. 42(b). If so, jurisdiction should ordinarily be refused.

The question of power will ordinarily be resolved on the pleadings. But the issue whether pendent jurisdiction has been properly assumed is one which remains open throughout the litigation. Pretrial procedures or even the trial itself may reveal a substantial hegemony of state law claims, or likelihood of jury confusion, which could not have been anticipated at the pleading stage. Although it will of course be appropriate to take account in this circumstance of the already completed course of the litigation, dismissal of the state claim might even then be merited. For example, it may appear that the plaintiff was well aware of the nature of his proofs and the relative importance of his claims; recognition of a federal court's wide latitude to decide ancillary questions of state law does not imply that it must tolerate a litigant's effort to impose upon it what is in effect only a state law case. Once it appears that a state claim constitutes the real body of a case, to which the federal claim is only an appendage, the state claim may fairly be dismissed.

We are not prepared to say that in the present case the District Court exceeded its discretion in proceeding to judgment on the state claim. We may assume for purposes of decision that the District Court was correct in its holding that the claim of pressure on Grundy to terminate the employment contract was outside the purview of § 303. Even so, the § 303 claims based on secondary pressures on Grundy relative to the haulage contract and on other coal operators generally were substantial. . . . The state and federal claims arose from the same nucleus of operative fact and reflected alternative remedies. Indeed, the verdict sheet sent in to the jury authorized only one award of damages, so that recovery could not be given separately on the federal and state claims.

It is true that the § 303 claims ultimately failed and that the only recovery allowed respondent was on the state claim. We cannot confidently say, however, that the federal issues were so remote or played such a minor role at the trial that in effect the state claim only was tried. Although the District Court dismissed as unproved the § 303 claims that petitioner's secondary activities included attempts to induce coal operators other than Grundy to cease doing business with respondent, the court submitted the § 303 claims relating to Grundy to the jury. The jury returned verdicts against petitioner on those § 303 claims, and it was only on petitioner's motion for a directed verdict and a judgment n.o.v. that the verdicts on those claims were set aside. . . . We thus conclude that although it may be that the District Court might, in its sound discretion, have dismissed the state claim, the circumstances show no error in refusing to do so.

[The Court went on to reverse the verdict of conspiracy under state law because Gibbs had not met his burden of proof.]

[The concurring opinion of Justice HARLAN is omitted.]

REVIEW QUESTIONS

1. Where does the Court find constitutional authority in Article III for "pendent jurisdiction"? Was there statutory authority at the time *Gibbs*

was decided? 28 U.S.C. § 1367 (discussed later in this chapter) is of much more recent vintage.

2. What are the pragmatic and judicial efficiency arguments that underlie the Court's endorsement of pendent jurisdiction? Consider a plaintiff in Gibbs's situation, with an injury that he believes gives rise to claims under *both* federal and state law. This could be a citizen alleging a police officer used excessive force to restrain him in violation of his federal civil rights (§ 1983) and also seeking recovery under state tort claims for assault and battery, and so forth. Or it could be an employee alleging sexual harassment in violation of both Title VII and the state tort law of intentional infliction of emotional distress. Absent recognition of pendent jurisdiction (and without diversity of citizenship), what forum options would they have?

3. What is the standard for the exercise of pendent jurisdiction under *Gibbs*? If this test is met, *must* the federal court exercise pendent jurisdiction? If not, under what circumstances does Justice Brennan envision a court declining jurisdiction over state claims that arise out of the same nucleus of facts as the federal claim?

4. If the justification for exercise of federal adjudicatory power over a state law claim is that the latter is appended to a federal claim being entertained, how can the court resolve the state claim even *after* the federal claim has failed (as it did in *Gibbs*)? Does this mean a plaintiff can use pendent jurisdiction to gain access to the federal forum for state claims merely by asserting *any* federal claim, no matter how frivolous? What does Justice Brennan mean when he writes that "assuming *substantiality* of the federal issues, there is power in federal courts to hear the whole [case]" (emphasis added)?

MORE TO PONDER

Timing can be a crucial issue in evaluating pendant jurisdiction. How late should it be in a case before a court will permit a supplemental claim to remain in the suit? What does it mean for plaintiffs when they have to refile and start anew? For example, in *Maguire v. Marquette University*, 814 F.2d 1213 (7th Cir. 1987), the plaintiff brought a federal action under Title VII alleging she was denied appointment to the Jesuit school's theology department because of her gender. After discovery she amended her complaint to add a pendent claim asserting breach of Wisconsin's law of academic freedom, asserting she was rejected because of her views favoring abortion. Defendant's motion for summary judgment on the Title VII count was granted because plaintiff's own submissions indicated that the motivating factor behind her rejection was not gender but her public statements regarding abortion. The district court went on to decide the state law claim on the merits.

On appeal, the Seventh Circuit reversed. Citing *Gibbs*, the court ruled that "[w]hen, as here, the federal claim is dismissed *before* trial, the district court should relinquish jurisdiction of any pendent state law claim unless there is some independent basis of federal jurisdiction." 814 F.2d at 1218 (emphasis added). As another court put it, "[w]here the federal element which is the basis for jurisdiction is disposed of early in the case, as on the pleadings, it smacks of the tail wagging the dog to continue with a federal hearing of the state claim." *McFaddin Express, Inc. v. Adley Corp.*, 346 F.2d 424, 427 (2d Cir. 1965).

Just as *pendent jurisdiction* stretches a federal court's authority over a federal claim to encompass a state law claim arising from the same facts, *ancillary jurisdiction* expands the authority of a federal court entertaining a diversity action, as explored in the next case.

Owen Equipment and Erection Co. v. Kroger
437 U.S. 365 (1978)

Justice STEWART delivered the opinion of the Court:

In an action in which federal jurisdiction is based on diversity of citizenship, may the plaintiff assert a claim against a third-party defendant when there is no independent basis for federal jurisdiction over that claim? The Court of Appeals for the Eighth Circuit held in this case that such a claim is within the ancillary jurisdiction of the federal courts. We granted *certiorari* because this decision conflicts with several recent decisions of other Courts of Appeals.

I

On January 18, 1972, James Kroger was electrocuted when the boom of a steel crane next to which he was walking came too close to a high-tension electric power line. The respondent (his widow, who is the administratrix of his estate) filed a wrongful-death action in the United States District Court for the District of Nebraska against the Omaha Public Power District (OPPD). Her complaint alleged that OPPD's negligent construction, maintenance, and operation of the power line had caused Kroger's death. Federal jurisdiction was based on diversity of citizenship, since the respondent was a citizen of Iowa and OPPD was a Nebraska corporation.

OPPD then filed a third-party complaint pursuant to Fed. Rule Civ. Proc. 14(a) against the petitioner, Owen Equipment and Erection Co. (Owen), alleging that the crane was owned and operated by Owen, and that Owen's negligence had been the proximate cause of Kroger's death.[3] OPPD later moved for summary judgment on the respondent's complaint against it. While this motion was pending, the respondent was granted leave to file an amended complaint naming Owen as an additional defendant. Thereafter, the District Court granted OPPD's motion for summary judgment in an unreported opinion. The case thus went to trial between the respondent and the petitioner alone.

The respondent's amended complaint alleged that Owen was "a Nebraska corporation with its principal place of business in Nebraska." Owen's answer admitted that it was "a corporation organized and existing under the laws of the State of Nebraska," and denied every other allegation of the complaint. On the third day of trial, however, it was disclosed that the petitioner's principal place of business was in Iowa, not Nebraska,[5] and that the petitioner and the respondent were thus both citizens of Iowa. The petitioner then moved to dismiss the complaint for lack of jurisdiction. The District Court reserved decision on the motion, and the jury thereafter returned a verdict in favor of the respondent. In an unreported opinion issued after the trial, the District Court denied the petitioner's motion to dismiss the complaint.

The judgment was affirmed on appeal. The Court of Appeals held that under this Court's decision in *Mine Workers v. Gibbs*, 383 U.S. 715, the District Court had jurisdictional power, in its discretion, to adjudicate the respondent's claim against the petitioner because that claim arose from the "core of 'operative facts' giving rise to both [respondent's] claim against OPPD and OPPD's claim against Owen." It further held that the District Court had properly exercised its discretion in proceeding to decide the case even after summary judgment had been granted to OPPD, because the petitioner had concealed its Iowa citizenship from the respondent. Rehearing en banc was denied by an equally divided court.

II

It is undisputed that there was no independent basis of federal jurisdiction over the respondent's state-law tort action against the petitioner, since both are citizens of Iowa. And although Fed. Rule Civ. Proc. 14(a) permits a plaintiff to assert a claim against a third-party defendant, it does not purport to say whether or not such a claim requires an independent basis of federal jurisdiction. Indeed, it could not determine that question, since it is axiomatic that the Federal Rules of Civil Procedure do not create or withdraw federal jurisdiction. Fed. Rule Civ. Proc. 82.

---

3. Under Rule 14(a), a third-party defendant may not be impleaded merely because he may be liable to the plaintiff. While the third-party complaint in this case alleged merely that Owen's negligence caused Kroger's death, and the basis of Owen's alleged liability to OPPD is nowhere spelled out, OPPD evidently relied upon the state common-law right of contribution among joint tortfeasors. The petitioner has never challenged the propriety of the third-party complaint as such.

5. The problem apparently was one of geography. Although the Missouri River generally marks the boundary between Iowa and Nebraska, Carter Lake, Iowa, where the accident occurred and where Owen had its main office, lies west of the river, adjacent to Omaha, Neb. Apparently the river once avulsed at one of its bends, cutting Carter Lake off from the rest of Iowa.

In affirming the District Court's judgment, the Court of Appeals relied upon the doctrine of ancillary jurisdiction, whose contours it believed were defined by this Court's holding in *Mine Workers v. Gibbs, supra.* The *Gibbs* case differed from this one in that it involved pendent jurisdiction, which concerns the resolution of a plaintiff's federal and state-law claims against a single defendant in one action. By contrast, in this case there was no claim based upon substantive federal law, but rather state-law tort claims against two different defendants. Nonetheless, the Court of Appeals was correct in perceiving that *Gibbs* and this case are two species of the same generic problem: Under what circumstances may a federal court hear and decide a state-law claim arising between citizens of the same state? But we believe that the Court of Appeals failed to understand the scope of the doctrine of the *Gibbs* case.

The plaintiff in *Gibbs* alleged that the defendant union had violated the common law of Tennessee as well as the federal prohibition of secondary boycotts. This Court held that, although the parties were not of diverse citizenship, the District Court properly entertained the state-law claim as pendent to the federal claim. The crucial holding was stated as follows:

> Pendent jurisdiction, in the sense of judicial power, exists whenever there is a claim "arising under [the] Constitution, the Laws of the United States, and Treaties made, or which shall be made, under their Authority. . . ." U.S. Const., Art. III, § 2, and the relationship between that claim and the state claim permits the conclusion that the entire action before the court comprises but one constitutional "case." . . . The state and federal claims must derive from a common nucleus of operative fact. But if, considered without regard to their federal or state character, a plaintiff's claims are such that he would ordinarily be expected to try them all in one judicial proceeding, then, assuming substantiality of the federal issues, there is power in federal courts to hear the whole.

It is apparent that *Gibbs* delineated the constitutional limits of federal judicial power. But even if it be assumed that the District Court in the present case had constitutional power to decide the respondent's lawsuit against the petitioner, it does not follow that the decision of the Court of Appeals was correct. Constitutional power is merely the first hurdle that must be overcome in determining that a federal court has jurisdiction over a particular controversy. For the jurisdiction of the federal courts is limited not only by the provisions of Art. III of the Constitution, but also by Acts of Congress.

[S]tatutory law as well as the Constitution may limit a federal court's jurisdiction over nonfederal claims. . . . [Thus] a finding that federal and nonfederal claims arise from a "common nucleus of operative fact," the test of *Gibbs*, does not end the inquiry into whether a federal court has power to hear the nonfederal claims along with the federal ones. Beyond this constitutional minimum, there must be an examination of the posture in which the nonfederal claim is asserted and of the specific statute that confers jurisdiction over the federal claim, in order to determine whether "Congress in [that statute] has . . . expressly or by implication negated" the exercise of jurisdiction over the particular nonfederal claim.

III

The relevant statute in this case, 28 U.S.C. § 1332(a)(1), confers upon federal courts jurisdiction over "civil actions where the matter in controversy exceeds the sum or value of $10,000* . . . and is between . . . citizens of different States." This statute and its predecessors have consistently been held to require complete diversity of citizenship. That is, diversity jurisdiction does not exist unless each defendant is a citizen of a different state from each plaintiff. Over the years Congress has repeatedly re-enacted or amended the statute conferring diversity jurisdiction, leaving intact this rule of complete diversity. Whatever may have been the original purposes of diversity-of-citizenship jurisdiction, this subsequent history clearly demonstrates a congressional mandate that diversity jurisdiction is not to be available when any plaintiff is a citizen of the same state as any defendant.

Thus it is clear that the respondent could not originally have brought suit in federal court naming Owen and OPPD as co-defendants, since citizens of Iowa would have been on both sides of the litigation. Yet the identical lawsuit resulted when she amended her complaint. Complete diversity was destroyed just as surely as if she had sued Owen initially. In either situation, in the plain language of the statute, the "matter in controversy" could not be "between . . . citizens of different States."

It is a fundamental precept that federal courts are courts of limited jurisdiction. The limits upon federal jurisdiction, whether imposed by the Constitution or by Congress, must be neither disregarded nor evaded. Yet under the reasoning of the Court of Appeals in this case, a plaintiff could defeat the statutory requirement of complete diversity by the simple expedient of suing only those defendants who were of diverse citizenship and waiting for them to implead non-diverse defendants.[17] If, as the Court of Appeals thought, a "common nucleus of operative fact" were the only requirement for ancillary jurisdiction in a diversity case, there would be no principled reason why the respondent in this case could not have joined her cause of action against Owen in her original complaint as ancillary to her claim against OPPD. Congress' requirement of complete diversity would thus have been evaded completely.

It is true, as the Court of Appeals noted, that the exercise of ancillary jurisdiction over nonfederal claims has often been upheld in situations involving

---

* *Eds.' Note:* In the original Judiciary Act of 1789, the amount in controversy requirement was $500. It was raised to $2,000 in 1887, to $3,000 in 1911, to $10,000 in 1958, to $50,000 in 1988, and to the current $75,000 in 1996.

17. This is not an unlikely hypothesis, since a defendant in a tort suit such as this one would surely try to limit his liability by impleading any joint tortfeasors for indemnity or contribution. Some commentators have suggested that the possible abuse of third-party practice could be dealt with under 28 U.S.C. § 1359, which forbids collusive attempts to create federal jurisdiction. The dissenting opinion today also expresses this view. But there is nothing necessarily collusive about a plaintiff's selectively suing only those tortfeasors of diverse citizenship, or about the named defendants' desire to implead joint tortfeasors. Nonetheless, the requirement of complete diversity would be eviscerated by such a course of events.

impleader, cross-claims or counterclaims. But in determining whether jurisdiction over a nonfederal claim exists, the context in which the nonfederal claim is asserted is crucial. And the claim here arises in a setting quite different from the kinds of nonfederal claims that have been viewed in other cases as falling within the ancillary jurisdiction of the federal courts.

First, the nonfederal claim in this case was simply not ancillary to the federal one in the same sense that, for example, the impleader by a defendant of a third-party defendant always is. A third-party complaint depends at least in part upon the resolution of the primary lawsuit. Its relation to the original complaint is thus not mere factual similarity but logical dependence. The respondent's claim against the petitioner, however, was entirely separate from her original claim against OPPD, since the petitioner's liability to her depended not at all upon whether or not OPPD was also liable. Far from being an ancillary and dependent claim, it was a new and independent one.

Second, the nonfederal claim here was asserted by the plaintiff, who voluntarily chose to bring suit upon a state-law claim in a federal court. By contrast, ancillary jurisdiction typically involves claims by a defending party haled into court against his will, or by another person whose rights might be irretrievably lost unless he could assert them in an ongoing action in a federal court. A plaintiff cannot complain if ancillary jurisdiction does not encompass all of his possible claims in a case such as this one, since it is he who has chosen the federal rather than the state forum and must thus accept its limitations. "[T]he efficiency plaintiff seeks so avidly is available without question in the state courts."

It is not unreasonable to assume that, in generally requiring complete diversity, Congress did not intend to confine the jurisdiction of federal courts so inflexibly that they are unable to protect legal rights or effectively to resolve an entire, logically entwined lawsuit. Those practical needs are the basis of the doctrine of ancillary jurisdiction. But neither the convenience of litigants nor considerations of judicial economy can suffice to justify extension of the doctrine of ancillary jurisdiction to a plaintiff's cause of action against a citizen of the same State in a diversity case. Congress has established the basic rule that diversity jurisdiction exists under 28 U.S.C. § 1332 only when there is complete diversity of citizenship. The policy of the statute calls for its strict construction. To allow the requirement of complete diversity to be circumvented as it was in this case would simply flout the congressional command.

Accordingly, the judgment of the Court of Appeals is reversed.

[Dissenting opinion of Justices WHITE and BRENNAN omitted.]

REVIEW QUESTIONS

1. Under the doctrine of ancillary jurisdiction, it had long been recognized that a federal district court could entertain an impleader against a third-party defendant even though addition of that party defeats complete diversity. In a products liability action against a dealership that allegedly

sold a defective automobile to the injured plaintiff, the dealer may implead the manufacturer asserting a "claim over" ("is or may be liable" for all or part of plaintiff's claim against the original defendant) despite the fact that the third-party defendant shares citizenship with either defendant or plaintiff. The rationale is that consolidation of the main and ancillary claims fosters judicial efficiency and avoids inconsistent results. Otherwise, the original defendant would have to seek contribution in a separate state proceeding following the federal litigation.

Ancillary jurisdiction has been available as well to accommodate compulsory counterclaims (Fed. R. Civ. P. 13(a)), cross-claims (Fed. R. Civ. P. 13(g)), and interventions (Fed. R. Civ. P. 24(a)). Can you see why?

2. How does *Owen Equipment Co. v. Kroger* distinguish the assertion of jurisdiction over plaintiff's claim against Owen Equipment from the well-established authority to entertain the original defendant's (OPPD's) impleader against Owen? What is the rationale for drawing the line here?

3. Given the Court's logic, would it have made a difference to the result if Kroger's original claim against OPPD had *not* been dismissed on summary judgment?

* * *

You have seen that *pendent jurisdiction* permits a federal court to entertain a related state law claim against a party already answering a federal claim. *Ancillary jurisdiction* permits the court to hear a related claim against a party impleaded by an original defendant. The following case involves a hybrid of the two, referred to as *pendent party* jurisdiction.

Finley v. United States
490 U.S. 545 (1989)

Justice SCALIA delivered the opinion of the Court:

On the night of November 11, 1983, a twin-engine plane carrying petitioner's husband and two of her children struck electric transmission lines during its approach to a San Diego, California, airfield. No one survived the resulting crash. Petitioner brought a tort action in state court, claiming that San Diego Gas and Electric Company had negligently positioned and inadequately illuminated the transmission lines, and that the city of San Diego's negligent maintenance of the airport's runway lights had rendered them inoperative the night of the crash. When she later discovered that the Federal Aviation Administration (FAA) was in fact the party responsible for the runway lights, petitioner filed the present action against the United States in the United States District Court for the Southern District of California. The complaint based jurisdiction upon the Federal Tort Claims Act (FTCA), 28 U.S.C. § 1346(b), alleging negligence in the FAA's operation and maintenance of the runway lights and performance of air traffic control functions. Almost a year later, she moved to amend the federal complaint to include claims against the original state-court defendants, as to which no independent basis for federal jurisdiction existed. The District Court granted petitioner's motion and asserted "pendent" jurisdiction under *Mine Workers v. Gibbs*, 383 U.S. 715 (1966), finding it "clear" that "judicial economy and efficiency" favored trying the actions together, and concluding that they arose "from a common nucleus of operative facts." The District Court certified an interlocutory appeal to the Court of Appeals for the Ninth Circuit under 28 U.S.C. § 1292(b). That court summarily reversed . . . , categorically reject[ing] pendent-party jurisdiction under the FTCA. We granted certiorari to resolve a split among the Circuits on whether the FTCA permits an assertion of pendent jurisdiction over additional parties.

The FTCA provides that "the district courts . . . shall have exclusive jurisdiction of civil actions on claims against the United States" for certain torts of federal employees acting within the scope of their employment. 28 U.S.C. § 1346(b). Petitioner seeks to append her claims against the city and the utility to her FTCA action against the United States, even though this would require the District Court to extend its authority to additional parties for whom an independent jurisdictional base—such as diversity of citizenship, 28 U.S.C. § 1332(a)(1)—is lacking.

In 1807 Chief Justice Marshall wrote for the Court that "courts which are created by written law, and whose jurisdiction is defined by written law, cannot transcend that jurisdiction." . . . It remains rudimentary law that "[a]s regards all courts of the United States inferior to this tribunal, two things are necessary to create jurisdiction, whether original or appellate. The Constitution must have given to the court the capacity to take it, and an act of Congress must have supplied it. . . . To the extent that such action is not taken, the power lies dormant."

Despite this principle, in a line of cases by now no less well established we have held, without specific examination of jurisdictional statutes, that federal courts have "pendent" claim jurisdiction—that is, jurisdiction over nonfederal claims between parties litigating other matters properly before the court—to the full extent permitted by the Constitution. *Mine Workers v. Gibbs*, which has come to stand for the principle in question, held that "[p]endent jurisdiction, in the sense of judicial power, exists whenever there is a claim 'arising under [the] Constitution, the Laws of the United States, and Treaties made, or which shall be made, under their Authority . . . ,' U.S. Const., Art. III, § 2, and the relationship between that claim and the state claim permits the conclusion that the entire action before the court comprises but one constitutional 'case.'" The requisite relationship exists, *Gibbs* said, when the federal and nonfederal claims "derive from a common nucleus of operative fact" and are such that a plaintiff "would ordinarily be expected to try them in one judicial proceeding." Petitioner contends that the same criterion applies here, leading to the result that her state-law claims against San Diego Gas and Electric Company and the city of San Diego may be heard in conjunction with her FTCA action against the United States.

Analytically, petitioner's case is fundamentally different from *Gibbs* in that it brings into question what has become known as pendent-party jurisdiction, that is, jurisdiction over parties not named in any claim that is independently cognizable by the federal court. We may assume, without deciding, that the constitutional criterion for pendent-party jurisdiction is analogous to the constitutional criterion for pendent-claim jurisdiction, and that petitioner's state-law claims pass that test. Our cases show, however, that with respect to the addition of parties, as opposed to the addition of only claims, we will not assume that the full constitutional power has been congressionally authorized, and will not read jurisdictional statutes broadly. . . .

[I]n *Owen Equipment & Erection Co. v. Kroger*, we held that the jurisdiction which § 1332(a)(1) confers over a "matter in controversy" between a plaintiff and defendant of diverse citizenship cannot be read to confer pendent jurisdiction over a different, nondiverse defendant, even if the claim involving that other defendant meets the *Gibbs* test. "*Gibbs*," we said, "does not end the inquiry into whether a federal court has power to hear the nonfederal claims along with the federal ones. Beyond this constitutional minimum, there must be an examination of the posture in which the non-federal claim is asserted and of the specific statute that confers jurisdiction over the federal claim."

The most significant element of "posture" or of "context" in the present case . . . is precisely that the added claims involve added parties over whom no independent basis of jurisdiction exists. While in a narrow class of cases a federal court may assert authority over such a claim "ancillary" to jurisdiction otherwise properly vested . . . we have never reached such a result solely on the basis that the *Gibbs* test has been met. And little more basis than that can be relied upon by petitioner here. As in *Kroger*, the relationship between petitioner's added claims and the original complaint is one of "mere factual similarity," which is of no consequence since "neither the convenience of the litigants nor considerations of judicial economy can suffice to justify extension of the doctrine of ancillary jurisdiction." It is true that here, unlike in *Kroger*, the party seeking to bring the added claims had little choice but to be in federal rather than state court, since the FTCA permits the Federal Government to be sued only there. But that alone is not enough. . . .

The second factor invoked by *Kroger*, the text of the jurisdictional statute at issue, likewise fails to establish petitioner's case. The FTCA, § 1346(b), confers jurisdiction over "civil actions on claims against the United States." It does not say "civil actions on claims that include requested relief against the United States," nor "civil actions in which there is a claim against the United States"—formulations one might expect if the presence of a claim against the United States constituted merely a minimum jurisdictional requirement, rather than a definition of the permissible scope of FTCA actions. Just as the statutory provision "between . . . citizens of different States" has been held to mean citizens of different states and no one else, so also here we conclude that "against the United States" means against the United States and no one else. "Due regard for the rightful independence of state governments . . . requires that [federal courts] scrupulously confine their own jurisdiction to the precise limits which the statute has defined." The statute here defines jurisdiction in a manner that does not reach defendants other than the United States. . . .

Because the FTCA permits the Government to be sued only in federal court, our holding that parties to related claims cannot necessarily be sued there means that the efficiency and convenience of a consolidated action will sometimes have to be forgone in favor of separate actions in state and federal courts. . . . [T]he present statute permits no other result. . . .

For the foregoing reasons, the judgment of the Court of Appeals is Affirmed.

Justice BLACKMUN, dissenting:

. . . Where, as here, Congress' preference for a federal forum for a certain category of claims makes the federal forum the only possible one in which the constitutional case may be heard as a whole, the sensible result is to permit the exercise of pendent-party jurisdiction. . . . I therefore dissent.

Justice STEVENS, with whom Justice BRENNAN and Justice MARSHALL join, dissenting:

The Court's holding is not faithful to our precedents and casually dismisses the accumulated wisdom of our best judges. As we observed more than 16 years ago, "numerous decisions throughout the courts of appeals since [*Mine Workers v. Gibbs*, 383 U.S. 715 (1966),] have recognized the existence of judicial power to hear pendent claims involving pendent parties where 'the entire action before the court comprises but one constitutional case' as defined in *Gibbs*." . . .

I would thus hold that the grant of jurisdiction to hear "civil actions on claims against the United States" authorizes the federal courts to hear state-law claims against a pendent party. [T]he fact that such claims are within the exclusive federal jurisdiction, together with the absence of any evidence of congressional disapproval of the exercise of pendent-party jurisdiction in FTCA cases, provides a fully sufficient justification for applying the holding in *Gibbs* to this case. . . .

The doctrine of pendent jurisdiction rests in part on a recognition that forcing a federal plaintiff to litigate his or her case in both federal and state courts impairs the ability of the federal court to grant full relief, and "imparts a fundamental bias against utilization of the federal forum owing to the deterrent effect imposed by the needless requirement of duplicate litigation if the federal forum is chosen." "The courts, by recognizing pendent jurisdiction, are effectuating Congress' decision to provide the plaintiff with a federal forum for litigating a jurisdictionally sufficient claim." This is especially the case when, by virtue of the grant of exclusive federal jurisdiction, "only in a federal court may all of the claims be tried together." In such circumstances, in which Congress has unequivocally indicated its intent that the federal right be litigated in a federal forum, there is reason to believe that Congress did not intend that the substance of the federal right be diminished by the increased costs in efficiency and convenience of litigation in two forums. No such special federal interest is present when federal jurisdiction is invoked on the basis of the diverse citizenship of the parties and the state-law claims may be litigated in a state forum.

I respectfully dissent.

* * *

In response to *Finley*, Congress enacted 28 U.S.C. § 1367. The statute, and some of its recorded legislative history, follows.

The Supplemental Jurisdiction Statute
28 U.S.C. § 1367

(a) Except as provided in subsections (b) and (c) or as expressly provided otherwise by Federal statute, in any civil action of which the district courts have original jurisdiction, the district courts shall have supplemental jurisdiction over all other claims that are so related to claims in the action within such original jurisdiction that they form part of the same case or controversy under Article III of the United States Constitution. Such supplemental jurisdiction shall include claims that involve the joinder or intervention of additional parties.

(b) In any civil action of which the district courts have original jurisdiction founded solely on section 1332 of this title, the district courts shall not have supplemental jurisdiction under subsection (a) over claims by plaintiffs against persons made parties under Rule 14, 19, 20, or 24 of the Federal Rules of Civil Procedure, or over claims by persons proposed to be joined as plaintiffs under Rule 19 of such rules, or seeking to intervene as plaintiffs under Rule 24 of such rules, when exercising supplemental jurisdiction over such claims would be inconsistent with the jurisdictional requirements of section 1332.

(c) The district courts may decline to exercise supplemental jurisdiction over a claim under subsection (a) if:
  (1) the claim raises a novel or complex issue of State law,
  (2) the claim substantially predominates over the claim or claims over which the district court has original jurisdiction,
  (3) the district court has dismissed all claims over which it has original jurisdiction, or
  (4) in exceptional circumstances, there are other compelling reasons for declining jurisdiction.

(d) The period of limitations for any claim asserted under subsection (a), and for any other claim in the same action that is voluntarily dismissed at the same time as or after the dismissal of the claim under subsection (a), shall be tolled while the claim is pending and for a period of 30 days after it is dismissed unless State law provides for a longer tolling period.

(e) As used in this section, the term "State" includes the District of Columbia, the Commonwealth of Puerto Rico, and any territory or possession of the United States.

* * *

The following are excerpts from the legislative history of § 1367.

House Report No. 101-734
1990 U.S. Code Congressional and Admin. News 6873

. . . The doctrines of pendent and ancillary jurisdiction, in this section jointly labeled supplemental jurisdiction, refer to the authority of the federal courts to adjudicate, without an independent basis of subject matter jurisdiction, claims that are so related to other claims within the district courts' original jurisdiction that they form part of the same cases or controversy under Article III of the United States Constitution.

Supplemental jurisdiction has enabled federal courts and litigants to take advantage of the federal procedural rules on claim and party joinder to deal economically in single rather than multiple litigation with related matters, usually those arising from the same transaction, occurrence, or series of transactions or occurrences. Moreover, the district court's exercise of supplemental jurisdiction, by making federal court a practical arena for the resolution of an entire controversy, has effectuated Congress' intent in the jurisdictional statutes to provide plaintiffs with a federal forum for litigating claims within original federal jurisdiction.

Recently, however, in *Finley v. United States*, the Supreme Court cast substantial doubt on the authority of the federal courts to hear some claims within supplemental jurisdiction. In *Finley* the Court held that a district court, in a Federal Tort Claims Act suit against the United States, may not exercise supplemental jurisdiction over a related claim by the plaintiff against an additional, nondiverse defendant. The Court's rationale that "with respect to the addition of parties, as opposed to the addition of only claims, we will not assume that the full constitutional power has been congressionally authorized, and will not read jurisdictional statutes broadly," threatens to eliminate other previously accepted forms of supplemental jurisdiction. Already, for example, some lower courts have interpreted *Finley* to prohibit the exercise of supplemental jurisdiction in formerly unquestioned circumstances.

Legislation, therefore, is needed to provide the federal courts with statutory authority to hear supplemental claims. Indeed, the Supreme Court has virtually invited Congress to codify supplemental jurisdiction by commenting in *Finley*, "Whatever we say regarding the scope of jurisdiction . . . can of course be changed by Congress. What is of paramount importance is that Congress be able to legislate against a background of clear interpretive rules, so that it may know the effect of the language it adopts." This section would authorize jurisdiction in a case like *Finley*, as well as essentially restore the pre-*Finley* understandings of the authorization for and limits on other forms of supplemental jurisdiction. In federal-question cases, it broadly authorizes the district courts to exercise supplemental jurisdiction over additional claims, including claims involving the joinder of additional parties. In diversity cases, the district courts may exercise supplemental jurisdiction, except when doing so would be inconsistent with the jurisdictional requirements of the diversity statute. In both cases, the district courts, as under current law, would have discretion to decline supplemental jurisdiction in appropriate circumstances.

[Section 1367(a)] generally authorizes the district court to exercise jurisdiction over a supplemental claim whenever it forms part of the same constitutional case or controversy as the claim or claims that provide the basis of the district court's original jurisdiction. In providing for supplemental jurisdiction over claims involving the addition of parties, subsection (a) explicitly fills the statutory gap noted in *Finley v. United States*.

[Section 1367(b)] prohibits a district court in a case over which it has jurisdiction founded solely on the general diversity provision, 28 U.S.C.

§ 1332, from exercising supplemental jurisdiction in specified circumstances. In diversity-only actions the district courts may not hear plaintiffs' supplemental claims when exercising supplemental jurisdiction would encourage plaintiffs to evade the jurisdictional requirement of 28 U.S.C. § 1332 by the simple expedient of naming initially only those defendants whose joinder satisfies § 1332's requirements and later adding claims not within original federal jurisdiction against other defendants who have intervened or been joined on a supplemental basis. In accord with case law, the subsection also prohibits the joinder or intervention of persons and plaintiffs if adding them is inconsistent with § 1332's requirements. . . .

[Section 1367(c)] codifies the factors that the Supreme Court has recognized as providing legitimate bases upon which a district court may decline jurisdiction over a supplemental claim, even though it is empowered to hear the claim. Subsection (c)(1)-(3) codifies the factors recognized as relevant under current law. Subsection (c)(4) acknowledges that occasionally there may exist other compelling reasons for a district court to decline supplemental jurisdiction, which the subsection does not foreclose a court from considering in exceptional circumstances. As under current law, subsection (c) requires the district court, in exercising its discretion, to undertake a case-specific analysis. . . .

[Section 1367(d)] provides a period of tolling of statutes of limitations for any supplemental claim that is dismissed under this section and for any other claims in the same action voluntarily dismissed at the same time or after the supplemental claim is dismissed. The purpose is to prevent the loss of claims to statutes of limitations where state law might fail to toll the running of the period of limitations while a supplemental claim was pending in federal court. It also eliminates a possible disincentive from such a gap in tolling when a plaintiff might wish to seek voluntary dismissal of other claims in order to pursue an entire matter in state court when a federal court dismisses a supplemental claim.

REVIEW QUESTIONS

1. House Report No. 101-734 notes elsewhere that "§ 1367 subsection (a) codifies the scope of supplemental jurisdiction first articulated by the Supreme Court in *United Mine Workers v. Gibbs*," and the "net effect of subsection (b) is to implement the principal rationale of *Owen Equipment & Erection Co.*" Can you identify the precise language that accomplishes these results? What precise language overturns *Finley*? How might you improve the drafting of § 1367 to achieve its stated purposes more clearly?

2. The language in § 1367(a) referring to claims so related that "they form part of the same case or controversy under Article III" codifies the *Gibbs* concept of federal and nonfederal claims deriving from "a common nucleus of operative fact." How broad is this concept? Consider the following hypothetical offered by Professor Martin Redish in a related context:

[A]ssume a traffic accident, followed by a fist fight between the drivers. Driver A sues driver B for negligence in causing the accident; driver B counterclaims for battery arising out of the postaccident fight. On a purely linguistic or conceptual level, these two incidents could be characterized as either being part of the same occurrence or not. Courts that define the phrase in terms of evidentiary overlap would probably decline to find these incidents to be part of the same occurrence, because there likely will be little, if any, evidentiary overlap. Yet courts that define the phrase in terms of the broader concept of "logical relationship" would quite probably find that the incidents are, in fact, part of the same occurrence.

Martin Redish, *Reassessing the Allocation of Judicial Business Between State and Federal Courts: Federal Jurisdiction and the "Martian Chronicles,"* 78 Va. L. Rev. 1769, 1822-1823 (1992). Given the policy underlying § 1367, which approach makes more sense? The problem of defining "same transaction or occurrence" is familiar to us from our look at joinder in Chapter 3, and will be encountered again with regard to the doctrine of finality in Chapter 10.

3. As noted earlier in Part C, § 1367 provides access to a federal forum for diversity cases in which joined plaintiffs lack the requisite amount in controversy provided *at least one plaintiff* satisfies it (and complete diversity exists). *Exxon Mobil Corp. v. Allapattah Services, Inc.*, 545 U.S. 546 (2005).

4. Try to answer the following questions based on the supplemental jurisdiction reading you have done so far:
   - A tenant who lives (and intends to reside permanently) in a building in New York sued her landlord in federal court for destruction of her baseball card collection valued at $100,000 when her apartment flooded. The landlord, who is domiciled in New Jersey, wants to implead his insurance company, which is incorporated and has its principal place of business in New York. May he do so? Under what authority?
     o If the insurance company is permitted to be impleaded, may the tenant file a claim against it as well?
     o The tenant realizes that the plumber, who has lived and worked his entire life in New York, was negligent and caused the leak. She wants to add the plumber as a defendant in her federal suit. May she do so? Under what authority?
   - An applicant who was denied an apartment has filed a suit in federal court under the Fair Housing Act, 42 U.S.C. §§ 3601 *et seq.*, alleging discrimination. She wants to add a claim for violation of the New York State Human Rights Law, which also prohibits discrimination in housing to her suit. May she do so? Under what authority?
     o Now imagine the applicant would like to add the real estate agent who facilitated her application to her lawsuit under Rule 20(a). The agent is a citizen of New York. She does not sue the agent for violation of the Fair Housing Act, but only under the New York Human Rights Law. Assume that liability for real estate agents under that law is ambiguous. Can she add this defendant? How is a court likely to analyze this problem?

PRACTICE EXERCISE NO. 36: CHALLENGING SUBJECT MATTER JURISDICTION IN *WARNER*

The plaintiffs in *Warner* pursue four counts in their Complaint. Counts One and Two are federal causes of action that arise under federal law. But Counts Three and Four are state-law claims between non-diverse parties. Would the federal court have supplemental jurisdiction over either or both of these state-law claims?

Now consider two hypothetical claims that build on facts described in the Complaint.

(A) During the incident involving the search of Warner outside his godmother's apartment in February 2008, a neighbor took a picture of the search and immediately posted it to her private blog with the tag line: "They caught the thief! Kudos to the NYPD." If Warner included the photographer/blogger as a defendant in this suit, would the federal court have subject matter jurisdiction of a state-law defamation claim against a non-diverse defendant?

(B) Less than an hour after the incident involving the search of Warner outside his godmother's apartment in February 2008, Warner, still shaken from the incident, inadvertently crossed a street against the traffic light and was hit by a speeding car in the pedestrian crosswalk. If Warner included the driver of the car as a defendant in this suit, would the federal court have subject matter jurisdiction of a state-law negligence claim against a non-diverse defendant?

PRACTICE EXERCISE NO. 37: CHALLENGING SUBJECT MATTER JURISDICTION IN *CARPENTER*

Review the amended complaint and third-party complaints in the *Carpenter* case. Assume for purposes of this exercise that Nancy Carpenter has always resided in New Hampshire and that her action is filed in federal district court in Massachusetts. She sues Dee and Ultimate Auto, both Massachusetts citizens;

Ultimate has impleaded McGill's Garage, also a Massachusetts corporation, and its sole owner, Dale McGill, a citizen of New Hampshire.

Nancy now seeks to amend her complaint to sue the Garage and McGill directly. The latter two parties have moved to dismiss both Ultimate's and Carpenter's claims for lack of subject matter jurisdiction. Students with last names beginning with A-F represent the Garage and McGill; G-M represent Ultimate Auto; and N-Z represent Nancy Carpenter in opposition to the motion.

E. REMOVAL

As we have seen, federal and state courts overlap considerably in their jurisdictional authority. Plaintiffs have the initial choice of federal or state court in federal question and diversity cases. If a plaintiff with such a choice opts for the state court, defendant may usually remove to federal court under 28 U.S.C. § 1441. We say "usually" because the defendant's right to remove to federal court is not completely coextensive with the plaintiff's right to initially choose the federal forum. Read § 1441(b)(2); this is often referred to as the "forum defendant rule." As the Supreme Court observed, the "scales are not evenly balanced" as an in-state plaintiff may invoke diversity jurisdiction but an in-state defendant may not. *Lincoln Property Co. v. Roche*, 546 U.S. 81 (2005). Why would Congress withhold the federal court option from a defendant sued in a diversity case in his home state? (Does Congress similarly withhold the federal court option from a plaintiff suing in a diversity case in her home state?)

A defendant who wants to remove an action from state to federal court does not make a motion. Rather, 28 U.S.C. § 1446(a) explains that the defendant simply files a notice of removal in the federal district embracing the place where the state action is pending. If removal is improper (i.e., if the federal court does not have jurisdiction), the plaintiff should file a motion to *remand* the case back to state court. 28 U.S.C. § 1447(c). Many of the disputes about the scope of § 1331 (e.g., does this cause of action arise under federal law?) or § 1332 (e.g., is the plaintiff a domiciliary of New York or New Jersey? or, does plaintiff's claim that seeks "$15,000 plus punitive damages" satisfy the amount in controversy?) arise in the context of removal of a case that is filed in state court. Indeed, sometimes plaintiffs are trying to establish federal subject matter jurisdiction, and sometimes they are trying to avoid it.

Next, notice the timing requirement for removal. 28 U.S.C. § 1446(b). Defendants must remove the action before the thirty-day window closes. In the ordinary case, the thirty days begins to run from service of the complaint. Accordingly, if there is federal question or diversity jurisdiction, the defendant must act promptly if he wishes to invoke the federal forum. Occasionally, a case that was not removable at the time that the complaint was served will become removable by subsequent events: A non-diverse party may be dropped or a federal cause of action may be added. 28 U.S.C. § 1446(b)(3). If the changed circumstance creates diversity jurisdiction, a thirty-day window opens, *provided* the removal occurs within one year of the commencement of the action; after one year, the action simply is not removable absent bad faith on the part of the plaintiff. *See* 28 U.S.C. § 1446(c)(1). If the changed circumstance creates federal question jurisdiction, however, a thirty-day window opens no matter how much time has passed since the commencement of the action.

Another important technical requirement of removal practice regards cases where there is more than one defendant. When more than one defendant is joined in the action, *all* must join in the notice of removal. 28 U.S.C. § 1446(b)(2)(A). Absent unanimity among the defendants about exercising the right to remove, then, the action will not be removed. There is one narrow exception to this rule about unanimity. 28 U.S.C. § 1441(c)(2). The exception regards situations where a civil action includes both removable and non-removable claims. And that is a phenomenon that we still need to address.

Occasionally a case will include some claims that are removable and some that are not. Consider, for example, a Kansas plaintiff who has two causes of action against a Kansas defendant—the first cause of action is a federal claim, and the second cause of action is an unrelated state law claim. When plaintiff files this action in state court, defendant might, for strategic reasons, prefer that the action be litigated in a federal court. But is this lawsuit removable to federal court?

The analysis of removability begins with 28 U.S.C. § 1441(a). Could a federal court have exercised original subject matter jurisdiction over this action? Although a federal court would have federal question subject matter jurisdiction over the count that raises the federal cause of action, the court would not have original subject matter jurisdiction over the state law claim. This second cause of action is not a federal question, and there is no diversity between the parties. Nor would there be supplemental jurisdiction over the state law claim under 28 U.S.C. § 1367, because we are told that this claim is *unrelated* to the federal question. (Remember 28 U.S.C. § 1367(a).) So a federal court would not have had original jurisdiction over the entire civil action.

But when a claim includes both a removable (federal question) claim and a non-removable (state law) claim, 28 U.S.C. § 1441(c) provides important guidance. The statutory schema contemplates that the entire action should be removed, the non-removable claims severed, and those non-removable claims remanded to the state court. In our hypothetical, then, if the Kansas defendant timely elects to remove the case, the federal question claim will be litigated in federal court, and the state law claim remanded to state court.

Now consider two variations of that hypothetical. (1) Everything in the hypothetical stays the same except that the state law claim is *related* to the federal question claim. Is this removable? (2) Everything in the hypothetical stays the same (including that the state law claim is *unrelated* to the federal question) except that the state law claim is asserted against the Kansas defendant and also a Missouri defendant). Is this removable?

We have focused only on the general removal provisions of the Code. We do not address specialized provisions for specific cases such as cases involving suits against federal officers, 28 U.S.C. § 1442, or torts by federal employees, 28 U.S.C. § 2679(d). Additional removal provisions have been added by CAFA and MMTJA, which are mentioned again in Chapter 11.

Strategic Considerations by Plaintiffs. Think about the strategy and ethics of drafting a complaint to invoke or to avoid federal jurisdiction. Occasionally state law will provide more protection in a particular context than will federal law. Imagine, for example, a state law that provides more protection than Title VII in the context of employment discrimination. Should you add a federal question under Title VII even when you don't need it just to get into federal court?

Or a plaintiff may structure her case to make it non-removable. Imagine your Texas client has a high-value products claim against a Delaware company, a manufacturer with a principal place of business in Florida. If this action is filed in state court, defendant may remove it: The amount in controversy is satisfied and there is complete diversity. Should you add a Texas defendant—say, the seller of the product—even though the substantive claim against the Texas defendant is weaker and even though you know that the Texas defendant is not able to pay any judgment even if you were able to recover?

Revisit the facts in *World-Wide Volkswagen* (from Chapter 7). What was the plaintiffs' domicile? And what were the states of citizenship of the various defendants? Were the plaintiffs pursuing federal or state law causes of action? Was the case removable? Would the case have been removable if World-Wide Volkswagen and Seaway were not named as additional defendants? Would the case have been removable if World-Wide Volkswagen and Seaway were dismissed for lack of personal jurisdiction?

Strategic Considerations by Defendants. In the ordinary course, the forum defendant rule prevents an in-state defendant from removing an action to federal court when the sole basis for federal court subject matter jurisdiction would be diversity jurisdiction. *See* 28 U.S.C. § 1441(b)(2). But savvy defendants found a loophole. As drafted, the forum defendant rule applies only to defendants who have been properly joined *and served.* Accordingly, an in-state defendant who removes the action to federal court before they have been served arguably falls outside the scope of the forum defendant rule. This practice is often referred to as *snap removal.* Defendants with the wherewithal and the resources to monitor state court dockets remove in a snap, before they are served. The propriety of snap removal is a wonderful example of textualism in conflict with purposivism. The plain meaning of the text authorizes snap removal. But the purpose of the forum defendant rule was to keep in-state defendants (who presumably would face no bias in their own state's state courts) from invoking the diversity jurisdiction of federal courts; the timing of service would have no bearing on that policy. The reason that the "properly joined and served" language appears in section 1441(b)(2) was to prevent a plaintiff from fraudulently joining an in-state defendant to prevent removal or from joining an in-state defendant and then simply not serving them. Only the U.S. Courts of Appeals for the Second and Third Circuits have squarely addressed the snap removal issue, and both of them allowed it. In the rest of the country, the federal district courts are rather evenly divided between allowing defendants to remove and remanding snap-removals back to state court. Proposals to close this "loophole" are pending as this book goes to press.

Federal Preemption.   In Part B, on federal question jurisdiction, we warned that there was an important exception to the well-pleaded complaint that arises in the context of plaintiffs who are trying to *avoid* stating a claim that arises under federal law. A case that pursues only a state-law claim (against a non-diverse party) would ordinarily not be removable. Indeed, applying § 1441(a) and the well-pleaded complaint rule, the district courts would not have had original jurisdiction over a state-law claim between non-diverse parties.

The pursuit of a state-law claim that is *completely preempted* by federal law may nevertheless be removable from state to federal court. This doctrine of complete preemption should not be confused with so-called *ordinary preemption*, which is a defense that exists where a federal law has superseded a state-law claim. *See, e.g., Nordegren v. Burlington N. R.R. Co.,* 101 F.3d 1246, 1248 (8th Cir. 1996). (We have known since *Mottley,* of course, that a *defense* raising an issue of federal law does not satisfy § 1331, a test that is incorporated by reference into § 1441(a).) By contrast, *complete preemption* exists only where federal preemption is so strong that "there is . . . no such thing as a state-law claim." *Beneficial National Bank v. Anderson,* 539 U.S. 1, 11 (2003).

> [We should] not conflate "complete preemption" with "conflict" or "ordinary" preemption. While these two concepts are linguistically related, they are not as close kin jurisprudentially as their names suggest. Complete preemption is a jurisdictional doctrine, while ordinary preemption simply declares the primacy of federal law, regardless of the forum or the claim. . . . Ordinary preemption has been categorized as a federal defense to the allegations. . . . And as a mere defense, the preemptive effect of a federal statute . . . will not provide a basis for removal. . . . Even if preemption forms the very core of the litigation, it is insufficient for removal. . . . By contrast, when complete preemption exists, there is no such thing as the state action . . . since the federal claim is treated as if it appears on the face of the complaint because it effectively displaces the state cause of action. Complete preemption thus transforms the plaintiff's state-law claims into federal claims.

Lontz v. Tharp, 413 F.3d 435, 440-441 (4th Cir. 2005).

The intent of Congress is the ultimate touchstone guiding preemption analysis. In determining whether a state-law claim is completely preempted, the court asks whether Congress intended a federal statute to provide "the exclusive cause of action for the claim asserted and also set forth procedures and remedies governing that cause of action." *Beneficial National Bank v. Anderson,* 539 U.S. 1, 8 (2003). If so, the cause of action necessarily *arises under* federal law and the case is therefore removable. The Supreme Court has recognized complete preemption in very few areas. *See, e.g., Avco Corp. v. Aero Lodge No. 735,* 390 U.S. 557 (1968) (recognizing complete preemption by § 301 of the Labor Management Relations Act); *Metro. Life Ins. Co. v. Taylor,* 481 U.S. 58 (1987) (recognizing complete preemption by § 502(a) of ERISA); *Beneficial Natl. Bank v. Anderson,* 539 U.S. 1 (2003) (recognizing complete preemption by §§ 85-86 of the National Bank Act).

Class Actions. The hospitality or hostility of a forum toward certain claims or litigants can raise the stakes when parties disagree about whether a state or federal court is the proper forum. Whether a class action belongs in federal or state court, for example, is often hotly contested. In *Dart Cherokee Basin Operating Co., LLC v. Owens,* 135 S. Ct. 547 (2014), the Court held that a party's notice of removal need include only a plausible allegation that the amount in controversy exceeds the jurisdictional threshold in 28 U.S.C. § 1332(d). If the plaintiff challenges that assertion, the court should decide whether there is a preponderance of evidence to support the removal. Because the class representatives cannot bind members of a proposed class before the class is certified, the plaintiffs cannot prevent removal of a class by representing that they will not seek damages in excess of the jurisdictional threshold. *Standard Fire Ins. Co. v. Knowles,* 133 S. Ct. 1345 (2013).

REVIEW QUESTIONS

Use the removal statutes, 28 U.S.C. § 1441 and 1446, to answer the following questions. For purposes of answering these questions, assume that Priya is a citizen of California, the *Star Newspaper* is incorporated and has its principal place of business in Florida, and *Celebrity Magazine* is incorporated and has its principal place of business in Nevada.

1. Priya sues the *Star Newspaper* for defamation in California state court. She claims damages of $1,000,000. Can the *Star Newspaper* remove to federal court? Under what authority?
2. What if Priya sues in Florida? Can the newspaper still remove?
3. Priya files a lawsuit against the *Star Newspaper* and *Celebrity Magazine* in Florida state court for defamation. Thirteen months later, the court dismisses claims against the *Star Newspaper*. Can the magazine remove? Under what authority?
4. Priya sues the *Star Newspaper* and *Celebrity Magazine* in Florida state court for both defamation and trademark infringement under 15 U.S.C. § 1114. She claims $2,000,000 in damages. Can the defendants remove to federal court? Under what authority?
5. Priya files a suit for defamation, seeking $1,000,000 against the *Star Newspaper* and *Celebrity Magazine* in California state court. The magazine does not agree to remove. Can the *Star Newspaper* remove the suit to federal court? On what authority do you base your answer?

REVIEW EXERCISE NO. 9

You have been consulted by the Very-Clean Vacuum Company regarding the following matter. Very-Clean has been served with a summons and complaint at its headquarters in St. Louis, Missouri. The complaint reads as follows:

UNITED STATES DISTRICT COURT
FOR THE SOUTHERN DISTRICT OF NEW YORK

Jane Whitecroft and John Whitecroft,
    Plaintiffs,
 	
                        v.
 	
Very-Clean Vacuum Company, Inc.,
    Defendants.
	Civil Action No. xxxx-yyyy
	COMPLAINT

1 Plaintiffs are husband and wife and residents of the State of Connecticut. Defendant is incorporated in the State of Delaware and has its principal place of business in Missouri. The matter in controversy exceeds $75,000.
2 On April 1, 2018, plaintiffs purchased a Very-Clean Model 500V Vacuum at the Ace Discount Store in White Plains, New York.
3 Soon after purchasing the Model 500V, plaintiff John Whitecroft was vacuuming the living room in his house shared with plaintiff Jane Whitecroft. The machine suddenly emitted a large electrical spark and exploded in flames.
4 As a result, plaintiff John Whitecroft was severely burned, suffering permanent and disabling injuries. The plaintiffs' home was destroyed by fire and all their personal belongings lost in the blaze.
5 Plaintiffs allege, upon information and belief, that the fire resulted from the negligence of defendant Very-Clean Vacuum Company, Inc., in the manufacture of the Model 500V and the subsequent negligent failure to warn consumers who had purchased the machines of the immediate danger, and/or that the Model 500V was a product in a defective condition, which was unreasonably dangerous to the user.

WHEREFORE, plaintiffs pray that judgment be rendered against defendant in the amount of $6,000,000, with interest and costs, and for such other relief as may be appropriate.

/s/
Daniel Z. Dugal,
Attorney for Plaintiffs
1001 3rd Avenue
New York, New York 10022

* * *

Very-Clean's general counsel, Jacinte Lavoie, informs you that the Company is very nervous about this action, especially given the amount of damages sought. The Company has a great safety record, but he concedes there have been other reported problems with the Model 500V. Very-Clean has received letters from several other purchasers reporting electrical problems with the same model, although none has suffered the type of catastrophic injuries that the White-crofts allege. Several of these purchasers have also threatened suit.

Nonetheless, the Company stands behind its product. The people in engineering believe that the accidents with the Model 500V have likely resulted because the consumers have plugged the machines into two-pronged, ungrounded electrical sockets instead of the three-pronged grounded sockets recommended in the instructions.

Very-Clean has always relied upon Second-Guess Testing Labs, located nearby in St. Louis, to assure the quality of its products. Very-Clean has retained them to put each of its prospective products through a series of grueling tests prior to placing them on the market. Second-Guess reported that it had tested the Model 500V and certified its safety and dependability to Very-Clean. If there is a defect in the product, Second-Guess apparently failed to detect it.

Corporate counsel is quite surprised that the Company's products are being sold in New York, since Very-Clean distributes only to retailers in the Midwest. (At one time about fifteen years ago, when the Company was just getting started, it did ship products to stores in New York, New Jersey, and Connecticut, but discontinued such sales because they proved unprofitable, given the high transportation costs.) It appears that one of the retail stores Very-Clean distributes to in the Midwest went out of business and its inventory was acquired by Ace Discount, a national chain, which explains how the Model 500V ended up on sale in White Plains, New York.

Very-Clean has learned that Jane Whitecroft has been enrolled for the past two years as a doctoral student at Washington University in St. Louis, Missouri. She subleases an apartment near the university, which she lives in while school is in session, but spends the rest of the year with her husband in Connecticut, where she is writing her dissertation.

Corporate counsel reports that after the accident the Whitecrofts engaged in a vicious publicity campaign against Very-Clean, appearing on talk shows and news programs and characterizing the Company as recklessly disregarding the public's safety. This has significantly hurt Very-Clean's reputation and business.

The New York State long-arm statute appears in Chapter 7.

Prepare a memorandum discussing:

1. How should Very-Clean respond to this complaint? Consider all possible procedural objections and defenses, including jurisdictional. For each, outline the manner in which it should be raised (by pleading or motion), the specific Federal Rule of Civil Procedure or other provision relied upon, and the likelihood of prevailing on the objection or defense in court. Include a list of any additional facts you may need to

investigate to complete your analysis, and explain how the information would be used.

2. What additional claims and parties should Very-Clean consider? For each, outline the manner in which it should be raised (by pleading or motion) and the specific provisions of the Federal Rules of Civil Procedure or Judicial Code relied upon. Include a discussion of the jurisdictional problems (if any) with each option.

Choice of Federal or State Law—The *Erie* Doctrine

W̶e learned in Chapter 8 that a federal court has subject matter jurisdiction of a civil action if the claim arises under federal law (28 U.S.C. § 1331), or if the parties are of diverse citizenship (28 U.S.C. § 1332). In the former case, the law that controls the rights and obligations of the parties is obviously the federal law from which the claim arises. Thus in an action brought under the Fair Housing Act of 1968 (42 U.S.C. §§ 3601 et seq.) alleging discrimination in the rental of an apartment, the federal statute (and decisional law interpreting it) will determine the elements of the claim, the defenses available to defendant, and the remedies plaintiff may be awarded if successful in the action.

For federal diversity cases, however, the question of what law applies has occupied courts and scholars for many years. After all, these are state law claims being entertained by courts of a different sovereign. Does the federal district court apply state or federal law in a personal injury action between citizens of different states? Even after the Supreme Court settled this question in favor of state *substantive* law, it faced an even more elusive issue: Is the federal court required to conform to the *procedural* rules that the state court would apply as well?

Choice of law issues arise because a court with jurisdictional power over a case does not necessarily also have authority to apply its own law to resolve the matter. A California court may have jurisdiction over a contract action based solely on service of process on the defendant while briefly present in that state (*see Burnham v. Superior Court* in Chapter 7). But if neither party is a forum resident and the events giving rise to the claim occurred elsewhere, would it be proper for the court to resolve the case by reference to California law of contract? What if plaintiff had "shopped" for the forum because its law is more favorable to her than the other jurisdictions more closely connected to the case?

The choice of law predicament has two dimensions in our federal system. The "vertical" choice, between federal and state law, raises fundamental issues of federalism and power-sharing and is the subject of this chapter. "Horizontal" choice issues arise when it is determined that state law applies, and the question becomes *which* state's law. This complex topic is covered in Conflict of Laws courses and will not be treated at length here.

As you read the landmark case below, consider how choice of law issues influenced the Pennsylvania plaintiff's strategic decision to file in federal district court in New York.

Erie Railroad Co. v. Tompkins
304 U.S. 64 (1938)

Justice BRANDEIS delivered the opinion of the Court:

The question for decision is whether the oft-challenged doctrine of *Swift v. Tyson* shall now be disapproved.

Tompkins, a citizen of Pennsylvania, was injured on a dark night by a passing freight train of the Erie Railroad Company while walking along its right of way at Hughestown in that State. He claimed that the accident occurred through negligence in the operation, or maintenance, of the train; that he was rightfully on the premises as licensee because on a commonly used beaten footpath which ran for a short distance alongside the tracks; and that he was struck by something which looked like a door projecting from one of the moving cars. To enforce that claim he brought an action in the federal court for southern New York, which had jurisdiction because the company is a corporation of that State. It denied liability; and the case was tried by a jury.

The Erie insisted that its duty to Tompkins was no greater than that owed to a trespasser. It contended, among other things, that its duty to Tompkins, and hence its liability, should be determined in accordance with the Pennsylvania law; that under the law of Pennsylvania, as declared by its highest court, persons who use pathways along the railroad right of way—that is a longitudinal pathway as distinguished from a crossing—are to be deemed trespassers; and that the railroad is not liable for injuries to undiscovered trespassers resulting from its negligence, unless it be wanton or wilful. Tompkins denied that any such rule had been established by the decisions of the Pennsylvania courts; and contended that, since there was no statute of the State on the subject, the railroad's duty and liability is to be determined in federal courts as a matter of general law.

The trial judge refused to rule that the applicable law precluded recovery. The jury brought in a verdict of $30,000; and the judgment entered thereon was affirmed by the Circuit Court of Appeals, which held that it was unnecessary to consider whether the law of Pennsylvania was as contended, because the question was one not of local, but of general, law and that "upon questions of general law the federal courts are free, in the absence of a local statute, to exercise their independent judgment as to what the law is; and it is well settled that the question of the responsibility of a railroad for injuries caused by its servants is one of general law. Where the public has made open and notorious use of a railroad right of way for a long period of time and without objection, the company owes to persons on such permissive pathway a duty of care in the operation of its trains. It is likewise generally recognized law that a jury may find that negligence exists toward a pedestrian using a permissive path on the railroad right of way if he is hit by some object projecting from the side of the train."

The Erie had contended that application of the Pennsylvania rule was required, among other things, by § 34 of the Federal Judiciary Act of September 24, 1789 [Rules of Decisions Act], which provides:

> The laws of the several States, except where the Constitution, treaties, or statutes of the United States otherwise require or provide, shall be regarded as rules of decision in trials at common law, in the courts of the United States, in cases where they apply.

Because of the importance of the question whether the federal court was free to disregard the alleged rule of the Pennsylvania common law, we granted certiorari.

First. *Swift v. Tyson* held that federal courts exercising jurisdiction on the ground of diversity of citizenship need not, in matters of general jurisprudence, apply the unwritten law of the State as declared by its highest court; that they are free to exercise an independent judgment as to what the common law of the State is—or should be; and that, as there stated by Mr. Justice Story:

> [T]he true interpretation of the thirty-fourth section limited its application to state laws strictly local, that is to say, to the positive statutes of the state, and the construction thereof adopted by the local tribunals, and to rights and titles to things having a permanent locality, such as the rights and titles to real estate, and other matters immovable and intraterritorial in their nature and character. It never has been supposed by us, that the section did apply, or was intended to apply, to questions of a more general nature, not at all dependent upon local statutes or local usages of a fixed and permanent operation, as, for example, to the construction of ordinary contracts or other written instruments, and especially to questions of general commercial law, where the state tribunals are called upon to perform the like functions as ourselves, that is, to ascertain upon general reasoning and legal analogies, what is the true exposition of the contract or instrument, or what is the just rule furnished by the principles of commercial law to govern the case.

The federal courts assumed, in the broad field of "general law," the power to declare rules of decision which Congress was confessedly without power to enact as statutes. Doubt was repeatedly expressed as to the correctness of the construction given § 34, and as to the soundness of the rule which it introduced. But it was the more recent research of a competent scholar, who examined the original document, which established that the construction given to it by the Court was erroneous; and that the purpose of the section was merely to make certain that, in all matters except those in which some federal law is controlling, the federal courts exercising jurisdiction in diversity of citizenship cases would apply as their rules of decision the law of the State, unwritten as well as written.[5]

Criticism of the doctrine became widespread after the decision of *Black & White Taxicab Co. v. Brown & Yellow Taxicab Co.*, 276 U.S. 518. There, Brown and Yellow, a Kentucky corporation owned by Kentuckians, and the Louisville and Nashville Railroad, also a Kentucky corporation, wished that the former should have the exclusive privilege of soliciting passenger and baggage transportation at the Bowling Green, Kentucky, railroad station; and that the Black and White, a competing Kentucky corporation, should be prevented from interfering with that privilege. Knowing that such a contract would be void under the common law of Kentucky, it was arranged that the Brown and Yellow reincorporate under the law of Tennessee, and that the contract with the railroad should be executed there. The suit was then brought by the Tennessee corporation in the federal court for western Kentucky to enjoin competition by the Black and White; an injunction issued by the District Court was sustained by the Court of Appeals; and this Court, citing many decisions in which the doctrine of *Swift v. Tyson* had been applied, affirmed the decree.

Second. Experience in applying the doctrine of *Swift v. Tyson* had revealed its defects, political and social; and the benefits expected to flow from the rule did not accrue. Persistence of state courts in their own opinions on questions of common law prevented uniformity; and the impossibility of discovering a satisfactory line of demarcation between the province of general law and that of local law developed a new well of uncertainties.

On the other hand, the mischievous results of the doctrine had become apparent. Diversity of citizenship jurisdiction was conferred in order to prevent apprehended discrimination in state courts against those not citizens of the State. *Swift v. Tyson* introduced grave discrimination by non-citizens against citizens. It made rights enjoyed under the unwritten "general law" vary according to whether enforcement was sought in the state or in the federal court; and the privilege of selecting the court in which the right should be determined was conferred upon the non-citizen. Thus, the doctrine rendered impossible equal protection of the law. In attempting to promote uniformity of law throughout the United States, the doctrine had prevented uniformity in the administration of the law of the State.

The discrimination resulting became in practice far-reaching. This resulted in part from the broad province accorded to the so-called "general law" as to which federal courts exercised an independent judgment. In addition to questions of purely commercial law, "general law" was held to include the obligations under contracts entered into and to be performed within the State, the extent to which a carrier operating within a State may stipulate for exemption from liability for his own negligence or that of his employee; the liability for torts

---

5. Charles Warren, *New Light on the History of the Federal Judiciary Act of 1789*, 37 Harv. L. Rev. 49, 51-52, 81-88, 108 (1923).

committed within the State upon persons resident or property located there, even where the question of liability depended upon the scope of a property right conferred by the State; and the right to exemplary or punitive damages. Furthermore, state decisions construing local deeds, mineral conveyances, and even devises of real estate were disregarded.

In part the discrimination resulted from the wide range of persons held entitled to avail themselves of the federal rule by resort to the diversity of citizenship jurisdiction. Through this jurisdiction individual citizens willing to remove from their own State and become citizens of another might avail themselves of the federal rule. And, without even change of residence, a corporate citizen of the State could avail itself of the federal rule by re-incorporating under the laws of another State, as was done in the *Taxicab* case.

The injustice and confusion incident to the doctrine of *Swift v. Tyson* have been repeatedly urged as reasons for abolishing or limiting diversity of citizenship jurisdiction. Other legislative relief has been proposed. If only a question of statutory construction were involved, we should not be prepared to abandon a doctrine so widely applied throughout nearly a century. But the unconstitutionality of the course pursued has now been made clear and compels us to do so.

Third. Except in matters governed by the Federal Constitution or by Acts of Congress, the law to be applied in any case is the law of the State. And whether the law of the State shall be declared by its Legislature in a statute or by its highest court in a decision is not a matter of federal concern. There is no federal general common law. Congress has no power to declare substantive rules of common law applicable in a State whether they be local in their nature or "general," be they commercial law or a part of the law of torts. And no clause in the Constitution purports to confer such a power upon the federal courts.

The fallacy underlying the rule declared in *Swift v. Tyson* is made clear by Mr. Justice Holmes. The doctrine rests upon the assumption that there is "a transcendental body of law outside of any particular State but obligatory within it unless and until changed by statute," that federal courts have the power to use their judgment as to what the rules of common law are; and that in the federal courts "the parties are entitled to an independent judgment on matters of general law": "[B]ut law in the sense in which courts speak of it today does not exist without some definite authority behind it. The common law so far as it is enforced in a State, whether called common law or not, is not the common law generally but the law of that State existing by the authority of that State."

Thus the doctrine of *Swift v. Tyson* is, as Mr. Justice Holmes said, "an unconstitutional assumption of powers by courts of the United States which no lapse of time or respectable array of opinion should make us hesitate to correct." In disapproving that doctrine we do not hold unconstitutional § 34 of the Federal Judiciary Act of 1789 or any other Act of Congress. We merely declare that in applying the doctrine this Court and the lower courts have invaded rights which in our opinion are reserved by the Constitution to the several States.

Fourth. The defendant contended that by the common law of Pennsylvania as declared by its highest court the only duty owed to the plaintiff was to refrain from wilful or wanton injury. The plaintiff denied that such is the Pennsylvania law. In support of their respective contentions the parties discussed and cited many decisions of the Supreme Court of the State. The Circuit Court of Appeals ruled that the question of liability is one of general law; and on that ground declined to decide the issue of state law. As we hold this was error, the judgment is reversed and the case remanded to it for further proceedings in conformity with our opinion. Reversed.

Justice CARDOZO took no part in the consideration or decision of this case.

Justice REED, concurring:

I concur in the conclusion reached in this case, in the disapproval of the doctrine of *Swift v. Tyson*, and in the reasoning of the majority opinion except in so far as it relies upon the unconstitutionality of the "course pursued" by the federal courts.

The "doctrine of *Swift v. Tyson*," as I understand it, is that the words "the laws," as used in §34, line one, of the Federal Judiciary Act of September 24, 1789, do not include in their meaning "the decisions of the local tribunals."

To decide the case now before us and to "disapprove" the doctrine of *Swift v. Tyson* requires only that we say that the words "the laws" include in their meaning the decisions of the local tribunals. As the majority opinion shows, by its reference to Mr. Warren's researches and the first quotation from Mr. Justice Holmes, that this Court is now of the view that "laws" includes "decisions," it is unnecessary to go further and declare that the "course pursued" was "unconstitutional," instead of merely erroneous. . . .

If the opinion commits this Court to the position that the Congress is without power to declare what rules of substantive law shall govern the federal courts, that conclusion also seems questionable. The line between procedural and substantive law is hazy but no one doubts federal power over procedure. The Judiciary Article and the "necessary and proper" clause of Article One may fully authorize legislation, such as this section of the Judiciary Act.

[In his dissenting opinion, Justice BUTLER, joined by Justice McREYNOLDS, argued for adherence to the long-standing *Swift v. Tyson* precedent.]

YOUR TAKEAWAY

Throughout this course you have studied our parallel system of courts—federal and state. The latter were the successors to the various colonial courts, the former the creation of Art. II in the U.S. Constitution. *Erie Railroad Co. v. Tompkins* arises at the intersection of these courts of different (and often competing) sovereigns. In the previous chapter, we examined the allocation of adjudicatory power—subject matter jurisdiction—between the two. Now we explore another power-sharing matter: which sovereign gets to apply its law to the resolution of the dispute.

Under the regime of *Swift v. Tyson*, federal law would apply in diversity cases, notwithstanding that the claims arose from state law (tort, contract, etc.), if the matter could be described as "general" as opposed to local law. This counterintuitive result came about because of *Swift*'s narrow reading of the state "laws" that federal courts were required to defer to by the Rules of Decision Act—only *statutory* laws, the "positive" enactments of a legislature, but not common law decisions of courts. Thus the lower courts ruled that Harry Tompkins could prevail on a showing of mere negligence, rather than the higher wanton/reckless standard applied by Pennsylvania's Supreme Court.

With Justice Brandeis's course correction in *Erie*, application-of-law power tacked from federal to state, at least as to "substantive" law like the standard of care owed in a tort action. Defining the elusive line between substance and procedure became the daunting task in Act II of the *Erie* drama.

REVIEW QUESTIONS

1. Identify the courts with both subject matter and personal jurisdiction in which Tompkins could have filed his action. Do you see why he chose the federal district in New York? Professor Edward A. Purcell, Jr. recounts the critical role Columbia Law student Aaron L. Danzig, as intern to Tompkins's lawyer, played in this choice of forum. *See The Story of* Erie: *How Litigants, Lawyers, Judges, Politics, and Social Change Reshape the Law*, in *Civil Procedure Stories* (Kevin M. Clermont ed. 2d ed. 2008), at 39.

2. In *Swift*, Justice Story construed § 34 of the Judiciary Act of 1789 (the Rules of Decision Act) to permit federal courts to ignore state "laws" when they appeared in the form of a common law decision, as opposed to *statutory*, law. Is this consistent with the plain meaning of the statutory language? If not, what might have motivated the Court to stray so far from the ordinary meaning of "laws"? Note that the first Judiciary Act had "the right answer" to the vertical choice of law quandary—it just took succeeding generations 150 years to rediscover it.

3. Louis D. Brandeis's critique of *Swift v. Tyson*, which had permitted the federal courts to apply (and indeed make up) their own "general common law" in cases like *Erie*, weaves several rhetorical threads. Identify the statutory, constitutional, and policy arguments Brandeis arrays against *Swift*.

4. What are the "mischievous results" of *Swift* referred to by Brandeis? How are these illustrated by the *Black & White Taxicab* case?

5. Imagine that Harry Tompkins was not walking alone on the fateful night, and that you are the personal injury attorney consulted by both Harry and his friend Jake (a citizen of New York) after they were simultaneously severely injured along the tracks in Hughestown. *Before* the *Erie* decision, how would you assess Jake's chances of recovery against the Erie Railroad, as compared to Harry's? How would you explain this to Jake? Can you see what Brandeis meant when he wrote that *Swift* "rendered impossible equal protection of the law"? Would

different standards of care apply to the friends' civil actions *after* the *Erie* decision?

6. What specific provision of the Constitution does Brandeis rely upon for the conclusion that *Swift* represented "an unconstitutional assumption of powers by the Courts of the United States"? The Tenth Amendment would have been a likely choice, as it provides: "The powers not delegated to the United States by the Constitution, nor prohibited by it to the States, are reserved to the States respectively, or to the people." But it is not mentioned.

    For one noted legal scholar, "*Erie*'s ambiguities are several and obvious. If the decision rests on statutory grounds, the constitutional portion may be unnecessary *dictum*. Even if it is constitutionally based, the Court confused the matter by failing to cite directly any provision of the Constitution and by placing some of the apparent constitutional analysis in the portion of the opinion that rests on other grounds. One can find in the opinion possible invocations of the doctrines of due process, equal protection, separation of powers, and federalism." George D. Brown, *The Ideologies of Forum Shopping—Why Doesn't a Conservative Court Protect Defendants?*, 71 U.N.C. L. Rev. 649, 657 (1993).

    Professor John Hart Ely finds no surprise in the Court's failure to indicate precisely what constitutional provision *Swift* had violated: "[T]he lack of a relevant provision was precisely the point. The [*Swift*] interpretation was unconstitutional, but not because the federal common law rules that had been developed under it were encroaching on areas of 'state substantive law.' . . . It was unconstitutional because nothing in the Constitution provided the central government with a general lawmaking authority of the sort the Court had been exercising under *Swift*." John Hart Ely, *The Irrepressible Myth of* Erie, 87 Harv. L. Rev. 693, 702-703 (1974).

7. Two distinctions drawn by Justice Reed in his concurrence play a very significant role in the post-*Erie* era. First, he reminds us that Congress may have the authority to declare substantive law that would govern in federal courts (as if, for example, it had enacted a Federal Railway Safety Act that applied to Tompkins's accident), even if a federal judge does not have this authority. Second, and more important from the perspective of the cases we take up next, Reed explicitly distinguishes between "substantive" and "procedural" law, observing that while the line between the two may be hazy, "*no one doubts federal power over procedure.*" Indeed, under established conflicts of law principles, a forum follows its own rules of procedure even while applying the substantive law of another jurisdiction. *See Restatement (Second) Conflicts* § 122. Brandeis makes only passing reference to this dichotomy when he notes that "no clause in the Constitution purports to confer [the power to declare substantive rules of common law applicable in a State] upon the federal courts."

    We will return to the elusive substance/procedure line shortly.

8. On Justice Reed's second point, note that the *Erie* decision and the adoption of the Federal Rules of Civil Procedure both occurred in the same momentous year of 1938. Prior to the Federal Rules of Civil Procedure, federal district courts were required by the Conformity Acts to follow the procedure of the state courts in the state in which they sat, creating what many federal court practitioners considered sheer chaos. In 1934 Congress, persuaded that a uniform body of federal procedure was desirable, set the rulemaking process in motion with the Rules Enabling Act* authorizing the Supreme Court to "prescribe by general rules, the forms of process, writs, pleadings, and motions, and the practice and procedure of the district courts and courts of appeals in the United States in civil actions." Significantly, the Act stipulated that "[s]uch rules shall not abridge, enlarge, or modify any substantive right."

   As Professor Mary Kay Kane has observed: "The year 1938 thus began a new era in the balance of power between state and federal courts—one that was to be controlled by the wavering (sometimes almost evanescent) line between substance and procedure." Mary Kay Kane, *The Golden Wedding Years:* Erie Railroad Company v. Tompkins *and the Federal Rules*, 63 Notre Dame L. Rev. 671, 673 (1988).

9. When *Erie Railroad v. Tompkins* resolved the vertical choice of law issue in favor of state over federal substantive law, it opened a second, horizontal choice between the tort law of Pennsylvania (where Tompkins's accident occurred) and New York (where the Railroad was incorporated and the federal court hearing the case sat). Conflicts of laws principles now seek to identify the state with "the most significant relationship" to the issue in question, but at the time of the *Erie* decision categorical rules pointed to the law of the state in which the accident occurred. *See generally* Russell J. Weintraub, *Commentary on the Conflict of Laws* (6th ed. 2010). Thus the *Erie* Court assumed Pennsylvania law would control, and remanded for determination of what duty of care was owed Tompkins under that law.

10. *Klaxon Co. v. Stentor Electric Mfg. Co.*, 313 U.S. 487 (1941), required federal courts in diversity actions to apply the same conflicts rule that would be applied by courts of the state in which they sit. "Otherwise, the accident of diversity of citizenship would constantly disturb equal administration of justice in coordinate state and federal courts sitting side by side." Thus in the *Klaxon* breach of contract action, the federal district court in Delaware was bound to apply the law of whatever state the Delaware state courts would look to if they were entertaining the action. As we will see in our next case, the goal was to conform results in federal diversity cases to those that would obtain if the case had been filed in state court.

---

* The current version is at 28 U.S.C. § 2072. For a more in-depth history of the Rules Enabling Act, see Chapter 4, Part E.4.

MORE TO PONDER

1. What if *Erie* commands application of state law, but that state's highest court has not pronounced on the subject? The Second Circuit Court of Appeals has answered:

> Absent law from a state's highest court, a federal court sitting in diversity has to predict how the state court would resolve an ambiguity in state law. In predicting how a state's highest court would rule on an issue, it is helpful to consider the decisions of the state's trial and appellate courts. The holding of an intermediate appellate state court . . . is a datum for ascertaining state law which is not to be disregarded by a federal court unless it is convinced by other persuasive data that the highest court of the state would decide otherwise. Other data include relevant case law from other jurisdictions on the same or analogous issues, scholarly writings in the field, and any other resources available to the state's highest court.

   Fieger v. Pitney Bowes Credit Corp., 251 F.3d 386, 399 (2d Cir. 2001). *See also Werwinski v. Ford Motor Co.,* 286 F.3d 661, 670 (3d Cir. 2002); *Iodice v. United States,* 289 F.3d 270, 275 (4th Cir. 2002). *See generally* Erwin Chemerinsky, *Federal Jurisdiction* § 5.3, at 363-365 (7th ed. 2016).

   Judge Henry Friendly put it more succinctly in *Nolan v. Transocean Air Lines,* 276 F.2d 280, 281 (2d Cir. 1960): "Our principal task, in this diversity of citizenship case, is to determine what the New York courts would think the California courts would think on an issue about which neither has thought." Henry Friendly, by the way, penned perhaps the most famous defense of Brandeis's *Erie* opinion against its critics. *See In Praise of* Erie—*And of the New Federal Common Law,* 39 N.Y.U. L. Rev. 383 (1964).

2. Justice Brandeis's assertion that "there is no federal general common law" is a bit of an overstatement. Indeed, the lead sentence in that paragraph contains the important caveat: "Except in matters governed by the Federal Constitution or by Acts of Congress. . . ." Federal courts have developed common law in such specialized areas as labor relations, antitrust, civil rights, and maritime disputes. *See generally* Charles A. Wright and Mary Kay Kane, *Law of Federal Courts* § 60, at 413-424 (6th ed. 2002); Erwin Chemerinsky, *supra*, §§ 6.1-6.3, at 353-380.

3. One scholar's take on *Erie* and the overruling of *Swift v. Tyson* is that it was part of a reaction against the dramatic expansion of federal power in the New Deal era:

> Brandeis also detected unwanted centralization in another area, far less significant politically, but more immediately relevant to the judicial system. In 1934, the Rules Enabling Act which [Brandeis] opposed, had authorized the Supreme Court to promulgate rules of procedure for both legal and equitable actions, and in December, 1937 the newly drafted Federal Rules of Civil procedure came before the Court for review. Brandeis alone dissented

from the Court's approval, and he cherished the hope that Congress might veto the new rules. He feared their potential rigidity; he felt that the Court should not take responsibility for a set of rules to which it could not give adequate consideration, and, likely most important, he believed that they represented yet another example of needless centralization. By overruling *Swift*, the Court would establish a new area of decentralized authority and counterbalance the new centralizing Federal Rules.

Edward A. Purcell, Jr., *Brandeis and the Progressive Constitution:* Erie, *the Judicial Power, and the Politics of the Federal Courts in Twentieth Century America* 135-136 (2000).

Another scholar suggests that Brandeis had become dismayed at the widespread tactic of corporate litigants removing personal injury cases to federal court in order to impose greater burdens on plaintiffs suing them: "*Erie* was a part of his overall campaign. Abolishing the general federal common law would eliminate a major incentive for intra-state forum shopping [to federal court] and reduce the utility of a variety of popular manipulative tactics." Stephen B. Burbank, Semtek, *Forum Shopping, and Federal Common Law*, 77 Notre Dame L. Rev. 1027, 1033 (2002) (citing Edward A. Purcell, Jr., *Brandeis,* Erie, *and the New Deal "Constitutional Revolution,"* 26 J. Sup. Ct. Hist. 257, 272-273 (2001)). Of course in *Erie*, it was Tompkins doing the forum shopping for more favorable federal law.

4. Soon after it was handed down, the usually reserved *New York Times* pronounced *Erie* a "transcendentally significant opinion." N.Y. Times, May 3, 1938, at 22, col. 5, as quoted in Irving Younger, *Observation: What Happened in* Erie, 56 Tex. L. Rev. 1011, 1029 (1978). It certainly had a devastating impact on Harry Tompkins, whose $30,000 jury verdict (a handsome sum at the time) was vacated. Tompkins died severely disabled and destitute. Bob Rizzi, Erie *Memoirs Reveal Drama, Tragedy*, 63 Harv. L. Rev. 2 (Sept. 24, 1976).

Was "justice" done to Harry Tompkins? How could one of the Court's great liberals, dubbed the "People's Attorney" for his earlier conscience-driven advocacy as a litigator, deliver this harsh result? Justice Brandeis apparently weighed the dismantling of *Swift* as more pressing than compensating this one plaintiff for his injury. Indeed, he felt so strongly about the need to restore state law to its rightful place in diversity cases that he insisted on characterizing *Swift* as unconstitutional, though as Reed noted it was unnecessary to reach that issue given that the reinterpretation of the Rules of Decision Act resolved the case on statutory grounds. Brandeis wanted to ensure that Congress could not restore *Swift* through legislation. *See* Lewis J. Paper, *Brandeis* (1983), at 383. He was a Justice on a mission. Harry Tompkins was, unfortunately, collateral damage.

5. How many civil procedure cases have their own official historical marker?

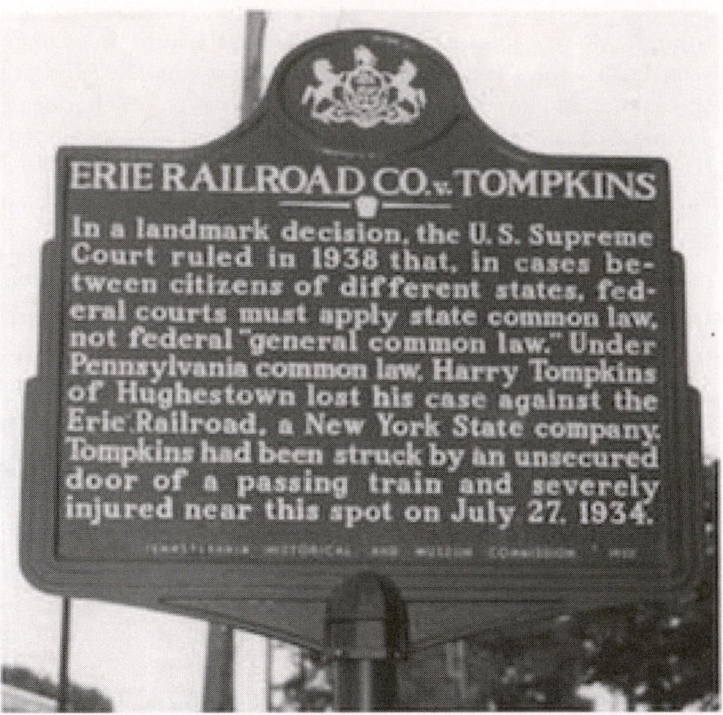

Used with permission of the Pennsylvania Historical and Museum Commission.

The challenge after *Erie Railroad Co. v. Tompkins* was distinguishing procedure from substance, as Justice Reed had perceptively foreseen. As you read the following case, compare your own intuitive characterizations with the Court's definitions. Is a statute of limitations procedural *or* substantive?

Guaranty Trust Co. v. York
326 U.S. 99 (1945)

Justice FRANKFURTER delivered the opinion of the Court:

[Guaranty Trust Co., acting as trustee, agreed to a buy-out plan in which note-holders received only 50 percent of the face value of their notes. The disgruntled among them brought a class action in federal court alleging state law claims of breach of trust, and invoking diversity jurisdiction. Guaranty Trust moved for summary judgment, which was granted on the grounds the action was time-barred by the New York statute of limitations. The Second Circuit Court of Appeals reversed, holding that the federal district court was not required to apply the state statute of limitations, but could exercise its own judgment as to timeliness.]

The importance of the question for the disposition of litigation in the federal courts led us to bring the case here. . . . Our only concern is with the holding that the federal courts in a suit like this are not bound by local law.

We put to one side the considerations relevant in disposing of questions that arise when a federal court is adjudicating a claim based on a federal law. Our problem only touches transactions for which rights and obligations are created by one of the States, and for the assertion of which, in case of diversity of the citizenship of the parties, Congress has made a federal court another available forum.

Our starting point must be the policy of federal jurisdiction which *Erie R. Co. v. Tompkins* embodies. In overruling *Swift v. Tyson*, *Erie R. Co. v. Tompkins* did not merely overrule a venerable case. It overruled a particular way of looking at law which dominated the judicial process long after its inadequacies had been laid bare. Law was conceived as a "brooding omnipresence" of Reason, of which decisions were merely evidence and not themselves the controlling formulations. Accordingly, federal courts deemed themselves free to ascertain what Reason, and therefore Law, required wholly independent of authoritatively declared State law, even in cases where a legal right as the basis for relief was created by State authority and could not be created by federal authority and the case got into a federal court merely because it was "between Citizens of different States" under Art. III, §2 of the Constitution of the United States.

This impulse to freedom from the rules that controlled State courts regarding State-created rights was so strongly rooted in the prevailing views concerning the nature of law, that the federal courts almost imperceptibly were led to mutilating construction even of the explicit command given to them by Congress to apply State law in cases purporting to enforce the law of a State. *See* § 34 of the Judiciary Act of 1789.

Since it was conceived that there was "a transcendental body of law outside of any particular State but obligatory within it unless and until changed by statute," State court decisions were not "the law" but merely someone's opinion—to be sure an opinion to be respected—concerning the content of this all-pervading law. Not unnaturally, the federal courts assumed power to find for themselves the content of such a body of law.

And so this case reduces itself to the narrow question whether, when no recovery could be had in a State court because the action is barred by the statute of limitations, a federal court in equity can take cognizance of the suit because there is diversity of citizenship between the parties.

Here we are dealing with a right to recover derived not from the United States but from one of the States. When, because the plaintiff happens to be a non-resident, such a right is enforceable in a federal as well as in a State court, the forms and mode of enforcing the right may at times, naturally enough, vary because the two judicial systems are not identic. But since a federal court adjudicating a State-created right solely because of the diversity of citizenship of the parties is for that purpose, in effect, only another court of the State, it cannot afford recovery if the right to recover is made unavailable by the State nor can it substantially affect the enforcement of the right as given by the State.

And so the question is not whether a statute of limitations is deemed a matter of "procedure" in some sense. The question is whether such a statute concerns merely the manner and the means by which a right to recover, as recognized by the State, is enforced, or whether such statutory limitation is a matter of substance in the aspect that alone is relevant to our problem, namely, does it significantly affect the result of a litigation for a federal court to disregard a law of a State that would be controlling in an action upon the same claim by the same parties in a State court?

Erie R. Co. v. Tompkins expressed a policy that touches vitally the proper distribution of judicial power between State and federal courts. In essence, the intent of that decision was to insure that, in all cases where a federal court is exercising jurisdiction solely because of the diversity of citizenship of the parties, the outcome of the litigation in the federal court should be substantially the same, so far as legal rules determine the outcome of a litigation, as it would be if tried in a State court. The nub of the policy that underlies *Erie R. Co. v. Tompkins* is that for the same transaction the accident of a suit by a non-resident litigant in a federal court instead of in a State court a block away should not lead to a substantially different result. And so, putting to one side abstractions regarding "substance" and "procedure," we have held that in diversity cases the federal courts must follow the law of the State as to burden of proof, *Cities Service Co. v. Dunlap*, 308 U.S. 208, as to conflict of laws, *Klaxon Co. v. Stentor Co.*, 313 U.S. 487, as to contributory negligence, *Palmer v. Hoffman*, 318 U.S. 109, 117. *Erie R. Co. v. Tompkins* has been applied with an eye alert to essentials in avoiding disregard of State law in diversity cases in the federal courts. A policy so important to our federalism must be kept free from entanglements with analytical or terminological niceties.

Plainly enough, a statute that would completely bar recovery in a suit if brought in a State court bears on a State-created right vitally and not merely formally or negligibly. As to consequences that so intimately affect recovery or non-recovery a federal court in a diversity case should follow State law. If a plea of the statute of limitations would bar recovery in a State court, a federal court ought not to afford recovery.

Diversity jurisdiction is founded on assurance to nonresident litigants of courts free from susceptibility to potential local bias. The Framers of the Constitution, according to Marshall, entertained "apprehensions" lest distant suitors be subjected to local bias in State courts, or, at least, viewed with "indulgence the possible fears and apprehensions" of such suitors. And so Congress afforded out-of-State litigants another tribunal, not another body of law. The operation of a double system of conflicting laws in the same State is plainly hostile to the reign of law. Certainly, the fortuitous circumstance of residence out of a State of one of the parties to a litigation ought not to give rise to a discrimination against others equally concerned but locally resident. The source of substantive rights enforced by a federal court under diversity jurisdiction, it cannot be said too often, is the law of the States. Whenever that law is authoritatively declared by a State, whether its voice be the legislature or its highest court, such law ought to govern in litigation founded on that law, whether the forum of application is a State or a federal court and whether the remedies be sought at law or may be had in equity.

The judgment is reversed and the case is remanded for proceedings not inconsistent with this opinion.

[The dissenting opinion of Justice RUTLEDGE is omitted.]

YOUR TAKEAWAY

Seven years after *Erie,* the Supreme Court tackled the classification of substance vs. procedure, which determines the choice between state or federal law. In Justice Frankfurter's reformulation, the distinction becomes a function of whether the difference between the two would significantly alter the outcome of the litigation. If so, the matter is deemed substantive and the federal court sitting in diversity must apply the state law. *Guaranty Trust* is an easy case under this analysis, as the New York State courts would have closed their doors to York's claim as the statute of limitations had run; Frankfurter concludes the federal court must dismiss accordingly.

REVIEW QUESTIONS

1. How did operation of a statute of limitations, which appears intuitively to be a matter of procedure, become "substantive"? How did "substantive" become defined as "outcome determinative"? What is Justice Frankfurter's reasoning behind these seemingly counterintuitive propositions? What lessons from *Erie* is he applying?

2. *Guaranty Trust* reads the intent of *Erie* "to insure that, in all cases where a federal court is exercising jurisdiction solely because of the diversity of citizenship of the parties, the outcome of the litigation in the federal court should be substantially the same, so far as legal rules determine the outcome of a litigation, as it would be if tried in a State court." Would Brandeis agree? What about Justice Reed's unrebutted assertion in *Erie* that "no one doubts federal power *over procedure*"?

3. What were the implications of the outcome test for the then newly adopted Federal Rules of Civil Procedure? After *Guaranty Trust*, the two pivotal civil procedure events of 1938—the *Erie* decision and the adoption of the Federal Rules—appeared to be on a collision course.

* * *

The Court was clearly troubled (as it was in *Erie*) by the operation of a "double system of conflicting laws in the same State." York must not be allowed to avoid the limitations rule merely because of the fortuity of diversity any more than Harry Tompkins should be able to shop for an easier standard of liability. The outcome test certainly solved that problem, by requiring conformity to state law whenever application of conflicting federal law would significantly alter the result of the litigation.

Do you see why Professor Charles E. Clark, principal draftsperson of the Federal Rules, remarked that *Guaranty Trust* reduced federal judges to "ventriloquists' dummies" mouthing state law? Quoted in Daniel J. Meador, *Transformation of the American Judiciary*, 46 Ala. L. Rev. 763, 765 (1995). Judge Jerome Frank used the same phrase in *Richardson v. C.I.R.*, 126 F.2d 562, 567 (2d Cir. 1942).

But was the cure (outcome conformity) more harmful to the operation of the judicial system than the disease (potentially different outcomes between federal and state courts)? One federal "practice and procedure" after another fell in the wake of the outcome-test juggernaut. *See, e.g., Ragan v. Merchants Transfer & Warehouse Co.*, 337 U.S. 530 (1949) (federal practice of deeming a case commenced for statute of limitations purposes upon filing of the complaint was displaced by state statute providing for tolling only upon service of process on defendant); *Cohen v. Beneficial Industrial Loan Corp.*, 337 U.S. 541 (1949) (state law requiring plaintiffs in shareholder derivative actions to post security to indemnify defendant for costs and attorneys' fees in event defendant prevails required dismissal of federal diversity action, even though the federal rule required no such security); *Bernhardt v. Polygraphic Co. of America*, 350 U.S. 198 (1956) (federal court could not enforce arbitration agreement contained in employment contract sued upon in diversity action in the face of state law rendering arbitration agreements revocable). *See also Palmer v. Hoffman*, 318 U.S. 109 (1943) (predating *Guaranty Trust*) (the question of who has the burden of proof on contributory negligence is a matter of state law, which in this case placed the burden on the plaintiff; thus federal courts in diversity cases must conform, notwithstanding that Fed. R. Civ. P. 8(c) makes it an affirmative defense).

Indeed, it is not hard to imagine virtually *any* conflict in rules having an outcome-determinative effect in the right circumstances. If a federal district court is hearing a diversity case arising from an accident in State *A*, and State *A*'s rules require that an answer be filed within ten days of service (rather than the twenty-one days allowed by Fed. R. Civ. P. 12(a)(1)), must the federal court default the defendant on Day 11 if an answer has not been filed? If State *A* requires that pleadings be on 8½″ × 14″ paper, and plaintiff files in federal court on 8½″ × 11″ paper at 5 p.m. on the very last day before the statute of limitations runs, must the federal court dismiss, as the state court would? If the courts in State *A* close at 4 p.m., and the plaintiff files her complaint at 4:45 p.m. in the federal court clerk's office, which is open until 5 P.M., must the clerk reject it?

Does it make sense to characterize paper size, days to file the answer, or courthouse hours as "substantive"? Are these matters of the same importance as the standard of care owed by the railroad in *Erie*? Do these matters really impact the constitutional allocation of powers between the two court systems?

It was left to the ingenuity of two renowned Justices to rescue federal procedure from the *Guaranty Trust* juggernaut in the two cases that follow.

Byrd v. Blue Ridge Rural Electric Cooperative, Inc.
356 U.S. 525 (1958)

Justice BRENNAN delivered the opinion of the Court:

This case was brought in the District Court for the Western District of South Carolina. Jurisdiction was based on diversity of citizenship. 28 U.S.C. § 1332.

The petitioner, a resident of North Carolina, sued respondent, a South Carolina corporation, for damages for injuries allegedly caused by the respondent's negligence. He had judgment on a jury verdict. The Court of Appeals for the Fourth Circuit reversed and directed the entry of judgment for the respondent. We granted certiorari.

The respondent is in the business of selling electric power to subscribers in rural sections of South Carolina. The petitioner was employed as a lineman in the construction crew of a construction contractor. The petitioner was injured while connecting power lines to one of the new substations.

One of respondent's affirmative defenses was that, under the South Carolina Workmen's Compensation Act,* the petitioner had the status of a statutory employee of the respondent and was therefore barred from suing the respondent at law because obliged to accept statutory compensation benefits as the exclusive remedy for his injuries. [The question before us is] whether petitioner, state practice notwithstanding, is entitled to a jury determination of the factual issues [whether Byrd was an "employee" within the meaning of the workers' compensation statute] raised by this defense.

A question is also presented as to whether on remand the factual issue is to be decided by the judge or by the jury. The respondent argues on the basis of the decision of the Supreme Court of South Carolina in *Adams v. Davison-Paxon Co.*, 230 S.C. 532, that the issue of immunity should be decided by the judge and not by the jury. That was a negligence action brought in the state trial court against a store owner by an employee of an independent contractor who operated the store's millinery department. The trial judge denied the store owner's motion for a directed verdict made upon the ground that [the workers compensation statute] barred the plaintiff's action. The jury returned a verdict for the plaintiff. The South Carolina Supreme Court reversed, holding that it was for the judge and not the jury to decide on the evidence whether the owner was a statutory employer, and that the store owner had sustained his defense.

The respondent argues that this state-court decision governs the present diversity case and "divests the jury of its normal function" to decide the disputed fact question of the respondent's immunity under [the statute]. This is to contend that the federal court is bound under *Erie R. Co. v. Tompkins* to follow the state court's holding to secure uniform enforcement of the immunity created by the State.

First. It was decided in *Erie R. Co. v. Tompkins* that the federal courts in diversity cases must respect the definition of state-created rights and obligations by the state courts. We must, therefore, first examine the rule in *Adams v. Davison-Paxon Co.* to determine whether it is bound up with these rights and

---

* *Eds.' Note:* Workers' compensation schemes, which date to the early twentieth century, operate as a kind of no-fault insurance: Employees collect benefits for workplace injuries without having to prove their employer was negligent, and in return the employer is exempt from tort suits, which carry the potential for far larger recoveries in compensatory and punitive damages.

obligations in such a way that its application in the federal court is required. The Workmen's Compensation Act is administered in South Carolina by its Industrial Commission. The South Carolina courts hold that, on judicial review of actions of the Commission, the question whether the claim of an injured workman is within the Commission's jurisdiction is a matter of law for decision by the court, which makes its own findings of fact relating to that jurisdiction. The South Carolina Supreme Court states no reasons in *Adams v. Davison-Paxon Co.* why, although the jury decides all other factual issues raised by the cause of action and defenses, the jury is displaced as to the factual issue raised by the affirmative defense under [the statute]. The decisions cited to support the holding are concerned solely with defining the scope and method of judicial review of the Industrial Commission. A State may, of course, distribute the functions of its judicial machinery as it sees fit. The decisions relied upon, however, furnish no reason for selecting the judge rather than the jury to decide this single affirmative defense in the negligence action. They simply reflect a policy that administrative determination of "jurisdictional facts" should not be final but subject to judicial review. The conclusion is inescapable that the *Adams* holding is grounded in the practical consideration that the question had theretofore come before the South Carolina courts from the Industrial Commission and the courts had become accustomed to deciding the factual issue of immunity without the aid of juries. We find nothing to suggest that this rule was announced as an integral part of the special relationship created by the statute. Thus the requirement appears to be merely a form and mode of enforcing the immunity, *Guaranty Trust Co. v. York*, and not a rule intended to be bound up with the definition of the rights and obligations of the parties.

Second. But cases following *Erie* have evinced a broader policy to the effect that the federal courts should conform as near as may be—in the absence of other considerations—to state rules even of form and mode where the state rules may bear substantially on the question whether the litigation would come out one way in the federal court and another way in the state court if the federal court failed to apply a particular local rule. *E.g., Guaranty Trust Co. v. York, supra.* Concededly the nature of the tribunal which tries issues may be important in the enforcement of the parcel of rights making up a cause of action or defense, and bear significantly upon achievement of uniform enforcement of the right. It may well be that in the instant personal-injury case the outcome would be substantially affected by whether the issue of immunity is decided by a judge or a jury. Therefore, were "outcome" the only consideration, a strong case might appear for saying that the federal court should follow the state practice.

But there are affirmative countervailing considerations at work here. The federal system is an independent system for administering justice to litigants who properly invoke its jurisdiction. An essential characteristic of that system is the manner in which, in civil common-law actions, it distributes trial functions between judge and jury and, under the influence—if not the command[10]—of the Seventh Amendment, assigns the decisions of disputed questions of fact to the jury. The policy of uniform enforcement of state-created rights and obligations cannot in every case exact compliance with a state rule—not bound up with rights and obligations—which disrupts the federal system of allocating functions between judge and jury. Thus the inquiry here is whether the federal policy favoring jury decisions of disputed fact questions should yield to the state rule in the interest of furthering the objective that the litigation should not come out one way in the federal court and another way in the state court.

We think that in the circumstances of this case the federal court should not follow the state rule. It cannot be gainsaid that there is a strong federal policy against allowing state rules to disrupt the judge-jury relationship in the federal courts. "[S]tate laws cannot alter the essential character or function of a federal court." In light of the influence of the Seventh Amendment the function assigned to the jury "is an essential factor in the process for which the Federal Constitution provides."

Third. We have discussed the problem upon the assumption that the outcome of the litigation may be substantially affected by whether the issue of immunity is decided by a judge or a jury. But clearly there is not present here the certainty that a different result would follow, *cf. Guaranty Trust Co. v. York, supra*, or even the strong possibility that this would be the case. There are factors present here which might reduce that possibility. The trial judge in the federal system has powers denied the judges of many States to comment on the weight of evidence and credibility of witnesses, and discretion to grant a new trial if the verdict appears to him to be against the weight of the evidence. We do not think the likelihood of a different result is so strong as to require the federal practice of jury determination of disputed factual issues to yield to the state rule in the interest of uniformity of outcome.

Reversed and remanded.

[The concurring and dissenting opinions of Justices WHITTAKER, FRANKFURTER, and HARLAN are omitted.]

YOUR TAKEAWAY

Swift v. Tyson allowed federal courts sitting in diversity to ignore the appropriate state's law and apply (or create) their own. *Erie* reset that balance, but especially together with *Guaranty Trust* pushed the pendulum too far in the other direction, as state law was now displacing much established federal practice. *Byrd* was the vehicle to readjust the federal-state relationship yet again. Justice Brennan recognized that some aspects of federal practice were so central to the character

---

10. Our conclusion makes unnecessary the consideration of—and we intimate no view upon—the constitutional question whether the right of jury trial protected in federal courts by the Seventh Amendment embraces the factual issue of statutory immunity when asserted, as here, as an affirmative defense in a common law negligence action.

of those courts—like maximizing the role of the jury under the influence of the Seventh Amendment—that such practice must prevail (notwithstanding potential outcome variances) as long as the displaced state practice (here assigning the judge the role to determine employee status) is not bound up with the substantive rights that the claim seeks to enforce.

REVIEW QUESTIONS

1. What are the strategic implications for the litigants here of having a jury instead of a judge decide whether Byrd was a statutory "employee" of the Cooperative? If you represented Byrd, which decisionmaker would you prefer? While the conventional wisdom is that individuals are usually better off in front of juries when suing corporate defendants, there is some contradictory data. *See generally* Chapter 5. *See also* Jeffrey J. Rachlinski, *Evidence Based Law*, 96 Cornell L. Rev. 901, 914-917 (2011).

2. Why doesn't the Seventh Amendment, protecting the right to civil jury trial in federal court, provide a simple answer to the judge versus jury issue in *Byrd*? Look at the Court's footnote 10 (in our version). What does the Court mean by "under the influence—if not the command—of the Seventh Amendment"?

3. Compare the extent to which the outcome of the litigation might be affected by the conflict in *Byrd* with the extent of outcome-determination in *Guaranty Trust* and in *Erie*. What are the implications of this comparison for the twin *Erie* concerns of discouraging forum shopping and avoiding inconsistent results? How does Justice Brennan utilize this comparison in his analysis?

4. How would you articulate the "test" adopted in *Byrd* to determine which practice will control in situations where the state rule vies with "affirmative [federal] countervailing considerations"? What are the elements of this analysis? The federal policy at stake here, maximizing jury participation in decision making, is said to reflect "*the essential character or function of a federal court.*" On the state practice side of the balance is a rule Brennan characterizes as one of mere administrative convenience, not "bound up" with state-created rights and obligations "in such a way that its application in the federal court is required." No surprise, given this view of the competing practices, that the federal practice is prevailing.

* * *

Byrd does not address the larger group of *Erie*-doctrine cases where the federal practice at stake does *not* embody the very character of federal litigation, like allocation of authority between judge and jury, but is far more mundane, such as the manner in which process is served on the defendant. What happens when such a practice, codified in the Fed. R. Civ. P., conflicts with state practice? The next case represented the second phase of the rescue of federal procedure.

Hanna v. Plumer
380 U.S. 460 (1965)

Chief Justice WARREN delivered the opinion of the Court:

The question to be decided is whether, in a civil action where the jurisdiction of the United States district court is based upon diversity of citizenship between the parties, service of process shall be made in the manner prescribed by state law or that set forth in Rule 4(d)(1)* of the Federal Rules of Civil Procedure.

On February 6, 1963, petitioner, a citizen of Ohio, filed her complaint in the District Court for the District of Massachusetts, claiming damages in excess of $10,000 for personal injuries resulting from an automobile accident in South Carolina, allegedly caused by the negligence of one Louise Plumer Osgood, a Massachusetts citizen deceased at the time of the filing of the complaint. Respondent, Mrs. Osgood's executor and also a Massachusetts citizen, was named as defendant. On February 8, service was made by leaving copies of the summons and the complaint with respondent's wife at his residence, concededly in compliance with Rule 4(d)(1), which provides:

> The summons and complaint shall be served together. The plaintiff shall furnish the person making service with such copies as are necessary. Service shall be made as follows:
>
> (1) Upon an individual other than an infant or an incompetent person, by delivering a copy of the summons and of the complaint to him personally or by leaving copies thereof at his dwelling house or usual place of abode with some person of suitable age and discretion then residing therein. . . .

Respondent filed his answer on February 26, alleging, inter alia, that the action could not be maintained because it had been brought "contrary to and in violation of the provisions of Massachusetts General Laws Chapter 197, Section 9." That section provides:

> [A]n executor or administrator shall not be held to answer to an action by a creditor of the deceased which is not commenced within one year from the time of his giving bond for the performance of his trust, or to such an action which is commenced within said year unless before the expiration thereof the writ in such action has been served by delivery in hand upon such executor or administrator. . . .

On October 17, 1963, the District Court granted respondent's motion for summary judgment, citing *Guaranty Trust Co. v. York*, 326 U.S. 99, in support of its conclusion that the adequacy of the service was to be measured by §9, with which, the court held, petitioner had not complied. On appeal, petitioner admitted non-compliance with §9, but argued that Rule 4(d)(1) defines the method by which service of process is to be effected in diversity actions. The Court of Appeals for the First Circuit, finding that "relatively recent amendments

---

* *Eds.' Note:* The Rule now appears as Fed. R. Civ. P. 4(e)(2)(B).

[to § 9] evince a clear legislative purpose to require personal notification within the year,"[1] concluded that the conflict of state and federal rules was over "a substantive rather than a procedural matter," and unanimously affirmed. Because of the threat to the goal of uniformity of federal procedure posed by the decision below, we granted certiorari.

We conclude that the adoption of Rule 4(d)(1), designed to control service of process in diversity actions, neither exceeded the congressional mandate embodied in the Rules Enabling Act nor transgressed constitutional bounds, and that the Rule is therefore the standard against which the District Court should have measured the adequacy of the service. Accordingly, we reverse the decision of the Court of Appeals.

The Rules Enabling Act, 28 U.S.C. § 2072, provides, in pertinent part:

> The Supreme Court shall have the power to prescribe, by general rules, the forms of process, writs, pleadings, and motions, and the practice and procedure of the district courts of the United States in civil actions. Such rules shall not abridge, enlarge or modify any substantive right and shall preserve the right of trial by jury.

Under the cases construing the scope of the Enabling Act, Rule 4(d)(1) clearly passes muster. Prescribing the manner in which a defendant is to be notified that a suit has been instituted against him, it relates to the "practice and procedure of the district courts." "The test must be whether a rule really regulates procedure,—the judicial process for enforcing rights and duties recognized by substantive law and for justly administering remedy and redress for disregard or infraction of them."

Thus were there no conflicting state procedure, Rule 4(d)(1) would clearly control. However, respondent, focusing on the contrary Massachusetts rule, calls to the Court's attention another line of cases, a line which—like the Federal Rules—had its birth in 1938. *Erie R. Co. v. Tompkins*, overruling *Swift v. Tyson*, held that federal courts sitting in diversity cases, when deciding questions of "substantive" law, are bound by state court decisions as well as state statutes. The broad command of *Erie* was therefore identical to that of the Enabling Act: federal courts are to apply state substantive law and federal procedural law. However, as subsequent cases sharpened the distinction between substance

---

1. Section 9 is in part a statute of limitations, providing that an executor need not "answer to an action . . . which is not commenced within one year from the time of his giving bond. . . ." This part of the statute, the purpose of which is to speed the settlement of estates, is not involved in this case, since the action clearly was timely commenced. (Respondent filed bond on March 1, 1962; the complaint was filed February 6, 1963; and the service—the propriety of which is in dispute—was made on February 8, 1963.) Section 9 also provides for the manner of service. Generally, service of process must be made by "delivery in hand," although there are two alternatives: acceptance of service by the executor, or filing of a notice of claim, the components of which are set out in the statute, in the appropriate probate court. The purpose of this part of the statute, which is involved here, is, as the court below noted, to insure that executors will receive actual notice of claims. Actual notice is of course also the goal of Rule 4(d)(1); however, the Federal Rule reflects a determination that this goal can be achieved by a method less cumbersome than that prescribed in §9. In this case the goal seems to have been achieved; although the affidavit filed by respondent in the District Court asserts that he had not been served in hand nor had he accepted service, it does not allege lack of actual notice.

and procedure, the line of cases following *Erie* diverged markedly from the line construing the Enabling Act. *Guaranty Trust Co. v. York* made it clear that *Erie*-type problems were not to be solved by reference to any traditional or common-sense substance-procedure distinction:

> And so the question is not whether a statute of limitations is deemed a matter of "procedure" in some sense. The question is . . . does it significantly affect the result of a litigation for a federal court to disregard a law of a State that would be controlling in an action upon the same claim by the same parties in a State court?

Respondent, by placing primary reliance on *York*, suggests that the *Erie* doctrine acts as a check on the Federal Rules of Civil Procedure, that despite the clear command of Rule 4(d)(1), *Erie* and its progeny demand the application of the Massachusetts rule. Reduced to essentials, the argument is: (1) *Erie*, as refined in *York*, demands that federal courts apply state law whenever application of federal law in its stead will alter the outcome of the case. (2) In this case, a determination that the Massachusetts service requirements obtain will result in immediate victory for respondent. If, on the other hand, it should be held that Rule 4(d)(1) is applicable, the litigation will continue, with possible victory for petitioner. (3) Therefore, *Erie* demands application of the Massachusetts rule. The syllogism possesses an appealing simplicity, but is for several reasons invalid.

In the first place, it is doubtful that, even if there were no Federal Rule making it clear that in-hand service is not required in diversity actions, the *Erie* rule would have obligated the District Court to follow the Massachusetts procedure. "Outcome-determination" analysis was never intended to serve as a talisman. *Byrd v. Blue Ridge Cooperative*. Indeed, the message of *York* itself is that choices between state and federal law are to be made not by application of any automatic, "litmus paper" criterion, but rather by reference to the policies underlying the *Erie* rule. The *Erie* rule is rooted in part in a realization that it would be unfair for the character or result of a litigation materially to differ because the suit had been brought in a federal court.

The decision was also in part a reaction to the practice of "forum-shopping" which had grown up in response to the rule of *Swift v. Tyson*. That the *York* test was an attempt to effectuate these policies is demonstrated by the fact that the opinion framed the inquiry in terms of "substantial" variations between state and federal litigation. Not only are nonsubstantial, or trivial, variations not likely to raise the sort of equal protection problems which troubled the Court in *Erie*; they are also unlikely to influence the choice of a forum. The "outcome-determination" test therefore cannot be read without reference to the twin aims of the *Erie* rule: discouragement of forum-shopping and avoidance of inequitable administration of the laws.

The difference between the conclusion that the Massachusetts rule is applicable, and the conclusion that it is not, is of course at this point "outcome-determinative" in the sense that if we hold the state rule to apply, respondent prevails, whereas if we hold that Rule 4(d)(1) governs, the litigation will continue. But in this sense every procedural variation is "outcome-determinative." For example, having brought suit in a federal court, a plaintiff cannot then insist on the right to file subsequent pleadings in accord with the time limits applicable in the state courts, even though enforcement of the federal timetable will, if he continues to insist that he must meet only the state time limit, result in determination of the controversy against him. So it is here. Though choice of the federal or state rule will at this point have a marked effect upon the outcome of the litigation, the difference between the two rules would be of scant, if any, relevance to the choice of a forum. Petitioner, in choosing her forum, was not presented with a situation where application of the state rule would wholly bar recovery; rather, adherence to the state rule would have resulted only in altering the way in which process was served.[11] Moreover, it is difficult to argue that permitting service of defendant's wife to take the place of in-hand service of defendant himself alters the mode of enforcement of state-created rights in a fashion sufficiently "substantial" to raise the sort of equal protection problems to which the *Erie* opinion alluded.

There is, however, a more fundamental flaw in respondent's syllogism: the incorrect assumption that the rule of *Erie R. Co. v. Tompkins* constitutes the appropriate test of the validity and therefore the applicability of a Federal Rule of Civil Procedure. The *Erie* rule has never been invoked to void a Federal Rule. It is true that there have been cases where this Court has held applicable a state rule in the face of an argument that the situation was governed by one of the Federal Rules. But the holding of each such case was not that *Erie* commanded displacement of a Federal Rule by an inconsistent state rule, but rather that the scope of the Federal Rule was not as broad as the losing party urged, and therefore, there being no Federal Rule which covered the point in dispute, *Erie* commanded the enforcement of state law. (Here, of course, the clash is unavoidable; Rule 4(d)(1) says—implicitly, but with unmistakable clarity—that in-hand service is not required in federal courts.) At the same time, in cases adjudicating the validity of Federal Rules, we have not applied the *York* rule or other refinements of *Erie*, but have to this day continued to decide questions concerning the scope of the Enabling Act and the constitutionality of specific Federal Rules.

When a situation is covered by one of the Federal Rules, the question facing the court is a far cry from the typical, relatively unguided *Erie* choice: the court has been instructed to apply the Federal Rule, and can refuse to do so only if the Advisory Committee, this Court, and Congress erred in their prima facie judgment that the Rule in question transgresses neither the terms of the Enabling Act nor constitutional restrictions.

---

11. We cannot seriously entertain the thought that one suing an estate would be led to choose the federal court because of a belief that adherence to Rule 4(d)(1) is less likely to give the executor actual notice than §9, and therefore, more likely to produce a default judgment. Rule 4(d)(1) is well designed to give actual notice, as it did in this case. *See* note 1, *supra*.

The opinion in *Erie*, which involved no Federal Rule and dealt with a question which was "substantive" in every traditional sense (whether the railroad owed a duty of care to Tompkins as a trespasser or a licensee), surely neither said nor implied that measures like Rule 4(d)(1) are unconstitutional. For the constitutional provision for a federal court system (augmented by the Necessary and Proper Clause) carries with it congressional power to make rules governing the practice and pleading in those courts, which in turn includes a power to regulate matters which, though falling within the uncertain area between substance and procedure, are rationally capable of classification as either. Neither *York* nor the cases following it ever suggested that the rule there laid down for coping with situations where no Federal Rule applies is coextensive with the limitation on Congress to which *Erie* had adverted.

Erie and its offspring cast no doubt on the long-recognized power of Congress to prescribe housekeeping rules for federal courts even though some of those rules will inevitably differ from comparable state rules. "When, because the plaintiff happens to be a non-resident, such a right is enforceable in a federal as well as in a State court, the forms and mode of enforcing the right may at times, naturally enough, vary because the two judicial systems are not identic." *Guaranty Trust Co. v. York, supra.* Thus, though a court, in measuring a Federal Rule against the standards contained in the Enabling Act and the Constitution, need not wholly blind itself to the degree to which the Rule makes the character and result of the federal litigation stray from the course it would follow in state courts, it cannot be forgotten that the *Erie* rule, and the guidelines suggested in *York*, were created to serve another purpose altogether. To hold that a Federal Rule of Civil Procedure must cease to function whenever it alters the mode of enforcing state-created rights would be to disembowel either the Constitution's grant of power over federal procedure or Congress' attempt to exercise that power in the Enabling Act. Rule 4(d)(1) is valid and controls the instant case.

Reversed.

Justice HARLAN, concurring:

Erie was something more than an opinion which worried about "forum-shopping and avoidance of inequitable administration of the laws," although to be sure these were important elements of the decision. I have always regarded that decision as one of the modern cornerstones of our federalism, expressing policies that profoundly touch the allocation of judicial power between the state and federal systems. *Erie* recognized that there should not be two conflicting systems of law controlling the primary activity of citizens, for such alternative governing authority must necessarily give rise to a debilitating uncertainty in the planning of everyday affairs. And it recognized that the scheme of our Constitution envisions an allocation of law-making functions between state and federal legislative processes which is undercut if the federal judiciary can make substantive law affecting state affairs beyond the bounds of congressional legislative powers in this regard. Thus, in diversity cases *Erie* commands that it be the state law governing primary private activity which prevails.

To my mind the proper line of approach in determining whether to apply a state or a federal rule, whether "substantive" or "procedural," is to stay close to basic principles by inquiring if the choice of rule would substantially affect those primary decisions respecting human conduct which our constitutional system leaves to state regulation. If so, *Erie* and the Constitution require that the state rule prevail, even in the face of a conflicting federal rule.

So long as a reasonable man could characterize any duly adopted federal rule as "procedural," the Court, unless I misapprehend what is said, would have it apply no matter how seriously it frustrated a State's substantive regulation of the primary conduct and affairs of its citizens. Since the members of the Advisory Committee, the Judicial Conference, and this Court who formulated the Federal Rules are presumably reasonable men, it follows that the integrity of the Federal Rules is absolute. Whereas the unadulterated outcome and forum-shopping tests may err too far toward honoring state rules, I submit that the Court's "arguably procedural, ergo constitutional" test moves too fast and far in the other direction.

It remains to apply what has been said to the present case. The Massachusetts rule provides that an executor need not answer suits unless in-hand service was made upon him or notice of the action was filed in the proper registry of probate within one year of his giving bond. The evident intent of this statute is to permit an executor to distribute the estate which he is administering without fear that further liabilities may be outstanding for which he could be held personally liable. If the Federal District Court in Massachusetts applies Rule 4(d)(1) of the Federal Rules of Civil Procedure instead of the Massachusetts service rule, what effect would that have on the speed and assurance with which estates are distributed? As I see it, the effect would not be substantial. It would mean simply that an executor would have to check at his own house or the federal courthouse as well as the registry of probate before he could distribute the estate with impunity. As this does not seem enough to give rise to any real impingement on the vitality of the state policy which the Massachusetts rule is intended to serve, I concur in the judgment of the Court.

YOUR TAKEAWAY

Nearly thirty years after their adoption, the Federal Rules of Civil Procedure finally found their protection from *Erie/Guaranty Trust* challenges. Chief Justice Earl Warren substituted a Rules Enabling Act analysis for the outcome determination hammer that was undoing the effort at uniform federal practice. Conflicts between the Federal Rules and state practice would be resolved by determining whether the particular Federal Rule truly regulates only "practice and procedure" and does not step on substantive toes ("[s]uch rules shall not abridge, enlarge or modify any substantive right"). In such cases, there is no unconstitutional interference with state prerogatives, nor a significant risk of forum shopping to the federal court.

REVIEW QUESTIONS

1. Note how Chief Justice Warren foreshadows the result early on in the *Hanna* decision when he observes: "Because of the threat to the goal of uniformity of federal procedure posed by the decision below, we granted certiorari."

2. Compare the extent to which the outcome of the litigation is affected by the rules conflict in *Hanna* with the extent of outcome-determination in (1) *Erie*; (2) *Guaranty Trust*; (3) *Byrd*. How does Warren use these comparisons to justify his decision in *Hanna*? What are the implications of this comparison for the "twin aims of *Erie*," i.e., discouraging forum shopping and avoiding inconsistent results?

3. What is the critical time juncture for assessing outcome determination—in *Hanna*, for example, is it on the day the case was filed, or at the point where defendant's motion for summary judgment was decided (and the one-year statute of limitations had passed)? Do you see the difference between using these competing points of reference? Why does the Chief Justice choose the former, the day the suit was filed? (Hint: When does forum shopping by a plaintiff occur? Look at the Court's footnote 11.) Note his observation that "petitioner, in choosing her forum, was not presented with a situation where application of the state rule would wholly bar recovery; rather, adherence to the state rule would have resulted only in altering the way in which process was served."

4. Mass. Gen. Laws ch. 197, § 9, required *both* that suit be filed against an executor within one year from his giving bond, *and* that suit be commenced by in-hand personal service. Regarding the one-year limitation, why was *Hanna* not controlled by the long-established rule of *Guaranty Trust* that a federal court sitting in diversity had to follow the statute of limitations of the state that created the claim? Look at the Court's footnote 1.

5. Can you see why the Court would grant more deference to a Federal Rule of Civil Procedure, which has the congressional imprimatur of the Rules Enabling Act and the elaborate rulemaking process behind it, *including its own approval* (look back at Chapter 4, Part E.4), than to a practice lacking that pedigree, such as the judge-made custom of extending the time for filing suits seeking equitable relief in *Guaranty Trust*? Do you see why a Court concerned about the uniformity of federal procedure, and the viability of the Fed. R. Civ. P., would have to reject defendant's outcome-determination syllogism?

6. *Erie* **Cases After** *Hanna*. *Hanna* has added an important initial step to the analysis of conflicts between state and federal practice in federal diversity cases, namely identification of *the source* of the federal side of the conflict. Different tracks (what Chief Justice Warren refers to as "the development of two separate lines of cases") are followed, depending on whether there is a Fed. R. Civ. P. on point or not. What is the test for determining whether to apply a Fed. R. Civ. P. when it *directly conflicts* with

state practice? Do you see why Justice Harlan characterizes this track as "the Court's 'arguably procedural, ergo constitutional' test"?

What is the test where the competing federal practice is *not* codified in the Fed. R. Civ. P., the so-called unguided *Erie* choice? Note that in this situation, the Rules of Decision Act (as construed in *Erie* and *Guaranty Trust*) is the controlling statute (usually pointing to the state's rule). In cases of direct and unavoidable conflicts with a Fed. R. Civ. P., it is the Rules Enabling Act (favoring application of the Fed. R. Civ. P.) that controls.

MORE TO PONDER

1. For reflections on *Hanna* by Earl Warren's law clerk at the time it was decided, *see* John Hart Ely, *The Irrepressible Myth of* Erie, 87 Harv. L. Rev. 693 (1974).

2. Given that the Supreme Court itself is the rulemaking authority that ultimately adopts and amends the Federal Rules of Civil Procedure under the Rules Enabling Act, does the Court have a conflict of interest when it later *judicially* considers the validity of a rule? Justices Black and Douglas thought so. Dissenting from the adoption of proposed amendments to the Federal Rules of Civil Procedure in 1963, they suggested that the responsibility for drafting should be shifted: "Transfer of the function to the Judicial Conference would relieve us of the embarrassment of having to sit in judgment on the constitutionality of rules which we have approved and which in given circumstances might have to be declared invalid." 374 U.S. 865, 869-870 (1963).

   Justice White joined this view in 1993, adding: "I did my share of litigating when in practice and once served on the Advisory Committee for the Civil Rules, but the trial practice is a dynamic profession, and the longer one is away from it the less likely it is that he or she should presume to second-guess the careful work of the active professionals manning the rulemaking committees, work that the Judicial Conference has approved." 146 F.R.D. 501, 504 (1993).

3. What alternative test would Justice Harlan impose for resolving the choice of law issue? Is his "primary decisions respecting human conduct" test workable, or too fuzzy?

4. Was Justice Harlan correct in arguing that the Court's analysis virtually immunizes the Federal Rules, and "it is hard to think of a case where a conflicting state rule would be allowed to operate, even though the state rule reflected policy considerations which, under *Erie*, would lie within the realm of state legislative authority"?

   Consider this prediction as you read our next case, and later on in the chapter after *Shady Grove Orthopedic Associates v. Allstate Ins. Co.*

Walker v. Armco Steel Corp.
446 U.S. 740 (1980)

Justice MARSHALL delivered the opinion of the Court:

This case presents the issue whether in a diversity action the federal court should follow state law or, alternatively, Rule 3 of the Federal Rules of Civil Procedure in determining when an action is commenced for the purpose of tolling the state statute of limitations.

I

According to the allegations of the complaint, petitioner, a carpenter, was injured on August 22, 1975, in Oklahoma City, Okla., while pounding a Sheffield nail into a cement wall. Respondent was the manufacturer of the nail. Petitioner claimed that the nail contained a defect which caused its head to shatter and strike him in the right eye, resulting in permanent injuries. The defect was allegedly caused by respondent's negligence in manufacture and design.

Petitioner is a resident of Oklahoma, and respondent is a foreign corporation having its principal place of business in a State other than Oklahoma. Since there was diversity of citizenship, petitioner brought suit in the United States District Court for the Western District of Oklahoma. The complaint was filed on August 19, 1977. Although summons was issued that same day, service of process was not made on respondent's authorized service agent until December 1, 1977.[2] On January 5, 1978, respondent filed a motion to dismiss the complaint on the ground that the action was barred by the applicable Oklahoma statute of limitations. Although the complaint had been filed within the 2-year statute of limitations, state law does not deem the action "commenced" for purposes of the statute of limitations until service of the summons on the defendant, Okla. Stat., Tit. 12, § 97 (1971). If the complaint is filed within the limitations period, however, the action is deemed to have commenced from that date of filing if the plaintiff serves the defendant within 60 days, even though that service may occur outside the limitations period. In this case, service was not effectuated until long after this 60-day period had expired. Petitioner in his reply brief to the motion to dismiss admitted that his case would be foreclosed in state court, but he argued that Rule 3 of the Federal Rules of Civil Procedure governs the manner in which an action is commenced in federal court for all purposes, including the tolling of the state statute of limitations.

The District Court dismissed the complaint as barred by the Oklahoma statute of limitations. The court concluded that Okla. Stat., Tit. 12, § 97 was "an

---

2. The record does not indicate why this delay occurred. The face of the process record shows that the United States Marshal acknowledged receipt of the summons on December 1, 1977, and that service was effectuated that same day. At oral argument counsel for petitioner stated that the summons was found "in an unmarked folder in the filing cabinet" in counsel's office some 90 days after the complaint had been filed. Counsel conceded that the summons was not delivered to the Marshal until December 1. It is unclear why the summons was placed in the filing cabinet.

integral part of the Oklahoma statute of limitations," and therefore under *Ragan v. Merchants Transfer & Warehouse Co.*, 337 U.S. 530 (1949), state law applied. The court rejected the argument that *Ragan* had been implicitly overruled in *Hanna v. Plumer*.

The United States Court of Appeals for the Tenth Circuit affirmed. That court concluded that Okla. Stat., Tit. 12, §97, was in "direct conflict" with Rule 3. However, the Oklahoma statute was "indistinguishable" from the statute involved in *Ragan*, and the court felt itself "constrained" to follow *Ragan*.

We granted certiorari, because of a conflict among the Courts of Appeals. We now affirm.

II

The question whether state or federal law should apply on various issues arising in an action based on state law which has been brought in federal court under diversity of citizenship jurisdiction has troubled this Court for many years. In the landmark decision of *Erie R. Co. v. Tompkins*, we overturned the rule expressed in *Swift v. Tyson* that federal courts exercising diversity jurisdiction need not, in matters of "general jurisprudence," apply the nonstatutory law of the State. The Court noted that "[diversity] of citizenship jurisdiction was conferred in order to prevent apprehended discrimination in state courts against those not citizens of the State." The doctrine of *Swift v. Tyson* had led to the undesirable results of discrimination in favor of noncitizens, prevention of uniformity in the administration of state law, and forum shopping. In response, we established the rule that "[except] in matters governed by the Federal Constitution or by Acts of Congress, the law to be applied in any [diversity] case is the law of the State."

In *Guaranty Trust Co. v. York*, we concluded that the state statute of limitations should be applied. "Plainly enough, a statute that would completely bar recovery in a suit if brought in a State court bears on a State-created right vitally and not merely formally or negligibly. As to consequences that so intimately affect recovery or non-recovery a federal court in a diversity case should follow State law."

The decision in *York* led logically to our holding in *Ragan v. Merchants Transfer & Warehouse Co., supra*. In *Ragan*, the applicable statute of limitations supplied by Kansas law was two years. Kansas had an additional statute which provided: "An action shall be deemed commenced within the meaning of [the statute of limitations], as to each defendant, at the date of the summons which is served on him. The defendant moved for summary judgment on the ground that the Kansas statute of limitations barred the action since service had not been made within either the 2-year period. It was conceded that had the case been brought in Kansas state court it would have been barred. Nonetheless, the District Court held that the statute had been tolled by the filing of the complaint. The Court of Appeals reversed because "the requirement of service of summons within the statutory period was an integral part of that state's statute of limitations."

We affirmed, relying on *Erie* and *York*. "We cannot give [the cause of action] longer life in the federal court than it would have had in the state court without adding something to the cause of action. We may not do that consistently with *Erie R. Co. v. Tompkins.*" We rejected the argument that Rule 3 of the Federal Rules of Civil Procedure governed the manner in which an action was commenced in federal court for purposes of tolling the state statute of limitations. Instead, we held that the service of summons statute controlled because it was an integral part of the state statute of limitations, and under *York* that statute of limitations was part of the state-law cause of action.

Ragan was not our last pronouncement in this difficult area, however. In 1965 we decided *Hanna v. Plumer*, holding that in a civil action where federal jurisdiction was based upon diversity of citizenship, Rule 4(d)(1) of the Federal Rules of Civil Procedure, rather than state law, governed the manner in which process was served. Massachusetts law required in-hand service on an executor or administrator of an estate, whereas Rule 4 permits service by leaving copies of the summons and complaint at the defendant's home with some person "of suitable age and discretion." The Court noted that in the absence of a conflicting state procedure, the Federal Rule would plainly control. We stated that the "outcome-determination" test of *Erie* and *York* had to be read with reference to the "twin aims" of *Erie*: "discouragement of forum-shopping and avoidance of inequitable administration of the laws." We determined that the choice between the state in-hand service rule and the Federal Rule "would be of scant, if any, relevance to the choice of a forum," for the plaintiff "was not presented with a situation where application of the state rule would wholly bar recovery; rather, adherence to the state rule would have resulted only in altering the way in which process was served." This factor served to distinguish that case from *York* and *Ragan*.

The Court in *Hanna*, however, pointed out "a more fundamental flaw" in the defendant's argument in that case. The Court concluded that the *Erie* doctrine was simply not the appropriate test of the validity and applicability of one of the Federal Rules of Civil Procedure:

> The *Erie* rule has never been invoked to void a Federal Rule. It is true that there have been cases where this Court had held applicable a state rule in the face of an argument that the situation was governed by one of the Federal Rules. But the holding of each such case was not that *Erie* commanded displacement of a Federal Rule by an inconsistent state rule, but rather that the scope of the Federal Rule was not as broad as the losing party urged, and therefore, there being no Federal Rule which covered the point in dispute, *Erie* commanded the enforcement of state law.

The Court cited *Ragan* as one of the examples of this proposition. The Court explained that where the Federal Rule was clearly applicable, as in *Hanna*, the test was whether the Rule was within the scope of the Rules Enabling Act, 28 U.S.C. § 2072, and if so, within a constitutional grant of power such as the Necessary and Proper Clause of Art. I.

III

The present case is indistinguishable from *Ragan*. The statutes in both cases require service of process to toll the statute of limitations, and in fact the predecessor to the Oklahoma statute in this case was derived from the predecessor to the Kansas statute in *Ragan*. Here, as in *Ragan*, the complaint was filed in federal court under diversity jurisdiction within the 2-year statute of limitations, but service of process did not occur until after the 2-year period and the 60-day service period had run. In both cases the suit would concededly have been barred in the applicable state court, and in both instances the state service statute was held to be an integral part of the statute of limitations by the lower court more familiar than we with state law. Accordingly, as the Court of Appeals held below, the instant action is barred by the statute of limitations unless *Ragan* is no longer good law.

Petitioner argues that the analysis and holding of *Ragan* did not survive our decision in *Hanna*. But *Hanna* analysis is premised on a "direct collision" between the Federal Rule and the state law. In *Hanna* itself the "clash" between Rule 4(d)(1) and the state in-hand service requirement was "unavoidable." The first question must therefore be whether the scope of the Federal Rule in fact is sufficiently broad to control the issue before the Court. It is only if that question is answered affirmatively that the *Hanna* analysis applies.[9]

The present case is an instance where "the scope of the Federal Rule [is] not as broad as the losing party [urges], and therefore, there being no Federal Rule which [covers] the point in dispute, *Erie* [commands] the enforcement of state law." Rule 3 simply states that "[a] civil action is commenced by filing a complaint with the court." There is no indication that the Rule was intended to toll a state statute of limitations, much less that it purported to displace state tolling rules for purposes of state statutes of limitations. In our view, in diversity actions Rule 3 governs the date from which various timing requirements of the Federal Rules begin to run, but does not affect state statutes of limitations.

In contrast to Rule 3, the Oklahoma statute is a statement of a substantive decision by that State that actual service on, and accordingly actual notice by, the defendant is an integral part of the several policies served by the statute of limitations. The statute of limitations establishes a deadline after which the defendant may legitimately have peace of mind; it also recognizes that after a certain period of time it is unfair to require the defendant to attempt to piece together his defense to an old claim. A requirement of actual service promotes both of those functions of the statute. It is these policy aspects which make the service requirement an "integral" part of the statute of limitations both in this case and in *Ragan*. As such, the service rule must be considered part and parcel of the statute of limitations. Rule 3 does not replace such policy determinations

---

9. This is not to suggest that the Federal Rules of Civil Procedure are to be narrowly construed in order to avoid a "direct collision" with state law. The Federal Rules should be given their plain meaning. If a direct collision with state law arises from that plain meaning, then the analysis developed in *Hanna v. Plumer* applies.

found in state law. Rule 3 and Okla. Stat., Tit. 12, §97, can exist side by side, therefore, each controlling its own intended sphere of coverage without conflict.

Since there is no direct conflict between the Federal Rule and the state law, the *Hanna* analysis does not apply. Instead, the policies behind *Erie* and *Ragan* control the issue whether, in the absence of a federal rule directly on point, state service requirements which are an integral part of the state statute of limitations should control in an action based on state law which is filed in federal court under diversity jurisdiction.

Although in this case failure to apply the state service law might not create any problem of forum shopping,[15] the result would be an "inequitable administration" of the law. There is simply no reason why, in the absence of a controlling federal rule, an action based on state law which concededly would be barred in the state courts by the state statute of limitations should proceed through litigation to judgment in federal court solely because of the fortuity that there is diversity of citizenship between the litigants. The policies underlying diversity jurisdiction do not support such a distinction between state and federal plaintiffs, and *Erie* and its progeny do not permit it.

The judgment of the Court of Appeals is Affirmed.

YOUR TAKEAWAY

Walker involves what Professor Burbank refers to as the "twilight zone" between substance and procedure that is not controlled by the Federal Rules. Stephen Burbank, Semtek, *Forum Shopping, and Federal Common Law*, 77 Notre Dame L. Rev. 1027, 1028 (2002). The key to resolving such cases is determining whether the Fed. R. Civ. P. and the state rule that are in *apparent* conflict are truly coextensive (i.e., cover the very same ground), and thus are in *direct unavoidable collision*.

If they are in direct conflict (as where the Massachusetts rule *required* in-hand service on the executor, but Fed. R. Civ. P. 4(d)(1) did *not*), *Hanna*'s Rules Enabling Act analysis controls, favoring application of the Fed. R. Civ. P. as long as it is arguably procedural. If there is *no* direct conflict with a Fed. R. Civ. P., and thus the federal practice at stake does not carry the imprimatur of the formal rulemaking process (where, for example, it is judge-made common law), *Walker* reverts to enforcing *Erie*'s twin aims of discouraging forum shopping and avoiding inconsistent results through *Guaranty Trust Co. v. York*'s outcome test, usually favoring state practice.

---

15. There is no indication that when petitioner filed his suit in federal court he had any reason to believe that he would be unable to comply with the service requirements of Oklahoma law or that he chose to sue in federal court in an attempt to avoid those service requirements.

REVIEW QUESTIONS

1. As in *Hanna*, Justice Marshall detected no indication that plaintiff had shopped for the federal forum in order to avoid the Oklahoma service requirements. *See* footnote 15. Why then the different result in the two cases—the federal rule trumps in *Hanna*, but not in *Walker*? The answer lies in the different tests applied to *direct and unavoidable* Fed. R. Civ. P. conflicts with state practice, and those in which the federal rule is not broad enough to cover the matter, as is the case with Fed. R. Civ. P. 3.

2. Does *Walker* reflect an inclination to read the Fed. R. Civ. P. narrowly so as to avoid direct conflicts whenever possible, notwithstanding the Court's explicit disavowal in footnote 9? Fed. R. Civ. P. 3's "commenced" language is read to simply refer to the starting point for the time periods set out elsewhere in the Rules, and *not* the tolling of the statute of limitations. This leaves only a conflict between the Oklahoma statute and the *federal custom* of tolling upon filing of the case.

   Critical of this approach, Professor Catherine Struve has argued that "[m]inimizing conflict with the Enabling Act is a worthy goal, but it can invite departure from a Rule's text and Notes." *See* Catherine T. Struve, *The Paradox of Delegation: Interpreting the Federal Rules of Civil Procedure*, 150 U. Pa. L. Rev. 1099, 1150 (2002). Another commentator argues that, in the interest of federalism and to respect important state policies, federal courts facing a potential conflict between a Fed. R. Civ. P. and state law should read the Rule to avoid the conflict if there is any such plausible reading. Joshua Zoffer, *An Avoidance Canon for* Erie: *Using Federalism to Resolve* Shady Grove's *Conflicts Analysis Problem*, 128 Yale L.J. 482, 488-89 (2018).

3. What does *Walker* do to the goal of uniformity of federal procedure articulated by Chief Justice Warren in *Hanna*? Does *Walker* undermine the rescue operation?

4. In *Harvey's Wagon Wheel, Inc. v. Van Blitter*, 959 F.2d 153 (9th Cir. 1992), a diversity action by a casino to collect on a gambling debt, defendant moved to dismiss because the plaintiff failed to bring the case to trial within five years, as required by Nev. R. Civ. P. 41(e). The casino countered that *Fed.* R. Civ. P. 41(b) should control in the federal court, and that rule *permits* dismissal for failure to prosecute but, unlike the Nevada rule, does not set a fixed time period. Defendant, seeking to come within *Walker* and thus application of the state rule, contended that there was "no direct collision here because the rules differ somewhat in scope. The federal rule does not require dismissal at any point; the Nevada rule requires dismissal after five years." The Ninth Circuit disagreed:

   > While not perfectly coextensive, the federal and Nevada involuntary dismissal rules conflict sufficiently to meet the *Hanna* standard. The federal rule is "sufficiently broad to cover the point in dispute" because it permits dismissal at (and before) the time that the Nevada rule requires dismissal. Additionally, both rules aim to promote judicial housekeeping

and diligent prosecution. Both rules also incorporate discretion, albeit in different degrees. Accordingly, we hold that the Federal Rule 41(b) and Nevada Rule 41(e) are coextensive.

959 F.2d at 156.

Observing that application of the federal rule would not raise forum shopping concerns ("No rational plaintiff would file in federal court based on the expectation that after five years without a trial, dismissal would be discretionary rather than mandatory"), the court applied Fed. R. Civ. P. 41(b) and affirmed the denial of defendant's motion to dismiss. *See also Burlington Northern Railroad v. Woods*, 480 U.S. 1 (1987) (Fed. R. App. P. 38, granting courts of appeals discretion to award costs in the case of frivolous appeals, displaces the Alabama penalty statute mandating damages for an unsuccessful appeal).

5. In *Stewart Organization, Inc. v. Ricoh Corp.*, 487 U.S. 22 (1988), the Court extended *Hanna*'s federal-friendly approach to federal statutory provisions as well as Rules. Defendant filed a motion under 28 U.S.C. § 1404(a) to transfer the diversity action from the Alabama federal district court to the Southern District of New York, invoking a forum selection clause in the dealership contract sued upon which required any litigation to be filed in New York City. The district court denied the motion because Alabama state law refused to enforce forum selection clauses. The Eleventh Circuit Court of Appeals reversed, holding that venue is a procedural matter properly controlled by § 1404(a), under which the forum selection clause was enforceable. (See Chapter 7, Part M.)

The Supreme Court agreed, holding that § 1404(a) properly addressed a matter of "practice and procedure" and was within the constitutional parameters of Congress to prescribe housekeeping rules for the federal courts. As it directly clashed with state law (by permitting the district court to weigh *all* factors of convenience and fairness, implicitly including the existence of a forum selection clause), § 1404(a) displaced the state rule and controlled the matter.

Justice Scalia dissented, viewing the conflict as similar to *Walker*, where the federal rule was *not* broad enough to cover the issue in dispute. Absent a direct conflict between federal and state practice, Scalia would apply the *Guaranty Trust Co. v. York* outcome test. He concluded that § 1404 should not displace the Alabama rule against enforcement of forum selection clauses because that would lead to forum shopping to federal court by litigants seeking to enforce such clauses, as well as inequitable administration of the laws—different outcomes in state and federal court. Scalia's observation that "[t]he decision of an important legal issue should not turn on the accident of diversity of citizenship" brings us back full circle to *Erie v. Tompkins*.

6. Synthesize the line of cases from *Erie* through *Walker*. Articulate the various "tests" for federal/state choice of law where:

   a. State practice conflicts *directly and unavoidably* with a Fed. R. Civ. P. or federal statute.

b. State practice conflicts with a judge-made federal practice *not* codified in a Fed. R. Civ. P. or federal statute (the "unguided *Erie* choice").

c. State practice conflicts with a federal practice that is not found in a Fed. R. Civ. P. or federal statute, but reflects (as in *Byrd*) an *"essential characteristic"* of federal litigation.

Note again the critical importance of *the source of the federal practice* in resolving federal-state conflicts. You should also be aware that where the U.S. Constitution supplies the federal law in contention, there is no *Erie* choice of law issue because any contrary state practice is displaced by operation of the Supremacy Clause. Thus, for example, if the Seventh Amendment had clearly mandated a jury trial on the issue of whether Byrd was an "employee" (look back again at footnote 10 in *Byrd*), that would have ended the conversation. *See generally* Kevin M. Clermont, *Reverse*-Erie, 82 Notre Dame L. Rev. 1, 9-10 (2006).

* * *

How does former Civil Procedure professor Ruth Bader Ginsburg employ all three routes of *Erie* analysis in the following case?

Gasperini v. Center for Humanities, Inc.
518 U.S. 415 (1996)

Justice GINSBURG delivered the opinion of the Court:

Under the law of New York, appellate courts are empowered to review the size of jury verdicts and to order new trials when the jury's award "deviates materially from what would be reasonable compensation." N.Y. Civ. Prac. Law and Rules (CPLR) § 5501(c). Under the Seventh Amendment, which governs proceedings in federal court, but not in state court, "the right of trial by jury shall be preserved, and no fact tried by a jury, shall be otherwise reexamined in any Court of the United States, than according to the rules of the common law." U.S. Const., Amdt. 7. The compatibility of these provisions, in an action based on New York law but tried in federal court by reason of the parties' diverse citizenship, is the issue we confront in this case. We hold that New York's law controlling compensation awards for excessiveness or inadequacy can be given effect, without detriment to the Seventh Amendment, if the review standard set out in CPLR § 5501(c) is applied by the federal trial court judge, with appellate control of the trial court's ruling limited to review for "abuse of discretion."

I

Petitioner William Gasperini, a journalist for CBS News and the Christian Science Monitor, began reporting on events in Central America in 1984. He earned his living primarily in radio and print media and only occasionally sold his photographic work. During the course of his seven-year stint in Central America,

Gasperini took over 5,000 slide transparencies, depicting active war zones, political leaders, and scenes from daily life. In 1990, Gasperini agreed to supply his original color transparencies to The Center for Humanities, Inc. (Center) for use in an educational videotape, Conflict in Central America. Gasperini selected 300 of his slides for the Center; its videotape included 110 of them. The Center agreed to return the original transparencies, but upon the completion of the project, it could not find them.

Gasperini commenced suit in the United States District Court for the Southern District of New York, invoking the court's diversity jurisdiction pursuant to 28 U.S.C. § 1332.[1] He alleged several state-law claims for relief, including breach of contract, conversion, and negligence. The Center conceded liability for the lost transparencies and the issue of damages was tried before a jury.

At trial, Gasperini's expert witness testified that the "industry standard" within the photographic publishing community valued a lost transparency at $1,500. This industry standard, the expert explained, represented the average license fee a commercial photograph could earn over the full course of the photographer's copyright, *i.e.*, in Gasperini's case, his lifetime plus 50 years. Gasperini estimated that his earnings from photography totaled just over $10,000 for the period from 1984 through 1993. He also testified that he intended to produce a book containing his best photographs from Central America.

After a three-day trial, the jury awarded Gasperini $450,000 in compensatory damages. This sum, the jury foreperson announced, "is [$]1500 each, for 300 slides." Moving for a new trial under Fed. R. Civ. P. 59, the Center attacked the verdict on various grounds, including excessiveness. Without comment, the District Court denied the motion.

The Court of Appeals for the Second Circuit vacated the judgment entered on the jury's verdict. Mindful that New York law governed the controversy, the Court of Appeals endeavored to apply CPLR § 5501(c), which instructs that, when a jury returns an itemized verdict, as the jury did in this case, the New York Appellate Division "shall determine that an award is excessive or inadequate if it deviates materially from what would be reasonable compensation." Surveying Appellate Division decisions that reviewed damage awards for lost transparencies, the Second Circuit concluded that testimony on industry standard alone was insufficient to justify a verdict; prime among other factors warranting consideration were the uniqueness of the slides' subject matter and the photographer's earning level.

Guided by Appellate Division rulings, the Second Circuit held that the $450,000 verdict "materially deviates from what is reasonable compensation." Some of Gasperini's transparencies, the Second Circuit recognized, were unique, notably those capturing combat situations in which Gasperini was the only photographer present. But others "depicted either generic scenes or events at which other professional photojournalists were present." No more than 50 slides merited a $1,500 award, the court concluded, after "giving Gasperini every benefit

---

1. Plaintiff Gasperini, petitioner here, is a citizen of California; defendant Center, respondent here, is incorporated, and has its principal place of business, in New York.

of the doubt." Absent evidence showing significant earnings from photographic endeavors or concrete plans to publish a book, the court further determined, any damage award above $100 each for the remaining slides would be excessive. Nevertheless, the Second Circuit set aside the $450,000 verdict and ordered a new trial, unless Gasperini agreed to an award of $100,000.

This case presents an important question regarding the standard a federal court uses to measure the alleged excessiveness of a jury's verdict in an action for damages based on state law. We therefore granted certiorari.

II

Before 1986, state and federal courts in New York generally invoked the same judge-made formulation in responding to excessiveness attacks on jury verdicts: courts would not disturb an award unless the amount was so exorbitant that it "shocked the conscience of the court." In both state and federal courts, trial judges made the excessiveness assessment in the first instance, and appellate judges ordinarily deferred to the trial court's judgment.

In 1986, as part of a series of tort reform measures,[3] New York codified a standard for judicial review of the size of jury awards. Placed in CPLR § 5501(c), the prescription reads:

> In reviewing a money judgment . . . in which it is contended that the award is excessive or inadequate and that a new trial should have been granted . . . the appellate division shall determine that an award is excessive or inadequate if it deviates materially from what would be reasonable compensation.

As stated in Legislative Findings and Declarations accompanying New York's adoption of the "deviates materially" formulation, the lawmakers found the "shock the conscience" test an insufficient check on damage awards; the legislature therefore installed a standard "invit[ing] more careful appellate scrutiny." In his signing statement, then-Governor Mario Cuomo emphasized that the CPLR amendments were meant to rachet up the review standard: "This will assure greater scrutiny of the amount of verdicts and promote greater stability in the tort system and greater fairness for similarly situated defendants throughout the State."

. . .

To determine whether an award "deviates materially from what would be reasonable compensation," New York state courts look to awards approved in similar cases.

III

In cases like Gasperini's, in which New York law governs the claims for relief, does New York law also supply the test for federal-court review of the size of the

---

3. The legislature sought, particularly, to curtail medical and dental malpractice, and to contain "already high malpractice premiums." Legislative Findings and Declaration, Ch. 266, 1986 N.Y. Laws 470 (McKinney).

verdict? The Center answers yes. The "deviates materially" standard, it argues, is a substantive standard that must be applied by federal appellate courts in diversity cases. The Second Circuit agreed. Gasperini, emphasizing that § 5501(c) trains on the New York Appellate Division, characterizes the provision as procedural, an allocation of decisionmaking authority regarding damages, not a hard cap on the amount recoverable. Correctly comprehended, Gasperini urges, § 5501(c)'s direction to the Appellate Division cannot be given effect by federal appellate courts without violating the Seventh Amendment's Reexamination Clause.

As the parties' arguments suggest, CPLR § 5501(c), appraised under *Erie R. Co. v. Tompkins* and decisions in *Erie*'s path, is both "substantive" and "procedural": "substantive" in that § 5501(c)'s "deviates materially" standard controls how much a plaintiff can be awarded; "procedural" in that § 5501(c) assigns decisionmaking authority to New York's Appellate Division. Parallel application of § 5501(c) at the federal appellate level would be out of sync with the federal system's division of trial and appellate court functions, an allocation weighted by the Seventh Amendment. The dispositive question, therefore, is whether federal courts can give effect to the substantive thrust of § 5501(c) without untoward alteration of the federal scheme for the trial and decision of civil cases.

A

Federal diversity jurisdiction provides an alternative forum for the adjudication of state-created rights, but it does not carry with it generation of rules of substantive law. As *Erie* read the Rules of Decision Act: "Except in matters governed by the Federal Constitution or by Acts of Congress, the law to be applied in any case is the law of the State." 304 U.S. at 78. Under the *Erie* doctrine, federal courts sitting in diversity apply state substantive law and federal procedural law.

Classification of a law as "substantive" or "procedural" for *Erie* purposes is sometimes a challenging endeavor.[7] *Guaranty Trust Co. v. York*, an early interpretation of *Erie,* propounded an "outcome-determination" test: "Does it significantly affect the result of a litigation for a federal court to disregard a law of a State that would be controlling in an action upon the same claim by the same parties in a State court?" A later pathmarking case, qualifying *Guaranty Trust*, explained that the "outcome-determination" test must not be applied mechanically to sweep in all manner of variations; instead, its application must

---

7. Concerning matters covered by the Federal Rules of Civil Procedure, the characterization question is usually unproblematic: It is settled that if the Rule in point is consonant with the Rules Enabling Act, 28 U.S.C. §2072, and the Constitution, the Federal Rule applies regardless of contrary state law. *See Hanna v. Plumer*, 380 U.S. 460 (1965). Federal courts have interpreted the Federal Rules, however, with sensitivity to important state interests and regulatory policies. *See, e.g., Walker v. Armco Steel Corp.*, 446 U.S. 740, 750-752 (1980) (state law rather than Rule 3 determines when a diversity action commences for the purposes of tolling the state statute of limitations; Rule 3 makes no reference to the tolling of state limitations, the Court observed, and accordingly found no "direct conflict").

be guided by "the twin aims of the *Erie* rule: discouragement of forum shopping and avoidance of inequitable administration of the laws." *Hanna v. Plumer*, 380 U.S. 460, 468.

Informed by these decisions, we address the question whether New York's "deviates materially" standard, codified in CPLR § 5501(c), is outcome affective in this sense: Would "application of the [standard] have so important an effect upon the fortunes of one or both of the litigants that failure to [apply] it would [unfairly discriminate against citizens of the forum State, or] be likely to cause a plaintiff to choose the federal court"?

We start from a point the parties do not debate. Gasperini acknowledges that a statutory cap on damages would supply substantive law for *Erie* purposes. Although CPLR § 5501(c) is less readily classified, it was designed to provide an analogous control.

New York's Legislature codified in § 5501(c) a new standard, one that requires closer court review than the common law "shock the conscience" test. More rigorous comparative evaluations attend application of § 5501(c)'s "deviates materially" standard. To foster predictability, the legislature required the reviewing court, when overturning a verdict under § 5501(c), to state its reasons, including the factors it considered relevant. We think it a fair conclusion that CPLR § 5501(c) differs from a statutory cap principally "in that the maximum amount recoverable is not set forth by statute, but rather is determined by case law." In sum, § 5501(c) contains a procedural instruction, but the State's objective is manifestly substantive.

It thus appears that if federal courts ignore the change in the New York standard and persist in applying the "shock the conscience" test to damage awards on claims governed by New York law, "substantial' variations between state and federal [money judgments]" may be expected. We therefore agree with the Second Circuit that New York's check on excessive damages implicates what we have called *Erie*'s "twin aims." Just as the *Erie* principle precludes a federal court from giving a state-created claim "longer life than [the claim] would have had in the state court," so *Erie* precludes a recovery in federal court significantly larger than the recovery that would have been tolerated in state court.

B

CPLR § 5501(c), as earlier noted, is phrased as a direction to the New York Appellate Division. Acting essentially as a surrogate for a New York appellate forum, the Court of Appeals reviewed Gasperini's award to determine if it "deviate[d] materially" from damage awards the Appellate Division permitted in similar circumstances. The Court of Appeals performed this task without benefit of an opinion from the District Court, which had denied "without comment" the Center's Rule 59 motion. Concentrating on the authority § 5501(c) gives to the Appellate Division, Gasperini urges that the provision shifts fact-finding responsibility from the jury and the trial judge to the appellate court. Assigning such responsibility to an appellate court, he maintains, is incompatible with the Seventh Amendment's Reexamination Clause, and therefore, Gasperini concludes, § 5501(c) cannot be given effect in federal court. Although we reach a different conclusion than Gasperini, we agree that the Second Circuit did not attend to "[a]n essential characteristic of [the federal court] system," *Byrd v. Blue Ridge Rural Elec. Cooperative, Inc.*, when it used § 5501(c) as "the standard for [federal] appellate review."

That "essential characteristic" was described in *Byrd*, a diversity suit for negligence in which a pivotal issue of fact would have been tried by a judge were the case in state court. The *Byrd* Court held that, despite the state practice, the plaintiff was entitled to a jury trial in federal court. In so ruling, the Court said that the *Guaranty Trust* "outcome-determination" test was an insufficient guide in cases presenting countervailing federal interests. The Court described the countervailing federal interests present in *Byrd* this way:

> The federal system is an independent system for administering justice to litigants who properly invoke its jurisdiction. An essential characteristic of that system is the manner in which, in civil common-law actions, it distributes trial functions between judge and jury and, under the influence—if not the command—of the Seventh Amendment, assigns the decisions of disputed questions of fact to the jury.

The Seventh Amendment, which governs proceedings in federal court, but not in state court, bears not only on the allocation of trial functions between judge and jury, the issue in *Byrd*; it also controls the allocation of authority to review verdicts, the issue of concern here. The Amendment reads:

> In Suits at common law, where the value in controversy shall exceed twenty dollars, the right of trial by jury shall be preserved, and no fact tried by a jury, shall be otherwise re-examined in any Court of the United States, than according to the rules of the common law.

Byrd involved the first Clause of the Amendment, the "trial by jury" Clause. This case involves the second, the "Reexamination" Clause. In keeping with the historic understanding, the Reexamination Clause does not inhibit the authority of trial judges to grant new trials "for any of the reasons for which new trials have heretofore been granted in actions at law in the courts of the United States." Fed. R. Civ. P. 59(a). That authority is large. "The trial judge in the federal system," we have reaffirmed, "has discretion to grant a new trial if the verdict appears to [the judge] to be against the weight of the evidence." This discretion includes overturning verdicts for excessiveness and ordering a new trial without qualification, or conditioned on the verdict winner's refusal to agree to a reduction (remittitur).

[When] courts of appeals engage in review of district court excessiveness determinations, "abuse of discretion" as their standard. Appellate review for abuse of discretion is reconcilable with the Seventh Amendment as a control necessary and proper to the fair administration of justice: "[N]othing in the Seventh Amendment precludes appellate review of the trial judge's denial of a motion to set aside [a jury verdict] as excessive."

C

In *Byrd*, the Court faced a one-or-the-other choice: trial by judge as in state court, or trial by jury according to the federal practice. In the case before us, a choice of that order is not required, for the principal state and federal interests can be accommodated. The Second Circuit correctly recognized that when New York substantive law governs a claim for relief, New York law and decisions guide the allowable damages. But that court did not take into account the characteristic of the federal-court system that caused us to reaffirm: "The proper role of the trial and appellate courts in the federal system in reviewing the size of jury verdicts is a matter of federal law." "The role of the district court is to determine whether the jury's verdict is within the confines set by state law. The court of appeals should then review the district court's determination under an abuse-of-discretion standard."

New York's dominant interest can be respected, without disrupting the federal system, once it is recognized that the federal district court is capable of performing the checking function, *i.e.*, that court can apply the State's "deviates materially" standard in line with New York case law evolving under CPLR § 5501(c).[22] We recall, in this regard, that the "deviates materially" standard serves as the guide to be applied in trial as well as appellate courts in New York.

Within the federal system, practical reasons combine with Seventh Amendment constraints to lodge in the district court, not the court of appeals, primary responsibility for application of § 5501(c)'s "deviates materially" check. Trial judges have the "unique opportunity to consider the evidence in the living courtroom context," while appellate judges see only the "cold paper record." District court applications of the "deviates materially" standard would be subject to appellate review under the standard the Circuits now employ when inadequacy or excessiveness is asserted on appeal: abuse of discretion.

IV

It does not appear that the District Court checked the jury's verdict against the relevant New York decisions demanding more than "industry standard" testimony to support an award of the size the jury returned in this case. As the Court of Appeals recognized, the uniqueness of the photographs and the plaintiff's earnings as photographer—past and reasonably projected—are factors relevant to appraisal of the award. Accordingly, we vacate the judgment of the Court of

---

22. Justice Scalia finds in Federal Rule of Civil Procedure 59 a "federal standard" for new trial motions in " 'direct collision' " with, and " 'leaving no room for the operation of,' " a state law like CPLR §5501(c). The relevant prescription, Rule 59(a), has remained unchanged since the adoption of the Federal Rules by this Court in 1937. Rule 59(a) is as encompassing as it is uncontroversial. It is indeed "Hornbook" law that a most usual ground for a Rule 59 motion is that "the damages are excessive." Whether damages are excessive for the claim-in-suit must be governed by some law. And there is no candidate for that governance other than the law that gives rise to the claim for relief— here, the law of New York. *See* 28 U.S.C. §2072(a) and (b) ("Supreme Court shall have the power to prescribe general rules of . . . procedure"; "[s]uch rules shall not abridge, enlarge or modify any substantive right").

Appeals and instruct that court to remand the case to the District Court so that the trial judge, revisiting his ruling on the new trial motion, may test the jury's verdict against CPLR § 5501(c)'s "deviates materially" standard.

[The dissenting opinions of Justices STEVENS and SCALIA (the latter joined by Chief Justice REHNQUIST and Justice THOMAS) are omitted.]

YOUR TAKEAWAY

Ruth Bader Ginsburg pens one of the great understatements in Supreme Court jurisprudence here: "Classification of a law as 'substantive' or 'procedural' for *Erie* purposes is sometimes a challenging endeavor." But *Gasperini* also illustrates another of *Erie*'s illusive distinctions in the post-*Hanna* world—*direct and unavoidable* conflicts between a Federal Rule and state practice, and situations where both can coexist.

Justice Ginsburg places *Gasperini* in the latter category, reading Fed. R. Civ. P. 59 as not supplying any substantive content or "federal standard" for the granting of new trials, but merely providing the mechanics of such a motion. Treating this as an unguided *Erie* conflict, she reverts to the outcome test and concludes (given the inconsistent results on damages) that the federal court must apply New York's standard for excessiveness.

Justice Scalia's dissent flows from his placement of the case in the other category—a direct and unavoidable clash between Fed. R. Civ. P. 59 and New York's "materially deviates" standard:

> [I]n my view, one does not even reach the *Erie* question in this case. The standard to be applied by a district court in ruling on a motion for a new trial is set forth in Rule 59 of the Federal Rules of Civil Procedure, which provides that "[a] new trial may be granted . . . for any of the reasons for which new trials have heretofore been granted in actions at law *in the courts of the United States*." (Emphasis added.) That is undeniably a federal standard. Federal District Courts in the Second Circuit have interpreted that standard to permit the granting of new trials where "it is quite clear that the jury has reached a seriously erroneous result" and letting the verdict stand would result in a "miscarriage of justice." Assuming (as we have no reason to question) that this is a correct interpretation of what Rule 59 requires, it is undeniable that the Federal Rule is "sufficiently broad to cause a direct collision with the state law or, implicitly, to control the issue before the court, thereby leaving no room for the operation of that law." It is simply not possible to give controlling effect both to the federal standard and the state standard in reviewing the jury's award. That being so, the court has no choice but to apply the Federal Rule, which is an exercise of what we have called Congress's "power to regulate matters which, though falling within the uncertain area between substance and procedure, are rationally capable of classification as either." *Hanna*.

518 U.S. at 467-468.

REVIEW QUESTIONS

1. Is Justice Scalia's dissent here consistent with his conclusion in *Stewart Organization, Inc. v. Ricoh* (Note following *Walker v. Armco Steel Corp.*, above) that § 1404 was *not* broad enough to displace the state rule against enforcement of forum selection clauses?

2. Can the Supreme Court give meaningful guidance in so complex an area if there is fundamental disagreement even about *which of the competing analyses applies*? Who has the better argument here, Scalia—that Fed. R. Civ. P. 59 is broad enough to displace the state law on the grounds for granting new trials—, or Ginsburg—that it is not the Federal Rule, but just judge-made practice, that bumps up against the state standard?

3. How does Justice Ginsburg invoke *Byrd*'s "essential characteristic" of federal litigation concept to untangle the intricate web of state and federal practice here?

The **Erie** *Epilogue.* *Gasperini v. Center for Humanities, Inc.* seemed an apt end to the *Erie* saga, as Justice Ginsburg was able to neatly divide the law-application authority between the state and federal sovereigns in a manner consistent with the three analyses developed since 1938. But the Supreme Court opted to jump back into the fray six years later, and produced a not-so-neat result.

Semtek International Inc. v. Lockheed Martin Corp., 531 U.S. 497 (2001), involved both vertical and horizontal choice of law issues, and prompted Professor Burbank to observe that it "would be difficult for even the most adept spinner of law school hypotheticals to devise a case more challenging." Stephen B. Burbank, Semtek, *Forum Shopping, and Federal Common Law*, 77 Notre Dame L. Rev. 1027 (2002).

Semtek's breach of contract action was dismissed by the federal district court in California as barred by that state's two-year statute of limitations. It then brought suit in a Maryland state court on the same claims, relying on Maryland's three-year statute. The Maryland court dismissed on grounds of *res judicata*, which (as covered in our next chapter) prevents a plaintiff from relitigating a claim that has already gone to final judgment on the merits. Semtek appealed, arguing that the *res judicata* effect of the federal court's dismissal of the first action should be controlled by California state court doctrine, which would not treat dismissal on statute of limitations grounds as "on the merits."

A unanimous Supreme Court held that federal (not state) law controls the issue, but (with a twist befitting the *Erie* puzzle) concluded that, absent a Fed. R. Civ. P. directly on point, federal law must incorporate state law, so that the same rule would apply whether the dismissal had been ordered by a federal or a state court:

> This is, it seems to us, a classic case for adopting, as the federally prescribed rule of decision, the law that would be applied by state courts in the State in which the federal diversity court sits. [A]ny other rule would produce the sort of "forum-shopping and inequitable administration of the laws" that *Erie* seeks

to avoid, since filing in, or removing to, federal court would be encouraged by the divergent effects that the litigants would anticipate from likely grounds of dismissal.

531 U.S. at 508.

We will have more to say about *Semtek* in Chapter 10.

* * *

The Supreme Court took another dive into the *Erie* pool (or swamp?) in our next case. Did the Court clarify the "murky waters"?

Shady Grove Orthopedic Associates v. Allstate Insurance Co.
559 U.S. 393 (2010)

Justice SCALIA announced the judgment of the Court and delivered the opinion of the Court with respect to Parts I and II-A, an opinion with respect to Parts II-B and II-D, in which THE CHIEF JUSTICE, Justice THOMAS, and Justice SOTOMAYOR join, and an opinion with respect to Part II-C, in which THE CHIEF JUSTICE and Justice THOMAS join.

New York law prohibits class actions in suits seeking penalties or statutory minimum damages.[1] We consider whether this precludes a federal district court sitting in diversity from entertaining a class action under Federal Rule of Civil Procedure 23.

I

The petitioner's complaint alleged the following: Shady Grove Orthopedic Associates, P. A., provided medical care to Sonia E. Galvez for injuries she suffered in an automobile accident. As partial payment for that care, Galvez assigned to Shady Grove her rights to insurance benefits under a policy issued in New York by Allstate Insurance Co. Shady Grove tendered a claim for the assigned benefits to Allstate, which under New York law had 30 days to pay the claim or deny it. Allstate apparently paid, but not on time, and it refused to pay the statutory interest that accrued on the overdue benefits (at two percent per month).

Shady Grove filed this diversity suit in the Eastern District of New York to recover the unpaid statutory interest. Alleging that Allstate routinely refuses to

---

1. N.Y. Civ. Prac. Law Ann. §901 (West 2006) provides:

(a) One or more members of a class may sue or be sued as representative parties on behalf of all if: 1. the class is so numerous that joinder of all members, whether otherwise required or permitted, is impracticable; 2. there are questions of law or fact common to the class which predominate over any questions affecting only individual members; 3. the claims or defenses of the representative parties are typical of the claims or defenses of the class; 4. the representative parties will fairly and adequately protect the interests of the class; and 5. a class action is superior to other available methods for the fair and efficient adjudication of the controversy.

(b) Unless a statute creating or imposing a penalty, or a minimum measure of recovery specifically authorizes the recovery thereof in a class action, an action to recover a penalty, or minimum measure of recovery created or imposed by statute may not be maintained as a class action.

pay interest on overdue benefits, Shady Grove sought relief on behalf of itself and a class of all others to whom Allstate owes interest. The District Court dismissed the suit for lack of jurisdiction. It reasoned that N.Y. Civ. Prac. Law Ann. § 901(b), which precludes a suit to recover a "penalty" from proceeding as a class action, applies in diversity suits in federal court, despite Federal Rule of Civil Procedure 23. Concluding that statutory interest is a "penalty" under New York law, it held that § 901(b) prohibited the proposed class action. And, since Shady Grove conceded that its individual claim (worth roughly $500) fell far short of the amount-in-controversy requirement for individual suits under 28 U.S.C. § 1332(a), the suit did not belong in federal court.[3]

The Second Circuit affirmed. The court did not dispute that a federal rule adopted in compliance with the Rules Enabling Act, would control if it conflicted with § 901(b). But there was no conflict because (as we will describe in more detail below) the Second Circuit concluded that Rule 23 and § 901(b) address different issues. Finding no federal rule on point, the Court of Appeals held that § 901(b) is "substantive" within the meaning of *Erie R. Co. v. Tompkins*, and thus must be applied by federal courts sitting in diversity.

II

The framework for our decision is familiar. We must first determine whether Rule 23 answers the question in dispute. If it does, it governs—New York's law notwithstanding—unless it exceeds statutory authorization or Congress's rulemaking power. See *Hanna v. Plumer*, 380 U.S. 460, 463-464 (1965). We do not wade into *Erie*'s murky waters unless the federal rule is inapplicable or invalid.

A

The question in dispute is whether Shady Grove's suit may proceed as a class action. Rule 23 provides an answer. It states that "[a] class action may be maintained" if two conditions are met: The suit must satisfy the criteria set forth in subdivision (a) (i.e., numerosity, commonality, typicality, and adequacy of representation), and it also must fit into one of the three categories described in subdivision (b). By its terms this creates a categorical rule entitling a plaintiff whose suit meets the specified criteria to pursue his claim as a class action. Thus, Rule 23 provides a one-size-fits-all formula for deciding the class-action question. Because § 901(b) attempts to answer the same question—i.e., it states that Shady Grove's suit "may not be maintained as a class action" (emphasis added) because of the relief it seeks—it cannot apply in diversity suits unless Rule 23 is *ultra vires*.

---

3. Shady Grove had asserted jurisdiction under 28 U.S.C. §1332(d)(2), which relaxes, for class actions seeking at least $5 million, the rule against aggregating separate claims for calculation of the amount in controversy. See *Exxon Mobil Corp. v. Allapattah Services, Inc.*, 545 U.S. 546, 571 (2005). [Discussed in Chapter 11.]

The Second Circuit believed that §901(b) and Rule 23 do not conflict because they address different issues. Rule 23, it said, concerns only the criteria for determining whether a given class can and should be certified; section 901(b), on the other hand, addresses an antecedent question: whether the particular type of claim is eligible for class treatment in the first place—a question on which Rule 23 is silent. Allstate embraces this analysis.

We disagree. To begin with, the line between eligibility and certifiability is entirely artificial. There is no reason, in any event, to read Rule 23 as addressing only whether claims made eligible for class treatment by some *other* law should be certified as class actions. Allstate asserts that Rule 23 neither explicitly nor implicitly empowers a federal court "to certify a class in each and every case" where the Rule's criteria are met. But that is *exactly* what Rule 23 does: It says that if the prescribed preconditions are satisfied "[a] class action *may be maintained*"—not "*a class action may be permitted*." Courts do not maintain actions; litigants do. The discretion suggested by Rule 23's "may" is discretion residing in the plaintiff: He may bring his claim in a class action if he wishes. And like the rest of the Federal Rules of Civil Procedure, Rule 23 *automatically* applies "in all civil actions and proceedings in the United States district courts," Fed. Rule Civ. Proc. 1.

Allstate next suggests that the structure of §901 shows that Rule 23 addresses only certifiability. Section 901(a), it notes, establishes class certification criteria roughly analogous to those in Rule 23 (wherefore it agrees that subsection is pre-empted). But §901(b)'s rule barring class actions for certain claims is set off as its own subsection, and where it applies §901(a) does not. . . . Rule 23 permits all class actions that meet its requirements, and a State cannot limit that permission by structuring one part of its statute to track Rule 23 and enacting another part that imposes additional requirements. Both of §901's subsections undeniably answer the same question as Rule 23: whether a class action may proceed for a given suit.

The dissent argues that §901(b) has nothing to do with whether Shady Grove may maintain its suit as a class action, but affects only the remedy it may obtain if it wins. Whereas "Rule 23 governs procedural aspects of class litigation" by "prescrib[ing] the considerations relevant to class certification and postcertification proceedings," §901(b) addresses only "the size of a monetary award a class plaintiff may pursue." Accordingly, the dissent says, Rule 23 and New York's law may coexist in peace.

We need not decide whether a state law that limits the remedies available in an existing class action would conflict with Rule 23; that is not what §901(b) does. By its terms, the provision precludes a plaintiff from "maintain[ing]" a class action seeking statutory penalties. Unlike a law that sets a ceiling on damages (or puts other remedies out of reach) in properly filed class actions, §901(b) says nothing about what remedies a court may award; it prevents the class actions it covers from coming into existence at all. Consequently, a court bound by §901(b) could not certify a class action seeking both statutory penalties and other remedies even if it announces in advance that it will refuse to award the penalties in the event the plaintiffs prevail; to do so would violate the statute's clear prohibition on "maintain[ing]" such suits as class actions.

The dissent's approach of determining whether state and federal rules conflict based on the subjective intentions of the state legislature is an enterprise destined to produce "confusion worse confounded." It would mean, to begin with, that one State's statute could survive pre-emption (and accordingly affect the procedures in federal court) while another State's identical law would not, merely because its authors had different aspirations. It would also mean that district courts would have to discern, in every diversity case, the purpose behind any putatively pre-empted state procedural rule, even if its text squarely conflicts with federal law. That task will often prove arduous. Many laws further more than one aim, and the aim of others may be impossible to discern. Moreover, to the extent the dissent's purpose-driven approach depends on its characterization of § 901(b)'s aims as substantive, it would apply to many state rules ostensibly addressed to procedure. Pleading standards, for example, often embody policy preferences about the types of claims that should succeed—as do rules governing summary judgment, pretrial discovery, and the admissibility of certain evidence. Hard cases will abound.

But while the dissent does indeed artificially narrow the scope of § 901(b) by finding that it pursues only substantive policies, that is not the central difficulty of the dissent's position. The central difficulty is that even artificial narrowing cannot render § 901(b) compatible with Rule 23. Whatever the policies they pursue, they flatly contradict each other. Allstate asserts (and the dissent implies) that we can (and must) interpret Rule 23 in a manner that avoids overstepping its authorizing statute. If the Rule were susceptible of two meanings— one that would violate § 2072(b) and another that would not—we would agree. But it is not. Rule 23 unambiguously authorizes any plaintiff, in any federal civil proceeding, to maintain a class action if the Rule's prerequisites are met. We cannot contort its text, even to avert a collision with state law that might render it invalid. See *Walker v. Armco Steel Corp.*, 446 U.S. 740, 750, n. 9 (1980).[8] What the dissent's approach achieves is not the avoiding of a "conflict between Rule 23 and § 901(b)," but rather the invalidation of Rule 23 (pursuant to § 2072(b) of the Rules Enabling Act) to the extent that it conflicts with the substantive policies of § 901. There is no other way to reach the dissent's destination. We must therefore confront head-on whether Rule 23 falls within the statutory authorization.

B

Erie involved the constitutional power of federal courts to supplant state law with judge-made rules. In that context, it made no difference whether the rule was technically one of substance or procedure; the touchstone was whether it

---

8. The cases chronicled by the dissent each involved a Federal Rule that we concluded could fairly be read not to "control the issue" addressed by the pertinent state law, thus avoiding a "direct collision" between federal and state law, see *Walker*. But here, as in *Hanna*, a collision is "unavoidable."

"significantly affect[s] the result of a litigation." *Guaranty Trust Co. v. York*. That is not the test for either the constitutionality or the statutory validity of a Federal Rule of Procedure. Congress has undoubted power to supplant state law, and undoubted power to prescribe rules for the courts it has created, so long as those rules regulate matters "rationally capable of classification" as procedure. *Hanna*. In the Rules Enabling Act, Congress authorized this Court to promulgate rules of procedure subject to its review, 28 U.S.C. § 2072(a), but with the limitation that those rules "shall not abridge, enlarge or modify any substantive right," § 2072(b).

We have long held that this limitation means that the Rule must "really regulat[e] procedure, the judicial process for enforcing rights and duties recognized by substantive law and for justly administering remedy and redress for disregard or infraction of them." The test is not whether the rule affects a litigant's substantive rights; most procedural rules do. What matters is what the rule itself regulates: If it governs only "the manner and the means" by which the litigants' rights are "enforced," it is valid; if it alters "the rules of decision by which [the] court will adjudicate [those] rights," it is not.

Applying that test, we have rejected every statutory challenge to a Federal Rule that has come before us. We have found to be in compliance with § 2072(b) rules prescribing methods for serving process (Fed. Rule Civ. Proc. 4(f)); (Fed. Rule Civ. Proc. 4(d)(1)), and requiring litigants whose mental or physical condition is in dispute to submit to examinations (Fed. Rule Civ. Proc. 35). Likewise, we have upheld rules authorizing imposition of sanctions upon those who file frivolous appeals (Fed. Rule App. Proc. 38), or who sign court papers without a reasonable inquiry into the facts asserted (Fed. Rule Civ. Proc. 11). Each of these rules had some practical effect on the parties' rights, but each undeniably regulated only the process for enforcing those rights; none altered the rights themselves, the available remedies, or the rules of decision by which the court adjudicated either.

Applying that criterion, we think it obvious that rules allowing multiple claims (and claims by or against multiple parties) to be litigated together are also valid. *See, e.g.*, Fed. Rules Civ. Proc. 18 (joinder of claims), 20 (joinder of parties), 42(a) (consolidation of actions). Such rules neither change plaintiffs' separate entitlements to relief nor abridge defendants' rights; they alter only how the claims are processed. For the same reason, Rule 23—at least insofar as it allows willing plaintiffs to join their separate claims against the same defendants in a class action—falls within § 2072(b)'s authorization. A class action, no less than traditional joinder (of which it is a species), merely enables a federal court to adjudicate claims of multiple parties at once, instead of in separate suits. And like traditional joinder, it leaves the parties' legal rights and duties intact and the rules of decision unchanged.

Allstate contends that the authorization of class actions is not substantively neutral: Allowing Shady Grove to sue on behalf of a class "transform[s] [the] dispute over a five hundred dollar penalty into a dispute over a five million dollar penalty." Allstate's aggregate liability, however, does not depend on whether the suit proceeds as a class action. Each of the 1,000-plus members of the putative class could (as Allstate acknowledges) bring a freestanding suit asserting his individual claim. It is undoubtedly true that some plaintiffs who would not bring individual suits for the relatively small sums involved will choose to join a class action. That has no bearing, however, on Allstate's or the plaintiffs' legal rights. The likelihood that some (even many) plaintiffs will be induced to sue by the availability of a class action is just the sort of "incidental effec[t]" we have long held does not violate § 2072(b).

As a fallback argument, Allstate argues that even if § 901(b) is a procedural provision, it was enacted "for *substantive reasons*." Its end was not to improve "the conduct of the litigation process itself" but to alter "the outcome of that process."

The fundamental difficulty with both these arguments is that the substantive nature of New York's law, or its substantive purpose, makes no difference. A Federal Rule of Procedure is not valid in some jurisdictions and invalid in others—or valid in some cases and invalid in others—depending upon whether its effect is to frustrate a state substantive law (or a state procedural law enacted for substantive purposes).

Hanna unmistakably expressed the same understanding that compliance of a Federal Rule with the Enabling Act is to be assessed by consulting the Rule itself, and not its effects in individual applications:

> "[T]he court has been instructed to apply the Federal Rule, and can refuse to do so only if the Advisory Committee, this Court, and Congress erred in their prima facie judgment that the Rule in question transgresses neither the terms of the Enabling Act nor constitutional restrictions."

In sum, it is not the substantive or procedural nature or purpose of the affected state law that matters, but the substantive or procedural nature of the Federal Rule. The validity of a Federal Rule depends entirely upon whether it regulates procedure. If it does, it is authorized by § 2072 and is valid in all jurisdictions, with respect to all claims, regardless of its incidental effect upon state-created rights.

D

We must acknowledge the reality that keeping the federal-court door open to class actions that cannot proceed in state court will produce forum shopping. That is unacceptable when it comes as the consequence of judge-made rules created to fill supposed "gaps" in positive federal law. See *Hanna*. For where neither the Constitution, a treaty, nor a statute provides the rule of decision or authorizes a federal court to supply one, "state law must govern because there can be no other law." But divergence from state law, with the attendant consequence of forum shopping, is the inevitable (indeed, one might say the intended) result of a uniform system of federal procedure. Congress itself has created the possibility that the same case may follow a different course if filed in federal instead of state court. The short of the matter is that a Federal Rule governing procedure is valid whether or not it alters the outcome of the case in a way that induces forum shopping. To hold otherwise would be to "disembowel either the Constitution's grant of power over federal procedure" or Congress's exercise of it.

The judgment of the Court of Appeals is reversed, and the case is remanded for further proceedings.

It is so ordered.

Justice STEVENS, concurring in part and concurring in the judgment.

The New York law at issue, N.Y. Civ. Prac. Law Ann. (CPLR) § 901(b), is a procedural rule that is not part of New York's substantive law. Accordingly, I agree with Justice Scalia that Federal Rule of Civil Procedure 23 must apply in this case and join Parts I and II-A of the Court's opinion. But I also agree with Justice Ginsburg that there are some state procedural rules that federal courts must apply in diversity cases because they function as a part of the State's definition of substantive rights and remedies.

Justice Ginsburg views the basic issue in this case as whether and how to apply a federal rule that dictates an answer to a traditionally procedural question (whether to join plaintiffs together as a class), when a state law that "defines the dimensions" of a state-created claim dictates the opposite answer. As explained above, I readily acknowledge that if a federal rule displaces a state rule that is " 'procedural' in the ordinary sense of the term," but sufficiently interwoven with the scope of a substantive right or remedy, there would be an Enabling Act problem, and the federal rule would have to give way. In my view, however, this is not such a case.

Because Rule 23 governs class certification, the only decision is whether certifying a class in this diversity case would "abridge, enlarge or modify" New York's substantive rights or remedies. § 2072(b). Although one can argue that class certification would enlarge New York's "limited" damages remedy, such arguments rest on extensive speculation about what the New York Legislature had in mind when it created § 901(b). But given that there are two plausible competing narratives, it seems obvious to me that we should respect the plain textual reading of § 901(b), a rule in New York's procedural code about when to certify class actions brought under any source of law, and respect Congress' decision that Rule 23 governs class certification in federal courts. In order to displace a federal rule, there must be more than just a possibility that the state rule is different than it appears.

Accordingly, I concur in part and concur in the judgment.

Justice GINSBURG, with whom Justice KENNEDY, Justice BREYER, and Justice ALITO join, dissenting.

The Court today approves Shady Grove's attempt to transform a $500 case into a $5,000,000 award, although the State creating the right to recover has proscribed this alchemy. If Shady Grove had filed suit in New York state court, the 2% interest payment authorized by New York Ins. Law Ann. § 5106(a), as a penalty for overdue benefits would, by Shady Grove's own measure, amount to no more than $500. By instead filing in federal court based on the parties' diverse citizenship and requesting class certification, Shady Grove hopes to recover, for the class, statutory damages of more than $5,000,000. The New York Legislature has barred this remedy, instructing that, unless specifically permitted, "an action to recover a penalty, or minimum measure of recovery created or imposed by statute may not be maintained as a class action." N.Y. Civ. Prac. Law Ann. § 901(b). The Court nevertheless holds that Federal Rule of Civil Procedure 23, which prescribes procedures for the conduct of class actions in federal courts, preempts the application of § 901(b) in diversity suits.

The Court reads Rule 23 relentlessly to override New York's restriction on the availability of statutory damages. Our decisions, however, caution us to ask, before undermining state legislation: Is this conflict really necessary? Had the Court engaged in that inquiry, it would not have read Rule 23 to collide with New York's legitimate interest in keeping certain monetary awards reasonably bounded. I would continue to interpret Federal Rules with awareness of, and sensitivity to, important state regulatory policies. Because today's judgment radically departs from that course, I dissent.

I

. . .

B

In our prior decisions in point, many of them not mentioned in the Court's opinion, we have avoided immoderate interpretations of the Federal Rules that would trench on state prerogatives without serving any countervailing federal interest. "Application of the *Hanna* analysis," we have said, "is premised on a 'direct collision' between the Federal Rule and the state law." *Walker v. Armco Steel Corp.*, 446 U.S. 740, 749-750 (1980) (quoting *Hanna*). To displace state law, a Federal Rule, "when fairly construed," must be " 'sufficiently broad' " so as "to 'control the issue' before the court, thereby leaving no room for the operation of that law."

The majority in *Hanna* recognized that "federal rules must be interpreted by the courts applying them, and that the process of interpretation can and should reflect an awareness of legitimate state interests." Following *Hanna*, we continued to "interpre[t] the federal rules to avoid conflict with important state regulatory policies." The Court veers away from that approach—and conspicuously, its most recent reiteration in *Gasperini*, in favor of a mechanical reading of Federal Rules, insensitive to state interests and productive of discord.

C

Section 901(a) allows courts leeway in deciding whether to certify a class, but § 901(b) rejects the use of the class mechanism to pursue the particular remedy of statutory damages. The limitation was not designed with the fair conduct or efficiency of litigation in mind. Indeed, suits seeking statutory damages are arguably best suited to the class device because individual proof of actual damages is unnecessary. New York's decision instead to block class-action proceedings for statutory damages therefore makes scant sense, except as a means to a manifestly substantive end: Limiting a defendant's liability in a single lawsuit in order to prevent the exorbitant inflation of penalties—remedies the New York Legislature created with individual suits in mind.

D

As the Second Circuit well understood, Rule 23 prescribes the considerations relevant to class certification and postcertification proceedings—but it does not command that a particular remedy be available when a party sues in a representative capacity. Section 901(b), in contrast, trains on that latter issue. Sensibly read, Rule 23 governs procedural aspects of class litigation, but allows state law to control the size of a monetary award a class plaintiff may pursue.

In other words, Rule 23 describes a method of enforcing a claim for relief, while §901(b) defines the dimensions of the claim itself. In this regard, it is immaterial that §901(b) bars statutory penalties in wholesale, rather than retail, fashion. The New York Legislature could have embedded the limitation in every provision creating a cause of action for which a penalty is authorized; §901(b) operates as shorthand to the same effect. It is as much a part of the delineation of the claim for relief as it would be were it included claim by claim in the New York Code.

Section 901(b) does not allow class members to recover statutory damages because the New York Legislature considered the result of adjudicating such claims *en masse* to be exorbitant. The fair and efficient conduct of class litigation is the legitimate concern of Rule 23; the remedy for an infraction of state law, however, is the legitimate concern of the State's lawmakers and not of the federal rulemakers.

. . .

The absence of an inevitable collision between Rule 23 and §901(b) becomes evident once it is comprehended that a federal court sitting in diversity can accord due respect to both state and federal prescriptions. Plaintiffs seeking to vindicate claims for which the State has provided a statutory penalty may pursue relief through a class action if they forgo statutory damages and instead seek actual damages or injunctive or declaratory relief; any putative class member who objects can opt out and pursue actual damages, if available, and the statutory penalty in an individual action. In this manner, the Second Circuit explained, "Rule 23's procedural requirements for class actions can be applied along with the substantive requirement of CPLR 901(b)." In sum, while phrased as responsive to the question whether certain class actions may begin, §901(b) is unmistakably aimed at controlling how those actions must end. On that remedial issue, Rule 23 is silent.

Any doubt whether Rule 23 leaves § 901(b) in control of the remedial issue at the core of this case should be dispelled by our *Erie* jurisprudence, including *Hanna*, which counsels us to read Federal Rules moderately and cautions against stretching a rule to cover every situation it could conceivably reach. The Court states that "[t]here is no reason . . . to read Rule 23 as addressing only whether claims made eligible for class treatment by some other law should be certified as class actions." To the contrary, [our precedents] provide good reason to look to the law that creates the right to recover. That is plainly so on a more accurate statement of what is at stake: Is there any reason to read Rule 23 as authorizing a claim for relief when the State that created the remedy disallows its pursuit on behalf of a class? None at all is the answer our federal system should give.

. . .

By finding a conflict without considering whether Rule 23 rationally should be read to avoid any collision, the Court unwisely and unnecessarily retreats from the federalism principles undergirding *Erie*. Had the Court reflected on the respect for state regulatory interests endorsed in our decisions, it would have found no cause to interpret Rule 23 so woodenly—and every reason not to do so.

II

Because I perceive no unavoidable conflict between Rule 23 and § 901(b), I would decide this case by inquiring "whether application of the [state] rule would have so important an effect upon the fortunes of one or both of the litigants that failure to [apply] it would be likely to cause a plaintiff to choose the federal court." *Hanna*, 380 U.S. at 468, n. 9.

When no federal law or rule is dispositive of an issue, and a state statute is outcome affective in the sense our cases on *Erie* (pre- and post-*Hanna*) develop, the Rules of Decision Act commands application of the State's law in diversity suits. As this case starkly demonstrates, if federal courts exercising diversity jurisdiction are compelled by Rule 23 to award statutory penalties in class actions while New York courts are bound by § 901(b)'s proscription, "substantial variations between state and federal [money judgments] may be expected." The "variation" here is indeed "substantial." Shady Grove seeks class relief that is ten thousand times greater than the individual remedy available to it in state court. As the plurality acknowledges, forum shopping will undoubtedly result if a plaintiff need only file in federal instead of state court to seek a massive monetary award explicitly barred by state law. The "accident of diversity of citizenship" should not subject a defendant to such augmented liability. We have long recognized the impropriety of displacing, in a diversity action, state-law limitations on state-created remedies.

The Court's erosion of *Erie*'s federalism grounding impels me to point out the large irony in today's judgment. Shady Grove is able to pursue its claim in federal court only by virtue of the recent enactment of the Class Action Fairness Act of 2005 (CAFA), 28 U.S.C. § 1332(d). In CAFA, Congress opened federal-court doors to state-law-based class actions so long as there is minimal diversity, at least 100 class members, and at least $5,000,000 in controversy. By providing a federal forum, Congress sought to check what it considered to be the over-readiness of some state courts to certify class actions. In other words, Congress envisioned fewer—not more—class actions overall. Congress surely never anticipated that CAFA would make federal courts a mecca for suits of the kind Shady Grove has launched: class actions seeking state-created penalties for claims arising under state law—claims that would be barred from class treatment in the State's own courts.

I would continue to approach *Erie* questions in a manner mindful of the purposes underlying the Rules of Decision Act and the Rules Enabling Act, faithful to precedent, and respectful of important state interests. I would therefore hold that the New York Legislature's limitation on the recovery of statutory damages applies in this case, and would affirm the Second Circuit's judgment.

YOUR TAKEAWAY

Shady Grove presents the oddity of one of the Court's most conservative (and states' rights oriented) members, Antonin Scalia, giving a broad reading to a Federal Rule and thereby displacing the state's judgment that class actions seeking such penalties should not proceed, while the liberal Ruth Bader Ginsburg would deprive plaintiffs of the class action device in deference to New York's statute. Does the *Erie* puzzle now transcend ideology?

Professor Jeffrey W. Stempel writes:

> Justice Ruth Bader Ginsburg's more functional approach, arguably too solicitous of state law, prevailed in *Gasperini* only to be relegated to a dissent in *Shady Grove*. By contrast, *Gasperini* dissenter Justice Antonin Scalia emerged victorious in a more formalist, perhaps overly federal court-empowering plurality opinion reminiscent of Chief Justice Earl Warren's *Hanna v. Plumer* majority opinion. Critics might term the Scalia plurality in *Shady Grove* as "*Hanna* on steroids" (or at least a pumped-up *Hanna*) in its aggressive view that federal procedural rules eject contrary state procedural codes, even where they embody substantive state law or policy, so long as the federal rule is actually procedural and on point.
>
> . . .
>
> *Shady Grove* was also a wonderful departure from the Court's seemingly predictable ideological divide that has characterized other close cases in recent years. The majority upholding Federal Rule 23 included conservatives Scalia, Chief Justice John Roberts and Justice Clarence Thomas combined with liberals Sotomayor and Stevens while the dissenters attempting to privilege the state law were liberals Ginsburg and Stephen Breyer joined by conservatives Anthony Kennedy and Samuel Alito. The division of the Court cut against type, which both illustrated the difficulty of *Erie* issues and provided a bit of reassurance that case outcomes are not completely predictable according to the Justices' overall ideology or outcome preferences. The conservative-led majority permitted the plaintiff considerably more leverage over a large commercial defendant

than it would have obtained under state law, a result opposed by the liberal-led dissenters.

Shady Grove *and the Potential Democracy-Enhancing Benefits of* Erie *Formalism*, 44 Akron L. Rev. 907, 908-911 (2011).

REVIEW QUESTIONS

1. Which opinion is more sympathetic to the concerns regarding federalism originally set forth in *Erie R. Co. v. Tompkins*—Justice Scalia's or Justice Ginsburg's? Or does each simply emphasize certain *Erie* policies over others?

2. Which opinion do you think Chief Justice Earl Warren (author of *Hanna v. Plumer*) would agree with? What about Justice Thurgood Marshall (author of *Walker v. Armco Steel Co.*)? Or Justice Harlan (concurring in *Hanna v. Plumer* with his "primary private activity" test)?

3. Is Scalia's opinion correct when it treats Fed. R. Civ. P. 23 as just another joinder device, like Fed. R. Civ. P. 18 (joinder of claims), 20 (joinder of parties), or 42(a) (consolidation of actions)? Are there "substantive" implications to allowing small claimants to aggregate their claims in a way that makes them financially feasible to bring?

4. What about *Erie*'s twin aims of discouraging forum shopping and avoiding inconsistent results between state and federal court? Note the apparent success of Shady Grove Orthopedic Associates in shopping for the federal forum, and thereby *transforming a $500 individual case into a $5 million class action*, as Justice Ginsburg notes in her dissent. Isn't this precisely what bothered Justice Brandeis about Harry Tompkins's gaming the system under the *Swift v. Tyson* regime?

5. Professors Stephen Burbank and Tobias Barrington Wolff view *Shady Grove* as a missed opportunity to clarify the murky area of conflicts between the Federal Rules and state law. *See Redeeming the Missed Opportunities of* Shady Grove, 159 U. Pa. L. Rev. 17 (2010). They complain that the Court's precedents "give some Federal Rules implausibly broad interpretations in order to apply federal law while emptying others of content in order to avoid an Enabling Act challenge." Can you annotate that assertion to the cases we have read?

PRACTICE EXERCISE NO. 38:
ANALYZING VERTICAL CHOICE OF LAW ISSUES IN *CARPENTER*

Assume there is diversity of citizenship among the parties in *Carpenter v. Dee*, making available either a federal or a state forum for the litigation. In weighing these options, we (as plaintiff's counsel) discover that Massachusetts has adopted a "tort reform" statute providing that a plaintiff seeking punitive damages in state court must:

1. "plead with particularity the facts and circumstances upon which any claim for punitive damages in based, and may not make any such allegations upon information and belief or on the assertion that there will likely be evidentiary support after reasonable opportunity for discovery."
2. "pay the reasonable attorneys' fees of defendant for defense of that claim if the claim for punitive damages is ultimately unsuccessful."
3. "post a security bond in the amount determined by the court to assure that such attorneys' fees will be paid, if so ordered."

The legislative history recites findings that claims for punitive damages are often made without merit to intimidate defendants into settling, and tend to substantially enlarge the time and expense of litigation.

It's been suggested that if we file in federal district court rather than state court, we would *not* be subject to the tort reform statute. Prepare for a brainstorming session on this strategy. Will it work? Where do *Twombly* and *Iqbal* fit into our discussion?

REVIEW EXERCISE NO. 10

You are law clerk to the judge trying a federal diversity action alleging negligence on the part of plaintiff's corporate landlord. The tenant claims he suffered debilitating injuries in a fall down a steep flight of outdoor stairs that had not been cleared of snow and ice.

During voir dire of prospective jurors, the judge asked the group whether they had any experience that would bias them against either party. Venireperson 6 answered that she had recently rented from a landlord who refused to make any necessary repairs. Venireperson 9 is a carpenter who informed the court that landlords have on occasion failed to pay his bills for work he performed at their request.

The judge excused both for cause, over the objection of plaintiff's counsel, who requested permission to ask the venirepersons follow-up questions to ascertain whether their objectivity would actually be compromised. Counsel pointed out that under state practice in that jurisdiction, a litigant has a statutory right to supplement the court's voir dire questions in such a situation to avoid unjustified exclusion of persons from jury service. The state supreme court has ruled that any violation of that statute is presumed to have been prejudicial to the party denied the right to question jurors, and requires reversal.

In effect, plaintiff's counsel argues, defendant has been given two additional peremptory challenges without having to show actual bias, affording the defense a distinct tactical advantage in shaping the jury, thus both infringing on plaintiff's Seventh Amendment right to a jury trial and carrying the risk of a less advantageous outcome than would obtain in state court.

Fed. R. Civ. P. 47 leaves this matter of juror questioning to the judge's discretion ("If the court examines the jurors, it must permit the parties or their attorneys to make any further inquiry *it considers proper*"), and she is inclined not to permit counsel follow-up questions because that would considerably slow down the selection process, especially as the issue may come up again with other members of the panel. It might also give plaintiff's counsel the opportunity to unduly influence the prospective jurors by the nature or manner in which the further questions are posed. But the judge is also concerned about the risk of reversal on this issue if the verdict goes against plaintiff and the matter is pressed on appeal.

The judge has called a recess, and asks for your advice as to whether state or federal practice should control. Be prepared to so advise.

"Reverse-Erie." The flip side of the vertical choice of law dilemma is the question of when a state court, entertaining a federal claim within its concurrent subject matter jurisdiction, is obligated to apply federal law in place of its own state rule—the so-called reverse-*Erie* scenario.

Assume an arrestee brings a § 1983 action against the police officers in state court, alleging use of excessive force. In such cases, the federal courts apply the usual standard of proof applicable in civil cases, namely preponderance of the evidence. But if the state courts impose on plaintiffs a heightened burden in tort actions against police officers—"clear and convincing" proof—which standard should the state court apply?

The Supreme Court of Wisconsin held that the federal standard must prevail:

> The United States Supreme Court has recognized that just as federal courts are constitutionally obligated to apply state law to state claims, *Erie R.R. Co. v. Tompkins*, so too the Supremacy Clause imposes on state courts a constitutional duty to proceed in such manner that all the substantial rights of the parties under controlling federal law [are] protected. Inasmuch as the burden of proof is substantive, we hold that under the Supremacy Clause, the lower federal burden of proof applies in § 1983 excessive force cases in state court.

Shaw v. Leatherberry, 286 Wis. 2d 380, 395 (2005). Burden of proof was not, the Wisconsin court concluded, "a mere incident" of procedure, but a "substantive aspect" of the cause of action, and the state court could not alter the "substantial rights" which Congress provided in § 1983. To read more about this topic, *see* Kevin M. Clermont, *Reverse-Erie*, 82 Notre Dame L. Rev. 1 (2006).

CHAPTER 10

Finality and Preclusion

A. INTRODUCTION

Suppose Joe and Sally collide in their automobiles at an intersection. Sally files a lawsuit alleging Joe's negligence caused the accident and seeking compensation for a broken left headlight. She litigates that case to conclusion, and a final judgment is entered. Sally then files a second negligence lawsuit against Joe arising from the very same accident, but this time seeking recovery for the broken *right* headlight. Could any dispute resolution system tolerate such inefficiency?

The doctrine of *res judicata* (or *claim preclusion*) prevents Sally from litigating successive suits against Joe arising from the same event (i.e., the same *claim*). Repetition would waste scarce judicial resources, be unfair to the harassed defendant, permit a plaintiff to spin the litigation roulette wheel until she hopefully finds a sympathetic jury, and risk inconsistent results from the same facts and evidence. "From the parties' perspective, finality creates a sense of repose—an assurance that, after a matter has been litigated once, the parties can consider it settled and adjust their real-world dealings accordingly." Riley T. Keenan, *Identity Crisis: Claim Preclusion in Constitutional Challenges to Statutes*, 20 U. Pa. J. Const. L. 371, 376 (2017).

Claim preclusion thus requires a plaintiff to assert *all* matters arising out of the *same incident or transaction,* and against the *same party,* in one lawsuit. The doctrine precludes repetitive litigation regardless of whether the plaintiff wins or loses the original case, and even if we now know that the decision *was wrong on the law or facts.* (The appeals process is the place to remedy such mistakes.) Subsequent litigation is categorically barred in the interest of finality.

But what if Sally also has a gripe against Joe for an unpaid loan that is *unrelated* to the accident? While Sally *could* join the two claims pursuant to Fed. R. Civ. P. 18 (*see* Chapter 3), finality doctrine does not require her to do so because the claims involve different events. Litigating these two cases separately would not involve a repetition of the same facts and evidence, nor would it constitute undue harassment of the defendant, nor would it risk inconsistent judgments from the very same set of circumstances.

Operation of the doctrine of claim preclusion will obviously depend on the breadth of our definition of *"same claim"*—the broader the definition, the more *inclusion* we are going to mandate at the time of the litigation, and the more *preclusion* that will follow later for matters that are left out.

Claim preclusion operates in two time frames of critical importance to lawyers and litigants. First, in planning the case, plaintiff's counsel must be careful to include in the complaint *all* matters that might be considered part of the *same claim* against that defendant, or risk preclusion of omitted matters in a future litigation. Second, once final judgment has been entered in a case, subsequent litigation between the same parties may require a determination of whether Case 2 represents impermissible "splitting" of a single claim into two lawsuits; if so, Case 2 will not be permitted to go forward.

Now suppose that Sally and Joe have executed a contract requiring Joe to clear timber from Sally's land every June for ten years. Joe performs on the contract for two years, but then is sued by Sally for failure to clear the land in Year 3. Joe defends by challenging the validity of the contract, asserting he was not of sufficient age and legal capacity to enter into the contract when it was signed. The case is tried and results in a jury verdict (and judgment) for Sally. Subsequently, Sally sues Joe again, this time for failure to clear the land in Year 7. This is a *different claim* because it arises out of a different breach (which obviously could not have been anticipated and litigated in Year 3), and thus is not foreclosed by claim preclusion. Here the doctrine of *collateral estoppel* (or *issue preclusion*) comes into play. If (as is likely) it is determined that the jury in the first case must have resolved the capacity issue against Joe in order to find for Sally, Joe will be foreclosed from asserting that same defense again in the later action. Once an issue has been adjudicated between adverse parties, that *identical issue* cannot be relitigated in another lawsuit between the same parties.

While claim preclusion prevents a second litigation from proceeding at all (usually by way of summary judgment), issue preclusion works more narrowly (usually through partial summary judgment) to foreclose litigation of an issue that has previously been litigated and resolved between the parties.

The influential American Law Institute (ALI) summarizes the finality doctrines as follows:

Restatement (Second) of Judgments
§ 17. Effects of Former Adjudication—General Rules

A valid and final personal judgment is conclusive between the parties, except on appeal or other direct review, to the following extent:*

 (1) If the judgment is in favor of the plaintiff, the claim is extinguished and merged in the judgment;

---

(2) If the judgment is in favor of the defendant, the claim is extinguished and the judgment bars a subsequent action on that claim;

(3) A judgment in favor of either the plaintiff or the defendant is conclusive, in a subsequent action between them on the same or a different claim, with respect to any issue actually litigated and determined if its determination was essential to that judgment.

COMMENT

d. *Erroneous judgment.* The general rules stated in this Section are applicable to a valid and final judgment, even if it is erroneous and subject to reversal. If the judgment is erroneous, the unsuccessful party's remedy is to have it set aside or reversed in the original proceedings. Such a remedy may be sought by a motion for a new trial or other relief in the court that rendered the judgment, or by an appeal or other proceedings for review of the judgment in an appellate court.

* * *

The doctrines of claim and issue preclusion must not be confused with the principle of *stare decisis*, by which courts generally follow past precedent in resolving questions of law. *Stare decisis* "is a basic self-governing principle within the Judicial Branch" designed to ensure that the law will not change erratically; it "permits society to presume that bedrock principles are founded in the law rather than in the proclivities of individuals." *Patterson v. McLean Credit Union*, 491 U.S. 164, 172 (1989). While precedents are not sacrosanct, the burden is on the party seeking reconsideration of an established principle.

In our *Sally v. Joe* collision hypothetical, decisional law holding that contributory negligence is a complete bar to recovery would control unless Sally's lawyers are successful in arguing for departure from precedent. Note that *stare decisis* widely applies to all litigants, whereas claim and issue preclusion constrain only the parties (and those "in privity" with them, as discussed later) from the prior case.

Two other doctrines should be noted: *Law of the case* dictates that once an issue of law has been determined in a case, that issue cannot generally be relitigated in subsequent stages of the same lawsuit. It is premised on obvious concerns of efficiency and consistency. *See* Larry L. Teply and Ralph U. Whitten, *Civil Procedure* 1113 (5th ed. 2013). *Double jeopardy* is a protection applicable only in criminal cases against being tried for the same offense twice; unlike preclusion on the civil side, it is derived from the Constitution, specifically the Fifth Amendment. *See generally Gamble v. United States*, 139 S. Ct. 1960 (2019) (holding that the dual-sovereignty doctrine permits successive prosecutions by different sovereigns, such as federal and state).

B. CLAIM PRECLUSION (*RES JUDICATA*)—"SPEAK NOW OR FOREVER HOLD YOUR PEACE"

To make out the defense of claim preclusion (which you will recall must be pled affirmatively under Fed R. Civ. P. 8(c)), three elements must be shown:

- A prior suit that proceeded to a ***final valid judgment on the merits***.
- The present suit arises out of the ***same claim*** as the prior suit.
- The ***parties in both suits are the same, or in privity***.

We will take these up separately, starting with the second.

1. What Constitutes the "Same Claim"?

The following excerpt elucidates the prevailing transactional definition of "claim." The Restatement uses the terms "merger" and "bar," which are vestiges of the common law. When the plaintiff prevailed in the earlier suit, everything within the scope of that claim was *merged* into the judgment. When the defendant prevailed in the earlier suit, everything within the scope of that claim was *barred*. In either situation, the prior judgment is given conclusive effect and there could be no subsequent litigation on that same claim.

Restatement (Second) of Judgments
§ 24. Dimensions of "Claim" for Purposes of Merger or Bar—General Rule Concerning "Splitting"

---

(1) When a valid and final judgment rendered in an action extinguishes the plaintiff's claim pursuant to the rules of merger or bar, the claim extinguished includes all rights of the plaintiff to remedies against the defendant with respect to all or any part of the transaction, or series of connected transactions, out of which the action arose.

(2) What factual grouping constitutes a "transaction," and what groupings constitute a "series," are to be determined pragmatically, giving weight to such considerations as whether the facts are related in time, space, origin, or motivation, whether they form a convenient trial unit, and whether their treatment as a unit conforms to the parties' expectations or business understanding or usage.

COMMENT

a. Rationale of a transactional view of claim. In defining claim to embrace all the remedial rights of the plaintiff against the defendant growing out of the relevant transaction (or series of connected transactions), this Section responds to modern procedural ideas which have found expression in the Federal Rules of Civil Procedure and other procedural systems.

"Claim," in the context of *res judicata*, has never been broader than the transaction to which it related. But in the days when civil procedure still bore the imprint of the forms of action and the division between law and equity, the courts were prone to associate claim with a single theory of recovery, so that with respect to one transaction, a plaintiff might have as many claims as there were theories of the substantive law upon which he could seek relief against the defendant. Thus, defeated in an action based on one theory, the plaintiff might be able to maintain another action based on a different theory, even though both actions were grounded upon the defendant's identical act or connected acts forming a single life-situation. In those earlier days there was also some adherence to a view that associated claim with the assertion of a single primary right as accorded by the substantive law, so that, if it appeared that the defendant had invaded a number of primary rights conceived to be held by the plaintiff, the plaintiff had the same number of claims, even though they all sprang from a unitary occurrence. There was difficulty in knowing which rights were primary and what was their extent, but a primary right and the corresponding claim might turn out to be narrow. Thus it was held by some courts that a judgment for or against the plaintiff in an action for personal injuries did not preclude an action by him for property damage occasioned by the same negligent conduct on the part of the defendant—this deriving from the idea that the right to be free of bodily injury was distinct from the property right. Still another view of claim looked to sameness of evidence; a second action was precluded where the evidence to support it was the same as that needed to support the first. Sometimes this was made the sole test of identity of claim; sometimes it figured as a positive but not as a negative test; that is, in certain situations a second action might be precluded although the evidence material to it varied from that in the first action. Even so, claim was not coterminous with the transaction itself.

The present trend is to see claim in factual terms and to make it coterminous with the transaction regardless of the number of substantive theories, or variant forms of relief flowing from those theories, that may be available to the plaintiff; regardless of the number of primary rights that may have been invaded; and regardless of the variations in the evidence needed to support the theories or rights. The transaction is the basis of the litigative unit or entity which may not be split.

A modern procedural system permits the presentation in the action of all material relevant to the transaction without artificial confinement to any single substantive theory or kind of relief and without regard to historical forms of action or distinctions between law and equity. The law of *res judicata* now reflects the expectation that parties who are given the capacity to present their "entire controversies" shall in fact do so.

b. Transaction: application of a pragmatic standard. The expression "transaction, or series of connected transactions," is not capable of a mathematically precise definition; it invokes a pragmatic standard to be applied with attention to the facts of the cases. And underlying the standard is the need to strike a delicate balance between, on the one hand, the interests of the defendant and of the courts in bringing litigation to a close and, on the other, the interest of the plaintiff in the vindication of a just claim.

It should be emphasized that the concept of a transaction is here used in the broad sense. In general, the expression connotes a natural grouping or common nucleus of operative facts. Among the factors relevant to a determination whether the facts are so woven together as to constitute a single claim are their relatedness in time, space, origin, or motivation, and whether, taken together, they form a convenient unit for trial purposes. Though no single factor is determinative, the relevance of trial convenience makes it appropriate to ask how far the witnesses or proofs in the second action would tend to overlap the witnesses or proofs relevant to the first. If there is a substantial overlap, the second action should ordinarily be held precluded. But the opposite does not hold true; even when there is not a substantial overlap, the second action may be precluded if it stems from the same transaction or series.

c. Transaction may be single despite different harms, substantive theories, measures or kinds of relief. A single transaction ordinarily gives rise to but one claim by one person against another. When a person by one act takes a number of chattels belonging to another, the transaction is single, and judgment for the value of some of the goods exhausts the claim and precludes the injured party from maintaining one action for the remainder. In the more complicated case where one act causes a number of harms to, or invades a number of different interests of the same person, there is still but one transaction; a judgment based on the act usually prevents the person from maintaining another action for any of the harms not sued for in the first action.

That a number of different legal theories casting liability on an actor may apply to a given episode does not create multiple transactions and hence multiple claims. This remains true although the several legal theories depend on different shadings of the facts, or would emphasize different elements of the facts, or would call for different measures of liability or different kinds of relief.

* * *

Consider the application of this transactional definition of "claim" in our next case.

Car Carriers, Inc. v. Ford Motor Co.
789 F.2d 589 (7th Cir. 1989)

Ripple, Circuit Judge:

In this case, we are asked to decide whether the present litigation is barred by an earlier lawsuit under the doctrine of *res judicata*. For the reasons which follow, we hold that the present suit is barred by the earlier judgment and, accordingly, affirm the judgment of the district court.

In 1982, Car Carriers, Inc. (Car Carriers) and six related entities brought an action against Ford Motor Company (Ford) and Nu-Car Carriers, Inc. (Nu-Car). Count I of the six count complaint (1982 Complaint) accused Ford and Nu-Car of conspiring in violation of the Sherman Act, 15 U.S.C. § 1. The remaining five counts asserted pendent state law claims.

The district court dismissed the entire action. The court found the antitrust claim lacking because the plaintiffs failed "to suffer the type of harm the antitrust laws were designed to recompense." Further, since the court found that this defect was "noncurable," the antitrust claim was dismissed with prejudice. Having dismissed the complaint's only federal claim, the district court declined to exercise pendent jurisdiction over the remaining state law claims and dismissed them without prejudice. On appeal, a panel of this court affirmed the district court's decision in all respects.

Undaunted by their first unfruitful journey through the federal courts, Car Carriers and its related entities filed the present action on October 25, 1983 (1983 Complaint). The 1983 Complaint consisted of twenty-four counts: Counts I-VI alleged violations of the Racketeer Influenced and Corrupt Organizations Act (RICO), 18 U.S.C. § 1961 *et seq.*; Count XXIV alleged a violation of the Interstate Commerce Act, 49 U.S.C. §§ 11902-11904; the remaining seventeen counts alleged violations of Illinois law.

The district court again dismissed the entire action. The court held that the federal claims arose from the same "basic fact situation" as that alleged in support of the 1982 Complaint's antitrust claim and, therefore, were barred by the doctrine of *res judicata*. This appeal followed.

I

Before addressing Car Carriers' substantive claims, it will be helpful to set out the occurrences which sparked the 1982 Complaint—the initial litigation in this matter. As set forth in that complaint, from 1968 until 1981, Car Carriers transported new Ford vehicles from Ford's plants and railheads in the Chicago area. According to Car Carriers, as early as 1975, Ford and its alleged co-conspirators entered into contracts and continuing combinations which were designed to restrain trade in the business of providing haulaway motor transportation for new Ford automobiles. Car Carriers accused Ford of employing the following method to implement its goal:

> First, the carrier selected for elimination (the so-called "target carrier") would be required to make substantial investments in new tractor-trailer equipment, real estate, and new terminal facilities. After the "target" carriers had made these investments, however, Ford would then prevent them from obtaining the rate increases necessary for profitable operations. Ford would apparently terminate its relationship with the target carrier at this point, thereby allowing the favored carriers to acquire the businesses and assets of the target carriers at distress prices or for less than fair market value as going business concerns.

In this litigation, the appellants present two issues for our review. First, they ask that we reject the district court's fact-oriented test for *res judicata* in favor of an analysis which would differentiate causes of action based on the rights, duties, and injuries allegedly redressed by each claim. Second, assuming we adopt the district court's approach, the appellants ask that we relieve them of their *res judicata* burden because some of their claims were based on facts which—while admittedly in existence prior to the 1982 Complaint—were unknown to them until after judgment on that complaint.

II

The district court found that the federal claims alleged in the 1983 Complaint arose out of the same factual context as described in the 1982 Complaint. Thus, the court dismissed these claims as barred by the doctrine of *res judicata*. The appellants do not disagree with the district court's finding that both complaints arose out of a common core of operative fact; rather, they attempt to overturn the district court's decision by persuading us to adopt an alternate formulation for determining the application of *res judicata*. Under this alternate test, *res judicata* would not bar a second lawsuit when "an analysis of the rights, duties, and injuries involved in the second lawsuit reveals that they are materially different from those in issue in the first." For the reasons which will be explained in the following section, we decline to adopt the appellants' suggested formulation.

Res judicata is designed to ensure the finality of judicial decisions. It is not "a mere matter of practice or procedure inherited from a more technical time than ours. It is a rule of fundamental and substantial justice, of public policy and of private peace, which should be cordially regarded and enforced by the courts." It "encourages reliance on judicial decisions, bars vexatious litigation, and frees the courts to resolve other disputes." "Its enforcement is essential to the maintenance of social order; for, the aid of judicial tribunals would not be invoked for the vindication of rights of person and property, if conclusiveness did not attend the judgments of such tribunals."

A

"Under *res judicata*, a final judgment on the merits bars further claims by parties or their privies based on the same cause of action." In determining the scope of a "cause of action," this circuit has utilized the "same transaction" test. Under this test, a "cause of action" consists of "a single core of operative facts which give rise to a remedy." This "same transaction" test is decidedly fact-oriented. Once a transaction has caused injury, all claims arising from that transaction must be brought in one suit or be lost. Thus, "a mere change in the legal theory does not create a new cause of action." Therefore, prior litigation acts as a bar not only to those issues which were raised and decided in the earlier litigation but also to those issues which could have been raised in that litigation.

As the commentators have noted, this approach is consistent with the general litigation scheme established by the Federal Rules of Civil Procedure. Litigants have great latitude in joining claims and amending pleadings. *See* Fed. R. Civ. P. 15, 18. Thus, to further the purpose of the rules, it is appropriate that *res judicata* be defined with sufficient breadth to encourage parties to present all their related claims at one time. Further, we note that the Federal Rules define compulsory counterclaims as those claims which have arisen out of the same transaction or occurrence that prompted the plaintiffs' action. *See* Fed. R. Civ. P. 13(a). By compelling defendants to bring their claims in the same action, the rule encourages the simultaneous and final resolution of all claims which arise from a common factual background. Thus, if the Federal Rules impose this obligation on defendants, we believe that it is appropriate to interpret the doctrine of *res judicata* in such a way as to further that same goal by imposing a similar obligation on plaintiffs.

The appellants argue that, while the "same transaction" test may be the primary test for defining a "cause of action," it is not the universal test. The appellants argue that a more appropriate test in this case would be one which scrutinized the theories of relief (RICO, Interstate Commerce Act, Sherman Act) in search of differences between the rights, duties and injuries addressed by each.

It is no accident that the "same transaction" test has become "the present trend among courts nationwide. It preserves—far more firmly than the alternate formulation—the fundamental policy concerns of the doctrine. In our view, these policy concerns counsel against using in this case the "right-duty" approach which the appellants have suggested. Indeed, an unsuccessful party ought not be able to "frustrate the doctrine of *res judicata* by cloaking the same cause of action in the language of a theory of recovery untried in the previous litigation." Therefore, the "right-duty" approach should not be used as a substitute for the "same transaction" test absent compelling circumstances and a clear showing that such a substitution will not undermine the policies of *res judicata*. Appellants have made absolutely no such showing in this case.

B

We turn now to an application of the "transactional" test to the facts of this case. We must decide whether these claims are part of the same cause of action which spawned the earlier Sherman Act claim. The three threshold requirements of *res judicata* are (1) an identity of the parties or their privies, (2) an identity of the causes of action, and (3) a final judgment on the merits.

In this appeal, neither party has contested the "final judgment" element. Further, neither party has questioned the identity of the parties in the two actions. Therefore, the only open question concerns the identity of the causes of action involved in both suits.

In concluding that both the 1982 and the 1983 Complaints alleged the same cause of action, the district court first relied on an analysis derived from the doctrine of pendent jurisdiction. As enunciated in *United Mine Workers v. Gibbs*, 383 U.S. 715 (1966), a federal court may exercise pendent jurisdiction over a state law claim if both the state and federal claims derive from a common nucleus of operative fact.

In this case, the alleged pendent claims were virtually identical to the state law claims alleged in the 1982 Complaint. Thus, according to the district court's reasoning, the appellants had admitted that the Sherman Act, RICO, and Interstate Commerce Act claims derived from a common nucleus of operative fact. Therefore, the district court concluded that *res judicata* was appropriate because the 1983 Complaint's RICO and Interstate Commerce Act claims arose out of the same set of facts as did the 1982 Complaint's Sherman Act claim.

As an alternate ground for its decision, the district court also specifically found that the RICO and Sherman Act counts arose out of the same underlying facts. The court stated: "Like the present RICO claims, the earlier antitrust claims alleged Ford induced Car Carriers to make investments it could not recoup. Like the earlier antitrust claims, the current RICO claims allege Car Carriers was terminated due to a sham and predatory bid, and Ford and Nu-Car refused to buy Car Carriers' assets upon its termination." We agree; the RICO and Sherman Act claims arose out of a single core of operative facts and, thus, were parts of the same cause of action.

The allegations in the present Complaint parallel the facts underlying the 1982 Complaint. Accordingly, the district court did not err by dismissing this count. In sum, we hold that the district court properly applied the "same transaction test" to dismiss all of Car Carriers' federal claims.

III

As a second ground for appeal, Car Carriers asks that we lift the *res judicata* bar for some of its claims because Car Carriers did not discover the facts supporting those claims until after the 1982 Complaint had been dismissed. In essence, Car Carriers claims that since *res judicata* will not bar actions based on facts occurring after the initial judgment,—presumably because those facts were unknown to the plaintiffs when they initiated their first action—*res judicata* should likewise not bar claims based on pre-judgment facts which were unknown to the plaintiffs when they filed. We find this contention to be absolutely without merit.

As we concluded in Part II, *supra*, all of the appellants' claims were part of the same cause of action; they all arose from a single core of operative fact. Since all claims arose from the same factual context and since the appellants had sufficient knowledge to sue on one claim, they also had sufficient knowledge to sue on the rest of their claims. When a litigant files a lawsuit, the courts have a right to presume that he has done his legal and factual homework. It would undermine the basic policies protected by the doctrine of *res judicata* to permit the appellants to once again avail themselves of judicial time and energy while another litigant, who has yet to be heard even once, waits in line behind them.

IV

In disposing of the 1983 Complaint, the district court properly analyzed the *res judicata* effect of its earlier decision. Therefore, the decision of the district court is Affirmed.

YOUR TAKEAWAY

As we noted in the hypothetical collision case between Sally and Joe, the efficiency rationales of the finality doctrines are incontestable. Car Carriers was viewed here as repackaging its unsuccessful case by simply changing the legal theories and statutes relied upon—but a comparison of the facts and circumstances revealed the obvious overlap between the two complaints. To permit such repetitive litigation would be to unjustly reward the ingenuity of counsel and their clients at the expense of the litigation system and the beleaguered defendants. The pragmatic transactional definition of "same claim" both avoids the consequences of narrower formulations such as the one proposed by Car Carriers—which would differentiate claims based on the rights, duties, and injuries pressed—and is consistent with the liberal rules of joinder in modern practice.

REVIEW QUESTIONS

1. Car Carriers also argued that *res judicata* should not apply because some of the facts supporting the 1983 complaint were not discovered by counsel until after the dismissal of the 1982 complaint. The court rejected this contention as "absolutely without merit." Why? Do you see the difference between *new events* giving rise to a *new claim* (look back at Sally and Joe's multi-year contract for clearing of timber), and *newly discovered facts* regarding the original claim? Could claim preclusion accommodate an exception of this kind without sacrificing its core purpose? Wouldn't such an exception reward lawyers for failing to do their "legal and factual homework"?

   It should be noted that Fed. R. Civ. P. 60(b) allows a district court to set aside a judgment on the basis of "newly discovered evidence that, with reasonable diligence, could not have been discovered in time to move for a new trial under Rule 59(b)." *See* Chapter 5, Part E.7.

2. What is the relationship between Fed. R. Civ. P. 13(a) and claim preclusion? If there were no compulsory counterclaim rule, would *res judicata* principles achieve the same result—i.e., preclusion of defendant's claim because it was not asserted in the prior case as a counterclaim arising from the same transaction or event as plaintiff's claim?

   In the absence of a compulsory rule (as in a few state jurisdictions) or where the rule is held not to apply (as where the counterclaim is not deemed sufficiently related to plaintiff's claim), a defendant in a previous action who now brings a claim against the former plaintiff (the parties have, in other words, switched roles) may nonetheless be foreclosed (1) by operation of issue preclusion from relitigating common issues that were determined in the prior action; or (2) from pursuing his claim at all by operation of claim preclusion if entertaining his claim would undermine the finality of the original judgment. *See* Larry L. Teply and Ralph U. Whitten, *Civil Procedure*, 1048-1049 (5th ed. 2013) (citing *Restatement (Second) of Judgments* § 22).

3. In *Heacock v. Heacock*, 402 Mass. 21 (1988), Carla filed a tort action in Superior Court seeking damages for injuries resulting from an assault allegedly committed by former husband Gregg while they were married. Gregg filed a motion to dismiss, asserting that her claim was precluded by a prior divorce judgment entered in the Probate Court, noting that in that proceeding, Carla had presented evidence of the assault and injuries to support her claim that the marriage should be dissolved because of irretrievable breakdown. The Superior Court judge agreed with Gregg and dismissed Carla's tort action "on the basis of issue preclusion, collateral estoppel, *res judicata*, or any one of those three, whichever happens to be the best one." (Warning: Don't try this approach on your Civil Procedure or Bar Examination.)

Can you help the judge determine *which* doctrine would apply? Here's what the Supreme Judicial Court said in reversing the dismissal on Carla's appeal:

> 1. Claim preclusion. The doctrine of claim preclusion makes a valid, final judgment conclusive on the parties and their privies, and bars further litigation of all matters that were or should have been adjudicated in the action. This is so even though the claimant is prepared in a second action to present different evidence or legal theories to support his claim, or seeks different remedies. The doctrine is a ramification of the policy considerations that underlie the rule against splitting a cause of action, and is based on the idea that the party to be precluded has had the incentive and opportunity to litigate the matter fully in the first lawsuit. As such, it applies only where both actions were based on the same claim.
>
> A tort action is not based on the same underlying claim as an action for divorce. The purpose of a tort action is to redress a legal wrong in damages; that of a divorce action is to sever the marital relationship between the parties, and, where appropriate, to fix the parties' respective rights and obligations with regard to alimony and support, and to divide the marital estate. Although a judge in awarding alimony and dividing marital property must consider, among other things, the conduct of the parties during the marriage, the purposes for which these awards are made do not include compensating a party in damages for injuries suffered. The purpose of an award of alimony is to provide economic support to a dependent spouse; that of the division of marital property is to recognize and equitably recompense the parties' respective contributions to the marital partnership. The plaintiff could not have recovered damages for the tort in the divorce action, as the Probate Court does not have jurisdiction to hear tort actions and award damages.* The policy considerations commonly advanced to justify the doctrine of claim preclusion are not implicated in the circumstances of this case. Maintenance of the tort

---

* *Eds.' Note:* Claim preclusion does not apply where the "plaintiff was unable to rely on a certain theory of the case or to seek a certain remedy or form of relief in the first action because of the limitations on the subject matter jurisdiction of the courts or restrictions on their authority to entertain multiple theories or demands for multiple remedies or forms of relief in a single action, and the plaintiff desires in the second action to rely on that theory or to seek that remedy or form of relief." *See Restatement (Second) of Judgments* § 26(1)(c).

claim will not subject the defendant and the courts to the type of piece-meal litigation that the doctrine of claim preclusion seeks to prevent. As such, nothing in the doctrine or in the policy considerations underlying it warrants its application in the circumstances of this case.

2. Issue preclusion. To defend successfully on the ground of issue preclusion, the defendant must establish that the issue of fact sought to be foreclosed actually was litigated and determined in a prior action between the parties or their privies, and that the determination was essential to the decision in the prior action. Because a judge in awarding alimony and dividing marital property must consider a number of factors, and the judge who presided over the Heacocks' divorce action did not make any findings of fact to support his judgment, we cannot say that the judge necessarily resolved any issue relating to the defendant's assault of the plaintiff. Accordingly, the doctrine of issue preclusion does not apply.

402 Mass. at 23-25.

The same result followed when Husband brought a defamation claim against Ex-Wife, the underlying facts of which had been part of the divorce proceedings and considered by the judge in the award of funds to Husband. *Kelso v. Kelso*, 15 N.E.3d 767 (Mass. App. Ct. 2014). And the Supreme Court of Connecticut agreed in *Delahunty v. Massachusetts Mutual Life Ins. Co.*, 236 Conn. 582, 674 A.2d 1290 (1996), where it refused to preclude a wife from bringing a postdivorce tort suit against her former husband for fraudulently converting the proceeds of her life insurance policy.

Had these decisions gone the other way, a divorce decree would in effect immunize the alleged tortfeasor from any litigation arising from acts committed during the marriage, notwithstanding the inability to seek specific recovery in the divorce proceeding.

MORE TO PONDER

1. *The Single Injury/Single Recovery Rule.* What happens if a plaintiff who has recovered in a lawsuit from an asbestos manufacturer after proving that his workplace exposure caused his asbestosis (a chronic inflammatory lung condition) later develops mesothelioma, a usually fatal malignant lung cancer also caused by the exposure? Can he file *a second suit* seeking damages for the far more serious ailment?

Under traditional claim preclusion principles, the answer is no. As the Fifth Circuit Court of Appeals explained:

> Once injury results there is but a single tort and not a series of separate torts, one for each resultant harm. The cause of action thus created is for all the damage caused by the single legal wrong, and a plaintiff may not split this cause of action by seeking damages for some of his injuries in one suit and for later-developing injuries in another. The cause of action inheres in the causative aspects of a breach of a legal duty, the wrongful act itself, and not in the various forms of harm

which result therefrom. He does not have a discrete cause of action for each harm.

Plaintiff has but one cause of action for all the damages caused by the defendants' legal wrong; the diseases that have developed *and will in probability develop* are included within this cause of action, for they are but part of the sequence of harms resulting from the alleged breach of legal duty. Plaintiff could not split his cause of action and recover damages for asbestosis, then later sue for damages caused by such other pulmonary disease as might develop, then still later sue for cancer should cancer appear. His claim includes, without limitation, all damages for future pain and suffering, inability to work in the future, reduced life expectancy, future medical expenses, and future disabilities and diseases that will probably develop from present injuries.

Gideon v. Johns-Manville Sales Corp., 761 F.2d 1129, 1136-1137 (5th Cir. 1985) (emphasis added). As a consequence, a plaintiff in this situation must present expert testimony that there is a reasonable medical probability of his developing and dying from cancer induced by the inhalation of asbestos fibers, and seek appropriate recovery for all present *and potential injuries. Id.* at 1138. *See also Restatement (Second) of Judgments* § 25 comment c.

Significantly, a few decisions have been willing to permit a later suit for a latent disease that had not developed at the time of the first trial. *See, e.g., Hagerty v. L & L Marine Services, Inc.*, 788 F.2d 315, 320-321 (5th Cir. 1986): "At least in the toxic chemical or asbestos cases, the disease of cancer should be treated as a separate cause of action for all purposes. There should be no cause of action or beginning of the running of limitations until the diagnosis of the disease. Nor should damages for that disease be recoverable unless and until that time. A prior but distinct disease, though the tortfeasor may have paid reparations, should not affect the cause of action and damages for the subsequent disease."

Which view best balances the interests of efficiency and just compensation?

2. In *Whole Woman's Health v. Hellerstedt*, 136 S. Ct. 2292 (2016), the Court waded into the "same claim" issue in the context of a challenge to abortion restrictions imposed by Texas requiring providers to have admitting privileges at a local hospital and to conform to the standards for ambulatory surgical centers. Justice Breyer's opinion allows the plaintiffs' *post*-enforcement challenge to the statute *as applied to two specific clinics* to proceed notwithstanding that they had previously litigated and lost a *pre*-enforcement *facial* challenge to its constitutionality. Breyer emphasizes that the second case was based on factual developments and promulgation of regulations that had occurred *since* the statute came into force ("changed circumstances"), and could not be fully anticipated in the first action.

Justice Breyer thus views the two cases as arising from different "transactions"—one the enactment of the statute, and the second its enforcement. For Justice Alito in dissent, these two are part of the very "same transaction" and set of operative facts, and plaintiffs thus improperly "split their claim," foreclosing the second suit. Which view is closer to *Car Carriers* and the Restatement (Second) of Judgments?

Is this situation analogous to the asbestosis cases discussed above, where the first suit is for injuries resulting from the chronic inflammatory lung condition, and the subsequent action may proceed in some courts for the deadly cancer that follows later?

One commentator argues the transactional approach is not a good fit in constitutional challenges like *Hellerstedt*:

> The genius of the transactional approach is that in most civil litigation, the facts that a plaintiff must prove to prevail on her claim form part of a larger factual narrative involving real-world interactions between the plaintiff and the defendant. Challenges to statutes are different. For one thing, not all constitutional challenges require the plaintiff to prove facts in order to prevail; many constitutional doctrines simply ask a court to use its tools of statutory interpretation to determine whether a statute is valid. In such cases, any "transaction" will have little to do with the substance of the plaintiff's challenge, because a transaction is a grouping of facts, and facts are not relevant to the merits of such challenges.
>
> Moreover, even when a plaintiff must prove facts to prevail on a constitutional challenge, those facts usually pertain to the characteristics of the challenged statute rather than to interactions between the plaintiff and the defendant government entity. For example, some constitutional doctrines require proof of a statute's effects; others require proof of the legislature's motive in enacting the statute; and still others require proof of the law's relationship to its aims. Thus, any real-world transaction between the plaintiff and the government defendant will poorly approximate the substantive relatedness of whatever constitutional claims that "arise" out of that transaction.

Riley T. Keenan, *Identity Crisis: Claim Preclusion in Constitutional Challenges to Statutes*, 20 U. Pa. J. Const. L. 371, 390 (2017).

2. What Constitutes a "Final Valid Judgment on the Merits"?

Restatement (Second) of Judgments
§ 20. Judgment for Defendant—Exceptions to the General Rule of Bar

(1) A personal judgment for the defendant, although valid and final, does not bar another action by the plaintiff on the same claim:

(a) When the judgment is one of dismissal for lack of jurisdiction, for improper venue, or for nonjoinder or misjoinder of parties; . . .

ILLUSTRATION

1. A brings an action against B for personal injuries, and the action is dismissed for improper venue on the ground that the judicial district in which suit was brought was not the district of defendant's residence as required by law. Although A is not barred from maintaining an action on the claim in another district, the rules of issue preclusion are applicable to the determination that venue was improper in the initial action.

2. A brings an action against B for personal injuries in a federal court, basing jurisdiction on diversity of citizenship. The action is dismissed on the ground that the alleged diversity does not in fact exist. A is not barred from bringing another action on the same claim in a court of competent jurisdiction.

* * *

Note that the *Restatement* does not use the phrase judgment "on the merits," but instead excludes from the operation of claim preclusion dismissals on jurisdictional or misjoinder grounds, in which instance the case can be refiled in an appropriate court with proper jurisdiction, or with the proper parties. Although the phrase connotes a decision on the substantive validity of the plaintiff's claim (such as summary judgment) rather than on a procedural ground (such as improper venue), it has not always been so interpreted. Fed. R. Civ. P. 41(b), for example, presumptively treats dismissals for failure of the plaintiff to prosecute the case or to comply with civil procedure rules as "an adjudication on the merits," even though such dismissals are obviously not directed at the "validity" of the claim. *See* Jack H. Friedenthal, Mary Kay Kane, and Arthur R. Miller, *Civil Procedure* § 14.7, at 646-648 (5th ed. 2015). *See generally* Bradley Scott Shannon, *Dismissing Federal Rule of Civil Procedure 41,* 52 U. Louisville L. Rev. 265 (2014); Bradley Scott Shannon, *Action Is an Action Is an Action Is an Action,* 77 Wash. L. Rev. 65 (2002).

Semtek International, Inc. v. Lockheed Martin Corp., 531 U.S. 497 (2001) (discussed in Chapter 9), dealt with the claim-preclusive effect of a dismissal on statute of limitations grounds. The California federal district court characterized its dismissal as "on the merits and with prejudice." Consequently, when Semtek refiled the claim in a state court in Maryland (where the statute had not yet run), that court dismissed on *res judicata* grounds. Reversing, a unanimous Court concluded that even though both Fed. R. Civ. P. 41(b) and the rendering federal court would treat the prior judgment as "on the merits," that was not conclusive as to whether the second lawsuit was precluded. Rather, California's law of claim preclusion would control the question, and the matter was remanded for that determination.

3. "The Parties Are the Same or Are in Privity"

Under what circumstances may someone be precluded from litigating on the basis of a prior decision in a case in which she was *not a party*? When, in other words, may a litigant be deprived of her day in court because *someone else* had it for her? The answer lies in what the common law called "privity."

Taylor v. Sturgell
553 U.S. 880 (2008)

Justice GINSBURG delivered the opinion of the Court.

"It is a principle of general application in Anglo-American jurisprudence that one is not bound by a judgment *in personam* in a litigation in which he is not designated as a party or to which he has not been made a party by service of process." *Hansberry v. Lee*, 311 U.S. 32, 40 (1940). Several exceptions, recognized in this Court's decisions, temper this basic rule. In a class action, for example, a person not named as a party may be bound by a judgment on the merits of the action, if she was adequately represented by a party who actively participated in the litigation. In this case, we consider for the first time whether there is a "virtual representation" exception to the general rule against precluding nonparties. Adopted by a number of courts, including the courts below in the case now before us, the exception so styled is broader than any we have so far approved.

The virtual representation question we examine in this opinion arises in the following context. Petitioner Brent Taylor filed a lawsuit under the Freedom of Information Act seeking certain documents from the Federal Aviation Administration. Greg Herrick, Taylor's friend, had previously brought an unsuccessful suit seeking the same records. The two men have no legal relationship, and there is no evidence that Taylor controlled, financed, participated in, or even had notice of Herrick's earlier suit. Nevertheless, the D.C. Circuit held Taylor's suit precluded by the judgment against Herrick because, in that court's assessment, Herrick qualified as Taylor's "virtual representative."

We disapprove the doctrine of preclusion by "virtual representation," and hold, based on the record as it now stands, that the judgment against Herrick does not bar Taylor from maintaining this suit.

I

The Freedom of Information Act (FOIA) accords "any person" a right to request any records held by a federal agency. No reason need be given for a FOIA request, and unless the requested materials fall within one of the Act's enumerated exemptions, the agency must "make the records promptly available" to the requester. If an agency refuses to furnish the requested records, the requester may file suit in federal court and obtain an injunction "order[ing] the production of any agency records improperly withheld."

The courts below held the instant FOIA suit barred by the judgment in earlier litigation seeking the same records. Because the lower courts' decisions turned on the connection between the two lawsuits, we begin with a full account of each action.

A

The first suit was filed by Greg Herrick, an antique aircraft enthusiast and the owner of an F-45 airplane, a vintage model manufactured by the Fairchild Engine and Airplane Corporation (FEAC) in the 1930's. In 1997, seeking information that would help him restore his plane to its original condition, Herrick filed a FOIA request asking the Federal Aviation Administration (FAA) for copies of any technical documents about the F-45 contained in the agency's records.

To gain a certificate authorizing the manufacture and sale of the F-45, FEAC had submitted to the FAA's predecessor, the Civil Aeronautics Authority, detailed specifications and other technical data about the plane. Hundreds of pages of documents produced by FEAC in the certification process remain in the FAA's records. The FAA denied Herrick's request, however, upon finding that the documents he sought are subject to FOIA's exemption for "trade secrets and commercial or financial information obtained from a person and privileged or confidential."

Herrick then filed suit in the U.S. District Court for the District of Wyoming. Challenging the FAA's invocation of the trade-secret exemption, Herrick placed heavy weight on a 1955 letter from FEAC to the Civil Aeronautics Authority. The letter authorized the agency to lend any documents in its files to the public "for use in making repairs or replacement parts for aircraft produced by Fairchild." This broad authorization, Herrick maintained, showed that the F-45 certification records held by the FAA could not be regarded as "secre[t]" or "confidential" within the meaning of [the exemption].

Rejecting Herrick's argument, the District Court granted summary judgment to the FAA. The 1955 letter, the court reasoned, did not deprive the certification documents of trade-secret status, for those documents were never in fact released pursuant to the letter's blanket authorization. The court also stated that even if the 1955 letter had waived trade-secret protection, Fairchild had successfully "reversed" the waiver by objecting to the FAA's release of the records to Herrick.

On appeal, the Tenth Circuit agreed with Herrick that the 1955 letter had stripped the requested documents of trade-secret protection. But the Court of Appeals upheld the District Court's alternative determination—i.e., that Fairchild had restored trade-secret status by objecting to Herrick's FOIA request. On that ground, the appeals court affirmed the entry of summary judgment for the FAA.

In so ruling, the Tenth Circuit noted that Herrick had failed to challenge two suppositions underlying the District Court's decision. First, the District Court assumed trade-secret status could be "restored" to documents that had lost protection. Second, the District Court also assumed that Fairchild had regained trade-secret status for the documents even though the company claimed that status only "after Herrick had initiated his request" for the F-45 records. The Court of Appeals expressed no opinion on the validity of these suppositions.

B

The Tenth Circuit's decision issued on July 24, 2002. Less than a month later, on August 22, petitioner Brent Taylor—a friend of Herrick's and an antique aircraft enthusiast in his own right—submitted a FOIA request seeking the same documents Herrick had unsuccessfully sued to obtain. When the FAA failed to respond, Taylor filed a complaint in the U.S. District Court for the District of Columbia. Like Herrick, Taylor argued that FEAC's 1955 letter had stripped the records of their trade-secret status. But Taylor also sought to litigate the two issues concerning recapture of protected status that Herrick had failed to raise in his appeal to the Tenth Circuit.

After Fairchild intervened as a defendant, the District Court in D.C. concluded that Taylor's suit was barred by claim preclusion; accordingly, it granted summary judgment to Fairchild and the FAA. The court acknowledged that Taylor was not a party to Herrick's suit, yet held that a nonparty may be bound by a judgment if she was "virtually represented" by a party.

The record before the District Court in Taylor's suit revealed the following facts about the relationship between Taylor and Herrick: Taylor is the president of the Antique Aircraft Association, an organization to which Herrick belongs; the two men are "close associate[s]"; Herrick asked Taylor to help restore Herrick's F-45, though they had no contract or agreement for Taylor's participation in the restoration; Taylor was represented by the lawyer who represented Herrick in the earlier litigation; and Herrick apparently gave Taylor documents that Herrick had obtained from the FAA during discovery in his suit.

Fairchild and the FAA conceded that Taylor had not participated in Herrick's suit. The D.C. District Court determined, however, that Herrick ranked as Taylor's virtual representative. Accordingly, the District Court held Taylor's suit, seeking the same documents Herrick had requested, barred by the judgment against Herrick.

The D.C. Circuit affirmed.

We granted certiorari to resolve the disagreement among the Circuits over the permissibility and scope of preclusion based on "virtual representation."

II

The preclusive effect of a federal-court judgment is determined by federal common law. *See Semtek Int'l Inc. v. Lockheed Martin Corp.*, 531 U.S. 497, 507-508 (2001). For judgments in federal-question cases—for example, Herrick's FOIA suit—federal courts participate in developing "uniform federal rule[s]" of res judicata, which this Court has ultimate authority to determine and declare. The federal common law of preclusion is, of course, subject to due process limitations.

Taylor's case presents an issue of first impression in this sense: Until now, we have never addressed the doctrine of "virtual representation" adopted (in varying forms) by several Circuits and relied upon by the courts below. Our inquiry, however, is guided by well-established precedent regarding the propriety of nonparty preclusion. We review that precedent before taking up directly the issue of virtual representation.

A

The preclusive effect of a judgment is defined by claim preclusion and issue preclusion, which are collectively referred to as "res judicata." Under the doctrine of claim preclusion, a final judgment forecloses "successive litigation of the very same claim, whether or not relitigation of the claim raises the same issues as the earlier suit." Issue preclusion, in contrast, bars "successive litigation of an issue of fact or law actually litigated and resolved in a valid court determination essential to the prior judgment," even if the issue recurs in the context of a different claim. By "preclud[ing] parties from contesting matters that they have had a full and fair opportunity to litigate," these two doctrines protect against "the expense and vexation attending multiple lawsuits, conserv[e] judicial resources, and foste[r] reliance on judicial action by minimizing the possibility of inconsistent decisions."

A person who was not a party to a suit generally has not had a "full and fair opportunity to litigate" the claims and issues settled in that suit. The application of claim and issue preclusion to nonparties thus runs up against the "deep-rooted historic tradition that everyone should have his own day in court." Indicating the strength of that tradition, we have often repeated the general rule that "one is not bound by a judgment *in personam* in a litigation in which he is not designated as a party or to which he has not been made a party by service of process." *Hansberry*, 311 U.S., at 40.

B

Though hardly in doubt, the rule against nonparty preclusion is subject to exceptions. For present purposes, the recognized exceptions can be grouped into six categories.

First, "[a] person who agrees to be bound by the determination of issues in an action between others is bound in accordance with the terms of his agreement." *Restatement (Second) of Judgments* § 40, p. 390 (1980) (hereinafter *Restatement*). For example, "if separate actions involving the same transaction are brought by different plaintiffs against the same defendant, all the parties to all the actions may agree that the question of the defendant's liability will be definitely determined, one way or the other, in a 'test case.'"

Second, nonparty preclusion may be justified based on a variety of preexisting "substantive legal relationship[s]" between the person to be bound and a party to the judgment. Qualifying relationships include, but are not limited to, preceding and succeeding owners of property, bailee and bailor, and assignee and assignor. *See* 2 Restatement §§ 43-44, 52, 55. These exceptions originated "as much from the needs of property law as from the values of preclusion by judgment."[1]

---

1. The substantive legal relationships justifying preclusion are sometimes collectively referred to as "privity." The term "privity," however, has also come to be used more broadly, as a way to express the conclusion that nonparty preclusion is appropriate on any ground. To ward off confusion, we avoid using the term "privity" in this opinion.

Third, we have confirmed that, "in certain limited circumstances," a nonparty may be bound by a judgment because she was "adequately represented by someone with the same interests who [wa]s a party" to the suit. Representative suits with preclusive effect on nonparties include properly conducted class actions, *see* Fed. Rule Civ. Proc. 23, and suits brought by trustees, guardians, and other fiduciaries.

Fourth, a nonparty is bound by a judgment if she "assume[d] control" over the litigation in which that judgment was rendered. Restatement § 39. Because such a person has had "the opportunity to present proofs and argument," he has already "had his day in court" even though he was not a formal party to the litigation. *Id.*, Comment a, p. 382.

Fifth, a party bound by a judgment may not avoid its preclusive force by relitigating through a proxy. Preclusion is thus in order when a person who did not participate in a litigation later brings suit as the designated representative of a person who was a party to the prior adjudication.

Sixth, in certain circumstances a special statutory scheme may "expressly foreclos[e] successive litigation by nonlitigants if the scheme is otherwise consistent with due process." Examples of such schemes include bankruptcy and probate proceedings. . . .

III

Reaching beyond these six established categories, some lower courts have recognized a "virtual representation" exception to the rule against nonparty preclusion.

The D.C. Circuit purported to ground its virtual representation doctrine in this Court's decisions stating that, in some circumstances, a person may be bound by a judgment if she was adequately represented by a party to the proceeding yielding that judgment. But the D.C. Circuit's definition of "adequate representation" strayed from the meaning our decisions have attributed to that term.

B

Fairchild and the FAA argue that preclusion is in order whenever "the relationship between a party and a non-party is 'close enough' to bring the second litigant within the judgment." Courts should make the "close enough" determination, they urge, through a "heavily fact-driven" and "equitable" inquiry.

We reject this argument for three reasons. First, our decisions emphasize the fundamental nature of the general rule that a litigant is not bound by a judgment to which she was not a party. Accordingly, we have endeavored to delineate discrete exceptions that apply in "limited circumstances." Respondents' amorphous balancing test is at odds with the constrained approach to nonparty preclusion our decisions advance. . . .

Our second reason for rejecting a broad doctrine of virtual representation rests on the limitations attending nonparty preclusion based on adequate representation. A party's representation of a nonparty is "adequate" for preclusion purposes only if, at a minimum: (1) the interests of the nonparty and her representative are aligned, *see Hansberry*, 311 U.S., at 43; and (2) either the party understood herself to be acting in a representative capacity or the original court took care to protect the interests of the nonparty. In addition, adequate representation sometimes requires (3) notice of the original suit to the persons alleged to have been represented.

In the class-action context, these limitations are implemented by the procedural safeguards contained in Federal Rule of Civil Procedure 23.

An expansive doctrine of virtual representation, however, would "recogniz[e], in effect, a common-law kind of class action." That is, virtual representation would authorize preclusion based on identity of interests and some kind of relationship between parties and nonparties, shorn of the procedural protections prescribed in *Hansberry* and Rule 23. These protections, grounded in due process, could be circumvented were we to approve a virtual representation doctrine that allowed courts to "create de facto class actions at will."

Third, a diffuse balancing approach to nonparty preclusion would likely create more headaches than it relieves. Most obviously, it could significantly complicate the task of district courts faced in the first instance with preclusion questions. An all-things-considered balancing approach might spark wide-ranging, time-consuming, and expensive discovery tracking factors potentially relevant under seven- or five-prong tests. And after the relevant facts are established, district judges would be called upon to evaluate them under a standard that provides no firm guidance. Preclusion doctrine, it should be recalled, is intended to reduce the burden of litigation on courts and parties. "In this area of the law," we agree, " 'crisp rules with sharp corners' are preferable to a round-about doctrine of opaque standards."

IV

For the foregoing reasons, we disapprove the theory of virtual representation on which the decision below rested. The preclusive effects of a judgment in a federal-question case decided by a federal court should instead be determined according to the established grounds for nonparty preclusion described in this opinion. *See* Part II-B, *supra*.

A

It is uncontested that four of the six grounds for non-party preclusion have no application here: There is no indication that Taylor agreed to be bound by Herrick's litigation, that Taylor and Herrick have any legal relationship, that Taylor exercised any control over Herrick's suit, or that this suit implicates any special statutory scheme limiting relitigation. Neither the FAA nor Fairchild contends otherwise.

It is equally clear that preclusion cannot be justified on the theory that Taylor was adequately represented in Herrick's suit. Nothing in the record indicates that Herrick understood himself to be suing on Taylor's behalf, that Taylor even knew of Herrick's suit, or that the Wyoming District Court took special care to protect Taylor's interests. Under our pathmarking precedent, therefore, Herrick's representation was not "adequate."

That leaves only the fifth category: preclusion because a nonparty to an earlier litigation has brought suit as a representative or agent of a party who is bound by the prior adjudication. Taylor is not Herrick's legal representative and he has not purported to sue in a representative capacity. He concedes, however, that preclusion would be appropriate if respondents could demonstrate that he is acting as Herrick's "undisclosed agent." . . .

We have never defined the showing required to establish that a nonparty to a prior adjudication has become a litigating agent for a party to the earlier case. Because the issue has not been briefed in any detail, we do not discuss the matter elaborately here. We note, however, that courts should be cautious about finding preclusion on this basis. A mere whiff of "tactical maneuvering" will not suffice; instead, principles of agency law are suggestive. They indicate that preclusion is appropriate only if the putative agent's conduct of the suit is subject to the control of the party who is bound by the prior adjudication. *See* 1 Restatement (Second) of Agency § 14, p. 60 (1957) ("A principal has the right to control the conduct of the agent with respect to matters entrusted to him.").

B

For the reasons stated, the judgment of the United States Court of Appeals for the District of Columbia Circuit is vacated, and the case is remanded for further proceedings consistent with this opinion.

YOUR TAKEAWAY

As Justice Ginsburg begins her opinion, "It is a principle of general application in Anglo-American jurisprudence that one is not bound by a judgment *in personam* in a litigation in which he is not designated as a party or to which he has not been made a party by service of process." *Taylor* underscores the presumption against non-party preclusion by allowing the prior plaintiff's friend Taylor, represented by the same attorney, to relitigate the matter, determining that the very narrow exceptions (denoted "privity" by the common law) did not apply here. *Taylor* removes "virtual representation" from the list. Remaining are six exceptions, most notably class actions and situations where there is a close *legal* relationship as between a successor property owner and his predecessor, or beneficiairy and trustee.

REVIEW QUESTIONS

The common law used the term "privity" (a label the *Taylor* Court explicitly eschews, see footnote 1) to describe a relationship between a past litigant and a current litigant such that the latter should be bound by the decision rendered in the former's prior action.

Examples of privity include the following:

- A person acquires an interest in property that has already been the subject of a lawsuit. Thus an heir who inherits land, or a successive buyer, is bound by a prior judgment regarding an easement.

- A party litigates in a representative capacity. A judgment in a suit brought by or against the trustee may, for example, bind the beneficiary in a subsequent action. *See, e.g., Cruickshank v. MAPFRE U.S.A.*, 116 N.E.3d 1233 (Mass. App. Ct. 2019) (trustee in bankruptcy was in privity with bankrupt and thus could not relitigate same factual issues which bankrupt had previously litigated and lost against the same insurance company).
- A close familial relationship exists between a party in the prior case and a litigant in the present case *whose claim is derivative of or closely aligned* with the former's. A wife was deemed bound by the outcome of her husband's prior bankruptcy proceeding, even though she was not a party to it, because the claims she asserted in the current action derived exclusively from claims asserted by her husband. *See, e.g., Eubanks v. FDIC*, 977 F.2d 166 (5th Cir. 1992).

It must be emphasized that family relationship and parallel interests are *not* in themselves sufficient to establish privity. For example, each member of a family injured in an automobile accident has an independent claim for his or her injuries that is *not* derivative of the others, and thus litigation by one family member will not foreclose actions by the others. *See, e.g., Freeman v. Lester Coggins Trucking, Inc.*, 771 F.2d 860 (5th Cir. 1985).

MORE TO PONDER

For more on privity, see Jack H. Friedenthal, Mary Kay Kane, and Arthur R. Miller, *Civil Procedure* § 14.13 (5th ed. 2015).

---

* * *

Consider the following excerpts from a pre-*Taylor v. Sturgell* decision taking on what Circuit Judge Bruce Selya describes as the "murky corner of the law" called "privity." A section on virtual representation has been deleted, as *Taylor* takes that concept off the table. Note that as a consequence of this decision, a seven-week jury trial in the district court may be repeated by a new group of plaintiffs asserting parallel claims, underscoring the tension between efficiency and fairness that lurks beneath any question of finality.

Gonzalez v. Banco Central Corp.
27 F.3d 751 (1st Cir. 1994)

SELYA, Circuit Judge:

This appeal raises tantalizing questions concerning the application of the doctrine of *res judicata* to nonparties. Because we conclude that appellants cannot lawfully be precluded from bringing their action in the circumstances at bar, we reverse the district court's order of dismissal and remand for further proceedings.

I. BACKGROUND

In the 1970s, a consortium of real estate developers sold subdivided lots of undeveloped land to approximately 3,000 purchasers, most of whom resided in Puerto Rico. Contrary to the promoters' glowing representations, the real estate proved to be Florida swampland, unsuitable for development.

In 1982, a gaggle of duped purchasers (whom we shall call "the Rodriguez plaintiffs") commenced a civil action in the United States District Court for the District of Puerto Rico. They sued the sellers, the banks that financed the project, and several related individuals. The Rodriguez plaintiffs alleged violations of the Interstate Land Sales Full Disclosure Act ("ILSFDA"), 15 U.S.C. § 1703, the Securities Exchange Act of 1934, 15 U.S.C. § 78j, Rule 10b-5 thereunder, 17 C.F.R. § 240.10b-5, and the Racketeering Influenced and Corrupt Organizations Act ("RICO"), 18 U.S.C. §§ 1961-1964.

After several years of discovery and numerous amendments to the pleadings, the Rodriguez plaintiffs, 152 strong, sought to convert their suit to a class action. In April of 1987, the district court refused either to certify a class or to permit additional plaintiffs to intervene. Almost immediately thereafter, several prospective plaintiffs who had tried in vain to join the Rodriguez litigation initiated the instant action. The new coalition of claimants (whom we shall call "the Gonzalez plaintiffs") were represented by the same lawyers who represented the Rodriguez plaintiffs. They sued the same defendants and their complaint mimicked a proposed amended complaint on file (but never allowed) in the Rodriguez litigation.

Despite strong evidence of skullduggery, the Rodriguez plaintiffs frittered away much of their case through a series of pretrial blunders. The Rodriguez plaintiffs ultimately lost what remained of their case after a seven-week jury trial when Judge Fuste directed verdicts for the defendants on the only surviving claims and this court upheld his ruling on appeal.

Following the interment of the Rodriguez litigation, renewed attention focused on the Gonzalez litigation. The Gonzalez plaintiffs were pressing certain claims that replicated those pressed and lost by the Rodriguez plaintiffs. [The case was dismissed in its entirety on grounds of *res judicata*.] The Gonzalez plaintiffs appeal.

II. ANALYSIS

Although appellants were not parties to the earlier litigation, the court below applied *res judicata* in bar of their claims under a theory of privity. The accepted formulation of *res judicata* for federal court use teaches that "a final judgment on the merits of an action precludes the parties or their privies from relitigating issues that were or could have been raised in that action." Accordingly, the elements of *res judicata* are (1) a final judgment on the merits in an earlier suit, (2) sufficient identicality between the causes of action asserted in the earlier and later suits, and (3) sufficient identicality between the parties in the two suits.

[The court found the first two prongs were met.]

IDENTICALITY OF PARTIES

Under federal law, *res judicata* can sometimes operate to bar the maintenance of an action by persons who, technically, were not parties to the initial action (to which preclusive effect is attributed). Nonetheless, we appreciate that this is a murky corner of the law and caution the district courts to tread gingerly in applying *res judicata* to nonparties.

PRIVITY

The most familiar mechanism for extending *res judicata* to nonparties without savaging important constitutional rights is the concept of privity—a concept that furnishes a serviceable framework for an exception to the rule that *res judicata* only bars relitigation of claims by persons who were parties to the original litigation. Although privity can be elusive, this case does not require us to build four walls around it. Here, the *res judicata* defense is based not on some exotic doctrinal refinement but on commonly accepted principles of how privity operates to bring about nonparty preclusion. The theory underlying defendants' iteration of the defense is that privity exists (and, therefore, nonparty preclusion potentially obtains) if a nonparty either substantially controlled a party's involvement in the initial litigation or, conversely, permitted a party to the initial litigation to function as his de facto representative. We accept defendants' theoretical premise, but, after close perscrutation of the record as a whole, we conclude that neither stripe of privity exists here.

SUBSTANTIAL CONTROL

The doctrine of *res judicata* rests upon the bedrock principle that, for claim preclusion to apply, a litigant first must have had a full and fair opportunity to litigate his claim. If a nonparty either participated vicariously in the original litigation by exercising control over a named party or had the opportunity to exert such control, then the nonparty effectively enjoyed his day in court, and it is appropriate to impute to him the legal attributes of party status for purposes of claim preclusion.

Substantial control means what the phrase implies; it connotes the availability of a significant degree of effective control in the prosecution or defense of the case—what one might term, in the vernacular, the power—whether exercised or not—to call the shots.

As the proverb suggests, a picture is sometimes worth a thousand words. Along these lines, we suspect that the concept of substantial control can be illustrated better by examples than by linguistic constructs. For instance, substantial control has been found in the case of a liability insurer that assumes the insured's defense, *see, e.g., Iacaponi v. New Amsterdam Cas. Co.*, 379 F.2d 311, 312

(3d Cir. 1967), *cert. denied*, 389 U.S. 1054 (1968), an indemnitor who partici-pates in defending an action brought against the indemnitee, *see, e.g., Bros., Inc. v. W.E. Grace Mfg. Co.*, 261 F.2d 428, 430-31 (5th Cir. 1958), and the owner of a close corporation who assumes control of litigation brought against the firm, *see, e.g., Kreager v. General Elec. Co.*, 497 F.2d 468, 471-72 (2d Cir.), *cert. denied*, 419 U.S. 1041 (1974). Conversely, courts have refused to find substantial con-trol merely because a nonparty retained the attorney who represented a party to the earlier action, *see Freeman v. Lester Coggins Trucking, Inc.*, 771 F.2d 860, 864 (5th Cir. 1985); *Ramey v. Rockefeller*, 348 F. Supp. 780, 785 (E.D.N.Y. 1972), or because the nonparty assisted in financing the earlier action, *see Rumford Chem.*, 215 U.S. at 159-60; *General Foods Corp. v. Massachusetts Dep't of Pub. Health*, 648 F.2d 784, 787-88 (1st Cir. 1981), or because the nonparty testified as a witness in the earlier action, *see Benson & Ford, Inc. v. Wanda Petroleum Co.*, 833 F.2d 1172, 1174-75 (5th Cir. 1987); *Ponderosa Devel. Corp. v. Bjordahl*, 787 F.2d 533, 536-37 (10th Cir. 1986), or because the nonparty procured witnesses or evidence, *see Carl Zeiss Stiftung v. V.E.B. Carl Zeiss, Jena*, 293 F. Supp. 892, 921 (S.D.N.Y. 1968), *modified*, 433 F.2d 686 (2d Cir. 1970), *cert. denied*, 403 U.S. 905 (1971), or because the nonparty furnished his attorney's assistance, *see Cofax Corp. v. Minn. Mining & Mfg. Co.*, 79 F. Supp. 842, 844 (S.D.N.Y. 1947).

In the last analysis, there is no bright-line test for gauging substantial control. The inquiry must be case-specific, and fact patterns are almost endlessly variable. The critical judgment cannot be based on isolated facts. Consequently, an inquir-ing court must consider the totality of the circumstances to determine whether they justify a reasonable inference of a nonparty's potential or actual involvement as a decisionmaker in the earlier litigation. The nonparty's participation may be overt or covert, and the evidence of it may be direct or circumstantial—so long as the evidence as a whole shows that the nonparty possessed effective control over a party's conduct of the earlier litigation as measured from a practical, as opposed to a purely theoretical, standpoint. The burden of persuasion ultimately rests with him who asserts that control (or the right to exercise it) existed to such a degree as would warrant invoking nonparty preclusion.

Applying this standard, there is no principled way in which it can be said that the *Gonzalez* plaintiffs substantially controlled the *Rodriguez* plaintiffs in regard to the original litigation. The only facts to which the district court alluded in ruling that nonparty preclusion loomed involve the similarity of the complaints at one point in time, the parties' common legal representation, and the planned use of some discovered materials in both litigations. In our view, these facts do not begin to show that the *Gonzalez* plaintiffs exercised any meaningful degree of control over the course of the *Rodriguez* litigation. Nor did they have either the right or the opportunity to demand such control.

III. CONCLUSION

We need go no further. Because the appellants were neither parties to the initial action nor in privity with the plaintiffs therein, the district court erred in dismissing their suit under principles of *res judicata*. Reversed and remanded for further proceedings. Costs to appellants.

REVIEW QUESTIONS

Given what you now know about the constitutional limitations on preclusion against nonparties, are you surprised by the following excerpt from a Supreme Court decision by Justice Anthony Kennedy in which white firefighters in New Haven successfully challenged the City's refusal to promote them from the civil service eligible list because of concerns regarding the discriminatory impact and validity of the tests?

> If, after it certifies the test results, the City faces a disparate-impact suit [from minority firefighters *who were not party to the litigation*], then in light of our holding today it should be clear that the City would avoid disparate-impact liability based on the strong basis in evidence that, had it not certified the results, it would have been subject to disparate-treatment liability.

Ricci v. DeStefano, 557 U.S. 557, 593 (2009).

An African-American firefighter who was neither a party in *Ricci*, nor represented by either party—the white plaintiffs or the City—filed his own discrimination case against the City, challenging the weighting of the test results which favored the written over the oral component, an issue not litigated in the earlier action. His case was dismissed on the basis of Justice Kennedy's paragraph in the preceding case, even though the district court judge admitted it deprived the plaintiff of his day in court. The Court of Appeals reversed. *Briscoe v. City of New Haven*, 654 F.3d 200 (2d Cir. 2011), *cert. denied*, 132 S. Ct. 2741 (2012).

As Justice Robert Jackson famously said, the Supreme Court is not final because it is infallible, it is infallible because it is final. Richard F. Lazarus, *The (Non) Finality of Supreme Court Opinions*, 128 Harv. L. Rev. 540 (2014). On the preclusion issue in *Ricci*, *see* Mark S. Brodin, Ricci v. DeStefano: *The* New Haven Firefighters *Case and the Triumph of White Privilege*, 20 S. Cal. Rev. L. Soc. Just. 161 (2011).

PRACTICE EXERCISE NO. 39:
APPLYING CLAIM PRECLUSION DOCTRINE IN *CARPENTER*

Assume that Twyla Burrell, the owner of the Jeep CJ-7, was in the vehicle with Randall and Charlie at the time of the accident. Shortly afterward, Twyla filed an action against Randall in Small Claims Court for property damage to the jeep, and recovered a judgment of $2,000, the maximum allowed in that court. Three months thereafter, Twyla hired your law firm. You promptly filed an action against Randall Dee in Superior Court seeking substantial damages for personal injuries she allegedly suffered as a result of the accident.

Randall's attorney has moved for a judgment on the pleadings, asserting claim preclusion.

The core principles of the doctrine are well established in this jurisdiction. But your research has yielded no case precedent for a situation like yours. Unfortunately, you found the following illustration in the *Restatement*:

> In an automobile collision, A is injured and his car damaged as a result of the negligence of B. Instead of suing in a court of general jurisdiction of the state, A brings his action for the damage to his car in a justice's court, which has jurisdiction in actions for damage to property but has no jurisdiction in actions for injury to the person. Judgment is rendered for A for the damage to the car. A cannot thereafter maintain an action against B to recover for the injury to his person arising out of the same collision.

Restatement (Second) of Judgments § 24, illustration 14. Courts in this state are inclined to follow the *Restatement*. Prepare to explain to the judge why she should find an exception on these facts and permit Twyla's suit to go forward. You are unlikely to prevail unless you can provide compelling policy reasons to support your argument. (Hint: Take a look at *Isaac v. Truck Service, Inc.*, 253 Conn. 416 (2000).)

C. ISSUE PRECLUSION (COLLATERAL ESTOPPEL)

1. Defined

If they were tools, claim preclusion might be analogized to a hammer and issue preclusion to a scalpel. As the analogy implies, the latter is a more targeted form of preclusion that forecloses from re-litigation issues that have been determined in a previous litigation. In contrast to claim preclusion, which forecloses further litigation of all matters that *were or should have been adjudicated* in the earlier action, issue preclusion operates to foreclose only those issues that *were actually litigated and resolved* in the prior action. Recall the story of Sally and Joe's contract. If in the first case, the issue of Joe's capacity to enter into the contract was asserted as a defense and determined by the outcome, then Joe is foreclosed from relitigating that specific issue in the subsequent litigation. There may be other issues that Joe can raise, but not the issue of his capacity.

The Restatement (Second) of Judgments § 27 (1982) defines the contours of collateral estoppel as follows:

> When an issue of fact or law is actually litigated and determined by a valid and final judgment, and the determination is essential to the judgment, the determination is conclusive in a subsequent action between the parties, whether on the same or a different claim.

Delineating the issue that is foreclosed by the prior judgment may prove difficult in a particular case. In making this determination, the court is balancing two important interests: everyone's right to a day in court on the one hand, and on the other, the system's need to prevent re-litigation of essentially the same matter in the interest of efficiency. Comment c explains:

> When there is a lack of total identity between the particular matter presented in the second action and that presented in the first, there are several factors that should be considered in deciding whether for purposes of the rule of this Section the "issue" in the two proceedings is the same, for example: Is there a substantial overlap between the evidence or argument to be advanced in the second proceeding and that advanced in the first? Does the new evidence or argument involve application of the same rule of law as that involved in the prior proceeding? Could pretrial preparation and discovery relating to the matter presented in the first action reasonably be expected to have embraced the matter sought to be presented in the second? How closely related are the claims involved in the two proceedings?

Restatement (Second) of Judgments § 27 (1982).

Suppose a person is arrested for possession of an unlawful firearm. At his criminal trial, he moves to suppress the evidence arguing that the police officers violated his Fourth Amendment right when they searched his car without consent. The judge denies the motion and he is convicted. He has also filed a civil suit against the police officers under § 1983 claiming damages for the unlawful search. The officers will argue that the issue of whether the search was unlawful was already decided in the criminal proceedings when the judge refused to suppress the evidence, and the plaintiff is not entitled to a second bite at the apple on that issue. *See, e.g., Allen v. McCurry*, 449 U.S. 90 (1980) [later in this chapter]; *Ayers v. City of Richmond*, 895 F.2d 1267, 1269 (9th Cir. 1990).

How does issue preclusion operate where the prior decision comes (as it typically does in a jury trial) in the form of a general verdict, opaque as to the underlying facts determined? Our next case is a "textbook example."

2. In Operation

David P. Hoult v. Jennifer Hoult
157 F.3d 29 (1st Cir. 1998)

BOUDIN, Circuit Judge:

In July 1988, when she was 27 years old, Jennifer Hoult brought suit in the district court against her father, David Hoult, alleging assault and battery, intentional infliction of emotional distress, and breach of fiduciary duty. To support these claims, she alleged that her father had sexually abused, raped and threatened her from the time that she was about four years old until she was about sixteen years old.

The statute of limitations presented an obvious obstacle. Jennifer Hoult sought to overcome it by showing that the alleged abuse caused her to repress her memory of the events until she began to recapture those memories during therapy sessions in October 1985. *See* M.G.L. 260 § 4C. The claim of repressed memory was supported at trial by testimony from a psychiatrist, Dr. Renee Brandt [sic. Brant], who appeared as an expert witness on repression caused by traumatic abuse.

In June 1993, the district court conducted an eight day jury trial in which Jennifer Hoult testified at length, giving detailed descriptions of extensive alleged abuse by her father; in addition to other forms of abuse, she testified to five specific episodes of rape. Supporting testimony was provided by her former therapist and by Dr. [Brant]. In defense, David Hoult testified on his own behalf, flatly denying the allegations, but presented no other witnesses.

On July 1, 1993, the jury returned a verdict in favor of Jennifer Hoult and ordered damages in the amount of $500,000. This verdict was preceded by a separate finding by the jury rejecting the statute of limitations defense; in effect the jury found that Jennifer Hoult had repressed memory of the abuse until it was rediscovered within the limitations period. David Hoult appealed both from the judgment against him and the denial of a motion for a new trial, but both appeals were ultimately dismissed for lack of prosecution.

Later, Jennifer Hoult wrote letters to several professional associations in which she repeated the charge that her father had raped her. David Hoult then brought the present action in the district court against Jennifer Hoult, claiming that her charge of rape against him was defamatory. Jennifer Hoult moved to dismiss on the ground that the jury verdict in her earlier assault action had determined that David Hoult had raped her and that David Hoult was barred by collateral estoppel from relitigating this finding.

Initially, the district court denied the motion to dismiss, saying that the evidence adduced at the trial could have led the jury to impose liability because David Hoult had sexually abused Jennifer Hoult "in ways that did not amount to rape" or could even have done so on the basis of Jennifer Hoult's testimony that David Hoult had "threatened her with murder, chased her around the house with a knife, and fondled her in a sexual manner, among other incidents of violence and assault."

By motion for reconsideration, Jennifer Hoult argued that the jury's finding of repression, in rejecting the statute of limitations defense, was necessarily based on Dr. [Brant's] expert opinion that the repression required "repeated acts" of sexual abuse; and the only repeated acts of sexual abuse (Jennifer Hoult argued) were her descriptions of five separate incidents of rape. Accepting this argument, the district court allowed Jennifer Hoult's motion to dismiss the action, and David Hoult now appeals.

The governing legal doctrine of collateral estoppel, which we briefly summarize, is largely undisputed; the problem is one of applying the doctrine to this case. Subject to certain exceptions, the general rule on "issue preclusion" is as follows: When an issue of fact or law is actually litigated and determined by a valid and final judgment, and the determination is essential to the judgment, the determination is conclusive in a subsequent action between the parties, whether on the same or a different claim. *Restatement (Second) of Judgments* § 27 (1982). Neither side disputes that this formulation sets forth the governing law.

David Hoult says—as did the district judge in his original order refusing to dismiss—that there is no proof that the jury ever determined that David Hoult had committed the alleged rapes. The burden is upon Jennifer Hoult, as the party invoking collateral estoppel, to establish that the jury did so determine in the original action.

Admittedly, the jury made no explicit finding that rapes occurred. Nevertheless, "an issue may be 'actually' decided [for collateral estoppel purposes] even if it is not explicitly decided, for it may have constituted, logically or practically, a necessary component of the decision reached." The court in the second case may examine the full record in the earlier one to decide "whether a rational jury could have grounded its verdict upon an issue other than that which the [moving party] seeks to foreclose from consideration."

Confronted with a general verdict in the earlier case, courts commonly ask whether a finding was "necessary" to the judgment, and answer the question by looking primarily to the instructions and the result. Here, the rape charges were the centerpiece of Jennifer Hoult's case. In the opening statement, her counsel said that Jennifer Hoult would have to live with her "memories of the rape, torture, and sexual abuse" by her father and that her father had had "intercourse" with her. Defense counsel answered that Jennifer Hoult could not have been "raped by her father some 3,000 times," as she had once claimed, and he promised evidence to show the unlikelihood that numerous rapes could have occurred without detection by other family members. Jennifer Hoult then testified specifically to five incidents of rape and said that there were other like rapes whose details she could not recollect.

A further consideration, stressed by the district court, is Dr. [Brant's] testimony and the jury's finding on the statute of limitations. Dr. [Brant] testified that repeated sexual abuse can cause repression of memory of the abuse and that Jennifer Hoult's symptoms "correlated" with such a syndrome. In finding that the statute of limitations had run, the only plausible explanation is that the jury accepted Jennifer Hoult's testimony as to the rapes, which were the salient and specific acts of repeated abuse to which she testified. In our view the jury necessarily decided that rapes had occurred.

The present law suit seeks, in the guise of a defamation action, to retry the central issue in the prior assault case between the same litigants. That issue—ultimately a credibility contest between the two opposing parties—was resolved by the jury at the first trial. Whether the jury was right or wrong, its decision about what happened is not now open to relitigation.

REVIEW QUESTIONS

1. How did Judge Boudin reconstruct what the jury had actually decided in reaching their general verdict in the first case? Note that it was accompanied by a separate jury finding rejecting David Hoult's statute of limitations defense. What role did this play in Judge Boudin's analysis of the preclusion question?

2. ***Alternative Defenses.*** The difficulty of determining what issues were necessarily resolved by a prior general verdict may be exacerbated where the defendant had raised alternative defenses. Take the example of Sally suing Joe for breach of the multi-year contract to clear her land every June. In the action for breach in Year 3, assume that Joe defended on two grounds: that he was not of sufficient age to enter a valid contract, *and*, in any event, that there was no breach. Sally offered evidence contradicting both defenses. A general verdict for Sally would mean that the jury must have resolved *all* the issues against Joe, and thus his legal capacity defense would be foreclosed if Joe tried to raise it again in the action for breach in Year 7.

But what if the verdict in the first case had been *in favor of Joe*? Since the jury could have reached a defendant's verdict by crediting *either* of his defenses, and thus may have found for Joe solely because there was no breach in Year 3, Joe should not be able to foreclose Sally from relitigating the issue of his legal capacity if he raises the defense again in the Year 7 case. As that issue was not clearly resolved in the first case, it is open to be litigated in the second case.

3. Fed. R. Civ. P. 49 authorizes the discretionary use of special verdicts, as well as interrogatories accompanying a general verdict (a variation of which was used in *Hoult v. Hoult*). What advantages do these alternatives to the general verdict provide insofar as the operation of issue preclusion is concerned? *See* Mark S. Brodin, *Accuracy, Efficiency, and Accountability in the Litigation Process—The Case for the Fact Verdict*, 59 U. Cin. L. Rev. 15 (1990).

4. ***Epilogue to*** **Hoult** ***Litigation.*** Winning a verdict of $500,000 and *collecting it* are two very different things. Shortly after the verdict, Jennifer sought and obtained a preliminary injunction to prevent her father (formerly a professor at MIT) from transferring his assets to protect them from the judgment in violation of the Massachusetts fraudulent conveyance statute (see the Case Files in the *Carpenter* case). After years of further proceedings in both district court and bankruptcy court, the First Circuit Court of Appeals in 2004 affirmed orders requiring David to deposit his income and pension benefits into a designated bank account to be used, minus modest living expenses, to pay toward the judgment. 373 F.3d 47 (1st Cir. 2004).

According to her Facebook page, Jennifer Hoult holds bachelor's degrees from both the Manhattan School of Music and Barnard College, and is a magna cum laude graduate of NYU School of Law. As a former prosecutor and children's law guardian, she has litigated hundreds of cases. She is now a public interest attorney who is licensed to practice in California, New Jersey, New York, and Massachusetts. *See also* Jennifer Hoult, J.D., *The Evidentiary Admissibility of Parental Alienation Syndrome: Science, Law, and Policy*, 26 Child. Legal Rts. J. 1 (2006).

Hoult **lists the requirements for issue preclusion as follows:**

- When an *issue of fact or law is actually litigated and determined,*
- by a *valid final judgment,*
- and the determination is *essential to the judgment,*
- then the determination is *conclusive on the identical issue in a subsequent action between the parties.*

Issue preclusion operates only where Case 1 and Case 2 share a common issue—the sexual assault in both *Jennifer v. David Hoult* and *David v. Jennifer Hoult*; the attorney-client relationship in both litigations in *Jarosz v. Palmer*, our next case; the misrepresentations in the proxy statement in the two litigations in *Parklane Hosiery*, the case that follows that. The diagram below may help you envision such situations, where Case 2 represents *a different claim* than Case 1 (and thus is not precluded by *res judicata*), but they share *a common issue* [D].

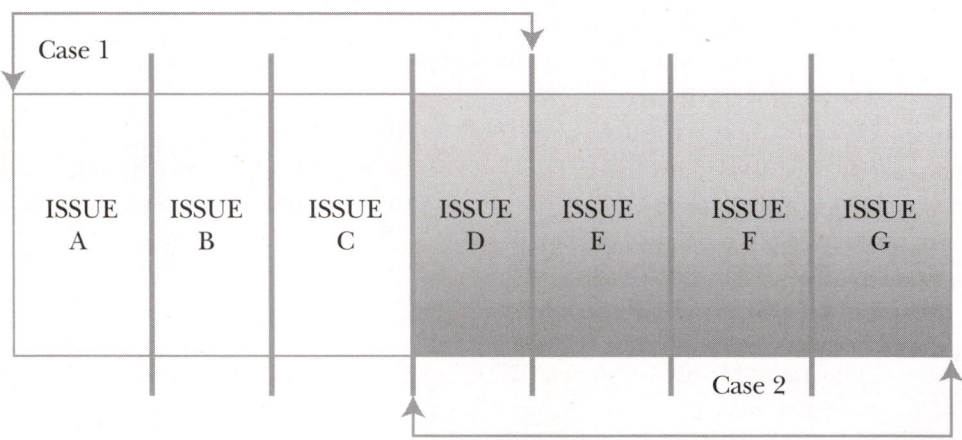

3. "Essential to the Judgment"

Jarosz v. Palmer
436 Mass. 526 (2002)

COWIN, J.:

The plaintiff, James Jarosz, appeals from an order of the Superior Court dismissing his claims against the defendants on the basis of issue preclusion. The plaintiff's claims against attorney Stephen L. Palmer and his law firm Warner & Stackpole LLP (Palmer) are premised on the contention that Palmer represented Jarosz individually in his acquisition of a corporation. A Superior Court judge granted the defendants' motion for judgment on the pleadings after concluding that Jarosz was precluded from arguing that Palmer had represented him individually because, in a separate case brought by Jarosz against his former business partners, another judge of the Superior Court had concluded that Palmer and Jarosz did not have an attorney-client relationship. We reverse the Superior Court's order and remand the case for further proceedings.

1. *Factual background and procedural history.* We summarize the relevant facts from the Superior Court's order on the defendants' motion for judgment on the pleadings. Jarosz and three business partners together agreed to acquire a company known as Union Products. Jarosz hired Palmer, an attorney, to assist in the acquisition and financing of the business. Jarosz and his partners successfully acquired the business and each became twenty-five per cent owners. The relationship between Jarosz and his partners eventually soured, and the partners terminated Jarosz from his position as employee and officer of Union Products. As a result, Jarosz filed suit against both the partners and the Union Products corporation, alleging wrongful termination and breach of fiduciary duty (the *Union Products* case). Palmer represented the three partners and the corporation in this suit.

Jarosz moved to disqualify Palmer from serving as the partners' attorney in the Union Products case on the basis that Palmer had represented Jarosz individually in his acquisition of Union Products, and therefore his continued representation of the partners and the corporation created a conflict of interest. The judge's order on Jarosz's disqualification motion in the Union Products case stated that, for Jarosz to succeed on his motion, "he must meet the threshold burden of establishing that an attorney-client relationship existed between himself and Palmer during the acquisition dealings." Having found that Jarosz failed to meet this burden, the judge denied the motion.

After the commencement of the *Union Products* case, Jarosz filed this suit against Palmer, alleging breach of contract, breach of fiduciary duty, legal malpractice, and violations of G.L. c. 93A. Palmer defended the suit on the ground, inter alia, that he had not represented Jarosz individually. Palmer filed a motion for judgment on the pleadings, claiming that the judge's ruling on Jarosz's motion for disqualification in the Union Products case precluded Jarosz from relitigating the issue whether Palmer had represented Jarosz individually. The judge in the instant case allowed the motion, finding that the three requirements for issue preclusion were met: the issue had been actually litigated, was the subject of a valid and final judgment, and was essential to the judge's decision. Jarosz filed a timely notice of appeal, claiming that the issue had not been actually litigated, was not the subject of a final judgment, and was not essential to the decision.

We conclude that issue preclusion's requirement that the issue decided be "essential to the judgment" requires that the issue be essential to the merits of the underlying case. Because this requirement was not met in this case, we reverse the Superior Court's judgment on this basis.

. . .

3. *Issue preclusion.* The doctrine of issue preclusion provides that when an issue has been "actually litigated and determined by a valid and final judgment, and the determination is essential to the judgment, the determination is conclusive

in a subsequent action between the parties whether on the same or different claim." Jarosz challenges the conclusion that the issue was both actually litigated and essential to the decision.

a. *Actually litigated*. The Appeals Court concluded correctly that the issue of Jarosz's attorney-client relationship with Palmer was actually litigated in the *Union Products* case. Jarosz claims that the issue was not actually litigated because the judge issued his decision without an evidentiary hearing or full trial, and he did not have the opportunity to conduct discovery or cross-examine witnesses. While it is true that "preclusive effect should not be given to issues or claims that were not actually litigated in [the] prior action," an evidentiary hearing or trial is not required before issue preclusion can apply. The appropriate question is whether the issue was " 'subject to an adversary presentation and consequent judgment' that was not 'a product of the parties' consent.' "

The issue of Jarosz's attorney-client relationship was briefed by the parties and, after a hearing, the judge determined the issue. Jarosz presented an affidavit detailing his contacts with Palmer. The judge considered the facts alleged by Jarosz and determined that, even if taken as true, they did not provide sufficient evidence of an individual attorney-client relationship.

The determination of an issue in a prior proceeding has no preclusive effect where "[t]he party against whom preclusion is sought had a significantly heavier burden of persuasion with respect to the issue in the initial action than in the subsequent action; the burden has shifted to his adversary; or the adversary has a significantly heavier burden than he had in the first action." Jarosz argues that because public policy considerations favor the rights of clients to choose their attorneys, the standard for disqualifying an opposing attorney in the initial action was very high, whereas, in the present case, he only needed to prove the attorney-client relationship by a preponderance of the evidence. However, the existence of the attorney-client relationship was the threshold determination in both instances, and the plaintiff's burden of proof was a preponderance of the evidence in both proceedings.

b. *Essential to the judgment*. The issue of Jarosz's attorney-client relationship with Palmer was clearly not essential to a determination of his breach of fiduciary duty and wrongful termination claims against the Union Products defendants; Jarosz could have prevailed on those claims regardless of the outcome of his motion to disqualify. However, the issue was obviously essential to the judge's decision to deny that motion. We therefore must determine whether the requirement that the issue be "essential to the judgment" necessitates that the issue be essential to the underlying case, or whether it is sufficient that the issue is essential to the decision at hand.

We conclude that, in this context, the term "judgment" refers to a final determination on the merits of the proceeding. For a ruling to have preclusive effect, it must have a bearing on the outcome of the case. "If issues are determined but the judgment is not dependent upon the determinations, relitigation of those issues in a subsequent action between the parties is not precluded." The use of the term "case" indicates that the finding must be regarded by the court and the party as essential to a determination on the merits, and not merely essential to a determination of the narrow issue before the court at that time.

The nature of Jarosz's attorney-client relationship with Palmer was clearly not essential to a determination on the merits of his underlying claim. Therefore, the issue was not essential to the judgment, and issue preclusion cannot apply.

REVIEW QUESTIONS

1. The requirement that resolution of the issue must have been *essential to the prior judgment* in order to be preclusive in a subsequent litigation is analogous to the rule that *dicta* is not binding precedent. The rationale is that only those matters central to the outcome will likely be given sufficient attention by the litigants and the court to justify according them finality. *See* Antonio Gidi, *Issue Preclusive Effect of Class Certification Orders,* 63 Hastings L.J. 1023, 1052 (2012) (citing Robert C. Casad and Kevin M. Clermont, *Res Judicata: A Handbook on Its Theory, Doctrine, and Practice* 127-129, 138-139 (2001)). Settlement of a lawsuit generally carries no issue preclusive effect because no issue has been *actually litigated and determined. See Arizona v. California*, 530 U.S. 392, 414 (2000).

2. *Burdens of Proof.* Note the significance of the comparative burdens of proof between the prior proceeding and one in which preclusion is sought. As a general rule (dictated by concerns for fairness), prior proceedings cannot have preclusive effect where the party against whom preclusion is now sought had a significantly heavier burden of persuasion with respect to the particular issue in the prior action, or his adversary has a significantly heavier burden now than in the first action. *See Restatement (Second) of Judgments* § 28(4). Thus a defendant in a criminal prosecution for arson—where proof must be beyond a reasonable doubt—cannot be precluded from litigating his guilt by a prior judgment of liability for destruction of the building in a civil action—where plaintiff prevailed upon a mere preponderance of the evidence.

   In the reverse sequence, where the criminal prosecution precedes the civil trial, conviction on proof beyond a reasonable doubt would usually preclude defendant from relitigating the issue in a subsequent civil action arising from the same events, where plaintiffs need only prove their case by a preponderance of the evidence. Thus a conviction for murder collaterally estopped defendant from contesting liability under the Massachusetts wrongful death statute in the subsequent civil action. *See Kowalski v. Gagne*, 914 F.2d 299 (1st Cir. 1990).

Issue preclusion and the Saga of O.J. Simpson. Following O. J. Simpson's acquittal of murdering Nicole Brown Simpson and Ronald Goldman in the so-called Trial of the Century in 1995, the victims' families filed a wrongful death civil action against him. Had Simpson been convicted, that decision on proof beyond a reasonable doubt would have precluded him from relitigating the issue of his responsibility for their deaths, as the families needed to prove the civil case by a mere preponderance of the evidence. Simpson could not of course use his actual acquittal *against* the plaintiffs in the wrongful death case, because they were neither parties nor in privity with the prosecution in the criminal case, and thus had not had their "day in court." Simpson was ultimately found liable and a verdict of $33 million was entered. *Rufo v. Simpson*, 103 Cal. Rptr. 2d 492 (Ct. App. 2001).

The issue of his responsibility for the murders came up yet again when Simpson filed an action to terminate the temporary guardianship that had been awarded to his children's maternal grandparents while he was incarcerated prior to his acquittal. The grandparents requested that the court await the result of the wrongful death action, hoping a finding against Simpson in that case would foreclose his relitigating the murder issue and assure their continued custody of the children. The court went ahead, however, ruling that the burden of proof was on the grandparents to establish Simpson's unfitness as a parent by "clear and convincing" evidence, a higher burden than "preponderance of the evidence" by which the families needed to prove his responsibility for the wrongful deaths. The grandparents lost custody under that standard, although the appeals court would later reverse and remand, holding that the burden should properly have been placed on Simpson. *Guardianship of Sydney Simpson, et al. v. O.J. Simpson*, 67 Cal. App. 4th 914 (Ct. App. 1998).

Following the murder trial, Johnnie Cochran, Simpson's defense lawyer who uttered the famous phrase "If it [the bloody glove found at the murder scene] doesn't fit [O.J.], you must acquit," brought a libel action against the *New York Post* over a column stating that "history reveals that [Cochran] will say or do just about anything to win, typically at the expense of the truth." The court dismissed the claim, concluding that the statement was a nonactionable opinion, not an assertion of fact. Suppose Cochran subsequently sued the columnist personally. Could she utilize defensive collateral estoppel to foreclose Cochran from relitigating the same libel issue he lost against *The Post*? In a similar situation, *Masson v. New Yorker Magazine, Inc.*, 85 F.3d 1394 (9th Cir. 1996) held that a prior judgment absolving the author of an allegedly libelous article collaterally estopped the plaintiff from relitigating his libel claims against *The New Yorker Magazine* for publishing the article.

One more: Now suppose that the column stated, "history reveals that Johnnie Cochran and Robert Kardashian [another member of the "Dream Team" that successfully defended O.J. Simpson in his murder trial] will say or do just about anything to win, typically at the expense of the truth." Had Cochran won his libel action against the newspaper, could Kardashian use offensive collateral estoppel against the newspaper in his own libel action? We will come back to this in *Parklane*, our next case.

Note: Issue Preclusion in Criminal Cases. As noted earlier in this chapter, the Double Jeopardy Clause of the Fifth Amendment, applicable in criminal cases, operates similarly to claim preclusion in civil litigation in that a defendant cannot be tried twice for the same offense. Issue preclusion also has an analogue in criminal cases. *Ashe v. Swenson*, 397 U.S. 436 (1970) involved a defendant accused of robbing a poker game with six players. After a jury acquitted him of robbing one player, the state sought to try him for robbing another of the players. The Court reasoned that the first jury must have found that he was not one of the robbers, and thus a second jury could not rationally convict him of robbing any of the other victims. A court must "examine the record and conclude whether a rational jury could have grounded its verdict upon an issue other than that which the defendant seeks to foreclose from consideration." *Ashe*, 397 U.S. at 444. Sound familiar? Look back at *Hoult v. Hoult*. For more, see Mark S. Brodin, *Case Note: Ashe v. Swenson: Collateral Estoppel, Double Jeopardy, and Inconsistent Verdicts*, 71 Colum. L. Rev. 321 (1971).

PRACTICE EXERCISE NO. 40: APPLYING PRECLUSION DOCTRINE IN *WARNER*

Your firm represents the plaintiffs in *Warner v. City of New York*. In a rambling telephone conversation earlier today, the City of New York indicated that it might move to strike paragraphs 48-50 of the Complaint and might seek a ruling that the *Daniels* suit is irrelevant to this case. Its lawyer mentioned "*res judicata*," among other things.

(1) Is *Daniels* relevant from the perspective of claim preclusion? (2) Is *Daniels* relevant from the perspective of issue preclusion?

4. Nonmutual Issue Preclusion

We know that (with the few narrow exceptions discussed in *Taylor v. Sturgell*) preclusion cannot operate *against* a litigant who was not a party in the prior case, as each party is entitled to his day in court. The next decision deals with the question of whether a nonparty can *invoke* preclusion against a litigant from the earlier case, a matter referred to as nonmutual estoppel.

Parklane Hosiery Co., Inc. v. Shore
439 U.S. 322 (1979)

Justice STEWART delivered the opinion of the Court:

This case presents the question whether a party who has had issues of fact adjudicated adversely to it in an equitable action may be collaterally estopped from relitigating the same issues before a jury in a subsequent legal action brought against it by a new party.

The respondent brought this stockholder's class action against the petitioners in a Federal District Court. The complaint alleged that the petitioners, Parklane Hosiery Co., Inc. (Parklane), and 13 of its officers, directors, and stockholders, had issued a materially false and misleading proxy statement in connection with a merger. The proxy statement, according to the complaint, had violated §§ 14(a), 10(b), and 20(a) of the Securities Exchange Act of 1934, as well as various rules and regulations promulgated by the Securities and Exchange Commission (SEC). The complaint sought damages, rescission of the merger, and recovery of costs.

Before this action came to trial, the SEC filed suit against the same defendants in the Federal District Court, alleging that the proxy statement that had been issued by Parklane was materially false and misleading in essentially the same respects as those that had been alleged in the respondent's complaint. Injunctive relief was requested. After a 4-day trial, the District Court found that the proxy statement was materially false and misleading in the respects alleged, and entered a declaratory judgment to that effect. The Court of Appeals for the Second Circuit affirmed this judgment. The respondent in the present case then moved for partial summary judgment against the petitioners, asserting that the petitioners were collaterally estopped from relitigating the issues that had been resolved against them in the action brought by the SEC.[2] The District Court denied the motion on the ground that such an application of collateral estoppel would deny the petitioners their Seventh Amendment right to a jury trial. The Court of Appeals for the Second Circuit reversed, holding that a party who has had issues of fact determined against him after a full and fair opportunity to litigate in a nonjury trial is collaterally estopped from obtaining a subsequent jury trial of these same issues of fact. Because of an intercircuit conflict, we granted certiorari.

I

The threshold question to be considered is whether, quite apart from the right to a jury trial under the Seventh Amendment, the petitioners can be precluded from relitigating facts resolved adversely to them in a prior equitable proceeding with another party under the general law of collateral estoppel. Specifically, we must determine whether a litigant who was not a party to a prior judgment may nevertheless use that judgment "offensively" to prevent a defendant from relitigating issues resolved in the earlier proceeding.[4]

---

2. A private plaintiff in an action under the proxy rules is not entitled to relief simply by demonstrating that the proxy solicitation was materially false and misleading. The plaintiff must also show that he was injured and prove damages. Since the SEC action was limited to a determination of whether the proxy statement contained materially false and misleading information, the respondent conceded that he would still have to prove these other elements of his prima facie case in the private action. The petitioners' right to a jury trial on those remaining issues is not contested.

4. In this context, offensive use of collateral estoppel occurs when the plaintiff seeks to foreclose the defendant from litigating an issue the defendant has previously litigated unsuccessfully in an action with another party. Defensive use occurs when a defendant seeks to prevent a plaintiff from asserting a claim the plaintiff has previously litigated and lost against another defendant.

A

Collateral estoppel, like the related doctrine of *res judicata*,[5] has the dual purpose of protecting litigants from the burden of relitigating an identical issue with the same party or his privy and of promoting judicial economy by preventing needless litigation. Until relatively recently, however, the scope of collateral estoppel was limited by the doctrine of mutuality of parties. Under this mutuality doctrine, neither party could use a prior judgment as an estoppel against the other unless both parties were bound by the judgment. Based on the premise that it is somehow unfair to allow a party to use a prior judgment when he himself would not be so bound,[7] the mutuality requirement provided a party who had litigated and lost in a previous action an opportunity to relitigate identical issues with new parties.

By failing to recognize the obvious difference in position between a party who has never litigated an issue and one who has fully litigated and lost, the mutuality requirement was criticized almost from its inception. "In any lawsuit where a defendant, because of the mutuality principle, is forced to present a complete defense on the merits to a claim which the plaintiff has fully litigated and lost in a prior action, there is an arguable misallocation of resources. . . . Permitting repeated litigation of the same issue as long as the supply of unrelated defendants holds out reflects either the aura of the gaming table or 'a lack of discipline and of disinterestedness on the part of the lower courts, hardly a worthy or wise basis for fashioning rules of procedure.' " *Blonder-Tongue Laboratories, Inc. v. University of Illinois Foundation*, 402 U.S. 313, 329 n.10.

B

The *Blonder-Tongue* case involved defensive use of collateral estoppel—a plaintiff was estopped from asserting a claim that the plaintiff had previously litigated and lost against another defendant. The present case, by contrast, involves offensive use of collateral estoppel—a plaintiff is seeking to estop a defendant from relitigating the issues which the defendant previously litigated and lost against another plaintiff. In both the offensive and defensive use situations, the party against whom estoppel is asserted has litigated and lost in an earlier action. Nevertheless, several reasons have been advanced why the two situations should be treated differently.

First, offensive use of collateral estoppel does not promote judicial economy in the same manner as defensive use does. Defensive use of collateral estoppel precludes a plaintiff from relitigating identical issues by merely "switching adversaries." Thus defensive collateral estoppel gives a plaintiff a strong incentive to

---

5. Under the doctrine of *res judicata*, a judgment on the merits in a prior suit bars a second suit involving the same parties or their privies based on the same cause of action. Under the doctrine of collateral estoppel, on the other hand, the second action is upon a different cause of action and the judgment in the prior suit precludes relitigation of issues actually litigated and necessary to the outcome of the first action.

7. It is a violation of due process for a judgment to be binding on a litigant who was not a party or a privy and therefore has never had an opportunity to be heard.

join all potential defendants in the first action if possible. Offensive use of collateral estoppel, on the other hand, creates precisely the opposite incentive. Since a plaintiff will be able to rely on a previous judgment against a defendant but will not be bound by that judgment if the defendant wins, the plaintiff has every incentive to adopt a "wait and see" attitude, in the hope that the first action by another plaintiff will result in a favorable judgment. Thus offensive use of collateral estoppel will likely increase rather than decrease the total amount of litigation, since potential plaintiffs will have everything to gain and nothing to lose by not intervening in the first action.

A second argument against offensive use of collateral estoppel is that it may be unfair to a defendant. If a defendant in the first action is sued for small or nominal damages, he may have little incentive to defend vigorously, particularly if future suits are not foreseeable. Allowing offensive collateral estoppel may also be unfair to a defendant if the judgment relied upon as a basis for the estoppel is itself inconsistent with one or more previous judgments in favor of the defendant.[14] Still another situation where it might be unfair to apply offensive estoppel is where the second action affords the defendant procedural opportunities unavailable in the first action that could readily cause a different result.[15]

C

We have concluded that the preferable approach for dealing with these problems in the federal courts is not to preclude the use of offensive collateral estoppel, but to grant trial courts broad discretion to determine when it should be applied. The general rule should be that in cases where a plaintiff could easily have joined in the earlier action or where, either for the reasons discussed above or for other reasons, the application of offensive estoppel would be unfair to a defendant, a trial judge should not allow the use of offensive collateral estoppel.

In the present case, however, none of the circumstances that might justify reluctance to allow the offensive use of collateral estoppel is present. The application of offensive collateral estoppel will not here reward a private plaintiff who could have joined in the previous action, since the respondent probably could not have joined in the injunctive action brought by the SEC even had he so desired. Similarly, there is no unfairness to the petitioners in applying offensive collateral estoppel in this case. First, in light of the serious allegations made in the SEC's complaint against the petitioners, as well as the foreseeability of

---

14. In Professor Currie's familiar example, a railroad collision injures 50 passengers all of whom bring separate actions against the railroad. After the railroad wins the first 25 suits, a plaintiff wins in suit 26. Professor Currie argues that offensive use of collateral estoppel should not be applied so as to allow plaintiffs 27 through 50 automatically to recover. Currie, *Mutuality of Estoppel: Limits of the Bernhard Doctrine*, 9 Stan. L. Rev. 281, 304 (1957).

15. If, for example, the defendant in the first action was forced to defend in an inconvenient forum and therefore was unable to engage in full scale discovery or call witnesses, application of offensive collateral estoppel may be unwarranted. Indeed, differences in available procedures may sometimes justify not allowing a prior judgment to have estoppel effect in a subsequent action even between the same parties, or where defensive estoppel is asserted against a plaintiff who has litigated and lost. The problem of unfairness is particularly acute in cases of offensive estoppel, however, because the defendant against whom estoppel is asserted typically will not have chosen the forum in the first action.

subsequent private suits that typically follow a successful Government judgment, the petitioners had every incentive to litigate the SEC lawsuit fully and vigorously.[18] Second, the judgment in the SEC action was not inconsistent with any previous decision. Finally, there will in the respondent's action be no procedural opportunities available to the petitioners that were unavailable in the first action of a kind that might be likely to cause a different result.[19]

We conclude, therefore, that none of the considerations that would justify a refusal to allow the use of offensive collateral estoppel is present in this case. Since the petitioners received a "full and fair" opportunity to litigate their claims in the SEC action, the contemporary law of collateral estoppel leads inescapably to the conclusion that the petitioners are collaterally estopped from relitigating the question of whether the proxy statement was materially false and misleading.

II

The question that remains is whether, notwithstanding the law of collateral estoppel, the use of offensive collateral estoppel in this case would violate the petitioners' Seventh Amendment right to a jury trial.[20] The party against whom estoppel is asserted has litigated questions of fact, and has had the facts determined against him in an earlier proceeding. There is no further fact-finding function for the jury to perform, since the common factual issues have been resolved in the previous action.

The judgment of the Court of Appeals is Affirmed.

Justice REHNQUIST, dissenting:

The right of trial by jury in civil cases at common law is fundamental to our history and jurisprudence. Today, however, the Court reduces this valued right, which Blackstone praised as "the glory of the English law," to a mere "neutral" factor and in the name of procedural reform denies the right of jury trial to defendants in a vast number of cases in which defendants, heretofore, have enjoyed jury trials. Over 35 years ago, Mr. Justice Black lamented the "gradual process of judicial erosion which in one-hundred-fifty years has slowly worn away a major portion of the essential guarantee of the Seventh Amendment." *Galloway v. United States*, 319 U.S. 372, 397 (1943) (dissenting opinion). Regrettably, the erosive process continues apace with today's decision.

---

18. After a 4-day trial in which the petitioners had every opportunity to present evidence and call witnesses, the District Court held for the SEC. The petitioners then appealed to the Court of Appeals for the Second Circuit, which affirmed the judgment against them. Moreover, the petitioners were already aware of the action brought by the respondent, since it had commenced before the filing of the SEC action.

19. It is true, of course, that the petitioners in the present action would be entitled to a jury trial of the issues bearing on whether the proxy statement was materially false and misleading had the SEC action never been brought—a matter to be discussed in Part II of this opinion. But the presence or absence of a jury as factfinder is basically neutral, quite unlike, for example, the necessity of defending the first lawsuit in an inconvenient forum.

20. The Seventh Amendment provides: "In Suits at common law, where the value in controversy shall exceed twenty dollars, the right to jury trial shall be preserved. . . ."

The founders of our Nation considered the right of trial by jury in civil cases an important bulwark against tyranny and corruption, a safeguard too precious to be left to the whim of the sovereign, or, it might be added, to that of the judiciary. Those who passionately advocated the right to a civil jury trial did not do so because they considered the jury a familiar procedural device that should be continued; the concerns for the institution of jury trial that led to the passages of the Declaration of Independence and to the Seventh Amendment were not animated by a belief that use of juries would lead to more efficient judicial administration. Trial by a jury of laymen rather than by the sovereign's judges was important to the founders because juries represent the layman's common sense, the "passional elements in our nature," and thus keep the administration of law in accord with the wishes and feelings of the community. O. Holmes, *Collected Legal Papers* 237 (1920). Those who favored juries believed that a jury would reach a result that a judge either could not or would not reach. It is with these values that underlie the Seventh Amendment in mind that the Court should, but obviously does not, approach the decision of this case.

I think it is clear that petitioners were denied their Seventh Amendment right to a jury trial in this case. In my view, it is "unfair" to apply offensive collateral estoppel where the party who is sought to be estopped has not had an opportunity to have the facts of his case determined by a jury. Since in this case petitioners were not entitled to a jury trial in the Securities and Exchange Commission (SEC) lawsuit, I would not estop them from relitigating the issues determined in the SEC suit before a jury in the private action.

Those who drafted the Declaration of Independence and debated so passionately the proposed Constitution during the ratification period, would indeed be astounded to learn that the presence or absence of a jury is merely "neutral," whereas the availability of discovery, a device unmentioned in the Constitution, may be controlling. It is precisely because the Framers believed that they might receive a different result at the hands of a jury of their peers than at the mercy of the sovereign's judges, that the Seventh Amendment was adopted. And I suspect that anyone who litigates cases before juries in the 1970's would be equally amazed to hear of the supposed lack of distinction between trial by court and trial by jury. The Court can cite no authority in support of this curious proposition. The merits of civil juries have been long debated, but I suspect that juries have never been accused of being merely "neutral" factors.

REVIEW QUESTIONS

1. The common law mutuality doctrine, effectively abrogated in federal litigation by *Parklane* (the states are free to continue to insist on mutuality), had limited the parties who could *invoke* issue preclusion against an adversary to those who were parties in the original case. The idea was that in fairness, only a party who had had "skin in the game" in the prior case should be allowed to benefit from the decision there. In contrast, the constitutional due process "day-in-court" safeguard prevents estoppel

from being *invoked against* a party who has not had a full and fair opportunity to litigate the matter in the previous case.

2. ***Issue Preclusion's Strategic Incentives.*** The demise of the mutuality requirement opened a whole new set of problems that the Court grapples with in *Parklane*, particularly regarding the offensive use of collateral estoppel, which, in contrast to defensive collateral estoppel, may actually encourage multiple litigation.

Take the following scenario. Alan collides with two vehicles on the highway, one driven by Bob and the other by Charlie. Each of the three drivers denies the accident was his fault. When contemplating an action to recover for his damages, Alan must consider that suing Bob or Charlie *separately* would run the risk that if he loses to one at trial, the other could use defensive collateral estoppel against him. If, for example, Bob successfully defends *Alan v. Bob* by asserting that Alan was the driver at fault, a jury verdict for Bob could foreclose Alan from relitigating the issue in *Alan v. Charlie*. Note that a verdict *in favor* of Alan could not be used by him in a subsequent suit against Charlie, who has not had his day in court. The incentive for Alan is therefore *to join* Bob and Charlie as co-defendants (Fed. R. Civ. P. 20), and take his best shot at each in a single trial, a result fully consistent with the goals of efficiency and avoiding the multiplicity of suits.

Now consider the very opposite incentive set up by offensive collateral estoppel. Suppose now that Alan was a passenger in Bob's car, which collided with Charlie. Bob sues Charlie for negligence. In contemplating whether to join as a co-plaintiff or intervenor, Alan knows that a decision *against* Bob on the issue of fault could not be used against him by Charlie if Alan brings his own separate action, as he has not had his day in court. Alan also knows, on the other hand, that he may be able to piggyback on the verdict if it goes *against* Charlie, by using offensive collateral estoppel to prevent Charlie from relitigating the fault issue common to both actions. Alan has, in short, "everything to gain and nothing to lose" by staying out of the first action. Multiple lawsuits from the same incident may thus be encouraged by the unrestricted use of offensive collateral estoppel.

Try creating your own hypotheticals to illustrate the contrast between offensive and defensive issue preclusion.

3. The discretionary constraints articulated by *Parklane* are designed to avoid such unfair exploitation of nonmutual offensive collateral estoppel. Thus a court in Case II is advised to decline its use if:
   - the plaintiff could have joined in the earlier case, but appears to have played the strategic waiting game;
   - the stakes in the earlier case were considerably smaller, so there was less incentive for the defendant to litigate the issue then than now;
   - the prior judgment relied upon is inconsistent with others in which the defendant has prevailed; or
   - the second action affords important procedural opportunities that were unavailable to the defendant in the first action.

4. How would Professor Currie's "familiar example" in the Court's footnote 14 be resolved under the *Parklane* analysis?

5. Note that the prior decision that was the source of preclusion in *Parklane* resulted from a bench trial before a judge, and therefore (unlike the jury's general verdict in *Hoult*) conveniently contained specific findings of fact and conclusions of law. *See* Fed. R. Civ. P. 52(a).

6. Given Justice Rehnquist's eloquent invocation of the Seventh Amendment in his *Parklane* dissent, has the Court not elevated the doctrine of finality above the cherished constitutional right to trial by jury? Could the interest in efficiency and streamlining dockets possibly justify this result?

QUESTIONS TO PONDER

1. Issue preclusion may operate when an administrative agency resolves issues in its judicial capacity and the losing party seeks to relitigate those issues in a federal court. *See University of Tennessee v. Elliott*, 478 U.S. 788 (1986). It also operates in the reverse, as where an attorney was precluded from relitigating, in state disbarment proceedings, the issue of whether he had intentionally overbilled a client, which had been resolved against him by summary judgment in the client's federal court action. *See In re Goldstone*, 445 Mass. 551 (2005). The Supreme Judicial Court of Massachusetts observed:

   > The application of offensive issue preclusion was fair in this case. First, the board was not involved in the initial civil litigation because it had neither a reason, nor an opportunity, to join the proceedings. Second, Goldstone had every incentive to defend the first action vigorously because he was confronting severe financial consequences if his client's allegations were found to be true. Third, the judgment relied on by bar counsel is not inconsistent with any previous judgments in favor of Goldstone—the civil case is the only relevant judgment here. Finally, contrary to Goldstone's contention, the bar discipline hearing would not afford him additional procedural opportunities unavailable in the first action that could "readily cause a different result."

   445 Mass. at 559-560. We will return to the application of issue preclusion from administrative to judicial proceedings when we take up *B & B Hardware, Inc. v. Hargis Industries, Inc.*, below.

2. The tug-of-war between finality and fairness also plays itself out with regard to postconviction relief in criminal cases. Dating back to the Magna Carta, the writ of habeas corpus has permitted collateral review of final convictions. *See generally* Wayne Lafave, Jerold Israel, and Nancy King, *Criminal Procedure* §§ 28.1 et seq. (5th ed. 2009). Proponents of expansive habeas review have argued that "[c]onventional notions of finality of litigation have no place where life or liberty is at stake and infringement of constitutional rights is alleged." *Sanders v. United States*, 373 U.S. 1, 8 (1963) (Brennan, J.).

But in sharp contrast to his dissent in *Parklane*, Justice Rehnquist came down firmly on the side of finality in habeas matters. *See Herrera v. Collins*, 506 U.S. 390 (1993), holding that a claim of *actual innocence* based on newly discovered evidence is not a valid ground for federal habeas relief absent a showing of a constitutional violation during the proceedings.

The tension between finality ("getting it *done*") and fairness ("getting it *right*"), or efficiency versus equity, is the subject of Part D, The Counterweights to Finality, later in this chapter, and arises perhaps most dramatically in the adjudication of mass torts, as is illustrated by our next case.

5. Issue Preclusion in Mass Tort Litigation

Hardy v. Johns-Manville Sales Corp.
681 F.2d 334 (5th Cir. 1982)

GEE, Circuit Judge:

This appeal arises out of a diversity action brought by various plaintiffs—insulators, pipefitters, carpenters, and other factory workers—against various manufacturers, sellers, and distributors of asbestos-containing products. The plaintiffs, alleging exposure to the products and consequent disease, assert various causes of action, including negligence, breach of implied warranty, and strict liability. The pleadings in each of the cases are substantially the same. No plaintiff names a particular defendant on a case-by-case basis but, instead, includes several—often as many as twenty asbestos manufacturers—in his individual complaint. The rationale offered for this unusual pleading practice is that, given the long latent period of the diseases in question, it is impossible for plaintiffs to isolate the precise exposure period or to identify the particular manufacturer's product responsible. The trial court accepted this rationale and opted for a theory of enterprise- or industry-wide liability (market share apportionment determines a manufacturer's liability unless a given manufacturer exculpates itself by proving that its product could not have caused the injury).

Defendants' interlocutory appeal is directed at the district court's order which applies collateral estoppel to this mass tort. The order is, in effect, a partial summary judgment for plaintiffs based on nonmutual offensive collateral estoppel derived from this court's opinion in *Borel v. Fibreboard Paper Products Corp.*, 493 F.2d 1076 (5th Cir. 1973) (henceforth *Borel*). *Borel* was a diversity lawsuit in which manufacturers of insulation products containing asbestos were held strictly liable to an insulation worker who developed asbestosis and mesothelioma and ultimately died. The trial court construed *Borel* as establishing as a matter of law and/or of fact that: (1) insulation products containing asbestos as a generic ingredient are "unavoidably unsafe products," (2) asbestos is a competent producing cause of mesothelioma and asbestosis, (3) no warnings were issued by any asbestos insulation manufacturers [during the relevant time period].

Under the terms of the order, the plaintiffs need not prove that the defendants either knew or should have known of the dangerous propensities of their products and therefore should have warned consumers of these dangers, defendants being precluded from showing otherwise. On appeal, the defendants contend that the order violates their rights to due process and to trial by jury. Because we conclude that the trial court abused its discretion in applying collateral estoppel, we reverse.

In *Parklane Hosiery Co. v. Shore*, 439 U.S. 322 (1979), the Supreme Court was asked to determine "whether a party who has had issues of fact adjudicated adversely to it in an equitable action may be collaterally estopped from relitigating the same issues before a jury in a subsequent legal action brought against it by a new party." The Court responded affirmatively, noting offensive collateral estoppel's "dual purpose of protecting litigants from the burden of relitigating an identical issue with the same party or his privy and of promoting judicial economy by preventing needless litigation." The Court reiterated that mutuality is not necessary to proper invocation of collateral estoppel under federal law, and further held that the use of offensive collateral estoppel does not violate a defendant's seventh amendment right to a jury trial. To avoid problems with the use of the doctrine, the Court adopted a general rule of fairness, stating "that in cases where plaintiff could easily have joined in the earlier action or where . . . for other reasons, the application of offensive collateral estoppel would be unfair to a defendant, a trial judge should not allow the use of offensive collateral estoppel."

While *Parklane* made the doctrine of mutuality effectively a dead letter under federal law, the case left undisturbed the requisite of privity, i.e., that collateral estoppel can only be applied against parties who have had a prior "full and fair opportunity to litigate their claims." The requirement that a person against whom the conclusive effect of a judgment is invoked must be a party or a privy to the prior judgment retains its full vigor after *Parklane*.

THE NON-*BOREL* DEFENDANTS

This is the first and, in our view, insurmountable problem with the trial court's application of collateral estoppel in the case *sub judice*. The omnibus order under review here does not distinguish between defendants who were parties to *Borel* and those who were not; it purports to estop all defendants because all purportedly share an "identity of interests" sufficient to constitute privity. The trial court's action stretches "privity" beyond meaningful limits.

Federal courts have deemed several types of relationships "sufficiently close" to justify preclusion. First, a nonparty who has succeeded to a party's interest in property is bound by any prior judgments against that party. Second, a nonparty who controlled the original suit will be bound by the resulting judgment. Third, federal courts will bind a nonparty whose interests were represented adequately by a party in the original suit. [Note: *Taylor v. Sturgell* has limited this exception.] The rationale for these exceptions is obviously that in these instances the nonparty has in effect had his day in court. In this case, the exceptions are inapplicable.

The fact that all the non-*Borel* defendants, like the *Borel* defendants, are engaged in the manufacture of asbestos-containing products does not evince privity among the parties. The plaintiffs did not demonstrate that any of the non-*Borel* defendants participated in any capacity in the *Borel* litigation—whether directly or even through a trade representative—or were even part of a trustee-beneficiary relationship with any *Borel* defendant. On the contrary, several of the defendants indicate on appeal that they were not even aware of the *Borel* litigation until those proceedings were over and that they were not even members of industry or trade associations composed of asbestos product manufacturers.

The court's omnibus order here amounts to collateral estoppel based on similar legal positions—a proposition that has been properly rejected. . . . "Privity is not established by the mere fact that persons may happen to be interested in the same question or in proving the same state of facts," and we hold that the trial court's actions here transgress the bounds of due process.

THE *BOREL* DEFENDANTS

The propriety of estopping the six defendants in this case who were parties to *Borel* poses more difficult questions. In ascertaining the precise preclusive effect of a prior judgment on a particular issue, [t]he party asserting the estoppel must show that: (1) the issue to be concluded is identical to that involved in the prior action; (2) in the prior action the issue was "actually litigated"; and (3) the determination made of the issue in the prior action must have been necessary and essential to the resulting judgment.

Appellants argue that *Borel* did not necessarily decide that asbestos-containing insulation products were unreasonably dangerous because of failure to warn. According to appellants, the general *Borel* verdict, based on general instructions and special interrogatories, permitted the jury to ground strict liability on the bases of failures to test, of unsafeness for intended use, of failures to inspect, or of unsafeness of the product. Strict liability on the basis of failure to warn, although argued to the jury by trial counsel for the plaintiff in *Borel*, was, in the view of the appellants, never formally presented in the jury instructions and therefore was not essential to the *Borel* jury verdict.

Appellants' view has some plausibility. The special interrogatories answered by the *Borel* jury were general and not specifically directed to failure to warn. General instructions to the *Borel* jury on the plaintiff's causes of action did not charge on failure to warn.

The court closely scrutinizes the evidence, theories of the parties, instructions to the jury, and the general verdict and special interrogatory answers. We must ultimately conclude that the judgment in *Borel* cannot estop even the *Borel* defendants in this case for three interrelated reasons.

First, after review of the issues decided in *Borel*, we conclude that *Borel* is ultimately ambiguous as to certain key issues. Even if we are wrong as to the ambiguities of the *Borel* judgment, there is a second, equally important, reason to deny collateral estoppel effect to it: the presence of inconsistent verdicts. In *Parklane*, the Court noted that collateral estoppel is improper and "unfair" to a defendant "if the judgment relied upon as a basis for the estoppel is itself inconsistent with one or more previous judgments in favor of the defendant." [The court noted that the asbestos manufacturers had prevailed in 35 of the 70 similar cases litigated.]

Finally, we conclude that even if the *Borel* verdict had been unambiguous and the sole verdict issued on point, application of collateral estoppel would still be unfair with regard to the *Borel* defendants because it is very doubtful that these defendants could have foreseen that their $68,000 liability to plaintiff Borel would foreshadow multimillion dollar asbestos liability. As noted in *Parklane*, it would be unfair to apply collateral estoppel "if a defendant in the first action is sued for small or nominal damages [since] he may have little incentive to defend vigorously, particularly if future lawsuits are not foreseeable." The omnibus order here involves 58 pending cases, and the many plaintiffs involved in this case are each seeking $2.5 million in damages. Such a staggering potential liability could not have been foreseen by the *Borel* defendants.

The trial court's application of issue preclusion to the "fact" that asbestos is in all cases a competent producing cause of mesothelioma and asbestosis involves similar problems. *Borel* dealt with the disease-causing aspects of asbestos dust generated by insulation materials. That case did not determine as a matter of fact that because airborne asbestos dust and fibers from thermal insulation materials are hazardous, all products containing asbestos—in whatever quantity or however encapsulated—are hazardous. The injustice in precluding the "fact" that the generic ingredient asbestos invariably and in every use or mode causes cancer is clearest in the case of appellant Garlock. Garlock points out that its products, unlike the loosely woven thermal insulation materials in *Borel* that, when merely handled, emitted large quantities of airborne asbestos dust and fibers, are linoleum-type products in which the asbestos is encapsulated in a rubber-like coating. According to Garlock, its gasket products do not release significant amounts of dust or fibers into the air and have never been demonstrated to be dangerous in installation, use, or removal. Certainly, defendants ought to be free, even after *Borel*, to present evidence of the scientific knowledge associated with their particular product without being prejudiced by a conclusive presumption that asbestos in all forms causes cancer.

We sympathize with the district court's efforts to streamline the enormous asbestos caseload it faces. None of what we say here is meant to cast doubt on any possible alternative ways to avoid reinventing the asbestos liability wheel (joint discovery and consolidation of appropriate groups of cases for trial of particular common issues are some of the possibilities). We hold today only that courts cannot read *Borel* to stand for the proposition that, as matters of fact, asbestos products are unreasonably dangerous or that asbestos as a generic element is in all products a competent producing cause of cancer. To do otherwise would be to elevate judicial expedience over considerations of justice and fair play.

REVIEW QUESTIONS

1. Given the press of tens of thousands of nearly identical asbestos cases on the docket, it is not surprising that trial judges would look to issue preclusion (claim preclusion of course being unavailable because each plaintiff is entitled to his or her own day in court) in an attempt to streamline the process. It is equally unsurprising that expansive privity theories like "identity of interests" would not survive constitutional scrutiny (refer back to *Taylor v. Sturgell*, above). *See generally* Michael D. Green, *The Inability of Offensive Collateral Estoppel to Fulfill Its Promise: An Examination of Estoppel in Asbestos Litigation*, 70 Iowa L. Rev. 141 (1984).

2. What if a prior decision was based on expert medical testimony that is now deemed unreliable, or discredited, or simply out of date? Should a court for example refuse to foreclose a pharmaceutical manufacturer from relitigating the issue of the hazardous nature of its product where, in the earlier decision against it in a similar case, plaintiffs had presented testimony of a medical researcher whose methods have since been discredited and rejected by other courts? Several decisions give an affirmative answer. *See Coburn v. Smithkline Beecham Corp.*, 174 F. Supp. 2d 1235, 1241 (D. Utah 2001) (alleging that antidepressant Paxil caused suicide): "As the scientific landscape changes concerning the evidence for or against the causal connection posited by Plaintiffs, GSK should be free to present—and juries free to evaluate—evidence that makes it more or less likely that Paxil does or does not cause violent reactions in some patients. Simply said, the prior verdict should not be—and will not be—the final word on the subject." *See also Rogers v. Ford Motor Co.*, 925 F. Supp. 1413 (N.D. Ind. 1996) (offensive collateral estoppel did not bar manufacturer of vehicle's seat belt assembly from relitigating issue of whether assembly was defective, where decision in prior case had been called into doubt by subsequent testing by the National Highway Traffic Safety Administration).

6. Issue Preclusion in Trademark Law

B & B Hardware, Inc. v. Hargis Industries, Inc.
135 S. Ct. 1293 (2015)

Justice ALITO delivered the opinion of the Court, in which Chief Justice ROBERTS, Justice KENNEDY, Justice GINSBURG, Justice BREYER, Justice SOTOMAYOR, and Justice KAGAN, joined.

Sometimes two different tribunals are asked to decide the same issue. When that happens, the decision of the first tribunal usually must be followed by the second, at least if the issue is really the same. Allowing the same issue to be decided more than once wastes litigants' resources and adjudicators' time, and it encourages parties who lose before one tribunal to shop around for another. The doctrine of collateral estoppel or issue preclusion is designed to prevent this from occurring.

This case concerns the application of issue preclusion in the context of trademark law. Petitioner, B & B Hardware, Inc. (B & B), and respondent Hargis Industries, Inc. (Hargis), both use similar trademarks; B & B owns SEALTIGHT while Hargis owns SEALTITE. Under the Lanham Act, 60 Stat. 427, as amended, 15 U.S.C. § 1051 et seq., an applicant can seek to register a trademark through an administrative process within the United States Patent and Trademark Office (PTO). But if another party believes that the PTO should not register a mark because it is too similar to its own, that party can oppose registration before the Trademark Trial and Appeal Board (TTAB). Here, Hargis tried to register the mark SEALTITE, but B & B opposed SEALTITE's registration. After a lengthy proceeding, the TTAB agreed with B & B that SEALTITE should not be registered.

In addition to permitting a party to object to the registration of a mark, the Lanham Act allows a mark owner to sue for trademark infringement. Both a registration proceeding and a suit for trademark infringement, moreover, can occur at the same time. In this case, while the TTAB was deciding whether SEALTITE should be registered, B & B and Hargis were also litigating the SEALTIGHT versus SEALTITE dispute in federal court. In both registration proceedings and infringement litigation, the tribunal asks whether a likelihood of confusion exists between the mark sought to be protected (here, SEALTIGHT) and the other mark (SEALTITE).

The question before this Court is whether the District Court in this case should have applied issue preclusion to the TTAB's decision that SEALTITE is confusingly similar to SEALTIGHT. Here, the Eighth Circuit rejected issue preclusion for reasons that would make it difficult for the doctrine ever to apply in trademark disputes. We disagree with that narrow understanding of issue preclusion. Instead, consistent with principles of law that apply in innumerable contexts, we hold that a court should give preclusive effect to TTAB decisions if the ordinary elements of issue preclusion are met. We therefore reverse the judgment of the Eighth Circuit and remand for further proceedings.

I

A

Trademark law has a long history, going back at least to Roman times. The principle underlying trademark protection is that distinctive marks—words, names, symbols, and the like—can help distinguish a particular artisan's goods from those of others. One who first uses a distinct mark in commerce thus acquires rights to that mark. Those rights include preventing others from using the mark.

Though federal law does not create trademarks, Congress has long played a role in protecting them. In 1946, Congress enacted the Lanham Act, the current federal trademark scheme. As relevant here, the Lanham Act creates at least two adjudicative mechanisms to help protect marks. First, a trademark owner can register its mark with the PTO. Second, a mark owner can bring a suit for infringement in federal court.

Registration is significant. The Lanham Act confers "important legal rights and benefits" on trademark owners who register their marks. Registration, for instance, serves as "constructive notice of the registrant's claim of ownership" of the mark. It also is "prima facie evidence of the validity of the registered mark and of the registration of the mark, of the owner's ownership of the mark, and of the owner's exclusive right to use the registered mark in commerce on or in connection with the goods or services specified in the certificate." And once a mark has been registered for five years, it can become "incontestable."

To obtain the benefits of registration, a mark owner files an application with the PTO. "Any person who believes that he would be damaged by the registration" may "file an opposition." Opposition proceedings occur before the TTAB (or panels thereof). The TTAB consists of administrative trademark judges and high-ranking PTO officials, including the Director of the PTO and the Commissioner of Trademarks.

Opposition proceedings before the TTAB are in many ways "similar to a civil action in a federal district court." These proceedings, for instance, are largely governed by the Federal Rules of Civil Procedure and Evidence. TTAB also allows discovery and depositions. The party opposing registration bears the burden of proof, and if that burden cannot be met, the opposed mark must be registered.

The primary way in which TTAB proceedings differ from ordinary civil litigation is that "proceedings before the Board are conducted in writing, and the Board's actions in a particular case are based upon the written record therein." In other words, there is no live testimony. Even so, the TTAB allows parties to submit transcribed testimony, taken under oath and subject to cross-examination, and to request oral argument.

When a party opposes registration because it believes the mark proposed to be registered is too similar to its own, the TTAB evaluates likelihood of confusion by applying some or all of the 13 factors set out in *In re E.I. DuPont DeNemours & Co.*, 476 F.2d 1357 (CCPA 1973). After the TTAB decides whether to register the mark, a party can seek review in the U.S. Court of Appeals for the Federal Circuit, or it can file a new action in district court. In district court, the parties can conduct additional discovery and the judge resolves registration de novo.

The Lanham Act, of course, also creates a federal cause of action for trademark infringement. The owner of a mark, whether registered or not, can bring suit in federal court if another is using a mark that too closely resembles the plaintiff's. The court must decide whether the defendant's use of a mark in commerce "is likely to cause confusion, or to cause mistake, or to deceive" with regards to the plaintiff's mark. In infringement litigation, the district court considers the full range of a mark's usages, not just those in the application.

B

Petitioner B & B and respondent Hargis both manufacture metal fasteners. B & B manufactures fasteners for the aerospace industry, while Hargis manufactures fasteners for use in the construction trade. Although there are obvious differences between space shuttles and A-frame buildings, both aerospace and construction engineers prefer fasteners that seal things tightly. Accordingly, both B & B and Hargis want their wares associated with tight seals. A feud of nearly two decades has sprung from this seemingly commonplace set of facts.

In 1993 B & B registered SEALTIGHT for "threaded or unthreaded metal fasteners and other related hardwar[e]; namely, self-sealing nuts, bolts, screws, rivets and washers, all having a captive o-ring, for use in the aerospace industry." In 1996, Hargis sought to register SEALTITE for "self-piercing and self-drilling metal screws for use in the manufacture of metal and post-frame buildings." B & B opposed Hargis' registration because, although the two companies sell different products, it believes that SEALTITE is confusingly similar to SEALTIGHT.

The twists and turns in the SEALTIGHT versus SEALTITE controversy are labyrinthine. The question whether either of these marks should be registered, and if so, which one, has bounced around within the PTO for about two decades; related infringement litigation has been before the Eighth Circuit three times; and two separate juries have been empaneled and returned verdicts. The full story could fill a long, unhappy book.

For purposes here, we pick up the story in 2002, when the PTO published SEALTITE in the Official Gazette. This prompted opposition proceedings before the TTAB, complete with discovery, including depositions. B & B argued that SEALTITE could not be registered because it is confusingly similar to SEALTIGHT. B & B explained, for instance, that both companies have an online presence, the largest distributor of fasteners sells both companies' products, and consumers sometimes call the wrong company to place orders. Hargis rejoined that the companies sell different products, for different uses, to different types of consumers, through different channels of trade.

Invoking a number of the DuPont factors, the TTAB sided with B & B. The Board considered, for instance, whether SEALTIGHT is famous (it's not, said the Board), how the two products are used (differently), how much the marks resemble each other (very much), and whether customers are actually confused (perhaps sometimes). Concluding that "the most critical factors in [its] likelihood of confusion analysis are the similarities of the marks and the similarity of the goods," the TTAB determined that SEALTITE—when "used in connection with 'self-piercing and self-drilling metal screws for use in the manufacture of metal and post-frame buildings' "—could not be registered because it "so resembles" SEALTIGHT when "used in connection with fasteners that provide leakproof protection from liquids and gases, fasteners that have a captive o-ring, and 'threaded or unthreaded metal fasteners and other related hardware for use in the aerospace industry' as to be likely to cause confusion." Despite a right to do so, Hargis did not seek judicial review in either the Federal Circuit or District Court.

All the while, B & B had sued Hargis for infringement. Before the District Court ruled on likelihood of confusion, however, the TTAB announced its decision. After a series of proceedings not relevant here, B & B argued to the District Court that Hargis could not contest likelihood of confusion because of the preclusive effect of the TTAB decision. The District Court disagreed, reasoning that the TTAB is not an Article III court. The jury returned a verdict for Hargis, finding no likelihood of confusion.

B & B appealed to the Eighth Circuit. Though accepting for the sake of argument that agency decisions can ground issue preclusion, the panel majority affirmed for three reasons: first, because the TTAB uses different factors than the Eighth Circuit to evaluate likelihood of confusion; second, because the TTAB placed too much emphasis on the appearance and sound of the two marks; and third, because Hargis bore the burden of persuasion before the TTAB, while B & B bore it before the District Court. Judge Colloton dissented, concluding that issue preclusion should apply. After calling for the views of the Solicitor General, we granted certiorari.

II

The first question that we must address is whether an agency decision can ever ground issue preclusion. The District Court rejected issue preclusion because agencies are not Article III courts. The Eighth Circuit did not adopt that view, and, given this Court's cases, it was right to take that course.

This Court has long recognized that "the determination of a question directly involved in one action is conclusive as to that question in a second suit." *Cromwell v. County of Sac*, 94 U.S. 351, 354 (1877). The idea is straightforward: Once a court has decided an issue, it is "forever settled as between the parties," *Baldwin v. Iowa State Traveling Men's Assn.*, 283 U.S. 522, 525 (1931), thereby "protect[ing]" against "the expense and vexation attending multiple lawsuits, conserv[ing] judicial resources, and foster[ing] reliance on judicial action by minimizing the possibility of inconsistent verdicts," *Montana v. United States*, 440 U.S. 147, 153-154 (1979). In short, "a losing litigant deserves no rematch after a defeat fairly suffered." *Astoria Fed. Sav. & Loan Assn. v. Solimino*, 501 U.S. 104, 107 (1991).

Although the idea of issue preclusion is straightforward, it can be challenging to implement. The Court, therefore, regularly turns to the Restatement (Second) of Judgments for a statement of the ordinary elements of issue preclusion. The Restatement explains that subject to certain well-known exceptions, the general rule is that "[w]hen an issue of fact or law is actually litigated and determined by a valid and final judgment, and the determination is essential to the judgment, the determination is conclusive in a subsequent action between the parties, whether on the same or a different claim." Restatement (Second) of Judgments § 27, p. 250 (1980); *see also id.*, § 28, at 273 (listing exceptions such as whether appellate review was available or whether there were "differences in the quality or extensiveness of the procedures followed").

Both this Court's cases and the Restatement make clear that issue preclusion is not limited to those situations in which the same issue is before two courts. Rather, where a single issue is before a court and an administrative agency, preclusion also often applies. "[W]hen an administrative agency is acting in a judicial capacity and resolves disputed issues of fact properly before it which the parties have had an adequate opportunity to litigate, the courts have not hesitated to apply res judicata to enforce repose." *University of Tenn. v. Elliott*, 478 U.S. 788, 797-798 (1986).

Hargis argues that we should not read the Lanham Act (or, presumably, many other federal statutes) as authorizing issue preclusion. Otherwise, Hargis warns, the Court would have to confront " 'grave and doubtful questions' as to the Lanham Act's consistency with the Seventh Amendment and Article III of the Constitution." We are not persuaded.

The Court has already held that the right to a jury trial does not negate the issue-preclusive effect of a judgment, even if that judgment was entered by a juryless tribunal. *See Parklane Hosiery Co. v. Shore*, 439 U.S. 322, 337 (1979). It would seem to follow naturally that although the Seventh Amendment creates a jury trial right in suits for trademark damages, TTAB decisions still can have preclusive effect in such suits.

IV

At last we turn to whether there is a categorical reason why registration decisions can never meet the ordinary elements of issue preclusion, e.g., those elements set out in § 27 of the Restatement (Second) of Judgments. Although many registrations will not satisfy those ordinary elements, that does not mean that none will. We agree with Professor McCarthy that issue preclusion applies where "the issues in the two cases are indeed identical and the other rules of collateral estoppel are carefully observed."

A

The Eighth Circuit's primary objection to issue preclusion was that the TTAB considers different factors than it does. Here, however, the same likelihood-of-confusion standard applies to both registration and infringement. The real question, therefore, is whether likelihood of confusion for purposes of registration is the same standard as likelihood of confusion for purposes of infringement. We conclude it is.

Moreover, the fact that the TTAB may have erred does not prevent preclusion. As Judge Colloton observed in dissent [in the Court of Appeals below], " 'issue preclusion prevent[s] relitigation of wrong decisions just as much as right ones.' " 716 F.3d 1020, 1029 (8th Cir. 2013) (quoting *Clark v. Clark*, 984

F.2d 272, 273 (C.A.8 1993)); *see also* Restatement (Second) of Judgments § 28, Comment j, at 284 (explaining that "refusal to give the first judgment preclusive effect should not . . . be based simply on a conclusion that [it] was patently erroneous").

B

No one disputes that the TTAB and district courts use different procedures. Most notably, district courts feature live witnesses. Procedural differences, by themselves, however, do not defeat issue preclusion. Equity courts used different procedures than did law courts, but that did not bar issue preclusion. Rather than focusing on whether procedural differences exist—they often will—the correct inquiry is whether the procedures used in the first proceeding were fundamentally poor, cursory, or unfair.

Here, there is no categorical "reason to doubt the quality, extensiveness, or fairness," of the agency's procedures. In large part they are exactly the same as in federal court. For instance, although "[t]he scope of discovery in Board proceedings . . . is generally narrower than in court proceedings"—reflecting the fact that there are often fewer usages at issue—the TTAB has adopted almost the whole of Federal Rule of Civil Procedure 26. It is conceivable, of course, that the TTAB's procedures may prove ill-suited for a particular issue in a particular case, e.g., a party may have tried to introduce material evidence but was prevented by the TTAB from doing so, or the TTAB's bar on live testimony may materially prejudice a party's ability to present its case. The ordinary law of issue preclusion, however, already accounts for those "rare" cases where a "compelling showing of unfairness" can be made. Restatement (Second) of Judgments § 28, Comments g and j, at 283-284.

C

Hargis also contends that the stakes for registration are so much lower than for infringement that issue preclusion should never apply to TTAB decisions. Issue preclusion may be inapt if "the amount in controversy in the first action [was] so small in relation to the amount in controversy in the second that preclusion would be plainly unfair." Restatement (Second) of Judgments § 28, Comment j, at 283-284. After all, "[f]ew . . . litigants would spend $50,000 to defend a $5,000 claim." Wright & Miller § 4423, at 612. Hargis is wrong, however, that this exception to issue preclusion applies to every registration. To the contrary: When registration is opposed, there is good reason to think that both sides will take the matter seriously.

V

For these reasons, the Eighth Circuit erred in this case. On remand, the court should apply the following rule: So long as the other ordinary elements of issue preclusion are met, when the usages adjudicated by the TTAB are materially the same as those before the district court, issue preclusion should apply.

The judgment of the United States Court of Appeals for the Eighth Circuit is reversed, and the case is remanded for further proceedings consistent with this opinion.

[Justice GINSBURG's concurrence is omitted.]

Justice THOMAS, with whom Justice SCALIA joins, dissenting. [The dissent challenged the Court's presumption that Congress intended agency decisions to have preclusive effect in this context.]

REVIEW QUESTIONS

1. Is Hargis's fate sealed with Justice Alito's apparent frustration?

> The twists and turns in the SEALTIGHT versus SEALTITE controversy are labyrinthine. The question whether either of these marks should be registered, and if so, which one, has bounced around within the PTO for about two decades; related infringement litigation has been before the Eighth Circuit three times; and two separate juries have been empaneled and returned verdicts. The full story could fill a long, unhappy book.

Issue preclusion finally puts the matter to rest.

2. How does the Court get around its acknowledgement that "Hargis bore the burden of persuasion before the TTAB, while B & B bore it before the District Court." And what about the procedural advantages Hargis would have had in the District Court, like live testimony? Aren't those usually deal-breakers for issue preclusion, as discussed above?

3. What would the late Chief Justice William Rehnquist have to say about the Court's dismissal of Hargis's Seventh Amendment right to jury trial here? (*See* his dissent in *Parklane Hosiery*, above.)

MORE TO PONDER

Underlying the dispute in *B & B Hardware* is the ongoing question of how much deference courts should give an agency's determination. Contending that the Federal Circuit should afford *greater* deference to the Trademark Office's decisions, Professor Melissa F. Wasserman writes: "[T]he Trademark Office possesses superior pathways to acquire consumer behavior and economic data, as well as the expertise to evaluate and analyze this information to craft substantive trademark law standards." Melissa F. Wasserman, *What Administrative Law Can Teach the Trademark System*, 93 Wash. U. L. Rev. 1511 (2016). Professor Deborah R. Gerhardt disagrees:

> Too much deference could result in decisions from a trademark echo chamber. The USPTO . . . cannot spend the amount of time that federal courts spend when making findings of fact. . . . [W]hile the USPTO does have significant trademark expertise, its own TTAB

> judges admit that they make decisions within their trademark paradigm and do not view their role as permitting review of overlapping doctrinal issues
>
> Deborah R. Gerhardt, *Beware the Trademark Echo Chamber: Why Federal Courts Should Not Defer to USPTO Decisions*, 33 Berkeley Tech. L.J. 644 (2018).

D. THE COUNTERWEIGHTS TO FINALITY

Are there any circumstances in which countervailing policy concerns outweigh the doctrines of finality? What if the decision in the prior case is based on what is now acknowledged to be an erroneous reading of the law? Does the interest in arriving at the correct result trump the interest in putting disputes to rest once and for all? Consider the following case.

Federated Department Stores, Inc. v. Moitie
452 U.S. 394 (1981)

Justice REHNQUIST delivered the opinion of the Court:

The only question presented in this case is whether the Court of Appeals for the Ninth Circuit validly created an exception to the doctrine of *res judicata*. The court held that *res judicata* does not bar relitigation of an unappealed adverse judgment where, as here, other plaintiffs in similar actions against common defendants successfully appeal the judgments against them. We disagree with the view taken by the Court of Appeals for the Ninth Circuit and reverse.

I

In 1976 the United States brought an antitrust action against petitioners, owners of various department stores, alleging that they had violated § 1 of the Sherman Act, 15 U.S.C. § 1, by agreeing to fix the retail price of women's clothing sold in northern California. Seven parallel civil actions were subsequently filed by private plaintiffs seeking treble damages on behalf of proposed classes of retail purchasers, including that of respondent Moitie in state court (*Moitie I*) and respondent Brown (*Brown I*) in the United States District Court for the Northern District of California. Each of these complaints tracked almost verbatim the allegations of the Government's complaint, though the *Moitie I* complaint referred solely to state law. All of the actions originally filed in the District Court were assigned to a single federal judge, and the *Moitie I* case was removed there on the basis of diversity of citizenship and federal-question jurisdiction. The District Court dismissed all of the actions "in their entirety" on the ground that plaintiffs had not alleged an "injury" to their "business or property" within the meaning of § 4 of the Clayton Act, 15 U.S.C. § 15.

Plaintiffs in five of the suits appealed that judgment to the Court of Appeals for the Ninth Circuit. The single counsel representing Moitie and Brown, however, chose not to appeal and instead refiled the two actions in state court, *Moitie II* and *Brown II*. Although the complaints purported to raise only state-law claims, they made allegations similar to those made in the prior complaints, including that of the Government. Petitioners removed these new actions to the District Court for the Northern District of California and moved to have them dismissed on the ground of *res judicata*. In a decision rendered July 8, 1977, the District Court first denied respondents' motion to remand. It held that the complaints, though artfully couched in terms of state law, were "in many respects identical" with the prior complaints, and were thus properly removed to federal court because they raised "essentially federal law" claims. The court then concluded that because *Moitie II* and *Brown II* involved the "same parties, the same alleged offenses, and the same time periods" as *Moitie I* and *Brown I*, the doctrine of *res judicata* required that they be dismissed. This time, Moitie and Brown appealed.

Pending that appeal, this Court on June 11, 1979, decided *Reiter v. Sonotone Corp.*, 442 U.S. 330, holding that retail purchasers can suffer an "injury" to their "business or property" as those terms are used in § 4 of the Clayton Act. On June 25, 1979, the Court of Appeals for the Ninth Circuit reversed and remanded the five cases which had been decided with *Moitie I* and *Brown I*, the cases that had been appealed, for further proceedings in light of *Reiter*. When *Moitie II* and *Brown II* finally came before the Court of Appeals for the Ninth Circuit, the court reversed the decision of the District Court dismissing the cases.[2] Though the court recognized that a "strict application of the doctrine of *res judicata* would preclude our review of the instant decision," it refused to apply the doctrine to the facts of this case. It observed that the other five litigants . . . had successfully appealed the decision against them. It then asserted that "non-appealing parties may benefit from a reversal when their position is closely interwoven with that of appealing parties," and concluded that "[because] the instant dismissal rested on a case that has been effectively overruled," the doctrine of *res judicata* must give way to "public policy" and "simple justice." We granted certiorari to consider the validity of the Court of Appeals' novel exception to the doctrine of *res judicata*.

---

2. The Court of Appeals also affirmed the District Court's conclusion that *Brown II* was properly removed to federal court, reasoning that the claims presented were "federal in nature." We agree that at least some of the claims had a sufficient federal character to support removal. As one treatise puts it, courts "will not permit plaintiff to use artful pleading to close off defendant's right to a federal forum . . . [and] occasionally the removal court will seek to determine whether the real nature of the claim is federal, regardless of plaintiff's characterization." 14 C. Wright, A. Miller, & E. Cooper, *Federal Practice and Procedure* § 3722, pp. 564-566 (1976). The District Court applied that settled principle to the facts of this case. After "an extensive review and analysis of the origins and substance of" the two Brown complaints, it found, and the Court of Appeals expressly agreed, that respondents had attempted to avoid removal jurisdiction by "[artfully]" casting their "essentially federal law claims" as state-law claims. We will not question here that factual finding.

II

There is little to be added to the doctrine of *res judicata* as developed in the case law of this Court. A final judgment on the merits of an action precludes the parties or their privies from relitigating issues that were or could have been raised in that action. Nor are the *res judicata* consequences of a final, unappealed judgment on the merits altered by the fact that the judgment may have been wrong or rested on a legal principle subsequently overruled in another case. As this Court explained in *Baltimore S.S. Co. v. Phillips*, 274 U.S. 316, 325 (1927), an "erroneous conclusion" reached by the court in the first suit does not deprive the defendants in the second action "of their right to rely upon the plea of *res judicata*. A judgment merely voidable because based upon an erroneous view of the law is not open to collateral attack, but can be corrected only by a direct review and not by bringing another action upon the same cause [of action]." We have observed that "[the] indulgence of a contrary view would result in creating elements of uncertainty and confusion and in undermining the conclusive character of judgments, consequences which it was the very purpose of the doctrine of *res judicata* to avert." *Reed v. Allen*, 286 U.S. 191, 201 (1932).

In this case, the Court of Appeals conceded that the "strict application of the doctrine of *res judicata*" required that *Brown II* be dismissed. By that, the court presumably meant that the "technical elements" of *res judicata* had been satisfied, namely, that the decision in *Brown I* was a final judgment on the merits and involved the same claims and the same parties as *Brown II*.[3] The court, however, declined to dismiss *Brown II* because, in its view, it would be unfair to bar respondents from relitigating a claim so "closely interwoven" with that of the successfully appealing parties. We believe that such an unprecedented departure from accepted principles of *res judicata* is unwarranted. Indeed, the decision below is all but foreclosed by our prior case law.

Indeed, this case presents even more compelling reasons to apply the doctrine of *res judicata* than did [prior cases]. Respondents here seek to be the windfall beneficiaries of an appellate reversal procured by other independent parties, who have no interest in respondents' case, not a reversal in interrelated cases procured by the same affected party. Moreover, it is apparent that respondents here made a calculated choice to forgo their appeals.

The Court of Appeals also rested its opinion in part on what it viewed as "simple justice." But we do not see the grave injustice which would be done by the application of accepted principles of *res judicata*. "Simple justice" is achieved when a complex body of law developed over a period of years is evenhandedly applied. The doctrine of *res judicata* serves vital public interests beyond any individual judge's ad hoc determination of the equities in a particular case. There is simply "no principle of law or equity which sanctions the rejection by a federal court of the salutary principle of *res judicata*." The Court of Appeals' reliance on "public

---

3. The dismissal for failure to state a claim under Federal Rule of Civil Procedure 12(b)(6) is a "judgment on the merits."

policy" is similarly misplaced. This Court has long recognized that "[public] policy dictates that there be an end of litigation; that those who have contested an issue shall be bound by the result of the contest, and that matters once tried shall be considered forever settled as between the parties." We have stressed that "[the] doctrine of *res judicata* is not a mere matter of practice or procedure inherited from a more technical time than ours. It is a rule of fundamental and substantial justice, of public policy and of private peace, which should be cordially regarded and enforced by the courts." Respondents argue that "the district court's dismissal on grounds of *res judicata* should be reversed, and the district court directed to grant respondent's motion to remand to the California state court." In their view, *Brown I* cannot be considered *res judicata* as to their state-law claims, since *Brown I* raised only federal-law claims and *Brown II* raised additional state-law claims not decided in *Brown I*, such as unfair competition, fraud, and restitution.

It is unnecessary for this Court to reach that issue. It is enough for our decision here that *Brown I* is *res judicata* as to respondents' federal-law claims. Accordingly, the judgment of the Court of Appeals is reversed, and the cause is remanded for proceedings consistent with this opinion. It is so ordered.

Justice BLACKMUN, with whom Justice MARSHALL joins, concurring in the judgment:

While I agree with the result reached in this case, I write separately to state my views on two points.

First, I, for one, would not close the door upon the possibility that there are cases in which the doctrine of *res judicata* must give way to what the Court of Appeals referred to as "overriding concerns of public policy and simple justice." Respondents were not "caught in a mesh of procedural complexities." Instead, they made a deliberate tactical decision not to appeal. Nor would public policy be served by making an exception to the doctrine in this case; to the contrary, there is a special need for strict application of *res judicata* in complex multiple party actions of this sort so as to discourage "break-away" litigation. Finally, this is not a case "where the rights of appealing and non-appealing parties are so interwoven or dependent on each other as to require a reversal of the whole judgment when a part thereof is reversed."

Second, and in contrast, I would flatly hold that *Brown I* is *res judicata* as to respondents' state-law claims. Like the District Court, the Court of Appeals found that those state-law claims were simply disguised federal claims; since respondents have not cross-petitioned from that judgment, their argument that this case should be remanded to state court should be itself barred by *res judicata*. More important, even if the state and federal claims are distinct, respondents' failure to allege the state claims in *Brown I* manifestly bars their allegation in *Brown II*. The dismissal of *Brown I* is *res judicata* not only as to all claims respondents actually raised, but also as to all claims that could have been raised. Since there is no reason to believe that it was clear at the outset of this litigation that the District Court would have declined to exercise pendent jurisdiction over state claims, respondents were obligated to plead those claims if they wished to preserve them. Because they did not do so, I would hold the claims barred.

Justice BRENNAN, dissenting:

In its eagerness to correct the decision of the Court of Appeals for the Ninth Circuit, the Court today disregards statutory restrictions on federal-court jurisdiction, and, in the process, confuses rather than clarifies long-established principles of *res judicata*. I therefore respectfully dissent.

I

Respondent Floyd R. Brown filed this class action (*Brown II*) against petitioners in California state court. The complaint stated four state-law causes of action: (1) fraud and deceit, (2) unfair business practices, (3) civil conspiracy, and (4) restitution. It alleged "not less than $600" damages per class member, and in addition sought "appropriate multiple damages," exemplary and punitive damages, interest from date of injury, attorney's fees and costs, and other relief. All four of the causes of action rested wholly on California statutory or common law; none rested in any fashion on federal law.

Nonetheless, petitioners removed the suit to the United States District Court for the Northern District of California, where respondent Brown filed a motion to remand on the ground that his action raised no federal question within the meaning of 28 U.S.C. § 1441(b). Respondent's motion was denied by the District Court, which stated that "[from] start to finish, plaintiffs have essentially alleged violations by defendants of federal antitrust laws." The court reasoned that "[artful] pleading" by plaintiffs cannot "convert their essentially federal law claims into state law claims," and held that respondent's complaint was properly removed "because [it] concerned federal questions which could have been originally brought in Federal District Court without satisfying any minimum amount in controversy." The court then dismissed the action, holding that, under the doctrine of *res judicata, Brown II* was barred by the adverse decision in an earlier suit in federal court (*Brown I*) involving "the same parties, the same alleged offenses, and the same time periods."

The Court of Appeals affirmed the District Court's decision not to remand, stating that "[the] court below correctly held that the claims presented were federal in nature." However, the Court of Appeals reversed the District Court's order of dismissal, and remanded for trial.

II

The provision authorizing removal of actions from state to federal courts on the basis of a federal question[2] is found in 28 U.S.C. § 1441(b):

---

2. As the District Court acknowledged, *Brown II* could not be removed on the basis of diversity of citizenship, because the amount in controversy did not exceed $10,000.

Any civil action of which the district courts have original jurisdiction founded on a claim or right arising under the Constitution, treaties or laws of the United States shall be removable without regard to the citizenship or residence of the parties.

Removability depends solely upon the nature of the plaintiff's complaint: an action may be removed to federal court only if a "right or immunity created by the Constitution or laws of the United States [constitutes] an element, and an essential one, of the plaintiff's cause of action." An action arising under state law may not be removed solely because a federal right or immunity is raised as a defense.

An important corollary is that "the party who brings a suit is master to decide what law he will rely upon and therefore does determine whether he will bring a 'suit arising under' the . . . [laws] of the United States" by the allegations in his complaint. Where the plaintiff's claim might be brought under either federal or state law, the plaintiff is normally free to ignore the federal question and rest his claim solely on the state ground. If he does so, the defendant has no general right of removal.

This corollary is well grounded in principles of federalism. So long as States retain authority to legislate in subject areas in which Congress has legislated without pre-empting the field, and so long as state courts remain the preferred forum for interpretation and enforcement of state law, plaintiffs must be permitted to proceed in state court under state law. It would do violence to state autonomy were defendants able to remove state claims to federal court merely because the plaintiff could have asserted a federal claim based on the same set of facts underlying his state claim.

This lawsuit concerns the area of antitrust in which federal laws have not displaced state law. Thus, respondent Brown had the option of proceeding under state or federal law, or both. So far as is apparent from the complaint, which was carefully limited to four California state-law causes of action, this case arises wholly without reference to federal law. Under settled principles of federal jurisdiction, therefore, respondent's lawsuit should not have been removed to federal court.

The Court today nonetheless sustains removal of this action on the ground that "at least some of the claims had a sufficient federal character to support removal." I do not understand what the Court means by this. Which of the claims are federal in character? Why are the claims federal in character? In my view, they are all predicated solely on California law. Certainly, none of them purports to state a claim under the federal antitrust laws, and the mere fact that plaintiffs might have chosen to proceed under the Clayton Act surely does not suffice to transmute their state claims into federal claims.

The Court relies on what it calls a "factual finding" by the District Court, with which the Court of Appeals agreed, that "respondents had attempted to avoid removal jurisdiction by '[artfully]' casting their 'essentially federal law claims' as state-law claims." But this amounts to no more than a pejorative characterization of respondents' decision to proceed under state rather than federal law. "Artful" or not, respondents' complaints were not based on any claim of a federal right or immunity, and were not, therefore, removable. . . .

Even assuming that this Court and the lower federal courts have jurisdiction to decide this case, however, I dissent from the Court's disposition of the *res judicata* issue. Having reached out to assume jurisdiction, the Court inexplicably recoils from deciding the case. The Court finds it "unnecessary" to reach the question of the *res judicata* effect of *Brown I* on respondents' "state-law claims." "It is enough for our decision here," the Court says, "that *Brown I* is *res judicata* as to respondents' federal-law claims." But respondents raised only state-law claims; respondents did not raise any federal-law claims. Thus, if the Court fails to decide the disposition of respondents' state-law claims, it decides nothing. And in doing so, the Court introduces the possibility—heretofore foreclosed by our decisions—that unarticulated theories of recovery may survive an unconditional dismissal of the lawsuit.

Like Justice Blackmun, I would hold that the dismissal of *Brown I* is *res judicata* not only as to every matter that was actually litigated, but also as to every ground or theory of recovery that might also have been presented. An unqualified dismissal on the merits of a substantial federal antitrust claim precludes relitigation of the same claim on a state-law theory. The Court's failure to acknowledge this basic principle can only create doubts and confusion where none were before, and may encourage litigants to split their causes of action, state from federal, in the hope that they might win a second day in court.

I therefore respectfully dissent, and would vacate the judgment of the Court of Appeals with instructions to remand to the District Court with instructions to remand to state court.

REVIEW QUESTIONS

1. *Moitie* demonstrates the very high priority our litigation system places on finality. In reaching the same result in a case invoking Fed. R. Civ. P. 60(b)(5)'s clause permitting a judgment to be reopened when it was "based on an earlier judgment that has been reversed or vacated," Judge Nancy Gertner wrote:

   > The Federal Rules of Civil Procedure place considerable importance on the finality of judgments, even as legal precedents come and go. Parties who complete litigation must be able to expect that a court's decision will continue to have effect. Accordingly, the Rules preclude reopening cases except in certain narrow circumstances not applicable here.

   Comfort ex rel. Neumyer v. Lynn School Committee, 541 F. Supp. 2d 429, 430 (D. Mass. 2008). The plaintiffs had argued unsuccessfully that an intervening Supreme Court decision declaring voluntary desegregation plans unconstitutional should change the result of their prior challenge to the plan, which had been dismissed.

2. Do you agree with the Court's explicit equation of finality and "simple justice"? When you read *United States v. Mendoza* in Note 7 below, and

Martin v. Wilks, reprinted later in this book, consider whether the Court is *always* consistent in treating adjudication as absolutely conclusive.

3. Can you reconcile the Court's suggestion at the end of the *Moitie* opinion—that *Brown I* may be *res judicata* only as to the *federal law* claims—with the established principle that claim preclusion operates as to *all* transactionally related claims that *could have been raised* in the prior proceeding? Do Justices Blackmun, Marshall, and Brennan stay closer to this principle in their analysis? Note Brennan's concern that the "Court introduces the possibility—heretofore foreclosed by our decisions—that unarticulated theories of recovery may survive an unconditional dismissal of the lawsuit." Why would the majority, which is so enthusiastic about finality, under-enforce *res judicata* in this way?

4. What is the relationship between the preclusion issue and the question of removal in *Moitie*? Is there not a contradiction between the Court's conclusion that *Brown II* was properly removed because of the "federal nature" of its assertedly state-law claims, and its suggestion nonetheless that *Brown II*'s state-law claims may not be precluded by *Brown I* because that case set out only federal claims? How could *Brown II* be a "disguised" federal claim for purposes of removal, yet avoid preclusion by the prior dismissal of that very federal claim? What does Justice Brennan say about this?

5. The Court's footnote 2 alludes to the so-called artful pleading doctrine, which prevents a plaintiff from depriving a defendant of the right to remove to a federal forum by cleverly pleading the case as a purely state-law claim, when in fact it is "federal in nature." Justice Brennan, harking back to the notion invoked in *Mottley* that the plaintiff is "the master" of his complaint and thus gets to decide what law to rely on, characterizes this artful pleading doctrine as a violation of the "principles of federalism" and an affront to "state autonomy."

   Also critical of the doctrine, Professor Arthur Miller concludes that the Supreme Court gave the removal question only "slight attention" in *Moitie*, and that subsequent decisions have raised serious question about the viability of the Court's reasoning in footnote 2. *See* Arthur R. Miller, *Artful Pleading: A Doctrine in Search of Definition*, 76 Tex. L. Rev. 1781 (1998).

6. Four years after *Moitie*, the Supreme Court returned to the claim preclusion question in the context of overlapping state and federal antitrust claims. In *Marrese v. American Academy of Orthopaedic Surgeons*, 470 U.S. 373 (1985), plaintiffs brought a Sherman Act case in federal court (which has exclusive jurisdiction over such claims) following unsuccessful litigation in state court challenging their exclusion from membership in the Academy. The Court held that the federal full faith and credit statute, 28 U.S.C. § 1738 (discussed in our next case), required that the federal court apply the state's law of claim preclusion to determine whether the

state court judgment barred the subsequent federal antitrust claim even though the latter could not have been raised in the state proceeding.

In so ruling, the Court rejected the position of Judge Cudahy who, dissenting from the Seventh Circuit's decision below barring the federal antitrust claim, argued in favor of the definition of claim preclusion embodied in the *Restatement (Second) of Judgments*, which requires that the prior court must have been able to exercise jurisdiction over the subsequent claim for preclusion to apply. Given exclusive federal jurisdiction, plaintiffs could not have litigated their Sherman Act claim in state court.

To read more about this topic, *see* Stephen B. Burbank, *Afterwords: A Response to Professor Hazard and a Comment on* Marrese, 70 Cornell L. Rev. 659 (1985) and David J. Schulte, *The Claim Preclusive Effect of State Court Judgments on Federal Antitrust Claims:* Marrese v. American Academy of Orthopaedic Surgeons, 71 Iowa L. Rev. 609 (1986).

How can plaintiffs avoid risking loss of their federal claim in the *Marrese* situation? What about filing the case in federal court in the first instance and seeking supplemental jurisdiction over the state claims?

7. Writing for the Court in *United States v. Mendoza*, 464 U.S. 154 (1984), Justice Rehnquist (who in *Moitie* insisted there were *no* exceptions to the doctrine of *res judicata*) carved out an exception to the use of issue preclusion against the U.S. government. Like Moitie and Brown, the government failed to appeal an adverse decision by a U.S. District Court holding that the due process rights of a group of Filipino World War II veterans had been violated when their citizenship naturalization process had been suspended. Mendoza (not a party to the earlier case) later brought a suit raising the same issue, and the Ninth Circuit held the government was estopped from relitigating it. The Supreme Court disagreed:

> A rule allowing nonmutual collateral estoppel against the Government in such cases would substantially thwart the development of important questions of law by freezing the first final decision rendered on a particular legal issue. Allowing only one final adjudication would deprive this Court of the benefit it receives from permitting several courts of appeals to explore a difficult question before this Court grants certiorari.

What happened to *strict* application of preclusion doctrine?

PRACTICE EXERCISE NO. 41: PRECLUSION AND NEW PRECEDENT IN *CARPENTER*

Assume that Nancy Carpenter filed an action in Superior Court against the City of Lowell based on the failure of the police officers who had stopped Randall Dee to advise him that the jeep had been illegally and dangerously modified. The action was dismissed on defendant's 12(b)(6) motion, the court relying on precedent holding that municipalities in the Commonwealth are not liable for the negligence of their employees. No appeal was filed, and a final judgment was entered for the City.

One month later, the Massachusetts Supreme Judicial Court, in an unrelated case, repudiated the prior precedent and announced a new rule rendering municipalities liable for the negligent acts of their employees. May Nancy Carpenter take advantage of this development and refile her suit against the City?

* * *

Should the usual rules of issue preclusion have been suspended as a matter of policy in the next case?

Allen v. McCurry
449 U.S. 90 (1980)

Justice STEWART delivered the opinion of the Court:

At a hearing before his criminal trial in a Missouri court, the respondent, Willie McCurry, invoked the Fourth and Fourteenth Amendments to suppress evidence that had been seized by the police. The trial court denied the suppression motion in part, and McCurry was subsequently convicted after a jury trial. The conviction was later affirmed on appeal. . . . [H]e sought federal-court redress for the alleged constitutional violation by bringing a damages suit under 42 U.S.C. § 1983 against the officers who had entered his home and seized the evidence in question. We granted certiorari to consider whether . . . the police officers [were precluded] from raising the state courts' partial rejection of McCurry's constitutional claim as a collateral estoppel defense to the § 1983 suit against them for damages.

I

In April 1977, several undercover police officers, following an informant's tip that McCurry was dealing in heroin, went to his house in St. Louis, Mo., to attempt a purchase. Two officers, petitioners Allen and Jacobsmeyer, knocked on the front door, while the other officers hid nearby. When McCurry opened the door, the two officers asked to buy some heroin "caps." McCurry went back into the house and returned soon thereafter, firing a pistol at and seriously wounding Allen and Jacobsmeyer. After a gun battle with the other officers and their reinforcements, McCurry retreated into the house; he emerged again when the police demanded that he surrender. Several officers then entered the house without a warrant, purportedly to search for other persons inside. One of the officers seized drugs and other contraband that lay in plain view, as well as additional contraband he found in dresser drawers and in auto tires on the porch.

McCurry was charged with possession of heroin and assault with intent to kill. At the pretrial suppression hearing, the trial judge excluded the evidence seized from the dresser drawers and tires, but denied suppression of the evidence found in plain view. McCurry was convicted of both the heroin and assault offenses.

McCurry subsequently filed the present § 1983 action for $1 million in damages against petitioners Allen and Jacobsmeyer, other unnamed individual police officers, and the city of St. Louis and its police department. The complaint alleged a conspiracy to violate McCurry's Fourth Amendment rights, an unconstitutional search and seizure of his house, and an assault on him by unknown police officers after he had been arrested and handcuffed. The petitioners moved for summary judgment. The District Court apparently understood the gist of the complaint to be the allegedly unconstitutional search and seizure and granted summary judgment, holding that collateral estoppel prevented McCurry from relitigating the search-and-seizure question already decided against him in the state courts.

The Court of Appeals reversed the judgment and remanded the case for trial and directed the trial court to allow him to proceed to trial unencumbered by collateral estoppel.

II

The federal courts have traditionally adhered to the related doctrines of *res judicata* and collateral estoppel. Under *res judicata*, a final judgment on the merits of an action precludes the parties or their privies from relitigating issues that were or could have been raised in that action. Under collateral estoppel, once a court has decided an issue of fact or law necessary to its judgment, that decision may preclude relitigation of the issue in a suit on a different cause of action involving a party to the first case. As this Court and other courts have often recognized, *res judicata* and collateral estoppel relieve parties of the cost and vexation of multiple lawsuits, conserve judicial resources, and, by preventing inconsistent decisions, encourage reliance on adjudication.

In recent years, this Court has reaffirmed the benefits of collateral estoppel in particular, finding the policies underlying it to apply in contexts not formerly recognized at common law. Thus, the Court has eliminated the requirement of mutuality in applying collateral estoppel to bar relitigation of issues decided earlier in federal-court suits, and has allowed a litigant who was not a party to a federal case to use collateral estoppel "offensively" in a new federal suit against the party who lost on the decided issue in the first case, *Parklane Hosiery Co. v. Shore*, 439 U.S. 322. But one general limitation the Court has repeatedly recognized is that the concept of collateral estoppel cannot apply when the party against whom the earlier decision is asserted did not have a "full and fair opportunity" to litigate that issue in the earlier case.

The federal courts generally have also consistently accorded preclusive effect to issues decided by state courts. *Res judicata* and collateral estoppel not only reduce unnecessary litigation and foster reliance on adjudication, but also promote the comity between state and federal courts that has been recognized as a bulwark of the federal system.

Indeed, though the federal courts may look to the common law or to the policies supporting *res judicata* and collateral estoppel in assessing the preclusive effect of decisions of other federal courts, Congress has specifically required all federal courts to give preclusive effect to state-court judgments whenever the courts of the State from which the judgments emerged would do so:

> [Judicial] proceedings [of any court of any State] shall have the same full faith and credit in every court within the United States and its Territories and Possessions as they have by law or usage in the courts of such State. . . .

III

This Court has never directly decided whether the rules of *res judicata* and collateral estoppel are generally applicable to § 1983 actions. The legislative history of § 1983 does not in any clear way suggest that Congress intended to repeal or restrict the traditional doctrines of preclusion. The main goal of the Act was to override the corrupting influence of the Ku Klux Klan and its sympathizers on the governments and law enforcement agencies of the Southern States, and of course the debates show that one strong motive behind its enactment was grave congressional concern that the state courts had been deficient in protecting federal rights. But in the context of the legislative history as a whole, this congressional concern lends only the most equivocal support to any argument that, in cases where the state courts have recognized the constitutional claims asserted and provided fair procedures for determining them, Congress intended to override § 1738 or the common-law rules of collateral estoppel and *res judicata*.

Collateral estoppel does not apply where the party against whom an earlier court decision is asserted did not have a full and fair opportunity to litigate the claim or issue decided by the first court. But [there is] no strength to any argument that Congress intended to allow relitigation of federal issues decided after a full and fair hearing in a state court simply because the state court's decision may have been erroneous.

The only conceivable basis for finding a universal right to litigate a federal claim in a federal district court is hardly a legal basis at all, but rather a general distrust of the capacity of the state courts to render correct decisions on constitutional issues. [This Court has emphatically rejected that position.]

The Court of Appeals erred in holding the doctrine of collateral estoppel inapplicable to his § 1983 suit. Accordingly, the judgment is reversed, and the case is remanded to the Court of Appeals for proceedings consistent with this opinion.

It is so ordered.

Justice BLACKMUN, with whom Justice BRENNAN and Justice MARSHALL join, dissenting:

The legal principles with which the Court is concerned in this civil case obviously far transcend the ugly facts of respondent's criminal convictions in the courts of Missouri for heroin possession and assault.

The Court today holds that notions of collateral estoppel apply with full force to this suit brought under 42 U.S.C. § 1983. In my view, the Court, in so ruling, ignores the clear import of the legislative history of that statute and disregards the important federal policies that underlie its enforcement. It also shows itself insensitive both to the significant differences between the § 1983 remedy and the exclusionary rule, and to the pressures upon a criminal defendant that make a free choice of forum illusory. I do not doubt that principles of preclusion are to be given such effect as is appropriate in a § 1983 action. In many cases, the denial of *res judicata* or collateral estoppel effect would serve no purpose and would harm relations between federal and state tribunals. Nonetheless, the Court's analysis in this particular case is unacceptable to me. It works injustice on this § 1983 plaintiff, and it makes more difficult the consistent protection of constitutional rights, a consideration that was at the core of the enacters' intent. Accordingly, I dissent.

In this case, the police officers seek to prevent a criminal defendant from relitigating the constitutionality of their conduct in searching his house, after the state trial court had found that conduct in part violative of the defendant's Fourth Amendment rights and in part justified by the circumstances. I doubt that the police officers, now defendants in this § 1983 action, can be considered to have been in privity with the State in its role as prosecutor. Therefore, only "issue preclusion" is at stake.

The process of deciding in a state criminal trial whether to exclude or admit evidence is not at all the equivalent of a § 1983 proceeding. The remedy sought in the latter is utterly different. In bringing the civil suit the criminal defendant does not seek to challenge his conviction collaterally. At most, he wins damages. In contrast, the exclusion of evidence may prevent a criminal conviction. A trial court, faced with the decision whether to exclude relevant evidence, confronts institutional pressures that may cause it to give a different shape to the Fourth Amendment right from what would result in civil litigation of a damages claim. Also, the issue whether to exclude evidence is subsidiary to the purpose of a criminal trial, which is to determine the guilt or innocence of the defendant, and a trial court, at least subconsciously, must weigh the potential damage to the truth-seeking process caused by excluding relevant evidence.

A state criminal defendant cannot be held to have chosen "voluntarily" to litigate his Fourth Amendment claim in the state court. The risk of conviction puts pressure upon him to raise all possible defenses. He also faces uncertainty about the wisdom of forgoing litigation on any issue, for there is the possibility that he will be held to have waived his right to appeal on that issue. The "deliberate bypass" of state procedures, which the imposition of collateral estoppel under these circumstances encourages, surely is not a preferred goal. To hold that a criminal defendant who raises a Fourth Amendment claim at his criminal trial "freely and without reservation submits his federal claims for decision by the state courts," is to deny reality. The criminal defendant is an involuntary litigant in the state tribunal, and against him all the forces of the State are arrayed. To force him to a choice between forgoing either a potential defense or a federal forum for hearing his constitutional civil claim is fundamentally unfair.

I would affirm the judgment of the Court of Appeals.

REVIEW QUESTIONS

1. What policy concerns are invoked by the dissenters to outweigh strict application of preclusion doctrine in the context of a federal civil rights action following on the heels of a state criminal prosecution? How does the Court answer these concerns?

2. Four years after *Allen v. McCurry*, the Court revisited the question of whether preclusion doctrine should be suspended in order to provide a federal forum for civil rights claims. Dr. Ethel D. Migra brought a state court breach of contract action against the Board of Education when it reneged on its earlier renewal of her contract as supervisor of elementary education. She prevailed, and was awarded reinstatement and compensatory damages. She subsequently filed a § 1983 action in federal court alleging that her nonrenewal was in retaliation for her role as an advocate of desegregation in the school district, thereby depriving her of constitutional rights. The district court granted summary judgment for the defendants on the basis of *res judicata*, and the Supreme Court affirmed. *Migra v. Warren City School District Board of Education*, 465 U.S. 75 (1984):

> The Court in *Allen* left open the possibility that the preclusive effect of a state-court judgment might be different as to a federal issue that a § 1983 litigant could have raised but did not raise in the earlier state-court proceeding. That is the central issue to be resolved in the present case. Petitioner did not litigate her § 1983 claim in state court, and she asserts that the state-court judgment should not preclude her suit in federal court simply because her federal claim could have been litigated in the state-court proceeding. Thus, petitioner urges this Court to interpret the interplay of § 1738 and § 1983 in such a way as to accord state-court judgments preclusive effect in § 1983 suits only as to issues actually litigated in state court.
>
> Petitioner suggests that to give state-court judgments full issue preclusive effect but not claim preclusive effect would enable litigants to bring their state claims in state court and their federal claims in federal court, thereby taking advantage of the relative expertise of both forums. Although such a division may seem attractive from a plaintiff's perspective, it is not the system established by § 1738. That statute embodies the view that it is more important to give full faith and credit to state-court judgments than to ensure separate forums for federal and state claims. This reflects a variety of concerns, including notions of comity, the need to prevent vexatious litigation, and a desire to conserve judicial resources. In the present litigation, petitioner does not claim that the state court would not have adjudicated her federal claims had she presented them

in her original suit in state court. Alternatively, petitioner could have obtained a federal forum for her federal claim by litigating it first in a federal court. Section 1983, however, does not override state preclusion law and guarantee petitioner a right to proceed to judgment in state court on her state claims and then turn to federal court for adjudication of her federal claims. We hold, therefore, that petitioner's state-court judgment in this litigation has the same claim preclusive effect in federal court that the judgment would have in the Ohio state courts.

465 U.S. at 83-85. *See also Kremer v. Chemical Constr. Corp.*, 456 U.S. 461 (1982) (a state court decision upholding on appeal an administrative agency's rejection of an employment discrimination claim precludes the subsequent filing of a federal Title VII claim in federal court). *But see University of Tennessee v. Elliott*, 478 U.S. 788 (1986) (where plaintiff has not sought review of the state administrative determinations, they do not have preclusive effect in a Title VII action; preclusive effect is, however, accorded to fact determinations made by a state agency in its judicial capacity when plaintiff seeks to relitigate them in a federal civil rights action under the Reconstruction statutes).

3. What are the lessons of *Allen v. McCurry*, *Migra v. Warren City School District Board of Education*, and *Kremer v. Chemical Constr. Corp.* for lawyers who represent plaintiffs in civil rights cases and seek to do so in federal court? Can supplemental jurisdiction (28 USC § 1367) play a useful role?

Summary Note on Cross-Jurisdictional Preclusion. As we have seen, the rules of finality operate expansively across many boundary lines—between State *A* and State *B*, between state and federal courts, between civil and criminal cases. A plaintiff cannot generally split her claim into transactionally related federal and state lawsuits. Issues litigated and resolved between litigants in state court are precluded from being relitigated in federal court, and vice versa. Issues resolved against a defendant in a criminal case will usually prelude relitigation by that party in a subsequent civil case. The following list summarizes the line-crossing nature of preclusion doctrine.

State → State. The Full Faith and Credit Clause of the Constitution mandates that a court in State *B* accord a judgment rendered in State *A* the same preclusive effect the judgment would have in State *A*.

State → Federal. 28 U.S.C. § 1738 imposes the same "full faith and credit" obligation on federal courts with regard to judgments of any state court. *See generally San Remo Hotel, L.P. v. City & County of San Francisco*, 545 U.S. 323 (2005).

Federal → State. The preclusive effect in state court of a prior federal court judgment was the subject of *Semtek International, Inc. v. Lockheed Martin Corp.*, 531 U.S. 497 (2001), discussed in Chapter 9. Where the judgment was entered in a federal question case (§ 1331), it is accorded the preclusive effect that federal common law provides. For diversity case judgments (§ 1332), *Semtek* mandates that federal common law incorporate the preclusion rules that would be applied by the state courts in the state in which the judgment was rendered. This is in order to avoid the forum shopping and inequitable administration of justice problems underlying the *Erie* doctrine. For a pre-*Semtek* treatment of the topic, see Stephen B. Burbank, *Interjurisdictional Preclusion, Full Faith and Credit and Federal Common Law: A General Approach*, 71 Cornell L. Rev. 733 (1986).

REVIEW EXERCISE NO. 11

To: Law Clerks
From: Trial Judge
Re: *Collector v. Gallery*

In *Charles Collector* (Collector) *v. Cape Gallery, Inc.* (Gallery), commenced June 10, 2019, both sides (subsequent to discovery) have moved for total or partial summary judgment, relying on preclusion law. Our state Supreme Court has, in other cases, affirmed the application of nonmutual collateral estoppel when deemed appropriate. Please tell me how to rule and why.

Collector's complaint alleges in relevant part: (1) On March 4, 2018, he purchased a painting ("Truro Fog") from Gallery for $7,200, which Sally Sales, while working for Gallery, and with authority, guaranteed him in writing was painted by Karl Knaths (Knaths) in 1962; (2) on May 4, 2019, Collector first realized the painting was a forgery; (3) if it were an original Knaths, the painting would be worth $30,000, but instead it is valueless; (4) Gallery owes Collector $30,000 as a result of breach of written guarantee. Gallery's answer admits all allegations in item; states, as to item 2, that it is without sufficient knowledge to answer when Collector realized anything and denies the allegation of forgery; and denies all allegations in items 3 and 4. Gallery asserts the affirmative defense of *res judicata*. Both parties demand a jury trial.

To support its partial summary judgment motion based on issue preclusion, Collector points to the pleadings and has filed three affidavits. One affidavit, signed by Collector, states that each allegation of his complaint is true; he is an experienced appraiser of oil paintings; he has had much experience buying and selling paintings by Knaths; if the Knaths was not a forgery it would be worth $30,000, but if the painting he bought is not a Knaths it is worthless. A second affidavit, signed by Carla Expert, says that she has been a professor of Modern Art at the Museum School for twenty-two years; she has compared "Wellfleet Sunset" and "Provincetown Pier" (both 1962 paintings allegedly by Knaths, which are in the Museum School Collection) with "Truro Fog" and there is no way that the painter of "Truro Fog" was the same painter who painted "Wellfleet Sunset" and "Provincetown Pier": The colors, brush strokes, types of paint, and sense of abstraction are too different. The third affidavit is signed by the clerk of the Superior Court and states that the attached docket, pleadings, complete transcript, and opinion are accurate copies. These documents show that in the earlier case of *The Museum School v. Gallery*, commenced January 3, 2016, in the Superior Court (with no jury), an action to rescind (for reason of mutual mistake or fraud) a contract to buy "Wellfleet Sunset" and "Provincetown Pier" on the grounds the paintings were not by Knaths, the judge found in favor of Gallery and wrote in her opinion that "I find in this hotly contested case that was tried for six days in September 2016, with many witnesses on both sides, that both paintings were painted in 1962 by Karl Knaths. Gallery's experts were persuasive as to the authenticity of the two Knaths." Final judgment was entered for Gallery on October 22, 2016, and no appeal was taken.

Gallery's motion for summary judgment based on claim preclusion is accompanied by an affidavit of the clerk of the Superior Court regarding another case of Collector against Gallery, commenced on August 1, 2019, with copies of the docket, pleadings, defendant's interrogatories, motions, and court order. The complaint stated that from January 1, 2018, through July 31, 2019, Collector had purchased three paintings on three different occasions from Gallery (all modern paintings but only one by Knaths, "Moon over Eastham," allegedly a 1960 painting), each with a separate written guarantee of authenticity, signed by different Gallery employees, and that Collector sought to rescind the purchases for fraud or mutual mistake, on the ground that none of the three were by their purported painters. Gallery admitted the sales and guarantees, denied the fraud and mistake, and alleged that each painting was authentic. The papers showed that, despite a court order, Collector had repeatedly refused to answer interrogatories or show up for depositions, and that the judge ordered the case dismissed with prejudice pursuant to the state counterpart of Fed. R. Civ. P. 37(b)(2)(A).

Gallery also filed an interrogatory answer submitted by Collector in the case presently before me, stating that Collector was paying Carla Expert $100 per hour for all work performed on this case, and an affidavit by Gallery's lawyer that she intended to cross-examine both Collector and Expert at the trial to show their bias, among other things.

CHAPTER 11

Aggregate Litigation: It All Comes Together

A. INTRODUCTION

Aggregate litigation describes a collection of procedural mechanisms that allow individual lawsuits to be grouped together. The core example is the class action, when one representative plaintiff sues on behalf of similarly situated people. In a class action, the class members cede control over their individual lawsuits in exchange for the benefits of collective action. These benefits include the ability to maintain a lawsuit in cases where the remedy is too inconsequential to merit individual litigation or the ability to reform institutions with class-wide injunctive relief.

There are ways to consolidate lawsuits to obtain efficiency gains other than the class action. For example, Rule 42 allows judges to consolidate separate suits for trial when they share "a common issue of law or fact." On a larger scale, the multidistrict litigation statute, 28 U.S.C. § 1407, allows a central panel of judges (called the Judicial Panel of Multidistrict Litigation or JPML) to transfer cases "involving one or more common questions of fact" for pretrial adjudication before a single district judge. Congress passed the multidistrict litigation statute very soon after the rulemakers promulgated the class action rule. The drafters of the statute understood that certain classes of cases likely to be brought would not be able to be adjudicated under the class action rule, but needed to be aggregated in some manner to avoid repetitive adjudication and waste of judicial resources. *See* Andrew D. Bradt, *Something Less and Something More: MDL's Roots as a Class Action Alternative*, 165 U. Pa. L. Rev. 1711, 1713 (2017). It was presented as more of a "housekeeping" rule than a rule that transformed litigation. But, in fact, it does transform litigation by moving cases before a single judge. As in a class action, individual plaintiffs may lose control over their cases to a plaintiffs' management committee and judicial rulings will affect all the cases in the multidistrict litigation.

You can find a list of multidistrict litigations currently pending at www .jpml.uscourts.gov. These aggregations are often referred to as "MDLs" and they have become increasingly controversial in recent years. As of this writing, between 20 and 40 percent of pending federal cases are part of MDLs. However, this does not mean that the bulk of cases brought in the federal courts are in MDLs. These aggregations of cases take much longer to resolve than the average case, and therefore tend to be in the system longer. Still, MDLs involve many thousands of plaintiffs and often significant litigation exposure for defendants, so they are important. It is worthwhile to remember that although the cases are aggregated, each case in the MDL keeps its own docket number and in theory is an individual lawsuit, even if in practice these suits are usually settled together. By contrast, a class action is one lawsuit with one docket number encompassing many class members. Any kind of lawsuit can be transferred to an MDL, such as for example a number of class actions alleging the same antitrust conspiracy or a large number of individual product liability suits.

In some ways, aggregate litigation is an extension of the simple joinder doctrines you learned about in Chapter 3. All forms of aggregation, from joinder under Rule 20 to complex aggregations such as MDLs or class actions, involve the same fundamental standard, which is whether the cases share a common question of law or fact. Yet, as you will see, these words have been interpreted very differently depending on context.

Larger aggregations of cases, where it is not expected that individual plaintiffs will be able to actively participate in the litigation, also raise three significant problems that make them different from litigation in binary cases. This is true whatever the form of the aggregation: a class action, an MDL, or some other consolidation. These problems are (1) the agent principal problem between plaintiffs and their representatives; (2) horizontal equity between plaintiffs; and (3) the desire for global resolution of the litigation, sometimes referred to by scholars as "global peace." We introduce these problems briefly here. Keep them in mind as you read on about class actions, the paradigm aggregation where many of these issues were noticed for the first time.

The Agent Principal Problem. The concern in the class action context is that the lawyer representing the class is the agent for the class, and economic theory would predict that the lawyer may have an incentive to settle early or cheaply to obtain a quicker or more lucrative payday for themselves at the expense of the class. Complaints about lawyers receiving a very high fee while class members receive only a few dollars are symptomatic of this concern. A similar problem arises in MDLs. For example, one small group of lawyers will be picked to be on the "Plaintiffs' Management Committee" or PMC, a group that coordinates the litigation. The concern is that these lawyers may be tempted to reach a settlement that is beneficial for themselves and their retained clients at the expense of the other lawsuits before the court. While the lawyer representing the class has a fiduciary duty to the class as a whole, there is no consensus on what duty the PMC lawyers owe to other lawyers or other clients.

Fairness Between Plaintiffs. A second issue raised by aggregation is fairness between plaintiffs. Do plaintiffs share enough of the same interests so that a small group can fairly represent the rest? Similar treatment of people different from one another can create problems. In one case, a class action brought by hemophiliacs who contracted HIV from tainted blood transfusions was settled for the same amount for each claimant. Judge Posner, who certified that class action, called the result "downright weird." *In re Factor VIII or IX Concentrate Blood Prods. Litig.*, 159 F.3d 1016, 1018 (7th Cir. 1998).

Aggregation also invites comparisons in outcomes between plaintiffs in a way individual litigation does not because all the class members or plaintiffs are before one court. We tolerate a great deal of inconsistency of outcomes in our system. This fact is obscured when cases are dispersed, and highlighted when they are consolidated. For example, in mass tort cases resolved under the auspices of the MDL or sometimes a class action, a settlement will set up a claims administration facility, essentially a form of ADR. Plaintiffs may question why another plaintiff received more than they did, if they think their injury is the same or worse. Or they may ask why the settlement money ran out after a certain date, and they were unable to collect. The aftermath of many of aggregate settlements seems to leave at least some plaintiffs unsatisfied.

Global Resolution for Defendants and the Judicial System. Resolving many cases together is more efficient than the alternative of individual litigation. A class action provides global peace by precluding any future claims by the class members. In an MDL, the parties may try to reach a global resolution either by creating a class action settlement to resolve the aggregated lawsuits or by conditioning settlement on a high participation rate. It is often beneficial to be able to tie up all litigation about a certain topic at once. The other side of the coin is that an aggregation may create additional pressure on a defendant to resolve the litigation globally because the size of the aggregation scares investors. This argument comes up most often in the context of class actions, as you will see in the cases below, but it also applies to MDLs and other aggregations. Even a trial of multiple plaintiffs at once under Rule 42 may be riskier for defendants than individual trials.

* * *

In this chapter, we mostly focus on the class action because it squarely presents the types of issues present in all aggregations, including more informal forms of aggregation, and it revisits a good deal of the civil procedure doctrine, concepts, and policies you have already studied in this course. Class actions are also one of the most debated procedural devices and for good reason. All of the anxiety-provoking issues in civil litigation are magnified in the class context, including questions of whether our system enables too much litigation, concerns about the cost of litigation to defendants and the economy, and concerns about trampling plaintiffs' individual rights in the name of efficiency. The doctrine of class actions and the practice of class action litigation also give rise to many questions about attorney incentives, individual rights, and access to justice that can only be understood in the political context of the times.

The chapter begins with a short historical overview and consideration of the policy debates surrounding class actions. These debates are applicable to most aggregations. We then consider the due process limitations on the class action, allowing us to review some of the material presented in Chapter 1. Then we turn to subject matter jurisdiction in aggregate litigation, for which Congress has established some special rules. After that we will reconsider the judicial role in such large-scale litigation. We end with a reconsideration of preclusion doctrine in the context of class actions. Throughout, keep in mind the policy issues raised above: fairness between litigants on the plaintiff side, the agent-principal problem, and the system's need for efficient resolution of disputes.

B. CLASS ACTION PRACTICE, POLICY, AND CONTEXT

1. Introduction

Because it can bind absent parties, the class action raises substantial due process concerns. The ordinary rule of civil litigation, as you have learned, is that parties cannot be bound by a judgment unless they have actually participated in the suit. Yet in the class action context individuals can be bound even though they have not had their day in court. How can this be? The first case in this chapter, *Hansberry v. Lee*, addresses this fundamental question, returning to the due process concerns raised in Chapter 1. The plaintiff class may also encompass individual class members from states outside the court's jurisdiction, even those who did not expressly consent to appear. The second case in this chapter, *Phillips Petroleum v. Shutts*, addresses the question of how a court can exercise personal jurisdiction over absent class members, returning to the due process concerns addressed in Chapter 7. Both of these cases were decided during a period when class action litigation was relatively new and rare, but the seeds of the current concerns about class actions had already been planted.

Even if the court's interpretation of due process allows a class action, this does not end the inquiry. In order for a lawsuit to proceed as a class action, it must be *certified* as a class action by a court. To do this, the court must find that the class action meets all the requirements of Rule 23. These requirements will be discussed in detail later in this chapter. As illustrated by the opinion in *Wal-Mart v. Dukes*, class certification is very difficult to achieve, especially in federal court, because the requirements have been tightened over time. Preclusion doctrine plays a critical role in understanding the reasons for the tightening of certification standards. If the class representative succeeds in certifying a class, the results of the class action litigation are binding on all the class members, even those who did not participate in the litigation and even those who did not actually *know* about the litigation.

2. Policy Concerns in Class Actions

Before delving into the doctrine, it is useful to consider the policy concerns that have driven the evolution of the law in this area. Class actions were a rarely used procedural device until the rule was liberalized in 1966. That year the rules drafters introduced a new structure to the class action rule, one which classified class actions based on remedies. After setting out basic requirements for sustaining a class action (numerosity, commonality, typicality, and adequate representation, to be discussed later in this chapter), the class action rule creates three types of class actions according to the type of remedy sought: (1) limited fund, (2) injunctive, and (3) money damages class actions. Limited fund class actions are brought, as their name suggests, when there is a limited pot of money to pay a group of individuals with claims against a defendant. Injunctive class actions are often civil rights cases. Money damages class actions can run the gamut from back pay claims in an employment discrimination suit to compensatory damages in a consumer protection suit.

One reason for the liberalization of the class action rule was the desegregation suits of the 1950s and 1960s. The ability to bring such suits was greatly expanded with the passage of the Civil Rights Act of 1964. Injunctive civil rights class actions have, until recently, been relatively non-controversial. The gender discrimination class action brought by female employees against Wal-Mart, excerpted later in this chapter, signals a change in the sanguine approach of the courts to civil rights class actions. By contrast, money damages class actions have always been very controversial. If you have ever been a member of a class action, most likely you were a member of a lawsuit brought under a consumer protection law or the securities laws seeking money damages. Concerns about this type of class action include the high attorneys' fees awards relative to the claims of individual class members and concerns that so much is at stake in a class action that it can unduly pressure a defendant to settle even non-meritorious claims.

Why permit one person to sue on behalf of others? There are three justifications for permitting class actions: efficiency, deterrence, and individual rights. Each of these arguments has corresponding counterarguments against this procedural device.

Efficiency. On the one hand, class actions permit the consolidation of what otherwise would be numerous smaller lawsuits so that courts can adjudicate them more efficiently, clear their dockets, and avoid duplicative motion practice. In doing so, class actions enable litigation, perhaps encouraging cases that would not otherwise be brought. How so? Class actions solve a collective action problem in situations where individuals have legal rights but the recovery is too small to merit a lawsuit. Because class actions aggregate claims and lawyers often receive a percentage of the total recovery, lawyers working on a contingency fee are able to leverage the class action device to garner very substantial fee awards, often in the millions of dollars. Class actions are lucrative for lawyers, and this encourages lawyers to sue. In the scholarly literature, these lawyers are sometimes referred to as "bounty hunters" and other times as "private attorneys general." *See* William B. Rubenstein, *On What a "Private Attorney General" Is—And Why It Matters*, 57 Vand. L. Rev. 2129 (2004). The benefit of this arrangement is that it encourages lawyers to sue (sometimes called "entrepreneurial litigation"). The criticism is similar: It encourages lawyers to bring risky or even meritless lawsuits on the chance that they can obtain a big payoff. For an article analyzing these issues that is as relevant today as when it was written, *see* John C. Coffee, Jr., *The Regulation of Entrepreneurial Litigation: Balancing Fairness and Efficiency in the Large Class Action*, 54 U. Chi. L. Rev. 877 (1987).

Deterrence. A closely related argument in favor of class actions is that this procedural device allows plaintiffs to hold defendants responsible for their misconduct. Where individual claims are very small, plaintiffs are unlikely to sue. This means that a large entity would be able to violate the rights of numerous plaintiffs only a little and get away with it. For example, imagine a financial services company overcharges its customers by $1. It would be a rare person who would sue for that dollar. But if the company has overcharged 5 million consumers, there is a potential class action lawsuit worth $5 million, which is a suit worth bringing. Many are concerned that class actions overdeter by encouraging litigation, sometimes without a good basis or on "technical" violations of the law that should not be pursued. Because defendants would rather pay a settlement with large fees to the lawyers than risk litigating a class action and face substantial damages at trial, the concern is that defendants will settle even meritless lawsuits. Although it is widely accepted that most class actions that are certified settle, there are no good empirical studies documenting settlement rates or the quality of settlements. There is some evidence that many of the plaintiffs filing complaints with class allegations never seek certification, and that actual certifications are rare, but the empirical data is limited.

Individual Rights. You have seen how complicated and expensive pre-trial practice, and especially discovery, can be. An ordinary person may not have sufficient funds to pay for such a lawsuit, and it would be unreasonable for that person to bring a lawsuit if the ultimate damages are less than the cost of litigating. Class actions, by aggregating small claims, make it worthwhile for lawyers to represent the class on a contingency basis, enabling individual class members to vindicate rights in a group setting that they could never do alone. At the same time, most commentators agree that class actions are really cases run by lawyers. Class members are largely absent from the litigation. Their rights of participation are limited to the right to opt out or to object at a fairness hearing late in the game. Because participation in them is limited, class actions can also be said to trample on individual rights. Some believe that class actions give lawyers the opportunity to extract rent from the class by settling for high attorneys' fees and lower compensation for class members. To the extent that this happens, as a practical matter it limits litigants' rights. Finally, there is an argument that class actions infringe on defendants' rights by encouraging "blackmail" litigation. This means that the defendant experiences pressure to settle not because the suit has merit, but instead because the defendant calculates that even a very small risk of losing a nonmeritorious suit is too great when the potential loss is very large. For an evaluation of the arguments in favor of and against the idea that class actions force defendants to settle, *see* Charles M. Silver, *"We're Scared to Death": Class Certification and Blackmail*, 78 N.Y.U. L. Rev. 1357 (2003).

3. History: Where Have We Been, Where Are We Going?

The evolution of class actions parallels the narrative of much of contemporary civil procedure. Early on, the Federal Rules of Civil Procedure were the embodiment of a philosophy that embraced access to courts through simplified pleading, ease of amendment, liberal discovery, broad joinder of parties, jury trials, and an invitation to lawyer creativity and innovative claims for relief. Over time, as you have seen throughout this book, there has been a retrenchment against the open approach to civil procedure. Courts and legislatures have demanded more particularized pleadings, sanctions have been invigorated, the discovery rules have been narrowed and limited, and jury trials have been replaced with summary judgment, case managers, and forms of alternative dispute resolution (ADR). Similarly, whereas in 1966, when the modern class action rule was ratified by Congress, the rule expressed the more liberal vision of the Federal Rules; it has since come to represent the excesses of our litigation system, and numerous attempts have been made to reform class actions. The length of the current version of Rule 23 and its numerous provisions is a reflection of the rulemakers' concern about the problems created by class action litigation. Courts and legislatures have tightened the requirements for certifying class actions and limited the remedies available in the context of class action litigation. For example, in 1996, Congress limited the ability of legal services providers who receive federal funds to represent clients in class actions. 42 U.S.C. § 2996e(d)(5). The Truth in Lending Act (TILA) limits the available remedies in class actions brought under that law to the lesser of $500,000 or 1 percent of the net worth of the defendant. 15 U.S.C. § 1640(a)(2)(B). The Public Securities Litigation Reform Act (PSLRA) imposed heightened pleading requirements for securities class actions, among other things. Pub. L. No. 104-67, 109 Stat. 737 (1995).

A similar phenomenon may occur with MDLs. Up until now, case management in MDLs has been pretty much left to judges, who have adjusted procedures to fit the cases before them. As of this writing, there are some groups advocating for specific rules for MDLs based on the same concerns articulated above: pressure to settle, fairness among claimants, and agent-principal problems. This raises a perennial question about the structure of the rules of procedure, which were written to apply to all cases, small and large, in all subject matter. Are the rules of procedure sufficiently flexible to adjust to any litigation, including MDLs, or should there be specific rules for different types of cases?

Class actions also differ from other areas of procedure you have studied. Many of the assumptions prevalent in the context of binary litigation are turned on their head in the class action context. For example, despite the prevailing view that the federal courts are inundated with cases and that access to the courthouse ought to be limited, Congress actually *expanded* federal subject matter jurisdiction over class actions by passing the Class Action Fairness Act of 2005. *See* 28 U.S.C § 1332(d). This legislation was largely understood to be a defendant-friendly reaction to concerns about state courts being too lenient in certifying national class actions. Similarly, although no defendant wants to be sued, in complex litigation defendants sometimes seek to have class actions certified so that they can preclude future suits and obtain global peace. Finally, while the policy debate about class actions has frequently centered on plaintiffs' rights—in other words, are class members getting their due?—defendants are often the ones expressing these concerns.

The next section explores the due process foundations of the class action. In addressing the due process issues, courts have largely been concerned with the implications of the class action for plaintiffs' individual rights. As you read the cases presented, consider how the various policy arguments in favor of and against class treatment play out.

C. DUE PROCESS FOUNDATIONS

In 1938, when the Federal Rules were adopted, the class action was a very seldom used procedural device that originated in English equity practice. *See* Stephen P. Yeazell, *From Medieval Group Litigation to the Modern Class Action* (1987). Today the class action rule is invoked much more often, although class actions still make up a tiny percentage of the federal docket, less than 1 percent by most estimates. The first problem posed by class action is the idea of representation. What does it mean for one person to "represent" the interests of another? This is a problem in political life as well as group litigation. The first case you will read, *Hansberry v. Lee*, addresses this question. We begin with some history behind the case.

1. Adequacy of Representation

Allen R. Kamp, *The History Behind* Hansberry v. Lee
20 U.C. Davis L. Rev. 481 (1987)

INTRODUCTION

This Article, investigating *Hansberry v. Lee*'s factual background, grew out of a student's comment after a civil procedure class. In teaching class actions, *Hansberry* is a classic, usually the first case in the class action section of civil procedure textbooks. My class session went according to plan. I initially explained racially restrictive covenants and their validity until *Shelley v. Kraemer* in 1948, and then began a Socratic examination of *Hansberry*. The case sought to enforce a racially restrictive covenant and the covenant's validity turned on the result of a prior case. The question then becomes whether Hansberry is bound by the prior case, *Burke v. Kleiman*, which was a class action. The Court held he was not bound because the class was composed of members with conflicting goals:

> It is quite another to hold that all those who are free alternatively either to assert rights or to challenge them are of a single class, so that any group, merely because it is of the class so constituted, may be deemed adequately to represent any others of the class in litigating their interests in either alternative.

Then the students realized that (a) it is constitutional to have a class action that binds the class members to the class judgment; (b) whether the prior class action binds the class members may be decided collaterally in a subsequent lawsuit; and (c) without "adequate representation" the class members are not bound. I discussed Rule 23's requirements of "adequate representation" and "typicality." Afterward, I upset the students' complacency by asking how much consistency between class members' views is required: what if some members in a prison suit are masochists and like cruel and unusual punishment? What if, in a school desegregation suit, some students do not want to be bussed? I discussed questions of opt-out rights and social policy concerning the advisability of representative lawsuits in general and class actions in particular, and then wrapped up.

This analysis of *Hansberry* was upset by one of my students, Mr. C. O. Travis, who, while working as a garbageman, was attending John Marshall Law School at night. "Professor, did you know that Hansberry in *Hansberry v. Lee* was Lorraine Hansberry's father and that *A Raisin in the Sun* was based on her family's experience?" Lorraine Hansberry had attended Mr. Travis' high school in Chicago. I did not know, and at first did not believe it. Some investigation, however, revealed that Mr. Travis was right. What was the history of the Hansberry family? The answer involves black, Chicago, and legal history, leads to a re-examination of the *Hansberry* case, and provides insights into the judicial process.

THE BACKGROUND OF THE *HANSBERRY* CASE

The conflict in *Hansberry*, caused by the Hansberrys' move into an all-white neighborhood, derived from Chicago's increasing black population. Between 1900 and 1934, the city's black population grew from 30,000 to 236,000. During this time, however, blacks were continuously more segregated. In 1910, 25% of blacks lived in areas of under 5% black population. None lived in areas of over 90% concentration. By 1934, less than 5% lived in areas of under 5% concentration, while 65% lived in areas that were 90% or more black. Geographically, blacks were concentrated in two narrow corridors stretching westward and southward from downtown Chicago.

This segregation was accomplished in two ways: violence and the racially restrictive covenant. After the violence of the 1910's and 1920's subsided, racially restrictive covenants were developed. "Around these black zones, an organized endeavor was put in place to subject the property to racially restrictive covenants. Although prior to the '20s, several individual owners and developers had placed race restrictions on their deeds, covenants covering entire neighborhoods were uncommon in Chicago." Such covenants were legal—in 1926, the Supreme Court dismissed for want of jurisdiction a case upholding a racially restrictive covenant in *Corrigan v. Buckley*.

After the *Corrigan* decision, the Chicago Real Estate Board started a program to cover neighborhoods with the covenants. They prepared a model covenant. (The *Hansberry* covenant was based on this model.) Then the Board sent out speakers and organizers across the city to get the covenants adopted. Organizing a neighborhood to adopt a covenant was a massive task. Legal descriptions and signatures had to be obtained, and then the covenants had to be filed with the Recorder of Deeds. Notary publics were hired to notarize and then record signatures. Subsequently, if any black persons moved into the area, they were reported, a suit filed against their occupancy, and an injunction obtained. By the late 1920's, black neighborhoods were hemmed in on all sides by the racial covenants. Up to 85 percent of Chicago was covered by such covenants.

The racially restrictive covenants legally prevented occupancy by blacks. They bound the signer and subsequent purchasers, showing up as an "objection" in any title search. Courts would routinely enforce the covenants, ordering vacation of the premises on pain of contempt. . . .

The covenant was useful only if most of the owners had signed it. Thus, a covenant's effectiveness required that a certain percentage of owners participate. Thus, the issue in dispute in *Hansberry*—actual percentage of the signatures in the affected area—was a key requirement:

> This agreement and the restrictions herein contained shall be of no force or effect unless this agreement or a substantially similar agreement, shall be signed by the owners above enumerated of ninety-five per cent of the frontage above described, or their heirs or assigns, and recorded in the office of the Recorder of Deeds of Cook County, Illinois, on or before December 31, 1928.

The covenant challenged by the Hansberrys covered a subdivision known as "South Park" or "Washington Park." This area was a three by four block rectangle bounded on the north by Washington Park, on the east by Cottage Grove, on the south by 63rd Street, and on the west by South Park Avenue. A race track, torn down in 1908, formerly occupied the land. This area was populated by whites, but surrounded on the west and south by black areas.

In 1940, only three black families lived in the area. West of the subdivision, the population went from 10% to 100% nonwhite. To the south, 90 to 100% of the population was nonwhite.

To the east, however, were the white areas of Hyde Park and Woodlawn, where the nonwhite population was only .1 to 9.9%. The South Park subdivision, therefore, was seen as a barrier between the black community and Woodlawn.

In 1928, a group of white businessmen, the Woodlawn Property Owners Association, organized a covenant to cover the South Park neighborhood. The covenant had the support of outside real estate organizations, institutions, banks, and mortgage companies. Contradictory evidence exists about the participation of the University of Chicago, located in Hyde Park. A 1937 article stated that the university was trying to establish a "buffer state," and had contributed funds to the Woodlawn Property Owners Association. The University did not deny this. Robert Hutchins, then president of the university, stated: "However unsatisfactory they [the covenants] may be they are the only means at present available by which the members of the associations [neighborhood associations] can stabilize the conditions under which they desire to live."

The effective system of segregation created by the racially restrictive covenants began to break down in the 1930's. Two phenomena contributed to this breakdown: the growth of Chicago's black population and the Depression. Together they produced an increased black demand for housing and a depressed market for white housing. Hansberry was able to buy his house because he was the only person who wanted it.

Chicago's black population grew in the first third of the twentieth century. In 1900, it was 30,000; in 1934, 236,000. At the same time, the process of continually increasing segregation restricted blacks to the ghetto. In 1910, 24% of the total black population lived in areas in which 95% of the people were white. In 1934, only 3% of the black population lived in such areas. In 1910, the highest concentration of blacks to the general population was between 60-69%; in 1934, 87% of blacks lived in areas that were over 70% black; 69% lived in areas that were 99% black. In 1937, it was estimated that there were 50,000 more black people than units available. Blacks had to pay 20 to 50% more than whites for comparable housing.

Contemporaneously, the Depression reduced the market for white housing. In the Washington Park subdivision, the population decreased by 13.8 percent between 1930 and 1934. In the 1930's, "there was no market among white people for property in the subdivision." The prior owner of the Hansberry home, Burke, had left the house vacant at the time he moved from the subdivision. Thus, most of those who wanted to rent or buy in white areas were blacks:

> The Supreme Court eventually ruled in favor of the blacks, but even before that ruling [Hansberry], other white property owners opened their buildings to blacks and extracted high rentals for accommodations which were unable to attract white tenants. Rather than suffer financial losses, they elected to violate existing covenants and fill their vacant units with blacks.

One of these owners was Burke, who was an officer in the Woodlawn Property Owners Association and whose wife, Olive Ida Burke, had successfully sued, in *Burke v. Kleiman*, to enforce the covenant. Burke afterwards "resigned his position and withdrew from the association with ill feelings, and stated several times that he would put negroes in every block of that property." In order to sell to the Hansberrys, Burke set up a dummy transaction in which Jay D. Crook bought the property to convey to the Hansberrys. In the suit to enforce the covenant against the Hansberrys, it was alleged that

> through fraudulent concealment on the part of the defendants James T. Burke and Harry A. Price, from the Bank [First National Bank of Englewood], of the fact that Hansberry was a negro and that the property was being purchased for him, a deed was produced from the bank to Jay D. Crook who, in fact, purchased for Hansberry.

Thus, Mr. Burke was one of the defendants in *Hansberry*, attacking the decree obtained in a prior suit by his wife, Olive.

The defendant, Carl A. Hansberry, was an active man who had had varied careers, including deputy United States Marshal, businessman, and unsuccessful Republican candidate for Congress. He distributed pamphlets on black civil rights under the name of "The Hansberry Foundation." His daughter Lorraine described him:

> My father was typical of a generation of Negroes who believed that the "American way" could successfully be made to work to democratize the United States. Thus, twenty-five years ago, he spent a small personal fortune, his considerable talents, and many years of his life fighting, in association with NAACP attorneys, Chicago's "restrictive covenants" in one of this nation's ugliest ghettos.
>
> That fight also required that our family occupy the disputed property in a hellishly hostile "white neighborhood" in which literally howling mobs surrounded our house. . . . One of these missiles almost took the life of the then eight-year old signer of this letter. My memories of this "correct" way of fighting white supremacy in America include being spat at, cursed and pummeled in the daily trek to and from school. And I also remember my desperate and courageous mother, patrolling our household all night with a loaded German luger, doggedly guarding her four children, while my father fought the respectable part of the battle in the Washington court.
>
> The fact that my father and the NAACP "won" a Supreme Court decision, in a now famous case which bears his name in the law books, is—ironically—the sort of "progress" our satisfied friends allude to when they presume to deride the more radical means of struggle. The cost, in emotional turmoil, time and money, which contributed to my father's early death as a permanently embittered exile in a foreign country when he saw that after such sacrificial efforts the Negroes of Chicago were as ghetto-locked as ever, does not seem to figure in their calculations.

The sale generated the lawsuit to enforce the covenant and evict the Hansberrys, *Lee v. Hansberry*. The complaint alleged a conspiracy on the part of the defendants to destroy the agreement by selling or leasing property in the restricted area to Negroes. Plaintiffs were successful below, the court restraining Burke "from leasing or selling any real estate within the restricted area to negroes, or to white persons for the purpose of selling or leasing to negroes, restraining . . . the Supreme Liberty Life Insurance company from making any further loans on real estate in the restricted area to negroes or for occupancy by negroes; declaring the conveyance to Hansberry and wife void and ordering them to remove from the premises, and holding the restrictive agreement valid and in full force and effect."

The main arguments considered by the Illinois Supreme Court concerned the covenant's interpretation and validity under its own terms. No constitutional objection was considered.

The evidentiary basis of the rulings against the defendants below were not challenged except as to one Israel Katz. The court found that his statement that "he would sell his property to anybody, including negroes," was sufficient evidence to enjoin him from doing so.

The appellants argued that enjoining the mortgage company from making loans in the restricted area to Negroes or for Negro occupancy was improper, because mortgages were exempted from the restrictive agreement. The Illinois Supreme Court ruled that the language merely provided that violating the restrictive agreement was an insufficient reason to invalidate a mortgage. "It does not give mortgagees a license to conspire to destroy the agreement, as the evidence shows this insurance company was doing."

The main argument in the case revolved around the question whether the requisite number of owners had signed the agreement. The agreement was to be "of no force or effect" unless signed by owners of 95 percent of the area's frontage. The plaintiffs in *Lee* argued that this question was *res judicata*, determined by the prior case of *Burke*. The trial court in *Hansberry* found that actually only 54 percent had signed the agreement, but that the question was *res judicata*.

The complainant's contention was "that unless an injunction is granted, said neighborhood will become mixed, both white and colored with its attendant evils." In *Burke*, the defense was that conditions had so changed in the area that enforcing the decree would be inequitable. Certain facts were stipulated, including that more than the required 95 percent of frontage owners had signed the covenants. The court in *Burke* found that the neighborhood had not changed materially and affirmed the decree, summarily rejecting the constitutional argument.

The Illinois Supreme Court, in *Lee v. Hansberry*, found that *Burke* "was a class or representative suit." Thus, "other members of the class are bound by the results in the case unless it is reversed or set aside on direct proceedings." That the finding was stipulated did not render the decree any less binding. The court found no evidence of fraud or collusion in procuring the stipulation. Thus the questions of execution and validity were *res judicata*, and *res judicata* extends to all matters that might have been raised. The covenant's validity could not be relitigated and the decree evicting the Hansberrys was affirmed.

Hansberry petitioned for *certiorari* to the Supreme Court. His lawyers hoped to have racially restrictive covenants declared unconstitutional. Their main arguments, however, went to the propriety of the class action—only their last argument went to the purported constitutional violation. . . .

Hansberry v. Lee
311 U.S. 32 (1940)

Justice STONE delivered the opinion of the Court:

The question is whether the Supreme Court of Illinois, by its adjudication that petitioners in this case are bound by a judgment rendered in an earlier litigation to which they were not parties, has deprived them of the due process of law guaranteed by the Fourteenth Amendment.

Respondents brought this suit in the Circuit Court of Cook County, Illinois, to enjoin the breach by petitioners of an agreement restricting the use of land within a described area of the City of Chicago, which was alleged to have been entered into by some five hundred of the land owners. The agreement stipulated that for a specified period no part of the land should be "sold, leased to or permitted to be occupied by any person of the colored race," and provided that it should not be effective unless signed by the "owners of 95 per centum of the frontage" within the described area. The bill of complaint set up that the owners of 95 per cent of the frontage had signed; that respondents are owners of land within the restricted area who have either signed the agreement or acquired their land from others who did sign and that petitioners Hansberry, who are Negroes, have, with the alleged aid of the other petitioners and with knowledge of the agreement, acquired and are occupying land in the restricted area formerly belonging to an owner who had signed the agreement.

To the defense that the agreement had never become effective because owners of 95 per cent of the frontage had not signed it, respondents pleaded that that issue was *res judicata* by the decree in an earlier suit. *Burke v. Kleiman*, 277 Ill. App. 519. To this petitioners pleaded, by way of rejoinder, that they were not parties to that suit or bound by its decree, and that denial of their right to litigate, in the present suit, the issue of performance of the condition precedent to the validity of the agreement would be a denial of due process of law guaranteed by the Fourteenth Amendment. It does not appear, nor is it contended that any of petitioners is the successor in interest to or in privity with any of the parties in the earlier suit.

The circuit court, after a trial on the merits, found that owners of only about 54 per cent of the frontage had signed the agreement, and that the only support of the judgment in the *Burke* case was a false and fraudulent stipulation of the parties that 95 per cent had signed. But it ruled that the issue of performance of the condition precedent to the validity of the agreement was *res judicata* as alleged and entered a decree for respondents. The Supreme Court of Illinois affirmed. We granted certiorari to resolve the constitutional question. . . .

It is a principle of general application in Anglo-American jurisprudence that one is not bound by a judgment in personam in a litigation in which he is not designated as a party or to which he has not been made a party by service of process. *Pennoyer v. Neff*, 95 U.S. 714; 1 *Freeman on Judgments*, 5th Ed., § 407. A judgment rendered in such circumstances is not entitled to the full faith and credit which the Constitution and statute of the United States, R.S. § 905, 28 U.S.C. § 687, 28 U.S.C.A. § 687, prescribe, *Pennoyer v. Neff, supra*; *Lafayette Ins. Co. v. French*, 18 How. 404, 15 L. Ed. 451; *Hall v. Lanning*, 91 U.S. 160; *Baker v. Baker, E. & Co.*, 242 U.S. 394, and judicial action enforcing it against the person or property of the absent party is not that due process which the Fifth and Fourteenth Amendments require. *Postal Telegraph-Cable Co. v. Neport*, 247 U.S. 464; *Old Wayne Mut. L. Ass'n v. McDonough*, 204 U.S. 8.

To these general rules there is a recognized exception that, to an extent not precisely defined by judicial opinion, the judgment in a "class" or "representative" suit, to which some members of the class are parties, may bind members of the class or those represented who were not made parties to it.

The class suit was an invention of equity to enable it to proceed to a decree in suits where the number of those interested in the subject of the litigation is so great that their joinder as parties in conformity to the usual rules of procedure is impracticable. Courts are not infrequently called upon to proceed with causes in which the number of those interested in the litigation is so great as to make difficult or impossible the joinder of all because some are not within the jurisdiction or because their whereabouts is unknown or where if all were made parties to the suit its continued abatement by the death of some would prevent or unduly delay a decree. In such cases where the interests of those not joined are of the same class as the interests of those who are, and where it is considered that the latter fairly represent the former in the prosecution of the litigation of the issues in which all have a common interest, the court will proceed to a decree.

It is evident that the considerations which may induce a court thus to proceed, despite a technical defect of parties, may differ from those which must be taken into account in determining whether the absent parties are bound by the decree or, if it is adjudged that they are, in ascertaining whether such an adjudication satisfies the requirements of due process and of full faith and credit. Nevertheless there is scope within the framework of the Constitution for holding in appropriate cases that a judgment rendered in a class suit is *res judicata* as to members of the class who are not formal parties to the suit. Here, as elsewhere, the Fourteenth Amendment does not compel state courts or legislatures to adopt any particular rule for establishing the conclusiveness of judgments in class suits; nor does it compel the adoption of the particular rules thought by this court to be appropriate for the federal courts. With a proper regard for divergent local institutions and interests, *cf. Jackson County v. United States*, 308 U.S. 343, 351, this Court is justified in saying that there has been a failure of due process only in those cases where it cannot be said that the procedure adopted, fairly insures the protection of the interests of absent parties who are to be bound by it. *Chicago, B. & Q.R. Co. v. Chicago*, 166 U.S. 226, 235.

It is familiar doctrine of the federal courts that members of a class not present as parties to the litigation may be bound by the judgment where they are in fact adequately represented by parties who are present, or where they actually participate in the conduct of the litigation in which members of the class are present as parties, *Plumb v. Goodnow (Plumb v. Crane)*, 123 U.S. 560; *Confectioners' Machinery Co. v. Racine Engine & Mach. Co.*, 7 Cir., 163 F. 914; *Id.*, 7 Cir., 170 F. 1021; *Bryant El. Co. v. Marshall, C.C.*, 169 F. 426, or where the interest of the members of the class, some of whom are present as parties, is joint, or where for any other reason the relationship between the parties present and those who are absent is such as legally to entitle the former to stand in judgment for the latter. *Smith v. Swormstedt, supra*; *cf. Christopher v. Brusselback, supra*, 302 U.S. at pages 503, 504, and cases cited.

In all such cases, so far as it can be said that the members of the class who are present are, by generally recognized rules of law, entitled to stand in judgment for those who are not, we may assume for present purposes that such procedure affords a protection to the parties who are represented though absent, which would satisfy the requirements of due process and full faith and credit. Nor do we find it necessary for the decision of this case to say that, when the only circumstance defining the class is that the determination of the rights of its members turns upon a single issue of fact or law, a state could not constitutionally adopt a procedure whereby some of the members of the class could stand in judgment for all, provided that the procedure were so devised and applied as to insure that those present are of the same class as those absent and that the litigation is so conducted as to insure the full and fair consideration of the common issue. We decide only that the procedure and the course of litigation sustained here by the plea of *res judicata* do not satisfy these requirements.

The restrictive agreement did not purport to create a joint obligation or liability. If valid and effective its promises were the several obligations of the signers and those claiming under them. The promises ran severally to every other signer. It is plain that in such circumstances all those alleged to be bound by the agreement would not constitute a single class in any litigation brought to enforce it. Those who sought to secure its benefits by enforcing it could not be said to be in the same class with or represent those whose interest was in resisting performance, for the agreement by its terms imposes obligations and confers rights on the owner of each plot of land who signs it. If those who thus seek to secure the benefits of the agreement were rightly regarded by the state Supreme Court as constituting a class, it is evident that those signers or their successors who are interested in challenging the validity of the agreement and resisting its performance are not of the same class in the sense that their interests are identical so that any group who had elected to enforce rights conferred by the agreement could be said to be acting in the interest of any others who were free to deny its obligation.

Because of the dual and potentially conflicting interests of those who are putative parties to the agreement in compelling or resisting its performance, it is impossible to say, solely because they are parties to it, that any two of them are of the same class. Nor without more, and with the due regard for the protection of the rights of absent parties which due process exacts, can some be permitted to stand in judgment for all.

It is one thing to say that some members of a class may represent other members in a litigation where the sole and common interest of the class in the litigation is either to assert a common right or to challenge an asserted obligation. *Smith v. Swormstedt, supra*; *Supreme Tribe of Ben-Hur v. Cauble, supra*; *Groves v. Farmers State Bank*, 368 Ill. 35, 12 N.E.2d 618. It is quite another to hold that all those who are free alternatively either to assert rights or to challenge them are of a single class, so that any group merely because it is of the class so constituted, may be deemed adequately to represent any others of the class in litigating their interests in either alternative. Such a selection of representatives for purposes of litigation, whose substantial interests are not necessarily or even probably the same as those whom they are deemed to represent, does not afford that protection to absent parties which due process requires. The doctrine of representation of absent parties in a class suit has not hitherto been thought to go so far. Apart from the opportunities it would afford for the fraudulent and collusive sacrifice of the rights of absent parties, we think that the representation in this case no more satisfies the requirements of due process than a trial by a judicial officer who is in such situation that he may have an interest in the outcome of the litigation in conflict with that of the litigants.

The plaintiffs in the *Burke* case sought to compel performance of the agreement in behalf of themselves and all others similarly situated. They did not designate the defendants in the suit as a class or seek any injunction or other relief against others than the named defendants, and the decree which was entered did not purport to bind others. In seeking to enforce the agreement the plaintiffs in that suit were not representing the petitioners here whose substantial interest is in resisting performance. The defendants in the first suit were not treated by the pleadings or decree as representing others or as foreclosing by their defense the rights of others, and even though nominal defendants, it does not appear that their interest in defeating the contract outweighed their interest in establishing its validity. For a court in this situation to ascribe to either the plaintiffs or defendants the performance of such functions on behalf of petitioners here, is to attribute to them a power that it cannot be said that they had assumed to exercise, and a responsibility which, in view of their dual interests it does not appear that they could rightly discharge.

REVIEW QUESTIONS

1. Describe the two lawsuits at issue in *Hansberry*. Who sued whom? Who wanted to bind whom and on what theory? What precisely was the constitutional question? How would you describe the holding of *Hansberry*?
2. *Hansberry* was decided before Rule 23 was promulgated. What procedural rule applied to the *Hansberry* case? Where is it codified?
3. Note that in *Hansberry*, the plaintiffs sought to preclude Mr. Hansberry on the basis of a stipulation from the previous case. Would that stipulation be sufficient to bind parties under modern federal preclusion doctrine? Under *Hansberry*, at what point in a class action lawsuit may the class no longer challenge the adequacy of the named plaintiffs who purported to represent them?

MORE TO PONDER

Why does it ever make sense for a suit to bind people other than the named parties? How representative must the interests of the class representative be vis-à-vis the rest of the class? The classic suit for which Rule 23 was written in 1966 was the school desegregation action. Yet, as Professor Kamp queried, "What if, in a school desegregation suit, some students do not want to be bussed?" For a discussion of this problem in the integration context, *see* Derek A. Bell, Jr., *Serving Two Masters: Integration Ideals and Client Interest in School Desegregation Litigation*, 85 Yale L.J. 470 (1976). Somewhat more recently, gay rights groups differed over litigation strategies with respect to gay marriage. Who should decide whether to go forward with such litigation? *See* William B. Rubenstein, *Divided We Litigate: Addressing Disputes Among Group Members and Lawyers in Civil Rights Campaigns*, 106 Yale L.J. 1623 (1997). In one school desegregation case in New York in the 1970s, Judge Jack Weinstein held community hearings to determine whether an injunction or some other form of relief would be appropriate, and how to structure that injunction. He did not think it was enough to rely on the class representatives alone and wanted input from the broader community. Do you think that some cases ought to require such hearings? What types of cases? For more on this, *see* Curtis J. Berger, *Away from the Court House and into the Field: The Odyssey of a Special Master*, 78 Colum. L. Rev. 707 (1978). Judge Weinstein appears later in this chapter as a model for active judicial involvement in settling large-scale litigation.

2. Participation

The biggest change made by the rules drafters in 1966 was to add a new type of class action that had never been available before: the money damages class action. Rule 23(b)(3) permits courts to certify a class action for money damages when the plaintiffs meet the requirements of the class action rule, which are described in more detail later. In keeping with the theme of this chapter, this case offers you the opportunity to revisit the doctrine of personal jurisdiction in a new context. As you read, consider the following questions:

1. Why does the Kansas court have personal jurisdiction over absent class members who have no connection with the state?
2. How are plaintiffs and defendants similarly (or differently) situated in class and individual litigation?
3. Do the due process standards articulated in *Hansberry* and *Shutts* differ, and if so, how? Do these cases, read together, indicate that different protections ought to be required to protect absent class members in injunctive as opposed to money damages class actions?

Phillips Petroleum Co. v. Shutts
472 U.S. 797 (1985)

Justice REHNQUIST delivered the opinion of the Court.

Petitioner is a Delaware corporation which has its principal place of business in Oklahoma. During the 1970's it produced or purchased natural gas from leased land located in 11 different States, and sold most of the gas in interstate commerce. Respondents are some 28,000 of the royalty owners possessing rights to the leases from which petitioner produced the gas; they reside in all 50 States, the District of Columbia, and several foreign countries. Respondents brought a class action against petitioner in the Kansas state court, seeking to recover interest on royalty payments which had been delayed by petitioner. They recovered judgment in the trial court, and the Supreme Court of Kansas affirmed the judgment over petitioner's contentions that the Due Process Clause of the Fourteenth Amendment prevented Kansas from adjudicating the claims of all the respondents, and that the Due Process Clause and the Full Faith and Credit Clause of Article IV of the Constitution prohibited the application of Kansas law to all of the transactions between petitioner and respondents. We reject petitioner's jurisdictional claim, but sustain its claim regarding the choice of law.

Because petitioner sold the gas to its customers in interstate commerce, it was required to secure approval for price increases from what was then the Federal Power Commission, and is now the Federal Energy Regulatory Commission. Under its regulations the Federal Power Commission permitted petitioner to propose and collect tentative higher gas prices, subject to final approval by the Commission. If the Commission eventually denied petitioner's proposed price increase or reduced the proposed increase, petitioner would have to refund to its customers the difference between the approved price and the higher price charged, plus interest at a rate set by statute. See 18 CFR § 154.102 (1984).

Although petitioner received higher gas prices pending review by the Commission, petitioner suspended any increase in royalties paid to the royalty owners because the higher price could be subject to recoupment by petitioner's customers. Petitioner agreed to pay the higher royalty only if the royalty owners would provide petitioner with a bond or indemnity for the increase, plus interest, in case the price increase was not ultimately approved and a refund was due to the customers. Petitioner set the interest rate on the indemnity agreements at the same interest rate the Commission would have required petitioner to refund to its customers. A small percentage of the royalty owners provided this indemnity and received royalties immediately from the interim price increases; these royalty owners are unimportant to this case.

The remaining royalty owners received no royalty on the unapproved portion of the prices until the Federal Power Commission approval of those prices became final. Royalties on the unapproved portion of the gas price were suspended three times by petitioner, corresponding to its three proposed price increases in the mid-1970's. In three written opinions the Commission approved all of petitioner's tentative price increases, so petitioner paid to its royalty owners the suspended royalties of $3.7 million in 1976, $4.7 million in 1977, and $2.9 million in 1978. Petitioner paid no interest to the royalty owners although it had the use of the suspended royalty money for a number of years.

Respondents Irl Shutts, Robert Anderson, and Betty Anderson filed suit against petitioner in Kansas state court, seeking interest payments on their suspended royalties which petitioner had possessed pending the Commission's approval of the price increases. Shutts is a resident of Kansas, and the Andersons live in Oklahoma. Shutts and the Andersons own gas leases in Oklahoma and Texas. Over petitioner's objection the Kansas trial court granted respondents' motion to certify the suit as a class action under Kansas law. The class as certified was comprised of 33,000 royalty owners who had royalties suspended by petitioner. The average claim of each royalty owner for interest on the suspended royalties was $100.

After the class was certified respondents provided each class member with notice through first-class mail. The notice described the action and informed each class member that he could appear in person or by counsel; otherwise each member would be represented by Shutts and the Andersons, the named plaintiffs. The notices also stated that class members would be included in the class and bound by the judgment unless they "opted out" of the lawsuit by executing and returning a "request for exclusion" that was included with the notice. The final class as certified contained 28,100 members; 3,400 had "opted out" of the class by returning the request for exclusion, and notice could not be delivered to another 1,500 members, who were also excluded. Less than 1,000 of the class members resided in Kansas. Only a minuscule amount, approximately one quarter of one percent, of the gas leases involved in the lawsuit were on Kansas land.

After petitioner's mandamus petition to decertify the class was denied, the case was tried to the court. The court found petitioner liable under Kansas law for interest on the suspended royalties to all class members. . . . The applicable interest rates were: 7% for royalties retained until October 1974; 9% for royalties retained between October 1974 and September 1979; and thereafter at the average prime rate. The trial court did not determine whether any difference existed between the laws of Kansas and other States, or whether another State's laws should be applied to non-Kansas plaintiffs or to royalties from leases in States other than Kansas.

Petitioner raised two principal claims in its appeal to the Supreme Court of Kansas. It first asserted that the Kansas trial court did not possess personal jurisdiction over absent plaintiff class members as required by *International Shoe Co. v. Washington*, 326 U.S. 310 (1945), and similar cases. Related to this first claim was petitioner's contention that the "opt-out" notice to absent class members, which forced them to return the request for exclusion in order to avoid the suit, was insufficient to bind class members who were not residents of Kansas or who did not possess "minimum contacts" with Kansas. Second, petitioner claimed that Kansas courts could not apply Kansas law to every claim in the dispute. The trial court should have looked to the laws of each State where the leases were located to determine, on the basis of conflict of laws principles, whether interest on the suspended royalties was recoverable, and at what rate.

The Supreme Court of Kansas held that the entire cause of action was maintainable under the Kansas class-action statute, and the court rejected both of petitioner's claims. 235 Kan. 195 (1984). . . .

I

As a threshold matter we must determine whether petitioner has standing to assert the claim that Kansas did not possess proper jurisdiction over the many plaintiffs in the class who were not Kansas residents and had no connection to Kansas. Respondents claim that a party generally may assert only his own rights, and that petitioner has no standing to assert the rights of its adversary, the plaintiff class, in order to defeat the judgment in favor of the class.

Standing to sue in any Article III court is, of course, a federal question which does not depend on the party's prior standing in state court. . . . One of [the] prudential limits on [Article III] standing is that a litigant must normally assert his own legal interests rather than those of third parties.

Respondents claim that petitioner is barred by the rule requiring that a party assert only his own rights; they point out that respondents and petitioner are adversaries and do not have allied interests such that petitioner would be a good proponent of class members' interests. They further urge that petitioner's interference is unneeded because the class members have had opportunity to complain about Kansas' assertion of jurisdiction over their claim, but none have done so.

Respondents may be correct that petitioner does not possess standing jus tertii, but this is not the issue. Petitioner seeks to vindicate its own interests. As a class-action defendant petitioner is in a unique predicament. If Kansas does not possess jurisdiction over this plaintiff class, petitioner will be bound to 28,100 judgment holders scattered across the globe, but none of these will be bound by the Kansas decree. Petitioner could be subject to numerous later individual suits by these class members because a judgment issued without proper personal jurisdiction over an absent party is not entitled to full faith and credit elsewhere and thus has no res judicata effect as to that party. Whether it wins or loses on the merits, petitioner has a distinct and personal interest in seeing the entire plaintiff class bound by res judicata just as petitioner is bound. The only way a class action defendant like petitioner can assure itself of this binding effect of the judgment is to ascertain that the forum court has jurisdiction over every plaintiff whose claim it seeks to adjudicate, sufficient to support a defense of res judicata in a later suit for damages by class members.

While it is true that a court adjudicating a dispute may not be able to predetermine the res judicata effect of its own judgment, petitioner has alleged that it would be obviously and immediately injured if this class-action judgment against it became final without binding the plaintiff class. We think that such an injury is sufficient to give petitioner standing on its own right to raise the jurisdiction claim in this Court. . . .

II

Reduced to its essentials, petitioner's argument is that unless out-of-state plaintiffs affirmatively consent, the Kansas courts may not exert jurisdiction over their claims. Petitioner claims that failure to execute and return the "request for exclusion" provided with the class notice cannot constitute consent of the out-of-state plaintiffs; thus Kansas courts may exercise jurisdiction over these plaintiffs only if the plaintiffs possess the sufficient "minimum contacts" with Kansas as that term is used in cases involving personal jurisdiction over out-of-state defendants. Since Kansas had no prelitigation contact with many of the plaintiffs and leases involved, petitioner claims that Kansas has exceeded its jurisdictional reach and thereby violated the due process rights of the absent plaintiffs.

In *International Shoe* we were faced with an out-of-state corporation which sought to avoid the exercise of personal jurisdiction over it as a defendant by a Washington state court. We held that the extent of the defendant's due process protection would depend "upon the quality and nature of the activity in relation to the fair and orderly administration of the laws. . . ." 326 U.S., at 319. We noted that the Due Process Clause did not permit a State to make a binding judgment against a person with whom the State had no contacts, ties, or relations. If the defendant possessed certain minimum contacts with the State, so that it was "reasonable and just, according to our traditional conception of fair play and substantial justice" for a State to exercise personal jurisdiction, the State could force the defendant to defend himself in the forum, upon pain of default, and could bind him to a judgment.

The purpose of this test, of course, is to protect a defendant from the travail of defending in a distant forum, unless the defendant's contacts with the forum make it just to force him to defend there. As we explained in [*World Wide Volkswagen v. Woodson*] the defendant's contacts should be such that "he should reasonably anticipate being haled" into the forum. 444 U.S., at 297.

Although the cases like *Shaffer* and *Woodson* which petitioner relies on for a minimum contacts requirement all dealt with out-of-state defendants or parties in the procedural posture of a defendant, petitioner claims that the same analysis must apply to absent class-action plaintiffs. In this regard petitioner correctly points out that a chose in action is a constitutionally recognized property interest possessed by each of the plaintiffs. *Mullane v. Central Hanover Bank & Trust Co.*, 339 U.S. 306 (1950). An adverse judgment by Kansas courts in this case may extinguish the chose in action forever through res judicata. Such an adverse judgment, petitioner claims, would be every bit as onerous to an absent plaintiff as an adverse judgment on the merits would be to a defendant. Thus, the same due process protections should apply to absent plaintiffs: Kansas should not be able to exert jurisdiction over the plaintiff's claims unless the plaintiffs have sufficient minimum contacts with Kansas.

We think petitioner's premise is in error. The burdens placed by a State upon an absent class-action plaintiff are not of the same order or magnitude as those it places upon an absent defendant. An out-of-state defendant summoned by a plaintiff is faced with the full powers of the forum State to render judgment against it. The defendant must generally hire counsel and travel to the forum to defend itself from the plaintiff's claim, or suffer a default judgment. The defendant may be forced to participate in extended and often costly discovery, and will be forced to respond in damages or to comply with some other form of remedy imposed by the court should it lose the suit. The defendant may also face liability for court costs and attorney's fees. These burdens are substantial, and the minimum contacts requirement of the Due Process Clause prevents the forum State from unfairly imposing them upon the defendant.

A class-action plaintiff, however, is in quite a different posture. The Court noted this difference in *Hansberry v. Lee*, 311 U.S. 32, 40-41 (1940), which explained that a "class" or "representative" suit was an exception to the rule that one could not be bound by judgment in personam unless one was made fully a party in the traditional sense. As the Court pointed out in *Hansberry*, the class action was an invention of equity to enable it to proceed to a decree in suits where the number of those interested in the litigation was too great to permit joinder. The absent parties would be bound by the decree so long as the named parties adequately represented the absent class and the prosecution of the litigation was within the common interest.

Modern plaintiff class actions follow the same goals, permitting litigation of a suit involving common questions when there are too many plaintiffs for proper joinder. Class actions also may permit the plaintiffs to pool claims which would be uneconomical to litigate individually. For example, this lawsuit involves claims averaging about $100 per plaintiff; most of the plaintiffs would have no realistic day in court if a class action were not available.

In sharp contrast to the predicament of a defendant haled into an out-of-state forum, the plaintiffs in this suit were not haled anywhere to defend themselves upon pain of a default judgment. As commentators have noted, from the plaintiffs' point of view a class action resembles a "quasi-administrative proceeding, conducted by the judge." 3B J. Moore & J. Kennedy, Moore's Federal Practice ¶23.45 (1984); Kaplan, *Continuing Work of the Civil Committee: 1966 Amendments to the Federal Rules of Civil Procedure* (I), 81 Harv. L. Rev. 356, 398 (1967).

A plaintiff class in Kansas and numerous other jurisdictions cannot first be certified unless the judge, with the aid of the named plaintiffs and defendant, conducts an inquiry into the common nature of the named plaintiffs' and the absent plaintiffs' claims, the adequacy of representation, the jurisdiction possessed over the class, and any other matters that will bear upon proper representation of the absent plaintiffs' interest. Unlike a defendant in a civil suit, a class-action plaintiff is not required to fend for himself. The court and named plaintiffs protect his interests. Indeed, the class-action defendant itself has a great interest in ensuring that the absent plaintiff's claims are properly before the forum. In this case, for example, the defendant sought to avoid class certification by alleging that the absent plaintiffs would not be adequately represented and were not amenable to jurisdiction.

The concern of the typical class-action rules for the absent plaintiffs is manifested in other ways. Most jurisdictions, including Kansas, require that a class action, once certified, may not be dismissed or compromised without the approval of the court. In many jurisdictions such as Kansas the court may amend the pleadings to ensure that all sections of the class are represented adequately.

Besides this continuing solicitude for their rights, absent plaintiff class members are not subject to other burdens imposed upon defendants. They need not hire counsel or appear. They are almost never subject to counterclaims or cross-claims, or liability for fees or costs. Absent plaintiff class members are not subject to coercive or punitive remedies. Nor will an adverse judgment typically bind an absent plaintiff for any damages, although a valid adverse judgment may extinguish any of the plaintiff's claims which were litigated.

Unlike a defendant in a normal civil suit, an absent class-action plaintiff is not required to do anything. He may sit back and allow the litigation to run its course, content in knowing that there are safeguards provided for his protection. In most class actions an absent plaintiff is provided at least with an opportunity to "opt out" of the class, and if he takes advantage of that opportunity he is removed from the litigation entirely. This was true of the Kansas proceedings in this case. The Kansas procedure provided for the mailing of a notice to each class member by first-class mail. The notice, as we have previously indicated, described the action and informed the class member that he could appear in person or by counsel, in default of which he would be represented by the named plaintiffs and their attorneys. The notice further stated that class members would be included in the class and bound by the judgment unless they "opted out" by executing and returning a "request for exclusion" that was included in the notice.

Petitioner contends, however, that the "opt out" procedure provided by Kansas is not good enough, and that an "opt in" procedure is required to satisfy the Due Process Clause of the Fourteenth Amendment. Insofar as plaintiffs who have no minimum contacts with the forum State are concerned, an "opt in" provision would require that each class member affirmatively consent to his inclusion within the class.

Because States place fewer burdens upon absent class plaintiffs than they do upon absent defendants in nonclass suits, the Due Process Clause need not and does not afford the former as much protection from state-court jurisdiction as it does the latter. The Fourteenth Amendment does protect "persons," not "defendants," however, so absent plaintiffs as well as absent defendants are entitled to some protection from the jurisdiction of a forum State which seeks to adjudicate their claims. In this case we hold that a forum State may exercise jurisdiction over the claim of an absent class-action plaintiff, even though that plaintiff may not possess the minimum contacts with the forum which would support personal jurisdiction over a defendant. If the forum State wishes to bind an absent plaintiff concerning a claim for money damages or similar relief at law,[3] it must provide minimal procedural due process protection. The plaintiff must receive notice plus an opportunity to be heard and participate in the litigation, whether in person or through counsel. The notice must be the best practicable, "reasonably calculated, under all the circumstances, to apprise interested parties of the pendency of the action and afford them an opportunity to present their objections." *Mullane*, 339 U.S., at 314-315, we hold that due process requires at a minimum that an absent plaintiff be provided with an opportunity to remove himself from the class by executing and returning an "opt out" or "request for exclusion" form to the court. Finally, the Due Process Clause of course requires that the named plaintiff at all times adequately represent the interests of the absent class members. *Hansberry*, 311 U.S., at 42-43, 45.

We reject petitioner's contention that the Due Process Clause of the Fourteenth Amendment requires that absent plaintiffs affirmatively "opt in" to the class, rather than be deemed members of the class if they do not "opt out." We think that such a contention is supported by little, if any precedent, and that it ignores the differences between class-action plaintiffs, on the one hand, and defendants in nonclass civil suits on the other. Any plaintiff may consent to jurisdiction. The essential question, then, is how stringent the requirement for a showing of consent will be.

We think that the procedure followed by Kansas, where a fully descriptive notice is sent first-class mail to each class member, with an explanation of the right to "opt out," satisfies due process. Requiring a plaintiff to affirmatively request inclusion would probably impede the prosecution of those class actions involving an aggregation of small individual claims, where a large number of claims are required to make it economical to bring suit. The plaintiff's claim may be so small, or the plaintiff so unfamiliar with the law, that he would not file suit individually, nor would he affirmatively request inclusion in the class if such a request were required by the Constitution. If, on the other hand, the plaintiff's claim is sufficiently large or important that he wishes to litigate it on his own, he will likely have retained an attorney or have thought about filing suit, and should be fully capable of exercising his right to "opt out."

In this case over 3,400 members of the potential class did "opt out," which belies the contention that "opt out" procedures result in guaranteed jurisdiction by inertia. Another 1,500 were excluded because the notice and "opt out" form was undeliverable. We think that such results show that the "opt out" procedure provided by Kansas is by no means pro forma, and that the Constitution does

---

3. Our holding today is limited to those class actions which seek to bind known plaintiffs concerning claims wholly or predominately for money judgments. We intimate no view concerning other types of class actions, such as those seeking equitable relief. Nor, of course, does our discussion of personal jurisdiction address class actions where the jurisdiction is asserted against a defendant class.

not require more to protect what must be the somewhat rare species of class member who is unwilling to execute an "opt out" form, but whose claim is nonetheless so important that he cannot be presumed to consent to being a member of the class by his failure to do so. . . .

We therefore hold that the protection afforded the plaintiff class members by the Kansas statute satisfies the Due Process Clause. The interests of the absent plaintiffs are sufficiently protected by the forum State when those plaintiffs are provided with a request for exclusion that can be returned within a reasonable time to the court. Both the Kansas trial court and the Supreme Court of Kansas held that the class received adequate representation, and no party disputes that conclusion here. We conclude that the Kansas court properly asserted personal jurisdiction over the absent plaintiffs and their claims against petitioner. . . .

We therefore affirm the judgment of the Supreme Court of Kansas insofar as it upheld the jurisdiction of the Kansas courts over the plaintiff class members in this case, and reverse its judgment insofar as it held that Kansas law was applicable to all of the transactions which it sought to adjudicate. We remand the case to that court for further proceedings not inconsistent with this opinion.

It is so ordered.

REVIEW QUESTIONS

1. Why is the *defendant* asserting the plaintiff class members' due process right not to be dragged into Kansas Court? A careful reading of the Court's rationale for permitting defendant to make the personal jurisdiction argument underscores the reasons that class certification is so important. Can you explain why certification is such an important motion for defendants? What are the effects on the defendant if a class is certified?

2. The Court explains in footnote 3 that the holding in *Shutts* that class members must be given the opportunity to opt out is limited to money damages class actions. In injunctive class actions, the court is not required to provide an opportunity for plaintiffs to opt out. Can you think of a policy rationale for the difference? Should plaintiffs be given an opportunity to opt out in injunctive class actions as well? You will want to revisit these questions after reading *Wal-Mart v. Dukes*, reproduced later in this chapter, in which the Court held (unanimously) that plaintiffs bringing injunctive class actions cannot seek back pay (a form of money damages) without certifying a money damages class action, with the greater due process protections money damages classes provide to class members and the heavier class certification burden imposed by Rule 23.

3. Is this case consistent or inconsistent with *Bristol Myers Squibb*, reproduced in Chapter 7? Lower courts have come out both ways on this question; can you articulate the potential arguments on both sides?

MORE TO PONDER

1. *Notice and Claims Rates in Class Actions.* What type of notice was afforded the class members in *Shutts*? Class action notices are notoriously unfriendly documents and difficult to decipher. You can see models for such notices on the Federal Judicial Center Web site: *www.fjc.gov*. When class notices are difficult to understand and claims forms difficult to fill out, response rates in class actions will predictably be lower than if notices and claims forms were more user friendly.

   There is little data on claiming rates in class actions because courts rarely require the parties to provide this information. The exception is coupon settlements. A coupon settlement is one in which class members receive the opportunity to purchase a product at a discounted price instead of cash. The Class Action Fairness Act of 2005 (CAFA) requires that in settlements offering coupons to class members, the attorneys' fees are to be calculated based on the coupons actually redeemed. 28 U.S.C. § 1712. This provision, combined with the increased scrutiny of coupon settlements mandated by CAFA, appears to have reduced the number of coupon settlements in the federal courts.

   The Court in *Shutts* also notes that 1,500 persons were excluded from the class action because their notices and opt-out forms were undeliverable. Does due process require that the notice be actually delivered in order to be adequate under *Mullane*? Today, undelivered notices are usually not considered by courts to require exclusion of those class members. Should they?

2. *Choice of Law Issues in Class Actions.* The second question presented in *Shutts* and not excerpted here concerned what substantive law ought to apply to that class action. In that case, the majority of the class members were citizens of five states: Texas, Oklahoma, Louisiana, New Mexico, and Wyoming. Which state's law should apply is a horizontal choice of law question. Originally the Kansas courts had applied Kansas law to all the gas leases. The Supreme Court struck down this holding on due process and full faith and credit grounds and explained that "for a State's substantive law to be selected in a constitutionally permissible manner, that State must have a significant contact or significant aggregation of contacts, creating state interests, such that choice of its law is neither arbitrary nor fundamentally unfair." *Shutts*, 472 U.S. at 818 (quoting *Allstate Ins. Co. v. Hague*, 449 U.S. 302 (1981)). The Court remanded to the Kansas Supreme Court. The Kansas Court subsequently analyzed the law of the relevant states and held that it was substantively the same as Kansas law. *Shutts v. Phillips Petroleum Co.*, 240 Kan. 764 (1987).

   In federal court, one of the biggest impediments to certifying national class actions has been the differing substantive laws of the various states. This problem has become more pronounced since the passage of CAFA, which effectively federalized most class actions and is discussed later in this chapter. *See* Linda Silberman, *The Role of Choice of Law in National Class Actions*, 156 U. Pa. L. Rev. 2001 (2008). Strictly speaking, this is not a choice of law problem, but rather a question of whether, under Rule 23, the class members from different states share enough in common to justify collective treatment. One proposed solution to this problem is to apply the law of the home state of the defendant to all the class members regardless of their home state. *See* Samuel Issacharoff, *Settled Expectations in a World of Unsettled Law: Choice of Law After the Class Action Fairness Act*, 106 Colum. L. Rev. 1839 (2006). How does this proposal square with the rationale of the *Erie* doctrine developed in Chapter 9?

D. THE CLASS ACTION RULE

In addition to the constitutional requirements imposed by the due process clause, class actions are governed by Federal Rule of Civil Procedure 23. Although the rule has been revised several times since its promulgation, the basic structure of the rule has remained the same. Many state class action rules mirror Rule 23, although judicial interpretations of these rules differ. Other states have more liberal or more restrictive class action rules. New York's rule, addressed in *Shady Grove v. Allstate* (reproduced in Chapter 9), prohibits class actions in cases seeking statutory remedies.

In order for a case to proceed collectively as a class action, a court must determine that the plaintiffs meet all the requirements of Rule 23. This process is called *class certification*.

1. The Contours of the Federal Rule

The first thing a plaintiff who wishes to bring a class action must do is define the class. Who is going to be included and who is not? The class definition will determine who is bound by the adjudication if the class is certified and is antecedent to the application of the remaining requirements of the rule. As you read the *Wal-Mart* case, see if you can identify how the class was defined— who would have been precluded by the class action had it been certified?

The plaintiff must also meet four requirements, set forth in Rule 23(a): (1) numerosity, (2) commonality, (3) typicality, and (4) adequacy of representation. First, she must demonstrate that the class is sufficiently numerous that joinder of all the plaintiffs is impracticable (called numerosity). Second, she must show that there are issues of law and fact in common for all class members (commonality). Third, the representative must be typical of the other class members such that she shared interests with them (typicality). Fourth and finally, the class representative must show that she can adequately represent the class (adequacy). These requirements apply regardless of the type of class action plaintiff seeks (injunctive or money damages, for example). Consider how these requirements overlap. For example, can a nontypical plaintiff be an adequate representative? If the class representative is "typical" of the class, does this not imply that the class members have something in common (otherwise, what would typicality mean)?

Courts have also added additional requirements through rule interpretation, but the requirements are not consistent across circuits. For example, some federal courts add an "ascertainability" requirement, requiring that the class members be objectively determinable by reference to the class definition. Some federal courts also require that the class definition not be contingent on liability. This means that a class cannot be defined as those whose rights defendant has violated; and if it is, some courts call this a "fail safe" class and it cannot be certified.

The class action rule provides for three different types of class actions, divided by the types of remedies plaintiffs seek. The first type is class actions where the defendant may be subject to incompatible legal standards or there is a limited fund from which plaintiffs seek recovery. Fed. R. Civ. P. 23(b)(1). This is the rarest type of class action. The second type of class action is an action where plaintiffs seek an injunction. Fed. R. Civ. P. 23(b)(2). This type of class action is often brought in the civil rights context, although not exclusively. The third type is available where plaintiffs seek money damages. Fed. R. Civ. P. 23(b)(3). Money damages class actions seem to be the most common type of class action, the most controversial, and the hardest to certify as a class action.

The requirements for each of these types of class actions are different, although they must all meet the numerosity, typicality, commonality, and adequacy requirements of 23(a). In class actions brought under 23(b)(1), the plaintiff must show that either there is a risk of inconsistent adjudication such that plaintiff would be subject to competing legal standards or that adjudication of some class members' interests would impede the interests of other class members (in other words, a limited fund such that if one plaintiff is paid and the fund runs out, a second plaintiff might get nothing although her claim is just as valid). These types of class actions resemble actions for interpleader and actions to which necessary joinder might apply. If a plaintiff certifies a 23(b)(1) class action, she need not notify the class and class members may not opt out. Why do you think the rulemakers decided to prohibit class members in these types of class actions from opting out? Think about what might happen if one class member were to opt out.

Actions certified under 23(b)(2) seek injunctive relief. Civil rights class actions seeking to change an institution's policy, such as the *Warner* case in the Case Files, would be certified under this provision. To certify a class under 23(b)(2) a plaintiff must show that "the party opposing the class has acted or refused to act on grounds that apply generally to the class, so that final injunctive relief or corresponding declaratory relief is appropriate respecting the class as a whole." 23(b)(2). In injunctive class actions, the court need not provide notice and cannot provide an opportunity to opt out. Ask yourself why an opt out would not be feasible in an injunctive class action against an institution—for example, would it be effective for a resident of New York City to opt out of the *Warner* class action against the city's stop-and-frisk practices?

Money damages class actions are certified under 23(b)(3) and have the most requirements. To certify a class for money damages, the plaintiff must show both that the issues common to the class predominate over individual issues and that the class action is a superior method for resolving the dispute. These are referred to as the *predominance* and *superiority* requirements. When you read Rule 23(b)(3), note the factors that courts may consider in determining predominance and superiority.

The predominance requirement is often a focus of dispute. In a case such as *Shutts*, where the absent class members are from different states and the claims arise under state law, common issues may not predominate over individual ones if state laws differ too much from another. Can a class member from California be governed by the same law as a class member from Kansas? The Kansas Supreme Court ruled that they could under Kansas choice of law, but the Supreme Court has not decided this question definitively. Many federal courts refuse to certify class actions when different state laws are implicated, holding that the common issues do not predominate over the questions created by different state laws. Similarly, many federal courts refuse to certify class actions in tort cases, finding that individual questions of causation predominate over common questions regarding a defendant's conduct.

In money damages class actions, the plaintiff must provide notice to class members and they must have an opportunity to opt out of the litigation. This differentiates money damages class actions from other forms of class actions to which these requirements do not attach. Note that the right to notice and opt out are both requirements of Rule 23 and due process requirements under *Shutts*.

The plaintiff must pay for the cost of notice. *Eisen v. Carlisle & Jacquelin*, 417 U.S. 156 (1974). This means that plaintiffs or their counsel must be well funded in order to maintain a class action, as the cost of notice can be very high. Such notice must meet the requirements that you read about in *Mullane v. Central Hanover Bank*, which is to say it must be reasonably calculated, under all the circumstances, to inform the absent class members about the pendency of the action and need not necessarily be by first class mail. Defendants will often pay the cost of notice when class actions are certified for settlement purposes.

Finally, sometimes a class action can be certified as to one issue only under Rule 23(c)(4). Often class actions certified under this provision will be certified for liability only, with the damages issues to be determined afterward in separate, individualized proceedings.

As you think about the additional requirements for money damages class actions, consider how they relate to the policy issues discussed at the start of this chapter—especially concern about defendants being subject to pressure to settle and individuals not having a full opportunity to participate in their lawsuit. What is the impetus for putting additional requirements on money damages class actions? Commentators and the rules drafters have expressed concern that there will be unresolvable conflicts of interest between class members in money damages suits. Should we be worried about the same conflicts of interest in injunctive actions, and if not, why not?

The class action rule also contains a series of provisions that mandate more procedures than those required for ordinary binary litigation to go forward. Consider these differences and what policy considerations justify them:

a. Settlement Approval

Rule 23(e) requires that before a class action is settled the parties receive court approval. By contrast, the decision to settle is determined by the parties in binary litigation. In a class action, the court must hold a hearing and determine whether the settlement is fair, reasonable, and adequate. If so, the court may approve the settlement.

b. Interlocutory Appeal

Rule 23(f) permits the losing party to appeal a certification decision prior to a final judgment (called an "interlocutory appeal"). This reflects the rulemakers' understanding of the importance of the certification decision. Interlocutory appeals are rare in litigation; ordinarily one needs a final judgment in order to appeal. Why are they available in class actions? This is largely because of arguments by defendants that the certification decision *determines* the litigation. If a class action is certified, then the value of the lawsuit, as compared with an individual suit, is very great. This means that the risk of loss for the defendant is also very great.

For example, compare the effect on a defendant of a series of $500 suits or one class action suit where the plaintiff class may recover $500 million if they win. First, not all the eligible plaintiffs are likely to bring their $500 suit, so even if he loses every case the defendant is not likely to be required to pay the full amount of damages that a class action might require. Second, in a series of individual lawsuits, the defendant may win some and lose some. The class action, by contrast, is an all-or-nothing proposition. Either the defendant loses and is liable for the entire amount or the defendant wins and is liable for nothing. Whether the risk of loss should be calculated differently in serial litigation as compared to a one-shot class suit is a question of probability theory that has important real-world implications for defendants. Defendants who are risk averse, risk neutral, or risk seeking will react differently to these probabilities.

c. Appointing the Class Counsel

Rule 23(g) requires that the *lawyer* demonstrate that he can adequately represent the class. This is largely because the class action is a lawyer-run litigation. Some people even go so far as to call it "entrepreneurial litigation." Lawyers often pick the class representatives, define the parameters of the class, and make all the decisions for the class members. This state of affairs is contrasted with binary litigation, where the lawyer (at least in theory) follows the directions of his client. Who is the client in the class action? Is it the class representative? Or is it the group of dispersed individuals who make up the class?

Plaintiff-side class action lawyers have been the subject of a great deal of criticism and many of the proposals for revising Rule 23 are driven by concerns over their conduct. This is largely because there is a lot of money to be made by lawyers in class suits. The lawyers' entrepreneurial role in class litigation creates an "agent-principal problem." This phrase refers to the idea that the lawyer may have interests that are not aligned with those of his client, the class. For example, it may be in the lawyer's interest to obtain a fee by quickly settling a case when a more protracted litigation would yield greater compensation for class members. A lot of scholarship has been devoted to solving the agent-principal problem in class actions. For a nice summary, *see* Bruce L. Hay and David Rosenberg, *"Sweetheart" and "Blackmail" Settlements in Class Actions: Reality and Remedy*, 75 Notre Dame L. Rev. 1377 (2000).

d. Attorneys' Fees

Rule 23(h) requires the attorneys to make a motion for fees and the court to determine what amount would be fair to award the attorneys for their work on the case. This provision is driven by the concern that class counsel would take advantage of the class if the lawyers were allowed to set their own fees.

There are two methods for calculating attorneys' fees in class actions. First, fees can be calculated on a percentage basis. The court may award a percentage of the fund that is to be awarded to class members rather than the (often much smaller) amount that is actually collected by class members at the end of the day. CAFA also set limits on attorneys' fees in certain situations such as when the class's recovery comes in the form of coupons rather than cash payments. A review of district and appellate opinions reveals that coupon settlements have become rarer in the federal courts since the passage of CAFA.

Second, fees can be calculated on a lodestar basis, that is, based on the number of hours the attorneys worked multiplied by an hourly rate. Courts may also add a "multiplier" when they calculate fees based on a lodestar method; multipliers increase the fees to reflect the risk that the attorneys took in pursuing the litigation. One study found that the mean and median fee awards in class actions are around 25 percent of the settlement fund. *See* Brian Fitzpatrick, *An Empirical Study of Class Action Settlements and Their Fee Awards*, 7 J. Empirical Legal Stud. 811 (2010).

2. The Rule in Application

The case brought by Betty Dukes and several other plaintiffs on behalf of all women employed by Wal-Mart garnered an extraordinary amount of publicity, even for a class action. *See* Liza Featherstone, *Selling Women Short: The Landmark Battle for Workers' Rights at Wal-Mart* (2005). This class action, which included from 500,000 to 3 million women (depending on who was doing the counting), projected the concerns about litigation generally and class actions in particular on a very big screen. At the time the suit was litigated, Wal-Mart was the nation's largest private employer. The size of the class action, and the plaintiffs' untested theory of liability, made the case extraordinary. Yet the Court's opinion, particularly its interpretation of the commonality requirement of Federal Rule 23(a), applies to all class actions.

Wal-Mart Stores, Inc. v. Dukes
564 U.S. 338 (2011)

Justice SCALIA delivered the opinion of the Court.

We are presented with one of the most expansive class actions ever. The District Court and the Court of Appeals approved the certification of a class comprising about one and a half million plaintiffs, current and former female employees of petitioner Wal-Mart who allege that the discretion exercised by their local supervisors over pay and promotion matters violates Title VII by discriminating against women. In addition to injunctive and declaratory relief, the plaintiffs seek an award of backpay. We consider whether the certification of the plaintiff class was consistent with Federal Rules of Civil Procedure 23(a) and (b)(2).

I

A

Petitioner Wal-Mart is the Nation's largest private employer. It operates four types of retail stores throughout the country: Discount Stores, Supercenters, Neighborhood Markets, and Sam's Clubs. Those stores are divided into seven nationwide divisions, which in turn comprise 41 regions of 80 to 85 stores apiece. Each store has between 40 and 53 separate departments and 80 to 500 staff positions. In all, Wal-Mart operates approximately 3,400 stores and employs more than one million people.

Pay and promotion decisions at Wal-Mart are generally committed to local managers' broad discretion, which is exercised "in a largely subjective manner." 222 F.R.D. 137, 145 (N.D. Cal. 2004). Local store managers may increase the wages of hourly employees (within limits) with only limited corporate oversight. As for salaried employees, such as store managers and their deputies, higher corporate authorities have discretion to set their pay within preestablished ranges.

Promotions work in a similar fashion. Wal-Mart permits store managers to apply their own subjective criteria when selecting candidates as "support managers," which is the first step on the path to management. Admission to Wal-Mart's management training program, however, does require that a candidate meet certain objective criteria, including an above-average performance rating, at least one year's tenure in the applicant's current position, and a willingness to relocate. But except for those requirements, regional and district managers have discretion to use their own judgment when selecting candidates for management training. Promotion to higher office—e.g., assistant manager, co-manager, or store manager—is similarly at the discretion of the employee's superiors after prescribed objective factors are satisfied.

B

The named plaintiffs in this lawsuit, representing the 1.5 million members of the certified class, are three current or former Wal-Mart employees who allege that the company discriminated against them on the basis of their sex by denying them equal pay or promotions, in violation of Title VII of the Civil Rights Act of 1964, 78 Stat. 253, as amended, 42 U.S.C. § 2000e-1 et seq. . . .

These plaintiffs, respondents here, do not allege that Wal-Mart has any express corporate policy against the advancement of women. Rather, they claim that their local managers' discretion over pay and promotions is exercised disproportionately in favor of men, leading to an unlawful disparate impact on female employees, see 42 U.S.C. § 2000e-2(k). And, respondents say, because Wal-Mart is aware of this effect, its refusal to cabin its managers' authority amounts to disparate treatment, see § 2000e-2(a). Their complaint seeks injunctive and declaratory relief, punitive damages, and backpay. It does not ask for compensatory damages.

Importantly for our purposes, respondents claim that the discrimination to which they have been subjected is common to all Wal-Mart's female employees. The basic theory of their case is that a strong and uniform "corporate culture" permits bias against women to infect, perhaps subconsciously, the discretionary decisionmaking of each one of Wal-Mart's thousands of managers—thereby making every woman at the company the victim of one common discriminatory practice. Respondents therefore wish to litigate the Title VII claims of all female employees at Wal-Mart's stores in a nationwide class action.

C

Class certification is governed by Federal Rule of Civil Procedure 23. Under Rule 23(a), the party seeking certification must demonstrate, first, that:

"(1) the class is so numerous that joinder of all members is impracticable,
"(2) there are questions of law or fact common to the class,
"(3) the claims or defenses of the representative parties are typical of the claims or defenses of the class, and
"(4) the representative parties will fairly and adequately protect the interests of the class" (paragraph breaks added).

Second, the proposed class must satisfy at least one of the three requirements listed in Rule 23(b). Respondents rely on Rule 23(b)(2), which applies when "the party opposing the class has acted or refused to act on grounds that apply generally to the class, so that final injunctive relief or corresponding declaratory relief is appropriate respecting the class as a whole."

Invoking these provisions, respondents moved the District Court to certify a plaintiff class consisting of " '[a]ll women employed at any Wal-Mart domestic retail store at any time since December 26, 1998, who have been or may be subjected to Wal-Mart's challenged pay and management track promotions policies and practices.' " 222 F.R.D., at 141-142. As evidence that there were indeed "questions of law or fact common to" all the women of Wal-Mart, as Rule 23(a)(2) requires, respondents relied chiefly on three forms of proof: statistical evidence about pay and promotion disparities between men and women at the company, anecdotal reports of discrimination from about 120 of Wal-Mart's female employees, and the testimony of a sociologist, Dr. William Bielby, who conducted a "social framework analysis" of Wal-Mart's "culture" and personnel practices, and concluded that the company was "vulnerable" to gender discrimination. 603 F.3d 571, 601 (9th Cir. 2010) (en banc).

Wal-Mart unsuccessfully moved to strike much of this evidence. It also offered its own countervailing statistical and other proof in an effort to defeat Rule 23(a)'s requirements of commonality, typicality, and adequate representation. Wal-Mart further contended that respondents' monetary claims for backpay could not be certified under Rule 23(b)(2), first because that Rule refers only to injunctive and declaratory relief, and second because the backpay claims could not be manageably tried as a class without depriving Wal-Mart of its right to present certain statutory defenses. With one limitation not relevant here, the District Court granted respondents' motion and certified their proposed class.

D

A divided en banc Court of Appeals substantially affirmed the District Court's certification order. 603 F.3d 571. The majority concluded that respondents' evidence of commonality was sufficient to "raise the common question whether Wal-Mart's female employees nationwide were subjected to a single set of corporate policies (not merely a number of independent discriminatory acts) that may have worked to unlawfully discriminate against them in violation of Title VII." Id., at 612 (emphasis deleted). It also agreed with the District Court that the named plaintiffs' claims were sufficiently typical of the class as a whole to satisfy Rule 23(a)(3), and that they could serve as adequate class representatives, see Rule 23(a)(4). Id., at 614-615. With respect to the Rule 23(b)(2) question, the Ninth Circuit held that respondents' backpay claims could be certified as part of a (b)(2) class because they did not "predominat[e]" over the requests for declaratory and injunctive relief, meaning they were not "superior in strength, influence, or authority" to the nonmonetary claims. Id., at 616 (internal quotation marks omitted).

Finally, the Court of Appeals determined that the action could be manageably tried as a class action because the District Court could adopt the approach the Ninth Circuit approved in *Hilao v. Estate of Marcos*, 103 F.3d 767, 782-787 (1996). There compensatory damages for some 9,541 class members were calculated by selecting 137 claims at random, referring those claims to a special master for valuation, and then extrapolating the validity and value of the untested claims from the sample set. The Court of Appeals "s[aw] no reason why a similar procedure to that used in *Hilao* could not be employed in this case." *Id.*, at 627. It would allow Wal-Mart "to present individual defenses in the randomly selected 'sample cases,' thus revealing the approximate percentage of class members whose unequal pay or nonpromotion was due to something other than gender discrimination." *Ibid.*, n.56 (emphasis deleted).

We granted certiorari.

II

The class action is "an exception to the usual rule that litigation is conducted by and on behalf of the individual named parties only." *Califano v. Yamasaki*, 442 U.S. 682, 700-701 (1979). In order to justify a departure from that rule, "a class representative must be part of the class and 'possess the same interest and suffer the same injury' as the class members." *East Tex. Motor Freight System, Inc. v. Rodriguez*, 431 U.S. 395, 403 (1977). Rule 23(a) ensures that the named plaintiffs are appropriate representatives of the class whose claims they wish to litigate. The Rule's four requirements—numerosity, commonality, typicality, and adequate representation—"effectively 'limit the class claims to those fairly encompassed by the named plaintiff's claims.' " *General Telephone Co. of Southwest v. Falcon*, 457 U.S. 147, 156 (1982).

A

The crux of this case is commonality—the rule requiring a plaintiff to show that "there are questions of law or fact common to the class." Rule 23(a)(2). That language is easy to misread, since "[a]ny competently crafted class complaint literally raises common 'questions.' " Nagareda, *Class Certification in the Age of Aggregate Proof*, 84 N.Y.U. L. Rev. 97, 131-132 (2009). For example: Do all of us plaintiffs indeed work for Wal-Mart? Do our managers have discretion over pay? Is that an unlawful employment practice? What remedies should we get? Reciting these questions is not sufficient to obtain class certification. Commonality requires the plaintiff to demonstrate that the class members "have suffered the same injury," *Falcon*, *supra*, at 157. This does not mean merely that they have all suffered a violation of the same provision of law. Title VII, for example, can be violated in many ways—by intentional discrimination, or by hiring and promotion criteria that result in disparate impact, and by the use of these practices on the part of many different superiors in a single company. Quite obviously, the mere claim by employees of the same company that they have suffered a Title VII injury, or even a disparate-impact Title VII injury, gives no cause to believe that all their claims can productively be litigated at once. Their claims must depend upon a common contention—for example, the assertion of discriminatory bias on the part of the same supervisor. That common contention, moreover, must be of such a nature that it is capable of classwide resolution—which means that determination of its truth or falsity will resolve an issue that is central to the validity of each one of the claims in one stroke.

"What matters to class certification . . . is not the raising of common 'questions'—even in droves—but, rather the capacity of a classwide proceeding to generate common answers apt to drive the resolution of the litigation. Dissimilarities within the proposed class are what have the potential to impede the generation of common answers." Nagareda, *supra*, at 132.

Rule 23 does not set forth a mere pleading standard. A party seeking class certification must affirmatively demonstrate his compliance with the Rule—that is, he must be prepared to prove that there are in fact sufficiently numerous parties, common questions of law or fact, etc. We recognized in *Falcon* that "sometimes it may be necessary for the court to probe behind the pleadings before coming to rest on the certification question," 457 U.S., at 160, and that certification is proper only if "the trial court is satisfied, after a rigorous analysis, that the pre-requisites of Rule 23(a) have been satisfied," *id.*, at 161. Frequently that "rigorous analysis" will entail some overlap with the merits of the plaintiff's underlying claim. That cannot be helped. . . . Nor is there anything unusual about that consequence: The necessity of touching aspects of the merits in order to resolve preliminary matters, e.g., jurisdiction and venue, is a familiar feature of litigation.

In this case, proof of commonality necessarily overlaps with respondents' merits contention that Wal-Mart engages in a pattern or practice of discrimination. That is so because, in resolving an individual's Title VII claim, the crux of the inquiry is "the reason for a particular employment decision," *Cooper v. Federal Reserve Bank of Richmond*, 467 U.S. 867, 876 (1984). Here respondents wish to sue about literally millions of employment decisions at once. Without some glue holding the alleged reasons for all those decisions together, it will be impossible to say that examination of all the class members' claims for relief will produce a common answer to the crucial question why was I disfavored.

B

[This Court's opinion in] *Falcon* suggested two ways in which [the] conceptual gap [between the individual's claim that she was denied higher pay on discriminatory grounds and the existence of a class of persons who have suffered the same injury] might be bridged. First, if the employer "used a biased testing procedure to evaluate both applicants for employment and incumbent employees, a class action on behalf of every applicant or employee who might have been prejudiced by the test clearly would satisfy the commonality and typicality requirements of Rule 23(a)." *Id.*, at 159, n. 15. Second, "[s]ignificant proof that an employer operated under a general policy of discrimination conceivably could justify a class of both applicants and employees if the discrimination manifested itself in hiring and promotion practices in the same general fashion, such as through entirely subjective decisionmaking processes." *Ibid*. We think that statement precisely describes respondents' burden in this case. The first manner of bridging the gap obviously has no application here; Wal-Mart has no testing procedure or other companywide evaluation method that can be charged with bias. The whole point of permitting discretionary decisionmaking is to avoid evaluating employees under a common standard.

The second manner of bridging the gap requires "significant proof" that Wal-Mart "operated under a general policy of discrimination." That is entirely absent here. Wal-Mart's announced policy forbids sex discrimination and as the District Court recognized the company imposes penalties for denials of equal employment opportunity. The only evidence of a "general policy of discrimination" respondents produced was the testimony of Dr. William Bielby, their sociological expert. Relying on "social framework" analysis, Bielby testified that Wal-Mart has a "strong corporate culture," that makes it " 'vulnerable' " to "gender bias." He could not, however, "determine with any specificity how regularly stereotypes play a meaningful role in employment decisions at Wal-Mart. At his deposition . . . Dr. Bielby conceded that he could not calculate whether 0.5 percent or 95 percent of the employment decisions at Wal-Mart might be determined by stereotyped thinking." . . . [E]ven if properly considered, Bielby's testimony does nothing to advance respondents' case. "[W]hether 0.5 percent or 95 percent of the employment decisions at Wal-Mart might be determined by stereotyped thinking" is the essential question on which respondents' theory of commonality depends. If Bielby admittedly has no answer to that question, we can safely disregard what he has to say. It is worlds away from "significant proof" that Wal-Mart "operated under a general policy of discrimination."

C

The only corporate policy that the plaintiffs' evidence convincingly establishes is Wal-Mart's "policy" of allowing discretion by local supervisors over employment matters. On its face, of course, that is just the opposite of a uniform employment practice that would provide the commonality needed for a class action; it is a policy against having uniform employment practices. It is also a very common and presumptively reasonable way of doing business—one that we have said "should itself raise no inference of discriminatory conduct."

To be sure, we have recognized that, "in appropriate cases," giving discretion to lower-level supervisors can be the basis of Title VII liability under a disparate-impact theory—since "an employer's undisciplined system of subjective decisionmaking [can have] precisely the same effects as a system pervaded by impermissible intentional discrimination." But the recognition that this type of Title VII claim "can" exist does not lead to the conclusion that every employee in a company using a system of discretion has such a claim in common. To the contrary, left to their own devices most managers in any corporation—and surely most managers in a corporation that forbids sex discrimination—would select sex-neutral, performance-based criteria for hiring and promotion that produce no actionable disparity at all. Others may choose to reward various attributes that produce disparate impact—such as scores on general aptitude tests or educational achievements. And still other managers may be guilty of intentional discrimination that produces a sex-based disparity. In such a company, demonstrating the invalidity of one manager's use of discretion will do nothing to demonstrate the invalidity of another's. A party seeking to certify a nationwide class will be unable to show that all the employees' Title VII claims will in fact depend on the answers to common questions.

Respondents have not identified a common mode of exercising discretion that pervades the entire company—aside from their reliance on Dr. Bielby's social frameworks analysis that we have rejected. In a company of Wal-Mart's size and geographical scope, it is quite unbelievable that all managers would exercise their discretion in a common way without some common direction. Respondents attempt to make that showing by means of statistical and anecdotal evidence, but their evidence falls well short. . . .

Even if they are taken at face value, these studies are insufficient to establish that respondents' theory can be proved on a classwide basis. . . . A regional pay disparity, for example, may be attributable to only a small set of Wal-Mart stores, and cannot by itself establish the uniform, store-by-store disparity upon which the plaintiffs' theory of commonality depends.

There is another, more fundamental, respect in which respondents' statistical proof fails. Even if it established (as it does not) a pay or promotion pattern that differs from the nationwide figures or the regional figures in all of Wal-Mart's 3,400 stores, that would still not demonstrate that commonality of issue exists. Some managers will claim that the availability of women, or qualified women, or interested women, in their stores' area does not mirror the national or regional statistics. And almost all of them will claim to have been applying some sex-neutral, performance-based criteria—whose nature and effects will differ from store to store. In the landmark case of ours which held that giving discretion to lower-level supervisors can be the basis of Title VII liability under a disparate-impact theory, the plurality opinion conditioned that holding on the corollary that merely proving that the discretionary system has produced a racial or sexual disparity is not enough. "[T]he plaintiff must begin by identifying the specific employment practice that is challenged." That is all the more necessary when a class of plaintiffs is sought to be certified. Other than the bare existence of delegated discretion, respondents have identified no "specific employment practice"—much less one that ties all their 1.5 million claims together. Merely showing that Wal-Mart's policy of discretion has produced an overall sex-based disparity does not suffice.

Respondents' anecdotal evidence suffers from the same defects, and in addition is too weak to raise any inference that all the individual, discretionary personnel decisions are discriminatory. In *Teamsters v. United States*, 431 U.S. 324 (1977), in addition to substantial statistical evidence of company-wide discrimination, the Government (as plaintiff) produced about 40 specific accounts of racial discrimination from particular individuals . . . [that] represented roughly one account for every eight members of the class. Moreover, the Court of Appeals noted that the anecdotes came from individuals "spread throughout" the company who "for the most part" worked at the company's operational centers that employed the largest numbers of the class members. Here, by contrast, respondents filed some 120 affidavits reporting experiences of discrimination—about 1 for every 12,500 class members—relating to only some 235 out of Wal-Mart's 3,400. . . . Even if every single one of these accounts is true, that would not demonstrate that the entire company "operate[s] under a general policy of discrimination," *Falcon, supra*, at 159, n. 15, which is what respondents must show to certify a companywide class.

The dissent misunderstands the nature of the foregoing analysis. It criticizes our focus on the dissimilarities between the putative class members on the ground that we have "blend[ed]" Rule 23(a)(2)'s commonality requirement with Rule 23(b)(3)'s inquiry into whether common questions "predominate" over individual ones. That is not so. We quite agree that for purposes of Rule 23(a)(2) " '[e]ven a single [common] question' " will do. We consider dissimilarities not in order to determine (as Rule 23(b)(3) requires) whether common questions predominate, but in order to determine (as Rule 23(a)(2) requires) whether there is "[e]ven a single [common] question." And there is not here. Because respondents provide no convincing proof of a companywide discriminatory pay and promotion policy, we have concluded that they have not established the existence of any common question. In sum, we agree with Chief Judge Kozinski that the members of the class:

> held a multitude of different jobs, at different levels of Wal-Mart's hierarchy, for variable lengths of time, in 3,400 stores, sprinkled across 50 states, with a kaleidoscope of supervisors (male and female), subject to a variety of regional policies that all differed. . . . Some thrived while others did poorly. They have little in common but their sex and this lawsuit.

603 F.3d, at 652 (dissenting opinion).

III

We also conclude that respondents' claims for backpay were improperly certified under Federal Rule of Civil Procedure 23(b)(2). Our opinion in *Ticor Title Ins. Co. v. Brown,* 511 U.S. 117, 121 (1994) (per curiam) expressed serious doubt about whether claims for monetary relief may be certified under that provision. We now hold that they may not, at least where (as here) the monetary relief is not incidental to the injunctive or declaratory relief.

A

Rule 23(b)(2) allows class treatment when "the party opposing the class has acted or refused to act on grounds that apply generally to the class, so that final injunctive relief or corresponding declaratory relief is appropriate respecting the class as a whole." One possible reading of this provision is that it applies only to requests for such injunctive or declaratory relief and does not authorize the class certification of monetary claims at all. We need not reach that broader question in this case, because we think that, at a minimum, claims for individualized relief (like the backpay at issue here) do not satisfy the Rule. The key to the (b)(2) class is "the indivisible nature of the injunctive or declaratory remedy warranted—the notion that the conduct is such that it can be enjoined or declared unlawful only as to all of the class members or as to none of them." Nagareda, 84 N.Y.U. L. Rev., at 132. In other words, Rule 23(b)(2) applies only when a single injunction or declaratory judgment would provide relief to each member of the class. It does not authorize class certification when each individual class member would be entitled to a different injunction or declaratory judgment against the defendant. Similarly, it does not authorize class certification when each class member would be entitled to an individualized award of monetary damages.

That interpretation accords with the history of the Rule. Because Rule 23 "stems from equity practice" that predated its codification, *Amchem Products, Inc. v. Windsor,* 521 U.S. 591, 613 (1997), in determining its meaning we have previously looked to the historical models on which the Rule was based. As we observed in *Amchem,* "[c]ivil rights cases against parties charged with unlawful, class-based discrimination are prime examples" of what (b)(2) is meant to capture. 521 U.S., at 614. In particular, the Rule reflects a series of decisions involving challenges to racial segregation—conduct that was remedied by a single classwide order. In none of the cases cited by the Advisory Committee as examples of (b)(2)'s antecedents did the plaintiffs combine any claim for individualized relief with their classwide injunction. *See* Advisory Committee's Note, 39 F.R.D. 69, 102 (1966) (citing cases).

Permitting the combination of individualized and classwide relief in a (b)(2) class is also inconsistent with the structure of Rule 23(b). Classes certified under (b)(1) and (b)(2) share the most traditional justifications for class treatment—that individual adjudications would be impossible or unworkable, as in a (b)(1) class, or that the relief sought must perforce affect the entire class at once, as in a (b)(2) class. For that reason these are also mandatory classes: The Rule provides no opportunity for (b)(1) or (b)(2) class members to opt out, and does not even oblige the District Court to afford them notice of the action. Rule 23(b)(3), by contrast, is an "adventuresome innovation" of the 1966 amendments, framed for situations "in which 'class-action treatment is not as clearly called for.'" It allows class certification in a much wider set of circumstances but with greater procedural protections. Its only prerequisites are that "the questions of law or fact common to class members predominate over any questions affecting only individual members, and that a class action is superior to other available methods for fairly and efficiently adjudicating the controversy." Rule 23(b)(3). And unlike (b)(1) and (b)(2) classes, the (b)(3) class is not mandatory; class members are entitled to receive "the best notice that is practicable under the circumstances" and to withdraw from the class at their option. *See* Rule 23(c)(2)(B).

Given that structure, we think it clear that individualized monetary claims belong in Rule 23(b)(3). The procedural protections attending the (b)(3) class—predominance, superiority, mandatory notice, and the right to opt out—are missing from (b)(2) not because the Rule considers them unnecessary, but because it considers them unnecessary to a (b)(2) class. When a class seeks an indivisible injunction benefitting all its members at once, there is no reason to undertake a case-specific inquiry into whether class issues predominate or whether class action is a superior method of adjudicating the dispute. Predominance and superiority are self-evident. But with respect to each class member's individualized claim for money, that is not so—which is precisely why (b)(3) requires the judge to make findings about predominance and superiority before allowing the class. Similarly, (b)(2) does not require that class members be given notice and optout rights, presumably because it is thought (rightly or wrongly) that notice has no purpose when the class is mandatory, and that depriving people of their right to sue in this manner complies with the Due Process Clause. In the context of a class action predominantly for money damages we have held that absence of notice and opt-out violates due process. *See Phillips Petroleum Co. v. Shutts,* 472 U.S. 797, 812 (1985). While we have never held that to be so where the monetary claims do not predominate, the serious possibility that it may be so provides an additional reason not to read Rule 23(b)(2) to include the monetary claims here.

B

Against that conclusion, respondents argue that their claims for backpay were appropriately certified as part of a class under Rule 23(b)(2) because those claims do not "predominate" over their requests for injunctive and declaratory relief. They rely upon the Advisory Committee's statement that Rule 23(b)(2) "does not extend to cases in which the appropriate final relief relates exclusively or predominantly to money damages." 39 F.R.D., at 102 (emphasis added). The negative implication, they argue, is that it does extend to cases in which the appropriate final relief relates only partially and nonpredominantly to money damages. Of course it is the Rule itself, not the Advisory Committee's description of it, that governs. And a mere negative inference does not in our view suffice to establish a disposition that has no basis in the Rule's text, and that does obvious violence to the Rule's structural features. The mere "predominance" of a proper (b)(2) injunctive claim does nothing to justify elimination of Rule 23(b)(3)'s procedural protections: It neither establishes the superiority of class adjudication over individual adjudication nor cures the notice and opt-out problems. We fail to see why the Rule should be read to nullify these protections whenever a plaintiff class, at its option, combines its monetary claims with a request—even a "predominating request"—for an injunction.

Respondents' predominance test, moreover, creates perverse incentives for class representatives to place at risk potentially valid claims for monetary relief.

In this case, for example, the named plaintiffs declined to include employees' claims for compensatory damages in their complaint. That strategy of including only backpay claims made it more likely that monetary relief would not "predominate." But it also created the possibility (if the predominance test were correct) that individual class members' compensatory-damages claims would be precluded by litigation they had no power to hold themselves apart from. If it were determined, for example, that a particular class member is not entitled to backpay because her denial of increased pay or a promotion was not the product of discrimination, that employee might be collaterally estopped from independently seeking compensatory damages based on that same denial. That possibility underscores the need for plaintiffs with individual monetary claims to decide for themselves whether to tie their fates to the class representatives' or go it alone—a choice Rule 23(b)(2) does not ensure that they have.

The predominance test would also require the District Court to reevaluate the roster of class members continually. The Ninth Circuit recognized the necessity for this when it concluded that those plaintiffs no longer employed by Wal-Mart lack standing to seek injunctive or declaratory relief against its employment practices. The Court of Appeals' response to that difficulty, however, was not to eliminate all former employees from the certified class, but to eliminate only those who had left the company's employ by the date the complaint was filed. That solution has no logical connection to the problem, since those who have left their Wal-Mart jobs since the complaint was filed have no more need for prospective relief than those who left beforehand. . . . Of course, the alternative (and logical) solution of excising plaintiffs from the class as they leave their employment may have struck the Court of Appeals as wasteful of the District Court's time. . . . What follows from this, however, is not that some arbitrary limitation on class membership should be imposed but that the backpay claims should not be certified under Rule 23(b)(2) at all.

Finally, respondents argue that their backpay claims are appropriate for a (b)(2) class action because a backpay award is equitable in nature. The latter may be true, but it is irrelevant. The Rule does not speak of "equitable" remedies generally but of injunctions and declaratory judgments. As Title VII itself makes pellucidly clear, backpay is neither.

C

. . . Contrary to the Ninth Circuit's view, Wal-Mart is entitled to individualized determinations of each employee's eligibility for backpay. . . .

. . . When the plaintiff seeks individual relief such as reinstatement or backpay after establishing a pattern or practice of discrimination, "a district court must usually conduct additional proceedings . . . to determine the scope of individual relief." *Teamsters,* 431 U.S., at 361. At this phase, the burden of proof will shift to the company, but it will have the right to raise any individual affirmative defenses it may have, and to "demonstrate that the individual applicant was denied an employment opportunity for lawful reasons." *Id.,* at 362.

The Court of Appeals believed that it was possible to replace such proceedings with Trial by Formula. A sample set of the class members would be selected, as to whom liability for sex discrimination and the backpay owing as a result would be determined in depositions supervised by a master. The percentage of claims determined to be valid would then be applied to the entire remaining class, and the number of (presumptively) valid claims thus derived would be multiplied by the average backpay award in the sample set to arrive at the entire class recovery—without further individualized proceedings. We disapprove that novel project. Because the Rules Enabling Act forbids interpreting Rule 23 to "abridge, enlarge or modify any substantive right," 28 U.S.C. § 2072(b), a class cannot be certified on the premise that Wal-Mart will not be entitled to litigate its statutory defenses to individual claims. And because the necessity of that litigation will prevent backpay from being "incidental" to the classwide injunction, respondents' class could not be certified even assuming, arguendo, that "incidental" monetary relief can be awarded to a 23(b)(2) class. . . .

The judgment of the Court of Appeals is [r]eversed.

Justice GINSBURG, with whom Justice BREYER, Justice SOTOMAYOR, and Justice KAGAN join, concurring in part and dissenting in part.

The class in this case, I agree with the Court, should not have been certified under Federal Rule of Civil Procedure 23(b)(2). The plaintiffs, alleging discrimination in violation of Title VII, 42 U.S.C. § 2000e et seq., seek monetary relief that is not merely incidental to any injunctive or declaratory relief that might be available. A putative class of this type may be certifiable under Rule 23(b)(3), if the plaintiffs show that common class questions "predominate" over issues affecting individuals—e.g., qualification for, and the amount of, backpay or compensatory damages—and that a class action is "superior" to other modes of adjudication.

Whether the class the plaintiffs describe meets the specific requirements of Rule 23(b)(3) is not before the Court, and I would reserve that matter for consideration and decision on remand. The Court, however, disqualifies the class at the starting gate, holding that the plaintiffs cannot cross the "commonality" line set by Rule 23(a)(2). In so ruling, the Court imports into the Rule 23(a) determination concerns properly addressed in a Rule 23(b)(3) assessment.

I

A

Rule 23(a)(2) establishes a preliminary requirement for maintaining a class action: "[T]here are questions of law or fact common to the class." . . .

A "question" is ordinarily understood to be "[a] subject or point open to controversy." American Heritage Dictionary 1483 (3d ed. 1992). *See also* Black's Law Dictionary 1366 (9th ed. 2009) (defining "question of fact" as "[a] disputed issue to be resolved . . . [at] trial" and "question of law" as "[a]n issue to be decided by the judge"). Thus, a "question" "common to the class" must be a dispute, either of fact or of law, the resolution of which will advance the determination of the class members' claims.[3]

B

The District Court, recognizing that "one significant issue common to the class may be sufficient to warrant certification," found that the plaintiffs easily met that test. Absent an error of law or an abuse of discretion, an appellate tribunal has no warrant to upset the District Court's finding of commonality.

The District Court certified a class of "[a]ll women employed at any Wal-Mart domestic retail store at any time since December 26, 1998." The named plaintiffs, led by Betty Dukes, propose to litigate, on behalf of the class, allegations that Wal-Mart discriminates on the basis of gender in pay and promotions. They allege that the company "[r]eli[es] on gender stereotypes in making employment decisions such as . . . promotion[s] [and] pay." Wal-Mart permits those prejudices to infect personnel decisions, the plaintiffs contend, by leaving pay and promotions in the hands of "a nearly all male managerial workforce" using "arbitrary and subjective criteria." Further alleged barriers to the advancement of female employees include the company's requirement, "as a condition of promotion to management jobs, that employees be willing to relocate." Absent instruction otherwise, there is a risk that managers will act on the familiar assumption that women, because of their services to husband and children, are less mobile than men. *See* Dept. of Labor, Federal Glass Ceiling Commission, *Good for Business: Making Full Use of the Nation's Human Capital* 151 (1995).

Women fill 70 percent of the hourly jobs in the retailer's stores but make up only "33 percent of management employees." "[T]he higher one looks in the organization the lower the percentage of women." The plaintiffs' "largely uncontested descriptive statistics" also show that women working in the company's stores "are paid less than men in every region" and "that the salary gap widens over time even for men and women hired into the same jobs at the same time."

The District Court identified "systems for . . . promoting in-store employees" that were "sufficiently similar across regions and stores" to conclude that "the manner in which these systems affect the class raises issues that are common to all class members." The selection of employees for promotion to in-store management "is fairly characterized as a 'tap on the shoulder' process," in which managers have discretion about whose shoulders to tap. Vacancies are not regularly posted; from among those employees satisfying minimum qualifications, managers choose whom to promote on the basis of their own subjective impressions.

Wal-Mart's compensation policies also operate uniformly across stores, the District Court found. The retailer leaves open a $2 band for every position's

---

3. The Court suggests Rule 23(a)(2) must mean more than it says. If the word "questions" were taken literally, the majority asserts, plaintiffs could pass the Rule 23(a)(2) bar by "[r]eciting . . . questions" like "Do all of us plaintiffs indeed work for Wal-Mart?" Sensibly read, however, the word "questions" means disputed issues, not any utterance crafted in the grammatical form of a question.

hourly pay rate. Wal-Mart provides no standards or criteria for setting wages within that band, and thus does nothing to counter unconscious bias on the part of supervisors.

Wal-Mart's supervisors do not make their discretionary decisions in a vacuum. The District Court reviewed means Wal-Mart used to maintain a "carefully constructed . . . corporate culture," such as frequent meetings to reinforce the common way of thinking, regular transfers of managers between stores to ensure uniformity throughout the company, monitoring of stores "on a close and constant basis," and "Wal-Mart TV," "broadcas[t] . . . into all stores."

The plaintiffs' evidence, including class members' tales of their own experiences, suggests that gender bias suffused Wal-Mart's company culture. Among illustrations, senior management often refer to female associates as "little Janie Qs." One manager told an employee that "[m]en are here to make a career and women aren't." A committee of female Wal-Mart executives concluded that "[s]tereotypes limit the opportunities offered to women."

Finally, the plaintiffs presented an expert's appraisal to show that the pay and promotions disparities at Wal-Mart "can be explained only by gender discrimination and not by . . . neutral variables." 222 F.R.D., at 155. Using regression analyses, their expert, Richard Drogin, controlled for factors including, inter alia, job performance, length of time with the company, and the store where an employee worked. The results, the District Court found, were sufficient to raise an "inference of discrimination."

C

The District Court's identification of a common question, whether Wal-Mart's pay and promotions policies gave rise to unlawful discrimination, was hardly infirm. The practice of delegating to supervisors large discretion to make personnel decisions, uncontrolled by formal standards, has long been known to have the potential to produce disparate effects. Managers, like all humankind, may be prey to biases of which they are unaware.[6] The risk of discrimination is heightened when those managers are predominantly of one sex, and are steeped in a corporate culture that perpetuates gender stereotypes. . . .

We have held that "discretionary employment practices" can give rise to Title VII claims, not only when such practices are motivated by discriminatory intent but also when they produce discriminatory results. . . .

The plaintiffs' allegations state claims of gender discrimination in the form of biased decisionmaking in both pay and promotions. The evidence reviewed by

---

6. An example vividly illustrates how subjective decisionmaking can be a vehicle for discrimination. Performing in symphony orchestras was long a male preserve. Goldin and Rouse, *Orchestrating Impartiality: The Impact of "Blind" Auditions on Female Musicians*, 90 Am. Econ. Rev. 715, 715-716 (2000). In the 1970's orchestras began hiring musicians through auditions open to all comers. *Id.*, at 716. Reviewers were to judge applicants solely on their musical abilities, yet subconscious bias led some reviewers to disfavor women. Orchestras that permitted reviewers to see the applicants hired far fewer female musicians than orchestras that conducted blind auditions, in which candidates played behind opaque screens. *Id.*, at 738.

the District Court adequately demonstrated that resolving those claims would necessitate examination of particular policies and practices alleged to affect, adversely and globally, women employed at Wal-Mart's stores. Rule 23(a)(2), setting a necessary but not a sufficient criterion for class-action certification, demands nothing further.

II

A

The Court gives no credence to the key dispute common to the class: whether Wal-Mart's discretionary pay and promotion policies are discriminatory. . . . "What matters," the Court asserts, "is not the raising of common 'questions,' " but whether there are "[d]issimilarities within the proposed class" that "have the potential to impede the generation of common answers."

The Court blends Rule 23(a)(2)'s threshold criterion with the more demanding criteria of Rule 23(b)(3), and thereby elevates the (a)(2) inquiry so that it is no longer "easily satisfied," 5 J. Moore et al., Moore's Federal Practice § 23.23[2], p. 23-72 (3d ed. 2011). Rule 23(b)(3) certification requires, in addition to the four 23(a) findings, determinations that "questions of law or fact common to class members predominate over any questions affecting only individual members" and that "a class action is superior to other available methods for . . . adjudicating the controversy."

The Court's emphasis on differences between class members mimics the Rule 23(b)(3) inquiry into whether common questions "predominate" over individual issues. And by asking whether the individual differences "impede" common adjudication, the Court duplicates 23(b)(3)'s question whether "a class action is superior" to other modes of adjudication. Indeed, Professor Nagareda, whose "dissimilarities" inquiry the Court endorses, developed his position in the context of Rule 23(b)(3). See 84 N.Y.U. L. Rev., at 131 (Rule 23(b)(3) requires "some decisive degree of similarity across the proposed class" because it "speaks of common 'questions' that 'predominate' over individual ones"). "The Rule 23(b)(3) predominance inquiry" is meant to "tes[t] whether proposed classes are sufficiently cohesive to warrant adjudication by representation." *Amchem Products, Inc. v. Windsor*, 521 U.S. 591, 623 (1997). If courts must conduct a "dissimilarities" analysis at the Rule 23(a)(2) stage, no mission remains for Rule 23(b)(3).

Because Rule 23(a) is also a prerequisite for Rule 23(b)(1) and Rule 23(b)(2) classes, the Court's "dissimilarities" position is far reaching. Individual differences should not bar a Rule 23(b)(1) or Rule 23(b)(2) class, so long as the Rule 23(a) threshold is met. . . .

B

The "dissimilarities" approach leads the Court to train its attention on what distinguishes individual class members, rather than on what unites them. Given the lack of standards for pay and promotions, the majority says, "demonstrating the invalidity of one manager's use of discretion will do nothing to demonstrate the invalidity of another's."

Wal-Mart's delegation of discretion over pay and promotions is a policy uniform throughout all stores. The very nature of discretion is that people will exercise it in various ways. A system of delegated discretion, *Watson* held, is a practice actionable under Title VII when it produces discriminatory outcomes. A finding that Wal-Mart's pay and promotions practices in fact violate the law would be the first step in the usual order of proof for plaintiffs seeking individual remedies for company-wide discrimination. That each individual employee's unique circumstances will ultimately determine whether she is entitled to backpay or damages, § 2000e-5(g)(2)(A) (barring backpay if a plaintiff "was refused . . . advancement . . . for any reason other than discrimination"), should not factor into the Rule 23(a)(2) determination.

. . .

The Court errs in importing a "dissimilarities" notion suited to Rule 23(b)(3) into the Rule 23(a) commonality inquiry. I therefore cannot join Part II of the Court's opinion.

REVIEW QUESTIONS

1. What is the definition of commonality articulated by the Court? Can you point to the language in the opinion that you would quote if you were writing a brief and needed to state the standard?

2. The case presents what appear to be two different interpretations of the "commonality" requirement of Rule 23(a). What are the differences between Justice Scalia's articulation of the "common questions" standard and Justice Ginsburg's?

3. How does the majority's interpretation of the words "common question of law or fact" differ from what you learned about the interpretation of that same language in the context of joinder under Rule 20?

4. In the segment entitled *How to Read a Rule* in Chapter 1, you were introduced to the controversy over interpretation of the Federal Rules and the role of the Advisory Committee Notes. What role do the Advisory Committee Notes play in the analysis in this case? How should the intention of the rule drafters be considered in the proper interpretation of the rule? How does the approach taken by the majority in *Wal-Mart* square with the Court's approach to rule interpretation in *Ashcroft v. Iqbal* (reproduced in Chapter 3)? Is the interpretive mode in the Court's modern jurisprudence consistent?

5. What are the assumptions of the Justices about how people behave in the workplace? Are they justified? How would you explain the relationship between these assumptions and the Justices' interpretation of Rule 23? In several other contexts, particularly pleadings, you have seen judicial assumptions driving doctrine. What limits should there be on judges using their common sense and personal observations of the world in framing doctrine? Is it possible to avoid this, even if we wanted to?

MORE TO PONDER

1. The commonality question is made more complicated by the relationship between the substantive merits and certification. In *Wal-Mart*, the plaintiffs pursued an innovative legal theory: that although Wal-Mart had no policy governing salary and promotions, the company's sexist corporate culture resulted in women receiving lower salaries than similarly situated men. One way to frame the "common question" at issue in the case is to ask whether that theory is viable. Although this was a class certification motion, not a motion to dismiss or a motion for summary judgment, the majority in effect ruled on the validity of this theory. Because the majority did not accept that the plaintiff's theory was viable, it found no common question. Scholars have debated both whether this theory is consistent with Title VII and whether it ought to be. *Compare* Melissa Hart and Paul M. Secunda, *A Matter of Context: Social Framework Evidence in Employment Discrimination Class Actions*, 78 Fordham L. Rev. 37 (2009), *and* Samuel Bagenstos, *Implicit Bias, "Science" and Antidiscrimination Law*, 1 Harv. L. & Pol'y Rev. 477 (2007), *with* John Monahan, Laurens Walker, and Gregory Mitchell, *Contextual Evidence of Gender Discrimination: The Ascendance of "Social Frameworks,"* 94 Va. L. Rev. 1715 (2008).

2. Another issue raised by this case is to what extent a court should consider the merits of the litigation on a certification motion. Some scholars have suggested that Rule 23 should be revised to include the litigants' likelihood of success on the merits, an analysis that parallels the test that courts apply in the preliminary injunction context, as part of class certification. What are the benefits and costs of requiring that class representatives prove that they are likely to prevail on the merits in order to certify a class? *See* Robert Bone, *Sorting Through the Certification Muddle*, 63 Vand. L. Rev. En Banc 105 (2010).

3. As noted earlier, *Wal-Mart v. Dukes* was an extraordinary case, yet the law made here applies to all class actions. Note that the Court unanimously agreed that the plaintiffs' back pay claims could not be certified as part of their injunctive class action. Do you think that class members seeking injunctive relief in an employment discrimination class action should have to meet the more onerous requirements of Rule 23(b)(3) in order to sustain their collective claims for back pay? What effect is this additional burden likely to have on the ability of class members to seek back pay in smaller employment discrimination class actions, if any? What effect will it have on lawyers who bring such class actions? Are plaintiffs like those in *Wal-Mart v. Dukes*, whose back pay claims average around $2,000, likely to bring individual actions? Why or why not? Is fee shifting enough to encourage such lawsuits? Should our society encourage such individual suits?

4. In this case, the plaintiffs were represented both by a prestigious private firm specializing in employment discrimination litigation, Cohen Milstein, and a well-regarded public interest organization, The Impact Fund. Should courts treat cases pursued by public interest organizations differently than those pursued for private gain? Why or why not?

PRACTICE EXERCISE NO. 42: CLASS CERTIFICATION IN *WARNER*

The judge in *Warner* has ordered a Rule 16 scheduling conference. One of the matters that needs to be discussed at the conference is a briefing schedule for the class certification motion. In order to establish an appropriate timetable for discovery and briefing on that motion, the judge has asked you to prepare answers to several of her questions.

1. Is the class definition here adequate?
2. Is this class likely to meet the commonality requirement of Rule 23(a) as it was interpreted in *Wal-Mart v. Dukes*?
3. Are the class representatives likely to satisfy the typicality and representativeness prerequisites of Rule 23(a)?
4. Will it possible to issue one injunction in this case that will be permissible under Rule 23(b)(2)? Or will there need to be individualized injunctions?
5. What discovery will be necessary?

At an earlier conference with the judge, she expressed doubt (based upon a reading of the Complaint) that the case could proceed as a class action. Her views may or may not have evolved since then. Students with last names beginning with the letters A through L represent the plaintiffs; students with last names beginning with the letters M through Z represent the defendants. You will be a lawyer at the conference with the judge. Be prepared to answer the questions the judge has asked.

E. SUBJECT MATTER JURISDICTION IN CLASS ACTION AND OTHER COMPLEX LITIGATION

In the first decade of the twenty-first century, Congress dramatically expanded the federal courts' jurisdiction over class actions and mass tort litigation. The two key statutes were the Class Action Fairness Act (CAFA), governing class actions, and the Multiparty, Multiforum Trial Jurisdiction Act (MMTJ), governing tort cases.

1. Subject Matter Jurisdiction over Class Actions

In 2005, Congress passed CAFA, which among other things amended 28 U.S.C. § 1332 by adding section (d). This section suspends the traditional requirements of complete diversity and the amount in controversy with respect to class actions. Now a class action may be filed in or removed to federal court so long as the total amount in controversy for the entire class is at least $5 million and the case meets a minimal diversity requirement—at least one plaintiff is a citizen of a different state than the defendant. This means that most class actions of any significance can end up in federal court.

In *Standard Fire Insurance v. Knowles,* 133 S. Ct. 1345 (2013), the Court considered whether the plaintiff can stipulate that its damages do not exceed $5 million to avoid federal jurisdiction. In binary litigation, a plaintiff can make such stipulations to avoid federal jurisdiction. The Court held that a plaintiff cannot do so in a class action. This is because the plaintiff's stipulation can bind them, but not the rest of the absent class members (at least, not until a class is certified). Accordingly, a district court cannot accept a class representative's stipulation as to the amount in controversy in determining jurisdiction under CAFA.

Several types of cases are exempt from CAFA. First, the Court has held that CAFA's removal provision does not apply to third-party defendants who are the subject of counterclaims. In *Home Depot U.S.A. v. Jackson*, 139 S. Ct. 1763 (2019), a debt collector, Citibank, filed an individual action against Mr. Jackson in state court seeking to recover the unpaid balance on a Home Depot credit card. Mr. Jackson filed a counterclaim, naming Home Depot in a class action. Home Depot then attempted to remove the case under CAFA. The Supreme Court held that the company could not remove because it was not an "original defendant" under 28 U.S.C. § 1441. In other words, the original complaint did not name Home Depot, and that was the operative complaint for determining removal. The dissent argued that this was merely a tactic that plaintiff was using to avoid federal jurisdiction and that congressional intent was more consistent with permitting removal of such cases.

Second, CAFA also contains exceptions for class actions that are entirely or largely local in character. The "local controversy exception" of CAFA limits the district court's removal jurisdiction in cases where more than two-thirds of the class are citizens of the state in which the action was originally filed, and one defendant is a citizen of the state in which the action was originally filed, the principal injuries allegedly caused by all the defendants occurred in the state in which the action was originally filed, and no other action was filed asserting the same or similar factual allegations. § 1332(d)(4)(A). CAFA also includes a "home state exception" providing that the district court "shall decline to exercise jurisdiction" when "two-thirds or more of the members of all proposed plaintiff classes in the aggregate, and the primary defendants, are citizens of the State in which the action was originally filed." § 1332(d)(4)(B).

A final provision leaves the exercise of subject matter jurisdiction at the discretion of the district court "in the interests of justice and looking at the totality of the circumstances" where "greater than one-third but less than two-thirds of the members of all proposed plaintiff classes in the aggregate and the primary defendants are citizens of the State in which the action was originally filed." In that case, the district court must consider these factors:

(A) whether the claims asserted involve matters of national or interstate interest;

(B) whether the claims asserted will be governed by laws of the State in which the action was originally filed or by the laws of other States;

(C) whether the class action has been pleaded in a manner that seeks to avoid Federal jurisdiction;

(D) whether the action was brought in a forum with a distinct nexus with the class members, the alleged harm, or the defendants;

(E) whether the number of citizens of the State in which the action was originally filed in all proposed plaintiff classes in the aggregate is substantially larger than the number of citizens from any other State, and the citizenship of the other members of the proposed class is dispersed among a substantial number of States; and

(F) whether, during the 3-year period preceding the filing of that class action, 1 or more other class actions asserting the same or similar claims on behalf of the same or other persons have been filed.

§ 1332(d)(3).

Unlike the Federal Rules of Civil Procedure, the Class Action Fairness Act is a statute passed by Congress. The politics of its enactment are summarized as follows:

> Defendants have long complained about the economic pressure that class actions place upon them. Consumer class actions, where individual damages may be minimal, but in the aggregate huge, have been of particular concern. Critics of class actions complained that in such cases consumers received little of value, while class counsel were awarded millions of dollars in fees. Although not specifically responding to these complaints, the federal judiciary, led by the United States Supreme Court in *Amchem Products, Inc. v. Windsor,* tightened up the class certification process, making federal court less attractive to plaintiffs in certain kinds of cases. Additionally, the Court's decisions in the 1986 Trilogy of Summary Judgment cases, together with its decision in *Daubert v. Merrell-Dow Pharmaceuticals* [forbidding the use of "junk science" evidence], have made it tougher for plaintiffs to survive motions for summary judgments in federal courts.

> These federal judicial developments led plaintiffs' lawyers to seek out state courts more amenable to class certification and jury trials. In response, defendants increasingly sought to remove cases from state court to federal court, where they hoped to defeat class certification, and more successfully defend their clients' interests. Plaintiffs learned to defeat the right to removal by naming non-diverse parties as defendants to destroy complete diversity, or by alleging an amount in controversy less than the amount required for federal diversity jurisdiction under 28 U.S.C. § 1332.

Neither side could be happy with these developments. While plaintiffs' attorneys complained of being deprived of their chosen state court forums, corporate defendants complained of being sued in "Judicial Hellholes." Although the problem might have been overstated, some state courts, and certain counties within some states, had become magnets for plaintiffs in certain forms of litigation. CAFA is a significant outgrowth of these dynamics. . . .

The purpose of CAFA, as Senator Arlen Specter, Chair of the Senate Judiciary Committee, put it, is

> . . . to prevent judge shopping to States and even counties where courts and judges have a prejudicial predisposition on cases. Regrettably, the history has been that there are some States in the United States and even some counties where there is forum shopping, which means that lawyers will look to that particular State, that particular county to get an advantage.

Georgene M. Vairo, *Developments in the Law: The Class Action Fairness Act of 2005*, 39 Loy. L.A. L. Rev. 979, 980-982 (2006).

2. Subject Matter Jurisdiction over Mass Torts

CAFA also has a role to play in federal cases involving mass torts. The statute's "mass action" provision permits removal of actions where at least 100 plaintiffs' cases are "proposed to be tried jointly." 28 U.S.C.A. § 1332(d)(11)(B)(i), (d)(11)(B)(ii)(II). The statute exempts cases in which the motion for a joint trial is brought by the defendant.

You have seen this provision in action before in this course. Looking back at the personal jurisdiction case *Bristol-Myers Squibb v. Superior Court of California*, reproduced in Chapter 7, you may notice that this was a mass tort case alleging injuries caused by the drug Plavix in which the plaintiffs—some California citizens, others citizens of other states such as Ohio—filed in groups of under 100. They likely did this to avoid federal jurisdiction under the mass action provision. The plaintiffs in that case also added a non-diverse defendant, apparently for the purpose of avoiding federal subject matter jurisdiction. Ultimately, while their suit structure might have been successful in avoiding federal jurisdiction, it did not survive the Court's personal jurisdiction analysis.

The Multiparty, Multiforum Trial Jurisdiction Act of 2002 (MMTJA), 28 U.S.C. § 1369, while more seldom used, also allows mass tort cases to be removed to federal court. That statute authorizes federal jurisdiction over mass tort cases deriving from a single accident killing at least seventy-five persons. As one judge described the provisions of this statute:

> This new jurisdictional statute, by its terms, expands the original jurisdiction of federal courts to include lawsuits arising from accidents where more than 75 natural persons die at a discrete location, provided that the other requirements of the statute are satisfied. The first part of the statute, § 1369(a), grants the federal district court original jurisdiction over any civil action stemming from such a tragedy with minimal diversity between the parties, provided that one of the

following factors is also present: (1) a defendant resides in a different state from where a substantial part of the accident took place, regardless of whether a substantial portion of the accident also took place in his or her own state; (2) any two defendants reside in different states, regardless of whether these defendants happen to reside in the same state as another defendant; or (3) substantial parts of the accident took place in different states. . . .

Section 1369(b), entitled, "Limitation of jurisdiction of district courts," mandates that a district court judge abstain from hearing any civil action meeting the requirements of § 1369(a) where two conditions are both satisfied: abstention is required when (1) "the substantial majority of plaintiffs are citizens of a single State of which the primary defendants are also citizens" and (2) "the claims asserted will be governed primarily by the laws of that State." 28 U.S.C. § 1369(b). . . .

[A]fter reviewing this legislative history, it is clear that in enacting § 1369, Congress intended to create a mechanism whereby litigation stemming from one major disaster could easily be consolidated in one federal court for discovery and trial. It is also clear that Congress' motivation in passing this legislation was to promote judicial efficiency while avoiding multiple lawsuits concerning the same subject matter strewn throughout the country in various state and federal courts. Thus, § 1369 was intended to address these concerns by creating a new statutory grant of original federal jurisdiction aimed exclusively at large accidents resulting in 75 or more deaths. . . .

Subsection (b) of new § 1369 creates an exception to the minimal diversity rule. In brief, a U.S. district court may not hear any case in which a "substantial majority" of the plaintiffs and the "primary" defendants are all citizens of the same state; and in which the claims asserted are governed primarily by the laws of that same state. In other words, only state courts may hear such cases. . . .

[I]t is clear that Congress was concerned about a small subset of disaster cases finding their way into federal court—cases where the substantial majority of the plaintiffs and the "primary" defendants are all from the same state, and where the claims asserted will be governed primarily by the laws of that same state. By creating § 1369(b), Congress attempted to create a statutory exception, or "safeguard" whereby these local disaster cases could continue to be heard in state court, even though more than 75 people died therein and minimal diversity existed between the parties. Thus, in an effort to achieve this balance, the statute directs the federal court to "abstain from accepting jurisdiction in primarily local actions," in favor of state courts. . . .

Passa v. Derderian, 308 F. Supp. 2d 43 (D.R.I. 2004) (interpreting the MMTJA in a case arising out of a fire at "The Station" nightclub in Rhode Island in which approximately 100 people died and 200 were injured). In addition to expanding federal subject matter authority by requiring only minimal diversity and no requisite amount in controversy, the MMTJA also provides for nationwide service of process and subpoena of witnesses, liberalized venue rules, and open-ended right for claimants to intervene.

The "single accident" at "a discrete location" requirement of the law has prevented frequent application of the MMTJA. For example, the numerous cases arising as a result of the multiple levee breaches caused by Hurricane Katrina were denied federal jurisdiction. *See Case v. ANPAC Louisiana Insurance Co.*, 466 F. Supp. 2d 781 (E.D. La. 2006) (action by homeowners against their insurance companies, removed to federal court by defendants, was remanded to state court).

Most mass tort cases in the federal courts are filed or removed under federal diversity jurisdiction. Often such cases are consolidated in the federal courts under the MDL statute, discussed at the beginning of this chapter. This statute does not give the federal courts subject matter jurisdiction over such suits. Once a case is in the federal system, however, it can be transferred under that law. Because transfer under the MDL statute is for pretrial purposes only, courts have not entertained challenges to personal jurisdiction. As the Judicial Panel on Multidistrict Litigation wrote: "Transfers under Section 1407 are simply not encumbered by considerations of in personam jurisdiction and venue." *In re FMC Corp. Patent Litig.*, 422 F. Supp. 1163, 1165 (J.P.M.L. 1976). The idea is that so long as there is personal jurisdiction in the original court where the action was filed (the transferor court) then the transferee court also has personal jurisdiction.

Some scholars have criticized this approach as an attempt to shoehorn jurisdiction. *See, e.g.,* Andrew D. Bradt, *The Long Arm of Multidistrict Litigation*, 59 Wm. & Mary L. Rev. 1165, 1225 (2018). So far, the courts do not see the weakness of the argument as much of a problem, but if they did, what solutions would you suggest? For example, Congress could pass a statute permitting nationwide personal jurisdiction for cases that fall under the federal subject matter jurisdiction. The courts might also hold that the Fifth Amendment's due process clause permits national jurisdiction, and/or the rulemakers could revise Rule 4(k). What you think is the best solution may turn on who you think the best decision maker is on these topics: the legislature, the courts through judicial opinions, or the courts through the rulemaking process.

F. REVISITING THE JUDICIAL ROLE IN AGGREGATE SETTLEMENTS

The doctrinal question of when and how to certify large-scale class actions is related to deeper questions about the limits of the judicial role. Limitations on the judicial role may be understood as an imposition of Article III and the idea of "separation of powers" or as a more common law requirement of the role of the judge in the adversarial system. Chapter 2 introduced these ideas in the context of *Brown v. Plata*, two class actions challenging the medical and mental health treatment provided prisoners in California's prison system. That litigation ended with a structural injunction that was affirmed by the Supreme Court. Now that you know a little more about class action doctrine, it is a good time to revisit these theoretical questions about the forms and limits of judging.

1. Background on Agent Orange

In the article reproduced below, Prof. Martha Minow discusses the role adopted by Judge Jack Weinstein in the Agent Orange litigation. His approach to that litigation seems to have been a model for many judges in aggregate litigation, and he adopted a very robust judicial role as settlement architect.

The case was brought by Vietnam veterans who believed that a number of illnesses they suffered were caused by exposure to the defoliant Agent Orange while serving in Vietnam. They brought the case as a class action, seeking compensation from the companies that produced the chemical. Judge Weinstein was committed to generating a settlement in the case from the moment it reached his courtroom, even though early settlement discussions had failed. He pressed for settlement by appointing an aggressive special master to push for one, by rejecting requests to bifurcate the trial or to delay it for more time for discovery, by issuing "tentative" rulings on the substantive law that made both sides worried about losing on the merits, and by directing all counsel to appear in chambers on the Saturday morning four days before trial was scheduled to begin for an around-the-clock negotiation session. Ultimately, the amount of settlement ($180 million) came from the judge himself. For a fascinating account of Judge Weinstein's activism and his unconventionally imaginative efforts to force the *Agent Orange* parties to settle, read Peter H. Schuck, *Agent Orange on Trial* (1986).

Years after the settlement of the Agent Orange litigation was administered and closed, potential claimants came forward arguing that they had not been adequately represented in the litigation because the settlement did not make adequate provision for people whose injuries had not yet manifested. They succeeded in reopening their case. *See Stephenson v. Dow Chemical Co.*, 273 F.3d 249 (2d Cir. 2001), *affirming judgment in part, vacating in part*, 539 U.S. 111 (2003). The success of the collateral attack on the *Agent Orange* settlement is one reason that class actions are no longer considered good vehicles for achieving "global peace" in mass torts. Ultimately these plaintiffs' suits failed. Once they were back in Judge Weinstein's courtroom, the plaintiffs lost on summary judgment. *See In re Agent Orange Product Liability Litigation*, 517 F.3d 76 (2008) (holding that government contractor defense barred plaintiffs' claims).

2. Rethinking the Judicial Role and the Adversarial System

Knowing a bit about the judge's approach, as you read the below, consider whether it fits with your idea of the judicial role. You may also wish to reread the Fuller and Chayes excerpts in Chapter 2. Do you think judges trying to resolve mass tort cases overstep the boundaries of the judicial role? When a judge creates an ADR process for resolving a large-scale dispute such as a mass tort, is this the kind of public dispute that Chayes had in mind? Is ADR a panacea in this context or does it create more problems than it solves?

Martha Minow, Judge for the Situation: Judge Jack Weinstein, Creator of Temporary Administrative Agencies
97 Colum. L. Rev. 2010, 2020-2026 (1997)

. . . Functionally, court-supervised settlements that establish systems for processing individual claims create temporary administrative agencies without proceeding through the legislative or executive branches. Even without the establishment of such claims facilities, judicial supervision of complex suits resembles administrative agency activity, especially in the use of masters and magistrates authorized to conduct fact-finding hearings, to manage parts of disputes, and to gather expert knowledge. Such solutions provide redress without destroying private defendants and construct flexible procedures and norms intended—by the judge and by the parties' lawyers—to suit particular circumstances. Sometimes, the court-created process is actually integrated into another prepackaged administrative procedure through the bankruptcy framework. At other times, the administrative dimensions of the court-supervised process are illustrated by the reactions of other players; other branches of government, government institutions such as schools, and private actors often send lobbyists to influence the court process, just as administrative agencies have inspired the development of vital advocacy organizations such as the AIDS Action Committee and the Natural Resources Defense Council. Judging for the situation, then, involves contextualized efforts to construct procedures tailored for a particular circumstance; judging for the situation involves generating temporary administrative structures responsive to the claims at hand. . . . Creation of claims processing facilities, use of public hearings, and consultation with community members and experts amount to the establishment of uniquely temporary and contextually specific administrative processes. These devices are framed around the parties to a litigation. The court, and the adjunct actors employed by the court, perform the work of processing claims under simplified procedures and management, seeking to fulfill party expectations swiftly. Exemplifying the range of administrative agencies in this country, some of the court-sponsored processes may be technically competent and efficient while others may be immersed in partisan debates. Typically, the claims-processing activity set up under court approval accomplishes the same shift from fault-based norms to compensation for harms that administrative agencies have adopted in contexts such as black lung disease and workers' compensation for injuries on the job. Yet, while it is fair to point to the similarities between these judicially created claims procedures and legislatively created administrative agencies, the differences between the two are also striking. Two important differences divide court-created administration systems from established administrative agencies: (1) the fact of court creation rather than legislative or executive authorization, and (2) their temporary, collapsible structure as compared to the more enduring, and at times entrenched, bureaucratic nature of traditional administrative agencies. The first invites intense scrutiny and potentially fatal objection on Article III and separation-of-powers grounds; the second may offer an intriguing challenge to other forms of administration. Both are, in my view, valuable contributions to American law and politics.

1. *Separation of Powers.* If a federal court, rather than the legislative or executive branches, creates an administrative agency, it is fair to inquire into the potential breach of separation-of-powers requirements and bounded authority for the judiciary. Has the court strayed into the domain of the executive to enforce the law or taken over the task of the legislature to devise prospective rules and establish government agencies? Have appointed judges stepped into the fray reserved for elected officials? Are the judges making political judgments that require accommodation, bargaining, and the accountability of the electoral sanction for democratic legitimacy and efficacy? Answers to these questions are bound to reflect the political preferences of the observer as much as considered theories of democratic governmental structures. Yet, seeing the inevitable infusion of politics into the question restates the problem. A judge who engages in the process of creating administrative responses to social problems is also inevitably immersed in political views, but lacks the tethering or camouflage of the traditional adjudicatory procedure. Judge Weinstein himself has not been shy in detailing his own support for compensatory, rather than fault-based, approaches to mass torts, and a cost-sharing approach toward defendants' liability. Similarly, Judge Weinstein has tried to reframe debates over the alleged litigation crisis and difficulties of access to the courts by labeling the issues as the challenge of responding to "the mass of cases working their way through the system." This is the language and conception of administration; it also reflects a choice in favor of redistribution and spreading the costs of injuries across broad communities, rather than other potential responses to harms in the world. For those who think these kinds of questions require the tangling and wrangling of legislative debate, such court actions amount to unchecked fiat, beyond the scope of legal authority and in violation of democratic principles.

Three modest defenses can be offered on behalf of Judge Weinstein and other judges who use judicial resources to respond to such social problems despite inaction by the elected branches: the vacuum created by their inaction leaves judges with properly filed, concrete claims, requiring some sort of response. Kenneth R. Feinberg, sometimes a special master in mass tort cases and always an expert in them, has concluded that no sweeping congressional reform is forthcoming on either the procedural or substantive sides of the field, "[s]o in effect the courts must do what they can with the tools at their disposal." These cases warrant utilization of untraditional means, like special masters, community input, and aggressive case management, because they encompass unanticipated problems with wide-ranging social and political ramifications. As Judge Weinstein insightfully notes, "[a] rigid and unresponsive judiciary, blind to the needs of various communities and of society at large, is far more likely to cause an erosion of public confidence in legal institutions than a judiciary perceived as overly interested in resolving the problems before it." Judicial action actually may trigger action by the other branches, and thereby promote the vision of overlapping and checking branches of government that lies behind the separation of powers. Judge Weinstein's *Agent Orange* settlement had this effect; Congress responded with a bill to aid veterans affected by exposure to dioxin, and the Veterans' Administration eventually interpreted its mandate to include responding to the needs of these veterans. Unlocking the logjam in the electoral branches may be a role uniquely assigned to the courts, and thus a basis for justifying judicial action that otherwise seems to interfere with legislative and executive prerogatives. Energetic judging thus may stimulate action by other branches that have been frozen and unresponsive.

Second, judicial action may be defended here as continuous, rather than discontinuous, with other forms of adjudication. There is not an obvious or steady line distinguishing the judicial role involved in selecting strict liability as the standard in a particular tort case from the judicial role involved in supervision of a settlement achieving a similar result. Of course, this line of defense may simply expose even more judicial action to critique as invasive of the ambit of legislative or executive authority. Moreover, if the costs of the administrative process include assessments to the government, and not just to private parties, obtaining public revenues and justifying their use calls for resort to the elected branches. Yet, all judicial action requires appropriations and expenditures of public funds, ranging from the salaries of judges and clerks to outlays for paper and computer disks. Enforcement of the simplest damages award requires the use of personnel to process forms and, at times, to execute liens on property. There is no sharp line separating the tasks of adjudication and the tasks of implementing the law. A separation-of-powers objection starts a debate about appropriate judicial behavior; it does not clinch the debate, nor provide an absolute bar to a temporary administrative apparatus. Third, exposure and defense of the boundaries between the branches are necessary for reasoned debate: The initiative of someone like Judge Weinstein can generate public debate and analysis to sharpen understandings of separation of powers, a crucial element of our governmental structure. Jack Weinstein's approach to judging renders immediate what otherwise can remain a remote debate about the proper relationship between law and justice. Weinstein's approach reminds lawyers, judges, and theorists that legal rules—ranging from the most technical procedures to the basic constitutional structure—were devised by human beings as means for governing with justice. In Judge Weinstein's court, it is no defense to argue "that's never been done before"; legitimacy and legality are to be measured as much by results as by concordance with precedent. Accordingly, if governing with justice requires bending the rules and altering precedents, then the rules and the precedents need to be bent and altered. Of course, this is only one of many vigorously competing views about the proper relation between justice and law. As a result, Judge Weinstein's landmark cases afford rich, real examples to test the typically abstract debates over this and other competing views of law. In this way, his decisions benefit even those who find his approach to law to be an appalling disregard of its constraints.

2. *Temporary Administration.*   An administrative agency established by the legislature or the executive may have an endpoint or sunset provision terminating its existence, but this is not the common practice. Instead, such administrative agencies, once established, tend to endure and require massive efforts to trim them, much less to close them down. The administrative processes established by courts, in contrast, have very specific time limitations, even if they endure for several years. A claims facility lasts only as long as the fund exists and claims remain to be processed; judicial supervision through masters and magistrates may extend longer than some would like, but it does come to an end when assigned tasks are fulfilled, when the parties complete their assigned duties or successfully move to modify their obligations, or when the judge involved concludes that no more can be done. These are not perfectly calibrated measures for termination, but they do yield endpoints to judicially sponsored administrative action. . . . Inventing flexible, responsive administrative practices may be the only alternative to big, blunt bureaucracies on the one hand, and private market mechanisms on the other.

REVIEW QUESTIONS

1. What is the argument that judicial involvement in structuring settlements in aggregate litigation violates separation of powers principles?

2. What are the three responses that Minow offers to these separation of powers concerns?

3. Many people think that mass tort class actions in which judges actively oversee settlements like the Agent Orange settlement could not be certified today because personal injury claims are too individualized. Can you put this argument into the language of the class action rule? (For example, do you think individual issues in personal injury cases predominate over common ones? What issues, and why? This requires you to think a bit about the requirements for proving a torts case, which include among other things causation and damages.)

MORE TO PONDER

If a class action cannot be certified, a case like Agent Orange will be consolidated in an MDL and likely a claims administration facility will be created to resolve the claims. Do you think that the issues that Prof. Minow raises are the same in that context as in a class action? Is there a meaningful difference between class members being bound by the settlement as a formal matter, and individual litigants feeling pressured to enter into a collective settlement in an MDL? The class action rule has a specific provision requiring judges to review settlement fairness to assuage concerns that there will be inequity among class members or that lawyers will take advantage of the class. *See* Fed. R. Civ. P. 23(e). Is such a rule required to give judges to power to review settlements? If not, what is the source of their power to review settlements? Finally, if judges do not take on this role, who will? The American Law Institute's Principles of the Law of Aggregate Litigation § 3.18 (2010) proposed that individuals who are subject to aggregate settlements be permitted to appeal to the judge for a fairness review. No rule has been promulgated to authorize such a procedure, however. The next practice exercise invites you to grapple with these problems in context.

PRACTICE EXERCISE NO. 43: THE JUDICIAL ROLE IN AGGREGATE LITIGATION

In the *In Re World Trade Center Disaster Site* litigation, approximately 9,900 plaintiffs were suing various defendants and the City of New York, which was covered by a federally-funded insurance policy, for damages arising out of their work in the immediate aftermath of the terror attack of September 11, 2001. All of the cases were consolidated before Judge Alvin K. Hellerstein of the Southern District of New York. The lead law firm and the defendants reached a settlement and presented it to the court. The judge found the settlement wanting. In particular, he thought that attorney's fees were too high (they were 33.33% for each individual, per their individual retainer contracts), that the settlement fund was too low, and that there was not enough information as to what each plaintiff would receive in the end. He announced his intention to (1) disapprove of the settlement; and (2) hold a fairness hearing about the settlement. The parties then filed a motion to appeal to the Second Circuit. Half of the class will be appointed to argue the motion for the parties who have filed the appeal, and the other half will be appointed to argue as *amici* on behalf of the judge in this highly irregular proceeding.

WANT TO KNOW MORE?

In the 9/11 First Responders case, the parties withdrew their appeal after presenting the judge with a revised settlement that assuaged his concerns. For an article arguing that judges do not have the power to hold a fairness hearing absent a rule, *see* Howard M. Erichson, *The Role of the Judge in Non-Class Settlements,* 90 Wash. U. L. Rev. 1015 (2013). For an article arguing that judges do have this power, *see* David M. Jaros & Adam S. Zimmerman, *Judging Aggregate Settlement,* 94 Wash. U. L. Rev. 545 (2017). And for the Judge's own perspective on this lawsuit *see* Alvin K. Hellerstein et al., *Managerial Judging: The 9/11 Responders' Tort Litigation,* 98 Cornell L. Rev. 127 (2012).

G. PRECLUSION IN CLASS ACTIONS

You have now reached the point where you should be able to grapple with a case that integrates almost all of the rules introduced in this chapter. Moreover, the case will force you to reconsider many of the underlying purposes of a procedural system, due process, and discrimination law. After you read *Martin v. Wilks*, study the applicable section of the Civil Rights Act of 1991 (which is printed after the case) and prepare for the final practice exercise.

Martin v. Wilks
490 U.S. 755 (1989)

Chief Justice REHNQUIST delivered the opinion of the Court:

A group of white firefighters sued the city of Birmingham, Alabama (City), and the Jefferson County Personnel Board (Board) alleging that they were being denied promotions in favor of less qualified black firefighters.* They claimed that the City and the Board were making promotion decisions on the basis of race in reliance on certain consent decrees, and that these decisions constituted impermissible racial discrimination in violation of the Constitution and federal statute. The District Court held that the white firefighters were precluded from challenging employment decisions taken pursuant to the decrees, even though these firefighters had not been parties to the proceedings in which the decrees were entered. We think this holding contravenes the general rule that a person cannot be deprived of his legal rights in a proceeding to which he is not a party.

The litigation in which the consent decrees were entered began in 1974, when the Ensley Branch of the National Association for the Advancement of Colored People and seven black individuals filed separate class-action complaints against the City and the Board. They alleged that both had engaged in racially discriminatory hiring and promotion practices in various public service jobs in violation of Title VII of the Civil Rights Act of 1964, 42 U.S.C. § 2000e *et seq.*, and other federal law. After a bench trial on some issues, but before judgment, the parties entered into two consent decrees, one between the black individuals and the City and the other between them and the Board. These proposed decrees set forth an extensive remedial scheme, including long-term and interim annual goals for the hiring of blacks as firefighters. The decrees also provided for goals for promotion of blacks within the fire department.

The District Court entered an order provisionally approving the decrees and directing publication of notice of the upcoming fairness hearings. Notice of the hearings, with a reference to the general nature of the decrees, was published in two local newspapers. At that hearing, the Birmingham Firefighters Association (BFA) appeared and filed objections as *amicus curiae*. After the hearing, but

---

* *Eds.' Note:* For more information about the history of race relations in Birmingham, see Chapter 2.

before final approval of the decrees, the BFA and two of its members also moved to intervene on the ground that the decrees would adversely affect their rights. The District Court denied the motions as untimely and approved the decrees. *United States v. Jefferson County*, 28 F.E.P. Cases 1834 (N.D. Ala. 1981). Seven white firefighters, all members of the BFA, then filed a complaint against the City and the Board seeking injunctive relief against enforcement of the decrees. The seven argued that the decrees would operate to illegally discriminate against them; the District Court denied relief.

Both the denial of intervention and the denial of injunctive relief were affirmed on appeal. *United States v. Jefferson County*, 720 F.2d 1511 (11th Cir. 1983). The District Court had not abused its discretion in refusing to let the BFA intervene, thought the Eleventh Circuit, in part because the firefighters could "institut[e] an independent Title VII suit, asserting specific violations of their rights." *Id.*, at 1518. And, for the same reason, petitioners had not adequately shown the potential for irreparable harm from the operation of the decrees necessary to obtain injunctive relief. *Id.*, at 1520.

A new group of white firefighters, the Wilks respondents, then brought suit against the City and the Board in District Court. They too alleged that, because of their race, they were being denied promotions in favor of less qualified blacks in violation of federal law. The Board and the City admitted to making race conscious employment decisions, but argued that the decisions were unassailable because they were made pursuant to the consent decrees. A group of black individuals, the Martin petitioners, were allowed to intervene in their individual capacities to defend the decrees.

The defendants moved to dismiss the reverse discrimination cases as impermissible collateral attacks on the consent decrees. The District Court denied the motions, ruling that the decrees would provide a defense to claims of discrimination for employment decisions "mandated" by the decrees, leaving the principal issue for trial whether the challenged promotions were indeed required by the decrees. After trial the District Court granted the motion to dismiss. The court concluded that "if in fact the City was required to [make promotions of blacks] by the consent decree, then they would not be guilty of [illegal] racial discrimination" and that the defendants had "establish[ed] that the promotions of the black individuals . . . were in fact required by the terms of the consent decree."

On appeal, the Eleventh Circuit reversed. It held that, "[b]ecause . . . [the Wilks respondents] were neither parties nor privies to the consent decrees, . . . their independent claims of unlawful discrimination are not precluded." . . .

We granted certiorari, and now affirm the Eleventh Circuit's judgment. All agree that "[i]t is a principle of general application in Anglo-American jurisprudence that one is not bound by a judgment in personam in a litigation in which he is not designated as a party or to which he has not been made a party by service of process." *Hansberry v. Lee*, 311 U.S. 32, 40 (1940). *See, e.g., Parklane Hosiery Co. v. Shore*, 439 U.S. 322, 327, n.7. This rule is part of our "deep-rooted historic tradition that everyone should have his own day in court." 18

C. Wright, A. Miller, & E. Cooper, *Federal Practice and Procedure* § 4449, p. 417 (1981) (18 Wright). A judgment or decree among parties to a lawsuit resolves issues as among them, but it does not conclude the rights of strangers to those proceedings.[2]

Petitioners argue that, because respondents failed to timely intervene in the initial proceedings, their current challenge to actions taken under the consent decree constitutes an impermissible "collateral attack." They argue that respondents were aware that the underlying suit might affect them, and if they chose to pass up an opportunity to intervene, they should not be permitted to later litigate the issues in a new action. The position has sufficient appeal to have commanded the approval of the great majority of the Federal Courts of Appeals, but we agree with the contrary view expressed by the Court of Appeals for the Eleventh Circuit in this case.

We begin with the words of Justice Brandeis in *Chase National Bank v. Norwalk*, 291 U.S. 431 (1934): "The law does not impose upon any person absolutely entitled to a hearing the burden of voluntary intervention in a suit to which he is a stranger. . . . Unless duly summoned to appear in a legal proceeding, a person not a privy may rest assured that a judgment recovered therein will not affect his legal rights." *Id.*, at 441. While these words were written before the adoption of the Federal Rules of Civil Procedure, we think the Rules incorporate the same principle; a party seeking a judgment binding on another cannot obligate that person to intervene; he must be joined. Against the background of permissive intervention set forth in *Chase Nat'l Bank*, the drafters cast Rule 24, governing intervention, in permissive terms. *See* Fed. R. Civ. P. 24(a) (intervention as of right) ("Upon timely application anyone shall be permitted to intervene"); Fed. R. Civ. P. 24(b) (permissive intervention) ("Upon timely application anyone may be permitted to intervene"). They determined that the concern for finality and completeness of judgments would be "better [served] by mandatory joinder procedures." 18 Wright § 4452, p. 453. Accordingly, Rule 19(a) provides for mandatory joinder in circumstances where a judgment rendered in the absence of a person may "leave . . . persons already parties subject to a substantial risk of incurring . . . inconsistent obligations. . . ." Rule 19(b) sets forth the factors to be considered by a court in deciding whether to allow an action to proceed in the absence of an interested party.

Joinder as a party, rather than knowledge of a lawsuit and an opportunity to intervene, is the method by which potential parties are subjected to the jurisdiction of the court and bound by a judgment or decree. The parties to a lawsuit presumably know better than anyone else the nature and scope of relief sought in the action, and at whose expense such relief might be granted. It makes sense,

---

2. We have recognized an exception to the general rule when, in certain limited circumstances, a person, although not a party, has his interests adequately represented by someone with the same interests who is a party. Additionally, where a special remedial scheme exists expressly foreclosing successive litigation by nonlitigants, as for example in bankruptcy or probate, legal proceedings may terminate preexisting rights if the scheme is otherwise consistent with due process. Neither of these exceptions, however, applies in this case.

therefore, to place on them a burden of bringing in additional parties where such a step is indicated, rather than placing on potential additional parties a duty to intervene when they acquire knowledge of the lawsuit. The linchpin of the "impermissible collateral attack" doctrine—the attribution of preclusive effect to a failure to intervene—is therefore quite inconsistent with Rule 19 and Rule 24 . . . preclusive effect might be attributed to a failure to intervene. 390 U.S., at 114-15.

Petitioners contend that a different result should be reached because the need to join affected parties will be burdensome and ultimately discouraging to civil rights litigation. Potential adverse claimants may be numerous and difficult to identify; if they are not joined, the possibility for inconsistent judgments exists. Judicial resources will be needlessly consumed in relitigation of the same question.

Even if we were wholly persuaded by these arguments as a matter of policy, acceptance of them would require a rewriting rather than an interpretation of the relevant Rules. But we are not persuaded that their acceptance would lead to a more satisfactory method of handling cases like this one. It must be remembered that the alternatives are a duty to intervene based on knowledge, on the one hand, and some form of joinder, as the Rules presently provide, on the other. No one can seriously contend that an employer might successfully defend against a Title VII claim by one group of employees on the ground that its actions were required by an earlier decree entered in a suit brought against it by another, if the later group did not have adequate notice or knowledge of the earlier suit.

The difficulties petitioners foresee in identifying those who could be adversely affected by a decree granting broad remedial relief are undoubtedly present, but they arise from the nature of the relief sought and not because of any choice between mandatory intervention and joinder. Rule 19's provisions for joining interested parties are designed to accommodate the sort of complexities that may arise from a decree affecting numerous people in various ways. We doubt that a mandatory intervention rule would be any less awkward. As mentioned, plaintiffs who seek the aid of the courts to alter existing employment policies, or the employer who might be subject to conflicting decrees, are best able to bear the burden of designating those who would be adversely affected if plaintiffs prevail; these parties will generally have a better understanding of the scope of likely relief than employees who are not named but might be affected. Petitioners' alternative does not eliminate the need for, or difficulty of, identifying persons who, because of their interests, should be included in a lawsuit. It merely shifts that responsibility to less able shoulders.

Nor do we think that the system of joinder called for by the Rules is likely to produce more relitigation of issues than the converse rule. The breadth of a lawsuit and concomitant relief may be at least partially shaped in advance through Rule 19 to avoid needless clashes with future litigation. And even under a regime of mandatory intervention, parties who did not have adequate knowledge of the suit would relitigate issues. Additional questions about the adequacy and timeliness of knowledge would inevitably crop up. We think that the system of joinder presently contemplated by the rules best serves the many interests involved in the run of litigated cases, including cases like the present one.

Petitioners also urge that the congressional policy favoring voluntary settlement of employment discrimination claims, referred to in cases such as *Carson v. American Brands, Inc.*, 450 U.S. 79 (1981), also supports the "impermissible collateral attack" doctrine. But once again it is essential to note just what is meant by "voluntary settlement." A voluntary settlement in the form of a consent decree between one group of employees and their employer cannot possibly "settle," voluntarily or otherwise, the conflicting claims of another group of employees who do not join in the agreement. This is true even if the second group of employees is a party to the litigation: "[P]arties who choose to resolve litigation through settlement may not dispose of the claims of a third party . . . without that party's agreement. A court's approval of a consent decree between some of the parties therefore cannot dispose of the valid claims of nonconsenting intervenors." *Firefighters v. Cleveland*, 478 U.S. 501, 529 (1986).

Insofar as the argument is bottomed on the idea that it may be easier to settle claims among a disparate group of affected persons if they are all before the court, joinder bids fair to accomplish that result as well as a regime of mandatory intervention.

For the foregoing reasons we affirm the decision of the Court of Appeals for the Eleventh Circuit. That court remanded the case for trial of the reverse discrimination claims. *In re Birmingham Reverse Discrimination*, 833 F.2d, at 1500-02. Petitioners point to language in the District Court's findings of fact and conclusions of law which suggests that respondents will not prevail on the merits. We agree with the view of the Court of Appeals, however, that the proceedings in the District Court may have been affected by the mistaken view that respondents' claims on the merits were barred to the extent they were inconsistent with the consent decree.

Affirmed.

Justice STEVENS with whom Justice BRENNAN, Justice MARSHALL, and Justice BLACKMUN join, dissenting:

As a matter of law there is a vast difference between persons who are actual parties to litigation and persons who merely have the kind of interest that may as a practical matter be impaired by the outcome of a case. Persons in the first category have a right to participate in a trial and to appeal from an adverse judgment; depending on whether they win or lose, their legal rights may be enhanced or impaired. Persons in the latter category have a right to intervene in the action in a timely fashion, or they may be joined as parties against their will. But if they remain on the sidelines, they may be harmed as a practical matter even though their legal rights are unaffected. One of the disadvantages of sideline-sitting is that the bystander has no right to appeal from a judgment no matter how harmful it may be.

In these cases the Court quite rightly concludes that the white firefighters who brought the second series of Title VII cases could not be deprived of their legal rights in the first series of cases because they had neither intervened nor been joined as parties. *See Firefighters v. Cleveland*, 478 U.S. 501, 529-530 (1986); *Parklane Hosiery Co. v. Shore*, 439 U.S. 322, 327, n.7 (1979). The consent decrees obviously could not deprive them of any contractual rights, such as seniority, *cf. W. R. Grace & Co. v. Rubber Workers*, 461 U.S. 757 (1983), or accrued vacation pay, *cf. Massachusetts v. Morash*, 490 U.S. 107 (1989), or of any other legal rights, such as the right to have their employer comply with federal statutes like Title VII, *cf. Firefighters v. Cleveland, supra*, 478 U.S., at 529. There is no reason, however, why the consent decrees might not produce changes in conditions at the white firefighters' place of employment that, as a practical matter, may have a serious effect on their opportunities for employment or promotion even though they are not bound by the decrees in any legal sense. The fact that one of the effects of a decree is to curtail the job opportunities of nonparties does not mean that the nonparties have been deprived of legal rights or that they have standing to appeal from that decree without becoming parties.

Persons who have no right to appeal from a final judgment—either because the time to appeal has elapsed or because they never became parties to the case—may nevertheless collaterally attack a judgment on certain narrow grounds. If the court had no jurisdiction over the subject matter, or if the judgment is the product of corruption, duress, fraud, collusion, or mistake, under limited circumstances it may be set aside in an appropriate collateral proceeding. *See Restatement (Second) of Judgments* §§ 69-72 (1982). This rule not only applies to parties to the original action, but also allows interested third parties collaterally to attack judgments. In both civil and criminal cases, however, the grounds that may be invoked to support a collateral attack are much more limited than those that may be asserted as error on direct appeal. Thus, a person who can foresee that a lawsuit is likely to have a practical impact on his interests may pay a heavy price if he elects to sit on the sidelines instead of intervening and taking the risk that his legal rights will be impaired.

In these cases there is no dispute about the fact that respondents are not parties to the consent decrees. It follows as a matter of course that they are not bound by those decrees. Those judgments could not, and did not, deprive them of any legal rights. The judgments did, however, have a practical impact on respondents' opportunities for advancement in their profession. For that reason, respondents had standing to challenge the validity of the decrees, but the grounds that they may advance in support of a collateral challenge are much more limited than would be allowed if they were parties prosecuting a direct appeal.

The District Court's rulings in this case have been described incorrectly by both the Court of Appeals and this Court. The Court of Appeals repeatedly stated that the District Court had "in effect" held that the white firefighters were "bound" by a decree to which they were not parties. And this Court's opinion seems to assume that the District Court had interpreted its consent decrees in the earlier litigation as holding "that the white firefighters were precluded from challenging employment decisions taken pursuant to the decrees." It is important, therefore, to make clear exactly what the District Court did hold and why its judgment should be affirmed.

I

The litigation in which the consent decrees were entered was a genuine adversary proceeding. In 1974 and 1975, two groups of private parties and the United States brought three separate Title VII actions against the city of Birmingham (City), the Personnel Board of Jefferson County (Board), and various officials, alleging discrimination in hiring and promotion in several areas of employment, including the fire department. After a full trial in 1976, the District Court found that the defendants had violated Title VII and that a test used to screen job applicants was biased. After a second trial in 1979 that focused on promotion practices—but before the District Court had rendered a decision—the parties negotiated two consent decrees, one with the City defendants and the other with the Board. The United States is a party to both decrees. The District Court provisionally approved the proposed decrees and directed that the parties provide notice "to all interested persons informing them of the general provisions of the Consent Decrees . . . and of their right to file objections." App. 695. Approximately two months later, the District Court conducted a fairness hearing, at which a group of black employees objected to the decrees as inadequate and a group of white firefighters—represented in part by the Birmingham Firefighters Association (BFA)—opposed any race-conscious relief. *Id.*, at 727. The District Court overruled both sets of objections and entered the decrees in August 1981.

In its decision approving the consent decrees, the District Court first noted "that there is no contention or suggestion that the settlements are fraudulent or collusive." *Id.*, at 238a. The court then explained why it was satisfied that the affirmative-action goals and quotas set forth in the decrees were "well within the limits upheld as permissible" in *Steelworkers v. Weber*, 443 U.S. 193 (1979), and other cases. It pointed out that the decrees "do not preclude the hiring or promotion of whites and males even for a temporary period of time," and that the City's commitment to promote blacks and whites to the position of fire lieutenant at the same rate was temporary and was subject both to the availability of qualified candidates and "to the caveat that the decree is not to be interpreted as requiring the hiring or promotion of a person who is not qualified or of a person who is demonstrably less qualified according to a job-related selection procedure." It further found that the record provided "more than ample reason" to conclude that the City would eventually be held liable for discrimination against blacks at high-level positions in the fire and police departments. Based on its understanding of the wrong committed, the court concluded that the remedy embodied in the consent decrees was "reasonably commensurate with the nature and extent of the indicated discrimination." The District Court then rejected other specific objections, pointing out that the decrees would not impinge on any contractual rights of the unions or their members. Finally, after noting that it had fully considered the white firefighters' objections to the settlement, it denied their motion to intervene as untimely.

Several months after the entry of the consent decrees, the Board certified to the City that five black firefighters, as well as eight whites, were qualified to full six vacancies in the position of lieutenant. A group of white firefighters then filed suit against the City and Board challenging their policy of "certifying candidates and making promotions on the basis of race under the assumed protection of consent settlements." The complaint alleged, in the alternative, that the consent decrees were illegal and void, or that the defendants were not properly implementing them. The plaintiffs filed motions for a temporary restraining order and a preliminary injunction. After an evidentiary hearing, the District Court found that the plaintiffs' collateral attack on the consent decrees was "without merit" and that four of the black officers were qualified for promotion in accordance with the terms of the decrees. Accordingly, it denied the motions, and, for the first time in its history, the City had a black lieutenant in its fire department.

The plaintiffs' appeal from that order was consolidated with the appeal that had been previously taken from the order denying the motion to intervene filed in the earlier litigation. The Court of Appeals affirmed both orders. *See United States v. Jefferson C.*, 720 F.2d 1511 (11th Cir. 1983). While that appeal was pending, in September 1983, the Wilks respondents filed a separate action against petitioners. The Wilks complaint alleged that petitioners were violating Title VII, but it did not contain any challenge to the validity of the consent decrees. After various preliminary proceedings, the District Court consolidated these cases, along with four other reverse discrimination actions brought against petitioners, under the caption *In re: Birmingham Reverse Discrimination Litigation*. In addition, over the course of the litigation, the court allowed further parties to intervene.

On February 18, 1985, the District Court ruled on the City's motion for partial summary judgment and issued an opinion that, among other things, explained its understanding of the relevance of the consent decrees to the issues raised in the reverse discrimination litigation. After summarizing the proceedings that led up to the entry of the consent decrees, the District Court expressly "recognized that the consent decrees might not bar all claims of 'reverse discrimination' since [the plaintiffs] had not been parties to the prior suits." The court then took a position with respect to the relevance of the consent decrees that differed from that advocated by any of the parties. The plaintiffs contended that the consent decrees, even if valid, did not constitute a defense to their action, and, in the alternative, that the decrees did not authorize the promotion of black applicants ahead of higher scoring white applicants and thus did not justify race-conscious promotions. The City, on the other hand, contended that the promotions were immunized from challenge if they were either required or permitted by the terms of the decrees. The District Court took the intermediate position that promotions required by—and made because of—the decrees were justified. However, it denied the City's summary judgment motion because it raised factual issues requiring a trial.

In December 1985, the court conducted a 5-day trial limited to issues concerning promotions in the City's fire and engineering departments. At that trial, respondents challenged the validity of the consent decrees; to meet that challenge, petitioners introduced the records of the 1976 trial, the 1979 trial, and the fairness hearing conducted in 1981. Respondents also tried to prove that they were demonstrably better qualified than the black firefighters who had been promoted ahead of them. At the conclusion of the trial, the District Court entered a partial final judgment dismissing portions of the plaintiffs' complaints. The judge explained his ruling in an oral opinion dictated from the bench, supplemented by the adoption, with some changes, of detailed findings and conclusions drafted by the prevailing parties.

In his oral statement, the judge adhered to the legal position he had expressed in his February ruling. He stated: "The conclusions there expressed either explicitly or implicitly were that under appropriate circumstances, a valid consent decree appropriately limited can be the basis for a defense against a charge of discrimination, even in the situation in which it is clear that the defendant to the litigation did act in a racially conscious manner. In that February order, it was my view as expressed then, that if the City of Birmingham made promotions of blacks to positions as fire lieutenant, fire captain and civil engineer, because the City believed it was required to do so by the consent decree, and if in fact the City was required to do so by the Consent Decree, then they would not be guilty of racial discrimination, either under Title 7, Section 1981, 1983 or the 14th Amendment. That remains my conclusion given the state of the law as I understand it." He then found as a matter of fact that petitioners had not promoted any black officers who were not qualified or who were demonstrably less qualified than the whites who were not promoted. He thus rejected respondents' contention that the City could not claim that it simply acted as required by terms of the consent decree.

> In this case, under the evidence as presented here, I find that even if the burden of proof be placed on the defendants, they have carried that proof and that burden of establishing that the promotions of the black individuals in this case were in fact required by the terms of the consent decree.

The written conclusions of law that he adopted are less clear than his oral opinion. He began by unequivocally stating: "The City Decree is lawful." He explained that "under all the relevant case law of the Eleventh Circuit and the Supreme Court, it is a proper remedial device, designed to overcome the effects of prior, illegal discrimination by the City of Birmingham." In that same conclusion, however, he did state that "plaintiffs cannot collaterally attack the Decree's validity." Yet, when read in context—and particularly in light of the court's finding that the decree was lawful under Eleventh Circuit and Supreme Court precedent—it is readily apparent that, at the extreme, this was intended as an alternative holding. More likely, it was an overstatement of the rule that collateral review is narrower in scope than appellate review. In any event, and regardless of one's reading of this lone sentence, it is absolutely clear that the court did not hold that respondents were bound by the decree. Nowhere in the District Court's lengthy findings of fact and conclusions of law is there a single word suggesting that respondents were bound by the consent decree or that the court intended to treat them as though they had been actual parties to that litigation and not merely as persons whose interests, as a practical matter, had been affected. Indeed, respondents, the Court of Appeals, and the majority opinion all fail to draw attention to any point in this case's long history at which the judge may have given the impression that any nonparty was legally bound by the consent decree.

II

Regardless of whether the white firefighters were parties to the decrees granting relief to their black co-workers, it would be quite wrong to assume that they could never collaterally attack such a decree. If a litigant has standing, he or she can always collaterally attack a judgment for certain narrowly defined defects. On the other hand, a district court is not required to retry a case—or to sit in review of another court's judgment—every time an interested nonparty asserts that some error that might have been raised on direct appeal was committed. Such a broad allowance of collateral review would destroy the integrity of litigated judgments, would lead to an abundance of vexatious litigation, and would subvert the interest in comity between courts. Here, respondents have offered no circumstance that might justify reopening the District Court's settled judgment.

The implementation of a consent decree affecting the interests of a multitude of nonparties, and the reliance on that decree as a defense to a charge of discrimination in hiring and promotion decisions, raise a legitimate concern of collusion. No such allegation, however, has been raised. Moreover, there is compelling evidence that the decrees were not collusive. In its decision approving the consent decrees over the objection of the BFA and individual white firefighters, the District Court observed that there had been "no contention or suggestion" that the decrees were fraudulent or collusive. The record of the fairness hearing was made part of the record of this litigation, and this finding was not contradicted. More significantly, the consent decrees were not negotiated until after the 1976 trial and the court's finding that the City had discriminated against black candidates for jobs as police officers and firefighters, and until after the 1979 trial, at which substantial evidence was presented suggesting that the City also discriminated against black candidates for promotion in the fire department. Like the record of the 1981 fairness hearing, the records of both of these prior proceedings were made part of the record in this case. Given this history, the lack of any indication of collusion, and the District Court's finding that "there is more than ample reason for . . . the City of Birmingham to be concerned that [it] would be in time held liable for discrimination against blacks at higher level positions in the police and fire departments," it is evident that the decree was a product of genuine arm's-length negotiations.

Nor can it be maintained that the consent judgment is subject to reopening and further litigation because the relief it afforded was so out of line with settled legal doctrine that it "was transparently invalid or had only a frivolous pretense to validity." *Walker v. Birmingham*, 388 U.S. 307, 315 (1967) (suggesting that a contemner might be allowed to challenge contempt citation on ground that underlying court order was "transparently invalid"). To the contrary, the type of race-conscious relief ordered in the consent decrees is entirely consistent with this Court's approach to affirmative action. Given a sufficient predicate of racial discrimination, neither the Equal Protection Clause of the Fourteenth Amendment nor Title VII of the Civil Rights Act of 1964 erects a bar to affirmative action plans that benefit non-victims and have some adverse effect on nonwrongdoers. As Justice O'Connor observed in *Wygant v. Jackson Bd. Of Educ.*, 476 U.S. 267 (1986): "This remedial purpose need not be accompanied by contemporaneous findings of actual discrimination to be accepted as legitimate as long as the public actor has a firm basis for believing that remedial action is required." *Id.*, at 286 (opinion concurring in part and concurring in judgment). Such a belief was clearly justified in these cases. After conducting the 1976 trial and finding against the City and after listening to the five days of testimony in the 1979 trial, the judge was well qualified to conclude that there was a sound basis for believing that the City would likely have been found to have violated Title VII if the action had proceeded to a litigated judgment.

Hence, there is no basis for collaterally attacking the judgment as collusive, fraudulent, or transparently invalid. Moreover, respondents do not claim—nor has there been any showing of—mistake, duress, or lack of jurisdiction. Instead, respondents are left to argue that somewhat different relief would have been more appropriate than the relief that was actually granted. Although this sort of issue may provide the basis for a direct appeal, it cannot, and should not, serve to open the door to relitigation of a settled judgment.

III

The facts that respondents are not bound by the decree and that they have no basis for a collateral attack, moreover, do not compel the conclusion that the District Court should have treated the decree as nonexistent for purposes of respondents' discrimination suit. That the decree may not directly interfere with any of respondents' legal rights does not mean that it may not affect the factual setting in a way that negates respondents' claim. The fact that a criminal suspect is not a party to the issuance of a search warrant does not imply that the presence of a facially valid warrant may not be taken as evidence that the police acted in good faith. Similarly, the fact that an employer is acting under court compulsion may be evidence that the employer is acting in good faith and without discriminatory intent. Indeed, the threat of a contempt citation provides as good a reason to act as most, if not all, other business justifications.

After reviewing the evidence, the District Court found that the City had in fact acted under compulsion of the consent decree. Based on this finding, the court concluded that the City carried its burden of coming forward with a legitimate business reason for its promotion policy, and, accordingly, held that the promotion decisions were "not taken with the requisite discriminatory intent" necessary to make out a claim of disparate treatment under Title VII or the Equal Protection Clause. For this reason, and not because it thought that respondents were legally bound by the consent decree, the court entered an order in favor of the City and defendant-intervenors.

Of course, in some contexts a plaintiff might be able to demonstrate that reference to a consent decree is pretextual. For example, a plaintiff might be able to show that the consent decree was collusive and that the defendants simply obtained the court's rubber stamp on a private agreement that was in no way related to the eradication of pervasive racial discrimination. The plaintiff, alternatively, might be able to show that the defendants were not bound to obey the consent decree because the court that entered it was without jurisdiction. Similarly, although more tenuous, a plaintiff might argue that the parties to the consent judgment were not bound because the order was "transparently invalid" and thus unenforceable. If the defendants were as a result not bound to implement the affirmative-action program, then the plaintiff might be able to show that the racial preference was not a product of the court order.

In a case such as this, however, in which there has been no showing that the decree was collusive, fraudulent, transparently invalid, or entered without jurisdiction, it would be "unconscionable" to conclude that obedience to an order remedying a Title VII violation could subject a defendant to additional liability. Rather, all of the reasons that support the Court's view that a police officer should not generally be held liable when he carries out the commands in a facially valid warrant apply with added force to city officials, or indeed to private employers, who obey the commands contained in a decree entered by a federal court. In fact, Equal Employment Opportunity Commission regulations concur in this assessment. They assert: "The Commission interprets Title VII to mean that actions taken pursuant to the direction of a Court Order cannot give rise to liability under Title VII." 29 C.F.R. § 1608.8 (1989). Assuming that the District Court's findings of fact were not clearly erroneous—which of course is a matter that is not before us—it seems perfectly clear that its judgment should have been affirmed. Any other conclusion would subject large employers who seek to comply with the law by remedying past discrimination to a never-ending stream of litigation and potential liability. It is unfathomable that either Title VII or the Equal Protection Clause demands such a counterproductive result.

IV

The predecessor to this litigation was brought to change a pattern of hiring and promotion practices that had discriminated against black citizens in Birmingham for decades. The white respondents in this case are not responsible for that history of discrimination, but they are nevertheless beneficiaries of the discriminatory practices that the litigation was designed to correct. Any remedy that seeks to create employment conditions that would have obtained if there had been no violations of law will necessarily have an adverse impact on whites, who must now share their job and promotion opportunities with blacks. Just as white employees in the past were innocent beneficiaries of illegal discriminatory practices, so is it inevitable that some of the same white employees will be innocent victims who must share some of the burdens resulting from the redress of the past wrongs.

There is nothing unusual about the fact that litigation between adverse parties may, as a practical matter, seriously impair the interests of third persons who elect to sit on the sidelines. Indeed, in complex litigation this Court has squarely held that a sideline-sitter may be bound as firmly as an actual party if he had adequate notice and a fair opportunity to intervene and if the judicial interest in finality is sufficiently strong.

There is no need, however, to go that far in order to agree with the District Court's eminently sensible view that compliance with the terms of a valid decree remedying violations of Title VII cannot itself violate that statute or the Equal Protection Clause. The city of Birmingham, in entering into and complying with this decree, has made a substantial step toward the eradication of the long history of pervasive racial discrimination that has plagued its fire department. The District Court, after conducting a trial and carefully considering respondents' arguments, concluded that this effort is lawful and should go forward. Because respondents have thus already had their day in court and have failed to carry their burden, I would vacate the judgment of the Court of Appeals and remand for further proceedings consistent with this opinion.

Civil Rights Act of 1991

Pub. L. No. 102-166, §402(a), 105 Stat. 1071, 1099, reprinted at
42 U.S.C. §2000e-2(n)(1) (Supp. V, 1993)

§108. [A]n employment practice that implements and is within the scope of a litigated or consent judgment or order that resolves a claim of employment discrimination under the Constitution or Federal civil rights laws may not be challenged . . . in a claim under the Constitution or Federal civil rights laws:

   (i) by a person who, prior to the entry of the judgment or order . . . had—

      (1) actual notice of the proposed judgment or order sufficient to apprise such person that such judgment or order might adversely affect the interests and legal rights of such person and that an opportunity was available to present objections to such judgment or order by a future date certain; and

(2) a reasonable opportunity to present objections to such judgment or order;

or

(ii) by a person whose interests were adequately represented by another person who had previously challenged the judgment or order on the same legal grounds and with a similar factual situation, unless there has been an intervening change in law or fact.

REVIEW QUESTIONS

1. It is noteworthy that *Martin v. Wilks* arose out of a dispute in Birmingham, Alabama. You will recall from Chapter 2 that Birmingham is the location from which Rev. Martin Luther King, Jr., penned his famous *Letter from Birmingham City Jail*. Reverend King referred to Birmingham as America's most segregated city, and it was among the cities that witnessed some of the most violent struggles of the civil rights movement.

2. As you reach the end of this course, revisit the question that we first addressed in Chapter 1: Is giving individuals their "day in court" an important procedural value? Does requiring parties who are aware of litigation that could potentially affect their interests to intervene adequately respect, protect, or advance that value? What other, competing values ought courts to consider?

PRACTICE EXERCISE NO. 44:
THE SUPREME COURT ADDRESSES THE CONSTITUTIONALITY OF PRECLUSION UNDER THE CIVIL RIGHTS ACT

Assume that the year is 2023 and that there are a number of new Justices on the Supreme Court of the United States. Moreover, the provisions of the Civil Rights Act of 1991 dealing with *Martin v. Wilks*, which are printed immediately after that case, are still in effect. Assume further that a lawsuit against the City of Cleveland, Ohio was filed by female firefighters alleging discrimination in hiring and promotions. That suit was commenced in January 2018 in federal court and resulted, after a full trial before a judge without a jury, in a verdict and judgment for the plaintiffs under Title VII and an injunction ordering the City of Cleveland to use a non-gender-biased written and physical examination in the future, which results in qualified women being hired for the Cleveland fire department, and granting them as of the hiring date (if they have previously taken the discriminatory tests, and now passed the new tests) seniority, pay, and the positions that they would have had if they had previously passed the test and been hired at that time. The judgment entered and decree ordered as a result of that suit were appealed to the Court of Appeals and affirmed. This decree has adversely affected some current male members of the fire department, who have, in effect, placed lower on the seniority scale and who have been prejudiced already, they argue, by a reduced opportunity to become officers in the department. Fifteen women have already been hired since the new nondiscriminatory tests have been administered, and three of these are already captains. Moreover, the women who were now hired at larger salaries left a diminished salary pool from which current male members could receive raises.

The current male members of the Cleveland Fire Department, claiming that they were prejudiced by the initial suit, brought a class action against the women on the Department and the City of Cleveland to void the judgment and the injunction on the grounds that they were indispensable parties to the initial suit brought in behalf of the women. The named white male class representatives admitted in depositions that within six months of the commencement of the 2018 suit they had read about it in the newspapers, but they also said that they did not realize the impact that "victory for the women" would have on them. They allege that the district court in the 2018 class action knew about them and their concerns at least by January 2020, three months before the trial commenced in that case, which is when they moved to intervene for the first time; their motion to intervene was denied, and that decision was affirmed by the appeals court, after hearing their argument. They further argued that they cannot be bound and harmed by a suit to which they were not a party. The district court granted summary judgment to the women on the force and to the City of Cleveland, on the grounds that the initial verdict and judgment were valid, the male firefighters were not necessary and indispensable parties, the *Martin v. Wilks* amendment found in the Civil Rights Act is dispositive, and that the trial judge in the initial suit acted within his appropriate discretion in denying the late attempt to intervene. The court of appeals affirmed on all points. The Supreme Court has granted certiorari.

The plaintiffs in the current class action suit, the male firefighters, argue that *Martin v. Wilks* governs, that the initial decree is invalid on Rule 19 and due process grounds, that they had a right to intervene and the denial to grant their motion was improper, and that the *Martin v. Wilks* amendment found in the Civil Rights Act of 1991 is unconstitutional on due process grounds for it purports to bind them without formal notice, service, and the right to be heard. The women firefighters and the City of Cleveland argue that this suit is in a procedurally incorrect posture, that *Martin v. Wilks* doesn't apply to their initial case or to this one because it is distinguishable, that the current court should decide the *Martin v. Wilks* issue differently for it was wrongly decided in 1989 (regardless of the Civil Rights Act of 1991), that the Civil Rights Act of 1991 does apply and is constitutional, and that the plaintiffs in the current suit lost any rights they might otherwise have had because of their tardy attempt to intervene in the first suit (the district court judge did not abuse her discretion in denying the motion to intervene and that preclusion law prevents their now appealing a motion denied in the prior lawsuit).

The women firefighters and the City of Cleveland have hired the same lawyer. Students with last names beginning with the letters A through M will argue for the appellees; all others will argue for the male appellants. Each student should be prepared to give a complete oral argument before the Supreme Court, unless you chose the option that follows. You will be picked at random. Appellants' counsel will be called upon first.

Option: You may wish to prepare your arguments as a team (of three or fewer). Make sure you team with students representing the same party (or parties). If any member of your team is selected, all should come forward to argue; divide the allotted time as you see fit.

CASE FILES

Carpenter v. Dee

Contents

Initial Memorandum	1142
Mass. Gen. Laws ch. 229 § 2 (Wrongful Death)	1144
Mass. Gen. Laws ch. 229 § 6 (Conscious Suffering)	1145
Mass. Gen. Laws ch. 109A §§ 1-10 (Fraudulent Conveyance)	1145
Complaint	1147
Dee's Motion to Dismiss	1152
Dee's Motion for a More Definite Statement	1154
Answer of Randall Dee (Counts I and II Only) and Jury Claim	1155
Motion to Amend and Amended Complaint	1158
U.C.C. § 2-314. Implied Warranty: Merchantability; Usage of Trade	1166
U.C.C. § 2-315. Implied Warranty: Fitness for Particular Purpose	1166
Mass. Gen. Laws ch. 90 § 7P. Height of Motor Vehicles; Alteration Restricted	1167
Mass. Gen. Laws ch. 231 § 85. Comparative Negligence; Limited Effect of Contributory Negligence as Defense	1167
Mass. Gen. Laws ch. 231B §§ 1-4. Contribution Among Joint Tortfeasors	1168
Walter VanBuskirk, "Lifting" a Truck	1170
Photographs	1173
Ultimate Auto's Motion to File a Third-Party Complaint	1175
Answer, Cross-Claims, and Jury Demand of Ultimate Auto	1178
Plaintiff's Request for Production of Documents	1182
Ultimate Auto's Response to Documents Request	1185
Ultimate Auto's Answers to Interrogatories	1187
Transcript: Deposition of Randall Dee	1190
Memorandum in Support of Third-Party Defendants' Motion for Summary Judgment	1212
Stipulation of Ultimate Auto, McGill, and McGill's Garage	1216
540 Mass. Regs. Code: Registry of Motor Vehicles	1218
Restatement (Second) of Contracts	1226
Restatement (Second) of Torts	1227
Letter from Economics Specialists of Boston, Inc.	1230

Initial Memorandum

To: Associates
From: Carol Coblentz (senior partner)
Re: Nancy Carpenter—potential client of Needham, Shaker & Coblentz

At 7:00 P.M. on August 31, 2019, 25-year-old Charlie Carpenter was riding as a passenger with his friend Randall Dee in Dee's Jeep CJ-7. They were on their way to pick up their swimming trunks so they could return to a friend's barbecue and pool party. On the corner of Palmer and Franklin Streets in Lowell, MA, Dee lost control of the jeep and it rolled over. Dee suffered only minor injuries, but Charlie Carpenter was pinned under the vehicle and killed.

Charlie Carpenter was survived by his wife Nancy who was pregnant and later delivered a premature but healthy son on January 10, 2020. She named the boy Charlie Jr. At the time of the accident Mr. Carpenter was employed as a custodian at Forsythe University, where he received benefits, which applied to his wife and would have covered his child as well. Charlie Sr. was killed just prior to qualifying for University-funded life insurance benefits. Prior to his custodian job, Charlie worked as an auto mechanic for a variety of local auto body shops.

Months prior to the incident Randall Dee had modified the jeep with a suspension lift kit and oversize tires. These modifications affected the jeep's handling characteristics and were a significant factor in the rollover of the jeep. Dee had been stopped by Lowell police on several occasions prior to the accident for various suspected motor vehicle offenses. However, we believe that the police never advised him that the jeep was illegally modified and that the authorities took no other action to prevent the jeep from being driven in its dangerously modified condition.

On July 28, 2020, Randall Dee was convicted in criminal court on four counts in relation to the incident on August 31, 2015: (1) negligent homicide; (2) failing to slow at an intersection; (3) speeding; and (4) altering the height of a motor vehicle. He received a one-year suspended sentence for the homicide count and was required to serve two years' probation and 200 hours of community service. Fines for the other charges amounted to $500.

The jeep that Dee was driving was owned by his ex-girlfriend, Twyla Burrell. Ms. Burrell maintained a minimum liability insurance policy on the jeep in the amount of $25,000. Ms. Burrell had lived with Dee for more than a year, and when she moved out, she left the jeep with Dee, ostensibly because he had done so much work on it.

We'll need to investigate further to discover the extent of the modifications made to the jeep, but Ms. Carpenter knows that they included a suspension lift and hugely oversized tires. I'm not entirely clear about the next bit, but Ms. Carpenter insists that the body of the jeep was lifted even further off the frame by using hockey pucks that were bolted to the frame at various points around the vehicle. A Massachusetts statute prohibits raising the height of a vehicle more than two inches off of the frame, and Ms. Carpenter says she's certain that the jeep was lifted at least a foot. Although she believes that the rollover was caused by the modifications—and from what I hear in the news about hiked-up vehicles, this sounds plausible—none of these modifications broke or were damaged as a part of the accident.

We know that Dee had been stopped by uniformed Lowell police officers previously and that on one prior occasion he was found guilty of the offense of driving while intoxicated (for which his license was suspended for thirty days). Further, we know that at some time prior to that conviction (but still subsequent to the modifications of the jeep) Dee was stopped by a uniformed Lowell police officer for driving without a side view mirror and instructed not to drive the jeep until he got a mirror. Dee was stopped on at least one other occasion by Lowell police for driving an unregistered, uninsured vehicle—at which time it was taken from him and towed away; Dee later proved that there was insurance on the jeep and was fined only for driving it unregistered.

From what we can tell, Randall Dee is not a wealthy man. He is unmarried and lives in his family home with his brother, Peter. Ms. Carpenter believes they bought the house from the estate of their deceased father. Ms. Carpenter says that she thought the brothers both owned the house, but a mutual friend told her recently that Peter says he owns the house alone. To date, we don't know where Randall Dee bought the parts he used to modify the jeep, nor do we know if he received any warnings from anyone about creating a dangerous propensity to tip over by raising the jeep off the frame. We also don't know if he knew the jeep was too high under the Mass. Code, nor do we know yet where he had his car inspected for its annual inspection sticker required under Massachusetts law.

Please be prepared to discuss with me who the parties might be in a lawsuit, and what the causes of action might be. Should we take the case?

Note—I advised Ms. Carpenter that if we take the case we would pursue it on a contingent fee basis.

[*Eds.' Note:* The names of the parties have been changed to protect their privacy. The dates of certain events (including the enactment and effective dates of certain Massachusetts regulations) have been modified for pedagogical reasons. With other minor exceptions, the pleadings, motions, and discovery in the Case Files are identical to those filed in the actual case.]

Mass. Gen. Laws Ch. 229 § 2 (Wrongful Death)

A person who[*]

(1) by his negligence causes the death of a person, or

(2) by willful, wanton or reckless act causes the death of a person under such circumstances that the deceased could have recovered damages for personal injuries if his death had not resulted, or

(3) operates a common carrier of passengers and by his negligence causes the death of a passenger, or

(4) operates a common carrier of passengers and by his willful, wanton or reckless act causes the death of a passenger under such circumstances that the deceased could have recovered damages for personal injuries if his death had not resulted, or

(5) is responsible for a breach of warranty arising under Article 2 of chapter one hundred and six which results in injury to a person that causes death, shall be liable in damages in the amount of:

(1) the fair monetary value of the decedent to the persons entitled to receive the damages recovered, as provided in section one, including but not limited to compensation for the loss of the reasonably expected net income, services, protection, care, assistance, society, companionship, comfort, guidance, counsel, and advice of the decedent to the persons entitled to the damages recovered;

(2) the reasonable funeral and burial expenses of the decedent;

(3) punitive damages in an amount of not less than five thousand dollars in such case as the decedent's death was caused by the malicious, willful, wanton or reckless conduct of the defendant or by the gross negligence of the defendant;

except that:

(1) the liability of an employer to a person in his employment shall not be governed by this section,

(2) a person operating a railroad shall not be liable for negligence in causing the death of a person while walking or being upon such railroad contrary to law or to the reasonable rules and regulations of the carrier and

(3) a person operating a street railway or electric railroad shall not be liable for negligence for causing the death of a person while walking or being upon that part of the street railway or electric railroad not within the limits of a highway.

A person shall be liable for the negligence or the willful, wanton or reckless act of his agents or servants while engaged in his business to the same extent and subject to the same limits as he would be liable under this section for his own act. Damages under this section shall be recovered in an action of tort by the executor or administrator of the deceased. An action to recover damages under this section shall be commenced within three years from the date of death or within such

---

[*] *Eds.' Note:* At common law, the death of the victim abated the victim's claim for personal injuries. Beginning in the mid-1800s, "wrongful death statutes" were enacted by states to prevent tortfeasors from escaping liability in circumstances where the victim happened to die.

time thereafter as is provided by section four, four B, nine or ten or chapter two hundred and sixty.

[The survivorship provisions of Mass. Gen. Laws ch. 229 § 1 are as follows:

(1) If the deceased shall have been survived by a wife or husband and no children or issue surviving, then to the use of such surviving spouse.

(2) If the deceased shall have been survived by a wife or husband and by one child or by the issue of one deceased child, then one half to the use of such surviving spouse and one half to the use of such child or his issue by right of representation.

(3) If the deceased shall have been survived by a wife or husband and by more than one child surviving either in person or by issue, then one third to the use of such surviving spouse and two thirds to the use of such surviving children or their issue by right of representation.

(4) If there is no surviving wife or husband, then to the use of the next of kin.]

Mass. Gen. Laws Ch. 229 § 6 (Conscious Suffering)

In any civil action brought under [the Wrongful Death section reprinted above], damages may be recovered for conscious suffering resulting from the same injury, but any sum so recovered shall be held and disposed of by the executors or administrators as assets of the estate of the deceased.

Mass. Gen. Laws Ch. 109A §§ 1-10 (Fraudulent Conveyance)

§ 1 Definitions.* In this chapter "Assets" of a debtor means property not exempt from liability for his debts. To the extent that any property is liable for any debts of the debtor, such property shall be included in his assets.

"Conveyance" includes every payment of money, assignment, release, transfer, lease, mortgage or pledge of tangible or intangible property, and also the creation of any lien or encumbrance.

"Creditor" is a person having any claim, whether matured or unmatured, liquidated or unliquidated, absolute, fixed or contingent.

"Debt" includes any legal liability, whether matured or unmatured, liquidated or unliquidated, absolute, fixed or contingent.

§ 2 Insolvency of persons. A person is insolvent within the meaning of this chapter when the present fair salable value of his assets is less than the amount that will be required to pay his probable liability on his existing debts as they become absolute and matured. . . .

---

*Eds.' Note: This was the law at the time the actual lawsuit was brought. Massachusetts has since adopted the Uniform Fraudulent Transfer Act, which has similar provisions. See Mass. Gen. Laws ch. 109A.

§ 3 Fair consideration. Fair consideration is given for property or obligation—

(a) When in exchange for such property or obligation, as a fair equivalent therefor, and in good faith, property is conveyed or an antecedent debt is satisfied, or

(b) When such property or obligation is received in good faith to secure a present advance or antecedent debt in amount not disproportionately small as compared with the value of the property or obligation obtained. . . .

§ 4 Conveyances by insolvent. Every conveyance made and every obligation incurred by a person who is or will be thereby rendered insolvent is fraudulent as to creditors without regard to his actual intent if the conveyance is made or the obligation is incurred without a fair consideration. . . .

§ 6 Conveyances by person about to incur debts beyond ability to pay. Every conveyance made and every obligation incurred without fair consideration when the person making the conveyance or entering into the obligation intends or believes that he will incur debts beyond his ability to pay as they mature is fraudulent as to both present and future creditors.

§ 7 Conveyances made with intent to defraud. Every conveyance made and every obligation incurred with actual intent, as distinguished from intent presumed in law, to hinder, delay or defraud either present or future creditors, is fraudulent as to both present and future creditors. . . .

§ 9 Rights of creditors; matured claims.

(1) Where a conveyance or obligation is fraudulent as to a creditor, such creditor, when his claim has matured, may, as against any person except a purchaser for fair consideration without knowledge of the fraud at the time of the purchase, or one who has derived title immediately or immediately from such a purchaser—

(a) Have the conveyance set aside or obligation annulled to the extent necessary to satisfy his claim, or

(b) Disregard the conveyance and attach or levy execution upon the property conveyed.

(2) A purchaser who without actual fraudulent intent has given less than a fair consideration for the conveyance or obligation may retain the property or obligation as security for repayment.

§10 Rights of creditors; immature claims. Where a conveyance made or obligation incurred is fraudulent as to a creditor whose claim has not matured, he may proceed in the supreme judicial or superior court against any person against whom he could have proceeded had his claim matured, and the court may—

(a) Restrain the defendant from disposing of his property,

(b) Appoint a receiver to take charge of the property,

(c) Set aside the conveyance or annul the obligation, or

(d) Make any order which the circumstances of the case may require.

COMMONWEALTH OF MASSACHUSETTS

MIDDLESEX, SS

SUPERIOR COURT DEPARTMENT OF
THE TRIAL COURT
CIVIL ACTION NO. 20-6144

NANCY CARPENTER, As
Administratrix of the Estate of
Charles Carpenter,
   Plaintiff

   vs.

RANDALL DEE and PETER DEE,
   Defendants.

COMPLAINT

PLAINTIFF CLAIMS
TRIAL BY JURY

PARTIES

1. The plaintiff Nancy Carpenter is a resident of Lowell, Middlesex County, Massachusetts. She brings this action in her capacity as the administratrix of the estate of Charles Carpenter, her late husband, of Lowell, Middlesex County, Massachusetts. She was duly appointed as administratrix by the Middlesex Probate Court, docket number 19P3875A.

2. The defendant Randall Dee is a resident of Lowell, Middlesex County, Massachusetts.

3. The defendant Peter Dee is a resident of Lowell, Middlesex County, Massachusetts.

FACTS

4. On or about August 31, 2019, the plaintiff's intestate, Charles Carpenter, was riding as a passenger in a 1986 Jeep CJ-7 (hereinafter "the jeep").

5. The jeep was owned by one Twyla Burrell, and operated by the defendant Randall Dee.

6. At or near the intersection of Palmer and Franklin Streets in Lowell, the operator lost control of the jeep, and it rolled over, pinning Charles Carpenter beneath it.

7. The loss of control and resulting accident was caused by the negligent and/or grossly negligent and/or wanton and willful, and reckless conduct of the defendant Randall Dee as operator of the jeep including, but not limited to, the following acts and omissions:

a. excessive speed;
b. failing to stop at an intersection; and
c. illegal and dangerous alteration of the chassis, causing unsafe handling characteristics.

COUNT I—WRONGFUL DEATH

8. The plaintiff repeats and incorporates herein the allegations of paragraphs 1 through 7.

9. As a result of the negligent and/or grossly negligent and/or wanton, willful, and reckless conduct of the defendant Randall Dee, the plaintiff's intestate was killed on August 31, 2019.

COUNT II—CONSCIOUS SUFFERING

10. The plaintiff repeats and incorporates herein the allegations of paragraphs 1 through 7.

11. As a result of the conduct of the defendant Randall Dee, as described above, the plaintiff's intestate sustained serious personal injuries, from which he suffered consciously, prior to his death on August 31, 2019.

COUNT III—FRAUDULENT CONVEYANCE

12. The plaintiff repeats and incorporates herein the allegations of paragraphs 1 through 7.

13. At the time of the accident on August 31, 2019, the defendant Randall Dee and the defendant Peter Dee owned as joint tenants a certain parcel of land at 91 Birch Hill Road, Lowell, Massachusetts, containing approximately 11,604 square feet.

14. The defendants Randall Dee and Peter Dee had purchased said property from the estate of their deceased father Rick Dee, for the amount of $140,000 on or about February 13, 2019.

15. On or about October 8, 2019, the defendant Randall Dee conveyed all his right, title and interest in the above property to Peter Dee for "nominal consideration."

16. On information and belief, the transfer of such interest was fraudulent as to creditors, including, but not limited to, the plaintiff, within the meaning of Mass. Gen. Laws ch. 109A, in that:

(a) The conveyance was made without fair consideration, and Randall Dee was thereby rendered insolvent, within the meaning of Mass. Gen. Laws ch. 109A, § 4; and/or

(b) The conveyance was made without fair consideration at a time when the defendant Randall Dee believed that he would incur debts beyond his ability to pay, within the meaning of Mass. Gen. Laws ch. 109A, § 6; and/or

(c) The transfer was made with an actual intent to hinder, delay, or defraud creditors, including but not limited to the plaintiff, within the meaning of Mass. Gen. Laws ch. 109A, § 7.

WHEREFORE, the plaintiff prays for the following relief:

1. Judgment on Count I against the defendant Randall Dee

(a) To compensate the survivors of the plaintiff's intestate for the fair monetary value of the deceased for reasonably expected net income lost, services, protection, care, assistance, society, companionship, comfort, guidance, counsel, and advice of the deceased;

(b) Reasonable funeral and burial expenses;

(c) Punitive damages in an amount of at least $5,000.00, pursuant to Mass. Gen. Laws ch. 229, § 2.

2. Judgment on Count II against the defendant Randall Dee to compensate the estate of Charles Carpenter for his pain and conscious suffering.

3. That the Court issue a temporary restraining order enjoining the defendant, Randall Dee, until further order of this court, from conveying, encumbering, or in any other manner transferring any interest, legal or equitable, in any of his assets, including but not limited to real estate, bank accounts, certificates of deposit, securities, valuables, and any other asset not immune from execution, except in the ordinary course of business.

4. That the Court issue a preliminary injunction enjoining the defendant Randall Dee, until the disposition of this action on the merits, from conveying, encumbering, or in any other manner transferring any interest, legal or equitable, in any of his assets, including but not limited to real estate, bank accounts, certificates of deposit, securities, valuables, and any other asset not immune from execution, except in the ordinary course of business.

5. That the Court issue a temporary restraining order enjoining the defendant Peter Dee, until further order of this court, from conveying, encumbering, or in any other manner transferring any interest, legal or equitable, in the real estate at 91 Birch Hill Road, Lowell, MA.

6. That the Court issue a preliminary injunction, enjoining the defendant Peter Dee, until the disposition of this action on the merits, from conveying, encumbering, or in any other manner transferring any interest, legal or equitable, in the real estate at 91 Birch Hill Road, Lowell, MA.

7. That the Court, under Count III, declare null and void the conveyance of the interest of Randall Dee in the property at 91 Birch Hill Road, Lowell, and/or allow satisfaction of any judgment in this action against Randall Dee to be satisfied against the interest he held in said property prior to the fraudulent conveyance.

8. That the Court issue a temporary restraining order enjoining the defendants, until further order of the Court, from selling, or transferring in any way the jeep vehicle involved or in any way modifying it, or changing its present condition.

9. That the Court issue a preliminary injunction enjoining the defendants, until the disposition of this action on the merits, from selling, or transferring in any way the jeep vehicle involved or in any way modifying it, or changing its present condition.

By her attorneys,

By: _____ /s/ Carol Coblentz _____
Carol Coblentz (BBO#304321)
Needham, Shaker and Coblentz
44 Park Place
Boston, MA 02100
(617) 555-5555

Dated: /d/

[*Eds.' Note:* Notice that at the beginning of this complaint, there is a civil action number, No. 20-6144. Practices vary among jurisdictions, but here the "20" represents the year this case was filed, 2020. The remainder of the number is a unique identification number issued by the clerk of the court upon filing of the complaint. This "docket number" will then appear on all subsequent court filings. Docket numbers may also include a letter or a set of initials that indicate to what judge or court session the case is assigned.

You will also notice another number in the signature block of the filing attorney. Upon admission to the bar in Massachusetts, new lawyers are issued a unique identification number by the Board of Bar Overseers (BBO). Here, attorney Carol Coblentz has a "BBO Number" of 304321. Various state (federal) rules may require lawyers to identify themselves with an identification number on documents filed with that court.]

COMMONWEALTH OF MASSACHUSETTS

MIDDLESEX, SS

SUPERIOR COURT DEPARTMENT
OF THE TRIAL COURT
CIVIL ACTION NO. 20-6144

NANCY CARPENTER, As
Administratrix of the Estate of
Charles Carpenter,
   Plaintiff

     vs.

RANDALL DEE and
PETER DEE,
   Defendants.

MOTION TO DISMISS

The defendant Randall Dee moves to dismiss Counts I, II, and III (Wrongful Death, Conscious Suffering, and Fraudulent Conveyance) of the Complaint against said defendant pursuant to Mass. R. Civ. P. 12(b)(6) for failure to state claims upon which relief can be granted.

In support thereof Randall Dee says that the Complaint alleges three causes of action against said defendant. It is further alleged that on August 31, 2019, the Plaintiff's intestate was injured and killed while a passenger in a Jeep CJ-7 that rolled over because said jeep was being driven at an excessive speed while failing to stop at an intersection and with illegal and dangerous alteration of the chassis. The specific allegations against the defendants include the following:

(a) On Count I, the defendant's conduct was negligent and/or grossly negligent and/or wanton, willful, and reckless;

(b) On Count II, the defendant's conduct resulted in serious personal injuries to the plaintiff's intestate which resulted in conscious suffering; and

(c) On Count III, the defendant fraudulently conveyed a certain parcel of land that was purchased for the amount of $140,000; and that defendant Randall Dee conveyed all his right, title, and interest in said property to Peter Dee for nominal consideration and that transfer of such interest was fraudulent.

All three counts should be dismissed for the two reasons hereunder set forth:

(1) Randall Dee was not the owner of said Jeep CJ-7.

(2) The complaint does not allege that Randall Dee owed a duty to Charles Carpenter.

Count III should also be dismissed for failure to plead the circumstances with particularity.

RANDALL DEE, by his attorney,

By: _____ /s/ Robert Orthwein _____
Robert Orthwein (BBO#627841)
Chaudhuri, Brown, Orthwein & Guinto
11 Boardwalk
Boston, MA 02100
(617) 555-1111

Dated: /d/

COMMONWEALTH OF MASSACHUSETTS

MIDDLESEX, SS

SUPERIOR COURT DEPARTMENT OF
THE TRIAL COURT
CIVIL ACTION NO. 20-6144

NANCY CARPENTER, As
Administratrix of the Estate of
Charles Carpenter,
  Plaintiff

    vs.

RANDALL DEE and PETER DEE,
  Defendants.

MOTION FOR MORE DEFINITE
STATEMENT

The defendant Randall Dee moves the Court to issue an order for a more definite statement pursuant to Mass. R. Civ. P. 12(e).

The complaint is so vague and ambiguous that defendant should not reasonably be required to prepare a responsive pleading. Plaintiff should be ordered to furnish a more definite statement of the nature of her claim as set forth in her complaint in the following respects:

1. With respect to the allegations contained in Paragraph 7, page 1 of the complaint, plaintiff should be required to state the facts supporting her conclusion that on August 31, 2019, Randall Dee lost control of the 1986 Jeep CJ-7 because of his negligent and/or grossly negligent and/or wanton and willful, conduct by stating the circumstances surrounding the accident: weather conditions, speed of vehicle, proximity to other vehicles, condition and experience of defendant-driver.

2. With respect to the prayer for relief, plaintiff has failed to provide the amount which she is claiming for loss of the value of the decedent's net income, services, protection, care, assistance, society, companionship, comfort, guidance, counsel, and advice of the deceased.

RANDALL DEE, by his attorney,

By: _____ /s/ Robert Orthwein _____
Robert Orthwein (BBO#627841)
Chaudhuri, Brown, Orthwein & Guinto
11 Boardwalk
Boston, MA 02100
(617) 555-1111

Dated: /d/

COMMONWEALTH OF MASSACHUSETTS

MIDDLESEX, SS

NANCY CARPENTER, As
Administratrix of the Estate of
Charles Carpenter,
    Plaintiff

    vs.

RANDALL DEE and PETER DEE,
    Defendants.

SUPERIOR COURT DEPARTMENT OF
THE TRIAL COURT
CIVIL ACTION NO. 20-6144

ANSWER OF RANDALL DEE
(AS TO COUNTS I AND II ONLY)

DEFENDANT RANDALL DEE
CLAIMS JURY TRIAL

PARTIES

1. The Defendant, Randall Dee, admits the allegations contained in Paragraph One of Plaintiff's Complaint.

2. The Defendant, Randall Dee, admits the allegations contained in Paragraph Two of Plaintiff's Complaint.

3. The Defendant, Randall Dee, admits the allegations contained in Paragraph Three of Plaintiff's Complaint.

FACTS

4. The Defendant, Randall Dee, admits the allegations contained in Paragraph Four of Plaintiff's Complaint.

5. The Defendant, Randall Dee, admits the allegations contained in Paragraph Five of Plaintiff's Complaint.

6. The Defendant, Randall Dee, denies each and every allegation contained in Paragraph Six of Plaintiff's Complaint.

7. The Defendant, Randall Dee, denies each and every allegation contained in Paragraph Seven of Plaintiff's Complaint.

COUNT I—WRONGFUL DEATH

8. The Defendant, Randall Dee, repeats and realleges his answers contained in Paragraphs One through Seven, as if fully stated herein.

9. The Defendant, Randall Dee, denies each and every allegation contained in Paragraph Nine of Plaintiff's Complaint.

COUNT II—CONSCIOUS SUFFERING

10. The Defendant, Randall Dee, repeats and realleges his answers contained in Paragraphs One through Seven, as if fully stated herein.

11. The Defendant, Randall Dee, denies each and every allegation contained in Paragraph Eleven of Plaintiff's Complaint.

FIRST DEFENSE

And further answering, the Defendant says that the Plaintiff's intestate's own negligence caused or contributed to the accident and damages alleged, and therefore the Plaintiff cannot recover.

SECOND DEFENSE

And further answering, the Defendant says that the Plaintiff's intestate was more than 50 percent negligent in causing or contributing to the accident and damages alleged, and therefore the Plaintiff either cannot recover or any verdict or finding in his favor must be reduced by the percentage of negligence attributed to the said Plaintiff's intestate.

THIRD DEFENSE

And further answering, the Defendant says that the Plaintiff's intestate assumed the risk of the accident and damages alleged, and therefore the Plaintiff cannot recover.

FOURTH DEFENSE

And further answering, the Defendant says that the Plaintiff's intestate was in violation of the law at the time and place of the alleged accident, which violation of the law caused or contributed to the happening of said accident, and therefore the Plaintiff cannot recover.

FIFTH DEFENSE

And further answering, the Defendant says that the Plaintiff's intestate's alleged injuries and subsequent death were caused by persons other than the Defendant, his agents, servants, or employees, and plaintiff's intestate's alleged injuries, if any, were caused by persons for whose conduct the defendant is not responsible, and therefore, the Plaintiff cannot recover.

SIXTH DEFENSE

And further answering, the Defendant says that the Plaintiff's intestate's alleged injuries, and subsequent death, do not come within one of the exceptions to the Massachusetts No-Fault Insurance Law, being Massachusetts General Laws, Chapter 231, Section 6D, and therefore the Plaintiff is barred from bringing this action and cannot recover.

SEVENTH DEFENSE

And further answering, the Defendant says that the alleged cause of action referred to in the Plaintiff's complaint falls within the purview of Massachusetts General Laws, Chapter 90, Section 34(m), and therefore this action is brought in violation of the law and the Plaintiff cannot recover.

WHEREFORE, the Defendant, Randall Dee, demands judgment against the Plaintiff and further demands that said action be dismissed.

AND FURTHER, the Defendant, Randall Dee, claims a trial by jury on all the issues.

RANDALL DEE, by his attorney,

By: _____ /s/ Robert Orthwein _____
Robert Orthwein (BBO#627841)
Chaudhuri, Brown, Orthwein & Guinto
11 Boardwalk
Boston, MA 02100
(617) 555-1111

Dated: /d/

[*Eds.' Note:* Randall Dee did not answer the allegations in Count III of the complaint. One possible explanation for this is that the parties may have reached an agreement on what to do about the alleged fraudulent conveyance pending a trial on the merits. It also is conceivable that Randall Dee intended later to answer Count III, but the parties then simply forgot. To be sure, unusual things happen during litigation.

We also wish to emphasize that Randall Dee's third defense, assumption of the risk, is not a defense under Massachusetts comparative negligence law. The sixth and seventh affirmative defenses are completely baseless. The statutory provisions cited relate to Massachusetts no-fault insurance, and the defenses do not apply in this case. We reprint the Answer in full, however, because we want you to see what was filed. It also is instructive to learn what happens when one blindly follows forms.]

COMMONWEALTH OF MASSACHUSETTS

MIDDLESEX, SS

SUPERIOR COURT DEPARTMENT
OF THE TRIAL COURT
CIVIL ACTION NO. 20-6144

NANCY CARPENTER, As
Administratrix of the Estate of
Charles Carpenter,
    Plaintiff

        vs.

RANDALL DEE and
PETER DEE,
    Defendants.

MOTION TO AMEND

    Now comes the plaintiff and moves for leave to file an Amended Complaint, a copy of which is attached hereto.

By her attorneys,

By: _____ /s/ Carol Coblentz _____
Carol Coblentz (BBO#304321)
Needham, Shaker and Coblentz
44 Park Place
Boston, MA 02100
(617) 555-5555

Dated: /d/

COMMONWEALTH OF MASSACHUSETTS

MIDDLESEX, SS	SUPERIOR COURT DEPARTMENT OF THE TRIAL COURT CIVIL ACTION NO. 20-6144
NANCY CARPENTER, As Administratrix of the Estate of Charles Carpenter, Plaintiff	AMENDED COMPLAINT
vs.	
RANDALL DEE, PETER DEE; ULTIMATE AUTO, INC; and CITY OF LOWELL, Defendants.	PLAINTIFF CLAIMS TRIAL BY JURY

PARTIES

1. The plaintiff Nancy Carpenter is a resident of Lowell, Middlesex County, Massachusetts. She brings this action in her capacity as the administratrix of the estate of Charles Carpenter, her late husband, of Lowell, Middlesex County, Massachusetts. She was duly appointed as administratrix by the Middlesex Probate Court, docket number 19P3875A.

2. The defendant Randall Dee is a resident of Lowell, Middlesex County, Massachusetts.

3. The defendant Peter Dee is a resident of Lowell, Middlesex County, Massachusetts.

4. Ultimate Auto, Inc. is a Massachusetts corporation, with a usual place of business in Lowell, Middlesex County, Massachusetts.

5. The City of Lowell ("the City"), is a body politic and corporate, with executive offices at 100 Main Street, Lowell, Middlesex County, Massachusetts.

FACTS

6. On or about August 31, 2019, the plaintiff's intestate, Charles Carpenter, was riding as a passenger in a 1986 Jeep CJ-7 (hereinafter "the jeep").

7. The jeep was owned by one Twyla Burrell, and operated by the defendant Randall Dee.

8. At or near the intersection of Palmer and Franklin Streets in Lowell, the operator lost control of the jeep, and it rolled over, pinning Charles Carpenter beneath it.

9. The loss of control and resulting accident was caused by the negligent and/or grossly negligent and/or wanton, willful, and reckless conduct of the defendant Randall Dee as operator of the jeep including, but not limited to, the following acts and omissions:

(a) Excessive speed;
(b) Failing to stop at an intersection; and
(c) Illegal and dangerous alteration of the chassis, causing unsafe handling characteristics.

10. The defendant Randall Dee modified the jeep, by means of a suspension lift kit and oversize tires. He purchased both items at a retail store owned and operated by the defendant Ultimate Auto.

11. The raised suspension and oversized tires markedly affected the handling characteristics (including, but not limited to, propensity to roll over) of the jeep, and such modifications were a substantial contributing cause to the accident on August 31, 2019.

12. On several occasions prior to August 31, 2019, police officers of the City of Lowell, acting within the scope of their employment, stopped the defendant Randall Dee while operating the jeep, in connection with suspected motor vehicle offenses. On no occasion, did any of the officers advise the defendant Dee that the vehicle was illegally modified, or take any other action to prevent the vehicle from being operated in its dangerous condition. The failure of the police to act was a substantial contributing cause to the accident on August 31, 2019.

COUNT I (Wrongful Death, Randall Dee)

13. The plaintiff repeats and incorporates herein the allegations of paragraphs 1-9.

14. As a result of the negligent and/or grossly negligent and/or wanton, willful, and reckless conduct of the defendant Randall Dee, the plaintiff's intestate was killed on August 31, 2019.

COUNT II (Conscious Suffering, Randall Dee)

15. The plaintiff repeats and incorporates herein the allegations of paragraphs 1-9.

16. As a result of the conduct of the defendant Randall Dee, as described above, the plaintiff's intestate sustained serious personal injuries, from which he suffered consciously, prior to his death on August 31, 2019.

COUNT III (Fraudulent Conveyance)

17. The plaintiff repeats and incorporates herein the allegations of paragraphs 1-9.

18. At the time of the accident on August 31, 2019, the defendant Randall Dee and the defendant Peter Dee owned as joint tenants a certain parcel of land at 91 Birch Hill Road, Lowell, Massachusetts, containing approximately 11,604 square feet.

19. The defendants Randall Dee and Peter Dee had purchased said property from the estate of their deceased father Richard Dee, for the amount of $140,000.00 on or about February 13, 2019.

20. On or about October 8, 2019, the defendant Randall Dee conveyed all his right, title, and interest in the above property to Peter Dee for "nominal consideration."

21. On information and belief, the transfer of such interest was fraudulent as to the creditors, including, but not limited to, the plaintiff, within the meaning of Mass. Gen. Laws ch. 109A, in that:

(a) The conveyance was made without fair consideration and Randall Dee was thereby rendered insolvent, within the meaning of Mass. Gen. Laws ch. 109A, § 4; and/or

(b) The conveyance was made without fair consideration at a time when the defendant Randall Dee believed that he would incur debts beyond his ability to pay, within the meaning of Mass. Gen. Laws ch. 109A, § 6; and/or

(c) The transfer was made with an actual intent to hinder, delay or defraud creditors, including but not limited to the plaintiff, within the meaning of Mass. Gen. Laws ch. 109A, § 7.

COUNT IV (Wrongful Death, Ultimate Auto)

22. The plaintiff repeats and incorporates herein the allegations of paragraphs 1-11.

23. The defendant Ultimate Auto as a retailer of automotive parts, owed a duty to Randall Dee (and to the public generally) to provide appropriate

technical advice with regard to the sale of products that could be used to modify vehicles.

24. In breach of that duty, the defendant Ultimate Auto was guilty of negligent and/or grossly negligent and/or wanton, willful, and reckless conduct, including, but not limited to, the following acts and omissions:

(a) Selling a suspension lift kit and oversized tires which, individually and in combination, altered the height of the jeep, affecting its handling characteristics (including, but not limited to, its propensity to roll over) and rendered it unsafe;

(b) Failing to give any kind of warning or instruction to Randall Dee, with respect to the effect of such parts on the handling characteristics of the jeep;

(c) Selling automotive parts which constituted per se a violation of Mass. Gen. Laws ch. 90, § 7P, with regard to modification of vehicle height;

(d) Failing to advise Randall Dee that the installation of the parts constituted a violation of Mass. Gen. Laws ch. 90, § 7P.

25. As a result of the above acts and omissions, the defendant Randall Dee installed the suspension lift kit and oversized tires, and the acts and omissions of Ultimate Auto were a substantial contributing cause to the loss of control and resulting accident on August 31, 2019.

26. As a result of the negligent and/or grossly negligent and/or wanton, willful, and reckless conduct of the defendant, Ultimate Auto, the plaintiff's intestate was killed on August 31, 2019.

COUNT V (Conscious Suffering, Ultimate Auto)

27. The plaintiff repeats and incorporates herein the allegations of paragraphs 1-11 and 23-26.

28. As a result of the conduct of the defendant Ultimate Auto, as described above, the plaintiff's intestate sustained serious personal injuries, from which he suffered consciously, prior to his death on August 31, 2019.

COUNT VI (Wrongful Death, Warranties, Ultimate Auto)

29. The plaintiff repeats and incorporates herein the allegations of paragraphs 1-11 and 23-26.

30. The defendant Ultimate Auto was a merchant with respect to sale of the suspension lift kit and oversized tires. The defendant Ultimate Auto breached implied warranties of merchantability and fitness for a particular

purpose, by selling to the defendant Randall Dee, a suspension lift kit and oversized tires which, individually and in combination, rendered the jeep unreasonably dangerous and/or by selling the suspension lift kit and over-sized tires, without adequate warning or instruction with regard to their dangerous propensity.

31. As a result of the said breaches of warranty, the defendant Randall Dee installed the suspension lift kit and oversized tires. The breaches of the defendant Ultimate Auto were a substantial contributing cause to the loss of control and resulting accident on August 31, 2019. As a result of the defendant's breaches of warranty, the plaintiff's intestate was killed on August 31, 2019.

COUNT VII (Conscious Suffering, Warranties, Ultimate Auto)

32. Plaintiff repeats and incorporates herein the allegations of paragraphs 1-11, 23-26, and 29-31.

33. As a result of the breaches of warranty of the defendant Ultimate Auto, as described above, the plaintiff's intestate sustained serious personal injuries, from which he suffered consciously, prior to his death on August 31, 2019.

COUNT VIII (Wrongful Death, City of Lowell)

34. Plaintiff repeats and incorporates herein the allegations of paragraphs 1-12.

35. On or about February 19, 2020, the year after the accident, the plaintiff, through her attorney and pursuant to Mass. Gen. Laws ch. 258, § 4, gave written notice of its claim to the City. No substantive response to that notice has been forthcoming.

36. The modification of the jeep represented an imminent danger to all persons who might be affected by it, in particular, its occupants, and a clear violation of Mass. Gen. Laws ch. 90, § 7P. As such, it created a special duty of care to those who might be affected by it, including the plaintiff's intestate.

37. Despite the obvious danger of immediate and foreseeable injury presented by the jeep, police officers of the City of Lowell failed to take any effective action to reduce or eliminate the danger.

38. As a result, the jeep was being operated in a condition of imminent danger on August 31, 2019, and the negligence of the City, through its police officers, was a substantial contributing cause to the loss of control and resulting accident on that date.

39. As a result of the negligence of the City, its agents and employees, the plaintiff's intestate was killed on August 31, 2019.

COUNT IX (City of Lowell, Conscious Suffering)

40. The plaintiff repeats and incorporates herein the allegations of paragraphs 1-12 and 34-39.

41. As a result of the conduct of the defendant City as described above, the plaintiff's intestate sustained serious personal injuries, from which he suffered consciously, prior to his death on August 31, 2019.

WHEREFORE the plaintiff prays for the following relief:

1. Judgment on Counts I, IV, VI, and VIII against the defendants Randall Dee, Ultimate Auto, and City of Lowell.

   (a) To compensate the survivors of the plaintiff's intestate for the fair monetary value of the deceased for reasonably expected net income lost, services, protection, care, assistance, society, companionship, comfort, guidance, counsel, and advice of the deceased.
   (b) Reasonable funeral and burial expenses.
   (c) Punitive damages in an amount of at least $5,000.00, pursuant to Mass. Gen. Laws ch. 229, § 2.

2. Judgment on Counts II, V, VII, and IX against the defendants Randall Dee, Ultimate Auto, and City of Lowell to compensate the estate of Charles Carpenter for his pain and conscious suffering.

3. That the Court issue a temporary restraining order enjoining the defendant, Randall Dee, until further order of this court, from conveying, encumbering, or in any other manner transferring any interest, legal or equitable, in any of his assets, including but not limited to real estate, bank accounts, certificates of deposit, securities, valuables, and any other asset not immune from execution, except in the ordinary course of business.

4. That the Court issue a preliminary injunction enjoining the defendant Randall Dee, until the disposition of this action on the merits, from conveying, encumbering, or in any other manner transferring any interest, legal or equitable, in any of his assets, including but not limited to real estate, bank accounts, certificates of deposit, securities, valuables, and any other asset not immune from execution, except in the ordinary course of business.

5. That the Court issue a Temporary Restraining Order enjoining the defendant Peter Dee, until further order of this court, from conveying, encumbering,

or in any other manner transferring any interest, legal or equitable, in the real estate at 91 Birch Hill Road, Lowell, Massachusetts.

6. That the Court issue a preliminary injunction enjoining the defendant, Peter Dee, until the disposition of this action on the merits, from conveying, encumbering, or in any other manner transferring any interest, legal or equitable, in the real estate at 91 Birch Hill Road, Lowell, Massachusetts.

7. That the Court, under Count III, declare null and void the conveyance of the interest of Randall Dee in the property at 91 Birch Hill Road, Lowell and/or allow satisfaction of any judgment in this action against Randall Dee to be satisfied against the interest he held in said property prior to the fraudulent conveyance.

8. That the Court issue a temporary restraining order enjoining the defendants, until further Order of the Court, from selling or transferring in any way the jeep vehicle involved or in any way modifying it or changing its present condition.

9. That the Court issue a preliminary injunction enjoining the defendants, until the disposition of this action on the merits, from selling or transferring in any way the jeep vehicle involved or in any way modifying it or changing its present condition.

10. PLAINTIFF CLAIMS TRIAL BY JURY.

By her attorneys,

By: _____ /s/ Carol Coblentz _____
Carol Coblentz (BBO#304321)
Needham, Shaker and Coblentz
44 Park Place
Boston, MA 02100
(617) 555-5555

Dated: /d/

Uniform Commercial Code § 2-314.
Implied Warranty: Merchantability; Usage of Trade

(1) Unless excluded or modified. . . , a warranty that the goods shall be merchantable is implied in a contract for their sale if the seller is a merchant with respect to goods of that kind. . . .

(2) Goods to be merchantable must be at least such as

(a) pass without objection in the trade under the contract description; and

(b) in the case of fungible goods, are of fair average quality within the description; and

(c) are fit for the ordinary purposes for which such goods are used; and

(d) run, within the variations permitted by the agreement, of even kind, quality and quantity within each unit and among all units involved; and

(e) are adequately contained, packaged, and labeled as the agreement may require; and

(f) conform to the promises or affirmations of fact made on the container or label if any.

(3) Unless excluded or modified . . . other implied warranties may arise from course of dealing or usage of trade.

COMMENT

1. The seller's obligation applies to present sales as well as to contracts. . . .

2. The question when the warranty is imposed turns basically on the meaning of the terms of the agreement as recognized in the trade. . . .

3. In an action based on breach of warranty, it is of course necessary to show not only the existence of the warranty but the fact that the warranty was broken and that the breach of the warranty was the proximate cause of the loss sustained. In such an action an affirmative showing by the seller that the loss resulted from some action or event following his own delivery of the goods can operate as a defense. Equally, evidence indicating that the seller exercised care in the manufacture, processing or selection of the goods is relevant to the issue of whether the warranty was in fact broken. Action by the buyer following an examination of the goods which ought to have indicated the defect complained of can be shown as matter bearing on whether the breach itself was the cause of the injury.

Uniform Commercial Code § 2-315. Implied Warranty:
Fitness for Particular Purpose

Where the seller at the time of contracting has reason to know any particular purpose for which the goods are required and that the buyer is relying on the seller's skill or judgment to select or furnish suitable goods, there is unless excluded or modified under the next section an implied warranty that the goods shall be fit for such purpose.

COMMENT

1. Whether or not this warranty arises in any individual case is basically a question of fact to be determined by the circumstances of the contracting. Under this section the buyer need not bring home to the seller actual knowledge of the particular purpose for which the goods are intended or of his reliance on the seller's skill and judgment, if the circumstances are such that the seller has reason to realize the purpose intended or that the reliance exists. . . .

2. A "particular purpose" differs from the ordinary purpose for which the goods are used in that it envisages a specific use by the buyer which is peculiar to the nature of his business whereas the ordinary purposes for which goods are used are those envisaged in the concept of merchantability and go to uses which are customarily made of the goods in question. For example, shoes are generally used for the purpose of walking upon ordinary ground, but a seller may know that a particular pair was selected to be used for climbing mountains.

A contract may of course include both a warranty of merchantability and one of fitness for a particular purpose. . . .

Mass. Gen. Laws Ch. 90 § 7P. Height of Motor Vehicles; Alteration Restricted

No person shall alter, modify or change the height of a motor vehicle with an original manufacturer's gross vehicle weight rating of up to and including ten thousand pounds, by elevating or lowering the chassis or body by more than two inches above or below the original manufacturer's specified height by use of so-called "shackle lift kits" for leaf springs or by use of lift kits for coil springs, tires, or any other means or device.

The registrar shall establish such rules and regulations for such changes in the height of motor vehicles beyond said two inches. No motor vehicle that has been so altered, modified or changed beyond the provisions of this section or the rules and regulations established by the registrar shall be operated on any way.

Mass. Gen. Laws Ch. 231B § 85. Comparative Negligence; Limited Effect of Contributory Negligence as Defense

Contributory negligence shall not bar recovery in any action by any person or legal representative to recover damages for negligence resulting in death or in injury to person or property, if such negligence was not greater than the total amount of negligence attributable to the person or persons against whom recovery is sought, but any damages allowed shall be diminished in proportion to the amount of negligence attributable to the person for whose injury, damage or death recovery is made. In determining by what amount the plaintiff's damages shall be diminished in such a case, the negligence of each plaintiff shall be compared to the total negligence of all persons against whom recovery is sought. The combined total of the plaintiff's negligence taken together with all of the negligence of all defendants shall equal one hundred per cent.

The violation of a criminal statute, ordinance or regulation by a plaintiff which contributed to said injury, death or damage, shall be considered as evidence of negligence of that plaintiff, but the violation of said statute, ordinance or regulation shall not as a matter of law and for that reason alone, serve to bar a plaintiff from recovery.

The defense of assumption of risk is hereby abolished in all actions hereunder.

The burden of alleging and proving negligence which serves to diminish a plaintiff's damages or bar recovery under this section shall be upon the person who seeks to establish such negligence, and the plaintiff shall be presumed to have been in the exercise of due care.

Mass. Gen. Laws Ch. 231B §§ 1-4. Contribution Among Joint Tortfeasors

§ 1. (a) Except as otherwise provided in this chapter, where two or more persons become jointly liable in tort for the same injury to person or property, there shall be a right of contribution among them even though judgment has not been recovered against all or any of them.

(b) The right of contribution shall exist only in favor of a joint tortfeasor, hereinafter called tortfeasor, who has paid more than his pro rata share of the common liability, and his total recovery shall be limited to the amount paid by him in excess of his pro rata share. No tortfeasor shall be compelled to make contribution beyond his own pro rata share of the entire liability.

(c) A tortfeasor who enters into a settlement with a claimant shall not be entitled to recover contribution from another tortfeasor in respect to any amount paid in a settlement which is in excess of what was reasonable.

(d) A liability insurer, who by payment has discharged in full or in part the liability of a tortfeasor and has thereby discharged in full its obligation as insurer, shall be subrogated to the tortfeasor's right of contribution to the extent of the amount it has paid in excess of the tortfeasor's pro rata share of the common liability. This provision shall not limit or impair any right of subrogation arising from any other relationship.

(e) This chapter shall not impair any right of indemnity under existing law. Where one tortfeasor is entitled to indemnity from another, the right of the indemnity obligee shall be for indemnity and not contribution, and the indemnity obligor shall not be entitled to contribution from the obligee for any portion of his indemnity obligation.

§ 2. In determining the pro rata shares of tortfeasors in the entire liability (a) their relative degrees of fault shall not be considered; (b) if equity requires, the collective liability of some as a group shall constitute a single share; and (c) principles of equity applicable to contribution generally shall apply.

§ 3. (a) Whether or not judgment has been entered in an action against two or more tortfeasors for the same injury, contribution may be enforced by separate action.

(b) Where a judgment has been entered in an action against two or more tortfeasors for the same injury, contribution may be enforced in that action by judgment in favor of one against other judgment defendants by motion upon notice to all parties to the action.

(c) If there is a judgment for the injury against the tortfeasor seeking contribution, any separate action by him to enforce contribution must be commenced within one year after the judgment has become final by lapse of time for appeal or after appellate review.

(d) If there is no judgment for the injury against the tortfeasor seeking contribution, his right of contribution shall be barred unless he has either (1) discharged by payment, the common liability within the statute of limitations period applicable to claimant's right of action against him and has commenced his action for contribution within one year after payment, or (2) agreed, while action is pending against him, to discharge the common liability and has, within one year after the agreement, paid the liability and commenced his action for contribution.

(e) The recovery of a judgment for an injury against one tortfeasor shall not, of itself, discharge the other tortfeasors from liability for the injury unless the judgment is satisfied. The satisfaction of the judgment shall not impair any right of contribution.

(f) The judgment of the court in determining the liability of the several defendants to the claimant for an injury shall be binding as among such defendants in determining their right to contribution.

§ 4. When a release or covenant not to sue or not to enforce judgment is given in good faith to one or two or more persons liable in tort for the same injury:

(a) It shall not discharge any of the other tortfeasors from liability for the injury unless its terms so provide; but it shall reduce the claim against the others to the extent of any amount stipulated by the release or the covenant, or in the amount of the consideration paid for it, whichever is the greater; and

(b) It shall discharge the tortfeasor to whom it is given from all liability for contribution to any other tortfeasor.

Walter VanBuskirk, "Lifting" a Truck

Driving around on the streets, it is not uncommon to see trucks that are higher off the ground and have larger tires than normal trucks. The process truck owners go through to achieve this effect is called "lifting" the truck. There are three basic ways to life a truck: body lifts, suspension lifts, and larger tires. Each of these types of lifts have different uses and have different effects on the center of gravity of the truck.

BODY LIFTS

All trucks and some cars have frames as the main structural member. The frame is the base which most everything else bolts onto. The body of the truck bolts onto the frame at numerous locations (apparently twelve locations on Randall Dee's jeep). Normally, there is a small rubber spacer approximately 1 inch in thickness, called a body mount, between the frame and the body at each of these locations. A body lift uses larger spacers between the body and the frame to raise the body up off the frame. This has the effect of raising the fenders up higher which allows the use of larger tires.

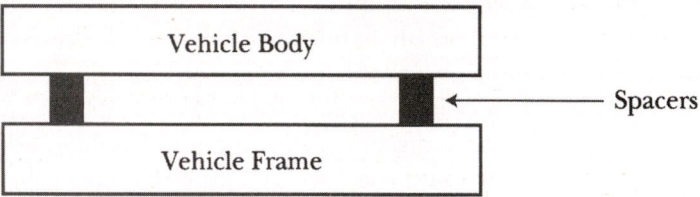

In the case, Randall Dee used hockey pucks as the spacers between the body and the frame. Although this may sound absurd, it is actually very common. However, most people will use spacers made of steel or some specially designed composite material when putting in more than 2 inches of lift. This approach is preferred, because the rubber hockey pucks are too compressible. Dee used four hockey pucks at each body mount location to achieve approximately 4 inches of lift.

SUSPENSION LIFTS

Between the truck's axle and frame is the suspension. The suspension is made up of four main components: the shackle, the leaf spring, the shock absorber, and the U-bolt. (Note that the following graphic does not have shock absorbers or U-Bolts.) The shackle attaches the leaf spring to the frame. The

---

* *Eds' Note:* Walter VanBuskirk wrote this while a student at Boston College Law School. After graduating in 1999, he joined and ultimately became a partner at Sullivan & Worcester; he is now in-house counsel for a company in Boston.

leaf spring is a series of "arched" strips of metal welded together, which flex to allow the vehicle to move somewhat independently of the tires. If left alone, after a vehicle hits a bump the leaf spring would continue to bounce. The shock absorber stops the leaf spring from bouncing. Finally, the U-bolt attaches the leaf spring to the axle.

To raise the suspension in a truck there are numerous options: longer shackles, larger leaf springs, or a spacer between the axle and the leaf spring (you would never use hockey pucks here). Randall Dee used larger leaf springs.

Typical Suspension of a Jeep CJ-7

Suspension of Dee's Jeep with New Leaf Springs and Relocated Axle

Suspension lifts are more desirable than body lifts. This type of lift actually raises the frame and everything attached to it further off the ground. Not only does that create additional tire clearance (by raising the fenders over the axle), it also raises the engine higher off the ground, which helps the truck in off-road situations. Dee used a 2-inch larger spring. This does not always give exactly a 2-inch lift; the spring is flexible, and the weight of the vehicle has a large effect on the actual lift. In this case Dee actually achieved a 3-inch lift. It should also be noted that jeeps are strange in that they are one of the only trucks that have the axle mounted on top of the leaf spring. Most other trucks mount the axle under the leaf spring, which allows the use of a spacer between the axle and leaf spring to lift the truck. Randall Dee remounted the axle under the leaf springs. This is a common step performed when lifting a jeep.

LARGER TIRES

Basically the major use of body lifts and suspension lifts is to allow the use of bigger tires. Bigger tires give the truck more total clearance (they can drive through deeper mud and over bigger rocks). Average tires are around 28 inches in diameter. The tires Randall Dee put on his jeep were 40 inches in diameter. This is a 12-inch increase in diameter, which leads to 6 inches of additional height over his previous tires.

DEE'S JEEP

In the case of Dee's jeep, he put in 4 inches of body lift, a 3-inch suspension lift replacing the leaf springs, 3 inches of additional suspension lift by remounting the axle, and larger tires adding 6 inches. In total, Dee's jeep is at least 16 inches higher than a regular jeep.

Randall Dee's CJ-7

16″ Minimum Difference

Stock CJ-7

PHOTOGRAPHS

Police Photographs of the Scene of the Accident

COMMONWEALTH OF MASSACHUSETTS

MIDDLESEX, SS

NANCY CARPENTER, As
Administratrix of the Estate
of Charles Carpenter,
    Plaintiff

        vs.

RANDALL DEE; PETER DEE;
CITY OF LOWELL,
    Defendants.

ULTIMATE AUTO, INC.,
Defendant and Third-Party
    Plaintiff

        vs.

DALE MCGILL and MCGILL'S
GARAGE, INC.,
    Third-Party Defendants.

SUPERIOR COURT DEPARTMENT OF
THE TRIAL COURT
CIVIL ACTION NO. 20-6144

MOTION OF DEFENDANT ULTIMATE
AUTO, INC.
TO FILE A THIRD-PARTY COMPLAINT

The defendant, Ultimate Auto, Inc., moves that the Court allow it to file the attached third-party complaint for contribution against Dale McGill and McGill's Garage, Inc.

In support thereof, the defendant Ultimate Auto, Inc. states that discovery has shown that the vehicle, which was allegedly in a defective condition at the time of the accident, had been issued an inspection sticker by the third-party defendants and that the issuance of said inspection sticker was in violation of applicable Massachusetts regulations. Accordingly, the third-party defendants would be liable as joint tortfeasors for the claims made by the plaintiff.

                    By its Attorneys,

                    _____ /s/ Bertram Cohen _____
                    Bertram Cohen (BBO#641311)
                    Roth, McKnight & Zimmerman
                    111 Milk Street
                    Boston, MA 02100
                    (617) 555-0000

Dated: /d/

COMMONWEALTH OF MASSACHUSETTS

MIDDLESEX, SS

SUPERIOR COURT DEPARTMENT
OF THE TRIAL COURT
CIVIL ACTION NO. 20-6144

NANCY CARPENTER, As
Administratrix of the Estate of
Charles Carpenter,
   Plaintiff

     vs.

RANDALL DEE; PETER DEE;
CITY OF LOWELL,
   Defendants.

THIRD-PARTY COMPLAINT OF
ULTIMATE AUTO, INC.

ULTIMATE AUTO, INC.,
   Defendant and Third-Party
   Plaintiff

vs.

DALE MCGILL and MCGILL'S
GARAGE, INC.,
   Third-Party Defendants.

COUNT I

1. The third-party defendant, Dale McGill, is an individual residing station doing business as McGill's Garage, Inc., in Watertown, Massachusetts.

2. The defendant/third-party plaintiff, Ultimate Auto, Inc., has been named as a party defendant in an action sounding in tort against it and in which it is alleged that the negligence of the defendant/third-party plaintiff entitled the plaintiff to recover for damages allegedly sustained as a result of a motor vehicle accident on August 31, 2019.

3. If the plaintiff did sustain injuries and damages as alleged, such injuries and damages occurred as a direct and proximate result of the negligence and carelessness of the third-party defendant, Dale McGill in approving an inspection sticker on the vehicle involved in the accident alleged in the plaintiff's complaint.

4. The third-party defendant is jointly liable for the injuries and damages allegedly sustained by the plaintiff pursuant to Mass. Gen. Laws ch. 231B, §§ 1-3.

WHEREFORE, the defendant/third-party plaintiff, Ultimate Auto, Inc., says that if it is found liable to the plaintiff, the third-party defendant, Dale McGill, is liable to the defendant/third-party plaintiff as a joint tortfeasor.

COUNT II

5. The third-party defendant, McGill's Garage, Inc., is a Massachusetts corporation with a usual place of business in Watertown, Massachusetts, and at all time material was in the business of conducting motor vehicle inspections.

6. The defendant/third-party plaintiff, Ultimate Auto, Inc., has been named as a party defendant in an action sounding in tort against it and in which it is alleged that the negligence of the defendant/third-party plaintiff entitled the plaintiff to recover for damages allegedly sustained as a result of a motor vehicle accident on August 31, 2019.

7. If the plaintiff did sustain injuries and damages as alleged, such injuries and damages occurred as a direct and proximate result of the negligence and carelessness of employees or agents of the third-party defendant, McGill's Garage, Inc., in approving or issuing an inspection sticker on the vehicle involved in the accident alleged in the plaintiff's complaint.

8. The third-party defendant is jointly liable for the injuries and damages allegedly sustained by the plaintiff pursuant to Mass. Gen. Laws ch. 231B, §§ 1-3.

WHEREFORE, the defendant/third-party plaintiff, says that if it is found liable to the plaintiff, the third-party defendant, McGill's Garage, Inc., is liable to the defendant/third-party plaintiff as a joint tortfeasor.

By its Attorneys,

_____ /s/ Bertram Cohen _____
Bertram Cohen (BBO 641311)
Roth, McKnight & Zimmerman
111 Milk Street
Boston, MA 02100
(617) 555-0000

Dated: /d/

COMMONWEALTH OF MASSACHUSETTS

MIDDLESEX, SS

SUPERIOR COURT DEPARTMENT
OF THE TRIAL COURT
CIVIL ACTION NO. 20-6144

NANCY CARPENTER, As
Administratrix of the Estate of
Charles Carpenter,
  Plaintiff

    vs.

RANDALL DEE; PETER DEE; CITY
OF LOWELL,
  Defendants.

ANSWER AND CROSS-CLAIMS OF
ULTIMATE AUTO, INC.

TRIAL BY JURY

ULTIMATE AUTO, INC.,
Defendant and Third-Party
  Plaintiff

    vs.

DALE MCGILL and
MCGILL'S GARAGE, INC.,
  Third-Party Defendants.

FIRST DEFENSE

The Defendant, Ultimate Auto, Inc. ("Ultimate Auto") addresses the separately numbered paragraphs of the Complaint as follows:

1. The Defendant is without knowledge or information sufficient to form a belief as to the truth of the allegations contained in Paragraph 1.

2. The Defendant is without knowledge or information sufficient to form a belief as to the truth of the allegations contained in Paragraph 2.

3. The Defendant is without knowledge or information sufficient to form a belief as to the truth of the allegations contained in Paragraph 3.

4. The Defendant admits the allegations contained in Paragraph 4.

5. The Defendant admits the allegations contained in Paragraph 5.

6. The Defendant is without knowledge or information sufficient to form a belief as to the truth of the allegations contained in Paragraph 6.

7. The Defendant is without knowledge or information sufficient to form a belief as to the truth of the allegations contained in Paragraph 7.

8. The Defendant is without knowledge or information sufficient to form a belief as to the truth of the allegations contained in Paragraph 8.

9. The Defendant denies the allegations contained in Paragraph 9.

10. The Defendant denies the allegations contained in Paragraph 10.

11. The Defendant denies the allegations contained in Paragraph 11.

12. The Defendant is without knowledge or information sufficient to form a belief as to the truth of the allegations contained in Paragraph 12.

13-21. The Defendant makes no answer to the allegations of these Paragraphs because they do not purport to make a claim against it.

22. The Defendant repeats and realleges its answers to Paragraphs 1-11.

23. The Defendant denies the allegations contained in Paragraph 23.

24. The Defendant denies the allegations contained in Paragraph 24.

25. The Defendant denies the allegations contained in Paragraph 25.

26. The Defendant denies the allegations contained in Paragraph 26.

27. The Defendant repeats and realleges its answers to Paragraphs 1-11 and 23-26.

28. The Defendant denies the allegations contained in Paragraph 28.

29. The Defendant repeats and realleges its answers to Paragraphs 1-11 and 23-26.

30. The Defendant denies the allegations contained in Paragraph 30.

31. The Defendant denies the allegations contained in Paragraph 31.

32. The Defendant repeats and realleges its answers to Paragraphs 1-11, 23-26, and 29-31.

33. The Defendant denies the allegations contained in Paragraph 33.

34-41. The Defendant makes no answer to the allegations of these Paragraphs because they do not purport to make a claim against it.

SECOND DEFENSE

This action is barred by operation of the applicable statute of limitations.

THIRD DEFENSE

If the Plaintiff is entitled to recover against the Defendant, any such recovery must be reduced in accordance with the comparative negligence statute as enacted in the Commonwealth, since the Plaintiff's own negligence was the proximate cause of the injury sustained.

FOURTH DEFENSE

Any loss sustained by the Plaintiff resulted from his own negligence, which was greater in degree than any negligence of the Defendant and therefore the Plaintiff is barred from recovery in this action.

FIFTH DEFENSE

The Defendant is exempt from liability to the extent provided by the Massachusetts "no fault" statutes, Mass. Gen. Laws ch. 90, § 34m, and Mass. Gen. Laws ch. 231 § 6d.

SIXTH DEFENSE

The Plaintiff has failed to give notice of breach of warranty, and the Defendant has thereby been prejudiced.

CROSS-CLAIM AGAINST RANDALL DEE, PETER DEE AND THE CITY OF LOWELL

1. If the Plaintiff's decedent was injured as alleged by the Plaintiff, he was injured as a result of the negligence of the Defendants, Randall Dee, Peter Dee, and/or the City of Lowell.

2. The Defendants, Randall Dee, Peter Dee, and the City of Lowell, are liable to the Defendant, Ultimate Auto, Inc. for contribution pursuant to Mass. Gen. Laws ch. 231B.

WHEREFORE, the Defendant Ultimate Auto, Inc., demands judgment for contribution against the Defendants, Randall Dee and Peter Dee.

THE DEFENDANT, ULTIMATE AUTO, INC., DEMANDS TRIAL BY JURY ON ALL CLAIMS.

By its Attorneys,

_____ /s/ Bertram Cohen _____
Bertram Cohen (BBO#641311)
Roth, McKnight & Zimmerman
111 Milk Street
Boston, MA 02100
(617) 555-0000

Dated: /d/

COMMONWEALTH OF MASSACHUSETTS

MIDDLESEX, SS	SUPERIOR COURT DEPARTMENT OF THE TRIAL COURT CIVIL ACTION NO. 20-6144
NANCY CARPENTER, As Administratrix of the Estate of Charles Carpenter, Plaintiff	
vs.	PLAINTIFF'S REQUEST FOR PRODUCTION OF DOCUMENTS BY ULTIMATE AUTO, INC.
RANDALL DEE; PETER DEE; ULTIMATE AUTO, INC.; and CITY OF LOWELL, Defendants.	

The plaintiff, Nancy Carpenter, hereby requests of defendant, Ultimate Auto, Inc., that the plaintiff be permitted to inspect and copy the originals and copies of the following designated documents, writings, photographs, or tangible things. Production, inspection and copying shall take place at the office of defendant's counsel, within thirty days of the receipt of this notice or at such other place and time as may be agreed upon by counsel for the parties.

If, in response to any of the following requests, production of a document is denied on the basis of attorney-client privilege or trial-preparation/work-product materials, kindly indicate sufficient information concerning said document and the claimed privilege to enable the court to assess the applicability of said privilege, including the nature of the document withheld, the identity of its author, the current custodian of the document, the date the document was prepared, and the exact privilege being asserted.

DEFINITIONS

A. "The accident" refers to the alleged accident described in plaintiff's complaint as occurring on or about August 31, 2019.

B. "The motor vehicle" means the jeep alleged to have caused the plaintiff's injuries and described in the plaintiff's complaint.

C. "Ultimate Auto, Inc." means the defendant Ultimate Auto, Inc., its officers, agents, and employees.

D. The term "documents" as used herein includes writings of any sort, drawings, graphs, charts, photographs, and other data compilations.

REQUESTS

1. All promotional and descriptive material in your possession relating in any way to oversize tires.

2. All promotional and descriptive material in your possession relating in any way to suspension lift kits.

3. All documents in your possession which comment upon, or relate in any way to, Mass. Gen. Laws ch. 90, § 7P.

4. A copy of all warnings and instructions which accompany suspension lift kits and/or oversize tires.

5. All warranties pertaining to the above products.

6. All complaints, letters, notices, claims or suit papers which constitute, reflect or relate to any claims as described in plaintiff's Interrogatory No. 11.*

7. All studies, reports, literature, research, or documents of any other kind and description, relating in any way to the alteration in vehicle handling or driving characteristics (including, but not limited to change in its propensity to roll over) as result of alteration of vehicle height.

8. Copies of all industry and trade standards which reflect, or relate in any way to, the design, construction, or configuration of automobile parts which have the purpose or effect of altering vehicle height.

9. Copies of all insurance policies (primary or excess) affording coverage to the defendant for this loss.

10. Copies of all statements secured at any time from plaintiff, or from any member of the plaintiff's family, and whether such statements be recorded or written, signed or unsigned.

Eds.' Note: Plaintiff's Interrogatory No. 11 can be found reprinted in Ultimate Auto's Answers to Interrogatories in these case files.

11. All written warnings or instructions, which you have ever furnished to any customer, relating in any way to alteration of the handling or driving characteristics of the vehicle (including, but not limited to, its propensity to roll over) as a result of modification of vehicle height.

By her Attorneys,

By: _____ /s/ Carol Coblentz _____
Carol Coblentz (BBO#304321)
Needham, Shaker and Coblentz
44 Park Place
Boston, MA 02100
(617) 555-5555

Dated: /d/

COMMONWEALTH OF MASSACHUSETTS

MIDDLESEX, SS

SUPERIOR COURT DEPARTMENT OF THE TRIAL COURT CIVIL ACTION NO. 20-6144

NANCY CARPENTER, As Administratrix of the Estate of Charles Carpenter,
    Plaintiff

    vs.

RANDALL DEE; PETER DEE; ULTIMATE AUTO, INC.; and CITY OF LOWELL,
    Defendants.

RESPONSE OF DEFENDANT ULTIMATE AUTO, INC. TO PLAINTIFF'S REQUEST FOR PRODUCTION OF DOCUMENTS

1. Catalogue and specification sheet to be produced.

2. Manufacturer's brochure to be produced.

3. Registry of Motor Vehicle regulation to be produced.

4. The defendant has no such documents in his possession, custody, or control other than the documents produced in response to requests no. 1 and 2.

5. The defendant has no such documents in his possession, custody, or control.

6. The defendant has no such documents in his possession, custody, or control.

7. The defendant has no such documents in his possession, custody, or control.

8. The defendant, by its attorney, objects to this request on the grounds that it is vague and does not specify with particularity the documents sought.

9. Insurance policy to be produced.

10. The defendant has no such documents in his possession, custody, or control.

11. The defendant has no such documents in his possession, custody, or control.

By its Attorneys,

_____ /s/ Bertram Cohen _____
Bertram Cohen (BBO#641311)
Roth, McKnight & Zimmerman
111 Milk Street
Boston, MA 02100
(617) 555-0000

Dated: /d/

COMMONWEALTH OF MASSACHUSETTS

MIDDLESEX, SS

SUPERIOR COURT DEPARTMENT OF THE TRIAL COURT CIVIL ACTION NO. 20-6144

NANCY CARPENTER, As
Administratrix of the Estate of
Charles Carpenter,
    Plaintiff

        vs.

RANDALL DEE; PETER DEE;
ULTIMATE AUTO, INC.; and
CITY OF LOWELL,
    Defendants.

ANSWERS OF DEFENDANT ULTIMATE AUTO, INC. TO PLAINTIFF'S INTERROGATORIES

1. Please identify yourself by stating your full name, residential address, business address, employer, occupation and job title.*

Adam Jenkins, 11 Weeping Willow Road, Lexington, MA, President of Ultimate Auto, Inc.

2. Before proceeding further, please consult with all necessary persons, and review all necessary documents, to answer the remaining interrogatories. Have you done so?

Yes.

3. If you are a member of any trade associations, related in any way in whole or in part to the design, manufacture, sale, or use of automotive parts, which have the purpose or effect of modifying the height of vehicles, please identify all such organizations including: (a) name; (b) address; (c) inclusive dates of your membership; and (d) the name of any publications which you regularly receive from such organizations.

Specialty Equipment Manufacturers Associations.

4. Were you, or anyone employed by your company, aware of the existence of Massachusetts General Laws ch. 90 section 7P. Unless the answer is in the unqualified negative, kindly state the name, residential address and position with your company of all persons who were so aware.

Yes. Cecil Sylvester.

---

*Eds.' Note: The local rules of many courts require that answers to interrogatories also contain the questions being answered. This makes it easier for judges and lawyers to comprehend and use the answers.

5. If you expect to call any person as an expert witness at the trial of this case, kindly state (a) the name and address of each person whom you expect to call as an expert witness at trial; (b) the subject matter on which each person whom you expect to call as an expert witness at trial is expected to testify, and his qualifications as an expert in that area; (c) the substance of the facts and opinions to which each expert is expected to testify and a summary of the grounds for each such opinion; and (d) the formal education (including the college and postgraduate education) of each such expert, each job or position such person has held in his area of expertise and the dates of such employment, membership in professional societies of each such expert, and identify all publications of each such subject in his field of expertise.

Unknown at the present time.

6. With respect to any primary or excess liability insurance applicable to the plaintiff's claim, please state the insurer, effective dates of the policy, and applicable coverage limits.

$500,000/$500,000 single limit bodily injury coverage, The Travelers Insurance Company, effective on the date of the loss alleged in the plaintiff's complaint.

7. Please identify all automotive parts ever purchased by the defendant, Randall Dee, at your company, including the exact description of such parts, date of purchase, and purchase price.

It is unknown what, if any, automotive parts were ever purchased by Randall Dee from Ultimate Auto. This question is presently being investigated by my attorney in connection with discovery in this action.

8. If you provided Randall Dee with any oral or written warning or instruction, relating in any way to change in the driving characteristics of modified vehicles (including, but not limited to, an increased propensity to roll over) please state (a) the exact content of such warning; (b) the date; and (c) the person or persons who gave such warning or instruction.

It is unknown what, if any, instructions were ever provided to Randall Dee by Ultimate Auto. This question is presently being investigated by my attorney in this action.

9. Are you, or is anyone in your company, aware that Monster Tire's 38 inch "Monster Mudder" tires (hereinafter "the Monster Tires") if mounted on a 1986 Jeep CJ7 (with necessary modifications to allow the mounting of such tires) could alter the driving and handling characteristics of the vehicle? Unless the answer is in the unqualified negative, kindly state (a) when you first became aware of this; (b) the name, address, and company position of all persons with

such awareness; and (c) in as much detail as possible, please describe what characteristics you were aware could be affected.

The defendant, by his attorney, objects to this interrogatory on the grounds that it is not clear what modifications are included in the term "necessary." Without waiving this objection the defendant states that both at, and after, the date of the accident, alleged in the plaintiff's complaint Adam Jenkins was aware that any modification to the center of gravity of a vehicle by the addition of tires could, depending on the vehicle, and other variables, affect the handling of the vehicle.

10. Are you, or is anyone in your company, aware that Rodeo Suspension lift kits, if mounted on a 1986 Jeep CJ7 could alter the driving and handling characteristics of the vehicle. Unless the answer is in the unqualified negative, kindly state (a) when you first became aware of this; (b) the name, address, and company position of all persons with such awareness; and (c) in as much detail as possible, please describe what characteristics you were aware could be affected.

No.

11. If you have ever received any claim or lawsuit, relating in any way to a vehicle rolling over, after the installation of any parts (including, but not limited to suspension lift kits and tires) purchased at your company, please state as to each such claim or lawsuit (a) the name of the person or persons involved in such claim or lawsuit; (b) name of plaintiff's attorney, if any; (c) date of receipt of the claim or lawsuit; (d) date of the incident; (e) the current status of such claim or lawsuit; and (f) the court, caption, and docket number of each such claim which resulted in litigation.

Not applicable.

12. Please identify the officers, directors, agent, servant, or employee of the defendant with the most knowledge as to each of the following topics, including such individuals' full name, residential address, business address and position; (a) training of your company's sales personnel; (b) warnings or instructions issued to customers with regard to changes in handling or driving characteristics as a result of altering the height of a vehicle; and (c) the status of any claims or lawsuits described in Interrogatory No. 11 above.

Cecil Sylvester.

Signed under the pains and penalties of perjury
ULTIMATE AUTO, INC.

By: _____ /s/ Adam Jenkins _____
Adam Jenkins

COMMONWEALTH OF MASSACHUSETTS

MIDDLESEX, SS	SUPERIOR COURT DEPARTMENT OF THE TRIAL COURT CIVIL ACTION NO. 20-6144
NANCY CARPENTER, As Administratrix of the Estate of Charles Carpenter, Plaintiff	TRANSCRIPT OF DEPOSITION OF DEFENDANT RANDALL DEE
vs.	
RANDALL DEE; PETER DEE; ULTIMATE AUTO, INC.; and CITY OF LOWELL, Defendants.	

Deposition of Randall Dee, taken on behalf of the Plaintiff, pursuant to Notice under the applicable Rules of the Massachusetts Rules of Civil Procedure, before Rochelle D. Baron, a Shorthand Reporter and Notary Public in and for the Commonwealth of Massachusetts, at the Offices of Needham, Shaker & Coblentz on Thursday, xxxxx, xx,* commencing at 10:30 A.M.

APPEARANCES
    ROSEMARY NEEDHAM, ESQ. and CAROL COBLENTZ, ESQ., For Plaintiff.
    GWENDOLYN FRANCIS, ESQ., For Defendant Randall Dee.
    BERTRAM COHEN, ESQ., For Defendant Ultimate Auto, Inc.
    CAITLIN TALBOT, ESQ., For Defendant City of Lowell.
. . .

Eds.' Note: In the actual case, this deposition was taken six months after the complaint was filed and prior to the addition of Ultimate Auto, Inc. and the City of Lowell as defendants.

MS. COBLENTZ: Let me propose the following stipulations. The witness will read and sign the deposition. We will waive the notarization, sealing and filing; reserve all objections, except as to form, and reserve all motions to strike, except as to form.

RANDALL DEE, a witness called by the plaintiff, having been first duly sworn, was examined and testified as follows:

DIRECT EXAMINATION BY *MS. COBLENTZ:* Mr. Dee, my name is Carol Coblentz. I represent the plaintiff in this action. I'm going to be asking you a series of questions. It is not my intent to trick you in any way. If you, therefore, don't understand a question or it's unclear to you, please let me know, and I'll rephrase it or repeat it. And if you don't ask me to do that, I will assume you understand it.

If you hear an objection from your attorney, you go ahead and answer unless I instruct you not to answer. And if you want a break at any time, just let me know about that as well. Would you state your name, please?

A: Randall Dee

Q: Where do you live, sir?

A: 91 Birch Hill Road, Lowell.

Q: And how long have you lived at that house?

A: Twenty-five years.

Q: And that's the house that you grew up in that your parents owned?

A: Yes.

Q: What's your Social Security number?

A: I'm not—I don't know it by heart.

Q: Do you have a driver's license with you today?

A: Yes.

Q: Is this your driver's license?

A: Yes.

Q: And is your Social Security number on your driver's license as well?

A: Yes.

Q: Mr. Dee, are your parents both deceased?

A: Yes.

Q: And what were their names?

A: Dorothy Dee and Richard Dee.

Q: And do you know approximately when they purchased the house that you live in now, approximately?

A: Twenty-five years ago—about twenty-five years ago.

[We have omitted three pages of deposition regarding the transfer of the Dee house to Randall and his three siblings.]

Q: Mr. Dee, tell me when you first got your driver's license, approximately.

A: Five years ago.

Q: And what's your current age?

A: Twenty-five.

Q: So it was several years after you were first entitled to apply that you got it.

A: Yes. I think it was about—it might have been two years after or—I'm not sure. I forget. I think I might have been nineteen.

Q: Did you take driver's education in school?

A: No.

Q: Did you graduate from high school?

A: Yes.

Q: Lowell?

A: Lowell Vocational High School.

Q: And what course did you take there?

A: Auto body.

Q: And you are presently employed?

A: Yes.

Q: By whom?

A: Raytheon of Waltham.

Q: And what do you do, sir?

A: I am a plater, metal finisher.

Q: And how long have you been at Raytheon?

A: Four years.

Q: And your present rate of pay is what?

A: What do you mean?

Q: Are you paid on an hourly basis?

A: Yes.

Q: What do you make an hour?

A: I think it's around $17 or something.

Q: And you work a forty-hour week?

A: Yes.

Q: Do you get overtime as well?

A: Very little but I do.

Q: And that's time and a half?

A: Yes.

Q: Did you take driving instruction from anyone?

A: No.

Q: Just kind of learned O.J.T., as they say?

A: Yes.

Q: Have you ever held a job in which driving was a part of your duties?

A: No.

Q: What was the first car that you owned?

A: I never owned a car. I had never actually owned a car.

Q: The jeep that you were driving at the time of this accident was registered to whom?

A: Twyla Burrell.

Q: And Burrell was an old girlfriend of yours?

A: Yes.

Q: And did you, in fact, live with her at some time?

A: Yes.

Q: Was her legal address 91 Birch Hill Road?

A: For a while before the accident.

Q: Now, when did you and she stop living together, approximately?

A: I'm not—

Q: It was before the accident?

A: Yes.

Q: A year or so before, something like that?

A: Yes.

Q: When was that vehicle purchased by Twyla Burrell?

A: Would have to be around 2017 or 2018, I'd say.

Q: And it was a 1986 Jeep CJ-7?

A: Yes.

Q: Where was it purchased from?

A: Some car auction, I think, in Concord maybe.

[We have omitted the portion of the deposition regarding Randall's acquisition of the jeep from Twyla Burrell.]

Q: Can you help me at all in terms of the specific date when the jeep was purchased?

A: I'm not too sure. It had to be late 2017 maybe. I could find out, but I'm not too sure.

Q: Now, were any modifications made to the jeep?

A: Yes.

Q: I want to talk about those in as much detail as we can and to talk about each of them separately. First of all, let me start with tires. When the jeep was purchased, what kind of tires did it have, if you know?

A: It had stock tires.

Q: And do you know the size of those tires?

A: Fifteen-inch.

Q: Would that be stock for a Jeep CJ-7?

A: Yes.

Q: At some point, much larger tires were put on, is that right?

A: Yes.

Q: Were the stock tires that were on it in good condition?

A: No. They were worn out.

Q: So they needed to be replaced anyway.

A: Yes.

Q: Did you immediately replace them with larger tires?

A: I had to lift the jeep before I could put the bigger tires on.

Q: And when you say "lift the jeep," you mean raise the suspension?

A: Yes.

Q: And we'll get to that. When and where did you purchase the larger tires?

A: I purchased them at Ultimate Auto, Inc.

Q: And these tires are called Monster Tires, is that right?

A: Yes.

Q: Is that a brand name, or do you know what the brand was?

A: That may be the brand. Though it might be technically something else.

Q: And what size tires were these?

A: They were 40 inch, 15's but 40 inch.

Q: In other words, the inner radius—

A: The rim was 15-inch rim.

Q: Fifteen-inch rim which is the same as the stock rim?

A: Yes.

Q: But the diameter of the tire is much larger.

A: Yes.

Q: And is 40-inch the diameter of the tire?

A: Yes.

Q: So it's over three feet. And the suspension needs to be raised to accommodate that.

A: Yes.

Q: Had you previously raised the suspension before you purchased the tires?

A: Yes.

Q: And tell me what you did to do that.

A: Well, I bought a lift kit, a suspension—a suspension lift kit from the same place, Ultimate Auto and then I—and that raised it, I think, 3 inches—

Q: The lift kit alone raised it 3 inches.

A: —and stiffened up the suspension. And then I raised the body from the frame 4 inches with spaces underneath the body of the jeep to the frame and that gave—

Q: So that was a total of 7 inches—

A: Yes.

Q: —which gave you enough clearance to fit the tires.

A: Fit the tires.

Q: And now, having raised it 7 inches, could the car then work? I mean I understand it would have looked silly. Would it have worked on stock tires?

A: Yes.

Q: And if it had stock tires, say, at the roof line, it still would have been 7 inches higher.

A: Yes.

Q: And with the Monster Tires, how much additional height was added?

A: It probably raised a foot?

Q: So that overall, it had been lifted as much as 1 foot 7 inches, am I right?

A: Approximately.

Q: What I want to do, Mr. Dee, is go into this in detail, and you have to bear with me because I'm not an auto mechanic. And I want to understand it as much as I can.

MS. FRANCIS: Can I just interject. I don't think there's anything to show that there's actual figures or that this is on his own estimate. I understand you've given us your best judgment about the height, and I understand you haven't measured them to the fraction of an inch.

A: Yes.

Q: Did you purchase the lift kit at the same time as you purchased tires to raise the body? Was that all done at the same time?

A: What do you mean?

Q: Okay. The lift kit contained some specific materials that are used to raise the suspension.

A: Are we talking about now the suspension or the body?

Q: The suspension.

A: They're just springs that are arced greater than a stock spring, and that's what gives you the lift.

Q: And you also purchased a kind of rubber disc as a spacer.

A: Not for the suspension; that's for the body.

Q: Did you do the work yourself?

A: Yes.

Q: Did anyone help you?

A: Charlie did a little bit, but it was mostly me.

Q: Charlie Carpenter?

A: Yes.

Q: Where did you do the work?

A: I did it in my backyard, my driveway.

Q: Did you need a lift to do any of this work?

A: Just a floor jack.

Q: And how long did it take you to do that work?

A: A couple of months, two months.

Q: Let's start by having you describe for me what parts you purchased from Ultimate Auto.

A: Okay. I purchased the Monster Tires, right—

Q: Four of them?

A: Four of them, yes—and—

Q: What was the cost of those? [Discussion off the record.]

Q: Is it your best memory that the tires were $500 each?

A: No. The tires were almost $400 each and the rims were maybe $60 each for a rim. So four—four rims was $250 and the tires were $400 each.

Q: So that's two thousand.

A: Yes, plus the tax or whatever. It came to roughly—I guess I got the receipt—$2400. Gee, and if I had gone to New Hampshire, I would have saved the tax.

Q: So it was about $2000 just for the tires and rims?

A: Yes.

Q: And with tax, excise tax and so forth.

A: Yes.

Q: Am I correct that you purchased those after you had already done the work to lift the car?

A: Yes.

Q: So the first thing you purchased was what?

A: The leaf spring, the suspension lift at Ultimate Auto.

MS. COBLENTZ: I have a pretty good idea what a leaf spring looks like but let's go off the record a minute. [Discussion off the record.]

Q: We're to do this by drawing of words as opposed to pictures.

A: Yes.

Q: The first thing that you did was you replaced the stock leaf spring with a more arced spring.

A: Yes.

Q: And the upper part of the spring connects to the frame of the jeep and the lower part connects to the axle.

A: Right.

Q: So that by increasing the arc, it has the effect of raising the frame relative to the axle, is that correct?

A: Yes.

Q: And the stiffer and more arced spring raises the frame relative to the axle by how much, approximately?

A: I think it was a 3-inch, 2-inch it says on the—2-inch suspension lift they call it.

Q: So there is a box that calls it a 2-inch lift.

A: Yes, Rodeo is the name.

Q: Rodeo?

A: Yes.

Q: Do you, by any chance, have any of the boxes or any of the instructions for that equipment?

A: Probably not.

Q: But it was called Rodeo?

A: Yes.

Q: And this was purchased at Ultimate Auto?

A: Yes.

Q: Now, did you purchase the body lift materials at the same time?

A: No.

Q: Did you buy four springs?

A: Yes.

Q: And what was the cost, approximately?

A: I think it cost between $400 and $500.

Q: So about $100 or $125 per spring, correct?

A: About that.

Q: Was that the first thing you purchased to do the modification?

A: Yes.

Q: And then at a subsequent time, you purchased the kit to lift the body relative to the frame.

A: Yes.

Q: And what is that called?

A: It's called a body lift.

Q: And is the term "hockey puck" sometimes used to describe that?

A: Well, what happened is I called Crazy Larry's, a place where they sell body lifts. I called the place to purchase it, and they—I don't know who the guy was, but he said, "Everybody's using hockey pucks. It's the hardest rubber in the world." He was buying hockey pucks and using them as body lifts so that's what I did. I went out and I bought a bunch of hockey pucks.

Q: An actual hockey puck in a sporting goods store?

A: Yes.

Q: Do you know where you bought them?

A: City Sports in Waltham.

Q: So you literally used hockey pucks.

A: Yes.

Q: Did you get this advice over the phone?

A: Yes.

Q: From Crazy Larry's?

A: Yes.

Q: Who gave you the advice about the body lifts?

A: I don't remember who it was because I was calling around a bunch of places looking for a body lift.

Q: Did Ultimate Auto sell body lifts?

A: Yes everybody did.

Q: Do you have any way of remembering who you talked to there?

A: No, no. I called so many locations. I forget who told me. I'm not too sure who said, but he said everybody's using hockey pucks so—

Q: Do you know what that body lift kit looks like?

A: Yes.

Q: Does it, in fact, consist of a rubber—

A: They are spacers; they're round; some are made out of aluminum; some are made out of steel. And they're just round pieces of metal with a hole through the middle. You just put—you just lift the body a little from the frame and fill it in and put body bolts back in.

Q: So it's just a cylinder really.

A: That's all.

Q: Okay. And does Ultimate Auto specialize in conversion of vehicles?

A: I don't know if—they don't do it themselves. They sell the parts, but they don't actually do any of the work.

Q: And they sell racing tires and so forth.

A: They sell everything.

Q: So it's a specialty store—

A: Yes.

Q: —for people who want to modify cars either in terms of racing them or speeding them up or things of that sort.

A: Or four-wheeling.

Q: Or four-wheeling. Now, when you bought the hockey pucks, what did you do, did you drill out a hole in them?

A: Yes.

Q: And you pile—

A: Four on—

Q: —four on top of each other.

A: Yes.

Q: So let's say a hockey puck's about an inch and a half thick.

A: No, an inch thick.

Q: So that raised it 4 inches.

A: Yes.

Q: When you purchased the hockey pucks, did you, by any chance, tell City Sports what you were going to use them for?

A: No. I told them I owned a hockey team.

Q: So you bought sixteen pucks.

A: I bought about fifty of them.

Q: Fifty of them?

A: Sure.

Q: Because they wear out?

A: No. You got—

Q: I thought you said four on each wheel.

A: No. We're talking about the body now. From the frame, you got—you got about twelve mount—twelve spots where the body bolts to the frame so you got to put four, four, four, and four.

Q: So at every point where the body bolts to the frame you put four hockey pucks as a spacer.

A: Yes.

Q: Is that something you had heard about before, the use—

A: Everybody was doing it.

Q: —the use of hockey pucks?

A: Everybody was doing it. They were cheaper, for one thing. And you are better off having rubber in between to absorb the shock rather than metal, metal to metal.

Everybody was using the hockey pucks.

MS. COBLENTZ: Off the record.

[Discussion off the record.]

Q: And then after you did that, you then went back and purchased the Monster Tires.

A: Yes.

Q: Do you remember the names of the persons you dealt with at Ultimate Auto?

A: No. They changed. He never gets the same salesmen. They come and go at that place. I wouldn't remember.

Q: Is the place still in existence?

A: Yes.

Q: Are Monster Tire tires designed specifically for jeeps?

A: No.

MS. FRANCIS: I don't know if he'd know that information anyway.

Q: If you know. Are they made for four-wheel-drive vehicles?

A: They're made for anything, any type of vehicle.

Q: Are they designed for off-road use?

A: Yes.

Q: They're pretty knobby?

A: Yes.

Q: But they will also operate on the road?

A: Yes.

Q: And I am correct that with a tire of that size that you would be unable to accommodate it without doing both the suspension lift and the body lift?

A: Yes.

Q: Had you ever had prior experience modifying vehicles?

A: No.

Q: Did you teach yourself to do this?

A: Yes.

Q: Did you use any printed materials to learn how to do it?

A: No. I looked in books, but like Off Road magazine or something. It was a fad. Everybody was lifting.

Q: Did you subscribe to any of those magazines?

A: No.

Q: You   just   purchased   them someplace?

A: Yes.

Q: Do you know the name of any specific ones that you used?

A: Magazine?

Q: Yes.

A: Off Road, I think it's called.

Q: Did you use an article in Off Road as a kind of "how to" or a manual to help you do this?

A: No.

Q: Had you gotten any instruction in this during your high school vocational training?

A: No.

Q: I take it that from a mechanical point of view it wasn't terribly complicated.

A: No.

Q: Now, did you ever learn in high school or from any source that jeeps were known to have a rollover problem?

A: Yes.

Q: And   where   did   you   first learn that?

A: I think I seen it on the TV, 20/20.

Q: On 20/20 or Sixty Minutes?

A: Something like that there was an article.

Q: Was that before this accident, if you know?

A: I think it was after. I'm not sure.

Q: Did you know at the time when you made the modifications that raising the height of a vehicle can affect its handling characteristics?

A: Yes.

Q: And did you know that raising the height of a vehicle can, among other things, affect its propensity to roll over?

A: I didn't know. I figured it would make it better because the tires were heavier. You got heavy tires at the bottom. Now you got more weight at the bottom of the vehicle now than the top so I figured it would roll less.

Q: You actually thought it would roll less because of the weight of the tires—

A: Yes.

Q: —even though the overall height was raised as much as it was?

A: Yes.

Q: When you purchased the Monster Tires at Ultimate Auto did the salesman give you any instructions concerning their use?

A: No.

Q: Did he tell you about anything to watch out for?

A: No.

Q: Did he ask you what vehicle you were putting them on?

A: No.

Q: Just sold them to you?

A: That's all.

Q: You paid the money and they went out.

A: You got it, right, yes.

Q: Same question with respect to the suspension raiser, suspension lift kit, did you get any warnings or instructions when you purchased that?

A: No, no.

Q: And were there any questions about what use you were going to put these parts to?

A: What do you mean, any questions?

Q: Did he give you any instructions?

A: Oh, the same man?

Q: Yes, the same man.

A: No, they just hand them to you and you give them the money.

Q: Were there any warnings or instructions in the suspension lift kits concerning their use?

A: Not that I know of. I didn't see any.

Q: I may have asked you and I forgot the answer, the manufacturer of the Monster Tires?

A: I think that's their name.

Q: Do they make other kinds of tires? It's not a name that's familiar to me.

A: I'm not too sure. It's not a familiar name. I'm not sure if that's all they make.

Q: Are these tires still on the car?

A: Yes.

Q: And the car is where?

A: It's in my driveway.

Q: And you know that you're not allowed to modify it.

A: I don't even think—it's rotting there.

Q: Did you do maintenance work on the jeep yourself?

A: Yes.

Q: Did you ever have maintenance work on it performed anywhere else?

A: No.

Q: Did you do all the work on it yourself?

A: Yes.

Q: Do you remember any of the maintenance you did on it?

A: Changed the oil, spark plugs.

Q: Did you do any engine work on it at all?

A: No. It's basically stock. I put a header on it, but other than that, it was all stock.

Q: So, to the best of your judgment, that car never saw the inside of an auto mechanic's door after you got it.

A: No.

Q: Do you remember where the vehicle was inspected?

A: Yes.

Q: Where was that?

A: McGill's.

Q: If I suggest to you December of 2018, does that sound about right as the last inspection?

A: I can't recall.

Q: But you know that it was inspected prior to the accident.

A: Yes.

Q: Now, by December 2018, had the modifications all been done?

A: That means before it's been inspected, you mean?

Q: Yes.

A: Oh, yes.

Q: So if, in fact, it was inspected in December of 2018, the inspector was looking at a very modified vehicle, correct—

A: Yes.

Q: —and with all of the modifications we've talked about.

A: Yes.

Q: I'd just like to talk about your driving history. You indicated that you started driving, you thought, about age nineteen, approximately.

A: I think it was nineteen.

Q: Prior to this accident, were you charged with any motor vehicle violations, excluding parking.

A: Yes.

Q: And I'd like to talk about them in order, starting with the earliest that you can recall.

A: Let me think. I think the only one was drunk driving.

Q: And do you recall when that was?

MS. FRANCIS: Approximate time.

A: I forget.

MS. FRANCIS: Do you want to go off the record to refresh your recollection?

[Discussion off the record.]

Q: I have some information suggesting that in April of 2019 you were charged with driving under the influence. Does that sound correct?

A: Yes.

Q: Do you know any of the officers involved?

A: Yes.

Q: And who were they? I'm talking about that stop now.

A: With the drunk driving?

Q: Drunk driving, right.

MS. FRANCIS: Do you want to go off the record to refresh your recollection?

A: Ricky Murdoch, the officer was Ricky Murdoch.

Q: M-U-R-D-O-C-H?

A: That's close enough.

Q: Do you know any other of the officers involved with that?

A: No.

Q: Were you driving the jeep at that time?

A: Yes.

Q: And it had, of course, been modified?

A: Yes.

Q: Did the officers at that time make any comments to you about the jeep?

A: No.

Q: What was the outcome of that charge?

A: What did they do to me?

Q: Yes.

A: I was found guilty of DWI and I lost my license—loss of license for thirty days, and I had to go to school, drunk driving school, for so many hours. I'm not sure how many hours.

Q: Now, when your license is pulled, do you physically give up your license?

A: Yes.

Q: You hand it, what, to the clerk or something in court?

A: Yes.

Q: And then you get it back later?

A: In thirty days from the date you give it to them, they'll give it back to you providing you go to that—

Q: Now, as I understand it, at the time of this accident, you didn't have your license in your possession, is that correct?

A: Yes.

Q: Am I correct?

A: Yes.

Q: But you did, in fact, have a license at that time.

A: Yes.

Q: It had been returned?

A: Oh, are we talking about—

Q: At the time of this accident that we're here for.

A: I didn't have it on me, but I did have a license.

Q: You mentioned another incident. There was something about there not being a side mirror.

A: Well, I was never cited for that.

Q: But were you pulled over for it?

A: Yes.

Q: Do you know the name of the officer who did that?

A: No.

Q: But it was a uniformed Lowell police officer?

A: Yes.

Q: And when was that, first of all?

A: It was prior to the accident. I'm not too sure.

Q: Was it prior to the drunk driving charge?

A: Yes.

Q: Was it in 2018?

A: Yes.

Q: So it was—and so at that time, the vehicle had been modified again.

A: Yes.

Q: And could you tell me what the officer said?

A: He told me to—he told me—he said, "Take the vehicle home and don't take it back out on the road till you get a mirror on it, a rear view mirror." So I took it home and I put a mirror on it.

Q: You're talking about a side mirror—

A: Yes.

Q: —not the inner rear view mirror.

A: No.

Q: The driver's side mirror.

A: Yes.

Q: And you did that?

A: Yes.

Q: And did that officer make any comment on the height of the vehicle or anything related to its height?

A: No.

Q: And again, that was in 2018?

A: Yes.

Q: Now, were there any other motor vehicle violations; that you have had up to this accident?

A: Yes.

Q: And what was that?

A: I was pulled over for being unregistered, uninsured in that jeep. What happened is it was insured, but the little sticker that goes on your plate there—you know how they send you a card, renewal-registration renewal, well, either I never got the card or something so I didn't notice that little sticker had expired. So I was pulled over in that jeep. They towed the vehicle, and they cited me for unregistered, uninsured.

Q: And when was that?

A: That was prior to the accident. It could have been in 2008 or 2009.

Q: You mean 2018.

A: I'm sorry, 2018.

Q: But it was after the vehicle had been modified.

A: Yes.

Q: Am I correct that you did the modification fairly shortly after you got the jeep?

A: Yes.

Q: So let me recap. On at least three occasions prior to the accident this vehicle, in its modified form, came under the scrutiny of the Lowell Police Department.

A: Yes.

Q: And on none of those occasions did the police officers comment to you at all about its height, am I correct?

A: Yes.

Q: Was there any court appearance involved with that unregistered, uninsured charge?

A: Yes.

Q: What was the outcome of that?

A: I proved that it was insured. I brought in proof that it was insured so he dismissed that charge, but he did fine me for being unregistered, and that's it.

Q: So, in fact, for whatever reason, you couldn't show that the car was registered.

A: It had expired.

Q: It had expired.

A: But it was insured.

Q: Okay. Were you fined?

A: Yes.

Q: So presumably there are court records relating to that.

A: Yes.

Q: Who was your insurance agent?

A: I don't remember.

Q: Is the jeep insured now?

A: No.

Q: Is it in a driveable condition?

A: No.

Q: Because?

A: The windshield broke, it's missing the hood and fender.

Q: So it hasn't been driven since the day of the accident.

A: No.

Q: How did it get from the accident site back to you house?

A: Towed.

Q: Do you know who towed it?

A: McGill's.

Q: Do you know how it was towed?

A: Just a normal—

Q: Was it dollied?

A: No. It was just towed, lift the front end.

Q: Towed on the rear wheels?

A: Yes.

Q: I'd like to turn to the happening of the accident itself. The date of

Q: the accident, sir, was what, do you recall?

A: August, 2019.

MS. COBLENTZ: Off the record.
    [Discussion off the record.]

Q: What day of the week was that, do you know?

A: Saturday.

Q: And what did you do that morning?

A: What did I do?

Q: Yes.

A: I got up—

Q: Do you remember anything special about the day?

A: No, just regular day.

Q: Did you have plans for the day?

A: Well, it was my brother's birthday.

Q: Peter's?

A: Yes. They invited a few friends over to his girlfriend's house. It was a hot day. She has a pool in the backyard, which is about a hundred—a hundred feet away from the accident where she lives.

Q: And her name is what?

A: Keisha Marcus-Jackson.

Q: How do you spell that?

A: K-E-I-S-H-A, M-A-R-C-U-S-J-A-C-K-S-O-N.

MS. COBLENTZ: Off the record.
    [Discussion off the record.]

Q: Does she still live there?

A: Yes.

Q: Do you know the address?

A: No.

Q: Does your brother still go out with her?

A: Yes.

Q: Who was present at the party?

A: There was myself, my wife, my brother, his girlfriend Keisha, her mother—was that—her brother-in-law with his two children.

Q: What's his name?

A: Stony; that's his last name, Stony. I'm not sure of his first name.

Q: And she has been here with us today.

A: Yes.

Q: When were you married?

A: [No response.]

Q: Nobody ever remembers that. Don't feel bad.

A: That's a toughie.

Q: Were you married at the time of this accident?

A: No.

Q: I should never have asked.

A: I'm in trouble now.

Q: It's just the pressure of the occasion. When did you arrive at the party?

A: I'd say around 4:30 or 5.

Q: And was Charlie invited to the party?

A: Yes.

Q: Did you invite him?

A: No, my brother did.

Q: Was Charlie more your friend or your brother's friend?

A: He was both.

Q: And you had known him for a long time?

A: Oh, yes. We were like brothers.

Q: Did Charlie arrive separately from you?

A: Yes.

Q: How did he get to the party?

A: His car.

Q: And what kind of car did he have?

A: I think he had a green Mustang.

Q: How long were you at the party?

A: About an hour before he came.

Q: You were there an hour before Charlie came?

A: About that.

Q: So Charlie would have come around 5:30 or so.

A: Yes.

Q: Was this party for a dinner?

A: It was a cookout, barbecue, whatever.

Q: And did you, in fact, have dinner?

A: Yes.

Q: Was there any alcohol served at this party?

A: There was beer.

Q: Did you have beer?

A: No.

Q: You had none?

A: No.

Q: How do you remember that?

A: I just was—just didn't drink. I wasn't drinking that day, I remember.

Q: How much did you drink then? Did you have an occasional beer?

A: That's all; on the weekends, maybe a Saturday.

Q: Have you ever had any kind of drinking problem?

A: No.

Q: Did Charlie have anything to drink?

A: I don't know.

Q: What time did you leave the party?

A: Let's see. I'd say around 6:30-7 or—we were just leaving to get our bathing suits to go swimming, me and Charlie.

Q: Were you going to go back to each of your houses to get suits?

A: Yes.

Q: And where were you on your way first, to your house or his?

A: Probably his; his was—let me think—yes, his house would be closer.

[Discussion off the record.]

Q: And the accident happened at the corner of Palmer and Franklin, is that right?

A: Yes.

Q: I'd like you to draw, just if you could, a little map showing the path from the party to where the accident happened.

A: Okay.
[Witness drawing.]

MS. FRANCIS: May I just inquire, are you intending to use this for future reference, this sketch, or is it just for questions?

MS. COBLENTZ: Well, I'll mark it.

MS. FRANCIS: Of course, it's completely out of scale.

MS. COBLENTZ: I want to get the relationship of one street to the other.

THE WITNESS: I'm not too sure of the spelling or whatever, but I think that's how it was, basically.

MS. COBLENTZ: Let me mark this sketch as the next exhibit.
[A sketch drawn by the witness was marked as Exhibit No. 4 for identification.]

Q: Exhibit 4 is your sketch indicating the house where—

A: Yes.

Q: And the accident happened in the course of the left turn onto Franklin Street; is that correct?

A: Yes.

Q: Now, before we get into that, in previous occasions when you had driven the vehicle, had there been any time when you felt it leaning or starting to roll over?

A: No.

Q: Had you driven it off the road at all?

A: Very little, a few times.

Q: Where did you drive it off road?

A: Prospect Hill.

Q: Prospect Hill in Waltham?

A: Yes.

Q: Did you drive up the hill there or just kind of around those grounds there?

A: Around the grounds.

Q: Had you ever driven it off road under conditions where you had any real need for the extra clearance that all the modifications had given you?

A: Yes.

Q: And are there, for example, rocks and boulders there that you need to clear?

A: There's rocks and boulders and muddy, and I took it up there in the snow. And you need the clearance or you'd get hung up in the snow. You know what I mean, you'd actually be stuck in the snow if you weren't that high.

Q: But the primary use that you made of the vehicle was on the road?

A: Yes.

Q: Now, is Palmer and Franklin a regulated intersection? Is there a stop sign or traffic light there?

A: No traffic light; I think there's a stop sign. I'm not sure, but not— I didn't have a stop sign. I think there is the stop sign.

Q: On Franklin?

A: On Franklin.

Q: Can you give me your best estimate of your speed as you were going down Palmer Street before you got to the corner?

A: I'd say it couldn't be no more than 20 because that jeep with the big tire, I didn't change the gear ratio so it didn't have no power. It took a long time to pick up speed so I say—the distance from about a hundred yards—

Q: Do you remember what gear you were in?

A: First gear, because it was a slight climb, like I said. When I put on the big tires, it took all the power away from it.

Q: You were in first gear all that time?

A: Yes, because it's real short. I don't think I got out of first gear.

Q: Were you in first gear as you made the corner?

A: Yes.

Q: When the jeep rolled, you were in first gear?

A: I'm pretty sure.

Q: Do you remember turning the corner excessively sharply?

MS. FRANCIS: I object.

Q: Let me rephrase it. Did you turn the corner more sharply than you usually turn a corner?

A: No.

Q: Tell me exactly what happened, as you remember it.

A: I was going down Palmer Street and then that intersection or that turn, it's real sharp—no. I wouldn't say sharp. It's a real dangerous turn or something. It dips and then—it dips toward— it's—I don't know. It's a bad— everybody cuts it. No one ever takes the turn. Everybody crosses the yellow line.

Q: In other words, you cut the corner a little bit onto Franklin.

A: You have to. That's the land of—

Q: Is it, for instance, a 90-degree turn?

MS. FRANCIS: I don't think he'd have any knowledge of that.

Q: If you know.

A: I don't know.

Q: You know what I mean when I say that? Is it more than like a square corner? Are you land of doubling back when you—

A: I don't think so.

Q: Is there something about the pitch on Franklin Road *that* creates any difficulty?

A: I would say there is, but—

Q: Have you ever heard about any other accidents at that corner?

A: I seen—the bushes that I hit, a couple of—maybe a month ago, the same bushes, the exact same spot, the bushes were dug up again.

Q: Okay. I'd like you to draw another diagram for me showing the same intersection in larger scale, and I'll draw the streets.

[Ms. Coblentz draws a diagram.]

Q: This is Palmer and this is Franklin. The jeep is coming from here and making this turn [indicating], correct?

A: Okay.

Q: Right?

A: Yes.

Q: First of all, describe it in words and then we'll figure out what we want on the sketch. You indicated that you had to cut the corner crossing the yellow line as you did so.

A: Yes, very—yes.

Q: And what was the first sensation you had of any problem?

A: I didn't. It just—I don't remember.

Q: Do you remember applying the brakes?

A: Yes, I think so. It happened—you know, I'd say so fast but just—I don't remember. I tried to, you know, block it out. I just can't recall.

Q: As you think back on it, do you have a memory of the vehicle rolling?

A: Barely.

Q: And I take it rolled—if you were looking at the vehicle from behind, it rolled clockwise? In other words, it rolled toward the right?

A: It rolled toward the passenger side.

Q: Right. And do you have any sense about when it started to roll in relation to where you were, on Palmer or Franklin?

A: No.

Q: It was shortly after you had started the turn though, is that right?

A: Oh, yes.

Q: Were you pretty much onto Franklin when it began to roll?

A: I was probably right in the middle of the turn maybe.

Q: What I'd like you to draw for me, as best you can, and try to get the jeep somewhat in scale, at least relative to the intersection itself, the position of the jeep at the moment when it first seemed to begin to turn. And the way we draw cars in the law business is like this with a "V" on the front end like that.

A: And what do you want me to do?

Q: I want you to draw the position of the jeep when it first started to roll.

MS. FRANCIS: Is that what he felt?

Q: When you felt that it first started to roll, as best you can. But I just want to get some sense of where it was in relation to the intersection.

A: I'm coming down here [indicating].

Q: Down here turning onto Franklin like that?

A: And there was a house here. There was bushes here, shrubs.

Q: Why don't you draw the shrubs.

A: How do you—

Q: Just kind of a wavy line to indicate the shrubs.
[Witness complies.]

Q: Those are the shrubs on that corner?

A: I'd say right about—maybe right there.

Q: And can you draw for me the final position that the jeep was in when it came to rest?

MS. FRANCIS: Can we mark that position with some kind of letter or something?

MS. COBLENTZ: Yes.

Q: Why don't you put "1" inside that. And then draw the position of the jeep when it came to rest.

MS. FRANCIS: The location, you mean?

MS. COBLENTZ: Yes, the position.

MS. FRANCIS: Because position means situation.
[Witness complies.]

A: Something like that.

Q: So it came to rest partly on the road in these bushes.

A: Yes.

MS. FRANCIS: Can we mark that position with a "2"?

MS. COBLENTZ: Yes.

Q: Can you put a "2" on there?

[Witness complies.]

Q: And at that point, the vehicle was completely flipped over.

A: Yes.

Q: And Charlie was pinned under the roll bar?

A: Yes.

Q: Did it have the roll bar when you got it?

A: Yes.

Q: Were you thrown out of the vehicle?

A: No.

Q: Were you belted in?

A: No.

Q: You were inside the vehicle?

A: Yes. I had the steering wheel, you know, to hold me in. So when it rolled, I slid out of it, like fell out toward the passenger side.

Q: And what did you do when you got out? First of all, you were conscious.

A: Yes.

Q: Were you hurt at all?

A: Yes.

Q: How had you gotten hurt?

A: I think I banged up my knee.

Q: But you weren't seriously hurt at all?

A: No.

Q: Were there people around?

A: Yes.

Q: What's the first thing you did?

A: I checked—I looked to see where Charlie was.

Q: And you saw him pinned under the roll bar.

A: Yes.

Q: What did you do next?

A: I flipped out. I tried to push the jeep. I just didn't know what to do.

Q: Did you get some people to help you?

A: Some—somebody came over. I just—I don't remember. I know—

Q: Do you remember at some point the vehicle being pushed onto its side?

A: I don't—I'm not sure. It must have been.

Q: Do you remember it being on its side when the police arrived?

A: Yes, I think so.

Q: Do you remember having any conversation with the police that night?

A: No.

Q: What do you mean, after the accident?

A: Yes. They put me in the traffic safety van and—

MS. FRANCIS: Do you remember talking to the police was the question.

A: Yes.

MS. FRANCIS: Was that the question, just talking to the police?

MS. COBLENTZ: Yes.

Q: Well, let me ask this. At some point, you knew you were being charged with some crime.

A: Correct, yes.

Q: Were you informed of it that night?

A: No.

Q: Were you taken to the hospital?

A: Yes.

Q: Was that Lowell's Community Hospital?

A: Yes.

Q: Were you treated and released?

A: What happened is I was waiting—I was waiting to be treated and then I heard that Charlie died. I just flipped out. I refused treatment, and I just walked out of the hospital and went home.

Q: You walked home?

A: Yes.

Q: How far is that?

A: About a mile.

Q: Was the car in the two-wheel drive or four-wheel drive position?

A: Two.

Q: Did you ever use four-wheel drive on the road?

A: Only in the winter in the snow.

Q: Did you tell the police that you had some steering difficulty?

A: I thought there was, but—I'm not sure. I said something about that.

Q: Is it your belief today that there was any steering difficulty?

A: I'm still not sure. I haven't touched the jeep. I don't know.

Q: Am I correct that at the moment when the vehicle began to roll over, up to that time, you had not been aware of any steering problem?

A: No.

Q: It began to negotiate the curve and accepted steering input as you made it, right?

A: Repeat that.

Q: Yes. You turned the wheel and the vehicle responded to your turning the wheel.

A: Yes, as far as I—yes.

Q: And you're not aware of any braking problem, is that right?

A: No.

Q: Do you remember the names of the officers you spoke to that night?

A: [No response.]

A: The officers?

Q: Yes.

A: No. I have it at home.

Q: Had you ever seen either of them before?

A: No.

Q: Were you or Charlie yelling anything just prior to the accident?

A: No.

Q: Did you ever hear any information of a witness that said you were?

A: Yes.

Q: How did you hear that?

A: He said it at the probable cause hearing.

Q: And your testimony is that you were not yelling?

A: No.

Q: Were there any repairs made to the jeep after the accident?

A: No.

Q: At what time was it towed back to your house, do you know?

A: I think it was two days after. It was towed to McGill's Garage, and it was stored back there, I think, for a couple of days, And then it was towed to my house.

Q: I just want to go through the charges and what happened. You were charged with a number of different offenses as a result of this, weren't you—

A: Right.

Q: —of which the most serious, of course, was motor vehicle homicide. You were found guilty of that.

A: I think so, yes.

MS. FRANCIS: Do you recall?

Q: And do you remember what your penalty was for that?

A: Two years suspended sentence.

Q: So that the two years has now elapsed.

A: No. I think it's—I got until May, I think.

Q: And the driving to endanger was dismissed and merged into the count for motor vehicle homicide.

A: Yes.

Q: And you were found not guilty of operating after license had been revoked.

A: Yes.

Q: And you were found guilty for failing to slow at the intersection.

A: Yes.

Q: And you were found guilty of speeding, right?

A: Yes.

Q: And you were found guilty of altering the height of a motor vehicle.

A: Yes.

Q: At the time, sir, when you deeded your interest in your house to your brother, did you have any other substantial property?

A: No.

Q: So it's fair to say that the house was really your sole significant asset.

A: That's it.

Q: And what was your motor vehicle liability insurance at the time of this accident?

A: What option, you mean?

Q: Yes.

A: I think it was option 3.

Q: Do you remember how much liability coverage you had?

A: I think it was 20/25, something like that.

MS. COBLENTZ: Off the record.
   [Discussion off the record.]

Q: So you knew that you had the minimum amount of liability insurance, correct?

A: Yes.

Q: And you knew at the time, did you not, that one who negligently causes the death of another can be responsible civilly as well as criminally for that?

MS. FRANCIS: I object to that. I don't think he even has the answer to that.

MS. COBLENTZ: I think it relates.

MS. FRANCIS: He knew at which time?

MS. COBLENTZ: At the time he conveyed the house. That's what this goes to.

MS. FRANCIS: That he knew—what was the question again?

Q: At the time when you conveyed the house, you knew that someone who is negligent and causes the death of another person can be responsible to the estate of that person civilly or criminally.

A: I didn't know that.

Q: You didn't know that?

A: No.

Q: You had no concerns whatever about possibly losing an asset?

A: No. I just needed money. I didn't have nowhere to turn. I don't have any credit at all. I needed money before he'd represent me.

Q: Does Raytheon have a credit union?

A: Yes.

Q: Had you gone to the credit union?

A: No.

Q: Did you ever ask?

A: No. I didn't think they'd lend you that much money.

Q: But you didn't inquire.

A: No.

MS. COBLENTZ: I'm done.

MS. FRANCIS: I have a couple of questions.

CROSS EXAMINATION BY MS. FRANCIS

Q: Was there any damage to the jeep that you described to us?

A: Right now? From the accident, you mean?

Q: From the accident.

A: The windshield broke and the nose—the nose is crushed, like the hood and the two fenders and that's—

Q: Was it driveable after the accident?

A: I don't think so.

Q: Was there any damage to this new suspension that you installed?

A: No, not that I know of.

Q: In other words, those hockey pucks were still in place?

A: Yes.

Q: Did you have to put separate bolts that you purchased to go through the center of those hockey pucks?

A: Did I, yes.

Q: Longer ones—

A: Yes.

Q: —than were there? Were they still intact after the accident?

A: Yes, yes.

Q: And the springs that you installed, were they still intact?

A: Yes. The whole undercarriage is intact?

Q: Was there any damage to any of the parts that you installed?

A: No, nothing; It didn't roll that hard.

MS. FRANCIS: I have no further questions.

REDIRECT EXAMINATION BY MS. COBLENTZ

Q: Where did you purchase the bolts?

A: A hardware store.

Q: But you didn't get them at a specialty auto store.

A: No.

MS. COBLENTZ: That's all I have.

MS. FRANCIS: We're all set.

[Whereupon, the deposition was concluded at 12:08 P.M.]

COMMONWEALTH OF MASSACHUSETTS

MIDDLESEX, SS

SUPERIOR COURT DEPARTMENT OF
THE TRIAL COURT CIVIL ACTION NO.
20-6144

NANCY CARPENTER, As
Administratrix of the Estate of
Charles Carpenter,
   Plaintiff

     vs.

RANDALL DEE; PETER DEE;
CITY OF LOWELL,
   Defendants.
ULTIMATE AUTO, INC.,
Defendant and Third-Party
   Plaintiff

vs.

DALE MCGILL and MCGILL'S
GARAGE, INC.,
   Third-Party Defendants.

THIRD-PARTY DEFENDANT DALE
MCGILL'S AND MCGILL'S GARAGE,
INC.'S MOTION FOR SUMMARY
JUDGMENT

Now come the third-party defendants, Dale McGill and McGill's Garage, Inc., by and through counsel and move this court pursuant to Rule 56 for Summary Judgment in their behalf on the basis that there is no genuine issue of material fact as to whether the third-party defendants owed a duty to Plaintiff's decedent, rather, this is a question of law to be decided by this court, as more fully set forth in the third-party defendants' memorandum filed in support of this motion.

Third-party defendants request oral argument of this motion.

Attorney for third-party defendants,

_____ /s/ Lisa Scottoline _____
Lisa Scottoline (BBO#393689)
Scottoline & Turow
One Federal Street
Boston, MA 02100
617/555-7777

Dated: /d/

COMMONWEALTH OF MASSACHUSETTS

MIDDLESEX, SS	SUPERIOR COURT DEPARTMENT OF THE TRIAL COURT CIVIL ACTION NO. 20-6144

NANCY CARPENTER, As
Administratrix of the Estate of
Charles Carpenter,
    Plaintiff

       vs.

RANDALL DEE; PETER DEE;
CITY OF LOWELL,
    Defendants.
ULTIMATE AUTO, INC.,
    Defendant and Third-Party
    Plaintiff

       vs.

DALE MCGILL and MCGILL'S
GARAGE, INC.,
    Third-Party Defendants.

MEMORANDUM IN SUPPORT OF THIRD-PARTY DEFENDANT DALE MCGILL'S AND MCGILL'S GARAGE, INC.'S MOTION FOR SUMMARY JUDGMENT

Now come the third-party defendants, Dale McGill and McGill's Garage, Inc., and in support of their Motion for Summary Judgment, pursuant to Rule 56 state as follows:

I. INTRODUCTION

This instant action arises out of a one-vehicle auto incident where a 1986 Jeep CJ-7 (hereinafter referred to as "the jeep"), operated by defendant, Randall Dee, "rolled-over," allegedly causing the death of plaintiff's decedent, Charles Carpenter, on August 31, 2019. Some time prior to August 31, 2019, Randall Dee allegedly modified the suspension on the jeep by installing oversize tires and a suspension kit manufactured and sold by the defendant, Ultimate Auto, Inc. It is alleged by the plaintiff that Ultimate Auto was negligent when it sold the tires and suspension kit which allegedly altered the height of the jeep and affected its handling characteristics rendering it unsafe. The plaintiff sets forth various specific allegations of negligence in support of its alleged cause of action. (Plaintiff's Complaint Count IV, ¶¶ 22-25.)

Ultimate Auto later added McGill's Garage, Inc., and Dale McGill as third-party defendants demanding contribution and alleging that Dale McGill, as agent or employee, of McGill's Garage, Inc. was negligent in approving an inspection sticker on said vehicle prior to the date of the accident. At the time alleged McGill's Garage, Inc., was a duly licensed inspection station for the Commonwealth of Massachusetts and engaged, among other things, in inspecting vehicles and either passing or rejecting said vehicles in accordance with the Code of Massachusetts Regulations, 540 Mass. Regs. Code, §§ 4.00 through 4.08 then in effect.

It is alleged that a safety inspection sticker was issued by McGill's Garage, Inc., to the Dee vehicle in December 2018, several months prior to the incident in question and after Dee had altered due jeep with the tires and suspension kit purchased from Ultimate Auto.

II. ARGUMENTS AND POINTS OF LAW

Neither Dale McGill (hereinafter called "McGill") nor McGill's Garage, Inc., (hereinafter called "McGill's Garage") are liable to Ultimate Auto as joint tortfeasor for contributions to any loss proved by the plaintiff against Ultimate Auto for the reason that at the time of the alleged incident no duty was owing by either Dale McGill or McGill's Garage to the plaintiff, plaintiff's decedent, or anyone else.

Without a duty owing by McGill and/or McGill's Garage to plaintiff or plaintiff's decedent, neither McGill or McGill's Garage are liable to plaintiff or plaintiff's decedent in tort. Because neither McGill nor McGill's Garage are liable in tort to plaintiff or plaintiff's decedent, neither is a joint tortfeasor against whom contribution can be had by Ultimate Auto.

Massachusetts General Laws, Chapter 231B, Section 1(a), inserted by Stat. 1962, Chapter 730, Section 1, provides in pertinent parts: "[W]here two or more persons become jointly liable in tort for the same injury to person or property, there shall be a right of contribution among them." The language of this statute requires that the potential contributor be directly liable to the plaintiff. Without liability in tort, there is no right to contribution.

It therefore follows that only if McGill's Garage and Dale McGill are directly liable to the plaintiff's decedent can the defendant/third-party plaintiff state a claim for contribution from McGill's Garage and Dale McGill.

At the time of the alleged issuance of the inspection sticker, December 2018, McGill's Garage, and its employee McGill were required to inspect vehicles in accordance with 540 Mass. Regs. Code, §§ 4.00 through 4.08 effective March 31, 2016.*

Eds.' Note: For this exercise we have changed the effective dates of these regulations in order to make this simulation conform with the sequence of events as they occurred in the actual case.

Said regulations did not require McGill's Garage, nor McGill, as employee acting within the scope of his employment when issuing the inspection sticker, to inspect and/or reject any vehicle for alleged violations of any height or suspension alteration requirement.

Although Mass. Gen. Laws, ch. 90, § 7P may have prohibited any person from modifying or changing the height of a motor vehicle, with some exceptions, as alleged by the plaintiff, neither McGill nor McGill's Garage altered the jeep and, therefore, they were not governed by that statute in the issuance of the December 2018 inspection sticker.

As 540 Mass. Regs. Code, §§ 4.00 through 4.08 effective March 31, 2016, did not require inspection for altered height, neither McGill nor McGill's Garage had a duty to do so. In fact, pursuant to 540 Mass. Regs. Code §§ 4.00 through 4.08, neither McGill nor McGill's Garage had any right to inspect and/or reject the subject jeep as the regulations set forth those specific areas only which were governed by the inspection procedure and did not authorize any inspection station to act beyond the specific directions of the regulations.

540 Mass. Regs. Code § 4.00 effective March 31, 2016, was not amended until May 27, 2020 [the year after the accident], after the death of Charlie Carpenter and after the issuance of the sticker in question. At that time the inspection guidelines were changed to include inspection and/or rejection of certain altered height vehicles. 540 Mass. Regs. Code § 4.04(13)(a).

III. CONCLUSION

There is only a question of law before this Court; that is, whether an inspection station, in December 2018 had a duty to, through its agents and/or employees, reject a 1986 Jeep CJ-7 vehicle which had been modified with a suspension kit and tires to alter the height of the vehicle. Dispositive questions of law are properly heard on Motion for Summary Judgment. Clearly, the answer is no. 540 Mass. Regs. Code § 4.00 effective March 31, 2016, through May 27, 2020, set forth the standards for vehicle inspection and was silent as to altered height vehicles. Therefore, neither Dale McGill nor McGill's Garage through any other agent and/or employee had a duty owing to plaintiff or plaintiff's decedent relative to Dee vehicle.

Having no duty owing to the plaintiff or plaintiff's decedent, neither McGill nor McGill's Garage can be held as a joint tortfeasor with Ultimate Auto and others regarding the loss claimed by plaintiff in this action. As neither McGill nor McGill's Garage can be held as joint tortfeasor, neither can be liable to Ultimate Auto for contribution as alleged in the Third-Party Complaint.

WHEREFORE, Dale McGill and McGill's Garage, Inc., move this Court for entry of summary judgment in their respective favors and against the third-party plaintiff, Ultimate Auto, Inc.

Attorney for third-party defendants,

_____ /s/ Lisa Scottoline _____
Lisa Scottoline (BBO#393689)
Scottoline & Turow
One Federal Street
Boston, MA 02100
617/555-7777

Dated: /d/

COMMONWEALTH OF MASSACHUSETTS

MIDDLESEX, SS

SUPERIOR COURT DEPARTMENT OF
THE TRIAL COURT CIVIL ACTION NO.
20-6144

NANCY CARPENTER, As
Administratrix of the Estate
of Charles Carpenter,
   Plaintiff

      vs.

RANDALL DEE; PETER DEE;
CITY OF LOWELL,
   Defendants.

ULTIMATE AUTO, INC.,
   Defendant and Third-Party
   Plaintiff

      vs.

DALE MCGILL and
MCGILL'S GARAGE, INC.,
   Third-Party Defendants.

STIPULATION OF THIRD-PARTY
PLAINTIFF, ULTIMATE AUTO, INC., AND
THIRD-PARTY DEFENDANTS, DALE
MCGILL AND MCGILL'S GARAGE, INC.

Defendant and Third-Party Plaintiff, Ultimate Auto, Inc., and Third-Party Defendants, Dale McGill and McGill's Garage, Inc., hereby stipulate as follows:

1. At all relevant times. McGill's Garage, Inc., was a duly licensed inspection station for the Commonwealth of Massachusetts, which was engaged in, among other things, passing or rejecting vehicles; and Dale McGill was a certified inspector.

2. A safety inspection sticker was issued by McGill's Garage, Inc., to the Dee vehicle in question in December 2018, several months prior to the incident in question and after Dee had altered the jeep with the tires and suspension kit purchased from Ultimate Auto. Randall Dee paid $35.00 for the inspection and sticker.

3. Dale McGill was at all relevant times the President of, and Chief Mechanic and Inspector at, McGill's Garage, Inc. As of December 2018, he had been a gas station owner for fifteen years; he worked in other gas stations as a mechanic and helper for eight years prior to that.

4. The Commonwealth of Massachusetts Periodic Annual Inspection of All Motor Vehicles regulations [reprinted in the Case Files] were in effect at the time of the December 2018 inspection. Mass. Gen. Laws ch. 90 § 7P [also in the Case Files] also was in effect at all relevant times, including at the time of the inspection.

5. At all relevant times, McGill's Garage had large external signs that said: "Full Service Center," "Gas Station," and "Massachusetts Inspection Station."

6. At several times during 2018 Randall Dee bought gas at McGill's Garage, and Dale McGill was often the individual who pumped the gas into the jeep. On at least one occasion prior to December 2018, Randall Dee got a change of oil and lubrication for the jeep at McGill's Garage.

7. The following discovery [not reprinted in the Case Files] has occurred:

(a) In a deposition, Randall Dee said that when he went to McGill's Garage for the December 2018 inspection, he said to Dale McGill words to the effect that "I want my jeep inspected for a safety sticker." He further states in that deposition that "I thought a safety sticker meant my jeep was safe."

(b) Randall Dee and Dale McGill both say in depositions that Dale McGill inspected the jeep in question in December 2018 and put the sticker showing that the vehicle had passed inspection on the front windshield of the jeep; both further say that neither Randall Dee nor Dale McGill mentioned the modifications to the jeep to each other in December 2018 or at any other time.

(c) Plaintiff's lawyers have provided an affidavit during the discovery process in this case from an engineer who states that she has had extensive education and experience in vehicle design and safety. The affidavit further says that in the expert's opinion, based on what she has learned through extensive discovery in the case, inspection of the jeep in question, and a visit to the relevant site, "a substantial cause of the accident in question was the elevated height of the modified jeep which made the jeep a good deal less stable than it would be without the modifications."

Executed by the parties as of this _____/d/_____ day of _____/ m/_____, _____/y/_____.

ULTIMATE AUTO, INC.,   DALE MCGILL and
Third-Party Plaintiff   MCGILL'S GARAGE, INC.,
                                          Third-Party Defendant

By its Attorney,   By its Attorney,
_____ /s/ Bertram Cohen _____   _____ /s/ Lisa Scottoline _____
Bertram Cohen (BBO#641311)   Lisa Scottoline (BBO#393689)
Roth, McKnight & Zimmerman   Scottoline & Turow
111 Milk Street   One Federal Street
Boston, MA 02100   Boston, MA 02100
(617) 555-0000   617/555-7777

The Commonwealth of Massachussetts, Secretary of State, Regulation Filing and Publication

1. **REGULATION CHAPTER NUMBER AND HEADING:** 540 Mass. Regs. Code § 4.00 Periodic Annual Staggered Safety and Combined Safety and Emissions Inspection of All Motor Vehicles.*

2. **NAME OF AGENCY: Registry of Motor Vehicles**

3. **READABLE LANGUAGE SUMMARY:** States the general purposes and requirements of this regulation as well as the persons, organizations and businesses affected.

The purpose of 540 Mass. Regs. Code § 4.00 is to provide for a periodic staggered safety and combined safety and emissions inspection of all motor vehicles registered in the Commonwealth of Massachusetts and to establish licensing procedures for inspection stations, fleet inspection stations and safety inspection stations only authorized to participate in the inspection program. 540 Mass. Regs. Code § 4.00 establishes regulations and procedures for the issuance of various certificates to owner/operators in accordance with inspection procedures. 540 Mass. Regs. Code § 4.00 shall affect all persons owning, operating, purchasing and selling automobiles in the Commonwealth and shall affect many businesses relating to motor vehicle industry.

CODE OF MASSACHUSETTS REGULATIONS: REGISTRY OF MOTOR VEHICLES

4.00 PERIODIC ANNUAL STAGGERED SAFETY AND COMBINED SAFETY AND EMISSION INSPECTION OF ALL MOTOR VEHICLES

. . . The purpose of 540 Mass. Regs. Code § 4.00 is to provide rules and regulations and to establish inspection procedures for a periodic annual staggered safety and combined safety and emissions inspection of all motor vehicles in accordance with the General Laws of the Commonwealth of Massachusetts.

4.01 SCOPE AND APPLICABILITY

540 Mass. Regs. Code § 4.00 is adopted by the Registrar of Motor Vehicles in accordance with the authority of Mass. Gen. Laws ch. 90 § 31 to establish rules and regulations governing the use and operation of motor vehicles and trailers. 540 Mass. Regs. Code § 4.00 establishes rules and regulations which provide for a periodic staggered safety and combined safety and emission inspection of all motor vehicles registered in the Commonwealth of Massachusetts under the

---

* Eds.' Note: These were the applicable regulations at the time of the inspection.

authority of Mass. Gen. Laws ch. 90 § 7A establishing regulations for issuance of various certificates in accordance with proper inspection of a motor vehicle pursuant to Mass. Gen. Laws ch. 90 § 7V(a)(b)(c) and establishes rules and regulations for licensing stations which are approved to perform safety or combined safety and emissions inspections on motor vehicles pursuant to Mass. Gen. Laws ch. 90 § 7W.

4.02 SPECIAL DEFINITIONS

In addition to the definitions set forth in Mass. Gen. Laws ch. 90 § 1, the following special definitions shall also apply. . . .

Certificate of Inspection shall mean a serially numbered, adhesive sticker, device or symbol, as may be prescribed by the registrar indicating a motor vehicle has met the inspection requirements established by the registrar for issuance of a certificate. The registrar may prescribe the use of one or more categories of certificate of inspection in accordance with Mass. Gen. Laws ch. 90 § 1.

Certified Inspector shall mean an individual certified by the commissioner as properly trained to perform an emissions inspection as delineated by the manufacturer of the emissions analyzer in accordance with Mass. Gen. Laws ch. 90 § 1. . . .

Exempt Vehicles shall mean motor vehicles whose curb weight exceeds eight thousand pounds, motorcycles, diesel powered vehicles, motor vehicles more than twenty-five model years old before the date of inspection, motor vehicles not capable of a speed greater than twenty-five miles per hour under any condition of operation or loading on a level surface and any class of vehicles exempted by the commissioner of Department of Environmental Quality Engineering which present prohibitive inspection problems. . . .

Inspection Station shall mean a proprietorship, partnership, or corporation licensed by the registrar to perform safety or combined safety and emissions inspections on motor vehicles. . . .

Safety Inspection Station Only shall mean a proprietorship, partnership or corporation whose principal business is unique to a particular exempt vehicle.

4.03 REQUIREMENTS FOR INITIAL AND SUBSEQUENT STAGGERED ANNUAL INSPECTION

(1) **General Provisions.** Every owner or person in control of a Massachusetts registered motor vehicle shall submit the vehicle for inspection under the following rules: . . .

(c) **Inspection upon Registration.** Every owner or person in control of a motor vehicle which is newly registered in the Commonwealth shall submit such motor vehicle for certificate of inspection within seven days of the date on which the motor vehicle is first registered to said owner in the Commonwealth. . . .

(2) **Subsequent Inspection.** Subsequent to initial inspection, every owner or person in control of a Massachusetts registered motor vehicle shall submit the vehicle for inspection annually during the monthly expiration of the previously issued Certificate of Inspection.

(3) **Validity of Certificates of Inspection.** Certificates of Inspection are valid until such time as they expire or ownership of the vehicle transferred.

4.04 PROCEDURES FOR INSPECTION OF ALL MOTOR VEHICLES

(1) **Prior to beginning inspection,** a visual check of the vehicle should be made to determine that ice and snow accumulation, condition of the suspension, etc., will not impede or interfere with the proper aiming of headlamps. Inspectors shall collect the established inspection fee and remove any inspection sticker from the wind-shield of the motor vehicle.

(2) **Check registration certificate** for date of expiration. . . .

(3) **Inspect number plate(s)** to see that they are undamaged, securely mounted, clean and clearly visible. No bumper, trailer hitch or other accessory may interfere with a clear view of them. The number plate must be mounted in the proper location on the rear of the vehicle if the vehicle has been issued one plate. Both number plates must be mounted in the proper location on the rear and front of the vehicle, if the vehicle has been issued two plates.

Any decorative number plate or number plate replica not issued by the Registry of Motor Vehicles on which the word Massachusetts appears must be removed from the vehicle.

(4) **Perform Emission Testing Requirements and Procedures.** . . .

(5) **Test Brakes.**

(a) The adjuster may operate the vehicle in the inspection bay and test the parking and service brake. The parking brake on all vehicles will be tested by accelerating the motor to approximately 1200 to 1300 RPMs with the vehicle in gear in both forward and reverse positions against the brake in the applied position. . . .

(b) Brakes shall be adequate to stop the vehicle from a speed of 20 MPH in not more than the following distances:

Service (foot) Brake	Pleasure Vehicles	25 feet
	Trucks and Buses	35 feet
Parking (hand) Brake	All Vehicles	75 feet

(6) **Examine Muffler and Exhaust System.** Accelerate motor to test for prevention of unnecessary noise and emission of any unreasonable amount of smoke. The exhaust system, exhaust manifold(s), exhaust pipe(s), muffler(s) and tailpipe(s), if designed to be so equipped, shall be tight and free of leaks.

(7) **Check Steering and Suspension**

(a) Check for free steering by turning the steering wheel through a full right and left turn. Reject a vehicle if binding or interference occurs during the procedure. With the front wheels in the straight ahead position (and the engine running on vehicle equipped with power steering) measure lash or lost movement at the steering wheel rim.

(b) Lash or lost movement on passenger cars and station wagons, as measured at the steering wheel rim, should not exceed 2 inches if the vehicle is equipped with manual steering. Lash or lost movement on antique motor vehicles, trucks, vans and buses will be measured in the same manner with the allowable tolerance on trucks, vans and buses to be determined by steering wheel diameter in accordance with the following schedule:

Steering Wheel Diameter	Lash (shall not exceed)
16″	2″
18″	2″
20″	2″
22″	2″

(c) The front end of all vehicles will be raised by jacking or hoisting and visually examined. Vehicles equipped with ball joints will be raised and checked in accordance with the instructions and recommendations of the Automobile Manufacturers Association. Ball joint tolerance shall not exceed those established by the vehicle manufacturer.

(d) Reject a vehicle with excessive wear or play in any part of the steering mechanism or of the vehicle that would affect proper steering. . . .

(8) **Sound Horn.** Sound horn to test for adequate signal. The horn must be securely fastened to the vehicle.

(9) **Examine Windshield and Rear Windows**

(a) **Clear Windshield**. . . .

(b) **Ornaments.** Ornaments forward of the operator's line of vision through the windshield must be removed. No poster or sticker shall be attached to the windshield in such a manner so as to obstruct the vision of the operator.

(c) **Rear Windows.** Rear windows must allow an unobstructed view to the rear. On convertible type vehicles, the rear window must be inspected and if clouded, the vehicle must be rejected.

(d) **Windshield Cleaner(s).** Test for proper operation. . . .

(10) **Examine Lighting Devices.**

(a) **Tail Lights.** Every motor vehicle, except a two wheeled motorcycle, an antique motor car and a farm tractor, shall be equipped with two red lights (tail lamps) mounted one at each side of the rear of the vehicle so as to show two red lights from behind and equipped with two stop lights (stop lamps) mounted and displayed in a like manner. A single lamp may combine both the above functions. Every motor vehicle shall be equipped with a white light so arranged as to illuminate the rear number plate so that it is plainly visible at sixty feet.

(b) **Directionals.** Front and rear directional signals will be operable on every vehicle originally equipped with such signals. Every motor vehicle registered in the Commonwealth which was manufactured for the model year 1967 and for subsequent model years, shall be equipped with a device to permit the front and rear directional signals to flash simultaneously.

(c) **Headlamps.** Headlamps shall be aimed in accordance with the Registrar's specifications. Said specifications shall be forwarded to licensees by the Registry of Motor Vehicles.

(11) **Examine Tires.**

(a) No tire mounted on a motor vehicle or trailer shall be deemed to be in safe operating condition unless it meets the visual and tread depth requirements set forth in these regulations.

1. **Tread Depth.** The amount of tread design on the tire. Tread depth includes both the original, retread and recap tread design; and, in respect to special mileage commercial tires, recut and regrooved tread design. Truck and bus tires having a wheel diameter over 16 inches, having sufficient original tread rubber above the breaker strip may be siped and classed as a siped tread design 2/32 of an inch siped depth shall be considered equal to 2/32 of an inch original tread depth, provided that the cords of the tire are not damaged by the process.

2. **Special Mileage Commercial Tire.** A tire manufactured with an extra layer of rubber between the cord body and original tread design, which extra layer is designed for the purpose of recutting or regrooving, and which tire is specifically labeled as a special mileage commercial tire.

3. **Visual Requirements.** No tire shall be deemed to be in safe operating condition if such tire has:

a. **Fabric Break.** A fabric break, or a cut in excess of one inch in any direction as measured on the outside of the tire and deep enough to reach the body cords, or has been repaired temporarily by the use of blowout patches or boots; or

b. **Bulges.** Any bump, bulge or knot related to separation or partial failure of the tire, structure; or

c. **Exposed Cord.** Any portion of the ply or cord structure exposed; or

d. **Worn Tread.** A portion of the tread design completely worn, provided such worn portion is of sufficient size to affect substantially the traction and stopping ability of the tire.

4. **Method of Measuring Tread Depth.** Tire tread depth shall be measured by a tread depth gauge which shall be of a type calibrated in thirty-seconds of an inch. Readings shall be taken in a major tread groove of the tire nearest the center at two points of the circumference at least fifteen inches apart. Readings for a tire which has the tread design running across the tire or for a siped tire, where such tread design is permitted, shall be taken at or near the center of the tire at two points of the circumference of at least fifteen inches apart.

5. **Tread Depth Requirements.** No tire shall be deemed to be in safe operating condition if such tire is worn to the point where less than two-thirty-seconds (2/32) of an inch of tread design remains at both points at which gauge readings are obtained.

6. **Tire Intermix.** The vehicle will be rejected if a radial ply tire is used on the same axle with a conventional non-radial tire. The vehicle will be rejected if bias or bias belted ply tires are used on the rear axle when non-radial tires are used on the front axle. . . .

(12) **Examine Bumpers, Fenders, External Sheet Metal and Fuel Tank.** Any motor vehicle will be rejected if any of the following conditions are evident:

(a) **Bumpers.** Broken or bent bumpers, fenders, exterior sheet metal or mouldings having sharp edges or abnormal protrusions extending beyond normal vehicle extremities so as to constitute a danger to pedestrians and other motor vehicle traffic. If bumper face plates are removed, bumper brackets must also be removed. The vehicle hood, door and luggage compartment lid and battery or engine compartment doors or lids, if so equipped, must fully and properly close and be capable of being firmly latched.

(b) **Fenders.** Front and rear fenders must be in place. . . .

(c) **Floor Pans.** Floor pans which are rusted through or otherwise would permit passage of exhaust gases into the passenger or trunk area.

(d) **Fuel Tanks.** Fuel tanks which are not securely attached to the vehicle's body or chassis. . . .

4.07 ISSUANCE OF CERTIFICATES OF INSPECTION, REJECTION, AND
WAIVER PROCEDURE

(1) **General Provisions.**

(a) A separate and distinct charge, as established by the Registrar and Commissioner, shall be made for each inspection.

(b) All required entries on certificates and periodic inspection reports must be legibly completed in ink, ball point pen or indelible pencil by the inspection station owner/operator or employee performing the inspection.

(2) **Certificate of Inspection.**

(a) Any motor vehicle subject to Safety Inspection Only or Combined Safety and Emissions Inspection, which, after inspection, is found to be in compliance with all safety or safety and emissions inspection requirements will be issued a Certificate of Inspection. . . .

(3) **Certificate of Rejection.**

(a) Any motor vehicle subject to the Combined Safety and Emissions Inspection which is not in compliance with all safety and emissions inspection requirements and any motor vehicle subject to Safety Inspection Only which is not in compliance with all safety inspection requirements, will be issued a Certificate of Rejection.

(b) **Requirements.** When a Certificate of Rejection is issued on a motor vehicle, entries pertaining to the date of inspection and vehicle registration number of the motor vehicle will be completed by the inspection station owner/operator or employee performing the inspection on the Certificate of Inspection, that would normally have been issued to the motor vehicle, and on the periodic inspection report. The certificate will be retained at the inspection station for a period of twenty days for potential issuance to the affected motor vehicle. If issued to the affected motor vehicle, all required entries on said certificate and on the periodic inspection report will be completed. At the expiration of the twenty day period, unissued certificates with partial entries will be held in an open file for return to the Registry of Motor Vehicles.

4.08 LICENSURE OF INSPECTION STATION

(1) **General Provisions: Licensing Requirements.** Effective April 1, 1983, all inspection stations, which shall include Inspection Stations for Combined Safety and Emissions Testing, Fleet Inspection Stations and Safety Inspection Stations Only shall be licensed by the Registry of Motor Vehicles to carry out the annual staggered Safety or Safety and Emissions Inspection Program. . . .

(g) **Requirements for Personnel Who Administer Inspections.** Inspections must be performed by the licensee or permanent employees of the licensee who are in possession of a Massachusetts Motor Vehicle Operators License. Persons performing inspections must be able to demonstrate their proficiency in inspecting motor vehicles and in operating, calibrating and maintaining items or equipment required for the inspection of motor vehicles, to personnel of the Registry of Motor Vehicles and the Massachusetts Department of Environmental Quality Engineering assigned to program administration and enforcement. Persons performing Emissions inspections must be certified by the Commissioner. A permanent employee is herein defined as a person carried on the payroll records of the applicant, regularly employed on the premises for a minimum of twenty hours a week. . . .

Restatement (Second) of Contracts

§ 201. WHOSE MEANING PREVAILS.

(1) Where the parties have attached the same meaning to a promise or agreement or a term thereof, it is interpreted in accordance with that meaning.

(2) Where the parties have attached different meanings to a promise or agreement or a term thereof, it is interpreted in accordance with the meaning attached by one of them if at the time the agreement was made

(a) that party did not know of any different meaning attached by the other, and the other knew the meaning attached by the first party; or

(b) that party had no reason to know of any different meaning attached by the other, and the other had reason to know the meaning attached by the first party. . . .

§ 202. RULES IN AID OF INTERPRETATION.

(1) Words and other conduct are interpreted in the light of all the circumstances, and if the principal purpose of the parties is ascertainable it is given great weight.

(2) A writing is interpreted as a whole, and all writings that are part of the same transaction are interpreted together.

(3) Unless a different intention is manifested,

(a) where language has a generally prevailing meaning, it is interpreted in accordance with that meaning;

(b) technical terms and words of art are given their technical meaning when used in a transaction within their technical field.

. . . (5) Wherever reasonable, the manifestations of intention of the parties to a promise or agreement are interpreted as consistent with each other and with any relevant course of performance, course of dealing, or usage of trade.

. . . § 207. INTERPRETATION FAVORING THE PUBLIC.

In choosing among the reasonable meanings of a promise or agreement or a term thereof, a meaning that serves the public interest is generally preferred.

Restatement (Second) of Torts

§ 299A. UNDERTAKING IN PROFESSION OR TRADE.

Unless he represents that he has greater or less skill or knowledge, one who undertakes to render services in the practice of a profession or trade is required to exercise the skill and knowledge normally possessed by members of that profession or trade in good standing in similar communities.

OFFICIAL COMMENTS

a. Skill, as the word is used in this Section, is something more than the mere minimum competence required of any person who does an act, under the rule stated in § 299. It is that special form of competence which is not part of the ordinary equipment of the reasonable man, but which is the result of acquired learning, and aptitude developed by special training and experience. All professions, and most trades, are necessarily skilled, and the word is used to refer to the special competence which they require.

b. Profession or trade. This Section is thus a special application of the rule stated in § 299. It applies to any person who undertakes to render services to another in the practice of a profession, such as that of physician or surgeon, dentist, pharmacist, oculist, attorney, accountant, or engineer. It applies also to any person who undertakes to render services to others in the practice of a skilled trade, such as that of airplane pilot, precision machinist, electrician, carpenter, blacksmith, or plumber. This Section states the minimum skill and knowledge which the actor undertakes to exercise, and therefore to have. If he has in fact greater skill than that common to the profession or trade, he is required to exercise that skill, as stated in § 299, Comment e.

c. Undertaking. In the ordinary case, the undertaking of one who renders services in the practice of a profession or trade is a matter of contract between the parties, and the terms of the undertaking are either stated expressly, or implied as a matter of understanding. The rule here stated does not, however, depend upon the existence of an enforceable contract between the parties. It applies equally where professional services are rendered gratuitously, as in the case of a physician treating a charity patient, or without any definite understanding, as in the case of one who renders services to a patient who is unconscious, in an emergency. The basis of the rule is the undertaking of the defendant, which may arise apart from contract.

This undertaking is not necessarily a matter of the requirements of the particular task undertaken, although that task will of course have its bearing upon what is understood. A highly skilled individual, as for example, a certified public accountant, may undertake to perform services which normally require little skill, as for example to do ordinary bookkeeping, and in performing those services he may, or may not, undertake to exercise his unusually high skill. On the other hand a bookkeeper with little or no accounting skill may undertake to do work which would normally call for a certified public accountant, and he may, or may not, undertake in doing it to exercise the skill of such an accountant. It is a matter of the skill which he represents himself to have, or is understood to undertake to have, rather than of the skill which he actually possesses, or which the task requires.

d. Special representation. An actor undertaking to render services may represent that he has superior skill or knowledge, beyond that common to his profession or trade. In that event he incurs an obligation to the person to whom he makes such a representation, to have, and to exercise, the skill and knowledge which he represents himself to have. Thus a physician who holds himself out as a specialist in certain types of practice is required to have the skill and knowledge common to other specialists. On the other hand the actor may make it clear that he has less than the minimum of skill common to the profession or trade; and in that case he is required to exercise only the skill which he represents that he has. Thus a layman who attempts to perform a surgical operation in an emergency, in the absence of any surgeon, and who makes it clear that he does not have the skill or knowledge of a surgeon, is not required to exercise such skill or knowledge. The rule stated in this Section applies only where there is no such special representation.

e. Standard normally required. In the absence of any such special representation, the standard of skill and knowledge required of the actor who practices a profession or trade is that which is commonly possessed by members of that profession or trade in good standing. It is not that of the most highly skilled, nor is it that of the average member of the profession or trade, since those who have less than median or average skill may still be competent and qualified. Half of the physicians of America do not automatically become negligent in practicing medicine at all, merely because their skill is less than the professional average. On the other hand, the standard is not that of the charlatan, the quack, the unqualified or incompetent individual who has succeeded in entering the profession or trade. It is that common to those who are recognized in the profession or trade itself as qualified, and competent to engage in it.

f. Schools of thought. Where there are different schools of thought in a profession, or different methods are followed by different groups engaged in a trade, the actor is to be judged by the professional standards of the group to which he belongs. The law cannot undertake to decide technical questions of proper practice over which experts reasonably disagree, or to declare that those who do not accept particular controversial doctrines are necessarily negligent in failing to do so. There may be, however, minimum requirements of skill applicable to all persons, of whatever school of thought, who engage in any profession or trade. Thus any person who holds himself out as competent to treat human ailments must have a minimum skill in diagnosis, and a minimum knowledge of possible methods of treatment. Licensing statutes, or those requiring a basic knowledge of science for the practice of a profession, may provide such a minimum standard.

g. Type of community. Allowance must be made also for the type of community in which the actor carries on his practice. A country doctor cannot be expected to have the equipment, facilities, experience, knowledge or opportunity to obtain it, afforded him by a large city. The standard is not, however, that of the particular locality. If there are only three physicians in a small town, and all three are highly incompetent, they cannot be permitted to set a standard of utter inferiority for a fourth who comes to town. The standard is rather that of persons engaged in similar practice in similar localities, considering geographical location, size, and the character of the community in general.

Such allowance for the type of community is most frequently made in professions or trades where there is a considerable degree of variation in the skill and knowledge possessed by those practicing it in different localities. It has commonly been made in the cases of physicians or surgeons, because of the difference in the medical skill commonly found in different parts of the United States, or in different types of communities. In other professions, such as that of the attorney, such variations either do not exist or are not as significant, and allowance for them has seldom been made. A particular profession may be so uniform, in different localities, as to the skill and knowledge of its members, that the court will not feel required to instruct the jury that it must make such allowance.

Economics Specialists of Boston, Inc.

282 Huntington Ave., Boston, MA 02115, (617) 555-0505*

/d/

Carol Coblentz, Esq.
Needham, Shaker and Coblentz   **CONFIDENTIAL**
44 Park Place
Boston, MA 02100

Re: Damages in Nancy Carpenter Case

Dear Carol,

Before we meet with you to discuss our final report in this case, I wanted to provide you with my current thinking about the damages resulting from the tragic death of Charles Carpenter. First, I should report that I have had no success in finding jury verdicts in Middlesex County, or even in Massachusetts, for similar cases during the past five years. No reported case has involved the tipping of a jeep or other car that had been raised. The tipped vehicle cases we have found in which there have been jury verdicts involved products liability with respect to an unaltered vehicle or alleged negligent work done by repair shops and plaintiffs who survived with severe injuries. There were four such cases in Middlesex County in the past five years: two resulted in defendants' verdicts, and the other two had plaintiffs' verdicts for $1,800,000 and $2,150,000, respectively; but again, these were plaintiffs who were still alive. Both of those cases, I am told, settled while still on appeal. The two plaintiffs' victories were plaintiffs with horrendous injuries, and each had a fairly large earning history and earning potential (one engineer and one accountant). On the other hand, those plaintiffs were older than Charles Carpenter at the time of his death, and none involved a retailer who sold parts or tires. There are wrongful death verdicts for plaintiffs in a number of cases in Middlesex during the past five years, but the circumstances of each case are so unique with respect to the deceased, surviving heirs, and the circumstances of death that we do not think they provide any real guidance. Those verdicts range from $180,000 to $7,125,000. You know better than we, but we do not think previous jury verdicts are very helpful in assessing the value of this case.

As you and I have discussed, the Massachusetts Wrongful Death Statute permits damages for categories of harm that are beyond the realm of our expertise

---

**Eds.' Note:* This document has been invented for this case in order to help students think about damages for various practice exercises. It does draw, in part, from economist reports, discovery, and other information in the actual case.

as economists. We can give you estimates for net lost earnings (after subtracting for direct personal consumption of the deceased, Charles Carpenter (hereafter "Charles")), as well as lost household services that would have been provided by Carpenter to his family. The statute also covers compensation for the loss of the "reasonably expected . . . protection, care, assistance, society, companionship, comfort, guidance, counsel and advice of the decedent to the persons entitled to the damages recovered. . . ." You (and a jury) will have to consider the value of those intangibles without the guidance of an economist.

Additional losses that we will not consider for purposes of our economic opinion (but you will undoubtedly wish to include) are the money paid to the hospital to which Carpenter was taken after the accident ($2,682.35); the ambulance charge ($663.00); funeral home expense ($2,950.00); monument company expense ($2,442.50); law firm charge for appointment of administratrix ($620.00); and uncertain additional expenses for the filling out and filing of the Massachusetts Department of Revenue estate tax return (this should probably run no more than $1,500.00 and perhaps as low as $750.00).

After interviewing the plaintiff widow and her sister, we ascertained that Charles was a very good high school student, involved in a number of extracurricular activities. He received training as an auto mechanic in high school, and after high school and before his job as a custodian at Forsythe University, he had two jobs as a mechanic: one at an auto dealer and one for a bus company. He took the job at Forsythe in order to be closer to home, and to work an evening shift so that when the baby arrived, his wife could work during the day, while he cared for the baby. He loved children, and was very close to his nieces and nephews; he worked with an autistic child while in high school. He adored his wife. So far as we can tell, the marriage was solid and they were very much in love and reliant on each other. He hoped eventually to have more schooling, and to get into the computer field.

His work as a custodian was covered by a union contract. His salary at Forsythe during the year he died would have been $31,662; in the following year, it would have been $33,562. We are assuming a forty-hour week, fifty-two weeks a year. We will assume that his benefits for retirement and insurance equal the average percent of wages for unionized employees in service industries nationally—16 percent.

His wages would have grown throughout his work life. We have made two alternative assumptions concerning the rate of growth of his wages: 1.5 percent in real, inflation-adjusted terms for the remainder of his life (based on raises in this type of work during the past twenty years) and 2.5 percent based on his above-average motivation and his future plan to move into the higher-paying computer field.

We have back-up for the following assumptions. He would work 27 more years, and live an additional 42 years. His effective average tax rate (state and federal combined) would be 15 percent over the course of his expected life. His personal consumption of his after-tax income would be 35.5 percent. Based on conversations with his wife, we assume he worked approximately twenty hours a week around the house, and would continue to do so. We use a conservative $5.00 per hour for that work, or an annual total of $5,200. We assume that the value of these services would remain constant in real terms over the remainder of his life.

Assuming the net lost earnings will be paid in a lump sum, which will be able to earn interest, future losses must be discounted to present value using a real discount rate. The real discount rate is estimated by subtracting the average historical inflation rate from the average historical long-term interest rate.

We'll give you a year by year chart, but here are the bottom lines. We estimate that the discounted net after-tax economic loss to Carpenter's wife and son resulting from his death would lie between $589,069 and $634,176, depending upon the assumptions concerning his future growth in wages. These figures are composed first of the total lost earnings calculated as I have described (having subtracted his anticipated personal consumption) of $428,139 (1.5 percent growth) or $473,246 (2.5 percent growth). To each of these one should add $160,931 for household services. The two figures added together are how we arrived at our total estimates.

Please give me a call if you want us to consider other variables or other figures before we meet.

Very truly yours,

/s/
Jocelyn Q. Russo

Warner v. City of New York

Contents

Initial Memorandum   1234

New York Times article   1243

New York Daily News article   1245

Complaint   1246

Answer of New York City Police Commissioner Raymond Kelly   1260

Defendants' Motion for Partial Summary Judgment   1268

Transcript: Deposition of Plaintiff Jacob Warner   1269

Transcript: Deposition of Defendant Richard Cannon   1274

Affidavit of Lauren Cassidy   1278

Affidavit of Detective Susan Stephens   1281

Initial Memorandum

To: Supervising Attorney
From: Legal intern
Matter: Initial Memorandum: *Warner v. City of New York*
Date: April 15, 2008*

OVERVIEW

Our office has filed a lawsuit against the City of New York, its mayor, its police commissioner, and three of its police officers. We filed a complaint with two named plaintiffs: Jacob Warner and William Moore. We will be asking the court to certify this case as a class action with the two named plaintiffs as class representatives. New York Police Department officers detained Warner and Moore for a period of time and patted down their outer clothes in what is known as a "stop and frisk." Our claim is that our clients and many other New Yorkers like them were stopped and searched because of their race. Our complaint alleges claims under the Fourth and Fourteenth Amendments of the United States Constitution, and New York state common law.

FACTS

I. *Plaintiffs*

Jacob Warner

Jacob Warner is a twenty-eight-year-old black man who lives in the Bronx. Warner has had two separate interactions with the NYPD that included a stop and frisk. The first incident occurred at midday on April 20, 2007 when one NYPD officer in a van told Warner to stop as he was walking on the sidewalk a few blocks from his home. After exiting the van, the officer cornered Warner, questioned him, and asked for identification. Warner replied that he was walking home and that no, he did not have any weapons. He gave the officers his driver's license. Warner asked why he was being stopped but received no reply. The officer then searched under Warner's shirt and put his hands in Warner's pants pockets. Warner informed the officer that he did not consent to the search. Upon failing to find any illegal item on Warner, the officer returned his driver's license and left. At no point did Warner see the officer fill out any paperwork.

The second incident occurred sometime in February 2008, around midday, when Warner was again stopped, frisked, and searched in his neighborhood. Warner was walking by his godmother's apartment building and saw that her

---

* *Eds' Note:* Notice the date. We are putting you at a particular moment in history so that you can appreciate the events as they unfolded in real time.

tenant Ron Belton, a thirty-year-old black male, was locked out of the building. Warner had a spare key but did not remember which key it was or which key chain it was on, so Warner and Belton were trying out various keys in the lock. Two NYPD officers saw them and asked Warner and Belton what they were doing, then quickly demanded they stand with their hands up against the wall with the wall in front of them. Officers frisked the men, and one officer put his hands inside Warner's pants pockets. After confirming Warner's and Belton's addresses, the officers left. Warner did not see either officer fill out paperwork.

William Moore

William Moore is a twenty-six-year-old black man who lives in Harlem (in the Borough of Manhattan in New York City). At 1:00 P.M. on a weekday in January 2006, two NYPD officers called out to Moore as he was leaving a bodega between the Subway restaurant where he was having lunch and the Charter School where he worked. Moore was in his work clothes: dress shirt, tie, and slacks. The officers backed Moore up against the bodega window, flashed their badges, and asked where he was coming from. Moore said he was on lunch break from his job at the Charter School. The officers told Moore that they saw him coming from the direction of a building known for drug activity. Moore again said he was on his lunch break from work at the Charter School. One officer then asked Moore three times if he had any contraband and whether they would find any if they searched him, raising his voice and stepping toward Moore the third time. Moore replied that he did not and that he did not consent to a search after each time he was asked those questions. When people from nearby stores emerged to witness the interrogation, the officers left. At no point did Moore see the officers fill out any paperwork.

II. NYPD Policies

A 2003 settlement in a similar stop and frisk lawsuit against the City of New York required the NYPD to adopt a written policy banning racial profiling. *Daniels v. City of New York*, 99 Civ. 1695 (SAS) (S.D.N.Y. 1999). Settlement of that suit led to a consent decree that required the NYPD to distribute that policy to all officers and to read it aloud at roll call. The NYPD's Quality Assurance Division was to routinely audit compliance by examining training materials and officer logs of stops and frisks. Further, the NYPD was to train officers in the legal standards governing a stop and frisk and hold public forums at which officers educated the community about their rights and remedies when stopped or frisked. Finally, the settlement required the NYPD to maintain a database of UF-250 forms documenting each stop and frisk. Officers must complete a UF-250 identifying the officer performing a stop, the person stopped, and the reason for a stop any time a suspect: (i) is stopped by use of force; (ii) is frisked or searched; (iii) is arrested; or (iv) refuses to provide identification when stopped. Officers must submit each UF-250 to their supervisors for review.

As part of its regular operations, the NYPD holds weekly CompStat meetings where each of precinct commanders must account for their precinct's crime statistics, and where UF-250s are considered evidence of productivity. In its 1999 investigation, the New York Office of the Attorney General (NYOAG) found some evidence that precinct commanders withheld employment perks unless officers fulfilled a monthly quota of stops, frisks, and arrests, to boost their precinct's CompStat numbers. The NYOAG found that while some officers believed UF-250s were completed fairly regularly, others estimated a UF-250 was completed for only one in five stops.

The NYOAG also analyzed 175,000 UF-250s from January 1998 to March 1999. That analysis revealed that blacks and Latinos together comprised 49.3% of NYC's population, but 83.6% of NYPD stops. Whites comprised 43.4% of NYC's population and 12.9% of NYPD stops. Arrest rates also differed by race: the NYPD stopped 9.5 blacks, 8.8 Latinos, and 7.9 whites for every one corresponding arrest. Regression analysis controlling for race-specific and crime-specific arrest rates by precinct demographics showed that blacks were stopped 2.1 times and Latinos 1.7 times more often than whites on suspicion of committing a violent crime. Although majority-minority precincts did see higher crime rates, the difference in stop rates exceeded the difference in crime rates, often by a factor of two.

The NYC Civilian Complaint Review Board reported that in 1999, 1240 people complained of being subjected to unlawful stops and frisks. In 2006, that number was 5089.

LEGAL ANALYSIS

I. Causes of Action Under 42 U.S.C. § 1983

Section 1983 provides a federal remedy for the deprivation of civil rights. 42 U.S.C. § 1983 (2006). It contains two elements.

The first element of a § 1983 claim is that the defendant acted under color of state law. Natural persons act under color of state law if they "carry a badge of authority of a State and represent it in some capacity, whether they act in accordance with their authority or misuse it." *Monroe v. Pape*, 365 U.S. 167, 172 (1961). Cities act under color of state law if the alleged violation implements either "official policy" or "'practices of state officials [that] could well be so permanent and well settled as to constitute a 'custom or usage' with the force of law'" *Monell v. Dep't of Soc. Servs.*, 436 U.S. 658, 690-91 (1978). Cities are not liable for their employees' acts under a respondeat superior theory, but are liable when the employees' execution of the government's policies or customs causes the injury. *Id.* at 694. Our complaint alleges § 1983 violations against both NYC and the relevant officials based on a theory of direct liability (i.e. their direct actions in the implementation, sanction, enforcement, and encouragement of unconstitutional stops and frisks, or their actions in the actual stop and frisk itself).

The second element of a § 1983 claim is the violation of a right secured by federal Constitution or federal statute. We are alleging violations of the Fourth Amendment right against unreasonable searches and seizures and of the Fourteenth Amendment right to equal protection of the laws.

A. Fourth Amendment—Search and Seizure

The Fourth Amendment protects people against "unreasonable searches and seizures." U.S. Const. amend. IV.[1] It governs stops and frisks because a stop is the "seizure" of a person and a frisk is the "search" of a person. *Terry v. Ohio*, 392 U.S. 1, 16 (1968). A stop occurs when an officer, "by means of physical force or show of authority" detains a civilian such that "a reasonable person would have believed that he was not free to leave." *United States v. Mendenhall*, 446 U.S. 544, 552, 554 (1980). A frisk occurs when an officer pats down the outer layer of a suspect's clothes. *Terry*, 392 U.S. at 16-17. An officer must have a "reasonable suspicion" that criminal activity is afoot to perform a stop and must have "reason to believe that he is dealing with an armed and dangerous individual" to perform a frisk. *United States v. Sokolow*, 490 U.S. 1, 7 (1989). The reasonableness standard does not include the officer's "inchoate and unparticularized suspicion or 'hunch,'" but does include the officer's "specific reasonable inferences which he is entitled to draw from the facts in light of his experience." *Terry*, 392 U.S. at 27.

In *Terry v. Ohio*, a police officer was patrolling downtown Cleveland at 2:30 P.M. when two men talking at a street corner caught his eye. *Terry*, 392 U.S. at 5. The officer had worked in the police force for thirty-nine years, as a detective for thirty-five years, and had patrolled this vicinity for thirty years. He did not recognize the two men and something seemed amiss. He watched one man leave, peer into a store, then walk a little more before turning, peering into the same store, and returning to the other man. *Id.* at 6. The two conferred. Then the second man did the same thing. Together, the two repeated this ritual a dozen times, at one point conferring with a third man who then left by a side street. At the end of ten minutes, the two men left by the same side street as had the third. The officer followed them and saw them confer with the third man in front of a different store. At this point the officer approached them, identified himself as an officer, and asked their names. *Id.* at 7. When the three mumbled something in reply, the officer grabbed one man, spun him around to face the other two, and patted down his outer clothing. *Id.* When he felt a pistol, he ordered the three into the store and up against a wall where, after removing the first man's gun, he patted down the other two. He found a second gun on the second man, which he removed, and no gun on the third man, whom he did not inspect further. He asked the storeowner to call the police and took all three men back to the station when back-up arrived.

---

1. The Fourth Amendment is enforceable against the States. *Mapp v. Ohio*, 367 U.S. 643, 655 (1961).

The Supreme Court held that these facts supported a reasonable suspicion that criminal activity was afoot at the time of the stop and to support a reasonable belief that the three men were armed and dangerous at the time of the frisk. *Id.* at 30.

Both the "reasonable suspicion" test and the "reason to believe. . ." test are objective reasonableness tests asking "would the facts available to the officer at the moment of the seizure or the search 'warrant a man of reasonable caution in the belief' that the action taken was appropriate?" *Id.* at 21-22. The Supreme Court has also held that an individual's presence in a "neighborhood frequented by drug users," *Brown v. Texas*, 443 U.S. 47, 52 (1979), or being in "an area of expected crime activity" *Illinois v. Wardlow*, 528 U.S. 119, 124 (2000), or an individual's refusal to answer police questions, *Florida v. Royer*, 460 U.S. 491, 498 (1983), or an individual's looking backwards, *Reid v. Georgia*, 448 U.S. 438, 441 (1980), cannot by themselves justify a reasonable suspicion.

B. Fourteenth Amendment—Equal Protection

The Fourteenth Amendment provides that "[n]o State shall . . . deny to any person within its jurisdiction the equal protection of the laws." U.S. Const. amend. XIV, § 1. It applies to all State actors, including local officials. *Vill. of Arlington Heights v. Metro. Hous. Dev. Corp.*, 429 U.S. 252 (1977). To sustain a claim of an equal protection violation, a plaintiff must prove discriminatory *intent* or *purpose*; discriminatory *effect* alone does not suffice. *Washington v. Davis*, 426 U.S. 229, 240 (1976). But discriminatory intent can be inferred "from the totality of the relevant facts, including the fact, if it is true, that the law bears more heavily on one race than another." *Id.* at 242. Factors that can be used to determine invidious intent include: impact of the action, specifically whether it "'bears more heavily on one race than another'" and including whether there was a clear pattern that shows racial motivation, historical background of the challenged decision, "specific sequence of events leading up to the challenged decision", "[d]epartures from the normal procedural sequence," substantive departures where the "factors usually considered important by decision-makers strongly favor a decision contrary to the one reached," and legislative or administrative history. *Vill. of Arlington Heights*, 429 U.S. at 266-68.

For instance, if the police frisk ninety per cent of black suspects and ten per cent white suspects, then that disproportionate effect cannot by itself sustain an equal protection claim. But if the reasons recorded on UF-250s for stopping black suspects are more often than not subjective, legally insufficient, or omitted entirely, and if officers change their testimony from that detailed in their UF-250s more often with black suspects, and if the UF-250s and other monitoring devices merely obscure the officer's conduct in practice, then a court may find that these factors, together with the disproportionate effect, indicate that the state police designed its official guidelines for stop and frisk as a proxy for race and intended the disproportionate effect.

If the plaintiff proves racially discriminatory intent, then the policy or practice can stand only if it passes strict scrutiny, meaning that the policy or practice must be narrowly tailored to meet a compelling government interest. *Adarand Constructors v. Pena*, 515 U.S. 200, 227 (1995).

II. New York State Claims and Respondeat Superior

As noted above, a municipality cannot be liable under § 1983 using a respondeat superior theory. *Monell v. Dep't of Soc. Servs.*, 436 U.S. 658, 691 (1978). However, it can be held liable for a state cause of action based on respondeat superior. We are bringing claims of assault and battery, based on the fact that the plaintiffs were touched by NYPD officers without a reasonable suspicion of criminal activity.

III. Qualified Immunity

There are two questions the court must resolve to determine if qualified immunity applies, although the order of this inquiry is up to the court's discretion. *Pearson v. Callahan*, 555 U.S. 223, 236 (2009). One question is, "[t]aken in the light most favorable to the party asserting the injury, do the facts alleged show the officer's conduct violated a constitutional right?" *Saucier v. Katz*, 533 U.S. 194, 201 (2001). The other question is whether the right was "clearly established" at the time the action was taken. *Id.*

A right is "clearly established" if the "contours of the right" are clear enough that a "reasonable official would understand that what he is doing violates that right." *Id.* at 202. In other words, the extent of that right must be established enough so that a reasonable official would know that they were violating the right. Law is "clearly established" when controlling authority has decided the issue or when there is a consensus among persuasive authority so that the officer couldn't have believed their actions were lawful, or when the case is so obvious as to be "open and shut." *Wilson v. Layne*, 526 U.S. 603, 615-17 (1999).

Even officials who "'reasonably but mistakenly conclude that probable cause is present' are entitled to immunity." *Hunter v. Bryant*, 502 U.S. 224, 227 (1991). Defendants often bring a summary judgment motion asserting qualified immunity in civil rights cases involving municipalities. In order to overcome qualified immunity and pursue his case to trial, the plaintiff must prove both elements.

The purpose of this immunity is to save public officials from the chore of endlessly defending legal claims, therefore questions regarding immunity should be resolved as early as possible in litigation. *Hunter v. Bryant*, 502 U.S. 224, 227 (1991). Qualified immunity is a question of law for the court to decide before the trial. *Id.* at 228. As noted, the court may determine either or both of the elements of qualified immunity at its discretion. *Pearson*, 555 U.S. at 232.

IV. Remedies

A plaintiff who prevails under § 1983 is entitled to appropriate injunctive relief, declaratory relief, and compensatory damages. Injunctive and declaratory relief are determined by a judge; damages are determined by a jury. Plaintiffs are not entitled to money damages merely for a violation of a constitutional right, but must demonstrate that they actually suffered such damages. *Carey v. Piphus*, 435 U.S. 247 (1978).

To obtain an award of punitive damages, a plaintiff must prove that an individual acted with "evil motive" or callous or "reckless indifference to the rights of others." *Smith v. Wade*, 461 U.S. 30, 47 (1983). Punitive damages are not available against municipalities under § 1983. *Newport v. Fact Concerts*, 453 U.S. 247, 271 (1981). The court also has discretion to permit "a reasonable attorney's fee as part of costs." 42 U.S.C. § 1988(b) (2006).

As for the claims under New York common law, a plaintiff can receive compensatory damages, which can include general damages for pain and suffering and emotional distress, as well as special damages such as medical expenses and lost earnings. Assault and Battery, 1 Am. Jur. Proof of Facts 3d 613, (2015). Even if we cannot show physical evidence of an injury, we can still request compensatory damages for emotional distress. *Id.* A plaintiff may receive punitive damages if the "intentional, malicious, outrageous, or otherwise aggravated beyond mere negligence." *McDougald v. Garber*, 73 N.Y.2d 246, 253 (N.Y. 1989). To prove malice, it may be sufficient to show that the actions were committed intentionally and without just cause. Malice is a question of fact, meaning a jury will be the one resolve whether a party acted with malice, and if so how much money should be awarded in punitive damages.

APPENDIX

42 U.S.C. § 1983

Every person who, under color of any statute, ordinance, regulation, custom or usage, of any State or Territory or the District of Columbia, subjects, or causes to be subjected, any citizen of the United States or other person within the jurisdiction thereof to the deprivation of any rights, privileges, or immunities secured by the Constitution and laws, shall be liable to the party injured in an action at law, suit in equity, or other proper proceeding for redress. . . .

U.S. Const. Amend. IV—Search and Seizure

The right of the people to be secure in their persons, houses, papers, and effects, against unreasonable searches and seizures, shall not be violated, and no Warrants shall issue, but upon probable cause, supported by Oath or affirmation, and particularly describing the place to be searched, and the persons or things to be seized.

U.S. Const. Amend. XIV, § 1, Cl. 1—Equal Protection

No State shall . . . deny to any person within its jurisdiction the equal protection of the laws.

FORM UF-250

(COMPLETE ALL CAPTIONS)

STOP, QUESTION AND FRISK REPORT WORKSHEET
PD344-151A (Rev. 11-02)

Pct.Serial No.		
Date		Pct. Of Occ.

Time Of Stop	Period Of Observation Prior To Stop	Radio Run/Sprint #

Address/Intersection Or Cross Streets Of Stop

☐ Inside ☐ Outside | ☐ Transit ☐ Housing | Type Of Location Describe:

Specify Which Felony/P.L. Misdemeanor Suspected	Duration Of Stop

What Were Circumstances Which Led To Stop?
(MUST CHECK AT LEAST ONE BOX)

☐ Carrying Objects In Plain View Used In Commission Of Crime e.g., Slim Jim/Pry Bar, etc.
☐ Fits Description.
☐ Actions Indicative Of "Casing" Victim Or Location.
☐ Actions Indicative of Acting As A Lookout.
☐ Suspicious Bulge/Object (Describe)
☐ Other Reasonable Suspicion Of Criminal Activity (Specify)

☐ Actions Indicative Of Engaging In Drug Transaction.
☐ Furtive Movements.
☐ Actions Indicative Of Engaging In Violent Crimes.
☐ Wearing Clothes/Disguises Commonly Used In Commission Of Crime.

Name Of Person Stopped	Nickname/ Street Name	Date Of Birth
Address	Apt. No.	Tel. No.

Identification: ☐ Verbal ☐ Photo I.D. ☐ Refused
☐ Other (Specify) _____

Sex:☐ Male ☐ Female | Race:☐ White ☐ Black ☐ White Hispanic ☐ Black Hispanic
☐ Asian/Pacific Islander ☐ American Indian/Alaskan Native

Age	Height	Weight	Hair	Eyes	Build

Other (Scars, Tattoos, Etc.)

Did Officer Explain Reason For Stop ☐ Yes ☐ No	If No, Explain:

Were Other Persons Stopped/ Questioned/Frisked? ☐ Yes ☐ No | If Yes, List Pct. Serial Nos.

If Physical Force Was Used, Indicate Type:
☐ Hands On Suspect
☐ Suspect On Ground
☐ Pointing Firearm At Suspect
☐ Handcuffing Suspect
☐ Suspect Against Wall/Car
☐ Drawing Firearm
☐ Baton
☐ Pepper Spray
☐ Other (Describe)

Was Suspect Arrested? ☐ Yes ☐ No	Offense	Arrest No.
Was Summons Issued? ☐ Yes ☐ No	Offense	Summons No.

Officer In Uniform? ☐ Yes ☐ No | If No, How Identified? ☐ Shield ☐ I.D. Card ☐ Verbal

Was Person Frisked? ☐ Yes ☐ No   **IF YES, MUST CHECK AT LEAST ONE BOX**

☐ Inappropriate Attire - Possibly Concealing Weapon
☐ Verbal Threats Of Violence By Suspect
☐ Knowledge Of Suspects Prior Criminal Violent Behavior/Use Of Force/Use Of Weapon
☐ Other Reasonable Suspicion of Weapons (Specify)

☐ Furtive Movements
☐ Actions Indicative Of Engaging In Violent Crimes

☐ Refusal To Comply With Officer's Direction(s) Leading To Reasonable Fear For Safety
☐ Violent Crime Suspected
☐ Suspicious Bulge/Object (Describe)

Was Person Searched? ☐ Yes ☐ No   **IF YES, MUST CHECK AT LEAST ONE BOX** ☐ Hard Object ☐ Admission Of Weapons Possession
☐ Outline Of Weapon ☐ Other Reasonable Suspicion of Weapons (Specify)

Was Weapon Found? ☐ Yes ☐ No   If Yes, Describe: ☐ Pistol/Revolver ☐ Rifle/Shotgun ☐ Assault Weapon ☐ Knife/Cutting Instrument
☐ Machine Gun ☐ Other (Describe)

Was Other Contraband Found? ☐ Yes ☐ No If Yes, Describe Contraband And Location _____
Demeanor Of Person After Being Stopped _____
Remarks Made By Person Stopped _____

Additional Circumstances/Factors: (Check All That Apply)

☐ Report From Victim/Witness
☐ Area Has High Incidence Of Reported Offense Of Type Under Investigation
☐ Time Of Day, Day Of Week, Season Corresponding To Reports Of Criminal Activity
☐ Suspect Is Associating With Persons Known For Their Criminal Activity
☐ Proximity To Crime Location
☐ Other (Describe)

☐ Evasive, False Or Inconsistent Response To Officer's Questions
☐ Changing Direction At Sight Of Officer/Flight
☐ Ongoing Investigations, e.g., Robbery Pattern
☐ Sights And Sounds Of Criminal Activity, e.g., Bloodstains, Ringing Alarms

Pct. Serial No. _____ | Additional Reports Prepared: Complaint Rpt.No. _____ Juvenile Rpt. No. _____ Aided Rpt. No. _____ Other Rpt. (Specify) _____

REPORTED BY: Rank, Name (Last, First, M.I.)   REVIEWED BY: Rank, Name (Last, First, M.I.)

Print _____ Tax# _____   Print _____ Tax# _____

Signature _____ Command _____   Signature _____ Command _____

City Police Stop Whites Equally But Frisk Them Less, A Study Finds

New York Times

By AL BAKER
Published: November 21, 2007

Whites and members of minorities have a roughly equal chance of being stopped by police officers and questioned on the street in New York City. But officers are more likely to frisk, search or arrest black and Hispanic people—or to use force against them—according to a study released yesterday.

The study by the Rand Corporation, commissioned in March after it was revealed that the police made 508,540 stops on the street last year, also found:

The pattern of whites and minorities being stopped equally, but the minorities being frisked more often, held up in white and black neighborhoods, but was most pronounced on Staten Island.

Slightly more than half of the 508,540 stops last year were made by 2,756 officers—an average of about 100 each.

Fifteen of those 2,756 officers—six of whom are assigned to precincts in the southern part of Queens—were disproportionately more likely to stop blacks and Hispanics, and an additional 13 officers were disproportionately more likely to stop whites.

The issue of stopping people on the street—known in department jargon as "stop and frisks"—has been a source of occasional tension in New York. It became an emotional flash point after the 1999 fatal police shooting of Amadou Diallo, an unarmed black street peddler. It came to light again after the fatal shooting in November 2006 of Sean Bell, when many people began to question why the number of stops had jumped to 508,540 from 97,296 in 2002, which was the last time that the department released a full year's worth of data.

The 59-page report by Rand, a private nonprofit organization, was commissioned by Police Commissioner Raymond W. Kelly after the department released the data. Of the 508,540 people stopped, about 10 percent were arrested or received summonses.

The report includes six recommendations for Mr. Kelly, such as refining paperwork to capture data on use of force and requiring officers to explain to people why they are being stopped.

"We're going to take an in-depth review of the six recommendations and study them, and obviously I think the report is well done," Mr. Kelly said. He added, "It seems to me that they all have merit, and we'll put in place what we think is appropriate as quickly as possible."

The other recommendations were to review the boroughs with the greatest disparities; to train newly hired officers in stop-and-frisk policies; to modify the internal audits of street stops; and to flag and investigate those officers who make more racially disparate stops.

The analysts, for the most part, did not explain why the racial disparities exist regarding stops, said Jack Riley, the associate director of the Rand division that did the study.

"There may be missing factors that are not collected by the officers that might help explain the small differences in what we would term adjusted frisk rates," Mr. Riley said.

"Certainly, resisting arrest or resisting interaction with an officer is not captured and that would be a factor that would influence whether the person is frisked or not."

Critics of the department's street-stop practices faulted Rand's methodology.

Donna Lieberman, the executive director of the New York Civil Liberties Union, called the report "hugely flawed," saying that the document was more striking for what it did not say than for what it said. She said the report relied on "inappropriate benchmarks" to reach its findings.

The phenomenon of a small number of officers doing most of the stops is roughly similar to patterns found in Oakland, Calif., and in Cincinnati, Mr. Riley said. Rand conducted similar studies there. "There are typically officers who are disproportionately involved in stops of all racial groups, not just minorities," Mr. Riley said. "Rand has found similar patterns."

In explaining why roughly 7 percent of the department's total patrol strength was responsible for 54 percent of all street stops last year, Paul J. Browne, the Police Department's chief spokesman, said it was generally based on their assignments to high-crime areas.

"In addition, it involves officers assigned to special units," he said. "Units that are encountering more suspects such as anticrime, narcotics, gang and other units."

Rand analysts left it to police officials to come up with an explanation for why blacks and Hispanics were more likely to be frisked, searched, arrested or to have force used against them—such as officers wielding a baton, spraying pepper spray or pointing a gun—on Staten Island compared with other boroughs.

Mr. Browne said the department would have to study why the disparities are most pronounced on Staten Island. "We don't know," he said. "It is something we will have to examine." Greg Ridgeway, the associate director at Rand, who wrote the report, said there were plausible reasons for the 508,540 stops in 2006, despite projections—based on data from national surveys on police and citizen contacts—that suggested 250,000 to 330,000 stops could be expected. This does not include traffic stops.

He said possible reasons included more 911 calls, more officers on the street—there are 44 officers per 10,000 residents in New York City, as opposed to roughly 29 officers per 10,000 residents around the country—more pedestrian traffic and more instances of violent crime than the national average.

The report stated that 69 percent of suspects in violent crimes were described by their victims as black whereas only 53 percent of all those stopped by police officers for stop-and-frisks were black. But the civil liberties group said only a fraction of the 508,540 people stopped last year were suspects in violent crimes, making the analysis flawed.

In one area—the use of force—the Rand study said, "If black suspects are likelier to flee or resist, the observed difference in rates of force may not be due to officer bias." But Christopher Dunn of the civil liberties group called this "an example of them not doing analysis and instead looking for justifications. It simply reflects the dishonesty that runs through this report."

http://www.nytimes.com/2007/11/21/nyregion/21rand.html

Cops: We Were Told to Profile. Frisk All Black Men at Subway Stop

New York Daily News
By MICHAEL SAUL, ALISON GENDAR

Tuesday, October 10, 2006, 12:00 AM

Five cops who heard an NYPD captain give a controversial order told the Daily News yesterday the message was crystal clear: Stop and frisk every black man at a robbery-plagued Brooklyn subway station. "The captain said the descriptions of the [suspects] vary a lot, so we were to stop all black males at the station, stop and frisk them because 'they have no reason being there,'" said one white officer who was outraged by the command. Capt. Michael Vanchieri, commander of Brooklyn Transit District 30, gave the orders at Thursday's 7 A.M. roll call, the cops said. A sergeant and a lieutenant opened the meeting, then turned the meeting over to Vanchieri, who described a series of robberies on the F line in Brooklyn, concentrated near the Seventh Ave.-Park Slope station. "All black men were to be stopped—no description other than that," the white officer said. "So some 30- to 40-year-old man who had every right to be at the station—he'd get frisked too."

The Daily News interviewed five of the 12 to 15 officers at the 7 A.M. briefing. All five—a mix of black and white, male and female cops, who spoke on condition of anonymity—gave consistent accounts. "Everybody was totally shocked," said a black officer who was present. "It was very clear. Stop and question and frisk. But no description of who we were looking for—just male blacks," he said. Vanchieri could not be reached. But Police Commissioner Raymond Kelly said Vanchieri has denied making any inappropriate comments, claiming any discussion of race was part of a broader description of the suspects. "He gave a description of those individuals and asked if anybody sees them, if anyone matched that description, to stop and speak to them," Kelly said. Kelly noted that the NYPD is the only major police department in the country to ban profiling. "All indications are that there was some sort of misunderstanding as to what his directions were," Kelly added. Victor Swinton, president of the Guardians Association, an association of black NYPD officers, said Vanchieri has offered to meet with him about the roll call order. msaul@nydailynews.com

http://www.nydailynews.com/archives/news/cops-told-profile-frisk-black-men-subway-stop-article-1.586382

UNITED STATES DISTRICT COURT
SOUTHERN DISTRICT OF NEW YORK

JACOB WARNER, and WILLIAM MOORE, Individually and on behalf of a class of all others similarly situated;	08 Civ. 01034 (SAS)
Plaintiffs,	CLASS ACTION COMPLAINT FOR DECLARATORY AND INJUNCTIVE RELIEF AND INDIVIDUAL DAMAGES
-against-	
THE CITY OF NEW YORK, NEW YORK CITY POLICE COMMISSIONER RAYMOND KELLY; MAYOR MICHAEL BLOOMBERG; OFFICER SCOTT MCDONALD; OFFICER THOMAS FOLEY; OFFICER RICHARD CANNON;	DEMAND FOR JURY TRIAL
Defendants.	

PARTIES

1. Plaintiff JACOB WARNER ("Warner") is an African-American male who lives in the Bronx in the City of New York.

2. Plaintiff WILLIAM MOORE ("Moore") is an African-American male who lives in Harlem in the City of New York.

3. Defendant CITY OF NEW YORK ("City") is a municipal entity in the State of New York. The City maintains the New York Police Department ("NYPD"). The City assumes the risks and liability of actions conducted by the NYPD.

4. Defendant New York City Police Commissioner RAYMOND KELLY ("Police Commissioner for the City" or "Commissioner Kelly") was and is, at all relevant times, the Commissioner of the New York City Police Department. Commissioner Kelly was and is responsible for implementing the relevant policies, practices and/or customs of the NYPD. Commissioner Kelly was and is in charge of training, monitoring, and disciplining NYPD officers.

5. Defendant MICHAEL BLOOMBERG ("Mayor Bloomberg") is the Mayor of the City of New York and is in charge of policy making for the City and all departments, including the NYPD.

6. Defendant SCOTT MCDONALD ("Officer McDonald" or "McDonald") is, and/or was, an officer with the New York Police Department during all relevant times. Officer McDonald is an employee and agent of the NYPD and is sued in his individual capacity.

7. Defendant THOMAS FOLEY ("Officer Foley" or "Foley") is, and/or was, an officer with the New York Police Department during all relevant times. Officer Foley is an employee and agent of the NYPD and is sued in his individual capacity.

8. Defendant RICHARD CANNON ("Officer Cannon" or "Cannon") is, and/or was, an officer with the New York Police Department during all relevant times. Officer Cannon is an employee and agent of the NYPD and is sued in his individual capacity.

CLASS ACTION ALLEGATIONS

9. The named Plaintiffs bring this action on their own behalf and on behalf of others similarly situated, pursuant to Rule 23(a) and (b)(2) of the Federal Rules of Civil Procedure. The class that the named Plaintiffs represent consists of all individuals who have been or will be subjected to NYPD officers stopping, or stopping and frisking individuals without a reasonable, articulable suspicion of criminal activity in violation of the Fourth Amendment. The NYPD officers' actions were and are enforced, encouraged, and/or sanctioned by the policies, practices and/or customs of Defendants City, Commissioner Kelly, and Mayor Bloomberg. This class includes all individuals who were stopped, or stopped and frisked based on racial or national origin profiling, in violation of the Equal Protection Clause of the Fourteenth Amendment.

10. The class is so numerous that joinder of all parties is impracticable. Based on publically available information provided by the NYPD, hundreds of thousands of individuals have been subjected to stops, or stops and frisks without a reasonable, articulable suspicion of criminal conduct every year by NYPD officers.

11. Upon information and belief, joinder is also impracticable because many class members are unaware that their constitutional rights have been violated and that they can seek redress in court, and/or do not bring individual claims for fear of retaliation by NYPD officers.

12. The class members share numerous facts and questions of law in common, including but not limited to:

a. whether the NYPD has policies, practices, and/or custom of stopping, and/or stopping and frisking class members without a reasonable, articulable suspicion of criminal conduct in violation of the Fourth Amendment;

b. whether the NYPD profiles on the basis of race and/or national origin in targeting members of the class for such stops and frisks, in violation of the Equal Protection Clause of the Fourteenth Amendment

c. whether the NYPD conducts searches and seizures, and uses excessive force, in violation of the Fourth Amendment, when conducting such stops and frisks;

d. whether Defendants City, Commissioner Kelly, and Mayor Bloomberg have failed to properly train, monitor, and discipline NYPD officers who are conducting such searches;

e. whether Defendants City, Commissioner Kelly, and Mayor Bloomberg have implemented, sanctioned, enforced, and encouraged NYPD officers to engage in unconstitutional stops and frisks, and whether their actions have caused class members' constitutional rights to be violated;

f. whether the failure of Defendants City, Commissioner Kelly, and Mayor Bloomberg remedy unconstitutional stops and frisks have caused class members' constitutional rights to be violated.

13. The named Plaintiff's claims are typical of the claims of the other members of the class. The named Plaintiffs, like other members of the class, have been victims of the NYPD's policies, practices and/or customs of stops and frisks without a reasonable, articulable suspicion of criminal conduct as required by the Fourth Amendment and on basis of their race and/or national origin. The named Plaintiffs likely will be victims again, as will other members of the class. The legal theories asserted by the named Plaintiffs in this action are the same or similar to the ones on which all other members of the class will rely. Furthermore, the named Plaintiffs suffered harms that are typical of the other class members.

14. The named Plaintiffs will fairly and adequately protect the interests of the class, and have a strong personal stake in the outcome of this action. The named Plaintiffs have no conflicts of interest with the other members of the class.

15. Pursuant to Rule 23(b)(2) of the Federal Rules of Civil Procedure, the Plaintiff class should be certified because the Defendants has acted on grounds that apply generally to the class, thereby making final injunctive relief and corresponding declaratory relief appropriate.

FACTS

Jacob Warner

16. On April 20, 2007, Plaintiff Jacob Warner, a 28 year old black man, was walking in the middle of the day in his neighborhood in the Bronx.

17. Warner was summoned by Officer McDonald, who was riding in a van next to the sidewalk where Warner was walking.

18. Officer McDonald told Warner to stop, without any basis for a reasonable, articulable suspicion that Warner had engaged in or was about to engage in criminal conduct. Officer McDonald exited the van, and cornered Warner. Officer McDonald asked Warner about what he was doing, where he was going, and if he had any weapons on him. Officer McDonald also asked Warner for identification. Warner asked Officer McDonald why he was being stopped, however Officer McDonald refused to answer his question nor did he provide any reason for the stop.

19. Without any basis for probable cause or a reasonable, articulable suspicion that Warner was armed or dangerous, Officer McDonald searched under Warner's shirt and also put his hands inside Warner's pants pockets. Warner told Officer McDonald that he did not consent to the search, and asked Officer McDonald what probable cause they had to search him. Officer McDonald refused to answer Warner's questions.

20. After conducting the unlawful stop and frisk and finding no weapons or illegal items on Warner, Officer McDonald questioned Warner about his out-of-state driver's license and told Warner that he could get arrested for not having a New York State license. Warner told the Officer McDonald that he did not drive in the State of New York. Officer McDonald then got into the van and Warner asked Officer McDonald for his name and badge numbers. Officer McDonald identified himself and jokingly asked the other officers in the van for their information before leaving without informing Warner why he was stopped and searched.

21. Warner did not witness Officer McDonald, who stopped and frisked him, or the other officers in the van fill out paperwork at any time.

22. Officer McDonald subjected Warner to a stop, frisk and search without a reasonable, articulable suspicion, based on his race and/or national origin.

23. In February 2008, NYPD officers again unlawfully stopped, questioned and searched Warner in his neighborhood. Warner was with acquaintance Ron Belton, a 30 year old black male, and the two men were trying to figure out which key went to the door of Warner's godmother's apartment at 146 Randall Ave in the Bronx.

24. Without any basis for probable cause or a reasonable, articulable suspicion that Warner was engaged in or was about to engage in criminal conduct, Officer Foley and Officer Cannon approached the men and asked what they were doing.

25. Without allowing Warner or Belton an opportunity to answer the question, the officers told both men to stand up against the wall with their hands spread on the wall in front of them.

26. Officer Foley put his hands inside Warner's pants pockets, thereby subjecting Warner to a search.

27. After the frisk and search, Warner explained that the apartment was owned by his godmother, and that Belton lived there and had locked himself out of the building. Warner explained that he was not sure which spare key went to the apartment door so he was trying various keys to figure it out.

28. Officer Cannon asked Warner and Belton for identification, and questioned Warner on the address on his license.

29. Belton's license was locked in the house, so Officer Foley and Belton used Warner's spare key to enter the building and confirm Belton's address.

30. Warner did not observe either officer that stopped and frisked him filling out paperwork.

31. Officers Foley and Cannon subjected Warner to a stop, frisk and search without a reasonable, articulable suspicion, based on his race and/or national origin.

William Moore

32. In January 2006 at 1:00 PM, Plaintiff William Moore, a 26 year old black male, was on his lunch break and bought food from Subway restaurant at W 134th Street and Frederick Douglass Boulevard in Harlem. Moore then walked to a bodega on the corner of W 134th Street and Adam Clayton Powell Jr. Boulevard, across from the Charter School where he worked.

33. Inside the bodega, Moore noticed two men, Officers McDonald and Cannon, in the bodega, both wearing plain clothes. Moore purchased food at the bodega and exited.

34. Without any basis for a reasonable, articulable suspicion that Moore had engaged in or was about to engage in criminal conduct, Officers McDonald and Cannon immediately followed Moore out of the bodega and called out to him. Moore stopped and turned. The officers walked over to Moore, flashed their police badges and backed Moore up against the bodega window. The officers, approximately half a foot taller than Moore, stood less than two feet away from Moore.

35. Officers McDonald and Cannon began to question Moore, without waiting for Moore to consent or object. Officer McDonald asked Moore where he was coming from, to which Moore responded that he was on his lunch break from his job at the Charter School across the street.

36. Officer Cannon told Moore that he had been observed coming from the direction of a building on Walton Avenue that was allegedly known as a center for drug activity. Moore explained that he had bought lunch at the Subway restaurant on 167th Street and Walton Avenue, and therefore had to pass by the building the officers mentioned on his way to work on 169th Street.

37. Officer Cannon asked Moore if he had any contraband on him, and whether the police would find any contraband if they were to search him. Moore replied that he did not have any contraband on him, and that he did not consent to a search.

38. Officer Cannon asked the question again, and Moore reaffirmed that he did not have any contraband on him and that he did not consent to a search.

39. Officer Cannon moved a couple of steps closer, and asked Moore the question a third time. Moore again reaffirmed that he did not have any contraband on him and that he did not consent to a search. At this time, several people had come out of stores in the area to witness the police interrogate and detain Moore.

40. Officers McDonald and Cannon left the scene after Moore refused to consent to the search a third time. Moore did not observe either officer fill out any paperwork.

41. Neither NYPD officer had a reasonable, articulable suspicion of criminal activity to stop Moore, and subjected him to a stop and detention based on his race and/or national origin.

NYPD's History of Stops and Frisks Without a Reasonable, Articulable Suspicion

42. The NYPD policy with regards to stop and frisk is facially neutral, although in practice has a disparate effect on minorities.

43. The NYPD's policy of stop and frisk started with the formation of the "Street Crime Unit" ("SCU") in the 1970s, and became a central part of NYPD's efforts to combat crime after Rudolph Giuliani ("Giuliani") became Mayor of the City of New York in 1994.

44. In 1999, the Office of the Attorney General ("OAG") investigated the NYPD's stop and frisk practices for January 1, 1998 through March 31, 1988. The study showed that there was evidence of a disparate impact based on race. The OAG found that Blacks and Hispanics made up 83.6% of all stops by the NYPD, although Blacks were only 25.6% and Hispanics 23.7% of the City's

population. On the other hand, Whites comprised only 12.9% of the stops but were 43.4% of the population.

45. The study also found that only 1 out of 9.5 stops of Blacks, 1 out of 8.8 stops of Hispanics and 1 out of 7.9 stops of Whites led to an arrest. These rates show that stops of Whites are more likely to lead to an arrest than stops of Blacks or Hispanics.

46. Blacks were stopped 23% more often than Whites. Hispanics were stopped 39% more often than Whites.

47. NYPD officers frequently failed to complete the UF-250 form to document the stop and frisk, and this required paperwork was only completed in 10%-20% of stops and frisks.

48. In 1999, the Center for Constitutional Rights filed a class action lawsuit, *Daniels et al. v. The City of New York, et al.*, ("*Daniels*") against the NYPD, challenging the NYPD's unconstitutional use of race and/or national origin to determine individuals to be stopped and frisked, instead of stopping individuals based on a reasonable articulable suspicion as required by the Fourth Amendment.

49. During litigation for *Daniels*, the NYPD claimed that the SCU was disbanded, however their unlawful practices have continued.

50. In 2003, a settlement was reached. The Stipulation required that the NYPD adopt a written policy banning racial profiling, and to create quarterly data of stop and frisk based on the information written on UF-250 forms.

51. The data gathered from the UF-250 forms for the last quarter of 2003, all quarters of 2004, 2005, 2006 and the first quarter of 2007 showed racial disparities in stop and frisk practices. This data demonstrates that NYPD officers have not complied with the written policy prohibiting racial profiling and therefore a continued violation of the United States and New York State Constitutions.

52. The UF-250 data reveals that in 2006, the NYPD stopped and frisked 506,491 people and 90% of those individuals were Black or Latino. In 2006, Blacks and Latinos made up only approximately 52% of the City's population. Only 10% of those stops led to arrests or summonses.

53. The UF-250 data also shows that the percentage of stops involving Blacks has been increasing. Blacks made up 48% of stops in 2003; 50% in 2004; 51% in 2005; and 53% in 2006.

54. Furthermore, Blacks who were stopped were more often frisked than Whites that were stopped. In 2004, 45% of Blacks who were stopped were

frisked by police officers, yet only 29% of Whites were. In 2005, 47% of Blacks who were stopped were frisked, and 27% of Whites were. In 2006, 46% of Blacks who were stopped were also frisked, compared with 29% of Whites. Of the Whites that were frisked in 2006, 13% were arrested compared with 7% of Blacks, meaning that stops of Whites were more likely to lead to an arrest. The lower percentage of frisks that led to an arrest for Blacks suggests that the police officers did not have a reasonable articulable suspicion for the stops and frisks of that group.

55. The UF-250 data shows a difference in the use of physical force by police officers based on race. In 2006, 15% of Whites were subject to physical force by the police compared with 21% of Blacks. However, Blacks who experienced physical force were less likely to be arrested afterwards. Blacks were only arrested in 14% of the cases where physical force was used, compared to Whites at 12%.

56. In the UF-250 data from 2006, the most common reason given for stopping Blacks was suspicion of a weapons crime, however only 2% of stops actually led to the discovery of a weapon. Significantly, Blacks and Latinos were frisked more often than Whites (45% compared to 29%) yet White suspects were 70% more likely than Black suspects to have a weapon. Only 29% of Whites were subjected to a frisk as compared with 45% of Blacks, although a police officer is twice as likely to find contraband on a White suspect than a Black suspect. Based on these statistics, searches of Whites were more productive, yet Blacks and Latinos were subject to searches more often.

57. Blacks were more likely to be stopped for subjective reasons, according to the UF-250 data, which allowed for differential treatment based on race. In 2006, 38% of Blacks were stopped for "furtive movements," as compared with 31% of Whites. A "suspicious bulge" was the reason given for 10% of Blacks stopped yet only 3% of Whites.

58. Public accounts, such as newspaper articles, further demonstrate unlawful stops and frisks. On October 10, 2006, the *Daily News* reported that officers had been ordered by their captain, in response to a series of robberies on the F subway line in Brooklyn, to stop, question and frisk all black males at the Seventh Avenue Park Slope subway station. This unlawful order directed police officers to stop and frisk all black males, regardless of whether the officer had a reasonable, articulable suspicion or not.

NYPD's Suspicionless Stops and Frisks Are Caused by the Policies, Practices and/or Customs of Defendants City, Commissioner Kelly, and Mayor Bloomberg

59. The Fourth Amendment protection against unreasonable searches and seizures requires officers to have a reasonable, articulable suspicion of criminal conduct in order to conduct a stop and frisk. Police officers may frisk a person

whom they have a reasonable belief is armed or dangerous. The police may not use excessive force while conducting policing activities and may not search or seize a person without probable cause. The Equal Protection Clause of the Fourteenth Amendment prohibits police officers from targeting an individual for stops and frisks based on their race or national origin.

60. Defendants implemented, sanctioned, enforced, and encouraged practices and policies that violate the U.S. Constitutional protections under the Fourth Amendment and the Equal Protection Clause of the Fourteenth Amendment.

61. The unconstitutional stop and frisks being conducted by NYPD officers is the direct and proximate result of policies, practices and/or customs created and sanctioned by Defendants City, Commissioner Kelly, and Mayor Bloomberg.

62. Defendants failed to properly train and supervise NYPD officers in the legal way to conduct stops and frisks in order to comply with the Fourth and Fourteenth Amendments, and this failure shows a deliberate indifference to protecting individuals' constitutional rights.

63. Defendants failed to properly monitor and supervise NYPD officers who engaged in, encouraged or concealed unconstitutional stops and frisks. Defendants purposefully, knowingly and recklessly failed to take disciplinary action against NYPD officers who conducted stops and frisks without a reasonable, articulable suspicion of criminal conduct, and/or monitor NYPD officers who were the subject of a substantial number of civilian complaints. Defendants purposefully, knowingly and recklessly failed to take sufficient steps to address NYPD officers' non-compliance with the requirement of filling out the UF-250 forms after each stop and frisk.

64. Defendants, on information and belief, created unwritten "productivity standards" which required NYPD officers to reach a certain number stops and frisks, and specific types of arrests, per month. On information and belief, NYPD officers who did not meet this quota faced adverse employment consequences and therefore engaged stops and frisks without a reasonable, articulable suspicion.

65. The Stipulation in *Daniels* required Defendant City and the NYPD to implement a written policy prohibiting racial or ethnic/national origin profiling because the practice violates the United States and New York State Constitutions. Defendants have violated that written policy, as described herein.

66. Pursuant to the Stipulation in *Daniels*, Defendant City and the NYPD were required to train NYPD officers that it was mandatory to fill out the UF-250 forms for every stop, question and frisk; supervise, monitor and train NYPD

officers in the policy banning racial profiling; and to determine how many stops and frisks were based on reasonable suspicion by an auditing system. On information and belief, Defendants failed to adhere to these requirements.

67. Tens of thousands of individuals have been subject to unconstitutional stops and frisks by the NYPD as a direct and proximate result of Defendants' policies, practices, customs, and failure to comply with the Stipulation in *Daniels*.

CAUSES OF ACTION

Count One

(Claims of Named Plaintiffs and Class Members Pursuant to 42 U.S.C. § 1983 Against All Defendants for Violations of the Fourth Amendment of the U.S. Constitution)

68. Plaintiffs repeat and reallege paragraphs "1" through "67" as if fully set forth herein.

69. Defendants implemented, enforced, and sanctioned policies, practices and/or customs of suspicionless stops and frisks in violation of Fourth Amendment requirement that such activities must be based on a reasonable, articulable suspicion of criminal conduct. Individuals that were subjected to stops and frisks without a reasonable, articulable suspicion of criminality were often also subjected to unconstitutional searches and seizures, as well as excessive force, by NYPD officers.

70. The NYPD's unconstitutional actions were and are the direct and proximate result of policies, practices and/or customs that were implemented, enforced, encouraged and/or sanctioned by the of Defendants City, Commissioner Kelly, and Mayor Bloomberg to: (a) properly train and monitor NYPD officers; (b) adequately discipline NYPD officers who violated NYPD policy and/or the U.S. Constitution; and (c) remedy the NYPD's practices that violate the Fourth Amendment.

71. Defendants acted under the color of law to deprive the named Plaintiffs and other members of the class of their Fourth Amendment rights in violation of 42 U.S.C. § 1983.

72. Due to the Defendants' policies, practices and/or customs of conducting stops and frisks without a reasonable, articulable suspicion of criminality, named Plaintiffs and other members of the class are unable to alter their behavior in order to prevent NYPD officers from violating their constitutional and civil rights.

73. The constitutional rights of the named Plaintiffs and other members of the class will continue to be harmed in the future unless Defendants are enjoined from permitting and enforcing the NYPD's policies, practices and/or customs of stops and frisks that violate the U.S. Constitution.

Count Two

(Claims of Named Plaintiffs and Class Members Pursuant to 42 U.S.C. § 1983 Against All Defendants for Violations of the Equal Protection Clause of the Fourteenth Amendment of the U.S. Constitution)

74. Plaintiffs repeat and reallege paragraphs "1" through "67" as if fully set forth herein.

75. Defendants' policies, practices and/or customs of conducting stops and frisks without a reasonable, articulable suspicion, as required by the Fourth Amendment, on the named Plaintiffs and other members of the class was based on their race and/or national origin.

76. NYPD officers, including but not limited to Officers McDonald, Foley, and Cannon, conducted stops and frisks predominantly on Black and Latino individuals based on their race and/or national origin, in violation of the Equal Protection Clause of the Fourteenth Amendment.

77. The NYPD's constitutional abuses were and are the direct and proximate result of policies, practices and/or customs that were implemented, enforced, encouraged and/or sanctioned by the failure of Defendants City, Commissioner Kelly, and Mayor Bloomberg to: (a) properly train and monitor NYPD officers; (b) adequately discipline NYPD officers who violated NYPD policy and/or the U.S. Constitution; and (c) remedy the NYPD's practices of using racial and/or national origin profiling in conducting stops and frisks.

78. Defendants' actions show a deliberate indifference to the Fourteenth Amendment rights of the named Plaintiffs and other members of the class.

79. Defendants acted under the color of law to deprive the named Plaintiffs and other members of the class of their Fourteenth Amendment rights in violation of 42 U.S.C. § 1983.

80. The Fourteenth Amendment rights of the named Plaintiffs and other members of the class will continue to be harmed in the future because of NYPD racial and/or national origin profiling unless Defendants are enjoined from

permitting and enforcing the NYPD's policies, practices and/or customs of stops and frisks that violate the U.S. Constitution.

81. Named Plaintiffs and other members of the class are unable to alter their behavior in order to prevent NYPD officers from violating their constitutional and civil rights, because of Defendants' policies, practices and/or customs of conducting stops and frisks on the basis of race and/or national origin without a reasonable, articulable suspicion of criminality.

Count Three

(Violation of Rights Under New York Law)

82. Plaintiffs repeat and reallege paragraphs "1" through "67" as if fully set forth herein.

83. As alleged above, every Defendant, jointly and severally, has committed assault and battery, both tortious acts, against the named Plaintiffs and other members of the class.

84. The conduct of Defendants was a direct and proximate cause of the injuries to the named Plaintiffs and other members of the class, in violation of New York State law.

Count Four

(Respondeat Superior Claim Against the City under New York Common Law)

85. Plaintiffs repeat and reallege paragraphs "1" through "67" as if fully set forth herein.

86. The conduct of NYPD officers occurred while they were on duty, and was within the scope and course of their duties as New York City police officers.

87. NYPD officers were acting as employees of Defendant City while they conducted stops and frisks without a reasonable, articulable suspicion.

88. Therefore, Defendant City is liable to the named Plaintiffs and members of the class under the doctrine of respondeat superior.

PRAYER FOR RELIEF

89. Plaintiffs repeat and reallege paragraphs "1" through "88" as if fully set forth herein.

90. WHEREFORE, the named Plaintiffs and other members of the class respectfully request that the Court will:

a. Pursuant to Rule 23(a) and (b)(2) of the Federal Rules of Civil Procedure, issue an order certifying this action as a class action with the named Plaintiffs as class representatives;

b. Declare that the NYPD's policies, practices and/or customs of stops and frisks without a reasonable, articulable suspicion challenged herein is unconstitutional as a violation of the Fourth and Fourteenth Amendments to the United States Constitution, and the laws of the State of New York, and that the unconstitutional actions of the NYPD is the direct and proximate result of Defendants City, Commissioner Kelly, and Mayor Bloomberg's:

i. failure to properly train and monitor NYPD officers

ii. failure to adequately discipline NYPD officers who violated NYPD policy and/or the U.S. Constitution

iii. failure to remedy the NYPD's practices of using racial and/or national origin profiling in conducting stops and frisks

iv. sanctioning and encouraging the NYPD's unconstitutional stops and frisks.

c. Issue an order for injunctive relief:

i. enjoining the NYPD from continuing its policies, practices and/or customs of stops and frisks without a reasonable, articulable suspicion;

ii. enjoining the NYPD from continuing its policies, practices and/ or customs of stops and frisks based on racial and/or national origin profiling;

iii. enjoining the use of productivity standards or other quotas, whether formal or informal, for arrests and/or stops and frisks by NYPD officers;

iv. requiring Defendants City, Commissioner Kelly, and Mayor Bloomberg to create and implement new policies and programs to train, discipline and promote NYPD officers in order to eliminate the NYPD's policies, practices and/or custom of stops and frisks without a reasonable, articulable suspicion of criminal conduct;

v. requiring Defendants City, Commissioner Kelly, and Mayor Bloomberg to create and implement adequate measures to ensure that UF-250's or other documentation, documenting all stops, frisks, searches, and arrests, are maintained in a computerized database that is kept up to date;

vi. requiring Defendants City, Commissioner Kelly, and Mayor Bloomberg to create and implement measures to regularly review the stop and frisk policies, practices and/or customs of the NYPD to determine whether the reported stops and frisks comply with constitutional requirements.

d. Award named Plaintiffs Warner and Moore compensatory and punitive damages that are fair and reasonable;

e. Pursuant to 28 U.S.C. § 1920 and 142 U.S.C. § 1988, award all Plaintiffs, including members of the class, costs of suit;

f. Pursuant to 42 U.S.C. § 1988, award all Plaintiffs, including members of the class, reasonable attorneys' fees;

g. Award any other relief as this Court decides is appropriate and in the interests of justice.

DATED: /d/ Respectfully Submitted
By Their Attorneys

By: _____/s/ Mark Goulding _____
By: _____/s/ Rebecca Newman _____

Mark Goulding (BBO#896531)
Rebecca Newman (BBO# 983421)
Goulding, Newman & Martin
103 W. 42nd Street
New York, NY 10119
(646) 555-5555

UNITED STATES DISTRICT COURT
SOUTHERN DISTRICT OF NEW YORK

JACOB WARNER, and WILLIAM MOORE, Individually and on behalf of a class of all others similarly situated; Plaintiffs, -against- THE CITY OF NEW YORK, NEW YORK CITY POLICE COMMISSIONER RAYMOND KELLY; MAYOR MICHAEL BLOOMBERG; OFFICER SCOTT MCDONALD; OFFICER THOMAS FOLEY; OFFICER RICHARD CANNON; Defendants.	08 Civ. 01034 (SAS) ANSWER TO CLASS ACTION COMPLAINT ON BEHALF OF DEFENDANT NEW YORK CITY POLICE COMMISSIONER RAYMOND KELLY DEMAND FOR JURY TRIAL

Defendant New York City Police Commissioner Raymond Kelly by his attorneys Hailey Roberts and Julia Grutzman for his answer to the Class Action Complaint allege, upon information and belief, the following:

1. Deny sufficient knowledge or information to form a belief as to the truth of the allegations set forth in paragraph "1" of the Class Action Complaint.

2. Deny sufficient knowledge or information to form a belief as to the truth of the allegations set forth in paragraph "2" of the Class Action Complaint.

3. Deny the allegations set forth in paragraph "3" of the Class Action Complaint, except admit that the City of New York is a municipal entity of the State of New York and admit that the City maintains a Police Department.

4. Deny the allegations set forth in paragraph "4" of the Class Action Complaint, except admit that Raymond Kelly is the Police Commissioner of the City of New York. Respectfully refer the Court to the New York City Charter and New York City Administrative Code for information about the role of the New York City Police Commissioner and the New York City Police Department.

5. Deny the allegations set forth in paragraph "5" of the Class Action Complaint, except admit that Michael Bloomberg is the Mayor of the City of

New York, and respectfully refer the Court to the New York City Charter and New York City Administrative Code for information about the role of the Mayor of New York City.

6. Defendant is without knowledge or information sufficient to form a belief as to the truth of the allegations set forth in paragraph "6" of the Class Action Complaint.

7. Defendant is without knowledge or information sufficient to form a belief as to the truth of the allegations set forth in paragraph "7" of the Class Action Complaint.

8. Defendant is without knowledge or information sufficient to form a belief as to the truth of the allegations set forth in paragraph "8" of the Class Action Complaint.

9. Deny the allegations set forth in paragraph "9" of the Class Action Complaint, except admit that the plaintiffs purport to proceed as stated therein.

10. Deny the allegations set forth in paragraph "10" of the Class Action Complaint.

11. Deny the allegations set forth in paragraph "11" of the Class Action Complaint.

12. Deny the allegations set forth in paragraph "12" of the Class Action Complaint and its subparts.

13. Deny the allegations set forth in paragraph "13" of the Class Action Complaint.

14. Deny the allegations set forth in paragraph "14" of the Class Action Complaint.

15. Deny the allegations set forth in paragraph "15" of the Class Action Complaint.

16. Defendant is without knowledge or information sufficient to form a belief as to the truth of the allegations set forth in paragraph "16" of the Class Action Complaint.

17. Defendant is without knowledge or information sufficient to form a belief as to the truth of the allegations set forth in paragraph "17" of the Class Action Complaint.

18. Deny the allegations set forth in paragraph "18" of the Class Action Complaint, except deny knowledge or information sufficient to form a belief as to the truth of the allegations regarding plaintiff's actions, officers' actions, and communications between plaintiff and the officers.

19. Deny the allegations set forth in paragraph "19" of the Class Action Complaint, except deny knowledge or information sufficient to form a belief as to the truth of the allegations regarding statements made to the officers.

20. Defendant is without knowledge or information sufficient to form a belief as to the truth of the allegations set forth in paragraph "20" of the Class Action Complaint.

21. Defendant is without knowledge or information sufficient to form a belief as to the truth of the allegations set forth in paragraph "21" of the Class Action Complaint.

22. Deny the allegations set forth in paragraph "22" of the Class Action Complaint.

23. Defendant is without knowledge or information sufficient to form a belief as to the truth of the allegations set forth in paragraph "23" of the Class Action Complaint, except deny that officers unlawfully stopped, questioned and frisked Warner in February 2008.

24. Deny the allegations set forth in paragraph "24" of the Class Action Complaint, except deny knowledge or information sufficient to form a belief as to the truth of the allegations regarding plaintiff's actions, officers' actions, and communications between the plaintiff and the officers.

25. Deny knowledge or information sufficient to form a belief as to the truth of the allegations set forth in paragraph "25" of the Class Action Complaint.

26. Deny knowledge or information sufficient to form a belief as to the truth of the allegations set forth in paragraph "26" of the Class Action Complaint.

27. Deny knowledge or information sufficient to form a belief as to the truth of the allegations set forth in paragraph "27" of the Class Action Complaint.

28. Deny knowledge or information sufficient to form a belief as to the truth of the allegations set forth in paragraph "28" of the Class Action Complaint.

29. Deny knowledge or information sufficient to form a belief as to the truth of the allegations set forth in paragraph "29" of the Class Action Complaint.

30. Deny knowledge or information sufficient to form a belief as to the truth of the allegations set forth in paragraph "30" of the Class Action Complaint.

31. Deny the allegations set forth in paragraph "31" of the Class Action Complaint.

32. Deny knowledge or information sufficient to form a belief as to the truth of the allegations set forth in paragraph "32" of the Class Action Complaint.

33. Deny knowledge or information sufficient to form a belief as to the truth of the allegations set forth in paragraph "33" of the Class Action Complaint.

34. Deny the allegations set forth in paragraph "34" of the Class Action Complaint, except deny knowledge or information sufficient to form a belief as to the truth of the allegations regarding plaintiff's actions, officers' actions, and communications between the plaintiff and the officers.

35. Deny knowledge or information sufficient to form a belief as to the truth of the allegations set forth in paragraph "35" of the Class Action Complaint.

36. Deny knowledge or information sufficient to form a belief as to the truth of the allegations set forth in paragraph "36" of the Class Action Complaint.

37. Deny knowledge or information sufficient to form a belief as to the truth of the allegations set forth in paragraph "37" of the Class Action Complaint.

38. Deny knowledge or information sufficient to form a belief as to the truth of the allegations set forth in paragraph "38" of the Class Action Complaint.

39. Deny knowledge or information sufficient to form a belief as to the truth of the allegations set forth in paragraph "39" of the Class Action Complaint.

40. Deny knowledge or information sufficient to form a belief as to the truth of the allegations set forth in paragraph "40" of the Class Action Complaint.

41. Deny the allegations set forth in paragraph "41" of the Class Action Complaint.

42. Deny the allegations set forth in paragraph "42" of the Class Action Complaint.

43. Deny the allegations set forth in paragraph "43" of the Class Action Complaint.

44. Deny the allegations set forth in paragraph "44" of the Class Action Complaint, except admit that the Office of the Attorney General issued a report regarding the NYPD's stop and frisk practices from January 1, 1998 to March 31, 1999.

45. Deny the allegations set forth in paragraph "45" of the Class Action Complaint.

46. Deny the allegations set forth in paragraph "46" of the Class Action Complaint.

47. Deny the allegations set forth in paragraph "47" of the Class Action Complaint.

48. Deny the allegations set forth in paragraph "48" of the Class Action Complaint, except admit the lawsuit *Daniels et al. v. The City of New York, et al.* was filed in 1999.

49. Deny the allegations set forth in paragraph "49" of the Class Action Complaint.

50. Deny the allegations set forth in paragraph "50" of the Class Action Complaint, except admit that a settlement was reached in *Daniels*.

51. Deny the allegations set forth in paragraph "51" of the Class Action Complaint.

52. Deny the allegations set forth in paragraph "52" of the Class Action Complaint.

53. Deny the allegations set forth in paragraph "53" of the Class Action Complaint.

54. Deny the allegations set forth in paragraph "54" of the Class Action Complaint.

55. Deny the allegations set forth in paragraph "55" of the Class Action Complaint.

56. Deny the allegations set forth in paragraph "56" of the Class Action Complaint.

57. Deny the allegations set forth in paragraph "57" of the Class Action Complaint.

58. Deny the allegations set forth in paragraph "58" of the Class Action Complaint.

59. Deny the allegations set forth in paragraph "59" of the Class Action Complaint and respectfully refer the Court to the United States Constitution and relevant case law.

60. Deny the allegations set forth in paragraph "60" of the Class Action Complaint.

61. Deny the allegations set forth in paragraph "61" of the Class Action Complaint.

62. Deny the allegations set forth in paragraph "62" of the Class Action Complaint.

63. Deny the allegations set forth in paragraph "63" of the Class Action Complaint.

64. Deny the allegations set forth in paragraph "64" of the Class Action Complaint.

65. Deny the allegations set forth in paragraph "65" of the Class Action Complaint.

66. Deny the allegations set forth in paragraph "66" of the Class Action Complaint.

67. Deny the allegations set forth in paragraph "67" of the Class Action Complaint.

68. In response to the allegations set forth in paragraph "68" of the Class Action Complaint, defendant repeats and realleges paragraphs "1" through "67" as if fully set forth herein.

69. Deny the allegations set forth in paragraph "69" of the Class Action Complaint.

70. Deny the allegations set forth in paragraph "70" of the Class Action Complaint.

71. Deny the allegations set forth in paragraph "71" of the Class Action Complaint.

72. Deny the allegations set forth in paragraph "72" of the Class Action Complaint.

73. Deny the allegations set forth in paragraph "73" of the Class Action Complaint.

74. In response to the allegations set forth in paragraph "74" of the Class Action Complaint, defendant repeats and realleges paragraphs "1" through "67" as if fully set forth herein.

75. Deny the allegations set forth in paragraph "75" of the Class Action Complaint.

76. Deny the allegations set forth in paragraph "76" of the Class Action Complaint.

77. Deny the allegations set forth in paragraph "77" of the Class Action Complaint.

78. Deny the allegations set forth in paragraph "78" of the Class Action Complaint.

79. Deny the allegations set forth in paragraph "79" of the Class Action Complaint.

80. Deny the allegations set forth in paragraph "80" of the Class Action Complaint.

81. Deny the allegations set forth in paragraph "81" of the Class Action Complaint.

82. In response to the allegations set forth in paragraph "82" of the Class Action Complaint, defendant repeats and realleges paragraphs "1" through "67" as if fully set forth herein.

83. Deny the allegations set forth in paragraph "83" of the Class Action Complaint.

84. Deny the allegations set forth in paragraph "84" of the Class Action Complaint.

85. In response to the allegations set forth in paragraph "85" of the Class Action Complaint, defendant repeats and realleges paragraphs "1" through "67" as if fully set forth herein.

86. Deny the allegations set forth in paragraph "86" of the Class Action Complaint.

87. Deny the allegations set forth in paragraph "87" of the Class Action Complaint.

88. Deny the allegations set forth in paragraph "88" of the Class Action Complaint.

89. In response to the allegations set forth in paragraph "89" of the Class Action Complaint, defendant repeats and realleges paragraphs "1" through "88" as if fully set forth herein.

AS FOR A FIRST AFFIRMATIVE DEFENSE

90. The Class Action Complaint fails to state a claim upon which relief can be granted.

AS FOR A SECOND AFFIRMATIVE DEFENSE

91. Defendant Commissioner Kelly has not violated any rights, privileges or immunities under the Constitution or laws under the United States or State of New York or any political subdivision thereof.

AS FOR A THIRD AFFIRMATIVE DEFENSE

92. Plaintiffs' claims are barred, in whole or in part, by relevant statutes of limitations.

AS FOR A FOURTH AFFIRMATIVE DEFENSE

93. NYPD officers had a reasonable, articulable suspicion for plaintiffs' stops and/or frisks.

AS FOR A FIFTH AFFIRMATIVE DEFENSE

94. Plaintiffs' claims are barred by the doctrines of *res judicata* and collateral estoppel.

DATED: /d/   Respectfully Submitted
                                    By His Attorneys

                                    By: _____/s/ Hailey Roberts _____
                                    By: _____/s/ Julia Grutzman _____

                                    Hailey Roberts (BBO#67903)
                                    Julia Grutzman (BBO# 76890)
                                    Roberts, Brennan & Grutzman
                                    701 7th Avenue
                                    New York, NY 10019
                                    (646) 555-0000

UNITED STATES DISTRICT COURT
SOUTHERN DISTRICT OF NEW YORK

JACOB WARNER, and WILLIAM MOORE, Individually and on behalf of a class of all others similarly situated;	08 Civ. 01034 (SAS)
Plaintiffs,	
-against-	
THE CITY OF NEW YORK, NEW YORK CITY POLICE COMMISSIONER RAYMOND KELLY; MAYOR MICHAEL BLOOMBERG; OFFICER SCOTT MCDONALD; OFFICER THOMAS FOLEY; OFFICER RICHARD CANNON;	DEFENDANTS' MOTION FOR PARTIAL SUMMARY JUDGMENT
Defendants.	

Defendants hereby move this Court under Rule 56 of the Federal Rules of Civil Procedure to grant Partial Summary Judgment on their behalf on the basis that there is no genuine dispute of two material facts relating to Plaintiff Warner's claims: first, whether the police stopped Warner while he was standing in front of an apartment door, trying numerous keys on the lock, and attempting to gain entry into the apartment; and second, that there was a burglary pattern in that neighborhood at that time of day.

Defendants request oral argument of this motion.

DATED: /d/

Respectfully Submitted
By His Attorneys

By: _____ /s/ Hailey Roberts _____
By: _____/s/ Julia Grutzman _____

Hailey Roberts (BBO#67903)
Julia Grutzman (BBO# 76890)
Roberts, Brennan & Grutzman
701 7th Avenue
New York, NY 10019
(646) 555-0000

UNITED STATES DISTRICT COURT
SOUTHERN DISTRICT OF NEW YORK

JACOB WARNER, and WILLIAM
MOORE, Individually and on behalf
of a class of all others similarly
situated;

    Plaintiffs,

    -against-

THE CITY OF NEW YORK,   TRANSCRIPT OF DEPOSITION OF
NEW YORK CITY POLICE   PLAINTIFF JACOB WARNER
COMMISSIONER RAYMOND
KELLY; MAYOR MICHAEL
BLOOMBERG; OFFICER SCOTT
MCDONALD; OFFICER THOMAS
FOLEY; OFFICER RICHARD
CANNON;

    Defendants.

Deposition of Jacob Warner, taken on behalf of the Defendants, pursuant to Notice under the applicable rules of the New York Civil Practice Law and Rules, before Claire Byron, a Shorthand Reporter and Notary Public in and for the State of New York, at the Offices of Roberts, Brennan & Gruztman on Friday, xxxx, xx, commencing at 10:00 A.M.

APPEARANCES
    HAILEY ROBERTS, ESQ. and JULIA GRUTZMAN, ESQ., For Defendants.
    MARK GOULDING, ESQ., For Plaintiff Jacob Warner.
    REBECCA NEWMAN, ESQ., For Plaintiff William Moore.

JACOB WARNER, a witness called by the defendants, having been first duly sworn, was examined and testified as follows:

DIRECT EXAMINATION BY *MS. ROBERTS*: Mr. Warner, my name is Hailey Roberts and I represent the defendants in this action. I'm going to ask you some questions. If you do not understand a question or need clarification, please let me know and I will repeat or rephrase the question. Otherwise, I will assume you understand the question.

If you hear an objection by your attorney, please answer the question anyways unless I tell you otherwise. Also, if you would like a break at any time let me know. Would you please state your name for the record?

A: Jacob Warner.

[We have omitted four pages of the deposition regarding Jacob Warner's personal information and about the first time he was stopped by police]

Q: And you said that you were stopped a second time by police, in February 2008, is that correct?

A: Yes.

Q: What date was that? Do you recall?

A: No, I don't remember the exact date.

Q: Okay. What were you doing when you were allegedly stopped by NYPD officers in February 2008?

A: No allegedly. I was stopped by police.

MR. GOULDING: Might I interject for a moment?

[Discussion off the record.]

Q: Mr. Warner, would you like me to repeat the question?

A: No, I remember it. I was at my godmother's apartment, trying to figure out which key went to the lock on her door.

Q: And what address is this?

A: 146 Randall Ave, in the Bronx.

Q: Were you with anyone else?

A: Yes.

Q: What is their name?

A: Ron Belton.

Q: Thank you. And back to what you were doing when you were allegedly stopped by police. Why were you trying to figure out which key opened the door to your godmother's apartment?

A: Ron lives with my godmother and locked himself out. He's her tenant. I saw that he was locked out of the apartment and I knew I had a spare key on my key chain but I couldn't remember which key it was.

Q: So you were trying multiple keys on the lock?

A: Yes.

Q: Do you recall how many keys you had with you at the time? Not just the keys you tried on the lock.

A: Maybe 7 to 10.

Q: Were these keys all on the same keychain?

A: No, I have a couple of different key chains and I couldn't remember which key chain the spare key was on.

Q: So you tried keys from two different key chains on the lock?

A: Yes. Oh yeah, and I had a couple of loose keys in my wallet, so I also tried those on the lock.

Q: So to reiterate, you tried keys from two different key chains and two loose keys from your wallet on the lock?

A: Yes.

Q: Were you the only one trying the keys on the lock, or was Mr. Belton also trying the keys on the lock?

A: Both of us. I tried a few keys on the lock and then lost track of which keys I had already tried, so Ron started to grab keys and we took turns.

Q: Did you end up finding the right key?

A: Yes.

Q: How many keys did you try before you found the right one?

A: About 5 or 6 keys.

Q: And how long were you at the door with Mr. Belton trying keys on the lock?

MR. GOULDING: Approximately.

A: Only a minute or two.

Q: Okay, and what happened when you found the right key?

A: I unlocked the door and two police officers came up and stopped me.

Q: Did they stop you before or after you opened the door?

A: Before. Like I said, I had just unlocked the door and they came up and stopped me before I could open it. I didn't even see them until they were right next to me, because I was unlocking the door and my back was to the street.

Q: You said that the officers stopped you. How?

A: They came up next to me and said something like we needed to stop what we were doing.

Q: And did you stop?

A: Yes.

Q: And then what happened?

A: The police asked Ron and I what we were doing and then frisked us.

Q: Did you tell officers what you were doing?

A: Well yeah, but they started to frisk us before we even had a chance to answer their question.

Q: Can you please describe in what way officers frisked you?

A: The officer that frisked me patted me up and down outside of my clothing and then reached into both of my front pockets.

Q: Which officer?

A: Not sure, I didn't know their names then. Plus I wasn't facing them.

Q: Did you have anything in your front pockets?

A: Yes.

Q: And what was that?

A: A phone and keys. Maybe some change too.

Q: Do you think it is possible that the officer felt the bulges in your pocket and thought you might have a weapon?

A: Well I don't know. I only had a phone and some keys.

Q: After the officers frisked you, what happened next?

A: The officers asked us what we were doing, and told us to show them some I.D.

Q: Do you remember which officer spoke?

A: Well I didn't know their names. Afterwards I asked for their names and he said his name was Officer Cannon.

Q: Can you describe him?

A: White, tall, strong looking. He was older than the other officer.

Q: Okay. So Officer Cannon asked you and Mr. Belton questions. Do you remember which questions and what you said back?

A: They asked us what we were doing, so I said that I lived in the area and was on my way home, passing by my god-mother's house and noticed that Ron her tenant was locked out so I tried to find the spare key I had.

Q: And then the officers asked for identification?

A: Yes. I handed over my license but Ron had left his inside of the house. Mine is from Massachusetts, and Officer Cannon questioned me about it.

Q: What did he ask?

A: He asked why I claimed to live in the area when my license was from Massachusetts. I said that I hadn't changed my license over to New York and he still didn't seem to believe me so I found an electricity bill in my backpack that showed my New York address.

Q: So Ron's I.D. was in the house?

A: Yes, so the other officer, who later told me his name was Officer Foley, went with Ron around the back of the apartment building and entered with the apartment so Ron could show him his license.

Q: And what happened while Mr. Belton and Officer Foley went to retrieve Mr. Belton's license?

A: Like I said, the officer questioned me about my address and I showed him the electricity bill. And I asked the officer why we were stopped. He told me that there were a number of burglaries in the area.

Q: What happened next?

A: The other officer and Ron came back to where Officer Cannon and I were standing and they started to leave, so I asked them for their names and badge numbers.

Q: Did they provide their names and badge numbers?

A: Yes.

Q: Thank you. That will be all. Oh no wait. One more question about the keys you had. Were all of the 7 to 10 keys you had on your person visible while you were trying keys on the lock? Let me rephrase for clarity. Could a person have seen 7 to 10 keys when you were trying out keys in the lock?

A: You mean were they in my hand or something? Yeah, the keys were all in my hand when I was trying keys out on the lock. Or Ron's hand.

MS. ROBERTS: I'm done—I don't have any more questions.

MR. GOULDING: I have a few questions.

CROSS EXAMINATION BY MR. GOULDING

Q: Did the officers instruct you on how to stand when they frisked you?

A: Yes, the officers told us to stand against the wall with our hands spread on front of us.

Q: Were you facing the officers or did you still have your back to them?

A: Both Ron and I had our backs to the police when they frisked us. We hadn't even seen them coming our way, and we had our backs to the street when they came by because we were trying to unlock the door.

Q: And back to the keys that were in your pockets when you were frisked? Were those the same keys that you had been trying on the lock?

A: Yes.

Q: So you tried the keys on the lock, and then put them back in your pocket the second before you opened the unlocked the door?

A: Yeah. When we found the right one, I put the rest back in my pocket right before the police stopped us.

Q: And when Ron and Officer Foley entered the apartment from the back, how did they get in?

A: I had given Officer Foley the spare key so they used that.

Q: Your spare key? The spare key from your key chain?

A: Well the one from my wallet, but yeah it was mine.

Q: Did you witness either officer fill out paperwork?

A: No.

Q: And is the neighborhood that your godmother lives in known for any gang or crime problems?

A: I don't think so. Not that I know of.

REDIRECT EXAMINATION BY MS. ROBERTS

Q: Are you an expert in crime rates? Do you have training?

A: No.

MS. ROBERTS: That's it. I don't have any more questions.

MR. GOULDING: We don't either.

[Whereupon, the deposition was concluded at 11:23 A.M.]

UNITED STATES DISTRICT COURT
SOUTHERN DISTRICT OF NEW YORK

JACOB WARNER, and WILLIAM MOORE, Individually and on behalf of a class of all others similarly situated;
 	
    Plaintiffs,
 	
    -against-
 	
THE CITY OF NEW YORK, NEW YORK CITY POLICE COMMISSIONER RAYMOND KELLY; MAYOR MICHAEL BLOOMBERG; OFFICER SCOTT MCDONALD; OFFICER THOMAS FOLEY; OFFICER RICHARD CANNON;
 	
    Defendants.
	TRANSCRIPT OF DEPOSITION OF DEFENDANT RICHARD CANNON

Deposition of Richard Cannon, taken on behalf of the Plaintiffs, pursuant to Notice under the applicable rules of the New York Civil Practice Law and Rules, before Stephen Clarke, a Shorthand Reporter and Notary Public in and for the State of New York, at the Offices of Goulding, Newman & Martin on Thursday, xxxx, xx, commencing at 11:30 A.M.

APPEARANCES
    MARK GOULDING, ESQ., For Plaintiff Jacob Warner.
    REBECCA NEWMAN, ESQ., For Plaintiff William Moore.
    HAILEY ROBERTS, ESQ. and JULIA GRUTZMAN, ESQ., For Defendants.

THOMAS FOLEY, a witness called by the plaintiffs, having been first duly sworn, was examined and testified as follows:

DIRECT EXAMINATION BY *MR. GOULDING:* Good morning Officer Cannon. My name is Mark Goulding and I represent the plaintiffs in this action. I am going to ask you some questions. If you do not understand a question or would like me to clarify one, please let me know and I will rephrase the question. If you need a question repeated, please let me know that as well. Should you want a break at any time, please let me know and we will take a break from questioning. You may hear objections from your attorney during the course of questioning. If you do, please answer the question anyways unless I tell you otherwise. Can you please state your name for the record?

A: Richard Cannon.

[We have omitted two pages of the deposition regarding Officer Foley's personal information and work history before and at the NYPD.]

Q: Did you stop Mr. Warner in February 2008 at 146 Randall Ave in the Bronx?

A: Yes, Officer Foley and I spotted Mr. Warner and a companion tinkering with a lock at the residence. We suspected a burglary, because there was a pattern of burglaries around that same time of day.

Q: And what time of day was the stop?

A: Noon. Same time frame as the burglaries were committed.

Q: What made you suspect they were about to commit a burglary?

A: Mr. Warner and his companion Mr. Belton repeatedly looked behind them and kept taking turns trying to open the lock to the door.

Q: Did you see them using any burglary tools to open the lock?

A: No, but their backs were blocking most of their actions so I couldn't see what was in their hands. There was a backpack next to them, which I thought might have had burglary tools in it.

Q: And did it?

A: No.

Q: So when you and Officer Foley saw Mr. Warner and Mr. Belton at the door, what did you do?

A: We approached and asked them what they were doing.

Q: Who asked?

A: Sorry?

Q: Did you ask the question or did Officer Foley?

A: Honestly I don't remember. The paperwork I filled out has it written down.

[Discussion off the record.]

A: I asked what they were doing.

Q: Did they respond?

A: No they did not, so I asked them to put their hands in front of them and we frisked them. I frisked Mr. Belton and Officer Foley frisked Mr. Warner.

Q: How long was the time between you asking them what they were doing and telling them to stand with their hands in front of them?

A: Probably a couple of minutes.

Q: Did you find any burglary tools or weapons when you frisked them?

A: No, we did not.

Q: What happened after you frisked them?

A: We asked them again what they were doing and Mr. Warner and Mr. Belton explained the situation.

Q: Which was?

A: That Mr. Belton lived there and locked himself out and that Mr. Warner was trying to figure out which key went to the lock.

Q: Did you believe them?

A: Once I saw that Mr. Warner had a bunch of keys in his hand and Mr. Belton's I.D. matched the address of the house, yes.

Q: So you asked them for I.D. after you frisked them?

A: Yeah. We asked them what they were doing and they explained the story, and we asked for I.D. to match it up.

Q: When Mr. Warner gave you his I.D., did you question Mr. Warner about his address?

A: Yes. When he was explaining what they were doing, Mr. Warner said that he lived in the area. But when he handed me his I.D., it was a Massachusetts license so his story didn't line up.

Q: Did Mr. Warner provide you with evidence to back up his story?

A: Yes, he gave me a copy of an electricity bill out of his backpack, which showed his address in New York.

Q: And what were Officer Foley and Mr. Belton doing during this time? Were they with you and Mr. Warner?

A: No, Mr. Belton said that his I.D. was inside the apartment, so he and Officer Foley went around the back of the apartment to get it.

Q: Okay, after you verified Mr. Warner's story did you and Mr. Warner have any more interaction?

A: You mean like did we talk?

Q: Yes, did you talk about anything else while Officer Foley and Mr. Belton were finding Mr. Belton's I.D.?

A: A little. Mr. Warner asked why we stopped him and I explained that there were a string of burglaries in the area so the police were on high alert.

Q: What happened next?

A: Officer Foley and Mr. Belton came back to where we were standing. Officer Foley said that Mr. Belton's I.D. matched and we said goodbye to the men.

Q: Did Mr. Warner or Mr. Belton ask for your names and badge numbers?

A: Yeah, Mr. Warner asked. So we gave the info to them and left. We then went back to our squad car and I filled out the UF-250 form.

Q: How many minutes after the stop ended did you fill out the form?

A: Less than 10 minutes later.

CROSS EXAMINATION BY MS. ROBERTS

Q: Can you describe how Mr. Warner and Mr. Belton acted when you stopped them?

A: They seemed nervous. Mr. Warner kept looking between

the street and Officer Foley and I, and Mr. Belton seemed a little jumpy.

Q: You said they were nervously looking behind them when they were trying to open the lock. Did they appear more or less nervous after you stopped them? Did their behavior change?

A: No, I would say about the same. They looked nervous before we stopped them and the same during the stop too.

MS. ROBERTS: I don't have any more questions.

MR. GOULDING: Me neither.

[Whereupon, the deposition was concluded at 12:06 P.M.]

UNITED STATES DISTRICT COURT
SOUTHERN DISTRICT OF NEW YORK

JACOB WARNER, and WILLIAM MOORE, Individually
and on behalf of a class of all others similarly situated;

Plaintiffs,

-against-

THE CITY OF NEW YORK, NEW YORK CITY
POLICE COMMISSIONER RAYMOND KELLY;
MAYOR MICHAEL BLOOMBERG; OFFICER SCOTT
MCDONALD; OFFICER THOMAS FOLEY; OFFICER
RICHARD CANNON;

Defendants.

AFFIDAVIT OF
LAUREN CASSIDY

LAUREN CASSIDY, having been duly sworn, deposes and says:

1. I am a Professor of Law at Columbia University.

2. I am neither a party nor counsel for a party in this action.

3. I submit this affidavit in support of Plaintiff's motion for class certification pursuant to Rule 23 of the Federal Rules of Civil Procedure.

4. I have been retained as a testifying expert for the plaintiffs in this case.

5. Through my role as an expert witness in this action, I have reviewed and analyzed electronic copies of the NYPD's criminal complaint report data for the years 2004 through 2009, which was provided by Defendants during discovery and then which the Plaintiffs' counsel provided to me. It is my understanding, based on representations made by Defendants' counsel, that the data includes information on all crimes reported to the NYPD during these years.

6. I used this data to determine the total number of reported crimes by category on specific individual precincts or census tracts for any given year, calendar quarter, month, week, or specific date.

7. Earlier this month, I was asked to determine the total number of reported burglaries in the vicinity of 146 Randall Avenue in the Bronx in January and February 2008.

8. According to the map of tracts from the 2000 census (the most recent available census at the time of my analysis), 146 Randall Avenue was located in Census Tract No. 66. However, Randall Avenue is the boundary between Census Tract No. 66 and 214, meaning that homes on the opposite side of the street from 146 Randall Avenue were in a different census tract. Therefore, I included crime totals for both Census Tracts 66 and 214 in my analysis of the January and February 2008 crime totals.

9. Together, Census Tracts 66 and 214 are nine city blocks from East to West, with Randall Avenue in the middle, and four city blocks from North to South. Total, the area comprises 36 square blocks and in 2008 was home to approximately 4,861 people. Census Tracts 66 and 214 are located entirely in NYPD's 43rd precinct.

10. The criminal complaint report data, taken from UF-250 forms, includes the following categories:

   a. Location of the crime (street address, intersection, and the latitude and longitude)

   b. Race of the suspect, if known

   c. Offense description (e.g., "robbery," "burglary," or a similar word/ abbreviation/phrase), and/or the N.Y. Penal Law Section

   d. NYPD precinct where the crime occurred

   e. Date (month, day, year) on which the crime occurred

   f. Time (hour, minute) at which the crime occurred

11. Using the information in the offense description category and the NYPD precinct field, I was able to determine the total number of crimes in any given offense category (e.g., burglary) that were reported in a given NYPD precinct.

12. Using the addresses and/or latitudinal and longitudinal information provided in the location field, I was able to locate each individual reported crime and match it up to where in the census tract it allegedly occurred.

13. As reflected in Exhibit A, there was only one reported burglary in Census Tract 66 between January 1, 2008 and February 28, 2008, and it occurred in

during the last ten days of January. In addition, there were no reported burglaries in Census Tract 214 during the same two month period.

xxxxx xx, xxxx

_____/s/ Lauren Cassidy_____

Lauren Cassidy

Sworn to before me this _____ day of xx, xxxx

_____

Notary Public

UNITED STATES DISTRICT COURT
SOUTHERN DISTRICT OF NEW YORK

JACOB WARNER, and WILLIAM MOORE, Individually and on behalf of a class of all others similarly situated;
 	
    Plaintiffs,
 	
    -against-
 	
THE CITY OF NEW YORK, NEW YORK CITY POLICE COMMISSIONER RAYMOND KELLY; MAYOR MICHAEL BLOOMBERG; OFFICER SCOTT MCDONALD; OFFICER THOMAS FOLEY; OFFICER RICHARD CANNON;
 	
    Defendants.
	AFFIDAVIT OF DETECTIVE SUSAN STEPHENS

DETECTIVE SUSAN STEPHENS, having been duly sworn, deposes and says:

1. I am a detective with the New York City Police Department ("NYPD") currently assigned to the Special Litigation Support Unit ("SLSU") within the Office of Deputy Commissioner, Legal Matters. I have been employed with SLSU since 2005 and have been with the NYPD as a whole since 1993.

2. I submit this affidavit in support of Defendants' motion for Partial Summary Judgment pursuant to Rule 56 of the Federal Rules of Civil Procedure.

3. As a part of my role at SLSU, I am in charge of investigating and answering inquiries that arise out of the course of litigation that involve the NYPD. In performing my duties, I reviewed all of the reports of burglaries in January and February 2008.

4. In January and February 2008, there were 66 complaints of burglaries in the 43rd Precinct. The 43rd Precinct includes all of Census Tract 66 and 214, and as of the 2000 Census was home to approximately 167,633 people.

5. Of the 66 complaints of burglaries, 62 occurred within one mile of Warner's home and 28 occurred within one half mile of his home.

6. In the six months between July 1, 2007 and December 31, 2007, there were 233 complaints of burglaries and 19 complaints of stolen property in the 43rd Precinct.

7. In January and February 2008, the entire borough of the Bronx had a reported 560 complaints of burglary, 116 complaints of stolen property, and 6 complaints of possession of burglar tools.

xxxxx xx, xxxx

_____/s/ Susan Stephens_____

Det. Susan Stephens

Sworn to before me this _____ day of xx, xxxx

_____

Notary Public

TABLE OF CASES

Principal cases are indicated by italics.

Abdelkarim v. Gonzales, 383
Acton Co. v. Bachman Foods, Inc., 405-406, 407, 411
Actos (Pioglitazone) Prods. Liab. Litig., In re, 431
Adams v. Davison-Paxon Co., 945-946
Adickes v. S.H. Kress & Co., 551, 558, 560, 562, 564, 566, 568, 569-571, 574
Advanced Tactical Ordnance Sys., LLC v. Real Action Paintball, Inc., 783
Aetna Cas. & Sur. Co. v. Yeatts, 594
Agent Orange Prod. Liab. Litig., In re, 1118, 1121
Airey v. Ireland, 102
Alabama v. White, 585
Albemarle Paper Co. v. Moody, 529
Albertini; United States v., 215
Al Daraji v. Monica, 381, 383, 384, 386
Alemite Mfg. Corp. v. Staff, 20
Alexander v. Turtur & Assocs., Inc., 880
Allen v. McCurry, 1016, *1054,* 1058, 1059
Alley v. MTD Prods., Inc., 462, 466-467, 469-470, 484
Allied-Bruce Terminix Cos. v. Dobson, 658
Allstate Ins. Co. v. Hague, 1089
Almazo v. M.A. Angeliades, Inc., 334
ALS Scan, Inc. v. Digital Serv. Consultants, Inc., 777, 778, 785
Alyeska Pipeline Serv. Co. v. Wilderness Soc'y, 187, 189, 191
Amchem Prods., Inc. v. Windsor, 1103, 1109, 1114
American Bank v. City of Menasha, 426
American Indoor Football Ass'n, Inc. v. Lockwood, 852
American Tel. & Tel. Co.; United States v., 135
American Tobacco Co. v. Patterson, 194
American Well Works Co. v. Layne & Bowler Co., 845, 879
Americold Realty Trust v. ConAgra Foods, Inc., 887
Amoco Prod. Co. v. Gambell, 126
Anderson v. Liberty Lobby, Inc., 565, 568, 571-572
Ankenbrandt v. Richards, 890
A-1 Premium Acceptance, Inc. v. Hunter, 659
Argersinger v. Hamlin, 90, 91

Arizona v. California, 1023
Armstrong v. Manzo, 82, 111
Armstrong v. Pomerance, 797
Arnett v. Kennedy, 41, 43, 46
Arnstein v. Porter, 574
Arrow Enter. Computing Solutions, Inc. v. BlueAlly, LLC, 456, 458, 459
Artis v. District of Columbia, 919
Asahi Metal Indus. Co. v. Superior Court of Cal., Solano Cty., 709, *720,* 727, 728, 729, 730, 731, 732, 733, 736, 742, 743, 744, 759, 781, 797, 805, 806, 808, 826
Ashbacker Radio Corp. v. FCC, 49
Ashcroft v. Iqbal, 273, *275,* 284, 286, 288, 289, 305, 311-312, 366, 372, 375, 520, 562, 563, 985
Ashe v. Swenson, 1025
Associated Gen. Contractors of Cal., Inc. v. Carpenters, 261
Astoria Fed. Sav. & Loan Ass'n v. Solimino, 1041
AT&T Mobility LLC v. Concepcion, 647-648, 655
Atlantic Marine Constr. Co. v. United States District Court, 844
Avco Corp. v. Aero Lodge No. 735, 924
Ayers v. City of Richmond, 1016

Bagg v. HighBeam Research, Inc., 844
Bailey Ford, Inc.; EEOC v., 198
Baker v. Baker, E. & Co., 1077
Baldwin v. Hale, 74
Baldwin v. Iowa State Traveling Men's Ass'n, 678, 1041
Ballew v. Georgia, 520
Balthazar v. Atlantic City Med. Ctr., 375
Baltimore & Carolina Line, Inc. v. Redman, 590
Baltimore S.S. Co. v. Phillips, 1047
B & B Hardware, Inc. v. Hargis Indus., Inc., 1032, *1037,* 1044
Baravati v. Josephthal, Lyon & Ross, Inc., 647
Barone v. Rich Bros. Interstate Display Fireworks Co., 729
Batson v. Kentucky, 541, 542, 543-544, 545, 547, 548
Beacon Theaters v. Westover, 525, 527, 532, 533, 535
Bell v. Burson, 41, 103, 108, 112
Bell v. Imperial Palace Hotel/Casino, Inc., 692

Bell Atl. Corp. v. Twombly, 257, 258, 273, 277, 278-281, 282-284, 287, 288, 289, 305, 311-312, 375, 520, 562, 563, 985

Bendectin Litig., In re, 622

Beneficial Nat'l Bank v. Anderson, 923, 924

Benitez v. JMC Recycling Sys., Ltd., 746

Benson & Ford, Inc. v. Wanda Petroleum Co., 1013

Bensusan Rest. Corp. v. King, 781

Bernhardt v. Polygraphic Co. of Am., 944

Berry, In re, 225

Betts v. Brady, 90, 94

Birmingham Reverse Discrimination Litig., In re, 1128, 1131

Bivens v. Six Unknown Fed. Narcotics Agents, 276, 282, 716

Black & White Taxicab Co. v. Brown & Yellow Taxicab Co., 932, 935

Blonder-Tongue Labs., Inc. v. University of Ill. Found., 1027

BMW v. Gore, 175, 176

BNSF Ry. Co. v. Tyrrell, 830, 834, 835

Boddie v. Connecticut, 80, 99, 113, 173, 364

Bonito Boats, Inc. v. Thunder Craft Boats, Inc., 881

Boomer v. Atlantic Cement Co., 132

Boothe v. TRW Credit Data, 290

Borel v. Fibreboard Paper Prods. Corp., 1033, 1035-1036

Boston & Mont. Consol. Copper & Silver Mining Co. v. Montana Ore Purchasing Co., 871

Bower v. Weisman, 289, 294-295

BP Chems. Ltd. v. Formosa Chem. & Fibre Corp., 697

BP Prods. v. Dagra, 852

Brand Energy & Infrastructure Servs. v. Irex Corp., 463

Brandon v. Chicago Bd. of Educ., 616

Braxton v. Board of Pub. Instruction for Duval Cty., 15, 18

Bray v. Alexandria Women's Health Clinic, 215

Bridgeport Music, Inc. v. Still N The Water Pub, 729

Briscoe v. City of New Haven, 1014

Bristol-Myers Squibb Co. v. Superior Court, 692, 749, 759, 760, 761, 1088, 1115

Brooke Group Ltd. v. Brown & Williamson Tobacco Corp., 260, 522

Brother, Inc. v. W.E. Grace Mfg. Co., 1013

Brothers Trading Co. v. Goodman Factors, 472

Brown v. Board of Educ. of Topeka, Kan., 15, 225

Brown v. Herbert, 312

Brown v. Plata, 134, *136,* 1117

Browning-Ferris Indus. of Vt. v. Kelco Disposal, Inc., 175

Bryant Elec. Co. v. Marshall, 1078

Buck v. Ford Motor Co., 481

Buckhannon Bd. & Care Home, Inc. v. West Va. Dep't of Health & Human Res., 198

Burdick v. Superior Court, 784

Burger King Corp. v. MacShara, 765

Burger King Corp. v. Rudzewicz, 718, 722, 725, 726, 727, 740, *762,* 772, 777, 797, 820, 823

Burke v. Kleiman, 1071, 1073, 1075, 1076, 1079

Burlington N. R.R. v. Wood, 963

Burnett v. Burnett, 676

Burnham v. Superior Court of Cal., Cty. of Marin, 733, *799,* 808, 827, 828, 845, 860, 929

Bushell's Case, 524

Byrd v. Blue Ridge Rural Elec. Coop., Inc., 944, 948, 951, 964, 969, 970, 972

Cable & Computer Tech., Inc. v. Lockheed Saunders, Inc., 483, 485

Cafeteria & Rest. Workers Union v. McElroy, 28, 42, 49, 90

Calder v. Jones, 710, *712-715,* 716, 718, 719, 720, 742, 767, 779, 783, 815

Calero-Toldeo v. Pearson Yacht Leasing Co., 115

Califano v. Yamasaki, 191, 1098

Caplan v. Donovan, 676

Car Carriers, Inc. v. Ford Motor Co., 261, *992,* 1001

Carefirst of Md., Inc. v. Carefirst Pregnancy Ctrs., Inc., 779, 780

Carey v. Piphus, 167, 179

Carl Zeiss Stiftung v. V.E.B. Carl Zeiss, Jena, 1013

Carnival Cruise Lines, Inc. v. Shute, 837, 841, 842, 845

Carpenter v. Dee, 165, 178, 214, 251, 296, 298, 309, 313, 318, 336, 386, 388, 392, 397, 402, 445-447, 492, 550, 583, 589, 625, 632, 663, 919, 984, 1014, 1019

Carson v. American Brands, Inc., 1128

Carusos v. Briarcliff, Inc., 131

Casavant v. Norwegian Cruise Line, Ltd., 842

Cascade Natural Gas Corp. v. El Paso Natural Gas Co., 414-415

Case v. ANPAC La. Ins. Co., 1117

Catlin v. United States, 635

Catrett v. Johns-Manville Sales Corp., 563, 571

Ceglia v. Zuckerberg, 888

Celotex Corp. v. Catrett, 558, 563, 571

Chaplin v. DuPont Advance Fiber Sys., 367, 373

Chase Nat'l Bank v. City of Norwalk, 20, 1126

Chauffeurs, Teamsters & Helpers, Local No. 391 v. Terry, 525

Chicago, B. & Q. R.R. Co. v. Chicago, 1077

Christian v. R. Wood Motors, Inc., 199

Christiansburg Garment Co. v. EEOC, 197

Christianson v. Colt Indus. Operating Corp., 879

Christopher v. Brusselback, 1078

Cities Serv. Co. v. Dunlap, 942

City of ___. *See name of city*

Clark v. Clark, 1042

Clausen & Sons, Inc. v. Hamm Brewing Co., 562
Cleveland Bd. of Educ. v. Loudermill, 35
Cleveland Demolition Co. v. Azcon Scrap Corp., 369, 370
C.M. Joiner Leasing Corp.; SEC v., 14
Coburn v. Smithkline Beecham Corp., 1037
Cofax Corp. v. Minnesota Mining & Mfg. Co., 1013
Cohen v. Beneficial Indus. Loan Corp., 944
Coleman v. Brown, 138, 139
Coleman v. Wilson, 138
Colgrove v. Battin, 520
Collins & Aikman Corp.; SEC v., 439
Comfort ex rel. Neumyer v. Lynn Sch. Comm., 1051
Confectioners' Mach. Co. v. Racine Engine & Mach. Co., 1078
Conley v. Gibson, 254, 260, 262, 268-269, 271, 277, 283, 284, 292, 305
Connecticut v. Doehr, 115
ConnectU LLC v. Zuckerberg, 888
Consolidated Rail Corp. v. Metz, 394
Cooper v. Federal Reserve Bank of Richmond, 1099
Cooper v. Fitzgerald, 379, 386, 388
Cooper Indus., Inc. v. Leatherman Tool Group, Inc., 636
Coopers & Lybrand v. Livesay, 635
Cooter & Gell v. Hartmarx Corp., 373
Copperweld Corp. v. Independence Tube Corp., 260
Corrigan v. Buckley, 1072
Cossaboon v. Maine Med. Ctr., 781
Costello Publ'g Co. v. Rotelle, 409
Coughlin v. Rogers, 381, 383, 385
Covey v. Town of Somers, 63, 68
Cox v. State of La., 219
Crocker v. Hilton Int'l Barbados, Ltd., 691
Cromwell v. County of Sac, 1041
Cruickshank v. MAPFRE U.S.A., 1010
Cruz v. Beto, 139
Cullen v. Nissan N. Am., Inc., 478
Cumba v. Merck & Co., 381, 383
Curran v. Price, 375
Curtis v. Loether, 529, 530

Daimler AG v. Bauman, 750, 754, 816, 817, *818,* 828, 829, 832, 834, 835
Dairy Queen, Inc. v. Wood, 533, 535
Daniels v. City of New York, 1025
Dart Cherokee Basin Operating Co. v. Owens, 924
Daubert v. Merrell-Dow Pharms., 610, 1114
Davidson v. New Orleans, 49
Davis v. Carl, 369
Daynard v. Ness, Motley, Loadholt, Richardson & Poole, P.A., 403

Dean Witter Reynolds, Inc. v. Byrd, 653
DeJesus; United States v., 547
Delahunty v. Massachusetts Mut. Life Ins. Co., 999
Delta Air Lines, Inc. v. August, 191, 192, 193, 195
Dery v. Wyer, 394
Detroit Coke Corp. v. NKK Chem. USA, Inc., 845
Dickerson v. Board of Educ. of Ford Heights, Ill., 618
Diebold; United States v., 557
Dimick v. Schiedt, 625, 626
Dioguardi v. Durning, 253
Dixon; United States v., 100
Doe v. ___. *See name of opposing party*
Donaldson v. United States, 415
D'Onofrio v. SFX Sports Group, Inc., 459
Dura Pharms., Inc. v. Broudo, 262
DuRocher v. Riddell, Inc., 285
Duro Textiles, LLC v. Sunbelt Corp., 842
Dusenbery v. United States, 67, 852
Dyer v. MacDougall, 610

East Tex. Motor Freight Sys., Inc. v. Rodriguez, 1098
eBay Inc. v. MercExchange, LLC, 127
Edmonson v. Leesville Concrete Co., 542
EEOC v. ___. *See name of opposing party*
Effron v. Sun Line Cruises, Inc., 842
E.I. DuPont DeNemours & Co., In re, 1039
Eisen v. Carlisle & Jacquelin, 1092
EIU Group, Inc. v. Citibank Del., Inc., 520
Ella R.B., In re, 99
Elmbrook Sch. Dist.; Doe v., 303
Elster v. Alexander, 291
Empire Healthchoice Assurance, Inc. v. McVeigh, 846, 879, 882
Epstein v. Balk, 681
Erie R.R. Co. v. Tompkins, 3, 903, *930,* 934, *937, 938, 939,* 940, 941, 942, 943, 945, 948, 950-954, 955-956, 958, 959, 960, 961, 964, 967, 968, 971, 972, 974, 976, 982-983, 984
Erlanger Mills, Inc. v. Cohoes Fibre Mills, Inc, 703
Eubanks v. FDIC, 1010
Evans v. Jeff D., 200-201
Evans v. Linden Research, Inc., 844
Exxon Mobil Corp. v. Allapattah Servs., Inc., 886, 894, 918, 974
Exxon Shipping Co. v. Baker, 178

Factor VIII or IX Concentrate Blood Prods. Litig., In re, 1065
Farquharson v. Metz, 784
FCC v. ___. *See name of opposing party*
Federated Dep't Stores, Inc. v. Moitie, 1045, 1051, 1052, 1053
FedEx Ground Package Sys., Inc.; EEOC v., 465
Feltner v. Columbia Pictures Television, Inc, 625

Fenster v. Schneider, 896
Fidelity & Deposit Co. v. United States, 575
Fieger v. Pitney Bowes Credit Corp., 938
Filartiga v. Pena-Irala, 810
Finley v. United States, 911, 914, 916
Finney v. Hutto, 134
Firefighters v. Cleveland, 1128, 1129
First Options of Chi. v. Kaplan, 647
First Time Videos, LLC v. FTV
    Programmgesellschaft MHB, 853
Flagg Bros., Inc. v. Brooks, 115
Flake v. Medline Indus., Inc., 845
FMC Corp. Patent Litig., In re, 1117
Foman v. Davis, 333
Ford Motor Co. v. Edgewood Props., Inc., 464
Foster v. Chatman, 542
Foulkes v. Hays, 134
Fowler Prop., Inc. v. Dowland, 199
Fox v. Vice, 187, 201
Franchise Tax Bd. of Cal. v. Construction
    Laborers Vacation Trust for S. Cal., 874, 879
Franchise Tax Bd. of Cal. v. Hyatt, 668
Frank; Doe v., 300
Freedom From Religion Found., Inc. v. Cherry
    Creek Sch. Dist., 302
Freedom From Religion Found., Inc. v. Emanuel Cty.
    Sch. Sys., 299
Freedom's Path at Dayton v. Dayton Metro. Hous.
    Auth., 470, 485
Freeman v. Lester Coggins Trucking, Inc.,
    1010, 1013
Friendfinder Network, Inc.; Doe v., 785
Fuentes v. Shevin, 41, 74, 108, 109, 114, 171
Fusari v. Steinberg, 43

Gagnon v. Scarpelli, 90, 93, 94, 96
Galloway v. United States, 588, 594, 609, 610, 1029
Gamble v. United States, 989
Gasperini v. Center for Humanities, Inc., 964, 971,
    980, 983
Gault, In re, 90
General Foods Corp. v. Massachusetts Dep't of
    Pub. Health, 1013
General Tel. Co. of S.W. v. Falcon, 1098,
    1099, 1102
Georgia v. Brailsford, 604
Georgia v. McCollum, 542
Gibson v. Chrysler Corp., 897
Gideon v. Johns-Manville Sales Corp., 1000
Gideon v. Wainwright, 90, 94, 100
Gitlitz v. Plankinton Bldg. Props., Inc., 133
Goettsch v. Goettsch, 534
Goldberg v. Kelly, 26, 27, 34, 39, 40, 41, 42, 43,
    44-45, 46-48, 53, 54, 95-96, 98, 108, 113
Golden State Bottling Co. v. NLRB, 16
Goldfarb v. Virginia State Bar, 883
Goldstein v. Malcolm G. Fries & Assocs., 370

Goldstone, In re, 1032
Gompers v. Buck's Stove & Range Co., 214
Gonzalez v. Banco Cent. Corp., 1010
Goodyear Dunlop Tires Operations, S.A. v. Brown,
    755, 811, 816, 818, 821, 822, 823, 828, 829,
    832, 834, 835
Goss v. Lopez, 94, 167
Grable & Sons Metal Prods., Inc. v. Darue Eng. &
    Mfg., 845-846, 878, 879, 880-881, 883
Grace v. MacArthur, 808
Graduate Mgmt. Admission Council v.
    Raju, 697
Grane Healthcare Co.; EEOC v., 463
Gray v. American Radiator & Standard Sanitary
    Corp., 704
Great Am. Ins. Co. v. Vegas Constr. Co., 481
Green v. Manhattanville Coll., 861
Green; People v., 548
Greenbaum v. United States, 311
Greene v. Lindsey, 851
Greenleaf v. Birth, 605
Gregory v. Ashcroft, 658
Greyhound Corp. v. Heitner, 795
Greyhound Corp.; United States v., 789
Griffin v. Illinois, 83, 84, 85
Griffin; United States v., 618
Griffis v. Luban, 714, 783
Gross v. Hanover Ins. Co., 393
Grove v. Guilfoyle, 852
Groves v. Farmers State Bank, 1079
GTE New Media Servs., Inc. v. BellSouth
    Corp., 782
Guaranty Trust Co. v. York, 940, 943, 944, 946, 947,
    948, 949, 951, 953, 954, 955-956, 958, 959,
    961, 963, 967, 969, 977
Guardianship of ___. See name of party
Gulf Oil Corp. v. Gilbert, 856, 858
Gunn v. Minton, 876, 877
Gunning v. Cooley, 606

Hackman v. One Brands, LLC, 895
Hagerty v. L & L Marine Servs., Inc., 1000
Halderman v. Pennhurst State Sch. & Hosp., 134
Hall v. Lanning, 1077
Hall; United States v., 1, 12, 13, 14, 17
Hallingby v. Hallingby, 889
Hall St. Assocs. LLC v. Mattel, Inc., 648
Hamdi v. Rumsfeld, 70, 79
Hannah v. Larche, 29
Hanna v. Plumer, 949, 955, 956, 959, 960, 961,
    962, 963, 967, 968, 971, 974, 977, 978, 980,
    982, 983, 984
Hansberry v. Lee, 1003, 1006, 1007-1008,
    1066, 1070-1075, 1076, 1079, 1080, 1085,
    1087, 1125
Hanson v. Denckla, 697, 699, 702, 704, 707, 717,
    722, 730, 731-732

Hardy v. Johns-Manville Sales Corp., 1033
Harlow v. Children's Hosp., 817
Harris v. Balk, 679, 689, 703, 792
Harris; United States v., 548
Harrods Ltd. v. Sixty Internet Domain
     Names, 799
Harvey's Wagon Wheel, Inc. v. Van Blitter, 962
H.D. Corp. v. Ford Motor Co., 406, 411
Heacock v. Heacock, 998
Hecht Co. v. Bowles, 131
Helicopteros Nacionales de Colombia v. Hall,
     814, 815, 816
Hensley v. Eckerhart, 190, 194, 203-205
Hernandez v. New York, 547
Herrera v. Collins, 1033
Hertz Corp. v. Friend, 887
Hess v. Pawloski, 682, 689, 690-691, 707, 836, 846
Hickman v. Taylor, 268, 421, 422, 447, 450, *493*
Hilao v. Estate of Marcos, 1098
Hogan v. Carter, 370
Holmes Group, Inc. v. Vornado Air Circulation
     Sys., Inc., 874
Home Depot U.S.A., Inc. v. Jackson, 874, 1113
Honda Motor Co. v. Oberg, *175*, 176
Hospital Bldg. Co. v. Trustees of Rex Hosp., 271
Hostrop v. Board of Junior Coll. Dist. No. 515, 169
Hoult v. Hoult, 1016, 1019, 1020, 1025, 1032
Howat v. Kansas, 225
Hudson v. Palmer, 154
Hunter v. Earthgrains Co. Bakery, 370
Hy Cite Corp. v. Badbusinessbureau.com, LLC, 782

Iacaponi v. New Amsterdam Cas. Co., 1012
iAccess, Inc. v. Webcard Techs., Inc., 781
Illinois v. Wardlow, 585
In re ___. *See name of party*
Insurance Corp. of Ireland, Ltd. v. Compagnie
     des Bauxites de Guinee, 710, 734
International Shoe Co. v. Washington, 669, *684,* 688,
     689, 690-691, 695, 697, 701, 702, 703, 704,
     705, 707, 709, 720, 724, 725, 731, 738, 741,
     742, 743, 744, 746, 753, 755, 760, 762, 765,
     766, 767, 771, 777, 790, 791, 792, 793, 794-
     795, 800-801, 802-803, 806, 808, 810, 811,
     813-814, 820-821, 822, 824, 828, 829, 832-
     833, 835, 1082, 1084
Iodice v. United States, 938
Iqbal v. Hasty, 276
Isaac v. Truck Serv., Inc., 1015
ISI Int'l, Inc. v. Borden Ladner Gervais LLP, 697
Islamic Shura Council of S. Cal. v. FBI, 372

Jackson v. Hall Cty. Gov't, Ga., 373
Jackson Cty. v. United States, 1077
James Daniel Good Real Prop.; United States
     v., 115
Jane Roes 1-2 v. SFBSC Mgmt., LLC, 304

Janney Montgomery Scott, Inc. v. Shepard Niles,
     Inc., 401, 406, 408-409, 411
Japanese Elec. Prods. Antitrust Litig., In re, 260,
     270, 521, 563, 572-573, 610
Jarosz v. Palmer, 1020
JBR, Inc. v. Café Don Paco, Inc., 853
J.E.B. v. Alabama ex rel. T.B., 542, 547
Jefferson Cty.; United States v., 1125, 1131
Jesner v. Arab Bank, PLC, 810
Jinks v. Richland Cty., S.C., 919
J. McIntyre Mach., Ltd. v. Nicastro, 709, *730, 745,*
     746, 748, 773, 780-781, 782, 828
Johnson v. Johnson, 464
Johnson v. Louisiana, 521
Johnson v. Smithsonian Inst., 409
Joint Anti-Fascist Refugee Comm. v. McGrath,
     25, 28, 34, 41, 46, 96, 111, 172, 173
Jones v. Flowers, 60, 852
Jones & Laughlin; NLRB v., 535

Kadic v. Karadzic, 810
Kasper v. Brittain, 224
Katchen v. Landy, 535
Keeton v. Hustler Magazine, Inc., 712-713, 718,
     767, 821
Kerr v. United States Dist. Court, 635
Kindred Nursing Ctrs. LP v. Clark, 653
Kiobel v. Royal Dutch Petroleum Co., 810, 824
Klaxon Co. v. Stentor Elec. Mfg. Co., 937, 942
K.M., State ex rel. v. West Virginia Dep't of
     Health & Human Res., 35
Kokkonen v. Guardian Life Ins. Co. of Am., 878
Kolstad v. American Dental Ass'n, 174
Koster v. Lumbermen's Mut. Cas. Co., 856
Kovacs v. Cooper, 95
Kowalski v. Gagne, 1023
Kras; United States v., 86
Krause v. Rhodes, 269
Kreager v. General Elec. Co., 1013
Kremer v. Chemical Constr. Corp., 1059
Krupski v. Costa Crociere S.P.A., 14, *328,* 334
Kulko v. Superior Court of Cal., City & Cty. of
     S.F., 689, 770, 804
Kumho Tire Co. Ltd. v. Carmichael, 611
Kunstler, In re, 369, 370
Kunz v. People of State of N.Y., 219
Kyreakakis v. Paternoster, 199

LaBrier v. State Farm Fire & Cas. Co., 458
Lafayette Ins. Co. v. French, 1077
Lamps Plus, Inc. v. Varela, 647
Lassiter, In re, 89
Lassiter v. Department of Soc. Servs. of Durham Cty.,
     N.C., 87, 99, 100
Leatherman v. Tarrant Cty. Narcotics
     Intelligence & Coordination Unit, 256-257,
     268, 269, 271, 273

Lee v. Hansberry, 1074, 1075
Leonard v. USA Petroleum Corp., 690
Lewin v. Cooke, 370
Lewis v. Sullivan, 87
Linardos v. Fortuna, 889
Lincoln Prop. Co. v. Roche, 920
Little v. Streater, 98
Little Hocking Water Ass'n, Inc. v. E.I. DuPont
     de Nemours & Co., 478
Liza Danielle, Inc. v. Jamko, Inc., 132
Lontz v. Tharp, 923
Lopez v. Martin Luther King, Jr., Hosp., 401
Lorillard v. Pons, 529
Louisville & Nashville R.R. Co. v. Mottley, 869, 873,
     875, 903, 923, 1052
Loving v. Virginia, 82

MacLeod v. MacLeod, 860
Maguire v. Marquette Univ., 905
Marek v. Chesny, 188, 196, 197-198, 199, 201
Margeson v. Boston & Me. R.R., 427
Markman v. Westview Instruments, Inc., 534
Marks v. United States, 79
Marrese v. American Acad. of Orthopaedic
     Surgeons, 1052
Marshall v. Marshall, 890
Martin v. Wilks, 135, 1052, *1124,* 1137-1138
Mas v. Perry, 887, 894
Massachusetts v. Morash, 1129
Masson v. New Yorker Magazine, Inc., 1024
Mathews v. Eldridge, 39, *40,* 46-47, 48-50, 48-54,
     57, 59, 73, 75, 77, 78, 91, 93, 95, 98, 127
May v. Anderson, 95
Mayer v. Allstate Vehicle & Prop. Ins. Co., 471
McClurg v. Mallinckrodt, Inc., 460
McDonnell Douglas Corp. v. Green, 270
McFaddin Express, Inc. v. Adley Corp., 906
McGee v. International Life Ins. Co., 694, 698,
     701-702, 709, 740, 766, 767, 768, 769
McLaughlin v. Biasucci, 394
Meadow Point Props. v. Nick Mazzoferro &
     Sons, 292
Mendoza; United States v., 1051, 1053
Mennonite Bd. of Missions v. Adams, 851
Mercury Air Group, Inc. v. Mansour, 373
Merrell Dow Pharms., Inc. v. Thompson, 845,
     846, 869
Metro-Goldwyn-Mayer Studios, Inc. v. Grokster,
     Ltd., 692
Metropolitan Life Ins. Co. v. Taylor, 924
Meyer v. Nebraska, 82, 95
Microsoft Corp.; United States v., 485
Migra v. Warren City Sch. Dist. Bd. of Educ.,
     1058, 1059
Miller v. Fenton, 581
Mims v. Duval Cty. Sch. Bd., 15, 18, 20, 22
Mine Workers v. Bagwell, 149

Mir v. L-3 Commc'ns Integrated Sys., LP, 455
Mitchell v. DeMario Jewelry, Inc., 529
Mitchell v. Neff, 676, 677
Mitsubishi Motors Corp. v. Soler Chrysler-
     Plymouth, Inc., 648
M.L.B. v. S.L.J., 86
Mohamad v. Palestinian Auth., 824
Monroe v. Pape, 169
Monsanto Co. v. Spray-Rite Serv. Corp., 260
Montana v. United States, 1041
Montgomery Ward & Co. v. Duncan, 612
Montiel v. Taylor, 478
Morrissey v. Brewer, 42, 90
Mt. Hood Stages, Inc. v. Greyhound
     Corp., 789
Muhammad v. Walmart Stores E., LP, 372
Mullane v. Central Hanover Bank & Trust Co., 60,
     62, 64, 66, 69, 82, *846,* 850-851, 852, 1084,
     1087, 1089, 1092
Mwani v. bin Laden, 697, 851

NAACP, Jacksonville Branch v. Duval Cty.
     Sch., 16
National Bank of Canada v. Artex Indus.,
     Inc., 394
National Licorice Co. v. NLRB, 402
Neely v. Martin K. Eby Constr. Co., 590
New Hampshire v. North Atl. Ref. Ltd., 728
New Marshall Engine Co. v. Marshall Engine
     Co., 883
New York Times Co. v. Sullivan, 625
Nicastro v. McIntyre Mach. Am., Ltd., 730
Nix v. Sword, 476
NLRB v. ___. *See name of opposing party*
Nolan v. Transocean Air Lines, 938
Noonan v. Winston Co., 772
Nordegren v. Burlington N. R.R. Co., 923
Northern Ind. Pub. Serv. Co.; United States v., 413

Ohralik v. Ohio State Bar Ass'n, 883
Olavarrieta; United States v., 396
Old Republic Ins. Co. v. Concast, Inc., 394
Old Wayne Mut. L. Ass'n v. McDonough, 1077
Oliner v. McBride's Indus., Inc., 394
Oppenheimer Fund, Inc. v. Sanders, 455
Osborn v. Bank of U.S., 878
Owen Equip. & Erection Co. v. Kroger, 906, 911,
     913, 917
*Oxbow Carbon & Minerals LLC v. Union Pac. R.R.
     Co.,* 453, 461, 468, 469-470
Oxford Global Res., LLC v. Hernandez, 861, 862

Pacific Mut. Life Ins. Co. v. Haslip, 174, 175
Palmer v. Hoffman, 942, 944
Panavision Int'l, LP v. Toeppen, 782
Parham v. J.R., 94
Park v. Ross, 605

Parklane Hosiery Co. v. Shore, 1024, *1025,*
    1030-1032, 1033, 1034, 1036, 1042,
    1044, 1055, 1125, 1129
Parsons v. Bedford, 525, 605
Passa v. Derderian, 1116
Patsy's Brand, Inc. v. I.O.B. Realty, Inc., 374
Patterson v. McLean Credit Union, 989
Payne v. Milwaukee Cty., 198
Penn, LLC v. Prosper Bus. Dev. Corp., 372
Pennoyer v. Neff, 668, 669, *670,* 675-677, 679, 681,
    682, 683, 684, 686, 688, 690, 701, 702, 746,
    788, 791, 795, 799, 800, 808, 821, 836, 846,
    1076-1077
Pennsylvania R.R. Co. v. Chamberlain, 610
People v. ___. *See name of opposing party*
Perez v. Boston Hous. Auth., 134
Perkins v. Benguet Consol. Mining Co., 694, 811,
    814, 815, 816, 821, 823, 833
Perrier Bottled Water Litig., In re, 727
Philip Morris USA v. Williams, 177
Phillips Petroleum v. Shutts, 1066, 1080, *1081,* 1088,
    1089, 1092, 1104
Pillar Title Agency v. Pei, 471
Piper Aircraft Co. v. Reyno, 854
Pizarro v. Hoteles Concorde Int'l, C.A., 692
Plaintiff B. v. Francis, 300
Plaintiffs #1-21 v. County of Suffolk, 304
Plata v. Brown, 138, 139
Plumb v. Goodnow, 1078
Plumhoff v. Rickard, 578, 579-580
Podhorn v. Paragon Group, Inc., 389, 865
Pogue v. NorthWestern Mut. Life Ins. Co., 477
Ponderosa Dev. Corp. v. Bjordahl, 1013
Porsche Cars N. Am. Inc. v. Porsche.net, 799
Postal Tel.-Cable Co. v. Neport, 1077
Pottsville Broad. Co.; FCC v., 45-46
Powell v. Alabama, 31
Powell v. McCormack, 878
Powers v. Ohio, 542
Price; United States v., 554
Proctor v. Fluor Enters., Inc., 312
Provident Tradesmens Bank & Trust Co. v.
    Patterson, 399, 410
Pujol v. Shearson/American Express, Inc., 406,
    407, 411
Purkett v. Elem, 543

Radovich v. National Football League, 271
Ragan v. Merchants Transfer & Warehouse Co.,
    944, 958, 959, 960, 961
Ramey v. Rockefeller, 1013
Rao v. Era Alaska Airlines, 774, 781, 782
Reed v. Allen, 1047
Reeves v. Sanderson Plumbing Prods., Inc., 611
Regal Knitwear Co. v. NLRB, 20
Reilly v. Phil Tolkan Pontiac, Inc., 703
Reiter v. Sonotone Corp., 1046

Relafen Antitrust Litig., In re, 520
Rennie & Laughlin, Inc. v. Chrysler Corp., 292
Republic of ___. *See name of republic*
Rhodes v. Chapman, 153
Ricci v. DeStefano, 1014
Richardson v. Belcher, 43
Richardson v. C.I.R., 943
Richardson v. Perales, 44
Riverside, City of v. Rivera, 202, 208
Roadway Express, Inc. v. Piper, 192, 194
Roberts v. Legendary Marine Sales, 781
Roberts v. T.H.E. Ins. Co., 841
Robinson v. Hanrahan, 63, 64, 68
Roch v. Mollica, 809
Rodriguez v. Mach, 102
Rogers v. Ford Motor Co., 1037
Ross v. Bernhard, 521, 522, 528, 533, 535
Rufo v. Inmates of the Suffolk Cty. Jail, 135
Rufo v. Simpson, 1024
Ruston Gas Turbines, Inc. v. Donaldson Co., 729

Saia v. People of State of N.Y., 219
St. Mary's Honor Ctr. v. Hicks, 611
St. Paul Mercury Indem. Co. v. Red Cab Co., 894
Salve Regina Coll. v. Russell, 141
Sanders v. United States, 1032
San Juan Dupont Plaza Hotel Fire Litig., In
    re, 423
San Remo Hotel, L.P. v. City & Cty. of S.F., 1059
Saria v. Massachusetts Mut. Life Ins. Co.,
    483, 485
Scales v. J.C. Bradford & Co., 471
Scheuer v. Rhodes, 269
Schiavone v. Fortune, 324
Schlagenhauf v. Holder, 442
Schneider v. State of N.J., 219
Schuylkill & Dauphin Improvement Co. v.
    Munson, 605
Scott v. Donald, 20
Scott v. Harris, 575-577, 579, 610
Scott v. Illinois, 91
SEC v. ___. *See name of opposing party*
Sellers v. O'Connell, 894
Semtek Int'l Inc. v. Lockheed Martin Corp., 972,
    1002, 1005, 1059-1060
Serrano v. Cintas Corp., 472
Shady Grove Orthopedic Assocs. v. Allstate Ins. Co.,
    956, *973,* 983, 984, 1090
Shaffer v. Heitner, 703, *788,* 796-797, 798-799,
    802-803, 805, 806, 808, 809, 822, 851, 1084
Shapiro v. Thompson, 28
Shaw v. Leatherberry, 986
Shelley v. Kraemer, 1071
Sherbert v. Verner, 28
Shoppers Food Warehouse v. Moreno, 692, 748
Shoshone Mining Co. v. Rutter, 879
Shrader v. Biddinger, 784

Shuttlewsorth v. City of Birmingham, 225
Sierra Club v. Watt, 402
Simpson, Guardianship of v. Simpson, 1024
Singletary v. Pennsylvania Dep't of Corrs., 319,
    327, 334
Sinochem Int'l Co. v. Malaysia Int'l Shipping
    Co., 860, 861
Skelly Oil Co. v. Phillips Petroleum Co., 874
Skinner v. Oklahoma, 82
Slochower v. Board of Higher Educ., 28
Slocum v. New York Life Ins. Co., 590, 605
Smith v. Doe, 842
Smith v. Kansas City Title & Trust Co., 881
Smith v. Swormstedt, 1078, 1079
Smith v. Times Publ'g Co., 594
Sniadach v. Family Fin. Corp., 41, 43, 108,
    112, 113
Snowney v. Harrah's Entm't, Inc., 692, 781
Sole v. Wyner, 198
Sosa v. Alvarez-Machain, 810
Southern Methodist Univ. Ass'n of Women Law
    Students v. Wynne & Jaffe, 300-301
Spano v. CSX Transp., Inc., 463
Specht v. Netscape Commc'ns Corp., 844
Speiser v. Randall, 28
Springer; United States v., 215
Standard Fire Ins. Co. v. Knowles, 924, 1113
Standard Process, Inc. v. KDealz Ltd. Co., 782
Stanley v. Illinois, 91, 95, 108
State ex rel. ___. *See name of relator*
State Farm Fire & Cas. Co. v. Tashire, 891
State Farm Mut. Auto. Ins. Co. v. Campbell, 176
State of ___. *See name of state*
Steel & Morris v. United Kingdom, 102
Steele v. Louisville & Nashville R. Co., 254
Steelworkers v. Weber, 1130
Stegall; Doe v., 300, 301, 302
Stephenson v. Dow Chemical Co., 1118
Stephenson v. Ercole, 336
Stewart Org., Inc. v. Ricoh Corp., 862, 963, 972
Strawbridge v. Curtiss, 886
Sudan, Republic of v. Harrison, 853
Supreme Tribe of Ben-Hur v. Cauble, 1079
Swann v. Charlotte-Mecklenburg Bd. of Educ.,
    15, 18, 134
Swierkiewicz v. Sorema, N.A., 257, 261, 266, 270,
    271, 273
Swift v. Tyson, 930, 931-936, 938, 939, 941, 947,
    951, 958, 984
Swiss Am. Bank, Ltd.; United States v., 696
Syngenta AG Mir162 Corn Litig., In re, 431

Tarter v. United States, 606
Tavoulareas v. The Washington Post Co., 623
Taylor v. Sturgell, 1003, 1009, 1025, 1034, 1037
Teamsters v. United States, 1101, 1105
Tellabs, Inc. v. Makor Issues & Rights, Ltd., 288

Temple v. Synthes Corp., 399, 400
Tennessee v. Union & Planters' Bank, 870, 871
Terrill v. Chao, 370
Terry v. Ohio, 585
Theatre Enters., Inc. v. Paramount Film Distrib.
    Corp., 260, 265
Thomas v. Holder, 87
Thompson v. C&H Sugar Co., 441
Ticor Title Ins. Co. v. Brown, 1102
Timbs v. Indiana, 115
Todd v. Oppenheimer & Co., 292
Tolan v. Cotton, 577-578
Tomalewski v. State Farm Life Ins. Co., 562
Tomelleri v. MEDL Mobile, Inc., 816
Torres v. Oakland Scavenger Co., 327
Trinity Church in the City of Bos. v. John
    Hancock Mut. Life Ins. Co., 174
Trump v. Hawaii, 23-24
Tull v. United States, 529, 531, 625
Turner v. Marshall, 542
Turner v. Rogers, 100, 214
Turner v. Safley, 151
Tutu Wells Contamination Litig., In re, 375
Twentieth Century-Fox Film Corp. v. Taylor &
    Burton, 892

Uffner v. La Reunion Francaise, S.A., 854
Union Carbide Corp. Gas Plant Disaster , In
    re, 860
United Mine Workers of Am. v. Gibbs, 902, 904, 905,
    906, 907, 908, 912-913, 914, 917, 995
United Mine Workers of Am.; United
    States v., 20
United Sav. Ass'n of Tex. v. Timbers of Inwood
    Forest Assocs., 14
United States v. ___. *See name of opposing party*
Unitherm Food Sys., Inc. v. Swift-Eckrich,
    Inc., 590
University of Tenn. v. Elliott, 1032, 1042, 1059
Urrutia v. Harriburg Cty. Police Dep't, 321
U.S. Fin. Sec. Litig., In re, 521
U.S. Gypsum Co.; United States v., 636
U.S. Term Limits, Inc. v. Thornton, 734

Vaca v. Sipes, 528
Varlack v. SWC Caribbean, Inc., 322, 325-326
Vasquez; United States v., 215
Venegas v. Mitchell, 209
Vermeulen v. Renault, 728
Village of ___. *See name of village*
Vitek v. Jones, 90, 96

Wade v. Goldschmidt, 415
Walden v. Fiore, 715, 753, 757, 781
Walgreen Co. v. Sara Creek Prop. Co., 130, 133
Walker v. Armco Steel Corp., 957, 961, 962, 963,
    967, 976, 980, 984

Walker v. Carnival Cruise Lines, 841
Walker v. City of Birmingham, 22, 216, *217*, 224, 225, 235, 867, 1134
Walker v. City of Hutchinson, 62, 851
Wal-Mart, Inc. v. Dukes, 1066, 1088, 1090, *1095*, 1110, 1111, 1112
Walsh v. U.S. Bank, N.A., 375
Warner v. City of New York, 165, 179, 214, 297-298, 377, 387, 398, 536, 585, 845, 919, 1025, 1091-1092, 1112
Warner Commc'ns Sec. Litig., In re, 644
Washington v. Washington State Commercial Passenger Fishing Vessel Ass'n., 16
Watson; United States v., 548
Weisgram v. Marley Co., 612
Wenche Siemer v. Learjet Acquisition Corp., 808
Werwinski v. Ford Motor Co., 938
Wesco Prods. Co. v. Alloy Auto. Co., 618, 619
Weston v. Cassata, 35
Whelan v. Heffler, Radetich & Saitta, LLP, 375
Whole Woman's Health v. Hellerstedt, 1000-1001
William A. Gross Constr. Assocs., Inc. v. American Mfrs. Mut. Ins. Co., 441
Williams v. BASF Catalysts, LLC, 455
Williams v. Florida, 520
Williams v. Philip Morris, Inc., 177-178

Winter v. Natural Res. Def. Council, 116, 127
Wireless Env't, LLC v. HooToo.com, Inc., 782
Wiwa v. Royal Dutch Petroleum Co., 817, 861
Wolff v. McDonnell, 41
Wonson; United States v., 525
Wood v. Strickland, 168
World Trade Ctr. Disaster Site Litig., In re, 1123
World-Wide Volkswagen Corp. v. Woodson, 699, 707, 708, 709, 710, 712, 717, 720, 722-723, 726, 727, 729, 732, 733, 736-737, 740, 742, 752, 753, 766, 777, 814, 815, 829, 867, 922, 1084
W. R. Grace & Co. v. Rubber Workers, 1129
Wygant v. Jackson Bd. of Educ., 1134

Xpedior Creditor Trust v. Credit Suisse First Bos. (USA), Inc., 459
Xuncax v. Gramajo, 809

Yakus v. United States, 131
Young v. New Haven Advocate, 779
Youngstown Sheet & Tube Co. v. Sawyer, 77

Zidon v. Pickrell, 784
Zielinski v. Philadelphia Piers, Inc., 310
Zippo Mfg. Co. v. Zippo Dot Com, Inc., 777, 778, 781, 782
Zubulake v. UBS Warburg, LLC, 459

TABLE OF STATUTES AND RULES

Federal Laws and Regulations

U.S. Constitution
Art. I, 77, 934, 959
Art. I, § 8, cl. 18, 919
Art. I, § 9, cl. 2, 76, 77
Art. II, 934
Art. III, 7, 120, 147, 149, 166, 239, 501, 865,
    873, 901, 904, 908, 915, 916, 1041, 1042,
    1083, 1117, 1119
Art. III, § 2, 604, 866, 868, 873, 891, 903, 908,
    912, 917, 941
Art. III, § 3, cl. 1, 76
Art. IV, 808, 1081
Art. IV, § 1, 7, 668
Art. VI, 349, 604
Amend. I, 203, 219, 220, 221, 222, 223, 224,
    225, 231, 276, 299, 300, 884
Amend. IV, 115, 165, 203, 304, 579, 716, 1016,
    1054, 1055, 1057, 1234, 1237, 1240, 1247,
    1248, 1252, 1253, 1254, 1255, 1258
Amend. V, 7, 25, 33, 40, 41, 47, 71, 73, 81, 115,
    276, 304, 448, 521, 522, 695, 696, 723, 754,
    870, 874, 989, 1025, 1117
Amend. VI, 89, 91, 94, 100, 604
Amend. VII, 7, 106, 508, 520, 521, 522,
    524-531, 526, 533, 534, 535, 548, 575, 590,
    595, 602, 603, 604, 606, 627, 628, 947, 948,
    964, 967, 969, 970, 985, 1026, 1029, 1030,
    1032, 1042, 1044
Amend. VIII, 115, 134, 135, 138, 139, 142, 145,
    148, 152, 153, 175, 320
Amend. X, 936
Amend. XI, 269, 321
Amend. XIV, 7, 25, 27, 32, 33, 41, 47, 60, 62,
    71, 73, 81, 82, 83, 84, 89, 91, 94, 95, 108,
    109, 112, 113, 114, 115, 136, 168, 171, 175,
    176, 191, 203, 219, 220, 221, 304, 535, 541,
    542, 551, 552, 553, 554, 558, 674, 675, 677,
    682, 683, 684, 688, 695, 696, 699, 701, 702,
    711, 721, 722, 751, 762, 788, 800, 803, 805,
    811, 814, 818, 820, 830, 846, 847, 848, 850,
    1054, 1076, 1077, 1081, 1086, 1087, 1132,
    1134, 1234, 1237, 1238, 1240, 1247, 1248,
    1254, 1256, 1258

U.S. Code
9 U.S.C.
    § 2, 649, 653, 655, 656, 657

§ 3, 657
§ 4, 657
§ 7, 648, 649
§ 8, 657
§ 9, 650
§ 10, 650
11 U.S.C.
    § 523(a), 135
15 U.S.C.
    § 1, 258-265, 270, 279, 282, 453,
        993, 1045
    § 2, 453
    § 4, 240
    § 15, 453, 457, 1045
    § 78j, 1011
    § 78u-4(b)(2), 288
    §§ 1051 et seq, 1038
    § 1114, 924
    § 1125(d), 798
    § 1125(d)(2), 798
    § 1640(a)(2)(B), 1069
    § 1693m(a), 187
    § 1693m(f), 187
    § 1703, 1011
16 U.S.C.
    § 1362(13), 118
    § 1371(f)(1), 118
    § 1372(a), 118
    § 1456(c)(1)(B), 119
18 U.S.C.
    §§ 1961 et seq., 993
    §§ 1961-1964, 1011
    § 3624(a), 135
    § 3626, 135, 136, 141
    § 3626(a), 142, 144
    § 3626(a)(1)(A), 140, 148, 149, 152
    § 3626(a)(3)(A)(i), 140
    § 3626(a)(3)(B), 140
    § 3626(a)(3)(E), 140
    § 3626(a)(3)(E)(i), 141
    § 3626(a)(3)(E)(ii), 141
    § 3626(b)(1)(A)(i), 136
    § 3626(b)(3), 136
    § 3626(g)(4), 140
    § 4001(a), 73
20 U.S.C.
    §§ 1071-1088, 396
    § 1415(e)(4)(B), 187

U.S. Code (*continued*)

26 U.S.C.
§ 6335(a), 876

28 U.S.C.
§ 331, 355, 504
§ 361, 414
§§ 471-482, 7, 355
§§ 631-639, 485
§ 651, 660
§ 687, 396, 1077
§§ 1253-1258, 246
§ 1257, 246, 637
§ 1292, 635
§ 1292(a), 246
§ 1292(b), 246, 912
§ 1295(a)(1), 881
§ 1331, 657, 696, 867, 868, 869, 872, 873, 875, 876, 878, 879, 894, 920, 923, 929, 1059
§ 1332, 240, 710, 867, 886, 891, 894, 898, 899, 910, 915, 916-917, 920, 929, 944, 965, 1060, 1113, 1114
§ 1332(a), 764, 895, 974
§ 1332(a)(1), 886, 887, 892, 909, 912, 913
§ 1332(a)(2), 891, 892
§ 1332(a)(3), 891, 892
§ 1332(b), 894
§ 1332(c)(1), 887
§ 1332(d), 924, 982, 1070
§ 1332(d)(2), 974
§ 1332(d)(2)(A), 891
§ 1332(d)(3), 1114
§ 1332(d)(4)(A), 1113
§ 1332(d)(4)(B), 1113
§ 1332(d)(10), 887
§ 1332(d)(11)(B)(i), 1115
§ 1332(d)(11)(B)(ii)(II), 1115
§§ 1333-1340, 869
§ 1335, 413, 696
§ 1335(a)(1), 891
§ 1338(a), 877, 878, 879, 880, 881
§§ 1343-1351, 869
§ 1343, 168
§ 1346(b), 911, 912, 913
§ 1350, 810, 819, 824
§ 1359, 869, 909
§§ 1361-1364, 869
§ 1367, 901, 905, 914, 915, 917, 918, 921, 1059
§ 1367(a), 916, 917, 921
§ 1367(b), 916
§ 1367(c), 917
§§ 1367(c)(1)-(3), 917
§ 1367(c)(4), 917
§ 1367(d), 917, 919
§ 1369, 1115, 1116
§ 1369(a), 1115, 1116
§ 1369(b), 1116
§ 1391, 853

§ 1391(c)(2), 853
§ 1397, 413
§ 1404, 807, 844, 854, 859, 862, 963, 972
§ 1404(a), 856, 963
§ 1406, 780, 854
§ 1407, 860, 1060
§ 1441, 920, 924, 1113
§ 1441(a), 921, 923
§ 1441(b), 1049
§ 1441(b)(2), 920, 922
§ 1441(c), 921
§ 1442, 922
§ 1446, 924
§ 1446(a), 920
§ 1446(b), 920
§ 1446(b)(2)(A), 921
§ 1446(b)(3), 920
§ 1446(c)(1), 921
§ 1446(c)(2), 921
§ 1447(c), 920
§ 1652, 349
§ 1658, 317
§ 1712, 1089
§ 1738, 1052, 1056, 1058, 1059
§ 1861, 540
§ 1862, 540
§ 1863, 540
§§ 1915(b)(1)-(4), 86
§§ 1915(g), 86
§ 1920, 191, 192, 194, 1259
§ 1927, 377
§ 1983, 257
§§ 2071-2072, 354
§§ 2072-2074, 269
§ 2072, 13, 191, 196, 304, 352, 355, 500, 503, 504, 505, 937, 950, 959, 967, 978
§ 2072(a), 970, 977
§ 2072(b), 6, 970, 977, 978, 979, 1106
§ 2073, 6, 503
§ 2073(b), 503
§ 2074, 6, 500
§ 2074(b), 504
§§ 2201-2202, 874
§ 2201, 166, 532
§ 2202, 166, 532
§ 2241, 71
§ 2361, 413
§ 2412(b), 187
§ 2679(d), 922

29 U.S.C.
§ 160(c), 529
§ 185, 526
§ 185(a), 526

35 U.S.C.
§ 102(b), 877
§ 120, 882
§ 134(a), 882
§ 141, 882

§ 145, 882
§ 271, 879
§ 281, 879
§ 285, 187
42 U.S.C.
  § 423, 40
  § 423(d)(3), 44
  § 423(g), 47
  §§ 601-610, 27
  § 1981, 203, 1132
  § 1983, 167, 168, 169-171, 172, 173, 188, 189-
    190, 194, 197, 203, 250, 299, 304, 319, 320,
    551, 552, 553, 554, 558, 562, 566, 569, 875,
    905, 986, 1016, 1054-1057, 1058-1059,
    1132, 1236, 1237, 1239-1240, 1255, 1256
  § 1985(3), 203
  § 1986, 203
  § 1988, 185, 187, 188-195, 196-198, 201, 202,
    203, 204, 206, 209, 1259
  § 1988(b), 1240
  §§ 2000e et seq., 250, 529, 1106, 1124
  §§ 2000e-1 et seq., 1096
  § 2000e-2(a), 1096
  § 2000e-2(k), 1096
  § 2000e-2(n)(1), 1136
  § 2000e-5(g), 529
  § 2000e-5(g)(2)(A), 1110
  §§ 2000e et seq., 367
  § 2996e(d)(5), 1069
  §§ 3601 et seq., 918, 929
  § 3601, 470
  § 4332, 125
  § 4332(2)(C), 118
  § 7064(b)(1)(B), 416
  § 7622(e)(2), 187
  § 12101, 470
45 U.S.C.
  §§ 51 et seq., 830
47 U.S.C.
  § 230, 785
  § 230(c)(1), 785
  § 230(e)(2), 785
  § 230(e)(3), 785
  § 230(e)(4), 785
49 U.S.C.
  §§ 11902-11904, 993

Federal Rules of Civil Procedure
  (Fed. R. Civ. P.)
1, 14, 192, 253, 372, 566
2, 527, 903
3, 253, 957, 960, 962
4, 695, 764, 959
4(a), 306
4(b), 306
4(c)(1), 852
4(c)(2), 852

4(d), 852
4(d)(1), 852, 949-954, 959, 960, 961, 977
4(d)(2), 852
4(d)(3), 852
4(e)(1), 852
4(e)(2)(B), 852
4(f), 852, 977
4(h), 852
4(i), 852
4(k)(1)(A), 695, 717, 771, 820
4(k)(1)(B), 696
4(k)(2), 696, 697, 836
4(m), 319, 321, 322, 330, 333
4(n), 798
5(d), 548
5(d)(1), 468
6, 435, 609
6(b), 305
7, 251, 397
7(a), 308, 310
7(b)(1)(A), 590
8, 251, 252, 257, 264, 268, 271, 278, 281, 284,
    291, 305, 872
8(a), 253, 257, 267, 307, 371, 397, 548
8(a)(1), 872
8(a)(2), 206, 253, 260, 266, 270, 278, 279,
    291, 315
8(b), 307, 309, 311, 397
8(b)(4), 310
8(b)(5), 310
8(b)(6), 309
8(c), 309, 311, 312, 397, 944, 990
8(d)(3), 295
8(e), 256
9, 251, 257, 264, 281, 282
9(b)-(c), 264
9(b), 257, 268, 270, 273, 281, 284, 291, 292, 295
9(g), 295
10, 251
10(a), 300, 304
10(c), 295
11, 187, 202, 309, 366, 367, 368-369, 372, 373,
    374, 375, 377, 427, 430, 563, 977
11(b), 368-369
11(b)(1), 374
11(b)(2), 370, 374
11(b)(3), 370-371, 374, 444
11(b)(4), 311, 366
11(c)(1)(A), 372
11(c)(2), 372
11(c)(3), 372
11(c)(4), 375
12, 252, 305
12(a), 305
12(a)(1), 944
12(a)(1)(A), 306
12(b), 306, 307, 308, 309, 313, 397, 678

Federal Rules of Civil Procedure
(Fed. R. Civ. P.) (continued)
12(b)(1), 306, 854, 872
12(b)(2), 306, 307, 678, 774
12(b)(3), 306, 307, 854
12(b)(4), 306, 307
12(b)(5), 306, 307
12(b)(6), 241, 251, 253, 255, 260, 266, 284, 289,
    292, 293, 294, 295, 296, 306, 308, 313, 338,
    368, 371, 418, 427, 444, 548, 549, 562, 608,
    807, 1047, 1053
12(b)(7), 307, 403, 404, 588
12(c), 308, 321, 608
12(e), 289, 290, 294, 296, 305
12(f), 297, 306, 309, 315
12(g), 307, 678
12(h), 307, 872
12(h)(1), 307, 678, 710, 836
12(h)(2), 308, 404, 412
12(h)(3), 308, 678, 710
12(i), 308
13, 309, 379, 388
13(a), 242, 391, 911, 995, 997
13(a)(2), 391
13(g), 242, 379, 389, 391, 392, 911
13(h), 309, 392
14, 242, 309, 379, 397, 584, 915
14(a), 394, 395, 397, 399, 906, 907
14(a)(1), 395
14(a)(2)(C), 397
15, 316, 317, 319, 328, 332, 397, 994
15(a), 316, 318, 333
15(a)(1)-(2), 333
15(a)(2), 316
15(b), 316
15(b)(1), 317
15(b)(2), 316
15(c), 316, 317, 318, 319, 321, 330, 333,
    378, 391
15(c)(1), 333
15(c)(1)(A), 337
15(c)(1)(B), 318, 330
15(c)(1)(C), 318, 319, 321, 322, 323, 324, 325,
    326, 327, 328, 330, 333
15(c)(1)(C)(i), 320, 321, 322, 330
15(c)(1)(C)(ii), 321, 322, 325, 326, 327, 330,
    331, 332, 333, 334
15(d), 316, 317
16, 245, 316, 495, 608, 1112
16(a)(5), 644
16(b), 435
16(b)(2), 435
16(c)(2)(I), 644
17(a), 298, 299
17(b), 299, 396
17(c), 299
18-20, 903
18, 378, 387, 388, 977, 984, 987, 994

18(a), 389
19, 242, 307, 398, 399, 400, 402, 404, 405, 406,
    410, 412, 416, 588, 915, 1127
19(a), 398, 399, 400, 401, 403, 404, 405, 406,
    407, 408, 409, 411, 1126
19(a)(1), 405, 406, 408
19(a)(1)(A), 398, 400, 401
19(a)(1)(B)(i), 398, 401, 405
19(a)(1)(B)(ii), 398, 402, 408
19(a)(2)(i) [earlier version], 405, 407, 408, 415
19(a)(2)(ii) [earlier version], 408, 409
19(b), 398, 399, 400, 403, 404, 405, 408, 409,
    410, 411, 1126
20, 378, 381, 385-386, 387, 388, 391, 915, 977,
    984, 1064, 1110
20(a), 380, 381, 382, 383, 384, 385, 386,
    387, 918
20(b), 378, 388
21, 309, 379, 380, 381, 384, 385
21(a), 381
22, 242, 413
23, 242, 973-977, 979-982, 983, 984, 1007,
    1008, 1066, 1071, 1079, 1080, 1088, 1090,
    1094, 1096, 1103, 1110, 1111, 1278
23(a), 1090, 1091, 1095, 1096, 1097, 1099,
    1106, 1109, 1110, 1112, 1247, 1258
23(a)(2), 1097, 1098, 1102, 1106, 1107,
    1109, 1110
23(a)(3), 1097
23(a)(4), 1097
23(b), 1096
23(b)(1), 1091, 1103, 1109
23(b)(2), 1091, 1095, 1096, 1097, 1102, 1103,
    1104, 1105, 1106, 1109, 1112, 1247,
    1248, 1258
23(b)(3), 1080, 1091, 1092, 1102, 1103, 1104,
    1106, 1109, 1110, 1111
23(c)(2)(B), 1103
23(c)(4), 1092
23(e), 1093, 1122
23(f), 635, 1093
23(g), 1093
23(h), 1094
24, 242, 309, 413, 415, 915, 1126, 1127
24(a), 414, 415, 416, 911, 1126
24(a)(2), 414, 415, 416
24(b), 415, 416
26-37, 493
26, 378, 436, 455, 456, 458, 459, 460, 468, 496,
    498, 1043
26 adv. comm. notes, 456, 457, 459, 460
26(a)(1)(A), 434, 435
26(a)(1)(B), 435
26(a)(1)(C), 435
26(a)(1)(E), 434
26(a)(2)(D), 435
26(a)(3)(B), 435
26(a)(4)(C), 198

26(b), 434, 439, 449, 452, 455, 460, 463, 464, 467, 495
26(b)(1), 438, 450, 451, 455, 456, 472, 473, 474
26(b)(1) adv. comm. note, 476
26(b)(2), 437, 438, 472
26(b)(2)(B), 440
26(b)(2)(C), 440
26(b)(5)(A), 450
26(b)(5)(B), 440
26(c), 452, 460, 463, 471, 807
26(c)(1)(B), 460
26(e), 435, 438, 439
26(f), 435, 467
26(f)(1), 435
26(f)(3), 440
26(g), 377, 430, 450, 451
27-32, 436
29-37, 242
29, 437
29(b), 435
30, 471, 476, 477, 481
30(a)(2)(A)(i), 437
30(b), 497
30(b)(1), 452, 467
30(b)(2), 436, 481
30(b)(6), 466-467, 469, 479, 480, 481, 482, 483
30(b)(7), 807
30(c), 437
30(c)(2), 478, 479, 483
30(d)(1), 437
30(d)(2), 483
30(d)(3), 477, 479, 481
30(e), 436
30(g), 436
31, 471, 807
33, 437-438, 807
33(a), 438
33(a)(1), 452
33(b), 438
34, 436, 438, 439
34(b), 438
34(b)(1)(A), 452
34(b)(2)(E)(i), 439
34(c), 439
35, 442, 977
35(a)(1), 452
35(b)(1), 443
36, 443, 611, 807
36(b), 443
37, 377
37(a), 452
37(a)(1), 452
37(a)(3)(B), 471
37(a)(4), 807
37(a)(5)(A), 461
37(b)-(d), 807
37(b)(2)(A), 1061
37(c)(1), 435

37(e)(1), 442
37(e)(2), 442
38, 963, 977
38(b), 548
38(d), 548
41(a)(1), 587
41(a)(2), 587
41(b), 588, 962, 963, 1002
41(c), 587
41(d), 587
42, 388, 903, 1063, 1065
42(a), 309, 387, 977, 984
42(b), 378, 620, 622, 903
45, 436, 439
47, 985
47(a), 538
48, 521
49, 587, 620, 1019
50, 588, 590, 603, 608, 611, 612
50(a), 243, 549, 565, 571, 589, 590, 591
50(a)(1), 591
50(a)(1)(B), 588
50(a)(2), 589, 590
50(b), 244, 589, 590, 591
51, 591, 623
52(a), 636, 1032
52(c), 589
53, 134
54(a), 165
54(d), 192, 193, 198
54(d) adv. comm. note, 189
56, 243, 270, 548, 557, 565, 567, 568, 569, 571, 574, 583, 608, 807, 820, 821, 1211, 1212, 1268, 1281
56(a), 550, 557, 565, 575
56(b), 565
56(c), 549, 557, 564, 565, 566, 568
56(c)(1)(A), 551
56(c)(1)(B), 551
56(d), 557, 574
56(e), 556, 557, 558, 564, 565, 566, 568
56(f), 557, 558, 568
58, 165, 179
59, 612, 965, 970, 971, 972
59(a), 969, 970
59(a)(1), 591
59(a)(1)(A), 591
59(a)(2), 591
59(b), 616, 618, 997
59(d), 591
60, 594, 615, 616, 617, 618
60(a), 618
60(b), 615, 616, 618, 619, 997
60(b)(1), 615, 616, 618, 619
60(b)(2), 616
60(b)(3), 616
60(b)(5), 1051
60(b)(6), 616, 618, 619

Federal Rules of Civil Procedure (Fed. R. Civ. P.) (*continued*)

60(c)(1), 616
60(d), 616
61, 591
64, 114
65, 13, 17, 21, 127, 165
65(b), 22, 116
65(d), 19, 21-22
65(d)(2), 23
65(d)(2)(A), 23
65(d)(2)(B), 23
68, 188-196, 197, 198, 199-200
68(a), 198
69, 179
70, 165
79(a), 179
82, 907
83, 365
Form 9, 268
Form 70, 179
Form 71, 179

Federal Rules of Appellate Procedure (Fed. R. App. P.)

38, 963, 977
52(a), 636

Federal Rules of Evidence (Fed. R. Evid.)

401, 445-446
403, 446
408, 662
501, 448
606(b), 593
701, 448
702, 448
801(c), 446
801(d)(2), 447

State Statutes and Rules

California

Cal. Code Civ. Proc. § 410.10, 693, 820

Connecticut

Conn. Gen. Stat., § 52-259, 80

Delaware

Del. Code Ann., Tit. 8, § 169, 789, 790
Del. Code Ann., Tit. 10, § 366, 789, 790, 795
Del. Code Ann., Tit. 10, § 366(a), 797
Del. Code Ann., Tit. 10, § 3114, 797

District of Columbia

D.C. Code § 28-3905(k)(2)(B), 897

Florida

Fla. Stat. Ann. § 48.19, 684
Fla. Stat. Ann. § 48.193(1)(g), 762, 771
Fla. Stat. Ann. § 78.01, 110
Fla. Stat. Ann. § 78.07, 110
Fla. Stat. Ann. § 78.08, 110
Fla. Stat. Ann. § 78.10, 110

Georgia

Code Ga. Ann. § 9-11-68(b)(1), 199

Kansas

Kan. Stat. Ann. 60-308(b)(11), 844

Maryland

Md. Code Ann., Cts. & Jud. Proc. § 3-2A-08A(f), 200
Md. Code Ann., Cts. & Jud. Proc. § 6-103(a), 775
Md. Code Ann., Cts. & Jud. Proc. § 6-103(b)(1), 776
Md. Code Ann., Cts. & Jud. Proc. § 6-103(b)(2), 776

Massachusetts

Mass. Gen. Laws, ch. 90, 682, 691
Mass. Gen. Laws, ch. 90, § 1, 1219
Mass. Gen. Laws, ch. 90, § 3A, 684
Mass. Gen. Laws, ch. 90, § 7A, 1219
Mass. Gen. Laws, ch. 90, § 7P, 337, 1162, 1163, 1167, 1183, 1187, 1214, 1215
Mass. Gen. Laws, ch. 90, § 7V(a)(b)(c), 1219
Mass. Gen. Laws, ch. 90, § 34(m), 1157, 1180
Mass. Gen. Laws, ch. 93A, 1021
Mass. Gen. Laws, ch. 109A, 1149, 1161
Mass. Gen. Laws, ch. 109A, §§ 1-10, 1145-1146
Mass. Gen. Laws, ch. 109A, § 4, 1149, 1161
Mass. Gen. Laws, ch. 109A, § 6, 1149, 1161
Mass. Gen. Laws, ch. 109A, § 7, 1149, 1161
Mass. Gen. Laws, ch. 197, § 9, 949-950, 952, 955
Mass. Gen. Laws, ch. 223, § 1, 853
Mass. Gen. Laws, ch. 223A, § 3, 748
Mass. Gen. Laws, ch. 223A, § 5, 861
Mass. Gen. Laws, ch. 229, § 2, 1144-1145, 1149, 1164
Mass. Gen. Laws, ch. 229, § 6, 1145
Mass. Gen. Laws, ch. 231, § 6D, 1157, 1180
Mass. Gen. Laws, ch. 231B, 1181
Mass. Gen. Laws, ch. 231B, §§ 1-4, 1168-1169
Mass. Gen. Laws, ch. 231B, §§ 1-3, 1177
Mass. Gen. Laws, ch. 231B, § 1(a), 1213
Mass. Gen. Laws, ch. 231B, § 85, 1167-1168
Mass. Gen. Laws, ch. 258, § 4, 1163
Mass. R. Civ. Proc. 12(b)(6), 1152
Mass. R. Civ. Proc. 12(e), 1154

Missouri

Mo. Rev. Stat. § 478.225.2(1), 390
Mo. Rev. Stat. § 517, 390
Mo. Rev. Stat. § 517.020.1(3), 390
Mo. Supreme Court Rule 55.32(a), 389

Montana

Mont. Rule Civ. Proc. 4(b)(1), 830, 832

Nevada
Nev. Rev. Stat. § 14.065, 717
Nev. R. Civ. P. 41(e), 962, 963

New Jersey
N.J. Ct. Rule 4:4-4(b)(1), 741

New York
N.Y. Banking Law, Consol. Laws, c. 2, 846
N.Y. Civ. Prac. Law and Rules, § 302, 691, 693
N.Y. Civ. Prac. Law and Rules, § 302(a), 784
N.Y. Civ. Prac. Law and Rules, § 302(a)(3)(ii),
    741
N.Y. Civ. Prac. Law and Rules, § 302(b), 676
N.Y. Civ. Prac. Law and Rules. §901, 973
N.Y. Civ. Prac. Law and Rules, §901(a), 980
N.Y. Civ. Prac. Law and Rules, §901(b),
    974-976, 978, 979-982
N.Y. Civ. Prac. Law and Rules, § 5501(c), 964,
    965-971
N.Y. Ins. Law Ann. § 5106(a), 979
N.Y. Laws 1848, c. 379,
    §120(2), 345
N.Y. Laws 1851, c. 479, §1, 345

North Carolina
N.C. Gen. Stat. § 7(b)-1109(b), 99
N.C. Gen. Stat. § 7A-289.24, 92
N.C. Gen. Stat. § 7A-289.25(6), 92
N.C. Gen. Stat. § 7A-289.27, 92
N.C. Gen. Stat. § 7A-289.28, 92
N.C. Gen. Stat. § 7A-289.29, 91, 92
N.C. Gen. Stat. § 7A-289.30, 92
N.C. Gen. Stat. § 7A-289.34, 92

Oklahoma
Okla. Stat., Tit. 12, § 97, 957-958, 961
Okla. Stat., Tit. 12, § 1701.03(a)(4), 700

Oregon
Or. Rev. Stat. § 14.080, 240
Or. R. Civ. Proc. Rule 4(c), 241

Pennsylvania
Pa. Rule Civ. Proc. 1073(a), 110-111
Pa. Rule Civ. Proc. 1076, 111

South Dakota
S.D. Cod. Laws § 15-7-13, 684

Texas
Tex. Civ. Proc. & Rem. Code § 42.004, 187, 200
Tex. Transp. Code Ann. § 708 et seq., 102

Washington
Unemployment Compensation Act § 14(c),
    685, 691

INDEX

ABA (American Bar Association)
  Model Rules of Professional Conduct. *See*
    Model Rules of Professional Conduct
  on promulgation of uniform procedural rules,
    351-352
Abuse of discretion, 133, 636
Access to justice, 79-103
  comparative view, 101-103
  to courts, 80-87
  donated legal services, 101
  to lawyers, 87-100
  overview, 79
  standard for, 100
  unbundling legal services, 101
Accounting (remedy), 129
Additur, 625-629
  defined, 592
Adickes, Sandra, 551-563
Adjudication
  settlements. *See* Settlements
  summary judgment. *See* Summary judgment
  verdicts. *See* Verdict
Admissions
  in answers, 309-311
  discovery requests for, 443
  interrogatory answers as, 438
  judgment as matter of law and, 611
  penalties for insufficient parsing and, 310
  in third-party answers, 397
ADR. *See* Alternative dispute resolution
Adversary system
  access to lawyers and, 91
  alternatives. *See* Alternative dispute resolution
  discovery and, 424, 486
  financing litigation and, 210
  judicial role in, 1118
Adverse claimants, 412
Advisory Committee on Civil Rules, 306,
    353, 548
  Notes, 13, 387, 1110
  role of, 354
Affirmative defenses, 311-315
  in answers, 309
  claim preclusion as, 391
  confession and avoidance as precursor to, 340
  defined, 241
  failure to plead, 312
  plausibility pleading and, 311-312
  statutes of limitations as, 309, 311

in third-party answers, 397
  unpleaded defenses, 307-308
  waiver of, 307-308, 312
Age discrimination, sufficiency of evidence and,
    611-612
Agent Orange, 1118, 1122
Aggregate litigation. *See* Class actions
Alabama
  collateral bar rule, 224
  forum selection clauses and, 963
  notice of hearing rule, 224
Alienage jurisdiction, 891-892
Alien Tort Statute (Alien Tort Claims Act), 697,
    810, 817, 861
Alternative dispute resolution
    (ADR), 641-666
  advantages of, 644-645
  arbitration, 645-666. *See also* Arbitration
  in business communities, 646
  disadvantages of, 644-645
  federal law preference for, 644
  history of, 643-644
  mediation, 643, 646. *See also* Mediation
  overview, 641-643
  in religious communities, 646
  stages of litigation and, 238-239
Alternative Dispute Resolution Act of
    1998, 660
Amazon, 782
Amendment of pleadings, 315-338
  ease of, 252
  Field Code and, 345
  implied consent to, 316
  mistake and, 327-328, 334
  relation back, 316-318, 328, 334
  state procedural rules on, 334-335
  statutes of limitations and, 317-318,
    335-338
  supplemental pleadings, 317
American Arbitration Association, 647
American Bar Association (ABA)
  Model Rules of Professional Conduct. *See*
    Model Rules of Professional Conduct
  on promulgation of uniform procedural rules,
    351-352
American Law Institute (ALI), 348, 988
American Rule for attorneys' fees, 185-186
Americans with Disabilities Act of 1990,
    471, 841

Amount in controversy, 5, 893-901
  aggregating claims to reach, 894
  in class actions, 895-898
  diversity jurisdiction and, 867
  non-monetary relief and, 894-895
  original setting of, 885
  punitive damages and, 895-898
  removal jurisdiction and, 924
  supplemental jurisdiction and, 918
Ancillary jurisdiction, 906-911. *See also*
  Supplemental jurisdiction
Anonymous parties, 299-305
Answers, 309
  admissions and denials in, 309-311
  affirmative defenses. *See* Affirmative defenses
  counterclaims. *See* Counterclaims
  cross-claims. *See* Cross-claims
  defined, 241
  Rule 11 applicability, 309
  to third-party complaints, 397
Anti-Cybersquatting Consumer Protection Act
  (ACPA), 798-799
Antitrust law
  claim preclusion, 993, 1052-1053
  damages, 166, 539
  discovery, 423
  injunctive relief, 130
  litigation costs, 261, 266
  plausibility pleading standard, 261, 262, 266,
    271, 273
  summary judgment, 573
Appeals, 634-639
  of arbitration awards, 648
  class certification orders, 1093
  federal circuit courts and, 5
  frivolous, 963
  interlocutory, 635, 1093
  mandamus, 635-636
  new trial motion rulings, 594
  parallel cases and issue preclusion
    in, 1045-1052
  stages of, 246
  Supreme Court jurisdiction and, 873
Appendix of Forms, abrogation of, 287
Arbitration, 645-666
  appealability of awards, 648
  class actions and, 647
  contracts and, 2, 647
  court-annexed arbitration, 647
  defined, 642-643
  forum selection clauses and, 845
  National Arbitration Forum
    (NAF), 658-659
  neutrals, selection of, 646-647
  policy issues in, 648-652
  procedure in, 647-648
  recent developments in, 658-666
  source of law for, 647

Arguments, closing. *See* Closing arguments
"Artful pleading" doctrine, 1052
Assault, 248
Attachment, 108
  due process and, 115
  personal jurisdiction based on, 798
Attorney-client privilege, 448
Attorneys
  access to justice and, 87-100
  class actions, appointment in, 1093-1094
  discovery, billing and, 208
  donated legal services, 101
  ethics. *See* Ethical considerations
  fees. *See* Attorneys' fee awards; Financing
    litigation
  number of, effect on litigation, 357
  privilege, 448
  standard for requiring appointment of, 99
  unbundling legal services, 101
  work-product privilege. *See* Work-product
    privilege
Attorneys' fee awards
  American Rule, 185-186
  authority to impose, sources of, 377
  calculating, 202-208
  in class actions, 1094
  conditional offers of settlement waiving,
    200-201
  deterrent effect of, 105
  English Rule, 185-186
  fee-shifting statutes, 185, 186-187, 196, 198,
    202, 209, 461
  injunctions and, 207, 208
  nominal damages and, 173
  prevailing plaintiff statutes, 5, 187
  public perception of, 208
  Rule 68 offers, 187-202. *See also* Rule 68
    offers
Auction sales, 179
Australia, law firm finance in, 213

Bankruptcy
  enforcement of judgments and, 180
  trustee in bankruptcy, privity of, 1010
Battery, 248
Bifurcation, 620-622
Breach of contract, 249
Browse-wrap forum selection clauses, 844
Burden of persuasion, 243, 312-313
  issue preclusion and, 1023-1024
  summary judgment and, 551
Burden of production, 243, 312
  judgment as matter of law
    and, 588, 608
  summary judgment and, 551
Burden of proof
  diversity jurisdiction and, 872
  issue preclusion and, 1023-1024

CAFA. *See* Class Action Fairness Act of 2005
California
    Field Code, adoption by, 345
    long-arm jurisdiction standard, 693, 797
    statute of limitations, 972, 1002
Canada, right to counsel and, 102
Capacity to sue or be sued, 299
Caption (pleadings), 298
Carter, Hodding, 558-559
Case management, 244-245
    institutionalization of, 357
Case or controversy requirement, 166
Cash advance industry, 210-211
Causes of action, 2, 247-251. *See also* Complaints
    common examples of, 248-250
    defined, 238, 247
Centers for Medicare and Medicaid Service, 658
Chamber of Commerce, U.S., 745
Chancery. *See* Equity
Chief Justice of the Supreme Court, 6
    committee appointment power of, 354
Choice of forum. *See* Forum selection clauses
Choice of law. *See* Conflict of laws
    in diversity actions. *See* Erie doctrine
Circumstantial evidence, 265, 270, 555,
    556, 1013
Citizenship. *See* Diversity jurisdiction
Civil forfeiture, 115
Civil Justice Reform Act of 1990, 7, 365, 644
Civil law systems, 340
Civil rights
    anonymous pleadings and, 304
    disparate impact liability, claim preclusion
        and, 1014
    federal common law and, 938
    forum selection and, 867
    heightened pleading requirements
        and, 256-257
    issue preclusion in suits over, 1053-1058
    pendent jurisdiction and, 905
    plausibility pleading and, 286
    school desegregation, class action cases, 1080
Civil Rights Act of 1964, 175-176, 250
    class actions, 1067, 1111
    passage of, 560
    pendent jurisdiction, 905
    sufficiency of evidence, 589
Civil Rights Act of 1991
    class actions and, 1124
    text of, 1136-1137
Civil Rights Attorneys' Fees Act of 1976, 187-196
Civil Service Commission, Loyalty Review
    Board of, 25
Claim preclusion, 990-1015
    abortion restrictions and, 1000-1001
    as affirmative defenses, 391
    antitrust law and, 1052-1053
    conflicts of law and, 972-973

counterclaims and, 997
defined, 246, 987
disparate impact liability and, 1014
divorce decree, tort claim distinguished,
    998-999
double jeopardy distinguished, 989
Erie doctrine and, 972-973
family members and, 1009
final valid judgment on merits standard,
    1001-1002
heirs and, 1009
involuntary dismissal and, 588
joinder of parties and, 387, 388
latent disease and, 999-1000
privity, 1002-1015
same claim standard, 990-1001
single injury/single recovery rule, 999-1000
splitting a claim, 991, 998, 999-1000, 1001
statutes of limitations and, 1002
successive buyers and, 1009
supplemental jurisdiction and, 1052-1053
transactional analysis, 990-997
trustees and, 1010
Claims. *See* Causes of action; Complaints
Clark, Charles E., 253, 352-353, 378, 387, 548,
    574, 943
Class Action Fairness Act of 2005 (CAFA), 922,
    1070, 1089, 1112-1115
    home state exception, 1113
    local controversy exception, 1113
    politics of enactment of, 1114-1115
Class actions, 5, 1063-1139
    adequacy of representation in, 1070-1080
    Agent Orange litigation, 1118, 1122
    agent principal problem and, 1064
    amount in controversy in, 895-898
    appeals from certification of classes, 1093
    arbitration and, 647
    attorneys' fee awards in, 1094
    certification of classes, 1066, 1088, 1090
    claim rates, 1089
    commonality requirement, 1094-1112
    conflict of laws, 1089-1090
    consumer contract waiver of, 647-648, 659
    counsel appointment in, 1093-1094
    counterclaims and, 1113
    defined, 242
    deterrence, 1068
    due process, 1066, 1070-1090
    efficiency issues, 1067-1068
    Erie doctrine and, 973-984
    fairness among plaintiffs in, 1065
    Federal Rules and, 1090-1112
    historical background, 1069-1070
    individual rights, 1068-1069
    injunctive, 1067, 1091-1092
    interlocutory appeals, 1093
    as joinder, 984, 1064

Class actions (*cont.*)
  local controversy exception, 1113
  mass torts, jurisdiction for, 1115-1117
  minimum contacts jurisdiction and, 761
  9/11 First Responders litigation, 1123
  notice, 1089
  numerosity, 974, 1067, 1090, 1091, 1098
  opting out, 1088
  overview, 1063-1066
  participation in, 1080-1090
  policy issues, 1067-1069
  preclusion, 1124-1139
  prerequisites, 1090-1093
  removal jurisdiction, 924
  representativeness, 1066, 1080, 1090-1091,
    1094, 1112-1113
  sample application of rules, 1094-1112
  settlement approval, 1093, 1117-1123
  settlement incentive and, 1065
  statistics, 1089
  subject matter jurisdiction over, 1070,
    1112-1117
  typicality, 974, 1067, 1071, 1090, 1091, 1097,
    1098, 1099
Claw-back of discovery, 440
Clean Air Act, 416
Clean Air Act Amendments of 1977, 187
Clear and convincing evidence
  standard, 571-572
Clearly erroneous standard, 636
Click-wrap forum selection clauses, 844
Closing arguments, 245, 629-634
  practice tips for, 633-634
Cognizability, 238
Collateral attack on judgments
  claim preclusion, 990-1015. *See also* Claim
    preclusion
  collateral order doctrine, 635
  issue preclusion, 1015-1045. *See also* Issue
    preclusion
  for lack of personal jurisdiction, 677-678
Collateral bar rule, 224, 225
Collateral estoppel. *See* Issue preclusion
Collateral order doctrine, 635
Common Good (advocacy group), 209-210
Common law
  American history of, 343-347
  contribution among joint tortfeasors, 907
  damages, 171-172, 174
  defined, 339-340, 525
  English procedure and equity, 339-342
  federal courts' development of, 938
  forum non conveniens. See Forum non conveniens
  joinder, 160
  king's motivations and, 358
  mutuality doctrine, 1030
  preclusion and *res judicata*, 7
  privity, 1009

  remedial powers of courts based on, 7, 22
  Seventh Amendment and, 524-534, 602-604.
    See also Jury trials
  writs. *See* Writs
Common Pleas (court), 340
Communications Decency Act, 785
Complaints, 2, 247-296
  abrogating forms, 287
  amendment of, 315-338. *See also* Amendment
    of pleadings
  class actions. *See* Class actions
  elements of claims, 247-251
  four-corners rule, 295-296
  fraud, pleading with particularity, 272
  frivolous litigation, 287-288
  heightened pleading requirements, 256-257
  legislation and, 288-289
  mistake, pleading with particularity, 272
  motions to dismiss, 289-295
  necessary and indispensable parties, 242, 307,
    398-412
  notice pleading, 252-257
  plausibility standard, 257-287
  purpose of, 252-296
  as stage of litigation, 241
Complete preemption, 923-924
Complex litigation
  class actions, 1063-1139. *See also* Class actions
  diversity jurisdiction in, 884-901. *See also*
    Diversity jurisdiction
  forum non conveniens, 854-863. *See also* Forum
    non conveniens
  impleader, 393-398. *See also* Impleader
  interpleader, 412-413. *See also* Interpleader
  intervention, 413-419. *See also* Intervention
  joinder of parties, 377-388. *See also* Joinder of
    parties
  removal jurisdiction in, 920-927. *See also*
    Removal jurisdiction
  supplemental jurisdiction in, 901-920. *See also*
    Supplemental jurisdiction
Compulsory counterclaims, 242
Computers
  electronic discovery, 440-442. *See also*
    Electronic discovery
  jurisdiction, 774-787. *See also* Cyberspace,
    personal jurisdiction in
Concurrent subject matter jurisdiction, 240, 867
Conflict of laws
  claim preclusion and, 972-973
  class actions, 1089-1090
  contracts, 2
  diversity actions, 929-986. *See also* Erie
    doctrine
  Erie Railroad case, 930-940. *See also* Erie
    doctrine
  horizontal conflicts, 930, 937, 972
Conformity Act of 1872, 349-350, 352, 937

Consent, personal jurisdiction based on, 683, 710, 836-845
  over foreign corporations, proposed, 835-836
Consent decrees, 134-135, 658
Consolidation
  compared to joinder, 387
  multidistrict, 860, 1063, 1064, 1117
Constitution, U.S. *See also specific amendments and clauses*
  Article I, 77, 934
  Article II, 934
  Article III, 7, 149, 166, 239, 501, 604, 865, 866-868, 901, 915, 917, 1117
  Article VI, 349
Contempt, 214-235
  criminal punishment for, 166
  proceedings, form of, 165-166
  right to counsel in hearings for, 100
  state proceedings, 179
Contingency fees, 185, 208-210
  third-party litigation financing, 212-213
Contracts
  arbitration and, 647
  minimum contacts jurisdiction and, 762-773
Conversion (cause of action), 249
Copyright infringement, 249
Corporations
  diversity jurisdiction and, 886-887
  foreign corporations, jurisdiction over, 835-836
Costs
  of due process, 39-60
  legal fees and costs. *See* Attorneys' fee awards; Legal costs
  of notice and hearing, 60-70
Counterclaims, 388-393
  ancillary jurisdiction and, 911
  answers, 309
  claim preclusion and, 997
  class actions, 1113
  cross-claims distinguished, 392-393
  defined, 242
  federal jurisdiction, creation of, 874
  motions to dismiss, 307
  overview, 388-389
  permissive vs. compulsory, 242, 388
  test for, 390, 391-392
  voluntary dismissal of, 587
Criminal cases
  issue preclusion, 1025, 1053-1058
  proliferation and judicial caseloads, 357
Criminal contempt, 166, 214
Cross-claims, 392-393
  ancillary jurisdiction and, 911
  answers, 309
  counterclaims distinguished, 392-393
  defined, 242
  limitations on, 389

  motions to dismiss, 307
  voluntary dismissal of, 587
  waiver, lack of, 389
Cross-examination, 245
Cummings, Homer, 352
Custodians of documents, 440
Cyberspace, personal jurisdiction in, 774-787
  defamation, 714-715, 783-785
  domain names, 798-799
  interactive websites, 774-783

Damages, 6, 166-180
  class actions seeking, 1088, 1092
  coupling with declaratory relief of, 166
  doctrine of presumed damages, 172
  enforcement of, 179-180
  fee-shifting and calculation of, 199
  nominal, 167-174
  overview, 166-167
  punitive, 174-179. *See also* Punitive damages
  valuation problems for, 174
Decision makers
  ADR. *See* Alternative dispute resolution
  judges. *See* Judges
  jury trials. *See* Jury trials
Declaratory judgment, 166
  amount in controversy, 894-895
  federal question jurisdiction, 874
Defamation
  cyberspace, personal jurisdiction in, 714-715, 783-785
  defined, 249
  issue preclusion and, 1024
  minimum contacts jurisdiction and, 711-715
Default judgment, 305
  vacating, 615
Defendants, 4-5
  John Doe defendants, 305
  jurisdiction over, 6. *See also* Personal jurisdiction
Defenses. *See also* Answers
  affirmative. *See* Affirmative defenses
  alternative, issue preclusion and, 1019
Deference to executive power, 23-24
Definition of civil procedure, 3-4
Delaware's long-arm statute, 797
Denials
  in answers, 309-311
  insufficient denials treated as admissions, 310
  in third-party answers, 397
Depositions, 436-437
  of corporate representatives, 466-467
  defined, 242
  Field Code and, 345
Derivative suits, 528, 533, 788, 794, 802
Design defect, 250
  plausibility pleading and, 285-286
Devitt, Edward, 510

Dicta, 1023
Digital data. *See* Electronic discovery
Directed verdict. *See* Judgment as matter of law
Direct evidence, 445
Direct examination, 245
Disabled persons
    benefits termination hearings, 47
    bifurcated trials, 622
    forum selection clauses, 841-842
    peremptory challenges, 547-548
Discovery, 2, 421-506
    abuse of, 486
    admissions, requests for, 443
    adversarial nature of, 424-426
    attorney billing and, 208
    attorney-client privilege and, 448
    civility and, 484-485
    claw-back provisions, 440
    conferences, 435
    cost of, 431-432
    depositions, 436-437. *See also* Depositions
    disputes over scope of, 452-461
    document production, 438-442
    electronic, 440-442. *See also* Electronic
        discovery
    ethical considerations in, 427-434
    experts, 444. *See also* Experts
    failure to disclose, consequences of, 435
    "fishing expeditions," 499-500
    framing requests, 469
    informal, 443-444
    interrogatories, 437-438. *See also*
        Interrogatories
    joinder of parties and, 387-388
    magistrate judges and, 485
    mandatory initial disclosures, 434-435
    mechanics of, 434-500
    mental examinations, 442-443
    motion practice and, 306
    necessity of, 426-427
    overbroad or objectionable requests, 469-470
    overview, 421-424
    party-controlled, 436-449
    perceived abuse of, 430-431
    physical examinations, 442-443
    plausibility pleading as barrier to, 356
    policy considerations in, 424-434
    procedural rulemaking and, 500-506
    produced in other lawsuits, 469
    production of documents and things, 438-442
    proportionality factors, 451, 460-462,
        467-469, 484
    protective orders, 452
    relevancy requirement, 450
    requests for admissions, 443
    rules of evidence, 445-449
    sanctions. *See* Sanctions
    scope of, 449-500

    strategic considerations in, 426
    supplementation of, 435, 438
    uniqueness of American law, 422
    work-product privilege. *See* Work-product
        privilege
    written interrogatories, 437-438. *See also*
        Interrogatories
Discovery Rule, 335
Discrimination. *See* Civil rights
Dismissal of actions, 585-619
    involuntary, 588
    voluntary, 587
Dispositions
    pretrial. *See* Pretrial dispositions
    settlements, 180-185. *See also* Settlements
    summary judgment, 548-585. *See also*
        Summary judgment
Diversity jurisdiction, 884-901, 929
    aggregation, 758, 1064, 1065-1066
    alienage, 891-892
    amount in controversy and, 867, 893-901
    citizens without domicile, 892
    complete diversity, 886-893
    constitutional grant of, 239
    corporations and, 886-887
    domicile. *See* Domicile
    Erie doctrine, 3, 929-986. *See also Erie* doctrine
    exceptions to complete diversity, 890-891
    foreign parties, 742, 891-892
    mass torts, 1117
    natural persons, 887-890
    overview, 884-886
    probate exception, 890-891
    rationale for, 884-885
    unincorporated associations, 887
Doctor-patient privilege, 448
Document production, 438-442
    cost of, 431
    defined, 242
    mandatory disclosure of, 435
    by nonparties, 439
    requests for, 439
Doe defendants, 305
Domain names, jurisdiction over, 798-799
Domicile
    alienage jurisdiction, 891-892
    citizens without, 892
    general jurisdiction, 693, 816, 823, 824, 864
    natural persons, 887
    personal jurisdiction, 672, 673, 675, 676, 690
    specific vs. general jurisdiction, 693
Double jeopardy, 989, 1025
Dual-sovereignty doctrine, 989
Due process, 4, 25-103
    access to justice, 79-103. *See also* Access to justice
    class actions and, 1070-1090
    Clauses. *See* Fifth Amendment; Fourteenth
        Amendment

costs of, 39-70
damages for violations of, 167-173
deterrence values, 79
dignity values, 79
enemy combatants, 70-79
enforcement of judgments, 180
ex parte relief, 127
hearings, 26-34
jurisdiction. *See* Jurisdiction; Minimum
    contacts jurisdiction
mass torts, issue preclusion in, 1033-1037
notice, 26-34
opportunity to be heard, 26-34
overview, 25-26
participation values, 79
preclusion, 7
provisional relief, 108-114
public assistance, 26-34
punitive damages, 175
service of process. *See* Service of process
tests for, 46-60
values of, 35-39
venue, 853-863. *See also* Venue
welfare reform, 26-34

Eighth Amendment, 115, 135, 175
Election of remedies as affirmative defense, 311
Electronically stored information (ESI). *See*
    Electronic discovery
Electronic discovery, 440-442
    careers in, 470
    metadata, 439
    preservation of ESI, 442
    Technology-Assisted Review (TAR), 441-442
Electronic Fund Transfer Act, 187
Electronic service of process, 853
Elements of claims, 247-251
    of affirmative defenses, 311
    defined, 238
E-mail
    discovery of. *See* Electronic discovery
    service of process by, 853
Enabling Acts, 351-352
Enemy combatants, 70-79
English Rule for attorneys' fees, 185-186
Equal Access to Justice Act of 1980, 187
Equal Protection Clause, 541-542
Equitable relief. *See* Injunctions;
    Provisional relief
Equity
    common law and, 339, 342-343
    merger of law and, 525, 534
Erie doctrine, 3, 929-986
    claim preclusion, 972-973
    class actions, 973-984
    forum selection clauses, 963
    jury trial right, 944-948
    new trial motions, 964-971

overview, 929-930
reverse, 986
service of process, 949-956
statutes of limitations, 940-944, 955, 959-964
venue, 963
ESI (Electronically stored information). *See*
    Electronic discovery
Ethical considerations
    conditional settlement offers, 200-201
    discovery, 427-434
    failure to disclose, consequences of, 435
    frivolous litigation, 201-202. *See also* Frivolous
        litigation
    padding billable hours, 208
    sanctions. *See* Sanctions
    zealous representation, 428-429
European Convention on Human Rights, 102
European Court of Human Rights, 101-102
Evers, Medgar, 559
Evidence
    circumstantial, 265, 270, 555, 556, 1013
    discovery. *See* Discovery
    experts. *See* Experts
    hearsay, 446-448
    newly discovered, 616
    spoliation, 250
    work product. *See* Work-product privilege
Examinations, physical and mental, 442-443
Exchequer (court), 340
Exclusive subject matter jurisdiction, 240, 867
Executive power, deference to, 23-24
Ex parte relief, 127
Experts
    discovery of, 444
    fee-shifting and, 198-199
    issue preclusion and, 1037
    judgment as matter of law and, 610-611
    mandatory disclosure of, 435
    opinions, admissibility of, 448
Exxon Valdez oil spill, 178

Fact, questions of, 31, 347, 581, 947, 969,
    1029, 1063
Failure to warn of product defect, 249
Fair Housing Act of 1968, 918, 929
Fair Housing Amendments Act of 1988, 471
Fair Labor Standards Act of 1938, 304
False imprisonment, 249
    pleading sufficient facts for, 295
Family law, complete diversity exception for, 890
F-cubed cases, 827-829
Federal Arbitration Act of 1925
    adoption of, 643
    application of, 649-653
    consumer contracts, 647
    judicial review, 648
    pre-emption of state law, 653-658
    procedural authority, 648

Federal Equity Rules of 1842, 350
Federal Equity Rules of 1912, 350, 353, 378
Federal question jurisdiction, 868-884, 929
    constitutional grant of, 239
    counterclaims as basis for, 874
    declaratory judgment actions, 874
    modern expansion of, 356-357
    patent cases, 877-884
    personal jurisdiction, 696
    railroads, 869-874
Federal Rules of Appellate Procedure (FRAP),
    634, 636. *See also* Appeals
Federal Rules of Civil Procedure (FRCP). *See also*
    specific topic
    adoption of, 348-355, 937, 943
    Advisory Committee Notes, 13, 387, 1110
    amendment of, 354-355, 956
    attachment jurisdiction and, 798
    case management under, 244-245
    discovery, views of drafters on, 421
    drafting of, 251, 350-354, 421
    enabling act, 350-354
    law and equity, combining of, 106-107
    lawsuit structure and, 5
    legal effect of, 355
    pre-FRCP statutes, 349-350
    reading rules of, 13
    role of, 363-365
    source of, 6-7
    state conformance to, 7, 375
    statutory construction and, 2-3
    trans-substantive procedure, 213, 354
Fees
    attorneys' fee awards. *See* Attorneys' fee awards
    legal costs. *See* Legal costs
Fee-shifting statutes, 185, 186-187, 196, 198,
    202, 209, 461
Field Code, 339, 344-348
    joinder and, 378
    political context for, 358
    state adoption of, 349
Fifth Amendment, 7, 47, 304, 448, 696, 989, 1117
Finality. *See* Preclusion
Final judgments, 246. *See also* Appeals; Judgment
Financing litigation, 185-214. *See also* Attorneys'
    fee awards
    calculating fee awards, 202-208
    contingency fees, 185, 208-210
    fee-shifting statutes, 186-187
    Rule 68 offers, 187-202. *See also* Rule 68 offers
    by third parties, 185, 210-214
Fines, excessive, 115
First Amendment, 225
Florida
    cruise ship forum selection clause, 841-842
    long-arm statute, 771
    non-resident aircraft and watercraft operators
      statute, 684

seizure statute, 114
Food, Drug, and Cosmetic Act (FDCA), 875
Foreign countries, service of process in, 853
Forfeiture, 115
Forum defendant rule, 920
Forum non conveniens, 807, 829, 854-863
    forum selection clauses and, 844-845
    transient jurisdiction and, 860
Forum selection clauses, 836-845
    arbitration and, 845
    browse-wrap, 844
    click-wrap, 844
    Erie doctrine and, 963
    forum non conveniens and, 844-845
    venue and, 862
Forum shopping, 712-713
    Erie doctrine and, 939, 948, 954, 961
Four-corners rule, 295-296
Fourteenth Amendment, 7, 25, 47, 108, 175,
    304, 675, 677, 694
    Bill of Rights application to states
      under, 535
Fourth Amendment, 115, 304
France's long-arm jurisdiction, 864
Franchise agreements, 762-773
Frank, Jerome, 574
Fraud
    by arbitrator, 648
    elements of, 249
    fraudulent conveyance, 249
    as grounds for vacating verdicts, 616
    heightened pleading and, 273, 295
FRCP. *See* Federal Rules of Civil Procedure
Freedom of Information Act of 1966, 443
Frivolous litigation
    "American Rule" as deterrent to, 186
    appeals, 963
    complaints, 287-288
    fee-shifting and, 201-202
    pendent jurisdiction and, 905
    sanctions for, 376-377
    summary judgment and, 563
Full Faith and Credit Clause, 7, 668, 1059

Garnishment, 179, 180
Gender discrimination class actions, 1067,
    1094-1112
General jurisdiction, 5
    federal, 810-836
    state, 239, 693-695
General verdict, 1016-1019
Georgia
    offer of settlement rule, 199
    Open Records Act, 542
Gift as affirmative defense, 311
Goldman, Ronald, 1023-1024
Griswold, Erwin, 509-510
Guardians *ad litem,* 99

Habeas corpus
  issue preclusion and, 1033
  suspension of, 79
Hague Convention, 853
Hamilton, Alexander, 524
Handicapped Children's Protection Act of
  1988, 187
Hearings
  damages for violations of requirement for,
    167-173
  disability benefits termination, 47
  due process and, 26-34. *See also* Due process
  wage garnishment, 108-114
Hearsay, 446-448
Heirs, claim preclusion and, 1009
High-low agreements, 185
Historical background of civil procedure, 339-365
  colonial period, 343-344
  common law procedure, 339-342, 358. *See also*
    Common law
  Enabling Acts, 351-352
  equity procedure, 342-343
  Federal Rules of Civil Procedure, 348-355. *See*
    also Federal Rules of Civil Procedure
  Field Code procedure, 344-348. *See also*
    Field Code
  post-trial era, 355-365
  Process Act of 1789, 349
  progressive politics and, 347-348
  Rules of Decision Act of 1789, 349-350, 935,
    939, 956
  transnational procedure, 348
  uniformity goals, 350-352, 365, 376
Hughes, Charles Evans, 351

Immigration and Naturalization Service, 274
Immunity from service of process, 809
Impleader, 393-398
  ancillary jurisdiction, 910-911
  in answers, 309
  defined, 242
  venue, 854
  voluntary dismissal of, 587
Indigent persons, right to counsel, 80-87
  termination of parental rights hearings, 99
Indispensable parties, 398-412
  defined, 242
  motion to dismiss for failure to join, 307
Injunctions, 6
  amount in controversy, 894-895
  civil disobedience, 235
  class actions, 1067, 1091-1092
  consent decrees, 134-135
  coupling with declaratory relief of, 166
  enforcement of, 165-166
  against federal government, 23-25
  fee award calculation, 207, 208
  fee-shifting, 198

  judicial role in, 135-155
  national or universal, 24
  permanent, 129-166
  preliminary, 116-129. *See also* Preliminary
    injunctions
  preventative, 134
  prisoner litigation, 135-155
  reparative, 134
  standard for, 129-133
  structural, 134
  temporary, 116-129. *See also* Preliminary
    injunctions
  theories of judicial power and, 155-165
  types of, 134-135
In personam jurisdiction. *See* Personal jurisdiction
In rem jurisdiction, 21, 668-675
  domain names and, 798-799
Instructions to jury, 586-587, 622-625
  model or panel instructions, 622-623
Intentional infliction of emotional distress, 249
  pendent jurisdiction and, 905
Interactive websites, personal jurisdiction and,
  774-783
Interlocutory appeals, 246
  in class actions, 1093
International law
  personal jurisdiction, 809, 863-864
  right to counsel, 101-102
  service of process in foreign countries, 853
Internet, jurisdiction and. *See* Cyberspace,
  personal jurisdiction in
Interpleader, 5, 412-413
  defined, 242
Interrogatories, 437-438
  accompanying general verdicts, 1019
  defined, 242
Intervention, 5, 413-419
  ancillary jurisdiction and, 911
  defined, 242
  in environmental litigation, 416
  joinder of parties compared, 416
  statutory authority for, 416
Investment funds
  law firm finance by, 212-213
  lawsuit participation by, 211-212
Issue preclusion, 1015-1045
  administrative adjudication and, 1032,
    1037-1045
  alternative defenses and, 1019
  burden of proof and, 1023
  criminal cases, 1025, 1053-1058
  defamation and, 1024
  defined, 247, 988, 1015-1016
  divorce decree, tort claim distinguished, 999
  essential to judgment standard, 1020-1025
  examples, 1016-1020
  expert testimony and, 1037
  full faith and credit clause and, 1059

Issue preclusion (*cont.*)
  general verdicts and, 1016-1019
  habeas relief and, 1032-1033
  jury trial right and, 1025-1033, 1044
  law of the case distinguished, 989
  litigation strategy, 1031
  mass tort cases, 759, 1033-1037
  nonmutuality of, 1025-1033
  nonparties and, 1025-1033
  trademark cases, 1037-1045

Jackson Piel, Eleanor, 563
JAMS Comprehensive Arbitration Rules and
  Procedures, 647
JMOL. *See* Judgment as matter of law
JNOV. *See* Judgment notwithstanding the verdict
John Doe defendants, 305
Joinder of claims. *See also* Joinder of parties
  defined, 241
  impleader, 393-398. *See also* Impleader
  indispensable parties, 242, 307, 398-412
  interpleader, 412-413. *See also* Interpleader
Joinder of parties, 5, 377-388
  claim preclusion and, 387, 388
  class actions as, 984, 1064
  consolidation contrasted, 387
  contribution among joint tortfeasors, 907
  counterclaims, 388-393. *See also*
    Counterclaims
  defined, 241
  discovery and, 387-388
  goals of rule drafters, 388
  impleader, 393-398. *See also* Impleader
  interpleader, 412-413. *See also* Interpleader
  intervention, 413-419. *See also* Intervention
  intervention compared, 416
  legal costs and, 388
  misjoinder, 309, 381, 419, 639, 1002
  motion to dismiss for failure to join
    indispensable party, 307
  permissive joinder, 378, 387. *See also*
    Permissive joinder
  personal jurisdiction and, 761
  public rights exception, 402
  strategy, 387-388
  test for, 387
Judges
  biases of, selection of juries and, 546-547
  contempt, powers regarding, 106, 214-235.
    See also Contempt
  election of, 519
Judgment
  default. *See* Default judgment
  defined, 245
  under Federal Rules of Civil Procedure
    (FRCP), 165, 179
  judgment as matter of law, 588-589, 594-615.
    See also Judgment as matter of law

motions to vacate, 615-619
notwithstanding the verdict. *See* Judgment
    notwithstanding the verdict
offer of judgment. *See* Offer of
    judgment
summary judgment, 548-585. *See also*
    Summary judgment
Judgment as matter of law (directed verdict),
    588-589, 594-615
  arguments for, 609-610
  burden of production and, 588, 608
  defined, 243
  evidentiary rules and, 610-611
  expert testimony and, 610-611
  plaintiff motions for, 611
  renewed. *See* Judgment notwithstanding the
    verdict
  Seventh Amendment and, 590
  sufficiency of evidence and, 611-612
  timing of, 589
Judgment notwithstanding the verdict (JNOV),
    589-591, 594-615
  defined, 244
  new trial motions and, 612
Judicature Acts, 106
Judicial Conference of the U.S., 6, 355
Judicial Improvements Act of
    1990, 644
Judicial Panel on Multidistrict Litigation
    (JPML), 1063
Judiciary Act of 1789, 349, 634, 810, 885, 931,
    933, 934, 935, 941
Jurisdiction, 667-927
  amount in controversy, 893-901. *See also*
    Amount in controversy
  ancillary jurisdiction. *See* Supplemental
    jurisdiction
  in cyberspace, 774-787. *See also* Cyberspace,
    personal jurisdiction in
  diversity jurisdiction, 884-901. *See also*
    Diversity jurisdiction
  federal question jurisdiction, 868-884. *See also*
    Federal question jurisdiction
  general jurisdiction, 5
  in personam jurisdiction. *See* Personal
    jurisdiction
  in rem jurisdiction, 668-669
  minimum contacts jurisdiction. *See* Minimum
    contacts jurisdiction
  overview, 5-6, 667-668
  products liability. *See* Products liability
  removal to federal court, 920-927. *See also*
    Removal jurisdiction
  subject matter jurisdiction, 865-927. *See also*
    Subject matter jurisdiction
  supplemental jurisdiction, 901-920. *See also*
    Supplemental jurisdiction
Jury instructions. *See* Instructions to jury

Jury trials, 507-639
    additur, 625-629
    ambivalence about, 508
    appeals from, 634-639
    bifurcation of, 620-622
    closing arguments, 629-634
    competence of jury, 518-519
    complexity exception, 521-522
    constitutional right to, 508
    directed verdicts, 588-589
    discrimination in composition of, 541-542
    dismissals, involuntary, 588
    dismissals, pre-trial, 585-619. *See also*
        Dismissal of actions
    dismissals, voluntary, 587
    diversity of jury pool and, 545-546
    Erie doctrine and right to, 944-948
    federal right to, 524-536
    historical background of, 341, 523-524
    instructions, 622-625. *See also* Instructions
        to jury
    international trends, 509
    involuntary dismissals, 588
    issue preclusion and right to, 1025-1033, 1044
    judgment as matter of law, 588-589. *See also*
        Judgment as matter of law
    judgment notwithstanding the verdict, 589-
        591, 594-615
    new trials, motions for, 591-615. *See also* New
        trial motions
    number of jurors, 520
    overview, 507-509
    patent infringement and, 534
    policy considerations, 509-523
    punitive damages and, 517-518
    reform proposals, 522-523
    remittitur, 625-629
    requesting in answers, 309
    selection of jurors, 536-548. *See also* Selection
        of jurors
    sequencing judicial determinations and, 534-
        535
    state courts, applicability of Seventh
        Amendment, 535
    statutes and, 535
    summary judgment and, 548-585. *See also*
        Summary judgment
    trifurcation of, 620-622
    unanimity requirement, 520-521
    vacating judgments, 615-619
    verdicts, 619-629. *See also* Verdict
    voluntary dismissals, 587
    waiver of right to, 548
Juvenile court, 5

Kentucky's clear statement rule, 656
King, Martin Luther, Jr., 215-217, 225
    Letter from Birmingham Jail, 226-235

Labor Management Relations Act of 1947,
    902, 924
Law, questions of
    appellate review, 133
    class action cases, 1096, 1097, 1098, 1103,
        1106, 1109
    fact-law distinction, 580-581
    federal jurisdiction, 870
Law of the case doctrine, 989
Lawsuit Abuse Reduction Act of 2011
    (proposed), 376
Lawsuit Abuse Reduction Act of 2017
    (proposed), 366, 376
Lawyers. *See* Attorneys
    access to justice. *See* Access to justice
Legal aid, 168, 186, 202
Legal costs, 105
    American Rule, 185-186
    attorneys' fees inclusion within, 187-199
    calculating fee awards, 202-208
    contingency fees, 208-210
    of depositions, 437
    of discovery, 431-432
    discovery motions, fee-shifting and, 461
    fee-shifting statutes, 186-187
    joinder of parties and, 388
    Rule 68 offers, 187-202. *See also*
        Rule 68 offers
Legal services. *See also* Attorneys' fee awards;
        Legal aid
    donated, 101
    unbundled, 101
Libel, 249
Lilly, Graham, 522
Limits of judicial power, 12-25
Lis pendens, 107
Litigation finance. *See* Financing
    litigation
Loadstar basis for fee calculation, 1094
Local controversy exception, 1113
Local rules, 242
    alternative dispute resolution, 660-663
    amendment of pleadings and, 319
Lodestar approach, 205, 825
Long-arm statutes, 240-241, 690-693. *See also*
        Minimum contacts jurisdiction
    federal, 696

Magistrate judges, 485
Mandatory initial disclosures, 434-435
    defined, 242
Manifest disregard of law standard, 648
Maritime law, punitive damages
    under, 178
Markman hearings, 534
Maryland
    offer of judgment statute, 200
    statute of limitations, 972

Massachusetts
forum non conveniens, 861
fraudulent conveyance statute, 1019
implied warranties rule, 337
long-arm statute, 748-749
minority attorneys study, 547
non-resident motorist statute, 683, 684, 846
relation back rule, 334
service of process as basis for personal
    jurisdiction, 809, 961
substantial conformance to FRCP, 375
Superior Court, 866
venue statute, 853
wrongful death statute, 1023
Mass torts. *See also* Class actions
Agent Orange litigation, 1118, 1122
issue preclusion, 1033-1037
minimum contacts jurisdiction, 749-761
9/11 First Responders litigation, 1123
subject matter jurisdiction over, 1115-1117
Material facts, 550
defining, 581-582
video evidence and, 575-580
Mediation. *See also* Alternative dispute resolution
defense and critiques of, 646
defined, 643
Medical malpractice
defined, 241
elements of, 249
Mental examinations, 442-443
Meredith, James, 558
Metadata, electronic discovery, 439
Minimum contacts jurisdiction, 684-690, 697-
774
contracts and, 762-773
cyberspace and, 774-787. *See also* Cyberspace,
    personal jurisdiction in
defamation and, 711-715
foreseeability and, 708, 727
intentional torts and, 715-720
mass torts and, 749-761
products liability and, 720-747. *See also*
    Products liability
purposeful availment test, 699-709
stream-of-commerce doctrine, 720-747, 771-
772
Minors, tolling statute of limitations for, 335
Misjoinder, 309, 381, 419, 639, 1002
Mississippi, civil rights movement in, 558-562
Missouri, arbiter consent decree, 658-659
Mitchell, William D., 353
Model Code of Professional Conduct
development and replacement of, 427
zealous representation under, 428-429
Model Rules of Professional Conduct
attorneys' duties under, 428-430
development of, 427
Monetary jurisdiction. *See* Amount in controversy

Motions
to amend pleadings. *See* Amendment of
    pleadings
to dismiss, 241, 251, 289-295, 306-309, 391
to dismiss for failure to join indispensable
    party, 307, 308
to dismiss for failure to state claim, 306, 308
to dismiss for improper venue, 306
to dismiss for insufficiency of process, 306
to dismiss for lack of jurisdiction, 306
for judgment as matter of law, 589-589, 594-
615
for judgment notwithstanding the verdict,
    589-591
for judgment on pleadings, 308-309
for more definite statement, 305
for new trial, 591-615, 964-971
preliminary, 305-306
sanctions and, 372
strategy for arguing, 338
to strike, 297, 306
to vacate judgments, 615-619
Multidistrict litigation (MDL), 1063-1064
Multiparty, Multiforum Trial Jurisdiction Act of
    2002, 922, 1112
mass torts and, 1115-1117
Multiplicity of suits as affirmative defense, 311
Mutuality, 227, 1027, 1030, 1031, 1034

National Arbitration Forum (NAF), 658-659
National Association for the Advancement of
    Colored People (NAACP), 559
National Bank Act, 924
Necessary and indispensable parties, 398-412
defined, 242
motion to dismiss for failure to join, 307
Negligence
affirmative defenses to, 311
elements of, 249
Negligent entrustment of vehicle, 249
Negotiation, 643
Nevada's failure to prosecute statute, 962
New Deal, 938-939
New Hampshire and statute of limitations, 713
New Jersey's long-arm statute, 741
Newly discovered facts, 997
New trial motions, 591-615
Erie doctrine and, 964-971
excessive verdicts and, 592, 626
judicial error and, 591-592
jury deliberations and, 592-593
verdict against weight of evidence, 593-594
New York
chancery court elimination, 344
class action rule, 983, 1090
federal trial court districts, 668
Field Code, adoption by, 344, 349
Human Rights Law, 918

long-arm statute, 691, 693
  new trial standard, 971
  pro bono bar requirement, 101
  Supreme Court, 866
Nexus
  class actions, 1114
  long-arm statutes, 691-692
  mass tort litigation, 760-761
9/11 First Responders litigation, 1123
Nominal damages, 167-174
  fee award calculation and, 207
Nonparties, depositions of, 436
Nonsuit. *See* Dismissal of actions
North Carolina
  indigent parents right to counsel statute, 99
  long-arm jurisdictional standard, 816
Notice
  class actions, 1089
  cost of, 60-70
  of depositions, 436
  due process and, 26-34. *See also* Due process
  joinder and, 387
  by mail, 851, 852
  personal jurisdiction and, 676, 846-853
  by publication, 851
  of removal, 920, 921
  service of process. *See* Service of process
  wage garnishment and, 108-114
Notice pleading, 252-256
Nuisance, 249
  pleading sufficient facts for, 295

Oakley, John, 375
Objections, rulings on, 245
Offer of judgment, 187-202
  conditional offers, 200-201
  contingency fees and, 209
  frivolous claims, 201-202
  state variations on, 199-200
Ohio
  Court of Common Pleas, 866
  Field Code, adoption by, 345
  substantial conformance to FRCP, 375
Oklahoma
  long-arm statute, 707
  service of process requirements, 962
  statute of limitations, 962
Opening statements, 245
Opinions, lay, 448
Opportunity to be heard. *See* Hearings
Oregon
  constitutional punitive damages review rule, 175, 177
  long-arm statute, 240-241

Parties
  impleader, 393-398. *See also* Impleader
  interpleader, 412-413. *See also* Interpleader
  intervention, 413-419. *See also* Intervention
  joinder of, 377-388. *See also* Joinder of parties
  necessary and indispensable, 242, 307, 398-412
  overview, 4-5
Patent and Trademark Office, U.S., 1044
Patent infringement
  elements of, 250
  federal question jurisdiction, 877-884
  jury trials, 534
Patent Infringement Act, 187
Pendent jurisdiction, 901-906. *See also* Supplemental jurisdiction
Pendent party jurisdiction, 911-914. *See also* Supplemental jurisdiction
Pennsylvania's seizure statute, 114
Peremptory challenges, 537, 541-548
Permanent injunctions. *See also* Injunctions
  defined, 245
Permissive counterclaims, 242
Permissive joinder, 378, 387
Personal jurisdiction, 4, 6, 667-864
  class actions, 1080-1088
  consent as basis of, 683, 710, 836-845
  in cyberspace, 774-787. *See also* Cyberspace, personal jurisdiction in
  defined, 239, 667
  in federal court, 695-697
  federal question jurisdiction and, 696
  foreign defendants, 697
  forum non conveniens and, 853-863
  general, 693-695, 810-836
  indispensable parties and, 307
  in personam jurisdiction, 669
  in rem jurisdiction, 668-675, 798-799
  international law and, 863-864
  joinder and, 387, 761
  long-arm statutes, 690-693
  minimum contacts jurisdiction, 684-690, 697-774. *See also* Minimum contacts jurisdiction
  motion to dismiss for lack of, 306
  nexus requirement, 691-692
  notice and, 676, 846-853
  overview, 667-668
  property, defendant's as basis for, 787-799
  quasi in rem jurisdiction, 669
  service of process as basis for, 799-810
  specific, 693-695
  traditional conception of, 669-684
  venue and, 853-863
  waiver of defense re, 668
Personal Responsibility and Work Opportunity Reconciliation Act (PRWORA) of 1996, 35
Persuasion burden. *See* Burden of persuasion
Physical examinations, 442-443
Plain meaning, 13-14, 196
Plaintiffs, 4-5. *See also* Parties
  anonymous, 299-305

Plato, 217
Plausibility pleading, 257-287
    informal discovery and, 444
    motion practice in light of, 305
    robust discovery, 499-500
Pleadings
    admissions and denials, 309-311
    affirmative defenses, 311-315
    amendment of, 315-338. *See also* Amendment
        of pleadings
    anonymous plaintiffs, 299-305
    answers, 309. *See also* Answers
    class actions. *See* Class actions
    complaints, 247-296. *See also* Complaints
    counterclaims. *See* Counterclaims
    cross-claims. *See* Cross-claims
    ethical considerations. *See* Ethical
        considerations
    heightened pleading requirements, 288, 311
    history of. *See* Historical background of civil
        procedure
    impleader, 393-398. *See also* Impleader
    interpleader, 412-413. *See also* Interpleader
    intervention, 413-419
    motions, preliminary, 305-306. *See also*
        Motions
    motions to dismiss, 306-309. *See also* Motions
    overview, 251-252
    plausibility pleading, 257-287, 305
    sanctions. *See* Sanctions
    single-issue, 340-341
    strategy behind, 296-298
    supplemental, 317
    technical requirements, 298-299
    third-party complaints, 397
    timing of, 305
Plurality rulings, 79
Poor persons, right to counsel. *See* Indigent
    persons, right to counsel
Pound, Roscoe, 351, 358
Pound Conference on Civil Justice Reform,
    358-363
Precedent, preclusive effect of, 989
Preclusion, 987-1061
    claim preclusion, 990-1015. *See also* Claim
        preclusion
    in class actions, 1124-1139
    counterweights to, 1045-1061
    issue preclusion, 1015-1045. *See also* Issue
        preclusion
    overview, 987-989
Preemption, federal, 923-924
Preliminary injunctions, 116-129
    defined, 245
    permanent injunctions contrasted, 129, 133
    test for, 127, 133
Preliminary motions, 305-306. *See also* Motions
Preponderance of the evidence, 243

Pretrial conferences, 315
Pretrial dispositions
    judgment as matter of law, 588-589, 594-615.
        See also Judgment as matter of law
    pretrial conferences, 315
    settlements, 180-185. *See also* Settlements
    summary judgment, 4, 548-585. *See also*
        Summary judgment
Prevailing plaintiff statutes, 5, 187
Preventative injunctions, 134
Priest-penitent privilege, 448
Prima facie case, 247. *See also* Elements of claims
Prisoners
    indigents, treatment in litigation as, 86-87
    injunctions and, 135-155
Prison Litigation Reform Act (PLRA) of 1996,
    86-87, 135-155
Private attorneys general suits, 186-187
Private Securities Litigation Reform Act of
    1995, 288
Privilege
    as affirmative defense, 311
    attorney-client privilege, 448
    in civil litigation, 448-449, 450
    work-product privilege. *See* Work-product
        privilege
Privilege logs, 450-451
Privity, 1002-1015
Probate, complete diversity exception for, 890-891
Pro bono legal services, 101
Process Act of 1789, 349
Production of documents and things, 438-442
Products liability
    ancillary jurisdiction, 911
    bifurcated trials, 621
    elements of, 249, 250
    minimum contacts jurisdiction, 720-747
    plausibility pleading, 285-286
Protective orders, 452, 469-483
Provisional relief, 106-129
    attachment, 108
    due process and, 108-115
    lis pendens, 107
    overview, 106-107
    replevy, 107
    repossession, 115
    securing judgments, 107-115
    sequestration, 107-108
    temporary injunctions, 116-129
    trustees, 108
Psychotherapist-patient privilege, 448
Public assistance
    due process and, 26-34
    legal aid, 168, 186, 202
    welfare reform, 35
Publication
    notice by, 851
    service of process by, 852

Public law litigation, judicial role
   in, 159-164
Public Securities Litigation Reform Act
   (PSLRA), 1069
Punitive damages, 174-179
   amount in controversy and, 895-898
   jury trials and, 517-518
   under maritime law, 178
Purposeful availment test, 699-709

Quasi in rem jurisdiction, 669
   anachronistic nature of, 798
Quotient verdict, 593

Race
   disparate impact liability, 1014
   minority representation on juries, 545-546
   peremptory challenges, 541-542
Railroads, federal question jurisdiction and,
   869-874
Real estate
   personal jurisdiction based on defendant's,
      787-799
   seizure of, 115
Real party in interest, 298-299
Receivers, 108
   actions for appointment of, 179
Reformation of contracts, 129
Relation-back amendment of
   pleadings, 316-318, 328, 334
Relevancy requirement in discovery, 445-446
Remand, 920
Remedies, 6, 105-235
   accounting, 129
   contempt, 214-235
   damages, 6, 166-180. *See also* Damages
   declaratory relief, 166
   equitable relief, 129-166. *See also* Injunctions
   financing litigation and, 185-214. *See also*
      Financing litigation
   injunctions, 6, 129-166. *See also* Injunctions
   overview, 105-106
   provisional relief, 106-129. *See also*
      Provisional relief
   rescission and reformation of contracts, 129
   settlements, 180-185
Remittitur, 625-629
   defined, 592
Removal jurisdiction, 920-927
   amount in controversy and, 924
   class actions, 924, 1113
   defendant's considerations, 922-923
   notice of removal, 920, 921
   overview, 920-922
   plaintiff's considerations, 922
   preemption and, 923-924
   remand, 920
   res judicata, 1045-1052

Renewed judgment as a matter of law. *See*
   Judgment notwithstanding the verdict
Reparative injunctions, 134
Replevin, 107, 108-114
Repossession, 115
Requests for admissions, 443
Rescission
   as affirmative defense, 311
   reformation of contracts, 129
Res judicata. See Claim preclusion; Issue
   preclusion
Responsive pleading. *See* Answers
Resting (party), 243
RICO (Racketeer Influenced and Corrupt
   Organizations) Act, 696
Rule 11 sanctions. *See* Sanctions
Rule 68 offers, 187-202
   conditional offers, 200-201
   contingency fees and, 209
   frivolous claims, 201-202
   state variations on, 199-200
Rules Enabling Act of 1934, 349, 500, 954, 955,
   956, 961
Rules of Decision Act of 1789, 349-350, 935,
   939, 956

Sanctions, 365-377
   authority for, 377
   bad faith and, 373-374
   chilling effect of, 374
   discovery, 377, 435
   for frivolous claims, 376-377
   inherent authority for, 377
   non-monetary sanctions, 374-375
   overview, 365-372
   safe harbor, 372-373
   state procedure of, 375-376
   statutory authority for, 377
School desegregation, class actions
   over, 1080
School suspensions, due process and, 167-173
Seizure of assets, 115
Selection of jurors, 536-548
   consultants for, 538
   equal protection, 541-542
   judicial biases, 546-547
   local practice and custom for, 537
   overview, 536
   peremptory challenges, 537, 541-548
   race of jurors, effect of, 545-546
   voir dire, 536-541
Sequestration, 107-108
Service of process
   defined, 241
   due process, 240
   electronic (e-mail), 853
   Erie doctrine, 949-956
   in foreign countries, 853

Service of process (cont.)
    motion to dismiss for insufficiency of, 306
    personal jurisdiction based on, 799-810
    plaintiff responsibility for, 852-853
    by publication, 852
Settlements, 180-185
    class actions, judicial approval of, 1093,
      1117-1123
    confidentiality in, 184-185
    incentive in class actions, 1065
    Rule 68 offers, 187-202. *See also* Rule 68 offers
    state fee-shifting statutes and, 199-200
Seventh Amendment, 106, 508, 520, 524-534,
    590, 602-604, 1044. *See also* Jury trials
    Erie doctrine and, 944-948
Sex discrimination. *See* Gender discrimination
    class actions
Shareholder derivative suits, 528, 533, 788
Shelton, Thomas Wall, 351
Simpson, O.J., 1023-1024
Single injury/single recovery rule, 999-1000
Single-issue pleadings, 340-341
Sixth Amendment, 100, 604
Small claims courts, subject matter jurisdiction,
    388-390, 865-866
Soldiers and Sailors Relief Act, 335
Sources of law, 6-7
South Africa, right to counsel in, 101-102
South Carolina, child support enforcement in,
    100, 214
South Dakota's non-resident hunter statute, 684
Specialized jurisdiction, 5
Special verdicts, 619-620
Speedy Trial Act of 1974, 357
Spoliation of evidence, 250
Spousal privilege, 448
Stages of litigation, 237-247
Stakeholders, 412
Standing Committee on Rules of Practice and
    Procedure, 354-355
Standing orders, 242
Stare decisis, 989
State courts. *See also specific states*
    class actions, 924
    diversity jurisdiction, 884-885, 886
    Erie doctrine. *See Erie* doctrine
    jurisdiction, 5-6, 239-240
    personal jurisdiction, 667-668, 690, 720-726
    removal to federal courts. *See* Removal
      jurisdiction
    sanctions, 375-376
    subject matter jurisdiction, 865-868, 872, 873,
      879, 882
Statutes of limitations
    as affirmative defense, 309, 311
    amendment of pleadings and, 317-318
    calculation of, 335-337
    claim preclusion and, 1002

    defined, 241
    under *Erie* doctrine, 940-944, 955, 959-964
    federal power and, 919
    John Doe defendants and, 305
    relation back, 316-318, 328, 334
    tolling of, 318, 959-964
Statutory interpretation, 13-14
    maxims of, 196
Stream-of-commerce doctrine, 720-747,
    771-772, 782
Strict products liability, 250
Strike, motion to, 297, 306
Structural injunctions, 134
Studying approach, 7-9
Subject matter jurisdiction, 865-927
    class actions, 1070, 1112-1115
    concurrent, 240, 668
    defined, 239, 667-668
    diversity jurisdiction, 884-901. *See also*
      Diversity jurisdiction
    exclusive, 240, 865
    federal question jurisdiction, 868-884. *See also*
      Federal question jurisdiction
    forum non conveniens and, 861
    general, 668
    indispensable parties, 307
    joinder, 387
    limited, 668, 865. *See also* Diversity
      jurisdiction; Federal question jurisdiction
    mass torts, 1115-1117
    motion to dismiss for lack of, 306
    overview, 865-868
    removal jurisdiction, 920-927. *See also*
      Removal jurisdiction
    small claims courts, 388-390, 865-866
    sources of, 866-868
    supplemental jurisdiction, 901-920. *See also*
      Supplemental jurisdiction
Subpoenas
    for nonparty depositions, 436
    for nonparty document requests, 439
Summary judgment, 4, 548-585
    burden of persuasion and, 551
    burden of production and, 551
    constitutionality of, 575
    defined, 243
    fact-law distinction and, 580-582
    as focal point in litigation, 356
    historical perspectives on, 551-563
    material facts and, 550, 575-580, 581-582
    motions to dismiss compared, 549
    new standard for, 563-580
    oral arguments on, 574
    original conception of, 562
    parties available to, 244, 550
    risks of, 548-549
    statistics on, 574
    strategic considerations, 582-585

Summary jury trials, 548-585
Supplemental jurisdiction, 901-920
    amount in controversy and, 894, 918
    ancillary jurisdiction, 906-911
    claim preclusion and, 1052-1053
    constitutional basis for, 904
    pendent jurisdiction, 901-906
    pendent party jurisdiction, 911-914
    statutory basis for, 901, 904-905
    substantiality standard for, 905
Supplemental Jurisdiction Statute, 901
    legislative history of, 915-917
    text of, 915
Supplemental pleadings, 317
Supremacy Clause, 349-350

Taft, William Howard, 351
Teapot Dome scandal, 352
Technology-Assisted Review (TAR), 441-442
Telecommunications Act of 1996, 257
Temporary injunctions. *See* Preliminary
    injunctions
Temporary restraining orders, 116, 245
Tenth Amendment, 936
Termination of parental rights, 87-99
Texas
    abortion restrictions, 1000
    District Court, 866
    offer of settlement rule, 199
    statute of limitations, 919
Theater, law as, 10-12
Third-party defendants, 393. *See also* Impleader
    class actions, 1113
Third-party litigation financing, 185, 210-214
    contingency fees and, 212-213
Third-party plaintiffs, 393. *See also* Impleader
Third-party practice. *See* Impleader
Tolling agreements, 318
Tortious interference, 250
Torture Victim Protection Act, 809-810, 819, 824
Trademark infringement, 250
    issue preclusion and, 1037-1045
Transaction or occurrence test, 242, 247, 330,
    364, 378-381, 383, 387, 391-392, 916, 918
Transfer. *See* Venue
Transient jurisdiction, 799-810
    forum non conveniens and, 860
Transnational procedure, 348
Trans-substantive procedure
    in complaints, 289
    politics and, 354
Trespass, 250
Trespass to chattel, 250
Trial courts, 5
Trials. *See also specific topic*
    infrequency of, 244, 356, 507
    jury trials, 507-639. *See also* Jury trials
    new trials. *See* New trial motions

Trifurcation, 620-622
Trustees, 108
    claim preclusion and, 1010
Truth as affirmative defense, 311
Truth in Lending At, 1069
Twain, Mark, 509

Uber, 659
Unbundling legal services, 101
UNIDROIT, 348
Uniform Commercial Code filings, 179
Uniform Rules of Evidence, 449
Unincorporated associations, diversity
    jurisdiction and, 887
Unjust enrichment, 250

Vacation of judgment, 615-619
Venue, 2, 853-863
    defined, 240
    Erie doctrine and, 963
    fallback provision, 854, 978
    federal courts, transfers of actions within, 963
    forum selection clauses and, 862
    impleader and, 854
    joinder and, 387
    motion to dismiss for impropriety of, 306
    personal jurisdiction and, 853-863
    transfer of, 854
    transient jurisdiction and, 860
Verdict, 619-629
    additur, 625-629
    bifurcation and trifurcation, 620-622
    directed verdict. *See* Judgment as matter of law
    general verdict, 1016-1019
    instructions to jury, 622-625
    interrogatories accompanying, 1019
    judgment notwithstanding, 589-591, 594-615
    overview, 619
    remittitur, 625-629
    special verdict, 619-620, 1019
    against weight of evidence, 593-594
Video evidence, 575-580
Virginia, *in rem* jurisdiction in, 798
Virtual representation, doctrine of, 1007-1008
Voir dire, 536-541
Voltaire, 105
Voluntary dismissal, 587

Wage garnishment, due process and, 108-114
Waiver
    of affirmative defenses, 307-308, 311-312
    class actions, 647-648, 659
    cross-claims and, 389
    of lack of personal jurisdiction defense, 668
    of service of process, 852-853
    of sufficiency of evidence challenge, 590-591
Walsh, Thomas, 352
"War on Poverty," 26

Washington (state)
  long-arm statute, 690
  product liability law, 286
Websites, interactive, personal jurisdiction and, 774-783
Welfare reform, 35
Well pleaded complaint rule, 872
  amount in controversy requirement compared, 894
  exceptions to, 875
William the Conqueror, 523
Wisconsin
  academic freedom law, 905
  prejudgment wage garnishment statute, 108
  privatization of welfare benefits administration, 35

Witnesses
  experts. *See* Experts
  mandatory disclosure of, 435
Work-product privilege
  disclosure and, 422
  discovery and, 450
  rationale for, 500
  scope of, 448
Writs
  of certiorari, 246, 637
  of execution, 179
  of habeas corpus, 79, 1033
  historical system of, 340-341
  of mandamus, 635-636
Wrongful death, 250